# The McGraw-Hill Reader

## Issues Across the Disciplines

### TENTH EDITION

**Gilbert H. Muller**
The City University of New York
LaGuardia

**McGraw-Hill
Higher Education**

Boston   Burr Ridge, IL   Dubuque, IA   New York   San Francisco   St. Louis
Bangkok   Bogotá   Caracas   Kuala Lumpur   Lisbon   London   Madrid   Mexico City
Milan   Montreal   New Delhi   Santiago   Seoul   Singapore   Sydney   Taipei   Toronto

# McGraw-Hill
# Higher Education

Published by McGraw-Hill, an imprint of The McGraw-Hill Companies, Inc., 1221 Avenue of the Americas, New York, NY 10020. Copyright © 2008, 2006, 2003, 2000, 1997, 1994, 1991, 1988, 1985, 1982. All rights reserved. No part of this publication may be reproduced or distributed in any form or by any means, or stored in a database or retrieval system, without the prior written consent of The McGraw-Hill Companies, Inc., including, but not limited to, in any network or other electronic storage or transmission, or broadcast for distance learning.

This book is printed on acid-free paper.

3 4 5 6 7 8 9 0 DOC/DOC 0 9 8

ISBN:   978-0-07-353313-1
MHID:   0-07-353313-0

Editor in Chief: *Michael Ryan*
Sponsoring Editor: *Christopher Bennem*
Marketing Manager: *Tamara Wederbrand*
Director of Development: *Carla Samodulski*
Developmental Editor: *Leah Snyder*
Editorial Coordinator: *Molly Meneely*
Production Editor: *Holly Paulsen*
Manuscript Editor: *Thomas L. Briggs*
Art Director: *Jeanne M. Schreiber*

Design Manager: *Cassandra Chu*
Cover Designer: *Adrian Morgan*
Art Editor: *Ayelet Arbel*
Photo Research Coordinator: *Natalia Peschiera*
Photo Research: *David Tietz, Editorial Image, LLC*
Production Supervisor: *Tandra Jorgensen*
Composition: *10/12 Palatino by Aptara, Inc.*
Printing: 45# *New Era Matte Plus,*
   *R. R. Donnelley & Sons*

Cover: (top) Earth from space, December 1992. Earth photographed by the spacecraft Galileo 11 from a distance of 1.2 million miles showing Antarctica and dawn rising over the Pacific Ocean. NASA photograph. Ann Ronan Picture Library, London, Great Britain. Photo: HIP/Art Resource, NY; (bottom) Celestial Globe, Islamic Art, Musee du Louvre, Paris. Photo © Peter Willi/SuperStock.

Credits: The credits section for this book begins on page C-1 and is considered an extension of the copyright page.

### Library of Congress Cataloging-in-Publication Data

The McGraw-Hill reader: issues across the disciplines / [edited by] Gilbert H. Muller. —10th ed.
   p. cm.
   Includes index.
   ISBN-13: 978-0-07-353313-1 (pbk.: acid-free paper)
   ISBN-10: 0-07-353313-0 (pbk.: acid-free paper)
   1. College readers. 2. Interdisciplinary approach in education--Problems, exercises, etc.
3. English language--Rhetoric--Problems, exercises, etc. 4. Academic writing--Problems, exercises, etc. I. Muller, Gilbert H.
PE1417.M44 2008
808′.0427--dc22

                                                    2007039569

The Internet addresses listed in the text were accurate at the time of publication. The inclusion of a Web site does not indicate an endorsement by the authors or McGraw-Hill, and McGraw-Hill does not guarantee the accuracy of the information presented at these sites.

www.mhhe.com

# About the Author

GILBERT H. MULLER, who received a PhD in English and American literature from Stanford University, is professor emeritus of English at the LaGuardia campus of the City University of New York. He has also taught at Stanford University, Vassar College, and several universities overseas. Dr. Muller is the author of the award-winning *Nightmares and Visions: Flannery O'Connor and the Catholic Grotesque; Chester Himes; New Strangers in Paradise: The Immigrant Experience and Contemporary American Fiction;* and other critical studies. His essays and reviews have appeared in *The New York Times, The New Republic, The Nation, The Sewanee Review, The Georgia Review,* and elsewhere. He is also a noted author and editor of textbooks in English and composition, including *The Short Prose Reader* with Harvey Wiener, and, with John A. Williams, *The McGraw-Hill Introduction to Literature* and *Ways In: Reading and Writing about Literature and Film.* Among Dr. Muller's awards are fellowships from the National Endowment for the Humanities, the Fulbright Commission, the Ford Foundation, and the Mellon Foundation.

*To Parisa and Darius*
*My favorite readers*

# Brief Contents

# Contents

## PART 2
## ISSUES ACROSS THE DISCIPLINES

## Chapter 13 Nature and the Environment: How Do We Relate to the Natural World?    792

# Contents of Essays
# by Rhetorical Mode

## NARRATION

## DESCRIPTION

## ILLUSTRATION

# COMPARISON AND CONTRAST

# ANALOGY

# DEFINITION

# CLASSIFICATION

# PROCESS ANALYSIS

# CAUSAL ANALYSIS

## ARGUMENTATION AND PERSUASION

## HUMOR, IRONY, AND SATIRE

# *Preface*

Through nine previous editions, *The McGraw-Hill Reader* has presented the finest classic and contemporary essays, works that span various ages, cultures, and disciplines, providing students with a range of quality prose works. Eudora Welty speaks of reading as "a sweet devouring." This anthology alerts students to the vast and varied pleasures of reading and writing while offering them opportunities to experience numerous perspectives on academic discourse.

Addressing the abiding national interest in core liberal arts programs, interdisciplinary issues, and multicultural perspectives, this tenth edition continues to offer students and instructors a full range of quality prose models important to writing courses, reading sequences, and key undergraduate disciplines. All of the selections have been chosen for their significance, vitality, and technical precision. With the high quality of its essays, its consistent humanistic emphases, and its clear organization, *The McGraw-Hill Reader* is a lively, sophisticated, and eminently flexible text for college composition and reading programs.

## Organization and Proven Features

Composed of 14 chapters, *The McGraw-Hill Reader* covers the major modes of writing and most of the disciplines that college students will encounter as undergraduates. Chapter 1 presents an extensive overview of the critical thinking, reading, and writing processes. Chapter 2 provides extensive coverage of argument and persuasion. Chapter 3 is a concise guide to research and documentation in the electronic age. Chapters 4–14 cover core liberal arts disciplines, including education, the social sciences, business and economics, the humanities, and the sciences. Each chapter asks a key question drawn from the disciplines it represents and designed to elicit constructive class discussion and sound critical writing. These disciplinary chapters offer prose models that allow students to practice skills they will need throughout college, including analysis, criticism, argumentation, and persuasion.

Throughout its previous editions, instructors and students have appreciated the following features of *The McGraw-Hill Reader:*

- **A rich selection of readings:** A distinct strength of *The McGraw-Hill Reader*—perhaps the primary one for teachers who prefer to create their own approaches to composition and reading courses—is the wide range of material and the varied constituencies represented in the text. The essays in this book have been selected carefully to embrace a rich assortment of authors, to achieve balance among constituencies, to cover major historical periods, and to provide prose models and styles for class analysis, discussion, and imitation. The authors in this text—whether Plato or Julia Alvarez, Jonathan Swift or Amy Tan—have high visibility as writers and thinkers of value. Some of these authors are represented by more than one essay. All the authors—writing from such vantage points as literature, journalism, anthropology, sociology, art history, biology, and philosophy—start from the perspective that ideas exist in the world, that we should be alert to them, and that we should be able to deal with them in our own discourse.

- **A text that works with a wide variety of levels and approaches.** Because the selections range from very simple essays to the most abstract and complex modes of prose, teachers and students will be able to use *The McGraw-Hill Reader* at virtually all levels of a program. Containing more than one hundred complete essays, *The McGraw-Hill Reader* thus is a flexible companion for composition courses. It can be used with any of the major pedagogical perspectives common to the practice of composition today: as a writing-across-the-curricula text, as the basis for a rhetorically focused course, as a thematic reader, as a multicultural anthology, or as an in-depth reader. An alternate table of contents, listing carefully selected essays in 11 rhetorical categories, also makes *The McGraw-Hill Reader* adaptable to an approach based on the rhetorical patterns. Above all, teachers can develop their own sequences of essays that will contribute not only to their students' reading and writing proficiency but also to their growing intellectual power.

- **Chapter introductions that encourage students to reflect on major issues in the discipline.** The introduction to each disciplinary chapter gives students a broad perspective on the field at hand by putting major issues and concerns in context. Each introduction ends with a previewing section that alerts students to strategies for reading, discussion, and writing.

- **Uniform apparatus that reinforces critical reading and writing.** Another major strength of *The McGraw-Hill Reader* is in the uniform apparatus that accompanies every essay. Much can be learned from any well-written essay, especially if the apparatus is systematic in design. Each selection in this text is preceded by a brief introduction that offers biographical information about the author. The questions that follow each essay are organized in a consistent format created to reinforce essential reading, writing, and oral communication skills. Arranged in three categories—Comprehension, Rhetoric, and Writing—these questions reflect current compositional theory as they move students from audience analysis to various modes and processes of composition. All specialized terms used in the questions are defined for students in an extensive Glossary of Terms at the end of the text. The integrated design of these questions makes each essay—simple or complex, short or long, old or new—accessible to college students who possess varied reading and writing abilities.

- **"Synthesis: Connections for Critical Thinking" sections.** The topics listed at the end of each chapter help students to gain practice in synthesis and critique, and make comparative assessments of various groups of essays. Students also are encouraged to use Internet resources.
- **A guide to research and documentation.** Chapter 3 offers guidance on the most current research writing processes and the documentation styles recommended by the Modern Language Association and the American Psychological Association.

## Highlights of the Tenth Edition

Informed by the comments and suggestions of instructors from across the country who reviewed the previous edition, this tenth edition of *The McGraw-Hill Reader* offers a number of new and significant features:

- **Two dozen new selections**. Fresh essays on topics of current and enduring interest such as the clash of civilizations, Wal-Mart, online social networking, dieting and obesity, the Patriot Act, the Iraq war, globalization, and terrorism will elicit effective student response and writing. Several longer, more demanding selections have been included, as well as readings that contain visuals. Most new selections are current—appearing in publications since 2000. New readings to this edition include essays by Julia Alvarez, P. J. O'Rourke, Amy Tan, Molly Ivins, Edward Said, Susan Sontag, Atul Gawande, Margaret Atwood, and other established and emerging writers.
- **Expanded treatment of argument, plagiarism, summary and précis, and electronic research.** The three chapters in Part 1 provide integrated guidelines on these topics. Additionally, argumentation is stressed throughout the text, with the last writing assignment following all selections asking students to compose an argumentative essay.
- **New sections on synthesis and critique.** For the first time, explanatory and argumentative synthesis and critique receive extensive treatment in Chapters 1 and 2 and in the apparatus appearing in all chapters.
- **New case studies.** Supplementing the fresh discussions of synthesis are essays by Virginia Woolf and Annie Dillard on literary influence and a set of essays on MySpace and young people's fascination with online social relationships.

- **New visuals throughout.** Provocative, high-quality images, with accompanying apparatus, add insight into essays and engage students while encouraging critical thought.
- **Readings with citations and footnotes.** An icon in the Table of Contents highlights a core of essays containing varieties of documentation.
- **A four-color insert on advertising and culture.** This insert encourages students to respond comparatively to advertisements as visual texts. New classic and contemporary visuals also appear at the beginning of each chapter. These visuals include photographs, paintings, cartoons, and other visual texts. Students are engaged by visual texts, and these provocative, high-quality images, along with the accompanying "Using a Critical Perspective" questions, will serve to interest them in the topic of the chapter and get them thinking and writing.

## Useful Supplements

The following supplements are designed to help instructors and students derive the full benefit from *The McGraw-Hill Reader:*

- **A powerful Online Learning Center powered by Catalyst 2.0.** The Web site for *The McGraw-Hill Reader* (www.mhhe.com/mhreader) features a wealth of online resources including additional resources that complement the readings in *The McGraw-Hill Reader,* tutorials for document design and visual rhetoric, guides for avoiding plagiarism and evaluating sources, Bibliomaker software for MLA, APA, Chicago, and CSE styles of documentation, and many more tools that support students with their writing at every stage of the process. Catalyst 2.0 features a full classroom management system that includes an online grade book and collaborative peer review environment.
- **A *Guide to the McGraw-Hill Reader.*** This supplement, by Gilbert H. Muller, offers well-considered strategies for teaching individual essays, sample rhetorical analyses, answers to questions, additional thought-provoking questions, comparative essay discussion formats, and tips for prewriting and guided writing activities. There is also a bibliography of criticism and research on the teaching of composition. This guide is available on the Online Learning Center at www.mhhe.com/mhreader.
- **Teaching Composition Faculty Listserv (www.mhhe.com/tcomp).** Moderated by Chris Anson at the University of North Carolina, Raleigh, and offered by McGraw-Hill as a service to the composition community, this listserv brings together senior members of the college composition community with newer members—junior faculty, adjuncts, and teaching assistants—in an online newsletter and accompanying discussion group to address issues of pedagogy, in theory and in practice.

## Acknowledgments

It is a pleasure to acknowledge the support, assistance, and guidance of numerous individuals who helped create *The McGraw-Hill Reader*. I want to thank the excellent McGraw-Hill family of assistants, editors, and executives who participated enthusiastically in the project from the outset and who encouraged me at every step. My editor, Christopher Bennem, has been an enthusiastic supporter of *The McGraw-Hill Reader*. Meg Botteon assisted in the revision of the chapter on research writing. Marguerite Newcomb helped with the preparation of the instructor's manual. I also want to thank Leah Snyder, my development editor; Thomas L. Briggs, my superlative copy editor; and Holly Paulsen, my production editor, who kept the train running on time.

The final content and design of *The McGraw-Hill Reader*, Tenth Edition, reflects the expertise and advice offered by college instructors across the country who gave generously of their time when asked to review the text:

Laurel Bollinger, University of Alabama in Huntsville
Bridget Boulton, Truckee Meadows Community College
Gina Burkart, University of Northern Iowa
Cheryl Cardoza, Truckee Meadows Community College
William Chalmers, Idaho State University
Rocky Colavito, Northwestern State University
Michael Davey, Valdosta State University
Carlen Donovan, Idaho State University
Richard Durocher, Saint Olaf College
Natasha Isadora Frank, American University in Beirut
Lawrence Gorman, East West University
Kimberly Greenfield, Lorain Community College
Chris Head, Cardinal Stritch University
Beth Huber, Western Carolina University
Erin Huskey, Valdosta State University
Trish Jenkins, University of Alaska, Anchorage
Lou Ann Karabel, Indiana University Northwest
H. Brown Miller, City College of San Francisco
Heather Milton, University of Florida
Michael Minassian, Broward Community College
Lee Moore, Austin Community College
Jen Nader, Bergen Community College
Jeff Nelson, University of Alabama in Huntsville
Marguerite Newcomb, University of Texas at San Antonio
Heather Olson, The Art Institute of Atlanta
Thomas Pfau, Bellevue Community College
Paula Sebastian, Bellevue Community College
Saundra Towns, Bernard Baruch College

Amy Ulmer, Pasadena City College
Tondalaya Van Lear, Dabney Lancaster Community College
Nathanial Wallace, South Carolina State University
Stacia Watkins, Middle Tennessee State University
Martha Willoughby, Pearl River Community College

I am pleased to acknowledge support from the Mellon Foundation, the Graduate Center of The City University of New York, and the United States Department of Education (Title III and Title IV) that enabled me to develop this text.

**Gilbert H. Muller**

## part 1

# An Overview of College Writing

# chapter 1

# Critical Thinking, Reading, and Writing

This book will help you read and write critically in college courses. Although we have entered the electronic information age, in which mastery of computer skills and visual literacy seem to be essential for understanding and maintaining our lives and careers, most college work still requires an ability to understand and reflect intelligently on written texts and, subsequently, to respond in writing to them. College courses typically involve the reading of challenging texts. As a college student, you will need to approach these texts with skills that go beyond those of casual reading, that is, the type of reading you may do for leisure, for pleasure, or for escapism, or simply to pass time. Even in courses in which a preponderance of work involves learning forms of knowledge and new technologies, such as computers, mathematics, and science, you are sure to find a healthy amount of reading that will supplement any other work done in the classroom or laboratory.

The reading and writing skills you develop during your college years will also help you in your future profession. Think of a lawyer reviewing legal history or preparing a legal brief, a doctor reviewing current literature on medical innovations or writing an article for a professional journal, or an environmental scientist reading and writing about issues regarding pollution and global warming. All these activities require the ability to think, read, and write about complex material. Learning the tools of critical reading and writing not only teaches you the "what" of an issue but also helps you think about and respond intelligently to the relative strength of the writer's opinions, ideas, and theories. Critical thinking, reading, and writing enable you to distinguish between informed ideas and pure speculation, rational arguments and emotional ones, and organized essays and structurally deficient ones.

As you hone your critical thinking, reading, and writing skills by tackling the essays in this anthology, you should soon understand how the written word is still the primary medium with which thinkers transmit the intricacies of controversial issues involving the family, society, politics, work, gender, and class. You will encounter complex texts that require you to extract maximum meaning from them, compare your own views with those of the authors you read, and respond to what you read in an informed and coherent manner. The reading selections in this textbook have been chosen specifically to assist you in developing such skills. As you tackle these texts, you will realize that sound reading habits permit you to understand the fine points of logic, reasoning, analysis, argumentation, and evaluation.

## STEPS TO READING CRITICALLY AND ACTIVELY

You can find numerous reasons to rationalize a failure to read carefully and critically. You have a headache. You're hungry. The material is boring. The writer puts you to sleep. Your roommates are talking. You have a date. In short, there are many internal and external barriers to critical reading. Fortunately, there are techniques—a critical reading process—to guide you through this maze of distractions. Consider these five strategies:

1. *Develop an attitude of "critical consciousness."* In other words, do not be passive, uncritical, or alienated from the writer or the text. Instead, be active, critical, and engaged with the writer and his or her text.
2. *Read attentively.* Give your full attention to the text in order to understand it. Do not let your mind wander.
3. *Paraphrase.* Periodically restate what you read. Learn to process bits of key information. Keep a running inventory of highlights. Take mental or actual notes on the text's main points. (More information on paraphrasing and summarizing appears in this chapter and in Chapter 3.)
4. *Ask questions.* If for any reason you are uncertain about any aspect of the text, pose a question about it and try to answer it yourself. You might seek immediate help from a friend or classmate. If you are unable to answer your question, ask for clarification from the instructor.
5. *Control your biases.* You must both control and correct any prejudices that might interfere with the claim, information, or tone of a text. You might, for example, have misgivings about a liberal or conservative writer, or about a feminist or a creationist, but such strong emotions can erode your ability to keep an open mind and your power to think critically about a subject or issue.

These five strategies will help you begin to overcome the barriers to critical reading.

One way to view critical reading is through the concept of active reading. Active reading suggests that you, as a reader, have an obligation to yourself and the author to bring an alert, critical, and responsive perspective to your encounter with the written word. Active reading means learning to annotate (a strategy discussed later in this chapter), to reflect on what you read, and to develop personal responses in order to prepare yourself for writing assignments that your instructor will present to you during the term. This process—reading critically in order to write critically—is not merely an "academic" exercise. It is a skill that can enrich you as a person throughout your life and career. It will teach you to respond critically to the admonitions of politicians or to the seductions of advertisements and, if you choose, to participate intelligently in the "national conversation," which can lead to a rewarding life and responsible citizenship.

When you read an essay or any other type of text, you create meaning out of the material the author has presented. If the essay is relatively simple, clear, and concise, the meaning that you construct from your reading may be very similar to what the author intended. Nevertheless, the way you interact with even the most comprehensible texts will never be identical to the way another reader interacts.

Consider an essay that you will encounter in this anthology, Langston Hughes's "Salvation." A chapter from his autobiography, *The Big Sea* (1940), this essay tells of a childhood incident in which the young Hughes's faith was tested. The essay focuses on a church revival meeting that Hughes was taken to and the increasing pressure he sensed at the meeting to "testify" to the presence of Jesus in his life. At first the young Hughes holds out against the fervor of the congregation, but ultimately he pretends to be converted, or "saved." That night, however, he weeps and then testifies to something entirely unexpected: the loss of faith he experienced because Jesus did not "save" him in a time of need.

As your class reads this essay, individuals among you may be struck by the compressed energy of the narration and the description of the event, by the swift characterization and revealing dialogue, or by the conflict and mounting tension. Moreover, the heightened personal and spiritual conflict will force class members to consider the sad irony inherent in the title "Salvation."

Even if your class arrives at a broad consensus on the intentions of the author, individual responses to the text will vary. Readers who have attended revival meetings will respond differently than those who have not. Evangelical Christians will see the text from a different perspective than will Catholics, Muslims, or Jews. African American readers (Hughes was black) may respond differently than white readers. Women may respond differently than men, and so on.

In this brief assessment of possible reader responses, we are trying to establish meaning from a shifting series of critical perspectives. Although we can establish a consensus of meaning as to what Hughes probably intended, our own interpretation and evaluation of the text will be conditioned by our personal experiences, backgrounds, attitudes, biases, and beliefs. In other words, even as the class attempts to construct a common reading, each member is also constructing a somewhat different meaning, one based on the individual's own interaction with the text.

## PREPARING TO READ

This textbook contains many essays covering a variety of subjects by writers from a wealth of backgrounds and historical periods. You may be familiar with some, unfamiliar with others. All, however, have something to say and a way of saying it that others have found significant. Hence, many have stood the test of time, whether a year, a decade, or centuries. Essays are a recognized genre, or form of literature, and the finest essays have staying power. As Ezra Pound said, "Literature is news that stays news," and the best examples of the essay convey this sense of permanent value. Thus, you have an obligation to be an active and critical reader to do justice to the work that was put into these texts. Most were written with care, over extended periods of time, and by people who themselves studied the art of writing and the topics of their discourse. During your first week of class, you may wish to read some of their brief biographies to understand these authors' personal and educational backgrounds, their beliefs and credos, and some of the significant moments of their lives. You will often find that there are logical connections between the stories of their lives and the topics they have written about.

Sharpening your reading skills will be important because you may not be able to personally choose the essays from the text. You may find some topics and essays more interesting than others. But if you are prepared to read critically, you will be able to bring the same set of skills to any selection your instructor assigns. With this principle in mind, we present an overview of the active reading process, which will culminate in a case study using this process with an essay titled "The Cult of Ethnicity," by Arthur M. Schlesinger Jr.

When you are given a reading assignment from the textbook, a good strategy in preparing to read is to locate the text as well as possible within its broader context. Read the biographical notes about the author. Focus on the title of the essay. What can you infer from the title? How long is the essay? Although many students delight at the thought of reading shorter texts rather than longer ones, you may find that this variable is not always the deciding one in determining how easily you "get through" the essay. Short essays can be intricate and difficult; long ones can be simpler and more transparent. A long essay on a topic in which you are interested may be more rewarding than a short essay that you find lacking in relevance. Other basic prereading activities include noting whether there are section breaks in the essay, whether there are subheadings, whether the author has used footnotes, and if so, how extensive they are. Other preliminary questions to answer could be, What is the date of the original publication of the essay? Is the essay a fully contained work, or is it an excerpt from a larger text? Are there visual or mathematical aids, such as graphs, charts, diagrams, or lists? Because authors often use typographical signals to highlight things or to help organize what they have written, you might ask, Does the author use quotation marks to "signal" certain words? Is italic type used, and if so, what is its purpose? Are other books and authors cited in the essay? Does the author use organizational tools such as Arabic or Roman numerals? Once you have answered these questions regarding mechanics, you will be prepared to deal more substantively with the essay as a unit of meaning and communication.

Preparing to read also means understanding that you bring your own knowledge, opinions, experiences, and attitudes to the text. You are not an empty glass to be filled with the knowledge and opinions of the authors, but rather a learner who can bring to bear your own reflections on what you read even if you think your knowledge is minimal. Often we do not know just how much ability we have in thinking about a topic until we actively respond to what others confront us with in their writings. By tackling the reading assignments in the text, you will not only learn new information and confront opinions that may challenge your own but also find that reading frees up your ability to express your own opinions. For this reason, most English teachers look upon reading as a two-way process: an exchange between writer and reader.

Although the credentials and experience of a professional writer may seem impressive, they should not deter you from considering your own critical talents as you read. But first, you must find a way to harness those abilities.

www.mhhe.com/ **mhreader**

For a student sample of preparing to read and an interactive previewing exercise, go to:

**More Resources > Ch. 1 Reading & Writing**

## CRITICAL READING

It should be evident to you by now that you are not a mere recipient of information who passively accepts what the writer conveys. Instead, you should feel comfortable about engaging the author as you might a friend in a lively conversation or argument. And just as a talk with a friend involves active listening, rebuttal, and the use of facts and logic, the interaction between yourself and the author needs to be a dynamic one as well. Active reading is so important in the learning process that one of America's most popular philosophers, Mortimer Adler, wrote an article that has become a classic on this topic. It is titled "How to Mark a Book" and appears beginning on page 57.

Among the essential elements of your close reading are annotating, note taking, and questioning the text.

### Annotating

Annotating refers to marking your text by making content notes, by using symbols such as question marks and exclamation points, and by recording personal reactions. Annotating is not, however, mere underlining or highlighting. These latter two methods often serve little purpose in helping you comprehend a text. Most likely, when you return to passages you've marked with these simple procedures, you will have forgotten why you felt they were important in the first place. If you do underline or highlight, you should be sure to link your marking with a note in the margin. Simply drawing attention to someone else's words does little in the way of expanding your own thoughts on a topic. Learning is best accomplished by restating ideas in your own words.

## Taking Notes

Many essays in your anthology will require more than simply jotting down marginal notes in order to comprehend them fully or to respond to them in depth. Just as you might take notes during a classroom lecture, you may find it useful to take notes to supplement your annotations. You may wish, for example, to write down quotations so that you can see them together. Or you may wish to summarize the essay by outlining its key points, a reversal of the process you would use to develop your own essay, wherein you begin with an outline and expand it into paragraphs. By collapsing an essay into an outline, you have a handy reference of the author's thesis (main idea) and supporting points, and the methods used to develop them. Another function of note taking is to overcome the simple habit most of us have of thinking we will remember things without jotting them down, only to find out later that we cannot recall significant information from memory. You will appreciate the benefits of taking notes when you tackle lengthy essays, which may run 15 or 20 pages.

## Questioning the Text

Posing key questions about a text and then answering them to the best of your ability is a helpful means of understanding an essay's substance and structure. Certain basic questions, like the ones below, are salient for nearly any text you confront, and answering them for yourself can be a powerful means of enhancing your comprehension. As you read the text, such questions help you spot the significant issues that lie within most essays, regardless of their form or length. It is a good habit to have these questions in mind as you read and then to return to them once you've thought through your responses. They serve as guideposts along the way of your reading experience and assist you in focusing on those issues that are most important to a text. When you become comfortable with them, you will probably find that your mind automatically poses them as you read, making your comprehension of difficult texts easier.

- What is the thesis or main point of the text?
- What methods does the author use to support these points, for instance, illustration, example, description, personal experience, or history? Does he or she site authorities or studies or statistics?
- What value position, if any, does the author present? In other words, is the author either directly or indirectly presenting her or his moral framework on an issue, or is she or he summarizing or describing an issue?
- Does the author use any special terms or expressions that need to be elucidated to understand the essay? You will find that authors, when addressing innovative or revolutionary ideas within the context of their times,

must use vocabulary that often needs to be defined. Take, for example, the term *multiculturalism*. Exactly what might an author mean by that word?
- What is the level of discourse of the essay? Or what is the audience's level of educational attainment the author presumes?
- Who is the implied audience for the essay? Is it written for a specialized profession (such as scientists or educators)? Is it written for individuals with a focus on their particular role in society, for example, as parents or consumers or citizens?

The following essay, "The Cult of Ethnicity," by the influential historian Arthur M. Schlesinger Jr., has been annotated to demonstrate how a student might respond to it. Schlesinger's essay also will be used to explain aspects of the reading and writing process as we move through this section.

The history of the world has been in great part the history of the mixing of peoples. Modern communication and transport accelerate mass migrations from one continent to another. Ethnic and racial diversity are more than ever a salient fact of the age.

But what happens when people of different origins, speaking different languages and professing different religions, inhabit the same locality and live under the same political sovereignty? Ethnic and racial conflict—far more than ideological conflict—is the explosive problem of our times.

*This seems like the thesis. Where are his supports? Or is it the thesis?*

On every side today ethnicity is breaking up nations. The Soviet Union, India, Yugoslavia, Ethiopia, are all in crisis. Ethnic tensions disturb and divide Sri Lanka, Burma, Indonesia, Iraq, Cyprus, Nigeria, Angola, Lebanon, Guyana, Trinidad—you name it. Even nations as stable and civilized as Britain and France, Belgium and Spain, face growing ethnic troubles. Is there any large multiethnic state that can be made to work?

*Look these up. Demonstrates knowledge on the part of the author.*

The answer to that question has been, until recently, the United States. "No other nation," Margaret Thatcher has said, "has so successfully combined people of different races and nations within a single culture." How have Americans succeeded in pulling off this almost unprecedented trick?

We have always been a multiethnic country. Hector St. John de Crevecoeur, who came from France in the 18th century, marveled at the astonishing diversity of the settlers—"a mixture of English, Scotch, Irish, French, Dutch, Germans and Swedes . . . this promiscuous breed." He propounded a famous question: "What then is the American, this new man?" And he gave a famous answer: "Here individuals of all nations are melted into a new race of men." *E pluribus unum.*

*Historical figure— who was he?*

The United States escaped the divisiveness of a multiethnic society by a brilliant solution: the creation of a brand-new national identity. The point of America was not to preserve old cultures but to *forge a new, American culture. "By an intermixture with our people," President George Washington told Vice

*Is this a partly American phenomenon? *prevents racial and ethnic conflict*

President John Adams, immigrants will "get assimilated to our customs, measures and laws: in a word, soon become one people." This was the ideal that a century later Israel Zangwill crystallized in the title of his popular 1908 play *The Melting Pot.* And no institution was more potent in molding Crevecoeur's "promiscuous breed" into Washington's "one people" than the American public school.

The new American nationality was <u>inescapably English in language</u>, ideas, and institutions. The pot did not melt everybody, not even all the white immigrants; deeply bred racism put black Americans, yellow Americans, red Americans and brown Americans well outside the pale. Still, the (infusion) of other (stocks,) even of nonwhite stocks, and the experience of the New World reconfigured the British legacy and made the United States, as we all know, a very different country from Britain.

*Why?—doesn't explain*

*Note S's use of historical process analysis*

In the 20th century, new immigration laws altered the composition of the American people, and a cult of ethnicity erupted both among non-Anglo whites and among nonwhite minorities. This had many healthy consequences. The American culture at last began to give shamefully overdue recognition to the achievements of groups subordinated and spurned during the high noon of Anglo dominance, and it began to acknowledge the great swirling world beyond Europe. Americans acquired a more complex and invigorating sense of their world—and of themselves.

*Vocab.: infusion
stocks
zeal
Eurocentric
apocalyptic
ferment
Kleagle
crucible*

But, pressed too far, the cult of ethnicity has unhealthy consequences. <u>It gives rise, for example, to the conception of the United States as a nation composed not of individuals making their own choices but of inviolable ethnic and racial groups</u>. It rejects the historic American goals of assimilation and integration.

*Signals a warning—danger*

And, in an excess of (zeal,) well-intentioned people seek to transform our system of education from a means of creating "one people" into a means of <u>promoting, celebrating and perpetuating separate ethnic origins and identities</u>. The balance is shifting from *unum* to *pluribus.*

*Is this thesis or related to thesis?*

That is the issue that lies behind the hullabaloo over "multiculturalism" and "political correctness," the attack on the ("Eurocentric") curriculum and the rise of the notion that history and literature should be taught not as disciplines but as therapies whose function is to raise minority self-esteem. <u>Group separatism crystallizes the differences, magnifies tensions, intensifies hostilities.</u> Europe—the unique source of the liberating ideas of democracy, civil liberties and human rights—<u>is portrayed as the root of all evil, and non-European cultures, their own many crimes deleted, are presented as the means of redemption</u>.

*Support against multiculturalism*

*General—where are the specific examples?*

I don't want to sound (apocalyptic) about these developments. Education is always in (ferment,) and a good thing too. The situation in our universities, I am confident, will soon right itself. But the impact of separatist pressures on our public schools is more troubling. If a (Kleagle) of the Ku Klux Klan wanted to use the schools to disable and handicap black Americans, he would hardly come up with anything more effective than the "Afrocentric" curriculum. And if separatist tendencies go unchecked, the result can only be the fragmentation, resegregation and tribalization of American life.

*Is this an exaggeration? How does he know?*

I remain optimistic. My impression is that the historic forces driving toward "one people" have not lost their power. The eruption of ethnicity is, I believe, a rather superficial enthusiasm stirred by romantic ideologues on the one hand and by unscrupulous con men on the other: self-appointed spokesmen whose claim to represent their minority groups is carelessly accepted by the media. Most American-born members of minority groups, white or nonwhite, see themselves primarily as Americans rather than primarily as members of one or another ethnic group. A notable indicator today is the rate of intermarriage across ethnic lines, across religious lines, even (increasingly) across racial lines. "We Americans," said Theodore Roosevelt, "are children of the (crucible.)"

*Who are these people? He doesn't mention them specifically.*

*Reality is stronger than "ideology"? Is this his "solution"?*

The growing diversity of the American population makes the quest for unifying ideals and a common culture all the more urgent. In a world savagely rent by ethnic and racial antagonisms, the United States must continue as an example of how a highly differentiated society holds itself together.

*A sharp conclusion → argument? United States must be example. This is the thesis.*

What has this annotating accomplished? It has allowed the reader/annotator to consider and think about what she has read, integrate her ideas with the ideas of the author, challenge those she may disagree with, raise issues for further study, find the seeds of ideas that may become the focus of an essay in response to the writing, review what she has read with more facility, and quickly and efficiently return to those parts of the essay she found the most salient.

The aforementioned strategies will assist you in responding intelligently in the classroom, remembering the main points of what you have read, and internalizing the critical reading skill so that it becomes automatic. However, such activities are not as challenging as the ultimate goal of most of your reading assignments, which will be to respond in formal writing to the works you've read. For this, you will need to enhance your study skills a bit further so that they will prepare you to write.

Formal writing assignments require you to demonstrate that you understood what you have read and are able to respond in an informed and intelligent manner to the material. They also require you to use appropriate form, organization, and exposition. Above all, regardless of what you want to express, you will have to communicate your ideas clearly and concisely. To this end, you will need to acquire skills that you can call on when it comes to writing at length about what you have read. To do so, you will find your ability to paraphrase, summarize, and quote directly from the original material particularly helpful.

When you move to this next phase, however, try to avoid a common practice among readers that causes them to waste time and effort. Many students think they have completed a reading assignment when they read the last word of an essay. They utter a sigh of relief, look inside the refrigerator for something to eat, call up friends, or go Web browsing. However, as a critical reader, you need to spend additional time reinforcing what you have read by thinking about the author's views, considering her or his rhetorical methods, and reviewing or adding to your notes and annotations. For example, one culminating activity at this point can be to either mentally or verbally summarize what you have read. You can summarize verbally by enlisting a classmate and simply stating in your own terms the main points of your reading assignment. This oral summarizing will prevent a common problem many readers experience: the natural tendency to forget most of what they read shortly after reading.

## BEYOND CONTENT: FOCUSING ON PROCESS

An essayist attempts to communicate a message to his or her audience. This message is the *content*. But "message making" is a process—the exchange of information through a shared system of verbal or visual symbols. Your goal in reading critically is to understand not just the informational content of a text but also how the writer shares meaning and typically tries to influence your beliefs and behavior. A good writer, to paraphrase Plato in *Phaedrus,* tries to "enchant" your mind.

From Plato to the present, theorists have stressed this interactional aspect of reading and writing. Someone constructs a message (for our purposes, a written text) and transmits it, and we have to receive it, decode it, and respond to it. Thus any "piece" of writing, whether designed to inform, persuade, or entertain, is the product of a complex process of actions and interactions by which we perceive, order, and verify (or make sense of) what we read. Whether we have the capacity to grasp the argument of a text, think logically about a thesis, or understand the cultural background of a writer and how it informs a text depends on how well we *perceive* the ways in which the writer creates meaning in the text.

Defined simply, *perception* is the process by which you create meaning for your world. As a process, it deals with the way you interpret the behavior of others as well as yourself. Thus, understanding perception helps to explain how we process information about self, others, and our world. Our senses—seeing, hearing, touching, tasting, smelling—provide us initial contact with the outside world, enabling us to establish our perceptual field of reference. However, we also perceive what we want to perceive, which we call *psychological selectivity*. Finally, there is a third form of perception known as *cultural selectivity:* from a cultural perspective, we are conditioned by our culture's code of values and modes of understanding. For example, the phenomenon of *binocular rivalry* demonstrates that people from two different cultures exposed to two pictures at the same time will remember elements compatible with their own culture. With critical reading, you can have diverging interpretations of passages or an entire text because you perceive them from different perspectives.

In addition to differences in perception, you should be mindful of how an author presents information. How an author presents her or his information is as important as what information the author presents. Strategies for writing may include the overall pattern of an essay—for example, is it an argument, an explanation, a definition, an evaluation, a comparison, or a contrast? While you may not think of essays in terms of genre, as you do literature (which may be presented in the form of poetry, the short story, the play, and so on), such forms can help you understand the motivation behind the writer's work and assist you as you seek out the more significant passages. For example, if the essay is argumentative, you should focus on the supporting points the author has provided, determining whether they offer adequate support for the author's point of view. In an essay arguing for the return to traditional family values, for instance, the use of one anecdote to prove a point would probably not be enough to persuade most readers.

As you read an essay, you should also consider the author's *purpose* for writing. An essay about a personal experience would probably contain physical description; at the same time, the author's purpose would probably be to communicate an element in his or her life that can provide insight into personal development in general. Among the more common purposes are the following: to inform, to persuade, to disprove, to describe, to narrate, to demonstrate, to compare and contrast, to seek a solution to a problem, to explain a process, to classify, to define, to warn, and to summarize. While most essays contain a variety of purposes, one often will stand out among the others.

## PARAPHRASING, SUMMARIZING, QUOTING, AND SYNTHESIZING

As you prepare to respond to the writing of others, you need to develop skills so that your own writing will reflect the hard work that went into the reading process. To this end, you can benefit from learning some shortcuts that will assist you in garnering information about what you have read. These skills include paraphrasing, summarizing, quoting directly from, and synthesizing another author's work.

### Paraphrasing

Paraphrasing means taking what you have read and putting it in your own words. Students occasionally complain about this process, using the argument that it is a waste of time to paraphrase when the author's own words are the best way to articulate his or her ideas. However, paraphrasing serves two main purposes. The more obvious one is that it prevents you from plagiarizing, even inadvertently, what you have read. In terms of learning, however, it is particularly helpful because it requires that you digest what you have read and then rewrite it. As you do so, you will develop writing patterns that over time will improve your ability to communicate. Paraphrasing forces you to truly think about what you have read and reinforces what you've read, since your mind has now been cognitively stimulated. You may find that paraphrasing often leads you to challenge the text or think more deeply about it simply because the paraphrasing process requires that you fully comprehend what you read.

It is important while paraphrasing to retain all the essential information of the original while not using any of the author's original vocabulary or style. One rule of thumb is to never use three or more words that appeared together in the original. However, you can keep words such as articles (*a, an, the*) and conjunctions (*and, for, but,* and so on).

The following are two examples of paraphrasing that demonstrate unsuccessful and successful application of the technique.

### Original

But, pressed too far, the cult of ethnicity has unhealthy consequences. It gives rise, for example, to the conception of the United States as a nation composed not of individuals making their own choices but of inviolable ethnic and racial groups. It rejects the historic American goals of assimilation and integration.

### Unsuccessful Paraphrase

But, pressed too far, the focus on ethnicity has dangerous consequences. It suggests that the United States is a nation made up of separate ethnic and racial groups rather than individuals. It goes against the American ideals of integration and assimilation.

There are several things wrong with paraphrase 1. Rather than change key words, the writer has merely rearranged them. The sentence structure is very similar to that of the original, as is the ordering of ideas. If the student were to incorporate this paraphrase into her or his own essay, the teacher would probably consider it a form of plagiarism. It is simply too close to the original. To truly paraphrase, you must substitute vocabulary, rearrange sentence structure, and change the length and order of sentences. These strategies are more evident in paraphrase 2.

### Successful Paraphrase

Our country is made up of both individuals and groups. The recent trend to focus on the idea that one's ethnic background should have a major influence on one's perspective as a citizen goes against the moral foundations of the United States. It is the very concept of accepting American culture as one's own that has made our country strong and relatively free from cultural conflict.

## Summarizing

A summary is a short, cohesive paragraph or paragraphs that are faithful to the structure and meaning of the original essay, but developed in your own words and including only the most essential elements of the original. Summaries are particularly helpful when you are planning to write lengthy assignments or assignments that require you to compare two or more sources. Because a good summary requires that you use many of the skills of active reading, it helps you to "imprint" the rhetorical features and content of what you have read in your memory, and also provides you with a means of communicating the essence of the essay to another person or group. To summarize successfully, you need to develop the ability to know what to leave out as much as what to include. As you review your source, the annotations and notes you made should help immensely. Since you want to deal with only the essentials of the original, you must delete all unimportant details and redundancies. Unlike paraphrasing, however, most summaries require that you stick to the general order of ideas as they are presented in a text. They also should not be mere retellings of what you have read, but should present the relationships among the ideas. It may be helpful to think of a summary as analogous to a news story, in which the essential details of what happened are presented in an orderly chronological fashion, because readers can best understand the gist of a story that way. It is simply the way the human mind—at least, the Western mind—operates. Another strategy in summarizing is to imagine that the audience you are summarizing for has not read the original. This places a strong responsibility on you to communicate the essentials of the text accurately.

The following six steps should help you in preparing a summary. After you've reviewed them, read the summary that follows and consider whether it seems to have fulfilled these suggestions.

1. Read the entire source at least twice and annotate it at least once before writing.
2. Write an opening sentence that states the author's thesis.
3. Explain the author's main supporting ideas, reviewing your notes to make sure you have included all of them. Be careful not to plagiarize, and use quotations only where appropriate.
4. Restate important concepts, key terms, main principles, and so on. Do not include your opinion or judge the essay in any way.
5. Present the ideas in the order in which they originally appeared. Note that in this sense summarizing is different from paraphrasing, in which staying too close to the original order of words may be detrimental to the process.
6. Review your summary once it has been completed. Consider whether someone who hasn't read the original would find your summary sufficient to understand the essence of the original work. You may also wish to have classmates or friends read the essay and furnish their verbal understanding of what you've written.

Now, review the following summary of Schlesinger's essay and determine whether it adheres to these points.

### Sample Summary

Schlesinger argues that the recent surge of interest in ethnic separatism that is being touted by some whom he considers self-styled spokespersons for various ethnic groups threatens the unifying principle of our country's founders and undermines the strength of our society. This principle is that the American identity that was forged by its creators would be adopted by all peoples arriving here through a process of assimilation to our culture, values, and system of government so that cultural conflict could be avoided. Although he finds some merit in the idea that recognizing the contributions of certain groups who have been kept out of the national focus, for example, "nonwhite minorities," is a positive move, he fears that this can be taken to an extreme. The result could be the development of antagonism between ethnic groups solely on the basis of overemphasizing differences rather than recognizing similarities. He further argues that efforts to fragment American culture into subgroups can have the effect of jeopardizing their own empowerment, the opposite of the movement's intention. He gives the example of "Afrocentric" schooling, which he claims would only harm students enrolled in its curriculum. Despite this new interest in the "cult of ethnicity," the author is optimistic that it is of limited effect. He claims that most Americans still strive toward unity and identify themselves as Americans first, members of ethnic or racial groups second. He buttresses this belief by explaining that intermarriage is growing across racial, religious, and ethnic lines. This striving toward unity and identification with America among groups is particularly important today since their diversity is continuously increasing.

## Quoting

Sayings and adages are extremely popular. You find them quoted in everyday speech, printed in calendars, rendered in calligraphy and framed and hung in homes, and spoken by public figures. These are, in effect, direct quotes, although the authors may be anonymous. Direct quotations often have a unique power because they capture the essence of an idea accurately and briefly. Another reason is that they are stylistically powerful. You may find in an essay a sentence or group of sentences that are worded so elegantly that you simply wish to savor them for yourself or plan to use them appropriately in a future writing assignment. Other times, you may wish to use direct quotations to demonstrate to a reader the effectiveness of an original essay or the authoritative voice of the author. And still other times, it may be necessary to quote an author because her or his vocabulary simply cannot be changed without injuring the meaning of the original. Review the following quotations taken from the Schlesinger essay, and consider how paraphrasing them would diminish their rhetorical power.

### Direct Quotations That Reflect the Conciseness of the Original
"The history of the world has been in great part the history of the mixing of peoples."

"On every side today ethnicity is breaking up nations."

"And if separatist tendencies go unchecked, the result can only be the fragmentation, resegregation and tribalization of American life."

### Direct Quotations That Have Particular Stylistic Strength
"The pot did not melt everybody."

"The balance is shifting from *unum* to *pluribus*."

### Direct Quotations That Establish the Writer's Authority

"The point of America was not to preserve old cultures but to forge a new, American culture. 'By an intermixture with our people,' President George Washington told Vice President John Adams, immigrants will 'get assimilated to our customs, measures and laws: in a word, soon become one people.'"

"A notable indicator today is the rate of intermarriage across ethnic lines, across religious lines, even (increasingly) across racial lines."

### Direct Quotation That Demonstrates Conceptual Power

"The eruption of ethnicity, is, I believe, a rather superficial enthusiasm stirred by romantic ideologues on the one hand and by unscrupulous con men on the other."

## Avoiding Plagiarism

When you employ summary, paraphrase, and quotation in an essay or a re-search paper, you must avoid *plagiarism*—the attempt to pass off the work of others as your own. The temptation to plagiarize is not only one of the oldest "crimes" in academe but also an unfortunate by-product of the computer revo-lution, for there are numerous opportunities for harried, enterprising, or—let's face it—dishonest students to download bits of information or entire texts and appropriate them without acknowledgment. At the same time, you should be aware that numerous Web sites and software programs allow your instructors to locate even the most inventive forms of plagiarism—right down to words and phrases—and that when writing research papers you may be required to attach all downloaded materials. Be warned: College teachers treat plagiarism as academic treason. If you plagiarize, you can fail a course, be suspended from college, and even be expelled.

We will treat plagiarism in greater detail in Chapter 3, which presents in-formation on writing research papers. For now, you can avoid plagiarism by following these basic rules:

- Cite (provide a reference for) all quoted, summarized, or paraphrased information in your paper, unless that information is commonly under-stood. (For example, you would not have to cite the information that two planes flew into the World Trade Center on September 11, 2001, because it is common knowledge.)
- Cite all special phrases or unique stylistic expressions that you derive from another writer's work. You might love a phrase by one of the famous writers in this book—say, E. B. White or Virginia Woolf—but that writer invented it, and it belongs to him or her. You cannot employ it without acknowledging the source.
- Work hard to summarize and paraphrase material in your own words. Constantly check your language and sentence structure against the

language and syntax in the source that you are using. If your words and sentences are too close to the original, change them.

Finally, it is perfectly legitimate to ask your instructor or a tutor in your college's writing center to look at your draft and render a verdict on any information you have summarized, paraphrased, or quoted. Whether this material has been taken intentionally or unintentionally from another source is immaterial. It is your responsibility to present honest written work.

| www.mhhe.com/ **mhreader** | For an interactive tutorial on avoiding plagiarism, go to: **Research > Avoiding Plagiarism** |

## Synthesis: Drawing Connections from Texts

The ability to summarize, paraphrase, or quote from a single source prepares you for successful academic reading and writing. However, critical reading in college courses typically requires you to think about relationships between and among essays, newspaper articles, sections in textbooks, research findings, interviews, or other types of texts. If, for example, your instructor assigns a block of essays, you probably will need to infer relationships among these texts. We call this process of inferring relationships among various works *synthesis*: drawing connections from two or more written or nonwritten sources.

You are probably already familiar with synthesis as an academic exercise. The act of reading two or more texts naturally prompts you to consider connections that link types of evidence, various ideas, or competing arguments. When you employ synthesis, you build strength in academic prose, skillfully condensing and connecting information, ideas, and arguments drawn from more than one text.

Any paper drawing on two or more sources requires you to construct relationships among materials that you quote, summarize, or paraphrase. (Remember that reading and writing are intimately connected, overlapping processes.) Suppose you paraphrase two complex passages from two texts. At the first level of critical response, you make the passages more intelligible. Then, at the next level, you convey the *essence* of the relationship between these two sources— whether it relates to the thesis or central argument, the accuracy of the data, or the structuring of materials.

In the process of synthesizing sources, you will often make judgments and arrive at conclusions about the validity of the information or arguments under consideration. In other words, you *critique* the texts—offering formalized, critical readings that express both your understanding of passages and your assessment of their content. With synthesis, what begins as an isolated moment (critically reading a single text) spirals into a series of moments (reading several texts), which demands your powers of comparative analysis and well-developed ability to evaluate relationships among sources.

**The Art of Synthesis**   With synthesis, you enter into a conversation with two or more writers, attempting to understand their main ideas or arguments, analyze the evidence they provide, and evaluate their conclusions. As with any academic conversation, you must present the writers' ideas with accuracy and respect—but also with an eye to the purpose or aim of your own writing. The noted writer and composition specialist Peter Elbow (see his essay in this chapter) calls this attempt to present fairly the ideas of other writers "the believing game." In other words, you enter into the minds of other writers in order to appreciate their ideas and critical perspectives, but you do not suspend your own beliefs or lose yourself entirely in the believing game. After all, you too have a specific purpose in writing: you merely want to exercise a degree of understanding and fairness as you synthesize the ideas of others.

It is relatively easy to consider two or more sources objectively when you use synthesis to explain the authors' ideas. (*Explanatory synthesis* is one of the two main types of synthesis. The second type, *argumentative synthesis,* will be treated briefly in this chapter and more fully in Chapter 2.) With explanatory synthesis, your purpose is to convey information using the tools of summary, paraphrase, and quotation to emphasize those aspects of certain texts that you find useful in constructing your own essay. In a sense, you are detached and objective, an observer or conveyer of information. Your purpose in using explanatory synthesis is to inform.

To illustrate the way that explanatory synthesis interweaves information from two sources, consider the following passage, which draws on essays by Peter Elbow and Donald Murray appearing in this chapter:

Both Peter Elbow and Donald Murray stress the importance of process in the craft of composition, but approach the process from different perspectives. For Elbow, freewriting or "automatic writing" is the best way to improve writing. Write for ten minutes or more without stopping to edit material, Elbow declares. On the other hand, Murray states that any first draft, whether it involves freewriting or any strategy, is not the essence of composition. Instead, Murray emphasizes that a first draft is only the "start of the writing process. When a draft is completed, the job of writing can begin." For Murray, revision stands at the center of the writing process.

Here the writer hints in the first sentence that her own agenda in providing this synthesis is to review at least two different theories of composition. But in synthesizing the ideas of Elbow and Murray at this point, she essentially wants to convey information objectively without necessarily agreeing or disagreeing with the writers' approaches or claims. Using paraphrase and quotation to construct her synthesis, she fairly, accurately, and objectively offers a baseline explanation of the theories of two prominent figures in the field of composition studies. The art of explanatory synthesis is to offer a balanced summary of two or more passages or complete texts without injecting too much of your own response into the materials.

With *argumentative synthesis,* your conversation or dialogue with other writers shifts from objective explanation to the use of source material to bolster your own *claim*—a major proposition or conclusion that other readers can agree or disagree with. You still might have to explain what others have said, but now you want to give a fair hearing to their arguments over a shared issue or topic while at the same time staking out your own position on the matter. To support your claim, you seek *evidence* (facts and expert opinions) from relevant sources, analyze and evaluate the merits of that evidence, and use it to support your own argument.

Suppose, for an introductory social science or economics course, you plan to argue that globalization has caused the dislocation of many factory workers in the United States. Clearly, this is a complex issue that can be argued from various perspectives—not just from pro/con viewpoints but from more nuanced positions. Of course, the issue of globalization is very broad; you will need to refine the focus and limit the topic, perhaps by concentrating on just one industry or one state or region. The clearer you are about the parameters of your topic and claim, the easier it will be to locate and synthesize those sources that will provide support for your argument.

When you use argumentative synthesis, try to locate expert testimony, reliable sources, and verifiable types of evidence to reinforce your claim. Use this evidence so that it informs and strengthens your viewpoint. At the same time, you should acknowledge alternative viewpoints, for one feature of successful argument is the willingness to present and refute opposing claims. The challenge is to use any evidence that strengthens your text—but not at the risk of misrepresenting another writer's position or engaging in a biased or unfair presentation of the evidence.

### Guidelines for Synthesis

1. *Consider your purpose.* Is your purpose to *explain* or to *argue*—or perhaps a combination of both? How will this purpose affect your search for sources?

2. *Select and identify your sources.* Where did the article first appear, and what might this publication tell you about the writer's perspective? Identify the author, noting his or her credentials, publications, and occupation. How does the title or subtitle reveal the writer's purpose? Does the title seem to conform to your own purpose? Why or why not?

3. *Read critically and actively.* Follow the steps and procedures outlined on pages 3–4. What is the writer's primary purpose? What is the main idea or argument? What are the minor points? How do the subpoints relate to the central point? What is the structure of the text—the introduction, middle sections, and conclusion? How does the text reinforce a key idea that you may have in mind for an essay?

4. *Take notes and summarize.* Use the techniques of annotation illustrated on pages 6–7. Identify the writer's main point and write it out in one or two sentences.

5. *Establish connections among readings.* What relationships do you detect as you move from text to text? How do major and minor points stressed by

the writers in their texts overlap or diverge? What elements of their arguments are similar and dissimilar? (Draw up a list of similar and dissimilar
points for handy reference.)

6. *Write your synthesis.* First, write down your main point (*thesis*) or argument (*claim*), and develop it in an introductory paragraph. Next, draft body
or middle paragraphs that offer support for the thesis or claim; write topic
sentences for all paragraphs; incorporate explanatory or argumentative details drawn from the sources that you synthesize; and document your
sources properly in order to avoid any charge of plagiarism. Finally, write
a conclusion that grows organically from the preceding paragraphs and
reinforces your main idea. And then revise your essay. (*Note:* You can find
information on the writing process, techniques of argumentation, and strategies for research in the pages and chapters that follow in Part 1.)

# Case Study for Synthesis
## ACKNOWLEDGING AND ESCAPING INFLUENCE

The question of "influence" often arises in literary and cultural criticism. We ask: How does a writer both acknowledge and escape from his or her predecessors and their work? As you read the two essays that follow—one by a classic author, Virginia Woolf, and the other by a contemporary writer, Annie Dillard—focus on the ways in which Woolf's "The Death of the Moth" influences Dillard's approach to the same subject in "The Death of a Moth."

# The Death of the Moth

### Virginia Woolf

*Virginia Woolf (1882–1941), English novelist and essayist, was the daughter of Sir Leslie Stephen, a famous critic and writer on economics. An experimental novelist, Woolf attempted to portray consciousness through a poetic, symbolic, and concrete style. Her novels include* Jacob's Room *(1922),* Mrs. Dalloway *(1925),* To the Lighthouse *(1927), and* The Waves *(1931). She was also a perceptive reader and critic, and her criticism appears in* The Common Reader *(1925) and* The Second Common Reader *(1933). The following essay, which demonstrates Woolf's capacity to find profound meaning even in commonplace events, appeared in* The Death of the Moth and Other Essays *(1942).*

Moths that fly by day are not properly to be called moths; they do not excite 1 that pleasant sense of dark autumn nights and ivy-blossom which the commonest yellow-underwing asleep in the shadow of the curtain never fails to rouse in us. They are hybrid creatures, neither gay like butterflies nor somber like their own species. Nevertheless the present specimen, with his narrow hay-colored wings, fringed with a tassel of the same color, seemed to be content with life. It was a pleasant morning, mid-September, mild, benignant, yet with a keener breath than that of the summer months. The plough was already scoring the field opposite the window, and where the share had been, the earth was pressed flat and gleamed with moisture. Such vigor came rolling in from the fields and the down beyond that it was difficult to keep the eyes strictly turned upon the book. The rooks too were keeping one of their annual festivities; soaring round the tree tops until it looked as if a vast net with thousands of black knots in it had been cast up into the air; which, after a few moments sank slowly down

21

upon the trees until every twig seemed to have a knot at the end of it. Then, suddenly, the net would be thrown into the air again in a wider circle this time, with the utmost clamor and vociferation, as though to be thrown into the air and settle down upon the tree tops were a tremendously exciting experience.

2      The same energy which inspired the rooks, the ploughmen, the horses, and even, it seemed, the lean bare-backed downs, sent the moth fluttering from side to side of this square of the windowpane. One could not help watching him. One was, indeed, conscious of a queer feeling of pity for him. The possibilities of pleasure seemed that morning so enormous and so various that to have only a moth's part in life, and a day moth's at that, appeared a hard fate, and his zest in enjoying his meager opportunities to the full, pathetic. He flew vigorously to one corner of his compartment, and, after waiting there a second, flew across to the other. What remained for him but to fly to a third corner and then to a fourth? That was all he could do, in spite of the size of the downs, the width of the sky, the far-off smoke of houses, and the romantic voice, now and then, of a steamer out at sea. What he could do he did. Watching him, it seemed as if a fibre, very thin but pure, of the enormous energy of the world had been thrust into his frail and diminutive body. As often as he crossed the pane, I could fancy that a thread of vital light became visible. He was little or nothing but life.

3      Yet, because he was so small, and so simple a form of the energy that was rolling in at the open window and driving its way through so many narrow and intricate corridors in my own brain and in those of other human beings, there was something marvelous as well as pathetic about him. It was as if someone had taken a tiny bead of pure life and decking it as lightly as possible with down and feathers, had set it dancing and zigzagging to show us the true nature of life. Thus displayed one could not get over the strangeness of it. One is apt to forget all about life, seeing it humped and bossed and garnished and cumbered so that it has to move with the greatest circumspection and dignity. Again, the thought of all that life might have been had he been born in any other shape caused one to view his simple activities with a kind of pity.

4      After a time, tired by his dancing apparently, he settled on the window ledge in the sun, and, the queer spectacle being at an end, I forgot about him. Then, looking up, my eye was caught by him. He was trying to resume his dancing, but seemed either so stiff or so awkward that he could only flutter to the bottom of the windowpane; and when he tried to fly across it he failed. Being intent on other matters I watched these futile attempts for a time without thinking, unconsciously waiting for him to resume his flight, as one waits for a machine, that has stopped momentarily, to start again without considering the reason of its failure. After perhaps a seventh attempt he slipped from the wooden ledge and fell, fluttering his wings, on to his back on the window sill. The helplessness of his attitude roused me. It flashed upon me that he was in difficulties; he could no longer raise himself; his legs struggled vainly. But, as I stretched out a pencil, meaning to help him to right himself, it came over me that the failure and awkwardness were the approach of death. I laid the pencil down again.

The legs agitated themselves once more. I looked as if for the enemy against 5 which he struggled. I looked out of doors. What had happened there? Presumably it was midday, and work in the fields had stopped. Stillness and quiet had replaced the previous animation. The birds had taken themselves off to feed in the brooks. The horses stood still. Yet the power was there all the same, massed outside, indifferent, impersonal, not attending to anything in particular. Somehow it was opposed to the little hay-colored moth. It was useless to try to do anything. One could only watch the extraordinary efforts made by those tiny legs against an oncoming doom which could, had it chosen, have submerged an entire city, not merely a city, but masses of human beings; nothing, I knew, had any chance against death. Nevertheless after a pause of exhaustion the legs fluttered again. It was superb this last protest, and so frantic that he succeeded at last in righting himself. One's sympathies, of course, were all on the side of life. Also, when there was nobody to care or to know, this gigantic effort on the part of an insignificant little moth, against a power of such magnitude, to retain what no one else valued or desired to keep, moved one strangely. Again, somehow, one saw life, a pure bead. I lifted the pencil again, useless though I knew it to be. But even as I did so, the unmistakable tokens of death showed themselves. The body relaxed, and instantly grew stiff. The struggle was over. The insignificant little creature now knew death. As I looked at the dead moth, this minute wayside triumph of so great a force over so mean an antagonist filled me with wonder. Just as life had been strange a few minutes before, so death was now as strange. The moth having righted himself now lay most decently and uncomplainingly composed. O yes, he seemed to say, death is stronger than I am.

## COMPREHENSION

1. Why is Woolf so moved by the moth's death? Why does she call the moth's protest "superb" (paragraph 5)?
2. What, according to Woolf, is the "true nature of life" (paragraph 3)?
3. What paradox is inherent in the death of the moth?

## RHETORIC

1. Examine Woolf's use of simile in paragraph 1. Where else in the essay does she use similes? Are any of them similar to the similes used in paragraph 1?
2. Why does Woolf personify the moth?
3. What sentences constitute the introduction of this essay? What rhetorical device do they use?
4. Divide the essay into two parts. Now explain why you divided the essay where you did. How are the two parts different? How are they similar?
5. Explain the importance of description in this essay. Where, particularly, does Woolf describe the setting of her scene? How does that description

contribute to the development of her essay? How does she describe the
moth, and how does this description affect tone?

**6.** How is narration used to structure the essay?

## WRITING

**1.** Woolf implicitly connects insect and human life. What else can we learn
about human development by looking at other forms of life? Analyze this
connection in an essay.

**2.** Write a detailed description of a small animal. Try to invest it with the importance that Woolf gives her moth.

**3.** **Writing an Argument:** Write a rebuttal of this essay, explaining why a moth,
or any other insect or animal, can tell us nothing about the human condition.

 **www.mhhe.com/ mhreader**       For more information on Virginia Woolf, go to:
**More Resources > Ch. 1 Reading & Writing**

# The Death of a Moth

### Annie Dillard

*Annie Dillard (b. 1945) was born in Pittsburgh and received her BA and MA degrees
from Hollins College in Roanoke, Virginia. Her first book,* Pilgrim at Tinker Creek, *won
the 1975 Pulitzer Prize for general nonfiction. Other published works of nonfiction include*
Teaching a Stone to Talk *(1982),* An American Childhood *(1987), and* The Writing
Life *(1989). She expanded her range of writing with a novel,* The Living *(1992), and
again with her most recent novel,* The Maytrees *(2007). She has received awards from the
National Endowment for the Arts and the Guggenheim Foundation as well as many other
sources. As an essayist, poet, memoirist, and literary critic, Dillard focuses on the relationships among the self, nature, religion, and faith. Her writing is recognizable by its observations on the minutia of life and its search for meaning in places as unlikely as a stone or an
insect. In this essay, Dillard works a variation on Virginia Woolf's title in order to create
a meditation on the process of creation and the nature of solitude.*

1   I live alone with two cats, who sleep on my legs. There is a yellow one, and a
black one whose name is Small. In the morning I joke to the black one, Do you
remember last night? Do you remember? I throw them both out before breakfast, so I can eat.

There is a spider, too, in the bathroom, of uncertain lineage, bulbous at the   2
abdomen and drab, whose six-inch mess of web works, works somehow, works
miraculously, to keep her alive and me amazed. The web is in a corner behind
the toilet, connecting tile wall to tile wall. The house is new, the bathroom im-
maculate, save for the spider, her web, and the sixteen or so corpses she's tossed
to the floor.

The corpses appear to be mostly sow bugs, those little armadillo creatures   3
who live to travel flat out in houses, and die round. In addition to sow-bug
husks, hollow and sipped empty of color, there are what seem to be two or
three wingless moth bodies, one new flake of earwig, and three spider carcasses
crinkled and clenched.

I wonder on what fool's errand an earwig, or a moth, or a sow bug, would   4
visit that clean corner of the house behind the toilet; I have not noticed any
blind parades of sow bugs blundering into corners. Yet they do hazard there, at
a rate of more than one a week, and the spider thrives. Yesterday she was working on the earwig, mouth on gut; today he's on the floor. It must take a certain
genius to throw things away from there, to find a straight line through that
sticky tangle to the floor.

Today the earwig shines darkly, and gleams, what there is of him: a dorsal   5
curve of thorax and abdomen, and a smooth pair of pincers by which I knew
his name. Next week, if the other bodies are any indication, he'll be shrunk and
gray, webbed to the floor with dust. The sow bugs beside him are curled and
empty, fragile, a breath away from brittle fluff. The spiders lie on their sides,
translucent and ragged, their legs drying in knots. The moths stagger against
each other, headless, in a confusion of arcing strips of chitin like peeling varnish, like a jumble of buttresses for cathedral vaults, like nothing resembling
moths, so that I would hesitate to call them moths, except that I have had some
experience with the figure Moth reduced to a nub.

Two summers ago I was camped alone in the Blue Ridge Mountains of Virginia.   6
I had hauled myself and gear up there to read, among other things, *The Day on
Fire*, by James Ullman, a novel about Rimbaud that had made me want to be a
writer when I was sixteen; I was hoping it would do it again. So I read every day
sitting under a tree by my tent, while warblers sang in the leaves overhead and
bristle worms trailed their inches over the twiggy dirt at my feet; and I read every
night by candlelight, while barred owls called in the forest and pale moths seeking
mates massed round my head in the clearing, where my light made a ring.

Moths kept flying into the candle. They would hiss and recoil, reeling up-   7
side down in the shadows among my cooking pans. Or they would singe their
wings and fall, and their hot wings, as if melted, would stick to the first thing
they touched—a pan, a lid, a spoon—so that the snagged moths could struggle
only in tiny arcs, unable to flutter free. These I could release by a quick flip with
a stick; in the morning I would find my cooking stuff decorated with torn flecks
of moth wings, ghostly triangles of shiny dust here and there on the aluminum.
So I read, and boiled water, and replenished candles, and read on.

8    One night a moth flew into the candle, was caught, burnt dry, and held. I must have been staring at the candle, or maybe I looked up when a shadow crossed my page; at any rate, I saw it all. A golden female moth, a biggish one with a two-inch wingspread, flapped into the fire, dropped abdomen into the wet wax, stuck, flamed, and frazzled in a second. Her moving wings ignited like tissue paper, like angels' wings, enlarging the circle of light in the clearing and creating out of the darkness the sudden blue sleeves of my sweater, the green leaves of jewelweed by my side, the ragged red trunk of a pine; at once the light contracted again and the moth's wings vanished in a fine, foul smoke. At the same time, her six legs clawed, curled, blackened, and ceased, disappearing utterly. And her head jerked in spasms, making a spattering noise; her antennae crisped and burnt away and her heaving mouthparts cracked like pistol fire. When it was all over, her head was, so far as I could determine, gone, gone the long way of her wings and legs. Her head was a hole lost to time. All that was left was the glowing horn shell of her abdomen and thorax—a fraying, partially collapsed gold tube jammed upright in the candle's round pool.

9    And then this moth-essence, this spectacular skeleton, began to act as a wick. She kept burning. The wax rose in the moth's body from her soaking abdomen to her thorax to the shattered hole where her head should have been, and widened into flame, a saffron-yellow flame that robed her to the ground like an immolating monk. That candle had two wicks, two winding flames of identical light, side by side. The moth's head was fire. She burned for two hours, until I blew her out.

10    She burned for two hours without changing, without swaying or kneeling—only glowing within, like a building fire glimpsed through silhouetted walls, like a hollow saint, like a flame-faced virgin gone to God, while I read by her light, kindled, while Rimbaud in Paris burnt out his brain in a thousand poems, while night pooled wetly at my feet.

11    So. That is why I think those hollow shreds on the bathroom floor are moths. I believe I know what moths look like, in any state.

12    I have three candles here on the table which I disentangle from the plants and light when visitors come. The cats avoid them, although Small's tail caught fire once; I rubbed it out before she noticed. I don't mind living alone. I like eating alone and reading. I don't mind sleeping alone. The only time I mind being alone is when something is funny; then, when I am laughing at something funny, I wish someone were around. Sometimes I think it is pretty funny that I sleep alone.

## COMPREHENSION

1. What is the link between the moth, its death, and Dillard's writing?
2. What is the significance of Dillard's reading material (paragraph 6) to the moth? What associations does it have?
3. Do we learn anything of Dillard's emotional response to the death of the moth? Why or why not?

# RHETORIC

1. Why do you think Dillard has written this essay?
2. How do images like "moth-essence" and "immolating monk" (in paragraph 9) help to enrich the meaning of the paragraph? What are other examples of Dillard's figurative language?
3. Comment on the use of transitions in paragraph 10 and the beginning of paragraph 11. How is repetition used effectively here? What impact does it have on the tone?
4. Note Dillard's use of similes in paragraph 10. What mood is she trying to evoke? How does the rest of the paragraph set off these images?
5. Dillard organizes this essay in three sections. What is the relationship of these sections to each other?
6. How well does Dillard's conclusion work? Does it serve to frame the essay? How does it relate to the paragraphs preceding it?

# WRITING

1. In a brief essay, explore what the moth represents to Dillard. Use support or examples from her piece to develop your theme.
2. Dillard explores the nature of solitude and introspection. In an essay, consider how the former can facilitate the latter. How do you feel about solitude? What do you think about when you're alone? Are your powers of observation and perception heightened by solitude? Is solitude at night different?
3. Have you ever witnessed the death of an insect or a small animal? How did you respond physically and emotionally? In a descriptive narrative, relate the experience and its effect on you.

www.mhhe.com/ **mhreader**

For more information on Annie Dillard, go to:
**More Resources > Ch. 1 Reading & Writing**

## Synthesis: Connections For Critical Thinking

1. Why is the moth central to the essays of Dillard and Woolf? Do the writers use the moth to symbolize the same concept? Why or why not? How does Dillard's use of a different article in her title (changing "the" in Woolf's title to "a") alter her focus and influence her analogy? Do the writers respond similarly to the moth's death? Justify your response.
2. How do Woolf and Dillard create a setting and evoke a specific mood in their essays? How do these strategies enrich and advance their respective theses?
3. What role does solitude play in establishing the writers' theses?

4.  Compare and contrast the levels of language used by Woolf and Dillard. Cite examples of their use of figurative language to enhance their narratives and advance their theses. Who is their intended audience, and how do they adjust style to this primary set of readers?
5.  In a brief essay, compare and contrast the writers' perspective on the central event—the death of the (a) moth. Does the fact that Woolf personifies the moth and attempts to rescue it reveal anything about her purpose? Does Dillard's reaction to the moth indicate a lack of compassion or philosophical depth? You might want to consider these questions in your synthesis.

## READING AND ANALYZING VISUAL TEXTS

In this new era of information technology, we seem to be immersed in a visual culture requiring us to contend with and think critically about the constant flow of images we encounter. From advertising, to film, to video, to the Internet, we must respond with increasing frequency not only to written but also to visual messages—images that typically are reinforced by verbal elements. Consequently, it is important to perceive the powerful linkages that exist in today's culture between visual and verbal experience.

Frequently in courses in engineering, social science, computer science, the humanities, fine arts, and elsewhere, you have to analyze and understand visual elements that are embedded in texts. Textbooks increasingly promote visuals as frames of reference that help readers comprehend and appreciate information. Some visual elements—charts, tables, and graphs—are integral to an understanding of verbal texts. Other visuals—comic art, drawings, photographs, paintings, and advertisements—offer contexts and occasions for enjoyment and deeper understanding of the reading, writing, and thinking processes. Visual images convey messages that often are as powerful as well-composed written texts. When they appear together, image and word are like French doors, both opening to reveal a world of heightened perception and understanding.

When visual elements stand alone, as in painting and photography, they often make profound statements about the human experience and frequently reflect certain persuasive purposes that are composed as skillfully as an argumentative essay. Consider, for example, the series that the great Spanish artist Francisco Goya painted, "The Disasters of War," a powerful statement of humankind's penchant for the most grotesque and violent cruelties. In the late 20th century, photographers of the Vietnam War, using a modern visual medium, similarly captured the pain and suffering of armed conflict, as in Eddie Adams's potent stills of the execution of a prisoner by the notorious chief of the Saigon national police, General Nguyen Ngoc Loan. In the framed sequence, the chief of police aims his pistol at the head of the prisoner and presses the trigger, and the viewer, in that captured instant, sees the jolt of the prisoner's head and a sudden spurt of blood. Reproduced widely in the American press in

February 1968, this single image did as much as any written editorial to transform the national debate over the Vietnam War. (Both images are reprinted on pages 152–153.)

Although paintings, photographs, advertisements, and other artistic and design forms that rely heavily on visual elements often function as instruments of persuasion, it would be simplistic to embrace uncritically the cliché "A picture is worth a thousand words." For instance, great literary artists from Homer to Norman Mailer have captured the horrors of war as vividly as artists in other media. Stephen Crane in *The Red Badge of Courage* illustrates the sordidness of America's Civil War in language as graphic as the images of the war's most noted photographer, Mathew Brady. Consider the visual impact of Crane's depiction of battlefield dead:

> The corpse was dressed in a uniform that once had been blue but was now faded to a melancholy shade of green. The eyes, staring at the youth, had changed to the dull hue to be seen on the side of a dead fish. The mouth was opened. Its red had changed to an appalling yellow. Over the grey skin of the face ran little ants. One was trundling some sort of a bundle along the upper lip.

Ultimately, the best verbal and visual texts construct meaning in vivid and memorable ways. When used in combination, visual and verbal texts can mix words and images to create uniquely powerful theses and arguments.

Just as you analyze or take apart a verbal text during the process of critical reading, you also have to think critically about visual images or elements. If you encounter charts, graphs, and tables in a text, you have to understand the information these visuals present, the implications of the numbers or statistics, the emphases and highlights that are conveyed, and the way the visual element—the picture, so to speak—shapes your understanding of the material and its relationship to the text. Sometimes the material presented in such visuals is technical, requiring you to carefully analyze, say, a bar graph: its structure, the relationship of parts to the whole, the assertions that are advanced, and the validity of the evidence conveyed. In short, critical reading of visual material is as demanding as critical reading of the printed word. Just as you often have to reread a verbal text, you also might have to return to charts, graphs, and tables, perhaps from a fresh perspective, in order to comprehend the content of the visual text.

The following questions can guide your critical analysis of such visual texts as charts, graphs, and tables:

- What is the design or structure of the visual?
- What information do you immediately notice?
- What is the purpose of the visual?
- What thesis or point of view does the information in the visual suggest?
- What is the nature of the evidence, and how can it be verified?
- What emphases and relationships do you detect among the visual details?
- How does the visual fit into the context of the verbal text surrounding it?

# Classic and Contemporary Images
## HOW DO WE COMMUNICATE?

*Using a Critical Perspective*   Carefully examine these two illustrations. What is your overall impression of these images? What details and objects in each scene capture your attention? What similarities and differences do you detect? How does each image communicate ideas and values about the culture that has produced it? Does one appeal to you more than the other? Why or why not?

Pulitzer Prize–winning combat photographer Joe Rosenthal captured this scene of U.S. Marines raising the American flag on the Pacific Island of Iwo Jima on February 25, 1945. The campaign to capture the island from Japanese troops cost nearly 7,000 American lives. Rosenthal's photo has been reproduced widely in the media and served as the model for the Marine Corps War Memorial in Washington, D.C.

Photographer Thomas E. Franklin captured a memorable moment in the wake of the terrorist attack on the World Trade Center in New York City in September 2001.

When responding to charts, tables, and graphs, you must develop the confidence to read such visual texts accurately and critically. This means taking nothing for granted and trusting your ability to sift through the evidence and the images with a critical eye in order to understand the strategies the author or graphic artist has employed to convey a specific message.

By and large, informative visuals such as tables and graphs rarely have the striking impact of the sort of graphics found in the best commercial and political advertising or in the illustrations we encounter in slick magazines or cutting-edge comic strips. The visual elements used by advertisers, for example, take advantage of our innate capacity to be affected by symbols—McDonald's Golden Arch, the president framed by American flags, a bottle of Coca-Cola beneath the word *America*. Such visual emblems convey unspoken ideas and have enormous power to promote products, personalities, and ideas. For example, the two powerful images on pages 30–31 convey important ideas about the cultures that produced them. Visual symbols achieve even more intense effects when they are reinforced by verbal elements.

When viewing art reproductions, photographs, advertisements, and cartoons from a critical perspective, you often have to detect the explicit and implicit messages being conveyed by certain images and symbols, and the design strategies that condition your response. Because these visuals combine many different elements, you have to consider all critical details: color, light, and shadow; the number and arrangement of objects and the relationships among them; the foregrounding and backgrounding of images within the frame; the impact of typography; the impact of language if it is employed; and the inferences and values that you draw from the overall composition. Learn to treat visuals in any medium as texts that need to be "read" critically. Every visual requires its own form of annotation, in which you analyze the selection and ordering of its parts and interpret the emotional effects and significant ideas and messages it presents. Throughout this text, paired "classic and contemporary" images such as the two on pages 30–31 give you opportunities to read visual texts with a critical eye.

## THE WRITING PROCESS

Whether you have been provided an assignment by your instructor or developed your own topic, the various tools for critical reading and analysis that you have mastered should now equip you with the foundation for what is necessary to embark on your own writing assignment. Essays are normally a three-part writing process: prewriting, drafting, and revising. To illuminate the writing process, we will examine strategies employed by several student and professional writers, including one student, Jamie Taylor, as she read and responded to Schlesinger. But first we require an overview of the writing process, starting with the origins and development of a writer's ideas.

Annie Dillard, one of today's preeminent essayists, stresses the primacy of the creative imagination in the writing process. Dillard uses the central metaphor of building a house to describe the three stages in the writing process: prewriting ("The line of words is a miner's pick, a woodcarver's gouge, a surgeon's probe. You wield it, and it digs a path you follow"), drafting ("You lay down the words carefully, watching all the angles"), and revising ("The part you must jettison is not only the best-written part; it is also, oddly, the part which was to have been the very point").

Think of the process of writing as a craft involving the planning, transcribing, polishing, and production of a text for an audience. In Old English, the word *craft* signifies strength and power. By treating writing as a craft, you empower yourself to make the most complex compositional tasks manageable. By thinking of the writing process habit of mind involving prewriting, writing, and revision, you can create effective essays and documents.

## Prewriting

Prewriting, which you have already been engaged in as you negotiated the reading-writing connection, is the discovery, exploration, and planning stage of the composing process. It is the stage in which you discover a reason to write, select and narrow a subject, consider audience and purpose, and engage in preliminary writing activities designed to generate textual material. During the prewriting process, you are free to let ideas incubate, to let thoughts and writing strategies ripen. You are also free to get in the mood to write. Ernest Hemingway used to sharpen all his pencils as preparation for a day's writing; the French philosopher Voltaire soaked his feet in cold water to get the creative juices flowing. Professional writers understand the importance of prewriting activities in the composing process, but college writers often undervalue or ignore them completely.

**Considering Purpose and Audience**   Any writing situation requires you to make choices and decisions about purpose, audience, planning, writing, revision, and transmission of your text. Determining your purpose or goal—the reason you are writing—at the outset of the composing process is one of the first steps. It prevents you from expending useless energy on thinking that is ultimately unimportant, misdirected, or unrelated to the problem because it forces you to ask, What do I hope to obtain from this text? With a specific purpose in mind, you start to anticipate the type of composing task ahead of you and to identify the problems that might be inherent in this task.

Traditionally, the main forms of writing—narration, description, exposition, and argumentation—help to guide or mold your purpose.

| Form | Purpose | Example |
|------|---------|---------|
| Narration | To relate a sequence of events | To tell about an accident |
| Description | To provide a picture or produce an impression | To describe a moth |
| Exposition | To explain, inform, or analyze | To compare two teachers |
| Argumentation | To convince or persuade | To oppose abortion |

Most writing actually combines more than one of these rhetorical modes or forms, but these basic categories help shape your text to a specific purpose.

Even as you determine your purpose, you must also create common ground between yourself and your audience. In fact, to define your audience is to define part of your problem. Think of your audience as the readers of your text. What do they know about the topic? How do they perceive you—your status, expertise, and credibility? In turn, what do you know about their opinions and backgrounds? Are they likely to agree or disagree with you? (This last question is especially important in argumentative writing, which will be discussed in the next chapter.) By defining your audience carefully, you can begin to tailor your text. Only by analyzing your readership will you be able to appeal to an audience.

**Freewriting and Brainstorming**   Two methods of getting in touch with what you already know or believe are freewriting and brainstorming. Freewriting is quite simple. Merely select a predetermined amount of time, say, from 5 to 15 minutes, and write down everything that you can think of regarding the subject at hand. Don't worry about punctuation or grammar. This activity is mainly to get your cognitive wheels rolling. Brainstorming is a variant of freewriting in which you jot down ideas and questions, often in numbered form. If you find freewriting and brainstorming helpful as techniques, you will probably find the length of time that suits you best. When you have finished, review what you have written. A well-known composition expert, Peter Elbow, explains the value of freewriting in the selection starting on page 68. The freewriting that Elbow describes can help any writer generate ideas, but freewriting and brainstorming can also help writers respond to others' ideas. For example, examine the following freewriting and brainstorming exercises by a student, James Moore, which he wrote after reading an excerpt from Schlesinger's "The Cult of Ethnicity."

### Freewriting Sample

This essay shows that the author really knows his history because he cites so many historical figures, places, and can quote word for word authorities that back up his argument. He makes a great argument that America's strength is in its diversity and at the same time its unity. I never thought of these two things as being able to complement one another. I always thought of them as being separate. It opens my mind to a whole new way of thinking. One thing that would have strengthened his argument, though, is the fact that although he criticizes people who want to separate themselves into subgroups, he doesn't really mention them by name. He's great when it comes to advancing his own argument but he seems to be a bit too general when he comes to attacking the opposition. I would have liked it if he had mentioned by name people who are undermining America's strengths and listen in their own words.

### Brainstorming Sample

1. The author says that ideological conflict isn't such a big problem, but what about the gap between rich and poor? Maybe if there were less of a gap, people wouldn't look for "false idols."

2. Schlesinger seems to be part of the white mainstream. Does this mean he is destined not to understand fully the reasons why people on the margins of society get so tempted to join "cults"?

3. He uses supporting points very well but doesn't exactly explain why "multiculturalism" and "political correctness" are happening now in our society. What is it about today that has opened the door to these ideas?

4. There are so many references to places with ethnic tensions around the world. It would be great to study one of them and see if they have any similarities to the ones that exist in the United States.

5. He seems to be writing for a very educated audience. I wonder really if he can reach the "common person" with this kind of sophisticated writing. I don't know about most of the places he mentions.

6. What's the solution? That could be the start of a topic for my paper. I don't think the author offers any.

Let's consider the benefits these processes can have. First, you can comment on the subject matter of the essay without censoring your thoughts. This prepares you for the second reading by marshaling a more coherent idea of your own perspective. Freewriting or brainstorming can be a tool that helps you understand how you can have something to contribute in the writer-reader "conversation" or helps you see a topic in a new way. For example, in the freewriting example, Moore discovered for himself the idea that the strength of American society is a combination of commonality and diversity. Second, during the brainstorming process, you might come up with a potential idea for a response essay, as the student did in the example.

Now let us return to the prewriting process that Jamie Taylor followed.

### Brainstorming Notes

1. Schlesinger seems to be saying that multiculturalism poses a danger because it threatens to create ethnic divisiveness rather than healthy identification.

2. This not only undermines us now, but threatens the very democratic principles upon which the United States was founded.

3. He says America must set an example for the rest of the world, which is torn with racial and ethnic strife.

4. He believes that there is a small group of individuals with a "hidden agenda" who are trying to create this divisiveness. These individuals are self-centered and have their own interests at heart, not the interests of the people they represent.

5. One flaw in the essay was that it seemed vague. He didn't mention any names or give specific examples. Only generalities.

6. He suggests the "battle" will be won by ordinary citizens; for example, he cites the many intermarriages occurring today.

7. Although he sees danger, he is optimistic because he thinks democracy is a strong institution.

8. He writes from a position of authority. He cites many historical figures and seems very well read.

9. The major problem I see in his essay is that he seems to lump everyone together in the same boat. He doesn't give enough credit to the average person to see through the hollowness of false idols. You don't need a Ph.D. to see the silliness of so many ideas floating around out there.

10. So many things to consider, how should I focus my essay??? What should be my theme??

11. Hmmm. Idea!!! Since I agree with his basic points, but find he doesn't provide specifics, and doesn't give the average person enough credit to see through the emptiness of cult rhetoric, why not use my personal observations to write a response paper in which I show just how reasonable we are in distinguishing mere rhetoric from substance?

**Outlining**   In addition to this brainstorming, Taylor developed a scratch outline—yet another prewriting strategy—to guide her into the drafting stage of the composing process.

### Outline
  I. Introduction: Summarize essay and thesis; provide counterthesis.
  II. University life as a demonstration of "ethnic" democracies.
  III. The emptiness and false promises of self-styled ethnic leaders.
  IV. The rejection of "home-grown" cults.
  V. Conclusion.

Although Taylor employed brainstorming and a scratch outline to organize her thoughts prior to writing her essay, not everyone uses these prewriting activities. Some students need to go through a series of prewriting activities, while others can dive into a first draft. Nevertheless, the process of discovering the materials and form for an essay includes a search for ideas, a willingness to discard ideas and strategies that don't work, an ability to look at old ideas in a fresh way, and a talent for moving back and forth across a range of composing activities. Rarely does that flash of insight or first draft produce the ideal flow of words resulting in a well-written and well-ordered essay.

Professional writers have their own unique approaches to the composing process. For example, Annie Dillard is a prolific keeper of journals, from which she extracts ideas for essays and books. She also jots down notes, often in rough outline form. Here are some notes she jotted down, based on journal entries, for her essay "The Death of a Moth."

Moth in candle:
the poet—materials of world, of bare earth at feet, sucked up, transformed,
    subsumed to spirit, to air, to light
the mystic—not through reason, but through emptiness
the martyr—virgin, sacrifice, death with meaning.

Her "moth essay," as she calls it, evolved from journal entries, doodles, and several drafts, and then fit into a much larger book that she was writing.

For more information on prewriting strategies, go to:
**Writing > Prewriting**

## Drafting

Everyone approaches the composing process differently. There are, however, certain basic principles for the drafting stage that you must consider. These principles are discussed in the following sections.

**Developing the Thesis**    Every essay requires a main idea or thesis that holds all your information together. What you seek is not just any idea relevant to the bulk of your topic, but the underlying idea that best expresses your purpose in writing the essay. Your thesis is the controlling idea for the entire essay.

The thesis requires you to take a stand on your topic. It is your reason for wanting to inform or persuade an audience. The noted teacher and scholar Sheridan Baker has expressed nicely this need to take a stand or assume an angle of interpretation: "When you have something to say about *cats*, you have found your underlying idea. You have something to fight about: not just 'Cats,' but 'The cat is really man's best friend.'" Not all thesis statements involve arguments or fights. Nevertheless, you cannot have a thesis unless you have something to demonstrate or prove.

The thesis statement, which normally appears as a single sentence near the beginning of your essay, serves several important functions:

- It introduces the topic to the reader.
- It limits the topic to a single idea.
- It expresses your approach to the topic—the opinion, attitude, or outlook that creates your special angle of interpretation for the topic.
- It may provide the reader with hints about the way the essay will develop.
- It should arouse the reader's interest by revealing your originality and your honest commitment to the topic.

Here is a typical thesis statement by a student:

*The automobile—America's metallic monster—takes up important public space, pollutes the environment, and makes people lazy, rude, and overweight.*

In this thesis, the writer has staked out a position, limited the topic, and given the reader some idea of how the essay will develop.

Your thesis cannot always be captured in a single sentence. Indeed, professional writers often offer an implied or unstated thesis or articulate a thesis statement that permeates an entire paragraph. Basically, you should ask if a thesis hooks you. Do you find it provocative? Do you know where the author is coming from? Does the author offer a map for the entire essay? These are some of the issues that you should consider as you compose your own thesis sentences.

www.mhhe.com/
**mhreader**

For more information on developing a thesis, go to:
**Writing > Thesis**

**Writing Introductory Paragraphs**   Your introduction should be like a door opening into the world of your essay. A good introduction entices readers into this world by arousing their curiosity about the topic and thesis with carefully chosen material and through a variety of techniques. The introduction, normally a single paragraph composed of a few sentences, serves several important functions:

- It introduces the topic.
- It states the writer's attitude toward the subject, normally in the form of a thesis statement.
- It offers readers a guide to the essay.
- It draws readers into the topic through a variety of techniques.

A solid introduction informs, orients, interests, and engages the audience. "Beginnings," wrote the English novelist George Eliot, "are always troublesome." Getting the introduction just right takes effort, considerable powers of invention, and often several revisions. Fortunately, there are special strategies that make effective introductions possible:

- Use a subject-clarification-thesis format. Present the essay's general subject, clarify and explain the topic briefly, and then present your attitude toward the topic in a thesis statement.
- Offer a brief story or incident that sets the stage for your topic and frames your thesis.
- Start with a shocking, controversial, or intriguing opinion.
- Begin with a comparison or contrast.
- Use a quotation or reference to clarify and illustrate your topic and thesis.
- Ask a question or series of questions directed toward establishing your thesis.
- Offer several relevant examples to support your thesis.
- Begin with a vivid description that supports your main idea.
- Cite a statistic or provide data.
- Correct a false assumption.

All these strategies should introduce your topic and state the thesis of the essay. They should be relatively brief and should direct the reader into the body of the essay. Finally, they should reveal your perspective and your tone or voice. In each introductory paragraph, the reader—your audience—should sense that you are prepared to address your topic in an honest and revealing manner.

www.mhhe.com/
**mhreader**

For more information on writing introductory paragraphs, go to:
**Writing > Introductions**

**Writing Body Paragraphs**   The body is the middle of the essay. Usually, the body consists of a series of paragraphs whose purpose is to satisfy your readers' expectations about the topic and thesis you presented in the introduction. The body of an essay gives substance, stability, and balance to your thesis. It offers facts, details, explanations, and claims supporting your main idea.

Body paragraphs reflect your ability to think critically, logically, and carefully about your topic. They are self-conscious units of expression whose indentations signal a new main point (or topic sentence) or unified and coherent unit of thought. The contour created by the series of body paragraphs that you design grows organically from the rhetorical or composing strategies that you select. As the English critic Herbert Read states in *English Prose Style,* "As thought takes shape in the mind, it takes *a* shape. . . . There is about good writing a visual actuality. It exactly reproduces what we should metaphorically call the contour of our thought. . . . The paragraph is the perception of this contour or shape." In other words, we see in the shape of an essay the shape of our thoughts. The contour created by the series of body paragraphs proceeds naturally from the material you include and the main point you use to frame this material in each paragraph.

Effective paragraph development depends on your ability to create a unit of thought that is *unified* and *coherent,* and that presents ideas that flesh out the topic sentence or controlling idea for the paragraph, thereby informing or convincing the reader. To achieve a sense of completeness as you develop body paragraphs, be sure to have enough topic sentences and sufficient examples or evidence for each key idea. College writers often have problems writing complete essays with adequately developed body paragraphs. Remember that topic sentences are relatively general ideas. Your primary task is to make readers understand what those ideas mean or why they are important. Your secondary task is to keep readers interested in those central thoughts. The only way to accomplish these two related goals is by explaining the central ideas through various kinds of evidence or support.

**Choosing Strategies for Development**   Different topics and paragraphs lend themselves to different types of development. These types of rhetorical approaches are essentially special writing and reasoning strategies designed to support your critical evaluation of a topic or hypothesis. Among the major rhetorical approaches are description, narration, illustration, process analysis, comparison and contrast, causal analysis, definition, classification, and argumentation. Each strategy might very well serve as your dominant approach to a topic. On the other hand, your essay might reflect a variety of methods. Remember, however, that any blending of rhetorical strategies should not be a random sampling of approaches but should contribute to your overall point.

*Description*   Good descriptive writing is often your best tool for explaining your observations about objects, people, scenes, and events. Simply, description is the creation of a picture using words. It is the translation of what the writer sees into what the writer wants the reader to imagine. Description has many applications in academic courses. For example, for a psychology course, you might need to describe the behavior of an autistic child. At an archeological dig or site, you might need to indicate accurately how a section of the excavated area looks. In a botany course, you might need to describe in detail a particular plant.

Effective description depends on several characteristics:

- It conveys ideas through images that appeal to our various senses: sight, hearing, touch, smell, and taste.
- It selects and organizes details carefully in a clearly identifiable spatial ordering—left to right, top to bottom, near to far, and so forth.
- It creates a dominant impression, a special mood or feeling.
- It is objective or subjective depending on the writer's purpose, the demands of an assignment, or the expectations of an audience.

In the following paragraph from her book *Spanish Harlem*, Patricia Cayo Sexton captures the sights, sounds, and rhythms of life in New York's East Harlem:

Later, when the children return from school, the sidewalks and streets will jump with activity. Clusters of men, sitting on orange crates on the sidewalks, will play checkers or cards. The women will sit on the stoop, arms folded, and watch the young at play; and the young men, flexing their muscles, will look for some adventure. Vendors, ringing their bells, will hawk hot dogs, orange drinks, ice cream; and the caressing but often jarring noise of honking horns, music, children's games, and casual quarrels, whistles, singing, will go on late into the night. When you are in it you don't notice the noise, but when you stand away and listen to a taped conversation, the sound suddenly appears as a background roar. This loud stimulation of the senses may produce some of the emotionalism of the poor.

*Narration*    Telling stories—or narration—is a basic pattern of organizing your thoughts. You employ narration on a daily basis—to tell what happened at work, in the cafeteria, or on Saturday night. Narration is also essential to many forms of academic writing, ranging from history, to sociology, to science. When planning and writing narration, keep in mind the following guidelines:

1. Present the events of your narration in a logical and coherent order. Make certain that you link events through the use of appropriate transitional words.
2. Select the narrative details carefully in order to suit the purpose of the essay. Narrate only those aspects of the event that serve to illustrate and support your thesis.
3. Choose a point of view and perspective suitable for your topic and audience. Narrative point of view may be either first or third person. A first-person narrative (*I*, *we*) is suitable for stories about yourself. A third-person narrative (*he*, *she*, *it*, *they*) conveys stories about others. The narrative perspective you use depends on your audience and purpose. Obviously, you

would use a different perspective and tone in narrating a laboratory experiment than you would narrating a soccer match you participated in.

4. Use dialogue, if appropriate to your topic, to add realism and interest to your narrative.

5. Limit the scope of the event you are narrating, and bring it to a suitable conclusion or climax.

When narration is used for informational or expository purposes, the story makes a point, illustrates a principle, or explains something. In other words, in expository narration, the event tends to serve as evidence in support of your thesis.

Here is a sample student paragraph based on narration:

Like most little girls I thought it would be very grown up to get my hair done in a beauty parlor instead of by my mother or older sister. For more than a month I cried and badgered my family. Finally, after hearing enough of my whining, my mother gave in and made an appointment for me. At the beauty parlor, I sat with my mother and a few older women, naively waiting for my transformation into another Shirley Temple. Finally the hairdresser placed me in a chair and began to chop a mass of hair onto the floor and then subject me to a burning sensation as rollers wound my remaining hair tight. The result was a classic example of the overworked permanent. At home later that day, I tried washing and rewashing my hair to remove the tangled mess. It took a week until I would see anyone without a scarf or hat over my head and a month before I could look at someone without feeling that they were making fun of me the minute I turned my back. In a way I feel that such a fruitless journey to the hairdresser actually helped me along the road to adulthood since it was a perfect example of a disappointment that only time and patience, rather than tantrums and senseless worrying, can overcome.

Narration answers the question, What happened? It can be used to tell real or fictional stories, to relate historical events, to present personal experience, or to support an analysis of events. It has broad utility in college as a critical writing skill.

***Illustration***   To make your paragraph or essay complete—without padding, repetition, or digression—be sure to have sufficient examples or illustrations to support key ideas. Different topics lend themselves to different types of examples or supporting evidence. Here are some types of illustration that will help you write well-developed paragraphs and essays:

- *Fact:* The Supreme Court ordered the desegregation of public schools in 1964.
- *Statistic:* A majority of schools in San Diego that were once 90 percent black are now almost 45 percent white.
- *Example:* One example of the success of San Diego's integration effort is its magnet schools.
- *Personal experience:* I attended the new computer science magnet school from 1996 to 1998. . . .
- *Quotation:* According to the *Phi Delta Kappan,* "On the first day of Los Angeles's mandatory desegregation program, 17,700 out of the total of 40,000 were not on the bus."

- *Process:* With the magnet concept, a school first creates a special theme and emphasis for its curriculum. Then it . . . .
- *Comparison and contrast:* By contrast, when Los Angeles announced its forced busing plan, an estimated 15.1 percent of the white population moved out of the system into private schools.
- *Case study:* Jamie, an eighth-grader, had seen very few black students at the Math-Science Center prior to the implementation of San Diego's desegregation plan. . . .

Illustrations develop your paragraph beyond the topic sentence. Such illustrations or examples may be short or extended. However, to make sure that your paragraphs are complete and properly developed, watch out for weak or poorly presented illustrations. For every main idea or topic sentence in a paragraph, use specific supporting evidence that sufficiently proves or amplifies your point. If you do not have the right evidence in the proper amount, your paragraph and essay will be underdeveloped, as in the following case:

The concept of choice does seem to appeal to students. On the first day of San Diego's new plan, the only people who were absent from the programs who had volunteered were those who were sick.

This two-sentence paragraph has promise but does not follow through with the main idea adequately. The concept at the heart of the topic sentence is clearer and more complete in the revised version:

The concept of choice does seem to appeal to San Diego's parents and students. On the first day of San Diego's new plan, the only people who were absent from the program who had volunteered were those who were sick. In contrast, on the first day of Los Angeles's mandatory desegregation program, 17,700 out of the total of 40,000 were not on the bus, according to the *Phi Delta Kappan*. Moreover, when Los Angeles announced its busing plan, an estimated 15.1 percent of the white population moved out of the district or into a private school. In San Diego, there was virtually no "white flight."

In the revision, the student chose to use contrasting evidence, highly specific in nature, to provide adequate support for the topic sentence. Other details and illustrative strategies might have been selected. In selecting illustrative material, you should always ask, Are there other examples that are more lively, specific, concrete, revealing, or interesting? It is not enough to just present examples. Illustration should be as effective as possible.

**Process Analysis**   When you describe how something works, how something is assembled, how something is done, or how something happens, you are explaining or analyzing a process. The complexity of your explanation will depend on how complex the process itself is, how detailed you want your explanation to be, and what you want your audience to be able to do or understand as a result of reading your explanation. Are you providing relatively simple how-to-do-it instructions for a relatively simple task, or are you attempting to explain a complicated laboratory experiment or computer program? The explanation of a process can make demands on your analytical and problem-solving abilities because you have to break down operations into component parts and actions. Process analysis always involves the systematic presentation of step-by-step or stage-by-stage procedures. You must show *how* the steps or parts in a process lead to its completion or resolution.

The explanation of processes is relevant to many college courses. Such topics as the stages of economic growth, Hobbes's view of the evolution of the state, the origins of the city, the development of the English lyric, the phenomenon of photosynthesis, and the history of abstract art could benefit from process analysis. Often process analysis can be combined with other writing strategies or even be subordinated to a more dominant writing strategy like narration, to which it bears a certain resemblance.

As with all other forms of mature and effective writing, you must assess your audience when writing process papers. You must decide whether you primarily want to inform or to give directions. When you give directions, you normally can assume that your audience wants to learn to do what you tell them about. If your primary purpose is to inform, you must assess the degree of interest of general readers and approach your subject from an objective perspective. Remember that there are natural, physical, mechanical, technical, mental, and historical types of processes. Certain topics might cut across these types, yet in each instance, your purpose is to direct the reader in how to do something or to inform the reader about the nature of the process.

Your analysis of a process can occur at the paragraph level, or it can control the development of an entire essay. Note how Laurence J. Peter, author of the book *The Peter Prescription*, uses process to structure the following paragraph:

> If you are inexperienced in relaxation techniques, begin by sitting in a comfortable chair with your feet on the floor and your hands resting easily in your lap. Close your eyes and breathe evenly, deeply, and gently. As you exhale each breath let your body become more relaxed. Starting with one hand direct your attention to one part of your body at a time. Close your fist and tighten the muscles of your forearm. Feel the sensation of tension in your muscles. Relax your hand and let your forearm and hand become completely limp. Direct all your attention to the sensation of relaxation as you continue to let all tension leave your hand and arm. Continue this practice once or several times each day, relaxing your other hand and arm, your legs, back, abdomen, chest, neck, face, and scalp. When you have this mastered and can relax completely, turn your thoughts to scenes of natural tranquility from your past. Stay with your inner self as long as you wish, whether thinking of nothing or visualizing only the loveliest of images. Often you will become completely unaware of your surroundings. When you open your eyes you will find yourself refreshed in mind and body.

Peter establishes his relationship and his purpose with his audience in the very first sentence, and then offers step-by-step procedures that move readers toward a full understanding of the process. Remember that you are the expert when writing about a process and that you have to think carefully about the degree of knowledge that your audience shares.

To develop a process paper, follow these guidelines:

1. Select an appropriate topic.
2. Decide whether your primary purpose is to direct or explain.
3. Determine the knowledge gap between you and your audience.
4. Explain necessary equipment or define special terms.
5. Organize paragraphs in a complete sequence of steps.
6. Explain each step clearly and completely.
7. State results or outcomes.

Numerous subjects lend themselves to process analysis. You must decide, especially for a particular course, which topic is most appropriate and which topic you know or want to learn about the most.

*Comparison and Contrast*    Comparison and contrast is an analytical method organizing thought to show similarities and differences between two persons, places, things, or ideas. Comparing and contrasting comes naturally to us. If, for example, you must decide on which candidate to vote for, you might compare the party affiliations, records, and positions on issues of both candidates to find the one who best meets your expectations. Comparison and contrast serves three useful purposes in writing:

- To evaluate the relative worth or performance of two things by comparing them point for point
- To increase understanding of two familiar things by exploring them for significant similarities and differences
- To explain something unfamiliar by comparing it with something familiar

The organization of comparison-and-contrast paragraphs and essays is fairly specialized and somewhat more prescribed than other methods of writing. The following are some basic guidelines for preparing comparison-and-contrast papers.

Most importantly, limit your comparison to only two subjects (from here on we'll refer to them as A and B). If you attempt to work with more, you may find that your writing becomes confused. In addition, subjects A and B should be from the same category of things. You would do better, for example, to compare two jazz pianists than to compare a jazz pianist and Dixieland jazz as a whole. Moreover, there needs to be a *purpose* for your comparison. Unless you explain your purpose, the comparison, which might otherwise be structurally sound, will ultimately seem meaningless.

The organization of comparison-and-contrast papers generally follows two basic patterns, or methods: the *block method* and the *alternating method*. The block method presents all material on subject A and then all material on subject B. With the block method, each subtopic must be the same for both subjects. The alternating method presents all the material on each subtopic together, analyzing these subtopics in an AB, AB, AB pattern. Although there is no hard-and-fast rule, the alternating method is probably the best choice for most essays in order to avoid the standard pitfalls of the block method. Unless you are an experienced writer, using the block method can lead to an insufficiently developed paper, with some subtopics receiving more attention than others. It can also lead to a paper that seems like two separate essays, with a big chunk about subject A followed by a second, disconnected chunk about subject B. Whether you are using the block or the alternating method, follow through in an orderly manner, stating clearly the main thesis or reason for establishing the comparison, and providing clear transitions as you move from idea to idea.

Consider the following paragraph, written by a student, John Shin:

> The story of Noah and the Great Flood is probably the best known story of a deluge in the Mesopotamian Valley. However, there are several other accounts of a large flood in the valley. Of these, the Akkadian story of Utnapishtim, as told by Gilgamesh, is the most interesting due to its similarities to the biblical story of Noah. Utnapishtim is a king who is forewarned of the coming of a great flood. He is advised to build an ark and does so. After many days the waters recede and Utnapishtim exits the ark and is turned into a god. The stories of Noah and Utnapishtim bear a striking resemblance in several parts: a god or gods cause a flood to punish men and women; arks, of certain dimensions, are built; animals are taken on board; birds are released to find land; and the arks come to rest on mountains. These parallels are so striking that many think the two to be the same tale.

Given the design of this paragraph, we can assume that Shin could develop body paragraphs that deal in detail with each of the key resemblances in the order they are mentioned: the coming of the flood, the building of the ark, the animals taken on board, the release of the birds, and the lodging of both arks on the mountaintop. By employing the alternating method, he constructs a well-organized comparative framework for his analysis of the story of Noah and the story of Utnapishtim.

**Causal Analysis**   Frequently in college writing, you must explain the causes or effects of some event, situation, or phenomenon. This type of investigation is termed *causal analysis*. When you analyze something, you divide it into its logical parts or processes for the purpose of close examination. Thus phenomena as diverse as divorce in America, the Civil War, carcinogens in asbestos, the death of Martin Luther King Jr., or the eruption of Mount St. Helens can be analyzed in terms of their causes and effects.

Cause-and-effect relationships are part of everyday thinking and living. Why did you select the college you now attend? Why did you stop dating Freddy or Barbara, and what effect has this decision had on your life? Why did the football team lose five straight games? You need causal analysis to explain why something occurred, to predict what will occur, and to make informed choices based on your perceptions. With causal analysis, you cannot simply tell a story, summarize an event, or describe an object or phenomenon. Instead, you must explain the *why* and *what* of a topic. The analysis of causes seeks to explain why a particular condition occurred. The analysis of effects seeks to explain what the consequences or results were, are, or will be.

Causal reasoning is common to writing in many disciplines: history, economics, politics, sociology, literature, science, education, and business, to list a few. Some essays and reports focus on causes, others on effects, and still others on both causes and effects. Sometimes even the simplest sort of causal reasoning based on personal experience does not admit to the complete separation of causes and effects but depends instead on the recognition that causes and effects are interdependent. For example, the following paragraph from a student's sociology paper focuses on a cause-and-effect relationship:

My parents came to New York with the dream of saving enough money to return to Puerto Rico and buy a home with some land and fruit trees. Many Puerto Ricans, troubled by the problem of life on the island, find no relief in migration to New York City. They remain poor, stay in the barrio, are unable to cope with American society and way of life, and experience the destruction of their traditionally close family life. My parents were fortunate. After spending most of their lives working hard, they saved enough to return to the island. Today they tend their orange, lemon, banana, and plantain trees in an area of Puerto Rico called "El Paraíso." It took them most of a lifetime to find their paradise—in their own backyard.

Here the writer blends personal experience with a more objective analysis of causes and effects, presenting the main cause-effect relationship in the first sentence, analyzing typical effects, providing an exception to this conventional effect, and describing the result.

Sometimes you will want to focus exclusively on causes or on effects. For example, in a history course, the topic might be to analyze why World War II occurred, as this student sought to do:

It is popularly accepted that Hitler was the major cause of World War II, but the ultimate causes go much deeper than one personality. There were long-standing German grievances against reparations levied on the nation following its defeat in World War I. Moreover, there were severe economic strains that caused resentment among the German people. Compounding these problems was the French and English reluctance to work out a sound disarmament policy and American noninvolvement in the matter. Finally, there was the European fear that Communism was a much greater danger than National Socialism. All these factors contributed to the outbreak of World War II.

Note that in his attempt to explain fully the causes of an event, the writer goes beyond *immediate* causes, that is, the most evident causes that trigger the event being analyzed. He tries to identify the *ultimate* causes, the deep-rooted reasons that completely explain the problem. In order to present a sound analysis of a problem, you need to be able to trace events logically to their underlying origins. Similarly, you have to engage in strategic thinking about immediate and ultimate effects in order to explain fully an event's results.

Writing about cause-and-effect relationships demands sound critical thinking skills with attention to logic and thorough preparation for the demands of the assignment. To write effective and logical essays of causal analysis, follow these guidelines:

1. Be honest, objective, and reasonable when establishing your thesis. As a critical thinker, you have to avoid prejudices and logical fallacies, including unsupportable claims, broad generalizations and overstatements, and false relationships. (For a discussion of logical fallacies, see pages 127–128.)
2. Distinguish between causes and effects, and decide whether you plan to focus on causes, effects, or both. As a prewriting strategy, draw up a list of causes and a corresponding list of effects. You can then organize your paper around the central causes and effects.
3. Distinguish clearly between immediate and ultimate causes and effects. Explore those causes and effects that best serve the purpose of your paper and your audience's expectations.
4. Provide evidence. Do not rely on simple assertions. Statistics and testimony from reliable authorities are especially effective types of evidence to support your analysis.
5. Try to establish links between causes or effects. Seek a logical sequence of related elements, a chain of causality that helps readers understand the totality of your topic.

Ultimately, there are many ways to write about causes and effects, depending on whether you are looking for explanations, reasons, consequences, connections, results, or any combination of these elements.

*Definition*   Concepts or general ideas often require careful definition if readers are to make sense of them or make intelligent decisions. Could you discuss supply and demand in economic theory without knowing the concept of the invisible hand? And isn't it best to know what a politician actually believes in before casting your vote? Concepts form the core of any discipline, line of inquiry, or problem. Because concepts are abstract, they may mean different things to different readers. In order to make ourselves understood, we must be able to specify their meaning in a particular context.

There are three types of definition. The simple *lexical* definition, or dictionary definition, is useful when briefly identifying concrete, commonplace, or uncontroversial terms for the reader. Many places, persons, and things can be defined in this manner. The *extended* definition is an explanation that might involve a paragraph or an entire essay. It is frequently used for abstract, complex, or controversial terms. The third form of definition is the *stipulative* definition, in which you offer a special definition of a term or set limitations on your use of the term. A solid definition, whether it is lexical, extended, or stipulative, involves describing the essential nature and characteristics of a concept that distinguish it from related ideas.

Consider the following paragraph by a student, Geeta Berrera:

The degree of loneliness that we feel can range from the mild or temporary case to a severe state which may eventually lead to depression or other psychological disorders. Being able to recognize the signs and signals of loneliness may help you to avoid it in the future. Do you find yourself unable to communicate with others? If so, you might be lonely. Do you find it difficult to put your faith in other human beings? If so, then you are setting up a situation that may be conducive to loneliness because you are preventing yourself from becoming too close to another person. Do you find yourself spending great amounts of time alone on a regular basis? Do you find that you are never invited to parties or other social events? Are you unable to love or care for another human being because you are afraid of permanent responsibilities and commitments? These are all signs and signals of either loneliness or situations that may eventually lead to loneliness. Loneliness is the feeling of sadness or grief experienced by a person at the realization that he or she lacks the companionship of other people.

Notice how Berrera introduces and emphasizes the central concept—loneliness—that is defined in this paragraph. She adds to the definition through a series of questions and answers—a strategy that permits her to analyze the qualities or manifestations of the concept. These symptoms serve as examples that reveal what is distinctive or representative about the condition of loneliness.

Definition can be used for several purposes. It may explain a difficult concept like phenomenology or a little-known activity like cricket. Definition can be used to identify and illustrate the special nature of a person, object, or abstract idea.

*Classification*   Classification is a mode of critical thinking and writing based on the division of a concept into groups and subgroups, and the examination of important elements within these groups. We have generalized ideas of classes of objects that help us organize and thereby understand the world. Many of these concepts lend themselves to classification. You think and talk frequently about types of college teachers, types of cars, types of boyfriends or girlfriends, and types of movies or music. When registering for courses, you know that English is in the humanities, psychology in the social sciences, and geology in the physical sciences; you select these courses on the basis of consistent classification principles, perhaps distribution requirements or the demands of your major. What you are doing is thinking about concepts within a class, sorting out and organizing information, and often evaluating possible alternatives. Classification, in short, is a basic mode of critical thought.

As a pattern of writing, classification enables you to make sense of large and potentially complex concepts. You divide a concept into groups and subgroups, and you classify elements within categories. Assume, for instance, that your politics professor asks for an analysis of the branches of the U.S. federal government. You divide the federal government into the executive, legislative, and judicial branches, and, depending on your purpose, you subdivide even further into departments, agencies, and so forth. Then, according to some consistent principle or thesis—say, a critical look at the erosion of the division of powers—you develop information for each category reflecting common characteristics. Essentially, if you classify in a rigorous and logical way, you sort out for analysis the parts and ideas within a scheme, progressing from general to specific in your treatment of the topic.

In developing a classification essay, you also have to determine the *system* of classification that works best for the demands of the assignment. The system you select would depend to an extent on your reader's expectations and the nature of the subject. Imagine that you have been asked to write an essay on sports by a physiology teacher, a psychology teacher, or a sociology teacher. Your system might be types of sports injuries for the physiology professor, behavior patterns of tennis players for your psychology professor, or levels of violence and aggression in team sports for your sociology professor. For a broad concept like sports, there are many possible classificatory systems depending on the purpose of your paper.

Although several classification and division strategies might be appropriate for any given concept, the following guidelines should be reviewed and applied for any classification essay:

1. Think about the controlling principle for your classification. *Why* are you classifying the concept? *What* is the significance? Create a thesis statement that gives your reader a clear perspective on your classification scheme.
2. Divide the subject into major categories and subdivide categories consistently. Make certain that you isolate all important categories and that these categories do not overlap excessively.
3. Arrange the classification scheme in an effective, emphatic order—as a chronology, in spatial terms, in order of importance, or from simple to complex.
4. Present and analyze each category in a clear sequence, proceeding through the categories until the classification scheme is complete.
5. Define or explain any difficult concepts within each category, providing relevant details and evidence.
6. Combine classification with other appropriate writing strategies—comparison and contrast, process analysis, definition, and so forth.

Examine the following student paragraph:

To many people, fishing is finding a "fishy-looking" spot, tossing a hooked worm into the water, and hoping that a hungry fish just happens to be nearby. Anyone who has used this haphazard method can attest to the fact that failures usually outnumber successes. The problem with the "bait and wait" method is that it is very limited. The bait has less chance of encountering a fish than it would if it were presented in different areas of water. A more intelligent approach to fishing is to use the knowledge that at any given moment fish can be in three parts of a lake. Assuming that a lake has fish, anglers will find them on the surface, in the middle, or on the bottom of the lake.

Fishing each of these areas involves the use of a separate technique. By fishing the surface, fishing the middle, or fishing the bottom, you greatly increase the chances of catching a fish.

This example is the student's introductory paragraph to a classification essay that blends description, process analysis, comparison and contrast, and the use of evidence to excellent effect. From the outset, however, the reader knows that this will be a classification essay.

*Argumentation*    Argumentation is a form of critical thinking in which you try to convince an audience to accept your position on a topic or persuade members of this audience to act in a certain way. In a sense, everything is an argument, for much of what you read and write, see and hear, is designed to elicit a desired response. Whether reading texts, viewing various media forms, or listening to the spoken word (especially of politicians), you know that just about anything is potentially debatable.

Argumentation in writing, however, goes beyond ordinary disagreements. With an argumentative essay, your purpose is to convince or persuade readers in a logical, reasonable, and appealing way. In other words, with formal argumentation, you must distinguish mere personal opinion from opinions based on reasons derived from solid evidence. An argumentative essay has special features and even step-by-step processes that will be treated in greater detail in the next chapter. For now, it is worth noting that solid argumentative writing can combine many of the forms and purposes that have been discussed in this chapter. Your understanding of such forms and purposes of discourse as narration, illustration, analysis, and comparison and contrast, and the ways these strategies can combine in powerful ways, will help you compose solid argumentative essays.

Above all, with argumentation, you must develop what Virginia Woolf called "some fierce attachment to an idea." Once you commit yourself to a viewpoint on a topic or issue, you will find it easy to bring an argumentative edge to your writing. Consider the following excerpt from a well-known essay by Caroline Bird that begins with the provocative title "College Is a Waste of Time and Money":

> A great majority of our 9 million college students are in school not because they want to be or because they want to learn. They are there because it has become the thing to do or because college is a pleasant place to be; because it's the only way they can get parents or taxpayers to support them without working at a job they don't like; because Mother wanted them to go, or some other reason entirely irrelevant to the course of studies for which college is supposedly organized.

Clearly, Bird's claim has that argumentative edge you encounter in essays designed to convince readers of a particular viewpoint or position on an issue. Do you agree or disagree with Bird's claim? How would you respond to her assertions? What evidence would you provide to support your own claim?

Argumentation is a powerful way to tap into the aspirations, values, and conduct of your audience. It makes demands on readers and writers to do something, believe something, or even become somebody different—say, a more tolerant person or a more active citizen. True, argument can provoke conflict, but it can also resolve it. In fact, many experts today emphasize the value of argument in solving problems and defusing or managing conflicts.

At the outset of any argument process, you must recognize that you have a problem to solve and decisions to make. Problem solving often is at the heart of argumentation; it is a process in which situations, issues, and questions are analyzed and debated, and decisions arrived at. The basic steps to problem solving in argumentation are these:

1. Define and analyze the problem. Examine all available information to identify the problem precisely.
2. Interpret the facts and review alternative approaches.
3. Make a claim or a decision—that is, assert the best course of action.
4. Implement the decision in order to persuade or convince your audience that the problem has been addressed and solved.
5. Evaluate the outcome in follow-up documents.

At times, it will be hard to diagnose a problem and find solutions for it. At other times, there is no ideal solution to a problem. Argumentation is not a simple academic exercise but rather an indispensable tool in personal and professional situations. It is indispensable in addressing increasingly complex political, economic, social, and technological trends on both a domestic and a global scale. Moreover, argument can produce ethically constructive and socially responsible results. Argument makes special demands on a writer that will be treated comprehensively in the next chapter.

**Writing End Paragraphs**   If an essay does not have a strong, appropriate ending, it may leave the reader feeling confused or dissatisfied, with the sense that the intention and promises built up in earlier parts of the essay have not been fulfilled. By contrast, an effective closing paragraph leaves the reader with the impression that the essay is complete and satisfying.

The techniques that follow permit you to end your essay emphatically and with grace:

- Use a full-circle pattern by echoing or repeating a phrase, idea, or detail that you presented in your introductory paragraph.
- State your conclusions, proofs, or theories based on the facts and supporting ideas of the essay. This strategy works especially well in papers for social science, science, and philosophy courses.
- Show the outcome or effects of the facts and ideas of the essay.
- Suggest a solution as a way to clarify your position on the problem you have discussed.
- Ask a question that sums up the main point of the essay.

- Offer an anecdote, allusion, or lighthearted point that sums up your thesis.
- Use a quotation that supports your main point or illuminates an aspect of the topic.

Other basic ways to end an essay include restating your thesis and main points, calling for action, providing a final summary evaluation, and looking at future consequences based on the essay's analysis or argument. A closing, like your introduction, should be brief. It is your one last attempt at clarity, your one last chance to illuminate your topic.

| | www.mhhe.com/ **mhreader** | For more information on writing endings, go to: **Writing > Conclusions** |

## Student Essay

Here is the essay that Jamie Taylor wrote in response to Schlesinger's "The Cult of Ethnicity." Consider the strategies that she used to make her composing process a success.

Jamie Taylor
Humanities 101, sec. 008
Professor Fred Segal
4 November 2007

Cultist Behavior or Doltish Behavior?

The introductory paragraph presents Schlesinger's main argument, amplifies Schlesinger's inferred claims, and then presents the writer's counterargument.

In Schlesinger's "The Cult of Ethnicity," the author warns that there are forces at work within our nation that undermine our principles of democracy. These forces come in the guise of individuals and groups who claim that they know what's right for the people whom they represent. Although he doesn't mention them all specifically, one can infer he means that certain leaders from the African American community, the Latino community, the Native American community, the Asian community, and so forth are advocating strong identification within groups to keep their identities alive since they claim Eurocentric culture has had a history of stealing and suppressing their own historic roots. But Schlesinger seems to fear that only divisiveness can result. In this regard, he does not give the individual enough credit. Rather than have a paternalistic attitude about what he fears these groups are doing, he should give more credit to the members of these groups to be able to discern which messages regarding ethnicity to accept as being benign and which to reject as being downright silly.

The first body paragraph presents Taylor's first point supported with evidence and examples.

Take, for example, the many clubs in the average college or university. Nearly every ethnic group is represented by one of these organizations. For example, my university has many groups that represent African Americans, Latinos, Asians, Native Americans, even subgroups like the Korean Society, the Chinese Student Association, and so on. Belonging to these groups gives students a healthy place to socialize, discuss common areas of interest and concern, and assist with community outreach. For example, many of these clubs sponsor programs to give demonstrations of cultural traditions such as cooking, dance, clothing, and so on to civic and business groups. They also assist the needy in gaining access to social services, particularly for shut-ins and the elderly who may not speak English. Also, there is strength in numbers, and the fact that these clubs are popular attests to the fact that they tolerate a range of ideas so that no one "ideology" is promoted over another. Besides, if that were to happen, it is the right of the organization to vote a person out of office or membership. To say that these clubs promote divisiveness would be like saying that the Newman Society for Catholic students or Hillel House for Jewish students promotes religious intolerance.

> The second point offers a unique slant on divisive ethnic and racial leaders and the ability of Americans to reject their claims. Again, specific examples and evidence buttress Taylor's argument.

Second, self-styled leaders of various racial and ethnic groups—in their efforts to be divisive—actually help people to see through their rhetoric, or at least, to apply only that which is reasonable and reject that which is intolerable. Because of today's media, such leaders cannot "hide" their views and thus can become their own worst enemies when presenting them in front of a national audience. For example, Louis Farrakhan has not only alienated Jewish individuals owing to his open anti-Semitism, and many among the gay population for his antigay sentiments, but many African Americans as well, particularly women, who often condemn him for his patriarchal views regarding the family and society. A simple proof of his lack of power is the fact that he has been presenting these antidemocratic ideals for decades now, and there is little evidence that anyone is listening to them. Another example is the late Rabbi Meyer Kahane, who advocated the expulsion of all Arabs from Israel. An open opponent of democracy, he was condemned by Jewish leaders in the United States to the point where he was shunned from any discussion regarding religious issues.

Finally, one can feel confident that even within the margins of mainstream white America, cultist groups are their own worst enemy. Take for example, the various groups of survivalists (primarily white Americans), white extremists and separatists, anti-gay groups, and radical anti-abortionists. The philosophy and tactics of these organizations are condemned by the vast majority of Americans owing to their antidemocratic postures, not to mention their often violent, even murderous activities. They may capture the headlines for a while, but they will never capture the hearts of Americans so long as we stay true to the "measures and laws" that Washington spoke of in his discussion with John Adams.

> The writer's third and final point encompasses a variety of "antidemocratic" groups and rejects their "postures."

The conclusion
returns to
Schlesinger, while
recapitulating
Taylor's main points.

In conclusion, the open democratic society we have created is just too strong a force to be weakened or undermined by "romantic ideologies" or "unscrupulous con men" as Schlesinger puts it. Mr. Schlesinger has little to worry about. Just look around your school or university cafeteria. There's no white section or Latino section or Asian section: Nowadays, it's just one big American section.

## Revising

Revising—the rethinking and rewriting of material—takes place during every stage of the composing process. It is integral to the quest for clarity and meaning. "Writing and rewriting are a constant search for what one's saying," declares celebrated American author John Updike. Similarly, the famous essayist E. B. White admits, "I rework a lot to make it clear." If these two great prose stylists revise material in order to seek clarity for their ideas, then you too should adopt the professional attitude that you can improve what you first say or think and what you first put down on paper. In fact, one trait that distinguishes experienced from inexperienced writers is that the professional writers understand fully the need to revise.

Revision is an art. It is the only way to make your writing match the vision of what you want to accomplish. Whether at word, sentence, paragraph, or essay level, you should develop a repertoire of choices that will permit you to solve writing problems and sharpen your ideas. You might also share your draft with another reader who can let you know what is or is not working and give you suggestions for improvement. To make the process of revision worthwhile, you should ask yourself the following questions during your prewriting and drafting activities (you can also give these questions to your reader):

- Is the essay long enough (or too long) to meet the demands of the assignment?
- Is the topic suitable for the assignment?
- Do you have a clear thesis statement?
- Does your writing make sense? Are you communicating with your reader instead of just with yourself?
- Have you included everything that is important to the development of your thesis or argument?
- Is there anything you should discard?
- Do you offer enough examples or evidence to support your key ideas?
- Have you ordered and developed paragraphs logically?
- Do you have a clear beginning, middle, and end?

Once you have answered these questions, you will be able to judge the extent to which you have to revise your first draft.

**Proofreading**   Proofreading is part of the revision process. You do not have final copy until you have carefully checked your essay for mistakes and inconsistencies. Proofreading differs from the sort of revision that moves you from an initial draft to subsequent versions of an essay in that it does not offer the opportunity to make major changes in content or organization. It does give you a last chance to correct minor errors that arise from carelessness, haste, or inaccuracy during writing, typing, or word processing.

When you proofread, do so word by word and line by line. Concentrate on spelling, punctuation, grammar, mechanics, and paragraph form. Read each sentence aloud—from the computer screen or your hard copy. If something sounds or looks wrong to you, consult a handbook, dictionary, or other reference work. Then make corrections accordingly.

Here are some basic guidelines for proofreading your essay:

1. Check the title. Are words capitalized properly?
2. Check all words in the essay that should be capitalized.
3. Check the spelling of any word you are uncertain about.
4. Check the meaning of any word you think you might have misused.
5. Check to see if you have unintentionally omitted or repeated any words.
6. Check paragraph form. Have you indented each paragraph?
7. Check to make certain you have smooth, grammatically correct sentences. This is your last chance to eliminate awkward and grammatically incorrect sentences.

**Responding to Editorial Comments**   Even when you submit what you *think* is the final version of your essay, your teacher might not agree that the essay has reached its best possible form. Teachers are experienced in detecting essays' strengths and weaknesses, pinpointing mistakes, and suggesting how material can be improved. Their comments are not attacks; they do want you to pay attention to them, to recognize and correct errors, and possibly to revise your essay once again—most likely for a higher grade. If you receive editorial comment in an objective manner and respond to it constructively, you will become a more effective writer.

When reading your essays, your instructor will use standard correction symbols that appear in English handbooks. He or she will make additional comments in the margins and compose an overall assessment of the paper at the end. Any worthwhile comment on your paper will blend supportive observations with constructive criticism. Often your instructor will offer concrete suggestions for revision. When you receive a graded paper, you typically are expected to make the necessary revisions and either add it to your portfolio or resubmit the essay.

Ultimately, refinement is integral to the entire writing process. From reading materials that you confront at the outset and respond to in various ways, you move through many composing stages to create a finished product. In *The Field of Vision,* the American novelist and critic Wright Morris refers to the important task of refinement that confronts the writer: "By raw material, I mean that comparatively crude ore that has not yet been processed by the imagination—what we refer to as *life*, or as experience, in contrast to art. By technique I mean the way the artist smelts this material down for human consumption." Your best writing is the result of this smelting process, which involves the many strategies covered in this introduction that are designed to help you acquire greater control over the art of critical reading and writing. Donald M. Murray's essay "The Maker's Eye: Revising Your Own Manuscripts," starting on page 72, offers one writer's summation of the stages of the revision process.

# A Portfolio on Writing and Communication

# How to Mark a Book

## Mortimer J. Adler

*Mortimer Jerome Adler (1902–2001) was born in New York City and received his PhD from Columbia University in 1928. A staunch advocate for classical philosophy, Adler believed that there are unshakable truths—an idea rejected by most contemporary philosophers. For this reason, Adler has not been taken seriously by the academic establishment. He was a champion of knowledge, believing that philosophy should be a part of everyone's life and that the great ideas in philosophy can be of value to everyone. Many of his over 75 books attempt to edify the general reader by explaining basic philosophical concepts in everyday language. He was also chairman of the editorial board of* the Encyclopedia Britannica. *To make knowledge more accessible to everyone, he also assumed editorship of the Encyclopedia Britannica's Great Books project, partly sponsored by the University of Chicago. This project, which has put 443 of the world's "classics" into a 54-volume set, graces the bookcases of many dens and studies in middle-class American homes. Despite his advancing years, Adler continued to work on many projects to promote his goal of universal education and enlightenment. "How to Mark a Book" is typical of his didactic, pragmatic approach to education.*

You know you have to read "between the lines" to get the most out of anything. 1 I want to persuade you to do something equally important in the course of your reading. I want to persuade you to "write between the lines." Unless you do, you are not likely to do the most efficient kind of reading.

I contend, quite bluntly, that marking up a book is not an act of mutilation 2 but of love.

You shouldn't mark up a book which isn't yours. Librarians (or your 3 friends) who lend you books expect you to keep them clean, and you should. If you decide that I am right about the usefulness of marking books, you will have to buy them. Most of the world's great books are available today, in reprint editions, at less than a dollar.

There are two ways in which one can own a book. The first is the property 4 right you establish by paying for it, just as you pay for clothes and furniture. But this act of purchase is only the prelude to possession. Full ownership comes only when you have made it a part of yourself, and the best way to

**57**

make yourself a part of it is by writing in it. An illustration may make the point clear. You buy a beefsteak and transfer it from the butcher's ice-box to your own. But you do not own the beefsteak in the most important sense until you consume it and get it into your bloodstream. I am arguing that books, too, must be absorbed in your bloodstream to do you any good.

5      Confusion about what it means to own a book leads people to a false reverence for paper, binding, and type—a respect for the physical thing—the craft of the printer rather than the genius of the author. They forget that it is possible for a man to acquire the idea, to possess the beauty, which a great book contains, without staking his claim by pasting his bookplate inside the cover. Having a fine library doesn't prove that its owner has a mind enriched by books; it proves nothing more than that he, his father, or his wife, was rich enough to buy them.

6      There are three kinds of book owners. The first has all the standard sets and best-sellers—unread, untouched. (This deluded individual owns woodpulp and ink, not books.) The second has a great many books—a few of them read through, most of them dipped into, but all of them as clean and shiny as the day they were bought. (This person would probably like to make books his own, but is restrained by a false respect for their physical appearance.) The third has a few books or many—every one of them dog-eared and dilapidated, shaken and loosened by continual use, marked and scribbled in from front to back. (This man owns books.)

7      Is it false respect, you may ask, to preserve intact and unblemished a beautifully printed book, an elegantly bound edition? Of course not. I'd no more scribble all over the first edition of *Paradise Lost* than I'd give my baby a set of crayons and an original Rembrandt! I wouldn't mark up a painting or a statue. Its soul, so to speak, is inseparable from its body. And the beauty of a rare edition or of a richly manufactured volume is like that of a painting or a statue.

8      But the soul of a book *can* be separated from its body. A book is more like the score of a piece of music than it is like a painting. No great musician confuses a symphony with the printed sheets of music. Arturo Toscanini reveres Brahms, but Toscanini's score of the C-minor Symphony is so thoroughly marked up that no one but the maestro himself can read it. The reason why a great conductor makes notations on his musical scores—marks them up again and again each time he returns to study them—is the reason why you should mark up your books. If your respect for magnificent binding or typography gets in the way, buy yourself a cheap edition and pay your respects to the author.

9      Why is marking up a book indispensable to reading it? First, it keeps you awake. (And I don't mean merely conscious; I mean wide awake.) In the second place, reading, if it is active, is thinking, and thinking tends to express itself in words, spoken or written. The marked book is usually the thought-through book. Finally, writing helps you remember the thoughts you had, or the thoughts the author expressed. Let me develop these three points.

10     If reading is to accomplish anything more than passing time, it must be active. You can't let your eyes glide across the lines of a book and come up with an understanding of what you have read. Now an ordinary piece of light

fiction, like say, *Gone with the Wind*, doesn't require the most active kind of reading. The books you read for pleasure can be read in a state of relaxation, and nothing is lost. But a great book, rich in ideas and beauty, a book that raises and tries to answer great fundamental questions, demands the most active reading of which you are capable. You don't absorb the ideas of John Dewey the way you absorb the crooning of Mr. Vallee. You have to reach for them. That you cannot do while you're asleep.

If, when you've finished reading a book, the pages are filled with your 11 notes, you know that you read actively. The most famous *active* reader of great books I know is President Hutchins, of the University of Chicago. He also has the hardest schedule of business activities of any man I know. He invariably reads with a pencil, and sometimes, when he picks up a book and pencil in the evening, he finds himself, instead of making intelligent notes, drawing what he calls "caviar factories" on the margins. When that happens, he puts the book down. He knows he's too tired to read, and he's just wasting time.

But, you may ask, why is writing necessary? Well, the physical act of writ- 12 ing, with your own hand, brings words and sentences more sharply before your mind and preserves them better in your memory. To set down your reaction to important words and sentences you have read, and the questions they have raised in your mind, is to preserve those reactions and sharpen those questions.

Even if you wrote on a scratch pad, and threw the paper away when you 13 had finished writing, your grasp of the book would be surer. But you don't have to throw the paper away. The margins (top and bottom, as well as side), the end-papers, the very space between the lines, are all available. They aren't sacred. And, best of all, your marks and notes become an integral part of the book and stay there forever. You can pick up the book the following week or year, and there are all your points of agreement, disagreement, doubt, and inquiry. It's like resuming an interrupted conversation with the advantage of being able to pick up where you left off.

And that is exactly what reading a book should be: a conversation between 14 you and the author. Presumably he knows more about the subject than you do; naturally, you'll have the proper humility as you approach him. But don't let anybody tell you that a reader is supposed to be solely on the receiving end. Understanding is a two-way operation; learning doesn't consist in being an empty receptacle. The learner has to question himself and question the teacher. He even has to argue with the teacher, once he understands what the teacher is saying. And marking a book is literally an expression of your differences, or agreements of opinion, with the author.

There are all kinds of devices for marking a book intelligently and fruit- 15 fully. Here's the way I do it:

1. Underlining: Of major points, of important or forceful statements.
2. Vertical lines at the margin: To emphasize a statement already underlined.
3. Star, asterisk, or other doo-dad at the margin: To be used sparingly, to emphasize the ten or twenty most important statements in the book. (You may

want to fold the bottom corner of each page on which you use such marks. It won't hurt the sturdy paper on which most modern books are printed, and you will be able to take the book off the shelf at any time and, by opening it at the folded-corner page, refresh your recollection of the book.)

4. Numbers in the margin: To indicate the sequence of points the author makes in developing a single argument.

5. Numbers of other pages in the margin: To indicate where else in the book the author made points relevant to the point marked; to tie up the ideas in a book, which, though they may be separated by many pages, belong together.

6. Circling of key words or phrases.

7. Writing in the margin, or at the top or bottom of the page, for the sake of: Recording questions (and perhaps answers) which a passage raised in your mind; reducing a complicated discussion to a simple statement; recording the sequence of major points right through the book. I use the end-papers at the back of the book to make a personal index of the author's points in the order of their appearance.

16      The front end-papers are, to me, the most important. Some people reserve them for a fancy bookplate. I reserve them for fancy thinking. After I have finished reading the book and making my personal index on the back end-papers, I turn to the front and try to outline the book, not page by page, or point by point (I've already done that at the back), but as an integrated structure, with a basic unity and an order of parts. This outline is, to me, the measure of my understanding of the work.

17      If you're a die-hard and anti-book-marker, you may object that the margins, the space between the lines, and the end-papers don't give you room enough. All right. How about using a scratch pad slightly smaller than the page-size of the book—so that the edges of the sheets won't protrude? Make your index, outlines, and even your notes on the pad, and then insert these sheets permanently inside the front and back covers of the book.

18      Or, you may say that this business of marking books is going to slow up your reading. It probably will. That's one of the reasons for doing it. Most of us have been taken in by the notion that speed of reading is a measure of our intelligence. There is no such thing as the right speed for intelligent reading. Some things should be read quickly and effortlessly, and some should be read slowly and even laboriously. The sign of intelligence in reading is the ability to read different things differently according to their worth. In the case of good books, the point is not to see how many of them you can get through, but rather how many can get through you—how many you can make your own. A few friends are better than a thousand acquaintances. If this be your aim, as it should be, you will not be impatient if it takes more time and effort to read a great book than it does a newspaper.

19      You may have one final objection to marking books. You can't lend them to your friends because nobody else can read them without being distracted by your notes. Furthermore, you won't want to lend them because a marked copy

is a kind of intellectual diary, and lending it is almost like giving your mind away.

If your friend wishes to read your *Plutarch's Lives*, "Shakespeare," or *The Federalist Papers*, tell him gently but firmly, to buy a copy. You will lend him your car or your coat—but your books are as much a part of you as your head or your heart. 20

## COMPREHENSION

1. Summarize what Adler means by "marking up a book."
2. In your own words, explain how you believe Adler would define the word *book*.
3. Adler mentions books throughout the essay. What particular type of book is he referring to?

## RHETORIC

1. What is the tone of the essay? What can you infer from this tone about Adler's emotional relationship to books?
2. Paragraphs 15 lists devices for marking a book. What is the function of enumerating them in this way? How would the tone of this section have been altered if Adler had summarized these devices in paragraph form?
3. The author makes reference to various intellectual and artistic figures and works in the essay. How does this help determine for whom the essay has been targeted?
4. Study the relationship between paragraph 9 and paragraphs 10–12. What is the rhetorical format of this section? What method of argumentation is Adler employing?
5. Adler uses the analogy that "reading a book should be: a conversation between you and the author." What other analogies can you find in the essay?
6. Adler raises objections to his argument and then refutes the objections. Where does he make use of this rhetorical device? How effective is it in advancing his argument?
7. Adler calls *Gone with the Wind* "light fiction." Is this opinion or fact? Is it a mere observation or a criticism of the book?

## WRITING

1. Mark up Adler's essay in the same manner he recommends that you mark up any good piece of writing. Then write an essay using process analysis to summarize the various methods you used.
2. Compare and contrast two books: one that Adler would regard as "light reading" and one that he would regard as worthy of marking up. Indicate

the primary differences between these books in terms of their diction, level of discourse, insight, purpose, and scholarship.

3. **Writing an Argument:** Argue for or against the proposition that this essay has lost its relevance owing to the introduction of new forms of educational media.

# Mother Tongue

## Amy Tan

*Amy Tan (b. 1952) was born in California, several years after her parents immigrated from China to San Francisco. She attended San Jose State University and the University of California, Berkeley. Before devoting herself full-time to the writing of fiction, Tan worked as a reporter and technical writer. Her fiction, deeply autobiographical, focuses on the lives of Chinese-American women trying to reconcile their traditional heritage with contemporary American culture. Tan's first novel,* The Joy Luck Club *(1989) catapulted her to fame. Her other books include* The Kitchen God's Wife *(1991),* The Hundred Secret Senses *(1996),* The Bonesetter's Daughter *(2001), and* Saving the Fish from Drowning *(2005). Tan's reflections on her career as a writer appear in* The Opposite of Fate *(2003). In "Mother Tongue," which first appeared in* The Threepenny Review *in 1990 and which has since become a contemporary classic, Tan considers the various languages or forms of communication she has used since childhood when conversing with her mother.*

1   I am not a scholar of English or literature. I cannot give you much more than personal opinions on the English language and its variations in this country or others.

2     I am a writer. And by that definition, I am someone who has always loved language. I am fascinated by language in daily life. I spend a great deal of my time thinking about the power of language—the way it can evoke an emotion, a visual image, a complex idea, or a simple truth. Language is the tool of my trade. And I use them all—all the Englishes I grew up with.

3     Recently, I was made keenly aware of the different Englishes I do use. I was giving a talk to a large group of people, the same talk I had already given to

half a dozen other groups. The nature of the talk was about my writing, my life, and my book, *The Joy Luck Club*. The talk was going along well enough, until I remembered one major difference that made the whole talk sound wrong. My mother was in the room. And it was perhaps the first time she had heard me give a lengthy speech, using the kind of English I have never used with her. I was saying things like, "The intersection of memory upon imagination" and "There is an aspect of my fiction that relates to thus-and-thus"—a speech filled with carefully wrought grammatical phrases, burdened, it suddenly seemed to me, with nominalized forms, past perfect tenses, conditional phrases, all the forms of standard English that I had learned in school and through books, the forms of English I did not use at home with my mother.

Just last week, I was walking down the street with my mother, and I again 4 found myself conscious of the English I was using, the English I do use with her. We were talking about the price of new and used furniture and I heard myself saying this: "Not waste money that way." My husband was with us as well, and he didn't notice any switch in my English. And then I realized why. It's because over the twenty years we've been together I've often used the same kind of English with him, and sometimes he even uses it with me. It has become our language of intimacy, a different sort of English that relates to family talk, the language I grew up with.

So you'll have some idea of what this family talk I heard sounds like, I'll 5 quote what my mother said during a recent conversation which I videotaped and then transcribed. During this conversation, my mother was talking about a political gangster in Shanghai who had the same last name as her family's, Du, and how the gangster in his early years wanted to be adopted by her family, which was rich by comparison. Later, the gangster became more powerful, far richer than my mother's family, and one day showed up at my mother's wedding to pay his respects. Here's what she said in part:

"Du Yusong having business like fruit stand. Like off the street kind. He is 6 Du like Du Zong—but not Tsung-ming Island people. The local people call putong, the river east side, he belong to that side local people. That man want to ask Du Zong father take him in like become own family. Du Zong father wasn't look down on him, but didn't take seriously, until that man big like become a mafia. Now important person, very hard to inviting him. Chinese way, came only to show respect, don't stay for dinner. Respect for making big celebration, he shows up. Mean gives lots of respect. Chinese custom. Chinese social life that way. If too important won't have to stay too long. He come to my wedding. I didn't see, I heard it. I gone to boy's side, they have YMCA dinner. Chinese age I was nineteen."

You should know that my mother's expressive command of English belies 7 how much she actually understands. She reads the *Forbes* report, listens to *Wall Street Week,* converses daily with her stockbroker, reads all of Shirley MacLaine's books with ease—all kinds of things I can't begin to understand. Yet some of my friends tell me they understand 50 percent of what my mother says. Some say they understand 80 to 90 percent. Some say they understand none of it, as if she were speaking pure Chinese. But to me, my mother's English is perfectly clear, perfectly natural. It's my mother tongue. Her language, as I hear it, is vivid, direct, full of observation and imagery. That was the language that helped shape the way I saw things, expressed things, made sense of the world.

8    Lately, I've been giving more thought to the kind of English my mother speaks. Like others, I have described it to people as "broken" or "fractured" English. But I wince when I say that. It has always bothered me that I can think of no way to describe it other than "broken," as if it were damaged and needed to be fixed, as if it lacked a certain wholeness and soundness. I've heard other terms used, "limited English," for example. But they seem just as bad, as if everything is limited, including people's perceptions of the limited English speaker.

9    I know this for a fact, because when I was growing up, my mother's "limited" English limited *my* perception of her. I was ashamed of her English. I believed that her English reflected the quality of what she had to say. That is, because she expressed them imperfectly her thoughts were imperfect. And I had plenty of empirical evidence to support me: the fact that people in department stores, at banks, and at restaurants did not take her seriously, did not give her good service, pretended not to understand her, or even acted as if they did not hear her.

10    My mother has long realized the limitations of her English as well. When I was fifteen, she used to have me call people on the phone to pretend I was she. In this guise, I was forced to ask for information or even to complain and yell at people who had been rude to her. One time it was a call to her stockbroker in New York. She had cashed out her small portfolio and it just so happened we were going to go to New York the next week, our very first trip outside California. I had to get on the phone and say in an adolescent voice that was not very convincing, "This is Mrs. Tan."

11    And my mother was standing in the back whispering loudly, "Why he don't send me check, already two weeks late. So mad he lie to me, losing me money."

12    And then I said in perfect English, "Yes, I'm getting rather concerned. You had agreed to send the check two weeks ago, but it hasn't arrived."

13    Then she began to talk more loudly. "What he want, I come to New York tell him front of his boss, you cheating me?" And I was trying to calm her down, make her be quiet, while telling the stockbroker, "I can't tolerate any more excuses. If I don't receive the check immediately, I am going to have to speak to your manager when I'm in New York next week." And sure enough, the following week there we were in front of this astonished stockbroker, and I was sitting there red-faced and quiet, and my mother, the real Mrs. Tan, was shouting at his boss in her impeccable broken English.

14    We used a similar routine just five days ago, for a situation that was far less humorous. My mother had gone to the hospital for an appointment, to find out about a benign brain tumor a CAT scan had revealed a month ago. She said she had spoken very good English, her best English, no mistakes. Still, she said, the hospital did not apologize when they said they had lost the CAT

scan and she had come for nothing. She said they did not seem to have any sympathy when she told them she was anxious to know the exact diagnosis, since her husband and son had both died of brain tumors. She said they would not give her any more information until the next time and she would have to make another appointment for that. So she said she would not leave until the doctor called her daughter. She wouldn't budge. And when the doctor finally called her daughter, me, who spoke in perfect English—lo and behold—we had assurances the CAT scan would be found, promises that a conference call on Monday would be held, and apologies for any suffering my mother had gone through for a most regrettable mistake.

I think my mother's English almost had an effect on limiting my possibili- 15 ties in life as well. Sociologists and linguists probably will tell you that a person's developing language skills are more influenced by peers. But I do think that the language spoken in the family, especially in immigrant families which are more insular, plays a large role in shaping the language of the child. And I believe that it affected my results on achievement tests, IQ tests, and the SAT. While my English skills were never judged as poor, compared to math, English could not be considered my strong suit. In grade school I did moderately well, getting perhaps B's, sometimes B-pluses, in English and scoring perhaps in the sixtieth or seventieth percentile on achievement tests. But those scores were not good enough to override the opinion that my true abilities lay in math and science, because in those areas I achieved A's and scored in the ninetieth percentile or higher.

This was understandable. Math is precise; there is only one correct answer. 16 Whereas, for me at least, the answers on English tests were always a judgment call, a matter of opinion and personal experience. Those tests were constructed around items like fill-in-the-blank sentence completion, such as, "Even though Tom was _____, Mary thought he was _____." And the correct answer always seemed to be the most bland combinations of thoughts, for example, "Even though Tom was shy, Mary thought he was charming," with the grammatical structure "even though" limiting the correct answer to some sort of semantic opposites, so you wouldn't get answers like, "Even though Tom was foolish, Mary thought he was ridiculous." Well, according to my mother, there were very few limitations as to what Tom could have been and what Mary might have thought of him. So I never did well on tests like that.

The same was true with word analogies, pairs of words in which you were 17 supposed to find some sort of logical, semantic relationship—for example, "*Sunset* is to *nightfall* as _____ is to _____." And here you would be presented with a list of four possible pairs, one of which showed the same kind of relationship: *red* is to *stoplight, bus* is to *arrival, chills* is to *fever, yawn* is to *boring*. Well, I could never think that way. I knew what the tests were asking, but I could not block out of my mind the images already created by the first pair, "*sunset* is to *nightfall*"—and I would see a burst of colors against a darkening sky, the moon rising, the lowering of a curtain of stars. And all the other pairs of words—red, bus, stoplight, boring—just threw up a mass of confusing images, making it impossible for me to sort out something as logical as saying: "A sunset precedes nightfall" is the same as "a chill precedes a fever." The only way I would have gotten that answer right would have been to imagine an associative situation, for example, my being disobedient and staying out past sunset, catching a chill at night, which turns into feverish pneumonia as punishment, which indeed did happen to me.

18   I have been thinking about all this lately, about my mother's English, about achievement tests. Because lately I've been asked, as a writer, why there are not more Asian Americans represented in American literature. Why are there few Asian Americans enrolled in creative writing programs? Why do so many Chinese students go into engineering? Well, these are broad sociological questions I can't begin to answer. But I have noticed in surveys—in fact, just last week—that Asian students, as a whole, always do significantly better on math achievement tests than in English. And this makes me think that there are other Asian-American students whose English spoken in the home might also be described as "broken" or "limited." And perhaps they also have teachers who are steering them away from writing and into math and science, which is what happened to me.

19   Fortunately, I happen to be rebellious in nature and enjoy the challenge of disproving assumptions made about me. I became an English major my first year in college, after being enrolled as pre-med. I started writing nonfiction as a freelancer the week after I was told by my former boss that writing was my worst skill and I should hone my talents toward account management.

20   But it wasn't until 1985 that I finally began to write fiction. And at first I wrote using what I thought to be wittily crafted sentences, sentences that would finally prove I had mastery over the English language. Here's an example from the first draft of a story that later made its way into *The Joy Luck Club*, but without this line: "That was my mental quandary in its nascent state." A terrible line, which I can barely pronounce.

21   Fortunately, for reasons I won't get into today, I later decided I should envision a reader for the stories I would write. And the reader I decided upon was my mother, because these were stories about mothers. So with this reader in mind—and in fact she did read my early drafts—I began to write stories using all the Englishes I grew up with: the English I spoke to my mother, which for lack of a better term might be described as "simple"; the English she used with me, which for lack of a better term might be described as "broken"; my translation of her Chinese, which could certainly be described as "watered down"; and what I imagined to be her translation of her Chinese if she could speak in perfect English, her internal language, and for that I sought to preserve the essence, but neither an English nor a Chinese structure. I wanted to capture what language ability tests can never reveal: her intent, her passion, her imagery, the rhythms of her speech and the nature of her thoughts.

22   Apart from what any critic had to say about my writing, I knew I had succeeded where it counted when my mother finished reading my book and gave me her verdict: "So easy to read."

## COMPREHENSION

1. Explain the pun in the title of Tan's essay. How does this pun echo throughout the essay?
2. Tan refers to "all the Englishes I grew up with" (paragraph 2). How many "Englishes" does she discuss, and how does she distinguish among them? According to the writer, what are the ways in which language can work?
3. What observations does Tan make about Asian Americans and standard test scores? Why does she introduce this topic into an essay that, after all, focuses on her mother?

## RHETORIC

1. Why does Tan begin her essay by confessing that she is "not a scholar of English or literature" (paragraph 1)? Does this disclaimer undermine her authority to speak about language? Why or why not?
2. Explain Tan's use of classification and division to organize her essay. Into what two main categories does she divide the languages she employs?
3. Identify places in the essay where Tan uses definition. What is her purpose in providing such basic definitions?
4. What is Tan's purpose in telling stories involving the use of language? How do these narrative moments affect the tone of the essay?
5. Do you detect an argument in this essay? If so, where does Tan present her claim, and how does she support it? If not, what is the thesis of the piece?
6. Analyze the conclusion. Why does Tan end with an image of her mother responding to her daughter's first novel? Do you think that her mother is Tan's intended audience? Why or why not?

## WRITING

1. Write an essay that classifies the "different Englishes" that people use in everyday life—at home, work, school, and elsewhere.
2. In an analytical paper, identify and evaluate the various rhetorical strategies that Tan employs to compose her essay.
3. **Writing an Argument:** Take a position on the proposition that the United States should be an "English only" nation.

www.mhhe.com/
**mhreader**

For more information on Amy Tan, go to:
**More Resources > Ch. 1 Reading & Writing**

# Freewriting

## Peter Elbow

*Peter Elbow (b. 1935) was born in New York and received degrees from Williams Col-*
*lege, Exeter College, Oxford, and Brandeis University. He has taught at the University*
*of Massachusetts at Amherst, the State University of New York at Stony Brook, the*
*Massachusetts Institute of Technology, Franconia College, and Evergreen State Col-*
*lege. He is considered by some writing teachers to have revolutionized the teaching of*
*writing through his popularization of the concept and practice called "freewriting." He*
*is the author or editor of more than 15 books on writing, including* Writing without
Teachers, Writing with Power, Embracing Contraries, What Is English? *and,*
*most recently,* Everyone Can Write: Essays toward a Hopeful Theory of Writing
and Teaching Writing (2000). *In "Freewriting," taken from* Writing without
Teachers, *Elbow explains an exercise for writing students that he helped popularize in*
*American colleges, universities, and writing workshops.*

1   The most effective way I know to improve your writing is to do freewriting
exercises regularly. At least three times a week. They are sometimes called
"automatic writing," "babbling," or "jabbering" exercises. The idea is simply
to write for ten minutes (later on, perhaps fifteen or twenty). Don't stop for
anything. Go quickly without rushing. Never stop to look back, to cross
something out, to wonder how to spell something, to wonder what word or
thought to use, or to think about what you are doing. If you can't think of a
word or a spelling, just use a squiggle or else write, "I can't think of it." Just
put down something. The easiest thing is just to put down whatever is in
your mind. If you get stuck it's fine to write "I can't think what to say, I can't
think what to say" as many times as you want; or repeat the last word you
wrote over and over again; or anything else. The only requirement is that
you *never* stop.

2       What happens to a freewriting exercise is important. It must be a piece of
writing which, even if someone reads it, doesn't send any ripples back to you.
It is like writing something and putting it in a bottle in the sea. The teacherless
class helps your writing by providing maximum feedback. Freewritings help
you by providing no feedback at all. When I assign one, I invite the writer to let
me read it. But also tell him to keep it if he prefers. I read it quickly and make
no comments at all and I do not speak with him about it. The main thing is that
a freewriting must never be evaluated in any way; in fact there must be no discussion or comment at all.

3       Here is an example of a fairly coherent exercise (sometimes they are very
incoherent, which is fine):

I think I'll write what's on my mind, but the only thing on my mind right now is what to write for ten minutes. I've never done this before and I'm not prepared in any way—the sky is cloudy today, how's that? now I'm afraid I won't be able to think of what to write when I get to the end of the sentence—well, here I am at the end of the sentence—here I am again, again, again, again, at least I'm still writing—Now I ask is there some reason to be happy that I'm still writing—ah yes! Here comes the question again—What am I getting out of this? What point is there in it? It's almost obscene to always ask it but I seem to question everything that way and I was gonna say something else pertaining to that but I got so busy writing down the first part that I forgot what I was leading into. This is kind of fun oh don't stop writing—cars and trucks speeding by somewhere out the window, pens clittering across people's papers. The sky is cloudy—is it symbolic that I should be mentioning it? Huh? I dunno. Maybe I should try colors, blue, red, dirty words—wait a minute—no can't do that, orange, yellow, arm tired, green pink violet magenta lavender red brown black green—now that I can't think of any more colors—just about done—relief? maybe.

Freewriting may seem crazy but actually it makes simple sense. Think of the difference between speaking and writing. Writing has the advantage of permitting more editing. But that's its downfall too. Almost everybody interposes a massive and complicated series of editings between the time words start to be born into consciousness and when they finally come off the end of the pencil or typewriter onto the page. This is partly because schooling makes us obsessed with the "mistakes" we make in writing. Many people are constantly thinking about spelling and grammar as they try to write. I am always thinking about the awkwardness, wordiness, and general mushiness of my natural verbal product as I try to write down words.

But it's not just "mistakes" or "bad writing" we edit as we write. We also 4 edit unacceptable thoughts and feelings, as we do in speaking. In writing there is more time to do it so the editing is heavier: when speaking, there's someone right there waiting for a reply and he'll get bored or think we're crazy if we don't come out with *something*. Most of the time in speaking, we settle for the catch-as-catch-can way in which the words tumble out. In writing, however, there's a chance to try to get them right. But the opportunity to get them right is a terrible burden: you can work for two hours trying to get a paragraph "right" and discover it's not right at all. And then give up.

Editing, *in itself,* is not the problem. Editing is usually necessary if we 5 want to end up with something satisfactory. The problem is that editing goes on *at the same time* as producing. The editor is, as it were, constantly looking ever the shoulder of the producer and constantly fiddling with what he's doing while he's in the middle of trying to do it. No wonder the producer gets nervous, jumpy, inhibited, and finally can't be coherent. It's an unnecessary burden to try to think of words and also worry at the same time whether they're the right words.

The main thing about freewriting is that it is *nonediting*. It is an exercise in 6 bringing together the process of producing words and putting them down on the page. Practiced regularly, it undoes the ingrained habit of editing at the same time you are trying to produce. It will make writing less blocked because words will come more easily. You will use up more paper, but chew up fewer pencils.

7      Next time you write, notice how often you stop yourself from writing down something you were going to write down. Or else cross it out after it's written. "Naturally," you say, "it wasn't any good." But think for a moment about the occasions when you spoke well. Seldom was it because you first got the beginning just right. Usually it was a matter of a halting or even garbled beginning, but you kept going and your speech finally became coherent and even powerful. There is a lesson here for writing: trying to get the beginning just right is a formula for failure—and probably a secret tactic to make yourself give up writing. Make some words, whatever they are, and then grab hold of that line and reel in as hard as you can. Afterwards you can throw away lousy beginnings and make new ones. This is the quickest way to get into good writing.

8      The habit of compulsive, premature editing doesn't just make writing hard. It also makes writing dead. Your voice is damped out by all the interruptions, changes, and hesitations between the consciousness and the page. In your natural way of producing words there is a sound, a texture, a rhythm—a voice—which is the main source of power in your writing. I don't know how it works, but this voice is the force that will make a reader listen to you, the energy that drives the meanings through his thick skull. Maybe you don't *like* your voice; maybe people have made fun of it. But it's the only voice you've got. It's your only source of power. You better get back into it, no matter what you think of it. If you keep writing in it, it may change into something you like better. But if you abandon it, you'll likely never have a voice and never be heard.

9      Freewritings are vacuums. Gradually you will begin to carry over into your regular writing some of the voice, force, and connectedness that creep into those vacuums.

## COMPREHENSION

1. What is the thesis of the essay? Is it implied or stated directly in the text?
2. In paragraph 5, Elbow refers to the "producer" and the "editor." Who are they? Where are they located? How did they develop?
3. In paragraph 8, the author makes a connection between one's personal "voice" and the idea of "power." Why does Elbow focus so strongly on this connection?

## RHETORIC

1. Elbow frequently uses the "imperative" (or command) sentence form in the opening paragraph. Why? What would have been the effect had he used the simple declarative form?

2.  Writers often use examples to help illustrate their point. Does the example of a freewriting exercise Elbow provides in paragraph 3 help you to understand the method? Why or why not?

3.  The author uses colloquial terms such as "squiggle" (paragraph 1), "crazy" and "mushiness" (paragraph 3), and "lousy" (paragraph 7). How does his use of such words affect the tone of the essay?

4.  Are there any elements in Elbow's own style that suggest his essay may have started as a freewriting exercise? Consider the reasons he provides for the importance of freewriting—for example, generating ideas, discovering one's own voice, or expressing oneself succinctly and naturally.

5.  Elbow is himself a college writing teacher. Based on your assessment of the tone of the essay, whom do you think is his intended audience? Is it broad or narrow? Specialized or general? Or could he have in mind more than one type of audience? Explain your answer.

6.  Note the number of times Elbow begins his sentences with coordinating conjunctions ("but," "and," "or"). For example, in paragraph 4, he does it three times. Many writing teachers frown on this method of structuring sentences. Why does Elbow employ it?

7.  Compare the essay's introduction to its conclusion. Note how the introduction is rather long and the conclusion is quite short (two sentences, in fact). How do these two elements contribute to the overall "pace" of the essay?

## WRITING

1.  During one week, complete three freewriting exercises. Wait one week, and then review what you have written. Explore any insights your freewriting gives you into your writer's "voice"— your concerns, interests, style, and "power."

2.  Write an expository paper explaining the difficulties you have when writing an essay homework assignment or writing an essay-length response during an exam.

3.  Write a comparison and contrast essay wherein you examine the similarities and differences of speaking and writing.

4.  **Writing an Argument:** Write an essay in which you support or discourage the act of freewriting.

www.mhhe.com/ **mhreader**

For more information on Peter Elbow, go to:
**More Resources > Ch. 1 Reading & Writing**

# The Maker's Eye: Revising Your Own Manuscripts

## Donald M. Murray

*Donald M. Murray (1917–2006) has combined a career as teacher, journalist, fiction writer, poet, and author of several important textbooks on writing. He has worked as a teacher, journalist, and editor for* Time *magazine. His books include* A Writer Teaches Writing, Write to Learn, Read to Write, *and more recently* Shoptalk: Learning to Write with Writers *(1991),* Crafting a Life in Essay, Story, Poem *(1996), and* The Craft of Revision *(1997). In this essay, originally published in the magazine* The Writer, *Murray argues for the absolute importance of the revision process to the writer. As he presents the stages of the revision process, Murray illustrates their usefulness to any writer—whether beginner or experienced—and offers his personal views and those of other authors.*

1   When students complete a first draft, they consider the job of writing done—and their teachers too often agree. When professional writers complete a first draft, they usually feel that they are at the start of the writing process. When a draft is completed, the job of writing can begin.

2    That difference in attitude is the difference between amateur and professional, inexperience and experience, journeyman and craftsman. Peter F. Drucker, the prolific business writer, calls his first draft "the zero draft"—after that he can start counting. Most writers share the feeling that the first draft, and all of those which follow, are opportunities to discover what they have to say and how best they can say it.

3    To produce a progression of drafts, each of which says more and says it more clearly, the writer has to develop a special kind of reading skill. In school we are taught to decode what appears on the page as finished writing. Writers, however, face a different category of possibility and responsibility when they read their own drafts. To them the words on the page are never finished. Each can be changed and rearranged, can set off a chain reaction of confusion or clarified meaning. This is a different kind of reading, which is possibly more difficult and certainly more exciting.

4    Writers must learn to be their own best enemy. They must accept the criticism of others and be suspicious of it; they must accept the praise of others and be even more suspicious of it. Writers cannot depend on others. They must detach themselves from their own pages so that they can apply both their caring and their craft to their own work.

5    Such detachment is not easy. Science fiction writer Ray Bradbury supposedly puts each manuscript away for a year to the day and then rereads it as a

stranger. Not many writers have the discipline or the time to do this. We must read when our judgment may be at its worst, when we are close to the euphoric moment of creation.

Then the writer, counsels novelist Nancy Hale, "should be critical of every- 6 thing that seems to him most delightful in his style. He should excise what he most admires, because he wouldn't thus admire it if he weren't . . . in a sense protecting it from criticism." John Ciardi, the poet, adds, "The last act of the writing must be to become one's own reader. It is, I suppose, a schizophrenic process, to begin passionately and to end critically, to begin hot and to end cold; and, more important, to be passion-hot and critic-cold at the same time."

Most people think that the principal problem is that writers are too proud 7 of what they have written. Actually, a greater problem for most professional writers is one shared by the majority of students. They are overly critical, think everything is dreadful, tear up page after page, never complete a draft, see the task as hopeless.

The writer must learn to read critically but constructively, to cut what is 8 bad, to reveal what is good. Eleanor Estes, the children's book author, explains: "The writer must survey his work critically, coolly, as though he were a stranger to it. He must be willing to prune, expertly and hard-heartedly. At the end of each revision, a manuscript may look . . . worked over, torn apart, pinned to-gether, added to, deleted from, words changed and words changed back. Yet the book must maintain its original freshness and spontaneity."

Most readers underestimate the amount of rewriting it usually takes to pro- 9 duce spontaneous reading. This is a great disadvantage to the student writer, who sees only a finished product and never watches the craftsman who takes the necessary step back, studies the work carefully, returns to the task, steps back, returns, steps back, again and again. Anthony Burgess, one of the most prolific writers in the English-speaking world, admits, "I might revise a page twenty times." Roald Dahl, the popular children's writer, states, "By the time I'm nearing the end of a story, the first part will have been reread and altered and corrected at least 150 times. . . . Good writing is essentially rewriting. I am positive of this."

Rewriting isn't virtuous. It isn't something that ought to be done. It is sim- 10 ply something that most writers find they have to do to discover what they have to say and how to say it. It is a condition of the writer's life.

There are, however, a few writers who do little formal rewriting, primarily 11 because they have the capacity and experience to create and review a large number of invisible drafts in their minds before they approach the page. And some writers slowly produce finished pages, performing all the tasks of revi-sion simultaneously, page by page, rather than draft by draft. But it is still pos-sible to see the sequence followed by most writers most of the time in rereading their own work.

Most writers scan their drafts first, reading as quickly as possible to catch 12 the larger problems of subject and form, then move in closer and closer as they read and write, reread and rewrite.

13    The first thing writers look for in their drafts is *information*. They know that a good piece of writing is built from specific, accurate, and interesting information. The writer must have an abundance of information from which to construct a readable piece of writing.

14    Next writers look for *meaning* in the information. The specifics must build a pattern of significance. Each piece of specific information must carry the reader toward meaning.

15    Writers reading their own drafts are aware of *audience.* They put themselves in the reader's situation and make sure that they deliver information which a reader wants to know or needs to know in a manner which is easily digested. Writers try to be sure that they anticipate and answer the questions a critical reader will ask when reading the piece of writing.

16    Writers make sure that the *form* is appropriate to the subject and the audience. Form, or genre, is the vehicle which carries meaning to the reader, but form cannot be selected until the writer has adequate information to discover its significance and an audience which needs or wants that meaning.

17    Once writers are sure the form is appropriate, they must then look at the *structure,* the order of what they have written. Good writing is built on a solid framework of logic, argument, narrative, or motivation which runs through the entire piece of writing and holds it together. This is the time when many writers find it most effective to outline as a way of visualizing the hidden spine by which the piece of writing is supported.

18    The element on which writers may spend a majority of their time is *development*. Each section of a piece of writing must be adequately developed. It must give readers enough information so that they are satisfied. How much information is enough? That's as difficult as asking how much garlic belongs in a salad. It must be done to taste, but most beginning writers underdevelop, underestimating the reader's hunger for information.

19    As writers solve development problems, they often have to consider questions of *dimension*. There must be a pleasing and effective proportion among all the parts of the piece of writing. There is a continual process of subtracting and adding to keep the piece of writing in balance.

20    Finally, writers have to listen to their own voices. *Voice* is the force which drives a piece of writing forward. It is an expression of the writer's authority and concern. It is what is between the words on the page, what glues the piece of writing together. A good piece of writing is always marked by a consistent, individual voice.

21    As writers read and reread, write and rewrite, they move closer and closer to the page until they are doing line-by-line editing. Writers read their own pages with infinite care. Each sentence, each line, each clause, each phrase, each word, each mark of punctuation, each section of white space between the type has to contribute to the clarification of meaning.

22    Slowly the writer moves from word to word, looking through language to see the subject. As a word is changed, cut, or added, as a construction is rearranged,

all the words used before that moment and all those that follow that moment must be considered and reconsidered.

Writers often read aloud at this stage of the editing process, muttering or 23 whispering to themselves, calling on the ear's experience with language. Does this sound right—or that? Writers edit, shifting back and forth from eye to page to ear to page. I find I must do this careful editing in short runs, no more than fifteen or twenty minutes at a stretch, or I become too kind with myself. I begin to see what I hope is on the page, not what actually is on the page.

This sounds tedious if you haven't done it, but actually it is fun. Making 24 something right is immensely satisfying, for writers begin to learn what they are writing about by writing. Language leads them to meaning, and there is the joy of discovery, of understanding, of making meaning clear as the writer employs the technical skills of language.

Words have double meanings, even triple and quadruple meanings. Each 25 word has its own potential for connotation and denotation. And when writers rub one word against the other, they are often rewarded with a sudden insight, an unexpected clarification.

The maker's eye moves back and forth from word to phrase to sentence to 26 paragraph to sentence to phrase to word. The maker's eye sees the need for variety and balance, for a firmer structure, for a more appropriate form. It peers into the interior of the paragraph, looking for coherence, unity, and emphasis, which make meaning clear.

I learned something about this process when my first bifocals were pre- 27 scribed. I had ordered a larger section of the reading portion of the glass because of my work, but even so, I could not contain my eyes within this new limit of vision. And I still find myself taking off my glasses and bending my nose towards the page, for my eyes unconsciously flick back and forth across the page, back to another page, forward to still another, as I try to see each evolving line in relation to every other line.

When does this process end? Most writers agree with the great Russian 28 writer Tolstoy, who said, "I scarcely ever reread my published writings, if by chance I come across a page, it always strikes me: all this must be rewritten; this is how I should have written it."

The maker's eye is never satisfied, for each word has the potential to ignite 29 new meaning. This article has been twice written all the way through the writing process, and it was published four years ago. Now it is to be republished in a book. The editors make a few small suggestions, and then I read it with my maker's eye. Now it has been re-edited, re-revised, re-read, re-re-edited, for each piece of writing to the writer is full of potential and alternatives.

A piece of writing is never finished. It is delivered to a deadline, torn out of 30 the typewriter on demand, sent off with a sense of accomplishment and shame and pride and frustration. If only there were a couple more days, time for just another run at it, perhaps then . . .

# COMPREHENSION

1. In paragraph 1, what does Murray mean by the statement "When a draft is completed, the job of writing can begin"? Isn't a draft a form of writing?
2. According to Murray, what are the major differences between student and professional writers? Why do the differences help make the "professional" more accomplished at his or her work?
3. What are the differences between the reading styles of novice and experienced writers? How do the differences affect their own writings?

# RHETORIC

1. Compare the introduction of this essay to that of Elbow's "Freewriting." How do they differ in tone and structure?
2. Murray begins to classify various aspects of the writer's concern in paragraph 13. Why does he wait so long to begin this analysis? Why are certain key words in paragraphs 13–20 italicized?
3. Murray uses analogy, comparing one thing with another, very different thing, to make the writing process concrete and familiar. Identify some of these analogies. Why are they models of clarity?
4. Murray refers to a writer as "the maker" several times in the essay. What does he imply by this usage? What other professions might be included in this category?
5. What is the purpose of the essay? Is it to inform? To persuade? To serve as a model? Anything else? Explain your response.
6. Murray ends the essay with an ellipses. Why?
7. Notice the sentence in paragraph 29 that has four consecutive words with the prefix "re-." What is the purpose and effect of this rhetorical device?

# WRITING

1. Murray focuses on the process, craft, and purpose of the writer, but he does not define "writer." Write an extended definition explaining what he means by this occupation or profession.
2. Write an essay explaining your own writing process. Do not be intimidated if it is not like the one described by Murray. Compare and contrast your method with that of one or more of your classmates.
3. **Writing an Argument:** Murray suggests that revision is actually "fun" (paragraph 24). Do you agree or disagree? Write an essay defending your position.

 **www.mhhe.com/ mhreader**   For more information on Donald M. Murray, go to: **More Resources > Ch. 1 Reading & Writing**

# The Blogs of War

## John Hockenberry

*John Hockenberry (b. 1956) is a novelist, journalist, and television commentator and anchor. Born in Dayton, Ohio, he attended the University of Chicago and, following a car accident that left him paralyzed from the chest down, the University of Oregon. A three-time Peabody Award and four-time Emmy Award winner, Hockenberry has worked for more than 20-years for National Public Radio, ABC, NBC, and MSNBC. He writes of his experience as a disabled person in a memoir,* Moving Violations: War Zones, Wheel Chairs, and Declarations of Independence *(1995). He has also written a novel,* A River out of Eden *(2001). In the following selection, which appeared in* Wired *in 2005 and which subsequently was selected for inclusion in* The Best American Essays 2006, *Hockenberry reports on the "milblogs" American troops maintain to report on their combat experiences in Iraq.*

The snapshots of Iraqi prisoners being abused at Abu Ghraib were taken by soldiers and shared in the digital military netherworld of Iraq. Their release to the world in May 2004 detonated a media explosion that rocked a presidential campaign, cratered America's moral high ground, and demonstrated how even a superpower could be blitzkrieged by some homemade downloadable porn. In the middle of it all, a lone reservist sergeant stationed on the Iraqi border posed a simple question: "I cannot help but wonder upon reflection of the circumstances, how much longer we will be able to carry with us our digital cameras, or take photographs and document the experiences we have had." 1

The writer was twenty-four-year-old Chris Missick, a soldier with the army's 319th Signal Battalion and author of the blog "A Line in the Sand." While balloon-faced cable pundits shrieked about the scandal, Missick was posting late at night in his army-issue "blacks," with a mug of coffee and a small French press beside him, his laptop blasting Elliott Smith's "Cupid's Trick" into his headphones. He quickly seized on perhaps the most profound and crucial implication of Abu Ghraib: 2

> Never before has a war been so immediately documented, never before have sentiments from the front scurried their way to the home front with such ease and precision. Here I sit, in the desert, staring daily at the electric fence, the deep trenches, and the concertina wire that separates the border of Iraq and Kuwait, and write home and upload my daily reflections and opinions on the war and my circumstances here, as well as some of the pictures I have taken along the way. It is amazing, and empowering, and yet the question remains, should I as a lower enlisted soldier have such power to express my opinion and broadcast to the world a singular soldier's point of view? To those outside the uniform who have never lived the military life, the question may seem absurd, and yet,

as an example of what exists even in the small following of readers I have here, the implications of thought expressed by soldiers daily could be explosive.

3    His sober assessments of the potential of free speech in a war zone began attracting a wider following, eventually logging somewhere north of 100,000 pageviews. No blogging record, but rivaling the wonkish audience for the Pentagon's daily briefing on C-Span or Department of Defense (DOD) press releases.

4    Missick is just one voice—and a very pro-Pentagon one at that—in an odd-ball online Greek chorus narrating the conflict in Iraq. It includes a core group of about one hundred regulars and hundreds more loosely organized activists, angry contrarians, jolly testosterone fuckups, self-appointed pundits, and would-be poets who call themselves milbloggers, as in military bloggers. Whether posting from inside Iraq on active duty, from noncombat bases around the world, or even from their neighborhoods back home after being dis-charged—where they can still follow events closely and deliver their often blunt opinions—milbloggers offer an unprecedented real-time, real-life window on war and the people who wage it. Their collective voice competes with and occasionally undermines the DOD's elaborate message machine and the much-loathed mainstream media, usually dismissed as MSM.

5    Milbloggers constitute a rich subculture with a refreshing candor about the war, expressing views ranging from far right to far left. They also offer helpful tips about tearing down an M-16, recipes for beef stew (hint: lots of red wine), reviews of the latest episode of 24, extremely technical discussions of Humvee armor configurations, and exceptionally raw accounts of field-hospital chaos, gore, and heroism.

6    For now, the Pentagon officially tolerates this free-form online journalism and in-house peanut gallery, even as the brass takes cautious steps to control it. A new policy instituted this spring requires all military bloggers inside Iraq to register with their units. It directs commanders to conduct quarterly reviews to make sure bloggers aren't giving out casualty information or violating opera-tional security or privacy rules. Commanding officers shut down a blog that reported on the medical response to a suicide bombing late last year in Mosul. The army has also created the Army Web Risk Assessment Cell to monitor com-pliance. And Wired has learned that a Pentagon review is under way to better understand the overall implications of blogging and other Internet communica-tions in combat zones.

7    "It's a new world out there," says Christopher Conway, a lieutenant colo-nel and DOD spokesperson. "Before, you would have to shake down your sol-diers for matches that might light up and betray a position. Today, every soldier has a cell phone, beeper, game device, or laptop, any one of which could pop off without warning. Blogging is just one piece of the puzzle."

8    Strong opinions throughout the military ranks, in and out of wartime, are nothing new. But online technology in the combat zone has suddenly given those opinions a mass audience and an instantaneous forum for the first time in

the history of warfare. On the twenty-first-century battlefield, the campfire glow comes from a laptop computer, and it's visible around the world.

"In World War II, letters basically didn't arrive for months," says Michael 9 Bautista, an Idaho National Guard corporal based in Kirkuk whose grandfather served in World War II and who blogs as Ma Deuce Gunner (named for the trusty M-2 machine gun he calls Mama). "What I'm doing and what my fellow bloggers are doing is groundbreaking."

If you're stuck in southern Baghdad in the dusty gray fortress called Camp 10 Falcon and find yourself in need of 50-caliber machine-gun ammo, chopper fuel, toilet paper, or M&M's, you call Danjel Bout, a thirty-two-year-old captain and logistics officer from the California National Guard who blogs as Thunder 6. He's been stationed here with the army's 3rd Infantry Division for most of 2005. When he's not chasing down requisitions of supplies or out on patrol hunting insurgents, Bout is posting about the details of army life in language evocative of literary warbloggers of yore like Thucydides, Homer, Thomas Paine, and John Donne.

> Sleep, blessed, blissful, wonderful sleep. Mother's milk. A full harvest in a time of famine. The storm that breaks the drought. It is the drug of choice here—assiduously avoided because of the never-ending chain of missions, but always craved. If rarity is the measure of a substance's worth, then here in Iraq, sleep carries a price beyond words. There is no more precious moment in my day than the sublime instant where my mind flickers between consciousness and the dreamworld. In that sliver of time the day seems to shimmer and melt like one of Dali's paintings—leaving only honey sweet dreams of my other life far from Arabia.

Bout's blog, "365 and a Wakeup," is unlikely to put you to sleep. It's one of 11 the most genuine accounts anywhere of what life is like for a soldier in Iraq. The captain can be spotted composing and editing his posts on his laptop from the roof of one of Camp Falcon's dusty buildings in the dark early-morning hours, or in a scarce patch of shade during a rare moment of daylight downtime. His posts are sharply rendered parables and small, often powerful scenes built on details of the violent world around him. "I just kind of bookmark the things I see during the day so I can reflect on them later. There's almost nothing about life here that isn't interesting in some way."

Thunder 6 is the oldest of eight siblings in a devout Catholic family. His 12 dad is a computer technician, his mom a horticulture therapist. This former altar boy and longtime reservist left the touchy-feely psychology Ph.D. program at the University of California, Davis, after September 11, grabbed an M-16 rifle and a Beretta 9-mm sidearm, and went all-infantry. Trained as an army ranger, he saw action in Kuwait and Bosnia and claims to have no yearning for his former scholarly life. "I was coasting through college," he says, "and the army spoke to honor and camaraderie and things I really believed in."

While Bout's blog is all about his emotional connection to the army and 13 very little about the daily bang-bang of Iraq, there are lots of milbloggers who will take you straight to the front lines, posting first-person accounts of the fighting and beating some newspaper reports of the same battle filed by embedded journalists. By the crude light of a small bulb and the backlit screen of his Dell laptop, Neil Prakash, a first lieutenant, posted some of the best descriptions of the fighting in Fallujah and Baquba last fall:

> Terrorists in headwraps stood anywhere from 30 to 400 meters in front of my tank. They stopped, squared their shoulders at us just like in an old-fashioned duel, and fired RPGs at our tanks. So far there hadn't been a single civilian in Task Force 2-2 sector. We had been free to light up the insurgents as we saw them. And because of that freedom, we were able to use the main gun with less restriction.

14      Prakash was awarded the Silver Star this year for saving his entire tank task force during an assault on insurgents in Iraq's harrowing Sunni Triangle. He goes by the handle Red 6 and is the author of "Armor Geddon." For him, the poetry of warfare is in the sounds of exploding weapons and the chaos of battle.

15      "It's mind-blowing what this stuff can do," Prakash tells me by phone from Germany, where his unit moved after rotating out of Iraq earlier this year. One of his favorite sounds is that of an F16 fighter on a strafing run. "It's like a cat in a blender ripping the sky open—if the sky was made out of a phone book." He is from India, the land of Gandhi, but he loves to talk about blowing things up. "It's just sick how badass a tank looks when it's killing."

16      Prakash is the son of two upstate New York dentists and has a degree in neuroscience from Johns Hopkins. He's a naturalized American citizen, born near Bangalore, and he describes growing up in the United States and his decision to join the military as something like *Bend It like Beckham* meets *The Terminator*. He says he admired the army's discipline and loved the idea of driving a tank. He knew that if he didn't join the army, he might end up in medical school or some windowless office in a high-tech company. With a bit of bluster, Prakash claims that for him, the latter would be more of a nightmare scenario than ending up in the line of fire of insurgents. "It was a choice between commanding the best bunch of guys in the world and being in a cubicle at Dell Computer in Bangalore right now helping people from Bum-fuck, USA, format their hard drives."

17      It's taken some adjustment, but Prakash says his parents basically support his army career, although his father can't conceal his anxiety about having a son in Iraq. Prakash says he blogs to assure the folks back home that he's safe, to let his friends all over the world know what's going on, and to juice up the morale in his unit. "The guys get really excited when I mention them."

18      By the time Prakash left Iraq early this year, the readers of "Armor Geddon" extended far beyond family and friends. He still posts from his base in Germany and is slowly trying to complete a blog memoir of his and his fellow soldiers' experiences in the battle for Fallujah.

19   The most widely read milbloggers engage in the twenty-first-century contact sport called punditry and, like their civilian counterparts, follow few rules of engagement. They mobilize sympathizers to ship body armor to reserve units in combat,

raise funds for families of wounded soldiers, deliver shoes to barefoot Afghani kids, and even take aim at media big shots. It was milblogger pundits who helped bring down Eason Jordan, a senior executive at CNN who resigned earlier this year over remarks he made that U.S. troops were targeting reporters in Iraq.

One important milblogger who weighed in on the Jordan affair is a secre-  20 tive twenty-year career army GI who goes by the handle Greyhawk. His blog, "The Mudville Gazette," investigated the incident and concluded that Iraq-based reporters disputed Jordan's claim. He's unhappy that a more thorough news investigation wasn't conducted. Other bloggers call Greyhawk "the father of us all" and credit him with coining the term *milblogger* shortly after he started "Mudville" in March 2003. In an e-mail interview—Greyhawk wouldn't agree to "voice-com" or a "face-to-face"—he writes proudly of his lifetime pageviews, which recently exceeded 1.7 million (700,000 of those have come in 2005): "Mudville is far and away the largest, oldest, widest-read active-duty MilBlog in the World. It's all in how you make the words line up and dance."

Then there's Blackfive: "I'm just a guy with a blog and I know how to use  21 it," says this modest former army intelligence officer and paratrooper, who gives his real name only as Matt. He prefers the nom de guerre of his popular site. His peers voted "Blackfive" the best military blog in the 2004 Weblog Awards, beating out such contenders as "Froggy Ruminations," "The Mudville Gazette," "2Slick," and "My War." "Blackfive" is a popular forum for analysis of the war and strident, argumentative warnings about media bias. It's nearly as cluttered with ads as "The Drudge Report," and the sales pitches mostly hawk "liberal-baiting merchandise." There are pictures of attractive women holding high-powered weapons, dozens of links to conservative books and films, and even the occasional big spender like Amazon.com. Blackfive also sells his own T-shirts to benefit military charities.

He says that milblogging is the result of an explosion of communications  22 technology throughout the military and an increase in brainpower among the lower ranks. "The educational level of sergeants and below is out of control." Blackfive himself has degrees in archaeology and computer science and avidly follows the postings of fellow bloggers. He describes Neil Prakash as "border-line Einstein" and Danjel Bout as "a real rock star." In his last deployment, Blackfive's unit had two such brainiacs, a sergeant with an M.B.A. and another with a master's in economics from the University of Chicago.

Blackfive is retired now, honorably discharged and working as an IT execu-  23 tive for a big civilian company. He blogs from Chicago and confidently claims he can mobilize thousands of people and their wallets, all from a wireless hot spot at his local Starbucks. He stays in the shadows because he believes that his company would not approve of his blog or of his unabashed support for the U.S. war.

The site has become a destination for thousands of information junkies and  24 influential opinion makers. According to "TruthLaid Bear," which tracks blog traffic for advertisers, "Blackfive" is regularly in the top one hundred blogs and averages five thousand unique visits a day. During the height of the war, traffic to "Blackfive" spiked when some high-profile conservatives linked to the site.

25   "My brother followed a link from *National Review* to me, and somebody, I think it was Jonah Goldberg"—a somebody who is only the editor of *National Review*—"told him that four or five of the biggest think tanks read my blog every day."

26   Goldberg confirms that at times he turns to military blogs to supplement and sometimes contradict information coming out of traditional media sources. "'Blackfive' was good, and in the blog world if you offer something unique, you make eyeballs sticky."

27   Since World War I the military has opened the letters soldiers sent back home from the battlefield and sometimes censored the dispatches of war correspondents. Now mail leaves the battlefield already open to the world. Anyone can publicly post a dispatch, and if the Pentagon reads these accounts at all, it's at the same time as the rest of us. The new policy requiring milbloggers to register their sites does not apply to soldiers outside Iraq, but nearly all of the bloggers contacted for this article say that the current system of few restrictions can't possibly last. Blackfive and Greyhawk wonder what the landscape will look like after the Pentagon finishes its review of global digital security. So far, the DOD is giving no hints.

28   Michael Cohen, a major and doctor with the 67th Combat Support Hospital based in Mosul, touched a nerve at the Pentagon late last year with his blog, "67cshdocs." Before he began posting, Cohen turned himself into a local private broadband provider in order to set up his own network outside the one provided to the field hospital. "Some of the docs suggested that life would be really good if we could get Internet into our nice trailers."

29   Cohen bought his network setup online and had it shipped directly to him in Mosul. For the oversize satellite dish, he had to get creative. He ordered it from Bentley Walker, a satellite broadband service provider, and they sent it to his wife's house in Germany. On a medical escort flight to Germany for a wounded soldier, Cohen persuaded the air force to let him hand-carry the dish onto a transport for the return trip. After about six weeks of agonized troubleshooting on a hot rooftop, the network was up and running. "We had pretty decent bandwidth," he says, "two meg downlink and one meg up. It was better than the hospital."

30   Cohen says the system supported webcams linking people back home, its own instant messaging system, live gaming, and, he theorizes, a robust trade in porn. "If you were to make the series *M\*A\*S\*H* about today's army, Radar would be an IT guy and he'd be more popular than Hawkeye."

31   Then Cohen started to blog on his homegrown network. Originally it was an attempt to stay in touch with family and friends, but when a suicide bomber killed twenty-two people last December in a mess tent, Cohen began detailing how doctors dealt with the carnage. His moving account drew attention from worldwide press as well as parents desperate to know the fate of their loved ones:

> The lab was running tests and doing a blood drive to collect more blood. The pharmacy was preparing intravenous medications and drips like crazy.

Radiology was shooting plain films and CT scans like nobody's business. We were washing out wounds, removing shrapnel, and casting fractures. We put in a bunch of chest tubes. Because of all the patients on suction machines and mechanical ventilators, the noise in the ICU was so loud everyone was screaming at each other just to communicate.

Here are some of our statistics. They are really quite amazing: 91 total patients arrived.

18 were dead on arrival.

4 patients dies of wounds shortly after arrival—all of these patients had non-survivable wounds.

Of the 69 remaining patients, 20 were transferred to military hospitals in other locations in Iraq.

This left 49 patients for us to treat and disposition.

Cohen posted mesmerizing details about the medical hardware and surgical procedures used to save lives on that bloody day. And then, without warning, it was over.   32

"My doctor boss came to me and said, hey, we need to talk. There are some people in the chain of command who believe there are things in your blog that violate army regulations." Cohen was shocked. He hadn't used names or talked about military operations. But his impression was that the information he provided about medical capability in the field worried senior officers at Central Command. At first the army asked Cohen to shut down his entire satellite network, which at its peak was serving forty-two families, but ultimately decided against it.   33

"I think they didn't want a hornet's nest," Cohen says. Instead, Cohen stopped blogging.   34

Back in Germany now, where he says he spends more time delivering the latest R-and-R babies than treating battlefield casualties, Cohen says that he was tempted to challenge the shutdown, but since he was close to going home anyway, he went along with the decision. The Pentagon will not comment specifically on Cohen's situation except to reiterate its policy that blogs should not reveal any casualty information that could upset next of kin or any details that might jeopardize operational security.   35

Army reservist Jason Hartley's popular and notoriously irreverent blog, "Just Another Soldier," also provoked the higher-ups; last summer, his commanding officer ordered him to shut it down. Hartley wrote with a fuck-you swagger that may partly explain why he's not blogging anymore: "Being a soldier is to live in a world of shit. From the pogues who cook my food and do my laundry to the Apache pilots and the Green Berets who do all the Hollywood stuff, our lives are in a constant state of suck."   36

Hartley got a lot of mileage out of a post about a soldier who was assembling a rifle blindfolded. Another soldier in his unit, as a joke, handed the assembler a certain piece of his anatomy instead of the tool he asked for.   37

"I told the story and asked the question, Who is more gay, the guy who touches a dick, or someone who allows a soldier to touch his dick?" This pressing infantry-level controversy hit a chord with the über-blogger and noted pundit-   38 of-all-things-queer Andrew Sullivan. "Sullivan was kind and wrote that he liked my site," Hartley recalls.

39      The Pentagon won't say why, but it ordered Hartley to shut down his blog. He did for a while. Then he resumed blogging a few months later, without asking permission, and was busted for defying a direct order and demoted from sergeant to specialist. He chose not to file an appeal and has returned to civilian life, though he's still in the reserves. His memoir about his time in Iraq will be published by HarperCollins.

40      If you read "A Line in the Sand," it's hard to imagine Chris Missick offending Pentagon brass. He is careful not to criticize his superiors and will tell you he has aspirations to run for Congress. While waiting for an early-morning plane to take him back home to southern California, Missick confesses that his biggest blog-related scandal is a romantic one. His stateside girlfriend when he left for Iraq was displaced by another woman, someone Missick says fell in love with him by reading his blog. "When I get home I kinda need to sort that out." (He kinda did and now has yet another girlfriend. Let's hope she likes Elliott Smith's music.)

41      Prakash remains in Germany, awaiting orders to jump back into his beloved tank, which he calls Ol' Blinky. He says he has no plans to resume his study of neuroscience, although it wasn't completely useless in Iraq. "Neuroscience actually came in handy when I had to explain to my guys exactly why doing Ecstasy in a tank when it's 140 degrees out on a road that's blowing up every day is a really bad idea."

42      Danjel Bout, aka Thunder 6, is looking to get home safely, keeping his head down on the streets of southern Baghdad and in his blog. He says the real value of milblogging may be that it brings to the United States the reality of what is becoming a long war. "I don't purposely leave out the moments when our bodies hit the adrenal dump switch, I just don't focus exclusively on them." More typical are his vignettes of Iraqi civilians interacting with U.S. soldiers, or the sad tale of the death of a guardsman who had the chance to go home and instead requested another tour of duty, only to be killed by an improvised explosive device.

43      "Americans are raised on a steady diet of action films and sound bites that slip from one supercharged scene to another," he says, "leaving out all the confusing decisions and subtle details where most people actually spend their lives. While that makes for a great story, it doesn't reveal anything of lasting value. For people to really understand our day-to-day experience here, they need more than the highlights reel. They need to see the world through our eyes for a few minutes."

44      Which suggests, at the very least, that this UC Davis psych-major dropout turned milblogger was perhaps paying more attention in class than he lets on.

## COMPREHENSION

1.  Why do you think Hockenberry begins his essay with a reference to the events at Abu Ghraib? How does reference to this prison in Iraq influence the tone of the essay?

2. What does Hockenberry say about the new digital universe that permits soldiers in combat to report on their experiences? Does he take sides on the issue of milblogging? Why or why not?
3. Hockenberry writes that milblogging raises interesting issues concerning censorship. Summarize the matter as he presents it.

## RHETORIC

1. How does Hockenberry frame or organize his essay? What are the major divisions and how are they organized?
2. Hockenberry includes excerpts from several blogs. What is his purpose? How effective are these illustrations?
3. Explain Hockenberry's style, including his level of diction. Would you say that the essay is a fine illustration of journalistic style? Explain. To what sort of audience would the following sentence appeal: "Missick is just one voice—and a very pro-Pentagon one at that—in an oddball online Greek chorus narrating the conflict in Iraq" (paragraph 4)?
4. Does Hockenberry have a thesis or claim? If so, is it stated or implied? Justify your response.
5. Identify instances where the writer expresses admiration for the milbloggers whom he describes. How does this affirmative tone radiate into the overall content of the essay?
6. Which paragraphs constitute the writer's conclusion? How effective are they, and why?

## WRITING

1. Go online and try to access one of the blogs that Hockenberry alludes to in this essay. Or connect with another milblog that you find to be especially compelling. Write a critique of your findings.
2. Write an essay in which you analyze the ways in which new forms of media and communications are affecting the ways we experience specific conflicts around the world.
3. **Writing an Argument:** Write an argumentative essay in which you either defend or criticize the right of American soldiers to maintain blogs that might be critical of the nation's military incursions. Synthesize information from at least two milblogs to support your position.

www.mhhe.com/
**mhreader**

For more information on John Hockenberry, go to:
**More Resources > Ch. 1 Reading & Writing**

# Sex, Lies and Conversation: Why Is It So Hard for Men and Women to Talk to Each Other?

### Deborah Tannen

*Deborah Tannen (b. 1945) born in Brooklyn, New York, holds a PhD in linguistics from the University of California at Berkeley. She is University Professor and Professor of Linguistics at Georgetown University. Tannen published numerous specialized articles and books on language and linguistics before becoming nationally known as a best-selling author. She publishes regularly in such magazines as* Vogue *and* New York, *and her book* That's Not What I Meant: How Conversational Style Makes or Breaks Your Relations with Others *(1986) drew national attention to her work on interpersonal communication. Her other popular books on communication include* You Just Don't Understand: Women and Men in Conversation *(1990),* Talking from 9 to 5: How Women's and Men's Conversational Styles Affect Who Gets Heard, Who Gets Credit, and What Gets Done at Work *(1994), and* I Only Say This Because I Love You: How the Way We Talk Can Make or Break Family Relationships Throughout Our Lives *(2001). The following essay was published in* The Washington Post *in 1990.*

1   I was addressing a small gathering in a suburban Virginia living room—a women's group that had invited men to join them. Throughout the evening, one man had been particularly talkative, frequently offering ideas and anecdotes, while his wife sat silently beside him on the couch. Toward the end of the evening, I commented that women frequently complain that their husbands don't talk to them. This man quickly concurred. He gestured toward his wife and said, "She's the talker in our family." The room burst into laughter; the man looked puzzled and hurt. "It's true," he explained. "When I come home from work I have nothing to say. If she didn't keep the conversation going, we'd spend the whole evening in silence."

2       This episode crystallizes the irony that although American men tend to talk more than women in public situations, they often talk less at home. And this pattern is wreaking havoc with marriage.

3       The pattern was observed by political scientist Andrew Hacker in the late '70s. Sociologist Catherine Kohler Riessman reports in her new book *Divorce Talk* that most of the women she interviewed—but only a few of the men—gave lack of communication as the reason for their divorces. Given the current divorce rate of nearly 50 percent, that amounts to millions of cases in the United States every year—a virtual epidemic of failed conversation.

In my own research, complaints from women about their husbands most 4 often focused not on tangible inequities such as having given up the chance for a career to accompany a husband to his, or doing far more than their share of daily life-support work like cleaning, cooking, social arrangements and errands. Instead, they focused on communication: "He doesn't listen to me," "He doesn't talk to me." I found, as Hacker observed years before, that most wives want their husbands to be, first and foremost, conversational partners, but few husbands share this expectation of their wives.

In short, the image that best represents the current crisis is the stereotypical 5 cartoon scene of a man sitting at the breakfast table with a newspaper held up in front of his face, while a woman glares at the back of it, wanting to talk.

## Linguistic Battle of the Sexes

How can women and men have such different impressions of communication in 6 marriage? Why the widespread imbalance in their interests and expectations?

In the April [1990] issue of *American Psychologist,* Stanford University's 7 Eleanor Maccoby reports the results of her own and others' research showing that children's development is most influenced by the social structure of peer interactions. Boys and girls tend to play with children of their own gender, and their sex-separate groups have different organizational structures and interactive norms.

I believe these systematic differences in childhood socialization make talk 8 between women and men like cross-cultural communication, heir to all the attraction and pitfalls of that enticing but difficult enterprise. My research on men's and women's conversations uncovered patterns similar to those described for children's groups.

For women, as for girls, intimacy is the fabric of relationships, and talk is 9 the thread from which it is woven. Little girls create and maintain friendships by exchanging secrets; similarly, women regard conversation as the cornerstone of friendship. So a woman expects her husband to be a new and improved version of a best friend. What is important is not the individual subjects that are discussed but the sense of closeness, of a life shared, that emerges when people tell their thoughts, feelings, and impressions.

Bonds between boys can be as intense as girls', but they are based less on 10 talking, more on doing things together. Since they don't assume talk is the cement that binds a relationship, men don't know what kind of talk women want, and they don't miss it when it isn't there.

Boys' groups are larger, more inclusive, and more hierarchical, so boys 11 must struggle to avoid the subordinate position in the group. This may play a role in women's complaints that men don't listen to them. Some men really don't like to listen, because being the listener makes them feel one-down, like a child listening to adults or an employee to a boss.

But often when women tell men, "You aren't listening," and the men protest, "I am," the men are right. The impression of not listening results from 12 misalignments in the mechanics of conversation. The misalignment begins as soon as a man and a woman take physical positions. This became clear when I studied videotapes made by psychologist Bruce Dorval of children and adults talking to their same-sex best friends. I found that at every age, the girls and women faced each other directly, their eyes anchored on each other's faces. At every age, the boys and men sat at angles to each other and looked elsewhere in the room, periodically glancing at each other. They were obviously attuned to each other, often mirroring each other's movements. But the tendency of men to face away can give women the impression they aren't listening even when they are. A young woman in college was frustrated: Whenever she told her boyfriend she wanted to talk to him, he would lie down on the floor, close his eyes, and put his arm over his face. This signaled to her, "He's taking a nap." But he insisted he was listening extra hard. Normally, he looks around the room, so he is easily distracted. Lying down and covering his eyes helped him concentrate on what she was saying.

13     Analogous to the physical alignment that women and men take in conversation is their topical alignment. The girls in my study tended to talk at length about one topic, but the boys tended to jump from topic to topic. The second-grade girls exchanged stories about people they knew. The second-grade boys teased, told jokes, noticed things in the room and talked about finding games to play. The sixth-grade girls talked about problems with a mutual friend. The sixth-grade boys talked about 55 different topics, none of which extended over more than a few turns.

## Listening to Body Language

14  Switching topics is another habit that gives women the impression men aren't listening, especially if they switch to a topic about themselves. But the evidence of the 10th-grade boys in my study indicates otherwise. The 10th-grade boys sprawled across their chairs with bodies parallel and eyes straight ahead, rarely looking at each other. They looked as if they were riding in a car, staring out the windshield. But they were talking about their feelings. One boy was upset because a girl had told him he had a drinking problem, and the other was feeling alienated from all his friends.

15     Now, when a girl told a friend about a problem, the friend responded by asking probing questions and expressing agreement and understanding. But the boys dismissed each other's problems. Todd assured Richard that his drinking was "no big problem" because "sometimes you're funny when you're off your butt." And when Todd said he felt left out, Richard responded, "Why should you? You know more people than me."

16     Women perceived such responses as belittling and unsupportive. But the boys seemed satisfied with them. Whereas women reassure each other by implying, "You shouldn't feel bad because I've had similar experiences," men do so by implying, "You shouldn't feel bad because your problems aren't so bad."

There are even simpler reasons for women's impression that men don't lis- 17 ten. Linguist Lynette Hirschman found that women make more listener-noise, such as "mhm," "uhuh," and "yeah," to show "I'm with you." Men, she found, more often give silent attention. Women who expect a stream of listener-noise interpret silent attention as no attention at all.

Women's conversational habits are as frustrating to men as men's are to 18 women. Men who expect silent attention interpret a stream of listener-noise as overreaction or impatience. Also, when women talk to each other in a close, comfortable setting, they often overlap, finish each other's sentences and antici- pate what the other is about to say. This practice, which I call "participatory listenership," is often perceived by men as interruption, intrusion and lack of attention.

A parallel difference caused a man to complain about his wife, "She just 19 wants to talk about her own point of view. If I show her another view, she gets mad at me." When most women talk to each other, they assume a conversation- alist's job is to express agreement and support. But many men see their conver- sational duty as pointing out the other side of an argument. This is heard as disloyalty by women, and refusal to offer the requisite support. It is not that women don't want to see other points of view, but that they prefer them phrased as suggestions and inquiries rather than as direct challenges.

In his book *Fighting for Life,* Walter Ong points out that men use "agonistic" 20 or warlike, oppositional formats to do almost anything; thus discussion be- comes debate, and conversation a competitive sport. In contrast, women see conversation as a ritual means of establishing rapport. If Jane tells a problem and June says she has a similar one, they walk away feeling closer to each other. But this attempt at establishing rapport can backfire when used with men. Men take too literally women's ritual "troubles talk," just as women mistake men's ritual challenges for real attack.

## The Sounds of Silence

These differences begin to clarify why women and men have such different 21 expectations about communication in marriage. For women, talk creates inti- macy. Marriage is an orgy of closeness: you can tell your feelings and thoughts, and still be loved. Their greatest fear is being pushed away. But men live in a hierarchical world, where talk maintains independence and status. They are on guard to protect themselves from being put down and pushed around.

This explains the paradox of the talkative man who said of his silent wife, 22 "She's the talker." In the public setting of a guest lecture, he felt challenged to show his intelligence and display his understanding of the lecture. But at home, where he has nothing to prove and no one to defend against, he is free to re- main silent. For his wife, being home means she is free from the worry that something she says might offend someone, or spark disagreement, or appear to be showing off; at home she is free to talk.

23      The communication problems that endanger marriage can't be fixed by mechanical engineering. They require a new conceptual framework about the role of talk in human relationships. Many of the psychological explanations that have become second nature may not be helpful, because they tend to blame either women (for not being assertive enough) or men (for not being in touch with their feelings). A sociolinguistic approach by which male-female conversation is seen as cross-cultural communication allows us to understand the problem and forge solutions without blaming either party.

24      Once the problem is understood, improvement comes naturally, as it did to the young woman and her boyfriend who seemed to go to sleep when she wanted to talk. Previously, she had accused him of not listening, and he had refused to change his behavior, since that would be admitting fault. But then she learned about and explained to him the differences in women's and men's habitual ways of aligning themselves in conversation. The next time she told him she wanted to talk, he began, as usual, by lying down and covering his eyes. When the familiar negative reaction bubbled up, she reassured herself that he really was listening. But then he sat up and looked at her. Thrilled she asked why. He said, "You like me to look at you when we talk, so I'll try to do it." Once he saw their differences as cross-cultural rather than right and wrong, he independently altered his behavior.

25      Women who feel abandoned and deprived when their husbands won't listen to or report daily news may be happy to discover their husbands trying to adapt once they understand the place of small talk in women's relationships. But if their husbands don't adapt, the women may still be comforted that for men, this is not a failure of intimacy. Accepting the difference, the wives may look to their friends or family for that kind of talk. And husbands who can't provide it shouldn't feel their wives have made unreasonable demands. Some couples will still decide to divorce, but at least their decisions will be based on realistic expectations.

26      In these times of resurgent ethnic conflicts, the world desperately needs cross-cultural understanding. Like charity, successful cross-cultural communication should begin at home.

## COMPREHENSION

1. What is the thesis or claim of this essay? Where does Tannen most clearly articulate it?
2. To advance her argument, the author cites political scientists and sociologists, while she herself is a linguist. What exactly is the nature of these three professions? What do professionals in the first two fields do? Why does Tannen use their observations in developing her argument?
3. Why does the author employ a question in her title? What other device does she employ in her title to capture the reader's attention? (*Hint:* It is a reference to the title of a movie.)

## RHETORIC

1. Tannen begins her essay with an anecdote. Is this an effective way of opening this particular essay? Why or why not?
2. Besides anecdotes, the author uses statistics, social science research, appeals to authority, and definition in advancing her argument. Find at least one example of each device. Explain the effectiveness or lack thereof.
3. Where and how does the author imply that she is an authority on the subject? How does this contribute to or detract from her ability to win the reader's confidence?
4. Tannen divides her essay into four sections: one untitled and three with headings. How does each section relate to the others structurally and thematically?
5. The author dramatically states that "given the current divorce rate of nearly 50 percent" the United States has a "virtual epidemic of failed conversation" (paragraph 3). Is this fact or opinion? Does it serve to heighten or weaken the import of her thesis?
6. Concerning the lack of proper communication between men and women, Tannen states, "Once the problem is understood, improvement comes naturally" (paragraph 24). Is this statement substantiated or backed up with evidence? Explain.
7. Explain the analogy the author employs in the final paragraph. Is it a good or poor analogy? Explain.

## WRITING

1. Another linguist has written an essay titled "The Communication Panacea," which argues that much of what is blamed on lack of communication actually has economic and political causes. Argue for or against this proposition in the light of the ideas advanced in Tannen's essay.
2. Using some of the observational methods described in the essay, conduct your own ethnographic research by observing a couple communicating. Write a report discussing your findings.
3. **Writing an Argument:** Tannen states, "Once the problem is understood, improvement comes naturally." Argue for or against this proposition.

www.mhhe.com/
**mhreader**

For more information on Deborah Tannen, go to:
**More Resources > Ch. 1 Reading & Writing**

# Politics and the English Language

## George Orwell

*George Orwell (1903–1950) was the pseudonym of Eric Arthur Blair, an English novelist, essayist, and journalist. Orwell served with the Indian Imperial Police from 1922 to 1927 in Burma, fought in the Spanish Civil War, and acquired from his experience a disdain of totalitarian and imperialistic systems. This attitude is reflected in the satiric fable* Animal Farm *(1945) and in the bleak, futuristic novel* 1984 *(1949). This essay, one of the more famous of the twentieth century, relates sloppy thinking and writing with political oppression.*

1   Most people who bother with the matter at all would admit that the English language is in a bad way, but it is generally assumed that we cannot by conscious action do anything about it. Our civilization is decadent, and our language—so the argument runs— must inevitably share in the general collapse. It follows that any struggle against the abuse of language is a sentimental archaism, like preferring candles to electric light or hansom cabs to airplanes. Underneath this lies the half-conscious belief that language is a natural growth and not an instrument which we shape for our own purposes.

2   Now, it is clear that the decline of a language must ultimately have political and economic causes: it is not due simply to the bad influence of this or that individual writer. But an effect can become a cause, reinforcing the original cause and producing the same effect in an intensified form, and so on indefinitely. A man may take to drink because he feels himself to be a failure, and then fail all the more completely because he drinks. It is rather the same thing that is happening to the English language. It becomes ugly and inaccurate because our thoughts are foolish, but the slovenliness of our language makes it easier for us to have foolish thoughts. The point is that the process is reversible. Modern English, especially written English, is full of bad habits which spread by imitation and which can be avoided if one is willing to take the necessary trouble. If one gets rid of these habits one can think more clearly, and to think clearly is a necessary first step towards political regeneration: so that the fight against bad English is not frivolous and is not the exclusive concern of professional writers. I will come back to this presently, and I hope that by that time the meaning of what I have said here will have become clearer. Meanwhile, here are five specimens of the English language as it is now habitually written.

3   These five passages have not been picked out because they are especially bad—I could have quoted far worse if I had chosen—but because they illustrate various of the mental vices from which we now suffer. They are a little below the average, but are fairly representative samples. I number them so that I can refer back to them when necessary:

1. I am not, indeed, sure whether it is not true to say the Milton who once seemed not unlike a seventeenth-century Shelley had not become, out of an experience even more bitter in each year, more alien (sic) to the founder of that Jesuit sect which nothing could induce him to tolerate.

    —Professor Harold Laski (essay in *Freedom of Expression*)

2. Above all, we cannot play ducks and drakes with a native battery of idioms which prescribes such egregious collocations of vocables as the basic *put up with* for *tolerate* or *put at a loss* for *bewilder*.

    —Professor Lancelot Hogben (*Interglossa*)

3. On the one side we have the free personality: by definition it is not neurotic, for it has neither conflict nor dream. Its desires, such as they are, are transparent, for they are just what institutional approval keeps in the forefront of consciousness; another institutional pattern would alter their number and intensity; there is little in them that is natural, irreducible, or culturally dangerous. But on the other side, the social bond itself is nothing but the mutual reflection of these self-secure integrities. Recall the definition of love. Is not this the very picture of a small academic? Where is there a place in this hall of mirrors for either personality or fraternity?

    —Essay on psychology in *Politics* (New York)

4. All the "best people" from the gentlemen's clubs, and all the frantic Fascist captains, united in common hatred of Socialism and bestial horror of the rising tide of the mass revolutionary movement, have turned to acts of provocation, to foul incendiarism, to medieval legends of poisoned wells, to legalize their own destruction to proletarian organizations, and rouse the agitated petty-bourgeoisie to chauvinistic fervor on behalf of the fight against the revolutionary way out of the crisis.

    —Communist pamphlet

5. If a new spirit is to be infused into this old country, there is one thorny and contentious reform which must be tackled, and that is the humanization and galvanization of the BBC. Timidity here will bespeak canker and atrophy for the soul. The heart of Britain may be sound and of strong beat, for instance, but the British lion's roar at present is like that of Bottom in Shakespeare's *Midsummer Night's Dream*—as gentle as any sucking dove. A virile new Britain cannot continue indefinitely to be traduced in the eyes, or rather ears, of the world by the effete languors of Langham Place, brazenly masquerading as "standard English." When the Voice of Britain is heard at nine o'clock, better far and infinitely less ludicrous to hear aitches honestly dropped than the present priggish, inflated, inhibited, schoolma'amish braying of blameless bashful mewing maidens!

    —Letter in *Tribune*

   Each of these passages has faults of its own, but, quite apart from avoid- 4
able ugliness, two qualities are common to all of them. The first is staleness of

imagery; the other is lack of precision. The writer either has a meaning and cannot express it, or he inadvertently says something else, or he is almost indifferent as to whether his words mean anything or not. This mixture of vagueness and sheer incompetence is the most marked characteristic of modern English prose, and especially of any kind of political writing. As soon as certain topics are raised, the concrete melts into the abstract and no one seems able to think of turns of speech that are not hackneyed: prose consists less and less of *words* chosen for the sake of their meaning, and more of *phrases* tacked together like the sections of a prefabricated henhouse. I list below, with notes and examples, various of the tricks by means of which the work of prose construction is habitually dodged:

## Dying Metaphors

5 A newly invented metaphor assists thought by evoking a visual image, while on the other hand a metaphor which is technically "dead" (e.g., *iron resolution*) has in effect reverted to being an ordinary word and can generally be used without loss of vividness. But in between these two classes there is a huge dump of wornout metaphors which have lost all evocative power and are merely used because they save people the trouble of inventing phrases for themselves. Examples are: *Ring the changes on, take up the cudgels for, toe the line, ride roughshod over, stand shoulder to shoulder with, play into the hands of, no axe to grind, grist to the mill, fishing in troubled waters, rift within the lute, on the order of the day, Achilles' heel, swan song, hotbed.* Many of these are used without knowledge of their meaning (what is a "rift," for instance?), and incompatible metaphors are frequently mixed, a sure sign that the writer is not interested in what he is saying. Some metaphors now current have been twisted out of their original meaning without those who use them even being aware of the fact. For example, *toe the line* is sometimes written *tow the line.* Another example is *the hammer and the anvil,* now always used with the implication that the anvil gets the worst of it. In real life it is always the anvil that breaks the hammer, never the other way about: a writer who stopped to think what he was saying would be aware of this, and would avoid perverting the original phrase.

## Operators, or Verbal False Limbs

6 These save the trouble of picking out appropriate verbs and nouns, and at the same time pad each sentence with extra syllables which give it an appearance of symmetry. Characteristic phrases are: *render inoperative, militate against, prove unacceptable, make contact with, be subjected to, give rise to, give grounds for, have the effect of, play a leading part (role) in, make itself felt, take effect, exhibit a tendency to, serve the purpose of,* etc. etc. The keynote is the elimination of simple verbs. Instead of being a single word, such as *break, stop, spoil, mend, kill,* a verb becomes a *phrase,* made up of a noun or adjective tacked on to some general-purposes verb such as *prove, serve, form, play, render.* In addition, the

passive voice is wherever possible used in preference to the active, and noun constructions are used instead of gerunds (*by examination of* instead of *by examining*). The range of verbs is further cut down by means of the *-ize* and *de-* formations, and banal statements are given an appearance of profundity by means of the *not un-* formation. Simple conjunctions and prepositions are replaced by such phrases as *with respect to, having regard to, the fact that, by dint of, in view of, in the interests of, on the hypothesis that;* and the ends of sentences are saved from anti-climax by such resounding commonplaces as *greatly to be desired, cannot be left out of account, a development to be expected in the near future, deserving of serious consideration, brought to a satisfactory conclusion,* and so on and so forth.

## Pretentious Diction

Words like *phenomenon, element, individual* (as noun), *objective, categorical, effec-* [7] *tive, virtual, basic, primary, promote, constitute, exhibit, exploit, utilize, eliminate, liquidate,* are used to dress up simple statements and give an air of scientific impartiality to biased judgments. Adjectives like *epoch-making, epic, historic, unforgettable, triumphant, age-old, inevitable, inexorable, veritable,* are used to dignify the sordid processes of international politics, while writing that aims at glorifying war usually takes on an archaic color, its characteristic words being: *realm, throne, chariot, mailed fist, trident, sword, shield, buckler, banner, jackboot, clarion.* Foreign words and expressions such as *cul de sac, ancien régime, deus ex machina, mutatis mutandis, status quo, Gleichschaltung, Weltanschauung,* are used to give an air of culture and elegance. Except for the useful abbreviations *i.e., e.g.,* and *etc.,* there is no real need for any of the hundreds of foreign phrases now current in English. Bad writers, and especially scientific, political and sociological writers, are nearly always haunted by the notion that Latin or Greek words are grander than Saxon ones, and unnecessary words like *expedite, ameliorate, predict, extraneous, deracinated, clandestine, subaqueous* and hundreds of others constantly gain ground from their Anglo-Saxon opposite numbers.[1] The jargon peculiar to Marxist writing (*hyena, hangman, cannibal, petty bourgeois, these gentry, lacquey, flunkey, mad dog, White Guard,* etc.) consists largely of words and phrases translated from Russian, German or French; but the normal way of coining a new word is to use a Latin or Greek root with the appropriate affix and, where necessary, the *-ize* formation. It is often easier to make up words of this kind (*deregionalize, impermissible, extramarital, non-fragmentatory* and so forth) than to think up the English words that will cover one's meaning. The result, in general, is an increase in slovenliness and vagueness.

---

[1]An interesting illustration of this is the way in which the English flower names which were in use till very recently are being ousted by Greek ones, *snapdragon* becoming *antirrhinum, forget-me-not* becoming *myosotis,* etc. It is hard to see any practical reason for this change of fashion: it is probably due to an instinctive turning-away from the more homely word and a vague feeling that the Greek word is scientific.

## Meaningless Words

8   In certain kinds of writing, particularly in art criticism and literary criticism, it is normal to come across long passages which are almost completely lacking in meaning.[2] Words like *romantic, plastic, values, human, dead, sentimental, natural, vitality,* as used in art criticism, are strictly meaningless, in the sense that they not only do not point to any discoverable object, but are hardly even expected to do so by the reader. When one critic writes, "The outstanding features of Mr. X's work is its living quality," while another writes, "The immediately striking thing about Mr. X's work is its peculiar deadness," the reader accepts this as a simple difference of opinion. If words like *black* and *white* were involved, instead of the jargon words *dead* and *living,* he would see at once that language was being used in an improper way. Many political words are similarly abused. The word *Fascism* has now no meaning except in so far as it signifies "something not desirable." The words *democracy, socialism, freedom, patriotic, realistic, justice,* have each of them several different meanings which cannot be reconciled with one another. In the case of a word like *democracy,* not only is there no agreed definition, but the attempt to make one is resisted from all sides. It is almost universally felt that when we call a country democratic we are praising it: consequently the defenders of every kind of régime claim that it is a democracy, and fear that they might have to stop using the word if it were tied down to any one meaning. Words of this kind are often used in a consciously dishonest way. That is, the person who uses them has his own private definition, but allows his hearer to think he means something quite different. Statements like *Marshal Pétain was a true patriot, The Soviet press is the freest in the world, The Catholic Church is opposed to persecution,* are almost always made with intent to deceive. Other words used in variable meanings, in most cases more or less dishonestly, are: *class, totalitarian, science, progressive, reactionary, bourgeois, equality.*

9   Now that I have made this catalogue of swindles and perversions, let me give another example of the kind of writing that they lead to. This time it must of its nature be an imaginary one. I am going to translate a passage of good English into modern English of the worst sort. Here is a well-known verse from *Ecclesiastes:*

> I returned, and saw under the sun, that the race is not to the swift, nor the battle to the strong, neither yet bread to the wise, nor yet riches to men of understanding, nor yet favor to men of skill; but time and chance happeneth to them all.

10   Here it is in modern English:

> Objective consideration of contemporary phenomena compels the conclusion that success or failure in competitive activities exhibits no tendency to be

---

[2]*Example:* "Comfort's catholicity of perception and image, strangely Whitmanesque in range, almost the exact opposite in aesthetic compulsion, continues to evoke that trembling atmospheric accumulative hinting at a cruel, an inexorably serene timelessness. . . . Wrey Gardiner scores by aiming at simple bullseyes with precision. Only they are not so simple, and through this contented sadness runs more than the surface bittersweet of resignation." (*Poetry Quarterly*)

commensurate with innate capacity, but that a considerable element of the unpredictable must invariably be taken into account.

This is a parody, but not a very gross one. Exhibit (3) above, for instance, 11 contains several patches of the same kind of English. It will be seen that I have not made a full translation. The beginning and ending of the sentence follow the original meaning fairly closely, but in the middle the concrete illustrations—race, battle, bread—dissolve into the vague phrase "success or failure in competitive activities." This had to be so, because no modern writer of the kind I am discussing—no one capable of using phrases like "objective consideration of contemporary phenomena"—would ever tabulate his thoughts in that precise and detailed way. The whole tendency of modern prose is away from concreteness. Now analyze these two sentences a little more closely. The first contains 49 words but only 60 syllables, and all its words are those of everyday life. The second contains 38 words of 90 syllables: 18 of its words are from Latin roots, and one from Greek. The first sentence contains six vivid images, and only one phrase ("time and chance") that could be called vague. The second contains not a single fresh, arresting phrase, and in spite of its 90 syllables it gives only a shortened version of the meaning contained in the first. Yet without a doubt it is the second kind of sentence that is gaining ground in modern English. I do not want to exaggerate. This kind of writing is not yet universal, and outcrops of simplicity will occur here and there in the worst-written page. Still, if you or I were told to write a few lines on the uncertainty of human fortunes, we should probably come much nearer to my imaginary sentence than to the one from *Ecclesiastes*.

As I have tried to show, modern writing at its worst does not consist in 12 picking out words for the sake of their meaning and inventing images in order to make the meaning clearer. It consists in gumming together long strips of words which have already been set in order by someone else, and making the results presentable by sheer humbug. The attraction of this way of writing is that it is easy. It is easier—even quicker, once you have the habit—to say *In my opinion it is a not unjustifiable assumption that* than to say *I think*. If you use ready-made phrases, you not only don't have to hunt about for words; you also don't have to bother with the rhythms of your sentences, since these phrases are generally so arranged as to be more or less euphonious. When you are composing in a hurry—when you are dictating to a stenographer, for instance, or making a public speech—it is natural to fall into a pretentious, latinized style. Tags like *a consideration which we should do well to bear in mind* or *a conclusion to which all of us would readily assent* will save many a sentence from coming down with a bump. By using stale metaphors, similes and idioms, you save much mental effort, at the cost of leaving your meaning vague, not only for your reader but for yourself. This is the significance of mixed metaphors. The sole aim of a metaphor is to call up a visual image. When these images clash—as in *The Fascist octopus has sung its swan song, the jackboot is thrown into the melting-pot*—can be taken as certain that the writer is not seeing a mental image of the objects he is naming; in other words he is not really thinking. Look again at the examples I gave at the beginning of this essay. Professor Laski (1) uses five negatives in 53 words. One of these is superfluous, making nonsense of the whole passage, and in addition there is the slip *alien* for akin, making further nonsense, and several avoidable pieces of clumsiness which increase the general vagueness. Professor Hogben (2) plays ducks and drakes with a battery which is able to write prescriptions, and, while disapproving of the everyday phrase *put up with,* is unwilling to look *egregious* up in the dictionary and see what it means. In (3), if one takes an uncharitable attitude towards it, [it] is simply meaningless: probably one could work out its intended meaning by reading the whole of the article in which it occurs. In (4) the writer knows more or less what he wants to say, but an accumulation of stale phrases chokes him like tealeaves blocking a sink. In (5) words and meaning have almost parted company. People who write in this manner usually have a general emotional meaning—they dislike one thing and want to express solidarity with another—but they are not interested in the detail of what they are saying. A scrupulous writer, in every sentence that he writes, will ask himself at least four questions, thus: What am I trying to say? What words will express it? What image or idiom will make it clearer? Is this image fresh enough to have an effect? And he will probably ask himself two more: Could I put it more shortly? Have I said anything that is avoidably ugly? But you are not obliged to go to all this trouble. You can shirk it by simply throwing your mind open and letting the ready-made phrases come crowding in. They will construct your sentences for you—even think your thoughts for you, to a certain extent—and at need they will perform the important service of partially concealing your meaning even from yourself. It is at this point that the special connection between politics and the debasement of language becomes clear.

13      In our time it is broadly true that political writing is bad writing. Where it is not true, it will generally be found that the writer is some kind of rebel, expressing his private opinions, and not a "party line." Orthodoxy, of whatever color, seems to demand a lifeless, imitative style. The political dialects to be found in pamphlets, leading articles, manifestos, White Papers and the speeches of Under-Secretaries do, of course, vary from party to party, but they are all alike in that one almost never finds in them a fresh, vivid, home-made turn of speech. When one watches some tired hack on the platform mechanically repeating the familiar phrases—*bestial atrocities, iron heel, blood-stained tyranny, free peoples of the world, stand shoulder to shoulder*—one often has a curious feeling that one is not watching a live human being but some kind of dummy: a feeling which suddenly becomes stronger at moments when the light catches the speaker's spectacles and turns them into blank discs which seem to have no eyes behind them. And this is not altogether fanciful. A speaker who uses that kind of phraseology has gone some distance towards turning himself into a machine. The appropriate noises are coming out of his larynx, but his brain is not involved as it would be if he were choosing his words for himself. If the speech he is making is one that he is accustomed to make over and over again, he may be almost unconscious of what he is saying, as one is when one utters

the responses in church. And this reduced state of consciousness, if not indispensable, is at any rate favorable to political conformity.

In our time, political speech and writing are largely the defense of the inde- 14 fensible. Things like the continuance of British rule in India, the Russian purges and deportations, the dropping of the atom bombs on Japan, can indeed be defended, but only by arguments which are too brutal for most people to face, and which do not square with the professed aims of political parties. Thus political language has to consist largely of euphemism, question-begging and sheer cloudy vagueness. Defenseless villages are bombarded from the air, the inhabitants driven out into the countryside, the cattle machine-gunned, the huts set on fire with incendiary bullets: this is called *pacification*. Millions of peasants are robbed of their farms and sent trudging along the roads with no more than they can carry: this is called *transfer of population or rectification of frontiers*. People are imprisoned for years without trial, or shot in the back of the neck or sent to die of scurvy in Arctic lumber camps: this is called *elimination of unreliable elements*. Such phraseology is needed if one wants to name things without calling up mental pictures of them. Consider for instance some comfortable English professor defending Russian totalitarianism. He cannot say outright, "I believe in killing off your opponents when you can get good results by doing so." Probably, therefore, he will say something like this:

> While freely conceding that the Soviet régime exhibits certain features which the humanitarian may be inclined to deplore, we must, I think, agree that a certain curtailment of the right to political opposition is an unavoidable concomitant of transitional periods, and that the rigors which the Russian people have been called upon to undergo have been amply justified in the sphere of concrete achievement.

The inflated style is itself a kind of euphemism. A mass of Latin words falls 15 upon the facts like soft snow, blurring the outlines and covering up all the details. The great enemy of clear language is insincerity. When there is a gap between one's real and one's declared aims, one turns as it were instinctively to long words and exhausted idioms, like a cuttlefish squirting out ink. In our age there is no such thing as "keeping out of politics." All issues are political issues, and politics itself is a mass of lies, evasions, folly, hatred and schizophrenia. When the general atmosphere is bad, language must suffer. I should expect to find—this is a guess which I have not sufficient knowledge to verify—that the German, Russian and Italian languages have all deteriorated in the last ten or fifteen years, as a result of dictatorship.

But if thought corrupts language, language can also corrupt thought. A bad 16 usage can spread by tradition and imitation, even among people who should and do know better. The debased language that I have been discussing is in some ways very convenient. Phrases like *a not unjustifiable assumption, leaves much to be desired, would serve no good purpose, a consideration which we should do well to bear in mind,* are a continuous temptation, a packet of aspirins always at one's elbow. Look back through this essay, and for certain you will find that I have again and again committed the very faults I am protesting against. By this morning's post I have received a pamphlet dealing with conditions in Germany. The author tells me that he "felt impelled" to write it. I open it at random, and here is almost the first sentence that I see: "(The Allies) have an opportunity not only of achieving a radical transformation of Germany's social and political structure in such a way as to avoid a nationalistic reaction in Germany itself, but at the same time of laying the foundations of a cooperative and unified Europe." You see, he "feels impelled" to write—feels, presumably, that he has something new to say—and yet his words, like cavalry horses answering the bugle, group themselves automatically into the familiar dreary pattern. This invasion of one's mind by ready-made phrases *(lay the foundations, achieve a radical transformation)* can only be prevented if one is constantly on guard against them, and every such phrase anaesthetizes a portion of one's brain.

17      I said earlier that the decadence of our language is probably curable. Those who deny this would argue, if they produced an argument at all, that language merely reflects existing social conditions, and that we cannot influence its development by any direct tinkering with words and constructions. So far as the general tone or spirit of a language goes, this may be true, but it is not true in detail. Silly words and expressions have often disappeared, not through any evolutionary process but owing to the conscious action of a minority. Two recent examples were *explore every avenue* and *leave no stone unturned*, which were killed by the jeers of a few journalists. There is a long list of fly-blown metaphors which could similarly be got rid of if enough people would interest themselves in the job; and it should also be possible to laugh the *not un-* formation out of existence,[3] to reduce the amount of Latin and Greek in the average sentence, to drive out foreign phrases and strayed scientific words, and, in general, to make pretentiousness unfashionable. But all these are minor points. The defense of the English language implies more than this, and perhaps it is best to start by saying what it does *not* imply.

18      To begin with, it has nothing to do with archaism, with the salvaging of obsolete words and turns of speech, or with the setting up of a "standard English" which must never be departed from. On the contrary, it is especially concerned with the scrapping of every word or idiom which has outworn its usefulness. It has nothing to do with correct grammar and syntax, which are of no importance so long as one makes one's meaning clear, or with the avoidance of Americanisms, or with having what is called a "good prose style." On the other hand it is not concerned with fake simplicity and the attempt to make written English colloquial. Nor does it even imply in every case preferring the Saxon word to the Latin one, though it does imply using the fewest and shortest words that will cover one's meaning. What is above all needed is to let the meaning choose the word, and not the other way about. In prose, the worst thing one can do with words is to surrender to them. When you think of a

---

[3]One can cure oneself of the *not un-* formation by memorizing this sentence: *A not unblock dog was chasing a not unsmall rabbit across a not ungreen field.*

concrete object, you think wordlessly, and then, if you want to describe the thing you have been visualizing, you probably hunt about till you find the exact words that seem to fit it. When you think of something abstract you are more inclined to use words from the start, and unless you make a conscious effort to prevent it, the existing dialect will come rushing in and do the job for you, at the expense of blurring or even changing your meaning. Probably it is better to put off using words as long as possible and get one's meaning as clear as one can through pictures or sensations. Afterwards one can choose—not simply *accept*—the phrases that will best cover the meaning, and then switch around and decide what impression one's words are likely to make on another person. This last effort of the mind cuts out all stale or mixed images, all prefabricated phrases, needless repetitions, and humbug and vagueness generally. But one can often be in doubt about the effect of a word or a phrase, and one needs rules that one can rely on when instinct fails. I think the following rules will cover most cases:

*i.* Never use a metaphor, simile or other figure of speech which you are used to seeing in print.
*ii.* Never use a long word where a short one will do.
*iii.* If it is possible to cut a word out, always cut it out.
*iv.* Never use the passive where you can use the active.
*v.* Never use a foreign phrase, a scientific word or a jargon word if you can think of an everyday English equivalent.
*vi.* Break any of these rules sooner than say anything outright barbarous.

These rules sound elementary, and so they are, but they demand a deep   19 change of attitude in anyone who has grown used to writing in the style now fashionable. One could keep all of them and still write bad English, but one could not write the kind of stuff that I quoted in those five specimens at the beginning of this article.

I have not here been considering the literary use of language, but merely   20 language as an instrument for expressing and not for concealing or preventing thought. Stuart Chase and others have come near to claiming that all abstract words are meaningless, and have used this as a pretext for advocating a kind of political quietism. Since you don't know what Fascism is, how can you struggle against Fascism? One need not swallow such absurdities as this, but one ought to recognize that the present political chaos is connected with the decay of language, and that one can probably bring about some improvement by starting at the verbal end. If you simplify your English, you are freed from the worst follies of orthodoxy. You cannot speak any of the necessary dialects, and when you make a stupid remark its stupidity will be obvious, even to yourself. Political language—and with variations this is true of all political parties, from Conservatives to Anarchists—is designed to make lies sound truthful and murder respectable, and to give an appearance of solidity to pure wind. One cannot change this all in a moment, but one can at least change one's own habits, and from time to time one can even, if one jeers loudly enough, send some worn-out and useless phrase—some *jackboot, Achilles' heel, hotbed, melting pot, acid test, veritable inferno* or other lump of verbal refuse—into the dustbin where it belongs.

## COMPREHENSION

1. What is Orwell's purpose? For what type of audience is he writing? Where does he summarize his concerns for readers?
2. According to Orwell, "thought corrupts language" and "language can also corrupt thought" (paragraph 16). Give examples of these assertions in the essay.
3. In what ways does Orwell believe that politics and language are related?

## RHETORIC

1. Orwell himself uses similes and metaphors. Locate five of them, and explain their relationship to the author's analysis.
2. Orwell claims that concrete language is superior to abstract language. Give examples of Orwell's attempt to write concretely.
3. One of the most crucial rhetorical devices in this essay is definition. What important concepts does Orwell define? What methods of definition does he tend to use?
4. Identify an example of hypothetical reasoning in the essay. How does it contribute to the thesis of the essay?
5. After having given five examples of bad English, why does Orwell, in paragraph 10, give another example? How does this example differ from the others? What does it add to the essay?
6. Explain the use of extended analogy in paragraph 14.

## WRITING

1. In an analytical essay, assess the state of language in politics today. Cite examples from newspapers and television reports.
2. Prepare an essay analyzing the use and abuse of any word that sparks controversy today—for example, *abortion, AIDS,* or *greed.*
3. **Writing an Argument:** Orwell claims that "the decline of a language must ultimately have political and economic causes" (paragraph 2). Is this claim true? Answer this question in an argumentative essay.

www.mhhe.com/
**mhreader**

For more information on George Orwell, go to:
**More Resources > Ch. 1 Reading & Writing**

## Synthesis: Connections For Critical Thinking

1. Examine the "how-to" aspect of the essays by Adler, Elbow, and Murray. What general strategies do they use to develop a comprehensive process analysis of an elusive subject—for example, reading or writing? Write an essay in which you compare the tactics these writers employ to demonstrate their processes.

2. Study the tone of Schlesinger's essay "The Cult of Ethnicity" (in the chapter introduction). How does he remain "civil" while arguing against a contemporary view he seems to abhor? Next, study Amy Tan's "Mother Tongue" and examine how she uses narration in addressing the complex subject of language(s). Can you make some general observations about how the stylistic elements of an essay contribute to the ability of the author to communicate difficult subjects in a manner that is appealing to the reader?

3. Synthesize the ideas in Elbow's "Freewriting" and those in Murray's "The Maker's Eye: Revising Your Own Manuscripts" so that you can write a coherent essay on writing that takes into account the transition from inspiration to craft.

4. Interview three fellow students to ascertain how they study. Compare and contrast their responses to the suggestions Adler makes in his essay.

5. Create an imaginary dialogue between Mortimer Adler and John Hockenberry in which the former lauds the joys of reading and the latter celebrates the blogs of American soldiers in Iraq.

6. Tannen and Tan write personal essays about the impact of language on their lives. Write a comparative essay in which you analyze the similarities and differences in their approach to the topic.

7. How do Orwell and Tannen treat the communication process? How are their topics similar and dissimilar? Write a comparative essay on this topic.

8. **Network:** Use a database or online search engine to locate at least three recent articles that provide perspectives on what John Hockenberry calls "milblogs." In an analytical essay, compare and contrast the different arguments for or against milblogging.

chapter *2*

# Reading and Writing Effective Arguments

You encounter various forms of argumentation in everyday situations—and most assuredly in many college courses. Consequently, it is important to learn more about this mode of thinking, reading, and writing. As a common form of academic writing, argumentation seeks to explore differences of opinion and attempts to promote agreement. As such, argument is useful not only in class-room situations but also in the realm of civic life and discourse, for it provides reasons for people to agree with a particular point of view or at least come to an understanding of an individual's or a group's perspective on an issue. Aristotle, who wrote the first major work on argument, thought that the best and most effective argumentative writing blends rational, emotional, and ethical appeals in order to move an audience—whether one person or an entire nation—to some desired action.

When you engage in *argumentation,* you offer reasons to support a position, belief, or conclusion. A typical argumentative essay presents a debatable thesis and defends it in logical fashion. Closely allied with argumentation is *persuasion,* in which the writer appeals to readers' intelligence, emotions, and beliefs in order to influence them to adopt a position or act in a certain way. Logic and persuasive appeal often combine when a writer tries to convince an audience that his or her position is valid and that other perspectives, while understandable perhaps, require reconsideration.

It is important to distinguish between oral arguments and written ones. Admittedly, both spoken and written arguments have a common purpose in their attempt to convince someone to agree with a particular position, make a certain decision, or take a specific action. In both your oral and written arguments, you will usually invoke reasons and attempt to manipulate language skillfully. However, with an oral argument, you rarely have access to the types of specific evidence needed to support your reasons, nor do you have the time or ability to martial reasons and evidence in well-organized and coherent ways. Oral arguments, as you well know, tend to involve excessive emotion; after all, oral arguments often erupt spontaneously and are rarely thoughtfully constructed and presented.

**104**

Unlike most oral arguments, effective written arguments are carefully and logically planned, organized, researched, and revised. The writer analyzes the audience and anticipates objections to the assertions being made. As she or he develops the argument, the writer considers and selects various rhetorical strategies—for example, analysis, definition, or comparison and contrast—to shape the presentation. Moreover, the writer has time to choose the appropriate language and style for the argument, exploring the use of striking diction, figurative language, rhythmic sentence patterns, and various tonalities and shades of meaning during the prewriting, drafting, and revision stages. Finally, especially when composing arguments for college courses, writers must attend to logic and the techniques of valid persuasive appeal.

## THE LANGUAGE OF ARGUMENT

Writers of argument often employ various modes of exposition like definition, comparison and contrast, illustration, and analysis, but they incorporate these modes of critical thinking as the means of justifying, or supporting, a logical position. The study of the special language, logic, and structure of argumentation fills volumes. For college writing, there is a core group of critical terms that you should know before you design an argumentative paper:

- A *claim* is a statement to be justified or upheld. It is the main idea or position that you plan to present in an argument.
- *Thesis, proposition, assertion,* and *premise* are all similar to a claim in that each is a positive statement or declaration to be supported with reasons and evidence. *Premise,* however, should be distinguished from the other terms: It is a statement or assumption that is established before an argument is begun and is important to an understanding of logic and various errors or fallacies in reasoning.
- *Grounds* are the reasons, support, and evidence presented to support your claim.
- A *warrant* is a stated or unstated belief, rule, or principle that underlies an argument. A *backing* is an even broader principle that serves as the foundation for a warrant.
- The *major proposition* is the main point of an argument, which is supported by the minor propositions.
- The *minor propositions* are the reasons you offer in support of the major proposition.
- *Evidence* is that part of the argument that supports the minor propositions. In argumentation, effective evidence is based either on facts, examples, statistics, and other forms of evidence or on accepted opinions. Without adequate evidence, the audience will not accept your major and minor propositions. Evidence in argument must be accurate and true.

- A *fact* is a verifiable statement. A valid *opinion* is a judgment based on the facts and careful deductive or inductive reasoning. *Induction* is a process of reasoning by which you develop evidence in order to reach a useful generalization. *Deduction* is a process of reasoning that proceeds from the general to the particular.
- A valid *conclusion* of an argument derives logically from the major and minor propositions. The logical conclusion is termed the *inference,* in which you arrive at a decision by reasoning from the previous evidence.
- A *fallacy* is a line of incorrect reasoning from premises.
- *Refutation* is the acknowledgment and handling of opposing viewpoints. You must anticipate opposing viewpoints and counter them effectively (what we term *rebuttal*) in order to convince or persuade readers.

Constructing an effective argument depends on the careful arrangement of major and minor propositions, evidence, and refutation. Like a lawyer, you build a position and subject your opponent's position to dissection in an effort to win the case.

## THE TEST OF JUSTIFICATION

Whatever its components, whether a writer can construct an argument or not essentially hinges on the concept of *justification*—the recognition that a subject lends itself to legitimate difference of opinion. Justification also involves proving or demonstrating that a claim is in accordance with the reasons and evidence offered to support it.

Not all statements require justification. A statement that is a verifiable fact or a commonly accepted assumption or belief—what we term a *warrant*—generally does not need justification. To test the concept of justification, consider the following four statements.

1. President John F. Kennedy was assassinated on November 22, 1963.
2. Children shouldn't smoke.
3. Abortion is the destruction of a human life.
4. African Americans should receive reparations for the damages caused by slavery.

Which of these statements require justification? The first statement about President Kennedy is a verifiable fact, and the second statement strikes any reasonable audience as common sense. Thus, the first two statements do not require justification and consequently could not be the subject of a useful argument, although the second statement could serve as the warrant for a more specific claim about smoking by children. By contrast, the third statement, concerning abortion, makes a critical assumption that would elicit either agreement or disagreement but in either case would demand substantiation. Similarly, the fourth statement, about reparations for slavery, is an issue that is debatable from a variety of positions. Therefore, statements 3 and 4 require justification: They are open to argumentation.

## READING AND ANALYZING ARGUMENTS

From the time of Aristotle to the present, numerous critical approaches to the study of argument have been devised. One of the most useful recent approaches to argument appears in *An Introduction to Reasoning* and *The Uses of Argument* by British logician and philosopher Stephen Toulmin. In his studies, Toulmin observes that any argument involves a *claim* supported by *reasons* and *evidence*. Whether writing a memo to your instructor contesting a certain grade, or a letter to the editor of your campus newspaper advocating a change in the cafeteria vendor because the food is terrible, or a petition to provide more parking spaces for commuting students, the argumentative method is the same. Essentially, you make a general assertion—a claim—and then offer the smaller propositions or supporting reasons along with the relevant facts, examples, statistics, and expert testimony to justify all claims. And underlying the nature of claims and evidence is recognition of the importance of *warrants*, those unstated beliefs that lead from evidence to claim.

Here is the way Toulmin presents his model:

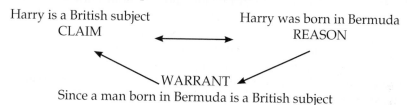

In truth, Toulmin's example is basic and perhaps too simplistic. The claims that you deal with when reading or writing arguments typically are more complex and controversial than Toulmin's diagram suggests, and the need for extensive evidence more demanding. Nevertheless, Toulmin's model offers a useful way to understand the nature of argumentative reasoning.

### Understanding Claims and Warrants

When you argue in writing, you make a specific claim, which is an assertion that you plan to prove. You present this claim or proposition as being true, and you support the claim with a series of logically related statements that are true. Think of the claim as the thesis or the main point of the argument that holds all other logically related statements together. The claim is the main idea that you set out to prove, and in a well reasoned argument, everything makes the claim seem inevitable. Any paper you write that fails to state a claim—your position in an argument—will leave readers shaking their heads and wondering if you actually have an argument to present.

Think of a claim as an arguable point, one that you can build a carefully reasoned paper around. By applying the test of justification, you can exclude numerous opinions, nonarguable propositions, and statements of taste and fact that might be common in everyday situations but not legitimate subjects for papers. To say "Turn down that rap music" to your roommate is the sort of command (containing perhaps an implied opinion) that doesn't in itself qualify as a claim but could get you involved in a heated conversation. To transform this command into a legitimate claim or an arguable point, you would have to state a proposition that expresses your main idea about rap.

Suppose, for example, that after reading the essay in this anthology by Henry Louis Gates Jr., "2 Live Crew, Decoded" (beginning on page 579), you *are* asked to write an argumentative paper on hip-hop or rap music. In his brief but provocative essay, Gates raises significant issues about obscenity and censorship, about "mainstream" and ethnic culture, and about white perceptions of black males. His claim is that we cannot address the complex, interrelated issues raised by the rap phenomenon unless we "become literate in the vernacular traditions of African Americans. To do less is to censor through the equivalent of intellectual prior restraint—and censorship is to art what lynching is to justice." Do you readily perceive the argumentative edge in Gates's claim? Do you agree or disagree with his main point that one cannot offer an informed critique of a cultural phenomenon without knowledge of the language of that culture? And what claim would you actually make about rap music and the culture, an increasingly "crossover" youth culture, that supports it? What reasons or grounds would you produce in support of your claim?

A complex, extended argument in essay form often reveals several types of claims that the writer advances. A *claim about meaning* (What is rap music?) is a proposition that defines or interprets a subject as it establishes an arguable point. A *claim about value* (Rap music is good or bad) advances an ideally open-minded view of the subject based on a coherent framework of aesthetic or ethical values. A *claim about policy* (Music stations should be forced to regulate the most offensive forms of rap music) advances propositions concerning laws, regulations, and initiatives designed to produce specific outcomes. Finally, *claims about consequences* (Children who listen to rap musicians begin to mimic their vulgar behavior) are rooted in propositions involving various forms of cause-and-effect relationships. Constructing an argument around one or more of these types of claims is essential to gaining an audience's assent.

Many claims, of course, cannot be presented as absolute propositions—certainly not as absolute as Aristotle's major premise in his famous syllogism (see page 112) that "all human beings are mortal." Writers must seek common ground with readers and foster a degree of trust by anticipating that some members of any audience will disagree with their claim, treat it with skepticism, and perhaps even respond with hostility. For this reason, it is important to qualify or clarify the nature of your claim. A *qualifier* restricts the absoluteness of a claim by using such cue words and phrases as *sometimes, probably, usually,* and *in most cases.*

Qualifiers can also explain certain circumstances or conditions under which the claim might not be true. The use of qualifiers enables the writer to anticipate certain audience reactions and handle them in an effective and subtle way.

Even more important than the possible need to qualify a claim is the need to justify it in a new way: by linking the claim with reasons and evidence in such a way that the audience sees the train of thinking that leads from the data to the claim. If you look again at the model that Toulmin provides, you see that the datum "Harry was born in Bermuda" does not completely support the claim "Harry is a British subject." What is required is what Toulmin calls a *warrant,* a form of justification—a general belief, principle, or rule—that links the claim and the data or support. Thus the warrant "Since a man born in Bermuda is a British subject" explains *why* the claim follows from the datum.

Another way of understanding this admittedly challenging concept of warrant is to treat it as the process of thinking that leads writers to hold the opinions they present. Thought of from this perspective, we can see that a weak or unclear warrant will undermine an argument and render it invalid. For example, the claim "Sara graduated from an excellent high school and consequently should do well in college" is based on the warrant or unstated (and untested) belief that all students who graduate from good high schools perform well at the college level. Obviously, this warrant is not satisfactory: To state that college success is based solely on the quality of one's high school education is to base the argument on a warrant that few readers would find acceptable. If, on the other hand, a writer claims that "Sara graduated from an excellent high school with a 3.97 cumulative average, the third highest in her class, and consequently should do well in college," we see that the warrant establishing the link between claim and conclusion becomes more acceptable. In fact, there is a consensus, or general belief, among experts that a person's grade point average in high school is a sound predictor—perhaps sounder than SAT scores—of his or her potential for success in college.

If you disagree with a writer's assumptions, you basically are questioning the warrants underlying the argument. An effective argument should rest on an acceptable warrant and also on the *backing*—some explanation or support—for it. Remember that even if a warrant, stated or unstated, is clear, understood, and backed with support, readers might still disagree with it. For example, one could argue that Sara might have obtained her lofty GPA in high school by taking easy courses and that consequently we cannot readily predict her success in college. Not everyone will accept even the most reasonable of warrants.

## Reasoning from Evidence

Evidence is the data, or *grounds,* used to make claims or general assertions clear, concrete, and convincing. In argumentation, the presentation of evidence must be examined from the perspective of logic or sound reasoning. Central to logic is the relationship of evidence to a *generalization,* a statement or conclusion that what is applicable in one situation also applies to similar situations. You cannot think and write clearly unless you test evidence to see that it supports your claims, assumptions, or general statements. Evidence in an argumentative essay creates a common ground of understanding that you and your reader can share.

You know that one of the keenest pleasures in reading mystery fiction or viewing whodunits on television or film is the quest for evidence. The great writers of crime and mystery fiction—Edgar Allan Poe, Sir Arthur Conan Doyle, Agatha Christie—were adept at creating a chain of clues, or evidence, leading with the inevitability of logic to the solution to the crime. Whether it is a letter lying on a desk in Poe's "The Purloined Letter" or a misplaced chair in Christie's *The Murder of Roger Ackroyd*, it is evidence that we seek in order to solve the crime.

In argumentative writing, evidence is used more to prove a point than to solve a mystery. College writers must know what constitutes evidence—examples, facts, statistics, quotations and information from authoritative sources, personal experience, careful reasoning—and how to use it to support certain claims. They must also determine if the evidence and assumptions surrounding the evidence are valid.

Here are some basic questions about evidence to consider when reading and writing argumentative essays:

- *Is the evidence typical and representative?* Examples must fairly represent the condition or situation if your claim is to be valid. If evidence is distorted or unrepresentative, a claim will not be logical or convincing.
- *Is the evidence relevant?* The evidence should speak directly to the claim. It should not utilize peripheral or irrelevant data.
- *Is the evidence specific and detailed?* In reading and writing arguments, do not trust broad, catchall statements presented as "evidence." Valid evidence should involve accurate quotations, paraphrases, and presentations of data from authoritative sources.
- *Is the evidence accurate and reliable?* A claim is only as valid as the data supporting it. Facts should come from reliable sources. (See page 123 for help with evaluating sources.) Current rather than outdated evidence should predominate in a current argument. Sources should be cited accurately for the convenience of the reader. Although personal observation and personal experience are admissible as types of evidence, such testimony rarely serves as conclusive proof for a claim.
- *Is the evidence sufficient?* There must be enough evidence to support claims and reasons. One extended piece of evidence, no matter how carefully selected, rarely is sufficient to win an argument.

Any argumentative essay should provide a clear, logical link between the writer's claim, assertion, generalization, or conclusion and the evidence. If an argumentative essay reveals false or illogical reasoning—that is, if the step from the evidence to the generalization is wrong, confusing, or deceptive—readers will not accept the truth of the claim or the validity of the evidence.

# THINKING CRITICALLY ABOUT ARGUMENTS

Whether you are reading another writer's argument or starting to plan one of your own, you need to consider the purposes of the argument. When you are reading an argument, you should also look for the appeals to reason, emotion, and ethics the writer is using and decide whether those appeals are effective for you, the writer's audience. In your own arguments, you will need to decide the types of appeals that will carry the most weight with *your* audience.

## The Purpose of Argumentation

As a college writer, your general aim is to communicate or convey messages in essay form to a literate and knowledgeable audience of teachers and scholars. When thinking about the subject for an essay, you also have to consider a more specialized *purpose*—the special nature or aim—behind your composition. You might have to report the result of an experiment in animal behavior, analyze a poem, compare and contrast Mario Puzo's novel *The Godfather* with its film adaptation, or assert the need for capital punishment. In each instance, your essay requires a key rhetorical strategy or set of strategies. These strategies reflect your purpose—your intention—in developing the essay.

An argumentative essay may serve one or more purposes:

- To present a position, belief, or conclusion in a rational and effective way
- To defend a position against critics or detractors
- To persuade people to agree with a position or take a certain action
- To attack a position without necessarily presenting an alternative or opposing viewpoint

An effective argumentative essay often combines a variety of forms and purposes. For example, an argumentative essay on legalizing marijuana might explain effects, analyze laws, or evaluate experiments, among a broad range of options. When you take time to consider your purpose before you even begin to write, the decisions you make will help you to think more clearly about both the design and intention of your essay.

## Appeals to Reason, Emotion, and Ethics

As the definitions of special terms and the discussion of justification presented earlier in the chapter suggest, argumentation places a premium on rational discourse. In fact, the *appeal to reason* is the fundamental purpose of argumentation. However, classical rhetorical theory acknowledges that the *appeal to emotion* and the *appeal to ethics* are also important elements in the construction of argument and the effort to persuade. A mere presentation of reasons is usually not an effective argument. For your argument to be effective, you need to pay attention to the value of strategic emotional and ethical appeals.

**Appeals to Reason**    The *appeal to reason* or logic is the primary instrument of effective argument. The most common way of developing an argument according to the principles of sound reasoning is *deduction,* which is most readily understood as an ordering of ideas from the general to the particular. With deduction, you move from a general assertion through reasons and support focused on the main assertion. Consider the following student paragraph, which uses the deductive method:

Anti-marijuana laws make people contemptuous of the legal system. This contempt is based in part on the key fact that there are too many contradictions and inconsistencies in criminal penalties for marijuana use. Laws vary radically from state to state. In Texas, you can be sentenced to life imprisonment for first-time use of marijuana. By contrast, in the District of Columbia, the same "crime" would most likely result in a suspended sentence.

Deduction is a convincing way of arranging ideas and information logically. By stating the proposition or generalization first, you present the most important idea. Then, as in the paragraph above, you move to more specific ideas and details. Examined more rigorously, deductive reasoning involves a process of critical thinking known as *syllogism,* in which you move from a major statement or premise, through another minor premise, to a third statement or conclusion. Aristotle's famous syllogism captures this mental process:

| | |
|---|---|
| Major premise: | All human beings are mortal. |
| Minor premise: | Socrates is a human being. |
| Conclusion: | Socrates is mortal. |

The soundness of any deductive argument rests on the *truth* of the premises and the *validity* of the syllogism itself. In other words, if you grant the truth of the premises, you must also grant the conclusion. The deductive method can be used effectively in many forms of expository as well as argumentative essays.

*Inductive* reasoning reverses the process of deduction by moving from particular ideas to general ones. In the paragraph that follows, from an essay by F. M. Esfandiary, "The Mystical West Puzzles the Practical East," the writer presents various ideas and evidence that lead to a major proposition at the end:

Twenty-five hundred years ago, Buddha, like other Eastern philosophers before him, said: "He who sits still, wins." Asia, then immobilized in primitive torpor, had no difficulty responding. It sat still. What it won for sitting still was the perpetuation of famines and terrorizing superstitions, oppression of children, subjugation of women, emasculation of men, fratricidal wars, persecutions, mass killings. The history of Asia, like the history of all mankind, is a horrendous account of human suffering.

By presenting his supporting—and provocative—ideas first, the author is able to interest us before we reach the climactic argument at the end of the paragraph. Of course, whether we accept Esfandiary's argument—his statement of truth—or are prepared to debate his claim depends on the strength of the reasons and evidence he offers.

Many of the argumentative essays you read and much of the argumentative writing you undertake will reflect the mental processes of deduction and induction. The novelist Robert M. Pirsig offers his version of these critical thinking strategies in his cult classic, *Zen and the Art of Motorcycle Maintenance:*

> If the cycle goes over a bump and the engine misfires, and then goes over another bump and the engine misfires, and then goes over another bump and the engine misfires, and then goes over a long smooth stretch of road and there is no misfiring, and then goes over a fourth bump and the engine misfires again, one can logically conclude that the misfiring is caused by the bumps. That is induction: reasoning from particular experiences to general truths.
>
> Deductive inferences do the reverse. They start with general knowledge and predict a specific observation. For example if, from reading the hierarchy of facts about the machine the mechanic knows the horn of the cycle is powered exclusively by electricity from the battery, then he can logically infer that if the battery is dead the horn will not work. That is deduction.

Constructing an argument through the use of logical reasoning is a powerful way to convince or persuade a particular audience about the validity of your claims.

**Appeals to Emotion**   In addition to developing your argument logically using the appeal to reason, you should consider the value of incorporating *appeals to emotion* into an argumentative paper. A letter home asking for more money would in all likelihood require a certain carefully modulated emotional appeal. Similarly, Martin Luther King Jr.'s famous "I Have a Dream" speech at the 1963 March on Washington, which begins on page 447 in this textbook, is one of the finest contemporary examples of emotional appeal. King's speech ends with this invocation:

> When we let freedom ring, when we let it ring from every village and every hamlet, from every state and every city, we will be able to speed up that day when all of God's children, black men and white men, Jews and Gentiles, Protestants and Catholics, will be able to join hands and sing in the words of the old Negro spiritual, "Free at last! Free at last! Thank God almighty, we are free at last!"

King's skillful application of balanced biblical cadences and connotative and figurative language, and a strong, almost prophetic tone demonstrates the value of carefully crafted emotional appeal in the hands of an accomplished writer of argument.

Of course, in constructing an argument, you should avoid the sort of cynical manipulation of emotion that is common in the world of spoken discourse and the media in general. (For a list of unfair emotional appeals, see page 126). But honest emotional appeal provides a human context for the rational ideas and evidence you present in an argumentative essay—ideas that might otherwise be uninteresting to your audience. Assuredly, if you want to persuade your audience to undertake a particular course of action, you must draw members of this audience closer to you as a person, and perhaps even inspire them by your feelings about the subject or issue. In truth, you *must* establish rapport with your reader in an argumentative essay. If you fail to engage the reader's feelings, the best-constructed rational appeal could fall flat.

**Appeals to Ethics**   For an emotional appeal to achieve maximum effectiveness, it must reinforce not only the rational strength of your argument but also the ethical basis of your ideas. When you use *ethical appeal,* you present yourself as a well-informed, fair-minded, honest person. Aristotle acknowledged the importance of *ethos,* or the character of the writer, in the construction of argument, for if you create a sense that you are trustworthy, your readers or listeners will be inspired or persuaded. The "sound" or "voice" of your essay, which you convey to the reader through your style and tone, and which can only be perfected through the process of careful drafting and revision, will help in convincing the audience to share your opinion.

In an appeal to ethics, you try to convince the reader that you are a person of sound character—that you possess good judgment and values. As a person of goodwill and good sense, you also demonstrate an ability to empathize with your audience, to understand their viewpoints and perspectives. The psychologist Carl Rogers suggests that a willingness to embrace a potentially adversarial audience, to treat this audience more like an ally in an ethical cause, is a highly effective way to establish goodwill and the credibility of your beliefs. In Rogerian argument, your willingness to understand an opposing viewpoint and actually rephrase it reflectively for mutual understanding enables you to further establish your ethical and personal qualities.

You can appreciate the powerful combination of rational, emotional, and ethical appeals in Abraham Lincoln's Gettysburg Address, which follows for analysis and discussion.

# The Gettysburg Address
### Abraham Lincoln

*Abraham Lincoln (1809–1865) was born the son of a pioneer in 1809 in Hodgesville, Kentucky, and moved to Illinois in 1831. After brief experiences as a clerk, postmaster, and county surveyor, he studied law and was elected to the state legislature in 1834. A prominent member of the newly formed Republican Party, Lincoln became president on the eve of the Civil War. In 1862, after the Union victory at Antietam, Lincoln issued the Emancipation Proclamation freeing the slaves—the crowning achievement of an illustrious presidency. Although he was an outstanding orator and debater throughout his political career, the Gettysburg Address is one of his greatest speeches—and certainly his most famous one. It was delivered at the dedication of the Gettysburg National Cemetery in 1863. Its form and content reflect the philosophical and moral views of the time as well as the rhetorical skill of its speaker. Lincoln was assassinated by John Wilkes Booth in 1865, shortly after Robert E. Lee's surrender and the end of the Civil War.*

Four score and seven years ago our fathers brought forth on this continent, a 1 new nation, conceived in Liberty, and dedicated to the proposition that all men are created equal.

Now we are engaged in a great civil war, testing whether that nation, or 2 any nation so conceived and so dedicated, can long endure. We are met on a great battlefield of that war. We have come to dedicate a portion of that field as a final resting-place for those who here gave their lives that that nation might live. It is altogether fitting and proper that we should do this.

But, in a larger sense, we cannot dedicate—we cannot consecrate—we can- 3 not hallow—this ground. The brave men, living and dead, who struggled here have consecrated it, far above our poor power to add or detract. The world will little note, nor long remember, what we say here, but it can never forget what they did here. It is for us the living, rather, to be dedicated here to the unfinished work which they who fought here have thus far so nobly advanced. It is rather for us to be here dedicated to the great task remaining before us—that from these honored dead we take increased devotion to that cause for which they gave the last full measure of devotion; that we here highly resolve that these dead shall not have died in vain; this nation, under God, shall have a new birth of freedom; and that government of the people, by the people, for the people, shall not perish from the earth.

## COMPREHENSION

**1.** Although this speech was supposed to be a "dedication," Lincoln states that "we cannot dedicate." What does he mean by this?

2. Lincoln uses abstract words such as "liberty," "freedom," and "nation." What does he mean specifically by each of these terms?
3. What exactly happened "four score and seven years ago" in the context of the speech? Why is this reference so significant to the purpose of Lincoln's address?

## RHETORIC

1. Note the progression of imagery from that of "death" to that of "birth." How does this structure contribute to the claim and coherence of the speech?
2. How do the syntax, punctuation, and choice of the first-person plural form of address contribute to our understanding that this message was intended to be spoken rather than written?
3. Note how Lincoln refers to the combatants as "brave" and "honored." How does he suggest that their struggle was distinguished from that of "us the living"? How does this comparison and contrast create clear similarities and differences between those who fought and those who are present to carry on the work of the soldiers?
4. The American Civil War was a battle between the North and the South as were the opponents at the Battle of Gettysburg. However, Lincoln does not mention this. What is the reason behind this omission? How does it make the speech focus on more comprehensive issues?
5. Besides being president, Lincoln was by definition a politician. In what ways can we determine that this is a political speech as well as a dedication?
6. Speeches are intended to be heard. What are some elements—for example, vocabulary, syntax, length or brevity of the sentences, and juxtaposition of sentences—that appeal to the sense of sound?
7. Does this speech appeal primarily to the intellect or the emotions, or equally to the two? What are two or three sentences that demonstrate one or both of these appeals? What was the rationale behind your selections? Does Lincoln include any ethical appeals?

## WRITING

1. Research the actual historical events that occurred during the Battle of Gettysburg. Write an argumentative essay in which you discuss the significance of this particular speech at this point in the Civil War. Use a minimum of three secondary source materials.
2. Read the speech three times. Then write a paraphrase of it. Examine your paraphrase to discover what elements you recalled. Then reread the speech and write an expository essay focusing on how the structure of the speech contributed to helping you recall the information you did remember.
3. Engage in an Internet search to find the rhetorical influences on the language and style of Abraham Lincoln. Try a search phrases such as "Lincoln,

rhetorical influences." Select three authoritative "hits" and write a research paper titled "Rhetorical Influences on Abraham Lincoln."

4. **Writing an Argument:** Richard Posner in his essay "Security versus Civil Liberties," which appears in the portfolio of argumentative essays at the end of this chapter, asserts that the Emancipation Proclamation "may . . . have been unconstitutional" (paragraph 7). Conduct research on this issue, and then write an argumentative essay in which you agree or disagree with Posner's claim.

## WRITING POWERFUL ARGUMENTS

One of the most common writing assignments in college courses, especially courses in the humanities and social sciences, is the argumentative essay. Unlike narrative and descriptive essays and the major forms of expository writing—comparison and contrast, definition, classification, process, and causal analysis—the argumentative paper requires the writer to take a stand and to support a position as effectively as possible. As mentioned earlier, the rhetorical strategies underlying expository or informative writing often appear in argumentative papers. However, given the purpose of the argumentative essay, you must present your ideas as powerfully as possible in order to advance your point of view and convince your readers to accept your position or take a specific course of action. For this reason, you must construct your argumentative paper carefully and effectively.

Argument, as stated in Chapter 1, is not a mere academic enterprise but rather an integral part of our personal, social, and professional lives. Whether you consider the 2004 presidential debates between George W. Bush and John Kerry, recent decisions of the Supreme Court, actions taken by the United States in the Middle East, or tax provisions enacted by Congress—argument determines in many ways the nature of life in the United States. More personally, argument—whether in the form of reviews or commercials—influences the films we watch, the music we download, the clothes we purchase, and the food we eat. And argument—the way you sell yourself in an interview—can get you a job or lose it.

In many other ways, argument impacts your professional life. It is most clearly in evidence in newspaper and television journalism and communications, where argument and persuasion express an institution's deepest convictions. Consider the role of editorials and the op-ed page of any newspaper (including your college newspaper) in the nation. Editorial writing offers carefully crafted debates and informed opinions on a variety of topics and issues. Many newspapers also develop guidelines to promote convincing but open-minded positions on the issues of the day.

A deputy editorial page director for the *Chicago Tribune* offers a series of questions for essays that, with slight modification, provide an excellent guide for writing an argument:

- *To whom are you writing?* Are you writing to authorities? Power elites? Professors? Average readers? Yourself?
- *What's your attitude?* Are you angry? Pleased? Perplexed? What tone will you project?
- *What, exactly, are you trying to accomplish?* An official response? A public change of attitude? An explanation? Entertainment?
- *What are you contributing to the debate?* What's the added value here? Just your opinion? New facts? New arguments, contexts, or dimensions to consider?
- *Do you have something new to say?* Are you advancing the conversation or just rehashing old facts, opinions, and wisdom? Aside from an opinion, do you have a solution?
- *Have you fiercely attacked your own premise?* Will your position survive scrutiny? How would your opponents answer your most compelling arguments? Are you correct or simply wrong?
- *Are you stirring up a "three-bowler"?* This borrowed phrase refers to the reader who is so bored with your writing that her face falls in the cereal bowl not once or twice but three times. You must compose your argument in such a way that the reader is hooked by your writing and persuaded by the force of your argument.

If you are further interested in tips for editorial writing, go to www.poynter .org, a Web site for journalists that offers excellent advice in composing articles for the press.

The process for writing powerful arguments that appears in this section is useful, but it is not a formula. Ultimately, you can construct powerful arguments in numerous ways, but you always must consider the relationship between your ideas, your purpose, and your audience.

## Identify an Issue

Remember that not every subject lends itself to useful or necessary argument. The notion that *"everything* is an argument" probably contains a grain of truth, but in reality some things make for more powerful arguments than others. Certain subjects—for example, stamp collecting—might appeal to you personally and powerfully, but are they worth arguing about? Consequently, your first step in writing an effective argumentative essay is to identify a subject that contains an issue—in other words, a subject that will elicit two or more differing opinions.

Clearly, there are certain subjects that touch on current problems and inspire strong opinions. President Lincoln's Gettysburg Address dealt with a monumental issue central to the very survival of the nation; for virtually everyone in the United States at that time, the issues raised by Lincoln were debatable. Similarly, the issue of the death penalty produces two diametrically opposed viewpoints in the essays by H. L. Mencken and Coretta Scott King that are reprinted in this chapter. Social and political issues tend to be ripe subjects for debate, fostering pro and con viewpoints. (Remember that there are often more than two sides to a complex issue.) Such issues, by their very nature, often raise powerful and conflicting systems of belief that place heavy burdens on the writer to provide convincing reasons and evidence to support a claim.

Not all issues in argumentative papers have to be of national or global concern, however. Indeed, issues like capital punishment, abortion, or global warming might not be of special interest to you. Of course, if an instructor requires an argumentative essay on one of these broad hot-button topics, you will need to prepare to write the paper by first establishing an argumentative perspective on it—in other words, by choosing your side on the issue. Fortunately, you often have opportunities to select issues of more immediate, personal, or local concern: Should fast-food franchises be permitted in the student cafeteria? Should there be a campus policy on hate language? Should sophomores be required to pass standardized tests in reading, writing, and mathematics before advancing to their junior year? Many powerfully constructed arguments can deal with issues close to home and with subjects that are of considerable personal interest. Whether dealing with an issue mandated by the instructor or selecting your own issue for an argumentative paper, ask yourself at the outset of this critical process what your position on the issue is and how it can be developed through logic and evidence.

## Take a Stand and Clarify Your Claim

Once you have identified an issue that lends itself to argumentation—an issue that people might reasonably disagree about—you must take a clear stand on this issue. In other words, your claim will advance your viewpoint over all other viewpoints. The aim is not to defeat an opponent but to persuade readers—your audience—to accept your opinion. Consequently, the first step at this stage is to establish as clearly as possible what your claim is going to be. You might want to experiment with one or more of the following strategies:

- Gather information on the issue from debates on radio, television, or the Internet. Electronic resources on the Web can be helpful as you begin to research what your position on an issue is going to be. (For help with critically evaluating Web sources, see page 185).
- Brainstorm or write informally about the issue, jotting down your immediate response to it—how it makes you feel or what you think about it. If the issue provokes an emotional response, what are the causes of this response? What are your more thoughtful or intellectual responses to the issue?
- List some preliminary reasons you respond to the issue in the way you do. By listing reasons, as well as the types of evidence you will need to support those reasons, you will be able to determine at an early stage whether you have enough material for a solid argumentative paper and what forms of research you will have to conduct.

- Jot down examples, facts, and ideas that might support your claim.
- Begin to think about possible objections to your position, and list these opposing viewpoints.

As this inventory of strategies suggests, there are numerous ways to think and write critically about your approach to an issue during the prewriting stage. Essentially, during prewriting, you want to begin to articulate and pinpoint your claim, and thereby start to limit, control, and clarify the scope of your argument.

Once you have developed a preliminary approach to an issue, you should be prepared to state your claim in the form of a thesis sentence. From your reading of the information on the thesis statement in the first chapter of this textbook (see page 37), you know that you must limit the scope and purpose of your thesis or claim. Too broad a claim will be hard to cover in convincing fashion in a standard argumentative paper. One useful way to limit and clarify your claim is to consider the purpose of your argument. Do you want to argue a position on a particular issue? Do you want to argue that a certain activity, belief, or situation is good or bad, harmful or beneficial, effective or ineffective? Do you want to persuade readers to undertake or avoid a particular course of action? Do you want readers to simply consider an issue in a new light? Do you want readers to endorse your interpretation or evaluation of an artistic or literary work? By sifting through the primary purposes of argument, which involve value judgments, policies, and interpretations, you will arrive at the main point of your argument—your claim.

## Analyze Your Audience

All writing can be considered a process of communication, a conversation with an audience of readers. In argumentative writing, it is especially important to establish a common ground of belief with your readers if you expect them to accept your claim or undertake a certain course of action. Of course, you cannot change your ideas and approaches to an issue merely to please a particular audience. However, you do not construct an argumentative paper in order to be misunderstood, disbelieved, or rejected. Within the limits set by who you are, what you believe, and what your purpose is, you can match your argumentative style and approach to audience expectations.

To establish common ground with your audience, it is important to know them well so that you can dispose them favorably to your claim and the reasons and evidence supporting it. Your audience might be a professor, a prospective employer, an admissions or financial aid officer, an editor, or a member of your family. If you determine the nature of your audience *before* you compose the first draft of your argumentative paper, you will be able to tailor style, content, and tone to a specific person or group.

Try to imagine and anticipate audience expectations by asking basic questions about your readers:

- What are the age, gender, professional background, educational level, and political orientation of most of the members of the audience?
- How much does the audience know about the issue? Is it an audience of experts or a general audience with only limited knowledge of the issue?
- What does the audience expect from you in terms of the purpose behind your claim? Does the audience expect you to prove your claim or persuade them to accept it, or both?
- Will the audience be friendly, hostile, or neutral toward your argument? What political, cultural, ethical, or religious factors contribute to the audience's probable position on this issue?
- What else do you know about the audience's opinions, attitudes, and values? How might these factors shape your approach to the argument?

Suppose you are planning to write an argumentative essay on pollution. What common expectations would an English professor, a sociology professor, and a chemistry professor have concerning your argument? What differences in approach and content would be dictated by your decision to write for one of these instructors? Or consider these different audiences for a paper on the topic of pollution: a group of grade school children in your home town, or the Environmental Protection Agency, or the manager of a landfill operation, or a relative in Missouri whose town has been experiencing chemical pollution. In each instance, the type and nature of the audience will influence your approach to the issue and even your purpose. Remember that through your *purpose* you find the proper context for your argument. Any writer who wants to communicate effectively with his or her audience will adjust the content and tone of an argument so as not to lose, confuse, or mislead the reader.

## Establish Your Tone

By *tone* we mean the attitude you take toward your subject. A word that often is used interchangeably with tone is *voice*. Tone is the personal voice that a reader "hears" in your writing. This voice may vary, depending on the situation, your purpose, and your audience. It may be personal or impersonal and range across a spectrum of attitudes: serious or humorous, subjective or objective, straightforward or ironic, formal or casual, and so forth. You adjust your tone to match your purpose in writing.

In argumentation an effective tone will be a true and trustworthy reflection of the writing situation. After all, you are writing an argumentative essay in order to convince and persuade, and consequently, you need to sound like a reasonable, well-organized, and rational individual. When writing for college instructors, that "community of scholars," you must be especially careful to maintain a reasonable tone. You do not have to sound scholarly, legalistic, or overly technical in presenting your argument, but you do have to employ a personal voice that is appropriate to the writing occasion and audience expectations.

To achieve an appropriate tone in argumentative writing, you will often need to be forceful in presenting your ideas. Remember that you are staking out a position, perhaps on a controversial issue, and you must seem willing to defend it. Try to maintain a consistent voice of authority, but do not be overbearing: Do not move from the lecture hall to the locker room, mixing voices in a way that will confuse or alienate your audience. A tone or voice that exceeds the limits of good taste and commonly accepted norms of argumentative style is likely to be ineffectual. A voice that is too emotional, overblown, or irrational will in all likelihood alienate the reader and erode your claim.

Your tone—your voice—is a revelation of yourself. It derives from your claims and supporting ideas, your language and sentence structure. Even if your audience is one person—typically, your professor—you certainly must present yourself to that audience as convincingly as possible. When your tone is adjusted to the issue, the claim, and the supporting evidence, and also to the nature of the opposition, you stand a good chance of writing an effective argumentative essay.

## Develop and Organize the Grounds for Your Claim

You establish the validity of your claim by setting out the reasons and evidence—the *grounds*—that support your main point. Whereas the claim presents your general proposition or point of view, as you develop your grounds you organize the argument into minor propositions, evidence, and refutation. By establishing the grounds for your claim, you explain the particular perspective or point of view you take on an issue. The grounds for your claim permit the reader to "see" the strength of your position.

There are numerous ways to state the primary reasons or grounds for holding your position. Think of these primary reasons as minor propositions underlying the basis of your claim—reasons that readers would find it difficult to rebut or reject. Three possible models for organizing claims and grounds in an essay can now be considered:

*Model 1*

    Introduction: statement and clarification of claim

    First minor proposition and evidence

    Second minor proposition and evidence

    Third minor proposition and evidence

    Refutation of opposing viewpoints for minor propositions

    Conclusion

*Model 2*

    Introduction: statement and clarification of claim

    First minor proposition and evidence; refutation

    Second minor proposition and evidence; refutation

    Third minor proposition and evidence; refutation

    Conclusion

*Model 3*

Statement and clarification of claim

Summary of opposing viewpoints and refutation

First minor proposition and evidence

Second minor proposition and evidence

Third minor proposition and evidence

Conclusion

In practice, arguments rarely adhere slavishly to these models. In fact, you can arrange your argument in numerous ways. However, the models can serve a useful purpose, especially in exams that require argumentative responses to a question, for they provide a handy template for your answer. In argument, to support your claim, you will need substantial reasons, sometimes more than the three minor propositions illustrated in these models. Remember that one reason generally will not provide sufficient grounds to prove an argument. Moreover, you should keep in mind the need to distinguish between your *opinions,* which in the broadest sense are beliefs that you cannot verify logically, and reasons, which are based on logic, evidence, and direct proof.

## Gather and Evaluate Your Evidence

Once you have established your claim and your reasons, you can turn your attention to developing evidence for your claim, a subject introduced in the first chapter. Collecting evidence is a bit like the strategies for successful fishing presented by the student in his classification paragraph in the first chapter (see page 49): You want to fish the top, the middle, and the bottom of your subject. Phrased somewhat differently, you want to cast a wide net as you seek evidence designed to support your claim and reasons.

At the outset, a carefully designed search of the Web can yield ample evidence. The Web will permit you to establish links to sites and listservs where you can download or print full or abstracted texts from periodicals, books, documents, and reports. Remember, however, that searching the Web is often like navigating a minefield: Useless "facts," hoaxes, and informational marketing ploys mix with serious research, honest reporting, and critical analysis. To guard against the pitfalls involved in relying exclusively on Web surfing, you should also make a trip to the college library. Research librarians can help you to evaluate Web sites and direct you to the best sources—both traditional and electronic—for the types of evidence you are seeking. (For more on library and Internet research, see Chapter 3.) Depending on your subject, you might consider interviewing individuals who can provide expert testimony designed to support your claim and reasons. Finally, your own personal experience and the experiences of your friends and acquaintances might provide useful evidence, although such kinds of anecdotal or firsthand support should be treated judiciously and not serve as the entire basis for your paper. For instance, you and your friends might claim that a current horror movie is great, but such personal evidence must be tempered by a willingness to consult established critics for additional support.

If you cast a wide net and fish the whole lake, you will almost always catch more than you require. Yet the very process of searching comprehensively for evidence can produce exciting, unintended consequences. You might, for example, discover that certain evidence suggests a need to revise or qualify your claim. Evidence can also help you to articulate or confirm the warrants that are the foundation of your argument, for experts writing on an issue often state the assumptions, principles, or beliefs that offer connections between a claim and its grounds. The insights gained by considering other evidence might cause you to develop a new reason for your claim that you had not considered initially. You might also discover evidence that helps you to refute the ideas of your anticipated opposition. Having a wealth of evidence at your disposal is an embarrassment of riches that you can exploit skillfully.

After you have collected adequate evidence to bolster your claim and the key reasons supporting that claim, the next necessary step is to evaluate and select the best evidence available to you. Writers who carefully evaluate and select their evidence produce effective arguments. At the outset, the nature of the writing situation—an exam, a term paper, a letter to the editor—will dictate to an extent the type of evidence you need to evaluate. In most instances, however, your evidence should be *credible, comprehensive,* and *current.* Your evidence is credible when your sources are reliable and the evidence itself is representative. Your evidence is comprehensive when you provide a broad range of facts, information, and data designed to cover all aspects of your argument. In presenting evidence comprehensively, you also make certain that there is sufficient support for each of your reasons— not too much evidence for one and too little for another, but an even balance between and among the minor propositions. Finally, always try to locate the most current evidence available to support your claim. Data and statistics often do not age well and tend to lose their relevance. However, in some arguments, older evidence can be compared with newer information. For example, a paper arguing that immigration to the United States is out of control could make skillful use of data from the 1960 Census *and* the 2000 Census.

Evidence is the heart of any argument. Without evidence, readers will not be interested in your claim and supporting reasons. Make certain that the evidence—the facts, examples, and details—you present is accurate and skillfully presented so that readers become interested in your more abstract propositions, identify with your position, and come away convinced of the validity of your argument.

## Consider Your Warrants

Even as you clarify your claim and assemble your reasons and evidence, you must also consider the assumptions underlying your argument. Think of the assumption or warrant as the link between a claim and the supporting evidence—the underlying set of beliefs or principles governing your essential perception of the world and the human condition. Warrants answer the question of *how* the data are connected to the claim. Sometimes these warrants are stated, but often they remain unstated. In either instance, they are not necessarily self-evident or universally accepted. They are significant nevertheless, for as generalizations that are far broader than claims and evidence, warrants serve as the bedrock of an argument.

Warrants help to guarantee that a reader will accept your argument, and consequently, it is important to consider them. When you are writing for a friendly or supportive audience, you can usually assume that your readers will accept the warrants supporting your claim, and so you might not even need to state them. For example, if you claim in a report for your biology professor that creationism should not be taught in high school science classrooms, your argument is based on several assumptions or warrants: that the Constitution, for example, requires the separation of church and state, or that there is no scientific basis for creationism. In fact, when making your claim about creationism before a scientist, you also are relying on certain *backings,* which are the principles underlying the warrants themselves—for instance, the idea that a scientist is concerned with scientific objectivity rather than literal interpretations of the Bible, or that scientists deal with the empirical reality and not matters of faith. But what if you were make your claim in a letter to a local school board, several of whose members want to revise the ninth-grade earth science curriculum to emphasize creationism and evolution equally? In this instance, you would be presenting your argument to a potentially skeptical or hostile audience, so you would have to state your warrants clearly, bolster them with adequate support, and establish solid causal links between your warrants and your backing.

Whether you are writing an argumentative paper or reading an argumentative essay critically, you need to develop the habit of looking for and evaluating the warrants and the backing behind the argument. If you are reading an argumentative essay, and the warrants are stated, it will make this task easier. If the warrants are unstated, you will have to detect and evaluate them. If you are writing an argumentative essay, you should consider whether your audience will probably understand and consent to the warrants that serve as the foundation of your paper. If you have any doubt, then you should include them.

## Deal with Opposing Viewpoints

To make your argument as effectively as possible, you need to acknowledge and deal with opposing viewpoints. Any controversial issue is going to have more than one viewpoint, and you must recognize contending claims and handle them fairly. As suggested in the section on audience analysis, you can enhance your credibility by describing these opposing viewpoints fully and accurately, with a respectful rather than hostile tone, even as you demonstrate that your position is the most reasonable and valid.

As a prewriting strategy for refutation, you might try dividing a sheet of paper or your computer screen into three columns, labeling them, from left to right, "Supporting Viewpoints," "Opposing Viewpoints," and "Refutation." Then list the main supporting points for your claim, thinking of possible opposing responses and writing them down as you go. Imagining how the opposition will respond to your supporting reasons will help you to develop refutations, or counterarguments. You can use the resulting chart as a guide to organize sections of your argumentative paper.

The listing technique for refutation forces you to acknowledge opposing viewpoints and also to refute them in a systematic way. It is perfectly appropriate—and even necessary—to demonstrate the weakness or insufficiency of opposing arguments, for refutation strengthens your own position. Any complex argument that you present will not be complete unless you skillfully refute all predictable opposing viewpoints, using one of the following techniques:

- Question the opposition's claim: Is it too flimsy or broad, overstated, or improperly grounded in minor propositions?
- Question the evidence: Is it insufficient, outdated, or inaccurate?
- Question the warrants and backing of an opposing argument—those assumptions and beliefs that underpin the opposition's claim.
- Concede some part of the opposition's viewpoint, a subtle but extremely attractive strategy that shows that you are a courteous and unbiased thinker and writer, and that therefore constitutes an appeal to ethics.

## Avoid Unfair Emotional Appeals and Errors in Reasoning

When you write and revise an argumentative essay, you need to avoid certain temptations and dangers that are unique to this form of discourse. You always have to make certain that your argumentative strategies are fair and appropriate and that you have avoided oversimplifying your argument. You also need to resist the temptation to include persuasive appeals that distort critical reasoning and to avoid errors in logical reasoning.

Emotional appeals are effective when used appropriately in argumentation, but used unfairly they can distort your logical reasoning. Such "loaded" arguments are filled with appeals to the reader's emotions, fears, and prejudices. Here are three of the most common fallacies of emotional distortion to avoid:

1. *Transfer* is the association of a proposition with a famous person. Transfer can be either positive ("In the spirit of President Franklin Delano Roosevelt, we should create a jobs program for the nation's unemployed") or negative ("President George W. Bush is the symbol of unbridled capitalism"). Another term for negative transfer is *name calling*. In both the positive and negative types of transfer, however, there is no logical basis for the connection.
2. *Argumentum ad hominem* (to the man) is a strategy that discredits a person in an effort to discredit his or her argument. It attacks the person rather

than the position: "Richards is a homosexual and consequently cannot understand the sanctity of heterosexual marriage." In this instance, the individual becomes a false issue.

3. *Argumentum ad populum* (to the people) deliberately arouses an audience's emotions about certain institutions and ideas. Certain words have strong positive or negative connotations. Such words as *patriotism* and *motherhood* are *virtue* words that often prompt the creation of *glittering generalities*. Suggestive words can be used to distort meaning by illogical association and to manipulate an audience to take a stand for or against a proposition: "USC should not take the *totalitarian* step of requiring athletes to maintain a full course load." A related strategy is the *bandwagon* approach, in which the writer generalizes falsely that the crowd or majority is always right: "Everyone is voting for Erikson and you should too."

These unfair emotional appeals are often found in political speech writing, advertising, and propaganda. When you write argumentative essays, you should use persuasive appeal to reinforce rather than distort the logical presentation of your ideas, blending reasonable claims and valid emotional and ethical appeals to convince rather than trick your audience into agreeing with you.

Equally important is the need to avoid errors in reasoning in the construction of an argument. Here are seven types of errors in reasoning, or *logical fallacies*, that are common in argumentative writing:

1. *Hasty generalizations.* A hasty generalization is a conclusion based on insufficient, unrepresentative, or untrue evidence: "The president of the college successfully raised 100 million dollars, so other college presidents should be able to do the same." When you indulge in hasty generalizations, you jump to false conclusions. Hasty generalizations are also at the heart of stereotyping—the uncritical application of an oversimplified generalization to a group or to individual members of the group. Make certain that you have adequate and accurate evidence to support any claim or conclusion.

2. *Broad generalizations.* A broad generalization typically employs words like *all, never,* and *always* to state something absolutely or categorically. It is actually a form of overstatement, as in the sentence "Freud always treated sexuality as the basis of human behavior." Usually, readers can easily find exceptions to such sweeping statements, so it is best to qualify them.

3. *Oversimplification.* Oversimplification reduces alternatives. Several forms of oversimplification can be distinguished:

   a. *Either/or.* Don't assume that there are only two sides to an issue, only two possibilities, only yes or no, only right or wrong: "Either we make English a one-year requirement or college students will not be able to write well."

   b. *No choice.* Don't assume that there is only one possibility: "The United States has no other alternative than to build the Star Wars missile defense system." Parents and politicians are prone to no-other-choice propositions.

    c. *No harm or cost.* Don't assume that a potential benefit will not have significant harms, consequences, or costs: "We should sell North Korea as much wheat as it needs." No-harm generalizations or arguments may overlook dangerous implications. Always consider alternative evidence.

    d. *One solution.* Don't assume that a complicated issue has only one solution: "Embryonic stem cells should not be used for research, for using them in this way will lead to the destruction of human life." Always consider evidence for other solutions or alternative approaches to issues and problems.

4. *Begging the question.* Do not assume in your premises or in your evidence what is to be proved in the conclusion. For example, if you argue that vandalism by teenagers is unavoidable because teenagers are young and irresponsible, you are begging the question because you are not proving your premise. Another form of begging the question is to take a conclusion for granted before it is proved.

5. *False cause-and-effect relationships.* Perhaps the most common error in trying to establish causal relationships is known as the *post hoc, ergo propter hoc* fallacy ("after this, therefore because of this). The fact that one event *follows* another is not proof that the first *caused* the second. If you maintain, for instance, that there is an increase in the crime rate every time there is a full moon, you are falsely identifying an unrelated event as a cause. Many superstitions—popular, political, and otherwise—illogically assume that one event somehow causes another.

6. *Disconnected ideas.* Termed in Latin *non sequitur* (It does not follow), this fault in reasoning arises when there is no logical connection between two or more ideas. Put differently, an argument's conclusion is not related to its premises: "George W. Bush makes a good president because he was a successful owner of a professional baseball team." Sometimes you think that a connection exists but you fail to state it in writing. For example, you may think that owners of baseball teams and presidents need to have strong people skills and be good judges of character. In other words, *you* may see the logical connection between your ideas about presidents and baseball team owners, but if you don't make it explicit, readers may think there is a non sequitur.

7. *Weak or false analogies.* An *analogy* is a type of comparison that explains a subject by comparing it to the features of another essentially dissimilar subject: "Unless we learn to think critically about the niagara of information that washes over us every day, we will be lost in a flood of rumors and gossip." Analogies can be used to illustrate a point, although they should always be used carefully and with discretion. More significantly, an analogy can *never* function as evidence or logical proof of a position.

    The hallmark of argumentation is sound critical thinking. If you present your claims, grounds, and evidence carefully; are willing to assemble the best and most objective data; treat the opposition with respect; and are flexible in responding to new ideas, you will be well on your way to constructing a solid argumentative essay. A successful argumentative paper reveals a writer who possesses an inquiring mind—who is able to judge opinions on the basis of evidence, reason well, and back up ideas and beliefs in a convincing and valid way.

## Argumentative Synthesis

Synthesis, you will recall from Chapter 1, is the process we use to combine information from two or more sources and infer relationships among them. Whereas the primary aim of explanatory synthesis is to convey information, the aim of argumentative synthesis is to convince readers that a claim is correct or valid. Whether we evaluate the relative quality of the readings (in other words, provide a *critique* of the texts) or draw material from readings to support a claim of our own, argumentative synthesis requires us to stake out a position on the materials at hand.

With explanatory synthesis, as we have seen, we try to accurately identify the key ideas and purposes of various writers, but we do not argue for or against a certain viewpoint. For example, here is the student's thesis based on the readings by Elbow and Murray from Chapter 1:

*Both Peter Elbow and Donald Murray stress the importance of process in the craft of composition, but approach the process from different perspectives.*

In this instance, the student makes a modest but useful attempt to convey information accurately through explanatory synthesis.

Consider the shift from explanation to argument as the writer now takes sides in presenting the ideas of Elbow and Murray:

*Although Peter Elbow's theory of freewriting might be useful to certain students with basic writing problems, Donald Murray in his stress on revision offers far more useful advice for mainstream college students who want to improve their writing.*

Observe how the writer moves from explanatory to argumentative synthesis as she critiques the two readings and their authors. She takes sides. She presents a claim (which she will have to support with convincing grounds or evidence). She wants us to agree with her interpretation and assessment.

**Critiquing**   As you prepare for argumentative synthesis, rely on the strategies for critical reading and writing that were outlined in Chapter 1 as well as the guidelines for argumentative synthesis presented in this chapter. At the outset, it would also be wise to focus your critical response on *critiquing*—the evaluation of each text's quality or worth based on a clearly defined set of guidelines. With critiquing, you cannot rely on a personal opinion or preference. Critiquing demands clear criteria and objective assessment of your text. It is a necessary aspect of successful argumentative synthesis.

When critiquing texts, you follow either *general academic standards* of evaluation (criteria that apply to many disciplines) or *discipline-specific standards* (for instance, criteria used by scholars in cognitive psychology or specialists in international law). In most cases, you will be working with general standards when critiquing sources in college composition courses. You will consider issues like the style, organization, importance of subject, effectiveness of a writer's claim, and quality of evidence as the evaluative criteria for your critique. Stated differently, you will agree, disagree, or (in certain cases) agree *and* disagree to varying degrees with a writer and his or her text—but doing so from the vantage point of informed judgment.

The formal demands of critiquing are neither mysterious, intimidating, or overwhelming. In everyday situations, we engage in critiquing: arguing over the merits of two recent films, evaluating the skills of various sports stars, praising our favorite musicians, supporting one candidate for political office over all others, or logging into a website to check and perhaps comment on the best (or worst) professors on campus. Writing a formal critique is perhaps more of a challenge than situations from everyday life, but if you follow basic steps the process of critiquing becomes manageable.

1. *Carefully read and evaluate each text.* Annotate the selection: Cite the source of the article and the author's intended audience, look for the writer's thesis or claim, identify his or her purpose (to inform, argue, or entertain), highlight the primary and secondary evidence, and consider the style and organization of the piece.
2. *Summarize your findings,* focusing on the author's main points.
3. *Evaluate the reading.* Consider the overall validity of the author's presentation: Has the writer achieved his or her purpose? What is the quality of the supporting evidence? Is the information or evidence convincing and representative? Has the author interpreted material correctly and argued logically?
4. *Write your response.* Establish your claim, focusing on specific aspects of the text that best illuminate your own thesis or argument. Explain to what extent you agree or disagree with the author and what standards you are applying. Offer examples to explain your judgments and support your interpretation.
5. *Revise the draft.* Clarify your position in relation to the author's text. Check the accuracy of your information about the text. Make certain that your assessment or interpretation is based on clear criteria. Refine and thoroughly develop your assertions, correcting any fallacies in reasoning and argumentation.

**Guidelines for Argumentative Synthesis**   As you read and respond to texts using argumentative synthesis, you might find certain essays easy to understand. However, you should be prepared to contend with challenging subjects— for instance, essays about genetic engineering or the Constitutional implications of electronic surveillance. In each instance, you will have to make complex topics intelligible for your primary and secondary audiences. Sometimes your instructor will provide clear guidelines; for example, he or she might assign essays on the Patriot Act (see pages 161–177) and tell you to determine the relative strengths and weaknesses of the texts. Or your instructor might ask you to formulate your own argument based on several assigned texts and/or your own research on the subject. Whether the instructor assigns the texts or you locate sources on your own, you must decide on how best to treat these texts fairly and accurately while at the same time positing a claim, organizing evidence and documenting sources (see Chapter 3), and presenting findings in a coherent way.

As you start to formulate a strategy, realize that there is no single solution to effective argumentative synthesis. In reality, argumentative synthesis, like any form of writing, is a recursive, or back-and-forth, process in which the strategies you employ can be drawn from a vast repertoire of rhetorical possibilities. For example, you could use the block method explained in the section in Chapter 1 on comparison and contrast (see page 44) to organize a paper in which you critique essays A and B, which present opposing viewpoints on a recent film. For a different assignment requiring you to defend a position on Wal-Mart, you might have to synthesize material from several sources, relying on the introduction to writing research papers that appears in Chapter 3. Even with the many strategies available to you, it is possible to establish a set of useful guidelines for argumentative synthesis:

1. *Analyze the assignment.* Determine whether your primary purpose will be to critique texts or to argue your own position based on several readings. (While it is easy to separate these goals, it should be evident that critiquing sources is relevant to both:)
2. *Select and carefully review the readings.* Perhaps your instructor will assign the readings—which should make your task easier. But if you have to find the readings, whether your purpose is to critique the texts or generate your own argument, you will have to highlight the key claims, warrants, and support in those texts that suit your essential aim.
3. *Take notes and formulate a claim or major proposition.* Critically read and reread passages, identifying key claims and presentation of ideas. Label and define terms that the author introduces. Write brief summaries, preferably in single sentences, of all texts. Formulate your claim, checking it against the texts you are critiquing to make certain it is accurate and conclusive. Decide on an organizational plan: Will you, for instance, rely on comparison and contrast, classification, or some other strategy to structure your claim?
4. *Write the first draft.* Establish your claim at the outset. Introduce the authors, texts, or passages that you will critique. Present the key definition, principle, or standard of evaluation you will apply to analyze and assess these texts. Evaluate the validity of each text, pointing to such elements as logic, evidence, weight or importance of the subject, and overall presentation. Agree or disagree with a text's assumptions and viewpoints. Document your sources. (See Chapter 3.)

5. *Revise your synthesis.* Refine the introduction so that your claim is clearly defined. Improve the organization of the main parts of your synthesis, making certain that support is well ordered, critical observations are compelling, transitions are strong, and information about the texts under consideration is presented in a fair and balanced way. Strengthen the conclusion by stating convincingly the importance of your insights and findings and the validity of your argument.

Argumentative synthesis, like all types of argumentative writing, presents a claim about which reasonable people might agree or disagree. The challenge is to formulate your synthesis in such a way that it convinces or persuades your audience to agree with your assessment and basic viewpoint.

# Case Study for Synthesis

## MySpace: Friend or Foe?

Following are three essays dealing with the impact of online communities on relationships. All three essays explore social networking, and all three authors treat MySpace as the focus for their analyses, arguments, and viewpoints. As you read the essays, consider how each author establishes a perspective on the topic, makes a claim, and organizes material to support that claim. Test your talent for engaging in argumentative synthesis by responding to the activities at the end of this case study.

# Fakesters

### Wade Roush

*Wade Roush is a contributing editor to* Technology Review, *where this essay appeared in November/December 2006.*

1 Web users have created more than 116 million profiles on MySpace, the social-networking site owned since 2005 by Rupert Murdoch's News Corp. As I will explain in a moment, many of these profiles are fake. Still, 116 million is more than the number of people in Mexico and the number of cable TV subscribers in the United States.

2      Parents and members of the U.S. Congress have begun to take note—and they don't like what they see. Conservative groups fomented a media panic this year over the supposed rash of sexual predators on MySpace and pushed a bill through the House of Representatives—the Delete Online Predators Act (DOPA)—that would cut off minors' ability to access this and other social-networking sites from federally funded facilities like schools and libraries.

3      In the opinion of experts such as Henry Jenkins, a professor of literature and director of the Comparative Media Studies Program at MIT, the threat of sexual solicitation on MySpace is not as great as many fear. The company has indeed been hit with a high-profile lawsuit over an incident in which an adult molester allegedly met his underage victim on the site. But teens who use the Internet have said in surveys that online "solicitations" often come from people under 25—and are simply ignored. Furthermore, MySpace is likely to get safer: an October Wired News report that as many as 744 registered sex offenders have MySpace profiles will likely push the company to cull such members.

4      But while MySpace's bad rap as a haven for sexual predators is probably undeserved, there's good reason to be disturbed by the site: it is devolving from a friends' network into a marketing madhouse.

5      If any social-networking company has found a way to rake in cash, it is MySpace; for example, Google recently agreed to pay $900 million for the exclusive right to provide Web searching and keyword-based text ads on the site. Of course, targeted advertisements distributed by Google and other companies provide the revenue that keeps many Web-based businesses afloat. But MySpace's venture into consumer marketing has gone far beyond traditional advertising. The site has given members the technological tools to "express themselves" by turning their own profiles into multimedia billboards for bands, movies, celebrities, and products. Think MTV plus user photos, bulletin boards, and instant messaging.

6      I realize that in criticizing a pop-culture mecca frequented by millions of people, I risk sounding just as out of touch as DOPA's supporters. But after spending

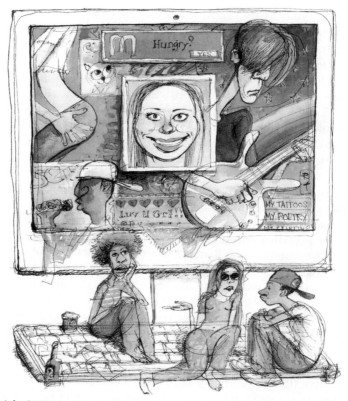

the last few years chronicling the emergence of social networking and other forms of social computing for this magazine, I had higher hopes for the technology. To me, the popularity of MySpace and other social-networking sites signals a demand for new, more democratic ways to communicate—a demand that's likely to remake business, politics, and the arts as today's young Web users enter the adult world and bring their new communications preferences with them. The problem is that MySpace's choice of business strategy threatens to divert this populist energy and trap its users in the old, familiar world of big-media commercialism.

My biggest worry about MySpace is that it is undermining the "social" in  7 social networking. The general expectation when one joins a social network is that its other members are actual people. On MySpace, this isn't always so. The movie *Jackass: Number Two* has a profile on the site, as do Pepsi, NASCAR, and Veronica Mars, the CW network's teen detective. The company interprets the idea of a "profile" so broadly that real people end up on the same footing as products, movies, promotional campaigns, and fictional characters—not exactly the conditions for a new flowering of authentic personal expression.

As a site organized around an enormous collection of profiles, MySpace  8 was modeled on Friendster and other earlier online social networks. Users are given pages where they can post self-descriptions, photos, short videos, blog entries, and the like. Every profile includes a list of the other members its creator has "friended," and a comment section where those friends leave feedback. (Most comments are encouraging, casual, and shallow: "Love the new look! How are you not married yet?")

9    But one feature that makes MySpace different from earlier sites, and evidently more appealing to users, is its friendliness toward independent artists. Cofounder Tom Anderson, who has a background in the Los Angeles arts scene, has said that he and business partner Chris DeWolfe started the site in 2003 because the older social networks didn't give musicians, photographers, digital filmmakers, and other artists adequate ways to promote themselves and their work. From its beginning, then, MySpace has functioned as a public stage. It lets bands and solo musicians create profiles, publicize upcoming shows, and upload their songs, which other members can then embed in their own profiles. Filmmakers can upload video clips. Indeed, the site has become one of the main places where unknown artists go to be discovered by major studios, or at least to develop a base of fans who'll attend shows and buy CDs and DVDs.

10    In the early days at Friendster, only real individuals could create profiles. Bands were lumped in with other "fakesters," the term coined by Fiendster users for profiles created by impostors or dedicated to someone other than the author, such as a pet or a celebrity. The company eventually relented, and fakester profiles became an accepted part of Friendster's culture, often taking on the function of fan clubs.

11    MySpace, however, has been hospitable to fakesters from the beginning—so much so that it's now perfectly kosher for a company (or one of its fans) to create a profile for a fast-food chain, a brand of soda, or an electronics product. Other MySpace members can friend these profiles just as if they represented people. As of early October, Burger King had more than 134,500 friends, and the Helio cell phone had 130,000.

12    The fakester phenomenon gives network members a way to declare their cultural affinities. These declarations are a huge part of a member's online identity, according to social-media researcher Danah Boyd, who is studying MySpace and other social-networking sites for her doctoral thesis at the University of California, Berkeley's School of Information. "It is important to be connected to all of your friends, your idols and the people you respect," Boyd writes. "Of course, a link does not necessarily mean a relationship. . . . The goal is to look cool and receive peer validation."

13    But profiles are about more than looking cool, in Boyd's view. She argues that social-networking sites are among the last unregimented environments for young people, places where they're free to explore issues of personal and group identity. Members of such sites "write themselves into being" through their profiles, Boyd says, trying out personalities and slowly coming to understand who they are and how they fit in.

14    Ideally, every networking site would be this liberating. Alas, MySpace tends to herd its users into niches created for them by the mass market. If MySpace members are writing themselves into being through the profiles they friend and the products they endorse, then today's 14-to-24-year-olds are

growing up into a generation of Whopper-eating, iPod-absorbed, Hollywood-obsessed Red Bull addicts.

Take BillyJ (not his real handle), an 18-year-old high-school graduate and 15 UPS employee in Louisville, KY. BillyJ smokes Kools, prefers Coke to Pepsi, counts *X-Men: The Last Stand* among his 393 friends, admires New Jersey Nets guard Jason Kidd, likes to work on car audio systems, doesn't have a girlfriend yet, and apparently covets a Ducati motorcycle (his profile features customized Ducati backgrounds, color schemes, and ads). BillyJ may have deeper, more personal interests, but you won't find them on his MySpace profile. It's unclear what he contributes to the network—but as a single 18-to-24-year-old male with his own income and lots of friends, he is a viral marketer's dream vector.

In fact, MySpace can be viewed as one huge platform for "personal product 16 placement"—one different from big-media-style product placement only in that MySpace members aren't paid for their services. There's nothing new, of course, about word-of-mouth marketing. What's sad about MySpace, though, is that the large supply of fake "friends," together with the cornucopia of ready-made songs, videos, and other marketing materials that can be directly embedded in profiles, encourages members to define themselves and their relationships almost solely in terms of media and consumption.

This can't be all that social computing has to offer. Older Web-based social 17 networks were launched with serious (or at least creative) missions: LinkedIn is about making business connections, Flickr and Fotolog are for sharing photographs, Meetup is for planning book clubs and campaign events. Of course, there's no requirement that a social network have high ideals. Like television and every other technology that started out as a shiny showroom prototype, social networking will inevitably accumulate some dings and scratches on the road to mass adoption. But if MySpace is to be the face of online social networking, it's fair to ask whether it's making our culture richer or poorer. To date, the only people who are profiting are Rupert Murdoch and his stockholders.

# Social Sites Are Becoming Too Much of a Good Thing

### Ellen Lee

*Ellen Lee, a journalist, wrote this report for the* San Francisco Chronicle. *The article appeared in the* Chronicle's *November 2, 2006, edition.*

Aarica Caro is sick of sharing. That is, sharing online. 1

She has shared the lives of her cats. She has shared a list of her favorite tele- 2 vision shows and movies ("Grey's Anatomy," chick flicks). She has shared her reviews of Bay Area haunts (two stars for the Old Spaghetti Factory in San Jose, five stars for the Starbucks in Morgan Hill). And she has been invited to share some more.

3    If you believe the buzz, the latest incarnation of the Web is all about sharing, connecting and community. Social networking sites such as MySpace and Palo Alto's Facebook have exploded in popularity, drawing new users into the fold each day. Users create profiles about themselves, link to their friends and post photos, messages and updates about their daily lives. Like instant messaging and chat rooms before it, social networking has become a powerful way for people to communicate via the Web and another place for people to spend their time online.

4    But even as the phenomenon continues to swell, the effort to maintain an active social life on the Web is taking its toll. Some have grown tired of what once was novel. Some feel bombarded by unsolicited messages, friend requests and advertisements. And some are cutting back.

5    This suggests that as much as people want to connect through the Internet, the practice also can have the opposite effect: social networking fatigue.

6    "You join a lot, but you don't keep up," said Dave Taylor, a 44-year-old Internet marketing consultant who complained about having social networking fatigue on his blog after joining about 15 sites.

7    Social networking sites have steadily attracted more people this year, according to Nielsen/NetRatings. But between August and September, traffic to almost all popular social networking sites fell: MySpace's audience dropped from 49.2 million to 47.2 million; Facebook from 8.9 million to 7.8 million; Microsoft's Windows Live Spaces from 8.2 million to 7.8 million. Although those losses could be attributed to students returning to school, the decline also comes as an increasing number of sites compete for attention and the newness has begun to fade.

8    Last year, Caro, a 28-year-old escrow officer who lives in Morgan Hill, stopped writing about the adventures of her three cats on Catster. She didn't have the time. Though she has been invited to join other online communities such as Yahoo 360, she hasn't bothered to sign up. She said her MySpace page is enough.

9    "It's getting pretty old," Caro said. "It makes no sense to have a million of those pages. I have one."

10    Caro kept an online cat diary for six months and hooked up her cats with about 50 friends each. "At that point, I though, 'Who cares?'" she said. "Who cares if my cats have friends?"

11    Her feelings highlight the challenge facing the social networking trend. Once someone has put together an elaborate profile online, connected with enough friends, found the love of her life, located old classmates and landed a job, what's next?

12    That depends. Teenagers and those in their 20s and 30s have been the early adopters, not just because they're Web-savvy but because they're at a time in their lives when they need to establish new ties, such as starting college, said Fred Stutzman, an Internet entrepreneur and graduate student at the University of North Carolina at Chapel Hill.

"Social networking Web sites are relevant to people at different times in 13 their lives," Stutzman said. "The more structure you have in your life, the less you need it as a crutch to understand the world around you. You already know what your friends are like. It's fun to look up their profile once in a while and check up on people, but it's not something you need every day."

Yet even as one group outgrows it, another comes on board. "There's a 14 whole generation, a younger subset, coming in," Stutzman said. "There is an exodus that goes on, but there are a ton of people just a couple of years younger who have those same needs."

Michigan State University Professor Nicole Ellison and her colleagues, who 15 are studying how college students use Facebook, found that, without much effort, Facebook users could keep in touch with a wider network of casual acquaintances than those who didn't use it.

"Checking Facebook is routine," she said. "When they first get on the computer, they check their e-mail. They log on to instant messaging. They check their Facebook." 16

Building a profile page also taps into the desire for self-expression. "They 17 want to go out there and state their case and talk about their lives," said Roni Ruddell, a teen-marketing consultant.

Social networking took off in 2002 with Friendster. MySpace, which has since 18 reached critical mass and was acquired by News Corp. last year for $580 million, and Facebook, born out of a Harvard dorm room, followed. And in the past year, the space has turned into a packed, wall-to-wall party: SnowboardGang for snowboarders, Pearl Harbor Stories for survivors and their friends and family, Zebo for people who like to list what they own, even Hamsterster for hamster owners.

Val Landi, co-founder of WiredBerries, a new site for women interested 19 in health, predicts the next step will be networks splintering off by people's interests.

"We're in the first-generation phase of social media," he said. "My sense 20 is you're going to find niche sites rather than these broad, general, catch-all platforms."

But success depends on whether members feel like their friends and the 21 people they want to meet use the same site. If not, they can move to a new one. When Friendster began experiencing technical problems and enforcing certain rules a few years ago, many members migrated to MySpace. In September, Facebook faced backlash after it introduced features that raised privacy concerns; the company responded and appeared to quell the uproar.

One in four who sign up for Catster, and its companion site Dogster, 22 become long-term members, said founder Ted Rheingold. But fostering an online community is more difficult than many entrepreneurs think, he said. "You can bring a person to a Web site, but you can't make them click" and interact, he said.

MySpace isn't immune, either. In recent months, Stephanie Chow, a 15- 23 year-old junior at Menlo School who used to spend hours on MySpace, has started to cut back.

24   "It was fun doing it at the beginning," said Chow, who now prefers Facebook over MySpace. "But it started getting time consuming. I was changing my layout instead of doing my homework."

25   She still maintains her MySpace page because not all her friends use Facebook. But the blinking advertisements on MySpace have become a turnoff, Chow said.

26   Her complaint is echoed by those who fear that, as large corporations such as News Corp. and Google take over independent sites, they will strip away what made them attractive.

27   "I just feel like it's becoming another way for companies to advertise their products," Chow said. "I just feel like I'm being used."

28   Her older sister, Tiffany Chow, a senior at Vassar who interned this summer at San Francisco's Six Apart, which runs the blogging site LiveJournal, also has curbed her use of MySpace and other sites. She has been a member, at one time or another, of MySpace, Facebook, Flickr, Vox, LiveJournal, deviantART, Mojizu, XuQa and Friendster. But she has canceled her account on Friendster and XuQa, and doesn't bother much with deviantART, Mojizu or MySpace.

29   "Weird people started messaging me," Tiffany Chow said about MySpace. The messages came from people she didn't know, asking to be friends and making comments about her looks. "That's when I made a decision. For me the best way to use these social networking engines is to keep track of my friends and people I know."

30   That's not to say members are abandoning MySpace. On a weekly basis between September and October, comScore Media Metrix, an independent source for tracking Internet traffic, showed its audience going back up.

31   "MySpace is an integral part of our members' lives," MySpace said in an e-mail response to questions. "There will always be anecdotes of people that love MySpace and people that don't, but we always like to rely on the numbers—both internal and third party—to show our continued, extraordinary growth. We are still experiencing enormous expansion domestically and abroad at an average rate of 320,000 worldwide new profiles added daily."

32   MySpace is also evolving beyond social networking by offering song downloads, movie trailers and television shows such as "Prison Break."

33   "It's already so big that even if people start abandoning it, it's still attracting new people," said David Card, senior analyst at Jupiter Research.

34   So where to next? Six Apart is betting that as the MySpace generation grows up, they will want to be more discerning; MySpace profiles are public unless users designate them as private. On Vox, which Six Apart launched last week, users determine what their friends and family see.

35   "I'm not sure MySpace is going to satisfy the needs of the next wave of your life," said Andrew Anker, executive vice president of Six Apart. "I'm not sure MySpace is the place where you want to post a picture of your kid."

36   The general expectation is that consumers ultimately will settle down with one or two social networks and that they will become a feature incorporated in more and more sites. You Tube, the popular online video-sharing

site, and Flickr, an online photo-sharing site, for instance, include social networking.

"I think it's been both overhyped and underestimated," Dogster's Rheingold ₃₇ said. Although some lofty expectations about how big of a business it could become won't pan out, "in the end it is going to be so much bigger than what people are seeing now."

# MySpace Is Not Responsible for Your Kids

### Greg Pivarnik

*This article appeared in* The Daily Campus *at the University of Connecticut on January 26, 2007.*

Four families from four separate states filed lawsuits against News Corp., the ₁ parent company of MySpace, because their underage daughters were sexually assaulted by people they met on the social-networking site. Though it may seem like a novel way for the parents to make some extra cash, MySpace is not responsible for the actions of its users. At some point individuals in this country have to start carrying some of the burden for their actions. These include parents, and yes, teenagers as well.

The families filing the lawsuits against News Corp. are holding nothing ₂ back. A lawyer from one of the firms representing multiple families says they are seeking millions of dollars in damages. Last June, in a separate incident, a mother of a 14-year-old who was sexually assaulted filed a lawsuit against News Corp. and MySpace, seeking $30 million in damages.

Apparently, litigiousness has replaced quality parenting as the way to ₃ raise the youth of this country. Parents often pass the buck when their children make poor choices. Whether they get arrested for possession of drugs, don't get playing time on a sports team or get poor grades in the school, the children are never to blame. Instead, parents blame society, coaches, teachers and other social influences instead of properly disciplining and raising the children themselves.

This is not meant to demean the horrific abuses that these girls suffered. ₄ Many of them are too young to maturely deal with a sexual relationship, and many were not seeking one in the first place. Rape and sexual assault is uncalled for and can be psychologically traumatizing for many years. Unfortunately, many adults use social sites such as MySpace, Facebook and Xanga to lure unsuspecting minors into potentially-harmful situations.

5   The popularity of MySpace has established it as one of the most utilized websites the world over. Many people use MySpace as a way to meet new people and make new friends. Many even use it almost like a free dating Web site, treating it is a place to go and meet a potential significant other. For many, this process goes smoothly and no problems arise. Knowing this fact, there is a question that needs to be raised—where were the parents? Unless they were living under a rock, they had to know that sexual predators scour the Internet searching for unsuspecting victims. Internet chat rooms and social-networking sites are notable tools that predators use to lure children under the guise of anonymity. The news is littered with warnings about sexual predators and their methods. Every week, for example, it seems that NBC's Dateline runs a new episode of "How to Catch a Predator."

6   Claiming ignorance and attempting to pass the responsibility onto MySpace is not a legitimate excuse to file a lawsuit. Responsible parents have to become familiar with the Internet and its benefits and dangers. It is also the job of the parents to sit down and discuss guidelines for Internet use with their children. Children are not born aware of potential dangers. Those are things they either learn from experience or are taught by another person, preferably a parent.

7   Teenagers also have to take responsibility for their actions. Yes, their hormones are spinning out of control, but they do have some semblance of a brain. The teenage girls who were victimized in these incidents still had to make the conscious choice to go and meet these men who sexually abused them. By simply ignoring these people, who they didn't even know, the girls could have saved themselves a lot of pain. This does not exonerate those men who have been accused of the abuse. That said, a little bit of rational thought on the part of the girls would have gone a long way in preventing this unfortunate outcome in the first place.

8   It is not the responsibility of MySpace to govern the actions of its users outside of their Web site. If they began instituting rules and regulations that infringed upon the privacy of their users, then many would just leave the website and join another network.

9   Despite this potential loss of clientele, MySpace already has policies instituted to prevent predators from taking advantage of underage children. First and foremost, they do not allow anybody under the age of 14 to even join the MySpace community. Users who are 14 or 15 can only share their full profile with people they are already friends with, which means it is not public information. Further, MySpace has recently developed a software program known as "Zephyr" that will let parents view the username, age and location their child lists on his or her profile. The software will also limit how adults can access the profiles of minors. On top of that, MySpace has developed tools to identify profiles registered to convicted sex offenders. By doing these things MySpace has developed all of these tools without greatly infringing on the privacy of their younger users.

The safety measures that MySpace has incorporated into its website should be  10
more than enough to protect them from frivolous lawsuits. It is understandable
that the parents of the children and the children themselves need somebody to
blame—they feel victimized and helpless. What happened to these girls was
horrific and deplorable. However, when all the emotional baggage is cast aside, it
is clearly evident that with more parental involvement, and improved decision
making on the part of the girls, this unfortunate situation could have been entirely
avoided.

## Synthesis: Connections for Argumentation

1. Annotate all three essays and then write brief, one-paragraph summaries of
   each.
2. Discuss with classmates the fascination that young people have with online
   social networking sites. Explore the reasons that Wade Roush, Ellen Lee,
   and Greg Pivarnik give to explain this trend, and their claims and viewpoints on the subject.
3. In an essay of argumentative synthesis, evaluate the relative effectiveness
   of each writer's claim. Using objective criteria, identify the author who you
   think is most successful in presenting his or her claim.
4. In an essay, argue that the overall impact of MySpace is either positive or
   negative. Incorporate relevant data and information from the articles by
   Roush, Lee, and Pivarnik that would be useful in making your case.
5. Go to at least three of the social networking sites mentioned by the writers
   in this case study or other sites that you know about. Compose an argumentative essay in which you assess the nature and content of these sites.
6. With one or two other class members, go online and investigate the subject
   of "cyberbullying." Locate at least three articles on this issue. Report your
   findings to the class, outlining strategies that parents, schools, groups,
   and Web sites can employ to discourage the practice. Compose your own
   essay, based on these sources, in which you state your own viewpoint on
   who is most responsible for discouraging cyberbullying: parents, schools,
   Web sites, the kids themselves, or perhaps a combination of these
   constituencies.
7. Argue for or against the proposition that trying to find love on the Internet is
   a futile endeavor. Research at least two sites to support your position on online romance. In addition, locate two or more articles on the subject, and incorporate the authors' viewpoints into your essay of argumentative synthesis.

www.mhhe.com/
**mhreader**

For an interactive tutorial on writing an argument, go to:
**Writing > Writing Tutor: Arguments**

# A Portfolio on Argumentation

## Classic and Contemporary Essays
### How Do We Argue?

We have all been in situations in which controversial issues arise. A friendly gathering may evolve into a spirited debate on abortion or cloning. Guests at a family dinner may turn their attention away from the host's expertly prepared cuisine toward a heated exchange over immigration. One issue that seems inevitably to arise when a conversation turns to issues of law and order is the death penalty or capital punishment. Arguments may range from cool statistical analysis of the value of this punishment as a "deterrent" to impassioned pleas regarding the sanctity of all human life. H. L. Mencken, in his classic essay "The Penalty of Death," provides a singular flavor to the argumentative stew by presenting the reasons for maintaining the death penalty; however, it appears evident from his style and tone that he is mocking its proponents by revealing their hypocrisy. He presents no fancy academic studies, nor does he draw on any experts or scholars. His approach is ironic. He contends in his disarming way that deterrence is merely an excuse for the exercise of the ultimate punishment; the true motive is revenge and retribution. Coretta Scott King, in her essay "The Death Penalty Is a Step Back," draws on sociology, law, psychology, morality, and logic to oppose capital punishment. Hers is a multipronged attack against the death penalty, and unlike Mencken, her tone is serious, straightforward, and unadorned. Is there *one* right way to address an issue of such seriousness? Perhaps it is not so much the style and methods one uses, but how well they are used.

# The Penalty of Death

## H. L. Mencken

*H(enry) L(ouis) Mencken (1880–1956) was an American editor, an author, and a critic. Born in Baltimore, he served as an editor for three Baltimore newspapers: the* Morning Herald, Evening Herald, *and* Baltimore Sun. *Noted for his pungent and iconoclastic criticism, he reveled in satirizing the middle classes. He was also a student of philology and published* The American Language, *which went through several editions with added supplements. The topics for his many books ranged from studies of dramatists to the defense of women's rights. He was also a champion for a whole generation of American realist fiction writers, including Theodore Dreiser, Sherwood Anderson, Sinclair Lewis, and Eugene O'Neill. The following well-known essay reveals the hypocrisy behind the rationale many people give for supporting the death penalty and the true reason they support it.*

Of the arguments against capital punishment that issue from uplifters, two are 1 commonly heard most often, to wit:

1. That hanging a man (or frying him or gassing him) is a dreadful business, degrading to those who have to do it and revolting to those who have to witness it.
2. That it is useless, for it does not deter others from the same crime.

The first of these arguments, it seems to me, is plainly too weak to need 2 serious refutation. All it says, in brief, is that the work of the hangman is unpleasant. Granted. But suppose it is? It may be quite necessary to society for all that. There are, indeed, many other jobs that are unpleasant, and yet no one thinks of abolishing them—that of the plumber, that of the soldier, that of the garbage-man, that of the priest hearing confessions, that of the sand-hog, and so on. Moreover, what evidence is there that any actual hangman complains of his work? I have heard none. On the contrary, I have known many who delighted in their ancient art, and practised it proudly.

In the second argument of the abolitionists there is rather more force, but 3 even here, I believe, the ground under them is shaky. Their fundamental error consists in assuming that the whole aim of punishing criminals is to deter other (potential) criminals—that we hang or electrocute A simply in order to so alarm B that he will not kill C. This, I believe, is an assumption which confuses a part with the whole. Deterence, obviously, is *one* of the aims of punishment, but it is surely not the only one. On the contrary, there are at least half a dozen, and some are probably quite as important. At least one of them, practically considered, is *more* important. Commonly, it is described as revenge, but revenge is really not the word for it. I borrow a better term from the late Aristotle: *katharsis*. *Katharsis*, so used, means a salubrious discharge of emotions, a healthy letting off of steam. A school-boy, disliking his teacher, deposits a tack upon the pedagogical chair; the teacher jumps and the boy laughs. This is *katharsis*. What I contend is that one of the prime objects of all judicial punishments is to afford the same grateful relief *(a)* to the immediate victims of the criminal punished, and *(b)* to the general body of moral and timorous men.

4       These persons, and particularly the first group, are concerned only indirectly with deterring other criminals. The thing they crave primarily is the satisfaction of seeing the criminal actually before them suffer as he made them suffer. What they want is the peace of mind that goes with the feeling that accounts are squared. Until they get that satisfaction they are in a state of emotional tension, and hence unhappy. The instant they get it they are comfortable. I do not argue that this yearning is noble; I simply argue that it is almost universal among human beings. In the face of injuries that are unimportant and can be borne without damage it may yield to higher impulses; that is to say, it may yield to what is called Christian charity. But when the injury is serious, Christianity is adjourned, and even saints reach for their sidearms. It is plainly asking too much of human nature to expect it to conquer so natural an impulse. A keeps a store and has a bookkeeper, B. B steals $700, employs it in playing at dice or bingo, and is cleaned out. What is A to do? Let B go? If he does so he will be unable to sleep at night. The sense of injury, of injustice, of frustration will haunt him like pruritus. So he turns B over to the police, and they hustle B to prison. Thereafter A can sleep. More, he has pleasant dreams. He pictures B chained to the wall of a dungeon a hundred feet underground, devoured by rats and scorpions. It is so agreeable that it makes him forget his $700. He has got his *katharsis*.

5       This same thing precisely takes place on a larger scale when there is a crime which destroys a whole community's sense of security. Every law-abiding citizen feels menaced and frustrated until the criminals have been struck down—until the communal capacity to get even with them, and more than even, has been dramatically demonstrated. Here, manifestly, the business of deterring others is no more than an afterthought. The main thing is to destroy the concrete scoundrels whose act has alarmed everyone, and thus made everyone unhappy. Until they are brought to book that unhappiness continues; when the law has been executed upon them there is a sigh of relief. In other words, there is *katharsis*.

6       I know of no public demand for the death penalty for ordinary crimes, even for ordinary homicides. Its infliction would shock all men of normal decency of feeling. But for crimes involving the deliberate and inexcusable taking of human life, by men openly defiant of all civilized order—for such crimes it seems, to nine men out of ten, a just and proper punishment. Any lesser penalty leaves them feeling that the criminal has got the better of society—that he is free to add insult to injury by laughing. That feeling can be dissipated only by a recourse to *katharsis*, the invention of the aforesaid Aristotle. It is more effectively

and economically achieved, as human nature now is, by wafting the criminal to realms of bliss.

The real objection to capital punishment doesn't lie against the actual extermination of the condemned, but against our brutal American habit of putting it off so long. After all, every one of us must die soon or late, and a murderer, it must be assumed, is one who makes that sad fact the cornerstone of his metaphysic. But it is one thing to die, and quite another thing to lie for long months and even years under the shadow of death. No sane man would choose such a finish. All of us, despite the Prayer Book, long for a swift and unexpected end. Unhappily, a murderer, under the irrational American system, is tortured for what, to him, must seem a whole series of eternities. For months on end he sits in prison while his lawyers carry on their idiotic buffoonery with writs, injunctions, mandamuses, and appeals. In order to get his money (or that of his friends) they have to feed him with hope. Now and then, by the imbecility of a judge or some trick of juridic science, they actually justify it. But let us say that, his money all gone, they finally throw up their hands. Their client is now ready for the rope or the chair. But he must still wait for months before it fetches him.

That wait, I believe, is horribly cruel. I have seen more than one man sitting in the death-house, and I don't want to see any more. Worse, it is wholly useless. Why should he wait at all? Why not hang him the day after the last court dissipates his last hope? Why torture him as not even cannibals would torture their victims? The common answer is that he must have time to make his peace with God. But how long does that take? It may be accomplished, I believe, in two hours quite as comfortably as in two years. There are, indeed, no temporal limitations upon God. He could forgive a whole herd of murderers in a millionth of a second. More, it has been done.

## COMPREHENSION

1. Based upon your reading of Mencken's essay, is the author for or against capital punishment? Explain.
2. Study the last three lines of the essay. Explain what they mean in your own words.
3. The author's facility with language is due partly to his impressive vocabulary. Define words such as *salubrious, timorous,* and *manifestly.*

## RHETORIC

1. Mencken uses symbolic logic, classification, and definition as devices in paragraphs 1–4. Cite examples of each of these rhetorical methods. What is each one's function?
2. What is the author's purpose in using a rather droll tone in discussing a subject that usually elicits strong emotional responses?

3. In paragraph 3, the author defines *katharsis* as "a healthy letting off of steam." In the light of the author's view that carrying out the death penalty results in a societal *katharsis,* what is the implicit irony in the definition?

4. What is Mencken's purpose in using both the placement of a tack on a teacher's seat and the execution of a human being as examples of *katharsis*?

5. What tone does Mencken use in describing humankind's desire for revenge? Does he support or deride this sentiment? Explain your conclusion by citing particular clues he provides in his writing.

6. In paragraph 4, the author states, "But when the injury is serious, Christianity is adjourned, and even saints reach for their sidearms." How does this statement relate to the theme of the essay?

## WRITING

1. For a creative writing project, pretend you are a legislator. Write an essay wherein you describe a crime and what its proper particular punishment should be. Be sure to fit the punishment to the crime.

2. There is some evidence to suggest that the death penalty may actually *increase* the murder rate. Study this line of inquiry, and write a research paper based on your findings that either supports or rejects the thesis.

3. **Writing an Argument:** Argue for or against the use of the death penalty in crimes other than murder.

| www.mhhe.com/ **mhreader** | For more information on H. L. Mencken, go to: **More Resources > Ch. 2 Arguments** |

# The Death Penalty Is a Step Back

## Coretta Scott King

*Coretta Scott King (1927–2006) is a civil rights activist, freelance journalist, and, since 1980, writer and commentator for CNN. Born in Alabama, she graduated from Antioch College and the New England Conservatory of Music. She first gained international prominence as the wife of Martin Luther King Jr., whom she married in 1953. She wrote about her experiences with the revered civil rights leader and orator in a book titled* My Life with Martin Luther King, Jr. *(1969). The following essay states in clear, thoughtful prose her feelings about the death penalty, which she considers both racist and immoral.*

When Steven Judy was executed in Indiana [in 1981] America took another step   1
backwards towards legitimizing murder as a way of dealing with evil in our
society.

Although Judy was convicted of four of the most horrible and brutal mur-   2
ders imaginable, and his case is probably the worst in recent memory for opponents of the death penalty, we still have to face the real issue squarely: Can
we expect a decent society if the state is allowed to kill its own people?

In recent years, an increase of violence in America, both individual and   3
political, has prompted a backlash of public opinion on capital punishment. But
however much we abhor violence, legally sanctioned executions are no deterrent and are, in fact, immoral and unconstitutional.

Although I have suffered the loss of two family members by assassination,   4
I remain firmly and unequivocally opposed to the death penalty for those convicted of capital offenses.

An evil deed is not redeemed by an evil deed of retaliation. Justice is never   5
advanced in the taking of a human life.

Morality is never upheld by legalized murder. Morality apart, there are a   6
number of practical reasons which form a powerful argument against capital
punishment.

First, capital punishment makes irrevocable any possible miscarriage of   7
justice. Time and again we have witnessed the specter of mistakenly convicted
people being put to death in the name of American criminal justice. To those
who say that, after all, this doesn't occur too often, I can only reply that if it happens just once, that is too often. And it has occurred many times.

Second, the death penalty reflects an unwarranted assumption that the   8
wrongdoer is beyond rehabilitation. Perhaps some individuals cannot be
rehabilitated; but who shall make that determination? Is any amount of academic training sufficient to entitle one person to judge another incapable of
rehabilitation?

Third, the death penalty is inequitable. Approximately half of the 711 per-   9
sons now on death row are black. From 1930 through 1968, 53.5 percent of those
executed were black Americans, all too many of whom were represented by
court-appointed attorneys and convicted after hasty trials.

The argument that this may be an accurate reflection of guilt, and homicide   10
trends, instead of a racist application of laws lacks credibility in light of a recent
Florida survey which showed that persons convicted of killing whites were
four times more likely to receive a death sentence than those convicted of killing
blacks.

Proponents of capital punishment often cite a "deterrent effect" as the main   11
benefit of the death penalty. Not only is there no hard evidence that murdering
murderers will deter other potential killers, but even the "logic" of this argument defies comprehension.

Numerous studies show that the majority of homicides committed in this   12
country are the acts of the victim's relatives, friends and acquaintances in the
"heat of passion."

13    What this strongly suggests is that rational consideration of future consequences are seldom a part of the killer's attitude at the time he commits a crime.

14    The only way to break the chain of violent reaction is to practice nonviolence as individuals and collectively through our laws and institutions.

## COMPREHENSION

1. On what grounds does King oppose capital punishment?
2. King calls the death penalty "immoral" and "unconstitutional." What does
   she mean by this?
3. Does King offer any solutions to the problem of crime and violence? What
   are they?

## RHETORIC

1. Where in the essay does King place her main proposition? In your own
   words, what is this claim?
2. What function do paragraphs 1–5 have in the essay?
3. What impact do the words *practical* and *powerful* (in paragraph 6) have on
   the reader? Who is King's intended audience?
4. Comment on the use of language in King's essay. Is it concrete or abstract?
   How would you characterize her writing style?
5. Trace King's use of transitions in paragraphs 7–9.
6. Where does the writer use refutation in her essay? How does she use it to
   strengthen her argument? How effective are her responses?
7. Is King's ordering of ideas inductive or deductive? Justify your answer.

## WRITING

1. If capital punishment doesn't deter crime, what will? Write an essay in
   which you offer detailed solutions to the problem of crime and violence.
   How can society take a step forward in its treatment of criminals?
2. King's essay makes a connection between the death penalty and racism.
   Develop this theme in an essay. Consider the roles of class, race, legal representation, and political empowerment in determining who goes to prison
   and who gets executed.
3. **Writing an Argument:** Write an essay for or against capital punishment,
   using quotes from King's essay either as support or as refutation. Provide
   examples and your own observations as proof.

www.mhhe.com/
**mhreader**

For more information on Coretta Scott King, go to:
**More Resources > Ch. 2 Arguments**

## Synthesis: Classic and Contemporary Questions for Comparison

1. Does Mencken's sarcasm and iconoclastic tone suggest he is writing for a different audience than the more austere and straightforward King? Consider that Mencken was writing at least a half-century before King. To what sorts of audiences would each of the essays appeal? Explain your view.

2. Study the language used in each of the essays. What is similar or different about the style and diction of the two pieces? Does one seem more accessible to the modern reader? Do any of Mencken's references seem dated? Consider such terms as *uplifters* (paragraph 1), *abolitionists* (paragraph 3), and *juridic science* (paragraph 7).

3. Both Mencken and King have had firsthand experience with gruesome events. Mencken mentions that he has observed men in the "death-house" prior to their execution, and Coretta Scott King's husband was assassinated. Does this lend authority to their grievances? Would you be less inclined to trust an opinion from a third arguer who had never had such personal experience?

# Classic and Contemporary Images
## WHAT IS AN ARGUMENT?

*Using a Critical Perspective*   What images and strategies do the Spanish artist Francisco de Goya and the American photographer Eddie Adams employ to construct an argument about war? What exactly is their argument? Comment on the nature and effectiveness of the details they use to illustrate their position. Which work do you find more powerful or engaging? Explain.

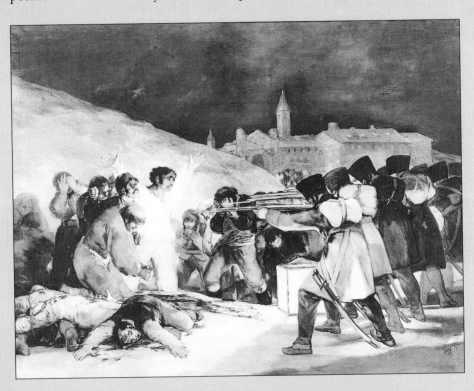

Horrified by the excesses of the Napoleonic invasion of his homeland and the Spanish war for independence, the Spanish artist Francisco de Goya (1746–1828) painted *The Third of May, 1808*, a vivid rendition of an execution during wartime.

Another wartime execution, this time captured on film by Eddie Adams
in an image that won the Pulitzer Prize for spot news photography
in 1969, brought home to Americans the horrors and
ambiguities of the war in Vietnam.

# Debate: Animal Research—Is It Ethical?

## Animal Research Saves Human Lives

Heloisa Sabin

*Heloisa Sabin* is honorary director of Americans for Medical Progress in Alexandria, Virginia. The wife of Albert Sabin, who discovered the oral vaccine for polio, she invokes her husband's name in the following essay to advance her position on animal experimentation. This essay appeared in The Wall Street Journal on October 18, 1995, shortly after Albert Sabin's death.

1  That scene in *Forrest Gump* in which young Forrest runs from his schoolmate tormentors so fast that his leg braces fly apart and his strong legs carry him to safety may be the only image of the polio epidemic of the 1950s etched in the minds of those too young to remember the actual devastation the disease caused. Hollywood created a scene of triumph far removed from the reality of the disease.

2  Some who have benefited directly from polio research, including that of my late husband, Albert, think winning the real war against polio was just as simple. They have embraced a movement that denounces the very process that enables them to look forward to continued good health and promising futures. This "animal rights" ideology—espoused by groups such as People for the Ethical Treatment of Animals, the Humane Society of the United States and the Fund for Animals—rejects the use of laboratory animals in medical research and denies the role such research played in the victory over polio.

3  The leaders of this movement seem to have forgotten that year after year in the early fifties, the very words *infantile paralysis* and *poliomyelitis* struck great fear in young parents that the disease would snatch their children as they slept. Each summer public beaches, playgrounds, and movie theaters were places to be avoided. Polio epidemics condemned millions of children and young adults to lives in which debilitated lungs could no longer breathe on their own and young limbs were left forever wilted and frail. The disease drafted tiny armies of children on crutches and in wheelchairs who were unable to walk, run, or jump. In the United States, polio struck down nearly 58,000 children in 1952 alone.

4  Unlike the braces on Forrest Gump's legs, real ones would be replaced only as the children's misshapen legs grew. Other children and young adults were

**154**

entombed in iron lungs. The only view of the world these patients had was through mirrors over their heads. These memories, however, are no longer part of our collective cultural memory.

Albert was on the front line of polio research. In 1961, thirty years after he  5 began studying polio, his oral vaccine was introduced in the United States and distributed widely. In the nearly forty years since, polio has been eradicated in the Western Hemisphere, the World Health Organization reports, adding that, with a full-scale effort, polio could be eliminated from the rest of the world by the year 2000.

Without animal research, polio would still be claiming thousands of lives  6 each year. "There could have been no oral polio vaccine without the use of innumerable animals, a very large number of animals," Albert told a reporter shortly before his death in 1993. Animals are still needed to test every new batch of vaccine that is produced for today's children.

Animal activists claim that vaccines really didn't end the epidemic—that,  7 with improvements in social hygiene, polio was dying out anyway, before the vaccines were developed. This is untrue. In fact, advanced sanitation was responsible in part for the dramatic *rise* in the number of paralytic polio cases in the fifties. Improvements in sanitation practices reduced the rate of infection, and the average age of those infected by the polio virus went up. Older children and young adults were more likely than infants to develop paralysis from their exposure to the polio virus.

Every child who has tasted the sweet sugar cube or received the drops contain-  8 ing the Sabin vaccine over the past four decades knows polio only as a word, or an obscure reference in a popular film. Thank heavens it's not part of their reality.

These polio-free generations have grown up to be doctors, teachers, busi-  9 ness leaders, government officials, and parents. They have their own concerns and struggles. Cancer, heart disease, strokes, and AIDS are far more lethal realities to them now than polio. Yet, those who support an "animal rights" agenda that would cripple research and halt medical science in its tracks are slamming the door on the possibilities of new treatments and cures.

My husband was a kind man, but he was impatient with those who refused  10 to acknowledge reality or to seek reasoned answers to the questions of life.

The pioneers of polio research included not only the scientists but also the  11 laboratory animals that played a critical role in bringing about the end of polio and a host of other diseases for which we now have vaccines and cures. Animals will continue to be as vital as the scientists who study them in the battle to eliminate pain, suffering, and disease from our lives.

That is the reality of medical progress.  12

## COMPREHENSION

1. Summarize Sabin's argument. Why does she begin the essay with a reference to the movie *Forrest Gump*, which starred Tom Hanks in an award-winning role as an American "hero"? Why does she refer repeatedly to "reality"?

2. What disease receives the major part of Sabin's attention? Where is it mentioned?
3. List all parts of the essay where the writer refers to her famous husband, Dr. Albert Sabin. What is her purpose? What is she implying?

## RHETORIC

1. What is Sabin's major proposition, and where does she place it? Is it effective where it is? Justify your answer.
2. What implied or stated warrants affect the writer's argument?
3. Where does the writer acknowledge the opposition? How does she refute those opposed to animal experimentation, and how effective do you think this strategy is? Explain.
4. How does Sabin limit her argument? Does this limitation strengthen or weaken her claim, and why?
5. Describe the logical, ethical, and emotional appeals that Sabin uses in this essay. Explain how each of these types of appeals advances her argument. What other logical appeals can you think of that might have strengthened her argument?
6. Analyze the conclusion. Is it effective? Why or why not?

## WRITING

1. Focusing on Sabin's article, write an essay explaining the importance of emotional appeal in argument. Does Sabin use excessive emotion or an appropriate amount? Does her relationship to her recently deceased husband weaken her use of emotion? Does she anticipate this question or ignore it, and why? These are some of the questions you might want to consider.
2. Imagine that you, a family member, or a friend is suffering from an incurable disease. How would you justify not pursuing animal research in an effort to find a cure? Write an essay responding to this question.
3. **Writing an Argument:** Select a disease other than polio—for example, cancer, AIDS, Parkinson's, or Alzheimer's—and argue that animal experimentation is necessary in order to find a cure for it. Conduct Internet research in order to familiarize yourself with the disease and current animal research dealing with it.

www.mhhe.com/
**mhreader**

For more information on Heloisa Sabin, go to:
**More Resources > Ch. 2 Arguments**

# A Question of Ethics

## Jane Goodall

*Jane Goodall (b. 1934) was born in London, England. In 1960, with no university degree or formal training, she began to study chimps in the Gombe Stream Reserve in Tanzania. Living in close proximity to the chimps and gaining their trust over the years, Goodall was the first scientist to discover that chimps are not strictly vegetarians and that the species uses tools—a trait thought previously to belong only to humans. Her books include* My Friends the Wild Chimpanzees *(1967) and* The Chimpanzee: The Living Link between Man and Beast *(1992). Goodall today is one of the world's foremost conservationists and animal rights activists. In the following essay, she asks whether it is ethical to use animals in laboratory research.*

David Greybeard first showed me how fuzzy the distinction between animals  1
and humans can be. Forty years ago I befriended David, a chimpanzee, during my first field trip to Gombe in Tanzania. One day I offered him a nut in my open palm. He looked directly into my eyes, took the nut out of my hand and dropped it. At the same moment he very gently squeezed my hand as if to say, I don't want it, but I understand your motives.

Since chimpanzees are thought to be physiologically close to humans, re-  2
searchers use them as test subjects for new drugs and vaccines. In the labs, these very sociable creatures often live isolated from one another in 5-by-5-foot cages, where they grow surly and sometimes violent. Dogs, cats and rats are also kept in poor conditions and subjected to painful procedures. Many people would find it hard to sympathize with rats, but dogs and cats are part of our lives. Ten or 15 years ago, when the use of animals in medical testing was first brought to my attention, I decided to visit the labs myself. Many people working there had forced themselves to believe that animal testing is the only way forward for medical research.

Once we accept that animals are sentient beings, is it ethical to use them in  3
research? From the point of view of the animals, it is quite simply wrong. From our standpoint, it seems ridiculous to equate a rat with a human being. If we clearly and honestly believe that using animals in research will, in the end, reduce massive human suffering, it would be difficult to argue that doing so is unethical. How do we find a way out of this dilemma?

One thing we can do is change our mind-set. We can begin by questioning  4
the assumption that animals are essential to medical research. Scientists have concluded that chimpanzees are not useful for AIDS research because, even though their genetic makeup differs from ours by about 1 percent, their immune systems deal much differently with the AIDS virus. Many scientists test drugs and vaccines on animals simply because they are required to by law

rather than out of scientific merit. This is a shame, because our medical technology is beginning to provide alternatives. We can perform many tests on cell and tissue cultures without recourse to systemic testing on animals. Computer simulations can also cut down on the number of animal tests we need to run. We aren't exploring these alternatives vigorously enough.

5      Ten or 15 years ago animal-rights activists resorted to violence against humans in their efforts to break through the public's terrible apathy and lack of imagination on this issue. This extremism is counterproductive. I believe that more and more people are becoming aware that to use animals thoughtlessly, without any anguish or making an effort to find another way, diminishes us as human beings.

## COMPREHENSION

1. Why does Goodall begin the essay with the anecdote about the chimpanzee named David Greybeard?
2. How, according to the writer, are laboratory animals treated? What are the physical and behavioral effects on these animals? Why does she visit a laboratory where these experiments are taking place, and what "ethical" conclusions does she draw?
3. According to Goodall, why is it important for people to change their "mindset" or hardened opinions about animal experimentation? What is her attitude toward animal rights extremists? Does she present any beneficial ways to change attitudes? Explain.

## RHETORIC

1. Locate Goodall's claim or major proposition. What are her warrants for this essay? Construct an outline of the argument.
2. Identify the forms of evidence that Goodall uses and where each type occurs. Does she present sufficient evidence to support her argument? Why or why not?
3. What assumptions (for example, about David Greybeard) does Goodall make in this essay? Do you find these assumptions reasonable? Explain.
4. What form of reasoning—deduction or induction—does Goodall employ in this essay? Does she strictly use logical appeal, or do ethical and emotional appeals appear? Explain.
5. In what way is this an argumentative essay that presents a problem and offers a solution? Point to specific passages to support your answer.

## WRITING

1. Goodall uses the word *ethical* in this essay. Write an essay in which you define *ethics* and analyze the ethical arguments for and against the use of animals in laboratory research.

2. How can you write about animal experimentation without having recourse to emotional appeals? Write an essay responding to this question. Explain how both Sabin and Goodall could have avoided emotional appeals and still constructed effective arguments.

3. **Writing an Argument:** Select either Sabin or Goodall's essay, and write a rebuttal to it. Use a combination of logical, ethical, and emotional appeals, as well as a variety of evidence, to support your claim.

www.mhhe.com/
**mhreader**

For more information on Jane Goodall, go to:

**More Resources > Ch. 2 Arguments**

# Debate: The Patriot Act—Should We Sacrifice Civil Liberties for Security?

# Security versus Civil Liberties

### Richard A. Posner

*Richard A. Posner (b. 1939), born in New York City, received a BA from Yale University (1959) and a law degree from Harvard University (1962), where he was editor of the* Harvard Law Review *and graduated first in his class. He is a federal appeals court judge for the Seventh Circuit in Chicago and a senior lecturer at the University of Chicago Law School. Termed a "thinking man's conservative," Posner is the author of several influential books, including* Frontiers of Legal Theory *(2001),* Public Intellectuals: A Study of Decline *(2001),* Law, Pragmatism, and Democracy *(2003), and* Catastrophe: Risk and Response *(2004). He has also published hundreds of articles in law journals and the popular press. In the following essay, published in* The Atlantic Monthly *shortly after the events of September 11, 2001, Posner offers a considered analysis of the tension between security and civil liberties and a logical argument favoring one over the other.*

1 In the wake of the September 11 terrorist attacks have come many proposals for tightening security; some measures to that end have already been taken. Civil libertarians are troubled. They fear that concerns about national security will lead to an erosion of civil liberties. They offer historical examples of supposed overreactions to threats to national security. They treat our existing civil liberties—freedom of the press, protections of privacy and of the rights of criminal suspects, and the rest—as sacrosanct, insisting that the battle against international terrorism accommodate itself to them.

2 I consider this a profoundly mistaken approach to the question of balancing liberty and security. The basic mistake is the prioritizing of liberty. It is a mistake about law and a mistake about history. Let me begin with law. What we take to be our civil liberties—for example, immunity from arrest except upon probable cause to believe we've committed a crime and from prosecution for violating a criminal statute enacted after we committed the act that violates it—were made legal rights by the Constitution and other enactments. The other enactments can be changed relatively easily, by amendatory legislation. Amending the Constitution is much more difficult. In recognition of this the Framers

**160**

left most of the constitutional provisions that confer rights pretty vague. The courts have made them definite.

Concretely, the scope of these rights has been determined, through an in- 3 teraction of constitutional text and subsequent judicial interpretation, by a weighing of competing interests. I'll call them the public-safety interest and the liberty interest. Neither, in my view, has priority. They are both important, and their relative importance changes from time to time and from situation to situation. The safer the nation feels, the more weight judges will be willing to give to the liberty interest. The greater the threat that an activity poses to the nation's safety, the stronger will the grounds seem for seeking to repress that activity, even at some cost to liberty. This fluid approach is only common sense.

Supreme Court Justice Robert Jackson gave it vivid expression many years 4 ago when he said, in dissenting from a free-speech decision he thought doctrinaire, that the Bill of Rights should not be made into a suicide pact. It was not intended to be such, and the present contours of the rights that it confers, having been shaped far more by judicial interpretation than by the literal text (which doesn't define such critical terms as "due process of law" and "unreasonable" arrests and searches) are alterable in response to changing threats to national security.

If it is true, therefore, as it appears to be at this writing, that the events of 5 September 11 have revealed the United States to be in much greater jeopardy from international terrorism than had previously been believed—have revealed it to be threatened by a diffuse, shadowy enemy that must be fought with police measures as well as military force—it stands to reason that our civil liberties will be curtailed. They *should* be curtailed, to the extent that the benefits in greater security outweigh the costs in reduced liberty. All that can reasonably be asked of the responsible legislative and judicial officials is that they weigh the costs as carefully as the benefits.

It will be argued that the lesson of history is that officials habitually exag- 6 gerate dangers to the nation's security. But the lesson of history is the opposite. It is because officials have repeatedly and disastrously underestimated these dangers that our history is as violent as it is. Consider such underestimated dangers as that of secession, which led to the Civil War; of a Japanese attack on the United States, which led to the disaster at Pearl Harbor; of Soviet espionage in the 1940s, which accelerated the Soviet Union's acquisition of nuclear weapons and emboldened Stalin to encourage North Korea's invasion of South Korea; of the installation of Soviet missiles in Cuba, which precipitated the Cuban missile crisis; of political assassinations and outbreaks of urban violence in the 1960s; of the Tet Offensive of 1968; of the Iranian revolution of 1979 and the subsequent taking of American diplomats as hostages; and, for that matter, of the events of September 11.

It is true that when we are surprised and hurt, we tend to overreact—but 7 only with the benefit of hindsight can a reaction be separated into its proper and excess layers. In hindsight we know that interning Japanese Americans did not shorten World War II. But was this known at the time? If not, shouldn't the

Army have erred on the side of caution, as it did? Even today we cannot say with any assurance that Abraham Lincoln was wrong to suspend habeas corpus during the Civil War, as he did on several occasions, even though the Constitution is clear that only Congress can suspend this right. (Another of Lincoln's wartime measures, the Emancipation Proclamation, may also have been unconstitutional.) But Lincoln would have been wrong to cancel the 1864 presidential election, as some urged: by November of 1864 the North was close to victory, and canceling the election would have created a more dangerous precedent than the wartime suspension of habeas corpus. This last example shows that civil liberties remain part of the balance even in the most dangerous of times, and even though their relative weight must then be less.

8      Lincoln's unconstitutional acts during the Civil War show that even legality must sometimes be sacrificed for other values. We are a nation under law, but first we are a nation. I want to emphasize something else, however: the malleability of law, its pragmatic rather than dogmatic character. The law is not absolute, and the slogan *"Fiat iustitia ruat caelum"* ("Let justice be done though the heavens fall") is dangerous nonsense. The law is a human creation rather than a divine gift, a tool of government rather than a mandarin mystery. It is an instrument for promoting social welfare, and as the conditions essential to that welfare change, so must it change.

9      Civil libertarians today are missing something else—the opportunity to challenge other public-safety concerns that impair civil liberties. I have particularly in mind the war on drugs. The sale of illegal drugs is a "victimless" crime in the special but important sense that it is a consensual activity. Usually there is no complaining witness, so in order to bring the criminals to justice the police have to rely heavily on paid informants (often highly paid and often highly unsavory), undercover agents, wiretaps and other forms of electronic surveillance, elaborate sting operations, the infiltration of suspect organizations, random searches and monitoring of airports and highways, the "profiling" of likely suspects on the basis of ethnic or racial identity or national origin, compulsory drug tests, and other intrusive methods that put pressure on civil liberties. The war on drugs has been a big flop; moreover, in light of what September 11 has taught us about the gravity of the terrorist threat to the United States, it becomes hard to take entirely seriously the threat to the nation that drug use is said to pose. Perhaps it is time to redirect law-enforcement resources from the investigation and apprehension of drug dealers to the investigation and apprehension of international terrorists. By doing so we may be able to minimize the net decrease in our civil liberties that the events of September 11 have made inevitable.

## COMPREHENSION

1. How, in general, does Posner view the debate over security and civil liberties? Why, as he indicates in paragraph 1, are civil libertarians troubled?

2. Posner's article was written in the wake of the September 11, 2001, attacks. Where does he refer to these events? What other "lessons of history" does he mention?
3. Posner writes of "the malleability of law, its pragmatic rather than dogmatic character" (paragraph 8). What does he mean by these words? How do they influence his analysis of the debate over security and civil liberties?

## RHETORIC

1. What is Posner's claim, and where does he state it most clearly? What forms of evidence does he provide to support his claim? Would you say that his argumentative method is inductive or deductive, and why?
2. Do you think that Posner's primary purpose is to change his audience's thinking, attack the opposition, justify his position, or perhaps a combination of these possibilities? Explain your conclusion.
3. Posner disagrees with conventional wisdom concerning war, freedom, security, and the Constitution. How does he defend these dissenting positions? What evidence does he provide from history?
4. Why does Posner refer to the drug war in his concluding paragraph? Do you consider this strategy to be effective or a distraction? Justify your response.

## WRITING

1. Select one of the historical events mentioned by Posner in his essay, conduct research of the subject, and then write an essay in which you demonstrate how the debate over security and civil liberties was reflected in this event.
2. Who or what is a "civil libertarian"? Form a group of four or five classmates, and discuss this question. Conduct research if necessary, and then write an extended definition of the term.
3. **Writing an Argument:** Posner claims that we often overreact to critical historical events, but overreaction is actually necessary and beneficial to our security, even if civil liberties have to be curtailed. Argue for or against his proposition in an essay. Cite some of Posner's own examples to support your position.

www.mhhe.com/
**mhreader**

For more information on Richard A. Posner, go to:
**More Resources > Ch. 2 Arguments**

# Acts of Resistance

## Elaine Scarry

*Elaine Scarry (b. 1946) was born in Summit, New Jersey. She attended Chatham College (BA, 1968) and received her doctorate from the University of Connecticut in 1974. She is an English professor at Harvard University. Best known for* The Body in Pain: The Making and Unmaking of the World *(1985), Scarry has also written* Resisting Representation *(1994) and* On Beauty and Being Just *(1999). In this essay, which appeared originally in the February/March 2004 issue of the* Boston Review *and was republished in* Harper's, *the noted scholar offers a detailed assessment of the problems raised by the Patriot Act.*

1   When the U.S.A. Patriot Act arrived in our midst in the fall of 2001, its very title seemed to deliver an injury: "Uniting and Strengthening America by Providing Appropriate Tools Required to Intercept and Obstruct Terrorism." One might have thought that "United States of America" would be a sufficient referent for the letters "U.S.A." and that no one would presume to bestow a new meaning on the word "patriot," with its heavy freight of history (Paul Revere, Patrick Henry, Emma Lazarus) and its always fresh aspiration ("O beautiful for patriot dream").

2   In the two and a half years since it was passed, the U.S.A. Patriot Act has become the locus of resistance against the unceasing injuries of the Bush-Rumsfeld-Ashcroft triumvirate, as first one community, then two, then eleven, then twenty-seven, and now 272 have passed resolutions against it, as have four state legislatures. The letters "U.S.A." and the word "patriot" are gradually reacquiring their earlier solidity and sufficiency as local and state governments reanimate the practice of self-rule by opposing the Patriot Act's assault on the personal privacy, free flow of information, and freedom of association that lie at the heart of democracy. Each of the resolutions affirms the town's obligation to uphold the constitutional rights of all persons who live there, and many of them explicitly direct police and other residents to refrain from carrying out the provisions of the Act, even when instructed to do so by a federal officer.

3   When the resistance was first beginning, in the winter of 2001–2002, it took five months for the first five resolutions to come into being; by the winter of 2003–2004, a new resolution was being drafted almost every day. The resolutions come from towns ranging from small villages—Wendell, Massachusetts (986), Riverside, Washington (348), Gaston, Oregon (620)—to huge cities—Philadelphia (1,517,550), Baltimore (651,000), Chicago (2,896,000), Detroit (951,000), Austin (656,300), San Francisco (777,000). Approximately a third of the resolutions come from towns and cities with populations between 20,000 and 200,000.

The fact that the Patriot Act has engendered such resistance may at first  4
seem puzzling. True, its legislative history is sordid: it was rushed through
Congress in several days; no hearings were held; it went largely unread; only a
few of its many egregious provisions were modified. But at least it *was* passed
by Congress: many other blows to civil liberties have been delivered as unmodified executive edicts, such as the formation of military tribunals and the
nullification of attorney-client privilege. True, the Patriot Act severed words
from their meanings (beginning with the letters "U.S.A."), but executive statements associating Iraq with nuclear weapons and with Al Qaeda severed words
from their basis in material fact, at the very great cost of a war that continues to
be materially and mortally destructive. True, the Patriot Act has degraded the
legal stature of the United States by permitting the executive branch to bypass
constitutional law, but our legal degradation outside the Patriot Act has gone
even further: Evidence indicates that the Bush Administration has created offshore torture centers in Bagram, Afghanistan, and on the British island of Diego
Garcia, and has sent prisoners to interrogation centers in countries with documented histories of torture such as Egypt, Jordan, Saudi Arabia, and Syria.

The executive edicts, the war against Iraq, and the alleged use of torture  5
have all elicited protest, but what differentiates the opposition to the Patriot Act
is the fact that it has enabled the population to move beyond vocalizing dissent
to retarding, and potentially reversing, the executive's inclination to carry out
actions divorced from the will of the people.

If many members of Congress failed to read the Patriot Act during its swift pas-  6
sage, it is in part because it is almost unreadable. The Patriot Act is written as an
extended sequence of additions to and deletions from previously existing statutes, instructing the bewildered reader to insert three words into paragraph X of
statute Y without ever providing the altered sentence in either its original or its
amended form. Only someone who had scores of earlier statutes open to the
relevant pages could step painstakingly through the revisions. Reading the Patriot Act is like standing outside the public library trying to infer the sentences in
the books inside by listening to hundreds of mice chewing away on the pages.

The Act does, however, have a coherent and unitary purpose: to increase  7
the power of the Justice Department and to decrease the rights of individual
persons. The constitutional rights abridged by the Patriot Act are enumerated
in the town resolutions, which most often specify violations of the First Amendment guarantee of free speech and assembly, the Fourth Amendment guarantee
against search and seizure, the Fifth and Fourteenth Amendment guarantees of
due process, and the Sixth and Eighth Amendment guarantees of a speedy and
public trial and of protection against cruel and unusual punishment.

The objective of the Patriot Act becomes even clearer if it is understood  8
concretely as making the population *visible* and the Justice Department *invisible*.
The Act inverts the constitutional requirement that people's lives be private
and the work of government officials be public; it instead crafts a set of conditions that make our inner lives transparent and the workings of the government

opaque. Either one of these outcomes would imperil democracy; together they not only injure the country but also cut off the avenues of repair.

9       When we say democracy requires that the people's privacy be ensured, we mean that we ourselves should control the degree to which, and the people to whom, our lives are revealed. Under the Patriot Act, the inner lives of people are made involuntarily transparent by provisions that increase the ability of federal officers to enter and search a person's house, to survey private medical records, business records, library records, and educational records, and to monitor telephone, email, and Internet use. The Fourth Amendment states: "The right of the people to be secure in their persons, houses, papers, and effects, against unreasonable searches and seizures, shall not be violated, and no Warrants shall issue, *but upon probable cause,* supported by Oath or affirmation, and *particularly describing the place to be searched, and the persons or things to be seized*" (emphasis added). The Patriot Act both explicitly lowers the "probable cause" requirement, thereby diminishing judicial review, and eliminates the specificity clause—"particularly describing the place to be searched, and the persons or things to be seized"— which, like "probable cause," puts severe restraints on the scope and duration of the search. The Act is a sweeping license to search and seize, everywhere and anywhere, guided not by court-validated standards of evidence but by Justice Department hunches and racially inflected intuitions.

10      As necessary to democracy as the nontransparency of persons is the transparency of government actions, and indeed the Constitution pauses again and again to insist upon open records: "Each house [of Congress] shall keep a Journal of its Proceedings, and from time to time publish the same" with "the Yeas and Nays of the Members . . . entered on the Journal"; "a regular Statement and Account of the Receipts and Expenditures of all public Money shall be published from time to time"; presidential objections to a piece of legislation must be forwarded to the house in which the legislation originated and published in its journal; the counting of the Electoral College votes must take place in the presence of the full Congress; treason proceedings will take place in "open Court" and criminal prosecutions in a "public trial," etc.

11      The obligation of each branch to make its actions public—to make them visible both to the people and to the other branches—is often construed as a right belonging to the populace, the right of "freedom of information." Indeed, it is hard to disagree with the argument that democratic deliberation is impossible without this access to information. Secrecy, the legal theorist Cass Sunstein writes, "is inconsistent with the principle of self-rule." He identifies citizen deliberation as the primary benefit of open government, but there are other benefits, including checks and balances (one branch cannot check the other if it does not know what the other is doing), and "sunlight as a disinfectant" (if deliberations are carried out in secret, "participants may be less careful to ensure that their behavior is unaffected by illegitimate or irrelevant considerations").

12      Because both the privacy of individual action and the publication of government action are necessary to democratic self-rule, the major complaint of the local resolutions has been the damage done to the liberties of persons and to the integrity

of our laws. The most forceful formulation of this worry comes at the conclusion of the Blount County, Tennessee, resolution, which calls upon all residents "to study the Bill of Rights so that they can recognize and resist attempts to undermine our Constitutional Republic . . . and declare null and void all future attempts to establish Martial Law, [or] Declared States of Emergency." Although most of the other resolutions are more measured in their language, they consistently register the view that both the people and the laws of this country are endangered.

The resolutions have a second, closely related focus. Although the Patriot Act enables the federal government to detain and investigate both citizens and non-citizens, and to carry out surveillance of both citizens and non-citizens, its blows fall most heavily on those who are not U.S. citizens.    13

Consider section 412. As summarized by the city of Ann Arbor, Michigan, it permits the incarceration of non-citizens for seven days without charge and "for six month periods indefinitely, without access to counsel" if the attorney general "determines release would endanger the security of the country or of a specific person." Before it was modified by Congress, the bill authorized the unlimited detention of immigrants, but the revision is less of an improvement than it seems, since various loopholes release the executive branch from the seven-day constraint.    14

The resolutions collectively work to prevent this imperilment of all residents of the United States. Almost without exception, the 272 resolutions celebrate their commitment to law and liberty for all "persons" or "residents," not only "citizens." This is expressed in part as a matter of constitutional conviction: The very first clause of the very first resolution (Ann Arbor) begins by echoing the 2001 Supreme Court decision *Zadvydas* v. *Davis*: "The due process and equal protection clauses of the Fifth and Fourteenth Amendments to the United States Constitution guarantee certain due process and equal protection rights to all residents of the United States regardless of citizenship or immigration status . . . " Other resolutions remind all residents that discrimination based on "citizenship status" is no more permissible than discrimination based on race or gender. They complain that the Patriot Act tries "to drive a wedge" between citizens and non-citizens, or between police and foreign nationals, a situation held to be intolerable because the town depends on the diversity of its population for its "vitality" and its "economy, culture, and civic character."    15

Almost the only time when "citizens" are singled out is when the documents place on them the burden of acting to ensure that all "persons" or "residents" enjoy the benefits of due process, protection from unwarranted search and seizure, freedom of speech, freedom of assembly, and privacy. If, in other words, citizens are unique, it is because they are the guardians of rights belonging to citizens and non-citizens alike, not the exclusive holders of those rights.    16

In addition to aiming blows at our legal framework of self-governance, the Patriot Act licenses the executive branch to harm other institutions—among them, financial markets and universities—and once again its blows appear to be structural.    17

18      Take, for example, the provisions that require bankers, broker-dealers, and trading advisers to file "suspicious activity reports" (SARs) when they notice their clients carrying out unusual transfers greater than $5,000. Failure to file is punishable by criminal and civil charges, with fines reaching $10,000. Furthermore, they are prohibited from telling their client about the SAR, which not only taints the client relationship but eliminates at the outset the possibility of determining whether the transfer has some sensible explanation that, if they only knew it, would convince them that the filing was preposterous.

19      Universities, too, are among the institutions the Patriot Act seeks to change, and the situation may be swiftly assessed by looking at the most widely discussed aspect of the Act, section 215, which applies to both college and public libraries (and, in many cases, bookstores). When approached by an FBI or CIA agent, librarians must turn over a record of the books a specified patron has taken out, and, like the bankers, they are prohibited from telling anyone of the intelligence gathering in which they have just participated.

20      In his fall 2003 tour of thirty cities to defend the Patriot Act, Attorney General John Ashcroft dismissed the idea that the Justice Department could conceivably care about librarians or library records. A University of Illinois study found, however, that by February 2002 (four months after the Patriot Act was passed) 4 percent of all U.S. libraries and 11 percent of libraries in communities of more than 50,000 people had already been visited by FBI agents requesting information about their patrons' reading habits. Ashcroft insisted that not-yet-released FBI records would demonstrate the indifference of the Justice Department to the libraries, but the Justice Department has in fact refused to release these very same records, despite Freedom of Information Act petitions filed by the American Civil Liberties Union and other organizations.

21      In distilled form, the logic of the Patriot Act and its defense involves four steps: Maximize the power of the Justice Department; erase the public record of Justice Department actions; respond with indignation if anyone protests that the Justice Department might actually be using its newly expanded powers; point out that the protesters are speaking without any hard evidence or facts without mentioning that the executive branch has withheld those very facts from the public.

22      From the founding of this country the phrase "a government of laws and not of men" has meant that the country cannot pass open-ended laws that will be good if the governors happen to be good and bad if the governors happen to be bad. The goal has always been to pass laws that will protect everyone regardless of the temperament and moral character of the individual governors. The country, as Justice Davis famously observed in the nineteenth century, "has no right to expect that it will always have wise and humane rulers." That's why it is crucial to pass good laws. And crucial, also, to repeal bad ones.

23      Despite impediments to resistance, 272 towns, cities, and counties have created a firewall against executive trespass in their communities. The resolutions

direct residents to decline to assist the federal government in any act that violates the Constitution: local police should abstain from assisting federal officers in house searches that violate the Fourth Amendment, and librarians should abstain from giving out private library records that violate the First and Fourth Amendments.

Here we have the key to why the Patriot Act—rather than the executive edicts—has become the focus of so much resistance. Since military tribunals do not require the assistance of the population, what we think about the military tribunals is a matter of indifference to the executive. Since the country has a standing army rather than a draft, the war against Iraq was neither ours to assist nor ours to decline to assist. If, without the population's assistance, 5,000 foreign nationals can be detained without charges (only three of whom were ever charged with terrorism-related acts), then the population's disapproval of this detention is like smoke rings in the wind. But since the aspirations encoded in the Patriot Act cannot come about without the help of police, bankers, and librarians, the refusal to assist provides a concrete brake on the actions of the federal government. 24

Although the Justice Department has tried to portray resistance to the Patriot Act as a liberal complaint, the resisters repeatedly assert that they occupy positions across the political spectrum. And, so far, both Congress and the courts appear to be listening. Various congressmen and senators have initiated bills to nullify or limit specific provisions of the Patriot Act. In July 2003 the House passed an amendment to the 2004 Appropriations Bill that withholds all federal funding from section 213—the provision that allows the Justice Department to search a house without notifying the resident. The courts, too, share the concerns of the local resolutions. In January a federal court in Los Angeles ruled one section of the Patriot Act unconstitutional: the judge objected to the provision making it a crime to provide "expert advice or assistance" to terrorists on the grounds that the phrasing is so vague as to license the Justice Department to interfere with First Amendment speech guarantees. In December two federal courts issued rulings declaring acts of detention carried out by the Bush Administration unlawful on grounds similar to those mentioned in the town resolutions. 25

Sorting out the legal status of the Patriot Act may take some time. The United States Constitution prohibits acts that the Patriot Act licenses, and, although constitutional provisions take legal precedence over contradictory legislation, for the time being the Act appears to empower the federal government not only to call upon the country's residents for assistance but also to impose criminal and civil penalties on those who fail to assist. 26

Whether the resistance to the Patriot Act gains momentum or is ultimately derailed, the town resolutions remind us that the power of enforcement lies not just with local police but with all those who reside in cities, towns, villages, isolated byways, and country lanes. Law—whether local, state, federal, or constitutional—is only real if, as Patrick Henry said, the rest of us will put our hands to it, put our hearts to it, stand behind it. 27

# COMPREHENSION

1. How does Scarry demonstrate that the Patriot Act "has become the locus of resistance against the unceasing injuries of the Bush-Rumsfeld-Ashcroft triumvirate" (paragraph 2)? How does she characterize the Bush administration? What examples does she provide to support this opinion?
2. According to Scarry, what constitutional rights has the Patriot Act abridged?
3. What does the writer mean by the "nontransparency of persons" and "transparency of government actions"? How do these concepts get to the core of Scarry's understanding of American democracy?

# RHETORIC

1. What is the tone of Scarry's introductory paragraph? How does she treat the title of the U.S.A. Patriot Act? Why does she refer to Paul Revere, Patrick Henry, and Emma Lazarus? What assumptions does she seem to be making about her audience?
2. What is Scarry's main proposition? What are her minor propositions? What forms of reasoning and evidence does she provide to support her claim?
3. The writer divides her essay into four sections. What is the purpose of each section? How does the sequence of sections serve to move the argument along?
4. Does Scarry deal effectively with opposing arguments? Why or why not?
5. Scarry's concluding paragraph consists of one lengthy sentence. How does it recapitulate some of the main ideas in the essay? How effective is this last paragraph? Justify your answer.

# WRITING

1. Write a 300-word summary of Scarry's essay. Try to capture all of the main features of her argument.
2. Imagine that you are Richard Posner, and compose a response to Scarry's article.
3. **Writing an Argument:** Write an essay in which you take two or three of Scarry's points and refute them, either by posing competing evidence or by demonstrating flaws in their logic.

| www.mhhe.com/ **mhreader** | For more information on Elaine Scarry, go to: <br> **More Resources > Ch. 2 Arguments** |

# Face Facts:
# Patriot Act Aids Security, Not Abuse

### Paul Rosenzweig

*Paul Rosenzweig (b. 1959), born in New York City, is a lawyer who received a BA from Haverford College (1981), an MA from the University of California at San Diego (1982), and a JD from the University of Chicago (1986). He has served in the United States Department of Justice and the Office of the United States Attorney for Washington, D.C. Rosenzweig is an adjunct professor of law at George Mason University and a senior legal research fellow at the Heritage Foundation. This defense of the Patriot Act appeared in the July 29, 2004, issue of* The Christian Science Monitor.

Falsehood, according to Mark Twain's famous dictum, gets halfway around the world before the truth even gets its shoes on. Time and again, outlandish stories seem to grow legs and find wide distribution before the truth can catch up. 1

A good example is the U.S.A. Patriot Act. It's so broadly demonized now, you'd never know it passed with overwhelming support in the days immediately after September 11, 2001. 2

Critics paint the Patriot Act as a caldron of abuse and a threat to civil liberties. Advocacy groups run ads depicting anonymous hands tearing up the Constitution and a tearful old man fearful to enter a bookstore. Prominent politicians who voted for the act call for a complete overhaul, if not outright repeal. 3

But the truth is catching up. And the first truth is that the Patriot Act was absolutely vital to protect America's security. 4

Before 9/11, U.S. law enforcement and intelligence agencies were limited by law in what information they could share with each other. The Patriot Act tore down that wall—and officials have praised the act's value. 5

As former Attorney General Janet Reno told the 9/11 commission, "Generally, everything that's been done in the Patriot Act has been helpful . . . while at the same time maintaining the balance with respect to civil liberties." 6

And as Attorney General John Ashcroft's recent report to Congress makes clear, this change in the law has real, practical consequences. Information-sharing facilitated by the Patriot Act, for example, was critical to dismantling terror cells in Portland, OR; Lackawanna, NY; and Virginia. Likewise, the act's information-sharing provisions assisted the prosecution in San Diego of those involved with an Al Qaeda drugs-for-weapons plot involving "Stinger" anti-aircraft missiles. 7

It also aided in the prosecution of Enaam Arnaout, who had a longstanding relationship with Osama bin Laden and who used his charity organization to obtain funds illicitly from unsuspecting Americans for terrorist groups and to serve as a channel for people to contribute knowingly to such groups. 8

9    These are not trivial successes. They're part of an enormous, ongoing effort to protect America from further terrorist attacks.

10   We cannot, of course, say that the Patriot Act alone can stop terrorism. But every time we successfully use the new tools at our disposal to thwart a terrorist organization, that's a victory.

11   Yet remarkably, some of these vital provisions allowing the exchange of information between law enforcement and intelligence agencies will expire at the end of next year. So here's a second truth: If Congress does nothing, then parts of the law will return to where they were on the day before 9/11—to a time when our government couldn't, by law, connect all the dots. Nobody wants a return to those days, but that is where we are headed if Congress does not set aside its partisan debates.

12   But what of the abuses? Time for a third truth: There is no abuse of the Patriot Act. None. The Justice Department's inspector general (who is required by the Patriot Act to examine its use and report any abuse twice a year) reported that there have been no instances in which the act has been invoked to infringe on civil rights or civil liberties. Others agree. For example, at a Judiciary Committee hearing on the Patriot Act, Sen. Dianne Feinstein (D) of California said: "I have never had a single abuse of the Patriot Act reported to me. My staff . . . asked [the ACLU] for instances of actual abuses. They . . . said they had none."

13   So the fiction of abuse can be laid to rest. The government is not, to take but one popular myth, invading libraries and scouring your book records. It's a convenient fiction that calls to mind, as Joseph Bottum, a contributor to *The Weekly Standard*, has written, the appealing image of "white-haired and apple-cheeked [librarians] resisting as best they can the terrible forces of McCarthyism, evangelical Christian bookburning, middle-class hypocrisy, and Big Brother government." But no matter how appealing the image, it has no more reality than a good Hollywood movie.

14   Government's obligation is a dual one: to provide security against violence and to preserve civil liberty. This is not a zero-sum game. We can achieve both goals if we empower government to do sensible things while exercising oversight to prevent any real abuses of authority. The Patriot Act, with its reasonable extension of authority to allow the government to act effectively with appropriate oversight rules, meets this goal.

15   And the truth eventually catches up to the fiction

## COMPREHENSION

1. Summarize Rosenzweig's position on the Patriot Act. What reasons does he give to support his position? What does he mean when he says that government's dual role is not a "zero-sum game" (paragraph 14)?

2. Explain the writer's reference to Mark Twain in your own words. Where else in the essay does Rosenzweig refer to the "truth"?

3. According to Rosenzweig, what are some of the objections to the Patriot Act?

## RHETORIC

1. Analyze the first four paragraphs in terms of the stylistic and argumentative strategies Rosenzweig employs. How does he introduce his subject? Why does he begin with refutation? What and where is his claim?
2. This article appeared as an op-ed essay in a daily newspaper. What formal features of editorial writing can you identify? How effective are they in conveying an argument?
3. What is the writer's tone? What kind of audience does he seem to be writing for? (It might be helpful to know that the *Christian Science Monitor* is a relatively progressive newspaper.)
4. What evidence does Rosenzweig use to support his claim? Is the evidence real or hypothetical? Does the writer provide sufficient evidence to make his case? Why or why not?
5. How does the writer employ concepts of "truth" and "fiction" to organize his essay?

## WRITING

1. Both Posner and Rosenzweig are trained in the law. Write a comparative essay in which you examine the "cases" that they develop in support of laws designed to protect our security, even if these laws provoke questions concerning civil liberties. Do they make the same points? How do they organize their material? What forms of evidence do they employ? Who makes the stronger case? These are some of the questions you might want to consider.
2. Write an op-ed essay telling readers what liberties you would be willing to give up in order to feel secure from the threat of terrorism.
3. **Writing an Argument:** Write a paper in which you refute Rosenzweig point by point, focusing on the three main "truths" that he mentions in his essay. Brainstorm with classmates to generate ideas, evidence, and other points of view. Refer to information provided by Scarry in her essay opposing the Patriot Act.

| www.mhhe.com/ **mhreader** | For more information on Paul Rosenzweig, go to: **More Resources > Ch. 2 Arguments** |

# The Patriot Act of the 18th Century

## Ishmael Reed

*Ishmael Reed (b. 1938), born in Chattanooga, Tennessee, is a well-known novelist, poet, essayist, and public commentator who also produces films, writes plays and songs, and edits and publishes other writers. Known for his advocacy of civil rights, especially for African Americans and other people of color, he has been in the forefront of progressive political movements for decades. Reed lives in Oakland, California; he has taught at the University of California at Berkeley and other universities. His impressive body of work includes* Mumbo Jumbo *(fiction, 1972),* Secretary to the Spirits *(poetry, 1975), and* Airing Dirty Laundry *(essays, 1993). In this essay, which appeared in the July 5, 2004, issue of* Time *magazine. Reed uses historical examples to develop a subtle commentary on the Patriot Act.*

1   Nations sometimes lose their bearings when confronted by an enemy. In a state of crisis or even panic, they implement measures that are later viewed as regrettable. From 1798 to 1800, the French were considered terrorists, pirating ships and making things uncomfortable for the fledgling American republic. The Federalist Party led a backlash against the French, and Thomas Jefferson and his Republican Party were seen as Francophiles. The XYZ Affair—a scandal centering on the fact that some French officials demanded bribes from American diplomats—brought relations between France and the U.S. to the breaking point. The Federalist Administration of President John Adams considered such solicitations to be grave insults. There were cultural differences as well. In the view of Abigail Adams, Frenchwomen were risque at best.

2   The reaction to the threat from France came in the form of the Alien and Sedition Acts, which were championed by the Federalists, passed by Congress and signed by Adams in 1798. The Alien Act required immigrants to reside in the U.S. for 14 years instead of 5 to qualify for citizenship. The act also gave the president the legal right to expel those the government considered "dangerous." The Sedition Act punished "false, scandalous and malicious" writings against the government with fines and imprisonment. Most of those arrested under the Sedition Act were Republican editors, and instead of sending boatloads of aliens back to France, it resulted in no one's deportation. In a foreshadowing of the climate that inspired today's U.S.A. Patriot Act, at the turn of the century 200 years ago, it was common practice to question the patriotism of citizens, immigrants and the political opposition.

3   Jefferson, who was vice president at the time, drafted his position in secret and wrote it into the Kentucky Resolutions of 1798. James Madison, in collaboration with Jefferson, subsequently authored the Virginia Resolutions. In the

second and fourth of the Kentucky Resolutions, Jefferson cited the Tenth Amendment, which gives the states powers not delegated to the government by the Constitution, to declare the Alien and Sedition Acts unconstitutional. Jefferson feared that a strong central government might put an end to slavery. Jefferson's fight against the Alien and Sedition Acts is often placed in the context of free speech, but it had unintended consequences beyond that. The Kentucky Resolutions were among the first to defend states' rights, and Jefferson had even threatened secession. Similar ideas helped spark the Civil War.

After Jefferson defeated Adams and was elected president in 1800, the Alien and Sedition Acts were allowed to expire. Adams, looking to distance himself from the mess, blamed the whole idea on Alexander Hamilton—who by then had been murdered by Aaron Burr. 4

The expiration of the acts did not end challenges to the First Amendment or the tendency on the part of some presidents to behave like monarchs, sometimes with the cooperation of Congress. The Espionage Act of 1917 prohibited "false statements" that might "impede military success." During World War II, FBI Director J. Edgar Hoover and President Franklin Roosevelt wanted to use sedition charges to suppress black newspapers, claiming they undermined the war effort with reports of racial dissension and demands for civil rights. It took Chief Justice Earl Warren's Supreme Court on March 9, 1964, in *The New York Times Co.* v. *Sullivan*, to finally declare unconstitutional the Sedition Act of the Adams administration. Though the act had expired under Jefferson's administration, the court's action buried that particular threat to free speech once and for all—or so people hoped. Writing for the majority, Justice William Brennan held that L. B. Sullivan, an Alabama official, had not been libeled in a *New York Times* ad that had been paid for by civil rights proponents. Brennan supported his arguments by citing Jefferson. 5

## COMPREHENSION

1. What parallel does Reed draw between the Alien and Sedition Acts and the Patriot Act? What does he assume about the reader's knowledge of the Patriot Act?
2. Why, according to Reed, were the Alien and Sedition Acts a danger to a democratic society? Why were they declared unconstitutional?
3. What other acts that endanger American society does Reed mention?

## RHETORIC

1. Who is Reed's intended audience for this essay? What does he assume about the knowledge and interests of this audience?
2. What is Reed's purpose in writing this article? What is his claim? Is this claim stated, implied, or perhaps a combination of both? Justify your answer.

3. The writer employs process analysis based on a sequence of historical events. Trace this sequence. Where is it complete, and where might it benefit from more evidence or detail?

4. Reed clearly draws parallels—some obvious and others less so—between earlier acts in American history and the Patriot Act. What minor propositions grow from these historical events? Do you feel that they strengthen Reed's argument or detract from it? Do you think that the essay is persuasive? Explain.

5. Evaluate Reed's conclusion. How effective do you find it, and why?

## WRITING

1. Go online and find out more about the Alien and Sedition Acts. Then write a paper in which you draw parallels between these earlier acts and the Patriot Act.

2. Write an essay in which you predict the outcome of the Patriot Act and how future historians might view its effects on American democracy.

3. **Writing an Argument:** Write an essay in which you argue for or against the proposition that there is a link, as Reed implies, between the Alien and Sedition Acts and the U.S.A. Patriot Act. Use information presented in the three previous essays in this section, library and online research, and notes from class discussion to construct this argumentative essay.

www.mhhe.com/ **mhreader**    For more information on Ishmael Reed, go to: **More Resources > Ch. 2 Arguments**

 chapter *3*

# Writing a Research Paper

A research paper is a report in which you synthesize information on your topic, contributing your own analysis and evaluation to the subject. Research writing is a form of problem solving. You identify a problem, form a hypothesis (an unproven thesis, theory, or argument), gather and organize information from various sources, assess and interpret data, evaluate alternatives, reach conclusions, and provide documentation.

Research writing is both exciting and demanding. American essayist and novelist Joan Didion states, "The element of discovery takes place, in nonfiction, not during the writing but during the research." Nowhere is the interplay of the stages in the composing process more evident than in writing research papers. Prewriting is an especially important stage, for the bulk of your research and bibliographical spadework is done before you actually sit down to draft your report. Moreover, strategic critical thinking skills are required at every step of research writing. Here you sense the active, questioning, reflective activity of the mind as it considers a problem and sifts through the evidence to reach a solution, proof, or conclusion. Developing the ability to do research writing thus represents an integration of problem-solving and composing skills.

Research writing is a skill to be developed rather than a trial to be borne. Contrary to conventional wisdom, research does not simply begin with the library catalog and end with the final bibliographic entry. (In fact, electronic searches and word processing have taken much of the drudgery out of writing research papers.) Nor does research writing exclusively report information in a bland and boring recitation of facts.

Research actually means the careful investigation of a subject in order to discover or revise facts, theories, or applications. Your purpose is to demonstrate how other researchers approach a problem, how you synthesize their most useful ideas, and how you treat that problem yourself. A good research paper subtly blends your ideas and synthesizes the attitudes or findings of others. In research writing, you are dealing with ideas that are already in the public domain, but you are also contributing to knowledge.

# RESEARCH WRITING:
# PRECONCEPTIONS AND PRACTICE

When your ideas—rather than the ideas of others—become the center of the research process, writing a research paper becomes dynamic instead of static. The standard preconception about preparing a research paper is that the researcher simply finds a subject and then assembles information from sources usually found in a library. This strategy does teach disciplined habits of work and thought, and it is a traditional way to conduct research for college courses. Yet, does this conventional preconception match the practices of professional researchers?

Consider the following tasks:

- Evaluating critical responses to a best-selling novel, a book of poetry, a CD, or an award-winning film
- Analyzing the impact of voter turnout on presidential politics during a recent decade
- Investigating a literary, political, or scientific scandal of the previous century
- Assessing the effectiveness of urban, suburban, and rural schools, comparing specific measures of student success
- Discussing the practical consequences of economic theory, examining work opportunities for men, women, recent immigrants, young people entering the workforce, former welfare recipients, or some other group
- Defining a popular dietary or health-related term, examining how it influences consumer behavior when shopping for food

How would a professional researcher view these projects? First, the researcher sees a subject as a *problem* rather than a mere topic. Often this problem is authorized or assigned by a collaborator, an editor, or a supervisor in the researcher's workplace. The researcher has the task of developing or testing a hypothesis stemming from the particular problem—for example, whether a vegetarian diet effectively wards off cancer. *Hypothesis formation* is at the heart of professional research.

Second, the researcher often conducts primary as well as secondary research. *Primary research* relies on analysis and synthesis of texts, letters, manuscripts, and other materials, whether written, visual, or aural. *Secondary research* relies on sources that comment on the primary sources. For example, a critic's commentary on *Citizen Kane* or a historian's analysis of the Cold War politics of the 1950s would be secondary sources; the film itself or a speech delivered by Senator Joseph McCarthy in 1950 would be primary sources. Because primary sources are not necessarily more reliable than secondary sources, you must always evaluate the reliability of both types of material. Critics can misinterpret, and experts often disagree, forcing you to weigh evidence and reach your own conclusions.

Third, all researchers face deadlines. The solution to a research problem is required to take action, to reach a decision, to influence policy, or to determine a business plan. Confronted with deadlines, professional researchers learn to *telescope* their efforts in order to obtain information quickly. Common strategies include networking (using personal and professional contacts as well as guides to organizations), browsing or searching online, conducting computerized bibliographical searches, and turning to annotated bibliographies (listing articles on the topic with commentaries on each item) and specialized indexes (focusing on a particular field or discipline). Other strategies include consulting review articles, which evaluate other resources, and browsing through current journals and periodicals, which may provide useful background as well as the most current thinking about the topic.

Finally, much professional researching cuts across academic subjects and disciplines, perhaps touching on literature, history, politics, psychology, economics, or more. The interdisciplinary nature of many research projects creates special problems for the researcher, especially in the use of bibliographical materials, which do tend to be subject-oriented. Good researchers know that they cannot confine their search for evidence to one subject area, such as history or physics. Knowledge in the contemporary era tends increasingly toward interdisciplinary concerns, and you must develop the training, discipline, and critical thinking skills necessary for any form of college research. Such research is not beyond your talents and abilities. Learn how to use library and electronic sources selectively and efficiently, but also learn how to view the world outside your library as a vast laboratory to be used fruitfully in order to solve your research problems.

## THE RESEARCH PROCESS

The research process involves thinking, searching, reading, writing, and rewriting. The final product—the research paper—is the result of your discoveries in and contributions to the realm of ideas about your topic. The process of researching and composing moves back and forth over a series of activities, and the actual act of writing remains unique to the individual researcher.

Writers with little experience in developing research papers do have to be more methodical than experienced researchers, who streamline and adjust the composing process to the scope and design of their projects. Despite the idiosyncrasies of individual writers, however, the research process tends to move through several interrelated phases.

---

### *Phases in the Research Process*

**Phase I: Defining Your Objective**

1. Choose a *researchable* topic.
2. Identify a *problem* inherent in the topic that gives you the reason for writing about the topic.

(*Phases in the Research Process* continued)

3. Examine the *purpose* of or the *benefits* to be gained from conducting research on the topic.
4. Think about the assumptions, interests, and needs of your *audience.*
5. Decide how you are going to *limit* your topic.
6. Establish a working *hypothesis* to guide and control the scope and direction of your research.

### Phase 2: Locating Your Sources

1. Decide on your *methodology*—the types or varieties of primary and secondary research you plan to conduct. Determine the method of collecting data.
2. Go to the library and skim a general article or conduct a computer search to *determine if your topic is researchable* and if your hypothesis is likely to stand up.
3. Develop a *tentative working bibliography,* a file listing sources that seem relevant to your topic.
4. Review your bibliography, and *reassess your topic and hypothesis.*

### Phase 3: Gathering and Organizing Data

1. *Obtain your sources,* taking notes on all information related directly to your thesis.
2. Analyze and organize your information. Design a *preliminary outline* with a tentative thesis if your findings support your hypothesis.
3. *Revise your thesis* if your findings suggest alternative conclusions.

### Phase 4: Writing and Submitting the Paper

1. Write a *rough draft* of the paper, concentrating on the flow of thoughts and integrating research findings into the texture of the report.
2. Write a *first revision* to tighten organization, improve style, and check on the placement of data. Prepare citations that identify the sources of your information. Assemble a list of the references you have cited in your paper.
3. *Prepare the manuscript* using the format called for by the course, the discipline, or the person authorizing the research project.

## Phase 1: Defining Your Objective

The first step in research writing is to select a topic that promises an adventure for you in the realm of ideas and that will interest, if not excite, your audience while meeting the expectations and requirements of your assignment.

You can reduce wasted time and effort if you approach the research project as a problem to be investigated and solved, a controversy to take a position on, or a question to be answered. As a basis, you need a strong hypothesis or working thesis (which may be little more than a hunch or a calculated guess). The point of your investigation is to identify, illustrate, explain, argue, or prove that thesis. Develop a hypothesis before you actually begin to conduct research; otherwise, you will discover that you are simply reading in or about a topic, instead of reading toward the objective of substantiating your thesis or proposition.

Of course, before you can formulate a hypothesis, you need to start with a general idea of what subject you want to explore, what your purpose is going to be, and how you plan to select and limit a topic from your larger subject area.

---

### FORMULATING A HYPOTHESIS

A topic will lead to a researchable hypothesis if it does the following:

- Meets the demands of your assignment
- Strongly interests you
- Engages knowledge you already possess
- Raises questions that will require both primary and secondary research to answer
- Provokes you toward an opinion or argument

---

To help you find and limit a research topic, try the following strategies:

- *Reflect on the assignment.* If your professor gave you a specific written assignment—even if it doesn't include a specific topic—review the assignment with an eye toward keywords that indicate the purpose of your research work. Highlight or underline key verbs such as *solve, argue, find, discover,* or *present.* Write out questions for your professor, and either ask them in class (other students probably share your questions) or arrange for a conference with her or him.
- *Ask questions.* Ask yourself, in writing, a series of specific questions about your subject. Combine questions that are related. Ask your questions in such a way as to pose problems that demand answers. Then try to determine which topic best fits the demands of the assignment.

- *Prewrite and brainstorm.* Idea generation strategies such as prewriting and brainstorming can help you to determine what you already know, or believe, about an assigned topic. If your assignment is to research gender roles in popular culture, you might begin by brainstorming on the last two or three movies that you saw and how male characters were depicted. For more information on prewriting strategies, see pages 33–36.
- *Do some background reading.* Your professor will probably assign a research topic that has something to do with the content of your class. Review the assigned readings for your course as well as your own notes. If your professor has suggested additional readings on the research topic or provided a bibliography, consult a few of those sources as well. Although the purpose of your background reading is to generate ideas, you should still use the note-taking strategies discussed in the following pages to ensure that you give proper credit later for any ideas you use from this preliminary reading.

Your purpose is to solve a *specific* problem, shed light on a *specific* topic, state an opinion on a *specific* controversy, or offer *specific* proofs or solutions. Your audience does not want a welter of general information, a bland summary of the known and the obvious, or free associations or meditations on an issue or problem. You know that your audience wants answers; consequently, a way to locate your ideal topic is to ask questions about it.

## Phase 2: Locating Your Sources

If you have a sufficiently narrowed topic and a working hypothesis, you should know what type of information will be most useful for your report. Not all information on a topic is relevant, of course; with a hypothesis, you can distinguish between useful and irrelevant material.

To use your time efficiently, you have to *streamline* your method for collecting data. Most research writing for college courses relies heavily on secondary research material available in libraries or online. To develop a preliminary list of sources, go directly to general reference works or a list of sources or reserved readings provided by your professor. If you already have some knowledge about the subject, begin with resources that permit you to find a continuing series of articles and books on a single issue—specifically, periodical indexes, newspaper indexes, and card catalogs. Again, you should be moving as rapidly as possible from the general to the specific.

**Should You Begin Your Research Online?**   The immense capabilities of the Internet make it very tempting to begin your search for information online, via a commercial search engine such as Yahoo! or Google. Although this method can be useful for background reading and idea generation, traditional research—both academic and professional—is generally more productive and efficient if begun in a library. However, if your research topic demands very contemporary and localized knowledge (a current political campaign, a recent medical breakthrough, a trend in popular culture), beginning your search online can be optimal. Research topics that require you to provide deeper contexts and backgrounds, or for which primary and secondary sources are restricted to academic journals and databases, are best begun in a library. Although we begin our discussion of locating sources with guidelines for searching online, only you can determine the most efficient and effective way of beginning your research. (Note, too, that "going to the library" on many campuses often begins at your personal computer with your own access, as a student, to the library's online catalog.)

**Finding Online Materials**   Your library, your college Web site, or your instructor's home page may list useful sites on the Web, organized by discipline or interest area. Online clearinghouses and print materials about the Web also identify especially useful sites for researchers. Depending on your topic, there are subject-specific Web pages on the Internet that link you to everything you could want, including both primary and secondary sources. "Findlaw" is a good example for law; most of the sciences and many of the liberal arts have useful pages like this. Once you have located an Internet address—a URL (universal resource locator)—for a site on the Web, you can go directly to that location. The end of the address can help you assess the kind of location you will reach:

.org  = nonprofit organizations, including professional groups

.edu  = colleges, universities, and other educational institutions

.com  = businesses and commercial enterprises

.gov  = government branches and agencies

.mil  = branches of the military

.net  = major computer networks

If you need to search the Internet for sources, try using one of the search engines supplied by your Internet access program. Search engines such as Google or Yahoo! hunt through vast numbers of pages at Web sites, seeking those that mention keywords that you specify. The search engine then supplies you with a list of those sites. Given the enormous number of Web sites and their component pages, you need to select your search terms carefully so that you locate reasonable numbers of pertinent sources.

A Web page may supply links to other useful sites. If you click on the link, usually highlighted or in color, you can go directly to that related site. For example, the following site *(www.fedworld.gov)*, sponsored by the federal government, includes links to federal databases and a keyword search that can lead to particular resources.

Following a chain of links requires critical thinking to assess whether each link seems reliable and current. This kind of research also can take a great deal of time, especially if you explore each link and then follow it to the next. As you move from link to link, keep your hypothesis in mind so that you are not distracted from your central purpose.

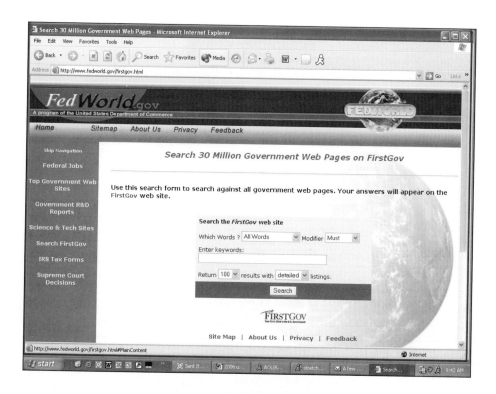

# EVALUATING ONLINE SOURCES

- Is the author identified? Is the site sponsored by a reputable business, agency, or organization? Does the site supply information so that you can contact the author or the sponsor?

- Does the site provide information comparable to that in other reputable sources, including print sources?

- Does the site seem accurate and authoritative or quirky and idiosyncratic?

- Does the site seem unbiased, or is it designed to promote a particular business, industry, organization, political position, or philosophy?

- Does the site supply appropriate, useful links? Do these links seem current and relevant? Do most of them work? Does the site document sources for the information it supplies directly?

- Has the site been updated or revised recently?

- Does the site seem carefully designed? Is it easy and logical to navigate? Are its graphics well integrated and related to the site's overall purpose or topic? Is the text carefully edited?

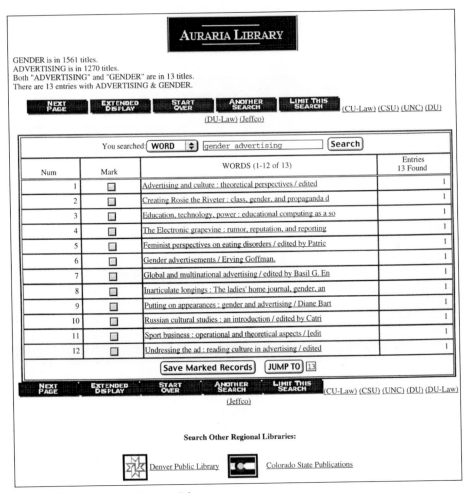

Reprinted by permission of Auraria Library.

**Using the Library Catalog**    The library online or card catalog lists information by author, title, subject, and keyword. Of the four, the subject listings are the best place to look for sources, but they are not necessarily the place to start your research. Begin by determining what your library offers. For instance, the online catalog may include all library materials or only holdings acquired fairly recently. The catalog also may or may not supply up-to-date information because books may take several years to appear in print and some weeks to be cataloged. Thus you may need to turn to separate indexes of articles, primary documents, and online materials for the most current material. Remember also that when you search by subject, you are searching the subject fields that are assigned by the cataloger. This differs from a keyword search in which the researcher—you, the writer—selects key terms that describe the research situation and enters them

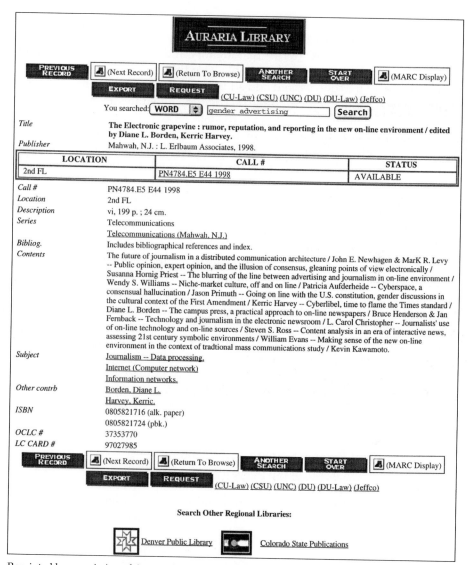

Reprinted by permission of Auraria Library.

into a search engine that will find these terms anywhere within the item record—whether they happen to be in the title, comments, notes, or subject fields.

On the other hand, if your library has a consolidated online system, you may have immediate access to materials available regionally and to extensive online databases. You may be able to use the same terminal to search for books shelved in your own library, materials available locally through the city or county library, and current periodicals listed in specialized databases. Such access can simplify and consolidate your search.

Subject indexing can be useful when you are researching a topic around which a considerable body of information and analysis has already developed. Identify as many keywords (terms that identify and describe your subject) or relevant subject classifications as possible. Use these same terms as you continue your search for sources, and add additional terms identified in the entries you find. The accompanying example on page 186 illustrates a keyword search for materials on gender issues and advertising.

Clicking on the Extended Display option for an item supplies full bibliographic information as well as the location of the book in the library and its availability. On page 187, you can see the wealth of information shown for the fourth item listed on the search screen from page 186.

There are two ways to make this search of the keywords *Gender* and *Advertising* more complete. First, think of alternate terms that might come into play; for example, *sex* is an synonym for *gender*, and *advertising* is only one form of the verb *to advertise*. A searcher would probably want to include *advertise* or *advertisement*. Using the truncation symbol (in this case, *, but it varies in different library catalogs) would help to catch these variations. The best course is to review the search tips that nearly always accompany any public catalog. Alternatively, select one of the titles you feel is most closely related to your subject, and pull up that record. For example, "Sex in advertising" and "Sex role in advertising" could yield fruitful links, directing you to other materials that have been assigned the same headings. This is a much more direct search than thumbing through the red Library of Congress Subject Headings volumes to find out what an appropriate subject heading might be, and it will catch those titles you might have missed when selecting your keywords.

**Checking General Reference Sources**    General reference sources include encyclopedias, dictionaries, handbooks, atlases, biographies, almanacs, yearbooks, abstracts, and annual reviews of scholarship within a field. Many of these sources are available both in print and in an electronic format, on CD-ROM or online. Begin your search for these sources in your library's reference room. General reference sources can be useful for background reading and for an introduction to your topic. The bibliographies they contain (such as those that end articles in an encyclopedia) are generally limited, however, and frequently out-of-date. Professional researchers do not rely exclusively on general reference sources to solve research problems, and neither should you.

**Searching Indexes and Databases**    Electronic and print indexes and databases include up-to-date articles in journals, magazines, and newspapers. Indexes usually list materials that you will then need to locate. Some databases, however, may include complete texts of articles or even books. Ask a reference librarian how to access materials on CD-ROM or online. If you need historical information or want to trace a topic back in time, however, you may need to use print indexes as well because electronic sources may date back only a few years or cover only a certain number of years.

The following indexes and databases are just a few of the many resources that are widely available. Some are general; others are specialized by discipline or field. Such indexes supply ready access to a wide array of useful materials, including articles, books, newspaper stories, statistics, and government documents. Ask the librarian in the reference area or the catalog area whether these are available in print or online.

Each index or database restricts the sources it lists in specific ways, based on the particular topics covered or the types of sources included. For example, the full title of the *MLA Bibliography* indicates that it lists "Books and Articles on the Modern Languages and Literatures." Besides books and articles, however, it includes essays or chapters collected in a book, conference papers, films, recordings, and other similar sources, but it does not list summaries or

---

## ELECTRONIC AND PRINT INDEXES AND DATABASES

### General Resources

*American Statistics Index*

*Congressional Information Service Index*

*Expanded Academic Index*

*FirstSearch Catalog*

*Magazine Index*

*National Newspaper Index*

*New York Times Index*

### Specialized Resources

*Applied Science and Technology Index*

*Biological and Agricultural Index*

*Business Periodicals Index*

*Education Index*

*ERIC (Educational Resources Information Center)*

*General Business File*

*Humanities Index*

*Index Medicus or Medline*

*MLA (Modern Language Association) International Bibliography*

*PsychLit*

*Public Affairs Information Service (PAIS)*

*Social Sciences Index*

encyclopedia articles. Its primary subjects include literary criticism, literary themes and genres, linguistics, and folklore. Thus you can search for an author's name, a title, a literary period, or subjects as varied as hoaxes, metaphysical poetry, and self-knowledge, all in relationship to studies in language and literature. This bibliography is available in print, on CD-ROM, online, or in other electronic versions. The print version is published every year, but the online version is updated 10 times during the year. A search of the *MLA Bibliography* 1/91–4/01 on CD-ROM for information on gender issues in advertising would turn up items such as the following:

TI: Gender Issues in Advertising Language
AU: *Artz,-Nancy; Munizer,-Jeanne; Purdy,-Warren*
SO: *Women-and-Language,* Fairfax, VA (W&Lang). 1999 Fall, 22:2, 20–26.
AN: 1999095570

TI: Anglicisms in German Car Advertising: The Problem of Gender  Assignment
AU: *Vesterhus,-Sverre-A.*
SO: *Moderna-Sprak,* Goteborg, Sweden (MSpr). 1998, 92:2, 160–70.
AN: 1999091717

TI: Ready or Not: Clothing, Advertising, and Gender in Late Nineteenth-Century America
AU: *Schorman,-Rob*
SO: *Dissertation-Abstracts-International,-Section-A:-The-Humanities-and-Social-Sciences,* Ann Arbor, MI (DAIA). 1999 Mar, 59:9, 3619 DAI No.: DA9907365. Degree granting institution: Indiana U, 1998.
AN: 1999079868

As your search progresses and your hypothesis evolves, you will find resources even more specifically focused on your interests.

---

## EVALUATING PRINT SOURCES

- Is the author a credible authority? Does the book jacket, preface, or byline indicate the author's background, education, or other publications? Do other writers refer to this source and accept it as reliable? Is the publisher or publication reputable?

- Does the source provide information comparable to that in other reputable sources?

- Does the source seem accurate and authoritative, or does it make claims that are not generally accepted?

- Does the source seem unbiased, or does it seem to promote a particular business, industry, organization, political position, or philosophy?

---

*(Evaluating Print Sources* continued)

- Does the source supply notes, a bibliography, or other information to document its sources?
- If the source has been published recently, does it include current information? Are its sources current or dated?
- Does the source seem carefully edited and printed?

---

**Using Nonprint Sources**   In the library and online, you have access to potentially useful nonprint materials of all kinds—videos, CD-ROMs, films, slides, works of art, records of performances, or other sources that might relate to your topic. When you search for these sources, you may find them in your library's main catalog or in a separate listing. In the catalog entry, be sure to note the location of the source and its access hours, especially if they are limited. If you need a projector or other equipment to use the material, ask the reference librarian where you go to find such equipment.

**Developing Field Resources**   You may want to *interview* an expert, *survey* the opinions of other students, *observe* an event or situation, or examine it over a long period of time as a *case study*. Ask your instructor's advice as you design questions for an interview or a survey or procedures for a short- or long-term observation. Also be sure to find out whether you need permission to conduct this kind of research on campus or in the community.

The questions you ask will determine the nature and extent of the responses that you receive; as a result, your questions should be developed after you have established clear objectives for your field research. You also need to plan how you will analyze the answers before, not after, you administer the questionnaire or conduct the interview. Once you have drafted interview or survey questions, test them by asking your friends or classmates to respond. Use these preliminary results to revise any ambiguous questions and to test your method of analysis. If you are an observer, establish in advance what you will observe, how you will record your observations, and how you will analyze them. Get permission, if needed, from the site where you will conduct your observation. Your field sources can help you expand your knowledge of the topic, see its applications or discover real-world surprises, or locate more sources, whether print, electronic, or field.

**Using Visuals in Your Paper**   Some of the nonprint sources you consult in your research might be useful to include, rather than just cite or refer to, in your own final paper. Technology has made it very easy to cut and paste visuals from sources into your own work, as well as to create and incorporate your own visuals. Be sure that when you incorporate other visuals into your own paper (or when you create a visual, such as a graph or chart, that draws on data from another source) you correctly and completely cite the source of the visual data. A caption that briefly describes the visual and gives its source information is usually sufficient.

---

## CONSIDERATIONS IN USING NONPRINT SOURCES IN YOUR RESEARCH

- Is a visual/nonprint source the most effective and useful way to present data? For example, if your paper is researching the ways in which photojournalists depict presidential candidates, you will probably want to include sample photographs in your paper. If your topic is trends in voter turnout, you might consult charts and graphs in your research but describe in words the evidence from those visuals rather than reproducing them in your paper.

- Can the visual be easily reproduced? What kinds of technology will you need to capture an image, import it into your own text, and print it legibly (and, if necessary, in color)? What capabilities will your audience need to access a visual? (For example, if you are submitting a paper electronically, remember that large visual files can take a *very* long time to download over a dial-up connection.)

- Have you gathered and noted all of the necessary source information, so that you can provide context (and, if necessary, a caption) for the visual as well as accurate bibliographical citation?

---

In order to gain expert information, you may wish to contact an informed individual directly by e-mail, following up on contact information supplied at a Web site or through other references. If your topic is of long-term interest to you and you have plenty of time to do your research, you may want to join a *listserv* or *e-mail conference,* a group of people interested in a particular topic, whose messages are sent automatically to all participants. Exchanges among those interested in a topic may also be posted on a *bulletin board server* or a *newsgroup,* where you can read both past and ongoing messages and exchanges. The information you receive from others may be very authoritative and reliable, but it may also represent the biased viewpoint of the individual. Assess it carefully by comparing it with information from other sources, print as well as electronic.

**Preparing a Working Bibliography**    The purpose of compiling a working bibliography is to keep track of possible sources, to determine the nature and extent of the information available, to provide a complete and accurate list of sources to be presented in the paper, and to make preparing the final bibliography much easier. Include in your working bibliography all sources that you have a hunch will be potentially useful. After all, you may not be able to obtain all the items listed, and some material will turn out to be useless, repetitious, or irrelevant to your topic. Such entries can easily be eliminated at a later stage when you prepare your final bibliography.

One way to simplify the task of preparing your final Works Cited or References section is to use a standard form for your working bibliography, whether you use cards or computer entries. The models given later in this chapter are based on two guides, abbreviated as MLA and APA. The *MLA Handbook for Writers of Research Papers* (New York: Modern Language Association of America, 2003; 6th ed.) is generally followed in English, foreign languages, and other fields in the humanities. Instructors in the social sciences, natural sciences, education, and business are likely to favor the style presented in the *Publication Manual of the American Psychological Association* (Washington, DC: American Psychological Association, 2001; 5th ed.). Because the preferred form of citation of sources varies considerably from field to field, check with your instructors to determine which of these two formats they prefer or if they recommend another style. Follow any specific directions from an instructor carefully.

As you locate relevant sources, take down complete information on each item on a 3 × 5 note card or start a bibliographic file on your computer. Complete information, properly recorded, will save you the trouble of having to scurry back to the library or back to a Web page for missing data when compiling your final bibliography. Be sure to list the source's call number and location in the library or its URL; then you can easily find the material once you are ready to begin reading and relocate it if you need to refer to it again. When preparing bibliography cards for entries listed in annotated bibliographies, citation indexes, and abstracts, you might want to jot down notes from any pertinent summaries that are provided. Complete a separate card or file entry for each item that you think is promising.

---

## INFORMATION FOR A WORKING BIBLIOGRAPHY

Record the following information for a book:

1. Name(s) of author(s)
2. Title of book, underlined
3. Place of publication
4. Publisher's name
5. Date of publication
6. Call number or location in library
7. URL and date of access online

*(continued)*

> (*Information For a Working Bibliography* continued)
>
> Record the following information for an article in a periodical:
>
> 1. Name(s) of author(s)
> 2. Title of article, in quotation marks
> 3. Title of periodical, underlined
> 4. Volume number or issue number
> 5. Date of publication
> 6. Page numbers on which article appears
> 7. Call number or location in library
> 8. URL and date of access online

| | |
|---|---|
| Author | Dvidhzi, Péter |
| Title | The Romantic cult of Shakespeare: Literary Reception in Anthropological Perspective |
| Place of publication | New York<br>St. Martin's Press |
| Date of publication | 1998 |
| Location | Call Number: PR 2979.H8.D38.1998 |

If you use your computer to record bibliographic information, you may want to find software designed for this purpose. Your software may provide database categories or options from which you can select the categories required by the style guide you need to use. You also can use the requirements of your style guide to help you develop your own, such as these for a book.

| | |
|---|---|
| Author's last name: | Pinker |
| Author's first name: | Steven |
| Book title: | The Language Instinct: How the Mind Creates Language |
| Publisher's location: | New York |
| Publisher (imprint): | HarperCollins Publishers (HarperPerennial) |
| Date published (original date): | 1995 (1994) |

Once you begin to build a bibliographic database, you can refer to your listings and supplement them each time you are assigned a paper.

**Reassessing Your Topic**   Once you have compiled your working bibliography, take the time to reassess the entire project before you get more deeply involved in it. Analyze your bibliography cards carefully to determine whether you should proceed to the next stage of information gathering.

Your working bibliography should send out signals that help you shape your thinking about the topic. The dominant signal should indicate that your topic is neither too narrow nor too broad. Generally, a bibliography of 10–15 promising entries for a 1,500-word paper indicates that your topic might be properly limited at this stage. A listing of only three or four entries signals that you must expand the topic or consider discarding it. Conversely, a listing of a hundred entries warns that you might be working yourself into a research swamp.

Another signal from your working bibliography should help you decide whether your hypothesis is on target or could be easily recast to make it more precise. Entry titles, abstracts, and commentaries on articles are excellent sources of confirmation. If established scholarship does not support your hypothesis, it would be best to discard your hypothesis and begin again.

Finally, the working bibliography should provide signals about the categories or parts of your research. Again, titles, abstracts, and commentaries are useful. In other words, as you compile the entries, you can begin to think through the problem and to perceive contours of thought that will dictate the organization of the paper even before you begin to do detailed research. Your working bibliography should be filled with such signals.

## Phase 3: Gathering and Organizing Data

If your working bibliography confirms the value, logic, and practicality of your research project, you can move to the next phase of the research process: taking notes and organizing information. Information shapes and refines your thinking; you move from an overview to a more precise understanding, analysis, and interpretation of the topic. By the end of this third phase, you should be able to transform your hypothesis into a thesis and your assembled notes into an outline.

**Plagiarism and Intellectual Property**   In this phase of the research process, it is especially critical that you maintain a clear distinction between ideas, opinions, information, words from other sources and your own interpretation of that information. *Plagiarism*, or the illicit appropriation of content and ideas, can result from sloppy note taking or poor study habits. Taking care to summarize, paraphrase, and quote from sources with scrupulous care—as well as ensuring that you have given yourself enough time to consider your own argument and write your own paper—will go a long way toward avoiding plagiarism.

The temptation to plagiarize is especially keen in an age when essays can easily be purchased online and when primary and secondary source information can be cut and pasted at the click of a button into your own work. Be aware that such behavior in the classroom may result in a failing grade or even suspension. In the professional world, however, plagiarism can result in the loss of a job, the destruction of a reputation, and even criminal charges. Plagiarism is a kind of theft. What a plagiarist steals is called, in legal terms, *intellectual property*—the ideas, opinions, inventions, and discoveries in which another writer or researcher has invested considerable time and resources.

When you are unsure of whether or how to give credit to another source, *always* assume that you should give credit (and ask your professor or a writing center instructor for help with citation guidelines). If you are tempted to buy or "borrow" another person's work because of extenuating circumstances, remember that it is *always* better to ask for a deadline extension (and for additional help with your paper). Just as there is never any excuse for the theft of property, there is never any excuse for the theft of ideas.

**Evaluating Sources**   As you move into the third phase, begin by skimming your source material to sort out the valuable sources from the not-so-valuable ones. For a book, check the table of contents and index for information on your topic; then determine whether the information is relevant to your problem. For an article, see if the abstract or topic sentences in the body of the essay confirm your research interests. The guidelines below can help you determine if a source will be useful.

---

## CRITERIA FOR ASSESSING THE VALUE OF A SOURCE FOR YOUR PROJECT

- Is it directly relevant to your topic?
- Does it discuss the topic extensively, uniquely, and authoritatively?
- Does it bear on your hypothesis, supporting, qualifying, or contradicting it?
- Does it present relatively current information, especially for research in the social and natural sciences?
- Does it meet the criteria for credibility discussed in "Evaluating Online Sources" (page 185) and "Evaluating Print Sources" (page 190)?

---

www.mhhe.com/ **mhreader**

For more information on evaluating sources, go to:
**Research > Source Evaluation Tutor**

**Taking Notes**   Once you have a core of valuable material, you can begin to read these sources closely and take detailed notes. Skillful note taking requires a subtle blend of critical thinking skills. It is not a matter of recording all the information available or simply copying long quotes. You want to select and summarize the general ideas that will form the outline of your paper, record specific evidence to support your ideas, and copy exact statements you plan to quote for evidence or interest. You also want to add your own ideas and evaluation of the material. All the notes you take must serve the specific purpose of your paper as stated in your hypothesis. It is essential that you record source information for *every* note that you take, whether that note is a summary, a paraphrase, or a direct quotation.

---

### GUIDELINES FOR TAKING NOTES ABOUT YOUR TOPIC

1. Write the author's last name, the title of the source, and the page number at the top of each card or entry. (Complete information on the source should already have been recorded on a bibliography card or listed in an entry in a computer file.)

2. Record only one idea or a group of closely related facts on each card or in each entry.

3. List a subtopic at the top of the card or entry. This will permit you to arrange your cards or entries from various sources into groups, and these groups can then serve as the basis of your outline.

4. List three types of information: (*a*) summaries of material, (*b*) paraphrases of material, in which you recast the exact words of the author, and (*c*) direct quotations, accurately transcribed.

5. Add your own ideas at the bottom of the card or following specific notes.

---

www.mhhe.com/
**mhreader**

For more information on taking notes, go to:
**Research > Taking Notes**

---

**Summarizing, Paraphrasing, and Quoting**   When you write a *summary* of a source, you focus on the main points of the source and restate them in your own words. Summary notes can be especially helpful to remind you, as you draft, of sources that you might want to revisit and look at more closely. Summaries can also be introduced into the body of your essay, especially in an argument research paper, to provide additional information and support for your thesis. Here is an example of a primary source text and a student's summary:

**Primary Source: Carl Elliott, "Humanity 2.0," The Wilson Quarterly, Autumn 2003**
Even technologies that unambiguously provide enhancements will raise issues of social justice not unlike those we currently face with ordinary medical technologies (wealthy Americans, for example, get liver transplants, while children in the developing world die from diarrhea). We live comfortably with such inequities, in part because we have so enthusiastically embraced an individualistic ethic. But to an outsider, a country's expenditure of billions of dollars on liposuction, face-lifts, and Botox injections while many of its children go without basic health care might well seem obscene.

**Student Summary**

| | |
|---|---|
| Topic label | "Transhumanism" and bioethics |
| Author of article | Elliott |
| Relevant pages/URL | http://wwics.si.edu |
| | |
| Summary | Bioethicist and philosopher Carl Elliott defines "transhumanism" and describes a conference of "transhumanists" that he attended. As a bioethicist, Elliott argues that we need to pay attention to the ethical implications of the medical "enhancements" currently practiced or being developed that might contribute to the "transhumanist" goal of creating perfect human beings. In particular, our society's emphasis on developing medical technologies to make us more beautiful or intelligent at the expense of those less fortunate is especially disturbing. |

A *paraphrase* focuses on one specific point or piece of information in an article and restates it in your own words. Writing a paraphrase of a source can help you to better understand it. When you paraphrase, follow the original writer's argument but do not mimic the writer's sentence structure or simply replace key words with synonyms.

| | |
|---|---|
| Topic label | "Transhumanism" and bioethics |
| Author of article | Elliott |
| Relevant pages/URL | http://wwics.si.edu |
| | |
| Unacceptable paraphrase | Even procedures designed for cosmetic purposes raise controversies over fairness (rich people get transplants while poor children die from basic diseases). Americans are fine with these inequalities because our culture values the individual. To non-Americans, the money we spend on plastic surgery even though many American children lack health insurance probably appears scandalous. |
| The sentence structure of the original is imitated, and synonyms replace the original terms (*scandalous* for *obscene*). | |

(continued)

Acceptable
paraphrase
Key terms from the
original source are
directly quoted, and
the source argument
is rephrased in the
student's own terms.

Elliott points out that our culture already seems to overlook the injustice of some individuals spending a great deal of money on cosmetic surgery (or "enhancements") while many lack access to basic health care. Elliott describes this as a uniquely American "individualist ethic" but points out that other cultures might see this inequality as "obscene." By extension, the willingness of the transhumanist movement to explore medical "enhancements" that will only benefit a very few wealthy people is also, ethically, "obscene."

As these examples demonstrate, an acceptable paraphrase shows that the researcher is genuinely engaged with the source's *argument*—not just the words—and has thought about how this particular component of the argument supports the original author's thesis.

When the language of source material is essential to understanding its argument, *quotation* is the most effective strategy. When you quote directly from a source, put quotation marks around the material that you are selecting.

Topic label
Author of article
Relevant pages/URL

Quotation

"Transhumanism" and bioethics
Elliott
http://wwics.si.edu

"But to an outsider, a country's expenditure of billions of dollars on liposuction, face-lifts, and Botox injections while many of its children go without basic health care might well seem obscene."

When you have completed all your research, organize your notes under the various subtopics or subheadings that you have established. Now is the time to establish your thesis. By reviewing your notes and assessing the data, you should be able to transform the calculated guess that was your hypothesis into a much firmer thesis. Focus your attention on your thesis by stating it at the top of the page where you are working on your outline. If possible or desirable, try to combine some subtopics and eliminate others so that you have three to five major categories for analysis and development. You are now ready to develop an outline for the research essay.

**Designing an Outline**   Because you must organize a lot of material in a clear way, an outline is especially valuable in a research essay. Spend as much time as is reasonable drafting an outline. Begin by creating a rough outline that simply lists your general subheadings and their supporting data. Next, work more systematically through your notes and fill in the rough outline with as much detail as possible, developing each point logically and in detail. If you are required to submit an outline with your research paper, you should begin to develop a full, formal outline at this stage. Such an outline would be structured like this:

I.
   A.
   B.
      1.
      2.
      3.
         a.
         b.
II.

Use roman numerals for your most important points, capital letters for the next most important points, arabic numbers for supporting points, and lowercase letters for pertinent details or minor points. If you are including visuals such as photographs or graphics, include them in the outline as well.

www.mhhe.com/ **mhreader**    For an interactive tutorial on creating outlines, go to: **Writing > Outline Tutor**

## Phase 4: Writing and Submitting the Paper

As you enter the fourth and final phase of the research process, keep in mind that a research paper is a formal essay, not a rag-tag compilation of notes. You should be prepared to take your research effort through several increasingly polished versions, most likely at least a rough draft, a revised draft, and a final manuscript.

**Writing the Rough Draft**    For your rough draft, concentrate on filling in the gaps in your outline. Take the time to rearrange your notes in the topic order that your outline assumes. In this way, you will be able to integrate notes and writing more efficiently and effectively.

Even as you adhere to your formal outline in beginning the rough draft, you should be open to alternate possibilities and prospects for presenting ideas and information. Although your primary task in writing a first draft is to rough out the shape and content of your paper, the flow of your ideas will often be accompanied by self-adjusting operations of your mind, all aimed at making your research effort even better than you thought it could be at the outline stage.

Whether you incorporate quotations from your notes into the rough draft is a matter of preference. Some writers prefer to transcribe quotations and paraphrases at this point in order to save time at a later stage. Other writers copy and insert these materials directly from entries in a computer file for notes. Still others believe that their thought processes are interrupted by having to write out summarized, quoted, and paraphrased material and to design transitions between their own writing and the transcribed material. They simply write "insert" in the draft with a reference to the appropriate notes. Whatever your strategy, it is essential that you keep track of the sources of summarized, quoted, and paraphrased material so that you can properly cite the sources and avoid plagiarism.

The need to integrate material from several sources will test your reasoning ability during the writing of the rough draft. For any given subtopic in your outline, you will be drawing together information from a variety of sources. To an extent, your outline will tell you how to arrange some of this information. At the same time, you must contribute your own commentary, arrange details in an effective order, and sort out conflicting claims and interpretations. A great deal of thinking as well as writing goes into the design of your first draft. You are not involved in a dull transcription of material when writing the rough draft of a research paper. Instead, you are engaged in a demanding effort to think your way through a problem of considerable magnitude, working in a logical way from the introduction and the statement of your thesis, through the evidence, to the outcome or conclusion that supports everything that has come before.

**Revising the Draft**   In the rough draft, you thought and wrote your way through the problem. Now you must rethink and rewrite in order to give better form and expression to your ideas. Use the guidelines outlined below to approach your revision. Consider every aspect of your paper, from the most general to the most specific. Look again at the over all organization, key topics, paragraphs, and sentences; read through for clarity of expression and details of grammar, punctuation, and spelling. A comprehensive revision effort will result in a decidedly more polished version of your paper.

---

CRITERIA FOR REVISING
YOUR RESEARCH WRITING

---

- Does your title illuminate the topic of the essay and capture the reader's interest?

- Have you created the proper tone to meet the expectations of your audience?

- Does your opening paragraph hook the reader? Does it clearly establish and limit the topic? Is your thesis statement clear, limited, and interesting?

*(continued)*

(*Criteria for Revising Your Research Writing* continued)

- Do all the body paragraphs support your thesis? Is there a single topic and main idea for each paragraph? Do you achieve unity, coherence, and proper development? Is there sufficient evidence in each paragraph to support the main idea?

- Are there clear and effective transitions linking your ideas within and between paragraphs?

- Have you selected the best strategies to meet the demands of the assignment and the expectations of your audience?

- Are your assertions clearly stated, defined, and supported? Do you use sound logic and avoid faulty reasoning? Do you acknowledge other peoples' ideas properly?

- Is your conclusion strong and effective?

- Are your sentences grammatically correct? Have you avoided errors in the use of verbs, pronouns, adjectives, and prepositions? Have you corrected errors of agreement?

- Are your sentences complete? Have you corrected all fragments, comma splices, and fused sentences?

- Have you varied your sentences effectively? Have you employed clear coordination and subordination? Have you avoided awkward constructions?

- If you include visual information, do you provide adequate context? Is the placement of the visual logical? Is the visual clearly reproduced?

- Are all words spelled correctly? Do your words mean what you think they mean? Are they specific? Are they concrete? Is your diction appropriate to college writing? Is your language free of clichés, slang, jargon, and euphemism? Do you avoid needless abstractions? Is your usage sound?

- Have you carefully attended to such mechanical matters as apostrophes, capitals, numbers, and word divisions?

- Does your manuscript conform to acceptable guidelines for submitting typewritten work?

- Are all of your summaries, paraphrases, and quotations appropriately cited?

**Preparing the Final Manuscript**    Leave time in your research effort to prepare a neat, clean, attractively designed manuscript. Store all of your files (notes, drafts, and final version) on a backup CD, and print or duplicate an extra copy of the report. Submit a neat, clear version, and keep the second copy. Consult your instructor for the desired format, and carefully follow the guidelines for manuscript preparation in your final version. Look also at the sample paper later in this chapter, which illustrates how to present the final version of a paper in accordance with MLA style (see pages 218–232).

## DOCUMENTING SOURCES

Documentation is an essential part of any research paper. Documenting your sources throughout the paper and in a Works Cited or References section tells your audience just how well you have conducted your research. It offers readers the opportunity to check on authorities, do further reading, and assess the originality of your contribution to an established body of opinion. Neglect of proper documentation can lead to charges of plagiarism (see page 195).

Quotations, paraphrases, and summaries obviously require credit, for they are the actual words or the theories or interpretations of others. Paraphrases and summaries also frequently offer statistics or data that are not well known, and this type of information requires documentation as well. Facts in a controversy (facts open to dispute or to varying interpretations) also fall within the realm of documentation. Visual information (maps, graphics, and photos) also require documentation, even if they show common knowledge (such as a map of Japan).

---

MATERIALS THAT REQUIRE DOCUMENTATION

---

- Direct quotations
- Paraphrased material
- Summarized material
- Any key idea or opinion adapted and incorporated into your paper
- Specific data (whether quoted, paraphrased, or tabulated)
- Disputed facts

---

Parenthetical documentation—briefly identifying sources within parentheses in the text—is the most common method of indicating sources. The purpose of a parenthetical citation is to identify a source briefly yet clearly enough that it can be located in the list of references at the end of the paper. In MLA style, the author's last name and the page number in the source are included. APA style uses the author's last name and the year of publication; page numbers are included primarily for direct quotations. Then complete information is listed, alphabetically by author or title (if a source has no specific author), in the Works Cited or References section following the text of the paper. The bibliographic information you have collected should provide you with the details needed for the preparation of both parenthetical documentation and a list of sources.

---

### GENERAL GUIDELINES FOR PARENTHETICAL DOCUMENTATION

1. Give enough information so that the reader can readily identify the source in the Works Cited (MLA) or References (APA) section of your paper.
2. Supply the citation information in parentheses placed where the material occurs in your text.
3. Give the specific information required by the documentation system you are using, especially when dealing with multivolume works, editions, newspapers, and legal documents.
4. Make certain that the sentence containing the parenthetical documentation is readable and grammatically correct.

---

With your parenthetical documentation prepared, turn your attention next to a final Works Cited or References section. To prepare this list of sources, simply transcribe those bibliography cards or entries that you actually used to write your paper, following the appropriate format.

---

### GENERAL GUIDELINES FOR PREPARING A LIST OF SOURCES

1. Use the title *Works Cited* (MLA) or *References* (APA).
2. Include only works actually cited in the research paper unless directed otherwise by your instructor.
3. Arrange all works alphabetically according to author's last name or according to the title of a work if there is no author. Ignore *A, An,* or *The*.
4. Begin each entry at the left margin. Indent everything in an entry that comes after the first line by five spaces or ½ inch (MLA style) or by five to seven spaces (following APA style for students, unless your instructor directs otherwise).
5. Double-space every line.
6. Punctuate with periods after the three main divisions in most entries—author, title, and publishing information.

---

In the following sections, you will find examples of MLA and APA documentation forms. Use these examples to help you cite your sources efficiently and clearly.

## MLA (Modern Language Association) Documentation

The following examples illustrate how to cite a source in the text and in the list of works cited at the end of a paper.

**MLA Parenthetical Documentation**   The simplest MLA entry includes the author's last name and the page number, identifying exactly where the quotation or information is located. If the author's name is included in the text, it does not need to be repeated in the citation.

### Page Number(s) for a Book

The play offers what many audiences have found a satisfying conclusion (Hansberry 265–76).

Garcia Marquez uses another particularly appealing passage as the opening of the story (105).

### Volume and Page Number(s) for One Volume of a Multivolume Work

A strong interest in this literature in the 1960s and 1970s inevitably led to "a significant reassessment of the aesthetic and humanistic achievements of black writers" (Inge, Duke, and Bryer 1: v).

### Page Number(s) for an Article in a Journal or Magazine

Barlow's description of the family members includes "their most notable strengths and weaknesses" (18).

### Section and Page Number(s) for a Newspaper Article

A report on achievement standards for high school courses found "significant variation among schools" (Mallory B1).

### Page Number(s) for a Work without an Author

Computerworld has developed a thoughtful editorial on the issue of government and technology ("Uneasy Silence" 54).

### Page Number(s) for a Work by a Group or an Organization

The Commission on the Humanities has concluded that "the humanities are inescapably bound to literacy" (69).

### Page Number(s) for Several Works by One Author

In The Coming Fury, Catton identifies the "disquieting omens" (6) which precede the Civil War.

As Catton concludes his history of the Civil War, he notes that "it began with one act of madness and it ended with another" (Never Call Retreat 457).

## Page Number(s) for One Work Quoted in Another

Samuel Johnson praises <u>She Stoops to Conquer</u> because Goldsmith's play achieves "the great end of comedy—making an audience merry" (qtd. in Boswell 171).

## Online Source

Most online sources do not have page numbers for easy parenthetical citation. When citing from an online source, the author's last name or the title of the article or Web page should be given.

Blackwelder observes that "Depp has [the central conflict of the movie] in his eyes in every scene."

**MLA List of Works Cited**   Following your paper, list the references you have cited in alphabetical order on a separate page titled "Works Cited." See the Works Cited page of the sample paper (page 232) for an illustration of how you should prepare this page. Use the following sample entries to help you format your references in MLA style. Pay special attention to abbreviated names of publishers, full names of authors, details of punctuation, and other characteristic features of MLA citations.

## Work with One Author

Notice the punctuation and underlining in the basic entry for a book.

Muller, Eddie. <u>Dark City: The Lost World of Film Noir</u>. New York: St. Martin's-Griffin, 1998.

Reynolds, David S. <u>John Brown, Abolitionist</u>. New York: Knopf, 2005.

## Several Works by One Author

If you use several books or articles by one author, list the author's name in the initial entry. In the next entry or entries, replace the name with three hyphens.

Said, Edward. <u>Humanism and Democratic Criticism</u>. New York: Columbia UP, 2004.

—. <u>Orientalism</u>. New York: Pantheon, 1978.

## Work with Two or Three Authors or Editors

List the names of several authors in the sequence in which they appear in the book or article. Begin with the last name of the author listed first because it is used to determine the alphabetical order for entries. Then identify the other authors by first and last names.

Oakes, Jill, and Rick Riewe. <u>Spirit of Siberia: Traditional Native Life, Clothing, and Footwear</u>. Washington: Smithsonian Inst. P, 1998.

Trueba, Henry T., Grace Pung Guthrie, and Kathryn Hu-Pei Au, eds. <u>Culture and the Bilingual Classroom: Studies in Classroom Ethnography</u>. Rowley: Newbury, 1981.

## Work with More than Three Authors or Editors

Name all those involved, or list only the first author or editor with *et al.,* for "and others."

Nordhus, Inger, Gary R. VandenBos, Stig Berg, and Pia Fromholt, eds. <u>Clinical Geropsychology.</u> Washington: APA, 1998.

Nordhus, Inger, et al., eds. <u>Clinical Geropsychology</u>. Washington: APA, 1998.

## Work with Group or an Organization as Author
Alphabetize by the name of the group or organization.

National PTA. <u>National Standards for Parent/Family Involvement Programs</u>. Chicago: National PTA, 1997.

## Work without an Author
<u>A Visual Dictionary of Art</u>. Greenwich, CT: New York Graphic Society, 1974.

## Work in an Anthology of Pieces by the Same Author
Munro, Alice. "Passion." <u>Runaway: Stories</u>. New York:Knopf, 2004. 159–196.

## Work in an Anthology of Different Authors
McCorkle, Jill. "Final Vinyl Days." <u>It's Only Rock and Roll: An Anthology of Rock and Roll Short Stories</u>. Ed. Janice Eidus and John Kastan. Boston: Godine, 1998. 19–33.

## Anthology Cited as a Whole
Weston-Lews, Aidan, ed. <u>Effigies and Ecstasies: Roman Baroque Sculpture and Design in the Age of Bernini</u>. Edinburgh: Natl. Gallery of Scotland, 1998.

## Work in Several Volumes
Smith, Andrew F. <u>The Oxford Encyclopedia of Food and Drink in America</u>. 2 vols. New York: Oxford UP, 2004.

## Work Translated from Another Language
The first entry below emphasizes the work of the original author by placing his name first. The next example shifts emphasis to the work of the translators by identifying them first.

Eco, Umberto. <u>On Literature</u>. Trans. Martin McLaughlin. New York: Harcourt, 2004.

Young, David, and Jiann I. Lin, trans. <u>The Clouds Float North: The Complete Poems of Du Xuanji</u>. Bilingual Edition. Hanover: Wesleyan UP, 1998.

## Work Appearing as Part of a Series
Rohn, Suzanne. <u>The Wizard of Oz: Shaping an Imaginary World</u>. Twayne's Masterwork Studies 167. New York: Twayne-Simon, 1998.

## New Edition of an Older Book
Wharton, Edith. <u>The Custom of the Country</u>. 1913. NY Public Library Collector's Edition. New York: Doubleday, 1998.

## Entry from a Reference Volume
Treat less common reference books like other books, including place of publication, publisher, and date. For encyclopedias, dictionaries, and other familiar

references, simply note the edition and its date. No page numbers are needed if the entries appear in alphabetical order in the reference volume.

"Cretaceous Period." <u>Encyclopedia Americana: International Edition</u>. 2003 ed.

Minton, John. "Worksong." <u>American Folklore: An Encyclopedia</u>. Ed. Jan Harold Brunvand. New York: Garland, 1996.

## Work Issued by a Federal, State, or Other Government Agency
Depending on the emphasis you intend, you can start with either the writer or the government agency responsible for the publication. "GPO" stands for "Government Printing Office," the publisher of most federal documents.

Brock, Dan W. "An Assessment of the Ethical Issues Pro and Con." <u>Cloning Human Beings</u>. National Bioethics Advisory Commission. Vol. 2. Rockville, MD: GPO, 1997. E1–E23.

National Bioethics Advisory Commission. <u>Cloning Human Beings</u>. 2 vols. Rockville, MD: GPO, 1997.

United States. Cong. House. Subcommittee on Oversight and Investigations of the Committee on Education and the Workforce. <u>Education at a Crossroads: What Works and What's Wasted in Education Today</u>. 105th Cong., 2nd sess. Washington: GPO, 1998.

US Const. Art. 9.

## Reference to a Legal Document
When you discuss court cases in your paper, underline their names. In your Works Cited, do not underline them.

Aguilar v. Felton. 473 US 402.1985.

## Article in a Journal with Continuous Pagination
Pistol, Todd A. "Unfinished Business: Letters from a Father to His Son, 1922–1928." <u>Journal of Men's Studies</u> 7 (1999): 215–31.

## Article in a Journal with Pagination Continuing Only through Each Issue
Add the issue number after the volume number.

Guyer, Jane I. "Traditions of Invention in Equatorial Africa." <u>African Studies Review</u> 39.3 (1996): 1–28.

## Article in a Weekly or Biweekly Periodical
Lemonick, Michael D. "The Biological Mother Lode." <u>Time</u> 16 Nov. 1998: 96–97.

Zakaria, Fareed. "In Search of the Real Iraq." <u>Newsweek</u> 2 May 2005: 35.

## Article in a Monthly or Bimonthly Periodical
If an article in a magazine or a newspaper does not continue on consecutive pages, follow the page number on which it begins with a plus sign.

Waters, Rob. "Medicating Aliah." <u>Mother Jones</u> May–June 2005: 50+.

## Article in a Daily Newspaper
Morson, Berny. "Tuft-eared Cats Make Tracks in Colorado." Denver Rocky Mountain News 4 Feb. 1999: 5A+.

## Article with No Author
"Machines That Think." New Scientist 25 April 2005: 32.

"Terrorism's Latest Report Card." US News & World Report 9 May 2005: 16.

## Editorial in a Periodical
Fogarty, Robert W. "Fictional Families." Editorial. Antioch Review 56 (1998): 388.

## Letter Written to the Editor of a Periodical
Posod, Melissa. "That Global Perspective." Letter. Ms. Spring 2005: 6.

## Review Article
If a review article has a title, add it after the author's name.

Swain, William N. Rev. of Getting Hits: The Definitive Guide to Promoting Your Website, by Don Sellers. Public Relations Review 24 (1998): 403–09.

## Presentation at a Professional Meeting or Conference
Ciardi, John. Address. National Council of Teachers of English Convention. Hilton Hotel, Washington. 19 Nov. 1982.

## Film, Slides, Videotape
Start with any actor, producer, director, or other person whose work you wish to emphasize. Otherwise, simply begin with the title of the recording. Note the form cited—DVD, videocassette, and so forth.

America in the Depression Years. Slide program. Laurel: Instructional Resources, 1979.

Olivier, Laurence, prod. and dir. Richard III. By William Shakespeare. Videocassette. London Film Productions, 1955.

Richard III. By William Shakespeare. Prod. and dir. Laurence Olivier. Videocassette. London Film Productions, 1955.

Visions of the Spirit: A Portrait of Alice Walker. By Elena Featherston. Videocassette. Women Make Films, 1989.

## Programs on Radio or Television
"Alone on the Ice." The American Experience. PBS. KRMA, Denver. 8 Feb. 1999.

The Life and Adventures of Nicholas Nickleby. By Charles Dickens. Adapt. David Edgar. Dir. Trevor Nunn and John Caird. Royal Shakespeare Co. Mobile Showcase Network. WNEW, New York. 10–13 Jan. 1983.

## CD or Other Recording
Identify the format if the recording is not on a CD.

Basie, Count. "Sunday at the Savoy." 88 Basie Street. Rec. 11–12 May 1983. LP. Pablo Records, 1984.

Cherry, Don. "When Will the Blues Leave?" Art Deco. A&M Records, 1989.

## Published or Personal Letter

Lasswell, Harold. Letter to the author. 15 July 1976.

Schneider, Alan. "To Sam from Alan." 3 Sept. 1972. <u>No Author Better Served: The Correspondence of Samuel Beckett and Alan Schneider</u>. Ed. Maurice Harmon. Cambridge: Harvard UP, 1998. 278–82.

Thackeray, William Makepeace. "To George Henry Lewes." 6 Mar. 1848. Letter 452 of <u>Letters and Private Papers of William Makepeace Thackery</u>. Ed. Gordon N. Ray. Cambridge: Harvard UP, 1946. 335–54.

## Published or Personal Interview

Freund, Nancy. Telephone interview. 18 June 2004.

Gerard, William. Personal interview. 16 May 2003.

Previn, Andre. Interview. "A Knight at the Keyboard." By Jed Distler. <u>Piano and Keyboard</u>. Jan.–Feb. 1999: 24–29.

## Computer Software

<u>Biblio-Link II for Windows: Powerful Data Transfer for ProCit</u>. Diskette. Ann Arbor: Personal Bibliographic Software, 1993.

Schwartz, Howard F., Robert Hamblen, and Mark S. McMillan, eds. <u>AG Photo CD-1</u>. Diskette. Fort Collins: Colorado State U and Advanced Digital Imaging, 1996.

## Database Available Online

<u>Bartleby Library</u>. Ed. Steven van Leeuwen. 1999. 27 Apr. 2005 <http://www.bartleby.com>.

## Book, Article, or Other Source Available Online

Besides author and title, add any translator or editor and the date of electronic publication or last update. Conclude with the date on which you visited the electronic site where the source is located and the site's address. If the URL is too long or does not lead directly to your source (as with some personal and subscription-based sites), provide the URL for the site's homepage or search page.

Land-Webber, Ellen. <u>To Save a Life: Stories of Jewish Rescue</u>. 1999. 5 Feb. 1999 <http://sorrel.humboldt/edu/rescuers>.

Latham, Ernest. "Conducting Research at the National Archives into Art Looting, Recovery, and Restitution." <u>National Archives Library</u>. 4 Dec. 1998. National Archives and Records Administration. 5 Feb. 1999 <http://www.nara.gov/research/assets/sympaper/latham.html>.

Marvell, Andrew. "Last Instructions to a Painter." <u>Poets' Corner</u>. 5 Sept. 2003. 12 Oct 2004 <http://www.theotherpages.org/poems/marvel04.html>.

Wollstonecraft, Mary. "A Vindication of the Rights of Women: With Strictures on Political and Moral Subjects." <u>Project Bartleby Archive</u>. Ed. Steven van Leeuwen. Jan. 1996. 27 Apr. 2005 <http://www.cc.columbia.edu/acis/bartleby/wollstonecraft>.

## Magazine Article Available Online

Chatsky, Jean Sherman. "Grow Your Own Employee Benefits." <u>Money</u>.com 30–31
Jan. 1999. 7 Feb. 1999 <http://www.pathfinder.com/money/moneytalk>.

## Newspaper Article Available Online

Wolf, Mark. "Finding Art in Albums."@ <u>The Post: World Wide Web Edition of
the Cincinnati Post</u> 5 Feb. 1999 <http://www.cincypost.com/living/
album020599.html>.

## Article from an Electronic Journal

Warren, W. L. "Church and State in Angevin Ireland." <u>Chronicon: An Electronic
History Journal</u> 1 (1997): 6 pars. 6 Feb. 1999 <http://www.ucc.ie/chronicon/
warren.htm>.

## Electronic Posting to a Group

Faris, Tommy L. "Tiger Woods." Online posting. 3 Sept. 1996. H-Net: Humanities &
Social Sciences Online Posting. 7 Feb. 1999 <http://www.h-net.msu.edu/arete/
archives/threads/tiger.html>.

## Review Available Online

Holden, Stephen. Rev. of <u>Anne Frank Remembered</u>. 22 Feb. 1996. 5 Feb. 1999
<http://www.english.upenn.edu/afilreis/Holocaust/anne-frank-film.html>.

## Public Web Site with Organizational Message

Raab, Jennifer J. "Greeting from Chairman Jennifer J. Raab." <u>Landmarks
Preservation Commission New York City</u>. 8 Sept. 1998. 7 Feb. 1999 <http://
www.ci.nyc.ny.us/html/lpc/home.html>.

## Database or Other Source Available on CD-ROM

Use *n.p.* to indicate either "no place" or "no publisher" if such information is
not available. Use *n.d.* to indicate "no date."

"Landforms of the Earth: Cause, Course, Effect, Animation." <u>Phenomena of the
Earth</u>. CD-ROM. n.p.: Springer Electronic Media/MMCD, 1998.

<u>Life in Tudor Times</u>. CD-ROM. Princeton: Films for the Humanities and Sciences, 1996.

| www.mhhe.com/ **mhreader** | For software that will help you format your citations, go to: **Research > Bibliomaker** |

## APA (American Psychological Association) Documentation

The samples below show how to use APA style for citing a source in the text
and in the References section at the end of a paper.

**APA Parenthetical Documentation**   The basic APA parenthetical citation includes the author's last name and the date of publication, information generally sufficient to identify the source in the reference list. Although researchers in the social sciences often cite works as a whole, the page number can be added to identify exactly where a quotation or other specific information is located. If the author's name is included in the text of your paper, it does not need to be repeated in the citation.

### Single Author

The city's most current traffic flow analysis (Dunlap, 1998) proposed two alternatives.

Nagle (1998) compared the costs and benefits of both designs.

### Two Authors

Use both names each time the source is cited. Use the word *and* to join them in the text; use an ampersand (&) within parentheses and the reference list.

Moll and Greenberg (1990) outline the advantages of a more flexible approach to social context.

An earlier study (Moll & Diaz, 1987) proposed classroom change as one research objective.

### Three to Five Authors

Supply all the names the first time the source is cited. If it is cited again, use only the name of the first author and *et al.,* for "and others."

Greene, Rucker, Zauss, and Harris (1998) maintain that anxiety is an important factor in communication.

Greene et al. (1998) address anxiety and communication directly.

### More than Five Authors

Use only the name of the first author with *et al.* in the paper. Supply the names of the first six authors in the list of references followed by *et al.* for any additional authors.

Heath et al. (1988) continue to address the problems involved in implementing this methodology.

### Group or Organization as Author

The Ford Foundation (1988) outlined several efforts to change decision-making processes.

### Work without an Author

"Challenging the Myths" (1995) identifies several traditional beliefs about teacher training.

### Page Numbers for a Work

The characteristics of successful charter schools follow an opening definition of the "charter school challenge" (Rowe, 1995, p. 34).

## Two or More Works in the Same Citation

If several citations are grouped in one pair of parentheses, arrange them alphabetically.

> Recent studies of small groups (Laramie & Nader, 1997; McGrew, 1996; Tiplett, 1999) concentrate on their interactions rather than their context.

## Letters, Telephone Calls, E-Mail Messages, and Similar Communications

These communications are personal and thus are cited only in the text, not in the references.

> This staffing pattern for nurses is used at four of the six major metropolitan hospitals (G. N. Prescott, personal communication, August 23, 1999).

**APA List of References**   As you examine the following illustrations, notice how capitalization, italics, punctuation, and other features change with the type of source noted. Note also that authors' names are listed with last names first, followed by initials only. Although the entries in an APA reference list follow very specific patterns, references in your paper—to titles, for instance—should use standard capitalization (that is, only the first word of titles and subtitles). Similarly, the word *and* should be spelled out in your paper (except in parenthetical citations) even though the ampersand (&) is used in the references. Note that the names of months (in periodical and online citations) are spelled out, not abbreviated.

For updated examples and further guidance on APA style, see the American Psychological Association Web site at www.apastyle.org.

## Book with One Author

> Blau, T. H. (1998). *The psychologist as expert witness* (2nd ed.). New York: Wiley.

> Nuckalls, C. W. (1998). *Culture: A problem that cannot be solved.* Madison: University of Wisconsin Press.

## Several Works by One Author

List the works by year of publication, with the earliest first.

> Muller, N. J. (1998). *Mobile telecommunications factbook.* New York: McGraw-Hill.

> Muller, N. J. (1999). *Desktop encyclopedia of the Internet.* Boston: Artech House.

## Book with Two Authors

> Arden, H., & Wall, S. (1998). *Travels in a stone canoe: The return to the wisdomkeepers.* New York: Simon & Schuster.

## Book with More than Two Authors or Editors

> Greenfield, L. A., Rand, M. R., Craven, D., Klaus, P. A., Perkins, C. A., et al. (1998). *Violence by intimates: Analysis of data on crimes by current or former spouses, boyfriends, and girlfriends* (NCJ-167237). Bureau of Justice Statistics Factbook. Washington, DC: U.S. Department of Justice.

> Hair, J. F., Jr., Anderson, R. E., Tatham, R. L., & Black, W. C. (1998). *Multivariate data analysis* (5th ed.). Upper Saddle River, NJ: Prentice-Hall, 1998.

## Work with a Group or an Organization as Author

When the author is also the publisher, *Author* is used as the publisher's name.

American Public Transit Association. (1986). *The 1986 rail transit report.* Washington, DC: Author.

Amnesty International. (1998). *Children in South Asia: Securing their rights.* New York: Author.

## Book without an Author

*Ultimate visual dictionary of science.* (1998). New York: Dorling Kindersley.

## Work in a Collection of Pieces by Different Authors

Ombaka, C. (1998). War and environment in African literature. In P. D. Murphy (Ed.), *Literature of nature: An international sourcebook* (pp. 327–336). Chicago: Fitzroy Dearborn.

## Collection of Pieces Cited as a Whole

Young, C. (Ed.). (1998). *Ethnic diversity and public policy.* New York: St. Martin's.

## Work in Several Volumes

AFL-CIO. (1960). *American Federation of Labor: History, encyclopedia, and reference book* (Vols. 1–3). Washington, DC: Author.

## Work Translated from Another Language

When you cite a translation in your paper, include both its original publication date and the date of the translation you have used, as in (Rousseau, 1762/1954).

Rousseau, J.-J. (1954). *The social contract.* (W. Kendall, Trans.) Chicago: Regnery. (Original work published 1762)

## Work Appearing as Part of a Series

Frith, K. T. (Vol. Ed.). (1997). *Counterpoints: Vol. 54. Undressing the ad: Reading culture in advertising.* New York: Peter Lang.

## New Edition of an Older Book

When you cite an older source in your paper, include the original publication date and the date of the new edition, as in (Packard, 1866/1969).

Packard, F. A. (1969). *The daily public school in the United States.* New York: Arno Press. (Original work published 1866)

## Article in a Reference Volume

Breadfruit (1994) In D. Crystal (Ed.), *The Cambridge encyclopedia* (2nd ed., p. 175). Cambridge: Cambridge University Press.

## Work Issued by a Federal, State, or Other Government Agency

Nelson, R. E., Ziegler, A. A., Serino, D. F., & Basner, P. J. (1987). Radioactive waste processing apparatus. *Energy research abstracts,* Vol. 12 (Abstract No. 34680).

Washington, DC: U.S. Department of Energy, Office of Scientific and Technical Information.

### Reference to a Legal Document

Individuals with Disabilities Education Act (IDEA), 20 U.S.C. 1400 *et seq.* (1996).

Turner Broadcasting System Inc. v. Federal Communications Commission, 95 U.S. 992 (1997).

### Article in a Journal with Pagination Continuing through Each Volume

Dinerman, T. (1998). The case for an American manned Mars mission. *The Journal of Social, Political and Economic Studies, 23,* 369–378.

Greene, J. O., Rucker, M. P., Zauss, E. S., & Harris, A. A. (1998). Communication anxiety and the acquisition of message-production skill. *Communication Education, 47,* 337–347.

### Article in a Journal with Pagination Continuing Only through Each Issue

Brune, L. H. (1998). Recent scholarship and findings about the Korean War. *American Studies International, 36*(3), 4–16.

### Special Issue of a Periodical

Larsen, C. S. (1994). In the wake of Columbus: Native population biology in the postcontact Americas. In A. T. Steegmann, Jr. (Ed.), *Yearbook of Physical Anthropology: Vol. 37* (pp. 109–154). New York: Wiley-Liss.

Riley, P., & Morse, P. R. (Eds.). (1998). Communication in the global community [Special issue]. *Communication Research, 25*(2).

### Article in a Weekly or Biweekly Periodical

Greenwald, J. (1998, November 23). Herbal healing. *Time, 152,* 58–67.

### Article in a Monthly or Bimonthly Periodical

Glausiusz, J. (1999, June). Creatures from the bleak lagoon. *Discover, 20,* 76–79.

Gordon, J. S. (1999, May/June). The great crash (of 1792). *American Heritage. 50,* 20–24.

### Article in a Daily Newspaper

Levine, S. (1999, January 30). Hearing loss touches a younger generation. *The Washington Post,* pp. A1, A8.

### Article with No Author

Fire and lightning. (1998, October 10). *New Scientist,* 25.

### Editorial in a Periodical

Zuckerman, M. B. (1999, February 8). Coming to Russia's rescue. *U.S. News & World Report,* p. 68.

### Letter Written to the Editor of a Periodical

Triebold, M. (1998, July/August). Digging bones for fun and $$$ [Letter to the editor]. *The Sciences,* 5.

### Review Article

Glaeser, E. L. (1997). [Review of the book *Policing space: Territoriality and the Los Angeles Police Department*]. *Contemporary Sociology: A Journal of Reviews, 26*, 750–751.

### Presentation at a Professional Meeting or Conference

Achilles, C. M., Keedy, J. L., & Zaharias, J. B. (1996, October). *If we're rebuilding education, let's start with a firm foundation.* Paper presented at the annual meeting of the University Council for Educational Administration, Louisville, KY.

### Film, Videotape

If sources do not mention a place of publication, use *n.p.* If no date is mentioned, use *n.d.*

CityTV and Sleeping Giant Productions (Producers). (1994). *Dalai Lama: A portrait in the first person* [Motion picture]. n.p.: Films for the Humanities and Sciences.

### Programs on Radio and Television

If appropriate, add the names of contributors or a specific episode before the series title.

*The New Detectives: Case Studies in Forensic Science.* (1999, February 9). Bethesda, MD: Discovery.

### CD or Other Recording

Use *n.d.* and *n.p.* if you need to indicate that a recording or other source does not note the date or place of publication.

Cleveland, J. (1993). Marching to Zion. On *The great gospel men* [CD]. Newton, NJ: Shanachie Records.

Jamal, A. (1961). Night mist blues. On *Ahmad Jamal at the Blackhawk* [Record]. Chicago: Argo.

### Letters, Interviews, and Personal Messages

If you have used a communication such as a letter in a print or other medium, follow the form for that type of citation. If the communication is a message or call not available to other researchers, cite it only in your text, not in your list of references. (See page 213.)

### Computer Software

Weiss, H. J. (1990). PC-POM: Software for Production and Operations Management (Version 2.10) [Computer software]. Boston: Allyn and Bacon.

### Database Available Online

*Academic Info: Your Gateway to Quality Internet Resources.* (1999, February 4). Retrieved February 5, 1999, from http://www.academicinfo.net

### Book, Article, or Other Source Available Online

Hornbeck, D. (1999, January 22). The past in California's landscape. Retrieved February 7, 1999, from California Mission Studies Association, http://www.camissions.org/hornbeck.html

*1695: Northwestern Indians at Quebec: Huron intrigues.* Retrieved February 5, 1999,
from State Historical Society of Wisconsin, http://memory.loc.gov/cgibin/
query/r?ammem/lhbum:@field (DOCID+Alit(M7689e42)

## Magazine Article Available Online

All hope gone for Hussein, power is passing to Abdullah. (1999, February 7). *Time
Daily.* Retrieved February 7, 1999, from http://cgi.pathfinder.com/time/
daily/0,2960,19381-101990206,00.html

Spragins, E. E. (1999, February 7). Patient power: How to beat job lock. *Newsweek.*
Retrieved February 7, 1999, from http://www.newsweek.com/nw-srv/ focus/
he/fohe0224_1.htm

## Newspaper Article Available Online

Harden, C., & Long, P. A. (1998, October 28). Grand jury begins work in bid probe.
*The Kentucky Post.* Retrieved February 5, 1999, from http://www.kypost.com/
news/bids102989.html

Sack, K. On the bipartisan bayou, a brouhaha. (1999, February 5). *New York Times.*
Retrieved February 5, 1999, from http://www.nytimes.com/yr/mo/day/news/
washpol/la-cooperate.html

## Article from an Electronic Journal

Peiss, K. L. (1998, Fall). American women and the making of modern consumer
culture. *Journal for MultiMedia History, 1*(1). Retrieved February 5, 1999, from
http://www.albany.edu/jmmh/vol1no1/peiss.html

## Abstract Available Online

Gay, H. (1998 August). East end, west end: Science education, culture and class in
mid-Victorian London. *Canadian Journal of History, 33.* Retrieved February 5, 1999,
from http://www.asask.ca/history/cjh/ABS_897.HTM

## Electronic Posting to a Group

French, M. (1996, February 21). Erie Canal? Message posted to http://www.h-net
.msu.edu/aseh/archives/threads/eriecanal.html

## Database or Other Source Available on CD-ROM

Real facts about the sun. (2000). *The Dynamic Sun.* Retrieved October 27, 2001, from
NASA database.

www.mhhe.com/
**mhreader**

For software that will help you format your citations, go to:
**Research > Bibliomaker**

## SAMPLE STUDENT PAPER (MLA STYLE)

Last name and page number ½ inch below top of page.

Lee 1

Heading 1 inch below top of page.

All lines double-spaced, including heading and title.

Clara Lee

Professor Paul Smith

Writing Workshop II

5 May 2007

Title centered. Title defines topic.

The Courage of Intimacy:

Movie Masculinity in the Nineties

Paragraph indented ½ inch or 5 spaces.

1-inch side margins.

Opening interests reader with detail from film.

Quotation from electronic source Support from print source.

Mike Newell's 1997 film Donnie Brasco begins and ends with an extreme close-up of Johnny Depp's eyes. Shot in wide-screen so that the eyes literally span the entire screen, the image is a black-and-white snapshot that appears during the opening credits and returns as a full-color close-up at the end of the movie. Depp's lustrous eyes are large and black and beautiful, and gazing at them up close gives the viewer a surprisingly intimate sensation. Even within the conventional narrative that makes up the body of the movie, they become noticeably important; Web-site critic Rob Blackwelder observes that "Depp has [the central conflict of the movie] in his eyes in every scene," and Susan Wloszczyna of USA Today notes, "It's all in the eyes. Depp's intense orbs focus like surveillance cameras, taking in each crime and confrontation. He's sucked into the brutal, bullying lifestyle, and so are we." The close-up image at the beginning and end is one of the

Lee 2

1-inch margin at the top.
Heading ½ inch below top of page continues last name and page numbering.

few instances in which the film draws blatant attention to its own style, but the device calls attention to the film's central focus, its constant probing into the character at the center of the movie.

Somehow, without restricting the film to a first-person narration by Depp's undercover FBI agent, the audience comes to identify with him and understand the many pressures increasing inside his head simply by watching his eyes. They reflect his watchfulness, his uncertainty, his frustration, and his guilt—all without drawing too much attention to himself from his unsuspecting wise guy companions. He is guarded with his words, causing his closest Mafioso friend to remark, "You never say anything without thinking about it

Quotation from film.

first." His quietness invites viewers to read his looks and expressions, to become intimately acquainted with a character who constantly has to hide part of himself from the people around him, until they can virtually feel every twinge of fear or

Thesis stated.

regret that the character feels. Seeing this man trapped in situations in which he faces crisis after crisis, unwillingly alienated from his family and eventually his employers, trying only to protect the people he loves, viewers can ultimately recognize him as a more sensitive, struggling, and courageous hero than those celebrated in the past.

Johnny Depp in the title role of <u>Donnie Brasco</u>.

**Past contrasted with present.**

Over the decades, Hollywood has glorified the gruff masculinity of actors from Humphrey Bogart to Sylvester Stallone. Joan Mellen notes in her 1977 book <u>Big Bad Wolves: Masculinity in the American Film</u> that in traditional Hollywood films, espe-

**Source identified in text.**

cially the stoic action films of the 1970s, "physical action unencumbered by effeminate introspection is what character-

**Quotation from book with page number.**

izes the real man" (5). In the 1990s, it seems that much has changed; introspection has become a central part of leading-male roles. Character-driven films of the past year alone have won accolades for such intimate roles as Robert Duvall's tor-

**Other examples noted.**

mented evangelical preacher in <u>The Apostle</u>, Matt Damon's

Lee 4

John Wayne, the
epitome of mid-
20th-century American
masculinity.

emotionally needy genius and Robin William's mourning

therapist in <u>Good Will Hunting</u>, and the unemployed guys strug-

gling over issues like impotence and child custody in <u>The Full</u>

<u>Monty</u>. Thoughtfulness, vulnerability, and the ability to handle

relationships have become virtual requirements for the male

"hero" in the 1990s. The old-fashioned masculinity of characters

played by Clint Eastwood or John Wayne in the past has come

to be regarded as emotionally repressed and overly macho.

    The change is partly cyclical. Mellen cites the 1930s and

1950s as eras in film in which leading men were given greater

Background tied to
thesis.

depth. She says, "despite the limitations imposed by a repressive

**Clarification added in brackets.**
**Quotation with page numbers.**

society [in the fifties], film recovered for men an individual self with

a distinctive identity and a flourishing ego" (191–92). Actors like

Marlon Brando and James Dean, in particular, played insecure,

emotionally torn rebels who express tenderness in their relation-

ships with women and with other men. However, in the sixties, "as

**Ellipses for words omitted added in brackets.**

the Vietnam War progressed [. . .] maleness itself appeared under

siege and in need of defense," and "traumatic events of the sixties

induced the Hollywood hero to tighten up, reveal as little about

himself as possible, and to find comfort in his own recalcitrance"

(248–49). Things scarcely got better when "glorification of the vig-

**Quotations and summary from source.**

ilante male [became] the dominant masculine myth of the seven-

ties" (295) with films like <u>Dirty Harry</u> and <u>Taxi Driver</u>. "In the

seventies film, people are allowed no option: they must meet force

with force" (307). Following two decades of grim testosterone,

there was a definite reaction in the bubble gum pop culture of the

eighties, with flashy cartoon violence starring Sylvester Stallone or

Arnold Schwarzenegger presenting highly unrealistic images of

masculinity, and lighter portrayals like Marty McFly and Indiana

Jones gaining in popularity. By the nineties, American audiences

were no longer taking tough guy masculinity seriously, leading to

a trend of ironic humor in action films from <u>True Lies</u> to <u>Indepen-</u>

<u>dence Day</u>. It is doubtful that Will Smith would have been a favor-

ite action hero in any other era but the 1990s.

Lee 6

However, the crucial underlying shift in American culture is the debilitation of the conventional white male hero in a country he once monopolized. Trends in society within the last thirty years have led to greater freedom for women, minorities, and homosexuals, and as pride and power among these groups have increased, there has been a backlash against the white male. Today's hero has to prove that he is sensitive and completely respectful of every group mentioned above in order to remain sympathetic, forcing his previous role of unquestioned dominance to change drastically. In addition, now that women are going to work and less is expected of men in terms of being the provider and protector of the family and society, more is expected of them in their personal relationships. As noted recently by Sylvester Stallone, a fitting symbol of the old macho masculinity who is now trying to change his image to a more sensitive one, "I think the leading man of the future will be one who is beleaguered by the need to constantly define on film the male-female relationship." He also notes, "People want to nurture the underdog. The day of the strongman is over" (94). The themes of inefficacy in society, sensitivity in relationships, and a reaction to the old strongman ideal show up clearly in <u>Donnie Brasco</u>.

In the movie, FBI agent Joe Pistone, alias Donnie Brasco, goes undercover in the belief that he is on the side of law and

*Transition back to present day.*

*Quotation from published interview.*

*Analysis of film.*

order, with the simple goal of booking some major criminals; instead he finds a bunch of endearing but disturbingly violent men who become his closest companions for several years.

Plot summary and interpretation.

Particularly perplexing is his relationship with Benjamin "Lefty" Ruggiero, the trod-upon hitman whose thirty years of faithful service are rewarded with dirty-work assignments while younger wise guys are promoted over him. Lefty is the one who notices Donnie and recruits him into the organization, and from the start his faith in Donnie is clear; as Pistone smugly reports to a contact early in the movie, "I got my hooks in this guy." However, Pistone's smugness wears off as Lefty repeatedly invites him into his home, confides in him with his complaints and his dreams, and says unexpectedly one day waiting

Character analysis.

in the hospital where his own son is in the E.R. for a drug overdose, "I love you, Donnie." It is appropriate that the fictional Donnie Brasco is an orphan, because Lefty essentially becomes a surrogate father to him. Pistone, concerned for Lefty's fate, becomes more and more reluctant to "pull out" of his undercover assignment, revealing Donnie Brasco as a spy and leaving the blame (and death sentence) on Lefty. At one point he stops meeting his FBI contacts because they are pressuring him to pull out. Instead, he lets himself take on his mob alter ego more and more, tearing both his professional and personal lives apart.

Lee 8

In a way, the film is an interesting commentary on how ide-

als have changed, because it is set in the 1970s but made with

a 1990s ideology. Because it is based on a book by the real

agent Joe Pistone, who is currently living under the Witness

Protection Program, one might think the portrayal would be

strictly fact-based and would not be affected by the recent ob-

session with the sensitive male; but of course, one must never

underestimate the power of filmmakers in any era to interpret

their material with their own contemporary vision (note the por-

trayal of the Three Musketeers as aging and vulnerable in the

recent screen adaptation of <u>The Man in the Iron Mask</u>; the sev-

enties version of the same book depicted the Musketeers as

brash and irreverent). There is plenty of traditional macho pos-

turing in the Mafia sequences of <u>Donnie Brasco</u>, but director

Mike Newell places special emphasis on Pistone's sensitive re-

lationship with Lefty Ruggiero, his mentor in the mob, and on his

imperiled relationship with his wife. Newell, a British director

most famous for his vastly different romantic comedy Four Wed-

dings and a Funeral, also boasted about <u>Donnie Brasco</u>'s "ab-

solutely novel point of view about the Mob," focusing on "the

lowest rung, the have-nots" (Schickel), rather than the rich and

powerful men at the top so often depicted in mob movies. The

film focuses on the soulful side of a male protagonist in a genre

in which sensitivity is rare.

Electronic source
cited by author's
name only.

In fact, <u>Donnie Brasco</u> has been recognized as "a different take on the mob," an evolutionary step in the genre of gangster films. <u>Time</u> calls it a "neo-Scorsesian study of lowlife Mob life" (Schickel), and Blackwelder says that it "rises above the mire of its shopworn genre by showing the cracks in its characters' armor." Chris Grunden sums up the difference when he says, "Newell eschews fancy camera-work and visual flair to remain tightly focused on the human drama—he's made an actors' picture in a genre obsessed with style (<u>GoodFellas</u>, <u>Heat</u>)." Conventional gangster films usually depict the rise and fall of a charismatic criminal. The gangster movies of the thirties and forties featured fast-talking tough guys like James Cagney and Humphrey Bogart; Francis Ford Coppola's 1972 epic <u>The God-father</u>, which revived the genre, depicted the same glamour, ruthlessness, and power of the Mafia, on an even greater romanticized scale. But after a spate of stylized mob movies in the past twenty years, many reviewers of <u>Donnie Brasco</u> welcomed a new approach in a genre that was growing old and stale. Put

**Contrasts lead back to thesis.**

another way, <u>Donnie Brasco</u> is the film that finally brings its genre into the nineties by replacing its tough, glamorous hero with a real guy who can't live up to the stereotypes.

**Analysis of main character.**

Almost in direct response to the ideal of masculinity presented in the past, Newell shows that although at first Pistone is doing everything right—fitting perfectly into his undercover

Lee 10

persona, doing top-rate work for the FBI, and sending checks

home regularly to his family—he cannot "be the man in the

f—kin' white hat" that he thought he could be, as he puts it late

in the movie. He knows how impossible it is to fulfill his male

responsibilities in all three of his very different worlds after he

has ditched the FBI, almost lost his marriage, and realized that

his undercover work, once revealed, will be the cause of Lefty's

death. He has failed his own expectations of himself to save the

day and make everything right. The contemporary audience

recognizes the realism of the situation. As Stallone stated in his

interview, "The male is [only] the illusion of the protector and

guardian, [. . . b]ecause in this day and age, there is no security

he can offer" (94). By now the audience realizes that a hero

cannot always save the day in a conventional sense. In an odd

way, viewers even appreciate his failure because it has knocked

all of his arrogance out of him and left only an exposed, vulner-

able character.

    A contemporary audience can especially relate to the is-

sues of family breakdown, recognizing in Donnie's situation the

roots of the culture of estrangement and divorce which is so

widespread today. Violating the conventional lone male gang-

ster/cop figure, Joe Pistone has not only a wife but three small

daughters hidden away in suburbia, and he can't tell them any-

thing about his job without putting them at risk. His visits home

Analysis of relationships with other characters.

are less and less frequent, sometimes months apart, due to the

consuming nature of his "job." Although viewers can see from

the start the tenderness and love he has for his wife and daugh-

ters, his prolonged absences and broken promises (he misses

his daughter's first Communion) lead to intensifying arguments

between him and his wife. As she constantly reminds him, his

job is tearing their home apart, and not knowing what he is do-

ing makes it all the more unbearable. Pistone knows, as his

identification with the Mafia grows deeper and deeper, that his

involvement has serious consequences for his family, and this

mounting pressure becomes impossible to resolve when

weighed against the life of Lefty Ruggiero.

Contrasting example.

Regarding the role of women in Mafia movies, Mellen points

out that "well into the seventies the male protagonist of films

from The Godfather (I or II) to Serpico uses women solely to

discard them" (327). Wives in The Godfather are cheated on,

lied to, and in one case, violently beaten. At a pivotal moment at

the end of the movie, the wife of Michael Corleone tearfully asks

him if he has ordered the death of his sister's husband, and he

looks directly into her eyes and lies, saying he did not. She

smiles and believes him. Her character is, in fact, constantly

under the thumb of her husband who misleads her, ignores her,

and coaxes her into marrying him after not contacting her for

over a year. She and the other women in the movie are not once

Lee 12

consulted or listened to, no matter how much their husbands'
actions affect their lives.

Donnie Brasco could have been made in precisely the
same way. Pistone's wife Maggie is, after all, left at home for
months at a time while her husband is off doing his job for the
FBI. However, Newell makes the relationship between them a
pivotal storyline in the movie. Repeatedly in the course of the
narrative, interrupting the Mafia sequences, the audience sees
Pistone call or visit home, reinforcing his identity as a husband
and father. Viewers also note the progression as his relationship
begins to sour. The lowest point comes when Pistone shows up
at his home in the middle of the night to retrieve a bag containing $3 million in cash and confronts Maggie, who has found it
and hidden it. When she tells him that he has become "like one
of them," he strikes her, and both recoil in surprise, less shocked
at the blow than at the realization of what their marriage has
become. At this critical moment, he tries to tell her the truth. He
awkwardly explains the situation with Lefty and his fear of being
responsible for his death. He tells her that he is not sure of what
is right anymore. He tells her, "I'm not like them. I am them." It is
evident that the troubles of Pistone's marriage hurt himself as
much as his wife, and in a sense, dealing with them takes more
courage than risking his life as an undercover agent in the Mafia. The film treats this relationship delicately, and the woman

Contrasting example
related to film.

Incident from film
substantiates
interpretation.

Quotation from film.

here is not merely discarded or lied to, but confronted and con-
fided in, with her concerns presented as clearly as his own.

What makes Pistone's situation so compelling is that he
starts out believing that he can be one of the traditional "solitary
heroes who solve all problems for themselves" (Mellen 23) and
instead comes up against situations that are too difficult to handle. Joe Pistone slaps his wife, not to exert his male dominance,
but because he has lost control. When he tries to make things
right, he doesn't sweep her into his arms (and probably have his
way with her, in the true tradition of male heroes); he is almost
frightened to make a move and instead makes a gesture—
kissing the back of her head—to try and reestablish the emotional (not sexual) intimacy between them. In his early scenes
with Lefty, Pistone is noticeably on his guard and detached from
the affection Lefty is developing for him; later, when he has the
opportunity to be promoted within the ranks of the mob and
Lefty feels betrayed, Pistone tries to express his devotion by
visiting him at the hospital where his son has overdosed. When
Lefty orders him to leave, he refuses.

These gestures are some of Pistone's most heroic acts,
at least as Newell presents it. Although he is given a medal
and a check for $500 at the end of the movie for his under-
cover work (which is enough to secure scores of convictions),
his feelings about it are clearly mixed; his loyalty to the FBI

**Source identified in citation**

**Detail from film supports interpretation**

Lee 14

has been disintegrating as he has lost faith in their good guy/
bad guy rhetoric, and his primary concern—Lefty's safety—is
now uncertain. His success in infiltrating a group of depressed
Brooklyn wise guys is now a cause for guilt. It is at this point
at the end of the movie, as Pistone accepts his reward and his
wife tells him it's all over, that Newell returns to the extreme
close-up of Depp's eyes, and the audience sees how troubled
they are. Viewers are left with that image, indicating that Newell intended for them to leave the theater asking themselves
what it was all for—whether doing his job was really the right
thing or not. True to life, there is no easy, happy ending, in
which a man can die in battle or save the day and thus fulfill
his "masculine" duties. What matters, however, as viewers return to that close-up, is that they have seen Joe Pistone/Don-
nie Brasco's vulnerability and his devotion within his
relationships. If he feels confused or uncertain at the end, it is
because he has faced these emotional issues, which are far
more subtle than the challenges related to his job. The audience has seen him show more courage in his private struggles
than John Wayne ever did out on the frontier and can applaud
him for that.

> Return to detail used
> in first paragraph.

> Return to thesis.

| | |
|---|---|
| All lines double-spaced, including title and entries. | **Works Cited** |
| Title 1 inch below top of page and centered. | Blackwelder, Rob. "<u>Donnie Brasco</u>." Rev. of <u>Donnie Brasco</u>, dir. Mike Newell. <u>The Fairfield [CA] Daily Republic</u> 3 Mar. 1997: |
| First line at margin. | D5+. <u>Spliced Online</u> Archives Mar. 1977. 23 Sept. 1998 |
| Next lines indented ½ inch or 5 spaces. | <http://www.splicedonline.com>. |
| Entries in alphabetical order. | <u>Donnie Brasco</u>. Dir. Mike Newell. Tristar, 1997.<br><br>Grunden, Chris. "<u>Donnie Brasco</u>." Rev. of <u>Donnie Brasco</u>, dir. Mike Newell. <u>Film Journal International Online</u> Mar. 1997. 20 Sept. 1998 <http://www.filmjournal.com/reviews/html/ mar977.html>.<br><br>Mellen, Joan. <u>Big Bad Wolves: Masculinity in American Film</u>. New York: Pantheon, 1977. |
| Article title in quotation marks. | Schickel, Richard. "Depp Charge." <u>Time Magazine Online</u> 3 Mar. 1977. 22 Sept. 1998 <http://cgi.pathfinder.com/time/ magazine/1997/dom/970303/deppcharge.html>.<br><br>Stallone, Sylvester. "Masculine Mystique." Interview. <u>Esquire</u>. Dec. 1996: 89–96. |
| Movie title underlined. | Wloszczyna, Susan. "<u>Donnie Brasco</u>: A High Point for Lowlifes." Rev. of <u>Donnie Brasco</u>, dir. Mike Newell. <u>USA Today</u> 28 Feb. 1997: 1D. |

# A Portfolio of Professional Research Papers

Your research project will likely serve as your introduction to professional and academic journals. Both in print and online, journals are like a public square or coffeehouse for researchers in a particular academic field or a profession. Unlike mainstream periodicals, which tend to be published for profit and supported by commercial advertising, journals are usually subscription-only and supported by membership dues, university presses, or professional organizations. Periodicals also usually have their own staff—reporters, columnists, cartoonists, and photographers. Journals, on the other hand, publish articles that have been submitted to an editorial board of experts in a field for comment and approval. Contributor to most journals are not paid for their contributions, but instead gain professional credibility and accolades for their journal articles. When you begin your research by delving into professional and academic journals, you are witnessing the creation of knowledge as well as listening to the most current conversation and debate in a field. By citing these journals to support your own hypothesis or claim, your own research is a contribution to this ongoing conversation.

Although individual journals have their own criteria for style, length, and citation, you will notice certain conventions reflected across the three disciplines represented in this portfolio. All journal articles draw upon and give credit to contemporary sources and include either a Works Cited or a References list (depending on the citation style). Most journal articles begin with a hypothesis, a problem, or a claim and end with a resolution, a proposal for action, or a suggestion for further research. Finally, journal articles (unlike articles in general-interest periodicals) make certain assumptions about their audience. For example, articles in medical journals presuppose an audience familiar with human anatomy and physiology. Articles in journals of literary criticism assume that the audience is familiar with canonical literature. And articles in social science journals assume that their audience is comfortable with statistics.

Does this mean that your own research paper needs to conform to the conventions of journal articles in your field? Probably not at this point. The journal articles presented in this portfolio, for example, all describe *original* research. In addition, you are probably not writing your research paper for an audience of specialists or for submission to a professional journal. That said, you can learn a great deal about how professional researchers in a field talk to each other and communicate their ideas and discoveries by closely examining the structure and design, as well as the content, of journal articles.

---

CRITERIA FOR READING JOURNAL ARTICLES

---

- What are the journal's submission guidelines and style expectations? Check the front or back pages of a journal issue, or go to the journal's Web site and look for information on submissions (or solicited/ unsolicited manuscripts). Who is eligible to write for this journal? How are articles selected?

- Does the article include an abstract or summary? Begin your reading here. Look up unfamiliar words or concepts, and ask your professor for assistance with any equations, statistics, or other unfamiliar numerical information. Remember that journal articles are written for an audience of experts in the field—you might not yet be an "expert," but you should consider this an opportunity to learn more key concepts and become familiar with your field's jargon.

- What is the hypothesis or claim of this article? Compare it to your own working hypothesis or claim. Does the article support or contradict your main idea? Just because an article contradicts your working hypothesis doesn't mean that you are "wrong," but it is an opportunity to reconsider your working thesis. In addition, if you are writing an argument, you will need to give fair and equal consideration to opposing points of view.

## HOW TO CITE AN ARTICLE FROM A JOURNAL OF LITERARY STUDIES OR HUMANITIES JOURNAL

If you are writing a paper about the poet Sylvia Plath, you are probably fulfilling an assignment for a literature course. The citation style used for research papers and journal articles in literature is MLA (see page 205). A reference to the following article by Dahlke on an MLA Works Cited list would use this format:

Dahlke, Laura Johnson. "Plath's Lady Lazarus." The Explicator 60.4 (2002): 234–36.

# Plath's "Lady Lazarus"

### Laura Johnson Dahlke

Sylvia Plath demonstrated a "long-standing" interest in the biblical story of Lazarus that peaked after her first attempt at suicide in 1953, when she felt she "had been on the other side of life like Lazarus" (qtd. in Sanazaro 55). A. Alvarez states that Plath's "Lady Lazarus," first published in *Ariel* (6–9), is autobiographical: "The deaths of Lady Lazarus correspond to her [Plath's] own crises" (64). This poem, like many others in *Ariel*, features "power not centered in a loving deity" but in a "subject[ion] to dominance by pure power" (McClanahan 168). Unlike the biblical story of Lazarus, in which a loving deity uses power for good, Plath's "Lady Lazarus" reveals a struggle for power with a cruel deity that ends in annihilation.

In the story of Lazarus of Bethany in the Gospel of John, Jesus raises Lazarus from the dead so that the "people standing [t]here [. . .] may believe" (John 11.42). This display of power does not merely advertise God's power, but also benefits Lazarus and his onlookers. Those who witnessed the new life given to Lazarus believed in Jesus and were offered the promise of eternal life in heaven.

In contrast, Lady Lazarus's raising by Herr Doktor produces a struggle for power between them that leads to her eventual destruction. Herr Doktor exploits his power and dominance over Lady Lazarus, and she must fight to control her life. As Theresa Collins points out, "'Lady Lazarus' can be interpreted as a struggle for control [. . .] a dominion prevented by her torturer, Herr Doktor."

Like Jesus, Herr Doktor displays his power in front of a crowd, but in contrast, he desires admiration and personal gain from the "peanut-crunching crowd" (28). He does not offer new life to the crowd or Lady Lazarus, but works for his own benefit. She is unwrapped by the male enemy and his assistants to exhibit his power. By calling it a "strip tease"(29) Plath adds "sexual flavour" (Wagner 52) and magnifies the male dominance over Lady Lazarus. As she is unwrapped, she is disembodied—becoming a hand, a knee, skin and bone. She becomes his "pure gold baby," a perfect image of male possession (69).

Readers know that Plath was a poet and that "Lady Lazarus" is a poem.   1

MLA in-text citation style.

Thesis statement.

2

3

Acknowledgment of other critics.

4

5   For this expression of male dominance, however, Lady Lazarus responds. During this strip tease she insists, "I am the same, identical woman" (34), giving the reader the sense she is "more than a collection of parts" (Wagner 52). She also speaks to Herr Doktor, inviting him to "Peel off the napkin/O my enemy" and smugly questions, "Do I terrify?—"(10–12). Lady Lazarus's aggressive tone suggests that she wants to see if her appearance startles or shocks him so that she might gain an advantage over him. Her language demonstrates her willingness to fight against this cruel deity.

6   As he makes a spectacle of her and "betray[s] the persona's trust in him" (Wagner 52), she expresses her anger and yet ironically resigns herself, saying, "I am your opus/I am your valuable" (67–68). This clear resignation of power is reminiscent of Plath's own life, as Laura Frost points out: "Even if she [Plath] rebels against the oppressive patriarchal father [in this poem, Herr Doktor] her anger is reactive and she does not succeed at freeing herself from him" (52). Being raised by a male figure produces a fight for power that is readily given up and ends in death, not freedom.

7   Moreover, Lady Lazarus makes herself vulnerable even as she takes control and charges the crowd for the "eyeing of [her] scars"(58). These wounds of vulnerability are symbols of pain caused by her male-dominated life. They symbolize Plath's own scars from her father's death and husband's betrayal. Try as she might to overcome them, she still "turns and burns" (71).

8   A cyclical pattern appears in the poem, with Lady Lazarus challenging the cruel deity, Herr Doktor, yet eventually submitting to his power. Lady Lazarus's attempts to excel in her male-dominated world lead her to a destructive art. She states, "Dying/Is an art, like everything else/I do it exceptionally well" (43–45).

9   At the end of the poem, Lady Lazarus's final attempt to gain power comes in apparently threatening words:

Beware
Beware.
Out of the ash
I rise with my red hair
And I eat men like air. (80–85)

10   As Collins states, "The revenge and immortality promised in the last two stanzas are taken out of God's

[Herr Doktor's] hands and attained by the speaker," implying that Plath takes control over her enemy at the end of the poem. This final statement of revenge and immortality, however, is not a true promise. The speaker uses the generic "men" rather than speaking directly to Herr Doktor. In the face of her enemy's power, she becomes incapable of confrontation. The men she promises to eat are abstract people, not the specific man. Had the threat been personalized by using the simple "you" or repeating "brute" or "enemy" she could have redeemed herself, but she chooses not to personalize her warning. This weakens her threat, and again she resigns her power. The poem ends on terms of defeat.

In the biblical story of Lazarus, Jesus' power generates joyous new life. Lazarus lives again on earth with the promise of heaven awaiting. For Lazarus, life is precious both now and in the hereafter. In "Lady Lazarus," the reader senses that life for the speaker is not worth living. Her struggle for power ends in destruction. A cruel deity imposes his power on Lady Lazarus, and she can do nothing but fall prey to his will.

11

## WORKS CITED

Alvarez, A. "Sylvia Plath." The Art of Sylvia Plath. Ed. Charles Newman. Bloomington: Indiana UP, 1970. 56–68.

Collins, Theresa. "Plath's 'Lady Lazarus.'" Explicator 56 (1998): 156–58.

The Concordia Self-Study Bible: New International Version. Gen. Ed. Robert G. Hoerber. St. Louis: Concordia, 1984.

Frost, Laura. "Woman Adores a Fascist: Feminist Visions of Fascism from Three Guineas to Fear of Flying." Women's Studies 29 (2000): 37–69.

McClanahan, Thomas. "Sylvia Plath." Dictionary of Literary Biography. Ed. Donald J. Greiner. Vol. 5. Detroit: Gale, 1980. 163–68.

Plath, Sylvia. Ariel. New York: Harper, 1966.

Sanazaro, Leonard. "Plath's 'Lady Lazarus.'" Explicator 41.3 (1983): 54–57.

Wagner, Linda W. "Plath's 'Lady Lazarus.'" Explicator 41.1 (1982): 50–52.

*Author Affiliation:* Laura Johnson Dahlke, University of Nebraska at Omaha.

MLA Works Cited list.

Academic and professional affiliations are included in journal articles.

## READING A LITERARY RESEARCH ARTICLE

1. Read Sylvia Plath's poem "Lady Lazarus." Is Dahlke's argument clear and persuasive? What additional information would you need to respond fully to her argument?
2. Summarize Dahlke's article. (See page 197 for guidance on summarizing.)
3. What can Dahlke assume about her audience's knowledge base, and how can you tell? Where does she provide additional context for her argument, and why?

 www.mhhe.com/ **mhreader**   For more information on Laura Johnson Dahlke, go to:
**More Resources > Ch. 3 Research**

## HOW TO CITE AN ARTICLE FROM A PUBLIC POLICY OR SOCIAL SCIENCES JOURNAL

A research paper for a political science course is likely to require APA citation style. Note that this article, like many journal articles, follows APA in-text citation style. Because this article was retrieved from an online database (ProQuest), the References list does not include the indentations or italics you would expect in a print journal. A reference to the following article by Gould on an APA References list would use this format:

Gould, Jon B. (2002). Playing with fire: The civil liberties implications of September 11th. *Public Administration Review, 62,* 74–80. Retrieved August 9, 2004, from ProQuest Newspapers database.

# Playing with Fire: The Civil Liberties Implications of September 11th

Jon B. Gould

| Subjects: | Public policy, Civil rights, Surveillance of citizens, National security, USA PATRIOT Act 2001-US |
|---|---|
| Classification Codes | 9190 United States, 9550 Public sector, 4320 Legislation |
| Locations: | United States, US |
| Author(s): | Jon B Gould |

Article types:
Publication title:



Supplement:
Source Type:
ISSN/ISBN:
ProQuest document ID:
Text Word Count
Article URL:

Feature
Public Administration Review.
Washington: Sep 2002. Vol.
62 pg. 74, 6 pgs
Special Issue
Periodical
00333352
156494591
4459
http://gateway.proquest.com/
openurl?url_ver=Z39.88-
2004& res_dat=xri:pqd&rft_
val_fmt=info:ofi/fmt:kev:mtx:
journal&genre=article&rft_
dat=xri:pqd:did=000

Articles accessed
through online or
CD-ROM databases
list all publication
data. This
information does not
appear in this form in
a print version.

## Abstract (Article Summary)

The aftermath of September 11th has seen a worrisome
rise in invasive surveillance measures. Both adopted by
statute and initiated by agencies, these provisions provide unprecedented powers for government agents to investigate suspects and search individuals, whether they
are directly involved in terrorism or not. The prevailing
wisdom has been that the American people will accept
these restrictions as the natural cost of heightened security, and initial evidence suggests the public has been
willing to tolerate greater limits on civil liberties. However, over time such support will erode, leaving in place
permanent restrictions on civil liberties that not only will
concern Americans, but also may turn them against government officials and civic participation. Thus, contrary
to many interpretations of September 11th, this article argues that the policy response has only sown the seeds for
greater detachment from and dissatisfaction with government as the public becomes increasingly separated from
the workings and operations of public policy.

APA style requires
an abstract.

## Full Text (4,459 words)

*Copyright American Society for Public Administration
Sept. 2002*

*[Headnote]*

The aftermath of September 11th has seen a worrisome ₁
rise in invasive surveillance measures. Both adopted by

statute and initiated by agencies, these provisions provide
unprecedented powers for government agents to investigate suspects and search individuals, whether they are
directly involved in terrorism or not. The prevailing wisdom has been that the American people will accept these
restrictions as the natural cost of heightened security, and
initial evidence suggests the public has been willing to
tolerate greater limits on civil liberties. However, over
time such support will erode, leaving in place permanent
restrictions on civil liberties that not only will concern
Americans, but also may turn them against government
officials and civic participation. Thus, contrary to many
interpretations of September 11th, this article argues that
the policy response has only sown the seeds for greater
detachment from and dissatisfaction with government as
the public becomes increasingly separated from the workings and operations of public policy.

### The Legislative Response

2  The horrors of September 11th have been covered extensively by the popular media, both by same-day reporting
of the attacks and lengthier analyses of the long-term
effects on victims' families. In response to the terrorist
threat—one that, interestingly, was interpreted as rising
after the initial attacks—Congress passed and President
Bush signed the U.S.A. Patriot Act. Described by Attorney General John Ashcroft as a "package of 'tools' urgently needed to combat terrorism" (McGee 2001), the
legislation raises domestic intelligence gathering to an
unprecedented level. Among its several provisions, the
act stipulates that:

APA author/year
citation.

- The standards for wiretapping may be lowered.
  Whereas previously, the FBI could obtain a court
  order only if its "primary purpose" was to gather
  intelligence through wiretapping, the new law
  permits wiretaps if "a significant purpose" involves
  intelligence gathering. As a result, people merely
  suspected of working with terrorists or spies may
  be wiretapped.
- The FBI may share sensitive grand jury and wiretap
  information with intelligence agencies without judicial review or any safeguards limiting its future use,
  so long as the information concerns foreign intelligence or international terrorism.

- Law enforcement may access an individual's internet communications if officials can certify to a court that the information is relevant to an ongoing criminal investigation. This standard is much lower than the showing of probable cause required for most search warrants.
- Financial institutions will be required to closely monitor daily financial transactions and share information with government intelligence services. The law also allows law enforcement agencies secret access to an individual's credit report without judicial review.
- A new crime of domestic terrorism is created, covering conduct that "involves acts dangerous to human life." Presumably, members of Operation Rescue or Greenpeace would be covered under this definition, permitting the FBI to wiretap the homes of individuals who provide lodging or other assistance to activists.
- Non-citizens facing deportation may be held indefinitely on the attorney general's certification that an individual endangers national security.

Even before this act was adopted, the federal government ₃ had stepped up security and surveillance, detaining roughly 1,200 people in the weeks following September 11th, proposing military tribunals for captured insurgents, and interviewing nearly 5,000 visa holders. On the home front, security was increased at public buildings and gatherings and, of course, at airports. Most of the public is now aware that a trip through airport security may involve some manner of disrobing.

## Balancing Civil Liberties

The first response to these heightened measures has been ₄ largely supportive. As Chief Justice William Rehnquist suggests in his book *All the Laws but One: Civil Liberties in Wartime,* national emergencies "shift the balance between freedom and order toward order—in favor of the government's ability to deal with the conditions that threaten the national well-being" (1998, 222). Initial public polling bears out that view. In February 2002, 62 percent of respondents in a Greenberg poll agreed that "Americans will have to accept new restrictions on their civil liberties if we are to win the war on terrorism." During the same

In APA style, book titles are italicized. Database articles do not usually include italics or paragraph indentations, but print journals (and your own papers) should conform to the appropriate style guide.

period, only 12 percent of respondents in a Newsweek poll feared the Bush administration's response to terrorism was "going too far in restricting civil liberties," a finding virtually unchanged from a similar poll conducted in November 2001. When asked about specific strategies to root out terrorists, 78 percent of respondents in a September 2001 NBC/Wall Street Journal poll said they would be willing to accept surveillance of internet communications, and 63 percent of participants in a similar Harris Poll said they would favor expanded camera surveillance on streets and in public places.

5      To read these responses as offering the federal government carte blanche to search and pry, however, misreads the public's calculus of civil liberties. At the same time respondents are expressing support for expanded surveillance measures, they also have reservations about the potential creep of government snooping. When asked whether they believed the "U.S. government might go too far in restricting civil liberties," 62 percent of respondents in a March 2002 Time/CNN poll expressed concerns, a result that is in line with the 58 percent of respondents who, in a November 2001 Investor's Daily poll, said they were concerned about sacrificing "certain civil liberties in light of recently passed anti-terrorism laws."

6      Still, the issue runs deeper than these potentially conflicting results. Historically, the American public has expressed generic support for civil liberties principles while at the same time backing restrictions against a clearly identified or understood "other"—particularly a group that is reviled. As Chong explains, the public views civil liberties by balancing on one hand "considerations of [legal] principles and rights" and on the other hand "considerations about the people or groups that are involved in the issue, including considerations about how the issue might affect oneself" (Chong 1993, 870; McClosky and Brill 1983). For this reason, vast majorities in the Harris Poll can simultaneously name individual freedom as "a major contributor to making America great," while at the same time recommending the Ku Klux Klan be placed under electronic surveillance. Respondents balance their attachment to civil liberties against the risk of—or their animosity toward—an "out group."

7      A similar point is true in the area of criminal procedure, where Americans seem willing to countenance

surveillance and searches so long as police activity is directed against individuals presumed to be criminals. Over 80 percent of Americans support the "frisking" of individuals who appear "suspicious," and large majorities would allow police officers to search a car for drugs or stolen goods following a stop (Lock 1999). Perhaps the public is balancing the perceived intrusion of the search against the likelihood of uncovering criminal activity, but the more likely answer is that Americans are willing to accept restrictions that do not "directly affect them or the groups to which they belong" (Chong 1993, 887). This is the classic example of the respondent who does not care what the police do to suspected drug dealers—because he is not one— but who opposes home searches because he might have something "embarrassing that would be found" (ibid.).

There is much in the survey data to support this notion. Americans largely accept dogs sniffing their luggage, but they are resistant to police rummaging through their garbage (Lock 1999). Similarly, they oppose warrantless searches of homes (although there are legal grounds to do so), as well as the government's opening of mail (McClosky and Brill 1983). The common denominator is heightened concern when the search or surveillance hits close to home—that is, when individuals fear they may actually be the target of law enforcement. Among other things, this dynamic explains the curious results found in both Canada and the United Kingdom, where elites, who generally are seen as the "carriers of the democratic creed," were much more supportive than the general public of electronic wiretapping (Fletcher 1989, 227; Sullivan and Barnum 1987). Although researchers speculated that the elites' support may be premised on their understanding of the legal safeguards built into wiretapping (Fletcher 1989), the better explanation is that elites, because they have greater social power, need not fear the exercise of government power. By contrast, the general public worries that elites will authorize the surveillance of them (Sullivan and Barnum 1987).

Closer to home, recent surveys identify concerns about the very kinds of surveillance now permitted by Congress. A month before September 11th, over 80 percent of respondents in a Harris Poll said it was extremely important that no one be allowed to watch or listen to them without their permission. Their responses echo previous surveys of internet users, who, by large margins,

8 Short for *ibidem*, which means "in the same place." Indicates that the information comes from the same source as the preceding citation (here, Chong 1993, 887).

want to control the information that is collected about them. Although the questions were asked in the context of commercial tracking, the answers paint a consumer—and citizen—base that value its privacy.

10     Of course, at a time of national emergency, Americans are likely to give government officials increased leeway in surveillance, but in some sense that is the point: Americans' attachment to civil liberties is a balancing test that, if mishandled operationally or politically by government officials, will only backfire. In this respect, I believe there are six factors that help to explain when the public will countenance restrictions—even against themselves—to uncover those individuals who pose a threat. None of these factors is either mutually exclusive or a sufficient condition, but together they provide a checklist of concerns that public administrators ought to consider carefully.

1.  When the search or surveillance is not intrusive or the least restrictive method possible.

11  For several years now, airline personnel have asked travelers whether they packed their bags themselves. Presumably this is a personal question, but it is accepted largely because the method is not intrusive. Were the Federal Aviation Administration to order so, a ticket agent could satisfy himself of the answer by prying open a passenger's suitcase and checking the contents against the passenger's memory, but, quite understandably, government officials recognize both the flying public and the airlines are much more likely to accept a simple question. So, too, courthouses and other public buildings use metal detectors to scan for weapons rather than strip searching each individual who enters. Although there are individuals who approach such machines with dread (consider the example of Congressman Dingell, whose artificial hip set off a detector), most of us tolerate the detectors because we recognize they are the least invasive method available to check for weapons.

2.  When the perceived threat is great.[1]

12  There is a long history in this country of restrictions on liberty during times of war or national emergency. Abraham Lincoln suspended habeas corpus during the Civil War; newspapers were censored during World War I; Japanese Americans were sent to concentration camps during World War II; and the CIA opened mail destined

for the USSR during the Cold War. When a national emergency exists, the public is likely to "rally 'round the flag" to support the country or the president and accept such restrictions (Bowen 1989). To reach this point, though, the public must come to see current events as constituting an emergency, a process that relies heavily on news coverage—and with it, the ability of public officials to frame issues as involving national security and not other concerns (Nelson, Clawson, and Oxley 1997). In the post–World War II era, rally effects can be short lived, averaging just under a year (Parker 1995).

3. When those responsible for the search or surveillance are seen as competent.

Interestingly, Attorney General John Ashcroft did not [13] support some of the same measures that are now in the U.S.A. Patriot Act when he served in the U.S. Senate, in part because he did not trust the Clinton administration to exercise the new powers properly.[2] Similarly, in reforming airport security, Congress and the Department of Transportation worried whether airline passengers would accept heightened security measures if those provisions continued to fall under the control of private, low-cost bidders, some of whom employ minimum-wage employees. In addition to providing better oversight, the federalization of airport security was considered necessary to reassure the flying public that screening is being handled competently.

Footnotes are found at the end of a database article. In print journals, they are placed either at the bottom of the relevant page or at the end of the article, before the References list.

4. When the method employed is considered effective.

People accept metal detectors at courthouses, not only be- [14] cause the intrusion is relatively minor, but also because they believe the systems are capable of identifying—and then stopping—armed individuals set on harm. We will remain content with such measures until the first suspect brings a plastic explosive into court and detonates himself, at which point there undoubtedly will be calls for more sensitive screening to catch explosive materials. At the same time, the public will reject heightened security if its effectiveness does not overcome the level of intrusiveness involved. For example, drivers may tolerate random sobriety checkpoints so long as drunk drivers do not shift their travels to unchecked roads. To accept stops, searches, or surveillance, the public seeks assurance that the invasive methods will be effective.

   5. When limiting the search or surveillance to more relevant suspects might smack of illegal discrimination.

15  Given the demographics of the September 11th hijackers, some might call for intensive screening of young, Middle Eastern men who seek to board an aircraft. Certainly, past experience suggests this profile is more likely to yield a terrorist than, say, an 88-year-old white grandmother from Iowa. But while some criticize current measures that randomly—and thus, equally—search airline passengers at the gate, even more worry that targeted searches would inevitably lead to ethnic or racial profiling. Indeed, one of the surprising findings following September 11th was that 68 percent of respondents in a Newsweek poll said it would be a mistake to "put Arabs and Arab-Americans in this country under special surveillance."

   6. When individuals are unaware that the search or surveillance is taking place.

16  When is a search not intrusive? Potentially when the target is unaware of it. Of course, this is a bit tongue-in-cheek, for liberties are never more at risk than when government agents can intrude without any outside check on their activities. But the public cannot object to surveillance about which it is unaware. This is what makes post–September 11th security so interesting, for the public may object to intrusive searches of which it is aware, but even greater surveillance may take place outside of its purview. On one hand, the U.S.A. Patriot Act has given the FBI and the intelligence community greater latitude to conduct surveillance without the public's knowledge—searches that, even if more intrusive, will likely persist without objection unless agents trip up and their activities are exposed. On the other hand, the public has begun to experience stepped-up security when entering public buildings, traveling by air, or attending notable public events. Such increasingly intrusive searches are probably the closest that members of the general public have come to the types of intrusions or surveillance that they have approved (at least tacitly) in other areas of American life, particularly in the criminal justice arena. As "average citizens" begin to taste the invasiveness of pat-down searches, of airport screeners with dirty plastic gloves "unzipping toiletries bag [and] picking through shoes and dirty laundry" (Hilkevitch 2002), of the newly

proposed low-level x-ray scan of passengers (Branom 2002), they may very well rebel against the application of heightened security to "innocent individuals" presumably themselves.

## The Aftermath of September 11th—An Increasingly Civil Libertarian Public

The challenge for government officials in the wake of 17 September 11th is that the public will become less supportive of extreme security measures as the perception of a terrorist threat drops. Unless the war in Afghanistan is expanded, or until another terrorist attack is leveled on U.S. soil, the immediate memories of September 11th's horrors will fade, to be replaced by an increasing sense of normalcy. News coverage will shift from a frame of warfare to geopolitics, and, in turn, Americans will rebalance the calculus between heightened surveillance and their own civil liberties. To the extent that major airports continue to grind to a halt from false alarms,[3] the flying public—and the rest of the American public who learn about such mistakes from the media—will begin to doubt the competence of federal agents whose new responsibilities extend to airport security. With these doubts will come an unwillingness to submit to heightened security.

Most important, enterprising reporters undoubtedly 18 will uncover cases in which surveillance measures intended for would-be terrorists extend outward and inadvertently ensnare an innocent, sympathetic individual. Maybe it will be the young mother whose credit dries up after her bank mistakenly turns her name over to intelligence authorities for unusual account activity; perhaps it will be the grandmother whose interest in Islamic history leads federal agents to track her Internet usage; or maybe it will be the young father on a green card who faces wiretapping, indefinite detention, and eventual deportation because he attended a meeting to plan protests against the International Monetary Fund. There assuredly will be mistakes in the application of new surveillance powers—there almost always are—and the media will be ready to cover the stories. To the extent that the immediate threat of terrorism has begun to recede, these stories will touch an American people tiring of added restrictions on their behavior.

19     This is not to say that September 11th will turn this country into a land of civil libertarians: Ultimately, Americans are willing to accept restrictions on "others," particularly if the targets are considered threatening. Nonetheless, as government surveillance moves out of the criminal justice arena and Americans begin to see that they, too, may be targeted or searched, we may well experience a renewed debate about the power of government and the wisdom of narrowing civil liberties protection in the name of generic security. In essence, government may actually have created its own backlash in its heightened response to September 11th.[4]

## Widening the Distance between Citizens and Government

20   That the U.S.A. Patriot Act may have raised civil libertarian sentiments is only one part of the equation. The stepped-up security following September 11th has widened the distance between citizen and government, potentially dampening citizen participation in government and with it reducing citizens' trust in public institutions and officials. The dynamic here is analogous to the creation of social capital. According to Paxton (1999), social capital is created when individuals share intensive associations and high levels of trust. Given a confluence between interpersonal connections and goodwill, the social capacity for action is increased, in turn facilitating the production of social good. The same is true for political capital. When citizens feel connected to their government or government officials, when they trust these institutions or leaders, citizens are more likely to participate in the governing function, and officials are allowed greater latitude and goodwill to take decisive action to address social problems. By the same token, when citizens feel disconnected from their government, they are far less likely to participate in any type of political activity—including voting—and diminished trust, in turn, strikes a blow at the underlying legitimacy of government institutions and public officials (Lipset and Schneider 1987).

21     To be sure, the immediate effects of September 11th were to "rally 'round the flag" and the U.S. government. In the first six months following the attack, Americans reflected overwhelming support for national leaders and government policy, a level not seen in more than 30 years

(Moore 2002). But it is worth asking whether such approval reflects support for government in general or for the war on terrorism, particularly since pollsters have not always used the correct question design to estimate the public's trust in government (ibid.).[5]

Apart from these issues of measurement, though, there [22] is a larger concern lurking, for the very security measures installed following the September 11th attacks present the grave risk of further separating Americans from government. Whether the barriers are concrete or merely symbolic, government sends an important message to citizens about their role in democratic self-rule when many of the institutions of government are closed to public access, when individuals must undergo intensive screening to enter public facilities or to interact personally with government officials. The message—that the public should be content to delegate government functions to those inside—is only intensified when ever-increasing security measures limit the number of people who have "passed" and thus are privileged to participate in certain government functions while leaving others to sit outside policy deliberations because they are not deemed sufficiently "secure."

Americans may tolerate these distinctions for a while, [23] seeing them as a necessary price to ensure the continued, safe working of American institutions of government. But ultimately, government, and indeed democratic citizenry, accepts a steep risk in accentuating the differences between those on the inside who run government and those on the outside who are subject to it. For years, scholars have noted that political participation turns partly on an individual's belief that his voice can be heard (Verba and Nie 1987). Indeed, trust in government depends on the citizenry's view that public institutions and government officials are accountable and attentive (Weatherford 1992). Yet, when the public is urged to remain silently supportive of an antiterrorism campaign that may extend indefinitely, when citizens are told they will be ministered to, not participate in the ministering of government, when resources are redirected to defense and surveillance and away from direct government services, those on the outside of government may ultimately extend less goodwill to public officials as they feel increasingly more distanced from government's operations.

This change is not likely in the midst of an immedi- [24] ate military campaign, for public institutions and leaders are viewed more positively in times of crisis. But as time passes and war passions wane and as government returns to its more traditional functions, it will face a citizenry that not only retains reservoirs of doubt about government—in particular, the federal government—but also it has added fuel to the fire by adopting security measures that further distance the public. Having enjoyed popular support during a time of national emergency, public officials may face a sinkhole that few would have predicted from the attack, a public that ultimately will be less supportive of government functions from which it has been kept at arms length.

## Acknowledgments

The author thanks Scott Keeter, Ann Springer, and David Rosenbloom for their assistance on this article.

Electronic text clearly indicates what is a footnote.

*[Footnote]*

## Notes

1. Presumably the threat was there all along, just inadequately detected. In times of emergency, the presumption seems to be that further attacks must be coming, if only because we could not predict the ones that just hit.
2. In a 1997 op-ed in the Washington Times, Ashcroft said, "The Clinton administration's paranoid and prurient interest in [monitoring] international e-mail is a wholly unhealthy precedent especially given this administration's track record on FBI files and IRS snooping. Every medium by which people communicate can be subject to exploitation by those with illegal or immoral intentions. Nevertheless, this is no reason to hand Big Brother the keys to unlock our e-mail diaries, open our ATM records or translate our international communications" (A15).
3. The FAA reported that, between February 17 and March 11, 2002, 22 airport terminals had been evacuated nationwide because of "security breaches" (AP 2002). In many of these cases, agents either failed to screen any passengers or were unable to stop an individual whom the x-ray detectors had identified as suspicious.

4. For this reason, Congress may have limited the U.S.A. Patriot Act to 2005 unless reauthorized. Any backlash, however, would likely start before then.

5. Examining an ABC News poll from January of this year, 69 percent of respondents said they trusted the federal government to handle issues of national security and terrorism at least "most of the time." By contrast, only 39 percent of respondents trusted the federal government to handle social issues. The latter numbers are similar to responses from a 2000 National Public Radio poll testing generic trust in government. Then, 5 percent of respondents "just about always" trusted the "federal government to do what is right," with 24 percent saying they agreed "most of the time."

*[Reference]*

## References

Ashcroft, John. 1997. Welcoming Big Brother. Washington Times, August 12, A15.

Associated Press. 2002. Logan Has Had Twice the Number of Evacuations as Similar Airports. April 7. Available at http/www2.bostonherald.com/news/local_regional//ap_logan04072002.htm. Accessed June 10, 2002.

Bowen, Gordon L. 1989. Presidential Action and Public Opinion about U.S. Nicaraguan Policy: Limits to the "Rally Round the Flag" Syndrome. PS: Political Science and Politics 24(4): 793–800.

Branom, Mike. 2002. New Security Devices at Fla. Airport. Associated Press, March 15. Available at http://www_i640.com/handel-newstory.html. Accessed June 10, 2002.

Chong, Dennis. 1993. How People Think, Reason, and Feel about Rights and Liberties. American Journal of Political Science 37(3): 867–99.

Fletcher, Joseph F. 1989. Mass and Elite Attitudes about Wiretapping in Canada: Implications for Democratic Theory and Politics. Public Opinion Quarterly 53(2): 225–45.

Hilkevitch, Jon. 2002. Where Pawing Dirty Laundry Is Part of the Job. Chicago Tribune (Internet edition), April 1. Available at http:/www.chicagotribune.com/classified/automotive/columnists/chi-0204010230 aprOcolumn. Accessed June 10, 2002.

Electronic texts sometimes do not strictly follow style guidelines for Works Cited or Reference lists but still provide all necessary information.

Lipset, Seymour Martin, and William Schneider. 1987. Confidence Gap: Business, Labor and Government in the Public Mind. Baltimore, MD: Johns Hopkins University Press.

Lock, Shmuel. 1999. Crime, Public Opinion, and Civil Liberties. Westport, CT: Praeger.

McClosky, Herbert, and Alida Brill. 1983. Dimensions of Tolerance: What Americans Believe about Civil Liberties. New York: Russell Sage.

McGee, Jim. 2001. An Intelligence Giant in the Making: Antiterrorism Law Likely to Bring Domestic Apparatus of Unprecedented Scope. Washington Post, November 4, A4.

Moore, David W. 2002. Just One Question: The Myth and Mythology of Trust in Government. Public Perspective (January/February): 7–11.

Nelson, Thomas E., Rosalee A. Clawson, and Zoe M. Oxley. 1997. Media Framing of a Civil Liberties Conflict and Its Effect on Tolerance. American Political Science Review 91(3): 567–83.

Parker, Suzanne L. 1995. Toward an Understanding of "Rally" Effects: Public Opinion in the Persian Gulf War. 1995. Public Opinion Quarterly 59(4): 526–46.

Paxton, Pamela. 1999. Is Social Capital Declining in the United States? A Multiple Indicator Assessment. American Journal of Sociology 105(1): 88–127.

Rehnquist, William. 1998. All the Laws but One: Civil Liberties in Wartime. New York: Knopf.

Sullivan, John, and David Barnum. 1987. Attitudinal Tolerance in the United Kingdom: A Comparison of Members of Parliament with the Mass Public. Paper presented at the annual meeting of the American Political Science Association, September 3–5, Chicago, Illinois.

Verba, Sidney, and Norman H. Nie. 1987. Participation in America: Political Democracy and Social Equality. Chicago: University of Chicago Press.

Weatherford, M. Stephen. 1992. Measuring Political Legitimacy. American Political Science Review 86(1): 149–66.

*[Author Affiliation]*

Jon B. Gould, George Mason University, is an assistant professor of public and international affairs and a visiting assistant professor of law at George Mason University where he is the assistant director of the Administration of Justice Program. Professor Gould has written on the First Amendment, hate speech, racial and sexual discrimination, the Fourth Amendment, and justice administration. Email: jbgould@gmu.edu.

## READING A POLITICAL SCIENCE ARTICLE

1. How would you characterize Gould's political perspective or bias, based on this article? In what ways does he establish and justify his opinion? (For example, what does the article's title tell you about his beliefs?)
2. How many different kinds of sources does Gould consult in his research? How recent are his sources? Do you consider his sources to be relevant and reliable? Spend some time online and at the library consulting some of these sources.
3. Ask your reference librarian how to look up additional articles, books, and reviews by and about Jon B. Gould. Although the "author affiliation" at the end of this article gives you a sense of a writer's qualifications, searching out additional work that a writer has published can give you a better sense of his or her place in the academic or professional community.

| www.mhhe.com/ **mhreader** | For more information on Jon B. Gould, go to: **More Resources > Ch. 3 Research** |

## HOW TO CITE AN ARTICLE FROM A SCIENCE OR MEDICINE JOURNAL

Publications in the sciences and medicine follow the CSE (Council of Science Editors) style guidelines. This is a highly specialized citation style and not one you will usually be expected to use in most undergraduate writing courses. However, scientific, medical, and technical journals are valuable sources of information for research in other fields. For example, you might consult the following paper by Ebbeling and colleagues if you were writing an argument for an education class about providing nutrition education and helpful meals for high-school students. Even though the article is written by and for medical specialists, and its style as well as some of its language is difficult for readers without specialized medical knowledge, the critical reading skills you are developing should help you to work through its argument and determine its key points. Assuming that you would cite this paper for a research project in an education or political science course requiring APA guidelines, you would include the following citation on your References page:

Ebbeling, C. B., Sinclair, K. B., Pereira, M. A., Garcia-Lago, E., Feldman, H. A., & Ludwig, D. S. (2004). Compensation for energy intake from fast food among overweight adolescents. *JAMA, 291,* 2828–2833.

# Compensation for Energy Intake from Fast Food among Overweight and Lean Adolescents

Cara B. Ebbeling, PhD
Kelly B. Sinclair, MS, RD
Mark A. Pereira, PhD
Erica Garcia-Lago, BA
Henry A. Feldman, PhD
David S. Ludwig, MD, PhD

A summary like this usually introduces a scientific article. It gives the hypothesis, the parameters of the experiment, and the outcome.

**Context**   Fast food consumption has increased greatly among children in recent years, in tandem with the obesity epidemic. Fast food tends to promote a positive energy balance and, for this reason, may result in weight gain. However, if fast food and obesity are causally related, the question arises of why some children who frequently eat fast food do not become overweight.

**Objective**   To test the hypothesis that overweight adolescents are more susceptible to the adverse effects of fast food than lean adolescents.

**Design and Setting**   In study 1, we fed participants an "extra large" fast food meal in a naturalistic setting (a food court). The participants were instructed to eat as much or little as desired during this 1-hour meal. In study 2, we assessed energy intake under free-living conditions for 2 days when fast food was consumed and 2 days when it was not consumed. Data were collected in Boston, Mass., between July 2002 and March 2003.

**Author Affiliations:** Division of Endocrinology, Department of Medicine, Children's Hospital, Boston, Mass. (Drs Ebbeling, Feldman, and Ludwig and Mss Sinclair and Garcia-Lago); and Division of Epidemiology, University of Minnesota, Minneapolis (Dr Pereira).
**Corresponding Author:** David S. Ludwig, MD, PhD, Department of Medicine, Children's Hospital, 300 Longwood Ave., Boston, MA 02115 (david.ludwig@childrens.harvard edu).

**Participants**   Overweight (n = 26) and lean (n = 28) adolescents aged 13 to 17 years. Overweight was defined as a body mass index exceeding sex- and age-specific 85th percentiles based on the 2000 Centers for Disease Control and Prevention growth charts.

**Main Outcome Measures**   Energy intake determined by direct observation in study 1 and by unannounced 24-hour dietary recalls, administered by telephone, in study 2.

**Results**   In study 1, mean (SEM) energy intake from the fast food meal among all participants was extremely large (1652 [87] kcal), accounting for 61.6% (2.2%) of estimated daily energy requirements. Overweight participants ate more than lean participants whether energy was expressed in absolute terms (1860 [129] vs. 1458 [107] kcal, $P = .02$) or relative to estimated daily energy requirements (66.5% [3.1%] vs. 57.0% [2.9%], $P = .03$). In study 2, overweight participants consumed significantly more total energy on fast food days than non–fast food days (2703 [226] vs. 2295 [162] kcal/d; +409 [142] kcal/d; $P = .02$), an effect that was not observed among lean participants (2575 [157] vs. 2622 [191] kcal/d; –47 [173] kcal/d; $P = .76$).

**Conclusions**   In this study, adolescents overconsumed fast food regardless of body weight, although this phenomenon was especially pronounced in overweight participants. Moreover, overweight adolescents were less likely to compensate for the energy in fast food, by adjusting energy intake throughout the day, than their lean counterparts.

Consumption of fast food has increased rapidly since the 1970s[1] among adolescents from all socioeconomic and racial/ethnic groups across the United States.[2,3] Fast food is ubiquitously available and heavily marketed to adolescents.[4] An estimated 75% of adolescents eat fast food 1 or more times per week.[5]

 1

Superscript numbers refer to the reference list at the end of the text.

The increase in fast food consumption parallels the escalating obesity epidemic,[6] raising the possibility that these 2 trends are causally related. Characteristics of fast food previously linked to excess energy intake or adiposity include enormous portion size,[7] high energy density,[8] palatability,[9] excessive amounts of refined starch and added sugars,[10] high fat content,[11] and low levels of dietary fiber.[12] Previous studies, which used between- and within-subject comparisons, consistently demonstrate

 2

that consumption of fast food is directly related to total energy intake and inversely related to diet quality.[2,5,13–16] Some studies,[13,14,17] although not all,[5,15] have found a direct association between fast food and body weight.

3     These studies raise a fundamental question: if most children eat fast food regularly, why do some become overweight, whereas others do not? Perhaps certain individuals are susceptible and others relatively resistant to the adverse effects of fast food. Therefore, we hypothesized that adolescents who eat fast food regularly but are not overweight compensate for the excessive energy in a fast food meal by commensurately decreasing energy intake throughout the day; in contrast, overweight adolescents do not have this tendency.

4     The purpose of this investigation, which was composed of 2 studies, was to evaluate the effects of fast food on energy intake in overweight vs. lean adolescents. In study 1, we assessed energy intake during a fast food meal consumed in a naturalistic setting. In study 2, we compared energy intake under free-living conditions on days when fast food was consumed and days when it was not consumed.

## Methods

Every detail of an experiment is carefully described. Notice the use of chronological arrangement, narrative, and description.

### Participants

5     We enrolled 54 adolescents (26 overweight, 28 lean) aged 13 to 17 years who reported eating fast food at least 1 time per week. Fifty-one (24 overweight, 27 lean) of the 54 participants enrolled in study 1 also completed study 2. Newspaper advertisements and fliers, stating that the purpose of the project was to collect information on why and how teenagers eat fast food, were used to recruit participants.

6     Weight and height were measured using an electronic scale (model 6702, Scale-Tronix, White Plains, NY) and a wall-mounted stadiometer (Holtain Limited, Crymych, Wales), respectively. Body mass index (BMI) was calculated as weight in kilograms divided by the square of height in meters. The Centers for Disease Control and Prevention defines childhood *overweight* as a BMI exceeding sex- and age-specific 95th percentiles and *at risk of overweight* as a BMI between the 85th and 95th percentiles, using the 2000 growth charts.[18] In this investigation, we grouped adolescents who were

*overweight* and *at risk of overweight* and herein refer to them as *overweight.*[18] Adolescents with a BMI not exceeding the 85th percentiles were considered *lean.* We did not enroll adolescents with a BMI below the 50th percentile or above the 98th percentile and also excluded those diagnosed as having any major medical illness or eating disorder. None of the participants was taking prescription medications or dieting for the purpose of weight loss. As incentive, we offered each participant two $30 gift certificates, one following completion of each study.

The protocol was approved by the institutional review board at Children's Hospital, Boston, Mass. Written informed consent and assent were obtained from parents and participants, respectively. Data were collected between July 2002 and March 2003. 7

### Study 1

Participation involved 1 study visit. We instructed the participants to eat a standard breakfast of cold cereal and milk at 8:30 AM on the day of the visit and then to refrain from eating and drinking (except water) until after the visit. At 1 PM, we fed the participants a fast food meal from a national chain at a food court. All feedings were conducted in groups of 4 participants, on average, to foster socializing that is often part of the fast food experience among adolescents. Participants were grouped by sex and weight status to avoid any self-consciousness about eating that may be associated with these variables (e.g., girls eating less in the presence of boys, overweight adolescents eating less in the presence of their lean peers). 8

The same meal, modeled after prevailing "extra large" fast food fare (Table 1), was served to each participant. The following standard instructions were read to the participants before the meal: "In a few minutes, we will bring each of you a meal. Eat as much or as little as you like, until you have had enough. There is more food available, and you may eat as much as you want. Please do not share your food with others in the group. If you need more of anything, just ask." The length of the meal was 1 hour. During this time, a research assistant discreetly monitored food intake to ensure that ample food was always available. 9

Tables clearly present data.

**Table 1**  Characteristics of Fast Food Meal Fed during Study 1

| Menu Item | "Extra Large" Meal | | Refill Portion | |
|---|---|---|---|---|
| | Portion | Energy, kcal* | Portion | Energy, kcal* |
| Chicken nuggets | 9 pieces, 162.45 g | 438 | 4 pieces, 72.29 g | 195 |
| French fries | 1 "extra large," 199.68 g | 584 | 1 small, 76.04 g | 223 |
| Cookies | 2 bags, 115.28 g | 460 | 1 bag, 57.64 g | 230 |
| Cola† | 1 bottle, 20 fl oz | 254 | 1 bottle, 20 fl oz | 254 |
| Ketchup | 4 packets, 34.40 g | 36 | Readily available on the table | . . . |
| Sweet and sour sauce | 2 packets, 56.84 g | 69 | Readily available on the table | . . . |

*Energy values represent data derived from the Nutrition Data System for Research Software and are based on the gram weights of the "reference units." The total energy value for the "extra large" meal was 1.841 kcal.
†A refrigerated bottle of cola, rather than a cup of soda, was provided to avoid measurement inaccuracies associsated with variable amounts of ice.

Let readers know when and where to consult visual information.

10    Whenever approximately three fourths of the meal portion of chicken nuggets, fries, or cookies was consumed, a refill portion of the item was added to the tray (Table 1).[5] Empty cola containers were immediately replaced with full containers. Participants could obtain ketchup and sweet and sour sauce from the middle of the table at any time during the meal. This standardized protocol allowed us to provide more of the items that each individual enjoyed the most and, thus, would be likely to order in large portions if given the option. Following the meal, each participant estimated the relative size of the meal consumed during the study compared with the size of fast food meals that he or she typically consumed, using a verbally anchored, 10-cm visual analog scale, ranging from "much smaller than usual" to "much larger than usual."

11    The difference in weight between the amount of each menu item provided and that remaining on the tray after the meal was used to calculate energy intake. In preparation for data collection, 20 reference units of each menu item were purchased and weighed to evaluate variability in portion sizes. Coefficients of variation, ranging from 0.8% for a packet of sweet and sour sauce to 9.2% for an order of "extra large" french fries, confirmed that portions are highly standardized. Thus, amounts of food provided during the feeding study were estimated based on mean weights of the reference units. Using this method, we were able to serve food immediately after purchasing it,

thereby maintaining the temperature, palatability, and visual appearance that are expected by consumers. Leftovers were weighed on an electronic scale (item E1D120, Ohaus Corporation, Florham Park, NJ). The Nutrition Data System for Research Software (NDS-R; versions 4.04 and 4.05, Nutrition Coordinating Center, University of Minnesota, Minneapolis) was used to convert the gram weight consumed to energy intake (in kilocalories). We relied on the NDS-R, rather than nutrition information available from the restaurant, to allow direct comparison with 24-hour dietary recall data collected for study 2.

*Study 2*

Four dietary and physical activity recall interviews, 2 for 12 fast food days and 2 for non–fast food days, were administered by telephone to assess energy intake under free-living conditions. We used the NDS-R multiple-pass, 24-hour dietary recall method, which prompted the participant to list in sequence what foods and beverages were consumed during the preceding day, identify gaps in the initial list, and then provide details concerning each reported item. At the end of each recall, participants were asked to confirm the information provided and categorize the amount of food intake for the day as "usual," "more than usual," or "less than usual." Physical activity was quantified using a 24-hour recall protocol modeled after the method of Pate et al.[19] In brief, participants were asked to recall the activity performed most during respective 15-minute time blocks throughout the day and then to rate the relative intensity of each activity as light, moderate, hard, or very hard. A metabolic equivalent (MET level) was assigned to each reported activity to calculate a physical activity factor. As points of reference, resting has a MET level of 1.0, and brisk walking has a level of 5.0.[20] Total energy expenditure (in kilocalories per day) was estimated by multiplying basal metabolic rate, calculated from validated Food and Agriculture Organization, World Health Organization, United Nations University equations that include weight and height as independent variables,[21] by the physical activity factor derived from the four 24-hour recalls.

   Two criteria were used to define a fast food day. Criterion 1 specified that the participant eat at 1 of the 5 leading fast food establishments: McDonald's, Burger King, KFC, Wendy's, or Taco Bell.[22] Criterion 2 specified that the participant consume at least 1 menu item containing meat (beef, pork), chicken, fish, beans, or egg plus 1 additional item (e.g., fries, beverage, dessert). A non–fast food day was one that did not meet criterion 1. Days when participants ate at other restaurants, including pizza and sandwich shops, were classified as non–fast food days. Because we were evaluating the effects of fast food meals, as opposed to single menu items, intake was not assessed on days when criterion 1 but not criterion 2 was satisfied. Recalls were unannounced, to avoid reactivity, and conducted on nonconsecutive days. On average, we contacted each participant a mean (SEM) of 6.9 (0.3) times to obtain data for 4 days, including 2 fast food days that satisfied both criteria.

### Interstudy Comparison to Evaluate Underreporting

14  Underreporting of dietary intake is a well-recognized phenomenon, particularly among overweight adolescents, but little is known regarding differential underreporting among foods.[23-25] This phenomenon could bias data in study 2 in either direction: against our primary hypothesis if energy intake from fast food were selectively underreported, or in favor of the hypothesis if energy intake from fast food were reported more completely than energy intake from other foods. To evaluate the potential for bias, we examined underreporting of total energy intake and energy intake from fast food in overweight and lean participants, using data from both studies. Recalled total daily energy intake (study 2), averaged across 2 fast food days and 2 non–fast food days, was expressed as a percentage of estimated total energy expenditure to assess the accuracy of self-report of total energy intake. Recalled energy intake from fast food (study 2), averaged across the 2 fast food days, was expressed as a percentage of observed energy intake during the fast food feeding (study 1) to assess the accuracy of self-report of fast food energy intake.

### Statistical Methods

15  Statistical analyses were conducted using SAS statistical software (release 8.2, SAS Institute Inc., Cary, NC). For study 1, 2-sample $t$ tests were used to compare energy intake during the meal between overweight and lean adolescents. For study 2, analysis of variance was performed using the mixed linear model procedure to evaluate whether the interaction between weight status (overweight

vs. lean) and type of day (fast food days vs. non–fast food days) influenced total daily energy intake. In an additional model, we adjusted for self-reported relative amount of food intake. Preplanned contrasts were estimated from the fitted models for overweight and lean adolescents to determine the effects of fast food on total daily energy intake within groups. For the interstudy comparison, a mixed linear model was used to compare the accuracy of self-report between overweight and lean participants. The model for evaluating self-report of fast food intake was adjusted for the relative meal size rating in study 1. Using a 5% type I error rate, we estimated that a sample of 50 participants (25 overweight, 25 lean) would provide 80% power to detect a between-group difference in energy intake of approximately 150 kcal in study 1 and a difference in effect of approximately 260 kcal between overweight and lean participants in study 2. All results are presented as mean (SEM). Statistical significance was defined as $P < .05$.

## Results

Participant characteristics are presented in Table 2. There were no significant differences in demographic variables (sex, race, age) or height between the overweight and lean participants. The overweight adolescents tended to be less [16]

**Table 2** Characteristics of Overweight and Lean Participants*

| Characteristic | Overweight | Lean | P Value† |
|---|---|---|---|
| No. of participants | 26 | 28 | |
| Male/female | 14/12 | 14/14 | .78 |
| White/nonwhite | 10/16 | 9/19 | .63 |
| Age, y | 15.4 (0.3) | 15.3 (0.2) | .95 |
| Height, cm | 170.0 (1.6) | 167.6 (1.6) | .49 |
| Weight, kg | 80.5 (2.4) | 60.7 (1.4) | <.001 |
| BMI‡ | 27.8 (0.7) | 21.6 (0.3) | <.001 |
| BMI percentile | 93.5 (0.8) | 65.9 (2.6) | <.001 |
| Physical activity factor, MET§ | 1.48 (0.03) | 1.56 (0.03) | .06 |
| Total energy expenditure, kcal/d§ | 2767 (113) | 2500 (87) | .07 |

Abbreviations: BMI, body mass index; MET, metabolic equivalent task.
*Values are expressed as frequency for categorical variables or mean (SEM) for continuous variables.
†$\chi^2$ Tests for categorical variables and $t$ tests for continuous variables were used to compare overweight with lean adolescents.
‡A measure of weight in kilograms divided by the square of height in meters.
§Values were calculated based on 4 days of physical activity recall data.

**Table 3** Energy Intake from Fast Food Meal, Study 1

| | Mean (SEM) | | |
| --- | --- | --- | --- |
| Variable | Overweight (n = 26) | Lean (n = 28) | P Value |
| Energy intake, kcal | 1860 (129) | 1458 (107) | .02 |
| Energy intake, % total energy expenditure | 66.5 (3.1) | 57.0 (2.9) | .03 |

**Table 4** Total Daily Energy Intake on Fast Food and Non–Fast Food Days, Study 2

| | Total Energy Intake, Mean (SEM), kcal/d | | | |
| --- | --- | --- | --- | --- |
| Group | Fast Food Day* | Non–Fast Food Day | Difference, kcal† | P Value‡ |
| Overweight (n = 24) | 2703 (226) | 2295 (162) | 409 (142) | .02 |
| Lean (n = 27) | 2575 (157) | 2622(191) | −47 (173) | .76 |

*Recalled energy intake from fast food was a mean (SEM) of 1107(80) kcal for overweight and 1047 (56) kcal for lean adolescents.
†Difference scores are for fast food day – non–fast food day.
‡The P value for the type of day (fast food vs. non–fast food) by obesity status (overweight vs. lean) interaction was .05 unadjusted and .04 after adjustment for self-reported relative amount of food intake.

physically active than their lean counterparts ($P = .06$) and tended to have a higher total energy expenditure ($P = .07$).

### Study 1

17 When instructed to eat as much or little fast food as desired, the participants consumed 1652 (87) kcal, amounting to 61.6% (2.2%) of the estimated total energy expenditure. Overweight participants ate more than lean participants, whether energy intake was expressed in absolute terms or relative to estimated needs (Table 3). Relative meal size ratings did not differ between the overweight and lean adolescents (8.5 [0.4] vs. 7.8 [0.5], $P = .22$).

### Study 2

18 There was a significant interaction between type of day (fast food vs. non–fast food day) and weight status (overweight vs. lean) for total daily energy intake ($P = .05$ unadjusted, $P = .04$ after adjustment for self-reported relative amount of food intake). Overweight participants consumed 409 (142) kcal/d more on fast food than non–fast food days. In contrast, energy intake was not significantly different on fast food and non–fast food days for the lean participants (Table 4). With regard to physical

**Table 5** Interstudy Comparison to Evaluate Underreporting*

| Variable | Overweight (n = 24) | Lean (n = 27) | Difference† | P Value |
|---|---|---|---|---|
| Recalled total energy intake, % of total energy expenditure | 91.6 (5.9) | 106.9 (6.6) | −15.3 (8.9) | .09 |
| Recalled fast food energy intake, % observed, unadjusted | 64.9 (4.9) | 82.2 (7.0) | −17.3 (8.7) | .05 |
| Recalled fast food energy intake, % observed, adjusted‡ | 66.1 (6.2) | 81.1 (5.9) | −15.0 (8.6) | .09 |

*Values are expressed as mean (SEM).
†Difference scores are for overweight − lean.
‡Values are adjusted for relative meal size rating in study 1.

activity, there was no interaction between type of day and weight status ($P = .46$).

### Interstudy Comparison to Evaluate Underreporting

We sought evidence for incomplete reporting of food in-  19
take by examining observed dietary intake data in study 1 and recalled intake data in study 2 (Table 5). Recalled total daily energy intake, expressed as a percentage of estimated total energy expenditure, tended to be lower for the overweight compared with lean participants (−15.3% [8.9%], $P = .09$). Recalled energy intake from fast food in study 2, compared with observed intake in study 1, was also lower for the overweight compared with lean participants (−17.3% [8.7%], $P = .05$). Adjustment for relative meal size rating in study 1 did not materially affect this difference (−15.0% [8.6%], $P = .09$). Thus, as expected, overweight participants tended to underreport total energy intake compared with lean participants; however, the group difference in reporting accuracy was similar for total and fast food energy intake (−15.3% vs. −17.3%, $P = .84$), providing evidence against the possibility of a false-positive result.

## Comment

In 1989, a published statement warned that a lifetime of  20
fast food consumption may place children at increased risk for obesity.[26] However, until recently, the potentially adverse effects of fast food in youth have received limited attention in the medical literature.[2,5] With increasing recognition that excess adiposity confers serious health risks and that environmental factors may be driving the

A "comment" or "discussion" in a scientific article explains and contextualizes the findings.

obesity epidemic,[27] the role of fast food in promoting obesity has emerged as a topic of great interest and debate. Some nutrition professionals argue that fast food is contributing to the obesity epidemic,[27,28] whereas others support industry claims that fast food can be part of a healthful diet.[29]

21   Herein, we present the first investigation, to our knowledge, designed to evaluate the effects of fast food on energy intake in overweight vs. lean adolescents. Assuming a dietary pattern of 3 meals and 1 or 2 snacks per day, average meal size to maintain energy balance should not exceed approximately 30% of daily energy requirements or approximately 790 kcal in our study sample. Compared with this figure, the participants in study 1 massively overate (1652 kcal or 61.6% of estimated total energy expenditure) in the naturalistic setting of a food court. Overeating, observed in both groups of participants, was especially pronounced among the overweight. Moreover, the overweight participants consumed more total energy on days with than without fast food, in contrast to the lean participants, who consumed virtually the same amount on both days. This observation suggests that overweight individuals do not compensate completely for the massive portion sizes characteristic of fast food today.

22   There are several ways that an individual could maintain energy balance throughout a day that included large portions of fast food: by decreasing food intake subsequent to a fast food meal, by decreasing food intake in anticipation of a fast food meal, or by adjusting the size of a fast food meal based on how much of other foods have been or will be consumed. Our study does not allow us to determine in which of these ways the lean and overweight participants differed. We also cannot determine whether the failure to compensate fully for energy from large fast food meals is an inherent trait, causing obesity in susceptible individuals, or a secondary event that occurs after development of obesity. Nevertheless, these findings suggest that, at least, fast food consumption serves to maintain or exacerbate obesity in susceptible individuals.

23   Although excess energy intake in response to large portions is not unique to fast food,[7,30–32] we focused on this dietary pattern because of its dominant position in adolescents' diets and the possibility of a causal link to

the obesity epidemic. Indeed, fast food is designed to promote consumption of a maximum of energy in a minimum of time, a precept of not only the business model but also the very name. Other dietary scenarios (e.g., a buffet) might also provoke overeating and incomplete energy compensation if they resembled fast food in critical respects, including high energy density, low fiber content, extensive food processing (facilitating rapid swallowing with minimal chewing), and low satiating value. In those scenarios, however, the distinction with fast food may be more one of terminology or marketing than physiology. By contrast, overeating to the magnitude observed in study 1 would be virtually impossible with satiating, low-energy-density, high-fiber foods that require much chewing before swallowing (e.g., fruits, vegetables, legumes, whole grain products).

Several issues that pertain to study design should be noted. Strengths include evaluation of energy intake in a naturalistic setting in study 1 and within-subject comparisons in study 2, reducing the possibility of confounding by demographic and behavioral factors. Limitations include a relatively small sample size, restricted generalizability, and reliance on self-report for assessment of energy intake in study 2 (a methodologic issue common to all studies that aim to assess diet under free-living conditions).

Consistent with previous studies[23,24] that show that overweight participants have a particularly strong tendency to underreport what they eat, self-reported energy intake on non–fast food days in study 2 was lower for the overweight compared with the lean adolescents. However, owing to the within-subject design, underreporting would lead to a false-positive result only if energy intake from fast food were reported more completely (i.e., less underreporting) than total energy intake by the overweight vs. lean adolescents. The interstudy comparison suggests that this was not the case. Total daily energy intake in study 2, expressed as a percentage of total energy expenditure, was lower for the overweight than the lean adolescents. Recalled energy intake from the fast food meals in study 2, expressed as a percentage of intake observed in study 1, was also lower for the overweight adolescents. However, the magnitude of underreporting of energy intake from fast food compared with total daily energy intake by the overweight vs. lean participants was similar, even after adjustment for meal size rating, suggesting that fast food was not reported more completely than other foods. Moreover, prior studies[33–35] suggest that the opposite is likely to occur: overweight individuals may report high-calorie foods perceived as "fattening" (e.g., fast food) less, rather than more, completely than other foods. This effect, if present, would bias the study toward the null hypothesis.

26     In conclusion, our investigation suggests that overweight adolescents are less likely to compensate for the energy in large portions of fast food than their lean counterparts. These findings do not imply that fast food is without detrimental effect in lean adolescents. Previous research has shown that fast food consumption among children in a nationally representative sample affects diet quality in ways that would plausibly increase risk for obesity, regardless of baseline body weight.[2] Although the causes of obesity are multifaceted (as emphasized by the fast food industry[22]), public health measures to limit fast food consumption in children may be warranted. Such measures could include nutrition education campaigns, legislation to regulate marketing of fast food to children, and elimination of fast food from schools.

*In some academic and professional fields, the contributions of each author are specifically identified in published papers.*

### Author Contributions

As principal investigator, Dr. Ludwig had full access to all of the data in the study and takes responsibility for the integrity of the data and the accuracy of the data analysis.

*Study concept and design:* Ebbeling, Sinclair, Pereira, Garcia-Lago, Ludwig.

*Acquisition of data:* Ebbeling, Sinclair, Garcia-Lago.

*Analysis and interpretation of data:* Ebbeling, Pereira, Feldman, Ludwig.

*Drafting of the manuscript:* Ebbeling, Ludwig.

*Critical revision of the manuscript for important intellectual content:* Sinclair, Pereira, Garcia-Lago, Feldman, Ludwig.

*Statistical expertise:* Ebbeling, Pereira, Feldman.

*Obtained funding:* Ludwig.

*Administrative, technical, or material support:* Sinclair, Garcia-Lago.

*Funding/Support*

This study was supported by grants R01 DK59240 and K01 DK62237 from the National Institute of Diabetes and Digestive and Kidney Diseases (Bethesda, MD); the Charles H. Hood Foundation (Boston, MA); and grant M01 RR02172 awarded by the National Institutes of Health (Bethesda, MD) to support the General Clinical Research Center at Children's Hospital (Boston, MA).

*Role of the Sponsors*

The funding organizations played no role in design and conduct of the study; collection, management, analysis, and interpretation of the data; nor preparation, review, or approval of the manuscript.

*References*

1. Guthrie JF, Lin B-H, Frazao E. Role of food prepared away from home in the American diet, 1977–78 versus 1994–96: changes and consequences. *J Nutr Educ Behav*. 2002;34:140–50.
2. Bowman BA, Gortmaker SL, Ebbeling CB, Pereira MA, Ludwig DS. Effects of fast food consumption on energy intake and diet quality among children in a national household survey. *Pediatrics*. 2004;113:112–118.
3. Nielsen SJ, Siega-Riz AM, Popkin BM. Trends in food locations and sources among adolescents and young adults. *Prev Med*. 2002;35:107–113.
4. Story M, Neumark-Sztainer D, French S. Individual and environmental influences on adolescent eating behaviors. *J Am Diet Assoc*. 2002;102:S40–S51.
5. French SA, Story M, Neumark-Sztainer D, Fulkerson JA, Hannan P. Fast food restaurant use among adolescents: associations with nutrient intake, food choices and behavioral and psychosocial variables. *Int J Obes Relat Metab Disord*. 2001;25:1823–1833.
6. Ogden CL, Flegal KM, Carroll MD, Johnson CL. Prevalence and trends in overweight among US children and adolescents, 1999–2000. *JAMA*. 2002;288:1728–1732.
7. Fisher JO, Rolls BJ, Birch LL. Children's bite size and intake of an entree are greater with large portions than with age-appropriate or self-selected portions. *Am J Clin Nutr*. 2003;77:1164–1170.

8. Rolls BJ, Bell EA, Castellanos VH, Chow M, Pelkman CL, Thorwart ML. Energy density but not fat content of foods affected energy intake in lean and obese women. *Am J Clin Nutr*. 1999;69:863–871.

9. McCrory MA, Suen VM, Roberts SB. Biobehavoral influences on energy intake and adult weight gain. *J Nutr*. 2002;132:3830S–3834S.

10. Ludwig DS. The glycemic index: physiological mechanisms relating to obesity, diabetes, and cardiovascular disease. *JAMA*. 2002;287:2414–2423.

11. Gazzaniga JM, Burns IL. Relationship between diet composition and body fatness, with adjustment for resting energy expenditure and physical activity, in preadolescent children. *Am J Clin Nutr*. 1993;58:21–28.

12. Pereira MA, Ludwig DS. Dietary fiber and body-weight regulation. *Pediatr Clin North Am*. 2001;48:969–980.

13. Binkley JK, Eales J, Jekanowski M. The relation between dietary change and rising US obesity. *Intl Obes Relat Metab Disord*. 2000;24:1032–1039.

14. French SA, Harnack L, Jeffrey RW. Fast food restaurant use among women in the Pound of Prevention study: dietary, behavioral and demographic correlates. *Intl Obes Relat Metab Disord*. 2000; 24:1353–1359.

15. Jeffery RW, French SA. Epidemic obesity in the United States: are fast foods and television viewing contributing? *Am J Public Health*. 1998;88:277–280.

16. McNutt SW, Hu Y, Schreiber GB, Crawford PB, Obarzanek E, Mellin L. A longitudinal study of the dietary practices of black and white girls 9 and 10 years old at enrollment: the NHLBI Growth and Health Study. *J Adolesc Health*. 1997;20:27–37.

17. Pereira MA, Kartashov AI, Ebbeling CB, et al. Fast food meal frequency and the incidence of obesity and abnormal glucose homeostasis in young black and white adults: the CARDIA study [abstract]. *Circulation*. 2003;107:35.

18. Kuczmarski RJ, Ogden CL, Grummer-Strawn LM, et al. CDC growth charts: United States. *Adv Data*. 2000;(314):1–27.

19. Pate RR, Ross R, Dowda M, Trost SG, Sirard JR. Validation of a 3-day physical activity recall instrument in female youth. *Pediatr Exerc Sci*. 2003;15:257–265.

20. Ainsworth BE, Haskell WL, Whitt MC, et al. Compendium of physical activities: an update of activity codes and MET intensities. *Med Sci Sports Exerc.* 2000;32:S498–S504.

21. Dietz WH, Bandini LG, Schoeller DA. Estimates of metabolic rate in obese and nonobese adolescents. *J Pediatr.* 1991;118:144–149.

22. Brownell KD, Horgen KB. *Food Fight: The Inside Story of the Food Industry, America's Obesity Crisis, and What We Can Do about It.* Chicago, Ill: Contemporary Books; 2004.

23. Bandini LG, Schoeller DA, Cyr HN, Dietz WH. Validity of reported energy intake in obese and nonobese adolescents. *Am J Clin Nutr.* 1990;52:421–425.

24. Bandini LG, Vu D, Must A, Cyr H, Goldberg A, Dietz WH. Comparison of high-calorie, low-nutrient-dense food consumption among obese and nonobese adolescents. *Obes Res.* 1999;7:438–443.

25. Krebs-Smith SM, Graubard BI, Kahle LL, Subar AF, Cleveland LE, Ballard-Barbash R. Low energy reporters vs. others: a comparison of reported food intakes. *Eur J Clin Nutr.* 2000;54:281–287.

26. Fast-food fare: consumer guidelines. *N Engl J Med.* 1989; 321:752–756.

27. Ebbeling CB, Pawlak DB, Ludwig DS. Childhood obesity: public-health crisis, common sense cure. *Lancet.* 2002;360:473–482.

28. St-Onge M-P, Keller KL, Heymsfield SB. Changes in childhood food consumption patterns: a cause for concern in light of increasing body weights. *Am J Clin Nutr.* 2003;78:1068–1073.

29. Freeland-Graves J, Nitzke S. Position of the American Dietetic Association: total diet approach to communicating food and nutrition information. *J Am Diet Assoc.* 2002;102:100–108.

30. Diliberti N, Bordi PL, Conklin MT, Roe LS, Rolls BJ. Increased portion size leads to increased energy intake in a restaurant meal. *Obes Res.* 2004;12:562–568.

31. Edelman B, Engell D, Bronstein P, Hirsch E. Environmental effects on the intake of overweight and normal-weight men. *Appetite.* 1986;7:71–83.

32. Rolls BJ, Roe LS, Kral TVE, Meengs JS, Wall DE. Increasing the portion size of a packaged snack increases energy intake in men and women. *Appetite.* 2004;42:63–69.

33. Heitmann BL, Lissner L. Dietary underreporting by obese individuals—is it specific or non-specific? *BMJ*. 1995;311:986–989.

34. Johansson L, Solvoll K, Bjorneboe G-EA, Drevon CA. Under- and overreporting of energy intake related to weight status and lifestyle in a nationwide sample. *Am J Clin Nutr*. 1998;68:266–274.

35. Goris AHC, Westerterp-Plantenga MS, Westerterp KR. Undereating and underrecording of habitual food intake in obese men: selective underreporting of fat intake. *Am J Clin Nutr*. 2000; 71:130–134.

## READING A SCIENTIFIC, MEDICAL, OR TECHNICAL ARTICLE

1. In your own words, restate the hypothesis that the authors of this article set out to test. In what ways is a hypothesis like an argument? In what ways is it different from other kinds of arguments you may have read or written?

2. Which parts of this article were especially difficult, technical, or specialized? How did you deal with those parts of the article? What kinds of references would you need to consult in order to better understand the methodology and conclusions described here?

3. What is the purpose of the "Comment" section of this article? In what ways does it support, complement, or build on the initial hypothesis?

4. If you were writing a letter to the editor of your local newspaper arguing for better nutrition in school lunchrooms, which portions of this article would you cite, and why?

www.mhhe.com/
**mhreader**

For more information on Cara B. Ebbeling et al., go to:
**More Resources > Ch. 3 Research**

## part 2

# Issues Across the Disciplines

 chapter *4*

# Education and Society

*How, What, and Why Do We Learn?*

In "Learning to Read and Write," a chapter from his autobiography, Frederick Douglass offers a spirited affirmation of the rights we all should have to pursue an education. For Douglass, who was born into slavery, knowledge began not only with experience but also with the need to articulate that experience through literacy. The ability to read and write should be the possession of all human beings, and Douglass was willing to risk punishment—even death—to gain that ability. Today, all over the globe, as ethnic and political conflicts arise, men and women face the same challenge of expressing themselves. For even with a tool like the Internet, if one does not have the tools to express oneself or if the expression of thought is suppressed, the vehicle for conveying ideas, no matter how powerful, is rendered useless.

Perhaps the struggle for an education always involves a certain amount of effort and risk, but the struggle also conveys excitement and the deep, abiding satisfaction that derives from achieving knowledge of oneself and of the world. Time and again in the essays in this chapter, we discover that there is always a price to be paid for acquiring knowledge, developing intellectual skills, and attaining wisdom. However, numerous task forces and national commissions tell us that students today are not willing to pay this price and that, as a consequence, we have become academically mediocre. Is it true that we no longer delight in educating ourselves through reading, as Richard Rodriguez recounts in "The Lonely Good Company of Books"? Is it true that we take libraries for granted—we expect them to be available but never visit them? A democratic society requires an educated citizenry, people who refuse to commit intellectual suicide or self-neglect. The writers in this chapter, who take many pathways to understanding, remind us that we cannot afford to be passive or compliant when our right to an education is challenged.

Today we are in an era of dynamic change in attitudes toward education. Such issues as sex education, multiculturalism, racism, sexism, and immigration suggest the liveliness of the educational debate on campus. Any debate over contemporary education touches on the themes of politics, economics, religion, or the social agenda, forcing us to recognize that configurations of power are at the heart of virtually all educational issues in society today.

Without education, many of our ideas and opinions can be stereotyped or prejudiced, bearing no relationship to the truth. It is easy to understand how such views can arise if we are merely passive vessels for others' uninformed opinions rather than active learners who seek true knowledge. If we judge the tenor of the essayists in this section, we discover that many of them are subversives, waging war against both ignorance *and* received dogma. These writers treat education as the key to upsetting the status quo and effecting change. Operating from diverse backgrounds, they challenge many assumptions about our educational system and invite us to think critically about its purpose.

## Previewing the Chapter

As you read the essays in this chapter and respond to them in discussion and writing, consider the following questions:

- What is the main educational issue that the author deals with?
- What tone does the author establish in treating the subject? Does the author take a positive or a negative position?
- Does the author define *education?* If so, how? If not, does the author suggest what he or she means by it?
- What is the impact of society at large on how education is perceived?
- What forms of evidence do the authors use to support their views on education?
- How do the rhetorical features of the essays that focus on personal experience differ from those of the essays that examine education from a more global perspective?
- What have you learned about the value of education from reading these selections?
- Which essays persuaded you the most? Which the least? Why?

# Classic and Contemporary Images

## DOES EDUCATION CHANGE OVER TIME?

*Using a Critical Perspective*   Consider these two photographs of students in science laboratories, the first from the 19th century and the second from the present. What is the setting of each laboratory like? Who are the people? What does each photographer frame and leave out of the scene? Which educational setting seems more conducive to scientific or educational inquiry? Why?

Founded in 1833, Oberlin College in Ohio was the first U.S. college
to grant undergraduate degrees to women. The photograph reprinted
here shows both male and female students in a zoology lab
at Oberlin sometime during the 1890s.

At the beginning of the 21st century, most colleges and universities in the United States are coeducational, and it is no longer unusual to see both male and female students in a laboratory setting, as shown in the contemporary photo of a food science lab at the University of Maine.

# Classic and Contemporary Essays

## WHAT IS THE VALUE OF EDUCATION?

A famous dictum proclaims that "the pen is mightier than the sword." In Frederick Douglass's narrative and the excerpt from the work of Richard Rodriguez, we get two portraits that demonstrate the truth of the adage. Douglass's efforts at becoming fully literate freed him from what would have been a life of slavery. No weapon could have done that for him. It is obvious that Douglass learned his lesson well, for his prose is stately, clear, direct, and precise. His story speaks of a determined youth and man who had a powerful motivation in learning to read and write. Would he have done so without this motivation? Perhaps, because he seems to be a very self-directed individual, as is evident from the anecdotes he relates. Rodriguez, too, has a strong motivation to master, and even to excel at, reading and writing. Writing nearly 150 years after Douglass, and at a time when he needn't fear slavery looming over him, Rodriguez nevertheless perceived that by emulating his teachers, who promoted book reading, his own reading would make him a better person. He, like Douglass, sensed that there was something about acquiring knowledge and about expanding one's view of the world by learning how others viewed it that would provide him with a certain amount of independence. As you read the following two essays, you may wish to consider whether the quiet, modest tone each author projects may have something to do with the subject matter. For reading, although active and mind-opening, is still a private and "lonely" activity.

# Learning to Read and Write

### Frederick Douglass

*Frederick Douglass (1817–1895) was an American abolitionist, orator, and journalist. Born of the union between a slave and a white man, Douglass later escaped to Massachusetts. An impassioned antislavery speech brought him recognition as a powerful orator; thereafter he was much in demand for speaking engagements. He described his experience as a black man in America in* Narrative of the Life of Frederick Douglass *(1845). After managing to buy his freedom, Douglass founded the* North Star, *a newspaper he published for the next 17 years. In the following excerpt from his stirring autobiography, Douglass recounts the tremendous obstacles he overcame in his efforts to become literate.*

I lived in Master Hugh's family about seven years. During this time, I succeeded 1 in learning to read and write. In accomplishing this, I was compelled to resort to various stratagems. I had no regular teacher. My mistress, who had kindly commenced to instruct me, had, in compliance with the advice and direction of her husband, not only ceased to instruct, but had set her face against my being instructed by any one else. It is due, however, to my mistress to say of her, that she did not adopt this course of treatment immediately. She at first lacked the depravity indispensable to shutting me up in mental darkness. It was at least necessary for her to have some training in the exercise of irresponsible power, to make her equal to the task of treating me as though I were a brute.

My mistress was, as I have said, a kind and tender-hearted woman; and in 2 the simplicity of her soul she commenced, when I first went to live with her, to treat me as she supposed one human being ought to treat another. In entering upon the duties of a slaveholder, she did not seem to perceive that I sustained to her the relation of a mere chattel, and that for her to treat me as a human being was not only wrong, but dangerously so. Slavery proved as injurious to her as it did to me. When I went there, she was a pious, warm, and tender-hearted woman. There was no sorrow or suffering for which she had not a tear. She had bread for the hungry, clothes for the naked, and comfort for every mourner that came within her reach. Slavery soon proved its ability to divest her of these heavenly qualities. Under its influence, the tender heart became stone, and the lamb-like disposition gave way to one of tiger-like fierceness. The first step in her downward course was in her ceasing to instruct me. She now commenced to practise her husband's precepts. She finally became even more violent in her opposition than her husband himself. She was not satisfied with simply doing as well as he had commanded; she seemed anxious to do better. Nothing seemed to make her more angry than to see me with a newspaper. She seemed to think that here lay the danger. I have had her rush at me with a face made all up of fury, and snatch from me a newspaper, in a manner that fully revealed her apprehension. She was an apt woman; and a little experience soon demonstrated, to her satisfaction, that education and slavery were incompatible with each other.

3      From this time I was most narrowly watched. If I was in a separate room any considerable length of time, I was sure to be suspected of having a book, and was at once called to give an account of myself. All this, however, was too late. The first step had been taken. Mistress, in teaching me the alphabet, had given me the *inch,* and no precaution could prevent me from taking the *ell.*

4      The plan which I adopted, and the one by which I was most successful, was that of making friends of all the little white boys whom I met in the street. As many of these as I could, I converted into teachers. With their kindly aid, obtained at different times and in different places, I finally succeeded in learning to read. When I was sent on errands, I always took my book with me, and by doing one part of my errand quickly, I found time to get a lesson before my return. I used also to carry bread with me, enough of which was always in the house, and to which I was always welcome; for I was much better off in this regard than many of the poor white children in our neighborhood. This bread I used to bestow upon the hungry little urchins, who, in return, would give me that more valuable bread of knowledge. I am strongly tempted to give the names of two or three of those little boys, a testimonial of the gratitude and affection I bear them; but prudence forbids—not that it would injure me, but it might embarrass them; for it is almost an unpardonable offence to teach slaves to read in this Christian country. It is enough to say of the dear little fellows, that they lived on Philpot Street, very near Durgin and Bailey's shipyard. I used to talk this matter of slavery over with them. I would sometimes say to them, I wished I could be as free as they would be when they got to be men. "You will be free as soon as you are twenty-one, *but I am a slave for life!* Have not I as good a right to be free as you have?" These words used to trouble them; they would express for me the liveliest sympathy, and console me with the hope that something would occur by which I might be free.

5      I was now about twelve years old, and the thought of being a *slave for life* began to bear heavily upon my heart. Just about this time, I got hold of a book entitled "The Colombian Orator." Every opportunity I got, I used to read this book. Among much of other interesting matter, I found in it a dialogue between a master and his slave. The slave was represented as having run away from his master three times. The dialogue represented the conversation which took place between them, when the slave was retaken the third time. In this dialogue, the whole argument in behalf of slavery was brought forward by the master, all of which was disposed of by the slave. The slave was made to say some very smart as well as impressive things in reply to his master—things which had the desired though unexpected effect; for the conversation resulted in the voluntary emancipation of the slave on the part of the master.

In the same book, I met with one of Sheridan's mighty speeches on and in  6
behalf of Catholic emancipation. These were choice documents to me. I read
them over and over again with unabated interest. They gave tongue to interesting thoughts of my own soul, which had frequently flashed through my mind,
and died away for want of utterance. The moral which I gained from the dialogue was the power of truth over the conscience of even a slaveholder. What I
got from Sheridan was a bold denunciation of slavery, and a powerful vindication of human rights. The reading of these documents enabled me to utter my
thoughts, and to meet the arguments brought forward to sustain slavery; but
while they relieved me of one difficulty, they brought on another even more
painful than the one of which I was relieved. The more I read, the more I was
led to abhor and detest my enslavers. I could regard them in no other light than
a band of successful robbers, who had left their homes, and gone to Africa, and
stolen us from our homes, and in a strange land reduced us to slavery. I loathed
them as being the meanest as well as the most wicked of men. As I read and
contemplated the subject, behold! that very discontentment which Master Hugh
had predicted would follow my learning to read had already come, to torment
and sting my soul to unutterable anguish. As I writhed under it, I would at
times feel that learning to read had been a curse rather than a blessing. It had
given me a view of my wretched condition, without the remedy. It opened my
eyes to the horrible pit, but to no ladder upon which to get out. In moments of
agony, I envied my fellow-slaves for their stupidity. I have often wished myself
a beast. I preferred the condition of the meanest reptile to my own. Any thing,
no matter what, to get rid of thinking! It was this everlasting thinking of my
condition that tormented me. There was no getting rid of it. It was pressed
upon me by every object within sight or hearing, animate or inanimate. The
silver trump of freedom had roused my soul to eternal wakefulness. Freedom
now appeared, to disappear no more forever. It was heard in every sound, and
seen in every thing. It was ever present to torment me with a sense of my
wretched condition. I saw nothing without seeing it, I heard nothing without
hearing it, and felt nothing without feeling it. It looked from every star, it smiled
in every calm, breathed in every wind, and moved in every storm.

I often found myself regretting my own existence, and wishing myself  7
dead; and but for the hope of being free, I have no doubt but that I should have
killed myself, or done something for which I should have been killed. While in
this state of mind, I was eager to hear anyone speak of slavery. I was a ready
listener. Every little while, I could hear something about the abolitionists. It was
some time before I found what the word meant. It was always used in such connections as to make it an interesting word to me. If a slave ran away and succeeded in getting clear, or if a slave killed his master, set fire to a barn, or did
any thing very wrong in the mind of a slaveholder, it was spoken of as the fruit
of *abolition*. Hearing the word in this connection very often, I set about learning
what it meant. The dictionary afforded me little or no help. I found it was "the
act of abolishing"; but then I did not know what was to be abolished. Here I
was perplexed. I did not dare to ask any one about its meaning, for I was

satisfied that it was something they wanted me to know very little about. After a patient waiting, I got one of our city papers, containing an account of the number of petitions from the north, praying for the abolition of slavery in the District of Columbia, and of the slave trade between the States. From this time I understood the words *abolition* and *abolitionist,* and always drew near when that word was spoken, expecting to hear something of importance to myself and fellow-slaves. The light broke in upon me by degrees. I went one day down on the wharf of Mr. Waters; and seeing two Irishmen unloading a scow of stone, I went, unasked, and helped them. When we had finished, one of them came to me and asked me if I were a slave. I told him I was. He asked, "Are ye a slave for life?" I told him that I was. The good Irishman seemed to be deeply affected by the statement. He said to the other that it was a pity so fine a little fellow as myself should be a slave for life. He said it was a shame to hold me. They both advised me to run away to the north; that I should find friends there, and that I should be free. I pretended not to be interested in what they said, and treated them as if I did not understand them; for I feared they might be treacherous. White men have been known to encourage slaves to escape, and then, to get the reward, catch them and return them to their masters. I was afraid that these seemingly good men might use me so; but I nevertheless remembered their advice, and from that time I resolved to run away. I looked forward to a time at which it would be safe for me to escape. I was too young to think of doing so immediately; besides, I wished to learn how to write, as I might have occasion to write my own pass. I consoled myself with the hope that I should one day find a good chance. Meanwhile, I would learn to write.

8      The idea as to how I might learn to write was suggested to me by being in Durgin and Bailey's ship-yard, and frequently seeing the ship carpenters, after hewing, and getting a piece of timber ready for use, write on the timber the name of that part of the ship for which it was intended. When a piece of timber was intended for the larboard side, it would be marked thus—"L." When a piece was for the starboard side, it would be marked thus—"S." A piece for the larboard side forward, would be marked thus—"L. F." When a piece was for starboard side forward would be marked thus—"S. F." For larboard aft, it would be marked thus—"L. A." For starboard aft, it would be marked thus—"S. A." I soon learned the names of these letters, and for what they were intended when placed upon a piece of timber in the ship-yard. I immediately commenced copying them, and in a short time was able to make the four letters named. After that, when I met with any boy who I knew could write, I would tell him I could write as well as he. The next word would be, "I don't believe you. Let me see you try it." I would then make the letters which I had been so fortunate as to learn, and ask him to beat that. In this way I got a good many lessons in writing, which it is quite possible I should never have gotten in any other way. During this time, my copy-book was the board fence, brick wall, and pavement; my pen and ink was a lump of chalk. With these, I learned mainly how to write. I then commenced and continued copying the Italics in Webster's Spelling Book, until I could make them all without looking on the book. By this

time, my little Master Thomas had gone to school, and learned how to write, and had written over a number of copy-books. These had been brought home, and shown to some of our near neighbors, and then laid aside. My mistress used to go to class meeting at the Wilk Street meetinghouse every Monday afternoon, and leave me to take care of the house. When left thus, I used to spend the time in writing in the spaces left in Master Thomas's copy-book, copying what he had written. I continued to do this until I could write a hand very similar to that of Master Thomas. Thus, after a long, tedious effort for years, I finally succeeded in learning how to write.

## COMPREHENSION

1. What strategies does Douglass use to continue his education after his mistress's abandonment?
2. Why did the author's mistress find his reading newspapers particularly threatening?
3. Why does Douglass call learning to read "a curse rather than a blessing" (paragraph 6)?

## RHETORIC

1. What is the thesis of Douglass's narration? How well is it supported and developed by the body paragraphs? Explain.
2. The first couple of sentences in the story, though simple, are very powerful. How do they serve to set up the mood of the piece and the reader's expectations?
3. Cite examples of Douglass's use of metaphors, and discuss why they work in those paragraphs.
4. How would you describe Douglass's writing style and level of language? Does it reveal anything about his character? Justify your response.
5. Explain the way in which the author uses comparison and contrast.
6. What is Douglass's definition of *abolition,* and how does he help the reader define it? How does this method contribute to the reader's understanding of the learning process?

## WRITING

1. What does Douglass mean when he writes that "education and slavery were incompatible with each other" (paragraph 2)? Write an essay in which you consider the relationship between the two.
2. Both Douglass and his mistress were in inferior positions to Master Hugh. Write an essay in which you compare and contrast their positions in society at the time.

3. Illiteracy is still a major problem in the United States. Write an account of what your day-to-day life would be like if you couldn't write or read. What impact would this deficiency have on your life? Use concrete examples to illustrate your narrative.

4. **Writing an Argument:** Write an essay in which you argue for or against the proposition that American education continues to discriminate against minority groups.

 www.mhhe.com/ **mhreader** | For more information on Frederick Douglass, go to: **More Resources > Ch. 4 Education**

# The Lonely, Good Company of Books

### Richard Rodriguez

*Richard Rodriguez (b. 1944) was born in San Francisco and received degrees from Stanford University and Columbia University. He also did graduate study at the University of California, Berkeley, and at the Warburg Institute, London. Rodriguez became a nationally known writer with the publication of his autobiography,* Hunger of Memory: The Education of Richard Rodriguez (1982). *In it, he describes the struggles of growing up biculturally—feeling alienated from his Spanish-speaking parents yet not wholly comfortable in the dominant culture of the United States. He opposes bilingualism and affirmative action as they are now practiced in the United States, and his stance has caused much controversy in educational and intellectual circles. Rodriguez continues to write about social issues such as acculturation, education, and language. In the following essay, Rodriguez records his childhood passion for reading.*

1   From an early age I knew that my mother and father could read and write both Spanish and English. I had observed my father making his way through what, I now suppose, must have been income tax forms. On other occasions I waited apprehensively while my mother read onion-paper letters air-mailed from Mexico with news of a relative's illness or death. For both my parents, however, reading was something done out of necessity and as quickly as possible. Never did I see either of them read an entire book. Nor did I see them read for pleasure. Their reading consisted of work manuals, prayer books, newspapers, recipes. . . .

2       In our house each school year would begin with my mother's careful instruction: "Don't write in your books so we can sell them at the end of the

year." The remark was echoed in public by my teachers, but only in part: "Boys and girls, don't write in your books. You must learn to treat them with great care and respect."

OPEN THE DOORS OF YOUR MIND WITH BOOKS, read the red and white poster ₃ over the nun's desk in early September. It soon was apparent to me that reading was the classroom's central activity. Each course had its own book. And the information gathered from a book was unquestioned. READ TO LEARN, the sign on the wall advised in December. I privately wondered: What was the connection between reading and learning? Did one learn something only by reading it? Was an idea only an idea if it could be written down? In June, CONSIDER BOOKS YOUR BEST FRIENDS. Friends? Reading was, at best, only a chore. I needed to look up whole paragraphs of words in a dictionary. Lines of type were dizzying, the eye having to move slowly across the page, then down, and across. . . . The sentences of the first books I read were coolly impersonal. Toned hard. What most bothered me, however, was the isolation reading required. To console myself for the loneliness I'd feel when I read, I tried reading in a very soft voice. Until: "Who is doing all that talking to his neighbor?" Shortly after, remedial reading classes were arranged for me with a very old nun.

At the end of each school day, for nearly six months, I would meet with her ₄ in the tiny room that served as the school's library but was actually only a storeroom for used textbooks and a vast collection of *National Geographics*. Everything about our sessions pleased me: the smallness of the room; the noise of the janitor's broom hitting the edge of the long hallway outside the door; the green of the sun, lighting the wall; and the old woman's face blurred white with a beard. Most of the time we took turns. I began with my elementary text. Sentences of astonishing simplicity seemed to me lifeless and drab: "The boys ran from the rain. . . . She wanted to sing. . . . The kite rose in the blue." Then the old nun would read from her favorite books, usually biographies of early American presidents. Playfully she ran through complex sentences, calling the words alive with her voice, making it seem that the author somehow was speaking directly to me. I smiled just to listen to her. I sat there and sensed for the very first time some possibility of fellowship between a reader and a writer, a communication, never *intimate* like that I heard spoken words at home convey, but one nonetheless *personal*.

One day the nun concluded a session by asking me why I was so reluc- ₅ tant to read by myself. I tried to explain; said something about the way written words made me feel all alone—almost, I wanted to add but didn't, as when I spoke to myself in a room just emptied of furniture. She studied my face as I spoke; she seemed to be watching more than listening. In an uneventful voice she replied that I had nothing to fear. Didn't I realize that reading would open up whole new worlds? A book could open doors for me. It could introduce me to people and show me places I never imagined existed. She gestured toward the bookshelves. (Bare-breasted African women danced, and the shiny hubcaps of automobiles on the back covers of the *Geographic* gleamed in my mind.) I listened with respect. But her words were not very influential. I was thinking then of another consequence of literacy, one I was too shy to admit but nonetheless trusted. Books were going to make me "educated." *That* confidence enabled me, several months later, to overcome my fear of the silence.

6    In fourth grade I embarked upon a grandiose reading program. "Give me the names of important books," I would say to startled teachers. They soon found out that I had in mind "adult books." I ignored their suggestion of anything I suspected was written for children. (Not until I was in college, as a result, did I read *Huckleberry Finn* or *Alice's Adventures in Wonderland.*) Instead, I read *The Scarlet Letter* and Franklin's *Autobiography.* And whatever I read I read for extra credit. Each time I finished a book, I reported the achievement to a teacher and basked in the praise my effort earned. Despite my best efforts, however, there seemed to be more and more books I needed to read. At the library I would literally tremble as I came upon whole shelves of books I hadn't read. So I read and I read and I read: *Great Expectations;* all the short stories of Kipling; *The Babe Ruth Story;* the entire first volume of the *Encyclopedia Britannica* (A–ANSTEY); the *Iliad; Moby Dick; Gone with the Wind; The Good Earth; Ramona; Forever Amber; The Lives of the Saints; Crime and Punishment; The Pearl.* . . . Librarians who initially frowned when I checked out the maximum ten books at a time started saving books they thought I might like. Teachers would say to the rest of the class, "I only wish the rest of you took reading as seriously as Richard obviously does."

7    But at home I would hear my mother wondering, "What do you see in your books?" (Was reading a hobby like her knitting? Was so much reading even healthy for a boy? Was it the sign of "brains"? Or was it just a convenient excuse for not helping around the house on Saturday mornings?) Always, "What do you see . . . ?"

8    What *did* I see in my books? I had the idea that they were crucial for my academic success, though I couldn't have said exactly how or why. In the sixth grade I simply concluded that what gave a book its value was some major idea or theme it contained. If that core essence could be mined and memorized, I would become learned like my teachers. I decided to record in a notebook the themes of the books that I read. After reading *Robinson Crusoe,* I wrote that its theme was "the value of learning to live by oneself." When I completed *Wuthering Heights,* I noted the danger of "letting emotions get out of control." Rereading these brief moralistic appraisals usually left me disheartened. I couldn't believe that they were really the source of reading's value. But for many years, they constituted the only means I had of describing to myself the educational value of books.

9    In spite of my earnestness, I found reading a pleasurable activity. I came to enjoy the lonely, good company of books. Early on weekday mornings, I'd read in my bed. I'd feel a mysterious comfort then, reading in the dawn quiet—the blue-gray silence interrupted by the occasional churning of the refrigerator motor a few rooms away or the more distant sounds of a city bus beginning its run. On weekends I'd go to the public library to read, surrounded by old men and women. Or, if the weather was fine, I would take my books to the park and read in the shade of a tree. Neighbors would leave for vacation and I would

water their lawns. I would sit through the twilight on the front porches or in backyards, reading to the cool, whirling sounds of the sprinklers.

I also had favorite writers. But often those writers I enjoyed most I was least 10 able to value. When I read William Saroyan's *The Human Comedy*, I was immediately pleased by the narrator's warmth and the charm of his story. But as quickly I became suspicious. A book so enjoyable to read couldn't be very "important." Another summer I determined to read all the novels of Dickens. Reading his fat novels, I loved the feeling I got—after the first hundred pages—of being at home in a fictional world where I knew the names of the characters and cared about was going to happen to them. And it bothered me that I was forced away at the conclusion, when the fiction closed tight, like a fortune-teller's fist—the futures of all the major characters neatly resolved. I never knew how to take such feelings seriously, however. Nor did I suspect that these experiences could be part of a novel's meaning. Still, there were pleasures to sustain me after I'd finish my books. Carrying a volume back to the library, I would be pleased by its weight. I'd run my fingers along the edge of the pages and marvel at the breadth of my achievement. Around my room, growing stacks of paperback books reinforced my assurance.

I entered high school having read hundreds of books. My habit of reading 11 made me a confident speaker and writer of English. Reading also enabled me to sense something of the shape, the major concerns, of Western thought. (I was able to say something about Dante and Descartes and Engels and James Baldwin in my high school term papers.) In these various ways, books brought me academic success as I hoped that they would. But I was not a good reader. Merely bookish, I lacked a point of view when I read. Rather, I read in order to acquire a point of view. I vacuumed books for epigrams, scraps of information, ideas, themes—anything to fill the hollow within me and make me feel educated. When one of my teachers suggested to his drowsy tenth-grade English class that a person could not have a "complicated idea" until he had read at least two thousand books, I heard the remark without detecting either its irony or its very complicated truth. I merely determined to compile a list of all the books I had ever read. Harsh with myself, I included only once a title I might have read several times. (How, after all, could one read a book more than once?) And I included only those books over a hundred pages in length. (Could anything shorter be a book?)

There was yet another high school list I compiled. One day I came across a 12 newspaper article about the retirement of an English professor at a nearby state college. The article was accompanied by a list of the "hundred most important books of Western Civilization." "More than anything else in my life," the professor told the reporter with finality, "these books have made me all that I am." That was the kind of remark I couldn't ignore. I clipped out the list and kept it for the several months it took me to read all of the titles. Most books, of course, I barely understood. While reading Plato's *Republic*, for instance, I needed to keep looking at the book jacket comments to remind myself what the text was about. Nevertheless, with the special patience and superstition of a scholarship boy, I looked at every word of the text. And by the time I reached the last word, relieved, I convinced myself that I had read *The Republic*. In a ceremony of great pride, I solemnly crossed Plato off my list.

## COMPREHENSION

1. What was Rodriguez's parents' attitude toward reading? Did it influence his attitude? Cite examples from the essay that support your opinion.
2. What does Rodriguez mean by "the fellowship between a reader and a writer" (paragraph 4)? Why does he differentiate between "intimate" and "personal" forms of communication?
3. Rodriguez hoped that reading would fill "the hollow" inside him. What was the cause of his emptiness? Did he succeed in filling the void? Why did he find reading a lonely experience? Did reading fulfill any of his expectations?

## RHETORIC

1. What is the thesis of Rodriguez's essay? Is it stated or implied? Explain.
2. How does the author's use of narrative advance his views on reading and education?
3. What is the writer's tone? How effective is it in conveying his point of view?
4. Rodriguez uses uppercase letters (small capitals) when referring to signs advocating reading. Why does he use this device? How does it support his point of view?
5. The essay ends with an ironic anecdote. Why did Rodriguez choose to conclude this way? Does it satisfactorily illustrate his attitude?
6. What words or phrases imply that there is an ethnic component in Rodriguez's conflict? Is the subtlety effective? Justify your response.

## WRITING

1. Rodriguez's parents had a pragmatic attitude toward reading. What was the attitude in your home as you were growing up? Did your parents encourage your interest in reading? Did they read themselves? What is the first book you remember reading by yourself? Write an essay in which you describe your reading history.
2. Is reading still a significant source of information and entertainment, or has it been usurped by television? Is it important (or necessary) to be a reader today?
3. **Writing an Argument:** Rodriguez believed reading would make him "educated." Do you agree or disagree? Is reading vital to a person's education? How do you define *education*? Can it be acquired only through reading, or are there other contributing factors? Write an argumentative essay on this topic.

## Synthesis: Classic and Contemporary Questions for Comparison

1. Both Rodriguez and Douglass were motivated to educate themselves in a society inimical to this achievement. Compare and contrast their struggles and attitudes in their quests for knowledge.
2. Pretend you are Rodriguez, and write a letter to Douglass addressing the issues of minorities and education in present-day America. What would Rodriguez say about the progress of minorities in our society?
3. Although Rodriguez and Douglass treat a similar theme, they communicate their messages differently. Which narration do you consider more powerful, and why?
4. Rodriguez explores the theme of isolation in his story. Is there any evidence that this feeling was shared by Douglass in his efforts to learn how to read? Use proof from both narratives to support your view.
5. Slavery was an obvious obstacle to Douglass's attempt to educate himself. What impeded Rodriguez's progress? Were similar forces at work? Cite examples from Rodriguez's narrative to prove your point.

# Little Asia on the Hill

### Timothy Egan

*Timothy Egan (b. 1954) is a* New York Times *correspondent based in Seattle, Washington, where he was born. Egan, who has a BA from the University of Washington, uses the Pacific Northwest as the basis for his nonfiction. His work includes* The Good Rain: Across Time and Travel in the Pacific Northwest *(1990) and* Lasso the Wind: Away to the New West *(1998). Egan's most recent book,* The Worst Hard Time: The Untold Story of Those Who Survived the Great American Dust Bowl *(2005), received the 2006 National Book Award for nonfiction. In this article, which appeared in a* Sunday New York Times *educational supplement in 2007, Egan reports on "the rise of the Asian campus."*

When Jonathan Hu was going to high school in suburban Southern Califor-   1
nia, he rarely heard anyone speaking Chinese. But striding through campus on his way to class at the University of California, Berkeley, Mr. Hu hears

Mandarin all the time, in plazas, cafeterias, classrooms, study halls, dorms and fast-food outlets. It is part of the soundtrack at this iconic university, along with Cantonese, English, Spanish and, of course, the perpetual jack-hammers from the perpetual construction projects spurred by the perpetual fund drives.

2      "Here, many people speak Chinese as their primary language," says Mr. Hu, a sophomore. "It's nice. You really feel like you don't stand out."

3      Today, he is iPod-free, a rare condition on campus, taking in the early winter sun at the dour concrete plaza of the Free Speech Movement Cafe, named for the protests led by Mario Savio in 1964, when the administration tried to muzzle political activity. "Free speech marks us off from the stones and stars," reads a Savio quote on the cafe wall, "just below the angels."

4      There are now mostly small protests, against the new chain stores invading Telegraph Avenue, just outside the campus entrance, and to save the old oak trees scheduled for removal so the football stadium can be renovated. The biggest buzz on Telegraph one week was the grand opening of a chain restaurant—the new Chipotle's, which drew a crowd of students eager to get in. The scent of patchouli oil and reefer is long gone; the street is posted as a drug-free zone.

5      And at least on this morning, there is very little speech of any kind inside the Free Speech Cafe; almost without exception, students are face-planted in their laptops, silently downloading class notes, music, messages. It could be the library but for the line for lattes. On mornings like this, the public university

beneath the towering campanile seems like a small, industrious city of über-students in flops.

I ask Mr. Hu what it's like to be on a campus that is overwhelmingly Asian— 6 what it's like to be of the demographic moment. This fall and last, the number of Asian freshmen at Berkeley has been at a record high, about 46 percent. The overall undergraduate population is 41 percent Asian. On this golden campus, where a creek runs through a redwood grove, there are residence halls with Asian themes; good dim sum is never more than a five-minute walk away; heaping, spicy bowls of pho are served up in the Bear's Lair cafeteria; and numerous social clubs are linked by common ancestry to countries far across the Pacific.

Mr. Hu shrugs, saying there is a fair amount of "selective self-racial segre- 7 gation," which is not unusual at a university this size: about 24,000 undergraduates. "The different ethnic groups don't really interact that much," he says. "There's definitely a sense of sticking with your community." But, he quickly adds, "People of my generation don't look at race as that big of a deal. People here, the freshmen and sophomores, they're pretty much like your average American teenagers."

Spend a few days at Berkeley, on the classically manicured slope overlooking 8 San Francisco Bay and the distant Pacific, and soon enough the sound of foreign languages becomes less distinct. This is a global campus in a global age. And more than any time in its history, it looks toward the setting sun for its identity.

The revolution at Berkeley is a quiet one, a slow turning of the forces of im- 9 migration and demographics. What is troubling to some is that the big public school on the hill certainly does not look like the ethnic face of California, which is 12 percent Asian, more than twice the national average. But it is the new face of the state's vaunted public university system. Asians make up the largest single ethnic group, 37 percent, at its nine undergraduate campuses.

The oft-cited goal of a public university is to be a microcosm—in this case, 10 of the nation's most populous, most demographically dynamic state—and to enrich the educational experience with a variety of cultures, economic backgrounds and viewpoints.

But 10 years after California passed Proposition 209, voting to eliminate 11 racial preferences in the public sector, university administrators find such balance harder to attain. At the same time, affirmative action is being challenged on a number of new fronts, in court and at state ballot boxes. And elite colleges have recently come under attack for practicing it—specifically, for bypassing highly credentialed Asian applicants in favor of students of color with less stellar test scores and grades.

In California, the rise of the Asian campus, of the strict meritocracy, has come 12 at the expense of historically underrepresented blacks and Hispanics. This year, in a class of 4809, there are only 100 black freshmen at the University of California at Los Angeles—the lowest number in 33 years. At Berkeley, 3.6 percent of freshmen are black, barely half the statewide proportion. (In 1997, just before the full force of Proposition 209 went into effect, the proportion of black freshmen matched the state population, 7 percent.) The percentage of Hispanic freshmen at

Berkeley (11 percent) is not even a third of the state proportion (35 percent). White freshmen (29 percent) are also below the state average (44 percent).

13      This is in part because getting into Berkeley—U.S. News & World Report's top-ranked public university—has never been more daunting. There were 41,750 applicants for this year's freshman class of 4,157. Nearly half had a weighted grade point average of 4.0 or better (weighted for advanced courses). There is even grumbling from "the old Blues"—older alumni named for the school color—"who complain because their kids can't get in," says Gregg Thomson, director of the Office of Student Research.

14      Mr. Hu applied to a lot of colleges, but Berkeley felt right for him from the start. "It's the intellectual atmosphere—this place is intense."

15      Mr. Hu says he was pressured by a professor to go into something like medicine or engineering. "It's a stereotype, but a lot of Asians who come here just study engineering and the sciences," he says. "I was never interested in that."

16      But as the only son of professionals born in China, Mr. Hu fits the profile of Asians at Berkeley in at least one way: they are predominantly first-generation American. About 95 percent of Asian freshmen come from a family in which one or both parents were born outside the United States.

17      He dashes off to class, and I wander through the serene setting of Memorial Glade, in the center of campus, and then loop over to Sproul Plaza, the beating heart of the university, where dozens of tables are set up by clubs representing every conceivable ethnic group. Out of nowhere, an a cappella group, mostly Asian men, appears and starts singing a Beach Boys song. Yes, tradition still matters in California.

18      Across the United States, at elite private and public universities, Asian enrollment is near an all-time high. Asian-Americans make up less than 5 percent of the population but typically make up 10 to 30 percent of students at the nation's best colleges: in 2005, the last year with across-the-board numbers, Asians made up 24 percent of the undergraduate population at Carnegie Mellon and at Stanford, 27 percent at the Massachusetts Institute of Technology, 14 percent at Yale and 13 percent at Princeton.

19      And according to advocates of race-neutral admissions policies, those numbers should be even higher.

20      Asians have become the "new Jews," in the phrase of Daniel Golden, whose recent book, "The Price of Admission: How America's Ruling Class Buys Its Way into Elite Colleges—and Who Gets Left outside the Gates," is a polemic against university admissions policies. Mr. Golden, a reporter for The Wall Street Journal, is referring to evidence that, in the first half of the 20th century, Ivy League schools limited the number of Jewish students despite their outstanding academic records to maintain the primacy of upper-class Protestants. Today, he writes, "Asian-Americans are the odd group out, lacking racial preferences enjoyed by other minorities and the advantages of wealth and lineage mostly accrued by upper-class whites. Asians are typecast in college admissions offices as quasi-robots programmed by their parents to ace math and science."

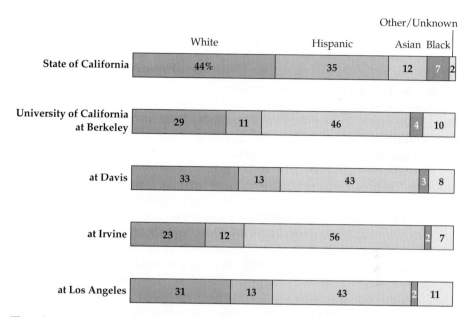

The ethnic breakdown of freshmen, fall 2006, at the four largest University of California campuses, compared with the population of the State of California.
Copyright © 2007 The New York Times Company. Reprinted by permission.

As if to illustrate the point, a study released in October by the Center for Equal   21
Opportunity, an advocacy group opposing race-conscious admissions, showed that in 2005 Asian-Americans were admitted to the University of Michigan, Ann Arbor, at a much lower rate (54 percent) than black applicants (71 percent) and Hispanic applicants (79 percent)—despite median SAT scores that were 140 points higher than Hispanics and 240 points higher than blacks.

To force the issue on a legal level, a freshman at Yale filed a complaint in   22
the fall with the Department of Education's Office of Civil Rights, contending he was denied admission to Princeton because he is Asian. The student, Jian Li, the son of Chinese immigrants in Livingston, N.J., had a perfect SAT score and near-perfect grades, including numerous Advanced Placement courses.

"This is just a very, very egregious system," Mr. Li told me. "Asians are   23
held to different standards simply because of their race."

To back his claim, he cites a 2005 study by Thomas J. Espenshade and Chang   24
Y. Chung, both of Princeton, which concludes that if elite universities were to disregard race, Asians would fill nearly four of five spots that now go to blacks or Hispanics. Affirmative action has a neutral effect on the number of whites admitted, Mr. Li is arguing, but it raises the bar for Asians. The way Princeton selects its entering class, Mr. Li wrote in his complaint, "seems to be a calculated move by a historically white institution to protect its racial identity while at the same time maintaining a facade of progressivism."

25    Private institutions can commit to affirmative action, even with state bans, but federal money could be revoked if they are found to be discriminating. Mr. Li is seeking suspension of federal financial assistance to Princeton. "I'm not seeking anything personally," he says. "I'm happy at Yale. But I grew up thinking that in America race should not matter."

26    Admissions officials have long denied that they apply quotas. Nonetheless, race is important "to ensure a diverse student body," says Cass Cliatt, a Princeton spokeswoman. But, she adds, "Looking at the merits of race is not the same as the opposite"—discrimination.

27    Elite colleges like Princeton review the "total package," in her words, looking at special talents, extracurricular interests and socioeconomics—factors like whether the applicant is the first in the family to go to college or was raised by a single mother. "There's no set formula or standard for how we evaluate students," she says. High grades and test scores would seem to be merely a baseline. "We turned away approximately half of applicants with maximum scores on the SAT, all three sections," Ms. Cliatt says of the class Mr. Li would have joined.

28    In the last two months, the nation has seen a number of new challenges to racial engineering in schools. In November, the United States Supreme Court heard a case questioning the legality of using race in assigning students to public schools in Seattle and Louisville, Ky. Voters are also sending a message, having thrown out racial preferences in Michigan in November, following a lead taken by California, Texas, Florida and Washington. Last month, Ward Connerly, the architect of Proposition 209, announced his next potential targets for a ballot initiative, including Arizona, Colorado, Missouri and Nebraska.

29    When I ask the chancellor at Berkeley, Robert J. Birgeneau, if there is a perfect demographic recipe on this campus that likes to think of itself as the world's finest public university—Harvard on the Hill—he demurs.

30    "We are a meritocracy," he says. And—by law, he adds—the campus is supposed to be that way. If Asians made up, say, 70 percent of the campus, he insists, there would still be no attempt to reduce their numbers.

31    Asian enrollment at his campus actually began to ramp up well before affirmative action was banned.

32    Historically, Asians have faced discrimination, with exclusion laws in the 1800s that kept them from voting, owning property or legally immigrating. Many were run out of West Coast towns by mobs. But by the 1970s and '80s, with a change in immigration laws, a surge in Asian arrivals began to change the complexion of California, and it was soon reflected in an overrepresentation at its top universities.

33    In the late 1980s, administrators appeared to be limiting Asian-American admissions, prompting a federal investigation. The result was an apology by the chancellor at the time, and a vow that there would be no cap on Asian enrollment.

34    University administrators and teachers use anguished words to describe what has happened since.

35    "I've heard from Latinos and blacks that Asians should not be considered a minority at all," says Elaine Kim, a professor of Asian-American studies at

Berkeley. "What happened after they got rid of affirmative action has been a disaster—for blacks and Latinos. And for Asians it's been a disaster because some people think the campus has become all-Asian."

The diminishing number of African-Americans on campus is a consistent ₃₆ topic of discussion among black students. Some say they feel isolated, without a sense of community. "You really do feel like you stand out," says Armilla Staley, a second-year law student. In her freshman year, she was one of only nine African-Americans in a class of 265. "I'm almost always the only black person in my class," says Ms. Staley, who favors a return to some form of affirmative action.

"Quite frankly, when you walk around campus, it's overwhelmingly ₃₇ Asian," she says. "I don't feel any tension between Asians and blacks, but I don't really identify with the Asian community as a minority either."

Walter Robinson, the director of undergraduate admissions, who is African- ₃₈ American, has the same impression. "The problem is that because we're so few, we get absorbed among the masses," he says.

Chancellor Birgeneau says he finds the low proportion of blacks and His- ₃₉ panics appalling, and two years into his tenure, he has not found a remedy. To broaden the pool, the U.C. system promises to admit the top 4 percent at each high school in the state and uses "comprehensive review"—considering an applicant's less quantifiable attributes. But the net results for a campus like Berkeley are disappointing. His university, Dr. Birgeneau says, loses talented black applicants to private universities like Stanford, where African-American enrollment was 10 percent last year—nearly three times that at Berkeley.

"I just don't believe that in a state with three million African-Americans ₄₀ there is not a single engineering student for the state's premier public university," says the chancellor, who has called for reinstating racial preferences.

One leading critic of bringing affirmative action back to Berkeley is David A. ₄₁ Hollinger, chairman of its history department and author of "Post-Ethnic America: Beyond Multiculturalism." He supported racial preferences before Proposition 209, but is no longer so sure. "You could argue that the campus is more diverse now," because Asians comprise so many different cultures, says Dr. Hollinger. A little more than half of Asian freshmen at Berkeley are Chinese, the largest group, followed by Koreans, East-Indian/Pakistani, Filipino and Japanese.

He believes that Latinos are underrepresented because many come from ₄₂ poor agrarian families with little access to the good schools that could prepare them for the rigors of Berkeley. He points out that, on the other hand, many of the Korean students on campus are sons and daughters of parents with college degrees. In any event, he says, it is not the university's job to fix the problems that California's public schools produce.

Dr. Birgeneau agrees on at least one point: "I think we're now at the point ₄₃ where the category of Asian is not very useful. Koreans are different from people from Sri Lanka and they're different than Japanese. And many Chinese-Americans are a lot like Caucasians in some of their values and areas of interest."

44    If Berkeley is now a pure meritocracy, what does that say about the future of great American universities in the post–affirmative action age? Are we headed toward a day when all elite colleges will look something like Berkeley: relatively wealthy whites (about 60 percent of white freshmen's families make $100,000 or more) and a large Asian plurality and everyone else underrepresented? Is that the inevitable result of color-blind admissions?

45    Eric Liu, author of "The Accidental Asian: Notes of a Native Speaker" and a domestic policy adviser to former President Bill Clinton, is troubled by the assertion that the high Asian makeup of elite campuses reflects a post-racial age where merit prevails.

46    "I really challenge this idea of a pure meritocracy," says Mr. Liu, who runs mentoring programs that grew out of his book "Guiding Lights: How to Mentor and Find Life's Purpose." Until all students—from rural outposts to impoverished urban settings—are given equal access to the Advanced Placement classes that have proved to be a ticket to the best colleges, then the idea of pure meritocracy is bunk, he says. "They're measuring in a fair way the results of an unfair system."

47    He also says Asian-Americans are tired of having to live up to—or defend— "that tired old warhorse of the model minority."

48    "We shouldn't be calling these studying habits that help so many kids get into good schools 'Asian values,'" says Mr. Liu, himself a product of Yale College and Harvard Law School. "These are values that used to be called Jewish values or Anglo-Saxon work-ethic values. The bottom line message from the family is the same: work hard, defer gratification, share sacrifice and focus on the big goal."

49    Hazel R. Markus lectures on this very subject as a professor of psychology at Stanford and co-director of its Research Institute for Comparative Studies in Race and Ethnicity. Her studies have found that Asian students do approach academics differently. Whether educated in the United States or abroad, she says, they see professors as authority figures to be listened to, not challenged in the back-and-forth Socratic tradition. "You hear some teachers say that the Asian kids get great grades but just sit there and don't participate," she says. "Talking and thinking are not the same thing. Being a student to some Asians means that it's not your place to question, and that flapping your gums all day is not the best thing."

50    One study at the institute looked at Asian-American students in lab courses, and found they did better solving problems alone and without conversations with other students. "This can make for some big problems," she says, like misunderstandings between classmates. "But people are afraid to talk about these differences. And one of the fantastic opportunities of going to a Stanford or Berkeley is to learn something about other cultures, so we should be talking about it."

51    As for the rise in Asian enrollment, the reason "isn't a mystery," Dr. Markus says. "This needs to come out and we shouldn't hide it," she says. "In Asian families, the No. 1 job of a child is to be a student. Being educated—that's the most honorable thing you can do."

Berkeley is "Asian heaven," as one student puts it. "When I went back ₅₂ East my Asian friends were like, 'Wow, you go to Berkeley—that must be great,'" says Tera Nakata, who just graduated and now works in the residence halls.

You need only go to colleges in, say, the Midwest to appreciate the Asian ₅₃ feel of this campus. But Berkeley is freighted with the baggage of stereotypes— that it is boring socially, full of science nerds, a hard place to make friends.

"About half the students at this school spend their entire career in the ₅₄ library," one person wrote in a posting on vault.com, a popular job and college search Web site.

Another wrote: "Everyone who is white joins the Greek system and every- ₅₅ one who isn't joins a 'theme house' or is a member of a club related to race."

There is some truth to the image, students acknowledge, but it does not do ₅₆ justice to the bigger experience at Berkeley. "You have the ability to stay with people who are like you and not get out of your comfort zone," says Ms. Na- kata. "But I learned a lot by mixing it up. I lived in a dorm with a lot of different races, and we would have these deep conversations all the time about race and our feelings of where we belong and where we came from." But she also says that the "celebrate diversity aspect" of Berkeley doesn't go deep. "We want to respect everyone's differences, but we don't mix socially."

Near the end of my stay at Berkeley I met a senior, Jonathan Lee, the son of a ₅₇ Taiwanese father and a mother from Hong Kong. He grew up well east of Los Angeles, in the New America sprawl of fast-growing Riverside County, where his father owned a restaurant. He went to a high school where he was a minority.

"When I was in high school," he says, "there was this notion that you're ₅₈ Chinese, you must be really good in math." But now Mr. Lee is likely to become a schoolteacher, much to the chagrin of his parents, "who don't think it will be very lucrative."

The story of Jon Lee's journey at Berkeley is compelling. As president of the ₅₉ Asian-American Association, he has tried to dispel stereotypes of "the Dragon Lady seductress or the idea that everybody plays the piano." His closest friends are in the club. It may seem that he has become more insular, that he has found his tribe. But Mr. Lee says he has been trying to lead other Asian students out of the university bubble. Once a week, they go into a mostly black and Hispanic middle school in the Bay Area to mentor students.

For the last five semesters, Mr. Lee has worked with one student. "I take ₆₀ him out for dim sum, or to Chinatown, or just talk about college and what it's like at Cal," he says. "We talk about race and we talk about everything. And he's taught me a lot."

The mentoring program came about not because of prodding by well- ₆₁ meaning advisers, teachers or student groups. It came about because Mr. Lee looked around at the new America—in California, the first state with no racial majority—and found that it looked very different from Berkeley. And much as he loves Berkeley, he knew that if he wanted to learn enough to teach, he needed to get off campus.

## COMPREHENSION

1. Egan focuses his essay on the University of California at Berkeley. What is the dominant impression that he gives of this campus? Does his report on UC Berkeley reflect the demographics on your campus? Why or why not?
2. What other colleges and universities does Egan refer to? What is his purpose?
3. According to the writer, what is the effect of "meritocracy" on affirmative action? Does Egan take sides on this controversy? Justify your response.

## RHETORIC

1. What is Egan's thesis, and where does he state it most clearly? What subtopics does he develop to support his thesis?
2. Egan organizes his article around the extended example of the University of California at Berkeley. What other types of examples does he use to lend authority to his report?
3. Explain the pattern of cause and effect that Egan weaves throughout this essay. What are some of the main and secondary causes and effects that he investigates?
4. How and where does the writer use comparison and contrast and classification to develop his article?
5. Two of the visuals from this richly illustrated article have been preserved. What do they add to your appreciation of the essay?
6. Egan begins his essay by profiling one student and ends it by profiling another one. Examine these passages and explain the strategy that the writer employs.

## WRITING

1. Write an essay about the student constituency on your campus. Incorporate some of the strategies and structures—for example, various forms of exemplification—that appear in Egan's article.
2. Go online and locate data on the student body at another college or university. Write a statistical report on your findings.
3. **Writing an Argument:** Write a persuasive essay defending or opposing the use of affirmative action to achieve racial and ethnic balance in undergraduate higher education.

www.mhhe.com/
**mhreader**

For more information on Timothy Egan, go to:
**More Resources > Ch. 4 Education**

# Sex Ed

## Anna Quindlen

*Anna Quindlen (b. 1953) was born in Philadelphia and educated at Barnard College
(BA, 1974). A journalist and novelist, she began her writing career as a reporter for the*
New York Post *and later moved on to* The New York Times, *where she was a
syndicated columnist. Quindlen has written a number of books, including* Living Out
Loud *(1986),* Object Lessons *(1991),* One True Thing *(1994), and* Black and Blue
*(1998). Quindlen received the Pulitzer Prize for Commentary in 1992. She is currently
a columnist for* Newsweek *magazine. In this essay, Quindlen focuses on the problem
of teenage pregnancy and suggests that children be given more than textbook information to help them cope with their sexuality.*

Several years ago I spent the day at a family planning clinic in one of New York   1
City's poorest neighborhoods. I sat around a Formica table with a half-dozen
sixteen-year-old girls and listened with some amazement as they showed off
their knowledge of human sexuality.

They knew how long sperm lived inside the body, how many women out   2
of a hundred using a diaphragm were statistically likely to get pregnant and
the medical term for the mouth of the cervix. One girl pointed out all the parts
of the female reproductive system on a placard; another recited the stages of the
ovulation cycle from day one to twenty-eight. There was just one problem with
this performance: although the results of their laboratory tests would not be
available for fifteen more minutes, every last one of them was pregnant.

I always think of that day when someone suggests that sex education at   3
school is a big part of the answer to the problem of teenage pregnancy. I happen
to be a proponent of such programs; I think human sexuality is a subject for
dispassionate study, like civics and ethics and dozens of other topics that have
a moral component. I'd like my sons to know as much as possible about how
someone gets pregnant, how pregnancy can be avoided, and what it means
when avoidance techniques have failed.

I remember adolescence about as vividly as I remember anything, however,   4
and I am not in the least convinced that that information alone will significantly
alter the rate of teenage pregnancy. It seemed to me that day in the clinic, and on
days I spent at schools and on street corners, that teenage pregnancy has a lot
more to do with what it means to be a teenager than with how someone gets
pregnant. When I was in high school, at the tail end of the sixties, there was a
straightforward line on sex among my friends. Boys could have it; girls couldn't.
A girl who was not a virgin pretended she was. A girl who was sleeping with her
boyfriend, no matter how long-playing the relationship, pretended she was not.

5       It is the nature of adolescence that there is no past and no future, only the present, burning as fierce, bright, and merciless as a bare light bulb. Girls had sex with boys because nothing seemed to matter except right now, not pregnancy, not parental disapprobation, nothing but those minutes, this dance, that face, those words. Most of them knew that pregnancy could result, but they assured themselves that they would be the lucky ones who would not get caught. Naturally, some of them were wrong, and in my experience they did one of three things: they went to Puerto Rico for a mysterious weekend trip; visited an aunt in some faraway state for three months and came back with empty eyes and a vague reputation, or got married, quickly, in Empire-waist dresses.

6       What seems to have changed most since then is that there is little philosophical counterpoint, hypocritical or not, to the raging hormones of adolescence, and that so many of the once-hidden pregnancies are hidden no more.

7       Not long after the day at the family planning clinic, I went to a public high school in the suburbs. In the girl's room was this graffito: Jennifer Is a Virgin. I asked the kids about it and they said it was shorthand for geek, nerd, weirdo, somebody who was so incredibly out of it that they were in high school and still hadn't had sex. If you were a virgin, they told me, you just lied about it so that no one would think you were that immature. The girls in the family planning clinic told me much the same thing—that everyone did it, that the boys wanted it, that not doing it made them seem out of it. The only difference, really, was that the girls in the clinic were poor and would have their babies, and the girls in the high school were well-to-do and would have abortions. Pleasure didn't seem to have very much to do with sex for either group. After she learned she was pregnant, one of the girls at the clinic said, without a trace of irony, that she hoped childbirth didn't hurt as much as sex had. Birth control was easily disposed of in both cases. The pill, the youngsters said, could give you a stroke; the IUD could make you sterile. A diaphragm was disgusting.

8       One girl told me the funniest thing her boyfriend—a real original thinker— had told her: they couldn't use condoms because it was like taking a shower with a raincoat on. She was a smart girl and pretty, and I wanted to tell her that it sounded as if she was sleeping with a jerk who didn't deserve her. But that is the kind of basic fact of life that must be taught not in the classroom, not by a stranger, but at home by the family. It is this that, finally, I will try to teach my sons about sex, after I've explained fertile periods and birth control and all the other mechanics that are important to understand but never really go to the heart of the matter: I believe I will say that when you sleep with someone you take off a lot more than your clothes.

## COMPREHENSION

1. Does Quindlen approve of sex education? Explain.
2. How does the writer characterize the attitude of adolescents regarding sex and pregnancy?
3. What advice or information about sex will the writer give her sons? Why?

## RHETORIC

1. Why did Quindlen choose "Sex Ed" as a title? What is its significance in relation to the thesis?
2. What is Quindlen's thesis? Where is it contained in the essay? Is it directly stated or implied?
3. Is Quindlen's writing an argumentative essay? Support your position with citations from the text.
4. What point is the writer making through use of accumulated details in paragraph 2?
5. What does Quindlen mean by the term "moral component" in paragraph 3? Where else in the essay does she allude to it? How does she employ definition in this essay?
6. What does Quindlen mean by her final statement that "when you sleep with someone you take off a lot more than your clothes"? How does this ending serve to underscore the thesis of the essay?

## WRITING

1. Write a paper analyzing the most common forms of birth control available and listing the advantages and disadvantages of each.
2. In an essay, consider possible solutions to the problem of teenage pregnancy. What role do you think sex education has in ameliorating the problem? Use support from the Quindlen essay if applicable.
3. **Writing an Argument:** Quindlen claims that sex education is like "civics" and "ethics" and should be taught in schools. Do you agree or disagree? Write an essay defending your position.

 www.mhhe.com/
**mhreader**

For more information on Anna Quindlen, go to:
**More Resources > Ch. 4 Education**

# Unplugged: The Myth of Computers in the Classroom

## David Gelernter

*David Gelernter (b. 1955) is a professor of computer science at Yale University. He is a leading figure in the field of human cognition and a seminal thinker in the field known as parallel computing. Gelernter, who was injured by a package sent by the Unabomber in 1993, is the author of* Mirror Worlds *(1991),* The Muse in the Machine *(1994),* 1939: The Lost World of the Fair *(1995), and* Machine Beauty *(1998). In the following essay, published in* The New Republic *in 1994, Gelernter offers a cogent analysis of the limits of technology in the classroom.*

1   Over the last decade an estimated $2 billion has been spent on more than 2 million computers for America's classrooms. That's not surprising. We constantly hear from Washington that the schools are in trouble and that computers are a godsend. Within the education establishment, in poor as well as rich schools, the machines are awaited with nearly religious awe. An inner-city principal bragged to a teacher friend of mine recently that his school "has a computer in every classroom . . . despite being in a bad neighborhood!"

2   Computers should be in the schools. They have the potential to accomplish great things. With the right software, they could help make science tangible or teach neglected topics like art and music. They help students form a concrete idea of society by displaying onscreen a version of the city in which they live— a picture that tracks real life moment by moment.

3   In practice, however, computers make our worst educational nightmares come true. While we bemoan the decline of literacy, computers discount words in favor of pictures and pictures in favor of video. While we fret about the decreasing cogency of public debate, computers dismiss linear argument and promote fast, shallow romps across the information landscape. While we worry about basic skills, we allow into the classroom software that will do a student's arithmetic or correct his spelling.

4   Take multimedia. The idea of multimedia is to combine text, sound and pictures in a single package that you browse on screen. You don't just *read* Shakespeare; you watch actors performing, listen to songs, view Elizabethan buildings. What's wrong with that? By offering children candy-coated books, multimedia is guaranteed to sour them on unsweetened reading. It makes the printed page look even more boring than it used to look. Sure, books will be available in the classroom, too—but they'll have all the appeal of a dusty piano to a teen who has a Walkman handy.

5   So what if the little nippers don't read? If they're watching Olivier instead, what do they lose? The text, the written word along with all of its attendant pleasures. Besides, a book is more portable than a computer, has a higher-resolution display, can be written on and dog-eared and is comparatively dirt cheap.

6   Hypermedia, multimedia's comrade in the struggle for a brave new classroom, is just as troubling. It's a way of presenting documents on screen without imposing a linear start-to-finish order. Disembodied paragraphs are linked by theme; after reading one about the First World War, for example, you might be able to choose another about the technology of battleships, or the life of Woodrow Wilson, or hemlines in the '20s. This is another cute idea that is good in minor ways and terrible in major ones. Teaching children to understand the orderly unfolding of a plot or a logical argument is a crucial part of education. Authors

don't merely agglomerate paragraphs; they work hard to make the narrative read a certain way, prove a particular point. To turn a book or a document into hypertext is to invite readers to ignore exactly what counts—the story.

The real problem, again, is the accentuation of already bad habits. Dyna- 7 miting documents into disjointed paragraphs is one more expression of the sorry fact that sustained argument is not our style. If you're a newspaper or magazine editor and your readership is dwindling, what's the solution? Shorter pieces. If you're a politician and you want to get elected, what do you need? Tasty sound bites. Logical presentation be damned.

Another software species, "allow me" programs, is not much better. These 8 programs correct spelling and, by applying canned grammatical and stylistic rules, fix prose. In terms of promoting basic skills, though, they have all the virtues of a pocket calculator.

In Kentucky, as *The Wall Street Journal* recently reported, students in grades 9 K–3 are mixed together regardless of age in a relaxed environment. It works great, the *Journal* says. Yes, scores on computation tests have dropped 10 percent at one school, but not to worry: "Drilling addition and subtraction in an age of calculators is a waste of time," the principal reassures us. Meanwhile, a Japanese educator informs University of Wisconsin mathematician Richard Akey that in his country, "calculators are not used in elementary or junior high school because the primary emphasis is on helping students develop their mental abilities." No wonder Japanese kids blow the pants off American kids in math. Do we really think "drilling addition and subtraction in an age of calculators is a waste of time"? If we do, then "drilling reading in an age of multimedia is a waste of time" can't be far behind.

Prose-correcting programs are also a little ghoulish, like asking a computer for 10 tips on improving your personality. On the other hand, I ran this article through a spell-checker, so how can I ban the use of such programs in schools? Because to misspell is human; to have no idea of correct spelling is to be semiliterate.

There's no denying that computers have the potential to perform inspiring 11 feats in the classroom. If we are ever to see that potential realized, however, we ought to agree on three conditions. First, there should be a completely new crop of children's software. Most of today's offerings show no imagination. There are hundreds of similar reading and geography and arithmetic programs, but almost nothing on electricity or physics or architecture. Also, they abuse the technical capacities of new media to glitz up old forms instead of creating new ones. Why not build a time-travel program that gives kids a feel for how history is structured by zooming you backward? A spectrum program that lets users twirl a frequency knob to see what happens?

Second, computers should be used only during recess or relaxation periods. 12 Treat them as fillips, not as surrogate teachers. When I was in school in the '60s, we all loved educational films. When we saw a movie in class, everybody won: teachers didn't have to teach, and pupils didn't have to learn. I suspect that classroom computers are popular today for the same reasons.

13　　　Most important, educators should learn what parents and most teachers already know: you cannot teach a child anything unless you look him in the face. We should not forget what computers are. Like books—better in some ways, worse in others—they are devices that help children mobilize their own resources and learn for themselves. The computer's potential to do good is modestly greater than a book's in some areas. Its potential to do harm is vastly greater, across the board.

## COMPREHENSION

1. State Gelernter's thesis or claim in one sentence.
2. In the final paragraph, Gelernter defines what he believes to be the most important shortcoming of the computer as a teaching tool. Explain the reason why this weakness is so significant.
3. In your own words, explain the author's dislike of hypermedia as a pedagogic tool (as expressed in paragraph 6) and why the orderly arrangement of paragraphs in a book is superior to this newer technological capability.

## RHETORIC

1. The introductory paragraph goes from a general fact to a specific quotation. What is the effect of this method of paragraph patterning?
2. Much of Gelernter's argument hinges on providing evidence that one medium is superior to another. Explain terms such as *linear argument* (paragraph 3), *agglomerate paragraphs* (paragraph 6), and *allow me programs* (paragraph 8). How do these terms help Gelernter prove his point?
3. The essay has a three-part structure, each section divided by space. How would you characterize the purpose of each section? How does the author use transitions to move from one section to the next?
4. Gelernter states that the overuse of computers in the classroom can hinder the development of clear thinking and reasoned argument. How clearly written is *his* essay? How reasoned is his argument? Gather evidence for your answer by reviewing the essay and determining whether each sentence seems to flow logically to the next and whether each paragraph seems to move reasonably to the next.
5. The author uses metaphors, similes, and other rhetorical devices. Explain the effectiveness of expressions such as "have all the appeal of a dusty piano to a teen who has a Walkman handy" (paragraph 4), "dynamiting documents" (paragraph 7), and "software species" (paragraph 8). Locate other unconventional descriptions.
6. Who is the intended audience for this essay? Educators? Parents? Students? Politicians? What evidence can you cite to back up your view?
7. What rhetorical device is Gelernter using in his title? What is the implicit meaning of the title?

## WRITING

1. Visit the writing or reading computer lab in your school. As an objective observer, study the interaction of student and computer. Write a descriptive essay focusing on the demeanor and behavior of the student and the atmosphere of the classroom. If you wish, compare it to a traditional classroom.

2. Copy a paragraph from the essay, and enter it into a word-processing program that has a grammar-check function. Record any comments that the program makes in response to its evaluation of the writing. Do the computer's responses to the author's sentence structure make sense?

3. **Writing an Argument:** Select one of the teaching capabilities of modern computers—multimedia, hypertext, or spell- and grammar-check programs. Argue for the benefits of one of these features.

| www.mhhe.com/ **mhreader** | For more information on David Gelernter, go to: **More Resources > Ch. 4 Education** |

# When Bright Girls Decide That Math Is "a Waste of Time"

### Susan Jacoby

*Susan Jacoby (b. 1945) has worked as an educator and as a reporter for* The Washington Post. *As a freelance journalist in the former Soviet Union (from 1969 to 1971), she produced two books about her experiences. Jacoby now contributes to* The Nation *and* McCall's; *her books include* The Possible She *(1979), a collection of autobiographical essays;* Wild Justice: The Evolution of Revenge *(1983); and* Half-Jew: A Daughter's Search for Her Buried Past *(2000). In this essay from* The New York Times, *Jacoby examines the reasons girls are often deficient in math and science.*

Susannah, a 16-year-old who has always been an A student in every subject    1
from algebra to English, recently informed her parents that she intended to drop physics and calculus in her senior year of high school and replace them with a drama seminar and a work-study program. She expects a major in art or history in college, she explained, and "any more science or math will just be a waste of my time."

2    Her parents were neither concerned by nor opposed to her decision. "Fine, dear," they said. Their daughter is, after all, an outstanding student. What does it matter if, at age 16, she has taken a step that may limit her understanding of both machines and the natural world for the rest of her life?

3    This kind of decision, in which girls turn away from studies that would give them a sure footing in the world of science and technology, is a self-inflicted female disability that is, regrettably, almost as common today as it was when I was in high school. If Susannah had announced that she had decided to stop taking English in her senior year, her mother and father would have been horrified. I also think they would have been a good deal less sanguine about her decision if she were a boy.

4    In saying that scientific and mathematical ignorance is a self-inflicted female wound, I do not, obviously, mean that cultural expectations play no role in the process. But the world does not conspire to deprive modern women of access to science as it did in the 1930s, when Rosalyn S. Yalow, the Nobel Prize–winning physicist, graduated from Hunter College and was advised to go to work as a secretary because no graduate school would admit her to its physics department. The current generation of adolescent girls—and their parents, bred on old expectations about women's interests—are active conspirators in limiting their own intellectual development.

5    It is true that the proportion of young women in science-related graduate and professional schools, most notably medical schools, has increased significantly in the past decade. It is also true that so few women were studying advanced science and mathematics before the early 1970s that the percentage increase in female enrollment does not yet translate into large numbers of women actually working in science.

6    The real problem is that so many girls eliminate themselves from any serious possibility of studying science as a result of decisions made during the vulnerable period of midadolescence, when they are most likely to be influenced—on both conscious and subconscious levels—by the traditional belief that math and science are "masculine" subjects.

7    During the teen-age years the well-documented phenomenon of "math anxiety" strikes girls who never had any problem handling numbers during earlier schooling. Some men, too, experience this syndrome—a form of panic, akin to a phobia, at any task involving numbers—but women constitute the overwhelming majority of sufferers. The onset of acute math anxiety during the teen-age years is, as Stalin was fond of saying, "not by accident."

8    In adolescence girls begin to fear that they will be unattractive to boys if they are typed as "brains." Science and math epitomize unfeminine braininess in a way that, say, foreign languages do not. High-school girls who pursue an advanced interest in science and math (unless they are students at special institutions like the Bronx High School of Science where everyone is a brain) usually find that they are greatly outnumbered by boys in their classes. They are, therefore, intruding on male turf at a time when their sexual confidence, as well as that of the boys, is most fragile.

A 1981 assessment of female achievement in mathematics, based on re- 9
search conducted under a National Institute for Education grant, found significant differences in the mathematical achievements of 9th and 12th graders. At
age 13 girls were equal to or slightly better than boys in tests involving algebra,
problem solving and spatial ability; four years later the boys had outstripped
the girls.

It is not mysterious that some very bright high-school girls suddenly decide 10
that math is "too hard" and "a waste of time." In my experience, self-sabotage
of mathematical and scientific ability is often a conscious process. I remember
deliberately pretending to be puzzled by geometry problems in my sophomore
year in high school. A male teacher called me in after class and said, in a baffled
tone, "I don't see how you can be having so much trouble when you got straight
A's last year in my algebra class."

The decision to avoid advanced biology, chemistry, physics and calculus 11
in high school automatically restricts academic and professional choices that
ought to be wide open to anyone beginning college. At all coeducational
universities women are overwhelmingly concentrated in the fine arts, social
sciences and traditionally female departments like education. Courses
leading to degrees in science- and technology-related fields are filled mainly
by men.

In my generation, the practical consequences of mathematical and scientific 12
illiteracy are visible in the large number of special programs to help professional women overcome the anxiety they feel when they are promoted into jobs
that require them to handle statistics.

The consequences of this syndrome should not, however, be viewed in nar- 13
rowly professional terms. Competence in science and math does not mean one
is going to become a scientist or mathematician any more than competence in
writing English means one is going to become a professional writer. Scientific
and mathematical illiteracy—which has been cited in several recent critiques by
panels studying American education from kindergarten through college— produces an incalculably impoverished vision of human experience.

Scientific illiteracy is not, of course, the exclusive province of women. In 14
certain intellectual circles it has become fashionable to proclaim a willed,
aggressive ignorance about science and technology. Some female writers specialize in ominous, uninformed diatribes against genetic research as a plot to
remove control of childbearing from women, while some well-known men of
letters proudly announce that they understand absolutely nothing about computers, or, for that matter, about electricity. This lack of understanding is nothing in which women or men ought to take pride.

Failure to comprehend either computers or chromosomes leads to a terrible 15
sense of helplessness, because the profound impact of science on everyday life is
evident even to those who insist they don't, won't, can't understand why the
changes are taking place. At this stage of history women are more prone to such
feelings of helplessness than men because the culture judges their ignorance less
harshly and because women themselves acquiesce in that indulgence.

16    Since there is ample evidence of such feelings in adolescence, it is up to parents to see that their daughters do not accede to the old stereotypes about "masculine" and "feminine" knowledge. Unless we want our daughters to share our intellectual handicaps, we had better tell them no, they can't stop taking mathematics and science at the ripe old age of 16.

## COMPREHENSION

1. What reasons does Jacoby give for girls' deficiency in math and science?
2. Why does Jacoby call it a "self-inflicted female disability" (paragraph 3)?
3. What are the consequences of being math- and science-illiterate?

## RHETORIC

1. Explain the main idea of Jacoby's essay in your own words.
2. Does the writer use abstract or concrete language in her essay? Cite examples to support your response.
3. What technique does Jacoby use in paragraphs 1 and 2? How does it aid in setting up her argument?
4. What rhetorical strategies does the writer use in her essay?
5. How does the use of dialogue aid in developing paragraph 10? What effect does the general use of dialogue have on Jacoby's point?
6. How is Jacoby's conclusion consistent in tone with the rest of the essay? Does it supply a sense of unity? Why or why not?

## WRITING

1. Write an essay describing a school-related phobia you once had or continue to have (for example, in math, writing, physical education or biology). Explain where you think that fear came from, how it affected your performance in school, and what you did (or are doing) to cope with the problem.
2. Write an essay about the need for math and science literacy in today's world. Use support from Jacoby's essay.
3. **Writing an Argument:** Write an argumentation essay proposing that math and science phobia is not "self-inflicted" but is caused primarily by the continued presence of sexism in society.

www.mhhe.com/ **mhreader**   |   For more information on Susan Jacoby, go to: **More Resources > Ch. 4 Education**

# Two Cheers for *Brown v. Board of Education*

### Clayborne Carson

*Clayborne Carson (b. 1944) is professor of history and director of the Martin Luther King Jr. Papers Project at Stanford University. He was born in Buffalo, New York, and educated at the University of California at Los Angeles, where he received his BA (1967), MA (1968), and PhD (1977). A specialist in African-American and civil rights history, Carson has written and edited numerous books, including* In Struggle: SNCC and the Black Awakening of the 1960s *(1981, rev. ed. 1995), which received the Frederick Jackson Turner Award;* Eyes on the Prize: America's Civil Rights Years *(1987); and* The Malcolm X File *(1991). Asked by Coretta Scott King to handle her late husband's literary estate, Carson is the lead editor of* The Papers of Martin Luther King Jr. *(University of California Press). "It was a job you couldn't say no to," Carson said. In this essay, published in the* Journal of American History *in 2004, Carson offers an evaluation of the impact of a major Supreme Court decision on school segregation.*

My gratuitous opinion of *Brown v. Board of Education* (1954) is somewhat ambiva-   1
lent and certainly arrives too late to alter the racial policies of the past fifty years. But for those of us who practice history, hindsight offers a far more reliable kind of wisdom than does foresight. We see clearly now that while the *Brown* decision informed the attitudes that have shaped contemporary American race relations, it did not resolve persistent disputes about the nation's civil rights policies. The Supreme Court's unanimous opinion in *Brown* broke decisively with the racist interpretations of traditional American values set forth in *Scott v. Sandford* (1857) and *Plessy v. Ferguson* (1896), offering instead the optimistic "American Creed" that Gunnar Myrdal saw as the solution to "the Negro problem."[1] Like the two earlier landmark decisions, *Brown* overestimated the extent of ideological consensus among Americans and soon exacerbated racial and regional conflicts instead of resolving them. The Court's ruling against school segregation encouraged African Americans to believe that the entire structure of white supremacy was illegitimate and legally vulnerable. But the civil rights struggles *Brown* inspired sought broader goals than the decision could deliver, and that gap fostered frustration and resentment among many black Americans. In short, the decision's virtues and limitations reflect both the achievements and the failures of the efforts made in the last half century to solve America's racial dilemma and to realize the nation's egalitarian ideals.

[1]*Scott v. Sandford,* 19 How. 393 (1857); *Plessy v. Ferguson,* 163 U.S. 537 (1896); *Brown v. Board of Education,* 347 U.S. 483 (1954); Gunnar Myrdal, *An American Dilemma: The Negro Problem and Modern Democracy* (2 vols., New York, 1944).

2      That the *Brown* decision spurred subsequent civil rights progress seems apparent, but its impact and its significance as a source of inspiration are difficult
to measure.[2] Although the Court's initial unwillingness to set firm timetables for
school desegregation undercut *Brown*'s immediate impact, African Americans
expanded the limited scope of the decision by individual and collective challenges to the Jim Crow system. Small-scale protests escalated during the decade
after 1954, becoming a sustained mass movement against all facets of segregation and discrimination in the North as well as the South. Civil rights protests
and litigation prompted Congress to pass the Civil Rights Act of 1964 and the Voting Rights Act of 1965, both of which extended the *Brown* decision's egalitarian
principles well beyond education. The historic mass struggle that followed
*Brown* ultimately destroyed the legal foundations of the Jim Crow system, and
their destruction prepared the way for a still more far-reaching expansion of
prevailing American conceptions of civil rights and of the role of government in
protecting those rights. During the past forty years, women and many minority
groups, including immigrants and people with disabilities, have gained new
legal protections modeled on the civil rights gains of African Americans.[3]

3      But the *Brown* decision also created racial aspirations that remain unreal-
ized. Although the decision may have been predicated on the notion of a shared
American creed, most white Americans were unwilling to risk their own racial
privileges to bring about racial equality. The decision was neither universally
accepted nor consistently enforced. "Instead, it provoked overwhelming resistance in the South and only tepid interest in the North," the historian John
Higham insisted. "In the South the decision released a tidal wave of racial hysteria that swept moderates out of office or turned them into demagogues. State
and local officials declined to obstruct a revival of the Ku Klux Klan. Instead,
they employed every conceivable device to maintain segregation, including harassment and dissolution of NAACP chapters."[4] By the 1970s, resistance to
school desegregation had become national. Northern whites in Boston and elsewhere demonstrated their unwillingness to send their children to predominantly black schools or to allow large-scale desegregation that would drastically
alter the racial composition of "their" schools in "their" neighborhoods. Voters

---

[2]On *Brown*'s direct and indirect consequences, see, for example, Michael J. Klarman, "How *Brown*
Changed Race Relations: The Backlash Thesis," *Journal of American History,* 81 (June 1994), 81–118.
Klarman correctly points out that *Brown* had limited impact on school desegregation, especially in
the Deep South, and stimulated southern white resistance to racial reform. He concludes that the
contributions of *Brown* to the broader civil rights struggle were mostly indirect.

[3]Cf. Hugh Davis Graham, *The Civil Rights Era: Origins and Development of National Policy, 1960–1972*
(New York, 1990); Hugh Davis Graham, *Collision Course: The Strange Convergence of Affirmative Ac-
tion and Immigration Policy in America* (New York, 2002); and John D. Skrentny, *The Minority Rights
Revolution* (Cambridge, Mass., 2002).

[4]John Higham, "Introduction: A Historical Perspective," in *Civil Rights and Civil Wrongs: Black-
White Relations since World War II,* ed. John Higham (University Park, 1997), 4. See also Klarman,
"How *Brown* Changed Race Relations"; Numan V. Bartley, *The Rise of Massive Resistance: Race and
Politics in the South in the 1950s* (Baton Rouge, 1969); and Neil McMillen, *The Citizens' Council: Or-
ganized Resistance to the Second Reconstruction, 1954–1964* (Urbana, 1971).

in the states of Washington and California passed initiatives to restrict the right of school boards (Washington) and state courts (California) to order busing to achieve school desegregation (the Supreme Court later held the Washington initiative unconstitutional). Nationwide, white racial resentments encouraged an enduring shift of white voters from the Democratic to the Republican party. The 1964 election would be the last presidential contest in which the majority of black voters and of white voters backed the same candidate. Since 1974, when the Supreme Court's *Milliken v. Bradley* decision set limits on busing, the legal meaning of desegregation has been scaled back to conform to American racial and political realities.[5]

African Americans generally applauded the *Brown* decision when it was   4 announced, but the Court's failure to realize *Brown*'s bold affirmation of egalitarian ideals fueled subsequent black discontent and disillusionment. *Brown* cited studies that demonstrated the harmful psychological impact of enforced segregation on black students, reporting, "To separate them from others of similar age and qualifications solely because of their race generates a feeling of inferiority as to their status in the community that may affect their hearts and minds in a way unlikely ever to be undone." Yet the Court did not offer an effective means to correct the problem it had identified. During the decades after *Brown*, most southern black children continued to suffer the psychological consequences of segregation, while a small minority assumed the often considerable psychological and physical risks of attending newly integrated public schools. Rather than bringing large numbers of black and white students together in public schools, the *Brown* decision—and the subsequent years of litigation and social conflict—enabled a minority of black students to attend predominantly white schools. Ten years after the *Brown* decision, according to data compiled by the U.S. Department of Education, almost 98 percent of southern black students still attended predominantly black schools. Now, at the beginning of the twenty-first century, the Court's ideal of educational opportunity as "a right which must be made available to all on equal terms" is still far from being realized. American schools, both public and private, are still highly segregated. According to a recent study, the typical Latino or black student in the United States still attends a school where members of minority groups are predominant.[6]

---

[5]See Ronald P. Formisano, *Boston against Busing: Race, Class, and Ethnicity in the 1960s and 1970s* (Chapel Hill, 1991); and J. Anthony Lukas, *Common Ground: A Turbulent Decade in the Lives of Three American Families* (New York, 1985). *Washington v. Seattle School District*, 458 U.S. 457 (1982); *Crawford v. Los Angeles Board of Education*, 458 U.S. 527 (1982); *Milliken v. Bradley*, 418 U.S. 717 (1974). See Gary Orfield and Susan E. Eaton, *Dismantling Desegregation: The Quiet Reversal of* Brown v. Board of Education (New York, 1996).

[6]*Brown v. Board of Education*, 347 U.S. at 494, 493; Gary Orfield and Chungmei Lee, "*Brown* at Fifty: King's Dream or Plessy's Nightmare?" Jan. 17, 2004, *The Civil Rights Project, Harvard University* <http://www.civilrightsproject.harvard.edu/research/reseg04/resegregation04.php> (April 4, 2004). In every region of the nation, at least 30% black students still attend schools with less than 10% white enrollment. *Ibid.*

5       Certainly, the *Brown* decision's most significant deficiency is its failure to address the concerns of the majority of African American students who have been unable or unwilling to seek better educational opportunities by leaving predominantly black schools for predominantly white ones. While it opened the door for the Little Rock Nine, who desegregated Central High School in 1957, the *Brown* decision offered little solace to the hundreds of students who remained at Little Rock's all-black Horace Mann High School. When Arkansas officials reacted to desegregation by closing all of Little Rock's high schools, those students were denied even segregated educational opportunities.[7] With the encouragement of the lawyers for the National Association for the Advancement of Colored People's (NAACP) Legal Defense and Education Fund, the Supreme Court largely abandoned previous efforts to enforce the separate but equal mandate in order to adopt a narrowly conceived strategy for achieving equal educational opportunity through desegregation. The pre-*Brown* equalization effort had encouraged social scientists to develop increasingly sophisticated ways of measuring differences in the quality of schools. But during the 1950s, pro–civil rights scholars shifted their focus from the educational environment of black students in black schools to the psychological state of black students experiencing desegregation. The NAACP's initial strategy of forcing southern states to equalize facilities at all-black schools had resulted in tangible improvements, whereas the removal of racial barriers in public schools was advertised as offering intangible psychological gains.

6       For Thurgood Marshall, who headed the NAACP legal staff, the equalization effort had always been a means of achieving the ultimate goal of desegregation. After the Supreme Court decided in *Sweatt v. Painter* (1950) that a makeshift segregated law school at a black college could not provide educational opportunities equal to those offered by the University of Texas Law School. Marshall exulted, "The complete destruction of *all* enforced segregation is now in sight." Despite having attended predominantly black schools at every stage of his academic career, he saw segregation as a racial stigma that could not be removed by increased state appropriations for Jim Crow schools. In the early 1950s he noted that social scientists were "almost in universal agreement that segregated education produces inequality." He therefore concluded "that segregated schools, perhaps more than any other single factor, are of major concern to the individual of public school age and contribute greatly to the unwholesomeness and unhappy development of the personality of Negroes which the color caste system in the United States has produced."[8]

[7]Cf. Melba Beals, *Warriors Don't Cry: A Searing Memoir of the Battle to Integrate Little Rock's Central High* (New York, 1995); and Melba Beals, *White Is a State of Mind: A Memoir* (New York, 1995).
[8]*Sweatt v. Painter*, 339 U.S. 629 (1950); *Baltimore Afro-American*, June 17, 1950, quoted in Juan Williams, *Thurgood Marshall: American Revolutionary* (New York, 1998), 195; Thurgood Marshall, "An Evaluation of Recent Efforts to Achieve Racial Integration in Education through Resort to the Courts," *Journal of Negro Education*, 21 (Summer 1952), 316–27, esp. 322.

Few African Americans would wish to return to the pre-*Brown* world of  7
legally enforced segregation, but in the half century since 1954, only a minority
of Americans has experienced the promised land of truly integrated public education. By the mid-1960s, with dual school systems still in place in many areas
of the Deep South, and with de facto segregation a recognized reality in urban
areas, the limitations of *Brown* had become evident to many of those who had
spearheaded previous civil rights struggles. The ideological gulf that appeared
in African American politics during the period was largely the result of efforts
to draw attention to the predominantly black institutions neglected in the drive
for racial integration. The black power movement arose in part as an effort by
African Americans to control and improve such institutions. Some black power
proponents exaggerated the benefits of racial separatism, but their extremism
can be best understood as a reaction against the unbalanced post-*Brown* strategy of seeking racial advancement solely through integration. Although James
S. Coleman's landmark 1966 study of equality of educational opportunity found
that black children attending integrated schools did better than students attending predominantly black schools, it was by no means clear that the gap was the
result of interracial interactions rather than of differences in the socioeconomic
backgrounds of the students involved. By the late 1960s, growing numbers of
black leaders had concluded that improvement of black schools should take
priority over school desegregation. In 1967, shortly before the National Advisory Commission on Civil Disorders warned that the United States was "moving toward two societies, one white, one black—separate and unequal," Martin
Luther King Jr. acknowledged the need to refocus attention, at least in the short
run, on "schools in ghetto areas." He also insisted that "the drive for immediate
improvements in segregated schools should not retard progress toward integrated education later." Even veterans of the NAACP's legal campaign had
second thoughts. "*Brown* has little practical relevance to central city blacks,"
Constance Baker Motley commented in 1974. "Its psychological and legal relevance has already had its effect."[9]

Black power advocates sometimes sought to replace the narrow strategy  8
of achieving racial advancement through integration with the equally narrow
strategy of achieving it through racial separatism. In both instances, claims of
psychological gains often substituted for measurable racial advancements,
but the continued popularity of Afrocentric educational experiments indicates
that many African Americans now see voluntary segregation as psychologically uplifting. Having personally experienced the burden of desegregating
numerous classrooms and having watched my son move with great success
from a predominantly black college to a predominantly white law school, I

[9]J. S. Coleman et al., *Equality of Educational Opportunity* (Washington, 1966), *passim; Report of the National Advisory Commission on Civil Disorders* (New York, 1968), 1; Martin Luther King Jr., *Where Do
We Go from Here: Chaos or Community?* (New York, 1967), 228. For Constance Baker Motley's statement (quoted from the *New York Times,* May 13, 1974), see James T. Patterson, Brown v. Board of
Education: *A Civil Rights Milestone and Its Troubled Legacy* (New York, 2001), 168.

am skeptical of sweeping claims about the impact of racial environment on learning. While believing that debates among African Americans during the last half century about their destiny have been useful, I regret that those debates have often exacerbated ideological conflict rather than encouraging us toward collective action. Rather than having to choose between overcoming racial barriers and improving black community institutions, we should be able to choose both.

9       In hindsight, the nation would have been better served if the *Brown* decision had evinced a more realistic understanding of the deep historical roots of America's racial problems—perhaps a little more familiarity with the writings of W. E. B. Du Bois and Carter C. Woodson as well as those of Myrdal and his colleagues. Rather than blandly advising that desegregation of public schools be achieved with "all deliberate speed," the Supreme Court—and the NAACP lawyers who argued before it—should have launched a two-pronged attack, not only against racial segregation but also against inferior schools, whatever their racial composition. Such an attack would have heeded the admonition that Du Bois offered in 1935, soon after his forced resignation as editor of the NAACP's journal, the *Crisis:*

> Theoretically, the Negro needs neither segregated schools nor mixed schools. What he needs is Education. . . . Other things being equal, the mixed school is the broader, more natural basis for the education of all youth. It gives wider contacts; it inspires great self-confidence; and suppresses the inferiority complex. But other things seldom are equal, and in that case, Sympathy, Knowledge, and the Truth, outweigh all that the mixed school can offer.[10]

10      Because the *Brown* decision was a decisive departure from *Plessy's* separate but equal principle, it was an important turning point in African American history. Nevertheless, fifty years later the Court's assumptions about the psychological consequences of legally enforced segregation seem dated. The Jim Crow system no longer exists, but most black American schoolchildren still attend predominantly black public schools that offer fewer opportunities for advancement than typical predominantly white public schools. Moreover, there is no contemporary civil rights movement able to alter that fact. Yet, if *Brown* represents a failed attempt to achieve comprehensive racial advancement, the opinion nonetheless still challenges us by affirming egalitarian ideals that remain relevant: "In these days, it is doubtful that any child may reasonably be expected to succeed in life if he is denied the opportunity of an education. Such an opportunity, where the state has undertaken to provide it, is a right which must be made available to all on equal terms."[11]

---

[10]*Brown v. Board of Education,* 349 U.S. 294 (1955); W. E. B. Du Bois, "Does the Negro Need Separate Schools?" *Journal of Negro Education,* 4 (July 1935), in *The Oxford W. E. B. Du Bois Reader,* ed. Eric J. Sundquist (New York, 1996), 431.
[11]*Brown v. Board of Education of Topeka:* Opinion on Segregation Laws," in *Civil Rights and African Americans: A Documentary History,* ed. Albert P. Blaustein and Robert I. Zangrando (Evanston, 1991), 436.

## COMPREHENSION

1. According to Carson, what are the benefits and shortcomings of the *Brown v. Board of Education* decision? Why does he give two cheers (instead of the traditional three cheers) for the Supreme Court's 1954 verdict?
2. What are the psychological effects of both segregation and desegregation on African American students?
3. Why does Carson say that the impact of the *Brown* decision is difficult to measure? What evidence does he provide to support this assessment?

## RHETORIC

1. Who is Carson's audience for this essay? How does he fit his style to the expectations he holds for this specific audience? Provide examples of vocabulary, syntax, and abstract language to support your response. Why would the article also be of interest to a more general audience?
2. Carson lays out a well-informed argument. What is his claim or major proposition? What are his warrants? What is his support? How does he deal with opposing viewpoints? What conclusions does he draw to convince the reader of his position?
3. Analyze the pattern of cause and effect that Carson presents in this essay.
4. Carson has very strong topic sentences at the start of virtually every paragraph. List these topic sentences, and then show how they control the flow of his thoughts within paragraphs while at the same time advancing his argument.
5. Examine the writer's footnotes. What are his sources? What range and variety of evidence do these notes suggest?

## WRITING

1. Using Carson's article as a reference point, write an essay describing the ethnic and racial composition of your former high school or the college you now attend. How does this demographic profile support some of Carson's key insights into *Brown v. Board of Education?*
2. Write an essay in which you offer your own analysis of the ways in which varieties of discrimination you encounter in education can have psychological consequences. Feel free to offer personal experience to support your analysis.
3. **Writing an Argument:** Unlike Carson, who argues both sides of the *Brown* decision in terms of the historical aftermath, write an argumentative essay in which you defend or criticize the results of *Brown v. Board* since 1954. Conduct research and collaborate with class members if you wish.

www.mhhe.com/
**mhreader**

For more information on Clayborne Carson, go to:
**More Resources > Ch. 4 Education**

## Synthesis: Connections For Critical Thinking

1. Compare and contrast the rhetoric of the personal essay as it is represented in Rodriguez's "The Lonely, Good Company of Books" with the rhetoric of such expository and argumentative essays as Quindlen's "Sex Ed" or Carson's "Two Cheers for *Brown v. Board of Education*."

2. Analyze an event in your education when you had a disagreement with a teacher or administrator. Explain and explore whether the differences in viewpoint were based on emotional perspective, intellectual perspective, or both.

3. Select the essay in this chapter you find most pertinent to your life as a student. Explain why you selected the essay, and explore your intellectual and emotional responses to it.

4. Does your college seem to support Jacoby's views regarding the educational lives of women? Explain why or why not.

5. Argue for or against the view that the publicized sexual activity of politicians and other celebrities makes the decision whether to keep sex education out of the schools entirely moot.

6. It is 2050. Write an essay in which you explore the demographics of a typical college classroom. Refer to the ideas contained in the Egan, Jacoby, and Carson essays.

7. Write an essay that classifies at least three educational issues that the authors in this chapter examine. Establish a clear thesis to unify the categories you establish.

8. Analyze the patterns and techniques used by Quindlen, Gelernter, and Jacoby to advance their claims about education today.

9. **Network:** Search the Web for *sex education* and *France* (or another country of your choice). Write an essay describing the policies of your chosen country toward the topic.

10. **Network:** Look up your college's or university's mission statement on its home Web page. Is the statement relevant? Is it truthful? Why or why not? Use personal observation and experience to support your view.

11. **Network:** Argue for or against the proposition that despite Gelernter's warnings about the purported shortcomings of computers in the classroom, in the future many students will prefer to obtain a bachelor of art degree completely via computer and the Internet. To support your viewpoint, research and report on at least three online sites that offer college degrees.

 chapter **5**

# Family Life and Gender Roles

*How Do We Become Who We Are?*

Every culture has its own ideas about what identity is, how it is formed, and where it comes from. What is the influence of family, of environment, of gender, and, as we saw in Chapter 4, of education on the creation of identity? Although it is challenging to reconcile these various cross-cultural ideas, the writers in this chapter attempt to make sense of identity from the perspectives of family and gender, and they invite readers to liberate themselves from the tyranny of stereotyping.

Families nourish us during childhood, and the values our families seek to maintain usually affect our identities in powerful ways, whether we adopt them wholly, modify them, or reject them outright. Writers have always been aware of the importance of the family in human development and behavior, and have written about it from various perspectives, using narration, sociological and psychological analysis, and cultural criticism, among other approaches. Tolstoy wrote that "happy families are all alike; every unhappy family is unhappy in its own way." But we shall discover that Tolstoy had a limited view of family life and its values—probably circumscribed by the mores of the time he lived in. Some of our finest essayists and observers of social life today demonstrate in this chapter that what constitutes the definition of a family is up for grabs as we begin the new millennium.

The family is one of the few institutions that we find in every society throughout the world, at least every thriving society. Anthropologists, sociologists, and psychologists tell us that family patterns are exceedingly diverse even in the same societies. In the past and even more so today, children grow up in many ways: in nuclear and in nontraditional households; in single-parent and in dual-parent arrangements; in extended families and in the new blended family; and in patriarchal and matriarchal, heterosexual and homosexual, monogamous and polygamous situations. And the dynamics of family life assume added dimension as we move across cultures, studying European families, African American families, Hispanic families, Asian families, and so forth. Even within these groups, we find variables that affect family life and values, such as economic class, social class, and educational levels.

Unlike in previous periods in our history, Americans today seem to be groping for a definition of what constitutes the happy family. With the influences of the media and of peer pressure on children, the rise in the number of latchkey children, and the fact that there is a growing diversity of cultures in America owing to the new wave of immigration, the family appears to be less of a traditional haven than it was even a generation ago. This chapter contains vivid accounts of the long-standing bonds within the family that have been treasured for their capacity to build values of love and sharing. It also contains essays that demonstrate how family life is filled with emotional complexities and conflicts that the child must negotiate as she or he finds meaning and attempts to construct an identity. Each writer, whether writing narration, exposition, or argumentation, shows how significant the family is for the development of our values, personalities, and lifestyles.

As much as our identities are shaped by powerful institutional forces like the family, what we are might be even more powerfully determined by the forces of sexuality and gender. Freud asserted that human behavior is rooted in sexuality, that gender (rather than family or school or any social institution) is destiny. Clearly, notions of what it means to be a man or a woman have an impact on the construction of our identities.

The identity issues discussed in this chapter might prove to be controversial, but they will encourage you to confront your own sense of identity. These essays are like a mirror in which you can see and evaluate what you really are.

## Previewing the Chapter

As you read the essays in this chapter and respond to them in discussion and writing, consider the following questions:

- What form of rhetoric is the author using: narration, exposition, or argumentation? Why is this form appropriate for the author's purpose?
- What perspective does the writer take on the subject of identity formation? Is the writer optimistic, pessimistic, or something else?
- What are the cultural, social, and economic issues addressed in the essay?
- How do you regard the authority of the author? Does she or he seem to be speaking from experience and knowledge? In essays that explain or argue, does the evidence appear substantial or questionable? Explain.
- What stylistic devices does the author employ to re-create a memory, explain a function, or argue a stance regarding an issue of identity?
- Which essays appear alike in purpose and method, and why?
- What have you learned or discovered about your own identity from reading these essays?
- Do you prefer one rhetorical form over another—for example, personal narration over argumentation? If so, why?

# Classic and Contemporary Images
## HOW DO WE RESPOND TO MARRIAGE?

*Using a Critical Perspective*   What was your first impression of Brueghel's *Rustic Wedding* and Elise Amendola's *Gay Marriage*? What details do you see? What senses do the artist and the photographer draw on to convey the atmosphere of the wedding? What does each want to say about the institution of marriage? How do you know?

The Flemish artist Pieter Brueghel the Elder (1525–1569) was one of the greatest painters of the 16th century and was renowned for his exuberant depictions of peasant life. His son Pieter Brueghel the Younger (1564–1638) copied many of his father's works and also painted religious subjects. He was responsible for *Rustic Wedding*, shown here.

Hillary, left, and Julie Goodridge, lead plaintiffs in the landmark Massachusetts gay marriage lawsuit, receive their wedding rings from their daughter, Annie, 8, as Unitarian Reverend William Sinkford presides over their marriage ceremony in Boston during the first day of state-sanctioned gay marriage in the United States on May 17, 2004.

# Classic and Contemporary Essays
## HOW MUCH DO FAMILIES MATTER?

E. B. White and Barbara Kingsolver represent two generations, each raised with different values regarding the function, structure, and role of the family. Both authors are master stylists, but each reflects a style of writing, an intellectual universe, and an external world that views the healthy family differently. White writes in clear, concise, elegiac prose. It marches on in a quiet, evenly patterned rhythm. Perhaps it is a metaphor of his view of life in general and family life in particular. Tradition is to be treasured; continuity is to be celebrated. He attends to the details of a nature outing and suggests that the sights, sounds, and smells that imbue the events he and his son experience are the same as those he experienced years before with his own father. For White, it seems, pleasure is derived from connectivity and permanence.

Kingsolver is passionate about her own perspective on what constitutes a healthy family structure, but it is a family transformed, reconfigured, and rearranged by contemporary events and values. Kingsolver's notion of family is various while White's view is archetypal. Kingsolver seems to believe that change in families creates security, particularly if one is moving from a dysfunctional environment to a more coherent one. Is White conservative in his views? Is Kingsolver a liberal? Perhaps a better way to get a sense of their differences is to inquire whether our amorphous contemporary world requires us to be more flexible and critical. And, of course, we must consider that Kingsolver adds a woman's voice to the conversation about family, a voice that was not as frequently heard by the members of White's generation.

320

# Once More to the Lake

## E. B. White

*E(lwyn) B(rooks) White (1899–1985), perhaps the finest American essayist of the 20th century, was at his most distinctive in his treatments of people and nature. A recipient of the National Medal for Literature, and associated for years with* The New Yorker, *White is the author of* One Man's Meat *(1942),* Here Is New York *(1949), and* The Second Tree from the Corner *(1954), among numerous other works. He was also one of the most talented writers of literature for children, the author of* Stuart Little *(1945),* Charlotte's Web *(1952), and* The Trumpet of the Swan *(1970). In this essay, White combines narration and description to make a poignant and vivid statement about past and present, youth and age, life and death.*

One summer, along about 1904, my father rented a camp on a lake in Maine and took us all there for the month of August. We all got ringworm from some kittens and had to rub Pond's Extract on our arms and legs night and morning, and my father rolled over in a canoe with all his clothes on; but outside of that the vacation was a success and from then on none of us ever thought there was any place in the world like that lake in Maine. We returned summer after summer—always on August 1st for one month. I have since become a saltwater man, but sometimes in summer there are days when the restlessness of the tides and the fearful cold of the sea water and the incessant wind which blows across the afternoon and into the evening make me wish for the placidity of a lake in the woods. A few weeks ago this feeling got so strong I bought myself a couple of bass hooks and a spinner and returned to the lake where we used to go, for a week's fishing and to revisit old haunts.

I took along my son, who had never had any fresh water up his nose and who had seen lily pads only from train windows. On the journey over to the lake I began to wonder what it would be like. I wondered how time would have marred this unique, this holy spot—the coves and streams, the hills that the sun set behind, the camps and the paths behind the camps. I was sure the tarred road would have found it out and I wondered in what other ways it would be desolated. It is strange how much you can remember about places like that once you allow your mind to return into the grooves which lead back. You remember one thing, and that suddenly reminds you of another thing. I guess I remembered clearest of all the early mornings, when the lake was cool and motionless, remembered how the bedroom smelled of the lumber it was made of and of the wet woods whose scent entered through the screen. The partitions in the camp were thin and did not extend clear to the top of the rooms, and as I was always the first up I would dress softly so as not to wake the others, and sneak out into the sweet outdoors and start out in the canoe, keeping close along the shore in the long shadows of the pines. I remembered being very careful never to rub my paddle against the gunwale for fear of disturbing the stillness of the cathedral.

3    The lake had never been what you would call a wild lake. There were cottages sprinkled around the shores, and it was in farming country although the shores of the lake were quite heavily wooded. Some of the cottages were owned by nearby farmers, and you would live at the shore and eat your meals at the farmhouse. That's what our family did. But although it wasn't wild, it was a fairly large and undisturbed lake and there were places in it which, to a child at least, seemed infinitely remote and primeval.

4    I was right about the tar: it led to within half a mile of the shore. But when I got back there, with my boy, and we settled into a camp near a farmhouse and into the kind of summertime I had known, I could tell that it was going to be pretty much the same as it had been before—I knew it, lying in bed the first morning, smelling the bedroom, and hearing the boy sneak quietly out and go off along the shore in a boat. I began to sustain the illusion that he was I, and therefore, by simple transposition, that I was my father. This sensation persisted, kept cropping up all the time we were there. It was not an entirely new feeling, but in this setting it grew much stronger. I seemed to be living a dual existence. I would be in the middle of some simple act, I would be picking up a bait box or laying down a table fork, or I would be saying something, and suddenly it would be not I but my father who was saying the words or making the gesture. It gave me a creepy sensation.

5    We went fishing the first morning. I felt the same damp moss covering the worms in the bait can, and saw the dragonfly alight on the tip of my rod as it hovered a few inches from the surface of the water. It was the arrival of this fly that convinced me beyond any doubt that everything was as it always had been, that the years were a mirage and there had been no years. The small waves were the same, chucking the rowboat under the chin as we fished at anchor, and the boat was the same boat, the same color green and the ribs broken in the same place, and under the floor-boards the same fresh-water leavings and débris—the dead hellgrammite, the wisps of moss, the rusty discarded fishhook, the dried blood from yesterday's catch. We stared silently at the tips of our rods, at the dragonflies that came and went. I lowered the tip of mine into the water, tentatively, pensively dislodging the fly, which darted two feet away, poised, darted two feet back, and came to rest again a little farther up the rod. There had been no years between the ducking of this dragonfly and the other one—the one that was part of memory. I looked at the boy, who was silently watching his fly, and it was my hands that held his rod, my eyes watching. I felt dizzy and didn't know which rod I was at the end of.

6    We caught two bass, hauling them in briskly as though they were mackerel, pulling them over the side of the boat in a businesslike manner without any landing net, and stunning them with a blow on the back of the head. When we got back for a swim before lunch, the lake was exactly where we had left it, the same

number of inches from the dock, and there was only the merest suggestion of a breeze. This seemed an utterly enchanted sea, this lake you could leave to its own devices for a few hours and come back to, and find that it had not stirred, this constant and trustworthy body of water. In the shallows, the dark, water-soaked sticks and twigs, smooth and old, were undulating in clusters on the bottom against the clean ribbed sand, and the track of the mussel was plain. A school of minnows swam by, each minnow with its small individual shadow, doubling the attendance, so clear and sharp in the sunlight. Some of the other campers were in swimming, along the shore, one of them with a cake of soap, and the water felt thin and clear and unsubstantial. Over the years there had been this person with the cake of soap, this cultist, and here he was. There had been no years.

Up to the farmhouse to dinner through the teeming, dusty field, the road 7 under our sneakers was only a two-track road. The middle track was missing, the one with the marks of the hooves and the splotches of dried, flaky manure. There had always been three tracks to choose from in choosing which track to walk in; now the choice was narrowed down to two. For a moment I missed terribly the middle alternative. But the way led past the tennis court, and something about the way it lay there in the sun reassured me; the tape had loosened along the backline, the alleys were green with plantains and other weeds, and the net (installed in June and removed in September) sagged in the dry noon, and the whole place steamed with midday heat and hunger and emptiness. There was a choice of pie for dessert, and one was blueberry and one was apple, and the waitresses were the same country girls, there having been no passage of time, only the illusion of it as in a dropped curtain—the waitresses were still fifteen; their hair had been washed, that was the only difference—they had been to the movies and seen the pretty girls with the clean hair.

Summertime, oh summertime, pattern of life indelible, the fade-proof lake, 8 the woods unshatterable, the pasture with the sweetfern and the juniper forever and ever, summer without end; this was the background, and the life along the shore was the design, the cottagers with their innocent and tranquil design, their tiny docks with the flagpole and the American flag floating against the white clouds in the blue sky, the little paths over the roots of the trees leading from camp to camp and the paths leading back to the outhouses and the can of lime for sprinkling, and at the souvenir counters at the store the miniature birch-bark canoes and the post cards that showed things looking a little better than they looked. This was the American family at play, escaping the city heat, wondering whether the newcomers in the camp at the head of the cove were "common" or "nice," wondering whether it was true that the people who drove up for Sunday dinner at the farmhouse were turned away because there wasn't enough chicken.

It seemed to me, as I kept remembering all this, that those times and those 9 summers had been infinitely precious and worth saving. There had been jollity and peace and goodness. The arriving (at the beginning of August) had been so big a business in itself, at the railway station the farm wagon drawn up, the first smell of the pine-laden air, the first glimpse of the smiling farmer, and the great importance of the trunks and your father's enormous authority in such matters, and the feel of the wagon under you for the long ten-mile haul, and at the top of the last long hill catching the first view of the lake after eleven months of not seeing this cherished body of water. The shouts and cries of the other campers when they saw you, and the trunks to be unpacked, to give up their rich burden. (Arriving was less exciting nowadays, when you sneaked up in your car and parked it under a tree near the camp and took out the bags and in five minutes it was all over, no fuss, no loud wonderful fuss about trunks.)

10      Peace and goodness and jollity. The only thing that was wrong now, really, was the sound of the place, an unfamiliar nervous sound of the outboard motors. This was the note that jarred, the one thing that would sometimes break the illusion and set the years moving. In those other summertimes all motors were inboard; and when they were at a little distance, the noise they made was a sedative, an ingredient of summer sleep. They were one-cylinder and two-cylinder engines, and some were make-and-break and some were jump-spark, but they all made a sleepy sound across the lake. The one-lungers throbbed and fluttered, and the twin-cylinder ones purred and purred, and that was a quiet sound too. But now the campers all had outboards. In the daytime, in the hot mornings, these motors made a petulant, irritable sound; at night, in the still evening when the afterglow lit the water, they whined about one's ears like mosquitoes. My boy loved our rented outboard, and his great desire was to achieve singlehanded mastery over it, and authority, and he soon learned the trick of choking it a little (but not too much), and the adjustment of the needle valve. Watching him I would remember the things you could do with the old one-cylinder engine with the heavy flywheel, how you could have it eating out of your hand if you got really close to it spiritually. Motor boats in those days didn't have clutches, and you would make a landing by shutting off the motor at the proper time and coasting in with a dead rudder. But there was a way of reversing them, if you learned the trick, by cutting the switch and putting it on again exactly on the final dying revolution of the flywheel, so that it would kick back against compression and begin reversing. Approaching a dock in a strong following breeze, it was difficult to slow up sufficiently by the ordinary coasting method, and if a boy felt he had complete mastery over his motor, he was tempted to keep it running beyond its time and then reverse it a few feet from the dock. It took a cool nerve, because if you threw the switch a twentieth of a second too soon you would catch the flywheel when it still had speed enough to go up past center, and the boat would leap ahead, charging bull-fashion at the dock.

11      We had a good week at the camp. The bass were biting well and the sun shone endlessly, day after day. We would be tired at night and lie down in the accumulated heat of the little bedrooms after the long hot day and the breeze would stir almost imperceptibly outside and the smell of the swamp drift in through the rusty screens. Sleep would come easily and in the morning the red squirrel would be on the roof, tapping out his gay routine. I kept remembering everything, lying in bed in the mornings—the small steamboat that had a long rounded stern like the lip of a Ubangi, and how quietly she ran on the moonlight sails, when the older boys played their mandolins and the girls sang and

we ate doughnuts dipped in sugar, and how sweet the music was on the water in the shining night, and what it had felt like to think about girls then. After breakfast we would go up to the store and the things were in the same place—minnows in a bottle, the plugs and spinners disarranged and pawed over by the youngsters from the boys' camp, the fig newtons and the Beeman's gum. Outside, the road was tarred and cars stood in front of the store. Inside, all was just as it had always been, except there was more Coca-Cola and not so much Moxie and root beer and birch beer and sarsaparilla. We would walk out with a bottle of pop apiece and sometimes the pop would backfire up our noses and hurt. We explored the streams, quietly, where the turtles slid off the sunny logs and dug their way into the soft bottom, and we lay on the town wharf and fed worms to the tame bass. Everywhere we went I had trouble making out which was I, the one walking at my side, the one walking in my pants.

One afternoon while we were there at that lake a thunderstorm came up. It 12 was like the revival of an old melodrama that I had seen long ago with childish awe. The second-act climax of the drama of the electrical disturbance over a lake in America had not changed in any important respect. This was the big scene, still the big scene. The whole thing was so familiar, the first feeling of oppression and heat and a general air around camp of not wanting to go very far away. In midafternoon (it was all the same) a curious darkening of the sky, and a lull in everything that had made life tick; and then the way the boats suddenly swung the other way at their moorings with the coming of a breeze out of the new quarter, and the premonitory rumble. Then the kettle drum, then the snare, then the bass drum and cymbals, then crackling light against the dark, and the gods grinning and licking their chops in the hills. Afterward the calm, the rain steadily rustling in the calm lake, the return of light and hope and spirits, and the campers running out in joy and relief to go swimming in the rain, their bright cries perpetuating the deathless joke about how they were getting simply drenched, and the children screaming with delight at the new sensation of bathing in the rain, and the joke about getting drenched linking the generations in a strong indestructible chain. And the comedian who waded in carrying an umbrella.

When the others went swimming my son said he was going in too. He 13 pulled his dripping trunks from the line where they had hung all through the shower, and wrung them out. Languidly, and with no thought of going in, I watched him, his hard little body, skinny and bare, saw him wince slightly as he pulled up around his vitals the small, soggy, icy garment. As he buckled the swollen belt suddenly my groin felt the chill of death.

## COMPREHENSION

1. At what point in the essay do you begin to sense White's main purpose? What is his purpose? What type of reader might his purpose appeal to?
2. What motivates White to return to the lake in Maine? Explain the "simple transposition" that he mentions in paragraph 4. List the illustrations that he gives of this phenomenon. What change does he detect in the lake?

3. Explain the significance of White's last sentence. Where are there foreshadowings of this statement?

## RHETORIC

1. Describe White's use of figurative language in paragraphs 2, 10, and 12.
2. Identify those words and phrases that White invokes to establish the sense of mystery about the lake. Why are these words and their connotations important to the nature of the illusion that he describes?
3. Explain the organization of the essay in terms of the following paragraph units: 1–4, 5–7, 8–10, and 11–13. Explain the function of paragraphs 8 and 12.
4. There are many vivid and unusual descriptive details in this essay—for example, the dragonfly in paragraph 5 and the two-track road in paragraph 7. How does White create symbolic overtones for these descriptive details and others? Why is the lake itself a complex symbol? Explain with reference to paragraph 6.
5. Describe the persona that White creates for himself in the essay. How does this persona function?
6. What is the relation between the introductory and concluding paragraphs, specifically in terms of irony of statement?

## WRITING

1. Explore in an essay the theme of nostalgia in "Once More to the Lake." What are the beauties and the dangers of nostalgia? Can the past ever be recaptured or relived? Justify your answer.
2. White consistently compares an outing with his father to one with his son. How does this structure help to emphasize the continuity of generations? Explain in an analytical and comparative essay.
3. Referring to revisiting a site on the lake that he had visited years before with his father, White remarks in paragraph 4, "I could tell that it was going to be pretty much the same as it had been before." How does this observation reflect the general sentiment White has about the role and function of the family? Respond to the question in an analytical essay.
4. **Writing an Argument**: Argue for or against the proposition that nostalgia can obscure the true nature of family relationships and even suppress painful memories that should be confronted.

# Stone Soup

## Barbara Kingsolver

*Barbara Kingsolver (b. 1955) was born in Annapolis, Maryland; grew up in rural Kentucky, and was educated at DePauw University and the University of Arizona. Her fiction includes* The Bean Trees *(1988);* Homeland *(1990);* Animal Dreams *(1991), for which she won a PEN fiction prize and an Edward Abbey Ecofiction Award;* Pigs in Heaven *(1993), which won a* Los Angeles Times *Book Award for Fiction; and* The Poisonwood Bible *(1998). She has also worked as a biologist, is active in the field of human rights, and plays keyboard with an amateur rock 'n' roll band. The following essay, first published in the January 1995 issue of* Parenting, *eschews the idea of the nuclear family as the standard by which the healthy family should be judged.*

In the catalog of family values, where do we rank an occasion like this? A curly-haired boy who wanted to run before he walked, age seven now, a soccer player scoring a winning goal. He turns to the bleachers with his fists in the air and a smile wide as a gap-toothed galaxy. His own cheering section of grown-ups and kids all leap to their feet and hug each other, delirious with love for this boy. He's Andy, my best friend's son. The cheering section includes his mother and her friends, his brother, his father and stepmother, a stepbrother and stepsister, and a grandparent. Lucky is the child with this many relatives on hand to hail a proud accomplishment. I'm there too, witnessing a family fortune. But in spite of myself, defensive words take shape in my head. I am thinking: I dare *anybody* to call this a broken home.

Families change, and remain the same. Why are our names for home so slow to catch up to the truth of where we live?

When I was a child, I had two parents who loved me without cease. One of them attended every excuse for attention I ever contrived, and the other made it to the ones with higher production values, like piano recitals and appendicitis. So I was a lucky child too. I played with a set of paper dolls called "The Family of Dolls," four in number, who came with the factory-assigned names of Dad, Mom, Sis, and Junior. I think you know what they looked like, at least before I loved them to death and their heads fell off.

Now I've replaced the dolls with a life. I knit my days around my daughter's survival and happiness, and am proud to say her head is still on. But we aren't the Family of Dolls. Maybe you're not, either. And if not, even though you are statistically no oddity, it's probably been suggested to you in a hundred ways that yours isn't exactly a real family, but an impostor family, a harbinger of cultural ruin, a slapdash substitute—something like counterfeit money. Here at the tail end of our century, most of us are up to our ears in the noisy business of trying to support and love a thing called family. But there's a current in the air with ferocious moral force that finds its way even into political campaigns, claiming there is only one right way to do it, the Way It Has Always Been.

5    In the face of a thriving, particolored world, this narrow view is so pickled and absurd I'm astonished that it gets airplay. And I'm astonished that it still stings.

6    Every parent has endured the arrogance of a child-unfriendly grump sitting in judgment, explaining what those kids of ours really need (for example, "a good licking"). If we're polite, we move our crew to another bench in the park. If we're forthright (as I am in my mind, only, for the rest of the day), we fix them with a sweet imperious stare and say, "Come back and let's talk about it after you've changed a thousand diapers."

7    But it's harder somehow to shrug off the Family-of-Dolls Family Values crew when they judge (from their safe distance) that divorced people, blended families, gay families, and single parents are failures. That our children are at risk, and the whole arrangement is messy and embarrassing. A marriage that ends is not called "finished," it's called *failed*. The children of this family may have been born to a happy union, but now they are called *the children of divorce*.

8    I had no idea how thoroughly these assumptions overlaid my culture until I went through divorce myself. I wrote to a friend: "This might be worse than being widowed. Overnight I've suffered the same losses—companionship, financial and practical support, my identity as a wife and partner, the future I'd taken for granted. I am lonely, grieving, and hard-pressed to take care of my household alone. But instead of bringing casseroles, people are acting like I had a fit and broke up the family china."

9    Once upon a time I held these beliefs about divorce: that everyone who does it could have chosen not to do it. That it's a lazy way out of marital problems. That it selfishly puts personal happiness ahead of family integrity. Now I tremble for my ignorance. It's easy, in fortunate times, to forget about the ambush that could leave your head reeling: serious mental or physical illness, death in the family, abandonment, financial calamity, humiliation, violence, despair.

10    I started out like any child, intent on being the Family of Dolls. I set upon young womanhood believing in most of the doctrines of my generation: I wore my skirts four inches above the knee. I had that Barbie with her zebra-striped swimsuit and a figure unlike anything found in nature. And I understood the Prince Charming Theory of Marriage, a quest for Mr. Right that ends smack dab where you find him. I did not completely understand that another whole story *begins* there, and no fairy tale prepared me for the combination of bad luck and persistent hope that would interrupt my dream and lead me to other arrangements. Like a cancer diagnosis, a dying marriage is a thing to fight, to deny, and finally, when there's no choice left, to dig in and survive. Casseroles would help. Likewise, I imagine it must be a painful reckoning in adolescence (or later on) to realize one's own true love will never look like the soft-focus fragrance ads because Prince Charming (surprise!) is a princess. Or vice versa. Or has skin the color your parents didn't want you messing with, except in the Crayola box.

It's awfully easy to hold in contempt the straw broken home, and that  11
mythical category of persons who toss away nuclear family for the sheer fun of
it. Even the legal terms we use have a suggestion of caprice. I resent the phrase
"irreconcilable differences," which suggests a stubborn refusal to accept a
spouse's little quirks. This is specious. Every happily married couple I know
has loads of irreconcilable differences. Negotiating where to set the thermostat
is not the point. A nonfunctioning marriage is a slow asphyxiation. It is waking
up despised each morning, listening to the pulse of your own loneliness before
the radio begins to blare its raucous gospel that you're nothing if you aren't
loved. It is sharing your airless house with the threat of suicide or other kinds
of violence, while the ghost that whispers, "Leave here and destroy your children," has passed over every door and nailed it shut. Disassembling a marriage
in these circumstances is as much *fun* as amputating your own gangrenous leg.
You do it, if you can, to save a life—or two, or more.

I know of no one who really went looking to hoe the harder row, especially  12
the daunting one of single parenthood. Yet it seems to be the most American of
customs to blame the burdened for their destiny. We'd like so desperately to
believe in freedom and justice for all, we can hardly name that rogue bad luck,
even when he's a close enough snake to bite us. In the wake of my divorce,
some friends (even a few close ones) chose to vanish, rather than linger within
striking distance of misfortune.

But most stuck around, bless their hearts, and if I'm any the wiser for my  13
trials, it's from having learned the worth of steadfast friendship. And also, what
not to say. The least helpful question is: "Did you want the divorce, or didn't
you?" Did I want to keep that gangrenous leg, or not? How to explain, in a culture that venerates choice: two terrifying options are much worse than none at
all. Give me any day the quick hand of cruel fate that will leave me scarred but
blameless. As it was, I kept thinking of that wicked third-grade joke in which
some boy comes up behind you and grabs your ear, starts in with a prolonged
tug, and asks, "Do you want this ear any longer?"

Still, the friend who holds your hand and says the wrong thing is made of  14
dearer stuff than the one who stays away. And generally, through all of it, you
live. My favorite fictional character, Kate Vaiden (in the novel by Reynolds
Price), advises: "Strength just comes in one brand—you stand up at sunrise and
meet what they send you and keep your hair combed."

Once you've weathered the straits, you get to cross the tricky juncture  15
from casualty to survivor. If you're on your feet at the end of a year or two,
and have begun putting together a happy new existence, those friends who
were kind enough to feel sorry for you when you needed it must now accept
you back to the ranks of the living. If you're truly blessed, they will dance at
your second wedding. Everybody else, for heavens sake, should stop throwing stones.

Arguing about whether nontraditional families deserve pity or tolerance is a  16
little like the medieval debate about left-handedness as a mark of the devil.

Divorce, remarriage, single parenthood, gay parents, and blended families simply are. They're facts of our time. Some of the reasons listed by sociologists for these family reconstructions are: the idea of marriage as a romantic partnership rather than a pragmatic one; a shift in women's expectations, from servility to self-respect and independence; and longevity (prior to antibiotics no marriage was expected to last many decades—in Colonial days the average couple lived to be married less than twelve years). Add to all this, our growing sense of entitlement to happiness and safety from abuse. Most would agree these are all good things. Yet their result—a culture in which serial monogamy and the consequent reshaping of families are the norm—gets diagnosed as "failing."

17      For many of us, once we have put ourselves Humpty-Dumpty–wise back together again, the main problem with our reorganized family is that other people think we have a problem. My daughter tells me the only time she's uncomfortable about being the child of divorced parents is when her friends say they feel sorry for her. It's a bizarre sympathy, given that half the kids in her school and nation are in the same boat, pursuing childish happiness with the same energy as their married-parent peers. When anyone asks how she feels about it, she spontaneously lists the benefits: our house is in the country and we have a dog, but she can go to her dad's neighborhood for the urban thrills of a pool and sidewalks for roller-skating. What's more, she has three sets of grandparents!

18      Why is it surprising that a child would revel in a widened family and the right to feel at home in more than one house? Isn't it the opposite that should worry us—a child with no home at all, or too few resources to feel safe? The child at risk is the one whose parents are too immature themselves to guide wisely; too diminished by poverty to nurture; too far from opportunity to offer hope. The number of children in the U.S. living in poverty at this moment is almost unfathomably large: twenty percent. There are families among us that need help all right, and by no means are they new on the landscape. The rate at which teenage girls had babies in 1957 (ninety-six per thousand) was twice what it is now. That remarkable statistic is ignored by the religious right— probably because the teen birth rate was cut in half mainly by legalized abortion. In fact, the policy gatekeepers who coined the phrase "family values" have steadfastly ignored the desperation of too-small families, and since 1979 have steadily reduced the amount of financial support available to a single parent. But, this camp's most outspoken attacks seem aimed at the notion of families getting too complex, with add-ons and extras such as a gay parent's partner, or a remarried mother's new husband and his children.

19      To judge a family's value by its tidy symmetry is to purchase a book for its cover. There's no moral authority there. The famous family comprised by Dad, Mom, Sis, and Junior living as an isolated economic unit is not built on historical bedrock. In *The Way We Never Were*, Stephanie Coontz writes, "Whenever people propose that we go back to the traditional family, I always suggest that they pick a ballpark date for the family they have in mind." Colonial families were tidily disciplined, but their members (meaning everyone but infants) labored incessantly and died young. Then the Victorian family adopted a new

division of labor, in which women's role was domestic and children were allowed time for study and play, but this was an upper-class construct supported by myriad slaves. Coontz writes, "For every nineteenth-century middle-class family that protected its wife and child within the family circle, there was an Irish or German girl scrubbing floors . . . a Welsh boy mining coal to keep the home-baked goodies warm, a black girl doing the family laundry, a black mother and child picking cotton to be made into clothes for the family, and a Jewish or an Italian daughter in a sweatshop making 'ladies' dresses or artificial flowers for the family to purchase."

The abolition of slavery brought slightly more democratic arrangements, in    20
which extended families were harnessed together in cottage industries; at the turn of the century came a steep rise in child labor in mines and sweat-shops. Twenty percent of American children lived in orphanages at the time; their parents were not necessarily dead, but couldn't afford to keep them.

During the Depression and up to the end of World War II, many millions of    21
U.S. households were more multigenerational than nuclear. Women my grandmother's age were likely to live with a fluid assortment of elderly relatives, in-laws, siblings, and children. In many cases they spent virtually every waking hour working in the company of other women—a companionable scenario in which it would be easier, I imagine, to tolerate an estranged or difficult spouse. I'm reluctant to idealize a life of so much hard work and so little spousal intimacy, but its advantage may have been resilience. A family so large and varied would not easily be brought down by a single blow: it could absorb a death, long-illness, an abandonment here or there, and any number of irreconcilable differences.

The Family of Dolls came along midcentury as a great American experi-    22
ment. A booming economy required a mobile labor force and demanded that women surrender jobs to returning soldiers. Families came to be defined by a single breadwinner. They struck out for single-family homes at an earlier age than ever before, and in unprecedented numbers they raised children in suburban isolation. The nuclear family was launched to sink or swim.

More than a few sank. Social historians corroborate that the suburban fam-    23
ily of the postwar economic boom, which we have recently selected as our definition of "traditional," was no panacea. Twenty-five percent of Americans were poor in the mid-1950s, and as yet there were no food stamps. Sixty percent of the elderly lived on less than $1,000 a year, and most had no medical insurance. In the sequestered suburbs, alcoholism and sexual abuse of children were far more widespread than anyone imagined.

Expectations soared, and the economy sagged. It's hard to depend on one    24
other adult for everything, come what may. In the last three decades, that amorphous, adaptable structure we call "family" has been reshaped once more by economic tides. Compared with fifties families, mothers are far more likely now to be employed. We are statistically more likely to divorce, and to live in blended families or other extranuclear arrangements. We are also more likely to plan and space our children, and to rate our marriages as "happy." We are less

likely to suffer abuse without recourse, or to stare out at our lives through a glaze of prescription tranquilizers. Our aged parents are less likely to be destitute, and we're half as likely to have a teenage daughter turn up a mother herself. All in all, I would say that if "intact" in modern family-values jargon means living quietly desperate in the bell jar, then hip-hip-hooray for "broken." A neat family model constructed to service the Baby Boom economy seems to be returning gradually to a grand, lumpy shape that human families apparently have tended toward since they first took root in the Olduvai Gorge. We're social animals, deeply fond of companionship, and children love best to run in packs. If there is a *normal* for humans, at all, I expect it looks like two or three Families of Dolls, connected variously by kinship and passion, shuffled like cards and strewn over several shoeboxes.

25    The sooner we can let go the fairy tale of families functioning perfectly in isolation, the better we might embrace the relief of community. Even the admirable parents who've stayed married through thick and thin are very likely, at present, to incorporate other adults into their families—household help and baby-sitters if they can afford them or neighbors and grandparents if they can't. For single parents, this support is the rock-bottom definition of family. And most parents who have split apart, however painfully, still manage to maintain family continuity for their children, creating in many cases a boisterous phenomenon that Constance Ahrons in her book *The Good Divorce* calls the "binuclear family." Call it what you will—when ex-spouses beat swords into plowshares and jump up and down at a soccer game together, it makes for happy kids.

26    Cinderella, look, who needs her? All those evil stepsisters? That story always seemed like too much cotton-picking fuss over clothes. A childhood tale that fascinated me more was the one called "Stone Soup," and the gist of it is this: Once upon a time, a pair of beleaguered soldiers straggled home to a village empty-handed, in a land ruined by war. They were famished, but the villagers had so little they shouted evil words and slammed their doors. So the soldiers dragged out a big kettle, filled it with water, and put it on a fire to boil. They rolled a clean round stone into the pot, while the villagers peered through their curtains in amazement.

27    "What kind of soup is that?" they hooted.

28    "Stone soup," the soldiers replied. "Everybody can have some when it's done."

29    "Well, thanks," one matron grumbled, coming out with a shriveled carrot. "But it'd be better if you threw this in."

30    And so on, of course, a vegetable at a time, until the whole suspicious village managed to feed itself grandly.

31    Any family is a big empty pot, save for what gets thrown in. Each stew turns out different. Generosity, a resolve to turn bad luck into good, and respect for variety—these things will nourish a nation of children. Name-calling and suspicion will not. My soup contains a rock or two of hard times, and maybe yours does too. I expect it's a heck of a bouillabaisse.

## COMPREHENSION

1. What is the essay's thesis?
2. According to Kingsolver, why is our society so apt to condemn divorce?
3. What is the author's view of family symmetry (paragraph 19)?

## RHETORIC

1. What rhetorical function does the opening anecdote serve in introducing the essay's subject matter?
2. What is Kingsolver's purpose in capitalizing, italicizing, and placing quotation marks around certain phrases—for example, "Way It Has Always Been" (paragraph 4), *failed* and *children of divorce* (paragraph 7), and "family values" (paragraph 18)?
3. What is the author's purpose in creating a gap between paragraphs 15 and 16? What is the focus of her argument after this break?
4. Compare the introductory paragraph with the concluding one. How do they differ? How are they similar? How do they help set the boundaries of the essay?
5. This essay contains personal observations, personal experiences, historical data, and anecdotes. How would you describe the author's overall method to a person who has not read the essay?
6. Unlike the titles of most essays, the title "Stone Soup" gives no hint at the essay's content. What is the rhetorical purpose in keeping the meaning of the title a mystery until the very end?
7. In paragraph 2, Kingsolver asks the question, "Why are our names for home so slow to catch up to the truth of where we live?" Does the author suggest an answer to this question either implicitly or explicitly during the course of the essay? If so, where?

## WRITING

1. Interview two individuals at least 25 years apart in age. Compare and contrast their views on divorce.
2. Describe the dynamics of a blended family with which you are familiar. It may be your own or a friend's.
3. **Writing an Argument:** Write an essay arguing that some negative outcomes could occur in the type of family the author celebrates.

www.mhhe.com/
**mhreader**

For more information on Barabara Kingsolver, go to:
**More Resources > Ch. 5 Family & Gender**

## Synthesis: Classic and Contemporary Questions for Comparison

1. Compare and contrast the tone of each writer. How does tone affect purpose? How does it affect mood? Select at least three passages from White and three from Kingsolver that demonstrate how their tones differ. Do they offer any hints as to the "voice" or personality of the writers? Why or why not?

2. What contemporary issues does Kingsolver address that White either ignores or is unaware of? Consider that White was born 58 years before Kingsolver, so his world was quite a different one. Are there other variables that might help us distinguish their concerns and outlooks—for example, gender, class, and environment?

3. What central values does each author have regarding the family? How are they similar? How do they differ? How do their values reflect their times?

# An American Childhood

### Annie Dillard

*Annie Dillard (b. 1945 in Pittsburgh) received her BA and MA degrees from Hollins College. Her first book,* Pilgrim at Tinker Creek *(1975), won the Pulitzer Prize for general nonfiction. Her other published works of nonfiction include* Teaching a Stone to Talk *(1982) and* An American Childhood *(1987). Dillard expanded her range of writing with the publication of her first novel,* The Living *(1992), and her latest novel,* The Maytrees *(2007). She has received awards from the National Endowment for the Arts and the Guggenheim Foundation as well as many other sources. As an essayist, poet, memoirist, and literary critic, she focuses her themes on the relationships among the self, nature, religion, and faith. Her writing is recognizable by its observations of the minutiae of life and its search for meaning in unlikely places, such as a stone or an insect. In this passage from* An American Childhood, *the author gives us a portrait of her mother by focusing on her small idiosyncrasies of speech, gesture, and attitude.*

1 One Sunday afternoon Mother wandered through our kitchen, where Father was making a sandwich and listening to the ball game. The Pirates were playing the New York Giants at Forbes Field. In those days, the Giants had a utility infielder named Wayne Terwilliger. Just as Mother passed through, the radio announcer cried—with undue drama—"Terwilliger bunts one!"

2 "Terwilliger bunts one?" Mother cried back, stopped short. She turned. "Is that English?"

3 "The player's name is Terwilliger," Father said. "He bunted."

"That's marvelous," Mother said. "'Terwilliger bunts one.' No wonder you ₄ listen to baseball. 'Terwilliger bunts one.'"

For the next seven or eight years, Mother made this surprising string of syl- ₅ lables her own. Testing a microphone, she repeated, "Terwilliger bunts one"; testing a pen or a typewriter, she wrote it. If, as happened surprisingly often in the course of various improvised gags, she pretended to whisper something else in my ear, she actually whispered, "Terwilliger bunts one." Whenever someone used a French phrase, or a Latin one, she answered solemnly, "Terwilliger bunts one." If Mother had had, like Andrew Carnegie, the opportunity to cook up a motto for a coat of arms, hers would have read simply and tellingly, "Terwilliger bunts one." (Carnegie's was "Death to Privilege.")

She served us with other words and phrases. On a Florida trip, she repeated ₆ tremulously, "That . . . is a royal poinciana." I don't remember the tree; I remember the thrill in her voice. She pronounced it carefully, and spelled it. She also liked to say "portulaca."

The drama of the words "Tamiami Trail" stirred her, we learned on the ₇ same Florida trip. People built Tampa on one coast, and they built Miami on another. Then—the height of visionary ambition and folly—they piled a slow, tremendous road through the terrible Everglades to connect them. To build the road, men stood sunk in muck to their armpits. They fought off cottonmouth moccasins and six-foot alligators. They slept in boats, wet. They blasted muck with dynamite, cut jungle with machetes; they laid logs, dragged drilling machines, hauled dredges, heaped limestone. The road took fourteen years to build up by the shovelful, a Panama Canal in reverse, and cost hundreds of lives from tropical, mosquito-carried diseases. Then, capping it all, some genius thought of the word Tamiami: they called the road from Tampa to Miami, this very road under our spinning wheels, the Tamiami Trail. Some called it Alligator Alley. Anyone could drive over this road without a thought.

Hearing this, moved, I thought all the suffering of road building was worth ₈ it (it wasn't my suffering), now that we had this new thing to hang these new words on—Alligator Alley for those who liked things cute, and, for connoisseurs like Mother, for lovers of the human drama in all its boldness and terror, the Tamiami Trail.

Back home, Mother cut clips from reels of talk, as it were, and played ₉ them back at leisure. She noticed that many Pittsburghers confuse "leave" and "let." One kind relative brightened our morning by mentioning why she'd brought her son to visit: "He wanted to come with me, so I left him." Mother filled in Amy and me on locutions we missed. "I can't do it on Friday," her pretty sister told a crowded dinner party, "because Friday's the day I lay in the stores."

(All unconsciously, though, we ourselves used some pure Pittsburghisms. ₁₀ We said "tele pole," pronounced "telly pole," for that splintery sidewalk post I loved to climb. We said "slippy"—the sidewalks are "slippy." We said, "That's all the farther I could go." And we said, as Pittsburghers do say, "This glass needs washed," or "The dog needs walked"—a usage our father eschewed; he knew it was not standard English, nor even comprehensible English, but he never let on.)

11 "Spell 'poinsettia,'" Mother would throw out at me, smiling with pleasure. "Spell 'sherbet.'" The idea was not to make us whizzes, but, quite the contrary, to remind us—and I, especially, needed reminding—that we didn't know it all just yet.

12 "There's a deer standing in the front hall," she told me one quiet evening in the country.

13 "Really?"

14 "No. I just wanted to tell you something once without your saying, 'I know.'"

15 Supermarkets in the middle 1950s began luring, or bothering, customers by giving out Top Value Stamps or Green Stamps. When, shopping with Mother, we got to the head of the checkout line, the checker, always a young man, asked, "Save stamps?"

16 "No," Mother replied genially, week after week, "I build model airplanes." I believe she originated this line. It took me years to determine where the joke lay.

17 Anyone who met her verbal challenges she adored. She had surgery on one of her eyes. On the operating table, just before she conked out, she appealed feelingly to the surgeon, saying, as she had been planning to say for weeks, "Will I be able to play the piano?" "Not on me," the surgeon said. "You won't pull that old one on me."

18 It was, indeed, an old one. The surgeon was supposed to answer, "Yes, my dear, brave woman, you will be able to play the piano after this operation," to which Mother intended to reply, "Oh, good, I've always wanted to play the piano." This pat scenario bored her; she loved having it interrupted. It must have galled her that usually her acquaintances were so predictably unalert; it must have galled her that, for the length of her life, she could surprise everyone so continually, so easily, when she had been the same all along. At any rate, she loved anyone who, as she put it, saw it coming, and called her on it.

19 She regarded the instructions on bureaucratic forms as straight lines. "Do you advocate the overthrow of the United States government by force or violence?" After some thought she wrote, "Force." She regarded children, even babies, as straight men. When Molly learned to crawl, Mother delighted in buying her gowns with drawstrings at the bottom, like Swee'pea's, because, as she explained energetically, you could easily step on the drawstring without the baby's noticing, so that she crawled and crawled and crawled and never got anywhere except into a small ball at the gown's top.

20 When we children were young, she mothered us tenderly and dependably; as we got older, she resumed her career of anarchism. She collared us into her gags. If she answered the phone on a wrong number, she told the caller, "Just a minute," and dragged the receiver to Amy or me, saying, "Here, take this, your name is Cecile," or, worse, just, "It's for you." You had to think on your feet.

But did you want to perform well as Cecile, or did you want to take pity on the wretched caller?

During a family trip to the Highland Park Zoo, Mother and I were alone for 21 a minute. She approached a young couple holding hands on a bench by the seals, and addressed the young man in dripping tones: "Where have you been? Still got those baby-blue eyes; always did slay me. And this"—a swift nod at the dumbstruck young woman, who had removed her hand from the man's— "must be the one you were telling me about. She's not so bad, really, as you used to make out. But listen, you know how I miss you, you know where to reach me, same old place. And there's Ann over there—see how she's grown? See the blue eyes?"

And off she sashayed, taking me firmly by the hand, and leading us around 22 briskly past the monkey house and away. She cocked an ear back, and both of us heard the desperate man begin, in a high-pitched wail, "I swear, I never saw her before in my life . . ."

On a long, sloping beach by the ocean, she lay stretched out sunning with 23 Father and friends, until the conversation gradually grew tedious, when without forethought she gave a little push with her heel and rolled away. People were stunned. She rolled deadpan and apparently effortlessly, arms and legs extended and tidy, down the beach to the distant water's edge, where she lay at ease just as she had been, but half in the surf, and well out of earshot.

She dearly loved to fluster people by throwing out a game's rules at a 24 whim—when she was getting bored, losing in a dull sort of way, and when everybody else was taking it too seriously. If you turned your back, she moved the checkers around on the board. When you got them all straightened out, she denied she'd touched them; the next time you turned your back, she lined them up on the rug or hid them under your chair. In a betting rummy game called Michigan, she routinely played out of turn, or called out a card she didn't hold, or counted backward, simply to amuse herself by causing an uproar and watching the rest of us do double-takes and have fits. (Much later, when serious suitors came to call, Mother subjected them to this fast card game as a trial by ordeal; she used it as an intelligence test and a measure of spirit. If the poor man could stay a round without breaking down or running out, he got to marry one of us, if he still wanted to.)

She excelled at bridge, playing fast and boldly, but when the stakes were 25 low and the hands dull, she bid slams for the devilment of it, or raised her opponents' suit to bug them, or showed her hand, or tossed her cards in a handful behind her back in a characteristic swift motion accompanied by a vibrantly innocent look. It drove our stolid father crazy. The hand was over before it began, and the guests were appalled. How do you score it, who deals now, what do you do with a crazy person who is having so much fun? Or they were down seven, and the guests were appalled. "Pam!" "Dammit, Pam!" He groaned. What ails such people? What on earth possesses them? He rubbed his face.

26    She was an unstoppable force; she never let go. When we moved across town, she persuaded the U.S. Post Office to let her keep her old address—forever—because she'd had stationery printed. I don't know how she did it. Every new post office worker, over decades, needed to learn that although the Doaks' mail is addressed to here, it is delivered to there.

27    Mother's energy and intelligence suited her for a greater role in a larger arena—mayor of New York, say—than the one she had. She followed American politics closely; she had been known to vote for Democrats. She saw how things should be run, but she had nothing to run but our household. Even there, small minds bugged her; she was smarter than the people who designed the things she had to use all day for the length of her life.

28    "Look," she said. "Whoever designed this corkscrew never used one. Why would anyone sell it without trying it out?" So she invented a better one. She showed me a drawing of it. The spirit of American enterprise never faded in Mother. If capitalizing and tooling up had been as interesting as theorizing and thinking up, she would have fired up a new factory every week, and chaired several hundred corporations.

29    "It grieves me," she would say, "it grieves my heart," that the company that made one superior product packaged it poorly, or took the wrong tack in its advertising. She knew, as she held the thing mournfully in her two hands, that she'd never find another. She was right. We children wholly sympathized, and so did Father; what could she do, what could anyone do, about it? She was Samson in chains. She paced.

30    She didn't like the taste of stamps so she didn't lick stamps; she licked the corner of the envelope instead. She glued sandpaper to the sides of kitchen drawers, and under kitchen cabinets, so she always had a handy place to strike a match. She designed, and hounded workmen to build against all norms, doubly wide kitchen counters and elevated bathroom sinks. To splint a finger, she stuck it in a lightweight cigar tube. Conversely, to protect a pack of cigarettes, she carried it in a Band-Aid box. She drew plans for an over-the-finger toothbrush for babies, an oven rack that slid up and down, and—the family favorite—Lendalarm. Lendalarm was a beeper you attached to books (or tools) you loaned friends. After ten days, the beeper sounded. Only the rightful owner could silence it.

31    She repeatedly reminded us of P. T. Barnum's dictum: You could sell anything to anybody if you marketed it right. The adman who thought of making Americans believe they needed underarm deodorant was a visionary. So, too, was the hero who made a success of a new product, Ivory soap. The executives were horrified, Mother told me, that a cake of this stuff floated. Soap wasn't supposed to float. Anyone would be able to tell it was mostly whipped-up air. Then some inspired adman made a leap: Advertise that it floats. Flaunt it. The rest is history.

32    She respected the rare few who broke through to new ways. "Look," she'd say, "here's an intelligent apron." She called upon us to admire intelligent control knobs and intelligent pan handles, intelligent andirons and

picture frames and knife sharpeners. She questioned everything, every pair of scissors, every knitting needle, gardening glove, tape dispenser. Hers was a restless mental vigor that just about ignited the dumb household objects with its force.

Torpid conformity was a kind of sin; it was stupidity itself, the mighty stream 33 against which Mother would never cease to struggle. If you held no minority opinions, or if you failed to risk total ostracism for them daily, the world would be a better place without you.

Always I heard Mother's emotional voice asking Amy and me the same 34 few questions: "Is that your own idea? Or somebody else's?" "*Giant* is a good movie," I pronounced to the family at dinner. "Oh, really?" Mother warmed to these occasions. She all but rolled up her sleeves. She knew I hadn't seen it. "Is that your considered opinion?"

She herself held many unpopular, even fantastic, positions. She was 35 scathingly sarcastic about the McCarthy hearings while they took place, right on our living-room television; she frantically opposed Father's wait-and-see calm. "We don't know enough about it," he said. "I do," she said. "I know all I need to know."

She asserted, against all opposition, that people who lived in trailer parks 36 were not bad but simply poor, and had as much right to settle on beautiful land, such as rural Ligonier, Pennsylvania, as did the oldest of families in the finest of hidden houses. Therefore, the people who owned trailer parks, and sought zoning changes to permit trailer parks, needed our help. Her profound belief that the country-club pool sweeper was a person, and that the department-store saleslady, the bus driver, telephone operator, and house-painter were people, and even in groups the steelworkers who carried pickets and the Christmas shoppers who clogged intersections were people—this was a conviction common enough in democratic Pittsburgh, but not altogether common among our friends' parents, or even, perhaps, among our parents' friends.

Opposition emboldened Mother, and she would take on anybody on any 37 issue—the chairman of the board, at a cocktail party, on the current strike; she would fly at him in a flurry of passion, as a songbird selflessly attacks a big hawk.

"Eisenhower's going to win," I announced after school. She lowered her 38 magazine and looked me in the eyes: "How do you know?" I was doomed. It was fatal to say, "Everyone says so." We all knew well what happened. "Do you consult this Everyone before you make your decisions? What if Everyone decided to round up all the Jews?" Mother knew there was no danger of cowing me. She simply tried to keep us all awake. And in fact it was always clear to Amy and me, and to Molly when she grew old enough to listen, that if our classmates came to cruelty, just as much as if the neighborhood or the nation came to madness, we were expected to take, and would be each separately capable of taking, a stand.

# COMPREHENSION

1. Dillard creates a picture of her mother's personality through a number of anecdotes and explanations. How would you sum up the mother's personality?
2. Dillard's mother appears to have a special appreciation for words and language. To what purpose does she apply this appreciation? What effect does it have on her family and acquaintances?
3. What values does the mother hold? What behaviors and attitudes does she abhor and discourage?

# RHETORIC

1. In paragraph 7, Dillard explains that the highway from Tampa to Miami is referred to either as "Tamiami Trail" or "Alligator Alley." What is the connotation of each of these terms? Why does her mother prefer to call it "Tamiami Trail"?
2. The author herself seems to have inherited a special fascination for language. Study her use of dashes and semicolons in paragraphs 26 and 27. How do they help contribute to energetic writing?
3. What are the functions of the spaces between paragraphs 19 and 20, 22 and 23, and 32 and 33? How do these divisions contribute to the structure of the essay as a whole?
4. How does Dillard use her writing talents to create paragraph 8 out of one long sentence? What other examples can you provide of long sentences in the essay? How do they contribute to the overall style of the writing?
5. What is the overall emotional "tone" of the writer toward her subject—admiring, or loving, or cautionary? What adjectives does she use in describing her mother that provides the reader with clues to the tone?
6. Dillard quotes her mother directly on several occasions. Can we assume that she is quoting precisely, given that the essay was written years after the incidents described? Does it matter?
7. The final paragraph not only provides closure to the essay but transmits a lesson the mother wants her family to learn. How do the style and structure of this paragraph contribute to the ultimate message of the essay? In other words, how does the form help convey the meaning?

# WRITING

1. Write a descriptive essay about someone you know, using at least five anecdotes from that person's life, so that by the end of the essay, we have a mental picture of your subject's personality, values, and attitudes.
2. Describe an incident in your life when the unexpected taught you an important lesson.

3. **Writing an Argument:** Argue for or against the proposition that an effective parent should have—at least—a touch of unconventionality.

www.mhhe.com/ **mhreader**

For more information on Annie Dillard, go to:
**More Resources > Ch. 5 Family & Gender**

# Love, Internet Style

### David Brooks

*David Brooks (b. 1961) is a columnist for the op-ed page of* The New York Times. *Prior to joining the* Times, *he was a senior editor at the* Weekly Standard, *an op-ed page editor at* The Wall Street Journal, *and a contributing editor to* Newsweek. *He is also a weekly guest on* The NewsHour with Jim Lehrer *on PBS. A graduate of the University of Chicago, Brooks writes on a wide range of topics, often from a conservative perspective; he has edited* Backward and Upward: The New Conservative Writing. *Brooks's recent books* Bobos in Paradise: The New Upper Class and How They Got There *(2000) and* On Paradise Drive *(2004), which explores the lives of people living in the suburbs, offer fascinating and often amusing insights into contemporary American culture. In this essay, which appeared in* The New York Times *in 2003, Brooks examines the ways in which the Internet facilitates personal relationships.*

The Internet slows things down. 1

If you're dating in the Age of the Hook-Up, sex is this looming possibility 2 from the first moment you meet a prospective partner. But couples who meet through online dating services tend to exchange e-mail for weeks or months. Then they'll progress to phone conversations for a few more weeks. Only then will there be a face-to-face meeting, almost always at some public place early in the evening, and the first date will often be tentative and Dutch.

Online dating puts structure back into courtship. For generations Americans 3 had certain courtship rituals. The boy would call the girl and ask her to the movies. He might come in and meet the father. After a few dates he might ask her to go steady. Sex would progress gradually from kissing to petting and beyond.

But over the past few decades that structure dissolved. And human beings, 4 who are really good at adapting, found that the Internet, of all places, imposes the restraints they need to let relationships develop gradually. So now 40 million Americans look at online dating sites each month, and we are seeing a revolution in the way people meet and court one another.

5   The new restraints are not like the old restraints. The online dating scene is like a real estate market where people go to fulfill their most sensitive needs. It is at once ruthlessly transactional and strangely tender.

6   It begins with sorting. Online daters can scan through millions of possible partners in an evening and select for age, education, height, politics, religion and ethnic background. JDate is a popular site for Jews. EHarmony insists that members fill out a long, introspective questionnaire, and thus is one of the few sites where most members are women. Vanity Date is for the South Beach crowd. "At Vanity Date," the Web site declares, "we have a vision of creating the largest database of the world's most good-looking, rich and superficial people."

7   Most of the sites have programs that link you up with people like yourself. One of the side effects of online dating is that it is bound to accelerate social stratification, as highly educated people become more efficient at finding and marrying one another.

8   Each member at a dating site creates his or her own Web page. The most important feature on the page is the photo; studies show that looks are twice as powerful as income in attracting mates.

9   But there are also autobiographical essays. If you judge by these essays, skinny-dipping with intellectuals is the most popular activity in America. All the writers try to show they are sensual yet smart.

10   The women on these sites are, or project themselves as being, incredibly self-confident. "I am a vivacious, intelligent, warm-hearted, attractive, cool chick, with a sharp, witty, and effervescent personality," writes one on Match. com. Another says: "I am a slender, radiantly beautiful woman on fire with passion and enthusiasm for life. I am articulate, intelligent and routinely given the accolade of being brilliant."

11   Still, men almost always make the first contact. Prospective partners begin a long series of e-mail interviews. Internet exchanges encourage both extreme honesty (the strangers-on-a-train phenomenon) and extreme dishonesty, as people lie about their ages, their jobs, whether they have kids and, most often, whether they are married. (About a fifth of online daters are married men.)

12   Whatever else has changed, men are more likely to be predators looking for sex, while women try to hold back. Men will ask women for more photos "from different angles." A woman, wanting to be reassured that this guy is not some rapist, will shut off anyone who calls her "hottie" or who mentions sex first. Women generally control the pace of the relationship.

13   But despite all the crass competition, all the marketing, all the shopping around, people connect. Studies by Katelyn McKenna at N.Y.U. and others indicate that Internet relationships are at least as powerful as relationships that begin face to face. Many people are better at revealing their true selves through the keyboard than through conversation. And couples who slow down and prolong the e-mail phase have a better chance of seeing their relationships last than people who get together more quickly.

14   The online dating world is superficially cynical. The word "love" will almost never appear on a member's page, because it is so heavy and intimidating.

But love is what this is all about. And the heart, even in this commercial age, finds a way.

## COMPREHENSION

1. How does Brooks describe Internet "love"? What does he mean by his opening sentence, "The Internet slows things down"?
2. What features of Internet culture does the writer identify as facilitating human relationships?
3. According to Brooks, how do men and women differ in their approach to online relationships?

## RHETORIC

1. What is Brooks's purpose in beginning his essay with a single-sentence paragraph? Is this sentence the thesis? Why or why not?
2. How would you describe the writer's stance? What is his attitude toward his subject? Is he an objective observer, or does he advance a particular point of view? Offer examples to support your answer.
3. What are Brooks's main reasons in support of his thesis or claim? What forms of evidence does he offer to support his claim?
4. How does the writer develop an extended definition of Internet "love"?
5. Brooks frequently structures his essay by means of comparison and contrast. Why do you think he uses this strategy? Do you find the method effective? Why or why not?
6. Does the final paragraph provide a solid conclusion? Justify your answer.

## WRITING

1. Narrate and describe your own experience with Internet relationships or online dating. Explain why the Internet has helped or hindered your relationships with other men or women.
2. Write a definition essay on "Internet love." Be certain to provide examples and utilize other rhetorical strategies like comparison and contrast to develop this extended definition.
3. **Writing an Argument:** Write a persuasive essay arguing that Internet dating is either dangerous or harmless. Provide at least three minor propositions and sufficient evidence to support your position.

www.mhhe.com/
**mhreader**

For more information on David Brooks, go to:
**More Resources > Ch. 5 Family & Gender**

# Family Values

### Richard Rodriguez

*Richard Rodriguez (b. 1944) received degrees from Stanford University and Colum-
bia University. He also did graduate study at the University of California, Berkeley,
and at the Warburg Institute in London. He is a writer and editor for* Pacifica News
Service *and a contributing editor and writer for many major American magazines and
journals including* Harper's *and the* Los Angeles Times. *His books include* Hunger
of Memory: The Education of Richard Rodriguez *(1982) and* Days of Obligation: An Argument with My Mexican Father *(1992). Both books have been profoundly influential in the public discussion on race, bilingualism, affirmative action,
and biculturalism. He has also made many appearances as a commentator on* The
NewsHour with Jim Lehrer. *In the following essay, originally published in the Sunday "Opinion" section of the* Los Angeles Times *in 1992, he addresses the concept of
"family values" and focuses on the controversial thesis that homosexuality—rather
than being a threat to family values—is actually a buttress against their dissolution.*

1   I am sitting alone in my car, in front of my parents' house—a middle-aged man
with a boy's secret to tell. What words will I use to tell them? I hate the word
*gay*, find its little affirming sparkle more pathetic than assertive. I am happier
with the less polite *queer*. But to my parents I would say *homosexual*, avoiding
the Mexican slang *joto* (I had always heard it said in our house with hints of
condescension), though *joto* is less mocking than the sissy-boy *maricon*.

2       The buzz on everyone's lips now: Family values. The other night on TV, the
vice president of the United States, his arm around his wife, smiled into the
camera and described homosexuality as "mostly a choice." But how would he
know? Homosexuality never felt like a choice to me.

3       A few minutes ago Rush Limbaugh, the radio guy with a voice that reminds me, for some reason, of a butcher's arms, was banging his console and
booming a near-reasonable polemic about family values. Limbaugh was not
very clear about which values exactly he considers to be family values. A divorced man who lives alone in New York?

4       My parents live on a gray, treeless street in San Francisco not far from the
ocean. Probably more than half of the neighborhood is immigrant. India lives
next door to Greece, who lives next door to Russia. I wonder what the Chinese
lady next door to my parents makes of the politicians' phrase *family values*.

5       What immigrants know, what my parents certainly know, is that when you
come to this country, you risk losing your children. The assurance of family—
continuity, inevitability—is precisely what America encourages its children to
overturn. *Become your own man.* We who are native to this country know this too,

of course, though we are likely to deny it. Only a society so guilty about its betrayal of family would tolerate the pieties of politicians regarding family values.

On the same summer day that Republicans were swarming in Houston 6 (buzzing about family values), a friend of mine who escaped family values awhile back and who now wears earrings resembling intrauterine devices, was complaining to me over coffee about the Chinese. The Chinese will never take over San Francisco, my friend said, because the Chinese do not want to take over San Francisco. The Chinese do not even see San Francisco! All they care about is their damn families. All they care about is double-parking smack in front of the restaurant on Clement Street and pulling granny out of the car—and damn anyone who happens to be in the car behind them or the next or the next.

Politicians would be horrified by such an American opinion, of course. But 7 then, what do politicians, Republicans or Democrats, really know of our family life? Or what are they willing to admit? Even in that area where they could reasonably be expected to have something to say—regarding the relationship of family life to our economic system—the politicians say nothing. Republicans celebrate American economic freedom, but Republicans don't seem to connect that economic freedom to the social breakdown they find appalling. Democrats, on the other hand, if more tolerant of the drift from familial tradition, are suspicious of the very capitalism that creates social freedom.

How you become free in America: Consider the immigrant. He gets a job. 8 Soon he is earning more money than his father ever made (his father's authority is thereby subtly undermined). The immigrant begins living a life his father never knew. The immigrant moves from one job to another, changes houses. His economic choices determine his home address—not the other way around. The immigrant is on his way to becoming his own man.

When I was broke a few years ago and trying to finish a book, I lived with 9 my parents. What a thing to do! A major theme of America is leaving home. We trust the child who forsakes family connections to make it on his own. We call that the making of a man.

Let's talk about this man stuff for a minute. America's ethos is anti-domestic. 10 We may be intrigued by blood that runs through wealth—the Kennedys or the Rockefellers—but they seem European to us. Which is to say, they are movies. They are Corleones. Our real pledge of allegiance: We say in America that nothing about your family—your class, your race, your pedigree—should be as important as what you yourself achieve. We end up in 1992 introducing ourselves by first names.

What authority can Papa have in a country that formed its identity in an act 11 of Oedipal rebellion against a mad British king? Papa is a joke in America, a stock sitcom figure—Archie Bunker or Homer Simpson. But my Mexican father went to work every morning, and he stood in a white smock, making false teeth, oblivious of the shelves of grinning false teeth mocking his devotion.

The nuns in grammar school—my wonderful Irish nuns—used to push 12 Mark Twain on me. I distrusted Huck Finn, he seemed like a gringo kid I would steer clear of in the schoolyard. (He was too confident.) I realize now, of course, that Huck is the closest we have to a national hero. We trust the story of a boy who has no home and is restless for the river. (Huck's Pap is drunk.) Americans are more forgiving of Huck's wildness than of the sweetness of the Chinese boy who walks to school with his mama or grandma. (There is no worse thing in America than to be a mama's boy, nothing better than to be a real boy—all boy—like Huck, who eludes Aunt Sally, and is eager for the world of men.)

13      There's a bent old woman coming up the street. She glances nervously as she passes my car. What would you tell us, old lady, of family values in America?

14      America is an immigrant country, we say. Motherhood—parenthood—is less our point than adoption. If I had to assign gender to America, I would note the consensus of the rest of the world. When America is burned in effigy, a male is burned. Americans themselves speak of Uncle Sam.

15      Like the Goddess of Liberty, Uncle Sam has no children of his own. He steals children to make men of them, mocks all reticence, all modesty, all memory. Uncle Sam is a hectoring Yankee, a skinflint uncle, gaunt, uncouth, unloved. He is the American Savonarola—hater of moonshine, destroyer of stills, burner of cocaine. Sam has no patience with mamas' boys.

16      You betray Uncle Sam by favoring private over public life, by seeking to exempt yourself, by cheating on your income taxes, by avoiding jury duty, by trying to keep your boy on the farm.

17      Mothers are traditionally the guardians of the family against America—though even Mom may side with America against queers and deserters, at least when the Old Man is around. Premature gray hair. Arthritis in her shoulders. Bowlegged with time, red hands. In their fiercely flowered housedresses, mothers are always smarter than fathers in America. But in reality they are betrayed by their children who leave. In a thousand ways. They end up alone.

18      We kind of like the daughter who was a tomboy. Remember her? It was always easier to be a tomboy in America than a sissy. Americans admired Annie Oakley more than they admired Liberace (who, nevertheless, always remembered his mother). But today we do not admire Annie Oakley when we see Mom becoming Annie Oakley.

19      The American household now needs two incomes, everyone says. Meaning: Mom is *forced* to leave home out of economic necessity. But lots of us know lots of moms who are sick and tired of being mom, or only mom. It's like the nuns getting fed up, teaching kids for all those years and having those kids grow up telling stories of how awful Catholic school was! Not every woman in America wants her life's work to be forgiveness. Today there are moms who don't want their husbands' names. And the most disturbing possibility: What happens when Mom doesn't want to be Mom at all? Refuses pregnancy?

20      Mom is only becoming an American like the rest of us. Certainly, people all over the world are going to describe the influence of feminism on women (all over the world) as their "Americanization." And rightly so.

21      Nothing of this, of course, will the politician's wife tell you. The politician's wife is careful to follow her husband's sentimental reassurances that nothing

has changed about America except perhaps for the sinister influence of deviants. Like myself.

I contain within myself an anomaly at least as interesting as the Republican 22 Party's version of family values. I am a homosexual Catholic, a communicant in a tradition that rejects even as it upholds me.

I do not count myself among those Christians who proclaim themselves 23 protectors of family values. They regard me as no less an enemy of the family than the "radical feminists." But the joke about families that all homosexuals know is that we are the ones who stick around and make families possible. Call on us. I can think of 20 or 30 examples. A gay son or daughter is the only one who is "free" (married brothers and sisters are too busy). And, indeed, because we have admitted the inadmissible about ourselves (that we are queer)—we are adepts at imagination—we can even imagine those who refuse to imagine us. We can imagine Mom's loneliness, for example. If Mom needs to be taken to church or to the doctor or ferried between Christmas dinners, depend on the gay son or lesbian daughter.

I won't deny that the so-called gay liberation movement, along with femi- 24 nism, undermined the heterosexual household, if that's what politicians mean when they say family values. Against churchly reminders that sex was for procreation, the gay bar as much as the birth-control pill taught Americans not to fear sexual pleasure. In the past two decades—and, not coincidentally, parallel to the feminist movement—the gay liberation movement moved a generation of Americans toward the idea of a childless adulthood. If the women's movement was ultimately more concerned about getting out of the house and into the workplace, the gay movement was in its way more subversive to puritan America because it stressed the importance of play.

Several months ago, the society editor of the morning paper in San Francisco 25 suggested (on a list of "must haves") that every society dame must have at least one gay male friend. A ballet companion. A lunch date. The remark was glib and incorrect enough to beg complaints from homosexual readers, but there was a truth about it as well. Homosexual men have provided women with an alternate model of masculinity. And the truth: The Old Man, God bless him, is a bore. Thus are we seen as preserving marriages? Even Republican marriages?

For myself, homosexuality is a deep brotherhood but does not involve do- 26 mestic life. Which is why, my married sisters will tell you, I can afford the time to be a writer. And why are so many homosexuals such wonderful teachers and priests and favorite aunts, if not because we are freed from the house? On the other hand, I know lots of homosexual couples (male and female) who model their lives on the traditional heterosexual version of domesticity and marriage. Republican politicians mock the notion of a homosexual marriage, but ironically such marriages honor the heterosexual marriage by imitating it.

"The only loving couples I know," a friend of mine recently remarked, "are 27 all gay couples."

This woman was not saying that she does not love her children or that she 28 is planning a divorce. But she was saying something about the sadness of

American domestic life: the fact that there is so little joy in family intimacy. Which is perhaps why gossip (public intrusion into the private) has become a national industry. All day long, in forlorn houses, the television lights up a freakish parade of husbands and mothers-in-law and children upon the stage of Sally or Oprah or Phil. They tell on each other. The audience ooohhhs. Then a psychiatrist-shaman appears at the end to dispense prescriptions—the importance of family members granting one another more "space."

29    The question I desperately need to ask you is whether we Americans have ever truly valued the family. We are famous, or our immigrant ancestors were famous, for the willingness to leave home. And it is ironic that a crusade under the banner of family values has been taken up by those who would otherwise pass themselves off as patriots. For they seem not to understand America, nor do I think they love the freedoms America grants. Do they understand why, in a country that prizes individuality and is suspicious of authority, children are disinclined to submit to their parents? You cannot celebrate American values in the public realm without expecting them to touch our private lives. As Barbara Bush remarked recently, family values are also neighborhood values. It may be harmless enough for Barbara Bush to recall a sweeter America—Midland, Texas, in the 1950s. But the question left begging is why we chose to leave Midland, Texas. Americans like to say that we can't go home again. The truth is that we don't want to go home again, don't want to be known, recognized. Don't want to respond in the same old ways. (And you know you will if you go back there.)

30    Little 10-year-old girls know that there are reasons for getting away from the family. They learn to keep their secrets—under lock and key—addressed to Dear Diary. Growing up queer, you learn to keep secrets as well. In no place are those secrets more firmly held than within the family house. You learn to live in closets. I know a Chinese man who arrived in America about 10 years ago. He got a job and made some money. And during that time he came to confront his homosexuality. And then his family arrived. I do not yet know the end of this story.

31    The genius of America is that it permits children to leave home, it permits us to become different from our parents. But the sadness, the loneliness of America, is clear too.

32    Listen to the way Americans talk about immigrants. If, on the one hand, there is impatience when today's immigrants do not seem to give up their family, there is also a fascination with this reluctance. In Los Angeles, Hispanics are considered people of family. Hispanic women are hired to be at the center of the American family—to babysit and diaper, to cook and to clean and to ease the dying. Hispanic attachment to family is seen by many Americans, I think, as the reason why Hispanics don't get ahead. But if Asians privately annoy us for being so family oriented, they are also stereotypically celebrated as the new "whiz kids" in school. Don't Asians go to college, after all, to honor their parents?

33    More important still is the technological and economic ascendancy of Asia, particularly Japan, on the American imagination. Americans are starting to wonder whether perhaps the family values of Asia put the United States at a disadvantage. The old platitude had it that ours is a vibrant, robust society

for being a society of individuals. Now we look to Asia and see team effort paying off.

In this time of national homesickness, of nostalgia, for how we imagine 34 America used to be, there are obvious dangers. We are going to start blaming each other for the loss. Since we are inclined, as Americans, to think of ourselves individually, we are disinclined to think of ourselves as creating one another or influencing one another.

But it is not the politician or any political debate about family values that 35 has brought me here on a gray morning to my parents' house. It is some payment I owe to my youth and to my parents' youth. I imagine us sitting in the living room, amid my mother's sentimental doilies and the family photographs, trying to take the measure of the people we have turned out to be in America.

A San Francisco poet, when he was in the hospital and dying, called a priest 36 to his bedside. The old poet wanted to make his peace with Mother Church. He wanted baptism. The priest asked why. "Because the Catholic Church has to accept me," said the poet. "Because I am a sinner."

Isn't willy-nilly inclusiveness the point, the only possible point to be de- 37 rived from the concept of family? Curiously, both President Bush and Vice President Quayle got in trouble with their constituents recently for expressing a real family value. Both men said that they would try to dissuade a daughter or granddaughter from having an abortion. But, finally, they said they would support her decision, continue to love her, never abandon her.

There are families that do not accept. There are children who are forced to 38 leave home because of abortions or homosexuality. There are family secrets that Papa never hears. Which is to say there are families that never learn the point of families.

But there she is at the window. My mother has seen me and she waves me 39 in. Her face asks: Why am I sitting outside? (Have they, after all, known my secret for years and kept it, out of embarrassment, not knowing what to say?) Families accept, often by silence. My father opens the door to welcome me in.

## COMPREHENSION

1. The title of this essay is "Family Values." What does Rodriguez mean by "family values"? According to the author, do Americans respect family values as they claim? Why or why not?
2. According to Rodriguez, do immigrants newly arrived to the United States possess a traditional allegiance to family values? Explain your answer.
3. In the conclusion, the author reflects—regarding his own homosexuality—that "families accept, often in silence." Is this an aspect of traditional family values? Why or why not?
4. Why does Rodriguez think that gay men and women are often the primary upholders of family values within their own families?
5. What is the thesis of the essay? Is it implicit or explicit? Explain.

## RHETORIC

1. Although much of this essay is expository, Rodriguez begins and ends with an event—that is, visiting his family to announce his homosexuality. Why has he shaped his essay in this way? What is problematic about his own relationship to the "gay" community? Why does he feel uncomfortable with the term "gay" to denote homosexual?
2. Rodriguez employs considerable irony in his essay. For example, in paragraph 15, he notes that two icons of American democracy, the Statue of Liberty and "Uncle Sam," are childless. Select two other ironic statements he makes in order to point out the contradiction between the "idea" of family values in America and the actual state of family values.
3. In paragraph 20, Rodriguez uses the term *Americanization*. What does he mean by this term? How is it central to his thesis?
4. Does Rodriguez suggest that much of what is said in public regarding "family values" in America is hypocritical? If so, what group or groups does he focus on? How does he support his argument?
5. Explain the meaning of the following stylistic flourishes: "the word *gay* . . . [is a] little affirming sparkle more pathetic than assertive" (paragraph 1), "America's ethos is anti-domestic" (paragraph 10), "Oedipal rebellion" (paragraph 11), "American Savonarola" (paragraph 15), "psychiatrist-shaman" (paragraph 28), "national homesickness" (paragraph 34), and "willy-nilly inclusiveness" (paragraph 37).
6. In paragraph 10, Rodriguez states that the Kennedys and Rockefellers "are movies." What does he mean?
7. Describe the emotional tone of this essay, considering that it is written by a man who is openly gay and understands that he is considered suspect and outside the mainstream of the American "value" system. Is it angry? Thoughtful? Defiant? Sympathetic? Select three or four passages that led you to your conclusion regarding tone.

## WRITING

1. Interview a member of your grandparents' generation, a member of your parents' generation, and a member of your own generation regarding their views on family values. Write an essay summarizing the similarities and differences among the three views.
2. Interview a counselor at your college or university. Ask the counselor to explain the various issues surrounding family conflict he or she comes across in the course of his or her job. Write an essay exploring your interview findings. Be sure to obtain permission from your interviewee and follow appropriate guidelines for protecting his or her anonymity.
3. For a creative writing project, imagine yourself 25 years from today. Write a letter to an old classmate, describing your family life.

4. **Writing an Argument:** In an essay, argue for or against the proposition that choosing to follow a tradition of "family values" is entirely the choice of the individual. Be sure to use at least three supporting points to advance your argument.

www.mhhe.com/
**mhreader**

For more information on Richard Rodriguez, go to:
**More Resources > Ch. 5 Family & Gender**

# Third Time's the Charm

## Julia Alvarez

*Julia Alvarez (b. 1950), a highly regarded novelist and poet, was born in New York City but raised until the age of 10 in the Dominican Republic. She was forced to flee with her family after her father was implicated in a plot to overthrow the dictator Rafael Trujillo, an event alluded to in her semiautobiographical novel.* How the Garcia Girls Lost Their Accents *(1991). Another novel,* Yo! *(1997), continues the Garcia/ Alvarez family saga. Alvarez attended Middlebury College (BA, 1971) and Syracuse University (MFA, 1975). She currently is on the English faculty at Middlebury College. In addition to her fiction, Alvarez has published books of poetry, including* Homecoming: New and Collected Poems *(1995); a collection of essays,* Something to Declare *(1998); nonfiction; and several books for children. Her newest book is* Saving the World *(2006), about the global attempt to eradicate smallpox. In this essay, published originally in* O: The Oprah Magazine *in 2006, Alvarez offers a revealing account of her thrice-married state.*

I didn't seem to have a problem getting married. Staying married was my prob-    1
lem. Happily ever after was a phrase that eluded me.

By age 30, 1 had been married and divorced twice. The first marriage lasted    2
a year; the second lasted three years, and then only because it took two years
after leaving my husband for us to agree we should divorce. I admit that for
years I sort of collapsed these two former husbands into one and said I'd been
married "before." Divorcing once in my generation wasn't such a big deal. But
twice! And after such short marriages! What would folks think? Wow, she must
be a horrible person to live with! Of course, what folks didn't know is that unlike most of my contemporaries in the sexually liberated America of the post-
sixties, I had only had sex with two men, and like a good Latina raised Catholic
by my mami and tías, I had married them.

3    Okay, by the second time around, I knew better. But I had to redeem myself to my family for the first marriage: I had dropped out of my last year of college to elope with a folksinger who had dropped out of high school. My second husband was a businessman, older, established, rich, British. (There was a title in the family, an uncle who was Sir Something or Other. "Lady Julia," my sisters teased me.) Mami, who had disowned me after my first marriage, fell in love with this second husband-to-be, who very winningly asked her and my father for my hand in marriage.

4    After the second divorce, I decided, enough! To never marry again unless I was really sure. Even Mami hinted it might not be a bad idea to get to know a man a little better before I married him. The way she said "know" I took as a nod and a wink in the biblical direction of the verb.

5    And so, fast-forward through ten years of loneliness, celibacy, a few getting-to-knows, and enter my third and present and "perfect husband," Bill. At least, that's what my sisters started calling him soon after we married.

6    I don't know what's worse: getting teased about being Lady Julia or about being married to a perfect husband. We're four sisters; we love each other fiercely. The gray areas of tact and restraint in other families are hung with green lights in my family. We stomp where angels fear to tread, comment and tease and get away with murder because down deep we all secretly believe we are the same person. Which means you'll never find such loving, passionate, and true hermanas. So, you pay your dues. I've paid my share in the husband-teasing department.

7    For the first few years of my marriage, my sisters teased me. How was my perfect husband? What did my perfect husband advise? And so on. Where did they get this idea? I wondered.

8    Well, he sure looked good, and not just on paper. The oldest in a poor, sharecropping family, at 9 Bill had taken over a lot of the chores at the farm in order for his dad to work the night shift at Continental Can. Meanwhile, Bill also studied hard, graduated first in his high school class, went to medical school, ended up buying his parents the farm they never owned, having farmed other people's land all their lives. He did get divorced (a fact my sisters seized on as proof of his humanhood), but he stayed fully involved in his daughters' lives. A devoted doctor, he answers calls at all hours. But farming is his first love. He comes home from the office, dons his work clothes, goes out on his tractor. He grows most of the food this vegetarian eats. He cooks and cans and freezes, too. He even wrote a cookbook for his daughters, a book I take credit for making him write out of not disinterested motives. (I learned to cook from it as well.) He has taken excellent, patient, loving care of my own parents. When Mami refused to talk to me after my first novel came out, and then again after my third novel, Bill stayed in touch with her; a couple of times, he even drove down to visit Mami in New York City to intercede for me. ("It's fiction, Mami, that's why there are so many 'lies' in her books." "Then why does she have to make the characters Dominicans? Why can't they be Scandinavians?") Bill reported

that he sat for several hours while my mother told him all about what an impossible, imperfect woman he had married, who would someday write about him. (Here I am proving Mami right!)

But my sisters, savvy girls that they are, know there is no such thing as a 9 perfect man or a perfect husband. Over the past 16 years that they've gotten to known and love Bill, they've seen what's wrong with this perfect husband of mine. Now any mention of "perfect Bill" is always accompanied by aerial quote marks, and I'm glad. This way I don't have to continue to feel guilty that I'm happily married to a perfectly wonderful man.

By now this epithet for Bill is one that I myself use to tease him and pretty 10 consistently get a rise out of him. (I said I wasn't perfect.) What I've discovered from staying married this last time around is a lot like what I've learned from writing novels: You have to work at it page by page, day by day. And if you stay with your story and characters, if you give your passion and talent and faith to the writing, and if after the bad days you still come back to the writing, well, you're going to end up not just writing a novel but learning and growing by doing it. So with marriage. And like the novels that end up being wonderful books because you tapped a subject and characters that deeply hold you, the marriages that last and are fairly successful are probably the ones in which you've found someone with whom the roots can go deep and the space can open wide and surprises can happen.

So I've come to give myself some credit as well for this good, third, charmed 11 marriage. I work hard to make it work. And so does Bill. We've had rough periods where we're on what I like to think of as a learning curve as a couple. One or the other of us—or both—is growing in ways that shift the balances and challenge us to come up with new and interesting ways to be together.

Here are some glitches on that learning curve, moments when we could 12 have broken up and didn't . . . because we kept learning and growing and surprising ourselves and each other.

How we almost didn't get married: It happens so serendipitously, it seems that 13 it is meant to be. I am a new person in town. I have an eye condition that has been giving me trouble for years. It flares up when I arrive looking for a place to live. I go to the eye doctor. He is intrigued to find this condition in someone in Vermont, as it is rare here but common in the Tropics. Oh, but I'm originally from the Tropics, I explain. Really? From where? he asks. The Dominican Republic. Really? he says, I was just there with an organization doing Third World ophthalmology in a free clinic. Wow, I say. Then he tells me where the clinic is, who it's run by. My cousin I grew up with! I tell him. Wow, he says. Yeah, I say, wow.

That's it. Eye condition improves. No reason to go back to see the eye doc- 14 tor. Except I'm looking for an apartment in town and the real estate agent suggests I think of buying a condo. Only problem is the condo is in the process of being built, but I could look at a finished condo. Call this number and ask if the owner could show it to me. Name seems familiar. I call. It's my eye doctor! He remembers me, too. Sure, stop by this evening. When I drop by, Bill and a woman who obviously lives there show me around their condo. I assume this is his wife. I thank them both and leave.

15     A few weeks into the school year, I am in the grocery store and I bump into my eye doctor. We chat. He learns that I didn't buy the condo. I tell him where I am living. Before we part, he asks if he can take me out to dinner sometime. I give him a sharp look. You two-timing sleazeball, I think. No, thank you, I tell him. This is a new job. I'm working toward tenure. I have to write a book to get tenure. For the next few years I am going to be very busy. But that same persistent, stubborn quality that will later drive me batty doesn't get deterred so easily. Fine, he says, but you're going to have to eat dinner sometime; here's my home number—give a call, okay?

16     Home number? Maybe the woman wasn't his wife, after all? Maybe she was a live-in girlfriend and they broke up and she moved out?

17     But I'm too embarrassed after the list of excuses I gave him to call him up. Too proud. Too stupid. So thank goodness for the sweet and lovely persistence of the man: One day when I come home from classes, there is a bouquet of flowers in front of my door with a little note. Welcome to your new hometown. And his number. I call to say thank you. And sure, I'd love to have dinner with him soon, like how about tomorrow?

18     I love you but I love being without you . . . at least part of my day: I used to think that I couldn't be married because I liked being alone so much. I'm a writer. I love solitude. Don't get me wrong; I love people, love being part of my noisy, impossibly crowded extended familia in the D.R. But solitude is my bread and butter. My sisters call it "working." Do you ever take a day off? they wonder. A day off from what? Does a nun take a day off from her vocation? Do mothers take a day off from being their children's mamis? It's a calling, a way of life.

19     I always tried to keep this part of me secret from people I became intimate with, even girlfriends. It seemed antisocial, a testament to how in a pinch I wouldn't be "there" for them. In my very social Latin culture, a person who went off, even with a valid excuse like reading a book, was considered rara. Se va enfermar, my grandmother used to say about my solitary, bookworm cousin Juan Tomas. He's going to get sick.

20     But what I didn't know until I married Bill is that you can be solitary together. Come to find out it's not just writers who love solitude. Farmers do, too. There is nothing Bill loves more than working on the land, letting the wind take him where it will. Sometimes as I sit at my writing desk and look out the window and see the tractor going by, Bill mowing the back pasture, I smile to myself. We're each doing the passionate work we love to do. Tonight at supper, he'll tell me what he got mowed, what is coming up, what he plans to do next year in the upper garden, and I'll tell him about what I'm working on, what I'm having trouble getting down on paper, what he might advise for a farmer character who is not him, I promise, as the guy is Scandinavian.

I am not going to make myself over into a beautiful woman to please you: 21
I worried that to keep a man, you had to be beautiful. If you weren't born
beautiful, well, you'd have to work at it. So long to not shaving your legs all
winter. So long to never putting on makeup except for special occasions. I had
read those articles waiting on line at the Grand Union. Women wondering
whether to wear mascara to bed. Women getting dressed up in something
sexy for when he came home. How to never have a bad hair day. How to always be sexy.

Since I was an independent, liberated woman, I could not openly worry 22
about any of this stuff. But it was there under my bluff. I had to be attractive to
him. Or else he'd lose interest in me. And so when he came home with gifts, little
dresses and sheer tops I would never have worn pre-him, I dressed up in those
clothes and felt like Halloween. I did it to please him for about a year, and then
I asked him what was wrong with my old way of dressing. Your one-size-fits-all
jersey period, he called it. Everything was black and looked like a hand-medown
I hadn't grown into. "You have a nice figure, you should show it off."

Vanity made me stick with it a few more months. And then one day we 23
were in a shop together. Bill and the young saleswoman were emoting over
some slinky little dress with spaghetti straps and practically no back. "She
would look fabulous in this!" the saleswoman said, holding it up in front of me.
The dress was also superexpensive. Besides, where on earth would I wear this
thing in small-town Vermont? I shook my head, no thanks. But the woman persisted and Bill chimed in. This dress was made for me.

I turned to my perfect husband and I said, "I am not your Barbie Doll! If 24
you don't like my black jerseys, marry somebody else!" And then I stomped
out of the store. A few days later, a close friend of Bill's asked if everything was
going all right for him. There was a rumor going around town that our marriage was on the rocks. We were getting divorced.

Bill's friend was right. There are a lot of little divorces that have to occur for 25
a good marriage to last. Barbie Doll and Fantasizing Hubby didn't last. We did
because we were able to discard them. I get to wear my comfortable, inexpen-
sive line of jersey clothes. And sometimes I dress up in one of those old sexy
numbers he paid too much money for.

Being the only step in the family: Coming into a marriage in which you're out- 26
numbered by blood kin ain't easy. My problem was that I thought it would be.
You see, when I married Bill, I thought of it as a plus that he came with two
girls. I would get not just a husband but daughters. I imagined them as younger
versions of my sisters. We'd stay up nights gabbing. We'd share everything,
tease Bill together, green lights left and right.

The trouble was these girls already had a mother. They didn't ask for me to 27
be in their family. Already it was not a clean transaction. But like old Gold-
ilocks, I stepped right in and made myself at home and then wondered why the
stepdaughters were not overjoyed that this interloper was sitting in the mama-
bear chair and sleeping with their father.

28　　I used to get so hurt and unload on Bill when we were first married. Couldn't he make them love me?

He could not.

29　　Bill is a father, and he and his former wife are the parents of two beautiful daughters I wish were mine. My jealousy and loss have been hard to acknowledge, to him, to myself. On the other side of that admission comes, I think, the possibility of a cleaner transaction: mutual respect, acceptance of whatever we can be for each other, a shared love for a lovely man who has not always been a perfect father, and a new shared love for their babies now being born, whom I claim as my full grandchildren. After all, I started out with everyone else from day one, cooing over their cribs.

30　　Mía, Naomi, my oldest grandgirl, calls me. That's Spanish for "mine." I'm hers, all right. And she is mine.

31　How we get over a fight: I didn't come into marriage with good fighting skills. I learned two ways of fighting growing up: threats (Mami) and departure (Papi). I didn't know until I was with Bill, and the time of pussyfooting around each other was over, that I didn't know how else to fight. Early on, I'd threaten divorce. And then I'd leave and have to sheepishly come back home to threaten to leave some more.

32　　And my husband would greet me at the door, not smug and ironical but stern and paternal. As soon as I stopped acting like a child, he would discuss the issue with me, he'd scold. Discussing the issue involved him telling me what was rational and right about his opinion and what was childish and unworkable about mine. If I was upset about something hurtful he'd done or said, I was told he hadn't done or said anything mean. I had misunderstood. But he was sorry that I had gotten upset. That was supposed to end the fight, and yet what I felt was anger I'd force myself to tamp down. The man had apologized. Why did I have to hold a grudge? And so fighting would "end" at this muddy, unsatisfying place.

33　　Then I got to see it from the outside. It happened that one of my stepdaughters got furious at her dad. We were at her apartment, and she departed to her room. A while later she came out and told him why she was upset with him. (I could see her point, but of course—I'm not that slow a learner—I kept my mouth shut.) She was crying as she went over what she was angry about. Out of the mouth of my beloved came that phrase I hear all the time, "I'm sorry you got upset at what I said. All I meant was . . ." And he proceeded very rationally to explain how what he said was nothing to get upset about.

34　　"So you're not sorry about what you said, just that I got upset! What kind of an apology is that?" my stepdaughter cried.

35　　I stood there in the middle of their fight with a huge lightbulb going on inside my head. What kind of an apology is that! Exactly. All these years, I knew down deep that he wasn't apologizing. No wonder I never felt the issue was really discussed, understood, resolved.

36　　Next time we had a fight, when he fed me that line I told him straight out: "What kind of an apology is that?" The fight with his daughter had been recent enough that a certain synergy happened in his brain. I could see it on his face. He got it. Something was wrong with his way of apologizing.

So how do we get over a fight? We now have ground rules: Nobody leaves ₃₇ the house. Threats are not okay We're going to stay together, and more important than one of us being right is both of us feeling understood. And you can only apologize for what you did, not for the other person being upset.

Of course, these rules go out the window when you get really mad, but ₃₈ hopefully, incrementally, they do start making a difference.

Our most recent bad fight took place in the Dominican Republic. We have a ₃₉ project there in which Bill is modeling sustainable farming methods with the help of some local NGOs and in conjunction with a group of local campesinos. The farm also hosts a school where adults and children learn to read and write. You can see our two passions coming together here. A perfect project for us. Well, not always. Like all perfect things, there is always something wrong with it.

So what's wrong with this picture? A pokey lawyer. For ten years we've ₄₀ been waiting for the local licenciado to acquire the titles to our land. Recently, as we turned over the farm to three NGOs to build a national green center there, acquiring those titles became important.

I had been in this lawyer's office countless times before. Since Bill was not ₄₁ willing to change lawyers, I finally gave up and said, Okay, then you handle it. This time Bill asked me to go with him. I was fluent in Spanish. I could state our case in no uncertain terms and we could finally move on.

Okay," I agreed, thinking that after ten years, Bill finally believed me that ₄₂ this lawyer was taking far too long.

And so I again found myself sitting inside the small, overly air-conditioned ₄₃ office, restating our case. The licenciado smiled graciously, asked after my writing, asked after my health, told me he'd seen the film version of *In the Time of the Butterflies* on cable TV, all smarmy and not getting to the point, Dona Julia this and Dona Julia that. I persisted. He then brought out the chart he always brings out, the wheel of the titling process, and he began to go over it. "Licenciado," I interrupted, "you've already explained this before, and we are going on ten years. We want the titles now."

The licendado's smile froze. "Oh, but Dona Julia, it sometimes takes much ₄₄ longer than that."

"It's taken long enough," I shot back. ₄₅

Into this moment of reckoning, my beloved husband, who'd asked me to ₄₆ come and be the barking dog, turned to me. "Honey, he's right. Remember how long it took us to get our permits in Vermont?"

"Don Bill understands," the lawyer beamed. "He is becoming a real ₄₇ Dominican."

I kept my temper until we had left the office, and then I got furious at Bill. ₄₈ Why had he set me up and, instead of covering my back, betrayed me by jumping on me in front of the lawyer?

"You misinterpreted," Bill said. "I just stepped in because I didn't want to ₄₉ see you getting upset with him."

50    "Who are you taking care of?" I confronted him. "Him or me?"

51    We were in the pickup headed down the mountain to my parents' house. We had an hour or more of traveling together. I wanted to jump out of the truck and walk the rest of the way to the capital. To show him. To make him feel sorry. But I couldn't. Our fighting rules say nobody leaves. A deal's a deal. Instead we fell into sullen silence.

52    Finally, Bill said, "I'm sorry that you got upset about what I said."

53    "There you go again," I pounced. "What kind of an apology is that? It's like you're not really sorry for what you did, you're sorry that I got upset. It's like you're perfect and never wrong, and it's always the other person's fault."

54    "I'm not perfect," he said, offended.

55    "Then act like it!" Sixteen years of marriage and I finally said it.

56    We were coming around a curve in the steepest part of the mountain road, a place where there have been a lot of accidents, and where, therefore, a little roadside altar to la Virgencita de la Altagracia has been built. Every time I pass her, I have to stop either on the way up or on the way down. We hadn't stopped on the way up in our hurry to get to the farm before darkness fell. But now I was in the middle of a fight and I'd be damned if I was going to remind Bill to stop so I could say goodbye. Most times when I ask, I get a sigh of indulgent impatience, and a little lecture on how Dominicans chose the worst places to set up their roadside shrines.

57    The pickup slowed, and Bill pulled onto the narrow shoulder.

58    He remembered, I thought, as I climbed out of the cab and headed up the steep steps. At the shrine, I touched the grate and asked la Virgencita de la Altagracia to help me not be so mad at this man in the pickup. This icon of the Virgencita is one in which she appears not as a solitary virgin but with Joseph behind her, the baby Jesus in a crib in front of her. I love it that my virgencita is a woman in a partnership. She understands what I am going through. She had a perfect son. A perfect, long-suffering husband. Please, help me be a better person, I pleaded, then headed down the steps, feeling a lot less angry at Bill. He had remembered to stop, and he hadn't even lectured me about the bad planning of Dominican shrine building.

59    "Did you ask her to help me be a better husband?" he asked as I climbed back in the pickup.

60    "Yeah," I said, trying hard not to smile.

61    A bus roared by on its way down the mountain. The pickup shook. We reached for each other at the same time. And all I could think was, he's right again! This is a bad place to build a shrine.

## COMPREHENSION

1.   After reading this selection, what is your response to the title? Is Alvarez being glib? Humorous? Straightforward? Does the title match the content and tone of the piece? Why or why not?

2. Offer a critique of Alvarez, focusing on her experience of marriage and attitude toward men, marriage, and divorce in general.
3. Alvarez speaks often of her Dominican family, and part of the narrative takes place in the Dominican Republic. What is Alvarez's purpose in providing these details about her Dominican background?

## RHETORIC

1. Although she writes in various literary modes, Alvarez is best known as a novelist. What elements of fiction do you detect in this essay? Identify specific passages to support your analysis. How effective are these strategies, and why?
2. What primary audience does Alvarez address? (Remember where the essay appeared.) How effective is she in tailoring the tone and content of the article to this audience? How does she present herself as an authority on the matter?
3. Alvarez interrupts her narrative from time to time in order to provide exposition. What does she explain to the reader, and why is this necessary?
4. Locate instances where Alvarez uses Spanish words, phrases, and locutions. What is her purpose?
5. Why does the narrator picture herself so often as an angry person? Cite instances of this strategy and how her anger reveals her mental state. Is there a cause-and-effect relationship operating here? Explain.
6. Do you think that by the end of this story Alvarez presents an argument or tries to persuade readers to follow a certain course of action concerning marriage? Justify your response.

## WRITING

1. Have you ever experienced a ruptured relationship or marriage? Or have you persisted through difficult times with someone because you realized that the person and the relationship were valuable? Write an essay combining narrative, description, and exposition to respond to either of these questions—or both.
2. Conduct research on the Internet or in the library, and find out more about Alvarez. Then write a brief account of her life, fitting this essay into your summary.
3. **Writing an Argument:** Argue for or against the proposition that serial marriage and divorce (until one finds Mister or Ms. Right) is beneficial for individuals and children, and healthy for society in general.

# Digital Scheherazades
# in the Arab World

## Fatema Mernissi

*Fatema Mernissi (b. 1940), a contemporary sociologist, university professor, and feminist scholar, was born in Fez, Morocco. She received a degree in political science at Mohammad V University and a degree in sociology at the Sorbonne in Paris. In 1973, she earned a PhD in sociology at Brandeis University. At present, she is a research scholar at the University Institute for Scientific Research in Rabat. Mernissi's work focuses on the intersection of gender and religion in Muslim society. Among her numerous publications are* The Veil and the Male Elite *(1975),* Islam and Democracy *(1992), and* Scheherazade Goes West *(2001). Two memoirs,* Dreams of Trespass *(1994) and* Harem Days *(1999), recount her life growing up as Muslim, Moroccan, and female. In this essay, published in* Current History *in 2006, Mernissi assesses the changing roles of women in the Arab Gulf as technology influences the thinking of a previously all-male elite.*

1 In May 2005, I listened attentively to the questions of the 30 journalists my Spanish publisher had scheduled to meet with me in Madrid to promote the translation of my book, *Les Sindbads marocains: Voyage dans le Maroc civique* (Moroccan Sinbads: Travels through Civic Morocco). From their questions, which all dealt with the veil and terrorism, it was clear that they had no clue about the strategic issue mobilizing the Arab world: *alfitna raqmiya* (digital chaos), the destruction of space frontiers by information technology.

2 The key problem that makes everyone anxious today in the Arab world—elites and masses, heads of state and street vendors, men and women—is the digital chaos induced by information technologies such as the Internet. These new technologies have destroyed the *hudud*, the frontier that divided the universe into a sheltered private arena, where women and children were supposed to be protected, and a public one where adult males exercised their presumed problem-solving authority.

3 Now, according to a best-selling book, *The Internet and Love* (Al Internet Wa I-Hub), by Imam Qaradawi, a star host on the Arab television network Al Jazeera, the satellite and the Internet have spawned apocalyptic chaos in Arab civilization by destroying that division of spheres. The imam's book, which is advertised on the popular IslamOnline website, is alerting crowds to the fact that Arab women and youth now navigate freely on the web and communicate intimately with strangers, escaping religious and parental censorship.

4 "Since the World Wide Web invaded our lives," explains Qaradawi, "we have been going through nonstop transformations. . . . The faraway has become

nearer with a simple push on the keyboard. This has deeply affected our societies, which have suffered from a lack of communication and the lack of educational quality entertainment. . . . Suddenly, the new technologies have provided opportunities to communicate and entertain oneself, and this without the supervision of a censoring authority or a controller to whom you are accountable. . . . This leaves individual responsibility as the sole controlling agency. And unfortunately, we have never cared to develop an educational system which focused on developing individual responsibility."

But what is also new is that even imams suggest we stop thinking about 5 static solutions like strengthening authority and reinforcing hudud and focus instead on inventing strategies that nurture a civilization of ethical nomadism, where individual responsibility creates order. The Arab world is a besieged place, but in many quarters the response to chaos is quietly shifting from crying to action. This shift helps explain the emergence of what I call "digital Scheherazades," after the fictional storyteller of *1,001 Nights*. Her successors are Arab women who take advantage of new communication strategies as the only initiatives likely to liberate both themselves and their countries.

## Digital Chaos

Imagine the anxiety of a parent reading "The Electronic Disfiguration of Our 6 Children," an article by an Egyptian psychoanalyst, Dr. Khalil Fadel, that appeared in the Kuwait-based *Al Arabi*, one of the most widely circulated cultural magazines in the region. Fadel identifies the child as the most vulnerable victim of the Western-made electronic war games that invade "our children's rooms and are available in the cyber-cafés which now exist on every street corner." According to Fadel, these war games are responsible for inciting violent behavior among Arab youth because they glorify "solitude, narcissism, and hatred of the other," all of which reflect the cultural choices of the Westerners who produce these games.

But if electronic war games are bad enough, sex is worse, according to an 7 article—"Electronic Sex Attack on the Arab World"—by Ahmed Mohamed Ali in the Saudi-based magazine *Al Majalla*. Ali, who believes this attack was first launched in 1999, describes "the unimaginable profit made from selling virtual prostitution or electronic sex on the Internet" to Arabs. Parents, he says, quoting Al-Hami Abdelaziz, an Egyptian psychology professor, are totally at a loss about what to do: "They know that the future of their children depends on their mastering such technologies, but they are afraid they will slip into these pornographic websites. The fact is that the parents are totally unarmed and ill-equipped to protect their children from such dangers."

Add to this the booming Arab satellite industry of erotic video-clips target- 8 ing youth. These clips constitute a terrifying challenge to the Islamic vision of the world, where sex belongs exclusively to the private sphere (which explains why no straightforward pornographic films are to be found on Arab satellite stations such as Arabsat and Nilesat). The video-clip is a tricky phenomenon, since its official objective is entertainment through music and songs. For Arabs, music and songs, just like poetry, have been regarded, even before Islam and since, as important sources of licit pleasure. Now they must confront the digital chaos induced by music video-clips that slip into explicit sex between unmarried people surrounding the singer. As Patricia Kabala has written, the video-clip "has without doubt become a symbol of access via satellite television stations and the Internet to the previously inaccessible sexually explicit material that state-controlled television channels in the Middle East censored and continue to censor."

9        Yet what is interesting once again is that instead of wasting time in complaints as Arabs usually do, a new attitude has appeared, the desire to invent solutions. Some ethically minded operators are trying to exploit that very video-clip technology to spread Islamic values among the youth. To counteract the sexual flood, investing in video-clips to promote young attractive religious singers as role models—such as Sami Yusuf Yusu, a British-born Muslim of Azeri origin—is one of the emerging positive responses to the previously frightening new information technologies. The lesson one gets from reading about the video-clip debate is that either you transform yourself into an agile digital surfer or you fade away.

10       It is this kind of immense civilizational shift in the Arab world, where men are finally embarking on becoming skilled digital nomads instead of decrying the frontier's collapse and dreaming of harems for their wives, that I tried to share with the Spanish journalists obsessed by the veil and terrorism during my Madrid encounter in May 2005. Although the Spanish city of Gibraltar is just 13 kilometers from the Moroccan port of Tangiers, I realized that Spaniards had no idea about the revolution that information technologies have produced in our part of the world. And one reason for this is the fact that in Madrid's plush hotel, which advertised itself as satellite-connected, I could not connect to my favorite, Al Jazeera, or to any one of the two hundred pan-Arab satellite channels beaming now in the Mediterranean.

11       At one point, I tried to illustrate this change by sharing with them the extraordinary emergence of women I saw in the Arab Gulf during a visit to Bahrain in March 2005. I tried to describe to them Mai al-Khalifa, a historian who in less than a decade has created modern spaces such as museums and cultural centers that encourage dialogue between the sexes and the generations. I tried to explain that this unexpected emergence of women in the oil-rich Arab Gulf is more significant than the question of the veil in the Muslim migrant community, but the Spanish journalists were trapped in their own veils and terror.

12       I left Madrid feeling guilty and helpless, an intellectual unable to carry out her job of facilitating dialogue. The journalists continued to haunt me after my return to Morocco, and when I saw al-Khalifa on a pan-Arab satellite television one day, I caught myself wishing they could share that experience with me.

## The Historian on TV

The café near University Mohamed V in Rabat was full of young students and    13
teachers when al-Khalifa appeared on Al Arabia, a new rival of Al Jazeera that
is financed by the Saudis. The manager of the café automatically turned up the
television's volume because he was a fan of Turki al-Dakhil, the show's anchor,
an electrifying young man who appears on the screen dressed in the Gulf
region's traditional white robes just to surprise you by his insolent remarks
toward all kinds of authorities.

At this moment, I noticed a striking change in the café: conversations came    14
to a half even though al-Khalifa was dressed like a professional woman in a
white suit and looked very much on guard, unlike belly dancers who blink
their eyes and sway hands and buttocks. The dynamics of what occurred in my
Rabat café were as important for me as what was happening on the television
screen. (When I was a child, the only women one could see in my hometown,
Fez, in movies or on television when it made its appearance in Morocco in the
1960s, were belly dancers and singers; intellectual women were not part of the
fare.)

It was by chance that I was in the café, because I am a rather homebound    15
creature. I was invited there by Kamal, one of my favorite colleagues, who is a
*1,001 Nights* expert. He was intrigued by what I had told him about my March
2005 Bahrain trip because there is very little cultural exchange between North
Africa and the Gulf. The gender ratio in the café was typical of Morocco: 10
women among 40 or so customers. Moroccan women, starting with myself, are
so exhausted by their daily chores that they rarely think about going out in the
evening.

One of al-Khalifa's best-known books deals with the Qarmatians, a contro-    16
versial group of Shiites who rebelled in the tenth century against the Sunni Abbasid caliphs, described as terrorists by some historians and as the founders of
the first republic in Islam by others. I thought this would be the topic al-Dakhil,
the Al Arabia host, would start with. To my great surprise, he opted for a very
personal angle instead: Why was al-Khalifa so controversial in her own country? One has to realize that the title of the show is *Idaat*, which literally means
"Flashes." The host is supposed to help the viewer discover some secret corner
of those he invites to his show.

Why, wondered al-Dakhil, was al-Khalifa generating so much debate in    17
Bahrain concerning the projects she promoted as one of the first women to hold
an official position? (Al-Khalifa was the first woman to be appointed in Bahrain
as assistant undersecretary for culture and national heritage.) Was it because
she was a woman, or because she was incompetent, coming from an academic
background and being thus unfit for practical work? Some people at the Ministry of Information, al-Dakhil argued, were saying that academics are too isolated in their ivory towers to be effective cultural operators.

"That intellectuals are unable to invent effective cultural strategies is a to-    18
tally wrong assumption," al-Khalifa responded brusquely, brushing her black

hair away from her face. Such statements, she added, are typical of bureaucrats who are in fact totally unfit to design the dynamic cultural strategies the Arab world needs to face the challenges posed by new technologies, and this for the simple reason that they lack vision. "I am an intellectual who has both a clear vision (*ruya*) of the future and the capacity to go ahead and act by undertaking successful innovative projects." Only intellectuals, she stressed, have *ruya*, a precious gift amid today's global chaos.

19    The reaction to al-Khalifa's response in the café was amazing. The crowd laughed merrily. One of the students stood up to declaim the Palestinian Mahmoud Darwish's poem about his compatriot Edward Said, in which he celebrates a strong vision rooted in one's reading of the past as the key allowing the Palestinian diaspora to survive and thrive: "If your past is a tough experience, make your future meaningful by developing a vision. . . . My dream directs my steps. And my vision places my dream in my lap like a friendly cat."

## The Vision Thing

20    The absence of a clear vision of the future has been identified by Arab intellectuals as a contributor to the dangerous political disengagement of Arab youth and their confusion, which makes them vulnerable to the violence spread on the Internet. The new voices of the Arab diaspora include the Palestinian Khaled Hroub, who lives in London but is extremely influential among young Arabs because he hosts a show on Al Jazeera. He argues in his recent book on Hamas that the generational gap is particularly explosive in Arab society.

21    Indeed, one of the causes of terrorism is the demographic split between the aging minority of decision makers and the youthful majority they are supposed to represent. In a burlesque article published in the very academic journal of the Arab League, Hroub notices that being "decadently old" (*chaykhoukha*) does not help Arab leaders design pertinent strategies for the majority of the population, which is young. The tiny minority that monopolizes political decisions, he says, "operates on a set of concepts and reasoning frameworks that have very little relevancy to the youth's own problems." It is this politico-demographic divide, he concludes, that explains "the disastrous scorn of our younger generations for politics." And this brings us to the enigma of why the café youth reacted so strongly when the word *ruya* came up on the television show.

22    To stop terrorism, Arab leaders have to provide Arab youth with a vision of a future in which they have a role to play as defenders of an ethical planet explains Nabil Abdel-Fattah of the Al Ahram Center for Political and Strategic Studies in Egypt. The frustration of Arab youth results from the elite's failure to articulate a clear ethical view of a future in which every individual has a mission and a purpose. It is this emergence of the *ruya* as the antidote to terrorism that explains the café crowd's response to al-Khalifa's defiant answer to her television host. She was reminding him that her *ruya* is the likely reason why some Bahrain government bureaucrats were angered by her audacious cultural

A woman in charge: Sheikha Lubna al-Qasimi, minister of economy and planning for the UAE, speaks during a meeting in Abu Dhabi.

projects such as museums and cultural centers that teach children to understand that diversity is the root of their identity.

Because Arabs in general and youth in particular are fed up with fanaticism 23 and censorship, neighborhood cafés are turning, thanks to the new culture-focus satellite television outlets such as Al Jazeera and Al Arabia, to debates over *ruya*, visions of the future as the key to empowerment.

Many men in the café followed the rough exchange between al-Dakhil and 24 his guest with beaming smiles, including my colleague Kamal. I asked him why he was smiling and he said because al-Khalifa's quick response to al-Dakhil was so spontaneous: "I think Arab intellectuals should create a fund to support this lady," he said, "because she is creating fantastic publicity for us. If she continues appearing on television shows making such statements, we, the poor marginalized intellectuals, will soon be receiving well-paid job offers to replace our vision-blind bureaucrats in all the 22 Arab states!"

Kamal was right, because very few Arab male intellectuals would have 25 dared to declare with so much self-confidence, as al-Khalifa did on television, that they are visionaries and that only far-sighted thinkers can invent futuristic strategies for an Arab world doubly assaulted by both new information technologies and the powerful American military. Yet one of the positive changes initiated by these assaults is that people have stopped complaining and are going one step further toward identifying concrete solutions: first defeat the bureaucrats who have monopolized power for decades.

It is a daring message that increasingly bold women, making use of the 26 new information technologies, are proclaiming to fellow Arabs. In the Arab Gulf, the amazing thing about this new breed of women is that growing numbers of them, like al-Khalifa, do not limit themselves to writing but manage to jump into action as well. "She, like Sheikha Hussa Al-Sabah from Kuwait, builds museums and cultural centers like other women turn out couscous tagines!" remarked my colleague, who always condemned my decision not to get involved in politics. For Kamal, who, unlike me, became

involved in politics and paid for it by having trouble with the Moroccan police, it is clear that now only intellectuals can help rulers to engineer power
and engage the future.

27       The challenge for the intellectuals is to help rulers equip the youth to navigate responsibly on the Internet. In particular, these solutions must help young
people navigate not only in space but also in time. In a globalized planet where
meeting strangers daily is the only way to make a living, mastering time is the
secret of graceful navigation. To travel in the past, that is, to navigate in time, is
the best way to teach oneself tolerace and respect for diversity.

28       Mobility is the name of the game, be they men or women, local or exiled,
Sunni or Shiite, upper-class or from modest backgrounds. We are seeing a sudden shift from complaining about the West and its technological superiority to
deciding to begin using the new information technologies to protect ourselves
by participating in building a more just and humanist planet. Oil wealth, which
makes it easy for visionaries to step quickly from vision to realization, has
helped fuel this shift in the Arab Gulf. But so has the emergence of women in a
region supposedly condemned to archaic conservatism.

## Women Can Play Too

29   Is it because the threats of destabilization and terrorism are so great in the oil-
rich Arab Gulf that emirs and sheikhs are keen on promoting e-government
and women as information technology and financial allies? Or is it because the
new information technologies are perceived by them as a fantastic opportunity
to get rid of American domination and empower themselves to become global
cybersurfers? What is certain is that electronic surfing has become a favorite
sport of the Gulf rulers, and they are discovering a secret rule of this game: that
it is essential for women to join in.

30       Al-Khalifa's emergence in Bahrain is impossible to understand if you do not
realize that Bahrain is one of the first Arab countries to invest in e-government.
The first step was the creation of an electronic visa system—an e-visa service—
that went into operation in mid-2004. The second was reported on the front
page of the *Bahrain Tribune* on March 9, 2005: "King Stresses Larger Role for
Women." The story explained that "His Majesty the King, Hamad bin Isa al-
Khalifa, yesterday requested all government and civil administrations and
organizations to help implement the National Strategy for the Advancement of
Bahraini Women."

31       To make sure that his routine-inclined bureaucrats grasped what he meant,
the king provided a detailed description: "The implementation of the National
Strategy, the first of its type in the country, will help us achieve our objective,
which is to see women assume their roles fully as dependable partners to men
and fully capable of contributing to building the family, the society, and the
state, and eventually, to be involved in making decisions in modern Bahrain."

32       It is important to note, in this context, that the number of women employed
in Bahrain has risen from just over 5 percent in 1971 to more than 40 percent

today. Now how can you explain this strange coincidence between the onset of e-government and women's invasion of the labor force and their promotion as public actors if not by a cataclysmic shift in the region's ideological references? Is there not a repudiation of fanatic conservatism to embark on new horizons where power implies feminization of decision making?

In a humorous 2004 article entitled "The 50 Most Powerful Arab Women," [33] which appeared in the Dubai-based Arabic version of *Forbes* magazine, the editor, Rasha Owais, and her team undertook a survey to answer that question. They came to the conclusion that, beyond the traditional profile of the wives and daughters of heads of state, a new breed of digitally literate and financially skilled women has emerged on the Arab scene.

Some of them do fit the profile of wives of leaders, but—unlike, say, Egypt's [34] Suzan Mubarak or Queen Rania of Jordan—the new Digital Scheherazades are themselves communication wizards. For example, Sheikha Muza, the wife of the emir of Qatar, the man who financed Al Jazeera, launched in September 2005 the first Arab children's channel. The ambitious objective, financed by a foundation she controls, is to snatch Arab kids from the foreign television influence by providing them with a new ethical content where education and entertainment mix.

Being from a royal family helps, of course, but not automatically: I know [35] many wives of powerful, rich men who spend their time swallowing antidepression pills. Self-confidence and ability seem to be key characteristics of the new Digital Scheherazades.

When you start looking for them instead of focusing on the veiled [36] women, as many Europeans do, you are amazed by their rapidly growing number. The minister of economy and planning for the United Arab Emirates, for example, is a woman: Lubna al-Qasimi. Before assuming this post, al-Qasimi, who has a computer science degree from the University of California, was a senior manager of the Information Systems department of the Dubai Port Authority and participated in the launch of her country as a planetary digital hub.

## Investing in Female Brains

Did al-Qasimi owe her success to her being the niece of Sheikh Sultan bin [37] Mohammed al-Qasimi, the ruler of Sharjah, one of the United Arab Emirate kingdoms? There are numerous nieces of powerful emirs and sheikhs in the Gulf who never manage to emerge as top players in the power game. One of her favorite slogans is "I have earned my desk."

Indeed, those who still identify the region with veiling women and tradi- [38] tional archaism miss the essential point: the Arab Gulf's previously all-male ruling elite is investing in female brains as the winning card for information-fueled power. "We have a system for our children whereby we encourage them to gain experience outside the group first," says Muhamed al-Sayer, the billionaire chairman of a Kuwait-based group of companies. "For example, my daughter Lulwa spent eight years with Gulf Bank and is its head of Treasury. Male and female family members are offered the same opportunities."

39      It is this fascinating paradox that explains the emergence of Digital Scheherazades. Because men in the Arab Gulf have chosen to invest in communication as a power base, we can understand why one of the most important modern museum initiatives in Kuwait was that of Hussa al-Sabah, who forced Saddam Hussein to give back the cultural heritage pieces stolen from Kuwait after Iraq's invasion, and whose main supporter was her husband. Kuwait is also home to the very young Maha al-Ghunaim, the vice chairwoman and managing director of Global Investment House, which had net profits of $73 million in 2004.

40      In Qatar, where the clever emir propelled his tiny capital of Doha into a global player by financing Al Jazeera, one would expect to find Digital Scheherazades taking advantage of the kingdom's new information technologies. Such is the case with Hanadi Nasser, a businesswoman who has become a key player as the managing director of Amwal, a well-funded Qatari investment company.

## The Caliph's Partner

41  According to my friend Kamal, Caliph Harun al-Rashid, who took power in Baghdad in 786 AD, is the key to elucidating the enigma of the Digital Scheherazades. The caliph's wife, Zubaida, made herself famous by digging wells along the Baghdad-Mecca road she had built to transform Muslims' yearly hajj into a comfortable and engaging trip.

42      Both Harun and Zubaida were heroes of the *1,001 Nights*, invented by eighth- and ninth-century Baghdad male street-storytellers who mirrored in their tales the fascination of Muslim elites and crowds with strangers as a source of magic diversity. And the primary fascinating strangers for men are indeed women. So, although Scheherazade, the storyteller of the *1,001 Nights*, was supposed to be Persian, it was Arab women like Princess Zubaida—who managed to seduce the Caliph Harun while digging wells and building walls to provide creature comforts during the hajj—who inspired our Baghdad storytellers.

43      These male storytellers forbade in their fiction the imaginary Scheherazade to speak during the day and condemned her to limit her activity to the night only, but modern historians are discovering that Zubaida exercised her power 24 hours a day.

44      Limiting women's power to the night while forbidding them from exercising authority during daylight—the monopoly of males—is a deep-seated reflex that goes back far into history. It is well condensed in the slogan-like sentence that ends mechanically each of the 1,001 stories: "When dawn overtook Scheherazade, she lapsed into silence." But limiting women's power to the private sphere has always been a male fiction. And the defensive fear of the feminine has always gone together with the fear of strangers. When the leaders of a nation embark on communication as their way to glory, welcoming the different other as a partner is the magic shift that explains their success.

To understand why modern Arab Gulf emirs are suddenly investing in in- ₄₅ formation technology as their power base and promoting women as their partners, we must go back to Harun, who did the same when he decided to invest in the paper industry to launch Islam as a communication-powered civilization whose main weapon was the Arabic language. Just as today, Arabs were scientifically backward in the eighth century, but their switch to communication enabled them to catch up with other nations by using language to navigate and conduct dialogue. Arabic, the language of illiterate pagans, was transformed into a medium of religion, the law, and sciences, promoting the Arabs to global prominence.

Are we witnessing once again the emergence of women as brainy allies ₄₆ when men opt for communication as their power base? Just to make sure you do not take me to be blindly optimistic, let me tell you that Western television companies such as the BBC and CBC are worried about competition in the United States from Al Jazeera, which has decided to launch an English language channel. As a woman, I will be more than thrilled if the competition between East and West switches from bombs and armies to communication strategies.

## COMPREHENSION

1. Who is Scheherazade? (If necessary, check Google or another site for information.) Where does she (or the connotations she evokes) appear in the essay?
2. What does Mernissi mean by "digital chaos"? What examples does she provide to illuminate this idea?
3. Explain the connections between digital chaos and the changing roles of women in Muslim society.

## RHETORIC

1. Is Mernissi's purpose to inform or to argue—or perhaps both? Justify your response by citing specific sentences and passages.
2. Mernissi's essay appeared in the journal *Current History*. What assumptions does she make about her primary audience? How does she establish her authority for this audience? How might the article appeal to a broader audience?
3. What is the effect of Mernissi's dividing the essay into sections? How does she manage transitions?
4. Analyze the ways in which Scheherazade serves as both symbol and organizing strategy in the essay.
5. Mernissi uses several forms of evidence to support her key ideas. Identify these various strategies of exemplification, and cite specific passages reflecting them.

6. The author is a noted feminist scholar. How do her feminist assumptions affect the tone of the essay? Where does she inject personal opinion? Where, if anywhere, does she make ethical and emotional appeals?

## WRITING

1. Although Mernissi writes about a part of the world that might not be familiar, she raises issues that have not just regional but global implications. Write an analytical essay in which you examine the ways in which "digital chaos" is changing gender relationships in the United States or elsewhere.
2. Write a comparative essay linking the articles by David Brooks and Fatema Mernissi appearing in this chapter.
3. **Writing an Argument:** Do you believe that "new communication strategies," as Mernissi terms it, can actually liberate women and reform society? Argue for or against this proposition.

| www.mhhe.com/ **mhreader** | For more information on Fatema Mernissi, go to: **More Resources > Ch. 5 Family & Gender** |

# Why Men Don't Last: Self-Destruction as a Way of Life

## Natalie Angier

*Natalie Angier (b. 1958) grew up in New York City and graduated from Barnard College in 1978. She has worked as a magazine staff writer for* Discover *and* Time *and became a reporter for* The New York Times *in 1990. Her work as a* Times *science correspondent led to a Pulitzer Prize in 1991. She is also a recipient of the Lewis Thomas Award and was one of only seven journalists to receive four stars in the* Forbes Media Guide *that rated 500 reporters. She has also published in* The Atlantic, Parade, Washington Monthly, *and* Reader's Digest. *Her books include* The Beauty of the Beastly: New Views on the Nature of Life *(1995) and* Women: An Intimate Geography *(1999). In the following essay, first published in* The New York Times *in 1999, Angier examines the biological, social, and psychological differences between men and women in order to explain why there is a marked difference in life expectancy between the genders.*

1 My father had great habits. Long before ficus trees met weight machines, he was a dogged exerciser. He did pushups and isometrics. He climbed rocks. He

went for long, vigorous walks. He ate sparingly and avoided sweets and grease. He took such good care of his teeth that they looked fake.

My father had terrible habits. He was chronically angry. He threw things 2 around the house and broke them. He didn't drink often, but when he did, he turned more violent than usual. He didn't go to doctors, even when we begged him to. He let a big, ugly mole on his back grow bigger and bigger, and so he died of malignant melanoma, a curable cancer, at 51.

My father was a real man—so good and so bad. He was also Everyman. 3

Men by some measures take better care of themselves than women do and 4 are in better health. They are less likely to be fat, for example; they exercise more, and suffer from fewer chronic diseases like diabetes, osteoporosis and arthritis.

By standard measures, men have less than half the rate of depression seen 5 in women. When men do feel depressed, they tend to seek distraction in an activity, which, many psychologists say, can be a more effective technique for dispelling the mood than is a depressed woman's tendency to turn inward and ruminate. In the United States and many other industrialized nations, women are about three times more likely than men to express suicidal thoughts or to attempt to kill themselves.

And yet . . . men don't last. They die off in greater numbers than women do 6 at every stage of life, and thus their average life span is seven years shorter. Women may attempt suicide relatively more often, but in the United States, four times more men than women die from the act each year.

Men are also far more likely than women to die behind the wheel or to kill 7 others as a result of their driving. From 1977 to 1995, three and a half times more male drivers than female drivers were involved in fatal car crashes. Death by homicide also favors men; among those under 30, the male-to-female ratio is 8 to 1.

Yes, men can be impressive in their tendency to self-destruct, explosively or 8 gradually. They are at least twice as likely as women to be alcoholics and three times more likely to be drug addicts. They have an eightfold greater chance than women do of ending up in prison. Boys are much more likely than girls to be thrown out of school for a conduct or antisocial personality disorder, or to drop out on their own surly initiative. Men gamble themselves into a devastating economic and emotional pit two to three times more often than women do.

"Between boys' suicide rates, dropout rates and homicide rates, and men's 9 self-destructive behaviors generally, we have a real crisis in America," said William S. Pollack, a psychologist at Harvard Medical School and co-director of the Center for Men at McLean Hospital in Belmont, Mass. "Until recently, the crisis has gone unheralded."

It is one thing to herald a presumed crisis, though, and to cite a ream of 10 gloomy statistics. It is quite another to understand the crisis, or to figure out where it comes from or what to do about it. As those who study the various forms of men's self-destructive behaviors realize, there is not a single, glib, overarching explanation for the sex-specific patterns they see.

11    A crude evolutionary hypothesis would have it that men are natural risk-takers, given to showy displays of bravado, aggression and daring all for the sake of attracting a harem of mates. By this premise, most of men's self-destructive, violent tendencies are a manifestation of their need to take big chances for the sake of passing their genes into the river of tomorrow.

12    Some of the data on men's bad habits fit the risk-taker model. For example, those who study compulsive gambling have observed that men and women tend to display very different methods and preferences for throwing away big sums of money.

13    "Men get enamored of the action in gambling," said Linda Chamberlain, a psychologist at Regis University in Denver who specializes in treating gambling disorders. "They describe an overwhelming rush of feelings and excitement associated with the process of gambling. They like the feeling of being a player, and taking on a struggle with the house to show that they can overcome the odds and beat the system. They tend to prefer the table games, where they can feel powerful and omnipotent while everybody watches them."

14    Dr. Chamberlain noted that many male gamblers engage in other risk-taking behaviors, like auto racing or hang gliding. By contrast, she said, "Women tend to use gambling more as a sedative, to numb themselves and escape from daily responsibilities, or feelings of depression or alienation. Women tend to prefer the solitary forms of gambling, the slot machines or video poker, where there isn't as much social scrutiny."

15    Yet the risk-taking theory does not account for why men outnumber women in the consumption of licit and illicit anodynes. Alcohol, heroin and marijuana can be at least as numbing and sedating as repetitively pulling the arm of a slot machine. And some studies have found that men use drugs and alcohol for the same reasons that women often overeat: as an attempt to self-medicate when they are feeling anxious or in despair.

16    "We can speculate all we want, but we really don't know why men drink more than women," said Enoch Gordis, the head of the National Institute on Alcohol Abuse and Alcoholism. Nor does men's comparatively higher rate of suicide appear linked to the risk-taking profile. To the contrary, Paul Duberstein, an assistant professor of psychiatry and oncology at the University of Rochester School of Medicine, has found that people who complete a suicidal act are often low in a personality trait referred to as "openness to experience," tending to be rigid and inflexible in their behaviors. By comparison, those who express suicidal thoughts tend to score relatively high on the openness-to-experience scale.

17    Given that men commit suicide more often than women, and women talk about it more, his research suggests that, in a sense, women are the greater risk-takers and novelty seekers, while the men are likelier to feel trapped and helpless in the face of changing circumstances.

18    Silvia Cara Canetto, an associate professor of psychology at Colorado State University in Fort Collins, has extensively studied the role of gender in suicidal behaviors. Dr. Canetto has found that cultural narratives may determine why

women attempt suicide more often while men kill themselves more often. She proposes that in Western countries, to talk about suicide or to survive a suicidal act is often considered "feminine," hysterical, irrational, and weak. To actually die by one's own hand may be viewed as "masculine," decisive, strong. Even the language conveys the polarized, weak-strong imagery: a "failed" suicide attempt as opposed to a "successful" one.

"There is indirect evidence that there is negative stigma toward men who 19 survive suicide," Dr. Canetto said. "Men don't want to 'fail,' even though failing in this case means surviving." If the "suicidal script" that identifies completing the acts as "rational, courageous and masculine" can be "undermined and torn to pieces," she said, we might have a new approach to prevention.

Dr. Pollack of the Center for Men also blames many of men's self-destructive 20 ways on the persistent image of the dispassionate, resilient, action-oriented male—the Marlboro Man who never even gasps for breath. For all the talk of the sensitive "new man,"he argues, men have yet to catch up with women in expanding their range of acceptable emotions and behaviors. Men in our culture, Dr. Pollack says, are pretty much limited to a menu of three strong feelings: rage, triumph, lust. "Anything else and you risk being seen as a sissy," he said.

In a number of books, most recently, *Real Boys: Rescuing Our Sons from the* 21 *Myths of Boyhood,* he proposes that boys "lose their voice, a whole half of their emotional selves," beginning at age 4 or 5. "Their vulnerable, sad feelings and sense of need are suppressed or shamed out of them," he said—by their peers, parents, the great wide televised fist in their face.

He added: "If you keep hammering it into a kid that he has to look tough 22 and stop being a crybaby and a mama's boy, the boy will start creating a mask of bravado."

That boys and young men continue to feel confused over the proper har- 23 monics of modern masculinity was revealed in a study that Dr. Pollack conducted of 200 eighth-grade boys. Through questionnaires, he determined their scores on two scales, one measuring their "egalitarianism"—the degree to which they think men and women are equal, that men should change a baby's diapers, that mothers should work and the like—and the other gauging their "traditionalism" as determined by their responses to conventional notions, like the premise that men must "stand on their own two feet" and must "always be willing to have sex if someone asks."

On average, the boys scored high on both scales. "They are split on what it 24 means to be a man," said Dr. Pollack.

The cult of masculinity can beckon like a siren song in baritone. Dr. Franklin 25 L. Nelson, a clinical psychologist at the Fairbanks Community Mental Health Center in Alaska, sees many men who get into trouble by adhering to sentimental notions of manhood. "A lot of men come up here hoping to get away from a wimpy world and live like pioneers by old-fashioned masculine principles of individualism, strength and ruggedness," he said. They learn that nothing is simple; even Alaska is part of a wider, interdependent world and they really do need friends, warmth and electricity.

26    "Right now, it's 35 degrees below zero outside," he said during a January interview. "If you're not prepared, it doesn't take long at that temperature to freeze to death."

## COMPREHENSION

1. What does the second sentence in the essay mean? What is Angier suggesting about modern life by including it?
2. Angier makes a number of comparisons between the lifestyles of men and women. Does she suggest one overriding principle regarding why "men don't last," or is it really a compilation of many factors? Explain.
3. Does Angier suggest that ideas of "masculinity" are hereditary or environmental, or both? Explain by using examples from the text.
4. Angier begins her essay with a personal anecdote about her father. She claims that he was "Everyman." Does he appear to you to have acted like the "typical male"?

## RHETORIC

1. Angier often mixes facts with theory. For example, in paragraph 11, she refers to a hypothesis that "men are natural risk-takers," while in other sections, she provides hard data about men's mortality rates. Does this combination make her argument more robust, or does it make it less convincing?
2. Describe Angier's tone. Is she sympathetic that men die younger, or does she seem to castigate them? Select three examples from her essay that support your view.
3. Writers will often mention opposing viewpoints to buttress their own arguments. Angier doesn't. Does this strengthen or weaken her main premise? Explain.
4. Angier is noted for her lively prose style. Examine the following phrases, and discuss what they mean and how they add "color" to her writing: "the great wide televised fist in their face" (paragraph 21), "the proper harmonics of modern masculinity" (paragraph 23), and "beckon like a siren song in baritone" (paragraph 25).
5. Compare and contrast the introduction and conclusion of the essay. How do they differ in imagery and tone? How does the subject matter of the conclusion help Angier achieve closure in her argument?
6. Angier often employs the "vocabulary of masculinity" in her argument. For example, she states, "My father was a real man" (paragraph 3); other masculine terms include "action-oriented" and "Marlboro man" (paragraph 20) and "away from a wimpy world" (paragraph 25). How does the use of this vocabulary contribute to her portrayal of the "masculine image"?
7. In paragraphs 5–14, Angier lists a number of statistics and behaviors that she attributes to male self-destructiveness. Is there a rationale behind the

order in which she lists them, or does it seem more like a compendium of facts? Regardless of your answer, what is the rhetorical effect?

## WRITING

1. Write an essay in the form of a process analysis with the title "How Men Can Live Longer." Be sure to provide examples and illustrations to support your report.
2. Write a narrative essay describing an event in which you took or witnessed an unnecessary risk. Reflect on why the risk was taken and what its consequences were—whether positive or negative.
3. For a research paper, compare and contrast the "masculine traits" of American males with those of males from a different country or culture. Include at least four secondary sources.
4. **Writing an Argument:** Respond to Angier, arguing for or against the idea that women are more self-destructive than men.

|  | For more information on Natalie Angier, go to: |
| www.mhhe.com/ **mhreader** | **More Resources > Ch. 5 Family & Gender** |

## Synthesis: Connections For Critical Thinking

1. Both Annie Dillard's "An American Childhood" and E. B. White's "Once More to the Lake" explore the experience of childhood from a different perspective. Do they share a common voice or mood? What is distinctive about each essay? Which essay do you prefer, and why? Consider the style and emotional impact of the writing.
2. Both Barbara Kingsolver's "Stone Soup" and Richard Rodriguez's "Family Values" attempt to alter stereotypes commonly held about contemporary families. What type of family does each author address? How do the authors differ in their rhetorical strategies and their use of supporting points to buttress their arguments? Who is the implied audience for each of the essays? How did you reach your conclusion?
3. Argue for or against the idea that Alvarez's portrayal of marriage and Angier's analysis of men are biased.
4. Argue for or against the idea that descriptions of the relatively new types of family relationships described by Kingsolver in "Stone Soup" or in Rodriguez's "Family Values" are presented in a biased, romanticized manner.
5. Argue for or against the view that changes in society and its norms—specifically, increased geographical mobility, an evolving workplace, ideas about economic class, individual liberties, and sexual preference—have

resulted in new forms of identity. Use examples from the work of Mernissi, Brooks, and Rodriguez.

6. Select the two more substantially argued essays in this chapter, Mernissi's "Digital Scheherazades in the Arab World," and Rodriguez's "Family Values." Compare and contrast their methods of argumentation.

7. Establish your own definition of what it means to be a male or a female. Refer to the essays of Mernissi, Angier, and Rodriguez.

8. **Network:** Search the Web for *family values*. Write an extended analysis of the results of your research.

9. **Network:** Join several newsgroups or chat rooms that focus on Internet dating. Compare and contrast the ideological focus of the conversations among members.

10. **Network:** Create your own home page, and develop an interface that includes a selected quote regarding the family taken from one of your essays. Create a link to the home page with a response page where fellow students can make comments regarding the quotation. At the end of the semester, write a report and summary of the responses you received. You may ask students to include their country of origin or their ethnicity to help you find possible connections between these factors and the responses.

chapter *6*

# History, Culture, and Civilization

*Are We Citizens of the World?*

At the start of a new century, the paroxysms caused by conflicts among peoples, nations, ethnic groups, and cultures continue to shake continents. The United States might have emerged from the cold war as the dominant superpower, but numerous local and global threats remain. We seem to be at a crossroads in history, culture, and civilization, but does the future hold great promise or equally great danger—or both?

The future assuredly holds significant peril as well as promise. History tells us that while there has never been complete absence of barbarism and nonrational behavior in human affairs, there have been societies, cultures, and nations committed to harmonious, or civil, conduct within various social realms. While it is clear that we have not attained an ideal state of cultural or world development, at the same time, we have advanced beyond the point in primitive civilization at which someone chipped at a stone in order to make a better tool.

As we consider the course of contemporary civilization, we must contend with our own personal histories and cultures as well as with the interplay of contradictory global forces. We have become increasingly concerned with finding a purpose beyond the parameters of our very limiting personal and nationalistic identities, something that the Czech writer and statesman Václav Havel calls the "divine revolution." Indeed, we have entered an era of renewed ethnic strife, in which a preoccupation with cultural difference seems stronger than the desire for universal civilization. The writers assembled here grapple with these contradictions; they search for those constituents of history and culture that might hasten the advent of a civilized world.

The idea of civilization suggests a pluralistic ethos whereby people of diverse histories and backgrounds can maintain cultural identities but also coexist with other cultural representatives in a spirit of tolerance and mutual respect. The wars, upheavals, and catastrophes of the 20th century were spawned by a narrow consciousness. Hopefully, as we enter a new century, all of us can advance the goal of a universal civilization based on the best that we have been able to create for humankind.

## Previewing the Chapter

As you read the essays in this chapter and respond to them in discussion and writing, consider the following questions:

- How does the author define *culture, history,* or *civilization?* Is this definition stated or implied? Is it broad or narrow? Explain.
- Is the writer hopeful or pessimistic about the state of culture and history?
- What values does the author seem to think are necessary to advance the idea of history and culture?
- Is the author's tone objective or subjective? What is his or her purpose? Does the author have a personal motive in addressing the topic in the way he or she does?
- Which areas of knowledge—for example, history, philosophy, and political science—does the author bring to bear on the subject?
- Do you agree or disagree with the author's view of the contemporary state of civilization?
- What cultural problems and historical conflicts are raised by the author in his or her treatment of the subject?
- Does the author have a narrow or a broad focus on the relationship of history and culture to the larger society?
- Which authors altered your perspective on a topic, and why?
- Based on your reading of these essays, how would you define *civilization?* Are you hopeful about the current state of civilization?

# Classic and Contemporary Images
## HOW DO WE BECOME AMERICANS?

*Using a Critical Perspective*   Compare the scene of early-20th-century immigrants at New York City's Ellis Island with the March 1999 X-ray photo taken by Mexican authorities of human forms and cargo in a truck. What mood is conveyed by each representation? Does each photograph have a thesis or argument? Explain. Which photo do you find more engaging and provocative, and why?

From the time of the first European settlers, the North American continent has experienced wave after wave of immigration from every part of the world. One period of heavy immigration occurred in the late 19th and early 20th centuries, when millions of people from eastern and southern Europe entered the United States through Ellis Island in New York City, as shown in this classic photograph.

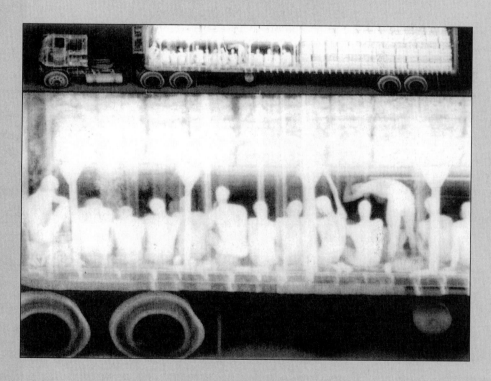

More recently, immigrants continue to come from all over the world, often
entering the country illegally. The X-ray photo shows a wide shot
and a close-up image of people being smuggled across
Mexico's border with Guatemala.

# Classic and Contemporary Essays
## ARE WE HEADING TOWARD A WORLD CULTURE?

Both of these essays address the issues of prejudice and national identification. As you read them, consider not only the differing styles and methods of discourse of their authors (to be expected of essays written more than two centuries apart) but also their themes and import. In addition, consider that Ishmael Reed is writing from the perspective of a racial and (to his mind) cultural minority, and may therefore be particularly aware of those who would claim that America's values, beliefs, doctrines, and cultural influences are homogeneous. Additionally, it may be ironic to note that Reed is writing within the context of a modern democratic state, while in 1762, the publication year of Oliver Goldsmith's essay, the United States did not even exist. Goldsmith's tone and style are immediately identifiable as being from another era. However, you should not confuse the formality of his rhetoric with the casual and intimate relationship to his reader. He addresses the reader quite directly, and the inspiration for his essay comes, he claims, from an informal conversation at a local tavern or coffeehouse. So, while his writing may appear abstruse, recall that Shakespeare wrote for an audience that had little formal education but understood his work with ease. Contemporary readers, on the other hand, often have trouble deciphering him because temporal distance often makes phrasing, vocabulary, and specific references obscure. Goldsmith uses no statistics, no historical record, and no ideological analysis in his testimony. Rather, he assumes the tone of the "gentleman observer," a common form of address in his era. He may sound formal, but his tone is friendly. He disputes his colleagues' views that the English character represents the height of human development, but he disarms his opponents through civility and deference. Reed is a contemporary African American writer of both fiction and nonfiction. From the perspective of a creative artist and keen observer of the modern intellectual and political scene, he combines personal experience and the historical record to demonstrate that much of "Western Civilization" draws its roots from a multiplicity of sources, not just European. Ironically, Reed, whose style is more colloquial than that of his distinguished predecessor, presents his argument using more of the traditional modes of support—for example, cultural analysis, appeals to authority, and historical evidence. Reed, however, unlike the courteous Goldsmith, is more forthright and direct in his disagreements. Can this be attributed to the reserved style of the English character versus the more direct discourse of the modern American? Or are we examining the reflections of two different personalities with different agendas?

# National Prejudices

## Oliver Goldsmith

*Oliver Goldsmith (1730–1774), the son of an Anglican curate, was an Anglo-Irish essayist, poet, novelist, dramatist, and journalist. His reputation as an enduring figure in English literature is based on his novel* The Vicar of Wakefield *(1766), his play* She Stoops to Conquer *(1773), his poem* The Deserted Village *(1770), and the essays and satiric letters collected in* The Bee *(1759) and* The Citizen of the World *(1762). In this essay from the latter, Goldsmith argues quietly for a new type of citizen, one who can transcend the xenophobia governing national behavior.*

As I am one of that sauntering tribe of mortals, who spend the greatest part of  1
their time in taverns, coffee houses, and other places of public resort, I have
thereby an opportunity of observing an infinite variety of characters, which, to
a person of a contemplative turn, is a much higher entertainment than a view
of all the curiosities of art or nature. In one of these, my late rambles, I accidentally fell into the company of half a dozen gentlemen, who were engaged in a
warm dispute about some political affair; the decision of which, as they were
equally divided in their sentiments, they thought proper to refer to me, which
naturally drew me in for a share of the conversation.

Amongst a multiplicity of other topics, we took occasion to talk of the dif-  2
ferent characters of the several nations of Europe; when one of the gentlemen,
cocking his hat, and assuming such an air of importance as if he had possessed
all the merit of the English nation in his own person, declared that the Dutch
were a parcel of avaricious wretches; the French a set of flattering sycophants;
that the Germans were drunken sots, and beastly gluttons; and the Spaniards
proud, haughty, and surly tyrants; but that in bravery, generosity, clemency,
and in every other virtue, the English excelled all the rest of the world.

This very learned and judicious remark was received with a general smile of  3
approbation by all the company—all, I mean, but your humble servant; who, endeavoring to keep my gravity as well as I could, and reclining my head upon my
arm, continued for some time in a posture of affected thoughtfulness, as if I had
been musing on something else, and did not seem to attend to the subject of conversation; hoping by these means to avoid the disagreeable necessity of explaining
myself, and thereby depriving the gentleman of his imaginary happiness.

But my pseudo-patriot had no mind to let me escape so easily. Not satis-  4
fied that his opinion should pass without contradiction, he was determined
to have it ratified by the suffrage of every one in the company; for which
purpose addressing himself to me with an air of inexpressible confidence, he
asked me if I was not of the same way of thinking. As I am never forward in

giving my opinion, especially when I have reason to believe that it will not be agreeable; so, when I am obliged to give it, I always hold it for a maxim to speak my real sentiments. I therefore told him that, for my own part, I should not have ventured to talk in such a peremptory strain, unless I had made the tour of Europe, and examined the manners of these several nations with great care and accuracy: that, perhaps, a more impartial judge would not scruple to affirm that the Dutch were more frugal and industrious, the French more temperate and polite, the Germans more hardy and patient of labor and fatigue, and the Spaniards more staid and sedate, than the English; who, though undoubtedly brave and generous, were at the same time rash, head-strong, and impetuous; too apt to be elated with prosperity, and to despond in adversity.

5   I could easily perceive that all the company began to regard me with a jealous eye before I had finished my answer, which I had no sooner done, than the patriotic gentleman observed, with a contemptuous sneer, that he was greatly surprised how some people could have the conscience to live in a country which they did not love, and to enjoy the protection of a government, to which in their hearts they were inveterate enemies. Finding that by this modest declaration of my sentiments I had forfeited the good opinion of my companions, and given them occasion to call my political principles in question, and well knowing that it was in vain to argue with men who were so very full of themselves, I threw down my reckoning and retired to my own lodgings, reflecting on the absurd and ridiculous nature of national prejudice and prepossession.

6   Among all the famous sayings of antiquity, there is none that does greater honor to the author, or affords greater pleasure to the reader (at least if he be a person of a generous and benevolent heart), than that of the philosopher, who, being asked what "countryman he was," replied, that he was, "a citizen of the world."—How few are there to be found in modern times who can say the same, or whose conduct is consistent with such a profession!—We are now become so much Englishmen, Frenchmen, Dutchmen, Spaniards or Germans, that we are no longer citizens of the world; so much the natives of one particular spot, or members of one petty society, that we no longer consider ourselves as the general inhabitants of the globe, or members of that grand society which comprehends the whole human kind.

7   Did these prejudices prevail only among the meanest and lowest of the people, perhaps they might be excused, as they have few, if any, opportunities of correcting them by reading, travelling, or conversing with foreigners; but the misfortune is, that they infect the minds, and influence the conduct, even of our gentlemen; of those, I mean, who have every title to this appellation but an exemption from prejudice, which however, in my opinion, ought to be regarded as the characteristical mark of a gentleman; for let a man's birth be ever so high, his station ever so exalted, or his fortune ever so large, yet if he is not free from national and other prejudices, I should make bold to tell him, that he had a low and vulgar mind, and had no just claim to the

character of a gentleman. And in fact, you will always find that those are most apt to boast of national merit, who have little or no merit of their own to depend on; than which, to be sure, nothing is more natural: the slender vine twists around the sturdy oak, for no other reason in the world but because it has not strength sufficient to support itself.

Should it be alleged in defense of national prejudice, that it is the natural 8 and necessary growth of love to our country, and that therefore the former cannot be destroyed without hurting the latter, I answer, that this is a gross fallacy and delusion. That it is the growth of love to our country, I will allow; but that it is the natural and necessary growth of it, I absolutely deny. Superstition and enthusiasm too are the growth of religion; but who ever took it in his head to affirm that they are the necessary growth of this noble principle? They are, if you will, the bastard sprouts of this heavenly plant, but not its natural and genuine branches, and may safely enough be lopped off, without doing any harm to the parent stock; nay, perhaps, till once they are lopped off, this goodly tree can never flourish in perfect health and vigor.

Is it not very possible that I may love my own country, without hating the 9 natives of other countries? that I may exert the most heroic bravery, the most undaunted resolution, in defending its laws and liberty, without despising all the rest of the world as cowards and poltroons? Most certainly it is; and if it were not—But why need I suppose what is absolutely impossible?—But if it were not, I must own, I should prefer the title of the ancient philosopher, viz. a citizen of the world, to that of an Englishman, a Frenchman, a European, or to any other appellation whatever.

## COMPREHENSION

1. Why does Goldsmith maintain that he is "a citizen of the world"? According to the author, could such an individual also be a patriot? Explain.
2. What connection does Goldsmith make between national prejudices and the conduct of gentlemen? Why does he allude to the manners of gentlemen?
3. Compare and contrast Goldsmith's observations with those of Schlesinger in "The Cult of Ethnicity" (page 8).

## RHETORIC

1. Locate in the essay examples of the familiar style in writing. What is the relationship between this style and the tone and substance of the essay?
2. Explain the metaphors at the end of paragraphs 7 and 8.
3. What is the relevance of the introductory narrative, with its description of characters, to Goldsmith's declaration of thesis? Where does he state his proposition concerning national prejudices?
4. Analyze the function of classification and contrast in paragraphs 2–5. How does the entire essay serve as a pattern of definition?

5. Examine the pattern of reasoning involved in the author's presentation of his argument in the essay, notably in paragraphs 6–8. What appeals to emotion and to reason does he make?
6. Assess the rhetorical effectiveness of Goldsmith's concluding paragraph.

### WRITING

1. Why has it been difficult to eliminate the problem that Goldsmith identified in 1762? Are we better able today to function as citizens of the world? In what ways? What role does the United Nations play in this issue? What factors contribute to a new world citizenry? Explore these questions in an essay.
2. Write a paper on contemporary national prejudices—from the viewpoint of an ingenious foreigner.
3. **Writing an Argument:** Write an argumentative essay on the desirability of world government or on the need to be a citizen of the world.

www.mhhe.com/
**mhreader**

For more information on Oliver Goldsmith, go to:
**More Resources > Ch. 6 History & Culture**

# America: The Multinational Society

## Ishmael Reed

*Ishmael Reed (b. 1938), an American novelist, poet, and essayist, is the founder and editor (along with Al Young) of* Quilt *magazine, begun in 1981. In his writing, Reed uses a combination of standard English, black dialect, and slang to satirize American society. He believes that African Americans must move away from identification with Europe in order to rediscover their African qualities. Reed's books include* Flight to Canada *(1976),* The Terrible Twos *(1982),* The Terrible Threes *(1989), and* Japanese by Spring *(1993). In addition, he has written volumes of verse, including* Secretary to the Spirits *(1975), and has published collections of his essays, including* Airing Dirty Laundry *(1993). In the following essay from* Writin' Is Fightin' *(1990), Reed seeks to debunk the myth of the European ideal and argues for a universal definition of culture.*

*At the annual Lower East Side Jewish Festival yesterday, a Chinese woman ate a pizza slice in front of Ty Thuan Duc's Vietnamese grocery store. Beside her a Spanish-speaking family patronized a cart with two signs: "Italian Ices" and "Kosher by Rabbi Alper." And after the pastrami ran out, everybody ate knishes.*
                                                    —The New York Times, *June 23, 1983*

On the day before Memorial Day, 1983, a poet called me to describe a city he   1
had just visited. He said that one section included mosques, built by the Islamic
people who dwelled there. Attending his reading, he said, were large numbers
of Hispanic people, forty thousand of whom lived in the same city. He was not
talking about a fabled city located in some mysterious region of the world. The
city he'd visited was Detroit.

A few months before, as I was leaving Houston, Texas, I heard it announced   2
on the radio that Texas's largest minority was Mexican American, and though a
foundation recently issued a report critical of bilingual education, the taped
voice used to guide the passengers on the air trams connecting terminals in
Dallas Airport is in both Spanish and English. If the trend continues, a day will
come when it will be difficult to travel through some sections of the country
without hearing commands in both English and Spanish; after all, for some
western states, Spanish was the first written language and the Spanish style
lives on in the western way of life.

Shortly after my Texas trip, I sat in an auditorium located on the campus of   3
the University of Wisconsin at Milwaukee as a Yale professor—whose original
work on the influence of African cultures upon those of the Americas has led to
his ostracism from some monocultural intellectual circles—walked up and
down the aisle, like an old-time southern evangelist, dancing and drumming
the top of the lectern, illustrating his points before some serious Afro-American
intellectuals and artists who cheered and applauded his performance and his
mastery of information. The professor was "white." After his lecture, he joined
a group of Milwaukeeans in a conversation. All of the participants spoke
Yoruban, though only the professor had ever traveled to Africa.

One of the artists told me that his paintings, which included African and   4
Afro-American mythological symbols and imagery, were hanging in the local
McDonald's restaurant. The next day I went to McDonald's and snapped pictures of smiling youngsters eating hamburgers below paintings that could grace
the walls of any of the country's leading museums. The manager of the local
McDonald's said, "I don't know what you boys are doing, but I like it," as he
commissioned the local painters to exhibit in his restaurant.

Such blurring of cultural styles occurs in everyday life in the United States   5
to a greater extent than anyone can imagine and is probably more prevalent
than the sensational conflict between people of different backgrounds that is
played up and often encouraged by the media. The result is what the Yale professor, Robert Thompson, referred to as a cultural bouillabaisse, yet members of
the nation's present educational and cultural Elect still cling to the notion that
the United States belongs to some vaguely defined entity they refer to as "Western civilization," by which they mean, presumably, a civilization created by the
people of Europe, as if Europe can be viewed in monolithic terms. Is Beethoven's
Ninth Symphony, which includes Turkish marches, a part of Western civilization, or the late nineteenth- and twentieth-century French paintings, whose creators were influenced by Japanese art? And what of the cubists, through whom
the influence of African art changed modern painting, or the surrealists, who

were so impressed with the art of the Pacific Northwest Indians that, in their map of North America, Alaska dwarfs the lower forty-eight in size?

6    Are the Russians, who are often criticized for their adoption of "Western" ways by Tsarist dissidents in exile, members of Western civilization? And what of the millions of Europeans who have black African and Asian ancestry, black Africans having occupied several countries for hundreds of years? Are these "Europeans" members of Western civilization, or the Hungarians, who originated across the Urals in a place called Greater Hungary, or the Irish, who came from the Iberian Peninsula?

7    Even the notion that North America is part of Western civilization because our "system of government" is derived from Europe is being challenged by Native American historians who say that the founding fathers, Benjamin Franklin especially, were actually influenced by the system of government that had been adopted by the Iroquois hundreds of years prior to the arrival of large numbers of Europeans.

8    Western civilization, then, becomes another confusing category like Third World, or Judeo-Christian culture, as man attempts to impose his small-screen view of political and cultural reality upon a complex world. Our most publicized novelist recently said that Western civilization was the greatest achievement of mankind, an attitude that flourishes on the street level as scribbles in public restrooms: "White Power," "Niggers and Spics Suck," or "Hitler was a prophet," the latter being the most telling, for wasn't Adolph [sic] Hitler the archetypal monoculturalist who, in his pigheaded arrogance, believed that one way and one blood was so pure that it had to be protected from alien strains at all costs? Where did such an attitude, which has caused so much misery and depression in our national life, which has tainted even our noblest achievements, begin? An attitude that caused the incarceration of Japanese-American citizens during World War II, the persecution of Chicanos and Chinese Americans, the near-extermination of the Indians, and the murder and lynchings of thousands of Afro-Americans.

9    Virtuous, hardworking, pious, even though they occasionally would wander off after some fancy clothes, or rendezvous in the woods with the town prostitute, the Puritans are idealized in our schoolbooks as "a hardy band" of no-nonsense patriarchs whose discipline razed the forest and brought order to the New World (a term that annoys Native American historians). Industrious, responsible, it was their "Yankee ingenuity" and practicality that created the work ethic. They were simple folk who produced a number of good poets, and they set the tone for the American writing style, of lean and spare lines, long before Hemingway. They worshiped in churches whose colors blended in with the New England snow, churches with simple structures and ornate lecterns.

10   The Puritans were a daring lot, but they had a mean streak. They hated the theater and banned Christmas. They punished people in a cruel and inhuman manner. They killed children who disobeyed their parents. When they came in contact with those whom they considered heathens or aliens, they behaved in such a bizarre and irrational manner that this chapter in the American history

comes down to us as a late-movie horror film. They exterminated the Indians, who taught them how to survive in a world unknown to them, and their encounter with the calypso culture of Barbados resulted in what the tourist guide in Salem's Witches' House refers to as the Witchcraft Hysteria.

The Puritan legacy of hard work and meticulous accounting led to the 11 establishment of a great industrial society; it is no wonder that the American industrial revolution began in Lowell, Massachusetts, but there was the other side, the strange and paranoid attitudes toward those different from the Elect.

The cultural attitudes of that early Elect continue to be voiced in everyday 12 life in the United States: the president of a distinguished university, writing a letter to the *Times,* belittling the study of African civilizations; the television network that promoted its show on the Vatican art with the boast that this art represented "the finest achievements of the human spirit." A modern up-tempo state of complex rhythms that depends upon contacts with an international community can no longer behave as if it dwelled in a "Zion Wilderness" surrounded by beasts and pagans.

When I heard a schoolteacher warn the other night about the invasion of the 13 American educational system by foreign curriculums, I wanted to yell at the television set, "Lady, they're already here." It has already begun because the world is here. The world has been arriving at these shores for at least ten thousand years from Europe, Africa, and Asia. In the late nineteenth and early twentieth centuries, large numbers of Europeans arrived, adding their cultures to those of the European, African, and Asian settlers who were already here, and recently millions have been entering the country from South America and the Caribbean, making Yale Professor Bob Thompson's bouillabaisse richer and thicker.

One of our most visionary politicians said that he envisioned a time when 14 the United States could become the brain of the world, by which he meant the repository of all of the latest advanced information systems. I thought of that remark when an enterprising poet friend of mine called to say that he had just sold a poem to a computer magazine and that the editors were delighted to get it because they didn't carry fiction or poetry. Is that the kind of world we desire? A humdrum homogeneous world of all brains but no heart, no fiction, no poetry; a world of robots with human attendants bereft of imagination, of culture? Or does North America deserve a more exciting destiny? To become a place where the cultures of the world crisscross. This is possible because the United States is unique in the world: The world is here.

## COMPREHENSION

1. Why does Reed believe that the notion of Western or European civilization is fallacious?
2. According to Reed, what are the origins of our monoculturalist view?
3. What are the dangers of such a narrow view? What historical examples does Reed allude to?

## RHETORIC

1. How do paragraphs 1–4 help set the stage for Reed's discourse? Does this section contain his thesis?
2. Does the computer analogy in Reed's conclusion work? Do his rhetorical questions underscore the thesis?
3. Comment on the author's extensive use of details and examples. How do they serve to support his point? Which examples are especially illuminating, and why?
4. What kind of humor does Reed use in his essay? Does its use contribute to the force of his essay? Why or why not?
5. Is Reed's reasoning inductive or deductive? Justify your answer.
6. How does Reed employ definitions to structure his essay?

## WRITING

1. How does America's insistence that it "belongs to . . . 'Western Civilization'" affect its dealings with other nations? How does it influence the way it treats its own citizens? Explore these questions in a causal-analysis essay, using support from Reed.
2. Write an essay in which you consider how a multinational United States affects you on a day-to-day basis. How does it enrich your life or the life of the country? Use specific examples and details to support your opinion.
3. **Writing an Argument:** Write an essay arguing that a multinational society is often riddled with complex problems. What are some of the drawbacks or disadvantages of such a society? What causes these conflicts? Explore these issues in your writing.

www.mhhe.com/
**mhreader**

For more information on Ishmael Reed, go to:
**More Resources > Ch. 6 History & Culture**

## Synthesis: Classic and Contemporary Questions for Comparison

1. How do the respective tones of Goldsmith's and Reed's essays differ? What clues are contained in the texts that make this difference evident? Use examples from both.
2. In his essay, Goldsmith argues against nationalism and professes to be a citizen of the world. Compare Goldsmith's view with Reed's argument that to be an "American" means to accept the variety of influences that have converged into a "multinational society." How do these arguments differ? How are they similar?

3. Discuss both Goldsmith's and Reed's essays in terms of formality of voice. Does one author speak with more authority than the other? Or are they equally authoritative, but employing the stylistic modes of their times? Use examples from both essays.

# The Myth of the Latin Woman: I Just Met a Girl Named Maria

### Judith Ortiz Cofer

*Judith Ortiz Cofer (b. 1952) was born in Puerto Rico and immigrated to the United States in 1956. Once a bilingual teacher in Florida public schools, Cofer has written two books of poetry; several plays; a novel,* The Line of the Sun *(1989); an award-winning collection of essays and poems,* Silent Dancing: A Partial Remembrance of a Puerto Rican Childhood *(1990); and a collection of short stories,* An Island like You: Stories of the Barrio *(1995). She is a professor of English and creative writing at the University of Georgia. In the following essay, she offers both personal insight and philosophical reflection on the theme of ethnic stereotyping.*

On a bus trip to London from Oxford University where I was earning some ₁ graduate credits one summer, a young man, obviously fresh from a pub, spotted me and as if struck by inspiration went down on his knees in the aisle. With both hands over his heart he broke into an Irish tenor's rendition of "Maria" from *West Side Story*. My politely amused fellow passengers gave his lovely voice the round of gentle applause it deserved. Though I was not quite as amused, I managed my version of an English smile: no show of teeth, no extreme contortions of the facial muscles—I was at this time of my life practicing reserve and cool. Oh, that British control, how I coveted it. But "Maria" had followed me to London, reminding me of a prime fact of my life: you can leave the island, master the English language, and travel as far as you can, but if you are a Latina, especially one like me who so obviously belongs to Rita Moreno's gene pool, the island travels with you.

This is sometimes a very good thing. It may win you that extra minute of ₂ someone's attention. But with some people, the same things can make *you* an island—not a tropical paradise but an Alcatraz, a place nobody wants to visit. As a Puerto Rican girl living in the United States and wanting like most children to "belong," I resented the stereotype that my Hispanic appearance called forth from many people I met.

Growing up in a large urban center in New Jersey during the 1960s, I suf- ₃ fered from what I think of as "cultural schizophrenia." Our life was designed by my parents as a microcosm of their *casas* on the island. We spoke in Spanish, ate Puerto Rican food bought at the *bodega,* and practiced strict Catholicism at a church that allotted us a one-hour slot each week for mass, performed in Spanish by a Chinese priest trained as a missionary for Latin America.

4      As a girl I was kept under strict surveillance by my parents, since my virtue and modesty were, by their cultural equation, the same as their honor. As a teenager I was lectured constantly on how to behave as a proper *senorita.* But it was a conflicting message I received, since the Puerto Rican mothers also encouraged their daughters to look and act like women and to dress in clothes our Anglo friends and their mothers found too "mature" and flashy. The difference was, and is, cultural; yet I often felt humiliated when I appeared at an American friend's party wearing a dress more suitable to a semiformal than to a playroom birthday celebration. At Puerto Rican festivities, neither the music nor the colors we wore could be too loud.

5      I remember Career Day in our high school, when teachers told us to come dressed as if for a job interview. It quickly became obvious that to the Puerto Rican girls "dressing up" meant wearing their mother's ornate jewelry and clothing, more appropriate (by mainstream standards) for the company Christmas party than as daily office attire. That morning I had agonized in front of my closet, trying to figure out what a "career girl" would wear. I knew how to dress for school (at the Catholic school I attended, we all wore uniforms), I knew how to dress for Sunday mass, and I knew what dresses to wear for parties at my relatives' homes. Though I do not recall the precise details of my Career Day outfit, it must have been a composite of these choices. But I remember a comment my friend (an Italian American) made in later years that coalesced my impressions of that day. She said that at the business school she was attending, the Puerto Rican girls always stood out for wearing "everything at once." She meant, of course, too much jewelry, too many accessories. On that day at school we were simply made the negative models by the nuns, who were themselves not credible fashion experts to any of us. But it was painfully obvious to me that to the others, in their tailored skirts and silk blouses, we must have seemed "hopeless" and "vulgar." Though I now know that most adolescents feel out of step much of the time, I also know that for the Puerto Rican girls of my generation that sense was intensified. The way our teachers and classmates looked at us that day in school was just a taste of the cultural clash that awaited us in the real world, where prospective employers and men on the street would often misinterpret our tight skirts and jingling bracelets as a "come-on."

6      Mixed cultural signals have perpetuated certain stereotypes—for example, that of the Hispanic woman as the "hot tamale" or sexual firebrand. It is a one-dimensional view that the media have found easy to promote. In their special vocabulary, advertisers have designated "sizzling" and "smoldering" as the adjectives of choice for describing not only the foods but also the women of Latin America. From conversations in my house I recall hearing about the harassment that Puerto Rican women endured in factories where the "boss-men" talked to

them as if sexual innuendo was all they understood, and worse, often gave them the choice of submitting to their advances or being fired.

It is custom, however, not chromosomes, that leads us to choose scarlet 7 over pale pink. As young girls it was our mothers who influenced our decisions about clothes and colors—mothers who had grown up on a tropical island where the natural environment was a riot of primary colors, where showing your skin was one way to keep cool as well as to look sexy. Most important of all, on the island, women perhaps felt freer to dress and move more provocatively since, in most cases, they were protected by the traditions, mores, and laws of a Spanish/Catholic system of morality and machismo whose main rule was: *You may look at my sister, but if you touch her I will kill you.* The extended family and church structure could provide a young woman with a circle of safety in her small pueblo on the island; if a man "wronged" a girl, everyone would close in to save her family honor.

My mother has told me about dressing in her best party clothes on Saturday 8 nights and going to the town's plaza to promenade with her girlfriends in front of the boys they liked. The males were thus given an opportunity to admire the women and to express their admiration in the form of *piropos:* erotically charged street poems they composed on the spot. (I have myself been subjected to a few *piropos* while visiting the island, and they can be outrageous, although custom dictates that they must never cross into obscenity.) This ritual, as I understand it, also entails a show of studied indifference on the woman's part; if she is "decent," she must not acknowledge the man's impassioned words. So I do understand how things can be lost in translation. When a Puerto Rican girl dressed in her idea of what is attractive meets a man from the mainstream culture who has been trained to react to certain types of clothing as a sexual signal, a clash is likely to take place. I remember the boy who took me to my first formal dance leaning over to plant a sloppy, overeager kiss painfully on my mouth; when I didn't respond with sufficient passion, he remarked resentfully: "I thought you Latin girls were supposed to mature early," as if I were expected to *ripen* like a fruit or vegetable, not just grow into womanhood like other girls.

It is surprising to my professional friends that even today some people, in- 9 cluding those who should know better, still put others "in their place." It happened to me most recently during a stay at a classy metropolitan hotel favored by young professional couples for weddings. Late one evening after the theater, as I walked toward my room with a colleague (a woman with whom I was coordinating an arts program), a middle-aged man in a tuxedo, with a young girl in satin and lace on his arm, stepped directly into our path. With his champagne glass extended toward me, he exclaimed "Evita!"

Our way blocked, my companion and I listened as the man half-recited, 10 half-bellowed "Don't Cry for Me, Argentina." When he finished, the young girl said: "How about a round of applause for my daddy?" We complied, hoping this would bring the silly spectacle to a close. I was becoming aware that our little group was attracting the attention of the other guests. "Daddy" must have perceived this too, and he once more barred the way as we tried to walk past him. He began to shout-sing a ditty to the tune of "La Bamba"—except the lyrics were about a girl named Maria whose exploits rhymed with her name and gonorrhea. The girl kept saying "Oh, Daddy" and looking at me with pleading eyes. She wanted me to laugh along with the others. My companion and I stood silently waiting for the man to end his offensive song. When he finished, I looked not at him but at his daughter. I advised her calmly never to ask her father what he had done in the army. Then I walked between them and to my room. My friend complimented me on my cool handling of the situation, but I confessed that I had really wanted to push the jerk into the swimming pool. This same man—probably a corporate executive, well-educated, even worldly by most standards—would not have been likely to regale an Anglo woman with a dirty song in public. He might have checked his impulse by assuming that she could be somebody's wife or mother, or at least *somebody* who might take offense. But, to him, I was just an Evita or a Maria: merely a character in his cartoon-populated universe.

11    Another facet of the myth of the Latin woman in the United States is the menial, the domestic—Maria the housemaid or countergirl. It's true that work as domestics, as waitresses, and in factories is all that's available to women with little English and few skills. But the myth of the Hispanic menial—the funny maid, mispronouncing words and cooking up a spicy storm in a shiny California kitchen—has been perpetuated by the media in the same way that "Mammy" from *Gone with the Wind* became America's idea of the black woman for generations. Since I do not wear my diplomas around my neck for all to see, I have on occasion been sent to that "kitchen" where some think I obviously belong.

12    One incident has stayed with me, though I recognize it as a minor offense. My first public poetry reading took place in Miami, at a restaurant where a luncheon was being held before the event. I was nervous and excited as I walked in with notebook in hand. An older woman motioned me to her table, and thinking (foolish me) that she wanted me to autograph a copy of my newly published slender volume of verse, I went over. She ordered a cup of coffee from me, assuming that I was the waitress. (Easy enough to mistake my poems for menus, I suppose.) I know it wasn't an intentional act of cruelty. Yet of all the good things that happened later, I remember that scene most clearly, because it reminded me of what I had to overcome before anyone would take me seriously. In retrospect I understand that my anger gave my reading fire. In fact, I have almost always taken any doubt in my abilities as a challenge, the result most often being the satisfaction of winning a convert, of seeing the cold, appraising eyes warm to my words, the body language change, the smile that indicates I have opened some avenue for communication. So that day as I read, I looked directly at that woman. Her lowered eyes told me she was embarrassed at her faux pas, and when I willed her to look up at me, she graciously allowed me to punish her with my full attention. We shook hands at the end of the reading and I never saw her again. She has probably forgotten the entire incident, but maybe not.

Yet I am one of the lucky ones. There are thousands of Latinas without the ₁₃ privilege of an education or the entrees into society that I have. For them life is a constant struggle against the misconceptions perpetuated by the myth of the Latina. My goal is to try to replace the old stereotypes with a much more interesting set of realities. Every time I give a reading, I hope the stories I tell, the dreams and fears I examine in my work, can achieve some universal truth that will get my audience past the particulars of my skin color, my accent, or my clothes.

I once wrote a poem in which I called all Latinas "God's brown daughters." ₁₄ This poem is really a prayer of sorts, offered upward, but also, through the human-to-human channel of art, outward. It is a prayer for communication and for respect. In it, Latin women pray "in Spanish to an Anglo God/with a Jewish heritage," and they are "fervently hoping/that if not omnipotent,/at least He be bilingual."

## COMPREHENSION

1. What is the theme of the essay?
2. What does Cofer mean by the expression "cultural schizophrenia" (paragraph 3)?
3. Define the following words: *coveted* (paragraph 1), *Anglo* (paragraph 4), *coalesced* (paragraph 5), *machismo* (paragraph 7), and *entrees* (paragraph 13).

## RHETORIC

1. Cofer uses many anecdotes in her discussion of stereotyping. How does this affect the tone of the essay?
2. Who is the implied audience for this essay? What aspects of the writing led you to your conclusion?
3. This essay is written in the first person, which tends to reveal a lot about the writer's personality. What adjectives come to mind when you think of the writer's singular voice?
4. Although this essay has a sociological theme, Cofer demonstrates that she has a poet's sensitivity toward language. What in the following sentence from paragraph 7 demonstrates this poetic style: "It is custom, however, not chromosomes, that leads us to choose scarlet over pale pink"? Select two other sentences from the essay that demonstrate Cofer's stylistic talent, and explain why they, too, are poetic.
5. In paragraph 8, Cofer contrasts cultural perceptions related to Hispanic and Anglo behavior. How is the paragraph structured so that this difference is demonstrated dramatically?
6. Cofer uses quotation marks to emphasize the connotation of certain words. Explain the significance of the following words: *mature* (paragraph 4), *hopeless* (paragraph 5), *hot tamale* (paragraph 6), *wronged* (paragraph 7), and *decent* (paragraph 8).

## WRITING

1. Write a problem-solution essay in which you discuss the reasons behind cultural stereotyping and provide suggestions on how to overcome stereotyped thinking.
2. Select an ethnic, racial, or cultural group, and explain how group members undergo stereotyping through their depiction in the media.
3. **Writing an Argument:** In an essay, argue for or against the proposition that stereotyping is excusable because it often is based on learned assumptions about which an individual cannot be expected to have knowledge.

| www.mhhe.com/ **mhreader** | For more information on Judith Ortiz Cofer, go to: **More Resources > Ch. 6 History & Culture** |

# Yellow Woman and a Beauty of the Spirit

### Leslie Marmon Silko

*Leslie Marmon Silko (b. 1948) was born in Albuquerque, New Mexico, and grew up on the Laguna Pueblo Reservation on the Rio Grande plateau. Of mixed Laguna, Mexican, and European American ancestry, Silko attended the University of New Mexico (BA, 1969) and briefly enrolled in law school before deciding to pursue a career as a writer. Associated with the Native American Renaissance, Silko has written stories, novels, essays, and poetry exploring Native American myths and traditions as well as the relationship of the tribes to contemporary culture. Silko has taught at the University of New Mexico and the University of Arizona, and has received numerous awards, including a prestigious five-year MacArthur Foundation grant. Her best-known work includes the novel* Ceremony *(1977); a collection of poetry,* Laguna Woman *(1974); a collection of short stories,* Storyteller *(1981); and an autobiography,* Sacred Water *(1993). Silko has also published a collection of essays,* Yellow Woman and a Beauty of the Spirit *(1996); in the title essay from this collection, Silko examines her mixed ancestry and explains traditional Pueblo culture.*

1   From the time I was a small child, I was aware that I was different. I looked different from my playmates. My two sisters looked different too. We didn't look quite like the other Laguna Pueblo children, but we didn't look quite white either. In the 1880s, my great-grandfather had followed his older brother west

from Ohio to the New Mexico Territory to survey the land for the U.S. government. The two Marmon brothers came to the Laguna Pueblo reservation because they had an Ohio cousin who already lived there. The Ohio cousin was involved in sending Indian children thousands of miles away from their families to the War Department's big Indian boarding school in Carlisle, Pennsylvania. Both brothers married full-blood Laguna Pueblo women. My great-grandfather had first married my great-grandmother's older sister, but she died in childbirth and left two small children. My great-grandmother was fifteen or twenty years younger than my great-grandfather. She had attended Carlisle Indian School and spoke and wrote English beautifully.

I called her Grandma A'mooh because that's what I heard her say whenever she saw me. *A'mooh* means "granddaughter" in the Laguna language. I remember this word because her love and her acceptance of me as a small child were so important. I had sensed immediately that something about my appearance was not acceptable to some people, white and Indian. But I did not see any signs of that strain or anxiety in the face of my beloved Grandma A'mooh. 2

Younger people, people my parents' age, seemed to look at the world in a more modern way. The modern way included racism. My physical appearance seemed not to matter to the old-time people. They looked at the world very differently; a person's appearance and possessions did not matter nearly as much as a person's behavior. For them, a person's value lies in how that person interacts with other people, how that person behaves toward the animals and the earth. That is what matters most to the old-time people. The Pueblo people believed this long before the Puritans arrived with their notions of sin and damnation, and racism. The old-time beliefs persist today; thus I will refer to the old-time people in the present tense as well as the past. Many worlds may coexist here. 3

I spent a great deal of time with my great-grandmother. Her house was next to our house, and I used to wake up at dawn, hours before my parents or younger sisters, and I'd go wait on the porch swing or on the back steps by her kitchen door. She got up at dawn, but she was more than eighty years old, so she needed a little while to get dressed and to get the fire going in the cook-stove. I had been carefully instructed by my parents not to bother her and to behave, and to try to help her any way I could. I always loved the early mornings when the air was so cool with a hint of rain smell in the breeze. In the dry New Mexico air, the least hint of dampness smells sweet. 4

My great-grandmother's yard was planted with lilac bushes and iris; there were four o'clocks, cosmos, morning glories, and hollyhocks, and old-fashioned rosebushes that I helped her water. If the garden hose got stuck on one of the big rocks that lined the path in the yard, I ran and pulled it free. That's what I came to do early every morning: to help Grandma water the plants before the heat of the day arrived. 5

Grandma A'mooh would tell about the old days, family stories about relatives who had been killed by Apache raiders who stole the sheep our relatives had been herding near Swahnee. Sometimes she read Bible stories that we kids 6 liked because of the illustrations of Jonah in the mouth of a whale and Daniel surrounded by lions. Grandma A'mooh would send me home when she took her nap, but when the sun got low and the afternoon began to cool off, I would be back on the porch swing, waiting for her to come out to water the plants and to haul in firewood for the evening. When Grandma was eighty-five, she still chopped her own kindling. She used to let me carry in the coal bucket for her, but she would not allow me to use the ax. I carried armloads of kindling too, and I learned to be proud of my strength.

7      I was allowed to listen quietly when Aunt Susie or Aunt Alice came to visit Grandma. When I got old enough to cross the road alone, I went and visited them almost daily. They were vigorous women who valued books and writing. They were usually busy chopping wood or cooking but never hesitated to take time to answer my questions. Best of all they told me the *hummah-hah* stories, about an earlier time when animals and humans shared a common language. In the old days, the Pueblo people had educated their children in this manner; adults took time out to talk to and teach young people. Everyone was a teacher, and every activity had the potential to teach the child.

8      But as soon as I started kindergarten at the Bureau of Indian Affairs day school, I began to learn more about the differences between the Laguna Pueblo world and the outside world. It was at school that I learned just how different I looked from my classmates. Sometimes tourists driving past on Route 66 would stop by Laguna Day School at recess time to take photographs of us kids. One day, when I was in the first grade, we all crowded around the smiling white tourists, who peered at our faces. We all wanted to be in the picture because afterward the tourists sometimes gave us each a penny. Just as we were all posed and ready to have our picture taken, the tourist man looked at me. "Not you," he said and motioned for me to step away from my classmates. I felt so embarrassed that I wanted to disappear. My classmates were puzzled by the tourists' behavior, but I knew the tourists didn't want me in their snapshot because I looked different, because I was part white.

9      In the view of the old-time people, we are all sisters and brothers because the Mother Creator made all of us—all colors and all sizes. We are sisters and brothers, clanspeople of all the living beings around us. The plants, the birds, fish, clouds, water, even the clay—they are all related to us. The old-time people believe that all things, even rocks and water, have spirit and being. They understood that all things want only to continue being as they are; they need only to be left as they are. Thus the old folks used to tell us kids not to disturb the earth unnecessarily. All things as they were created exist already in harmony with one another as long as we do not disturb them.

10     As the old story tells us, Tse'itsi'nako, Thought Woman, the Spider, thought of her three sisters, and as she thought of them, they came into being. Together with Thought Woman, they thought of the sun and the stars and the moon. The Mother Creators imagined the earth and the oceans, the animals and the people, and the *ka'tsina* spirits that reside in the mountains. The Mother Creators

imagined all the plants that flower and the trees that bear fruit. As Thought Woman and her sisters thought of it, the whole universe came into being. In this universe, there is no absolute good or absolute bad; they are only balances and harmonies that ebb and flow. Some years the desert receives abundant rain, other years there is too little rain, and sometimes there is so much rain that floods cause destruction. But rain itself is neither innocent nor guilty. The rain is simply itself.

My great-grandmother was dark and handsome. Her expression in photo- 11 graphs is one of confidence and strength. I do not know if white people then or now would consider her beautiful. I do not know if the old-time Laguna Pueblo people considered her beautiful or if the old-time people even thought in those terms. To the Pueblo way of thinking, the act of comparing one living being with another was silly, because each being or thing is unique and therefore incomparably valuable because it is the only one of its kind. The old-time people thought it was crazy to attach such importance to a person's appearance. I understood very early that there were two distinct ways of interpreting the world. There was the white people's way and there was the Laguna way. In the Laguna way, it was bad manners to make comparisons that might hurt another person's feelings.

In everyday Pueblo life, not much attention was paid to one's physical ap- 12 pearance or clothing. Ceremonial clothing was quite elaborate but was used only for the sacred dances. The traditional Pueblo societies were communal and strictly egalitarian, which means that no matter how well or how poorly one might have dressed, there was no social ladder to fall from. All food and other resources were strictly shared so that no one person or group had more than another. I mention social status because it seems to me that most of the defini- tions of beauty in contemporary Western culture are really codes for determin- ing social status. People no longer hide their face-lifts and they discuss their liposuctions because the point of the procedures isn't just cosmetic, it is social. It says to the world, "I have enough spare cash that I can afford surgery for cosmetic purposes."

In the old-time Pueblo world, beauty was manifested in behavior and in 13 one's relationships with other living beings. Beauty was as much a feeling of harmony as it was a visual, aural, or sensual effect. The whole person had to be beautiful, not just the face or the body; faces and bodies could not be separated from hearts and souls. Health was foremost in achieving this sense of well- being and harmony; in the old-time Pueblo world, a person who did not look healthy inspired feelings of worry and anxiety, not feelings of well-being. A healthy person, of course, is in harmony with the world around her; she is at peace with herself too. Thus an unhappy person or spiteful person would not be considered beautiful.

In the old days, strong, sturdy women were most admired. One of my most 14 vivid preschool memories is of the crew of Laguna women, in their forties and fifties, who came to cover our house with adobe plaster. They handled the lad- ders with great ease, and while two women ground the adobe mud on stones and added straw, another woman loaded the hod with mud and passed it up to the two women on ladders, who were smoothing the plaster on the wall with their hands. Since women owned the houses, they did the plastering. At Laguna, men did the basket making and the weaving of fine textiles; men helped a great deal with the child care too. Because the Creator is female, there is no stigma on being female; gender is not used to control behavior. No job was a man's job or a woman's job; the most able person did the work.

15    My Grandma Lily had been a Ford Model A mechanic when she was a teenager. I remember when I was young, she was always fixing broken lamps and appliances. She was small and wiry, but she could lift her weight in rolled roofing or boxes of nails. When she was seventy-five, she was still repairing washing machines in my uncle's coin-operated laundry.

16    The old-time people paid no attention to birthdays. When a person was ready to do something, she did it. When she no longer was able, she stopped. Thus the traditional Pueblo people did not worry about aging or about looking old because there were no social boundaries drawn by the passage of years. It was not remarkable for young men to marry women as old as their mothers. I never heard anyone talk about "women's work" until after I left Laguna for college. Work was there to be done by any able-bodied person who wanted to do it. At the same time, in the old-time Pueblo world, identity was acknowledged to be always in a flux; in the old stories, one minute Spider Woman is a little spider under a yucca plant, and the next instant she is a sprightly grandmother walking down the road.

17    When I was growing up, there was a young man from a nearby village who wore nail polish and women's blouses and permed his hair. People paid little attention to his appearance; he was always part of a group of other young men from his village. No one ever made fun of him. Pueblo communities were and still are very independent, but they also have to be tolerant of individual eccentricities because survival of the group means everyone has to cooperate.

18    In the old Pueblo world, differences were celebrated as signs of the Mother Creator's grace. Persons born with exceptional physical or sexual differences were highly respected and honored because their physical differences gave them special positions as mediators between this world and the spirit world. The great Navajo medicine man of the 1920s, the Crawler, had a hunchback and could not walk upright, but he was able to heal even the most difficult cases.

19    Before the arrival of Christian missionaries, a man could dress as a woman and work with the women and even marry a man without any fanfare. Likewise, a woman was free to dress like a man, to hunt and go to war with the men, and to marry a woman. In the old Pueblo worldview we are all a mixture of male and female, and this sexual identity is changing constantly. Sexual inhibition did not begin until the Christian missionaries arrived. For the old-time people, marriage was about teamwork and social relationships, not about sexual excitement. In the days before the Puritans came, marriage did not mean an end to sex with people other than your spouse. Women were just as likely as men to have a *si'ash*, or lover.

New life was so precious that pregnancy was always appropriate, and  20
pregnancy before marriage was celebrated as a good sign. Since the children
belonged to the mother and her clan, and women owned and bequeathed the
houses and farmland, the exact determination of paternity wasn't critical.
Although fertility was prized, infertility was no problem because mothers with
unplanned pregnancies gave their babies to childless couples within the clan in
open adoption arrangements. Children called their mother's sisters "mother"
as well, and a child became attached to a number of parent figures.

In the sacred kiva ceremonies, men mask and dress as women to pay hom-  21
age and to be possessed by the female energies of the spirit beings. Because
differences in physical appearance were so highly valued, surgery to change
one's face and body to resemble a model's face and body would be unimaginable. To be different, to be unique was blessed and was best of all.

The traditional clothing of Pueblo women emphasized a woman's sturdiness.  22
Buckskin leggings wrapped around the legs protected her from scratches and
injuries while she worked. The more layers of buckskin, the better. All those
layers gave her legs the appearance of strength, like sturdy tree trunks. To demonstrate sisterhood and brotherhood with the plants and animals, the old-time
people make masks and costumes that transform the human figures of the
dancers into the animal beings they portray. Dancers paint their exposed skin;
their postures and motions are adapted from their observations. But the motions are stylized. The observer sees not an actual eagle or actual deer dancing,
but witnesses a human being, a dancer, gradually changing into a woman/buf-
falo or a man/deer. Every impulse is to reaffirm the urgent relationships that
human beings have with the plant and animal world.

In the high desert plateau country, all vegetation, even weeds and thorns,  23
becomes special, and all life is precious and beautiful because without the
plants, the insects, and the animals, human beings living here cannot survive.
Perhaps human beings long ago noticed the devastating impact human activity
can have on the plants and animals; maybe this is why tribal cultures devised
the stories about humans and animals intermarrying, and the clans that bind
humans to animals and plants through a whole complex of duties.

We children were always warned not to harm frogs or toads, the beloved  24
children of the rain clouds, because terrible floods would occur. I remember in
the summer the old folks used to stick bog bolls of cotton on the outside of their
screen doors as bait to keep the flies from going in the house when the door was
opened. The old folks staunchly resisted the killing of flies because once, long,
long ago, when human beings were in a great deal of trouble, a Green Bottle Fly
carried the desperate messages of human beings to the Mother Creator in the
Fourth World, below this one. Human beings had outraged the Mother Creator
by neglecting the Mother Corn altar while they dabbled with sorcery and magic.
The Mother Creator disappeared, and with her disappeared the rain clouds,
and the plants and the animals too. The people began to starve, and they had no
way of reaching the Mother Creator down below. Green Bottle Fly took the

message to the Mother Creator, and the people were saved. To show their gratitude, the old folks refused to kill any flies.

25    The old stories demonstrate the interrelationships that the Pueblo people have maintained with their plant and animal clanspeople. Kochininako, Yellow Woman, represents all women in the old stories. Her deeds span the spectrum of human behavior and are mostly heroic acts, though in at least one story, she chooses to join the secret Destroyer Clan, which worships destruction and death. Because Laguna Pueblo cosmology features a female Creator, the status of women is equal with the status of men, and women appear as often as men in the old stories as hero figures. Yellow Woman is my favorite because she dares to cross traditional boundaries of ordinary behavior during times of crisis in order to save the Pueblo; her power lies in her courage and in her uninhibited sexuality, which the old-time Pueblo stories celebrate again and again because fertility was so highly valued.

26    The old stories always say that Yellow Woman was beautiful, but remember that the old-time people were not so much thinking about physical appearances. In each story, the beauty that Yellow Woman possesses is the beauty of her passion, her daring, and her sheer strength to act when catastrophe is imminent.

27    In one story, the people are suffering during a great drought and accompanying famine. Each day, Kochininako has to walk farther and farther from the village to find fresh water for her husband and children. One day she travels far, far to the east, to the plains, and she finally locates a freshwater spring. But when she reaches the pool, the water is churning violently as if something large had just gotten out of the pool, Kochininako does not want to see what huge creature had been at the pool, but just as she fills her water jar and turns to hurry away, a strong, sexy man in buffalo skin leggings appears by the pool. Little drops of water glisten on his chest. She cannot help but look at him because he is so strong and so good to look at. Able to transform himself from human to buffalo in the wink of an eye, Buffalo Man gallops away with her on his back. Kochininako falls in love with Buffalo Man, and because of this liaison, the Buffalo People agree to give their bodies to the hunters to feed the starving Pueblo. Thus Kochininako's fearless sensuality results in the salvation of the people of her village, who are saved by the meat the Buffalo People "give" to them.

28    My father taught me and my sisters to shoot .22 rifles when we were seven; I went hunting with my father when I was eight, and I killed my first mule deer buck when I was thirteen. The Kochininako stories were always my favorite because Yellow Woman had so many adventures. In one story, as she hunts rabbits to feed her family, a giant monster pursues her, but she has the courage and presence of mind to outwit it.

29    In another story, Kochininako has a fling with Whirlwind Man and returns to her husband ten months later with twin baby boys. The twin boys grow up to be great heroes of the people. Once again, Kochininako's vibrant sexuality benefits her people.

The stories about Kochininako made me aware that sometimes an individ- 30 ual must act despite disapproval, or concern for appearances or what others may say. From Yellow Woman's adventures, I learned to be comfortable with my differences. I even imagined that Yellow Woman had yellow skin, brown hair, and green eyes like mine, although her name does not refer to her color, but rather to the ritual color of the east.

There have been many other moments like the one with the camera-toting 31 tourist in the schoolyard. But the old-time people always say, remember the stories, the stories will help you be strong. So all these years I have depended on Kochininako and the stories of her adventures.

Kochininako is beautiful because she has the courage to act in times of great 32 peril, and her triumph is achieved by her sensuality, not through violence and destruction. For these qualities of the spirit, Yellow Woman and all women are beautiful.

## COMPREHENSION

1. Silko devotes part of this essay to recollections of her great-grandmother, Grandma A'mooh. What is her great-grandmother like? What does the writer learn from Grandma A'mooh? Why is the essay more about Pueblo women than men?
2. Explain what you learned about traditional Pueblo culture from this essay. What values does the writer associate with this "old-time" culture? According to Silko, how does this culture contrast both explicitly and implicitly with modern Anglo culture? How did this traditional culture sustain her as a young girl?
3. Silko summarizes several Pueblo stories. What are the main ones? Why does she especially like the story of Kochininako or Yellow Woman?

## RHETORIC

1. What is Silko's thesis? Does this thesis appear in a single sentence? If so, what is it? If not, what is the implied thesis?
2. What strategy does the writer use to both start and conclude this essay? Is this strategy effective? Justify your response.
3. Silko provides an extended definition of Pueblo culture in this selection. Explain how she uses description, narration, comparison and contrast, and analysis to develop this definition.
4. While Silko's primary purpose is to define or explain Pueblo culture, she also provides several supporting definitions. Identify them, and explain how they contribute to the broader definition.
5. Is the diction in this essay concrete or abstract? Specific or general? Identify specific passages to support your answer.

6. Consider the essay as an argument. What is the claim? What is the supporting evidence? What warrants underpin the argument? How effective is the argument, and why?

### WRITING

1. Working in a group, create a list of all the features of traditional Pueblo culture that Silko discusses. Choose two or three and write brief summaries of each.
2. Using Silko's essay as a frame of reference, write a comparative essay in which you discuss contemporary American cultural values in relationship to "old-time" Pueblo values and traditions.
3. **Writing an Argument:** Argue for or against the proposition that traditional Pueblo culture is superior to contemporary American culture. Use at least three topics drawn from Silko's essay—for example, approach to diversity and difference, treatment of women, or respect for the environment—to develop your argumentative essay.

www.mhhe.com/ **mhreader**

For more information on Leslie Marmon Silko, go to: **More Resources > Ch. 6 History & Culture**

# A World Not Neatly Divided

### Amartya Sen

*Amartya Sen (b. 1933), born in Santiniketan, India, was awarded the Nobel Prize in Economics in 1988 for his groundbreaking work on welfare economics. Educated at Presidency College in Calcutta and Cambridge University (PhD, 1959), Sen has taught at Harvard University, the London School of Economics, and Oxford University; currently, he is a professor at Trinity College, Cambridge University. His major works, all of which investigate the role of poverty and inequality in the world,* include Collective Choice and Social Welfare *(1970),* On Economic Inequality *(1973),* Poverty and Famines: An Essay on Entitlement and Deprivation *(1981),* Commodities and Capabilities *(1985), and* Development as Freedom *(1999). In the following essay, which appeared in* The New York Times *in 2001, Sen suggests that generalizations about "civilization" tend to blur the realities of complex cultures.*

When people talk about clashing civilizations, as so many politicians and aca-  1
demics do now, they can sometimes miss the central issue. The inadequacy of
this thesis begins well before we get to the question of whether civilizations
must clash. The basic weakness of the theory lies in its program of categorizing
people of the world according to a unique, allegedly commanding system of
classification. This is problematic because civilizational categories are crude
and inconsistent and also because there are other ways of seeing people (linked
to politics, language, literature, class, occupation, or other affiliations).

   The befuddling influence of a singular classification also traps those who  2
dispute the thesis of a clash: To talk about "the Islamic world" or "the Western
world" is already to adopt an impoverished vision of humanity as unalterably
divided. In fact, civilizations are hard to partition in this way, given the diver-
sities within each society as well as the linkages among different countries and
cultures. For example, describing India as a "Hindu civilization" misses the
fact that India has more Muslims than any other country except Indonesia and
possibly Pakistan. It is futile to try to understand Indian art, literature, music,
food, or politics without seeing the extensive interactions across barriers of
religious communities. These include Hindus and Muslims, Buddhists, Jains,
Sikhs, Parsees, Christians (who have been in India since at least the fourth century, well before England's conversion to Christianity), Jews (present since the
fall of Jerusalem), and even atheists and agnostics. Sanskrit has a larger atheistic literature than exists in any other classical language. Speaking of India as a
Hindu civilization may be comforting to the Hindu fundamentalist, but it is an
odd reading of India.

   A similar coarseness can be seen in the other categories invoked, like "the  3
Islamic world." Consider Akbar and Aurangzeb, two Muslim emperors of the
Mogul dynasty in India. Aurangzeb tried hard to convert Hindus into Muslims
and instituted various policies in that direction, of which taxing the non-
Muslims was only one example. In contrast, Akbar reveled in his multiethnic
court and pluralist laws, and issued official proclamations insisting that no one
"should be interfered with on account of religion" and that "anyone is to be
allowed to go over to a religion that pleases him."

   If a homogeneous view of Islam were to be taken, then only one of these  4
emperors could count as a true Muslim. The Islamic fundamentalist would
have no time for Akbar; Prime Minister Tony Blair, given his insistence that
tolerance is a defining characteristic of Islam, would have to consider excom-
municating Aurangzeb. I expect both Akbar and Aurangzeb would protest, and
so would I. A similar crudity is present in the characterization of what is called
"Western civilization." Tolerance and individual freedom have certainly been
present in European history. But there is no dearth of diversity here, either.
When Akbar was making his pronouncements on religious tolerance in Agra,
in the 1590s, the Inquisitions were still going on; in 1600, Giordano Bruno was
burned at the stake, for heresy, in Campo dei Fiori in Rome.

   Dividing the world into discrete civilizations is not just crude. It propels us  5
into the absurd belief that this partitioning is natural and necessary and must

overwhelm all other ways of identifying people. That imperious view goes not only against the sentiment that "we human beings are all much the same," but also against the more plausible understanding that we are diversely different. For example, Bangladesh's split from Pakistan was not connected with religion, but with language and politics.

6      Each of us has many features in our self-conception. Our religion, important as it may be, cannot be an all-engulfing identity. Even a shared poverty can be a source of solidarity across the borders. The kind of division highlighted by, say, the so-called "antiglobalization" protesters—whose movement is, incidentally, one of the most globalized in the world—tries to unite the underdogs of the world economy and goes firmly against religious, national, or "civilizational" lines of division.

7      The main hope of harmony lies not in any imagined uniformity, but in the plurality of our identities, which cut across each other and work against sharp divisions into impenetrable civilizational camps. Political leaders who think and act in terms of sectioning off humanity into various "worlds" stand to make the world more flammable—even when their intentions are very different. They also end up, in the case of civilizations defined by religion, lending authority to religious leaders seen as spokesmen for their "worlds." In the process, other voices are muffled and other concerns silenced. The robbing of our plural identities not only reduces us; it impoverishes the world.

## COMPREHENSION

1. According to Sen, what is the "basic weakness" underlying the idea that the world is composed of "clashing civilizations" (paragraph 1)?
2. What does the writer mean by "singular classification" (paragraph 2)? Why is classifying people in terms of their civilization "crude and inconsistent"? Why is applying singular classification to religions and other features of society wrong?
3. What, according to Sen, is "the main hope of harmony" (paragraph 7) in the world?

## RHETORIC

1. What argumentative strategy does Sen employ in the introductory paragraph? What point of view is he arguing against?
2. While arguing against a certain type of classification, Sen actually uses classification as a rhetorical strategy. How, precisely, does he employ classification to organize his argument?
3. What examples does Sen use to support his argument? Why does he use them? Why does he decide not to provide illustrations near the end of the selection?
4. What transitional devices serve to unify the essay?

5. How effective is Sen's concluding paragraph? Does it serve to confirm his claim? Why or why not?

## WRITING

1. Write an essay about the problems you see in your community or on campus. Explain how singular classification might explain some of these problems.
2. In an analytical essay, explain how singular classification might help explain the events of September 11, 2001.
3. **Writing an Argument:** Write an essay in which you demonstrate that singular classification actually can be helpful in framing public discourse about groups, nations, or civilizations.

 **www.mhhe.com/ mhreader** | For more information on Amartya Sen, go to: **More Resources > Ch. 6 History & Culture**

# Andalusia's Journey

### Edward Said

*Edward Said (1935–2003), an influential literary and cultural critic and provocative political commentator, was born in Palestine and grew up in Egypt before moving to the United States with his parents in 1951. After receiving degrees from Princeton University (BA, 1957) and Harvard University (PhD, 1964), Said began a distinguished and frequently stormy career in higher education and public affairs. As University Professor of English and comparative literature at Columbia University, Said commented frequently on the plight of the Palestine people while at the same time carving out a reputation as one of the most distinguished literary critics of his generation. His major literary criticism includes* Orientalism *(1978) and* Culture and Imperialism *(1993). Among his books on politics are* The Question of Palestine *(1979),* Covering Islam *(1981), and* The Politics of Dispossession: The Struggle for Palestinian Self-Determination *(1994). In the essay that follows, published in* Travel and Leisure *in 2002, Said examines a crossroads of civilization that might reveal something promising for us today.*

*Poverty turns our country into a foreign land, and riches our place of exile into our home. For the whole world, in all its diversity, is one. And all its inhabitants our brothers and neighbors.*

—*Abu Muhammad al-Zubaydi, Seville,* A.D. *926–989*

A 16th-century pouring vessel from Valencia (once part of the Caliphate of Cordova), on which Arabic and Spanish designs merge.

1    For an Arab, such as myself, to enter Granada's 13th-century Alhambra palace is to leave behind a modern world of disillusionment, strife, and uncertainty. In this, the calmest, most harmonious structure ever built by Arab Muslims, the walls are covered with dizzying arabesques and geometric patterns, interspersed with Arabic script extolling God and his regents on earth. The repetition of a basically abstract series of motifs suggests infinity, and serves to pull one through the palace's many rooms. The palace's Generalife gardens, punctuated by cooling streams, are a miracle of balance and repose. The Alhambra, like the great ninth-century mosque-cum-cathedral of Cordova, La Mezquita, invites believer and nonbeliever alike with opulence and rigorous discipline of ornament, and almost imperceptible changes in perspective from one space to the next. The whole composition is always in evidence—always changing yet always somehow the same—a unity in multiplicity.

2    I have been traveling for four decades to southern Spain, Andalucía as it is called by Spaniards, al-Andalus by Arabs, drawn there by its magnificent architecture, and the amazingly mixed Arab, Jewish, and Latin cultural centers of Cordova, Granada, and Seville. The turmoil of Andalusia's extraordinary past seems to hover just beneath the surface of its pleasant landscapes and generally small-scaled urban life. In its medieval heyday, Andalusia, established by the Arab general Tariq bin Ziyad and continuously fought over by numerous Muslim sects (among them Almoravids, Nasrids, and Almohads) and by Catholics as far north as Galicia, was a particularly lively instance of the dialogue, much more than the clash, of cultures. Muslims, Jews, and Christians co-existed with astonishing harmony. Today its periods of fruitful cultural diversity may provide a model for the co-existence of people, a model quite different from the ideological battles, local chauvinism, and

The Alhambra's repeating arches.

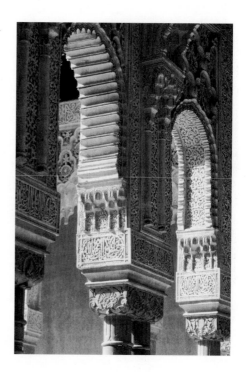

ethnic conflict that finally brought it down—and which ironically enough threaten to engulf our own 21st-century world.

When I first visited, in the summer of 1966, Franco-era Andalusia seemed like a forgotten, if wonderfully picturesque, province of Catholic Spain. Its fierce sun accentuated the area's rigors: the scarcity of good accommodations, the difficulty of travel, the heaviness of the cuisine, the unyielding spirit of a people living in relative poverty and obdurate pride, the political and religious repression under which the country suffocated. The splendor of its great buildings was evident but seemed part of a distant backdrop to more urgent and more recent times: the Civil War of 1936–39 and Hemingway's sentimentalized view of it; the burgeoning and quite sleazy mass tourist trade that had put down roots in Málaga (not to mention the ghastly neighboring village of Torremolinos) and that was creeping slowly westward toward Portugal's Algarve (from the Arabic *al-gharb min al-Andalus*, "west of Andalusia").

Even in the summer of 1979, when I spent a few weeks in the area with my wife and two young children, the Alhambra was all but deserted. You could stroll into it as you would into a public park. (Today, visiting the place is more like going to Disneyland. There are five gigantic parking lots and you must reserve well in advance.) For its part, Seville was a pleasant, somewhat subdued city of modest restaurants and family-style hotels. Franco had disappeared in 1975, of course, but the prosperous Spain of solidly based, open

The palace's Generalife gardens.

democracy had not yet arrived. You could still feel the Church's cold impress and the vestiges of the fascist dictatorship. Europe was a long distance away, beyond the Pyrenees, to the north.

5    In the 1980's and 90's Spain awakened into modernity and globalization. NATO's Spain, the EU's Spain, took over the peninsula's identity. There is now no shortage of excellent hotels or good restaurants, although it must again be admitted, as the Michelin Guide put it in the 1960's, that for the most part "Spanish cuisine is more complicated than it is refined." But for me, and indeed for many Arabs, Andalusia still represents the finest flowering of our culture. That is particularly true now, when the Arab Middle East seems mired in defeat and violence, its societies unable to arrest their declining fortunes, its secular culture so full of almost surreal crisis, shock, and nihilism.

6    A spate of recent Arabic and Muslim writing has redirected attention to Andalusia as a mournful, tantalizing emblem of what a glorious civilization was lost when Islamic rule ended. This literature serves only to accentuate the conditions of decline and loss that have so diminished modern Arab life—and the conquests that have dominated it. Thus, for instance, the 1992 appearance of Palestinian poet Mahmud Darwish's great *qasida*, or ode, *Ahd Ashr Kawkaban Ala Akhir Almashad Al-Andalusi* (Eleven Stars over the Last Moments of Andalusia). The poem was written about—and served to clarify—what the Palestinians felt they had lost not just once but time after time. The Palestinian national poet seems to be asking, What do we do after the last time, after the new conquerors

Gunsmiths at the Palace of Alhambra, as imagined by Filippo Baratti, one of many 19th-century European artists captivated by Andalusia's history.

have entered our palaces and consumed our still hot tea and heard our mellifluous music? Does it mean that as Arabs we exist only as a footnote to someone else's history?

> Our tea is green and hot: drink it. Our pistachios are fresh; eat them.
> The beds are of green cedar, fall on them,
> following this long siege, lie down on the feathers of our dream.
> The sheets are crisp, perfumes are ready by the door, and there are plenty of mirrors:
> Enter them so we may exist completely. Soon we will search
> In the margins of your history, in distant countries,
> For what was once our history. And in the end we will ask ourselves:
> Was Andalusia here or there? On the land . . . or in the poem?

It is difficult to overestimate the searing poignancy of these lines. They recall not only the self-destructive demise of the Andalusian kings and their *tawai'f* but also present-day Arab disunity and consequent weakness. (*Tawai'f* is the plural of the Arabic *ta'ifa*, used to refer both to the independent Muslim kingdoms that began in 1023, and also to modern-day confessional sects, of the sort common in Lebanon during its recent civil war. The references are lost on

The Iberian Peninsula and
North Africa.
Copyright © 2002 by Josh Kibble.
Reprinted by permission of the
illustrator.

no one whose language is Arabic.) For a visitor from either North Africa or the
Arab countries east of Suez, including Egypt, Andalusia is idealized as a kind
of lost paradise, which fell from the brilliance of its medieval apex into terrible
squabbles and petty jealousies. This perhaps makes a rather too facile moral
lesson of the place.

8      Andalusia's unthreatening landscape—tranquil hills, agreeable towns, and
rich green fields—survived a turbulent and deeply unsavory history. Running
through its convoluted past was a steady current of unrest, of trust betrayed. It
seems to have been made up of composite or converted souls, Mozarabs (Ara-
bized Christians) and *muwallads* (Christian converts to Islam). Nothing and no
one is simple. Several of its city-states (there were no fewer than 12 at the height
of the internecine conflict) were occasionally ruled by poets and patrons of the
arts, such as Seville's 11th-century al-Mutamid, but they were often jealous and
even small-minded schemers. Andalusia multiplies in the mind with its contradictions and puzzles; its history is a history of the masks and assumed identities it has worn.

9      Was Andalusia largely Arab and Muslim, as it certainly seems to have been,
and if so why was it so very different from, say, Syria, Egypt, and Iraq, themselves
great centers of civilization and power? And how did the Jews, the Visigoth
Catholics, and the Romans who colonized it before the Arabs play their role in
Andalusia's makeup and identity? However all these components are sorted out,
a composite Andalusian identity anchored in Arab culture can be discerned in its
striking buildings, its tiles and wooden ceilings, its ornate pottery and neatly constructed houses. And what could be more Andalusian than the fiery flamenco
dancer, accompanied by hoarse *cantaores*, martial hand-clapping, and hypnotically
strummed guitars, all of which have precedents in Arabic music?

Seville's Alcázar palace, one of the best surviving examples
of Mudejar architecture, a late Andalusian style.

On this trip I wanted to discover what Andalusia was from my perspective 10
as a Palestinian Arab, as someone whose diverse background might offer a way
of seeing and understanding the place beyond illusion and romance. I was born
in Jerusalem, Andalusia's great Eastern antipode, and raised as a Christian.
Though the environment I grew up in was both colonial and Muslim, my university education and years of residence in the United States and Europe allow
me to see my past as a Westerner might. Standing before the monumental por-
tal of Seville's Alcázar (the Hispanicized word for *al-qasr*, "castle"), every inch
of which is covered in raised florid swirls and interlocking squares, I was reminded of similar surfaces from my earlier year in Cairo, Damascus, and Jerusalem, strangely present before me now in southern Europe, where Arab

Muslims once hoped to set up an Umayyad empire in the West to rival the one in Syria. The Arabs journeyed along the shores of the Mediterranean though Spain, France, and Italy, all of which now bear their traces, even if those traces are not always acknowledged.

11      Perhaps the most striking feature of Andalusia historically was the care lavished on such aspects of urban life as running water, leafy gardens, viewing places (*miradores*), and graceful wall and ceiling designs. Medieval Europe, all rough skins, drafty rooms, and meaty cuisine, was barbaric by comparison. This is worth noting, since the interiors of Andalusia's palaces today are presented as out of time, stripped of their luxurious silks and divans, their heady perfumes and spices, their counterpoint of din and lyrical poetry.

12      Except for Cordova's immense Mezquita, the choice spaces of what has been known historically as Muslim Spain are generally not very large. Even Seville's Alcázar, big enough as a castle or palace, doesn't dominate at all. The Arabs who gave Andalusia its characteristic features generally used architecture to refashion and enhance nature, to create symmetrical patterns that echo Arabic calligraphy. Streets are pleasant to saunter in, rather than utilitarian thoroughfares. Curved ornaments—such as highly patterned vases and metal utensils—abound, all part of a wonderfully relaxed worldliness.

13      That worldliness, which reached its apex between the 9th and 12th centuries, testifies to the extraordinary diversity of Islam itself, so often thought of today as a monolithic block of wild-eyed terrorists, bent on destruction and driven by fanaticism. Yes, there were feuding factions, but rarely before or after did the Islamic kings and princes produce a civilization of such refinement with so many potentially warring components. Consider that in Cordova's heyday the Jewish sage Maimonides and Islam's greatest thinker, Ibn Rushd (Averroës), lived in Cordova at the same time, each with his own disciples and doctrines, both writing and speaking in Arabic. Part of the Damascus-based Umayyad empire that had fallen to the Baghdad-based Abbasids in 750, the Spanish territories always retained an eagerness to be recognized by, and an ambition to surpass the achievements of, their Eastern cousin.

14      Quite soon, Andalusia became a magnet for talent in many arenas: music, philosophy, mysticism, literature, architecture, virtually all of the sciences, jurisprudence, religion. The monarchs Abd ar-Rahman I (731–788) and Abd ar-Rahman III (891–961) gave Cordova its almost mythic status. Three times the size of Paris (Europe's second-largest city in the 10th century), with 70 libraries, Cordova also had, according to the historian Salma Kahdra Jayyusi, "1,600 mosques, 900 baths, 213,077 homes for ordinary people, 60,300 mansions for notables, officials, and military commanders, and 80,455 shops." The mystics and poets Ibn Hazm and Ibn Arabi, Jewish writers Judah ha-Levi and Ibn Gabirol, the colloquial but lyrical *zajals* and wonderful strophic songs, or *muwashshah*, that seemed to emerge as if from nowhere and later influenced the troubadors, provided al-Andalus with verse, music, and atmosphere such as Europe had never had before.

The Arab general Tariq bin Ziyad and his desert army streamed across 15
the Gibraltar straits in 711; on later forays he brought with him many North
African Berbers, Yemenis, Egyptians, and Syrians. In Spain they encountered
Visigoths and Jews, plus the remnants of a once thriving Roman community,
all of whom at times co-existed, and at times fought with one another. No
harmony was stable for very long—too many conflicting elements were always in play. Andalusia's reign of relative tolerance (three monotheistic faiths
in complex accord with one another) abruptly ended when King Ferdinand
and Queen Isabella seized the region and imposed a reign of terror on non-
Christians. Significantly, one of the towering figures of the Andalusian cultural synthesis, Ibn Khaldun, a founder of sociology and historiography, came
from a prominent Seville family, and was perhaps the greatest analyst of how
nations rise and fall.

The last king of Granada, the luckless Boabdil (Abu Abd Allah Muham- 16
mad), was expelled along with the Jews in 1492, weeping or sighing—choose
your version. The unhappy Moor quickly became the emblem of what the
Arabs had lost. Yet most people who are gripped by the pathos of the king's
departure may not know that Boabdil negotiated very profitable surrender
terms—some money, and land outside Granada—before he left the city to the
Castilian monarchs.

Despite the richness of Andalusia's Islamic past and its indelible presence 17
in Spain's subsequent history after the Reconquista, for years the Church and
royalist ideologues stressed the purgation of Spain's Islamic and Jewish heritage, insisting that Christian Spain was restored in 1492 as if little had happened to disturb its ascendancy in the seven preceding centuries. Not for
nothing has the cult of Santiago (Saint James) been highlighted in Catholic
Spain: St. James was, among other things, the patron saint of the Spanish in
their battles against the Moors, hence his nickname Matamoros, "Killer of
Moors." Yet, classical Mudejar art, with its typically florid arabesques and geo-
metrical architecture, was produced after the Muslims were defeated. As far
away as Catalonia, Gaudí's obsession with botanical motifs shows the Arab
influence at its most profound. Why did it linger so if Arabs had represented
only a negligible phase in Spanish history?

The Jews and Muslims who weren't thrown out or destroyed by the Inqui- 18
sition remained as conversos and Moriscos, men and women who had converted to Catholicism to preserve their lives. No one will ever know whether
the identity they abandoned was really given up or whether it continued underground. Miguel de Cervantes's magnificent novel *Don Quixote* draws attention to its supposed author, the fictional Arab Sidi Hamete Benengeli, which—it
is plausibly alleged—was a way of masking Cervantes's own secret identity as
an unrepentant converso. The wars between Muslims and Catholics turn up
again and again in literature, including of course the *Chanson de Roland* (in
which Charlemagne's Frankish army is defeated in 778 by Abd ar-Rahman's
men) and Spain's national epic, *El Poema del Cid*. About 60 percent of the Spanish language is made up of Arabic words and phrases: *alcalde* (mayor), *barrios*

(quarters of a city), *aceite* (oil), *aceitunas* (olives). Their persistence indicates that Spain's identity is truly, if perhaps also uneasily, bicultural.

19     It took the great Spanish historian and philologist Américo Castro, who taught for many years at Princeton, to establish the enduring pervasiveness of the country's repressed past in his monumental work *The Structure of Spanish History* (1954). One of Spain's finest contemporary novelists, Juan Goytisolo, has also inspired interest in Andalusia's Arab and Muslim origins, and done much to reassert Spain's non-European past. His *Count Julian*, which centers on the treacherous Catholic whom Spaniards hold responsible for bringing in the Moors, challenges the myth that Visigoth Spain's rapid fall in 711 can be explained by nothing other than the nobleman's betrayal.

20     Andalusia's identity was always in the process of being dissolved and lost, even when its cultural life was at its pinnacle. Every one of its several strands—Arabic, Muslim, Berber, Catholic, Jewish, Visigothic, Roman—calls up another. Cordova was a particularly wonderful case in point. A much smaller city today than under Abd ar-Rahman I, it is still dominated by the mosque that he began in 785. Erected on the site of a Christian church, it was an attempt to assert his identity as a Umayyad prince fleeing Damascus, to make a cultural statement as a Muslim exiled to a place literally across the world from where he had come.

21     The result is, in my experience, the greatest and most impressive religious structure on earth. The mosque-cathedral, La Mezquita, stretches effortlessly for acres in a series of unending double arches, whose climax is an incredibly ornate mihrab, the place where the muezzin or prayer leader stands. Its contours echo those of the great mosque in Damascus (from which Abd ar-Rahman I barely managed to escape when his Umayyad dynasty fell), while its arches are conscious quotations of Roman aqueducts. So assiduous was its architect in copying Damascus that the Cordovan mihrab actually faces south, rather than east—toward Mecca—as it should.

22     The great mosque was later barbarically seized by a Christian monarch who turned it into a church. He did this by inserting an entire cathedral into the Muslim structure's center, in an aggressive erasure of history and statement of faith. He may also have had in mind the legend that Muslims had stolen the bells of the Cathedral of Santiago de Compostela, melted them down, and used them in the mosque, which also housed the Prophet Muhammad's hand. Today, though the Muslim idea of prayer remains dominant, the building exudes a spirit of inclusive sanctity and magnanimity of purpose.

23     Beyond the mosque's imposing walls, Cordova retains its memorial splendor and inviting shelter. To this day, the houses communicate a sense of welcome: inner courtyards are often furnished with a fountain, and the rooms are dispersed around it, very much as they are in houses in Aleppo thousands of miles to the east. Streets are narrow and winding because, as in medieval Cairo, the idea is to cajole the pedestrian with promises of arrival. Thus one walks along without having to face the psychologically intimidating distance of the long, straight avenue. Moreover, Cordova is one of the few cities in the

Mediterranean where the intermingling of Arab and Jewish quarters doesn't immediately suggest conflict. Just seeing streets and squares named after Averroës and Maimonides in 21st-century Cordova, one gets an immediate idea of what a universal culture was like a thousand years ago.

Only five miles outside Cordova stand the partially restored ruins of 24 what must have been the most lavish, and certainly the most impressive, royal city in Europe, Madinat al-Zahra (City of the Flower). Begun by Abd ar-Rahman III in 936, it, too, was a vast echo of palace-cities in the Arab East, which it almost certainly overshadowed for a time. It is as if Andalusia's rulers and great figures were unable ever to rid their minds of the East. They relived its prior greatness on their terms, nowhere with more striving for effect than in Madinat al-Zahra.

Now an enormous excavation, Madinat al-Zahra is slowly being restored. 25 You can stand looking down on the symmetrical array of stables, military barracks, reception rooms, courtyards—all pointing at the great central hall in which the king received his guests and subjects. According to some scholars, Abd ar-Rahman wanted not only to assume the mantle of the caliphate, thereby wresting it from the Abbasid king in Baghdad (who couldn't have paid much attention to Abd ar-Rahman's posturings), but also to establish political authority as something that belonged in the West but had meaning only if snatched from the East. For an Arab visitor, it is hard not to be struck by the rather competitive Andalusian reference to the better-known Eastern Muslim empires, mainly those of the Abbasids and Fatimids, who to this day form the core of what is taught and propagated as Arab culture.

A special poignancy hangs over Andalusia's impressively animated spaces. 26 It derives not only from a pervasive sense of former grandeur but also from what, because so many people hoped to possess it, Andalusia tried to be—and what it might have been. Certainly Granada's Alhambra is a monument to regret and the passage of time. Next to the wonderful 13th- to 14th-century Nasrid palace and superb Generalife gardens looms the ponderous 16th-century castle of the Spanish king and Holy Roman Emperor Charles V, who obviously wanted his rather ostentatious abode to acquire some of the luster of the Arab complex. Yet, despite the Alhambra's opulence and its apparently hedonistic celebration of the good life (for rulers, mainly), its arabesque patterns can seem like a defense against mortality or the ravages of human life. One can easily imagine the beleaguered and insecure Boabdil using it as a place of perfumed forgetfulness—perhaps even at times reexperiencing the studied oblivion cultivated by Sufi masters such as Ibn Arab.

The schizophrenia inherent in Spain's identity is more apparent in 27 Granada than anywhere else in Andalusia. Because the Alhambra sits on one of several hills high above the city, Granada proper has paid the price in clogged streets and overbuilt residential and commercial quarters through which the Arab palace must be approached. Granada as a whole embodies this tension between high and low. A mazelike system of one-way streets connects the Alhambra to Albaicín, the old Muslim quarter. Despite the wonders of the Alhambra, being in Albaicín is like feeling the fantasy of summer and the realities of a grim winter very close to each other. The resemblances between Albaicín and Cordova's barrios are striking, except that, as the name suggests, Albaicín—Arabic for "the downtrodden and hopeless"—was indeed an area for the poor and, one can't help feeling, where the last Arabs and Jews huddled together before their eviction in 1492. Nothing evokes Granada's riven history more superbly than the "Albaicín" movement in Isaac Albéniz's greatest musical work, the redoubtably difficult-to-perform piano collection *Iberia*.

28      By contrast, Seville's spirit is very much of this world—part feline, part macho, part dashing sparkle, part somber colonialism. Seville contains Spain's finest *plaza de toros* and also its largest cathedral. And it is here that all the archives of Spain's imperial conquests are housed. But before 1492, Seville was the administrative capital of the Arab monarchy that held sway over Andalusia. Where the Catholic empire-builders set their sights on the New World, the Arabs were taken up with the Old: Morocco, which before the final Reconquista was considered to be part of Andalusia. Similarities in metal, leather, and glazed pottery design between Spain and North Africa reinforce a prevailing unity of vision and religious discourse.

29      If Seville is a city where Catholic and Muslim cultures interact, it is to the decided advantage of the former—though given Seville's special status in the Western romantic imagination as an extension of the Orient, it's probably truer to say that Seville is the triumph of Andalusian style. This, after all, is the city of Mérimée's and Bizet's *Carmen*, the heart of Hemingway's bullfighting obsession, and a favorite port of call for northern European poets and writers for whom citrus blossoms represent the salutary opposite of their dreary climates. Stendhal's *espagnolisme* derives from Sevillian themes, and the city's Holy Week parades and observances have gripped many peregrinating artists.

30      Not that the Arabs haven't made their own indelible mark on the city. Standing watch over the landscape is the four-sided Giralda, a minaret built by an Almohad (basically an austere fundamentalist sort of Islam) king in the late 12th century. Its upper third was added to, for purposes of "improvement," by zealous Christians 400 years later. Despite some unnecessary flourishes, the tower was so magnetic that a contemporary chronicler observed, "From a distance it would appear that all the stars of the Zodiac had stopped in the heart of Seville." Incorporated into the cathedral, whose awesome bulk testifies to Catholic ambition and consolidation of power (Christopher Columbus's tomb is inside), the Giralda leads an independent existence as an ornate symbol of how even the harshest of ideologies can be filled with grace.

31      In the long run, and almost in spite of its kings and magistrates, the Andalusian style seems to have fostered movement and discovery rather than monumentality and stability. It enacted an earlier version of our own hybrid world, one whose borders were also thresholds, and whose multiple identities formed an enriched diversity.

## COMPREHENSION

1. Why, according to Said, is Andalusia a place worth traveling to and understanding?
2. How does Said distinguish between the clash of civilizations and a dialogue among civilizations? Point to specific information in the essay to support your understanding of this core distinction.
3. How does Said explain the Spanish identity in light of the history of Andalusia?

## RHETORIC

1. What is Said's claim? What tone does he take in advancing his key idea? Where does he employ logical, ethical, and emotional appeals?
2. Said published this essay in a travel magazine. How does he slant his material to appeal to his primary audience? How do illustrations augment the appeal of the essay? In what ways might this piece be of general and even academic interest?
3. Examine the introductory and concluding paragraphs. How do they offer a frame for the entire essay?
4. Mood or atmosphere is important in certain forms of writing. How does Said create a specific mood in this essay? Identify passages that contribute to the creation of atmosphere. How does mood reinforce Said's claim?
5. Said uses causal and process analysis to advance his argument. Identify the stages in this dual process in the essay.
6. Explain how Said creates a definition of culture and civilization in this article. What types of evidence does he offer to flesh out this definition?

## WRITING

1. Using Said's article as a guide, write a reflective essay on the ways in which a dialogue of civilizations might be possible today.
2. Select a place you have visited (or a place you would like to visit), and in an expository essay, explain why that place and its people reveal something important about the current state of culture or civilization.
3. **Writing an Argument:** Said claims that civilizations do not necessarily have to clash. In an argumentative essay that employs logical, ethical, and emotional appeals, either agree or disagree with Said's main proposition.

www.mhhe.com/
**mhreader**

For more information on Edward Said, go to:
**More Resources > Ch. 6 History & Culture**

# The Arab World

### Edward T. Hall

*Edward T. Hall (b. 1914) was born in Missouri and earned a master's degree at the University of Arkansas and a PhD in anthropology at Columbia University. He was a professor of anthropology at the Illinois Institute of Technology and at Northwestern University.* Hall is also the author of many books on anthropology and culture, among the most famous of which are The Silent Language *(1959),* The Hidden Dimension *(1966),* The Dance of Life *(1983),* Hidden Differences: Doing Business with the Japanese *(1987), and* Understanding Cultural Differences: Germans, French and Americans *(1990). In this selection from* The Hidden Dimension, *Hall demonstrates how such basic concepts as public and private space are perceived far differently depending upon one's culture of origin.*

1 In spite of over two thousand years of contact, Westerners and Arabs still do not understand each other. Proxemic research reveals some insights into this difficulty. Americans in the Middle East are immediately struck by two conflicting sensations. In public they are compressed and overwhelmed by smells, crowding, and high noise levels; in Arab homes Americans are apt to rattle around, feeling exposed and often somewhat inadequate because of too much space! (The Arab houses and apartments of the middle and upper classes which Americans stationed abroad commonly occupy are much larger than the dwellings such Americans usually inhabit.) Both the high sensory stimulation which is experienced in public places and the basic insecurity which comes from being in a dwelling that is too large provide Americans with an introduction to the sensory world of the Arab.

## Behavior in Public

2 Pushing and shoving in public places is characteristic of Middle Eastern culture. Yet it is not entirely what Americans think it is (being pushy and rude) but stems from a different set of assumptions concerning not only the relations between people but how one experiences the body as well. Paradoxically, Arabs consider northern Europeans and Americans pushy, too. This was very puzzling to me when I started investigating these two views. How could Americans who stand aside and avoid touching be considered pushy? I used to ask Arabs to explain this paradox. None of my subjects was able to tell me specifically what particulars of American behavior were responsible, yet they all agreed that the impression was widespread among Arabs. After repeated unsuccessful attempts to gain insight into the cognitive world of the Arab on this particular point, I filed

it away as a question that only time would answer. When the answer came, it was because of a seemingly inconsequential annoyance.

While waiting for a friend in a Washington, D.C., hotel lobby and wanting ₃ to be both visible and alone, I had seated myself in a solitary chair outside the normal stream of traffic. In such a setting most Americans follow a rule, which is all the more binding because we seldom think about it, that can be stated as follows: as soon as a person stops or is seated in a public place, there balloons around him a small sphere of privacy which is considered inviolate. The size of the sphere varies with the degree of crowding, the age, sex, and the importance of the person, as well as the general surroundings. Anyone who enters this zone and stays there is intruding. In fact, a stranger who intrudes, even for a specific purpose, acknowledges the fact that he has intruded by beginning his request with "Pardon me, but can you tell me . . . ?"

To continue, as I waited in the deserted lobby, a stranger walked up to ₄ where I was sitting and stood close enough so that not only could I easily touch him but I could even hear him breathing. In addition, the dark mass of his body filled the peripheral field of vision on my left side. If the lobby had been crowded with people, I would have understood his behavior, but in an empty lobby his presence made me exceedingly uncomfortable. Feeling annoyed by this intrusion, I moved my body in such a way as to communicate annoyance. Strangely enough, instead of moving away, my actions seemed only to encourage him, because he moved even closer. In spite of the temptation to escape the annoyance, I put aside thoughts of abandoning my post, thinking, "To hell with it. Why should I move? I was here first and I'm not going to let this fellow drive me out even if he is a boor." Fortunately, a group of people soon arrived whom my tormentor immediately joined. Their mannerisms explained his behavior, for I knew from both speech and gestures that they were Arabs. I had not been able to make this crucial identification by looking at my subject when he was alone because he wasn't talking and he was wearing American clothes.

In describing the scene later to an Arab colleague, two contrasting patterns ₅ emerged. My concept and my feelings about my own circle of privacy in a "public" place immediately struck my Arab friend as strange and puzzling. He said, "After all, it's a public place, isn't it?" Pursuing this line of inquiry, I found that in Arab thought I had no rights whatsoever by virtue of occupying a given spot; neither my place nor my body was inviolate! For the Arab, there is no such thing as an intrusion in public. Public means public. With this insight, a great range of Arab behavior that had been puzzling, annoying, and sometimes even frightening began to make sense. I learned, for example, that if *A* is standing on a street corner and *B* wants his spot, *B* is within his rights if he does what he can to make *A* uncomfortable enough to move. In Beirut only the hardy sit in the last row in a movie theater, because there are usually standees who want seats and who push and shove and make such a nuisance that most people give up and leave. Seen in this light, the Arab who "intruded" on my space in the hotel lobby had apparently selected it for the very reason I had: it was a good place to watch two doors and the elevator. My show of annoyance, instead of driving him away, had only encouraged him. He thought he was about to get me to move.

6      Another silent source of friction between Americans and Arabs is in an area that Americans treat very informally—the manners and rights of the road. In general, in the United States we tend to defer to the vehicle that is bigger, more powerful, faster, and heavily laden. While a pedestrian walking along a road may feel annoyed he will not think it unusual to step aside for a fast-moving automobile. He knows that because he is moving he does not have the right to the space around him that he has when he is standing still (as I was in the hotel lobby). It appears that the reverse is true with the Arabs who apparently *take on rights to space as they move.* For someone else to move into a space an Arab is also moving into is a violation of his rights. It is infuriating to an Arab to have someone else cut in front of him on the highway. It is the American's cavalier treatment of moving space that makes the Arab call him aggressive and pushy.

## Concepts of Privacy

7    The experience described above and many others suggested to me that Arabs might actually have a wholly contrasting set of assumptions concerning the body and the rights associated with it. Certainly the Arab tendency to shove and push each other in public and to feel and pinch women in public conveyances would not be tolerated by Westerners. It appeared to me that they must not have any concept of a private zone outside the body. This proved to be precisely the case.

8      In the Western world, the person is synonymous with an individual inside a skin. And in northern Europe generally, the skin and even the clothes may be inviolate. You need permission to touch either if you are a stranger. This rule applies in some parts of France, where the mere touching of another person during an argument used to be legally defined as assault. For the Arab the location of the person in relation to the body is quite different. The person exists somewhere down inside the body. The ego is not completely hidden, however, because it can be reached very easily with an insult. It is protected from touch but not from words. The dissociation of the body and the ego may explain why the public amputation of a thief's hand is tolerated as standard punishment in Saudi Arabia. It also sheds light on why an Arab employer living in a modern apartment can provide his servant with a room that is a boxlike cubicle approximately 5 by 10 by 4 feet in size that is not only hung from the ceiling to conserve floor space but has an opening so that the servant can be spied on.

9      As one might suspect, deep orientations toward the self such as the one just described are also reflected in the language. This was brought to my attention one afternoon when an Arab colleague who is the author of an Arab English dictionary arrived in my office and threw himself into a chair in a state of obvious exhaustion. When I asked him what had been going on, he said: "I have spent the entire afternoon trying to find the Arab equivalent of the English word 'rape.' There is no such word in Arabic. All my sources, both written and

spoken, can come up with no more than an approximation, such as 'He took her against her will.' There is nothing in Arabic approaching your meaning as it is expressed in that one word."

Differing concepts of the placement of the ego in relation to the body are  10
not easily grasped. Once an idea like this is accepted, however, it is possible to understand many other facets of Arab life that would otherwise be difficult to explain. One of these is the high population density of Arab cities like Cairo, Beirut, and Damascus. According to the animal studies described in the earlier chapters [of *The Hidden Dimension*], the Arabs should be living in a perpetual behavioral sink. While it is probable that Arabs are suffering from population pressures, it is also just as possible that continued pressure from the desert has resulted in a cultural adaptation to high density which takes the form described above. Tucking the ego down inside the body shell not only would permit higher population densities but would explain why it is that Arab communications are stepped up as much as they are when compared to northern European communication patterns. Not only is the sheer noise level much higher, but the piercing look of the eyes, the touch of the hands, and the mutual bathing in the warm moist breath during conversation represent stepped up sensory inputs to a level which many Europeans find unbearably intense.

The Arab dream is for lots of space in the home, which unfortunately many  11
Arabs cannot afford. Yet when he has space, it is very different from what one finds in most American homes. Arab spaces inside their upper middle-class homes are tremendous by our standards. They avoid partitions because Arabs *do not like to be alone.* The form of the home is such as to hold the family together inside a single protective shell, because Arabs are deeply involved with each other. Their personalities are intermingled and take nourishment from each other like the roots and soil. If one is not with people and actively involved in some way, one is deprived of life. An old Arab saying reflects this value: "Paradise without people should not be entered because it is Hell." Therefore, Arabs in the United States often feel socially and sensorially deprived and long to be back where there is human warmth and contact.

Since there is no physical privacy as we know it in the Arab family, not  12
even a word for privacy, one could expect that the Arabs might use some other means to be alone. Their way to be alone is to stop talking. Like the English, an Arab who shuts himself off in this way is not indicating that anything is wrong or that he is withdrawing, only that he wants to be alone with his own thoughts or does not want to be intruded upon. One subject said that her father would come and go for days at a time without saying a word, and no one in the family thought anything of it. Yet for this very reason, an Arab exchange student visiting a Kansas farm failed to pick up the cue that his American hosts were mad at him when they gave him the "silent treatment." He only discovered something was wrong when they took him to town and tried forcibly to put him on a bus to Washington, D.C., the headquarters of the exchange program responsible for his presence in the U.S.

## Arab Personal Distances

13  Like everyone else in the world, Arabs are unable to formulate specific rules for their informal behavior patterns. In fact, they often deny that there are any rules, and they are made anxious by suggestions that such is the case. Therefore, in order to determine how the Arab sets distances, I investigated the use of each sense separately. Gradually, definite and distinctive behavioral patterns began to emerge.

14      Olfaction occupies a prominent place in the Arab life. Not only is it one of the distance-setting mechanisms, but it is a vital part of a complex system of behavior. Arabs consistently breathe on people when they talk. However, this habit is more than a matter of different manners. To the Arab good smells are pleasing and a way of being involved with each other. To smell one's friend is not only nice but desirable, for to deny him your breath is to act ashamed. Americans, on the other hand, trained as they are not to breathe in people's faces, automatically communicate shame in trying to be polite. Who would expect that when our highest diplomats are putting on their best manners they are also communicating shame? Yet this is what occurs constantly, because diplomacy is not only "eyeball to eyeball" but breath to breath.

15      By stressing olfaction, Arabs do not try to eliminate all the body's odors, only to enhance them and use them in building human relationships. Nor are they self-conscious about telling others when they don't like the way they smell. A man leaving his house in the morning may be told by his uncle, "Habib, your stomach is sour and your breath doesn't smell too good. Better not talk too close to people today." Smell is even considered in the choice of a mate. When couples are being matched for marriage, the man's go-between will sometimes ask to smell the girl, who may be turned down if she doesn't "smell nice." Arabs recognize that smell and disposition may be linked.

16      In a word, the olfactory boundary performs two roles in Arab life. It enfolds those who want to relate and separates those who don't. The Arab finds it essential to stay inside the olfactory zone as a means of keeping tab on changes in emotion. What is more, he may feel crowded as soon as he smells something unpleasant. While not much is known about "olfactory crowding," this may prove to be as significant as any other variable in the crowding complex because it is tied directly to the body chemistry and hence to the state of health and emotions. . . . It is not surprising, therefore, that the olfactory boundary constitutes for the Arabs an informal distance-setting mechanism in contrast to the visual mechanisms of the Westerner.

## Facing and Not Facing

17  One of my earliest discoveries in the field of intercultural communication was that the position of the bodies of people in conversation varies with the culture. Even so, it used to puzzle me that a special Arab friend seemed unable to walk and talk at the same time. After years in the United States, he could not bring himself to stroll along, facing forward while talking. Our progress would be arrested while

he edged ahead, cutting slightly in front of me and turning sideways so we could see each other. Once in this position, he would stop. His behavior was explained when I learned that for the Arabs to view the other person peripherally is regarded as impolite, and to sit or stand back-to-back is considered very rude. You must be involved when interacting with Arabs who are friends.

One mistaken American notion is that Arabs conduct all conversations at close 18 distances. This is not the case at all. On social occasions, they may sit on opposite sides of the room and talk across the room to each other. They are, however, apt to take offense when Americans use what are to them ambiguous distances, such as the four- to seven-foot social-consultative distance. They frequently complain that Americans are cold or aloof or "don't care." This was what an elderly Arab diplomat in an American hospital thought when the American nurses used "professional" distance. He had the feeling that he was being ignored, that they might not take good care of him. Another Arab subject remarked, referring to American behavior, "What's the matter? Do I smell bad? Or are they afraid of me?"

Arabs who interact with Americans report experiencing a certain flatness 19 traceable in part to a very different use of the eyes in private and in public as well as between friends and strangers. Even though it is rude for a guest to walk around the Arab home eyeing things, Arabs look at each other in ways which seem hostile or challenging to the American. One Arab informant said that he was in constant hot water with Americans because of the way he looked at them without the slightest intention of offending. In fact, he had on several occasions barely avoided fights with American men who apparently thought their masculinity was being challenged because of the way he was looking at them. As noted earlier, Arabs look each other in the eye when talking with an intensity that makes most Americans highly uncomfortable.

## Involvement

As the reader must gather by now, Arabs are involved with each other on many 20 different levels simultaneously. Privacy in a public place is foreign to them. Business transactions in the bazaar, for example, are not just between buyer and seller, but are participated in by everyone. Anyone who is standing around may join in. If a grownup sees a boy breaking a window, he must stop him even if he doesn't know him. Involvement and participation are expressed in other ways as well. If two men are fighting, the crowd must intervene. On the political level, *to fail to intervene* when trouble is brewing is to take sides, which is what our State Department always seems to be doing. Given the fact that few people in the world today are even remotely aware of the cultural mold that forms their thoughts, it is normal for Arabs to view *our* behavior as though it stemmed from *their* own hidden set of assumptions.

## Feelings about Enclosed Spaces

In the course of my interviews with Arabs the term "tomb" kept cropping up in 21 conjunction with enclosed space. In a word, Arabs don't mind being crowded by people but hate to be hemmed in by walls. They show a much greater overt sensitivity to architectural crowding than we do. Enclosed space must meet at least three requirements that I know of if it is to satisfy the Arabs: there must be plenty of unobstructed space in which to move around (possibly as much as a thousand square feet); very high ceilings—so high in fact that they do not normally impinge on the visual field; and, in addition, there must be an unobstructed view. It was spaces such as these in which the Americans referred to earlier felt so uncomfortable. One sees the Arab's need for a view expressed in many ways, even negatively, for to cut off a neighbor's view is one of the most effective ways of spiting him. In Beirut one can see what is known locally as the "spite house." It is nothing more than a thick, four-story wall, built at the end of a long fight between neighbors, on a narrow strip of land for the express purpose of denying a view of the Mediterranean to any house built on the land behind. According to one of my informants, there is also a house on a small plot of land between Beirut and Damascus which is completely surrounded by a neighbor's wall built high enough to cut off the view from all windows!

## Boundaries

22   Proxemic patterns tell us other things about Arab culture. For example, the whole concept of the boundary as an abstraction is almost impossible to pin down. In one sense, there are no boundaries. "Edges" of towns, yes, but permanent boundaries out in the country (hidden lines), no. In the course of my work with Arab subjects I had a difficult time translating our concept of a boundary into terms which could be equated with theirs. In order to clarify the distinctions between the two very different definitions, I thought it might be helpful to pinpoint acts which constituted trespass. To date, I have been unable to discover anything even remotely resembling our own legal concept of trespass.

23       Arab behavior in regard to their own real estate is apparently an extension of, and therefore consistent with, their approach to the body. My subjects simply failed to respond whenever trespass was mentioned. They didn't seem to understand what I meant by this term. This may be explained by the fact that they organize relationships with each other according to closed social systems rather than spatially. For thousands of years Moslems, Marinites, Druses, and Jews have lived in their own villages, each with strong kin affiliations. Their hierarchy of loyalties is: first to one's self, then to kinsman, townsman, or tribesman, co-religionist and/or countryman. Anyone not in these categories is a stranger. Strangers and enemies are very closely linked, if not synonymous, in Arab thought. Trespass in this context is a matter of who you are, rather than a piece of land or a space with a boundary that can be denied to anyone and everyone, friend and foe alike.

24       In summary, proxemic patterns differ. By examining them it is possible to reveal hidden cultural frames that determine the structure of a given people's perceptual world. Perceiving the world differently leads to differential definitions of what constitutes crowded living, different interpersonal relations, and a different approach to both local and international politics.

## COMPREHENSION

1. This excerpt is from Hall's book *The Hidden Dimension*. What is the hidden dimension, according to the author?
2. In paragraph 10, Hall explains that "differing concepts of the placement of the ego in relation to the body are not easily grasped." What does he mean by this statement? How is it relevant to the theme of his essay?
3. The title of this essay is "The Arab World." What does the term *world* mean within the context of the essay?
4. Define the following words: *proxemic* (paragraph 1), *paradox* (paragraph 2), *inviolate* (paragraph 3), *defer* (paragraph 6), *olfaction* (paragraph 14), and *peripherally* (paragraph 17).

## RHETORIC

1. Anthropology is often thought of as an intellectual pursuit. How would you characterize Hall's voice, considering his style of language and method of analysis?
2. How does Hall develop his comparison and contrast of the American versus the Arab perception of manners and driving?
3. People often favor their own perspective of life over a foreign perspective. Is Hall's comparison value-free, or does he seem to prefer one cultural system to another? Explain by making reference to his tone.
4. Who is the implied audience for this essay? Explain your view.
5. Hall makes use of personal anecdote in explaining his theme. What other forms of support does he offer? Cite at least two others and provide an example of each.
6. Writers often have various purposes in writing—for example, to entertain, to inform, to effect change, to advise, or to persuade. What is Hall's purpose or purposes in writing this essay? Explain your view.

## WRITING

1. Write an expository essay in which you explain the use and interpretation of personal space by observing students in social situations at your college or university.
2. Write a personal anecdote about a time in your life when cultural perception caused a conflict between yourself and another person.
3. **Writing an Argument:** In a persuasive essay, argue for or against the proposition that some cultures are better than others.

www.mhhe.com/
**mhreader**

For more information on Edward T. Hall, go to:
**More Resources > Ch. 6 History & Culture**

# Strangers from a Distant Shore

### Ronald Takaki

*Ronald Takaki (b. 1939) was born in Honolulu, Hawaii. He earned his BA from the College of Wooster in 1961 and his MA and PhD from the University of California, Berkeley, where he is currently a professor of ethnic studies. He also taught American history at the College of San Mateo from 1965 to 1967. Takaki feels that American history is still viewed from a predominantly white perspective and is devoted to more accurately representing all Americans in our society. He has written a number of books:* A Pro-Slavery Crusade: The Agitation to Reopen the African Slave Trade *(1971),* Strangers from a Distant Shore: A History of Asian Americans *(1989),* Hiroshima: Why America Dropped the Bomb *(1996),* Iron Cages: Race and Culture in 19th Century America *(1999), and* Double Victory: A Multicultural History of America in World War II *(2000). He is a frequent lecturer and a frequent contributor to history journals as well as other publications. In the following essay, he reflects on the internment of Japanese citizens during World War II and describes his attempts to establish a connection with his Japanese relatives.*

1   To confront the current problems of racism, Asian Americans know they must remember the past and break its silence. This need was felt deeply by Japanese Americans during the hearings before the commission reviewing the issue of redress and reparations for Japanese Americans interned during World War II. Memories of the internment nightmare have haunted the older generation like ghosts. But the former prisoners have been unable to exorcise them by speaking out and ventilating their anger.

> When we were children,
> you spoke Japanese
> in lowered voices
> between yourselves.
> Once you uttered secrets
> which we should not know,
> were not to be heard by us.
> When you spoke
> of some dark secret
> you would admonish us,
> "Don't tell it to anyone else."
> It was a suffocated vow of silence.[1]

[1]Richard Oyama, poem published in *Transfer 38* (San Francisco, 1979), p. 43, reprinted in Elaine Kim, *Asian American Literature: An Introduction to the Writings and Their Social Context* (Philadelphia, 1982).

"Stigmatized," the ex-internees have been carrying the "burden of  2
shame" for over forty painful years. "They felt like a rape victim," explained
Congressman Norman Mineta, a former internee of the Heart Mountain internment camp. "They were accused of being disloyal. They were the victims
but they were on trial and they did not want to talk about it." But Sansei, or
third-generation Japanese Americans, want their elders to tell their story.
Warren Furutani, for example, told the commissioners that young people
like himself had been asking their parents to tell them about the concentration camps and to join them in pilgrimages to the internment camp at Manzanar. "Why? Why!" their parents would reply defensively. "Why would
you want to know about it? It's not important, we don't need to talk about
it." But, Furutani continued, they need to tell the world what happened
during those years of infamy.[2]

Suddenly, during the commission hearings, scores of Issei and Nisei came  3
forward and told their stories. "For over thirty-five years I have been the stereotype Japanese American," Alice Tanabe Nehira told the commission. "I've kept
quiet, hoping in due time we will be justly compensated and recognized for our
years of patient effort. By my passive attitude, I can reflect on my past years to
conclude that it doesn't pay to remain silent." The act of speaking out has enabled the Japanese-American community to unburden itself of years of anger
and anguish. Sometimes their testimonies before the commission were long and
the chair urged them to conclude. But they insisted the time was theirs. "Mr.
Commissioner," protested poet Janice Mirikitani,

> So when you tell me my time is
> up I tell you this.
> Pride has kept my lips
> pinned by nails,
> my rage coffined.
> But I exhume my past
> to claim this time.[3]

The former internees finally had spoken, and their voices compelled the  4
nation to redress the injustice of internment. In August 1988, Congress passed a
bill giving an apology and a payment of $20,000 to each of the survivors of the
internment camps. When President Ronald Reagan signed the bill into law, he
admitted that the United States had committed "a grave wrong," for during
World War II, Japanese Americans had remained "utterly loyal" to this country. "Indeed, scores of Japanese Americans volunteered for our Armed Forces—
many stepping forward in the internment camps themselves. The 442nd

[2]Congressman Robert Matsui, speech in the House of Representatives on bill 442 for redress and
reparations, September 17, 1987, *Congressional Record* (Washington, 1987), p. 7584; Congressman
Norman Mineta, interview with author, March 26, 1988; Warren Furutani, testimony, reprinted in
*Amerasia*, vol. 8, no. 2 (1981), p. 104.
[3]Alice Tanabe Nehira, testimony, reprinted in *Amerasia*, vol. 8, no. 2 (1981), p. 93; Janice Mirikitani,
"Breaking Silences," reprinted ibid., p. 109.

Regimental Combat Team, made up entirely of Japanese Americans, served with immense distinction to defend this nation, their nation. Yet, back at home, the soldiers' families were being denied the very freedom for which so many of the soldiers themselves were laying down their lives." Then the president recalled an incident that happened forty-three years ago. At a ceremony to award the Distinguished Service Cross to Kazuo Masuda, who had been killed in action and whose family had been interned, a young actor paid tribute to the slain Nisei soldier. "The name of that young actor," remarked the president, who had been having trouble saying the Japanese names"—I hope I pronounce this right—was Ronald Reagan." The time had come, the president acknowledged, to end "a sad chapter in American history."[4]

5      Asian Americans have begun to claim their time not only before the commission on redress and reparations but elsewhere as well, in the novels of Maxine Hong Kingston and Milton Murayama, the plays of Frank Chin and Philip Gotanda, the scholarly writings of Sucheng Chan and Elaine Kim, the films of Steve Okazaki and Wa Wang, and the music of Hiroshima and Fred Houn. Others, too, have been breaking silences. Seventy-five-year-old Tomo Shoji, for example, had led a private life, but in 1981 she enrolled in an acting course because she wanted to try something frivolous and to take her mind off her husband's illness. In the beginning, Tomo was hesitant, awkward on the stage. "Be yourself," her teacher urged. Then suddenly she felt something surge through her, springing from deep within, and she began to tell funny and also sad stories about her life. Now Tomo tours the West Coast, a wonderful wordsmith giving one-woman shows to packed audiences of young Asian Americans. "Have we really told our children all we have gone through?" she asks. Telling one of her stories, Tomo recounts: "My parents came from Japan and I was born in a lumber camp. One day, at school, my class was going on a day trip to a show, and I was pulled aside and told I would have to stay behind. All the white kids went." Tomo shares stories about her husband: "When I first met him, I thought, wow. Oh, he was so macho! And he wanted his wife to be a good, submissive wife. But then he married me." Theirs had been at times a stormy marriage. "Culturally we were different because he was Issei and I was American, and we used to argue a lot. Well, one day in 1942 right after World War II had started he came home and told me we had to go to an internment camp. 'I'm not going to one because I'm an American citizen,' I said to him. 'You have to go to camp, but not me.' Well, you know what, that was one time my husband was right!" Tomo remembers the camp: "We were housed in barracks, and we had no privacy. My husband and I had to share a room with another couple. So we hanged a blanket in the middle of the room as a partition. But you could hear everything from the other side. Well, one night, while we were in bed, my husband and I got into an argument, and I dumped him out of the bed. The other couple thought we were making violent love." As she stands on the

---

[4]Text of Reagan's remarks: reprinted in *Pacific Citizen*, August 19–26, 1988, p. 5; *San Francisco Chronicle*, August 5 and 11, 1988.

stage and talks stories excitedly, Tomo cannot be contained: "We got such good, fantastic stories to tell. All our stories are different."[5]

Today, young Asian Americans want to listen to these stories—to shatter images of themselves and their ancestors as "strangers" and to understand who they are as Asian Americans. "What don't you know?" their elders ask. Their question seems to have a peculiar frame: it points to the blank areas of collective memory. And the young people reply that they want "to figure out how the invisible world the emigrants built around [their] childhoods fit in solid America." They want to know more about their "no name" Asian ancestors. They want to decipher the signs of the Asian presence here and there across the landscape of America—railroad tracks over high mountains, fields of cane virtually carpeting entire islands, and verdant agricultural lands.

> Deserts to farmlands
> Japanese-American
> Page in history.[6]

They want to know what is their history and "what is the movies." They want to trace the origins of terms applied to them. "Why are we called 'Oriental'?" they question, resenting the appellation that has identified Asians as exotic, mysterious, strange, and foreign. "The word 'orient' simply means 'east.' So why are Europeans 'West' and why are Asians 'East'? Why did empire-minded Englishmen in the sixteenth century determine that Asia was 'east' of London? Who decided what names would be given to the different regions and peoples of the world? Why does 'American' usually mean 'white'?" Weary of Eurocentric history, young Asian Americans want their Asian ancestral lives in America chronicled, "given the name of a place." They have earned the right to belong to specific places like Washington, California, Hawaii, Puunene, Promontory Point, North Adams, Manzanar, Doyers Street. "And today, after 125 years of our life here," one of them insists, "I do not want just a home that time allowed me to have." Seeking to lay claim to America, they realize they can no longer be indifferent to what happened in history, no longer [be] embarrassed by the hardships and humiliations experienced by their grandparents and parents.

> My heart, once bent and cracked, once
> ashamed of your China ways.
> Ma, hear me now, tell me your story
> again and again.[7]

---

[5]Tomo Shoji, "Born Too Soon . . . It's Never Too Late: Growing Up Nisei in Early Washington," presentations at the University of California, Berkeley, September 19, 1987, and the Ohana Cultural Center, Oakland, California, March 4, 1988.

[6]Maxine Hong Kingston, *The Woman Warrior*, p. 6; poem in Kazuo Ito, *Issei: A History of Japanese Immigrants in North America* (Seattle, 1973), p. 493.

[7]Kingston, *The Woman Warrior*, p. 6; Robert Kwan, "Asian v. Oriental: A Difference That Counts," *Pacific Citizen*, April 25, 1980; Sir James Augustus Henry Murry (ed.), *The Oxford English Dictionary* (Oxford, 1933), vol. 7, p. 200; Aminur Rahim, "Is Oriental an Occident?" in *The Asiandian*, vol. 5, no. 1, April 1983, p. 20; Shawn Wong, *Homebase* (New York, 1979), p. 111; Nellie Wong, "From a Heart of Rice Straw," in Nellie Wong, *Dreams in Harrison Railroad Park* (Berkeley, 1977), p. 41.

8        As they listen to the stories and become members of a "community of memory," they are recovering roots deep within this country and the homelands of their ancestors. Sometimes the journey leads them to discover rich and interesting things about themselves. Alfred Wong, for example, had been told repeatedly for years by his father, "Remember your Chinese name. Remember your village in Toisha. Remember you are Chinese. Remember all this and you will have a home." One reason why it was so important for the Chinese immigrants to remember was that they never felt sure of their status in America. "Unlike German and Scottish immigrants, the Chinese immigrants never felt comfortable here," Wong explained. "So they had a special need to know there was a place, a home for them somewhere."[8]

9        But Wong had a particular reason to remember. His father had married by mutual agreement two women on the same day in China and had come to America as a merchant in the 1920s. Later he brought over one of his wives. But she had to enter as a "paper wife," for he had given the immigration authorities the name of the wife he had left behind. Born here in 1938, Wong grew up knowing about his father's other wife and the other half of the family in China; his parents constantly talked about them and regularly sent money home to Quangdong. For years the "family plan" had been for him to see China someday. In 1984 he traveled to his father's homeland, and there in the family home—the very house his father had left decades earlier—Alfred Wong was welcomed by his *Chunk Gwok Ma* ("China Mama"). "You look just like I had imagined you would look," she remarked. On the walls of the house, he saw hundreds of photographs—of himself as well as sisters, nieces, nephews, and his own daughter—that had been placed there over the years. He suddenly realized how much he had always belonged there, and had a warm connectedness. "It's like you were told there was this box and there was a beautiful diamond in it," Wong said. "But for years and years you couldn't open the box. Then finally you got a chance to open the box and it was as wonderful as you had imagined it would be."[9]

10       Mine is a different yet similar story. My father, Toshio Takaki, died in 1945, when I was only five years old; my mother married Koon Keu Young about a year later, and I grew up knowing very little about my father. Many years later, in 1968, after my parents had moved to Los Angeles, my mother passed away and I had to clear out her room after the funeral. In one of her dresser drawers, I found an old photograph of my father as a teenager: it was his immigration photograph. I noticed some Japanese writing on the back. Later a friend translated: "This is Toshio Takaki, registered as an emigrant in Mifune, Kumamoto Prefecture, 1918." I wondered how young Toshio managed to come to the United States. Why did he go to Hawaii? Did he go alone? What dreams burned within the young boy? But a huge silence stood before me, and I could only

[8]Robert Bellah, et al., *Habits of the Heart: Individualism and Commitment in American Life* (Berkeley, 1985), p. 153; Alfred Wong, interviewed by Carol Takaki, April 6 and 13, 1988.
[9]Ibid.

speculate that he must have come alone and entered as a student, since the 1908 Gentlemen's Agreement had prohibited the immigration of Japanese laborers. In Hawaii, he met and married my mother, Catherine Okawa, a Nisei. I had no Takaki relatives in Hawaii, I thought.

Ten years later, while on a sabbatical in Hawaii, I was "talking story" 11 with my uncle Richard Okawa. I was telling him about the book I was then writing—*Iron Cages*, a study of race and culture in America. Suddenly his eyes lit up as he exclaimed: "Hey, why you no go write a book about us, huh? About the Japanese in Hawaii. After all, your grandparents came here as plantation workers and your mother and all your aunts and uncles were born on the plantation." Smiling, I replied: "Why not?" I went on to write a history of the plantation laborers. The book was published in 1983, and I was featured on television news and educational programs in Hawaii. One of the programs was aired in January 1985; a plantation laborer on the Puunene Plantation, Maui, was watching the discussion on television when he exclaimed to his wife: "Hey, that's my cousin, Ronald!" "No joke with me," she said, and he replied: "No, for real, for real."

A few months later, in July, I happened to visit Maui to give a lecture on 12 the plantation experience. While standing in the auditorium shortly before my presentation, I noticed two Japanese men approaching me. One of them draped a red carnation lei around my shoulders and smiled: "You remember me, don't you?" I had never seen this man before and was confused. Then he said again. "You remember me?" After he asked for the third time, he pulled a family photograph from a plastic shopping bag. I saw among the people in the picture my father as a young man, and burst out excitedly: "Oh, you're a Takaki!" He replied: "I'm your cousin, Minoru. I saw you on television last January and when I found out you were going to come here I wanted to see you again. You were five years old when I last saw you. I was in the army on my way to Japan and I came by your house in Palolo Valley. But I guess you don't remember. I've been wondering what happened to you for forty years." Our families had lost contact with each other because of the war, the isolation of the plantation located on another island, my father's death, and my mother's remarriage. Minoru introduced me to his brother Susumu and his son, Leighton, who works on the Puunene Plantation and represents the fourth generation of Takaki plantation workers. Afterward they took me to the Puunene Plantation, showing me McGerrow Camp, where my branch of the Takaki family had lived, and filling me with stories about the old days. "You also have two cousins, Jeanette and Lillian in Honolulu," Minoru said, "and a big Takaki family in Japan."

A year later I visited my Takaki family in Japan. On the day I arrived, my 13 cousin Nobuo showed me a box of old photographs that had been kept for decades in an upstairs closet. "We don't know who this baby is," he said, pointing to a picture of a baby boy. "That's me!" I exclaimed in disbelief. The box contained many photographs of my father, mother, sister, and me. My father had been sending pictures to the family in Kumamoto. I felt a part of me had been there all along and I had in a sense come home. Nobuo's wife Keiko told me that I was *Kumamoto kenjin*—"one of the people of Kumamoto." During my visit, I was taken to the farm where my father was born. We drove up a narrow winding road past waterfalls and streams, tea farms, and rice paddies, to a village nestled high in the mountains. The scene reminded me of old Zen paintings of Japanese landscapes and evoked memories of my mother telling me the story of Momotaro. Toshino Watanabe, an old woman in her eighties, gave me a family portrait that her sister had sent in 1915; there they were in fading sepia—my uncle Teizo, grandfather Santaro, aunt Yukino, cousin Tsutako, uncle Nobuyoshi, and father Toshio, just fourteen years old—in McGerrow Camp on the Puunene Plantation.

14    The stories of Alfred Wong and myself branch from the late history of Asian Americans and America itself—from William Hooper and Aaron Palmer, westward expansion, the economic development of California and Hawaii, the Chinese Exclusion Act, the Gentlemen's Agreement. The history of America is essentially the story of immigrants, and many of them, coming from a "different shore" than their European brethren, had sailed east to this new world. After she had traveled across the vast Pacific Ocean and settled here, a woman captured the vision of the immigrants from Asia in haiku's seventeen syllables:

> All the dreams of youth
> Shipped in emigration boats
> To reach this far shore.[10]

15    In America, Asian immigrants and their offspring have been actors in history—the first Chinese working on the plantations of Hawaii and in the gold fields of California, the early Japanese immigrants transforming the brown San Joaquin Valley into verdant farmlands, the Korean immigrants struggling to free their homeland from Japanese colonialism, the Filipino farm workers and busboys seeking the America in their hearts, the Asian-Indian immigrants picking fruit and erecting Sikh temples in the West, the American-born Asians like Jean Park and Jade Snow Wong and Monica Sone trying to find an identity for themselves as Asian Americans, the second-wave Asian immigrants bringing their skills and creating new communities as well as revitalizing old communities with culture and enterprise, and the refugees from the war-torn countries of Southeast Asia trying to put their shattered lives together and becoming our newest Asian Americans. Their dreams and hopes unfurled here before the wind, all of them— from the first Chinese miners sailing through the Golden Gate to the last Vietnamese boat people flying into Los Angeles International Airport—have been making history in America. And they have been telling us about it all along.

## COMPREHENSION

1. Why does Takaki think it important for younger Asian Americans to know about their culture?

[10]Poem by Shigeko, in Kazuo Ito, *Issei*, p. 40.

2. Why were the adults reluctant to talk about their experiences in the internment camps?
3. What does the writer mean when he says, "Asian Americans have begun to claim their time" (paragraph 5)?

## RHETORIC

1. Takaki uses poetry and dialogue in his essay. How do these devices help to advance his point of view?
2. What is the main idea of the essay? Where in the writing does it appear?
3. What use does Takaki make of historical facts and details? Cite some examples of these in the essay, and discuss what effect they have on the theme?
4. How does Takaki organize his essay? Trace his ideas through the first five paragraphs. What transitions does he use to shift focus? What is the reasoning behind this strategy?
5. Much of the information Takaki provides comes from individuals. What makes this a powerful technique? Cite examples from the essay to support your response.
6. Examine the conclusion. Why does Takaki crowd so much information into it? How does it work to reinforce his thesis?

## WRITING

1. Photographs play an important role in Takaki's essay as reminders of the past. Find an old family photograph (preferably one taken before your birth), and describe it in detail: the people in it, their relation to you, the setting, the year it was taken, and its significance to you and your family. Use details and sensory images.
2. Write a research paper about one of the major historical events mentioned in Takaki's essay (the internment of Asian Americans during WWII or the building of railroads across the United States).
3. **Writing an Argument:** Takaki claims that ethnic groups in the United States, especially Asian Americans, "must remember the past and break its silence." In an essay, argue that this effort has already been accomplished— or argue the opposite, that the effort to explore one's ethnic or racial identity must continue.

www.mhhe.com/
**mhreader**

For more information on Ronald Takaki, go to:
**More Resources > Ch. 6 History & Culture**

# Synthesis: Connections For Critical Thinking

1. Cofer writes about Latino culture and Silko about Native American culture in their respective essays. What connections do they make between their subjects and cultural affiliation and alienation? How do they present their ideas? How are their tones similar? How are they different?

2. Write an essay exploring the topic of culture and civilization in the essays by Said, Sen, and Silko.

3. Consider the current position of women in our culture. Refer to any three essays in this chapter to support your main observations.

4. How does one's experience of being an outsider or stranger to a culture affect one's understanding of that culture? Use essays from this chapter to support your key points.

5. Write an essay exploring the shape of contemporary civilization as it is reflected in the essays in this chapter. Cite specific support from at least three of the selections you have read.

6. How does a nation maintain a strong sense of self and still remain open to outside influences? Is a national identity crucial to a nation's survival? Use the opinions of representative authors in this chapter to address the question.

7. Is there such a thing as ethnic character, something that distinguishes Native Americans from African Americans, or Latinos from Asian Americans? What factors contribute to identification with culture and with nation? Cite at least three essays in this chapter.

8. Argue for or against the proposition that Americans are ignorant of both the contributions and the values of non-Western cultures in our country. Refer specifically to Reed, Hall, Said, and Takaki.

9. **Network:** Design a chat room with five class members, and discuss the differences in cultural perspectives among the writers in this chapter.

10. **Network:** Search the Web for information on Judith Ortiz Cofer and Ishmael Reed. Download appropriate material, and then write a brief research paper on their perceptions of ethnicity and the American experience.

chapter **7**

# Government, Politics, and Social Justice

*How Do We Decide What Is Fair?*

Recent studies indicate that American students have an extremely limited understanding of government and politics. In fact, one-third of all high school juniors cannot identify the main purpose of the Declaration of Independence or say in which century it was signed. This document is one of the selections in this chapter. If we are ignorant of such a basic instrument in the making of our history and society, what might that say about our concepts of citizenship? Do we now see ourselves purely as economic units—that is, in terms of our ability or potential to make money—or as consumers—that is, in terms of the roles we play in spending it? Other notable essays on government, politics, and social justice in this chapter will help us understand our cultural legacies and what has traditionally been thought of as the impetus in developing America as a country.

Skilled writers can bring politics and issues of social justice to life, enabling us to develop a sense of the various processes that have influenced the development of cultures over time. By studying the course of history and politics, we develop causal notions of how events are interrelated and how traditions have evolved. The study of history and politics can be an antidote to the continuous "present tense" of the media, which often have the power to make us believe we live from moment to moment, discouraging reflection on serious issues such as why we live the way we do and how we came to be the people we are. Essays, speeches, documents, biographies, narratives, and many other literary forms capture events and illuminate the past while holding up a mirror to the present. On the one hand, our political story can be brought to life out of the plain but painfully eloquent artifacts of oral culture. On the other, Thomas Jefferson employs classical rhetorical structures—notably argumentation—in outlining democratic vistas in the Declaration of Independence.

Even the briefest reflection will remind us of how important political processes and institutions are. Put simply, a knowledge of government and politics, and of our quest for social justice, validates our memory, a remembrance of

**438**

how important the past is to our current existence. When, for example, Martin Luther King Jr. approaches the subject of oppression from a theological perspective, we are reminded of how important the concept of freedom is to our heritage and the various ways it can be addressed. Indeed, had we been more familiar with chapters in human history, we might have avoided some of the commensurate responses to the crises in our own era. The essays in this chapter help remind us—as the philosopher Santayana warned—that "those who forget the lessons of history are doomed to repeat them."

Only with a knowledge of government and politics can we make informed choices. Through a study of government and politics, we learn about challenges and opportunities, conflicts and their resolutions, and the use and abuse of power across time in numerous cultures and civilizations. It is through the study of historical processes and political institutions that we seek to define ourselves and to learn how we have evolved.

## Previewing the Chapter

As you read the selections in this chapter and respond to them in discussion and writing, consider the following questions:

- On what specific events does the author concentrate? What is the time frame?
- What larger historical and political issues concern the author?
- From what perspective does the author treat the subject—from that of participant, observer, commentator, or some other role?
- What is the author's purpose in treating events and personalities—to explain, to instruct, to amuse, to criticize, or to celebrate?
- What does the author learn about history and politics from his or her inquiry into events?
- What sorts of conflicts—historical, political, economic, social, religious— emerge in the essay?
- Are there any correspondences among the essays? What analogies do the authors themselves draw?
- What is the relationship of people and personalities to the events under consideration?
- Which biases and ideological positions do you detect in the authors' works?
- How has your understanding of history and politics been challenged by the essays in this chapter?

# Classic and Contemporary Images

## HAVE WE MADE ADVANCES IN CIVIL RIGHTS?

*Using a Critical Perspective*   Are you optimistic or skeptical about the lofty words in the Declaration of Independence announcing that everyone is created equal? How do these two visual texts, one advertising a slave auction and the other presenting Dr. Martin Luther King Jr. and a young friend, affect your response? What aspects of these visual texts stand out? What is your emotional and ethical response to the images? What do the two illustrations tell us about the evolution of equal rights and justice in the United States?

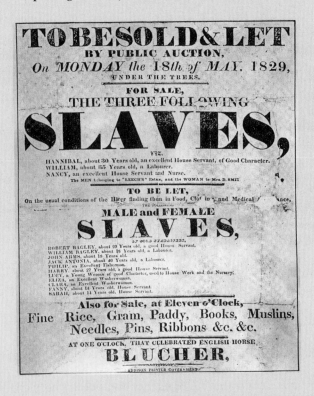

Advertisement of slaves for sale by the company Hewlett & Bright,
May 13, 1835.

Six-year-old Robin Arrington, daughter of a Miami Southern Christian
Leadership Conference attorney, leans on Dr. Martin Luther King's
shoulder as he holds a press conference, April 11, 1966, in Miami,
Florida. Dr. King arrived in Miami for a meeting
to establish a local chapter of his SCLC.

# Classic and Contemporary Essays
## WHAT IS THE AMERICAN DREAM?

Both Thomas Jefferson and Martin Luther King Jr. are now safely ensconced within the pantheon of American historical figures. The following two writing samples help indicate why. Both are concerned with perhaps the most significant issue that concerns contemporary humankind: freedom. Jefferson creates a doctrine that is powerful owing to his use of concise and powerful language, which he employs both to enumerate British offenses and to call upon his fellow Americans to revolt if need be. While his list of grievances may seem unquestionably correct to the contemporary mind, one must consider that Jefferson was a product of the Enlightenment, when philosophers had finally turned their attention to the primacy of individual rights after millennia of living under monarchic rule. King also provides us with the powerful theme of freedom in his famous speech; while his reflections address the peculiarly American racial divide, his style contains many biblical references, and his rhetoric is that of the sermon. You should consider why these two documents, regardless of their historical context, seem to be milestones in our nation's history.

# The Declaration of Independence

In Congress, July 4, 1776

## Thomas Jefferson

*Thomas Jefferson (1743–1826) was governor of Virginia during the American Revolution, America's first secretary of state, and the third president of the United States. He had a varied and monumental career as politician, public servant, scientist, architect, educator (he founded the University of Virginia), and man of letters. Jefferson attended the Continental Congress in 1775, where he wrote the rough draft of the Declaration of Independence. Other hands made contributions to the document that was signed on July 4, 1776, but the wording, style, structure, and spirit of the final version are distinctly Jefferson's. Like Thomas Paine, Benjamin Franklin, James Madison, and other major figures of the Revolutionary era, Jefferson was notable for his use of prose as an instrument for social and political change. In the Declaration of Independence, we see the direct, precise, logical, and persuasive statement of revolutionary principles that makes the document one of the best-known and best-written texts in world history. Jefferson died in his home at Monticello on July 4, 50 years to the day from the signing of the Declaration of Independence.*

When in the Course of human events it becomes necessary for one people to 1 dissolve the political bands which have connected them with another, and to assume among the powers of the earth, the separate and equal station to which the Laws of Nature and of Nature's God entitle them, a decent respect to the opinions of mankind requires that they should declare the causes which impel them to the separation.

We hold these truths to be self-evident, that all men are created equal, that 2 they are endowed by their Creator with certain unalienable Rights, that among these are Life, Liberty and the pursuit of Happiness.—That to secure these rights, Governments are instituted among Men, deriving their just powers from the consent of the governed.—That whenever any Form of Government becomes destructive of these ends, it is the Right of the People to alter or to abolish it, and to institute new Government, laying its foundation on such principles and organizing its powers in such form, as to them shall seem most likely to effect their Safety and Happiness. Prudence, indeed, will dictate that Governments long established should not be changed for light and transient causes; and accordingly all experience hath shewn that mankind are more disposed to suffer, while evils are sufferable, than to right themselves by abolishing the forms to which they are accustomed. But when a long train of abuses and usurpations, pursuing invariably the same Object evinces a design to reduce them under absolute Despotism, it is their right, it is their duty, to throw off such

Government, and to provide new Guards for their future security.—Such has been the patient sufferance of these Colonies; and such is now the necessity which constrains them to alter their former Systems of Government. The history of the present King of Great Britain is a history of repeated injuries and usurpations, all having in direct object the establishment of an absolute Tyranny over these States. To prove this, let Facts be submitted to a candid world.

3      He has refused his Assent to Laws, the most wholesome and necessary for the public good.

4      He has forbidden his Governors to pass Laws of immediate and pressing importance, unless suspended in their operation till his Assent should be obtained; and when so suspended, he has utterly neglected to attend to them.

5      He has refused to pass other Laws for the accommodation of large districts of people, unless those people would relinquish the right of Representation in the Legislature, a right inestimable to them and formidable to tyrants only.

6      He has called together legislative bodies at places unusual, uncomfortable, and distant from the depository of their public Records, for the sole purpose of fatiguing them into compliance with his measures.

7      He has dissolved Representative Houses repeatedly, for opposing with manly firmness his invasions on the rights of the people.

8      He has refused for a long time, after such dissolutions, to cause others to be elected; whereby the Legislative powers, incapable of Annihilation, have returned to the People at large for their exercise; the State remaining in the mean time exposed to all the dangers of invasion from without, and convulsions within.

9      He has endeavored to prevent the population of these States; for that purpose obstructing the Laws for Naturalization of Foreigners; refusing to pass others to encourage their migrations hither, and raising the conditions of new Appropriations of Lands.

10     He has obstructed the Administration of Justice, by refusing his Assent to Laws for establishing Judiciary powers.

11     He has made Judges dependent on his Will alone, for the tenure of their offices, and the amount and payment of their salaries.

12     He has erected a multitude of New Offices, and sent hither swarms of Officers to harass our people, and eat out their substance.

13     He has kept among us, in times of peace, Standing Armies without the Consent of our legislatures.

14     He has affected to render the Military independent of and superior to the Civil power.

15     He has combined with others to subject us to a jurisdiction foreign to our constitution, and unacknowledged by our laws; giving his Assent to their Acts of pretended Legislation:

For quartering large bodies of armed troops among us:

For protecting them, by a mock Trial, from punishment for any Murders which they should commit on the Inhabitants of these States:

For cutting off our Trade with all parts of the world:

For imposing Taxes on us without our Consent:

For depriving us in many cases, of the benefits of Trial by jury:

For transporting us beyond Seas to be tried for pretended offences:

For abolishing the free System of English Laws in a neighboring Province, establishing therein an Arbitrary government, and enlarging its Boundaries so as to render it at once an example and fit instrument for introducing the same absolute rule into these Colonies:

For taking away our Charters, abolishing our most valuable Laws and altering fundamentally the Forms of our Governments:

For suspending our own Legislatures, and declaring themselves invested with power to legislate for us in all cases whatsoever.

He has abdicated Government here, by declaring us out of his Protection 16 and waging War against us.

He has plundered our seas, ravaged our Coasts, burnt our towns, and de- 17 stroyed the lives of our people.

He is at this time transporting large Armies of foreign Mercenaries to com- 18 plete the works of death, desolation and tyranny, already begun with circumstances of Cruelty & Perfidy scarcely paralleled in the most barbarous ages, and totally unworthy the Head of a civilized nation.

He has constrained our fellow Citizens taken Captive on the high Seas to 19 bear Arms against their Country, to become the executioners of their friends and Brethren, or to fall themselves by their Hands.

He has excited domestic insurrections amongst us, and has endeavored to 20 bring on the inhabitants of our frontiers, the merciless Indian Savages, whose known rule of warfare, is an undistinguished destruction of all ages, sexes and conditions.

In every stage of these Oppressions We have Petitioned for Redress in the 21 most humble terms: Our repeated Petitions have been answered only by repeated injury. A Prince, whose character is thus marked by every act which may define a Tyrant, is unfit to be the ruler of a free people.

Nor have We been wanting in attentions to our British brethren. We have 22 warned them from time to time of attempts by their legislature to extend an unwarrantable jurisdiction over us. We have reminded them of the circumstances of our emigration and settlement here. We have appealed to their native justice and magnanimity, and we have conjured them by the ties of our common kindred to disavow these usurpations, which would inevitably interrupt our connections and correspondence. They too have been deaf to the voice of justice and of consanguinity. We must, therefore, acquiesce in the necessity, which denounces our Separation, and hold them, as we hold the rest of mankind, Enemies in War, in Peace Friends.

We, therefore, the Representatives of the United States of America, in 23 General Congress, Assembled, appealing to the Supreme Judge of the world for the rectitude of our intentions, do, in the Name, and by Authority of the good

People of these Colonies, solemnly publish and declare, That these United Colonies are, and of Right ought to be Free and Independent States; that they are Absolved from all Allegiance to the British Crown, and that all political connection between them and the State of Great Britain, is and ought to be totally dissolved; and that as Free and Independent States, they have full Power to levy War, conclude Peace, contract Alliances, establish Commerce, and to do all other Acts and Things which Independent States may of right do. And for the support of this Declaration, with a firm reliance on the protection of divine Providence, we mutually pledge to each other our Lives, our Fortunes and our sacred Honor.

## COMPREHENSION

1. Explain Jefferson's main and subordinate purposes in this document.
2. What is Jefferson's key assertion or argument? Mention several reasons that he gives to support his argument.
3. Summarize Jefferson's definition of human nature and government.

## RHETORIC

1. There are many striking words and phrases in the Declaration of Independence, notably in the beginning. Locate three such examples, and explain their connotative power and effectiveness.
2. Jefferson and his colleagues had to draft a document designed for several audiences. What audiences did they have in mind? How do their language and style reflect their awareness of multiple audiences?
3. The Declaration of Independence is a classic model of syllogistic reasoning and deductive argument (see the Glossary). What is its major premise, and where is this premise stated? The minor premise? The conclusion?
4. What sort of inductive evidence does Jefferson offer?
5. Why is the middle portion, or body, of the Declaration of Independence considerably longer than the introduction or conclusion? What holds the body together?
6. Explain the function and effect of parallel structure in this document.

## WRITING

1. Discuss the relevance of the Declaration of Independence to politics today.
2. Explain in an essay why the Declaration of Independence is a model of effective prose.
3. Write your own declaration of independence—from family, employer, required courses, or the like. Develop this declaration as an op-ed piece for a newspaper.

4. **Writing an Argument:** Do you believe that "all men are created equal"? Justify your answer in an argumentative essay.

|  www.mhhe.com/ **mhreader** | For more information on Thomas Jefferson, go to: **More Resources > Ch. 7 Government & Politics** |

# I Have a Dream

## Martin Luther King Jr.

*Martin Luther King Jr. (1929–1968) was born in Atlanta, Georgia, and received degrees from Morehouse College, Crozer Theological Seminary, Boston University, and Chicago Theological Seminary. As Baptist clergyman, civil rights leader, founder and president of the Southern Christian Leadership Conference, and 1964 Nobel Peace Prize winner, King was a celebrated advocate of nonviolent resistance to achieve equality and racial integration in the world. King was a gifted orator and a highly persuasive writer. His books include* Stride toward Freedom *(1958),* Letter from Birmingham City Jail *(1963),* Strength to Love *(1963),* Why We Can't Wait *(1964), and* Where Do We Go from Here: Chaos or Community? *(1967), a book published shortly before he was assassinated on April 4, 1968, in Memphis, Tennessee. This selection, a milestone of American oratory, was the keynote address at the March on Washington, August 28, 1963.*

I am happy to join with you today in what will go down in history as the greatest demonstration for freedom in the history of our nation.   1

Fivescore years ago, a great American, in whose symbolic shadow we stand   2
today, signed the Emancipation Proclamation. This momentous decree came as a great beacon light of hope to millions of Negro slaves who had been seared in the flames of withering injustice. It came as a joyous daybreak to end the long night of their captivity.

But one hundred years later, the Negro still is not free; one hundred years   3
later, the life of the Negro is still sadly crippled by the manacles of segregation and the chains of discrimination; one hundred years later, the Negro lives on a lonely island of poverty in the midst of a vast ocean of material prosperity; one hundred years later, the Negro is still languishing in the corners of American society and finds himself in exile in his own land.

So we've come here today to dramatize a shameful condition. In a sense   4
we've come to our nation's capital to cash a check. When the architects of our republic wrote the magnificent words of the Constitution and the Declaration of Independence, they were signing a promissory note to which every American

was to fall heir. This note was the promise that all men, yes, black men as well as white men, would be guaranteed the unalienable rights of life, liberty, and the pursuit of happiness.

5    It is obvious today that America has defaulted on this promissory note in so far as her citizens of color are concerned. Instead of honoring this sacred obligation, America has given the Negro people a bad check; a check which has come back marked "insufficient funds." We refuse to believe that there are insufficient funds in the great vaults of opportunity of this nation. And so we've come to cash this check, a check that will give us upon demand the riches of freedom and the security of justice.

6    We have also come to this hallowed spot to remind America of the fierce urgency of now. This is no time to engage in the luxury of cooling off or to take the tranquilizing drug of gradualism. Now is the time to make real the promises of democracy; now is the time to rise from the dark and desolate valley of segregation to the sunlit path of racial justice; now is the time to lift our nation from the quicksands of racial injustice to the solid rock of brotherhood; now is the time to make justice a reality for all God's children. It would be fatal for the nation to overlook the urgency of the moment. This sweltering summer of the Negro's legitimate discontent will not pass until there is an invigorating autumn of freedom and equality.

7    Nineteen sixty-three is not an end, but a beginning. And those who hope that the Negro needed to blow off steam and will now be content, will have a rude awakening if the nation returns to business as usual.

8    There will be neither rest nor tranquility in America until the Negro is granted his citizenship rights. The whirlwinds of revolt will continue to shake the foundations of our nation until the bright day of justice emerges.

9    But there is something that I must say to my people who stand on the warm threshold which leads into the palace of justice. In the process of gaining our rightful place we must not be guilty of wrongful deeds.

10   Let us not seek to satisfy our thirst for freedom by drinking from the cup of bitterness and hatred. We must forever conduct our struggle on the high plane of dignity and discipline. We must not allow our creative protest to degenerate into physical violence. Again and again we must rise to the majestic heights of meeting physical force with soul force.

11   The marvelous new militancy which has engulfed the Negro community must not lead us to a distrust of all white people, for many of our white brothers, as evidenced by their presence here today, have come to realize that their destiny is tied up with our destiny and they have come to realize that their freedom is inextricably bound to our freedom. This offense we share mounted to storm the battlements of injustice must be carried forth by a biracial army. We cannot walk alone.

12   And as we walk, we must make the pledge that we shall always march ahead. We cannot turn back. There are those who are asking the devotees of civil rights, "When will you be satisfied?" We can never be satisfied as long as the Negro is the victim of the unspeakable horrors of police brutality.

13   We can never be satisfied as long as our bodies, heavy with fatigue of travel, cannot gain lodging in the motels of the highways and the hotels of the cities.

We cannot be satisfied as long as the Negro's basic mobility is from a smaller ghetto to a larger one.

We can never be satisfied as long as our children are stripped of their self-  14 hood and robbed of their dignity by signs stating "for whites only." We cannot be satisfied as long as a Negro in Mississippi cannot vote and a Negro in New York believes he has nothing for which to vote. No, we are not satisfied, and we will not be satisfied until justice rolls down like waters and righteousness like a mighty stream.

I am not unmindful that some of you have come here out of excessive trials  15 and tribulation. Some of you have come fresh from narrow jail cells. Some of you have come from areas where your quest for freedom left you battered by the storms of persecution and staggered by the winds of police brutality. You have been the veterans of creative suffering. Continue to work with the faith that unearned suffering is redemptive.

Go back to Mississippi; go back to Alabama; go back to South Carolina; go  16 back to Georgia; go back to Louisiana; go back to the slums and ghettos of the northern cities, knowing that somehow this situation can, and will be changed. Let us not wallow in the valley of despair.

So I say to you, my friends, that even though we must face the difficul-  17 ties of today and tomorrow, I still have a dream. It is a dream deeply rooted in the American dream that one day this nation will rise up and live out the true meaning of its creed—we hold these truths to be self-evident, that all men are created equal.

I have a dream that one day on the red hills of Georgia, sons of former  18 slaves and sons of former slave-owners will be able to sit down together at the table of brotherhood.

I have a dream that one day, even the state of Mississippi, a state sweltering  19 with the heat of injustice, sweltering with the heat of oppression, will be transformed into an oasis of freedom and justice.

I have a dream my four little children will one day live in a nation where  20 they will not be judged by the color of their skin but by the content of their character. I have a dream today!

I have a dream that one day, down in Alabama, with its vicious racists,  21 with its governor having his lips dripping with the words of interposition and nullification, that one day, right there in Alabama, little black boys and black girls will be able to join hands with little white boys and white girls as sisters and brothers. I have a dream today!

I have a dream that one day every valley shall be exalted, every hill and  22 mountain shall be made low, the rough places shall be made plain, and the crooked places shall be made straight and the glory of the Lord will be revealed and all flesh shall see it together.

This is our hope. This is the faith that I go back to the South with.  23

With this faith we will be able to hear out of the mountain of despair a  24 stone of hope. With this faith we will be able to transform the jangling discords of our nation into a beautiful symphony of brotherhood.

25    With this faith we will be able to work together, to pray together, to struggle together, to go to jail together, to stand up for freedom together, knowing that we will be free one day. This will be the day when all of God's children will be able to sing with new meaning—"my country 'tis of thee; sweet land of liberty; of thee I sing; land where my fathers died, land of the pilgrims' pride; from every mountain side, let freedom ring"—and if America is to be a great nation, this must become true.

26    So let freedom ring from the prodigious hilltops of New Hampshire.

27    Let freedom ring from the mighty mountains of New York.

28    Let freedom ring from the heightening Alleghenies of Pennsylvania.

29    Let freedom ring from the snow-capped Rockies of Colorado.

30    Let freedom ring from the curvaceous slopes of California.

31    But not only that.

32    Let freedom ring from Stone Mountain of Georgia.

33    Let freedom ring from Lookout Mountain of Tennessee.

34    Let freedom ring from every hill and molehill of Mississippi, from every mountainside, let freedom ring.

35    And when we allow freedom to ring, when we let it ring from every village and hamlet, from every state and city, we will be able to speed up that day when all of God's children—black men and white men, Jews and Gentiles, Catholics and Protestants—will be able to join hands and to sing in the words of the old Negro spiritual, "Free at last, free at last; thank God Almighty, we are free at last."

## COMPREHENSION

1. What is the main purpose of this speech? Where does King state this purpose most clearly?
2. Why does King make use of "fivescore years ago" (paragraph 2)? How is this more appropriate than simply saying "a hundred years ago"?
3. Who is King's audience? Where does he acknowledge the special historical circumstances influencing his speech?

## RHETORIC

1. From what sources does King adapt phrases to give his work allusive richness?
2. What do the terms *interposition* and *nullification* (paragraph 21) mean? What is their historical significance?
3. Why does King make use of repetition? Does this technique work well in print? Explain.
4. What is the purpose of the extended metaphor in paragraphs 4 and 5? Which point in paragraph 3 does it refer to?
5. In which paragraphs does King address the problems of African Americans?
6. Why is this selection titled "I Have a Dream"? How do dreams serve as a motif for this speech?

## WRITING

1. "I Have a Dream" is considered by many people to be among the greatest speeches delivered by an American. Do you think it deserves to be? Explain in an essay.
2. Write a comparative essay analyzing King's assessment of black Americans' condition in 1963 and their condition today. What do you think King would say if he knew of contemporary conditions?
3. Write your own "I Have a Dream" essay, basing it on your vision of America or of a special people.
4. **Writing an Argument:** Prepare a newspaper editorial advocating a solution to one aspect of racial, ethnic, or sexual injustice.

 **www.mhhe.com/ mhreader** | For more information on Martin Luther King Jr., go to: **More Resources > Ch. 7 Government & Politics**

### Synthesis:  Classic  and  Contemporary Questions  for  Comparison

1. Compare the Declaration of Independence with King's speech in terms of language, style, and content. Are they equally powerful and resonant? Cite specific passages from the essays to illustrate your response.
2. Rewrite the Declaration of Independence in modern English as you believe Dr. King might, reflecting his concerns about the African American and other minorities in this country. Include a list of grievances similar to the ones concerning British rule.
3. Write a research paper about the lives and times of King and Jefferson. Compare and contrast any significant events or pertinent biographical data in their backgrounds.

# Is Texas America?

## Molly Ivins

*Molly Ivins (1944–2007), a humorous and typically irreverent newspaper commentator whose syndicated column appeared in about 350 newspapers, was born in California but grew up in Texas. The Lone Star State—and especially the Bush family—animated Ivins's writing and prompted her satirical assessment of Texas;*

*its people, politics, and culture. She called Texas the Great State, "reactionary, can-
tankerous, and hilarious." Growing up in an affluent family, she learned to confront
her conservative Republican father, arguing with him over civil rights and the
Vietnam War. Ivins attended Smith College and the Institute for Political Science in
Paris before earning a master's degree at the Columbia Graduate School of Journalism. She worked for several newspapers, including* The New York Times *and the
monthly* Texas Observer, *and published six books, among them* Molly Ivins Can't
Say That, Can She? *(1991) and two books on George Bush,* Shrub: The Short but
Happy Life of George Bush *(2000) and* Bushwacked *(2003). "There are two
kinds of humor," Ivins once observed; one "makes us chuckle about our foibles and
shared humanity. The other kind holds people up to public contempt and ridicule.
That's what I do." In fact, the following essay, published in* The Nation *in 2003,
indicates that Ivins is adept at both kinds of humor.*

1    Well, sheesh. I don't know whether to warn you that because George Dubya
Bush is President the whole damn country is about to be turned into Texas (a
singularly horrible fate: as the country song has it: "Lubbock on Everythang")
or if I should try to stand up for us and convince the rest of the country we're
not all that insane.

2    Truth is, I've spent much of my life trying, unsuccessfully, to explode the
myths about Texas. One attempts to explain—with all good will, historical evidence, nasty statistics and just a bow of recognition to our racism—that Texas is
not *The Alamo* starring John Wayne. We're not *Giant*, we ain't a John Ford western. The first real Texan I ever saw on TV was *King of the Hill's* Boomhauer, the
guy who's always drinking beer and you can't understand a word he says.

3    So, how come trying to explode myths about Texas always winds up reinforcing them? After all these years, I do not think it is my fault. The fact is, it's a
damned peculiar place. Given all the horseshit, there's bound to be a pony in
here somewhere. Just by trying to be honest about it, one accidentally under-
lines its sheer strangeness.

4    Here's the deal on Texas. It's big. So big there's about five distinct and different places here, separated from one another geologically, topographically, botani-
cally, ethnically, culturally and climatically. Hence our boring habit of specifying
East, West and South Texas, plus the Panhandle and the Hill Country. The majority of the state's blacks live in East Texas, making it more like the Old South than
the Old South is anymore. West Texas is, more or less, like *Giant*, except, like every
place else in the state, it has an incurable tendency toward the tacky and all the
cowboys are brown. South Texas is 80 percent Hispanic and a weird amalgam of
cultures. You get names now like Shannon Rodriguez, Hannah Gonzalez and Tiffany Ruiz. Even the Anglos speak English with a Spanish accent. The Panhandle,
which sticks up to damn near Kansas, is High Plains, like one of those square
states, Nebraska or the Dakotas, except more brown folks. The Hill Country,
smack dab in the middle, resembles nothing else in the state.

5    Plus, plopped on top of all this, we have three huge cities, all among the ten
largest in the country. Houston is Los Angeles with the climate of Calcutta,

Copyright © 2002 by Karen Caldicott.

Dallas is Dutch (clean, orderly and conformist), while San Antonio is Monterrey North. Many years ago I wrote of this state: "The reason the sky is bigger here is because there aren't any trees. The reason folks here eat grits is because they ain't got no taste. Cowboys mostly stink and it's hot, oh God, is it hot. . . . Texas is a mosaic of cultures, which overlap in several parts of the state, with the darker layers on the bottom. The cultures are black, Chicano, Southern, freak, suburban and shitkicker. (Shitkicker is dominant.) They are all rotten for women." All that's changed in thirty years is that suburban is now dominant, shitkicker isn't so ugly as it once was and the freaks are now Goths or something. So it could be argued we're becoming more civilized.

In fact, it was always easy to argue that: Texas has symphony orchestras 6 and great universities and perfect jewels of art museums (mostly in Fort Worth, of all places). It has lots of people who birdwatch, write PhD theses on esoteric subjects and speak French, for chrissake. But what still makes Texas Texas is that it's ignorant, cantankerous and ridiculously friendly. Texas is still resistant to Howard Johnsons, Interstate highways and some forms of phoniness. It is the place least likely to become a replica of everyplace else. It's authentically awful, comic and weirdly charming, all at the same time.

Culturally, Texans rather resemble both Alaskans (hunt, fish, hate govern- 7 ment) and Australians (drink beer, hate snobs). The food is quite good— Mexican, barbecue, chili, shrimp and chicken-fried steak, an acquired taste. The music is country, blues, folk mariachi, rockabilly and everything else you can think of. Mexican music—norteño, ranchero—is poised to cross over, as black music did in the 1950s.

If you want to understand George W. Bush—unlike his daddy, an unfortu- 8 nate example of a truly Texas-identified citizen—you have to stretch your imagination around a weird Texas amalgam: religion, anti-intellectualism and machismo. All big, deep strains here, but still an odd combination. Then add that Bush is just another li'l upper-class white boy out trying to prove he's tough.

9  The politics are probably the weirdest thing about Texas. The state has gone from one-party Democrat to one-party Republican in thirty years. Lyndon said when he signed the Civil Rights Act in 1964 that it would take two generations and cost the Democrats the South. Right on both counts. We like to think we're "past race" in Texas, but of course East Texas remains an ugly, glaring exception. After James Byrd Jr. was dragged to death near Jasper, only one prominent white politician attended his funeral—US Senator Kay Bailey Hutchison. Dubya, then governor, put the kibosh on the anti–hate crimes bill named in Byrd's memory. (The deal-breaker for Bush was including gays and lesbians. At a meeting last year of the Texas Civil Liberties Union board, vicious hate crimes against gays in both Dallas and Houston were discussed. I asked the board member from Midland if they'd been having any trouble with gay-bashing out there. "Hell, honey," she said, with that disastrous frankness one can grow so fond of, "there's not a gay in Midland would come out of the closet for fear people would think they're a Democrat.")

10     Among the various strains of Texas right-wingism (it is factually incorrect to call it conservatism) is some leftover loony John Birchism, now morphed into militias; country-club economic conservatism, à la George Bush *père*; and the usual batty antigovernment strain. Of course Texas grew on the tender mercies of the federal government—rural electrification, dams, generations of master pork-barrel politicians and vast subsidies to the oil and gas industry. But that has never interfered with Texans' touching but entirely erroneous belief that this is the Frontier, and that in the Old West every man pulled his own weight and depended on no one else. The myth of rugged individualism continues to afflict a generation raised entirely in suburbs with names like "Flowering Forest Hills of Lubbock."

11     The Populist movement was born in the Texas Hill Country, as genuinely democratic an uprising as this country has ever known. It produced legendary politicians for generations, including Ralph Yarborough, Sam Rayburn, Lyndon and even into the 1990s, with Agriculture Commissioner Jim Hightower. I think it is not gone, but only sleeping.

12  Texans retain an exaggerated sense of state identification, routinely identifying themselves when abroad as Texans, rather than Americans or from the United States. That aggravated provincialism has three sources. First, the state is so big (though not so big as Alaska, as they are sure to remind us) that it can take a couple of days hard travel just to get out of it. Second, we reinforce the sense of difference by requiring kids to study Texas history, including roughly ten years as an independent country. In state colleges, the course in Texas government is mandatory. Third, even national advertising campaigns pitch brands with a Texas accent here and certain products, like the pickup truck, are almost invariably sold with a Texas pitch. (Makes sense: Texas leads the nation with more than four million registered pickups.)

13     The founding myth is the Alamo. I was raised on the Revised Standard Version, which holds that while it was stupid of Travis and the gang to be there at

all (Sam Houston told them to get the hell out), it was still an amazing last stand. Stephen Harrigan in *The Gates of the Alamo* is closer to reality, but even he admits in the end there was something romantic and even noble about the episode, like having served in the Abraham Lincoln Brigade during the Spanish Civil War.

According to the demographers at Texas A&M (itself a source of much Texas 14 lore), Texas will become "majority minority" in 2008. Unfortunately, we won't see it in the voting patterns for at least a generation, and by then the Republicans will have the state so tied up by redistricting (recently the subject of a massive standoff, now over, in the legislature), it's unlikely to shift for another generation beyond that. The Christian right is heavily dominant in the Texas Republican Party. It was the genius of Karl Rove/George W. Bush to straddle the divide between the Christian right and the country club conservatives, which is actually a significant class split. The politics of resentment plays a large role on the Christian right: Fundamentalists are perfectly aware that they are held in contempt by "the intellectuals." (William Brann of Waco once observed, "The trouble with our Texas Baptists is that we do not hold them under water long enough." He was shot to death by an irate Baptist.) In Texas, "intellectual" is often used as a synonym for "snob." George W. Bush perfectly exemplifies that attitude.

Here in the National Laboratory for Bad Government, we have an anti- 15 quated and regressive tax structure—high property, high sales, no income tax. We consistently rank near the bottom by every measure of social service, education and quality of life (leading to one of our state mottoes, "Thank God for Mississippi"). Yet the state is incredibly rich in more than natural resources. The economy is now fully diversified, so plunges in the oil market can no longer throw the state into the bust cycle.

It is widely believed in Texas that the highest purpose of government is to 16 create "a healthy bidness climate." The legislature is so dominated by special interests that the gallery where the lobbyists sit is called "the owners' box." The consequences of unregulated capitalism, of special interests being able to buy government through campaign contributions, are more evident here because Texas is "first and worst" in this area. That Enron was a Texas company is no accident: Texas was also Ground Zero in the savings-and-loan scandals, is continually the site of major ripoffs by the insurance industry and has a rich history of gigantic chicanery going way back. Leland Beatty, an agricultural consultant, calls Enron "Billie Sol Estes Goes to College." Economists call it "control fraud" when a corporation is rotten from the head down. I sometimes think Texas government is a case of control fraud too.

We are currently saddled with a right-wing ideologue sugar daddy, James 17 Leininger out of San Antonio, who gives immense campaign contributions and wants school vouchers, abstinence education and the like in return. The result is a crew of breathtakingly right-wing legislators. This session, Representative Debbie Riddle of Houston said during a hearing, "Where did this idea come from that everybody deserves free education, free medical care, free whatever? It comes from Moscow, from Russia. It comes straight out of the pit of hell."

18   Texans for Lawsuit Reform, *a k a* the bidness lobby, is a major player and has
     effectively eviscerated the judiciary with a two-pronged attack. While round
     after round of "tort reform" was shoved through the legislature, closing off ac-
     cess to the courts and protecting corporations from liability for their misdeeds,
     Karl Rove was busy electing all nine state Supreme Court justices. So even if
     you should somehow manage to get into court, you are faced with a bench
     noted for its canine fidelity to corporate special interests.

19       Here's how we make progress in Texas. Two summers ago, Governor
     Goodhair Perry (the man has a head of hair every Texan can be proud of, re-
     gardless of party) appointed an Enron executive to the Public Utilities Commis-
     sion. The next day, Governor Goodhair got a $25,000 check from Ken Lay. Some
     thought there might be a connection. The guv was forced to hold a press confer-
     ence, at which he explained that the whole thing was "totally coincidental." So
     that was a big relief.

20       We don't have a sunshine law in Texas; it's more like a partly cloudy law.
     But even here a major state appointee has to fill out a bunch of forms that are
     then public record. When the governor's office put out the forms on the Enron
     guy, members of the press, that alert guardian watchdog of democracy, noticed
     that the question about any unfortunate involvement with law enforcement
     looked funny. The governor's office had whited out the answers. A sophisti-
     cated cover-up. The alert guardian watch dogs were on the trail. We soon un-
     covered a couple of minor traffic violations and the following item: While out
     hunting a few years ealier, the Enron guy accidentally shot a whooping crane.
     As a result he had to pay a $15,000 fine under what is known in Texas as the In
     Danger Species Act. We print this. A state full of sympathetic hunters reacted
     with, "Hell, anybody could accidentally shoot a whooper." But the press stayed
     on the story and was able to report that the guy shot the whooper while on a
     goose hunt. Now the whooper is a large bird—runs up to five feet tall. The
     goose—short. Now we have a state full of hunters saying, "Hell, if this boy is
     too dumb to tell a whooper from a goose, maybe he shouldn't be regulatin'
     public utilities." He was forced to resign.

21       As Willie Nelson sings, if we couldn't laugh, we would all go insane. This
     is our redeeming social value and perhaps our one gift to progressives outside
     our borders. We do laugh. We have no choice. We have to have fun while try-
     ing to stave off the forces of darkness because we hardly ever win, so it's the
     only fun we get to have. We find beer and imagination helpful. The Billion
     Bubba March, the Spam-o-rama, the time we mooned the Klan, being embed-
     ded with the troops at the Holiday Inn in Ardmore, Oklahoma, singing "I'm
     Just an Asshole from El Paso" with Kinky Friedman and the Texas Jewboys,
     and "Up Against the Wall, Redneck Mother" with Ray Wylie Hubbard laugh-
     ing at the loonies in the lege—does it get better than this? The late Bill Kugle of
     Athens is buried in the Texas State Cemetery. On the front of his stone are listed
     his service in the Marines in World War II, his years in the legislature, other
     titles and honors. On the back of the stone is, "He never voted for a Republican
     and never had much to do with them either."

We have lost some great freedom fighters in Texas during the past year.  22
Billie Carr, the great Houston political organizer (you'd've loved her: She got
invited to the White House during the middle of the Monica mess, sashayed
through the receiving line, looked Bill Clinton in the eye and said, "You dumb
son of a bitch"), always said she wanted her funeral to be like her whole life in
politics: It should start half an hour late, she wanted a balanced delegation of
pallbearers—one black, one brown, two women—and she wanted an open cas-
ket and a name tag stuck over her left tit that said, "Hi there! My name is Billie
Carr." We did it all for her.

At the funeral of Malcolm McGregor, the beloved legislator and bibliophile  23
from El Paso, we heard "The Eyes of Texas" and the Aggie War Hymn played
on the bagpipes. At the service for Maury Maverick Jr. of San Antonio, and at
his request, J. Frank Dobie's poem "The Mustangs" was read by the poet Naomi
Shihab Nye. The last stanza is:

> So sometimes yet, in the realities of silence and solitude,
> For a few people unhampered a while by things,
> The mustangs walk out with dawn, stand high, then
> Sweep away, wild with sheer life, and free, free, free—
> Free of all confines of time and flesh.

## COMPREHENSION

1. How does Ivins answer the question posed by her title? In other words,
   what does Texas have that the United States in general possesses? What,
   according to Ivins, is unique about Texas?
2. In paragraph 9, Ivins writes, "The politics are probably the weirdest thing
   about Texas." What examples does she give to support her statement?
3. Ivins seems to warn us about the excesses of Texas life and politics, but
   clearly she is also fascinated by her home state. Does she reconcile these
   conflicting perspectives? Why or why not?

## RHETORIC

1. What is Ivins's claim or main proposition? What are her minor propositions?
   Do you think that her argument is sound or valid? Justify your response.
2. How does Ivins establish herself as an authority on Texas? Would you ac-
   cuse her of bias? Why or why not? Why might her opinions be congenial to
   an audience reading *The Nation*?
3. Ivins uses phrases like "Well, sheesh" (paragraph 1), "plopped on
   top"(paragraph 5), and "for crissake" (paragraph 6) in the essay. What is
   the effect of this colloquial style and tone? What is her purpose?
4. Locate varieties of humor in the essay. Do you think that Ivins employs
   humor effectively to advance her argument? Explain your response.

5. The essay contains four main sections. What is the core topic of each section? How do these topics overlap? What transitions serve to link the parts?
6. Throughout the essay, Ivins alludes to many aspects of Texas life, culture, people, and politics that we might not be familiar with. Do these allusions detract from the essay or make it too topical? Why, for instance, would Ivins want to end her essay with reference to the deaths of two Texans and an allusion to a poem by J. Frank Dobie?

### WRITING

1. Write a humorous essay on the state in which you grew up. Decide in advance what varieties of humor and what tone you want to use.
2. Go online or to a library and find out more about a Texan (for instance, George W. Bush), a Texas trait (like *machismo*), or a Texas institution (for example, the state legislature), and then write an essay that seeks to either confirm or refute Ivins's presentation of the subject.
3. **Writing an Argument:** In an essay, argue for or against the proposition that Ivins is too biased and cruel in her exposé of Texas. Defend or refute her argument on a point-by-point basis.

---

www.mhhe.com/ **mhreader**     For more information on Molly Ivins, go to:
**More Resources > Ch. 7 Government & Politics**

---

# Cyberspace: If You Don't Love It, Leave It

## Esther Dyson

*Esther Dyson (b. 1951) was born in Zurich, Switzerland; grew up in Princeton, New Jersey; and received a BA in economics from Harvard University. She is the daughter of Freeman Dyson, a physicist prominent in arms control. She is the editor and publisher of the widely respected computer newsletter* Release 1.0, *which is circulated to many computer industry leaders. She is also chairperson of the Electronic Frontier Foundation and on the board of the Santa Fe Institute, the Global Business Network, and the Institute for East/West Studies. She served as a reporter for* Forbes *magazine for four years. The following essay appeared in* The New York Times Magazine *in July 1995. In it, Dyson defends the free-market approach to cyberspace content, arguing that regulation of the Internet is simply impossible and counterproductive.*

Something in the American psyche loves new frontiers. We hanker after wide-open spaces; we like to explore; we like to make rules instead of follow them. But in this age of political correctness and other intrusions on our national cult of independence, it's hard to find a place where you can go and be yourself without worrying about the neighbors.

There is such a place: cyberspace. Lost in the furor over porn on the Net is the exhilarating sense of freedom that this new frontier once promised—and still does in some quarters. Formerly a playground for computer nerds and techies, cyberspace now embraces every conceivable constituency: schoolchildren, flirtatious singles, Hungarian-Americans, accountants—along with pederasts and porn fans. Can they all get along? Or will our fear of kids surfing for cyberporn behind their bedroom doors provoke a crackdown?

The first order of business is to grasp what cyberspace *is*. It might help to leave behind metaphors of highways and frontiers and to think instead of real estate. Real estate, remember, is an intellectual, legal, artificial environment constructed *on top of* land. Real estate recognizes the difference between parkland and shopping mall, between red-light zone and school district, between church, state and drugstore.

In the same way, you could think of cyberspace as a giant and unbounded world of virtual real estate. Some property is privately owned and rented out; other property is common land; some places are suitable for children, and others are best avoided by all but the kinkiest citizens. Unfortunately, it's those places that are now capturing the popular imagination: places that offer bomb-making instructions, pornography, advice on how to procure stolen credit cards. They make cyberspace sound like a nasty place. Good citizens jump to a conclusion: Better regulate it.

The most recent manifestation of this impulse is the Exon-Coats Amendment, a well-meaning but misguided bill drafted by Senators Jim Exon, Democrat of Nebraska, and Daniel R. Coats, Republican of Indiana, to make cyberspace "safer" for children. Part of the telecommunications reform bill passed by the Senate and awaiting consideration by the House, the amendment would outlaw making "indecent communication" available to anyone under 18.[1] Then there's the Amateur Action bulletin board case, in which the owners of a porn service in Milpitas, Calif., were convicted in a Tennessee court of violating "community standards" after a local postal inspector requested that the material be transmitted to him.

Regardless of how many laws or lawsuits are launched, regulation won't work.

---

[1] The Communications Decency Act (CDA) was passed by Congress, but the Supreme Court ruled that it was unconstitutional in 1996.

7     Aside from being unconstitutional, using censorship to counter indecency and other troubling "speech" fundamentally misinterprets the nature of cyberspace. Cyberspace isn't a frontier where wicked people can grab unsuspecting children, nor is it a giant television system that can beam offensive messages at unwilling viewers. In this kind of real estate, users have to *choose* where they visit, what they see, what they do. It's optional, and it's much easier to bypass a place on the Net than it is to avoid walking past an unsavory block of stores on the way to your local 7-Eleven.

8     Put plainly, cyberspace is a voluntary destination—in reality, many destinations. You don't just get "onto the net"; you have to go someplace in particular. That means that people can choose where to go and what to see. Yes, community standards should be enforced, but those standards should be set by cyberspace communities themselves, not by the courts or by politicians in Washington. What we need isn't Government control over all these electronic communities: We need self-rule.

9  What makes cyberspace so alluring is precisely the way in which it's *different* from shopping malls, television, highways and other terrestrial jurisdictions. But let's define the territory:

10     First, there are private e-mail conversations, akin to the conversations you have over the telephone or voice mail. These are private and consensual and require no regulation at all.

11     Second, there are information and entertainment services, where people can download anything from legal texts and lists of "great new restaurants" to game software or dirty pictures. These places are like bookstores, malls and movie houses—places where you go to buy something. The customer needs to request an item or sign up for a subscription; stuff (especially pornography) is not sent out to people who don't ask for it. Some of these services are free or included as part of a broader service like Compuserve or America Online; others charge and may bill their customers directly.

12     Third, there are "real" communities—groups of people who communicate among themselves. In real-estate terms, they're like bars or restaurants or bathhouses. Each active participant contributes to a general conversation, generally through posted messages. Other participants may simply listen or watch. Some are supervised by a moderator; others are more like bulletin boards—anyone is free to post anything. Many of these services started out unmoderated but are now imposing rules to keep out unwanted advertising, extraneous discussions or increasingly rude participants. Without a moderator, the decibel level often gets too high.

13     Ultimately, it's the rules that determine the success of such places. Some of the rules are determined by the supplier of content; some of the rules concern prices and membership fees. The rules may be simple: "Only high-quality content about oil-industry liability and pollution legislation: $120 an hour." Or: "This forum is unmoderated, and restricted to information about copyright issues. People who insist on posting advertising or unrelated material

will be asked to desist (and may eventually be barred)." Or: "Only children 8 to 12, on school-related topics and only clean words. The moderator will decide what's acceptable."

Cyberspace communities evolve just the way terrestrial communities do: people with like-minded interests band together. Every cyberspace community has its own character. Overall, the communities on Compuserve tend to be more techy or professional; those on America Online, affluent young singles; Prodigy, family oriented. Then there are independents like Echo, a hip, downtown New York service, or Women's Wire, targeted to women who want to avoid the male culture prevalent elsewhere on the Net. There's Surf-Watch, a new program allowing access only to locations deemed suitable for children. On the Internet itself, there are lots of passionate noncommercial discussion groups on topics ranging from Hungarian politics (Hungary-Online) to copyright law.  14

And yes, there are also porn-oriented services, where people share dirty pictures and communicate with one another about all kinds of practices, often anonymously. Whether these services encourage the fantasies they depict is subject to debate—the same debate that has raged about pornography in other media. But the point is that no one is forcing this stuff on anybody.  15

What's unique about cyberspace is that it liberates us from the tyranny of government, where everyone lives by the rule of the majority. In a democracy, minority groups and minority preferences tend to get squeezed out, whether they are minorities of race and culture or minorities of individual taste. Cyberspace allows communities of any size and kind to flourish; in cyberspace, communities are chosen by the users, not forced on them by accidents of geography. This freedom gives the rules that preside in cyberspace a moral authority that rules in terrestrial environments don't have. Most people are stuck in the country of their birth, but if you don't like the rules of a cyberspace community, you can just sign off. Love it or leave it. Likewise, if parents don't like the rules of a given cyberspace community, they can restrict their children's access to it.  16

What's likely to happen in cyberspace is the formation of new communities, free of the constraints that cause conflict on earth. Instead of a global village, which is a nice dream but impossible to manage, we'll have invented another world of self-contained communities that cater to their own members' inclinations without interfering with anyone else's. The possibility of a real market-style evolution of governance is at hand. In cyberspace, we'll be able to test and evolve rules governing what needs to be governed—intellectual property, content and access control, rules about privacy and free speech. Some communities will allow anyone in; others will restrict access to members who qualify on one basis or another. Those communities that prove self-sustaining will prosper (and perhaps grow and split into subsets with ever-more-particular interests and identities). Those that can't survive—either because people lose interest or get scared off—will simply wither away.  17

In the near future, explorers in cyberspace will need to get better at defining and identifying their communities. They will need to put in place—and  18

accept—their own local governments, just as the owners of expensive real estate often prefer to have their own security guards rather than call in the police.
But they will rarely need help from any terrestrial government.

19      Of course, terrestrial governments may not agree. What to do, for instance, about pornography? The answer is labeling—not banning—
questionable material. In order to avoid censorship and lower the political
temperature, it makes sense for cyberspace participants themselves to agree
on a scheme for questionable items, so that people or automatic filters can
avoid them. In other words, posting pornography in "alt.sex.bestiality"
would be OK; it's easy enough for software manufacturers to build an automatic filter that would prevent you—or your child—from ever seeing that
item on a menu. (It's as if all the items were wrapped with labels on the
wrapper.) Someone who posted the same material under the title "Kid-Fun"
could be sued for mislabeling.

20      Without a lot of fanfare, private enterprises and local groups are already
producing a variety of labeling and ranking services, along with kid-oriented
sites like Kidlink, EdWeb and Kids' Space. People differ in their tastes and values and can find services or reviewers on the Net that suit them in the same
way they select books and magazines. Or they can wander freely if they prefer,
making up their own itinerary.

21      In the end, our society needs to grow up. Growing up means understanding that there are no perfect answers, no all-purpose solutions, no government-
sanctioned safe havens. We haven't created a perfect society on earth and we
won't have one in cyberspace either. But at least we can have individual
choice—and individual responsibility.

## COMPREHENSION

1. The title of the essay is a variation of a phrase popularized in the 1960s.
   What is the original expression, and what was its significance? What is its
   relevance to this essay?
2. What is Dyson's thesis? Is it stated explicitly? If so, where in the essay does
   it occur? If it is merely suggested, how is it suggested, and where?
3. There are many forms of new media that are not considered communities.
   Why does Dyson refer to cyberspace as a community?
4. According to Dyson, what distinguishes cyberspace from physical space?
5. What does Dyson mean when she states that cyberspace needs "self-rule"
   (paragraph 8)?

## RHETORIC

1. How does Dyson use her introduction to foreshadow her main concerns
   about censorship in cyberspace?

2. How does Dyson use metaphor in paragraphs 11–13 to help us understand the structure of cyberspace? Why is metaphor a particularly useful literary device when explaining a new concept?
3. Key to Dyson's views on cyberspace is that it is a "voluntary destination" (paragraph 8). What evidence does Dyson present that it is voluntary? What argument can be made that it is not always "voluntary"?
4. Who is the implied audience for this essay? What level of education does one need to have and how sophisticated about the world of cyberspace does one need to be in order to comprehend and process the author's views? Explain your answer.
5. Dyson refers to laws, rules, and regulations as strategies that various interest groups may use to determine access to content in cyberspace. How does Dyson distinguish these three related tactics? What significance does differentiating these methods have in her presentation of her argument?
6. Dyson concludes her essay with an analogy between human society and cyberspace culture. Why does she save this final support for last? How does it extend her argument rather than merely restate it?

## WRITING

1. In a comparison-and-contrast essay, select three cyberspace communities and describe each one's character (refer to Dyson's reference to cyberspace character in paragraph 14).
2. In paragraph 17, Dyson refers to the "global village," a term coined by the media critic Marshall McLuhan. For a research project, study McLuhan's views on the nature of the global village, and compare and contrast them to Dyson's views of the nature of cyberspace.
3. **Writing an Argument:** Dyson argues that technology can create filters, labeling and ranking services to prevent children from viewing inappropriate material. In an essay, argue for or against the proposition that there can be a nontechnological solution to this issue—for example, instilling values in children or developing a society that does not create a mystique about taboo subject matter.

www.mhhe.com/
**mhreader**

For more information on Esther Dyson, go to:
**More Resources > Ch. 7 Government & Politics**

# The Circle of Governments

## Niccolò Machiavelli

*Niccolò Machiavelli (1469–1527), Italian patriot, statesman, and writer, is one of the seminal figures in the history of Western political thought. His inquiries into the nature of the state, the amoral quality of political life, and the primacy of power are distinctly modernist in outlook. He began his studies of political and historical issues after being forced to retire from Florentine politics in 1512. Exiled outside the city, Machiavelli wrote* The Prince *(1513),* The Discourses *(1519),* The Art of War *(1519–1520), and* The Florentine History *(1525). The following selection from* The Discourses *(conceived by the author as commentaries on the first 10 books of Livy's* History of Rome*) analyzes the varieties of government and their political implications in history.*

1 Having proposed to myself to treat of the kind of government established at Rome, and of the events that led to its perfection, I must at the beginning observe that some of the writers on politics distinguished three kinds of government, vis. the monarchical, the aristocratic, and the democratic; and maintain that the legislators of a people must choose from these three the one that seems to them most suitable. Other authors, wiser according to the opinion of many, count six kinds of governments, three of which are very bad, and three good in themselves, but so liable to be corrupted that they become absolutely bad. The three good ones are those which we have just named; the three bad ones result from the degradation of the other three, and each of them resembles its corresponding original, so that the transition from the one to the other is very easy. Thus monarchy becomes tyranny; aristocracy degenerates into oligarchy; and the popular government lapses readily into licentiousness. So that a legislator who gives to a state which he founds either of these three forms of government, constitutes it but for a brief time; for no precautions can prevent either one of the three that are reputed good from degenerating into its opposite kind; so great are in these the attractions and resemblances between the good and the evil.

2 Chance has given birth to these different kinds of governments amongst men; for at the beginning of the world the inhabitants were few in number and lived for a time dispersed, like beasts. As the human race increased, the necessity for uniting themselves for defense made itself felt; the better to attain this object they chose the strongest and most courageous from amongst themselves and placed him at their head promising to obey him. Thence they began to know the good and the honest, and to distinguish them from the bad and vicious; for seeing a man injure his benefactor aroused at once two sentiments in every heart, hatred against the ingrate and love for the benefactor. They blamed the first, and

on the contrary honored those the more who showed themselves grateful, for each felt that he in turn might be subject to a like wrong; and to prevent similar evils, they set to work to make laws, and to institute punishments for those who contravened them. Such was the origin of justice. This caused them, when they had afterwards to choose a prince, neither to look to the strongest nor bravest, but to the wisest and most just. But when they began to make sovereignty hereditary and non-elective, the children quickly degenerated from their fathers; and, so far from trying to equal their virtues, they considered that a prince had nothing else to do than to excel all the rest in luxury, indulgence, and every other variety of pleasure. The prince consequently soon drew upon himself the general hatred. An object of hatred, he naturally felt fear; fear in turn dictated to him precautions and wrongs, and thus tyranny quickly developed itself. Such were the beginning and causes of disorders, conspiracies, and plots against the sovereigns, set on foot, not by the feeble and timid, but by those citizens who, surpassing the others in grandeur of soul, in wealth, and in courage, could not submit to the outrages and excesses of their princes.

Under such powerful leaders the masses armed themselves against the tyrant, 3 and after having rid themselves of him, submitted to these chiefs as their liberators. These, abhorring the very name of prince, constituted themselves a new government; and at first bearing in mind the past tyranny, they governed in strict accordance with the laws which they had established themselves; preferring public interests to their own, and to administer and protect with greatest care both public and private affairs. The children succeeded their fathers, and ignorant of the changes of fortune, having never experienced its reverses, and indisposed to remain content with this civil equality, they in turn gave themselves up to cupidity, ambition, libertinage, and violence, and soon caused the aristocratic government to degenerate into an oligarchic tyranny, regardless of all civil rights. They soon, however, experienced the same fate as the first tyrant; the people, disgusted with their government, placed themselves at the command of whoever was willing to attack them, and this disposition soon produced an avenger, who was sufficiently well seconded to destroy them. The memory of the prince and the wrongs committed by him being still fresh in their minds, and having overthrown the oligarchy, the people were not willing to return to the government of a prince. A popular government was therefore resolved upon, and it was so organized that the authority would not again fall into the hands of a prince or a small number of nobles. And as all governments are at first looked up to with some degree of reverence, the popular state also maintained itself for a time, but which was never of long duration, and lasted generally only about as long as the generation that had established it; for it soon ran into that kind of licence which inflicts injury upon public as well as private interests. Each individual only consulted his own passions, and a thousand acts of injustice were daily committed, so that, constrained by necessity, or directed by the counsels of some good man, or for the purpose of escaping from this anarchy, they returned anew to the government of a prince, and from this they generally lapsed again into anarchy, step-by-step, in the same manner and from the same causes as we have indicated.

4      Such is the circle which all republics are destined to run through. Seldom, however, do they come back to the original form of government, which results from the fact that their duration is not sufficiently long to be able to undergo these repeated changes and preserve their existence. But it may well happen that a republic lacking strength and good counsel in its difficulties becomes subject after a while to some neighboring state, that is better organized than itself; and if such is not the case, then they will be apt to revolve indefinitely in the circle of revolutions. I say, then, that all kinds of government are defective; those three which we have qualified as good because they are too short-lived, and the three bad ones because of their inherent viciousness. Thus sagacious legislators, knowing the vices of each of these systems of government by themselves, have chosen one that should partake of all of them, judging that to be the most stable and solid. In fact, when there is combined under the same constitution a prince, a nobility, and the power of the people, then these three powers will watch and keep each other reciprocally in check.

## COMPREHENSION

1. Where in the essay does Machiavelli state his thesis? What is his thesis?
2. Explain in your own words the three types of government Machiavelli describes, their origins, and their pitfalls.
3. Ultimately, who determines what system of government a country will have—the governed or the legislators? Explain your view.

## RHETORIC

1. In paragraph 1, Machiavelli states the motivation for writing his essay. How does he create a transition from explaining this motivation to addressing his subject directly?
2. Machiavelli explains the three forms of government in a particular order. What is the unifying rhetoric behind the order in which he describes them? How does it relate to the theme of the essay?
3. Both paragraphs 2 and 3 describe the process by which governments are formed. What methods does the author use to create coherent paragraphs in providing a step-by-step description of these formations?
4. Would you consider this essay descriptive, narrative, expository, or a combination of two or more of these methods? Explain your answer.
5. Define *oligarchy* (paragraph 1), *benefactor* (paragraph 2), *cupidity* and *libertinage* (paragraph 3), and *sagacious* (paragraph 4). What does the use of these words in the essay suggest about the author and his intended audience?
6. From what vantage point does Machiavelli appear to view his subject matter—as participant, reporter, critic, or teacher? Explain your view.

## WRITING

1. Using the terms *monarchy, oligarchy,* and *democracy,* describe the various governing bodies of your school, their functions, and their place in Machiavelli's taxonomy.
2. **Writing an Argument:** Argue for or against the proposition that the United States has an ideal form of government, according to Machiavelli's view of what a government should be.
3. **Writing an Argument:** Argue for or against *one* of the forms of government Machiavelli describes in his essay.

www.mhhe.com/ **mhreader** | For more information on Niccolò Machiavelli, go to: **More Resources > Ch. 7 Government & Politics**

# Grant and Lee:
# A Study in Contrasts

### Bruce Catton

*Bruce Catton (1899–1978) was born in Petosky, Michigan. After serving in the Navy during World War I, he attended Oberlin College but left in his junior year to pursue a career in journalism. From 1942 to 1952, Catton served in the government, first on the War Production Board and later in the departments of Commerce and the Interior. He left government to devote himself to literary work as a columnist for* The Nation *and a historian of the Civil War. His many works include* A Stillness at Appomattox *(1953), which won the 1954 Pulitzer Prize;* Mr. Lincoln's Army *(1951);* The Centennial History of the Civil War *(1961–1965); and* Prefaces to History *(1970). In the following selection, Catton presents vivid portraits of two well-known but little understood figures from American history.*

When Ulysses S. Grant and Robert E. Lee met in the parlor of a modest house at 1 Appomattox Court House, Virginia, on April 9, 1865, to work out the terms for the surrender of Lee's Army of Northern Virginia, a great chapter in American life came to a close, and a great new chapter began.

These men were bringing the Civil War to its virtual finish. To be sure, 2 other armies had yet to surrender, and for a few days the fugitive Confederate government would struggle desperately and vainly, trying to find some way to go on living now that its chief support was gone. But in effect it was all over when Grant and Lee signed the papers. And the little room where they wrote out the terms was the scene of one of the poignant, dramatic contrasts in American history.

3      They were two strong men, these oddly different generals, and they represented the strengths of two conflicting currents that, through them, had come into final collision.

4      Back of Robert E. Lee was the notion that the old aristocratic concept might somehow survive and be dominant in American life.

5      Lee was tidewater Virginia, and in his background were family, culture, and tradition . . . the age of chivalry transplanted to a New World which was making its own legends and its own myths. He embodied a way of life that had come down through the age of knighthood and the English country squire. America was a land that was beginning all over again, dedicated to nothing much more complicated than the rather hazy belief that all men had equal rights and should have an equal chance in the world. In such a land Lee stood for the feeling that it was somehow of advantage to human society to have a pronounced inequality in the social structure. There should be a leisure class, backed by ownership of land; in turn, society itself should be keyed to the land as the chief source of wealth and influence. It would bring forth (according to this ideal) a class of men with a strong sense of obligation to the community; men who lived not to gain advantage for themselves, but to meet the solemn obligations which had been laid on them by the very fact that they were privileged. From them the country would get its leadership; to them it could look for the higher values—of thought, of conduct, of personal deportment—to give it strength and virtue.

6      Lee embodied the noblest elements of this aristocratic ideal. Through him, the landed nobility justified itself. For four years, the Southern states had fought a desperate war to uphold the ideals for which Lee stood. In the end, it almost seemed as if the Confederacy fought for Lee; as if he himself was the Confederacy . . . the best thing that the way of life for which the Confederacy stood could ever have to offer. He had passed into legend before Appomattox. Thousands of tired, underfed, poorly clothed Confederate soldiers, long since past the simple enthusiasm of the early days of the struggle, somehow considered Lee the symbol of everything for which they had been willing to die. But they could not quite put this feeling into words. If the Lost Cause, sanctified by so much heroism and so many deaths, had a living justification, its justification was General Lee.

7      Grant, the son of a tanner on the Western frontier, was everything Lee was not. He had come up the hard way and embodied nothing in particular except the eternal toughness and sinewy fiber of the men who grew up beyond the mountains. He was one of a body of men who owed reverence and obeisance to no one, who were self-reliant to a fault, who cared hardly anything for the past but who had a sharp eye for the future.

8      These frontier men were the precise opposites of the tidewater aristocrats. Back of them, in the great surge that had taken people over the Alleghenies and

into the opening Western country, there was a deep, implicit dissatisfaction with a past that had settled into grooves. They stood for democracy, not from any reasoned conclusion about the proper ordering of human society, but simply because they had grown up in the middle of democracy and knew how it worked. Their society might have privileges, but they would be privileges each man had won for himself. Forms and patterns meant nothing. No man was born to anything, except perhaps to a chance to show how far he could rise. Life was competition.

Yet along with this feeling had come a deep sense of belonging to a national community. The Westerner who developed a farm, opened a shop, or set up in business as a trader, could hope to prosper only as his own community prospered—and his community ran from the Atlantic to the Pacific and from Canada down to Mexico. If the land was settled, with towns and highways and accessible markets, he could better himself. He saw his fate in terms of the nation's own destiny. As its horizons expanded, so did his. He had, in other words, an acute dollars-and-cents stake in the continued growth and development of his country. 9

And that, perhaps, is where the contrast between Grant and Lee becomes most striking. The Virginia aristocrat, inevitably, saw himself in relation to his own region. He lived in a static society which could endure almost anything except change. Instinctively, his first loyalty would go to the locality in which that society existed. He would fight to the limit of endurance to defend it, because in defending it he was defending everything that gave his own life its deepest meaning. 10

The Westerner, on the other hand, would fight with an equal tenacity for the broader concept of society. He fought so because everything he lived by was tied to growth, expansion, and a constantly widening horizon. What he lived by would survive or fall with the nation itself. He could not possibly stand by unmoved in the face of an attempt to destroy the Union. He would combat it with everything he had, because he could only see it as an effort to cut the ground out from under his feet. 11

So Grant and Lee were in complete contrast, representing two diametrically opposed elements in American life. Grant was the modern man emerging; beyond him, ready to come on the stage, was the great age of steel and machinery, of crowded cities and a restless burgeoning vitality. Lee might have ridden down from the old age of chivalry, lance in hand, silken banner fluttering over his head. Each man was the perfect champion of his cause, drawing both his strengths and his weaknesses from the people he led. 12

Yet it was not all contrast, after all. Different as they were—in background, in personality, in underlying aspiration—these two great soldiers had much in common. Under everything else, they were marvelous fighters. Furthermore, their fighting qualities were really very much alike. 13

Each man had, to begin with, the great virtue of utter tenacity and fidelity. Grant fought his way down the Mississippi Valley in spite of acute personal discouragement and profound military handicaps. Lee hung on in the trenches 14 at Petersburg after hope itself had died. In each man there was an indomitable quality . . . the born fighter's refusal to give up as long as he can still remain on his feet and lift his two fists.

15     Daring and resourcefulness they had, too; the ability to think faster and move faster than the enemy. These were the qualities which gave Lee the dazzling campaigns of Second Manassas and Chancellorsville and won Vicksburg for Grant.

16     Lastly, and perhaps greatest of all, there was the ability, at the end, to turn quickly from war to peace once the fighting was over. Out of the way these two men behaved at Appomattox came the possibility of a peace of reconciliation. It was a possibility not wholly realized, in the years to come, but which did, in the end, help the two sections to become one nation again . . . after a war whose bitterness might have seemed to make such a reunion wholly impossible. No part of either man's life became him more than the part he played in their brief meeting in the McLean house at Appomattox. Their behavior there put all succeeding generations of Americans in their debt. Two great Americans, Grant and Lee—very different, yet under everything very much alike. Their encounter at Appomattox was one of the great moments of American history.

## COMPREHENSION

1.  What is the central purpose of Catton's study? Cite evidence to support your view. Who is his audience?
2.  What is the primary appeal to readers of describing history through the study of individuals rather than through the recording of events? How does Catton's essay reflect this appeal?
3.  According to Catton, what special qualities did Grant and Lee share, and what qualities set them apart?

## RHETORIC

1.  What role does the opening paragraph play in setting the tone for the essay? Is the tone typical of what you would expect of an essay describing military generals? Explain your view. How does the conclusion echo the introductory paragraph?
2.  Note that the sentence "Two great Americans, Grant and Lee—very different, yet under everything very much alike" (paragraph 16) has no verb. What does this indicate about Catton's style? What other sentences contain atypical syntax? What is their contribution to the unique quality of the writing?
3.  Although this essay is about a historical era, there is a notable lack of specific facts—dates, statistics, and events. What has Catton focused on instead?
4.  What is the function of the one-sentence paragraph 3?

5. Paragraphs 9, 10, 12, and 13 begin with coordinating conjunctions. How do these transitional words give the paragraphs their special coherence? How would more typical introductory expressions, such as *in addition, furthermore,* or *moreover,* have altered this coherence?
6. What strategy does Catton use in comparing and contrasting the two generals? Study paragraphs 5–16. Which are devoted to describing each man separately, and which include aspects of both men? What is the overall effectiveness of the comparisons?

## WRITING

1. Does Lee's vision of society exist in the United States today? If not, why not? If so, where do you find this vision? Write a brief essay on this topic.
2. Select two well-known individuals in the same profession—for example, politics, entertainment, or sports. Make a list for each, enumerating the different aspects of their character, behavior, beliefs, and background. Using this as an outline, devise an essay comparing and contrasting the two.
3. **Writing an Argument:** Apply, in an argumentative essay, Catton's observation about "two diametrically opposed elements in American life" (paragraph 12) to the current national scene.

 **www.mhhe.com/**
**mhreader**

For more information on Bruce Catton, go to:
**More Resources > Ch. 7 Government & Politics**

# American Dreamer

### Bharati Mukherjee

*Bharati Mukherjee (b. 1940) was born in Calcutta, India, and learned to read and write by the age of three. In 1947, she moved to Britain with her family. After receiving her BA from the University of Calcutta and her MA in English and ancient Indian culture from the University of Boroda, she came to the United States, where she received an MFA in creative writing and a PhD in English and comparative literature at the University of Iowa. Mukherjee is the author of* Jasmine *(1989) and* The Middleman and Other Stories, *which won the 1988 National Book Critic's Circle Award for Fiction. Her more recent work includes the novels* The Holder of the World *(1993) and* Leave It to Me *(1997). She is currently a professor at the University of California, Berkeley. Mukherjee is often interested in and writing about issues of cultural identity. In the following essay, which first appeared in the magazine* Mother Jones *in 1997, she examines why "hyphenated Americans" always seem to be members of nonwhite groups.*

1 The United States exists as a sovereign nation. "America," in contrast, exists as a myth of democracy and equal opportunity to live by, or as an ideal goal to reach.

2 I am a naturalized U.S. citizen, which means that, unlike native-born citizens, I had to prove to the U.S. government that I merited citizenship. What I didn't have to disclose was that I desired "America," which to me is the stage for the drama of self-transformation.

3 I was born in Calcutta and first came to the United States—to Iowa City, to be precise—on a summer evening in 1961. I flew into a small airport surrounded by cornfields and pastures, ready to carry out the two commands my father had written out for me the night before I left Calcutta: Spend two years studying creative writing at the Iowa Writers' Workshop, then come back home and marry the bridegroom he selected for me from our caste and class.

4 In traditional Hindu families like ours, men provided and women were provided for. My father was a patriarch and I a pliant daughter. The neighborhood I'd grown up in was homogeneously Hindu, Bengali-speaking, and middle-class. I didn't expect myself to ever disobey or disappoint my father by setting my own goals and taking charge of my future.

5 When I landed in Iowa 35 years ago, I found myself in a society in which almost everyone was Christian, white, and moderately well-off. In the women's dormitory I lived in my first year, apart from six international graduate students (all of us were from Asia and considered "exotic"), the only non-Christian was Jewish, and the only nonwhite an African-American from Georgia. I didn't anticipate then, that over the next 35 years, the Iowa population would become so diverse that it would have 6,931 children from non-English-speaking homes registered as students in its schools, nor that Iowans would be in the grip of a cultural crisis in which resentment against immigrants, particularly refugees from Vietnam, Sudan, and Bosnia, as well as unskilled Spanish-speaking workers, would become politicized enough to cause the Immigration and Naturalization Service to open an "enforcement" office in Cedar Rapids in October for the tracking and deporting of undocumented aliens.

6 In Calcutta in the '50s, I heard no talk of "identity crisis"—communal or individual. The concept itself—a person not knowing who he or she is—was unimaginable in our hierarchical, classification-obsessed society. One's identity was fixed, derived from religion, caste, patrimony, and mother tongue. A Hindu Indian's last name announced his or her forefathers' caste and place of origin. A Mukherjee could only be a Brahmin from Bengal. Hindu tradition forbade intercaste, interlanguage, interethnic marriages. Bengali tradition even discouraged emigration: To remove oneself from Bengal was to dilute true culture.

7 Until the age of 8, I lived in a house crowded with 40 or 50 relatives. My identity was viscerally connected with ancestral soil and genealogy. I was who I was because I was Dr. Sudhir Lal Mukherjee's daughter, because I was a

Hindu Brahmin, because I was Bengali-speaking, and because my *desh*—the Bengali word for homeland—was an East Bengal village called Faridpur.

The University of Iowa classroom was my first experience of coeducation. And 8 after not too long, I fell in love with a fellow student named Clark Blaise, an American of Canadian origin, and impulsively married him during a lunch break in a lawyer's office above a coffee shop.

That act cut me off forever from the rules and ways of upper-middle-class 9 life in Bengal, and hurled me into a New World life of scary improvisations and heady explorations. Until my lunch-break wedding, I had seen myself as an Indian foreign student who intended to return to India to live. The five-minute ceremony in the lawyer's office suddenly changed me into a transient with conflicting loyalties to two very different cultures.

The first 10 years into marriage, years spent mostly in my husband's native 10 Canada, I thought of myself as an expatriate Bengali permanently stranded in North America because of destiny or desire. My first novel, *The Tiger's Daughter*, embodies the loneliness I felt but could not acknowledge, even to myself, as I negotiated the no man's land between the country of my past and the continent of my present. Shaped by memory, textured with nostalgia for a class and culture I had abandoned, this novel quite naturally became an expression of the expatriate consciousness.

It took me a decade of painful introspection to put nostalgia in perspective 11 and to make the transition from expatriate to immigrant. After a 14-year stay in Canada, I forced my husband and our two sons to relocate to the United States. But the transition from foreign student to U.S. citizen, from detached onlooker to committed immigrant, has not been easy.

The years in Canada were particularly harsh. Canada is a country that offi- 12 cially, and proudly, resists cultural fusion. For all its rhetoric about a cultural "mosaic," Canada refuses to renovate its national self-image to include its changing complexion. It is a New World country with Old World concepts of a fixed, exclusivist national identity. Canadian official rhetoric designated me as one of the "visible minority" who, even though I spoke the Canadian languages of English and French, was straining "the absorptive capacity" of Canada. Canadians of color were routinely treated as "not real" Canadians. One example: In 1985 a terrorist bomb, planted in an Air-India jet on Canadian soil, blew up after leaving Montreal, killing 329 passengers, most of whom were Canadians of Indian origin. The prime minister of Canada at the time, Brian Mulroney, phoned the prime minister of India to offer Canada's condolences for India's loss.

Those years of race-related harassments in Canada politicized me and 13 deepened my love of the ideals embedded in the American Bill of Rights. I don't forget that the architects of the Constitution and the Bill of Rights were white males and slaveholders. But through their declaration, they provided us with the enthusiasm for human rights, and the initial framework from which other empowerments could be conceived and enfranchised communities expanded.

14     I am a naturalized U.S. citizen and I take my American citizenship very seriously. I am not an economic refugee, nor am I a seeker of political asylum. I am a voluntary immigrant. I became a citizen by choice, not by simple accident of birth.

15     Yet these days, questions such as who is an American and what is American culture are being posed with belligerence, and being answered with violence. Scapegoating of immigrants has once again become the politicians' easy remedy for all that ails the nation. Hate speeches fill auditoriums for demagogues willing to profit from stirring up racial animosity. An April [1996] Gallup poll indicated that half of Americans would like to bar almost all legal immigration for the next five years.

16     The United States, like every sovereign nation, has a right to formulate its immigration policies. But in this decade of continual, large-scale diasporas, it is imperative that we come to some agreement about who "we" are, and what our goals are for the nation, now that our community includes people of many races, ethnicities, languages, and religions.

17     The debate about American culture and American identity has to date been monopolized largely by Eurocentrists and ethnocentrists whose rhetoric has been flamboyantly divisive, pitting a phantom "us" against a demonized "them."

18   All countries view themselves by their ideals. Indians idealize the cultural continuum, the inherent value system of India, and are properly incensed when foreigners see nothing but poverty, intolerance, strife, and injustice. Americans see themselves as the embodiments of liberty, openness, and individualism, even as the world judges them for drugs, crime, violence, bigotry, militarism, and homelessness. I was in Singapore in 1994 when the American teenager Michael Fay was sentenced to caning for having spraypainted some cars. While I saw Fay's actions as those of an individual, and his sentence as too harsh, the overwhelming local sentiment was that vandalism was an "American" crime, and that flogging Fay would deter Singapore youths from becoming "Americanized."

19     Conversely, in 1994, in Tavares, Florida, the Lake County School Board announced its policy (since overturned) requiring middle school teachers to instruct their students that American culture, by which the board meant European-American culture, is inherently "superior to other foreign or historic cultures." The policy's misguided implication was that culture in the United States has not been affected by the American Indian, African-American, Latin-American, and Asian-American segments of the population. The sinister implication was that our national identity is so fragile that it can absorb diverse and immigrant cultures only by recontextualizing them as deficient.

20     Our nation is unique in human history in that the founding idea of "America" was in opposition to the tenet that a nation is a collection of like-looking, like-speaking, like-worshipping people. The primary criterion for nationhood in Europe is homogeneity of culture, race, and religion—which has contributed to blood-soaked balkanization in the former Yugoslavia and the former Soviet Union.

America's pioneering European ancestors gave up the easy homogeneity of  21
their native countries for a new version of Utopia. Now, in the 1990s, we have
the exciting chance to follow that tradition and assist in the making of a new
American culture that differs from both the enforced assimilation of a "melting
pot" and the Canadian model of a multicultural "mosaic."

The multicultural mosaic implies a contiguity of fixed, self-sufficient,  22
utterly distinct cultures. Multiculturalism, as it has been practiced in the United
States in the past 10 years, implies the existence of a central culture, ringed by
peripheral cultures. The fallout of official multiculturalism is the establishment
of one culture as the norm and the rest as aberrations. At the same time, the
multiculturalist emphasis on race- and ethnicity-based group identity leads to a
lack of respect for individual differences within each group, and to vilification
of those individuals who place the good of the nation above the interests of
their particular racial or ethnic communities.

We must be alert to the dangers of an "us" vs. "them" mentality. In  23
California, this mentality is manifesting itself as increased violence between minority, ethnic communities. The attack on Korean-American merchants in South
Central Los Angeles in the wake of the Rodney King beating trial is only one
recent example of the tragic side effects of this mentality. On the national level,
the politicization of ethnic identities has encouraged the scapegoating of legal
immigrants, who are blamed for economic and social problems brought about
by flawed domestic and foreign policies.

We need to discourage the retention of cultural memory if the aim of that  24
retention is cultural balkanization. We must think of American culture and nationhood as a constantly reforming, transmogrifying "we."

In this age of diasporas, one's biological identity may not be one's only  25
identity. Erosions and accretions come with the act of emigration. The experience of cutting myself off from a biological homeland and settling in an adopted homeland that is not always welcoming to its dark-complexioned citizens
has tested me as a person, and made me the writer I am today.

I choose to describe myself on my own terms, as an American, rather than as an  26
Asian-American. Why is it that hyphenation is imposed only on nonwhite
Americans? Rejecting hyphenation is my refusal to categorize the cultural landscape into a center and its peripheries; it is to demand that the American nation
deliver the promises of its dream and its Constitution to all its citizens equally.

My rejection of hyphenation has been misrepresented as race treachery by  27
some India-born academics on U.S. campuses who have appointed themselves
guardians of the "purity" of ethnic cultures. Many of them, though they reside
permanently in the United States and participate in its economy, consistently
denounce American ideals and institutions. They direct their rage at me because, by becoming a U.S. citizen and exercising my voting rights, I have invested in the present and not the past; because I have committed myself to help
shape the future of my adopted homeland; and because I celebrate racial and
cultural mongrelization.

28      What excites me is that as a nation we have not only the chance to retain those values we treasure from our original cultures but also the chance to acknowledge that the outer forms of those values are likely to change. Among Indian immigrants, I see a great deal of guilt about the inability to hang on to what they commonly term "pure culture." Parents express rage or despair at their U.S.-born children's forgetting of, or indifference to, some aspects of Indian culture. Of those parents I would ask: What is it we have lost if our children are acculturating into the culture in which we are living? Is it so terrible that our children are discovering or are inventing homelands for themselves?

29      Some first-generation Indo-Americans, embittered by racism and by unofficial "glass ceilings," construct a phantom identity, more-Indian-than-Indians-in-India, as a defense against marginalization. I ask: Why don't you get actively involved in fighting discrimination? Make your voice heard. Choose the forum most appropriate for you. If you are a citizen, let your vote count. Reinvest your energy and resources into revitalizing your city's disadvantaged residents and neighborhoods. Know your constitutional rights, and when they are violated, use the agencies of redress the Constitution makes available to you. Expect change, and when it comes, deal with it!

30      As a writer, my literary agenda begins by acknowledging that America has transformed me. It does not end until I show that I (along with the hundreds of thousands of immigrants like me) am minute by minute transforming America. The transformation is a two-way process: It affects both the individual and the national-cultural identity.

31      Others who write stories of migration often talk of arrival at a new place as a loss, the loss of communal memory and the erosion of an original culture. I want to talk of arrival as a gain.

## COMPREHENSION

1. What is the significance of the title? In what way is Mukherjee a "dreamer"? In what way does the United States inspire "dreaming"?

2. In paragraph 6, Mukherjee states that in India she had a strong sense of identity. Why was it difficult for her to feel at ease with her "American identity"?

3. A country is a geographical area with national boundaries as well as an underlying concept and ideal. Does Mukherjee focus on these aspects of the United States and Canada equally, or does she emphasize one more than the other? Explain.

## RHETORIC

1. The essay is divided into four parts. Why did the author adopt this structure? What is the focus of each? How does each section function rhetorically in relation to the other three?

2. Mukherjee introduces her essay with her own explanations of the terms "America" and "the United States." What is her purpose, considering that this is an autobiographical essay?

3. Mukherjee explores her transition from "expatriate" to "immigrant" to "U.S. citizen" in paragraphs 10 and 11. Explain the significance of each term in general and each term's particular role in the author's cultural metamorphosis.

4. Mukherjee rejects and condemns the belligerence toward and scapegoating of immigrants. How would you characterize the effect of these attacks on Mukherjee, an immigrant herself? Note, in particular, her statements in paragraphs 13 and 26.

5. How does Mukherjee employ irony in paragraph 12 to demonstrate the double standard imposed on individuals who do not fit the stereotypical mold of what it means to be a "citizen"?

6. In paragraph 14, the author states, "I take my American citizenship very seriously." Is the tone of the essay serious? Explain your view.

7. As you define the following words, identify the intended audience for this essay: *exclusivist* (paragraph 12), *demagogues* (paragraph 15), *diasporas* (paragraph 16), *ethnocentrists* and *demonized* (paragraph 17), and *balkanization* (paragraph 24).

## WRITING

1. In a personal essay, write about a time in your life when your allegiance, honesty, or integrity was unfairly questioned. Be sure to use specifics such as the circumstances of who, what, when, where, and why. Also describe your feelings at the time and the emotional outcome.

2. Write an essay based on personal experience or observation, explaining whether Mukherjee is correct in stating that "hyphenation is imposed only on nonwhite Americans" (paragraph 26). A variation on this theme might be an exploration why "hyphenated" terms used to describe certain white American groups have a different tone and purpose than terms used for nonwhites.

3. **Writing an Argument:** In an essay, argue for or against the proposition that a course on cultural diversity should be taught at your college or university. Consider whether other ways of approaching the subject would be more profitable, or whether the subject needs to be addressed at all.

4. **Writing an Argument:** In her conclusion, Mukherjee criticizes "guardians of the 'purity' of ethnic cultures." Is there such a thing as a "pure" ethnic culture? Write an essay arguing your viewpoint.

www.mhhe.com/
**mhreader**

For more information on Bharati Mukherjee, go to:
**More Resources > Ch. 7 Government & Politics**

# Stranger in the Village

### James Baldwin

*James Baldwin (1924–1988), a major American essayist, novelist, short-story writer, and playwright, was born and grew up in Harlem. He won a Eugene Saxon Fellowship and lived in Europe from 1948 to 1956. Always an activist in civil rights causes, Baldwin focused in his essays and fiction on the black search for identity in modern America and on the myth of white superiority. Among his principal works are* Go Tell It on the Mountain *(1953),* Notes of a Native Son *(1955),* Giovanni's Room *(1956),* Nobody Knows My Name *(1961),* Another Country *(1962), and* If Beale Street Could Talk *(1974). One of the finest contemporary essayists, Baldwin had a rare talent for portraying the deepest concerns about civilization in an intensely personal style, as the following essay indicates.*

1   From all available evidence no black man had ever set foot in this tiny Swiss village before I came. I was told before arriving that I would probably be a "sight" for the village; I took this to mean that people of my complexion were rarely seen in Switzerland, and also that city people are always something of a "sight" outside of the city. It did not occur to me—possibly because I am an American—that there could be people anywhere who had never seen a Negro.

2   It is a fact that cannot be explained on the basis of the inaccessibility of the village. The village is very high, but it is only four hours from Milan and three hours from Lausanne. It is true that it is virtually unknown. Few people making plans for a holiday would elect to come here. On the other hand, the villagers are able, presumably, to come and go as they please—which they do: to another town at the foot of the mountain, with a population of approximately five thousand, the nearest place to see a movie or go to the bank. In the village there is no movie house, no bank, no library, no theater; very few radios, one jeep, one station wagon; and, at the moment, one typewriter, mine, an invention which the woman next door to me here had never seen. There are about six hundred people living here, all Catholic—I conclude this from the fact that the Catholic church is open all year round, whereas the Protestant chapel, set off on a hill a little removed from the village, is open only in the summertime when the tourists arrive. There are four or five hotels, all closed now, and four or five *bistros,* of which, however, only two do any business during the winter. These two do not do a great deal, for life in the village seems to end around nine or ten o'clock. There are a few stores, butcher, baker, *épicerie,* a hardware store, and a money-changer—who cannot change travelers' checks, but must send them down to the bank, an operation which takes two or three days. There is something called the *Ballet Haus,* closed in the winter and used for God knows what, certainly not

ballet, during the summer. There seems to be only one schoolhouse in the village, and this for the quite young children; I suppose this to mean that their older brothers and sisters at some point descend from these mountains in order to complete their education—possibly, again, to the town just below. The landscape is absolutely forbidding, mountains towering on all four sides, ice and snow as far as the eye can reach. In this white wilderness, men and women and children move all day, carrying washing, wood, buckets of milk or water, sometimes skiing on Sunday afternoons. All week long boys and young men are to be seen shoveling snow off the rooftops, or dragging wood down from the forest in sleds.

The village's only real attraction, which explains the tourist season, is the  3
hot spring water. A disquietingly high proportion of these tourists are cripples, or semi-cripples, who come year after year—from other parts of Switzerland, usually—to take the waters. This lends the village, at the height of the season, a rather terrifying air of sanctity, as though it were a lesser Lourdes. There is often something beautiful, there is always something awful, in the spectacle of a person who has lost one of his faculties, a faculty he never questioned until it was gone, and who struggles to recover it. Yet people remain people, on crutches or indeed on deathbeds; and wherever I passed, the first summer I was here, among the native villagers or among the lame, a wind passed with me—of astonishment, curiosity, amusement, and outrage. The first summer I stayed two weeks and never intended to return. But I did return in the winter, to work; the village offers, obviously, no distractions whatever and has the further advantage of being extremely cheap. Now it is winter again, a year later, and I am here again. Everyone in the village knows my name, though they scarcely ever use it, knows that I come from America—though this, apparently, they will never really believe: black men come from Africa—and everyone knows that I am the friend of the son of a woman who was born here, and that I am staying in their chalet. But I remain as much a stranger today as I was the first day I arrived, and the children shout *Neger! Neger!* as I walk along the streets.

It must be admitted that in the beginning I was far too shocked to have any  4
real reaction. In so far as I reacted at all, I reacted by trying to be pleasant—it being a great part of the American Negro's education (long before he goes to school) that he must make people "like" him. This smile-and-the-world-smiles-with-you routine worked about as well in this situation as it had in the situation for which it was designed, which is to say that it did not work at all. No one, after all, can be liked whose human weight and complexity cannot be, or has not been, admitted. My smile was simply another unheard-of phenomenon which allowed them to see my teeth—they did not, really, see my smile and I began to think that, should I take to snarling, no one would notice any difference. All of the physical characteristics of the Negro which had caused me, in America, a very different and almost forgotten pain were nothing less than miraculous—or infernal—in the eyes of the village people. Some thought my hair was the color of tar, that it had the texture of wire, or the texture of cotton. It was jocularly suggested that I might let it all grow long and make myself a

winter coat. If I sat in the sun for more than five minutes some daring creature was certain to come along and gingerly put his fingers on my hair, as though he were afraid of an electric shock, or put his hand on my hand, astonished that the color did not rub off. In all of this, in which it must be conceded there was the charm of genuine wonder and in which there was certainly no element of intentional unkindness, there was yet no suggestion that I was human: I was simply a living wonder.

5     I knew that they did not mean to be unkind, and I know it now; it is necessary, nevertheless, for me to repeat this to myself each time I walk out of the chalet. The children who shout *Neger!* have no way of knowing the echoes this sound raises in me. They are brimming with good humor and the more daring swell with pride when I stop to speak with them. Just the same, there are days when I cannot pause and smile, when I have no heart to play with them; when, indeed, I mutter sourly to myself, exactly as I muttered on the streets of a city these children have never seen, when I was no bigger than these children are now: *Your* mother *was a nigger.* Joyce is right about history being a nightmare—but it may be the nightmare from which no one *can* awaken. People are trapped in history and history is trapped in them.

6     There is a custom in the village—I am told it is repeated in many villages—of "buying" African natives for the purpose of converting them to Christianity. There stands in the church all year round a small box with a slot for money, decorated with a black figurine, and into this box the villagers drop their francs. During the *carnaval* which precedes Lent, two village children have their faces blackened—out of which bloodless darkness their blue eyes shine like ice—and fantastic horsehair wigs are placed on their blond heads; thus disguised, they solicit among the villagers for money for the missionaries in Africa. Between the box in the church and the blackened children, the village "bought" last year six or eight African natives. This was reported to me with pride by the wife of one of the *bistro* owners and I was careful to express astonishment and pleasure at the solicitude shown by the village for the souls of black folk. The *bistro* owner's wife beamed with a pleasure far more genuine than my own and seemed to feel that I might now breathe more easily concerning the souls of at least six of my kinsmen.

7     I tried not to think of these so lately baptized kinsmen, of the price paid for them, or the peculiar price they themselves would pay, and said nothing about my father, who having taken his own conversion too literally never, at bottom, forgave the white world (which he described as heathen) for having saddled him with a Christ in whom, to judge at least from their treatment of him, they themselves no longer believed. I thought of white men arriving for the first time in an African village, strangers there, as I am a stranger here, and tried to imagine the astounded populace touching their hair and marveling at the color of their skin. But there is a great difference between being the first white man to be seen by Africans and being the first black man to be seen by whites. The white man takes the astonishment as tribute, for he arrives to conquer and to convert the natives, whose inferiority in relation to himself is not even to be

questioned; whereas I, without a thought of conquest, find myself among a people whose culture controls me, has even, in a sense, created me, people who have cost me more in anguish and rage than they will ever know, who yet do not even know of my existence. The astonishment with which I might have greeted them, should they have stumbled into my African village a few hundred years ago, might have rejoiced their hearts. But the astonishment with which they greet me today can only poison mine.

And this is so despite everything I may do to feel differently, despite my 8 friendly conversations with the *bistro* owner's wife, despite their three-year-old son who has at last become my friend, despite the *saluts* and *bonsoirs* which I exchange with people as I walk, despite the fact that I know that no individual can be taken to task for what history is doing, or has done. I say that the culture of these people controls me—but they can scarcely be held responsible for European culture. America comes out of Europe, but these people have never seen America nor have most of them seen more of Europe than the hamlet at the foot of their mountain. Yet they move with an authority which I shall never have; and they regard me, quite rightly, not only as a stranger in their village but as a suspect latecomer, bearing no credentials, to everything they have—however unconsciously—inherited.

For this village, even were it incomparably more remote and incredibly 9 more primitive, is the West, the West onto which I have been so strangely grafted. These people cannot be, from the point of view of power, strangers anywhere in the world; they have made the modern world, in effect, even if they do not know it. The most illiterate among them is related, in a way that I am not, to Dante, Shakespeare, Michelangelo, Aeschylus, da Vinci, Rembrandt, and Racine; the cathedral at Chartres says something to them which it cannot say to me, as indeed would New York's Empire State Building, should anyone here ever see it. Out of their hymns and dances come Beethoven and Bach. Go back a few centuries and they are in their full glory—but I am in Africa, watching the conquerors arrive.

The rage of the disesteemed is personally fruitless, but it is also absolutely 10 inevitable; this rage, so generally discounted, so little understood even among the people whose daily bread it is, is one of the things that makes history. Rage can only with difficulty, and never entirely, be brought under the domination of the intelligence and is therefore not susceptible to any arguments whatever. This is a fact which ordinary representatives of the *Herrenvolk*, having never felt this rage and being unable to imagine it, quite fail to understand. Also, rage cannot be hidden, it can only be dissembled. This dissembling deludes the thoughtless, and strengthens rage and adds, to rage, contempt. There are, no doubt, as many ways of coping with the resulting complex of tensions as there are black men in the world, but no black man can hope ever to be entirely liberated from this internal warfare—rage, dissembling, and contempt having inevitably accompanied his first realization of the power of white men. What is crucial here is that, since white men represent in the black man's world so heavy a weight, white men have for black men a reality which is far from being reciprocal; and hence all black men have toward all white men an attitude which is designed, really, either to rob the white man of the jewel of his naïveté, or else to make it cost him dear.

11      The black man insists, by whatever means he finds at his disposal, that the white man cease to regard him as an exotic rarity and recognize him as a human being. This is a very charged and difficult moment, for there is a great deal of will power involved in the white man's naïveté. Most people are not naturally reflective any more than they are naturally malicious, and the white man prefers to keep the black man at a certain human remove because it is easier for him thus to preserve his simplicity and avoid being called to account for crimes committed by his forefathers, or his neighbors. He is inescapably aware, nevertheless, that he is in a better position in the world than black men are, nor can he quite put to death the suspicion that he is hated by black men therefore. He does not wish to be hated, neither does he wish to change places, and at this point in his uneasiness he can scarcely avoid having recourse to those legends which white men have created about black men, the most usual effect of which is that the white man finds himself enmeshed, so to speak, in his own language which describes hell, as well as the attributes which lead one to hell, as being as black as night.

12      Every legend, moreover, contains its residuum of truth, and the root function of language is to control the universe by describing it. It is of quite considerable significance that black men remain, in the imagination, and in overwhelming numbers in fact, beyond the disciplines of salvation; and this despite the fact the West has been "buying" African natives for centuries. There is, I should hazard, an instantaneous necessity to be divorced from this so visibly unsaved stranger, in whose heart, moreover, one cannot guess what dreams of vengeance are being nourished; and, at the same time, there are few things on earth more attractive than the idea of the unspeakable liberty which is allowed the unredeemed. When, beneath the black mask, a human being begins to make himself felt one cannot escape a certain awful wonder as to what kind of human being it is. What one's imagination makes of other people is dictated, of course, by the laws of one's own personality and it is one of the ironies of black-white relations that, by means of what the white man imagines the black man to be, the black man is enabled to know who the white man is.

13      I have said, for example, that I am as much a stranger in this village today as I was the first summer I arrived, but this is not quite true. The villagers wonder less about the texture of my hair than they did then, and wonder rather more about me. And the fact that their wonder now exists on another level is reflected in their attitudes and in their eyes. There are the children who make those delightful, hilarious, sometimes astonishingly grave overtures of friendship in the unpredictable fashion of children; other children, having been taught that the devil is a black man, scream in genuine anguish as I approach. Some of the older women never pass without a friendly greeting, never pass, indeed, if it seems that they will be able to engage me in conversation; other women look down or look away or rather contemptuously smirk. Some of the men drink with me and suggest that I learn how to ski—partly, I gather, because they

cannot imagine what I would look like on skis—and want to know if I am married, and ask questions about my *métier*. But some of the men have accused *le
sale négre*—behind my back—of stealing wood and there is already in the eyes
of some of them that peculiar, intent, paranoiac malevolence which one sometimes surprises in the eyes of American white men when, out walking with
their Sunday girl, they see a Negro male approach.

There is a dreadful abyss between the streets of this village and the streets  14
of the city in which I was born, between the children who shout *Neger!* today
and those who shouted *Nigger!* yesterday—the abyss is experience, the
American experience. The syllable hurled behind me today expresses, above
all, wonder: I am a stranger here. But I am not a stranger in America and the
same syllable riding on the American air expresses the war my presence has
occasioned in the American soul.

For this village brings home to me this fact: that there was a day, and not  15
really a very distant day, when Americans were scarcely Americans at all but
discontented Europeans, facing a great unconquered continent and strolling,
say, into a marketplace and seeing black men for the first time. The shock this
spectacle afforded is suggested, surely, by the promptness with which they decided that these black men were not really men but cattle. It is true that the necessity on the part of the settlers of the New World of reconciling their moral
assumptions with the fact—and the necessity—of slavery enhanced immensely
the charm of this idea, and it is also true that this idea expresses, with a truly
American bluntness, the attitude which to varying extents all masters have had
toward all slaves.

But between all former slaves and slave owners and the drama which be-  16
gins for Americans over three hundred years ago at Jamestown, there are at
least two differences to be observed. The American Negro slave could not suppose, for one thing, as slaves in past epochs had supposed and often done, that
he would ever be able to wrest the power from his master's hands. This was a
supposition which the modern era, which was to bring about such vast changes
in the aims and dimensions of power, put to death; it only begins, in unprecedented fashion, and with dreadful implications, to be resurrected today. But
even had this supposition persisted with undiminished force, the American
Negro slave could not have used it to lend his condition dignity, for the reason
that this supposition rests on another: that the slave in exile yet remains related
to his past, has some means—if only in memory—of revering and sustaining
the forms of his former life, is able, in short, to maintain his identity.

This was not the case with the American Negro slave. He is unique among  17
the black men of the world in that his past was taken from him, almost literally,
at one blow. One wonders what on earth the first slave found to say to the first
dark child he bore. I am told that there are Haitians able to trace their ancestry
back to African kings, but any American Negro wishing to go back so far will
find his journey through time abruptly arrested by the signature on the bill of
sale which served as the entrance paper for his ancestor. At the time—to say
nothing of the circumstances—of the enslavement of the captive black man who

was to become the American Negro, there was not the remotest possibility that he would ever take power from his master's hands. There was no reason to suppose that his situation would ever change, nor was there, shortly, anything to indicate that his situation had ever been different. It was his necessity, in the words of E. Franklin Frazier, to find a "motive for living under American culture or die." The identity of the American Negro comes out of this extreme situation, and the evolution of this identity was a source of the most intolerable anxiety in the minds and the lives of his masters.

18      For the history of the American Negro is unique also in this: that the question of his humanity, and of his rights therefore as a human being, became a burning one for several generations of Americans, so burning a question that it ultimately became one of those used to divide the nation. It is out of this argument that the venom of the epithet *Nigger!* is derived. It is an argument which Europe has never had, and hence Europe quite sincerely fails to understand how or why the argument arose in the first place, why its effects are so frequently disastrous and always so unpredictable, why it refuses until today to be entirely settled. Europe's black possessions remained—and do remain—in Europe's colonies, at which remove they represented no threat whatever to European identity. If they posed any problem at all for the European conscience, it was a problem which remained comfortingly abstract: in effect, the black man, *as a man,* did not exist for Europe. But in America, even as a slave, he was an inescapable part of the general social fabric and no American could escape having an attitude toward him. Americans attempt until today to make an abstraction of the Negro, but the very nature of these abstractions reveals the tremendous effects the presence of the Negro has had on the American character.

19      When one considers the history of the Negro in America it is of the greatest importance to recognize that the moral beliefs of a person, or a people, are never really as tenuous as life—which is not moral—very often causes them to appear; these create for them a frame of reference and a necessary hope, the hope being that when life has done its worst they will be enabled to rise above themselves and to triumph over life. Life would scarcely be bearable if this hope did not exist. Again, even when the worst has been said, to betray a belief is not by any means to have put oneself beyond its power; the betrayal of a belief is not the same thing as ceasing to believe. If this were not so there would be no moral standards in the world at all. Yet one must also recognize that morality is based on ideas and that all ideas are dangerous—dangerous because ideas can only lead to action and where the action leads no man can say. And dangerous in this respect: that confronted with the impossibility of becoming free of them, one can be driven to the most inhuman excesses. The ideas on which American beliefs are based are not, though Americans often seem to think so, ideas which originated in America. They came out of Europe. And the establishment of democracy on the American continent was scarcely as radical a break with the past as was the necessity, which Americans faced, of broadening this concept to include black men.

20      This was, literally, a hard necessity. It was impossible, for one thing, for Americans to abandon their beliefs, not only because these beliefs alone seemed

able to justify the sacrifices they had endured and the blood that they had spilled, but also because these beliefs afforded them their only bulwark against a moral chaos as absolute as the physical chaos of the continent it was their destiny to conquer. But in the situation in which Americans found themselves, these beliefs threatened an idea which, whether or not one likes to think so, is the very warp and woof of the heritage of the West, the idea of white supremacy.

Americans have made themselves notorious by the shrillness and the brutal-  21 ity with which they have insisted on this idea, but they did not invent it; and it has escaped the world's notice that those very excesses of which Americans have been guilty imply a certain, unprecedented uneasiness over the idea's life and power, if not, indeed, the idea's validity. The idea of white supremacy rests simply on the fact that white men are the creators of civilization (the present civilization, which is the only one that matters; all previous civilizations are simply "contributions" to our own) and are therefore civilization's guardians and defenders. Thus it was impossible for Americans to accept the black man as one of themselves, for to do so was to jeopardize their status as white men. But not so to accept him was to deny his human reality, his human weight and complexity, and the strain of denying the overwhelmingly undeniable forced Americans into rationalizations so fantastic that they approached the pathological.

At the root of the American Negro problem is the necessity of the American  22 white man to find a way of living with the Negro in order to be able to live with himself. And the history of this problem can be reduced to the means used by Americans—lynch law and law, segregation and legal acceptance, terrorization and concession—either to come to terms with this necessity, or to find a way around it, or (most usually) to find a way of doing both these things at once. The resulting spectacle, at once foolish and dreadful, led someone to make the quite accurate observation that "the Negro-in-America is a form of insanity which overtakes white men."

In this long battle, a battle by no means finished, the unforeseeable effects  23 of which will be felt by many future generations, the white man's motive was the protection of his identity; the black man was motivated by the need to establish an identity. And despite the terrorization which the Negro in America endured and endures sporadically until today, despite the cruel and totally inescapable ambivalence of his status in his country, the battle for his identity has long ago been won. He is not a visitor to the West, but a citizen there, an American; as American as the Americans who despise him, the Americans who fear him, the Americans who love him—the Americans who became less than themselves, or rose to be greater than themselves by virtue of the fact that the challenge he represented was inescapable. He is perhaps the only black man in the world whose relationship to white men is more terrible, more subtle, and more meaningful than the relationship of bitter possessed to uncertain possessor. His survival depended, and his development depends, on his ability to turn his peculiar status in the Western world to his own advantage and, it may be, to the very great advantage of that world. It remains for him to fashion out of his experience that which will give him sustenance, and a voice.

24    The cathedral at Chartres, I have said, says something to the people of this village which it cannot say to me; but it is important to understand that this cathedral says something to me which it cannot say to them. Perhaps they are struck by the power of the spires, the glory of the windows; but they have known God, after all, longer than I have known him, and in a different way, and I am terrified by the slippery bottomless well to be found in the crypt, down which heretics were hurled to death, and by the obscene, inescapable gargoyles jutting out of the stone and seeming to say that God and the devil can never be divorced. I doubt that the villagers think of the devil when they face a cathedral because they have never been identified with the devil. But I must accept the status which myth, if nothing else, gives me in the West before I can hope to change the myth.

25    Yet, if the American Negro has arrived at his identity by virtue of the absoluteness of his estrangement from his past, American white men still nourish the illusion that there is some means of recovering the European innocence, of returning to a state in which black men do not exist. This is one of the greatest errors Americans can make. The identity they fought so hard to protect has, by virtue of that battle, undergone a change: Americans are as unlike any other white people in the world as it is possible to be. I do not think, for example, that it is too much to suggest that the American vision of the world—which allows so little reality, generally speaking, for any of the darker forces in human life, which tends until today to paint moral issues in glaring black and white—owes a great deal to the battle waged by Americans to maintain between themselves and black men a human separation which could not be bridged. It is only now beginning to be borne in on us—very faintly, it must be admitted, very slowly, and very much against our will—that this vision of the world is dangerously inaccurate, and perfectly useless. For it protects our moral high-mindedness at the terrible expense of weakening our grasp of reality. People who shut their eyes to reality simply invite their own destruction, and anyone who insists on remaining in a state of innocence long after that innocence is dead turns himself into a monster.

26    The time has come to realize that the interracial drama acted out on the American continent has not only created a new black man, it has created a new white man, too. No road whatever will lead Americans back to the simplicity of this European village where white men still have the luxury of looking on me as a stranger. I am not, really, a stranger any longer for any American alive. One of the things that distinguishes Americans from other people is that no other people has ever been so deeply involved in the lives of black men, and vice versa. This fact faced, with all its implications, it can be seen that the history of the American Negro problem is not merely shameful, it is also something of an achievement. For even when the worst has been said, it must also be added that the perpetual challenge posed by this problem was always, somehow, perpetually met. It is precisely this black-white experience which may prove of indispensable value to us in the world we face today. This world is white no longer, and it will never be white again.

## COMPREHENSION

1. According to Baldwin, what distinguishes Americans from other people? What is his purpose in highlighting these differences?
2. What connections between Europe, Africa, and America emerge from this essay? What is the relevance of the Swiss village to this frame of reference?
3. In the context of the essay, explain what Baldwin means by his statement "People are trapped in history and history is trapped in them" (paragraph 5).

## RHETORIC

1. Analyze the effect of Baldwin's repetition of "there is" and "there are" constructions in paragraph 2. What does the parallelism at the start of paragraph 8 accomplish? Locate other examples of parallelism in the essay.
2. Analyze the image of winter in paragraph 3 and its relation to the rest of the essay.
3. Where in the essay is Baldwin's complex thesis condensed for the reader? What does this placement of thesis reveal about the logical method of development in the essay?
4. How does Baldwin create his introduction? What is the focus? What key motifs does he present that will inform the rest of the essay? What is the relationship of paragraph 5 to paragraph 6?
5. What paragraphs constitute the second section of the essay? What example serves to unify this section? What major shift in emphasis occurs in the third part of the essay? Explain the cathedral of Chartres as a controlling motif between these two sections.
6. What comparisons and contrasts help structure and unify the essay?

## WRITING

1. Examine the paradox implicit in Baldwin's statement in the final paragraph that the history of the American Negro problem is "something of an achievement."
2. Describe a time when you felt yourself a "stranger" in a certain culture.
3. **Writing an Argument:** Write an argumentative essay on civilization based on the last sentence in Baldwin's essay: "This world is white no longer, and it will never be white again."

www.mhhe.com/
**mhreader**

For more information on James Baldwin, go to:
**More Resources > Ch. 7 Government & Politics**

# Some Reflections
# on American Manners

### Alexis de Tocqueville

*Alexis Charles Henri Clerél de Tocqueville (1805–1859), descended from an aristocratic Norman family, was a French lawyer, politician, statesman, and historian. Sent to the United States in 1831 to study the American penal system, he wrote instead one of the most penetrating inquiries into the nature of the American system,* Democracy in America *(1835). In this chapter from his study, Tocqueville compares and contrasts manners as manifested in the political and social contexts of democracy and aristocracy.*

1  Nothing, at first sight, seems less important than the external formalities of human behavior, yet there is nothing to which men attach more importance. They can get used to anything except living in a society which does not share their manners. The influence of the social and political system on manners is therefore worth serious examination.

2  Manners, speaking generally, have their roots in mores; they are also sometimes the result of an arbitrary convention agreed between certain men. They are both natural and acquired.

3  When some see that, without dispute or effort of their own, they stand first in society; when they daily have great aims in view which keep them occupied, leaving details to others; and when they live surrounded by wealth they have not acquired and do not fear to lose, one can see that they will feel a proud disdain for all the petty interests and material cares of life and that there will be a natural grandeur in their thoughts that will show in their words and manners.

4  In democracies there is generally little dignity of manner, as private life is very petty. Manners are often vulgar, as thoughts have small occasion to rise above preoccupation with domestic interests.

5  True dignity in manners consists in always taking one's proper place, not too high and not too low; that is as much within the reach of a peasant as of a prince. In democracies everybody's status seems doubtful; as a result, there is often pride but seldom dignity of manners. Moreover, manners are never well regulated or well thought out.

6  There is too much mobility in the population of a democracy for any definite group to be able to establish a code of behavior and see that it is observed. So everyone behaves more or less after his own fashion, and a certain incoherence of manners always prevails, because they conform to the feelings and ideas of each individual rather than to an ideal example provided for everyone to imitate.

7  In any case, this is much more noticeable when an aristocracy has just fallen than when it has long been destroyed.

New political institutions and new mores then bring together in the same 8
places men still vastly different in education and habits and compel them to a
life in common; this constantly leads to the most ill-assorted juxtapositions.
There is still some memory of the former strict code of politeness, but no one
knows quite what it said or where to find it. Men have lost the common standard of manners but have not yet resolved to do without it, so each individual
tries to shape, out of the ruins of former customs, some rule, however arbitrary
and variable. Hence manners have neither the regularity and dignity frequent
in aristocracies nor the qualities of simplicity and freedom which one sometimes finds in democracies; they are both constrained and casual.

But this is not a normal state of things. 9

When equality is complete and old-established, all men, having roughly the 10
same ideas and doing roughly the same things, do not need to come to an understanding or to copy each other in order to behave and talk in the same way;
one sees a lot of petty variations in their manners but no great differences. They
are never exactly alike, since they do not copy one pattern; they are never very
unlike, because they have the same social condition. At first sight one might be
inclined to say that the manners of all Americans are exactly alike, and it is only
on close inspection that one sees all the variations among them.

The English make game of American manners, but it is odd that most of 11
those responsible for those comic descriptions belong themselves to the English
middle classes, and the cap fits them very well too. So these ruthless critics generally themselves illustrate just what they criticize in America; they do not notice that they are abusing themselves, to the great delight of their own
aristocracy.

Nothing does democracy more harm than its outward forms of behavior; 12
many who could tolerate its vices cannot put up with its manners.

But I will not admit that there is nothing to praise in democratic manners. 13

In aristocracies, all within reach of the ruling class are at pains to imitate it, 14
and very absurd and insipid imitations result. Democracies, with no models of
high breeding before them, at least escape the necessity of daily looking at bad
copies thereof.

In democracies manners are never so refined as among aristocracies, but 15
they are also never so coarse. One misses both the crude words of the mob and
the elegant and choice phrases of the high nobility. There is much triviality of
manner, but nothing brutal or degraded.

I have already said that a precise code of behavior cannot take shape in 16
democracies. That has its inconveniences and its advantages. In aristocracies
rules of propriety impose the same demeanor on all, making every member of
the same class seem alike in spite of personal characteristics; they bedizen and
conceal nature. Democratic manners are neither so well thought out nor so regular, but they often are more sincere. They form, as it were, a thin, transparent
veil through which the real feelings and personal thoughts of each man can be
easily seen. Hence there is frequently an intimate connection between the form
and the substance of behavior; we see a less decorative picture, but one truer to

life. One may put the point this way: democracy imposes no particular manners, but in a sense prevents them from having manners at all.

17      Sometimes the feelings, passions, virtues, and vices of an aristocracy may
reappear in a democracy, but its manners never. They are lost and vanish past
return when the democratic revolution is completed. It would seem that nothing
is more lasting than the manners of an aristocratic class, for it preserves them for
some time after losing property and power, nor more fragile, for as soon as they
have gone, no trace of them is left, and it is even difficult to discover what they
once were when they have ceased to exist. A change in the state of society works
this marvel, and a few generations are enough to bring it about.

18      The principal characteristics of the aristocracy remain engraved in history
after its destruction, but the slight and delicate forms of its manners are lost to
memory almost immediately after its fall. No one can imagine them when they
are no longer seen. Their disappearance is unnoted and unfelt. For the heart
needs an apprenticeship of custom and education to appreciate the refined
pleasure derived from distinguished and fastidious manners; once the habit is
lost, the taste for them easily goes too.

19      Thus, not only are democratic peoples unable to have aristocratic manners,
but they cannot even conceive or desire them. As they cannot imagine them,
from their point of view it is as if they had never existed.

20      One should not attach too much importance to this loss, but it is permissible to regret it.

21      I know it has happened that the same men have had very distinguished
manners and very vulgar feelings; the inner life of courts has shown well
enough what grand appearances may conceal the meanest hearts. But though
the manners of an aristocracy by no means create virtue, they may add grace to
virtue itself. It was no ordinary sight to see a numerous and powerful class
whose every gesture seemed to show a constant and natural dignity of feeling
and thought, an ordered refinement of taste and urbanity of manners.

22      The manners of the aristocracy created a fine illusion about human nature;
though the picture was often deceptive, it was yet a noble satisfaction to look on it.

## COMPREHENSION

1. Summarize Tocqueville's observations about American manners, and explain why he believes they got that way.
2. Explain the positive and negative aspects that Tocqueville finds in both
   aristocratic manners and democratic ones.
3. Why are manners the one element in the transition from an aristocracy to a
   democracy that cannot be transmitted?

## RHETORIC

1. Tocqueville makes a number of points concerning the nature of manners.
   What method, if any, does he use to reach his conclusions?

2. The author seems quite concerned about the concepts of formality and informality. Would you rate his writing as formal or informal? What educational level does he assume his intended audience has attained? Explain your answer.

3. Paragraph 3 is one long sentence. What punctuation devices does Tocqueville use to achieve this? How does his use of the word *when* help give the paragraph a logical structure?

4. We ordinarily think of rhythm as a component of music, yet, by mixing long and short sentences, the author is able to establish a rhythm to his prose. How do the short sentences help keep the prose moving? How do they function as transitional devices?

5. One commonly learns in school not to begin a sentence with the word *but*. Tocqueville breaks this convention three times in his essay—in paragraphs 9, 13, and 21. Explain why this is or is not effective.

6. The author uses comparison and contrast in many of his sentences. For example, in paragraph 15, he lists three distinctions between democratic manners and aristocratic ones. How often does he use this device in the essay? What is the overall effect of using it so consistently?

7. Paragraph 13 offers a rare example of the double negative in English. How does this reflect upon the style of the writing? How would the tone be different if the sentence were "But I will admit there is something to praise in democratic manners"?

## WRITING

1. Select an aspect of American behavior or perspective—such as language, attire, or taste—and write a brief essay explaining your subject, using Tocqueville's writing style.

2. For a research project, use anthropological, cultural, and historical source materials in your library to write an essay about daily life in one American city during the early 19th century.

3. All cultures have rituals concerning things such as conversation, comfort zones, and greeting and leave-taking signals. Browse through a book featuring photographs of a range of people from another era or culture, and write a brief descriptive essay describing their gestures or expressions.

4. **Writing an Argument:** Argue for or against the proposition that manners have nothing to do with democracy.

www.mhhe.com/ **mhreader**   | For more information on Alexis de Tocqueville, go to: **More Resources > Ch. 7 Government & Politics**

# Synthesis: Connections For Critical Thinking

1. Discuss the views that Mukherjee and Baldwin have in common regarding the refusal of American culture to accept the "otherness" of those it perceives as not behaving like or looking like the conventional "American." Expand your discussion to present your own views about the similarities and differences in the ways "white" America views immigrants and African Americans.

2. Compare and contrast the diction, level of discourse, style, and vocabulary of Ivins and Baldwin.

3. Both Thomas Jefferson and Martin Luther King Jr. made powerful appeals to the government in power on behalf of their people. Write a comparison-and-contrast essay that examines the language, style, and content of both essays.

4. Select the three essays you find the most and the least appealing or compelling in this chapter. Discuss why you selected them, and explore the way you developed your viewpoint.

5. Compare and contrast the narrative style of Catton with the more analytical style of Machiavelli.

6. Compare and contrast the difficulties Baldwin had in attempting to "fit in" to an alien European culture with the experiences Mukherjee describes of a nonwhite American trying to assimilate into the dominant culture.

7. Interview five parents who have children under the age of 10, and ask them if and how they control the Internet content their children view. Report your findings to your class.

8. Discuss with a nonnative student Tocqueville's "Reflections on American Manners." Explore to what degree your interviewee agrees with his classic assessments and to what degree his views pertain today.

9. **Network:** Create a "group" chat room with three students from different sections of your course, and discuss Dyson's views on cyberspace regulation. Provide a summary of your discussion to your classmates.

10. **Network:** Conduct online research on Ivins, Mukherjee, and Baldwin. Write an analysis of how their sense of place influences their ideas.

 chapter **8**

# Business and Economics

*How Do We Earn Our Keep?*

Work is central to the human experience; in fact, it is work and its economic and social outcomes that provide us with the keys to an understanding of culture and civilization. Work tells us much about scarcity and abundance, poverty and affluence, the haves and have-nots in any society, as well as a nation's economic imperatives. Whether it is the rise and fall of cities, the conduct of business and corporations, or the economic policies of government, we see in the culture of work an attempt to impose order on nature. Work is our handprint upon the world.

The work we perform and the careers we pursue also define us in very personal ways. "I'm a professor at Harvard" or "I work for IBM" serve as identity badges. (Robert Reich, a contributor to this chapter, did work at Harvard.) For what we do explains, at least in part, what and who we are. The very act of looking for work illuminates one's status in society, one's background, one's aspirations. Jonathan Swift, in his classic essay "A Modest Proposal," written in 1729, demonstrates how labor reveals economic and political configurations of power. Over 250 years later, Reich tells us the same thing in his analysis of the changing nature of work and the way these changes create an even broader gap between rich and poor.

Work is not merely an important human activity but an essential one for social and psychological health. You might like your work, or you might loathe it; be employed or unemployed; enjoy the reputation of a workaholic or a person who lives for leisure time; view work as a curse or as a duty. Regardless, it is work that occupies a central position in your relationship to society. In fact, Sigmund Freud spoke of work as the basis of one's social reality.

Regardless of your perspective on the issue, it is important to understand the multiple dimensions of work. In both traditional and modern societies, work prepares us for economic and social roles. It affects families, school curricula, and public policy. Ultimately, as many authors here suggest, it determines our self-esteem. Through work we come to terms with ourselves and our environment. The nature and purpose of the work we do provide us with a powerful measure of our worth.

494

## Previewing the Chapter

As you read the essays in this chapter and respond to them in discussion and writing, consider the following questions:

- What are the significant forms of support the author uses in viewing the world of work: observation, statistics, personal experience, history, and so on?
- What assumptions does the author make about the value of work?
- Does the author discuss work in general or focus on one particular aspect of work?
- How does the writer define *work*? In what ways, if any, does she or he expand on the simple definition of *work* as "paid employment"?
- What issues of race, class, and gender does the author raise?
- What is the relationship of work to the changing social, political, and economic systems depicted in the author's essay?
- What tone does the writer take in his or her presentation of the work experience?
- What psychological insights does the author offer into the culture of work?
- What does the writer's style reveal about her or his attitude toward work?

✳

# Classic and Contemporary Images
## WILL WORKERS BE DISPLACED BY MACHINES?

*Using a Critical Perspective*   Diego Rivera's mural and George Haling's photograph present industrial scenes that reveal the impact of technology on workers. What details are emphasized in each illustration? How are these two images similar and dissimilar? What, for example, is the relation of human beings to the machines that are the centerpiece of each photograph? Are the artist and photographer objective or subjective in the presentation of each scene? Explain.

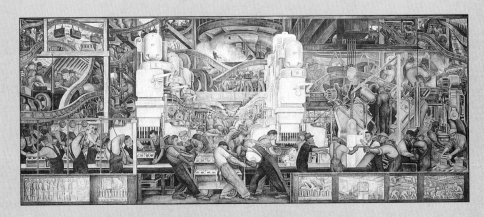

In the era known as the "Machine Age," 1918–1941, many artists, industrial
designers, and architects in the United States and Europe evoked the
mechanisms and images of industry in their works. During this time,
the Mexican painter Diego Rivera (1886–1957) created a mural
for the Detroit Institute of Arts (1932–33),
a portion of which is reprinted here.

Today, computers are used to help control assembly lines,
as shown in this recent photo of a Chrysler assembly line.

# Classic and Contemporary Essays

## DOES EQUAL OPPORTUNITY EXIST?

Virginia Woolf's "Professions for Women" is ironic from the start as she readily admits she can speak expertly of only one profession, her own, which is writing. But her message is clear regarding the effect of living in a male-dominated society. Simply put, it is very difficult to break the shackles of conditioning that one acquires from being told over and over again by one's culture that gender is destiny, regardless of what one aspires to. The author—through personal experience—demonstrates how this discrimination has a profound effect on the ability to see with one's own eyes and to think with one's own head. Henry Louis Gates Jr. presents an interesting variation on this theme. Although the outcome is the same, the premise is reversed. He demonstrates how correlating supposedly positive attributes to a group—that is, superior athletic performance and race—results in the same deadening of the sense of personal ambition and a limiting of the scope of what one can aspire to. The thoughtful reader should be able to learn valuable lessons from comparing and contrasting these essays—one of which is that misguided perception all too often can be a self-fulfilling prophecy.

# Professions for Women

### Virginia Woolf

*Virginia Woolf (1882–1941), novelist and essayist, was the daughter of Sir Leslie Stephen, a famous critic and writer on economics. An experimental novelist, Woolf attempted to portray consciousness through a poetic, symbolic, and concrete style. Her novels include* Jacob's Room *(1922),* Mrs. Dalloway *(1925),* To the Lighthouse *(1927), and* The Waves *(1931). She was also a perceptive reader and critic; her criticism appears in* The Common Reader *(1925) and* The Second Common Reader *(1933). In the following essay, which was delivered originally as a speech to the Women's Service League in 1931, Woolf argues that women must overcome several "angels," or phantoms, in order to succeed in professional careers.*

When your secretary invited me to come here, she told me that your Society is  1
concerned with the employment of women and she suggested that I might tell you something about my own professional experiences. It is true I am a woman; it is true I am employed; but what professional experiences have I had? It is difficult to say. My profession is literature; and in that profession there are fewer experiences for women than in any other, with the exception of the stage—fewer, I mean, that are peculiar to women. For the road was cut many years ago—by Fanny Burney, by Aphra Behn, by Harriet Martineau, by Jane Austen, by George Eliot—many famous women, and many more unknown and forgotten, have been before me, making the path smooth, and regulating my steps. Thus, when I came to write, there were very few material obstacles in my way. Writing was a reputable and harmless occupation. The family peace was not broken by the scratching of a pen. No demand was made upon the family purse. For ten and sixpence one can buy paper enough to write all the plays of Shakespeare—if one has a mind that way. Pianos and models, Paris, Vienna and Berlin, masters and mistresses, are not needed by a writer. The cheapness of writing paper is, of course, the reason why women have succeeded as writers before they have succeeded in the other professions.

But to tell you my story—it is a simple one. You have only got to figure to  2
yourselves a girl in a bedroom with a pen in her hand. She had only to move that pen from left to right—from ten o'clock to one. Then it occurred to her to do what is simple and cheap enough after all—to slip a few of those pages into an envelope, fix a penny stamp in the corner, and drop the envelope into the red box at the corner. It was thus that I became a journalist; and my effort was rewarded on the first day of the following month—a very glorious day it was for me—by a letter from an editor containing a check for one pound ten shillings and sixpence. But to show you how little I deserve to be called a professional

woman, how little I know of the struggles and difficulties of such lives, I have to admit that instead of spending that sum upon bread and butter, rent, shoes and stockings, or butcher's bills, I went out and bought a cat—a beautiful cat, a Persian cat, which very soon involved me in bitter disputes with my neighbors.

3      What could be easier than to write articles and to buy Persian cats with the profits? But wait a moment. Articles have to be about something. Mine, I seem to remember, was about a novel by a famous man. And while I was writing this review, I discovered that if I were going to review books I should need to do battle with a certain phantom. And the phantom was a woman, and when I came to know her better I called her after the heroine of a famous poem, "The Angel in the House." It was she who used to come between me and my paper when I was writing reviews. It was she who bothered me and wasted my time and so tormented me that at last I killed her. You who come of a younger and happier generation may not have heard of her—you may not know what I mean by the Angel in the House. I will describe her as shortly as I can. She was intensely sympathetic. She was immensely charming. She was utterly unselfish. She excelled in the difficult arts of family life. She sacrificed herself daily. If there was a chicken, she took the leg; if there was a draught she sat in it—in short she was so constituted that she never had a mind or a wish of her own, but preferred to sympathize always with the minds and wishes of others. Above all—I need not say it—she was pure. Her purity was supposed to be her chief beauty—her blushes, her great grace. In those days—the last of Queen Victoria— every house had its Angel. And when I came to write I encountered her with the very first words. The shadow of her wings fell on my page; I heard the rustling of her skirts in the room. Directly, that is to say, I took my pen in hand to review that novel by a famous man, she slipped behind me and whispered: "My dear, you are a young woman. You are writing about a book that has been written by a man. Be sympathetic; be tender; flatter; deceive; use all the arts and wiles of our sex. Never let anybody guess that you have a mind of your own. Above all, be pure." And she made as if to guide my pen. I now record the one act for which I take some credit to myself, though the credit rightly belongs to some excellent ancestors of mine who left me a certain sum of money—shall we say five hundred pounds a year—so that it was not necessary for me to depend solely on charm for my living. I turned upon her and caught her by the throat. I did my best to kill her. My excuse, if I were to be had up in a court of law, would be that I acted in self-defense. Had I not killed her she would have killed me. She would have plucked the heart out of my writing. For, as I found, directly I put pen to paper, you cannot review even a novel without having a mind of your own, without expressing what you think to be the truth about human relations, morality, sex. And all these questions, according to the Angel in the House, cannot be dealt with freely and openly by women; they must charm, they must conciliate, they must—to put it bluntly—tell lies if they are to succeed. Thus, whenever I felt the shadow of her wing or the radiance of her halo upon my page, I took up the inkpot and flung it at her. She died hard. Her fictitious nature was of great assistance to her. It is far harder to kill a phantom than

a reality. She was always creeping back when I thought I had dispatched her. Though I flatter myself that I killed her in the end, the struggle was severe; it took much time that had better have been spent upon learning Greek grammar; or in roaming the world in search of adventures. But it was a real experience; it was an experience that was bound to befall all women writers at that time. Killing the Angel in the House was part of the occupation of a woman writer.

But to continue my story. The Angel was dead; what then remained? You may say that what remained was a simple and common object—a young woman in a bedroom with an inkpot. In other words, now that she had rid herself of falsehood, that young woman had only to be herself. Ah, but what is "herself"? I mean, what is a woman? I assure you, I do not know. I do not believe that you know. I do not believe that anybody can know until she has expressed herself in all the arts and professions open to human skill. That indeed is one of the reasons why I have come here—out of respect for you, who are in process of showing us by your experiments what a woman is, who are in process of providing us, by your failures and successes, with that extremely important piece of information.

But to continue the story of my professional experiences. I made one pound 5 ten and six by my first review; and I bought a Persian cat with the proceeds. Then I grew ambitious. A Persian cat is all very well, I said; but a Persian cat is not enough. I must have a motor car. And it was thus that I became a novelist— for it is a very strange thing that people will give you a motor car if you will tell them a story. It is a still stranger thing that there is nothing so delightful in the world as telling stories. It is far pleasanter than writing reviews of famous novels. And yet, if I am to obey your secretary and tell you my professional experiences as a novelist, I must tell you about a very strange experience that befell me as a novelist. And to understand it you must try first to imagine a novelist's state of mind. I hope I am not giving away professional secrets if I say that a novelist's chief desire is to be as unconscious as possible. He has to induce in himself a state of perpetual lethargy. He wants life to proceed with the utmost quiet and regularity. He wants to see the same faces, to read the same books, to do the same things day after day, month after month, while he is writing, so that nothing may break the illusion in which he is living—so that nothing may disturb or disquiet the mysterious nosings about, feelings round, darts, dashes and sudden discoveries of that very shy and illusive spirit, the imagination. I suspect that this state is the same both for men and women. Be that as it may, I want you to imagine me writing a novel in a state of trance. I want you to figure to yourselves a girl sitting with a pen in her hand, which for minutes, and indeed for hours, she never dips into the inkpot. The image that comes to my mind when I think of this girl is the image of a fisherman lying sunk in dreams on the verge of a deep lake with a rod held out over the water. She was letting her imagination sweep unchecked round every rock and cranny of the world that lies submerged in the depths of our unconscious being. Now came the experience, the experience that I believe to be far commoner with women writers than with men. The line raced through the girl's fingers. Her imagination had rushed away. It had sought the pools, the depths, the dark places where the largest fish slumber.

And then there was a smash. There was an explosion. There was foam and confusion. The imagination had dashed itself against something hard. The girl was
roused from her dream. She was indeed in a state of the most acute and difficult
distress. To speak without figure she had thought of something, something
about the body, about the passions which it was unfitting for her as a woman to
say. Men, her reason told her, would be shocked. The consciousness of what
men will say of a woman who speaks the truth about her passions had roused
her from her artist's state of unconsciousness. She could write no more. The
trance was over. Her imagination could work no longer. This I believe to be a
very common experience with women writers—they are impeded by the
extreme conventionality of the other sex. For though men sensibly allow themselves great freedom in these respects, I doubt that they realize or can control the
extreme severity with which they condemn such freedom in women.

6　　　These then were two very genuine experiences of my own. These were two of
the adventures of my professional life. The first—killing the Angel in the House—
I think I solved. She died. But the second, telling the truth about my own experiences as a body, I do not think I solved. I doubt that any woman has solved it yet.
The obstacles against her are still immensely powerful—and yet they are very difficult to define. Outwardly, what is simpler than to write books? Outwardly, what
obstacles are there for a woman rather than for a man? Inwardly, I think, the case
is very different; she has still many ghosts to fight, many prejudices to overcome.
Indeed it will be a long time still, I think, before a woman can sit down to write a
book without finding a phantom to be slain, a rock to be dashed against. And if
this is so in literature, the freest of all professions for women, how is it in the new
professions which you are now for the first time entering?

7　　　Those are the questions that I should like, had I time, to ask you. And indeed, if I have laid stress upon these professional experiences of mine, it is because I believe that they are, though in different forms, yours also. Even when
the path is nominally open—when there is nothing to prevent a woman from
being a doctor, a lawyer, a civil servant—there are many phantoms and obstacles, as I believe, looming in her way. To discuss and define them is I think of
great value and importance; for thus only can the labor be shared, the difficulties be solved. But besides this, it is necessary also to discuss the ends and the
aims for which we are fighting, for which we are doing battle with these formidable obstacles. Those aims cannot be taken for granted; they must be perpetually questioned and examined. The whole position, as I see it—here in this hall
surrounded by women practicing for the first time in history I know not how
many different professions—is one of extraordinary interest and importance.
You have won rooms of your own in the house hitherto exclusively owned by
men. You are able, though not without great labor and effort, to pay the rent.
You are earning your five hundred pounds a year. But this freedom is only a
beginning; the room is your own, but it is still bare. It has to be furnished; it has
to be decorated; it has to be shared. How are you going to furnish it, how are
you going to decorate it? With whom are you going to share it, and upon what
terms? These, I think, are questions of the utmost importance and interest. For

the first time in history you are able to ask for them; for the first time you are able to decide for yourselves what the answers should be. Willingly would I stay and discuss those questions and answers—but not tonight. My time is up; and I must cease.

## COMPREHENSION

1. This essay was presented originally as a speech. What internal evidence indicates that it was intended as a talk? How do you respond to it today as a reader?
2. Who or what is the "angel" that Woolf describes in this essay? Why must she kill it? What other obstacles does a professional woman encounter?
3. Paraphrase the last two paragraphs of this essay. What is the essence of Woolf's argument?

## RHETORIC

1. There is a significant amount of figurative language in the essay. Locate and explain examples. What does the figurative language contribute to the tone of the essay? Compare and contrast the figurative language in this essay with that in Woolf's "The Death of the Moth" in Chapter 1.
2. How do we know that Woolf is addressing an audience of women? Why does she pose so many questions, and what does this strategy contribute to the rapport she wants to establish? Explain the effect of the last two sentences.
3. How does Woolf use analogy to structure part of her argument?
4. Why does Woolf rely on personal narration? How does it affect the logic of her argument?
5. Evaluate Woolf's use of contrast to advance her argument.
6. Where does Woolf place her main proposition? How emphatic is it, and why?

## WRITING

1. How effectively does Woolf use her own example as a professional writer to advance a broader proposition concerning all women entering professional life? Answer this question in a brief essay.
2. Discuss the problems and obstacles that you anticipate when you enter your chosen career.
3. **Writing an Argument:** Argue for or against the proposition that Woolf's essay has little relevance for women planning careers today.

www.mhhe.com/
**mhreader**

For more information on Virginia Woolf, go to:
**More Resources > Ch. 8 Business & Economics**

# Delusions of Grandeur

## Henry Louis Gates Jr.

*Henry Louis Gates Jr. (b. 1950) is an educator, writer, and editor. He was born in West Virginia and educated at Yale and at Clare College in Cambridge. Gates has had a varied career, working as a general anesthetist in Tanzania and as a staff correspondent for* Time *magazine in London. His essays have appeared in such diverse publications as* Black American Literature Forum, Yale Review, The New York Times Book Review, *and* Sports Illustrated. *He is also the author of* Figures in Black: Words, Signs and the Racial Self *(1987) and* The Signifying Monkey: A Theory of Afro-American Literary Criticism *(1988) and is the editor, with Nellie Y. McKey, of* The Norton Anthology of African American Literature *(1996). In this article from* Sports Illustrated, *Gates turns his attention to the limited career choices presented as viable to African American youth and to public misconceptions about blacks in sports.*

1    Standing at the bar of an all-black VFW post in my hometown of Piedmont, W.Va., I offered five dollars to anyone who could tell me how many African-American professional athletes were at work today. There are 35 million African-Americans, I said.

2    "Ten million!" yelled one intrepid soul, too far into his cups.

3    "No way . . . more like 500,000," said another.

4    "You mean *all* professional sports," someone interjected, "including golf and tennis, but not counting the brothers from Puerto Rico?" Everyone laughed.

5    "Fifty thousand, minimum," was another guess.

6    Here are the facts:

There are 1,200 black professional athletes in the U.S.

There are 12 times more black lawyers than black athletes.

There are 2½ times more black dentists than black athletes.

There are 15 times more black doctors than black athletes.

7    Nobody in my local VFW believed these statistics; in fact, few people would believe them if they weren't reading them in the pages of *Sports Illustrated*. In spite of these statistics, too many African-American youngsters still believe that they have a much better chance of becoming another Magic Johnson or Michael Jordan than they do of matching the achievements of Baltimore Mayor Kurt Schmoke or neurosurgeon Dr. Benjamin Carson, both of whom, like Johnson and Jordan, are black.

8    In reality, an African-American youngster has about as much chance of becoming a professional athlete as he or she does of winning the lottery. The tragedy for our people, however, is that few of us accept that truth.

Let me confess that I love sports. Like most black people of my generation— 9
I'm 40—I was raised to revere the great black athletic heroes, and I never tired
of listening to the stories of triumph and defeat that, for blacks, amount to a collective epic much like those of the ancient Greeks: Joe Louis's demolition of
Max Schmeling; Satchel Paige's dazzling repertoire of pitches; Jesse Owens's
in-your-face performance in Hitler's 1936 Olympics; Willie Mays's over-
the-shoulder basket catch; Jackie Robinson's quiet strength when assaulted by
racist taunts; and a thousand other grand tales.

Nevertheless, the blind pursuit of attainment in sports is having a devastat- 10
ing effect on our people. Imbued with a belief that our principal avenue to fame
and profit is through sport, and seduced by a win-at-any-cost system that corrupts even elementary school students, far too many black kids treat basketball
courts and football fields as if they were classrooms in an alternative school
system. "O.K., I flunked English," a young athlete will say. "But I got an A plus
in slamdunking."

The failure of our public schools to educate athletes is part and parcel of the 11
schools' failure to educate almost everyone. A recent survey of the Philadelphia
school system, for example, stated that "more than half of all students in the third,
fifth and eighth grades cannot perform minimum math and language tasks." One
in four middle school students in that city fails to pass to the next grade each
year. It is a sad truth that such statistics are repeated in cities throughout the
nation. Young athletes—particularly young black athletes—are especially ill-
served. Many of them are functionally illiterate, yet they are passed along from
year to year for the greater glory of good old Hometown High. We should not be
surprised to learn, then, that only 26.6 percent of black athletes at the collegiate
level earn their degrees. For every successful educated black professional athlete,
there are thousands of dead and wounded. Yet young blacks continue to aspire
to careers as athletes, and it's no wonder why; when the University of North
Carolina recently commissioned a sculptor to create archetypes of its student
body, guess which ethnic group was selected to represent athletes?

Those relatively few black athletes who do make it in the professional ranks 12
must be prevailed upon to play a significant role in the education of all of our
young people, athlete and nonathlete alike. While some have done so, many
others have shirked their social obligations: to earmark small percentages of
their incomes for the United Negro College Fund; to appear on television for
educational purposes rather than merely to sell sneakers; to let children know
the message that becoming a lawyer, a teacher or a doctor does more good for
our people than winning the Super Bowl; and to form productive liaisons with
educators to help forge solutions to the many ills that beset the black community. These are merely a few modest proposals.

A similar burden falls upon successful blacks in all walks of life. Each of 13
us must strive to make our young people understand the realities. Tell them
to cheer Bo Jackson but to emulate novelist Toni Morrison or businessman
Reginald Lewis or historian John Hope Franklin or Spelman College president Johnetta Cole—the list is long.

14      Of course, society as a whole bears responsibility as well. Until colleges stop using young blacks as cannon fodder in the big-business wars of so-called nonprofessional sports, until training a young black's mind becomes as important as training his or her body, we will continue to perpetuate a system akin to that of the Roman gladiators, sacrificing a class of people for the entertainment of the mob.

## COMPREHENSION

1. What does Gates suggest is the general assumption made about African Americans in sports?
2. Why do American schools continue to perpetuate the myth that Gates is writing about?
3. According to Gates, what should successful African American athletes do to help guide the career choices of young black males?

## RHETORIC

1. What is Gates's thesis? Where does it appear?
2. How does the introductory paragraph work to set up the writer's focus?
3. State Gates's purpose in using statistics in his essay.
4. What is the tone of Gates's essay? Cite specific sections where this tone seems strongest.
5. Examine the accumulation of facts in paragraph 11. How does this technique underscore Gates's point?
6. Explain Gates's allusion to Roman gladiators in his conclusion. How does it aid in emphasizing his main point?

## WRITING

1. Write a brief essay in which you analyze your personal reaction to Gates's statistics. Were you surprised by them? What assumptions did you have about the number of black athletes? Why do you think most Americans share these assumptions?
2. Write a biographical research paper on the life and career of an African American athlete.
3. **Writing an Argument:** Pretend you are addressing a group of young African Americans at an elementary school. Argue that sports and entertainment should (or should not) be their career choices.

www.mhhe.com/
**mhreader**

For more information on Henry Louis Gates Jr., go to:
**More Resources > Ch. 8 Business & Economics**

## Synthesis:  Classic  and  Contemporary Questions  for  Comparison

1. Examine the argumentative styles of Woolf and Gates. What are their main propositions? Their minor propositions? What evidence do they provide?
2. Woolf first presented her paper as a speech before an audience of women. Gates wrote his essay as an opinion piece for *Sports Illustrated*. Write a comparative audience analysis of the two selections. Analyze purpose, tone, style, and any other relevant aspects of the two essays.
3. Argue for or against the proposition that white women and African American men face the same barriers to employment in today's professions. Refer to the essays by Woolf and Gates to support your position.

# Manna from Hell

### Liza Featherstone

*Liza Featherstone (b. 1969), an investigative reporter and columnist, is the author of* Selling Women Short: The Landmark Battle for Workers' Rights at Wal-Mart *(2005). She has also published* Students against Sweatshop Labor *(1991). As a syndicated columnist and contributing editor to* The Nation, *Featherstone is a forceful advocate for the rights of women and working-class individuals. In this essay, Featherstone, who acknowledges the research efforts of colleagues Laura Starecheski and Meleiza Figueroa, exposes the use of Wal-Mart charitable dollars to promote a conservative agenda.*

With a combined fortune of more than $90 billion, the Waltons—the immediate   1
heirs of Wal-Mart founder Sam Walton—are the richest family in the world. Five of the country's ten richest individuals are members of Sam's immediate family: his wife, Helen, and their three surviving children—Rob, Jim and Alice—as well as his late son John's widow, Christy (John Walton died in June when his private plane crashed). Until recently, however, they gave away little of their fortune. As Sam Walton explained in his 1992 autobiography, *Made in America*, he didn't believe in giving "any undeserving stranger a free ride." Nor did he believe in being generous with company profits. "We feel very strongly," he wrote, "that Wal-Mart really is *not*, and *should not* be, in the charity business." Money that Wal-Mart donated to charity, he reasoned, would only come out of the pockets of "either our share holders or our customers." (He didn't mention workers, perhaps a tacit acknowledgment that picking their pockets was just business as usual.) As for politics, Sam couldn't stand the stuff. At a 1988 Mother's Day "toast and roast" honoring Helen Walton, then-Senator Dale

Bumpers of Arkansas quipped that waiting for big campaign contributions from the Waltons was like "leaving landing lights on for Amelia Earhart."

2      All that has changed. Since Sam died in 1992, both the Bentonville, Arkansas–based company and the family have dramatically escalated their charitable giving, becoming far more influential in the worlds of philanthropy and politics. It is hardly a coincidence that this transformation occurred after Wal-Mart became the nation's largest private employer and a flytrap for much-deserved criticism. The company is battling numerous employee rights lawsuits in court, the biggest of these being *Betty Dukes v. Wal-Mart Stores*, a sex-discrimination class action representing 1.6 million women. Communities around the nation, charging that the company is a stingy low-wage employer with an arrogant disregard for local and national laws, are battling to keep Wal-Mart from opening or expanding stores. Several labor unions have made fighting Wal-Mart a top priority. This year two major national organizations, Wal-Mart Watch and Wake Up Wal-Mart, formed to lead a citizens' movement to pressure the company to change its ways.

3      The National Committee for Responsive Philanthropy (NCRP), a watch-dog group, released a report in September, *The Waltons and Wal-Mart: Self-Interested Philanthropy*, detailing the recent increase in Wal-Mart and Walton philanthropy and noting its likely relationship to the company's image problems. Indeed, the increase has been staggering. The Walton Family Foundation (WFF) gave away $106.9 million in 2003—the most recent year for which data are available—twice as much as in 2000. Wal-Mart's company PAC, now the third-largest corporate PAC and the second-largest corporate donor to the GOP, gave away $2.1 million in 2004, compared with just $100,000 in 1994. The Walton family, too, has greatly increased its political giving; in 2004, for example, Alice donated $2.6 million to the influential Republican PAC Progress for America, which supported the sleazy Swift Boat Veterans for Truth and gave Bush a critical push in the election's final months. Since 1999 the Wal-Mart Foundation (WMF)—a company-controlled entity with no direct connection to the WFF—has tripled its giving and by the end of this year will have doled out more than $200 million in cash and merchandise, according to spokeswoman Melissa O'Brien.

4      The company also donated $20 million in cash and merchandise to the Hurricane Katrina relief effort, garnering extensive—and partially justified—praise. To antigovernment zealots like *New York Times* columnist John Tierney and the wing nuts running the *Wall Street Journal* editorial page, Wal-Mart's impressive response to the hurricane showed that the private sector is simply more effective than the government. It is true that when you starve government by draining its resources and electing officials who don't believe in it, nothing seems to work. But Wal-Mart played a major role in that eviscerating process. Much of Wal-Mart's philanthropy (as well as that of the Walton family) has been directed toward promoting antigovernment politics, whether by lobbying against high taxes for the rich or contributing to Republican candidates, conservative think tanks and efforts to privatize education.

Jeff Krehely, who co-wrote the NCRP report, says that for his organization, 5
such a sharp increase in giving, coupled with the company's obvious desire to
spin itself as a better corporate citizen, "raises red flags. We wonder, What's the
agenda here? What's happening?" The WMF's Melissa O'Brien told *The Nation*
that criticisms of the company come from "special-interest groups" and do not
influence its giving. She also told the *New York Sun* that the NCRP report was
funded by Target, a charge Krehely calls "ludicrous." (Dayton Hudson, Target's
former parent company, contributed to the NCRP in the 1990s. In 2000 the company reorganized as the Target Corporation and hasn't contributed to the
watchdog group since.)

Each Walton heir has philanthropic projects of his or her own—Alice, for 6
example, is building a world-class art museum in northwest Arkansas—but the
family fortune should be considered as one because most of the money is managed together. The giving is also largely administered together, through the
Walton Family Foundation, as well as through close communication among its
family members. (At least twice a year, the family meets to talk about how to
spend its money.) The Waltons own about 40 percent of Wal-Mart's stock, making Wal-Mart essentially a family business—highly unusual for a large multinational company. (Both the Wal-Mart Family Foundation and Walton
Enterprises—the company that represents the Walton family's interests—
declined to cooperate with this article, or to make any of the notoriously press-
shy Waltons available for interviews.)

Philanthropy obscures the often unseemly process by which the money 7
was made—and for Wal-Mart that's at least part of the point. Stephen Copley,
a United Methodist Church pastor who serves on the board of the Arkansas
Single Parents Scholarship Fund, a Springdale, Arkansas, charity that has benefited from Walton dollars, says that the program has "an incredible success
rate. One lady even got a PhD. [The Walton money] does a tremendous amount
of good." However, he adds, "it's great to help single parents go to school, but
those same single parents might be working for Wal-Mart, and they can't afford
health insurance." Copley, also head of the Arkansas Interfaith Committee for
Worker Justice, is troubled that in his home state, Walton and Wal-Mart generosity "gets great media . . . they look so good even though in reality their business practices are very bad."

The Wal-Mart Foundation gives a staggering number of gifts, apparently in 8
order to buy goodwill in as many communities as possible, rather than, as Krehely points out, "giving to sustain organizations." The WMF's 2003 IRS 990
form is 2,239 pages long, far longer than that of the Ford Foundation, which has
billions more in assets. That's because most WMF gifts are tiny: thousands or
even hundreds of dollars to churches and Lions clubs and Boys and Girls clubs,
$500 to the YMCA of Nashville and Middle Tennessee and to the Tulip Trace
(Indiana) Girl Scouts Council and so on. Communities where Wal-Mart faced a
particular battle over opening a new store—Inglewood, California, or New
York City—enjoyed especially generous largesse. Like the flowers and other
tokens of courtship from a suitor who later becomes a wife-beater, such gifts

are often followed by demands for public subsidies and tax breaks. In this way Wal-Mart is repeating the strategy that has served it so well in Arkansas, where Wal-Mart and the Waltons' charitable gifts are many and company critics are relatively few. Says Lindsay Brown, president of the Central Arkansas Labor Council, "It's a hell of a plan, and it works."

9  We are supposed to applaud philanthropy—the very word connotes altruism and "giving back"—but Walton and Wal-Mart giving serves as a reminder that philanthropy provides an alternative to taxation, a way for rich people and corporations to decide what to do with their extra money, as opposed to letting the rest of us decide through our elected governments. Since charitable donations are a tax write-off, as Krehely points out, "they are supposed to benefit the public good." He thinks it is reasonable to ask whether a family's—or a company's—philanthropy serves the common good, or at least enough good "to make up for the public revenue that we're losing."

10       Funny he should mention taxes: Wal-Mart and the Waltons have, after all, been notably reluctant to pay them. Not only has the company lobbied for tax breaks in communities all over the nation, the Waltons—the family that former Wal-Mart board member Hillary Clinton has called "the best America has to offer"—have campaigned vigorously against the estate tax. They have donated money to its opponents, Republicans like John Thune of South Dakota and David Vitter of South Carolina, and enlisted one of Washington's top lobbying firms, Patton Boggs—a leading anti–estate tax lobbyist—to represent their interests.

11       Chuck Collins of Responsible Wealth, a group of well-off people who strongly favor the estate tax, observes that the Waltons sometimes say the estate tax is not a priority for the family. "That may be true from their perspective," he says, "but it's a bit like an elephant saying it's really not interested in stepping on anthills. When you're America's wealthiest family, you are a philanthropic and lobbying heavyweight even on your minor interests." For instance, Senator Blanche Lincoln of Arkansas, one of a handful of Democrats who draw checks from the Waltons, supports estate-tax repeal (or crippling "reform"). "Senator Lincoln will wax eloquent about the small farmers of Arkansas," Collins says, "but what's really on her mind is Walton."

12  In addition to campaigning specifically against the estate tax, the Waltons also give money to groups that generally favor tax giveaways to the rich, like Americans for Tax Reform. And the Waltons have already reaped the benefits of tax policies enacted by the conservatives they helped put in office: This year Bush's dividend tax cut will save the family $51 million, according to Lee Farris, an estate-tax expert with the Boston-based United for a Fair Economy.

13       The Waltons' philanthropy—and their hostility to paying their fair share of taxes—also needs to be viewed in the context of tax subsidies Wal-Mart has received for building new stores, which Good Jobs First places at more than $1 billion, an estimate that does not include the many other ways taxpayers subsidize Wal-Mart stores, for instance, through numerous forms of public

assistance—Medicaid, Food Stamps, public housing—that often allow workers to subsist on Wal-Mart's low wages. A report by the House Education and
Workforce Committee conservatively places the latter at $420,750 per store;
the Wal-Mart Foundation's per-store charitable giving is just 11 percent of
that amount ($47,222).

In addition to spending on Republican candidates, the Waltons have lav- 14
ished funds on right-wing ideological institutions—organizations that serve the
interest of wealthy individuals and lawless antiunion companies like Wal-Mart.
From 1998 through 2003 the WFF contributed $25,000 to the Heritage Founda-
tion, $15,000 to the Cato Institute, $125,000 to the Hudson Institute, $155,000 to
the Goldwater Institute, $70,000 to the National Right to Work Legal Defense
Foundation, $300,000 to the Mackinac Center for Public Policy, $185,000 to the
Pacific Research Institute for Public Policy and $350,000 to the Evergreen Free-
dom Foundation.

Both the family and the company have made education a major funding 15
priority. Many of the WFF's education gifts have a distinct ideological tilt, emphasizing a "free market" approach to education reform, a vision the late John
Walton embraced with particular enthusiasm. The WFF funds advocacy groups
promoting conservative school "reform"—otherwise known as privatization—
like the Center for Education Reform and the Black Alliance for Educational
Options, as well as the actual programs these groups champion: charter schools
and voucher programs. (The BAEO did not return calls for this article.)

Among such projects, the Waltons tend to fund the most mind-numbing 16
and cultish, giving in 2003 alone nearly $3 million to Knowledge Is Power (KIPP)
schools and millions more to other schools using the KIPP curriculum, which
emphasizes regimented recitation rather than critical or creative thinking. Particularly widespread in low-income neighborhoods, such schools seem bent on
disciplining and exhorting the poor rather than developing human potential
(much like Wal-Mart as a workplace, with its relentless company cheers and
dead-end jobs.) Several years ago the principal of New York City's John A. Rei-
senbach Charter School, which uses the KIPP curriculum and received $118,000
from the Waltons in 2003, told me proudly, as we watched fidgety second graders chant meaningless slogans, "We are getting them ready for business."

The WFF has become the single largest source of funding for the voucher 17
and charter school movement. Walton funding allows some charter schools to
spend more per pupil than "competing" public schools. The ironic result is that
while these projects are supposed to demonstrate to the public the wonders of
a marketized approach to education, the WFF's money gives its grantees an
advantage over other schools, allowing them to perform better than they would
otherwise. "[The Waltons] claim to support competition and the free market,"
says Paul Dunphy, a policy analyst for Citizens for Public Schools, a Boston-
based coalition, "but actually they are manipulating the market, conferring advantage on their pet projects."

It's a fitting paradox, since the Wal-Mart economic model, like almost any- 18
thing held up as an example of the beauty of the free market, contains so many

contradictions (yes, it's extremely profitable, but look at all those tax subsidies). Because so much Walton and Wal-Mart philanthropy is crudely self-interested, it's tempting to find an equally crude motive for the Walton family's interest in education; many Wal-Mart critics have assumed that the Waltons must be planning to reap several more fortunes through for-profit education companies. That's not completely baseless: John Walton was briefly involved in such a venture. However, he backed out, realizing such profiteering was hurting the credibility of his education reform efforts. And so far, for-profit education is still not a very profitable industry—especially when compared with retail.

19   The Waltons' motives for supporting the privatization of education seem—at this writing, anyway—to be ideological, even idealistic, rather than an elaborate backdrop to a new money-making scheme. Like many rich Americans who have helped to finance the far right's rise to power, they have embraced a worldview in which what's good for the wealthy is good for everyone else. And greater cultural acceptance of the unfettered market—through an increasing tolerance for privatization of all kinds—will certainly make the world safer for a family business that thrives on weak government and lack of regulation. But it's also likely that the Waltons, like most right-wingers, sincerely believe that their ideas have the potential to improve people's lives. Why wouldn't the Waltons genuinely believe in the free market? Look how well it has served them.

20       Helen Walton, now 85 and in poor health, is expected to donate almost all of her personal fortune—worth $18 billion—to the WFF upon her death, which, as the NCRP points out, will make that entity the richest foundation in the world. This should disturb progressives, since so much Walton money goes to support conservative causes. Yet although the current direction and political leanings of Walton "philanthropy" are clear, the future is a mystery. As Krehely observes, nothing is known about the politics or interests of Sam Walton's grandchildren. This matters in a family foundation; this fall the Olin Foundation closed its doors, having spent down its endowment because the older generation did not trust the younger Olins to carry on the family's right-wing traditions. Since the Waltons don't say much about their future plans, or about their internal family politics, it's unclear what lies in store for this—currently—right-wing fortune.

21       "The Waltons could be an enormous force for good," says Responsible Wealth's Chuck Collins. "As the company's biggest shareholders, they could decide that Wal-Mart could pay a living wage. They could use their charitable dollars not to undermine public education but to boost educational opportunity. They could become major contributors to social good. But they're not."

22       One item in the Walton Family Foundation's most recent IRS filing shown how uninterested this family is in true social responsibility: a measly $6,000 to something called the Wal-Mart Associates in Need Fund. Contrast that with the millions the family spends promoting right-wing causes, and it becomes painfully clear that the Waltons value conservative ideology far more than they value the human beings who have made them the richest family on earth. Told

about these figures, Kathleen MacDonald, a Wal-Mart candy department clerk in Aiken, South Carolina, responded bluntly, "All I have to say about that is, it doesn't surprise me. Like Bush, they don't have a clue what working families go through." MacDonald would like to see *The Simple Life* do a show about working at Wal-Mart. "I could see Paris Hilton on a register at Christmastime, or stocking shelves," she says. Or perhaps Alice Walton as a greeter, on her feet all day, thanking us for shopping at Wal-Mart.

## COMPREHENSION

1. What is the main point of Featherstone's argument? How well do you think she makes it, and why? Justify your response.
2. Summarize the philanthropic projects of the Walton family as Featherstone presents them. What is your own impression of these charitable projects?
3. According to Featherstone, what are the links between charitable giving and politics? Do you think that the Walton family is unique in this respect or symptomatic of a broader connection between money and politics? Explain.

## RHETORIC

1. How does the title capture Featherstone's tone, scope, and method in this essay?
2. What is the purpose of the first two introductory paragraphs? Why does Featherstone provide quotations from the founder of Wal-Mart, Sam Walton?
3. Featherstone traces a chain of causality in her article. Explain the pattern of cause and effect governing the essay's organization.
4. Argument is supposed to be balanced rather than biased—even as it is convincing and persuasive in its claim. Does Featherstone follow this prescription for argument? Why or why not? For example, does she present opposing viewpoints? Does she avoid logical and emotional fallacies? Are her ethical charges and appeals fair? Justify your response to these questions and other issues that you cite.
5. What forms of evidence does Featherstone introduce to support her major and minor propositions?
6. How does Featherstone use irony and satire to advance her claim, and what is the effect?

## WRITING

1. Write a précis (concise summary) of Featherstone's essay, capturing the essential points in her argument.

2. Collaborating with one or two classmates, conduct your own research on Wal-Mart, and then write a report on your findings.
3. **Writing an Argument:** Write a counterclaim to Featherstone's argument, advancing the proposition that Wal-Mart is actually good for America.

www.mhhe.com/ **mhreader**

For more information on Liza Featherstone, go to: **More Resources > Ch. 8 Business & Economics**

# Mapping Innovation

## P. J. O'Rourke

*P(atrick) J(ake) O'Rourke (b. 1947), a celebrated conservative humorist and commentator, is noted for his ability to parody and satirize contemporary life while at the same time offering unique insights into the human condition. Born in Toledo, Ohio, he received a BA from Miami University (1969) and an MA from Johns Hopkins University (1970). A frequent contributor to such magazines as* Harper's, Playboy, American Spectator, *and* The Weekly Standard, *O'Rourke has also served as an editor at* The National Lampoon *and* Rolling Stone. *He has written more than a dozen books, among them* Modern Manners: An Etiquette Book for Rude People *(1983),* Holidays in Hell *(1988),* Give War a Chance *(1992),* Peace Kills *(2004), and* On the Wealth of Nations *(2006). O'Rourke currently is a correspondent for* The Atlantic Monthly, *where the following essay on innovation appeared in 2007.*

1 Predicting innovation is something of a self-canceling exercise: the most probable innovations are probably the least innovative. The history of humankind's development can be summed up as the story of surprise. Adam Smith failed to forecast the Industrial Revolution despite his friendship with James Watt, inventor of the steam engine that powered it. And who would have prophesied MySpace, Oprah, or a TSA ban on hair-styling gel in quantities greater than three ounces?

2    But even if we can't see what innovations are around the corner, maybe we can at least predict what places are likely to be the most innovative in the future. And an innovative tool called Worldmapper might help.

3    Worldmapper was created by geographers from the University of Sheffield's Social and Spatial Inequalities Research Group (*there's* an innovative college major) and by Mark Newman, a physicist at the University of Michigan. It allows them to turn all sorts of obscure statistical information into vivid

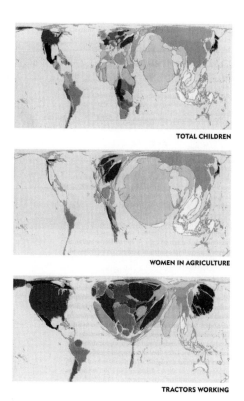

TOTAL CHILDREN

WOMEN IN AGRICULTURE

TRACTORS WORKING

pictures. Countries look skinny or fat according to their share of wealth or trade or population, but retain their familiar national boundary shapes. The results are often cartoonish, but nonetheless scientifically precise. Perhaps a decidedly unscientific tour through a few of Worldmapper's more than 200 maps will help us see which countries are best endowed with the stuff of future innovation—and whether the United States has a fat or a skinny future.

## Mother is the Necessity of Invention

No place can be innovative without children. This is not because of the plati-    4
tudinous link between youth and creativity; the children's art on my refrigerator suggests there isn't any. Ben Franklin was no kid when he invented bifocals. Henry Ford, by all accounts, seems never to have been youthful. But countries with children, demographers predict, will have adults. India, China, and the nations of Africa and South Asia are in the lead, as the **Total Children** map shows. Note, however, that there are adequate numbers of children elsewhere, even in supposedly child-proof Europe and Japan, and plenty in the United States. And not every child will grow up to be an innovative adult.

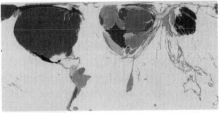

FEMALE MANAGERS

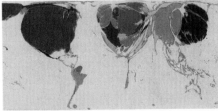

TOTAL R&D EXPENDITURES

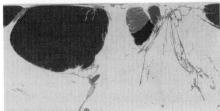

ROYALTIES AND LICENSE FEE EXPORTS

5    Each child is biologically required to have a mother. Fatherhood is a well-regarded theory, but motherhood is a fact. What kind of woman is best at lovingly fostering the potential in children? Let us sidestep sociological, economic, and feminist arguments and posit simply a woman who is herself beloved. Quantification of that is difficult, and Worldmapper hasn't tried. But two of its maps, one almost the exact inverse of the other, are nonetheless telling: **Women in Agriculture** (the number of female farm laborers) and **Tractors Working.** It's good when a society values women, not so good when it values women because they are cheaper than a John Deere.

6    The United States and Western Europe excel in the ratio of farm machinery to women farmworkers. They also excel—as do Japan, South Korea, and South Africa—in another statistic: **Female Managers.** A country is more likely to be innovative when 100 percent of its population, instead of 50 percent, has an opportunity to innovate. Whether the girls and boys of that country are better off with executive moms is sometimes debated. But whether women should have an influence on children is not debatable, and a country with influential women is, perforce, a country with women who influence.

## Obviously Innovative

There is a kind of thinker known as a MOTO, a "Master of the Obvious." MOTOS   7
are hired by the hundreds as editorial writers and news commentators.
Though always boring, they aren't always wrong. And it would be a violation of MOTO principles to ignore research and development as a predictor of
innovation.

In per capita R&D spending, the United States, the wealthier Western   8
European nations, Israel, Japan, and South Korea are giants. In gross spending
(see **Total R&D Expenditures),** China is Brobdingnagian enough, and Brazil
and South Africa are midsized titans on otherwise rather un-innovative
continents.

But what are the researchers researching and the developers developing?   9
Cold fusion or YouTube? A cure for malaria or for flatulence? We can't know
the future worth of a country's R&D. We can, however, inspect that country's
track record. The map of **Royalties and License Fee Exports** gives a picture of
where past R&D has been valuable enough that other countries buy it. Gang-
way for the United States of America! Sorry about that, Japan. Way to go, feisty
runners-up Great Britain, Sweden, and France.

## A Little Education . . .

Education is another MOTO indicator, albeit an occasionally dubious one. More   10
years of education do not always yield more innovative thinking, as anyone
who has suffered through a Harvard cocktail party can attest. Thomas Edison
dropped out of school at age seven. Whoever invented the wheel had no school
out of which to drop. Socrates didn't go to a university; he was one.

Education, however, does change minds. And a new mentality is more   11
significant invention than the moldboard plow or the semiconductor. Not
much was really invented during the Renaissance, if you don't count modern
civilization.

Currently, spending on education lines up about as you'd expect: rich   12
countries spend more than poor ones. But for purposes of futurism, *growth* in
educational spending may be more to the point. The **Secondary Education
Spending Growth** map shows total increases for children aged eleven to seventeen—the time when kids start getting a mind of their own (necessary to innovation, however annoying it is to parents). Here the future seems to belong to
Western Europe, South Korea, Thailand, Malaysia, China, Latin America, the
northern and southern (but not the central) parts of Africa, and New Zealand.
By comparison, America and Australia are idling or stalled.

But another map, **Primary Education Spending Growth,** gives Yanks and   13
Aussies some hope. Expenditures shown here include preschool programs.
Some educators claim that that's when the mind is truly formed. But do you
want to hear the engineers building your high-speed particle accelerator say,
"Everything I need to know I learned in kindergarten"?

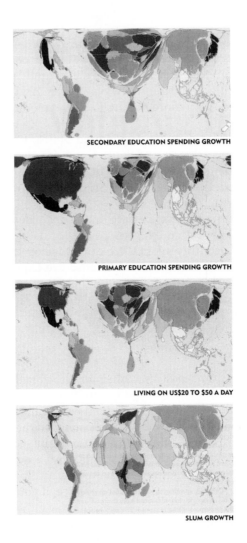

SECONDARY EDUCATION SPENDING GROWTH

PRIMARY EDUCATION SPENDING GROWTH

LIVING ON US$20 TO $50 A DAY

SLUM GROWTH

## Blessed are the Innovative in Spirit

14  Innovation is necessary to progress, and progress is, we tend to think, necessarily linked to prosperity. But if we look at the most innovative nation in history to date—our own—we see that the most distinctive American innovations were the products of poverty. Bluegrass, gospel, jazz, rhythm and blues, country and western, rock and roll, and hip-hop are the music of poor people. American slang, American style, American fashions and fads have their sources among the least affluent. America's car culture, teen culture, sports culture (and drug culture and gun culture) were shaped by what, in other countries, would be called the lower classes.

15      One secret to this sort of innovation is rich poor people. To be on the poverty threshold in the United States ($9,973 per year for a single adult) is to be

richer than most people in the rest of the world (per capita global average GDP is $8,229). A nation's poor can't be innovative if they're famished. Famine takes too much time and energy.

The other secret is what sociologists would call agglomeration and what 16 we'd call a ghetto, inner city, or slum. Poor people are creative by themselves, but put a lot of them together and the result is brilliant—African American artistic genius in the Harlem Renaissance, Jewish intellectual genius on New York's Lower East Side, Irish political genius among the ward heelers and block captains of Boston's South End.

The **Living on US$20 to $50 a Day** map shows where people are poor but 17 not so miserably poor that they're sunk in inertia and despair. The world is well supplied with folks of modest means even in Russia, which has previously been inconspicuous on our innovation maps. Such places as central Africa, Madagascar, Haiti, Pakistan, Bangladesh, and Burma seem too poor too harbor innovative forces. And only Scandinavia seems too rich.

But the "Living on US$20 to $50 a Day" map needs to be correlated with the 18 **Slum Growth** map. It then becomes clear that the greatest potential for innovation from below is in Central America, Peru, Turkey, the Gaza Strip and the West Bank, China, South Korea, and the Philippines. Be on the lookout for an Incan/Mayan/Muslim/Confucian Manila dance craze.

## Innovating with Their Feet

The poor are an especially important resource for innovation when they have 19 the bravery and pluck to get out of the poor places in which they're living. Moving around may be the single most innovative thing that humans do—for good or ill. Our species spread from Africa into the cradle of civilization (a very messy crib at the moment). The scruffy hill tribes of the Tiber conquered the world. The scruffier barbarians conquered them. Mongols with nothing but a few horses to their name swept across Asia. Hungry mammoth-hunters migrated to America from one end of the earth, and their gold-hungry cousins "discovered" if from the other. The results have been innovative in the extreme.

The **Net Immigration** map gives a fairly predictable predication of future 20 innovation. People are moving to places that have the good life from places where life is not so good. The United States, Canada, Western Europe, Israel, and the posher and more peaceful areas of the Arabian Peninsula account for almost 80 percent of the world's net immigration. Hong Kong, Singapore, and Australia are also gainers. And certain umprepossessing countries in even less prepossessing regions—Venezuela, Costa Rica, Russia, South Africa, and Tanzania—are acquiring brave, plucky innovators.

But other movements in human populations are far less innovative. These are 21 the waves of tourists. To be a tourist is to express rank conservatism. Tourists seek the "unspoiled." No one is as offended as a tourist when a warren of crumbling adobe is leveled to make way for a KFC or when a colorful peasant woman is replaced by a working tractor. The **Net In-Tourism** map shows places where visits

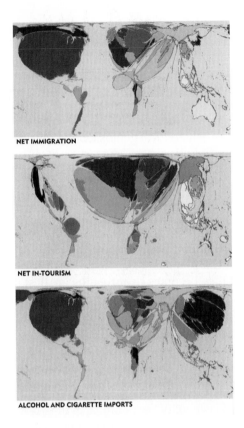

**NET IMMIGRATION**

**NET IN-TOURISM**

**ALCOHOL AND CIGARETTE IMPORTS**

from tourists exceed the tourist travel of the residents. Thus is sapped the innovative potential of France, Spain, Austria, Italy, Mexico, the Caribbean, southern Africa, Thailand, Hong Kong, Singapore, the United Arab Emirates, and China.

## Attitude-Adjustment Hour

22   Given all the very rigorous research compiled by Worldmapper, what totally un-rigorous conclusions can we draw? A rough tally of quick impressions of arbitrarily chosen criteria indicates that only about a dozen countries or regions are likely to be innovative in the near future. Perhaps unsurprisingly, the United States and Europe loom largest. But South Korea and South Africa keep popping up strongly as well, and so do Japan, Australia, New Zealand, and a few other places.

23       All of which is mirrored, at least tolerably closely, by the **Alcohol and Cig-arette Imports** map. That's one more thing about innovation: it's very stressful. And who, among the world's innovators, are so stressed that they have to bring in stress relief from overseas? That would be the Americans, the Japanese, the Taiwanese, the South Koreans, and the Continentals in Western Europe. You folks look like you need a drink. Innovation is a damn big job. Congratulations. Have a cigar.

# COMPREHENSION

1. According to O'Rourke, why is innovation important? What nations or regions seem best poised to be innovative leaders in the future?
2. Is O'Rourke arguing that innovation is a necessary corollary to progress, or is he merely presenting a series of informative points about global innovation? Explain.
3. Just how serious is O'Rourke in presenting the data drawn from Worldmapper? Justify your response.

# RHETORIC

1. Where does this essay begin and end? How are the introduction and conclusion interconnected?
2. Cite specific instances of O'Rourke's use of humor in this essay, noting especially the two main levels of diction. Does this overall strategy strengthen his analysis or weaken it, in your opinion? Why?
3. On what authority or grounds does O'Rourke accept the statistical data presented by Worldmapper? How does he turn data from these maps to his own purpose?
4. How does O'Rourke create the impression that he is a credible authority on "mapping innovation"?
5. Explain O'Rourke's use of comparison and contrast, classification, and causal analysis to organize the materials in his essay.
6. What line of reasoning does O'Rourke present in this essay? Does he appeal to ethics or emotion? Explain.

# WRITING

1. Access Worldmapper online, and write a paper summarizing its contents.
2. Compose an extended definition of innovation. If you choose, try to use humor to support your thesis or claim.
3. **Writing an Argument:** O'Rourke raises the question of whether all countries and regions will benefit from innovation in the future. (After all, as he comments waggishly in the concluding sentence, innovation "is a damn big job.") Write a persuasive essay in which you take a stand on the issue that innovation will inevitably produce a few winners but many more losers as the century advances.

www.mhhe.com/
**mhreader**

For more information on P. J. O' Rourke, go to:
**More Resources > Ch. 8 Business & Economics**

# Globalization: The Super-Story

## Thomas L. Friedman

*Thomas L. Friedman (b. 1953) was born in Minneapolis, Minnesota. He majored in Mediterranean studies at Brandeis University (BA 1975) and received an MA in modern Middle Eastern studies from Oxford University in 1978. As journalist, author, television commentator, and op-ed contributor to* The New York Times, *Friedman tries to provide unbiased viewpoints on cultural, political, and economic issues. From 1979 to 1984 he was the* Times *correspondent in Beirut, Lebanon, and subsequently until 1988 served as bureau chief in Jerusalem. His book recounting his 10 years in the Middle East,* From Beirut to Jerusalem *(1983), received the National Book Award for nonfiction. Friedman also has published* The Lexus and the Olive Tree: Understanding Globalization *(2000) and a collection of essays,* Longitudes and Attitudes: Explaining the World after September 11 *(2002), which contains the following selection.*

1   I am a big believer in the idea of the super-story, the notion that we all carry around with us a big lens, a big framework, through which we look at the world, order events, and decide what is important and what is not. The events of 9/11 did not happen in a vacuum. They happened in the context of a new international system—a system that cannot explain everything but *can* explain and connect more things in more places on more days than anything else. That new international system is called globalization. It came together in the late 1980s and replaced the previous international system, the cold war system, which had reigned since the end of World War II. This new system is the lens, the super-story, through which I viewed the events of 9/11.

2       I define globalization as the inexorable integration of markets, transportation systems, and communication systems to a degree never witnessed before—in a way that is enabling corporations, countries, and individuals to reach around the world farther, faster, deeper, and cheaper than ever before, and in a way that is enabling the world to reach into corporations, countries, and individuals farther, faster, deeper, and cheaper than ever before.

3       Several important features of this globalization system differ from those of the cold war system in ways that are quite relevant for understanding the events of 9/11. I examined them in detail in my previous book, *The Lexus and the Olive Tree,* and want to simply highlight them here.

4       The cold war system was characterized by one overarching feature—and that was *division*. That world was a divided-up, chopped-up place, and whether you were a country or a company, your threats and opportunities in the cold war system tended to grow out of who you were divided from.

Appropriately, this cold war system was symbolized by a single word—*wall*, the Berlin Wall.

The globalization system is different. It also has one overarching feature— 5 and that is *integration*. The world has become an increasingly interwoven place, and today, whether you are a company or a country, your threats and opportunities increasingly derive from who you are connected to. This globalization system is also characterized by a single word—*web*, the World Wide Web. So in the broadest sense we have gone from an international system built around division and walls to a system increasingly built around integration and webs. In the cold war we reached for the hotline, which was a symbol that we were divided but at least two people were in charge—the leaders of the United States and the Soviet Union. In the globalization system we reach for the Internet, which is a symbol that we are all connected and nobody is quite in charge.

Everyone in the world is directly or indirectly affected by this new system, 6 but not everyone benefits from it, not by a long shot, which is why the more it becomes diffused, the more it also produces a backlash by people who feel overwhelmed by it, homogenized by it, or unable to keep pace with its demands.

The other key difference between the cold war system and the globalization 7 system is how power is structured within them. The cold war system was built primarily around nation-states. You acted on the world in that system through your state. The cold war was a drama of states confronting states, balancing states, and aligning with states. And, as a system, the cold war was balanced at the center by two superstates, two superpowers: The United States and the Soviet Union.

The globalization system, by contrast, is built around three balances, which 8 overlap and affect one another. The first is the traditional balance of power between nation-states. In the globalization system, the United States is now the sole and dominant superpower and all other nations are subordinate to it to one degree or another. The shifting balance of power between the United States and other states, or simply between other states, still very much matters for the stability of this system. And it can still explain a lot of the news you read on the front page of the paper, whether it is the news of China balancing Russia, Iran balancing Iraq, or India confronting Pakistan.

The second important power balance in the globalization system is be- 9 tween nation-states and global markets. These global markets are made up of millions of investors moving money around the world with the click of a mouse. I call them the Electronic Herd, and this herd gathers in key global financial centers—such as Wall Street, Hong Kong, London, and Frankfurt— which I call the Supermarkets. The attitudes and actions of the Electronic Herd and the Supermarkets can have a huge impact on nation-states today, even to the point of triggering the downfall of governments. Who ousted Suharto in Indonesia in 1998? It wasn't another state, it was the Supermarkets, by withdrawing their support for, and confidence in, the Indonesian economy. You also will not understand the front page of the newspaper today unless you bring the Supermarkets into your analysis. Because the United States can destroy you by dropping bombs, but the Supermarkets can destroy you by downgrading your bonds. In other words, the United States is the dominant player in maintaining the globalization game board, but it is hardly alone in influencing the moves on that game board.

10      The third balance that you have to pay attention to—the one that is really the newest of all and the most relevant to the events of 9/11—is the balance between individuals and nation-states. Because globalization has brought down many of the walls that limited the movement and reach of people, and because it has simultaneously wired the world into networks, it gives more power to *individuals* to influence both markets and nation-states than at any other time in history. Whether by enabling people to use the Internet to communicate instantly at almost no cost over vast distances, or by enabling them to use the Web to transfer money or obtain weapons designs that normally would have been controlled by states, or by enabling them to go into a hardware store now and buy a five-hundred-dollar global positioning device, connected to a satellite, that can direct a hijacked airplane—globalization can be an incredible force-multiplier for individuals. Individuals can increasingly act on the world stage directly, unmediated by a state.

11      So you have today not only a superpower, not only Supermarkets, but also what I call "super-empowered individuals." Some of these super-empowered individuals are quite angry, some of them quite wonderful—but all of them are now able to act much more directly and much more powerfully on the world stage.

12      Osama bin Laden declared war on the United States in the late 1990s. After he organized the bombing of two American embassies in Africa, the U.S. Air Force retaliated with a cruise missile attack on his bases in Afghanistan as though he were another nation-state. Think about that: on one day in 1998, the United States fired 75 cruise missiles at bin Laden. The United States fired 75 cruise missiles, at $1 million apiece, at a person! That was the first battle in history between a superpower and a super-empowered angry man. September 11 was just the second such battle.

13      Jody Williams won the Nobel Peace Prize in 1997 for helping to build an international coalition to bring about a treaty outlawing land mines. Although nearly 120 governments endorsed the treaty, it was opposed by Russia, China, and the United States. When Jody Williams was asked, "How did you do that? How did you organize one thousand different citizens' groups and nongovernmental organizations on five continents to forge a treaty that was opposed by the major powers?" she had a very brief answer: "E-mail." Jody Williams used e-mail and the networked world to super-empower herself.

14      Nation-states, and the American superpower in particular, are still hugely important today, but so too now are Supermarkets and super-empowered individuals. You will never understand the globalization system, or the front page of the morning paper—or 9/11—unless you see each as a complex interaction between all three of these actors: states bumping up against states, states bumping up against Supermarkets, and Supermarkets

and states bumping up against super-empowered individuals—many of whom, unfortunately, are super-empowered angry men.

## COMPREHENSION

1. What is Friedman's "super-story"? How does he define it?
2. What are the main features of globalization? How does globalization differ from the system characterized by the cold war? Explain the "three balances" (paragraph 8) that Friedman writes about.
3. What does Friedman mean by "super-empowered" individuals (paragraph 11)?

## RHETORIC

1. What is Friedman's thesis or claim in this essay? Where does it appear?
2. How and why does Friedman create a personal voice as well as a colloquial style in this selection? What is the effect?
3. What definitions does Friedman establish? Are the definitions too abstract, or does he provide sufficient explanations and evidence? Explain.
4. Locate instances of classification and of comparison and contrast. Why does Friedman use these rhetorical strategies? How do the two methods complement each other?
5. Friedman uses several metaphors in this essay. What are they, and how do they function to enhance meaning?
6. Why does the writer introduce 9/11 in the final three paragraphs? What is the effect on the overall message and purpose of the essay?

## WRITING

1. In groups of three or four, use Friedman's essay to brainstorm about globalization. Construct a list of ideas and attributes. Using this list, write a definition essay exploring the subject of globalization. Include comparison and contrast or classification, or both, to help organize the essay.
2. Write a personal essay on how you think globalization is affecting your life.
3. **Writing an Argument:** Write a letter to Friedman, either agreeing or disagreeing with his opinions concerning globalization, supporting or refuting his ideas, or offering alternative views.

www.mhhe.com/ **mhreader**    For more information on Thomas L. Friedman, go to: **More Resources > Ch. 8 Business & Economics**

# Nickel and Dimed

### Barbara Ehrenreich

*Barbara Ehrenreich (b. 1941) was born in Butte, Montana. The daughter of working-class parents, she attended Reed College (BA 1963) and Rockefeller University, where she received a PhD in biology in 1968. After deciding not to pursue a career in science, Ehrenreich turned to political causes, using her scientific training to investigate a broad range of social issues. A prolific writer, Ehrenreich has contributed to* Time, The New Republic, The Progressive, *and other magazines. She also has written several books, including* The American Health Empire *(1970),* Complaints and Disorders: The Sexual Politics of Sickness *(1978), and* Nickel and Dimed: On (Not) Getting By in America *(2001). In the following excerpt from* Nickel and Dimed, *Ehrenreich recounts her experience working for a large cleaning agency.*

1   I am rested and ready for anything when I arrive at The Maids' office suite Monday at 7:30 A.M. I know nothing about cleaning services like this one, which, according to the brochure I am given, has over three hundred franchises nationwide, and most of what I know about domestics in general comes from nineteenth-century British novels and *Upstairs, Downstairs.* Prophetically enough, I caught a rerun of that very show on PBS over the weekend and was struck by how terribly correct the servants looked in their black-and-white uniforms and how much wiser they were than their callow, egotistical masters. We too have uniforms, though they are more oafish than dignified—ill-fitting and in an overloud combination of kelly-green pants and a blinding sunflower-yellow polo shirt. And, as is explained in writing and over the next day and a half of training, we too have a special code of decorum. No smoking anywhere, or at least not within fifteen minutes of arrival at a house. No drinking, eating, or gum chewing in a house. No cursing in a house, even if the owner is not present, and—perhaps to keep us in practice—no obscenities even in the office. So this is Downstairs, is my chirpy first thought. But I have no idea, of course, just how far down these stairs will take me.

2       Forty minutes go by before anyone acknowledges my presence with more than a harried nod. During this time the other employees arrive, about twenty of them, already glowing in their uniforms, and breakfast on the free coffee, bagels, and doughnuts The Maids kindly provides for us. All but one of the others are female, with an average age I would guess in the late twenties, though the range seems to go from prom-fresh to well into the Medicare years. There is a pleasant sort of bustle as people get their breakfasts and fill plastic buckets with rags and bottles of cleaning fluids, but surprisingly little conversation outside of a few references to what people ate (pizza) and drank

(Jell-O shots are mentioned) over the weekend. Since the room in which we gather contains only two folding chairs, both of them occupied, the other new girl and I sit cross-legged on the floor, silent and alert, while the regulars get sorted into teams of three or four and dispatched to the day's list of houses. One of the women explains to me that teams do not necessarily return to the same houses week after week, nor do you have any guarantee of being on the same team from one day to the next. This, I suppose, is one of the advantages of a corporate cleaning service to its customers: there are no sticky and possibly guilt-ridden relationships involved, because the customers communicate almost entirely with Tammy, the office manager, or with Ted, the franchise owner and our boss. The advantage to the cleaning person is harder to determine, since the pay compares so poorly to what an independent cleaner is likely to earn—up to $15 an hour, I've heard. While I wait in the inner room, where the phone is and Tammy has her desk, to be issued a uniform, I hear her tell a potential customer on the phone that The Maids charges $25 per person-hour. The company gets $25 and we get $6.65 for each hour we work? I think I must have misheard, but a few minutes later I hear her say the same thing to another inquirer. So the only advantage of working here as opposed to freelancing is that you don't need a clientele or even a car. You can arrive straight from welfare or, in my case, the bus station—fresh off the boat.

At last, after all the other employees have sped off in the company's eye-  3 catching green-and-yellow cars, I am led into a tiny closet-sized room off the inner office to learn my trade via videotape. The manager at another maid service where I'd applied had told me she didn't like to hire people who had done cleaning before because they were resistant to learning the company's system, so I prepare to empty my mind of all prior house-cleaning experience. There are four tapes—dusting, bathrooms, kitchen, and vacuuming—each starring an attractive, possibly Hispanic young woman who moves about serenely in obedience to the male voiceover: For vacuuming, begin in the master bedroom; when dusting, begin with the room directly off the kitchen. When you enter a room, mentally divide it into sections no wider than your reach. Begin in the section to your left and, within each section, move from left to right and top to bottom. This way nothing is ever overlooked.

I like *Dusting* best, for its undeniable logic and a certain kind of austere  4 beauty. When you enter a house, you spray a white rag with Windex and place it in the left pocket of your green apron. Another rag, sprayed with disinfectant, goes in the middle pocket, and a yellow rag bearing wood polish in the right-hand pocket. A dry rag, for buffing surfaces, occupies the right-hand pocket of your slacks. Shiny surfaces get Windexed, wood gets wood polish, and everything else is wiped dust-free with disinfectant. Every now and then Ted pops in to watch with me, pausing the video to underscore a particularly dramatic moment: "See how she's working around the vase? That's an accident waiting to happen." If Ted himself were in a video, it would have to be a cartoon, because the only features sketched onto his pudgy face are brown buttonlike eyes and a tiny pug nose; his belly, encased in a polo shirt, overhangs the waistline of his

shorts. "You know, all this was figured out with a stopwatch," he tells me with
something like pride. When the video warns against oversoaking our rags with
cleaning fluids, he pauses it to tell me there's a danger in undersoaking too,
especially if it's going to slow me down. "Cleaning fluids are less expensive
than your time." It's good to know that *something* is cheaper than my time, or
that in the hierarchy of the company's values I rank above Windex.

5      *Vacuuming* is the most disturbing video, actually a double feature beginning with an introduction to the special backpack vacuum we are to use. Yes,
the vacuum cleaner actually straps onto your back, a chubby fellow who introduces himself as its inventor explains. He suits up, pulling the straps tight
across and under his chest and then says proudly into the camera: "See, I *am* the
vacuum cleaner." It weighs only ten pounds, he claims, although, as I soon find
out, with the attachments dangling from the strap around your waist, the total
is probably more like fourteen. What about my petulant and much-pampered
lower back? The inventor returns to the theme of human/machine merger: when
properly strapped in, we too will be vacuum cleaners, constrained only by the
cord that attaches us to an electrical outlet, and vacuum cleaners don't have
backaches. Somehow all this information exhausts me, and I watch the second
video, which explains the actual procedures for vacuuming, with the detached
interest of a cineast. Could the model maid be an actual maid and the model
home someone's actual dwelling? And who are these people whose idea of decorating is matched pictures of mallard ducks in flight and whose house is perfectly characterless and pristine even before the model maid sets to work?

6      At first I find the videos on kitchens and bathrooms baffling, and it takes
me several minutes to realize why: there is no *water*, or almost no water, involved. I was taught to clean by my mother, a compulsive housekeeper who
employed water so hot you needed rubber gloves to get into it and in such
Niagara-like quantities that most microbes were probably crushed by the force
of it before the soap suds had a chance to rupture their cell walls. But germs are
never mentioned in the videos provided by The Maids. Our antagonists exist
entirely in the visible world—soap scum, dust, counter crud, dog hair, stains,
and smears—and are to be attacked by damp rag or, in hard-core cases, by
Dobie (the brand of plastic scouring pad we use). We scrub only to remove im-
purities that might be detectable to a customer by hand or by eye; otherwise
our only job is to wipe. Nothing is said about the possibility of transporting
bacteria, by rag or by hand, from bathroom to kitchen or even from one house
to the next. It is the "cosmetic touches" that the videos emphasize and that Ted,
when he wanders back into the room, continually directs my eye to. Fluff up all
throw pillows and arrange them symmetrically. Brighten up stainless steel
sinks with baby oil. Leave all spice jars, shampoos, etc., with their labels facing
outward. Comb out the fringes of Persian carpets with a pick. Use the vacuum
cleaner to create a special, fernlike pattern in the carpets. The loose ends of toilet paper and paper towel rolls have to be given a special fold (the same one
you'll find in hotel bathrooms). "Messes" of loose paper, clothing, or toys are to be
stacked into "neat messes." Finally, the house is to be sprayed with the cleaning

service's signature floral-scented air freshener, which will signal to the owners, the moment they return home, that, yes, their house has been "cleaned."

After a day's training, I am judged fit to go out with a team, where I soon 7 discover that life is nothing like the movies, at least not if the movie is *Dusting*. For one thing, compared with our actual pace, the training videos were all in slow motion. We do not walk to the cars with our buckets full of cleaning fluids and utensils in the morning, we run, and when we pull up to a house, we run with our buckets to the door. Liza, a good-natured woman in her thirties who is my first team leader, explains that we are given only so many minutes per house, ranging from under sixty for a 1½-bathroom apartment to two hundred or more for a multibathroom "first timer." I'd like to know why anybody worries about Ted's time limits if we're being paid by the hour but hesitate to display anything that might be interpreted as attitude. As we get to each house, Liza assigns our tasks, and I cross my fingers to ward off bathrooms and vacuuming. Even dusting, though, gets aerobic under pressure, and after about an hour of it—reaching to get door tops, crawling along floors to wipe baseboards, standing on my bucket to attack the higher shelves—I wouldn't mind sitting down with a tall glass of water. But as soon as you complete your assigned task, you report to the team leader to be assigned to help someone else. Once or twice, when the normal process of evaporation is deemed too slow, I am assigned to dry a scrubbed floor by putting rags under my feet and skating around on it. Usually, by the time I get out to the car and am dumping the dirty water used on floors and wringing out rags, the rest of the team is already in the car with the motor running. Liza assures me that they've never left anyone behind at a house, not even, presumably, a very new person whom nobody knows.

In my interview, I had been promised a thirty-minute lunch break, but this 8 turns out to be a five-minute pit stop at a convenience store, if that. I bring my own sandwich—the same turkey breast and cheese every day—as do a couple of the others; the rest eat convenience store fare, a bagel or doughnut salvaged from our free breakfast, or nothing at all. The two older married women I'm teamed up with eat best—sandwiches and fruit. Among the younger women, lunch consists of a slice of pizza, a "pizza pocket" (a roll of dough surrounding some pizza sauce), or a small bag of chips. Bear in mind we are not office workers, sitting around idling at the basal metabolic rate. A poster on the wall in the office cheerily displays the number of calories burned per minute at our various tasks, ranging from about 3.5 for dusting to 7 for vacuuming. If you assume an average of 5 calories per minute in a seven-hour day (eight hours minus time for travel between houses), you need to be taking in 2,100 calories in addition to the resting minimum of, say, 900 or so. I get pushy with Rosalie, who is new like me and fresh from high school in a rural northern part of the state, about the meagerness of her lunches, which consist solely of Doritos—a half-bag from the day before or a freshly purchased small-sized bag. She just didn't have anything in the house, she says (though she lives with her boyfriend and his mother), and she certainly doesn't have any money to buy lunch, as I find out when I offer to fetch her a soda from a Quik Mart and she has to admit she doesn't have eighty-nine cents. I treat her to the soda, wishing I could force her, mommylike, to take milk instead. So how does she hold up for an eight- or even nine-hour day? "Well," she concedes, "I get dizzy sometimes."

9      How poor are they, my coworkers? The fact that anyone is working this job at all can be taken as prima facie evidence of some kind of desperation or at least a history of mistakes and disappointments, but it's not for me to ask. In the prison movies that provide me with a mental guide to comportment, the new guy doesn't go around shaking hands and asking, "Hi there, what are you in for?" So I listen, in the cars and when we're assembled in the office, and learn, first, that no one seems to be homeless. Almost everyone is embedded in extended families or families artificially extended with housemates. People talk about visiting grandparents in the hospital or sending birthday cards to a niece's husband; single mothers live with their own mothers or share apartments with a coworker or boyfriend. Pauline, the oldest of us, owns her own home, but she sleeps on the living room sofa, while her four grown children and three grandchildren fill up the bedrooms.

10      But although no one, apparently, is sleeping in a car, there are signs, even at the beginning, of real difficulty if not actual misery. Half-smoked cigarettes are returned to the pack. There are discussions about who will come up with fifty cents for a toll and whether Ted can be counted on for prompt reimbursement. One of my teammates gets frantic about a painfully impacted wisdom tooth and keeps making calls from our houses to try to locate a source of free dental care. When my—or, I should say, Liza's—team discovers there is not a single Dobie in our buckets, I suggest that we stop at a convenience store and buy one rather than drive all the way back to the office. But it turns out I haven't brought any money with me and we cannot put together $2 between the four of us.

11      The Friday of my first week at The Maids is unnaturally hot for Maine in early September—95 degrees, according to the digital time-and-temperature displays offered by banks that we pass. I'm teamed up with the sad-faced Rosalie and our leader, Maddy, whose sullenness, under the circumstances, is almost a relief after Liza's relentless good cheer. Liza, I've learned, is the highest-ranking cleaner, a sort of supervisor really, and said to be something of a snitch, but Maddy, a single mom of maybe twenty-seven or so, has worked for only three months and broods about her child care problems. Her boyfriend's sister, she tells me on the drive to our first house, watches her eighteen-month-old for $50 a week, which is a stretch on The Maids' pay, plus she doesn't entirely trust the sister, but a real day care center could be as much as $90 a week. After polishing off the first house, no problem, we grab "lunch"—Doritos for Rosalie and a bag of Pepperidge Farm Goldfish for Maddy—and head out into the exurbs for what our instruction sheet warns is a five-bathroom spread and a first-timer to boot. Still, the size of the place makes us pause for a moment, buckets in hand, before searching out an appropriately humble entrance. It sits there like a beached ocean liner, the prow cutting through swells of green turf, windows without number. "Well, well," Maddy says, reading the owner's

name from our instruction sheet. "Mrs. W. and her big-ass house. I hope she's going to give us lunch."

Mrs. W. is not in fact happy to see us, grimacing with exasperation when    12
the black nanny ushers us into the family room or sunroom or den or whatever kind of specialized space she is sitting in. After all, she already has the nanny, a cooklike person, and a crew of men doing some sort of finishing touches on the construction to supervise. No, she doesn't want to take us around the house, because she already explained everything to the office on the phone, but Maddy stands there, with Rosalie and me behind her, until she relents. We are to move everything on all surfaces, she instructs during the tour, and get underneath and be sure to do every bit of the several miles, I calculate, of baseboards. And be mindful of the baby, who's napping and can't have cleaning fluids of any kind near her.

Then I am let loose to dust. In a situation like this, where I don't even know    13
how to name the various kinds of rooms, The Maids' special system turns out to be a lifesaver. All I have to do is keep moving from left to right, within rooms and between rooms, trying to identify landmarks so I don't accidentally do a room or a hallway twice. Dusters get the most complete biographical overview, due to the necessity of lifting each object and tchotchke individually, and I learn that Mrs. W. is an alumna of an important women's college, now occupying herself by monitoring her investments and the baby's bowel movements. I find special charts for this latter purpose, with spaces for time of day, most recent fluid intake, consistency, and color. In the master bedroom, I dust a whole shelf of books on pregnancy, breastfeeding, the first six months, the first year, the first two years—and I wonder what the child care–deprived Maddy makes of all this. Maybe there's been some secret division of the world's women into breeders and drones, and those at the maid level are no longer supposed to be reproducing at all. Maybe this is why our office manager, Tammy, who was once a maid herself, wears inch-long fake nails and tarty little outfits—to show she's advanced to the breeder caste and can't be sent out to clean anymore.

It is hotter inside than out, un-air-conditioned for the benefit of the baby, I    14
suppose, but I do all right until I encounter the banks of glass doors that line the side and back of the ground floor. Each one has to be Windexed, wiped, and buffed—inside and out, top to bottom, left to right, until it's as streakless and invisible as a material substance can be. Outside, I can see the construction guys knocking back Gatorade, but the rule is that no fluid or food item can touch a maid's lips when she's inside a house. Now, sweat, even in unseemly quantities, is nothing new to me. I live in a subtropical area where even the inactive can expect to be moist nine months out of the year. I work out, too, in my normal life and take a certain macho pride in the *V*s of sweat that form on my T-shirt after ten minutes or more on the StairMaster. But in normal life fluids lost are immediately replaced. Everyone in yuppie-land—airports, for example—looks like a nursing baby these days, inseparable from their plastic bottles of water. Here, however, I sweat without replacement or pause, not in individual drops but in continuous sheets of fluid soaking through my polo shirt, pouring down the

backs of my legs. The eyeliner I put on in the morning—vain twit that I am—has long since streaked down onto my cheeks, and I could wring my braid out if I wanted to. Working my way through the living room(s), I wonder if Mrs. W. will ever have occasion to realize that every single doodad and *objet* through which she expresses her unique, individual self is, from another vantage point, only an obstacle between some thirsty person and a glass of water.

15    When I can find no more surfaces to wipe and have finally exhausted the supply of rooms, Maddy assigns me to do the kitchen floor. OK, except that Mrs. W. is *in* the kitchen, so I have to go down on my hands and knees practically at her feet. No, we don't have sponge mops like the one I use in my own house; the hands-and-knees approach is a definite selling point for corporate cleaning services like The Maids. "We clean floors the old-fashioned way—*on our hands and knees*" (emphasis added), the brochure for a competing firm boasts. In fact, whatever advantages there may be to the hands-and-knees approach—you're closer to your work, of course, and less likely to miss a grimy patch—are undermined by the artificial drought imposed by The Maids' cleaning system. We are instructed to use less than half a small bucket of lukewarm water for a kitchen and all adjacent scrubbable floors (breakfast nooks and other dining areas), meaning that within a few minutes we are doing nothing more than redistributing the dirt evenly around the floor. There are occasional customer complaints about the cleanliness of our floors—for example, from a man who wiped up a spill on his freshly "cleaned" floor only to find the paper towel he employed for this purpose had turned gray. A mop and a full bucket of hot soapy water would not only get a floor cleaner but would be a lot more dignified for the person who does the cleaning. But it is this primal posture of submission—and of what is ultimately anal accessibility—that seems to gratify the consumers of maid services.

16    I don't know, but Mrs. W.'s floor is hard—stone, I think, or at least a stone-like substance—and we have no knee pads with us today. I had thought in my middle-class innocence that knee pads were one of Monica Lewinsky's prurient fantasies, but no, they actually exist, and they're usually a standard part of our equipment. So here I am on my knees, working my way around the room like some fanatical penitent crawling through the stations of the cross, when I realize that Mrs. W. is staring at me fixedly—so fixedly that I am gripped for a moment by the wild possibility that I may have once given a lecture at her alma mater and she's trying to figure out where she's seen me before. If I were recognized, would I be fired? Would she at least be inspired to offer me a drink of water? Because I have decided that if water is actually offered, I'm taking it, rules or no rules, and if word of this infraction gets back to Ted, I'll just say I thought it would be rude to refuse. Not to worry, though. She's just watching that I don't leave out some stray square inch, and when I rise painfully to my feet again, blinking through the sweat, she says, "Could you just scrub the floor in the entryway while you're at it?"

17    I rush home to the Blue Haven at the end of the day, pull down the blinds for privacy, strip off my uniform in the kitchen—the bathroom being too small

for both a person and her discarded clothes—and stand in the shower for a good ten minutes, thinking all this water is *mine*. I have paid for it, in fact, I have earned it. I have gotten through a week at The Maids without mishap, injury, or insurrection. My back feels fine, meaning I'm not feeling it at all; even my wrists, damaged by carpal tunnel syndrome years ago, are issuing no complaints. Coworkers warned me that the first time they donned the backpack vacuum they felt faint, but not me. I am strong and I am, more than that, good. Did I toss my bucket of filthy water onto Mrs. W.'s casual white summer outfit? No. Did I take the wand of my vacuum cleaner and smash someone's Chinese porcelain statues or Hummel figurines? Not once. I was at all times cheerful, energetic, helpful, and as competent as a new hire can be expected to be. If I can do one week, I can do another, and might as well, since there's never been a moment for job-hunting. The 3:30 quitting time turns out to be a myth; often we don't return to the office until 4:30 or 5:00. And what did I think? That I was going to go out to interviews in my soaked and stinky postwork condition? I decide to reward myself with a sunset walk on Old Orchard Beach.

On account of the heat, there are still a few actual bathers on the beach, but 18 I am content to sit in shorts and T-shirt and watch the ocean pummel the sand. When the sun goes down I walk back into the town to find my car and am amazed to hear a sound I associate with cities like New York and Berlin. There's a couple of Peruvian musicians playing in the little grassy island in the street near the pier, and maybe fifty people—locals and vacationers—have gathered around, offering their bland end-of-summer faces to the sound. I edge my way through the crowd and find a seat where I can see the musicians up close—the beautiful young guitarist and the taller man playing the flute. What are they doing in this rinky-dink blue-collar resort, and what does the audience make of this surprise visit from the dark-skinned South? The melody the flute lays out over the percussion is both utterly strange and completely familiar, as if it had been imprinted in the minds of my own peasant ancestors centuries ago and forgotten until this very moment. Everyone else seems to be as transfixed as I am. The musicians wink and smile at each other as they play, and I see then that they are the secret emissaries of a worldwide lower-class conspiracy to snatch joy out of degradation and filth. When the song ends, I give them a dollar, the equivalent of about ten minutes of sweat.

## COMPREHENSION

1. Why do women work for The Maids when they could earn more money as independent cleaners? How does Ehrenreich distinguish her cleaning practices from her coworkers'? Why do the maids emphasize "cosmetic touches" (paragraph 6)?
2. Describe the plight of Ehrenreich's coworkers. What "signs . . . of real difficulty if not actual misery" (paragraph 10) does she detect? What, if anything, does she do to help them?

3. Who is Mrs. W? What is her lifestyle like, and what does she expect of the maids? How does she treat Ehrenreich?

## RHETORIC

1. How does Ehrenreich structure her narrative? How much time elapses? What elements of conflict develop? What transitional devices does she employ to unify the action?
2. Where does the writer employ description, and for what purpose? What descriptive details seem most striking to you? How, for example, does Ehrenreich bring her coworkers and Mrs. W. to life?
3. Identify those instances where the writer uses process analysis and comparison and contrast to organize her essay. Why does she select these strategies?
4. Explain the tone of this selection. What elements of irony and sarcasm do you detect?
5. Do you think this essay provides a straightforward account of Ehrenreich's experience working for The Maids, or does she have an argumentative point? Justify your response.
6. How does the writer conclude this selection? What elements in the last paragraph capture the main purpose behind her account?

## WRITING

1. Write a narrative and descriptive essay of a job you have held that involved menial labor. Establish a time frame. Describe any colleagues who worked with you. Have a thesis or an argument that you either state explicitly or permit to emerge from the account.
2. Compare and contrast a bad job that you have held and a job that provided you with a degree of satisfaction.
3. **Writing an Argument:** In *Nickel and Dimed,* Ehrenreich set out to find minimum-wage jobs in several parts of the United States, including a Wal-Mart in Minnesota and a restaurant in Florida. However, she knew at the outset that these jobs were temporary and that she had the luxury of going back to her comfortable life and her career as a writer and activist. Argue for or against the proposition that Ehrenreich was being unethical and exploitative in her behavior. Refer to this selection to support your position.

www.mhhe.com/
**mhreader**

For more information on Barbara Ehrenreich, go to:
**More Resources > Ch. 8 Business & Economics**

# Why the Rich Are Getting Richer and the Poor, Poorer

### Robert Reich

*Robert Reich (b. 1946) is a University Professor in the Heller Graduate School at Brandeis University. He served as secretary of labor in the first Clinton administration and, before that, as a professor of economics at Harvard University. He has written numerous books on economics and has been a prominent lecturer for a dozen years. His books include* The Next American Frontier *(1983) and* The Work of Nations *(1991), which takes its title from Adam Smith's classic work on economics* The Wealth of Nations, *written in 1776. Reich is known for his ability to "think outside the box," in other words, to see things from a unique and original perspective. Here he warns of what exists—perhaps in front of our very noses—but that we are too caught up in the moment to consider.*

*The division of labor is limited by the extent of the market.*
—*Adam Smith,* An Inquiry into the Nature and Causes of the Wealth of
Nations *(1776)*

Regardless of how your job is officially classified (manufacturing, service, man-  1
agerial, technical, secretarial, and so on), or the industry in which you work
(automotive, steel, computer, advertising, finance, food processing), your real
competitive position in the world economy is coming to depend on the function
you perform in it. Herein lies the basic reason why incomes are diverging. The
fortunes of routine producers are declining. In-person servers are also becoming poorer, although their fates are less clear-cut. But symbolic analysts—who
solve, identify, and broker new problems—are, by and large, succeeding in the
world economy.

All Americans used to be in roughly the same economic boat. Most rose or  2
fell together as the corporations in which they were employed, the industries
comprising such corporations, and the national economy as a whole became
more productive—or languished. But national borders no longer define our
economic fates. We are now in different boats, one sinking rapidly, one sinking
more slowly, and the third rising steadily.

The boat containing routine producers is sinking rapidly. Recall that by mid-  3
century routine production workers in the United States were paid relatively well.
The giant pyramidlike organizations at the core of each major industry coordinated their prices and investments—avoiding the harsh winds of competition and
thus maintaining healthy earnings. Some of these earnings, in turn, were reinvested

in new plants and equipment (yielding ever-larger-scale economies); another portion went to top managers and investors. But a large and increasing portion went to middle managers and production workers. Work stoppages posed such a threat to high-volume production that organized labor was able to exact an ever-larger premium for its cooperation. And the pattern of wages established within the core corporations influenced the pattern throughout the national economy. Thus the growth of a relatively affluent middle class, able to purchase all the wondrous things produced in high volume by the core corporations.

4       But, as has been observed, the core is rapidly breaking down into global webs which earn their largest profits from clever problem-solving, -identifying, and brokering. As the costs of transporting standard things and of communicating information about them continue to drop, profit margins on high-volume, standardized production are thinning, because there are few barriers to entry. Modern factories and state-of-the-art machinery can be installed almost anywhere on the globe. Routine producers in the United States, then, are in direct competition with millions of routine producers in other nations. Twelve thousand people are added to the world's population every hour, most of whom, eventually, will happily work for a small fraction of the wages of routine producers in America.[1]

5       The consequence is clearest in older, heavy industries, where high-volume, standardized production continues its ineluctable move to where labor is cheapest and most accessible around the world. Thus, for example, the Maquiladora factories cluttered along the Mexican side of the U.S. border in the sprawling shanty towns of Tijuana, Mexicali, Nogales, Agua Prieta, and Ciudad Juárez—factories owned mostly by Americans, but increasingly by Japanese—in which more than a half million routine producers assemble parts into finished goods to be shipped into the United States.

6       The same story is unfolding worldwide. Until the late 1970s, AT&T had depended on routine producers in Shreveport, Louisiana, to assemble standard telephones. It then discovered that routine producers in Singapore would perform the same tasks at a far lower cost. Facing intense competition from other global webs, AT&T's strategic brokers felt compelled to switch. So in the early 1980s they stopped hiring routine producers in Shreveport and began hiring cheaper routine producers in Singapore. But under this kind of pressure for ever lower high-volume production costs, today's Singaporean can easily end up as yesterday's Louisianan. By the late 1980s, AT&T's strategic brokers found that routine producers in Thailand were eager to assemble telephones for a small fraction of the wages of routine producers in Singapore. Thus, in 1989, AT&T stopped hiring Singaporeans to make telephones and began hiring even cheaper routine producers in Thailand.

---

[1]The reader should note, of course, that lower wages in other areas of the world are of no particular attraction to global capital unless workers three are sufficiently productive to make the labor cost of producing *each unit* lower there than in higher-wage regions. Productivity in many low-wage areas of the world has improved due to the ease with which state-of-the-art factories and equipment can be installed there.

The search for ever lower wages has not been confined to heavy indus- ⁷ try. Routine data processing is equally footloose. Keypunch operators located anywhere around the world can enter data into computers, linked by satellite or transoceanic fiber-optic cable, and take it out again. As the rates charged by satellite networks continue to drop, and as more satellites and fiber-optic cables become available (reducing communication costs still further), routine data processors in the United States find themselves in ever more direct competition with their counterparts abroad, who are often eager to work for far less.

By 1990, keypunch operators in the United States were earning, at most, ⁸ $6.50 per hour. But keypunch operators throughout the rest of the world were willing to work for a fraction of this. Thus, many potential American data-processing jobs were disappearing, and the wages and benefits of the remaining ones were in decline. Typical was Saztec International, a $20-million-a-year data-processing firm headquartered in Kansas City, whose American strategic brokers contracted with routine data processors in Manila and with American-owned firms that needed such data-processing services. Compared with the average Philippine income of $1,700 per year, data-entry operators working for Saztec earn the princely sum of $2,650. The remainder of Saztec's employees were American problem-solvers and -identifiers, searching for ways to improve the worldwide system and find new uses to which it could be put.[2]

By 1990, American Airlines was employing over 1,000 data processors in ⁹ Barbados and the Dominican Republic to enter names and flight numbers from used airline tickets (flown daily to Barbados from airports around the United States) into a giant computer bank located in Dallas. Chicago publisher R. R. Donnelley was sending entire manuscripts to Barbados for entry into computers in preparation for printing. The New York Life Insurance Company was dispatching insurance claims to Castleisland, Ireland, where routine producers, guided by simple directions, entered the claims and determined the amounts due, then instantly transmitted the computations back to the United States. (When the firm advertised in Ireland for twenty-five data-processing jobs, it received six hundred applications.) And McGraw-Hill was processing subscription renewal and marketing information for its magazines in nearby Galway. Indeed, literally millions of routine workers around the world were receiving information, converting it into computer-readable form, and then sending it back—at the speed of electronic impulses—whence it came.

The simple coding of computer software has also entered into world com- ¹⁰ merce. India, with a large English-speaking population of technicians happy to do routine programming cheaply, is proving to be particularly attractive to global webs in need of this service. By 1990, Texas Instruments maintained a software development facility in Bangalore, linking fifty Indian programmers

---

[2]John Maxwell Hamilton, " A Bit Player Buys into the Computer Age," *New York Times Business World*, December 3, 1989, p. 14.

by satellite to TI's Dallas headquarters. Spurred by this and similar ventures, the Indian government was building a teleport in Poona, intended to make it easier and less expensive for many other firms to send their routine software design specifications for coding.[3]

11   This shift of routine production jobs from advanced to developing nations is a great boon to many workers in such nations who otherwise would be jobless or working for much lower wages. These workers, in turn, now have more money with which to purchase symbolic-analytic services from advanced nations (often embedded within all sorts of complex products). The trend is also beneficial to everyone around the world who can now obtain high-volume, standardized products (including information and software) more cheaply than before.

12   But these benefits do not come without certain costs. In particular the burden is borne by those who no longer have good-paying routine production jobs within advanced economies like the United States. Many of these people used to belong to unions or at least benefited from prevailing wage rates established in collective bargaining agreements. But as the old corporate bureaucracies have flattened into global webs, bargaining leverage has been lost. Indeed, the tacit national bargain is no more.

13   Despite the growth in the number of new jobs in the United States, union membership has withered. In 1960, 35 percent of all nonagricultural workers in America belonged to a union. But by 1980 that portion had fallen to just under a quarter, and by 1989 to about 17 percent. Excluding government employees, union membership was down to 13.4 percent.[4] This was a smaller proportion even than in the early 1930s, before the National Labor Relations Act created a legally protected right to labor representation. The drop in membership has been accompanied by a growing number of collective bargaining agreements to freeze wages at current levels, reduce wage levels of entering workers, or reduce wages overall. This is an important reason why the long economic recovery that began in 1982 produced a smaller rise in unit labor costs than any of the eight recoveries since World War II—the low rate of unemployment during its course notwithstanding.

14   Routine production jobs have vanished fastest in traditional unionized industries (autos, steel, and rubber, for example), where average wages have kept up with inflation. This is because the jobs of older workers in such industries are protected by seniority; the youngest workers are the first to be laid off. Faced with a choice of cutting wages or cutting the number of jobs, a majority of union members (secure in the knowledge that there are many who are junior to them who will be laid off first) often have voted for the latter.

15   Thus the decline in union membership has been most striking among young men entering the work force without a college education. In the early

[3]Udayan Gupta, "U.S.-Indian Satellite Link Stands to Cut Software Costs," *Wall Street Journal,* March 6, 1989, p. B2.
[4]*Statistical Abstract of the United States* (Washington, D.C.: U.S. Government Printing Office, 1989), p. 416, table 684.

1950s, more than 40 percent of this group joined unions; by the late 1980s, less than 20 percent (if public employees are excluded, less than 10 percent).[5] In steelmaking, for example, although many older workers remained employed, almost half of all routine steelmaking jobs in America vanished between 1974 and 1988 (from 480,000 to 260,000). Similarly with automobiles: During the 1980s, the United Auto Workers lost 500,000 members—one-third of their total at the start of the decade. General Motors alone cut 150,000 American production jobs during the 1980s (even as it added employment abroad). Another consequence of the same phenomenon: the gap between the average wages of unionized and nonunionized workers widened dramatically—from 14.6 percent in 1973 to 20.4 percent by end of the 1980s.[6] The lesson is clear. If you drop out of high school or have no more than a high school diploma, do not expect a good routine production job to be awaiting you.

Also vanishing are lower- and middle-level management jobs involving  16 routine production. Between 1981 and 1986, more than 780,000 foremen, supervisors, and section chiefs lost their jobs through plant closings and layoffs.[7] Large numbers of assistant division heads, assistant directors, assistant managers, and vice presidents also found themselves jobless. GM shed more than 40,000 white-collar employees and planned to eliminate another 25,000 by the mid-1990s.[8] As America's core pyramids metamorphosed into global webs, many middle-level routine producers were as obsolete as routine workers on the line.

As has been noted, foreign-owned webs are hiring some Americans to do  17 routine production in the United States. Philips, Sony, and Toyota factories are popping up all over—to the self-congratulatory applause of the nation's governors and mayors, who have lured them with promises of tax abatements and new sewers, among other amenities. But as these ebullient politicians will soon discover, the foreign-owned factories are highly automated and will become far more so in years to come. Routine production jobs account for a small fraction of the cost of producing most items in the United States and other advanced nations, and this fraction will continue to decline sharply as computer-integrated robots take over. In 1977, it took routine producers thirty-five hours to assemble an automobile in the United States; it is estimated that by the mid-1990s, Japanese-owned factories in America will be producing finished automobiles using only eight hours of a routine producer's time.[9]

The productivity and resulting wages of American workers who run  18 such robotic machinery may be relatively high, but there may not be many

[5]Calculations from Current Population Surveys by L. Katz and A. Revenga, "Changes in the Structure of Wages: U.S. and Japan," National Bureau of Economic Research, September 1989.
[6]U.S. Department of Commerce, Bureau of Labor Statistics, "Wages of Unionized and Nonunionized Workers," various issues.
[7]U.S. Department of Labor, Bureau of Labor Statistics, "Reemployment Increases among Displaced Workers," *BLS News*, USDL 86-414, October 14, 1986, table 6.
[8]*Wall Street Journal*, February 16, 1990, p. A5.
[9]Figures from the International Motor Vehicles Program, Massachusetts Institute of Technology, 1989.

such jobs to go around. A case in point: in the late 1980s, Nippon Steel joined with America's ailing Inland Steel to build a new $400 million cold-rolling mill fifty miles west of Gary, Indiana. The mill was celebrated for its state-of-the-art technology, which cut the time to produce a coil of steel from twelve days to about one hour. In fact, the entire plant could be run by a small team of technicians, which became clear when Inland subsequently closed two of its old cold-rolling mills, laying off hundreds of routine workers. Governors and mayors take note: your much-ballyhooed foreign factories may end up employing distressingly few of your constituents.

19    Overall, the decline in routine jobs has hurt men more than women. This is because the routine production jobs held by men in high-volume metal bending manufacturing industries had paid higher wages than the routine production jobs held by women in textiles and data processing. As both sets of jobs have been lost, American women in routine production have gained more equal footing with American men—equally poor footing, that is. This is a major reason why the gender gap between male and female wages began to close during the 1980s.

20    The second of the three boats, carrying in-person servers, is sinking as well, but somewhat more slowly and unevenly. Most in-person servers are paid at or just slightly above the minimum wage and many work only part-time, with the result that their take-home pay is modest, to say the least. Nor do they typically receive all the benefits (health care, life insurance, disability, and so forth) garnered by routine producers in large manufacturing corporations or by symbolic analysts affiliated with the more affluent threads of global webs.[10] In-person servers are sheltered from the direct effects of global competition and, like everyone else, benefit from access to lower-cost products from around the world. But they are not immune to its indirect effects.

21    For one thing, in-person servers increasingly compete with former routine production workers, who, no longer able to find well-paying routine production jobs, have few alternatives but to seek in-person service jobs. The Bureau of Labor Statistics estimates that of the 2.8 million manufacturing workers who lost their jobs during the early 1980s, fully one-third were rehired in service jobs paying at least 20 percent less.[11] In-person servers must also compete with high school graduates and dropouts who years before had moved easily into routine production jobs but no longer can. And if demographic predictions about the American work force in the first decades of the twenty-first century are correct (and they are likely to be, since most of the people who will comprise the work force are already identifiable), most new entrants into the job market will be black or Hispanic men, or women—groups that in years past

[10]The growing portion of the American labor force engaged in in-person services, relative to routine production, thus helps explain why the number of Americans lacking health insurance increased by at least 6 million during the 1980s.

[11]U.S. Department of Labor, Bureau of Labor Statistics, "Reemployment Increases among Disabled Workers," October 14, 1986.

have possessed relatively weak technical skills. This will result in an even larger number of people crowding into in-person services. Finally, in-person servers will be competing with growing numbers of immigrants, both legal and illegal, for whom in-person services will comprise the most accessible jobs. (It is estimated that between the mid-1980s and the end of the century, about a quarter of all workers entering the American labor force will be immigrants.[12])

Perhaps the fiercest competition that in-person servers face comes from 22 labor-saving machinery (much of it invented, designed, fabricated, or assembled in other nations, of course). Automated tellers, computerized cashiers, automatic car washes, robotized vending machines, self-service gasoline pumps, and all similar gadgets substitute for the human beings that customers once encountered. Even telephone operators are fast disappearing, as electronic sensors and voice simulators become capable of carrying on conversations that are reasonably intelligent and always polite. Retail sales workers—among the largest groups of in-person servers—are similarly imperiled. Through personal computers linked to television screens, tomorrow's consumers will be able to buy furniture, appliances, and all sorts of electronic toys from their living rooms— examining the merchandise from all angles, selecting whatever color, size, special features, and price seem most appealing, and then transmitting the order instantly to warehouses from which the selections will be shipped directly to their homes. So, too, with financial transactions, airline and hotel reservations, rental car agreements, and similar contracts, which will be executed between consumers in their homes and computer banks somewhere else on the globe.[13]

Advanced economies like the United States will continue to generate siz- 23 able numbers of new in-person service jobs, of course, the automation of older ones notwithstanding. For every bank teller who loses her job to an automated teller, three new jobs open for aerobics instructors. Human beings, it seems, have an almost insatiable desire for personal attention. But the intense competition nevertheless ensures that the wages of in-person servers will remain relatively low. In-person servers—working on their own, or else dispersed widely amid many small establishments, filling all sorts of personal-care niches— cannot readily organize themselves into labor unions or create powerful lobbies to limit the impact of such competition.

In two respects, demographics will work in favor of in-person servers, 24 buoying their collective boat slightly. First, as has been noted, the rate of growth of the American work force is slowing. In particular, the number of young workers is shrinking. Between 1985 and 1995, the number of the eighteen- to twenty-four-year-olds will have declined by 17.5 percent. Thus, employers will have more incentive to hire and train in-person servers whom they might previously have avoided. But this demographic relief from the competitive pressures will be only temporary. The cumulative procreative energies of the

[12]Federal Immigration and Naturalization Service, *Statistical Yearbook* (Washington, D.C.: U.S. Government Printing Office, 1986, 1987).
[13]See Claudia H. Deutsch, "The Powerful Push for Self-Service," *New York Times*, April 9, 1989, section 3, p. 1.

postwar baby-boomers (born between 1946 and 1964) will result in a new surge of workers by 2010 or thereabouts.[14] And immigration—both legal and illegal—shows every sign of increasing in years to come.

25      Next, by the second decade of the twenty-first century, the number of Americans aged sixty-five and over will be rising precipitously, as the baby-boomers reach retirement age and live longer. Their life expectancies will lengthen not just because fewer of them will have smoked their way to their graves and more will have eaten better than their parents, but also because they will receive all sorts of expensive drugs and therapies designed to keep them alive—barely. By 2035, twice as many Americans will be elderly as in 1988, and the number of octogenarians is expected to triple. As these decaying baby-boomers ingest all the chemicals and receive all the treatments, they will need a great deal of personal attention. Millions of deteriorating bodies will require nurses, nursing-home operators, hospital administrators, orderlies, home-care providers, hospice aides, and technicians to operate and maintain all the expensive machinery that will monitor and temporarily stave off final disintegration. There might even be a booming market for euthanasia specialists. In-person servers catering to the old and ailing will be in strong demand.[15]

26      One small problem: the decaying baby-boomers will not have enough money to pay for these services. They will have used up their personal savings years before. Their Social Security payments will, of course, have been used by the government to pay for the previous generation's retirement and to finance much of the budget deficits of the 1980s. Moreover, with relatively fewer young Americans in the population, the supply of housing will likely exceed the demand, with the result that the boomers' major investments—their homes—will be worth less (in inflation-adjusted dollars) when they retire than they planned for. In consequence, the huge cost of caring for the graying boomers will fall on many of the same people who will be paid to care for them. It will be like a great sump pump: in-person servers of the twenty-first century will have an abundance of health-care jobs, but a large portion of their earnings will be devoted to Social Security payments and income taxes, which will in turn be used to pay their salaries. The net result: no real improvement in their standard of living.

27      The standard of living of in-person servers also depends, indirectly, on the standard of living of the Americans they serve who are engaged in world commerce. To the extent that *these* Americans are richly rewarded by the rest of the world for what they contribute, they will have more money to lavish upon in-person services. Here we find the only form of "trickle-down" economics that has a basis in reality. A waitress in a town whose major factory has just been closed is unlikely to earn a high wage or enjoy much job security; in a swank resort populated by film producers and banking moguls, she is apt

---

[14]U.S. Bureau of the Census, Current Population Reports, Series P-23, no. 138, tables 2-1, 4-6. See W. Johnson, A. Packer, et al., *Workforce 2000: Work and Workers for the 21st Century* (Indianapolis: Hudson Institute, 1987).

[15]The Census Bureau estimates that by the year 2000, at least 12 million Americans will work in health services—well over 6 percent of the total work force.

to do reasonably well. So, too, with nations. In-person servers in Bangladesh may spend their days performing roughly the same tasks as in-person servers in the United States, but have a far lower standard of living for their efforts. The difference comes in the value that their customers add to the world economy.

Unlike the boats of routine producers and in-person servers, however, the vessel containing America's symbolic analysts is rising. Worldwide demand for their insights is growing as the ease and speed of communicating them steadily increases. Not every symbolic analyst is rising as quickly or as dramatically as every other, of course; symbolic analysts at the low end are barely holding their own in the world economy. But symbolic analysts at the top are in such great demand worldwide that they have difficulty keeping track of all their earnings. Never before in history has opulence on such a scale been gained by people who have earned it, and done so legally. [28]

Among symbolic analysts in the middle range are American scientists and researchers who are busily selling their discoveries to global enterprise webs. They are not limited to American customers. If the strategic brokers in General Motors' headquarters refuse to pay a high price for a new means of making high-strength ceramic engines dreamed up by a team of engineers affiliated with Carnegie Mellon University in Pittsburgh, the strategic brokers of Honda or Mercedes-Benz are likely to be more than willing. [29]

So, too, with the insights of America's ubiquitous management consultants, which are being sold for large sums to eager entrepreneurs in Europe and Latin America. Also, the insights of America's energy consultants, sold for even larger sums to Arab sheikhs. American design engineers are providing insights to Olivetti, Mazda, Siemens, and other global webs; American marketers, techniques for learning what worldwide consumers will buy; American advertisers, ploys for ensuring that they actually do. American architects are issuing designs and blueprints for opera houses, art galleries, museums, luxury hotels, and residential complexes in the world's major cities; American commercial property developers, marketing these properties to worldwide investors and purchasers. [30]

Americans who specialize in the gentle art of public relations are in demand by corporations, governments, and politicians in virtually every nation. So, too, are American political consultants, some of whom, at this writing, are advising the Hungarian Socialist Party, the remnant of Hungary's ruling Communists, on how to salvage a few parliamentary seats in the nation's first free election in more than forty years. Also at this writing, a team of American agricultural consultants is advising the managers of a Soviet farm collective employing 1,700 Russians eighty miles outside Moscow. As noted, American investment bankers and lawyers specializing in financial circumnavigations are selling their insights to Asians and Europeans who are eager to discover how to make large amounts of money by moving large amounts of money. [31]

Developing nations, meanwhile, are hiring American civil engineers to advise on building roads and dams. The present thaw in the Cold War will no [32] doubt expand these opportunities. American engineers from Bechtel (a global firm notable for having employed both Caspar Weinberger and George Shultz for much larger sums than either earned in the Reagan administration) have begun helping the Soviets design and install a new generation of nuclear reactors. Nations also are hiring American bankers and lawyers to help them renegotiate the terms of their loans with global banks, and Washington lobbyists to help them with Congress, the Treasury, the World Bank, the IMF, and other politically sensitive institutions. In fits of obvious desperation, several nations emerging from communism have even hired American economists to teach them about capitalism.

33      Almost everyone around the world is buying the skills and insights of Americans who manipulate oral and visual symbols—musicians, sound engineers, film producers, makeup artists, directors, cinematographers, actors and actresses, boxers, scriptwriters, songwriters, and set designers. Among the wealthiest of symbolic analysts are Steven Spielberg, Bill Cosby, Charles Schulz, Eddie Murphy, Sylvester Stallone, Madonna, and other star directors and performers—who are almost as well known on the streets of Dresden and Tokyo as in the Back Bay of Boston. Less well rewarded but no less renowned are the unctuous anchors on Turner Broadcasting's Cable News, who appear daily, via satellite, in places ranging from Vietnam to Nigeria. Vanna White is the world's most-watched game-show hostess. Behind each of these familiar faces is a collection of American problem-solvers, -identifiers, and brokers who train, coach, advise, promote, amplify, direct, groom, represent, and otherwise add value to their talents.[16]

34      There are also the insights of senior American executives who occupy the world headquarters of global "American" corporations and the national or regional headquarters of global "foreign" corporations. Their insights are duly exported to the rest of the world through the webs of global enterprise. IBM does not export many machines from the United States, for example. Big Blue makes machines all over the globe and services them on the spot. Its prime American exports are symbolic and analytic. From IBM's world headquarters in Armonk, New York, emanate strategic brokerage and related management services bound for the rest of the world. In return, IBM's top executives are generously rewarded.

35  The most important reason for this expanding world market and increasing global demand for the symbolic and analytic insights of Americans has been the dramatic improvement in worldwide communication and transportation technologies. Designs, instructions, advice, and visual and audio symbols can be communicated more and more rapidly around the globe, with ever greater precision and at ever-lower cost. Madonna's voice can be transported to billions

[16]In 1989, the entertainment business summoned to the United States $5.5 billion in foreign earnings—making it among the nation's largest export industries, just behind aerospace. U.S. Department of Commerce, International Trade Commission, "Composition of U.S. Exports," various issues.

of listeners, with perfect clarity, on digital compact discs. A new invention emanating from engineers in Battelle's laboratory in Columbus, Ohio, can be sent
almost anywhere via modem, in a form that will allow others to examine it in
three dimensions through enhanced computer graphics. When face-to-face
meetings are still required—and videoconferencing will not suffice—it is relatively easy for designers, consultants, advisers, artists, and executives to board
supersonic jets and, in a matter of hours, meet directly with their worldwide
clients, customers, audiences, and employees.

With rising demand comes rising compensation. Whether in the form of 36
licensing fees, fees for service, salaries, or shares in final profits, the economic
result is much the same. There are also nonpecuniary rewards. One of the best-
kept secrets among symbolic analysts is that so many of them enjoy their work.
In fact, much of it does not count as work at all, in the traditional sense. The
work of routine producers and in-person servers is typically monotonous; it
causes muscles to tire or weaken and involves little independence or discretion.
The "work" of symbolic analysts, by contrast, often involves puzzles, experiments, games, a significant amount of chatter, and substantial discretion over
what to do next. Few routine producers or in-person servers would "work" if
they did not need to earn the money. Many symbolic analysts would "work"
even if money were no object.

At mid-century, when America was a national market dominated by core 37
pyramid-shaped corporations, there were constraints on the earnings of people
at the highest rungs. First and most obviously, the market for their services was
largely limited to the borders of the nation. In addition, whatever conceptual
value they might contribute was small relative to the value gleaned from large
scale—and it was dependent on large scale for whatever income it was to summon. Most of the problems to be identified and solved had to do with enhancing the efficiency of production and improving the flow of materials, parts,
assembly, and distribution. Inventors searched for the rare breakthrough revealing an entirely new product to be made in high volume; management consultants, executives, and engineers thereafter tried to speed and synchronize its
manufacture, to better achieve scale efficiencies; advertisers and marketers
sought then to whet the public's appetite for the standard item that emerged.
Since white-collar earnings increased with larger scale, there was considerable
incentive to expand the firm; indeed, many of America's core corporations grew
far larger than scale economies would appear to have justified.

By the 1990s, in contrast, the earnings of symbolic analysts were limited 38
neither by the size of the national market nor by the volume of production of
the firms with which they were affiliated. The marketplace was worldwide, and
conceptual value was high relative to value added from scale efficiencies.

There had been another constraint on high earnings, which also gave way 39
by the 1990s. At mid-century, the compensation awarded to top executives and
advisers of the largest of America's core corporations could not be grossly out
of proportion to that of low-level production workers. It would be unseemly for

executives who engaged in highly visible rounds of bargaining with labor unions, and who routinely responded to government requests to moderate prices, to take home wages and benefits wildly in excess of what other Americans earned. Unless white-collar executives restrained themselves, moreover, blue-collar production workers could not be expected to restrain their own demands for higher wages. Unless both groups exercised restraint, the government could not be expected to forbear from imposing direct controls and regulations.

40    At the same time, the wages of production workers could not be allowed to sink too low, lest there be insufficient purchasing power in the economy. After all, who would buy all the goods flowing out of American factories if not American workers? This, too, was part of the tacit bargain struck between American managers and their workers.

41    Recall the oft-repeated corporate platitude of the era about the chief executive's responsibility to carefully weigh and balance the interests of the corporation's disparate stakeholders. Under the stewardship of the corporate statesman, no set of stakeholders—least of all white-collar executives—was to gain a disproportionately large share of the benefits of corporate activity; nor was any stakeholder—especially the average worker—to be left with a share that was disproportionately small. Banal though it was, this idea helped to maintain the legitimacy of the core American corporation in the eyes of most Americans, and to ensure continued economic growth.

42    But by the 1990s, these informal norms were evaporating, just as (and largely because) the core American corporation was vanishing. The links between top executives and the American production worker were fading: an ever-increasing number of subordinates and contractees were foreign, and a steadily growing number of American routine producers were working for foreign-owned firms. An entire cohort of middle-level managers, who had once been deemed "white collar," had disappeared; and, increasingly, American executives were exporting their insights to global enterprise webs.

43    As the American corporation itself became a global web almost indistinguishable from any other, its stakeholders were turning into a large and diffuse group, spread over the world. Such global stakeholders were less visible, and far less noisy, than national stakeholders. And as the American corporation sold its goods and services all over the world, the purchasing power of American workers became far less relevant to its economic survival.

44    Thus have the inhibitions been removed. The salaries and benefits of America's top executives, and many of their advisers and consultants, have soared to what years before would have been unimaginable heights, even as those of other Americans have declined.

## COMPREHENSION

1. To what does the title allude? Why is this allusion significant to the meaning of the title?

2. To whom does Reich refer when he mentions "symbolic analysts"? Regardless of their occupation, what do all symbolic analysts have in common regarding the nature of their work?

3. What has traditionally been the image of and the nature of work among the white-collar workers to whom Reich alludes? Why are they now one of the groups in danger of losing employment opportunities?

## RHETORIC

1. Reich uses the central metaphor of the "boat" in describing the state of economics and employment. Why? What connotations are associated with this image in regard to financial security?

2. How does Reich's introduction prepare you for the major themes he addresses in the body of his essay?

3. Examine the section breaks at the start of paragraphs 3, 11, 20, 35, and 37. How does each section relate to the theme of the essay as a whole? What transitional devices does Reich use to bridge one section to the next?

4. Paragraphs 5, 6, 9, and 16 cite specific and detailed examples of the effects of the changing global economy. How does this contribute to conveying Reich's authority regarding the subject he is discussing?

5. Reich describes a dire situation for the American worker. How would you characterize the tone of this description? Is it angry, resigned, impartial, or accusatory? You may use these or any other adjectives as long as you explain your view.

6. Why does Reich open his essay with an epigraph from Adam Smith? What is the relationship of the quotation to the overall theme of the essay? How does the tone of the epigraph contrast with the tone of the title?

7. What is the author's purpose? Is it to inform, to explain, to warn, to enlighten, to offer solutions, or a combination of any of these? Explain your view.

## WRITING

1. In a classification essay, describe three areas of academic concentration at your college or university that can help prepare one for a job as a symbolic analyst.

2. In an expository essay, explain whether you believe the discrepancy between high-wage and low-wage workers will increase, decrease, or remain the same.

3. **Writing an Argument:** In an essay, argue for or against the proposition that as long as one knows which careers command the highest salaries, it is up to the individual to decide whether he or she should pursue a job in those fields.

www.mhhe.com/
**mhreader**

For more information on Robert Reich, go to:
**More Resources > Ch. 8 Business & Economics**

# A Modest Proposal
## Preventing the Children of Poor People in Ireland from Being a Burden to Their Parents or Country, and for Making Them Beneficial to the Public

### Jonathan Swift

*Jonathan Swift (1667–1745) is best known as the author of three satires:* A Tale of a Tub *(1704),* Gulliver's Travels *(1726), and* A Modest Proposal *(1729). In these satires, Swift pricks the balloon of many of his contemporaries' and our own most cherished prejudices, pomposities, and delusions. He was also a famous churchman, an eloquent spokesman for Irish rights, and a political journalist. The following selection, perhaps the most famous satiric essay in the English language, offers modest advice to a nation suffering from poverty, overpopulation, and political injustice.*

1   It is a melancholy object to those who walk through this great town or travel in the country, when they see the streets, the roads, and cabin doors, crowded with beggars of the female-sex, followed by three, four, or six children, all in rags and importuning every passenger for an alms. These mothers, instead of being able to work for their honest livelihood, are forced to employ all their time in strolling to beg sustenance for their helpless infants, who, as they grow up, either turn thieves for want of work, or leave their dear native country to fight for the Pretender in Spain, or sell themselves to the Barbadoes.

2   I think it is agreed by all parties that this prodigious number of children in the arms, or on the backs, or at the heels of their mothers, and frequently of their fathers, is in the present deplorable state of the kingdom a very great additional grievance; and therefore whoever could find out a fair, cheap, and easy method of making these children sound, useful members of the commonwealth would deserve so well of the public as to have his statue set up for a preserver of the nation.

3   But my intention is very far from being confined to provide only for the children of professed beggars; it is of a much greater extent, and shall take in the whole number of infants at a certain age who are born of parents in effect as little able to support them as those who demand our charity in the streets.

4   As to my own part, having turned my thoughts for many years upon this important subject, and maturely weighted the several schemes of other projectors, I have always found them grossly mistaken in their computation. It is true,

a child just dropped from its dam may be supported by her milk for a solar year, with little other nourishment; at most not above the value of two shillings, which the mother may certainly get, or the value in scraps, by her lawful occupation of begging; and it is exactly at one year old that I propose to provide for them in such a manner as instead of being a charge upon their parents or the parish, or wanting food and raiment for the rest of their lives, they shall on the contrary contribute to the feeding, and partly to the clothing, of many thousands.

There is likewise another great advantage in my scheme, that it will pre- 5 vent those voluntary abortions, and that horrid practice of women murdering their bastard children, alas, too frequent among us, sacrificing the poor inno- cent babes, I doubt, more to avoid the expense than the shame, which would move tears and pity in the most savage and inhuman breast.

The number of souls in this kingdom being usually reckoned one million 6 and a half, of these I calculate there may be about two hundred thousand cou- ples whose wives are breeders; from which number I subtract thirty thousand couples who are able to maintain their own children, although I apprehend there cannot be so many under the present distresses of the kingdom; but this being granted, there will remain an hundred and seventy thousand breeders. I again subtract fifty thousand for those women who miscarry, or whose chil- dren die by accident or disease within the year. There only remain an hundred and twenty thousand children of poor parents annually born. The question therefore is, how this number shall be reared and provided for, which, as I have already said, under the present situation of affairs, is utterly impossible by all the methods hitherto proposed. For we can neither employ them in handicraft or agriculture; we neither build houses (I mean in the country) nor cultivate land. They can very seldom pick up a livelihood by stealing till they arrive at six years old, except where they are of towardly parts; although I confess they learn the rudiments much earlier, during which time they can however be looked upon only as probationers, as I have been informed by a principal gen- tleman in the county of Cavan, who protested to me that he never knew above one or two instances under the age of six, even in a part of the kingdom so re- nowned for the quickest proficiency in that art.

I am assured by our merchants that a boy or girl before twelve years old is 7 no salable commodity; and even when they come to this age they will not yield above three pounds, or three pounds and half a crown at most on the Exchange; which cannot turn to account either to the parents or the kingdom, the charge of nutriment and rags having been at least four times that value.

I shall now therefore humbly propose my own thoughts, which I hope will 8 not be liable to the least objection.

I have been assured by a very knowing American of my acquaintance in 9 London, that a young healthy child well nursed is at a year old a most deli- cious, nourishing, and wholesome food, whether stewed, roasted, baked or boiled; and I make no doubt that it will equally serve in a fricassee or a ragout.

I do therefore humbly offer it to public consideration that of the hundred 10 and twenty thousand children, already computed, twenty thousand may be reserved for breed, whereof only one fourth part to be males, which is more than we allow to sheep, black cattle, or swine; and my reason is that these children are seldom the fruits of marriage, a circumstance not much regarded by our savages, therefore one male will be sufficient to serve four females. That the remaining hundred thousand may at a year old be offered in sale to the persons of quality and fortune through the kingdom, always advising the mother to let them suck plentifully in the last month, so as to render them plump and fat for a good table. A child will make two dishes at an entertainment for friends; and when the family dines alone, the fore or hind quarter will make a reasonable dish, and seasoned with a little pepper or salt will be very good boiled on the fourth day, especially in winter.

11    I have reckoned upon a medium that a child just born will weigh twelve pounds, and in a solar year if tolerably nursed increaseth to twenty-eight pounds.

12    I grant this food will be somewhat dear, and therefore very proper for landlords, who, as they have already devoured most of the parents, seem to have the best title to the children.

13    Infant's flesh will be in season throughout the year, but more plentiful in March, and a little before and after. For we are told by a grave author, an eminent French physician, that fish being a prolific diet, there are more children born in Roman Catholic countries about nine months after Lent than at any other season: therefore, reckoning a year after Lent, the markets will be more glutted than usual, because the number of popish infants is at least three to one in this kingdom; and therefore it will have one other collateral advantage, by lessening the number of Papists among us.

14    I have already computed the charge of nursing a beggar's child (in which list I reckon all cottagers, laborers, and four fifths of the farmers) to be about two shillings per annum, rags included: and I believe no gentleman would repine to give ten shillings for the carcass of a good fat child, which, as I have said, will make four dishes of excellent nutritive meat, when he hath only some particular friend or his own family to dine with him. Thus the squire will learn to be a good landlord, and grow popular among the tenants; the mother will have eight shillings net profit, and be fit for work till she produces another child.

15    Those who are more thrifty (as I must confess the times require) may flay the carcass; the skin of which artificially dressed will make admirable gloves for ladies, and summer boots for fine gentlemen.

16    As to our city of Dublin, shambles may be appointed for this purpose in the most convenient parts of it, and butchers we may be assured will not be wanting; although I rather recommend buying the children alive, and dressing them hot from the knife as we do roasting pigs.

17    A very worthy person, a true lover of his country, and whose virtues I highly esteem, was lately pleased in discoursing on this matter to offer a refinement upon my scheme. He said that many gentlemen of this kingdom, having of late destroyed their deer, he conceived that the want of venison might be

well supplied by the bodies of young lads and maidens, not exceeding fourteen years of age nor under twelve, so great a number of both sexes in every county being now ready to starve for want of work and service; and these to be disposed of by their parents, if alive, or otherwise by their nearest relations. But with due deference to so excellent a friend and so deserving a patriot, I cannot be altogether in his sentiments; for as to the males, my American acquaintance assured me from frequent experience that their flesh was generally tough and lean, like that of our schoolboys, by continual exercise, and their taste disagreeable; and to fatten them would not answer the charge. Then as to the females, it would, I think with humble submission, be a loss to the public, because they soon would become breeders themselves: and besides, it is not improbable that some scrupulous people might be apt to censure such a practice (although indeed very unjustly) as a little bordering upon cruelty; which, I confess, hath always been with me the strongest objection against any project, how well so ever intended.

But in order to justify my friend, he confessed that this expedient was put 18 into his head by the famous Psalmanazar, a native of the island Formosa, who came from thence to London above twenty years ago, and in conversation told my friend that in his country when any young person happened to be put to death, the executioner sold the carcass to persons of quality as a prime dainty; and that in his time the body of a plump girl of fifteen, who was crucified for an attempt to poison the emperor, was sold to his Imperial Majesty's prime minister of state, and other great mandarins of the court, in joints from the gibbet, at four hundred crowns. Neither indeed can I deny that if the same use were made of several plump young girls in this town, who without one single groat to their fortunes cannot stir abroad without a chair, and appear at the playhouse and assemblies in foreign fineries which they never will pay for, the kingdom would not be the worse.

Some persons of a desponding spirit are in great concern about that vast 19 number of poor people who are aged, diseased, or maimed, and I have been desired to employ my thoughts what course may be taken to ease the nation of so grievous an encumbrance. But I am not in the least pain upon that matter, because it is very well known that they are every day dying and rotting by cold and famine, and filth and vermin, as fast as can be reasonably expected. And as to the younger laborers, they are now in almost as hopeful a condition. They cannot get work, and consequently pine away for want of nourishment to a degree that if at any time they are accidentally hired to common labor, they have not strength to perform it; and thus the country and themselves are happily delivered from the evils to come.

I have too long digressed, and therefore shall return to my subject. I think 20 the advantages by the proposal which I have made are obvious and many, as well as of the highest importance.

For first, as I have already observed, it would greatly lessen the number 21 of Papists, with whom we are yearly overrun, being the principal breeders of the nation as well as our most dangerous enemies; and who stay at home on purpose to deliver the kingdom to the Pretender, hoping to take their advantage by the absence of so many good Protestants, who have chosen rather to leave their country than to stay at home and pay tithes against their conscience to an Episcopal curate.

22      Secondly, the poorer tenants will have something valuable of their own, which by law may be made liable to distress, and help to pay their landlord's rent, their corn and cattle being already seized and money a thing unknown.

23      Thirdly, whereas the maintenance of an hundred thousand children, from two years old and upwards, cannot be computed at less than ten shillings a piece per annum, the nation's stock will be thereby increased fifty thousand pounds per annum, besides the profit of a new dish introduced to the tables of all gentlemen of fortune in the kingdom who have any refinement in taste. And the money will circulate among ourselves, the goods being entirely of our own growth and manufacture.

24      Fourthly, the constant breeders, besides the gain of eight shillings sterling per annum by the sale of their children, will be rid of the charge of maintaining them after the first year.

25      Fifthly, this food would likewise bring great custom to taverns, where the vintners will certainly be so prudent as to procure the best receipts for dressing it to perfection, and consequently have their houses frequented by all the fine gentlemen, who justly value themselves upon their knowledge in good eating; and a skillful cook, who understands how to oblige his guests, will contrive to make it as expensive as they please.

26      Sixthly, this would be a great inducement to marriage, which all wise nations have either encouraged by rewards or enforced by laws and penalties. It would increase the care and tenderness of mothers toward their children, when they were sure of a settlement for life to the poor babes, provided in some sort by the public, to their annual profit instead of expense. We should see an honest emulation among the married women, which of them could bring the fattest child to the market. Men would become as fond of their wives during the time of their pregnancy as they are now of their mares in foal, their cows in calf, or sows when they are ready to farrow; nor offer to beat or kick them (as is too frequent a practice) for fear of a miscarriage.

27      Many other advantages might be enumerated. For instance, the addition of some thousand carcasses in our exportation of barreled beef, the propagation of swine's flesh, and improvement in the art of making good bacon, so much wanted among us by the great destruction of pigs, too frequent at our tables, which are no way comparable in taste or magnificence to a well-grown, fat yearling child, which roasted whole will make a considerable figure at a lord mayor's feast or any other public entertainment. But this and many others I omit, being studious of brevity.

28      Supposing that one thousand families in this city would be constant customers for infants' flesh, besides others who might have it at merry meetings, particularly weddings and christenings, I compute that Dublin would take off annually about twenty thousand carcasses, and the rest of the kingdom

(where probably they will be sold somewhat cheaper) the remaining eighty thousand.

I can think of no one objection that will possibly be raised against this pro- 29 posal, unless it should be urged that the number of people will be thereby much lessened in the kingdom. This I freely own, and it was indeed one principal design in offering it to the world. I desire the reader will observe, that I calculate my remedy for this one individual kingdom of Ireland and for no other that ever was, is, or I think ever can be upon earth. Therefore let no man talk to me of other expedients: of taxing our absentees at five shillings a pound: of using neither clothes nor household furniture except what is of our own growth and manufacture: of utterly rejecting the materials and instruments that promote foreign luxury: of curing the expensiveness of pride, vanity, idleness, and gaming in our women: of introducing a vein of parsimony, prudence, and temperance: of learning to love our country, in the want of which we differ even from Laplanders and the inhabitants of Topinamboo: of quitting our animosities and factions, nor acting any longer like the Jews, who were murdering one another at the very moment their city was taken: of being a little cautious not to sell our country and conscience for nothing: of teaching landlords to have at least one degree of mercy toward their tenants: lastly, of putting a spirit of honesty, industry, and skill into our shopkeepers; who, if a resolution could be now taken to buy only our native goods, would immediately unite to cheat and exact upon us in the price, the measure and the goodness, nor could ever yet be brought to make one fair proposal of just dealing, though often and earnestly invited to it.

Therefore I repeat, let no man talk to me of these and the like expedients, 30 till he hath at least some glimpse of hope that there will ever be some hearty and sincere attempt to put them in practice.

But as to myself, having been wearied out for many years with offering 31 vain, idle, visionary thoughts, and at length utterly despairing of success, I fortunately fell upon this proposal, which, as it is wholly new, so it hath something solid and real, of no expense and little trouble, full in our own power, and whereby we can incur no danger in disobliging England. For this kind of commodity will not bear exportation, the flesh being of too tender a consistence to admit a long continuance in salt, although perhaps I could name a country which would be glad to eat up our whole nation without it.

After all, I am not so violently bent upon my own opinion as to reject any 32 offer proposed by wise men, which shall be found equally innocent, cheap, easy, and effectual. But before something of that kind shall be advanced in contradiction to my scheme, and offering a better, I desire the author or authors will be pleased maturely to consider two points. First, as things now stand, how they will be able to find food and raiment for an hundred thousand useless mouths and backs. And secondly, there being a round million of creatures in human figure throughout this kingdom, whose sole subsistence put into a common stock would leave them in debt two millions of pounds sterling, adding those who are beggars by profession to the bulk of farmers, cottagers, and laborers, with their wives and children who are beggars in effect; I desire those politicians who dislike my overture, and may perhaps be so bold to attempt an answer, that they will first ask the parents of these mortals whether they would not at this day think it a great happiness to have been sold for food at a year old in the manner I prescribe, and thereby have avoided such a perpetual scene of misfortunes as they have since gone through by the oppression of landlords, the impossibility of paying rent without money or trade, the want of common sustenance, with neither house nor clothes to cover them from the inclemencies of the weather, and the most inevitable prospect of entailing the like or greater miseries upon their breed forever.

33      I profess, in the sincerity of my heart, that I have not the least personal interest in endeavoring to promote this necessary work, having no other motive than the public good of my country, by advancing our trade, providing for infants, relieving the poor, and giving some pleasure to the rich. I have no children by which I can propose to get a single penny; the youngest being nine years old, and my wife past childbearing.

## COMPREHENSION

1. Who is Swift's audience for this essay? Defend your answer.
2. Describe the persona in this essay. How is the unusual narrative personality (as distinguished from Swift's personality) revealed by the author in degrees? How can we tell that the speaker's opinions are not shared by Swift?
3. What are the major propositions behind Swift's modest proposal? What are the minor propositions?

## RHETORIC

1. Explain the importance of the word *modest* in the title. What stylistic devices does this "modesty" contrast with?
2. What is the effect of Swift's persistent reference to people as "breeders," "dams," "carcass," and the like? Why does he define *children* in economic terms? Find other words that contribute to this motif.
3. Analyze the purpose of the relatively long introduction, consisting of paragraphs 1–7. How does Swift establish his ironic-satiric tone in this initial section?
4. What contrasts and discrepancies are at the heart of Swift's ironic statement in paragraphs 9 and 10? Explain both the subtlety and savagery of the satire in paragraph 12.
5. Paragraphs 13–20 develop six advantages of Swift's proposal, while paragraphs 21–26 list them in enumerative manner. Analyze the progression of these propositions. What is the effect of the listing? Why is Swift parodying argumentative techniques?

**6.** How does the author both sustain and suspend the irony in paragraph 29? How is the strategy repeated in paragraph 32? How does the concluding paragraph cap his satiric commentary on human nature?

## WRITING

**1.** Discuss Swift's social, political, religious, and economic views as they are revealed in the essay.
**2.** Write a comprehensive critique of America's failure to address the needs of its poor.
**3.** **Writing an Argument:** Write a modest proposal—on, for example, how to end the drug problem—advancing an absurd proposition through various argumentative techniques.

 www.mhhe.com/ **mhreader**   For more information on Jonathan Swift, go to: **More Resources > Ch. 8 Business & Economics**

## Synthesis: Connections For Critical Thinking

**1.** Using the essays of Ehrenreich and Reich, compare the effects of work on human relationships.
**2.** Write a definition essay titled "What Is Work?" Refer to any of the selections in this chapter to substantiate your opinions.
**3.** Describe the potential effect of the global marketplace as described by O'Rourke, Reich, and Friedman.
**4.** Compare the writings of Swift, Ehrenreich, and Reich in terms of the options of those on the lowest rungs of the economic system in Western society.
**5.** Woolf and Swift are considered to be "classic" writers. What makes their essays "classics"?
**6.** Monitor and videotape three business news television shows that focus on analysis and commentary. Analyze the discourse of the moderators, hosts, and guests. As an alternative method, review selected business news Web sites, and subject them to the same process.
**7.** To what extent is American society guided by a business ethic? For example, have Americans historically been so preoccupied with wealth that the quest for money has actually become a distinguishing mark of the national character? Or does the merging of business and religion (what social scientists term the Protestant work ethic) reflect a uniquely American trait? Discuss these issues in an analytical and argumentative essay.

8. **Network:** Locate the Web sites of three major newspapers in three different large cities in America. Review their classified sections, and compare and contrast the types of jobs advertised in the three cities. Do a similar search and comparison for federal and state government jobs.

9. **Network:** Examine your own college or university's Web site, and review its philosophy regarding the relationship of college studies to the world of work.

10. **Network:** Join a newsgroup with a special interest in the global economy. Post a general question to its members, asking whether they agree with Reich's analysis of the changing job market. Collect the responses.

11. **Network:** Locate several Web sites for job seekers—for example, Monster .com. Enter the job classification you are interested in, and compare and contrast the number and types of jobs advertised for three cities. Do a similar search and comparison for federal and state government jobs advertised on the Web.

# chapter 9

# Media and Popular Culture

*What Is the Message?*

We are surrounded today as never before by images, sounds, and texts—by what Todd Gitlin, who has an essay in this chapter, terms a "media torrent." Radio and television programs, newspapers and Internet sites, MTV and video games, iPods and cell phone gadgetry increasingly mold our place in culture and society. Indeed, the power of media in our waking and subliminal lives might very well condition our understanding (or misunderstanding) of reality. Today, we can download "reality."

Today's media universe, fueled by new technology, is transforming our sense of the world. Consider the ways in which computers permit us to enter the media stream, making us willing, even compulsive participants in and consumers of popular culture. Video games, streaming advertisements, wraparound music, newsgroups, chat rooms, and more—all provide data and sensation at warp computer speed. Some slow down the torrent: Bloggers (a word that didn't exist until recently) interrogate their lives and the "facts," even holding newspapers and television news channels accountable for information. But if, as Marshall McLuhan declared, the medium is the message, then any medium, whether old or new, has the power to reflect or construct versions of reality.

Perhaps Americans have moved from a print-based culture to an aural/visual one, preferring electronic media for information, distraction, and entertainment. For centuries books were the molders of popular taste and culture. Tocqueville in *Democracy in America* was amazed by the fact that in the rudest pioneer's hut there was a copy of Shakespeare—and probably, we might add, a copy of the best seller of all time, the Bible. Today's typical household might have more media for DVD players, VCRs, MP3 players, and PlayStations than books in a library. Of course, print media—say, a book on the ways in which major political parties manipulate the media—offer us the opportunity to scrutinize facts and sources in ways that shock jocks on radio, or talk show hosts on television, or participants in chat rooms cannot. The *medium* or *source* from which we receive sounds, images, and text—the place from which we enter the media torrent—determines the version of reality we carry with us. We can even drown in this torrent, as people who have been captured in "virtual reality" can attest.

The writers in this chapter invite us to enter the media torrent from a variety of places. They ask broad cultural questions about how we conduct our everyday lives and what choices we make. These questions have both local and worldwide implications, because media and their technological helpmates have created a global village permitting the instant transmission of ideas and images, as well as a subtle transfer of culture—typically American—to the remotest parts of the planet. Whether we navigate the torrent intelligently or succumb passively to the images and sounds washing over us, it is clear that the media in this century will have a significant impact on human experience.

## Previewing the Chapter

As you read the essays in this chapter and respond to them in discussion and writing, consider the following questions:

- What is the main media form and issue on which the author focuses?
- What tone or attitude does the author take toward the subject?
- How does the author fit his or her analysis into the context of popular culture? What social, economic, psychological, or political problems or controversies are treated?
- Which areas of expertise does the author bring to bear on the subject?
- What form of rhetoric—narration and description, exposition, argument—does the writer use? If argument, what is the author's claim? What evidence does she or he provide to support this claim?
- Which essays are similar in subject, thesis, style, purpose, or method, and why?
- What have you learned about the media and popular culture from reading these essays?
- Which essays did you find the most compelling or persuasive? The least? Why?

# Classic and Contemporary Images
## WHAT DO GANGSTER FILMS REVEAL ABOUT US?

*Using a Critical Perspective*   The best gangster films—like *Little Caesar, The Godfather,* and the *Sopranos* series—challenge viewers to form ethical opinions about and interpretations of the tale of crime that unfolds. Even if you haven't seen these two films, what do you think is happening in each frame? What details do you focus on? Do the two characters capture the essence of the gangster life, and why? What aspects of film art—framing, the use of close-up or distance shots, the handling of light, shadow, and color—convey an ethical statement? More broadly, in what ways can film art serve as a commentary on American life?

During the 1930s, the first decade of sound films, actors such as Edward G. Robinson, James Cagney, and Paul Muni created the classic portrait of the gangster as a tough-talking, violent outlaw in films such as *Little Caesar* (1930), *The Public Enemy* (1931), and *Scarface* (1932).

HBO's award-winning program *The Sopranos* provided a more nuanced
portrait of the gangster as a member of a corrupt, and corrupting,
organization with shifting loyalties. For example, Tony Soprano,
the character played by James Gandolfini in the series,
is a family man beset by so many problems that
he must seek psychiatric help.

# Classic and Contemporary Essays
## WHY ARE WE FASCINATED BY GANGSTERS?

Both Robert Warshow and Ellen Willis examine the portrayal of the gangster in modern culture, although each has a somewhat different interpretive slant. Warshow sees the gangster as a "tragic hero" at odds with—although at times admired by—our value system. Willis, on the other hand, sees him as a representation of a flawed mythology, a world doomed from the start owing to its own internal inadequacies. Warshow demonstrates that the gangster is ill-fated because he is compelled to operate in an "outlawed" system that ultimately must be squashed by the dominant one. Willis demonstrates—through her analysis of the HBO series *The Sopranos*—that the gangster is destined to failure because at heart his system is intrinsically corrupt, and it is the very system to which he has pledged his allegiance that is responsible for his anxiety. Both critics acknowledge that the mythological gangster exists outside of "real time," and although he may be surrounded by family and acquaintances—in fact, embroiled with them in an alternative social structure—he is ultimately alone. Warshow's gangster is doomed because he must die, because as the author states, "The gangster's whole life is an effort to assert himself as an individual, to draw himself out of the crowd, and he always dies *because* he is an individual." For Willis, Tony Soprano, while always conscious of the reality of death and in fact perpetrating it against his adversaries, wills himself to survive in a split culture. Tony's dilemma, which causes him to seek psychiatric help, is that he exists simultaneously in a "dying tribal culture" and in mainstream American popular culture. If gangsters are doomed, the reason is that in the end, corruption, by its very nature, cannot renew itself. Each of these highly articulate essays demonstrates that an observant writer can glean issues of major moral significance from what the general public views as mere "entertainment."

562

# The Gangster as Tragic Hero

### Robert Warshow

*Robert Warshow (1917–1955) attended the University of Michigan and worked for the U.S. Army Security Agency from 1942 to 1946. After the war, he served as an editor of* Commentary, *writing film criticism for this magazine and also for* Partisan Review. *Before his untimely death from a heart attack, Warshow had written several brilliant essays on film and on popular culture. Writing of Warshow, Lionel Trilling observed, "I believe that certain of his pieces establish themselves in the line of Hazlitt, a tradition in which I would place only one other writer of our time, George Orwell." One of these brilliant essays, focusing on the interrelation of film and society, is "The Gangster as Tragic Hero," which appeared in* The Immediate Experience: Movies, Games, Theatre and Other Aspects of Popular Culture *(1962).*

America, as a social and political organization, is committed to a cheerful view of  1
life. It could not be otherwise. The sense of tragedy is a luxury of aristocratic societies, where the fate of the individual is not conceived of as having a direct and legitimate political importance, being determined by a fixed and supra-political—that is, non-controversial—moral order or fate. Modern equalitarian societies, however, whether democratic or authoritarian in their political forms, always base themselves on the claim that they are making life happier; the avowed function of the modern state, at least in its ultimate terms, is not only to regulate social relations, but also to determine the quality and possibilities of human life in general. Happiness thus becomes the chief political issue—in a sense, the only political issue—and for that reason it can never be treated as an issue at all. If an American or a Russian is unhappy, it implies a certain reprobation of his society, and therefore, by a logic of which we can all recognize the necessity, it becomes an obligation of citizenship to be cheerful; if the authorities find it necessary, the citizen may even be compelled to make a public display of his cheerfulness on important occasions, just as he may be conscripted into the army in time of war.

Naturally, this civic responsibility rests most strongly upon the organs of  2
mass culture. The individual citizen may still be permitted his private unhappiness so long as it does not take on political significance, the extent of this tolerance being determined by how large an area of private life the society can accommodate. But every production of mass culture is a public act and must conform with accepted notions of the public good. Nobody seriously questions the principle that it is the function of mass culture to maintain public morale, and certainly nobody in the mass audience objects to having his

morale maintained.[1] At a time when the normal condition of the citizen is a state of anxiety, euphoria spreads over our culture like the broad smile of an idiot. In terms of attitudes towards life, there is very little difference between a "happy" movie like *Good News,* which ignores death and suffering, and a "sad" movie like *A Tree Grows in Brooklyn,* which uses death and suffering as incidents in the service of a higher optimism.

3      But, whatever its effectiveness as a source of consolation and a means of pressure for maintaining "positive" social attitudes, this optimism is fundamentally satisfying to no one, not even to those who would be most disoriented without its support. Even within the area of mass culture, there always exists a current of opposition, seeking to express by whatever means are available to it that sense of desperation and inevitable failure which optimism itself helps to create. Most often, this opposition is confined to rudimentary or semi-literate forms: in mob politics and journalism, for example, or in certain kinds of religious enthusiasm. When it does enter the field of art, it is likely to be disguised or attenuated: in an unspecific form of expression like jazz, in the basically harmless nihilism of the Marx Brothers, in the continually reasserted strain of hopelessness that often seems to be the real meaning of the soap opera. The gangster film is remarkable in that it fills the need for disguise (though not sufficiently to avoid arousing uneasiness) without requiring any serious distortion. From its beginnings, it has been a consistent and astonishingly complete presentation of the modern sense of tragedy.[2]

4      In its initial character, the gangster film is simply one example of the movies' constant tendency to create fixed dramatic patterns that can be repeated indefinitely with a reasonable expectation of profit. One gangster film follows another as one musical or one Western follows another. But this rigidity is not necessarily opposed to the requirements of art. There have been very successful types of art in the past which developed such specific and detailed conventions as almost to make individual examples of the type interchangeable. This is true, for example, of Elizabethan revenge tragedy and Restoration comedy.

5      For such a type to be successful means that its conventions have imposed themselves upon the general consciousness and become the accepted vehicles of a particular set of attitudes and a particular aesthetic effect. One goes to any individual example of the type with very definite expectations, and originality is to be welcomed only in the degree that it intensifies the expected experience without fundamentally altering it. Moreover, the relationship between the

---

[1]In her testimony before the House Committee on Un-American Activities, Mrs. Leila Rogers said that the movie *None But the Lonely Heart* was un-American because it was gloomy. Like so much else that was said during the unhappy investigation of Hollywood, this statement was at once stupid and illuminating. One knew immediately what Mrs. Rogers was talking about; she had simply been insensitive enough to carry her philistinism to its conclusion.

[2]Efforts have been made from time to time to bring the gangster film into line with the prevailing optimism and social constructiveness of our culture; *Kiss of Death* is a recent example. These efforts are usually unsuccessful; the reasons for their lack of success are interesting in themselves, but I shall not be able to discuss them here.

conventions which go to make up such a type and the real experience of its audience or the real facts of whatever situation it pretends to describe is of only secondary importance and does not determine its aesthetic force. It is only in an ultimate sense that the type appeals to its audience's experience of reality; much more immediately, it appeals to previous experience of the type itself: it creates its own field of reference.

Thus the importance of the gangster film, and the nature and intensity of its emotional and aesthetic impact, cannot be measured in terms of the place of the gangster himself or the importance of the problem of crime in American life. Those European moviegoers who think there is a gangster on every corner in New York are certainly deceived, but defenders of the "positive" side of American culture are equally deceived if they think it relevant to point out that most Americans have never seen a gangster. What matters is that the experience of the gangster *as an experience of art* is universal to Americans. There is almost nothing we understand better or react to more readily or with quicker intelligence. The Western film, though it seems never to diminish in popularity, is for most of us no more than the folklore of the past, familiar and understandable only because it has been repeated so often. The gangster film comes much closer. In ways that we do not easily or willingly define, the gangster speaks for us, expressing that part of the American psyche which rejects the qualities and the demands of modern life, which rejects "Americanism" itself.

The gangster is the man of the city, with the city's language and knowledge, with its queer and dishonest skills and its terrible daring, carrying his life in his hands like a placard, like a club. For everyone else, there is at least the theoretical possibility of another world—in that happier American culture which the gangster denies, the city does not really exist; it is only a more crowded and more brightly lit country—but for the gangster there is only the city; he must inhabit it in order to personify it: not the real city, but that dangerous and sad city of the imagination which is so much more important, which is the modern world. And the gangster—though there are real gangsters—is also, and primarily, a creature of the imagination. The real city, one might say, produces only criminals; the imaginary city produces the gangster: he is what we want to be and what we are afraid we may become.

Thrown into the crowd without background or advantages, with only those ambiguous skills which the rest of us—the real people of the real city—can only pretend to have, the gangster is required to make his way, to make his life and impose it on others. Usually, when we come upon him, he has already made his choice or the choice has already been made for him, it doesn't matter which: we are not permitted to ask whether at some point he could have chosen to be something else than what he is.

The gangster's activity is actually a form of rational enterprise, involving, fairly definite goals and various techniques for achieving them. But thus rationality is usually no more than a vague background; we know, perhaps, that the gangster sells liquor or that he operates a numbers racket; often we are not given even that much information. So his activity becomes a kind of pure criminality: he hurts people. Certainly our response to the gangster film is most consistently and most universally a response to sadism; we gain the double satisfaction of participating vicariously in the gangster's sadism and then seeing it turned against the gangster himself.

10     But on another level the quality of irrational brutality and the quality of rational enterprise become one. Since we do not see the rational and routine aspects of the gangster's behavior, the practice of brutality—the quality of unmixed criminality—becomes the totality of his career. At the same time, we are always conscious that the whole meaning of this career is a drive for success: the typical gangster film presents a steady upward progress followed by a very precipitate fall. Thus brutality itself becomes at once the means to success and the content of success—a success that is defined in its most general terms, not as accomplishment or specific gain, but simply as the unlimited possibility of aggression. (In the same way, film presentations of businessmen tend to make it appear that they achieve their success by talking on the telephone and holding conferences and that success *is* talking on the telephone and holding conferences.)

11     From this point of view, the initial contact between the film and its audience is an agreed conception of human life: that man is a being with the possibilities of success or failure. This principle, too, belongs to the city; one must emerge from the crowd or else one is nothing. On that basis the necessity of the action is established, and it progresses, by inalterable paths to the point where the gangster lies dead and the principle has been modified: there is really only one possibility—failure. The final meaning of the city is anonymity and death.

12     In the opening scene of *Scarface*, we are shown a successful man; we know he is successful because he has just given a party of opulent proportions and because he is called Big Louie. Through some monstrous lack of caution, he permits himself to be alone for a few moments. We understand from this immediately that he is about to be killed. No convention of the gangster film is more strongly established than this: it is dangerous to be alone. And yet the very conditions of success make it impossible not to be alone, for success is always the establishment of an *individual* pre-eminence that must be imposed on others, in whom it automatically arouses hatred; the successful man is an outlaw. The gangster's whole life is an effort to assert himself as an individual, to draw himself out of the crowd, and he always dies *because* he is an individual; the final bullet thrusts him back, makes him, after all, a failure. "Mother of God," says the dying Little Caesar, "is this the end of Rico?"—speaking of himself thus in the third person because what has been brought low is not the undifferentiated *man*, but the individual with a name, the gangster, the success; even to himself he is a creature of the imagination. (T. S. Eliot has pointed out that a number of Shakespeare's tragic heroes have this trick of looking at themselves dramatically; their true identity, the thing that is destroyed when they die, is something outside themselves—not a man, but a style of life, a kind of meaning.)

13     At bottom, the gangster is doomed because he is under the obligation to succeed, not because the means he employs are unlawful. In the deeper layers of the modern consciousness, *all* means are unlawful, every attempt to succeed is an act

of aggression, leaving one alone and guilty and defenseless among enemies: one is *punished* for success. This is our intolerable dilemma: that failure is a kind of death and success is evil and dangerous, is—ultimately—impossible. The effect of the gangster film is to embody this dilemma in the person of the gangster and resolve it by his death. The dilemma is resolved because it is *his* death, not ours. We are safe; for the moment, we can acquiesce in our failure, we can choose to fail.

## COMPREHENSION

1. What are the "organs of mass culture" (paragraph 2)? What properties do they all have in common?
2. Define the term *tragic hero* as Warshow uses it in his title.
3. Compare and contrast Warshow's concepts of the "real city" with those of the "imaginary city" as they relate to modern life and mass culture.

## RHETORIC

1. Although the ultimate focus of the essay is on the "gangster," the subject is not referred to until paragraph 4. Why does Warshow need so much exposition before focusing on his main topic?
2. What do terms such as *supra-political* (paragraph 1), *harmless nihilism* (paragraph 3), and *general consciousness* (paragraph 5) suggest about the tone of the essay? What do they imply concerning the target audience for the essay?
3. Study the topic sentence of each paragraph. Are the topic sentences successful in setting up the material that follows? How does this strategy enhance or detract from the coherence of the author's argument?
4. Essayists usually provide their thesis at the beginning of their essays. Where does Warshow provide the thesis in his essay? What is the purpose and effect of placing it where he does?
5. The author explains the nature of the gangster film genre—its function, characters, themes, plots, meanings, and so on—*before* he cites specific films. Is this a rhetorical weakness in the essay, or does it give the essay particular potency? Explain.
6. Does the conclusion summarize the main points of the essay, bolster them, or provide new insights into them? Or does it do a combination of these things? Explain.
7. Study the introductory paragraph and the conclusion. What themes are reiterated or complemented? How do these two paragraphs serve to provide both thematic and structural coherence?

## WRITING

1. Select a genre of television show or movie. Analyze its conventions and the degree to which these conventions transgress the implicit values of our society.

2. Select a contemporary gangster movie or television program. Using Warshow's criteria, demonstrate—via reference to its characters, plot, and theme—how your selection reinforces the author's thesis.
3. **Writing An Argument:** Argue for or against the proposition that genre movies are a form of escapism that distorts the individual's concept of the actual society he or she lives in and its citizens.

| www.mhhe.com/ **mhreader** | For more information on Robert Warshow, go to: **More Resources > Ch. 9 Media & Pop Culture** |

# Our Mobsters, Ourselves:
# Why *The Sopranos* Is Therapeutic TV

## Ellen Willis

*Ellen Willis (b. 1941) was born in New York City; she received a BA from Barnard College in 1962 and was enrolled for graduate study at the University of California at Berkeley in 1962–63. Willis has been a freelance writer and editor for four decades, contributing articles on the media and popular culture to* The New Yorker, Ms., Rolling Stone, The Village Voice, *and other periodicals. She also has been a fellow at the Nation Institute and has directed the cultural reporting and criticism program at New York University. Her books include* Beginning to See the Light: Pieces of a Decade *(1981),* Beginning to See the Light: Sex, Hope, and Rock-and-Roll *(1992),* No More Nice Girls: Countercultural Essays *(1992), and* Don't Think, Smile! Notes on a Decade of Denial *(1999). In the following essay, published in* The Nation *in 2001, Willis places the popular HBO series* The Sopranos *in a broad cultural context.*

1   Midway through the first season of *The Sopranos,* the protagonist's psychotherapist, Jennifer Melfi, has a not-exactly-traditional family dinner with her middle-class Italian parents, son and ex-husband Richard. She lets slip (hmm!) that one of her patients is a mobster, much to Richard's consternation. An activist in Italian anti-defamation politics, he is incensed at the opprobrium the Mafia has brought on all Italians. What is the point, he protests, of trying to help such a person? In a subsequent scene he contemptuously dismisses Jennifer and her profession for purveying "cheesy moral relativism" in the face of evil. His challenge boldly proclaims what until then has been implicit: The richest and most compelling piece of television—no, of popular culture—that I've encountered in the past twenty years is a meditation on the nature of morality, the possibility of redemption and the legacy of Freud.

To be sure, *The Sopranos* is much else as well. For two years (the third sea- 2
son began March 4) David Chase's HBO series has served up a hybrid genre of
post-Godfather decline-of-the-mob movie and soap opera, with plenty of sex,
violence, domestic melodrama and comic irony; a portrait of a suburban landscape that does for northern New Jersey what film noir did for Los Angeles,
with soundtrack to match; a deft depiction of class and cultural relations among
various subgroups and generations of Italian-Americans; a gloss on the manners and mores of the fin-de-siècle American middle-class family; and perfect-
pitch acting, especially by James Gandolfini as Tony Soprano; Edie Falco as his
complicated wife, Carmela; Lorraine Bracco as Dr. Melfi; and the late Nancy
Marchand as the Sopranos' terrifying matriarch, Livia.

Cumulatively, these episodes have the feel of an as yet unfinished 3
nineteenth-century novel. While the sheer entertainment and suspense of the
plot twists are reminiscent of Dickens and his early serials, the underlying
themes evoke George Eliot: The world of Tony Soprano is a kind of postmodern
*Middlemarch,* whose inhabitants' moral and spiritual development (or devolu-
tion) unfolds within and against the norms of a parochial social milieu. This era
being what it is, however, the Sopranos' milieu has porous boundaries, and the
norms that govern it are a moving target. In one scene, the family is in mid-
breakfast when Tony and Carmela's teenage daughter, Meadow, apropos a recent scandal brought on by a high school classmate's affair with her soccer
coach, declaims about the importance of talking openly about sex. Yes, Tony
agrees, but not during breakfast. "Dad, this is the 1990s," Meadow protests.
"Outside it may be the 1990s," Tony retorts, "but in this house it's 1954." It's
wishful thinking, and Tony knows it. What 1950s gangster would take Prozac
and make weekly visits to a shrink or, for that matter, have a daughter named
Meadow?

In fact, contemporary reality pervades the Sopranos' suburban manse. A 4
school counselor tries to persuade them that their son, Anthony Jr., has attention deficit disorder. Meadow hosts a clandestine party in her grandmother's
empty house that gets busted for drugs and alcohol. Tony's sister Janice, who
years ago decamped to Seattle, became a Buddhist and changed her name to
Parvati, shows up at his door flaunting her postcounterculture reinvented self.
And while Tony displays some of the trappings of the stereotypical Italian
patriarch—he is proud of supporting his family in style, comes and goes as he
pleases, leaves the running of the household to Carmela and cheats on her with
the obligatory goombah—his persona as fear-inspiring gangster does not translate to his home life. Carmela is his emotional equal; she does what she likes,
tells him off without hesitation and, unlike old-style mob wives, knows plenty
about the business. Nor, despite periodic outbursts of temper, is Tony an intimidating father. Caught between empathy for their children and the urge to
whip them into line, the Sopranos share the dirty little secret of nineties middle-
class parenthood: You can't control teenagers' behavior without becoming full-
time prison guards. "Let's not overplay our hand," Tony cautions after
Meadow's party caper, "'cause if she knows we're powerless, we're fucked."

5      In Tony's other "house"—represented by his office in the Bada Bing strip club—1954 is also under siege. Under pressure of the RICO laws, longtime associates turn government witness. Neophytes chafe at their lowly status in the hierarchy, disobey their bosses, take drugs, commit gratuitous freelance crimes and in general fail to understand that organized crime is a business, not a vehicle for self-expression or self-promotion. The line between reality and media image has become as tenuous here as elsewhere: Tony and his men love *Good-Fellas* and the first two *Godfathers* (by general agreement III sucks) and at the same time are objects of fantasy for civilians steeped in the same movies. Tony accepts an invitation to play golf with his neighbor Dr. Cusamano, who referred him to Melfi, and finds that his function is to titillate the doctor's friends; during a falling out with Jennifer he tries to connect with another therapist, who demurs, explaining that he has seen *Analyze This* ("It's a fucking comedy," Tony protests). Tony's fractious nephew Christopher, pissed because press coverage of impending mob indictments doesn't mention him, reprises *GoodFellas* by shooting an insufficiently servile clerk in the foot. He aspires to write screenplays about mob life, and in pursuit of this dream is used for material and kicks by a Hollywood film director and his classy female assistant. Meanwhile Jennifer's family debates whether wiseguy movies defame Italians or rather should be embraced as American mythology, like westerns. *The Sopranos*, of course, has provoked the same argument, and its continual reflection of its characters in their media mirrors is also a running commentary on the show itself.

6      Self-consciousness, then, is a conspicuous feature of Tony Soprano's world even aside from therapy; in fact, it's clear that self-consciousness has provoked the anxiety attack that sends him to Jennifer Melfi. It's not just a matter of stressful circumstances. Tony's identity is fractured, part outlaw rooted in a dying tribal culture, part suburbanite enmeshed in another kind of culture altogether—a split graphically exemplified by the famous episode in which Tony, while taking Meadow on a tour of colleges in Maine, spots a mobster-turned-informer hiding in the witness protection program and manages to juggle his fatherly duties with murder. Despite his efforts at concealment, his criminal life is all too evident to his children (after all, they too have seen *The Godfather*), a source of pain and confusion on both sides. Tony's decision to seek therapy also involves an identity crisis. In his first session, which frames the first episode, he riffs on the sad fate of the strong and silent Gary Cooper: Once they got him in touch with his feelings, he wouldn't shut up. "I have a semester and a half of college," he tells Dr. Melfi, "so I understand Freud. I understand therapy as a concept, but in my world it does not go down." In his wiseguy world, that is: Carmela thinks it's great idea.

7      Richard Melfi's charge of moral relativism is highly ironic, for Jennifer finds that her task is precisely to confront the tribal relativism and cognitive dissonance that keep Tony Soprano from making sense of his life. He sees his business as the Sicilians' opportunity to get in on the American Dream, the violence that attends it as enforcement of rules known to all who choose to play the game: Gangsters are soldiers, whose killing, far from being immoral,

is impelled by positive virtues—loyalty, respect, friendship, willingness to put one's own life on the line. It does not strike Tony as inconsistent to expect his kids to behave or to send them to Catholic school, any more than he considers that nights with his Russian girlfriend belie his reverence for the institution of the family. Nor does he see a contradiction in his moral outrage at a sadistic, pathologically insecure associate who crushes a man with his car in fury over an inconsequential slight.

In its original literal sense, "moral relativism" is simply moral complexity.   8 That is, anyone who agrees that stealing a loaf of bread to feed one's children is not the moral equivalent of, say, shoplifting a dress for the fun of it, is a relativist of sorts. But in recent years, conservatives bent on reinstating an essentially religious vocabulary of absolute good and evil as the only legitimate framework for discussing social values have redefined "relative" as "arbitrary." That conflation has been reinforced by social theorists and advocates of identity politics who argue that there is no universal morality, only the value systems of particular cultures and power structures. From this perspective, the psychoanalytic—and by extension the psychotherapeutic—worldview is not relativist at all.

Its values are honesty, self-knowledge, assumption of responsibility for the   9 whole of what one does, freedom from inherited codes of family, church, tribe in favor of a universal humanism: in other words, the values of the Enlightenment, as revised and expanded by Freud's critique of scientific rationalism for ignoring the power of unconscious desire. What eludes the Richard Melfis is that the neutral, unjudging stance of the therapist is not an end in itself but a strategy for pursuing this moral agenda by eliciting hidden knowledge.

Predictably, the cultural relativists have no more use for Freud than the re-   10 ligious conservatives. Nor are the devotees of "rational choice" economics and of a scientism that reduces all human behavior to genes or brain chemistry eager to look below the surface of things, or even admit there's such a thing as "below the surface." Which is why, in recent years, psychoanalysis has been all but banished from the public conversation as a serious means of discussing our moral and cultural and political lives. And as the Zeitgeist goes, so goes popular culture: Though a continuing appetite for the subject might be inferred from the popularity of memoirs, in which psychotherapy is a recurring theme, it has lately been notably absent from movies and television. So it's more than a little interesting that *The Sopranos* and *Analyze This* plucked the gangster-sees-therapist plot from the cultural unconscious at more or less the same time and apparently by coincidence. In *The Sopranos,* however, therapy is no fucking comedy, nor does it recycle old Hollywood cliches about shamanlike shrinks and sudden cathartic cures. It's a serious battle for a man's soul, carried on in sessions that look and sound a lot like the real thing (at least as I've experienced it)—full of silence, evasive chatter, lies, boredom and hostility, punctuated by outbursts of painful emotion, moments of clarity and insights that almost never sink in right away. Nor is it only the patient's drama; the therapist is right down there in the muck, sorting out her own confusions, missteps, fantasies and fears, attraction and repulsion, as she struggles to understand.

11    The parallels between psychotherapy and religion are reinforced by the adventures of the other *Sopranos* characters, who are all defined by their spiritual state. Some are damned, like Livia, whose nihilism is summed up in her penchant for smiling at other people's misfortunes and in her bitter remark to her grandson, "It's all a big nothing. What makes you think you're so special?" Some are complacent, like the respectable bourgeois Italian-Americans, or the self-regarding but fatally unself-aware Father Phil, Carmela's young spiritual adviser, who feeds (literally as well as metaphorically) on the neediness of the mob wives. The older, middle-level mobsters see themselves as working stiffs who expect little from life and for whom self-questioning is a luxury that's out of their class. (One of them is temporarily jolted when Tony's nephew Christopher is shot and has a vision of himself in hell; but the crisis passes quickly.) Charmaine Bucco, a neighborhood girl and old friend of Carmela's who with her husband, Artie, owns an Italian restaurant, is the embodiment of passionate faith in the virtues of honesty, integrity and hard work; she despises the mobsters, wishes they would stop patronizing the restaurant and does her best to pull the ambivalent Artie away from his longtime friendship with Tony. And then there are the strugglers, like Christopher, who inchoately wants something more out of life but also wants to rise in the mob, and Big Pussy, Tony's close friend as well as crew member, who rats to the Feds to ward off a thirty-year prison term, agonizes over his betrayal and ultimately takes refuge in identifying with his FBI handlers.

12    Carmela Soprano is a struggler, an ardent Catholic who feels the full weight of her sins and Tony's and lets no one off the hook. She keeps hoping Tony will change but knows he probably will not; and despite the many discontents of her marriage, anger at Tony's infidelity and misgivings about her complicity in his crimes, she will not leave him. Though she rationalizes her choice on religious grounds ("The family is a sacred institution"), she never really deceives herself: She still loves Tony, and furthermore she likes the life his money provides. Nor does she hesitate to trade on his power in order to do what she feels is a mother's duty: She intimidates Cusamano's lawyer sister-in-law into writing Meadow a college recommendation. Guilt and frustration drive her to Father Phil, who gives her books on Buddhism, foreign movies and mixed sexual signals, but after a while she catches on to his bullshit, and in a scene beloved of *Sopranos* fans coolly nails him: "He's a sinner, Father. You come up here and you eat his steaks and use his home entertainment center . . . I think you have this MO where you manipulate spiritually thirsty women, and I think a lot of it's tied up with food somehow, as well as the sexual tension game." Compromised as she is, Carmela is a moral touchstone because of her clear eye.

13    But Tony's encounters with Melfi are the spiritual center of the show. The short version of Tony's psychic story is this: His gangster persona provides him with constant excitement and action, a sense of power and control, a definition of masculinity. Through violence rationalized as business or impersonal soldiering he also gets to express his considerable unacknowledged rage without encroaching on his alter ego as benevolent husband and father. But when the

center fails to hold, the result is panic, then—as Melfi probes the cracks—depression, self-hatred, sexual collapse and engulfing, ungovernable anger. There are glimmers along the way, as when Tony sees the pointlessness of killing the sexually wayward soccer coach, calls off the hit and lets the cops do their job (after which he feels impelled to get so drunk he passes out). But the abyss always looms.

Tony's heart of darkness is personified by Livia Soprano, who at first seems 14 peggable as a better-done-than-usual caricature of the overbearing ethnic mother but is gradually revealed as a monstrous Medea. Furious at Tony for consigning her to a fancy "retirement community," Livia passes on some well-chosen pieces of information—including the fact that he's seeing a shrink—to Tony's malleable Uncle Junior, who orders him killed. When the hit is botched, she suddenly begins to show symptoms of Alzheimer's. Jennifer Melfi puts it together; worried that Tony's life is in danger, she breaks the therapeutic rule that patients must make their own discoveries and confronts him with her knowledge. He reacts with a frightening, hate-filled paroxysm of denial—for the first time coming close to attacking Jennifer physically—but is forced to admit the truth when he hears a damning conversation between Livia and Junior, caught on tape by the FBI.

This is a turning point in the story, but not, as the standard psychiatric 15 melodrama would have it, because the truth has made Tony free. The truth has knocked him flat. "What kind of person can I be," he blurts to Carmela, "where his own mother wants him dead?" Afraid that Junior will go after Jennifer, he orders her to leave town; when she comes back she is angry and fearful and tells him to get out of her life. He is lost, his face a silent Munchian scream. Later Jennifer has a change of heart, but things are not the same: The trust is gone. And yet, paradoxically, her rejection has freed him to be more honest, throwing the details of his gang's brutality in her face, railing at her for making him feel like a victim, at himself for becoming the failed Gary Cooper he once mocked, at the "happy wanderers" who still seem in control.

Jennifer encourages him to feel the sadness under the rage, but what comes 16 through is hard and bleak. He tells anyone who mentions his mother, "She's dead to me," but it's really he who feels dead. During this time, Anthony Jr. shocks his mother by announcing that God is dead; "Nitch" says so. (At its most serious, the show never stops being funny.) Tony mentions this to Jennifer, who gives him a minilecture on existential angst: When some people realize they're solely responsible for their lives, and all roads lead to death, they feel "intense dread" and conclude that "the only absolute truth is death." "I think the kid's onto something," Tony says.

As if to validate Richard Melfi's contempt, he uses what he's learned in 17 therapy—that you can't compartmentalize your life—to more fully accept his worst impulses. Against his more compassionate instincts, he allows an old friend who is the father of a classmate of Meadow's and a compulsive gambler to join his high-stakes card game. When David inevitably piles up a debt he can't pay, Tony moves in on his business, sucking it dry and draining his son's college fund.

Amid a torrent of self-pity, David asks why Tony let him in the game. Tony answers jocularly that it's his nature—you know, as in the tale of the frog and the scorpion. In the last episode of season two Tony whacks Pussy, whose perfidy has been revealed, choosing his mob code over his love and sorrow for the man. He then walks out on Jennifer, as if to say, this is who I am and will be.

18        Jennifer's trip is also a rocky one. In her person, the values of Freud and the Enlightenment are filtered through the cultural radical legacy of the 1960s: She is a woman challenging a man whose relationship to both legitimate and outlaw patriarchal hierarchies is in crisis. It's a shaky and vulnerable role, the danger of physical violence an undercurrent from the beginning, but there are also bonds that make the relationship possible. Tony chooses her over a Jewish male therapist because "you're a paisan, like me," and she is drawn to the outlaw, no doubt in rebellion against the safe smugness of her own social milieu. Predictably, Tony loses all sexual interest in his wife and girlfriend and falls in love with his doctor (if there is any answering spark, it stays under the professional surface), but after the initial "honeymoon" of therapy, trouble, as always, begins. Tony gives Jennifer "gifts" like stealing her car and getting it fixed; it's his way of assuring her, and himself, that his power is benevolent, but of course she only feels violated. Wanting to find out about her life, he has her followed by a corrupt con who harasses her boyfriend, thinking he's doing Tony a favor; she can't help but be suspicious. By inviting her family to object to her criminal patient, she gives voice to her own doubts: Perhaps she is not only endangering herself but abetting evil.

19        Her conflict intensifies when she tells Tony she must charge for a missed session, and he throws the money at her, calling her a whore. It explodes in the aftermath of the attempt on his life. But then the other side of her ambivalence reasserts itself; she feels she has irresponsibly abandoned a patient and takes him back against the advice of her own (Jewish male) therapist. Now it is Jennifer who is in crisis, treating her anxiety with heavy drinking. She is frightened and morally repulsed by Tony's graphic revelations, yet also feels an erotically tinged fascination (it's like watching a train wreck, she tells her shrink). She still cares about Tony but seems to have lost faith in her ability to exorcise the demonic by making contact with the suffering human being. In the last episode, with Tony closed as a clam, she admits that she blew it, that she stopped pushing him because she was afraid. But he can't hear her.

20        No false optimism here. Yet it's no surprise that by the second hour of the third season premiere Tony is back in Jennifer Melfi's office. The requirements of the show's premise aside, his untenable situation has not changed. Having glimpsed the possibility of an exit from despair, it would be out of character for him simply to close that door and walk away. For the same reason, I suspect our culture's flight from psychoanalysis is not permanent. It's grandiose, perhaps, to see in one television series, however popular, a cultural trend; and after all *The Sopranos* is on HBO, not CBS or NBC. But ultimately the show is so gripping because, in the words of Elaine Showalter, it's a "cultural Rorschach test." It has been called a parable of corruption and hypocrisy in the postmodern middle class, and it is that; a critique of sexuality, the family and male-

female relations in the wake of feminism, and it's that too. But at the primal level, the inkblot is the unconscious. The murderous mobster is the predatory lust and aggression in all of us; his lies and cover-ups are ours; the therapist's fear is our own collective terror of peeling away those lies. The problem is that we can't live with the lies, either. So facing down the terror, a little at a time, becomes the only route to sanity, if not salvation.

In the tumultuous last episode of *The Sopranos'* first season, another in-   21 former is killed. Tony finds out about his mother and sends Jennifer into hiding. Uncle Junior and two of his underlings are arrested, arousing fears that one of them will flip. Artie Bucco nearly kills Tony after being told—by Livia—that Tony is responsible for the fire that destroyed his restaurant (the idea was to help the Buccos by heading off a planned mob hit in the restaurant, which would have ruined the business—this way they could get the insurance and rebuild), but Tony swears "on my mother" it isn't true. Carmela tells off Father Phil. At the end, Tony, Carmela and the kids are caught in a violent storm in their SUV; they can't see a thing but suddenly realize they're in front of the Buccos' (rebuilt) restaurant. There's no power, but Artie graciously ushers them in, lights a candle and cooks them a meal. Tony proposes a toast: "To my family. Someday soon you're gonna have families of your own. And if you're lucky, you'll remember the little moments. Like this. That were good." The moment feels something like sanity. The storm, our storm, goes on.

## COMPREHENSION

1. In her introduction, Willis states that HBO's *Sopranos* series is "a meditation of the nature of morality, the possibility of redemption and the legacy of Freud." In the context of the overall essay, what does she mean by this statement?
2. What observations does Willis make about "self-consciousness" or "self-knowledge" as a crucial aspect of our understanding of *The Sopranos*?
3. According to Willis, what does *The Sopranos* tell us about contemporary American culture? Why is the program, in the words of a critic whom the writer quotes, "a cultural Rorschach test"?

## RHETORIC

1. Throughout the essay, Willis summarizes various plot lines in *The Sopranos* and describes certain main characters. Why does she devote so much space to this type of overview? What assumptions is she making about her audience? What information does she disclose that the average viewer might not be likely to know?
2. How does the author make a case for considering *The Sopranos* "a gloss on the manners and mores of the fin-de-siècle American middle-class family" (paragraph 2)? What evidence does she provide to support this premise?

3. What comparative elements appear in this essay? How do they serve to bolster the author's main critical points and advance her argument?

4. Is Willis's reference to Freud consistent with your understanding of him? If not, how would you clarify her references to Freud?

5. Identify these allusions and explain what they contribute to the writer's analysis: Dickens and Eliot (paragraph 3), *GoodFellas* and *Analyze This* (paragraph 5), Gary Cooper (paragraph 6), the American Dream (paragraph 7), "heart of darkness" (paragraph 14), the Enlightenment (paragraph 18).

6. Willis makes a number of assertions regarding moral and cultural relativism, psychotherapy, and religion. Are these facts or opinions? Explain your view.

7. How does the writer bring this essay to a conclusion? Is the final paragraph effective? Why or why not?

## WRITING

1. Write a review of any gangster film or television series that you are familiar with, referring to aspects of Willis's essay to support your commentary and analysis.

2. Why is *The Sopranos* so popular? Write an essay in response to this question.

3. **Writing an Argument:** It could be argued that movies and television programs like *The Sopranos* engage in stereotyping of Italian Americans. Which side of the argument do you take? Write an argumentative essay on this topic. Evaluate core premises, offer evidence, and structure the argument carefully.

www.mhhe.com/ **mhreader** | For more information on Ellen Willis, go to: **More Resources > Ch. 9 Media & Pop Culture**

## Synthesis: Classic and Contemporary Questions for Comparison

1. Warshow critiques the function and role of the gangster in the popular media, whereas Willis focuses on an analysis of one television series in which the life of the gangster is articulated. How do these different focuses determine the themes of each essay? What are the positive and negative consequences of addressing the general issue of "The Gangster as Tragic Hero" without an in-depth explication of an example, as in the essay by Warshow, as opposed to the detailed analysis of one cable TV series without a discussion of the gangster genre, as in Willis's essay?

2. Warshow explores the significance of the gangster film within the greater context of American culture. If you were to ascribe a genre to his essay, what would you call it: Cultural criticism? Media analysis? Genre definition?

There need not necessarily be one correct response, but be sure to support your answer with examples from the essay. On the other hand, is Willis's essay a review, a critique, or an analysis of a television series, or is it more than one of these? Explain your view.

3. Willis introduces her essay with a summary of a scene from *The Sopranos*. War-show, on the other hand, begins by making general observations on the nature of society, the modern state, and politics. How do these different rhetorical strategies set up the mode of analysis, tone, and purpose of the two essays?

4. Is it fair to say that Willis's essay is about "television" while Warshow's is about society at large? Explain your view.

# Loose Ends

## Rita Dove

*Rita Dove (b. 1953) grew up in Akron, Ohio, and graduated from Miami University of Ohio and the University of Iowa. She later studied at Tübingen University in West Germany on a Fulbright scholarship and received fellowships from the Guggenheim Foundation and the National Endowment for the Arts. In 1987, she received the Pulitzer Prize for her third book of poetry,* Thomas and Beulah. *In 1993, Dove was named Poet Laureate, the first African American and, at 40 years of age, the youngest person ever to hold that post. Rita Dove continues to write and to teach at the University of Virginia, where she is Commonwealth Professor of English. About her writing, she has said: "I am concerned with race but certainly not every poem of mine mentions the fact of being black. They are poems about humanity and sometimes humanity happens to be black. I cannot run from, I won't run from, any kind of truth." Her most recent book of poems is* American Smooth *(2004). The following essay is from* The Poet's World *(1995).*

For years the following scene would play daily at our house: Home from school,  1 my daughter would heave her backpack off her shoulder and let it thud to the hall floor, then dump her jacket on top of the pile. My husband would tell her to pick it up—as he did every day—and hang it in the closet. Begrudgingly with a snort and a hrrumph, she would comply. The ritual interrogation began:

"Hi, Aviva. How was school?"                                                                       2

"Fine."                                                                                            3

"What did you do today?"                                                                           4

"Nothing."                                                                                         5

And so it went, every day. We cajoled, we pleaded, we threatened with  6 rationed ice cream sandwiches and new healthy vegetable casseroles, we attempted subterfuges such as: "What was Ms. Boyers wearing today?" or: "Any new pets in science class?" but her answer remained the same: I dunno.

7       Asked, however, about that week's episodes of "MathNet," her favorite series on Public Television's "Square One," or asked for a quick gloss of a segment of "Lois and Clark" that we happened to miss, and she'd spew out the details of a complicated story, complete with character development, gestures, every twist and backflip of the plot.

8       Is TV greater than reality? Are we to take as damning evidence the soap opera stars attacked in public by viewers who obstinately believe in the onscreen villainy of Erica or Jeannie's evil twin? Is an estrangement from real life the catalyst behind the escalating violence in our schools, where children imitate the gun-'em-down pyrotechnics of cop-and-robber shows?

9       Such a conclusion is too easy. Yes, the influence of public media on our perceptions is enormous, but the relationship of projected reality—i.e., TV—to imagined reality—i.e., an existential moment—is much more complex. It is not that we confuse TV with reality, but that we prefer it to reality—the manageable struggle resolved in twenty-six minutes, the witty repartee within the family circle instead of the grunts and silence common to most real families; the sharpened conflict and defined despair instead of vague anxiety and invisible enemies. "Life, my friends, is boring. We must not say so," wrote John Berryman, and many years and "Dream Songs" later he leapt from a bridge in Minneapolis. But there is a devastating corollary to that statement: Life, friends, is ragged. Loose ends are the rule.

10      What happens when my daughter tells the television's story better than her own is simply this: the TV offers an easier tale to tell. The salient points are there for the plucking—indeed, they're the only points presented—and all she has to do is to recall them. Instant Nostalgia! Life, on the other hand, slithers about and runs down blind alleys and sometimes just fizzles at the climax. "The world is ugly, / And the people are sad," sings the country bumpkin in Wallace Stevens's "Gubinnal." Who isn't tempted to ignore the inexorable fact of our insignificance on a dying planet? We all yearn for our private patch of blue.

## COMPREHENSION

1. What is the thesis or claim of the essay?
2. What is the meaning of the title as it pertains to the essay's argument?
3. Define the following terms: *subterfuge* (paragraph 6), *existential* (paragraph 9), *corollary* (paragraph 9), and *salient* (paragraph 10).

## RHETORIC

1. What is the tone of the essay? How does Dove's use of language suggest this tone?
2. Where and how does Dove make the transition from the opening anecdote to her more general conclusions about television?
3. The author uses dashes, semicolons, and colons in her essay. Locate them. What is their stylistic effect and function?

4. Dove talks of television shows as exhibiting only the "salient points." How can this same observation be made of her writing?
5. Dove states of television that "we prefer it to reality" (paragraph 9). Who is the "we" in that statement?

## WRITING

1. Observe a family watching a television drama or comedy. Note their body language, demeanor, responses, and gestures. Write an essay describing your observations.
2. Ask five students on your campus to write one-paragraph responses to this question: "What is the function of television, and what is your purpose in watching television?" Compare and contrast the responses with Dove's argument regarding the purpose and function of television.
3. **Writing an Argument:** Argue for or against the proposition that watching television is a passive activity.

www.mhhe.com/
**mhreader**

For more information on Rita Dove, go to:
**More Resources > Ch. 9 Media & Pop Culture**

# 2 Live Crew, Decoded

## Henry Louis Gates Jr.

*Henry Louis Gates Jr. (b. 1950) was born in Keyser, West Virginia, and was educated at Yale University and Clare College, Cambridge, where he received his PhD in 1979. He now teaches at Harvard University. Gates has edited numerous books addressing the issues of race, identity, and African American history and has contributed to over a dozen periodicals and journals, including* Critical Inquiry, Black World, The Yale Review, *and* The Antioch Review. *His work attempts to apply contemporary literary theories, such as structuralism and poststructuralism, to African and African American literature so that readers can develop a deep understanding of the structure, significance, methods, and meanings of this body of work. Many of his theoretical insights are summed up in his book* The Signifying Monkey: Towards a Theory of Afro-American Literary Criticism *(1988). Among his awards and honors have been a Carnegie Foundation fellowship, a MacArthur Prize fellowship, and a Mellon fellowship from Yale University. In the following essay, published in* The New York Times *in 1990, Gates offers a keen analysis of the rap music phenomenon.*

1 The rap group 2 Live Crew and their controversial hit recording, "As Nasty as They Wanna Be," may well earn a signal place in the history of First Amendment rights. But just as important is how these lyrics will be interpreted and by whom.

2      For centuries, African Americans have been forced to develop coded ways of communicating to protect them from danger. Allegories and double meanings, words redefined to mean their opposites ("bad" meaning "good," for instance), even neologisms ("bodacious") have enabled blacks to share messages only the initiated understand.

3      Many blacks were amused by the transcripts of Marion Barry's sting operation, which reveals that he used the traditional black expression about one's "nose being opened." This referred to a love affair and not, as Mr. Barry's prosecutors have suggested, to the inhalation of drugs. Understanding this phrase could very well spell the difference (for the Mayor) between prison and freedom.

4      2 Live Crew is engaged in heavy-handed parody, turning the stereotypes of black and white American culture on their heads. These young artists are acting out, to lively dance music, a parodic exaggeration of the age-old stereotypes of the oversexed black female and male. Their exuberant use of hyperbole (phantasmagoric sexual organs, for example) undermines—for anyone fluent in black cultural codes—a too literal-minded hearing of the lyrics.

5      This is the street tradition called "signifying" or "playing the dozens," which has generally been risqué, and where the best signifier or "rapper" is the one who invents the most extravagant images, the biggest "lies," as the culture says. (H. "Rap" Brown earned his nickname in just this way.) In the face of racist stereotypes about black sexuality, you can do one of two things: you can disavow them or explode them with exaggeration.

6      2 Live Crew, like many "hip-hop" groups, is engaged in sexual carnivalesque. Parody reigns supreme; from a take-off of standard blues to a spoof of the black power movement, their off-color nursery rhymes are part of a venerable Western tradition. The group even satirizes the culture of commerce when it appropriates popular advertising slogans ("Tastes great!" "Less filling!") and puts them in a bawdy context.

7      2 Live Crew must be interpreted within the context of black culture generally and of signifying specifically. Their novelty, and that of other adventuresome rap groups, is that their defiant rejection of euphemism now voices for the mainstream what before existed largely in the "race record" market—where the records of Redd Foxx and Rudy Ray Moore once were forced to reside.

8      Rock songs have always been about sex but have used elaborate subterfuges to convey that fact. 2 Live Crew uses Anglo-Saxon words and is self-conscious about it: a parody of a white voice in one song refers to "private personal parts," as a coy counterpart to the group's bluntness.

9      Much more troubling than its so-called obscenity is the group's overt sexism. Their sexism is so flagrant, however, that it almost cancels itself out in a hyperbolic war between the sexes. In this, it recalls the inter-sexual jousting in Zora Neale Hurston's novels. Still, many of us look toward the emergence of more female rappers to redress sexual stereotypes. And we must not allow

ourselves to sentimentalize street culture: the appreciation of verbal virtuosity does not lessen one's obligation to critique bigotry in all of its pernicious forms.

Is 2 Live Crew more "obscene" than, say, the comic Andrew Dice Clay? 10 Clearly, this rap group is seen as more threatening than others that are just as sexually explicit. Can this be completely unrelated to the specter of the young black male as a figure of sexual and social disruption, the very stereotypes 2 Live Crew seem determined to undermine?

This question—and the very large question of obscenity and the First 11 Amendment—cannot even be addressed until those who would answer them become literate in the vernacular traditions of African Americans. To do less is to censor through the equivalent of intellectual prior restraint—and censorship is to art what lynching is to justice.

## COMPREHENSION

1. What is the author's thesis?
2. According to Gates, what must one know before engaging in a critique of 2 Live Crew?
3. Does Gates consider 2 Live Crew's music obscene? Why or why not?

## RHETORIC

1. The paragraphs in this essay are fairly short. How does this affect Gates's argument?
2. How does the author use definition to decode certain aspects of African American culture? Why is definition an important strategy in his argument?
3. Gates uses the word *hyperbole* in paragraph 4 and the word *hyperbolic* in paragraph 9. Why is it necessary for him to emphasize this concept to develop his argument?
4. Does the author appear to use a particular tone toward his subject matter? Does he appear to support the art of his subject, condemn it, explain it, or provide a mixture of all three approaches?
5. For whom is this essay written? What is its intended purpose? Explain your view.
6. Examine the final sentence of the essay. Does it provide an effective closure? Why is it particularly pertinent considering 2 Live Crew is an African American music group? Explain your view.

## WRITING

1. In an essay, explain your position on rap music as (in Gates's words) "sexual carnivalesque."

2. For a research project, write a paper on your favorite singer or music group, and how this artist or group mirrors contemporary patterns of culture.
3. **Writing an Argument:** Argue for or against the proposition that the music of 2 Live Crew or any more contemporary rap artist or group is obscene, basing your argument on the points raised in the article by Gates.

www.mhhe.com/ **mhreader**  | For more information on Henry Louis Gates Jr., go to: **More Resources > Ch. 9 Media & Pop Culture**

# My Creature from the Black Lagoon

### Stephen King

*Stephen King (b. 1947) was born in Portland, Maine. Raised by his mother, he spent parts of his childhood in Indiana, Connecticut, Massachusetts, and Maine. He graduated from the University of Maine at Orono in 1970 with a degree in English. During his early writing career, he sold several stories to mass market men's magazines and taught English in Hampden, Maine. In 1973, his novel* Carrie *sold enough copies that he could devote his energies to writing full-time. He is the author of about 100 books, most focusing on horror and the occult. A number have been adapted for film and television, including* Carrie, The Dead Zone, The Shining, Christine, Pet Sematary, Stand by Me, *and* The Green Mile. *Besides writing, he belongs to an all-writers rock and roll band (with Dave Barry and Amy Tan) and is a major contributor to local and national charities. In the following selection, taken from* Danse Macabre *(1981), King compares and contrasts the responses of adults and children to horror movies.*

1   The first movie I can remember seeing as a kid was *Creature from the Black Lagoon.* It was at the drive-in, and unless it was a second-run job I must have been about seven, because the film, which starred Richard Carlson and Richard Denning, was released in 1954. It was also originally released in 3-D, but I cannot remember wearing the glasses, so perhaps I did see a rerelease.

2       I remember only one scene clearly from the movie, but it left a lasting impression. The hero (Carlson) and the heroine (Julia Adams, who looked absolutely spectacular in a one-piece white bathing suit) are on an expedition somewhere in the Amazon basin. They make their way up a swampy, narrow waterway and into a wide pond that seems an idyllic South American version of the Garden of Eden.

3       But the creature is lurking—naturally. It's a scaly, batrachian monster that is remarkably like Lovecraft's half-breed, degenerate aberrations—the crazed

and blasphemous results of liaisons between gods and human women (it's difficult to get away from Lovecraft). This monster is slowly and patiently barricading the mouth of the stream with sticks and branches, irrevocably sealing the party of anthropologists in.

I was barely old enough to read at that time, the discovery of my father's  4 box of weird fiction still years away. I have a vague memory of boyfriends in my mom's life during that period—from 1952 until 1958 or so; enough of a memory to be sure she had a social life, not enough to even guess if she had a sex life. There was Norville, who smoked Luckies and kept three fans going in his two-room apartment during the summer; and there was Milt, who drove a Buick and wore gigantic blue shorts in the summertime; and another fellow, very small, who was, I believe, a cook in a French restaurant. So far as I know, my mother came close to marrying none of them. She'd gone that route once. Also, that was a time when a woman, once married, became a shadow figure in the process of decision-making and bread-winning. I think my mom, who could be stubborn, intractable, grimly persevering and nearly impossible to discourage, had gotten a taste for captaining her own life. And so she went out with guys, but none of them became permanent fixtures.

It was Milt we were out with that night, he of the Buick and the large blue  5 shorts. He seemed to genuinely like my brother and me, and to genuinely not mind having us along in the back seat from time to time (it may be that when you have reached the calmer waters of your early forties, the idea of necking at the drive-in no longer appeals so strongly . . . even if you have a Buick as large as a cabin cruiser to do it in). By the time the Creature made his appearance, my brother had slithered down onto the floor of the back and had fallen asleep. My mother and Milt were talking, perhaps passing a Kool back and forth. They don't matter, at least not in this context; nothing matters except the big black-and-white images up on the screen, where the unspeakable Thing is walling the handsome hero and the sexy heroine into . . . into . . . the Black Lagoon!

I knew, watching, that the Creature had become *my* Creature; I had bought  6 it. Even to a seven-year-old, it was not a terribly convincing Creature. I did not know then it was good old Ricou Browning, the famed underwater stuntman, in a molded latex suit, but I surely knew it was some guy in some kind of a monster suit . . . just as I knew that, later on that night, he would visit me in the black lagoon of my dreams, looking much more realistic. He might be waiting in the closet when we got back; he might be standing slumped in the blackness of the bathroom at the end of the hall, stinking of algae and swamp rot, all ready for a post-midnight snack of small boy. Seven isn't old, but it is old enough to know that you get what you pay for. You own it, you bought it, it's yours. It is old enough to feel the dowser suddenly come alive, grow heavy, and roll over in your hands, pointing at hidden water.

My reaction to the Creature on that night was perhaps the perfect reaction,  7 the one every writer of horror fiction or director who has worked in the field hopes for when he or she uncaps a pen or a lens: total emotional involvement, pretty much undiluted by any real thinking process—and you understand, don't you, that when it comes to horror movies, the only thought process really necessary to break the mood is for a friend to lean over and whisper, "See the zipper running down his back?"

8    I think that only people who have worked in the field for some time truly understand how fragile this stuff really is, and what an amazing commitment it imposes on the reader or viewer of intellect and maturity. When Coleridge spoke of "the suspension of disbelief" in his essay on imaginative poetry, I believe he knew that disbelief is not like a balloon, which may be suspended in air with a minimum of effort; it is like a lead weight, which has to be hoisted with a clean and a jerk and held up by main force. Disbelief isn't light; it's heavy. The difference in sales between Arthur Hailey and H. P. Lovecraft may exist because everyone believes in cars, and banks, but it takes a sophisticated and muscular intellectual act to believe, even for a little while, in Nyarlathotep, the Blind Faceless One, the Howler in the Night. And whenever I run into someone who expresses a feeling along the lines of, "I don't read fantasy or go to any of those movies; none of it's real," I feel a kind of sympathy. They simply can't lift the weight of fantasy. The muscles of the imagination have grown too weak.

9    In this sense, kids are the perfect audience for horror. The paradox is this: children, who are physically quite weak, lift the weight of unbelief with ease. They are the jugglers of the invisible world—a perfectly understandable phenomenon when you consider the perspective they must view things from. Children deftly manipulate the logistics of Santa Claus's entry on Christmas Eve (he can get down small chimneys by making himself small, and if there's no chimney there's the letter slot, and if there's no letter slot there's always the crack under the door), the Easter Bunny, God (big guy, sorta old, white beard, throne), Jesus ("How do you think he turned the water into wine?" I asked my son Joe when he—Joe, not Jesus—was five; Joe's idea was that he had something "kinda like magic Kool-Aid, you get what I mean?"), the devil (big guy, red skin, horse feet, tail with an arrow on the end of it, Snidely Whiplash moustache), Ronald McDonald, the Burger King, the Keebler Elves, Dorothy and Toto, the Lone Ranger and Tonto, a thousand more.

10    Most parents think they understand this openness better than, in many cases, they actually do, and try to keep their children away from anything that smacks too much of horror and terror—"Rated PG (or G in the case of *The Andromeda Strain*), but may be too intense for younger children," the ads for *Jaws* read—believing, I suppose, that to allow their kids to go to a real horror movie would be tantamount to rolling a live hand grenade into a nursery school.

11    But one of the odd Döppler effects that seems to occur during the selective forgetting that is so much a part of "growing up" is the fact that almost *everything* has a scare potential for the child under eight. Children are literally afraid of their own shadows at the right time and place. There is the story of the four-year-old who refused to go to bed at night without a light on in his closet. His parents at last discovered he was frightened of a creature he had heard his father speak of often; this creature, which had grown large and dreadful in the child's imagination, was the "twi-night double-header."

Seen in this light, even Disney movies are minefields of terror, and the ani-  12
mated cartoons, which will apparently be released and rereleased even unto the
end of the world,[1] are usually the worst offenders. There are adults today, who,
when questioned, will tell you that the most frightening thing they saw at the
movies as children was Bambi's father shot by the hunter, or Bambi and his
mother running before the forest fire. Other Disney memories which are right up
there with the batrachian horror inhabiting the Black Lagoon include the marching brooms that have gone totally out of control in *Fantasia* (and for the small
child, the real horror inherent in the situation is probably buried in the implied
father-son relationship between Mickey Mouse and the old sorcerer; those
brooms are making a terrible mess, and when the sorcerer/father gets home,
there may be PUNISHMENT. . . . This sequence might well send the child of strict
parents into an ecstasy of terror); the night on Bald Mountain from the same film;
the witches in *Snow White* and *Sleeping Beauty*, one with her enticingly red poisoned apple (and what small child is not taught early to fear the idea of POISON?),
the other with her deadly spinning wheel; this holds all the way up to the relatively innocuous *One Hundred and One Dalmatians* which features the logical
granddaughter of those Disney witches from the thirties and forties—the evil
Cruella DeVille, with her scrawny, nasty face, her loud voice (grownups sometimes forget how terrified young children are of loud voices, which come from
the giants of their world, the adults), and her plan to kill all the dalmatian pup-
pies (read "children," if you're a little person) and turn them into dogskin coats.

Yet it is the parents, of course, who continue to underwrite the Disney pro-  13
cedure of release and rerelease, often discovering goosebumps on their own
arms as they rediscover what terrified them as children . . . because what the
good horror film (or horror sequence in what may be billed a "comedy" or an
"animated cartoon") does above all else is to knock the adult props out from
under us and tumble us back down the slide into childhood. And there our
own shadow may once again become that of a mean dog, a gaping mouth, or a
beckoning dark figure.

Perhaps the supreme realization of this return to childhood comes in David  14
Cronenberg's marvelous horror film *The Brood*, where a disturbed woman is
literally producing "children of rage" who go out and murder the members of
her family, one by one. About halfway through the film, her father sits dispirit-
edly on the bed in an upstairs room, drinking and mourning his wife, who has
been the first to feel the wrath of the brood. We cut to the bed itself . . . and
clawed hands suddenly reach out from beneath it and dig into the carpeting

---

[1]In one of my favorite Arthur C. Clarke stories, this actually happens. In this vignette, aliens from
space land on earth after the Big One has finally gone down. As the story closes, the best brains of
this alien culture are trying to figure out the meaning of a film they have found and learned how
to play back. The film ends with the words *A Walt Disney Production*. I have moments when I
really believe that there would be no better epitaph for the human race, or for a world where the
only sentient being absolutely guaranteed of immortality is not Hitler, Charlemagne, Albert
Schweitzer, or even Jesus Christ—but is, instead, Richard M. Nixon, whose name is engraved on a
plaque placed on the airless surface of the moon.

near the doomed father's shoes. And so Cronenberg pushes us down the slide; we are four again, and all of our worst surmises about what might be lurking under the bed have turned out to be true.

15    The irony of all this is that children are better able to deal with fantasy and terror *on its own terms* than their elders are. You'll note I've italicized the phrase "on its own terms." An adult is able to deal with the cataclysmic terror of something like *The Texas Chainsaw Massacre* because he or she understands that it is all make-believe, and that when the take is done the dead people will simply get up and wash off the stage blood. The child is not so able to make this distinction, and *Chainsaw Massacre* is quite rightly rated R. Little kids do not need this scene, any more than they need the one at the end of *The Fury* where John Cassavetes quite literally blows apart. But the point is, if you put a little kid of six in the front row at a screening of *The Texas Chainsaw Massacre* along with an adult who was temporarily unable to distinguish between make-believe and "real things" (as Danny Torrance, the little boy in *The Shining* puts it)—if, for instance, you had given the adult a hit of Yellow Sunshine LSD about two hours before the movie started—my guess is that the kid would have maybe a week's worth of bad dreams. The adult might spend a year or so in a rubber room, writing home with Crayolas.

16    A certain amount of fantasy and horror in a child's life seems to me a perfectly okay, useful sort of thing. Because of the size of their imaginative capacity, children are able to handle it, and because of their unique position in life, they are able to put such feelings to work. They understand their position very well, too. Even in such a relatively ordered society as our own, they understand that their survival is a matter almost totally out of their hands. Children are "dependents" up until the age of eight or so in every sense of the word; dependent on mother and father (or some reasonable facsimile thereof) not only for food, clothing, and shelter, but dependent on them not to crash the car into a bridge abutment, to meet the school bus on time, to walk them home from Cub Scouts or Brownies, to buy medicines with childproof caps, dependent on them to make sure they don't electrocute themselves while screwing around with the toaster or while trying to play with Barbie's Beauty Salon in the bathtub.

17    Running directly counter to this necessary dependence is the survival directive built into all of us. The child realizes his or her essential lack of control, and I suspect it is this very realization which makes the child uneasy. It is the same sort of free-floating anxiety that many air travelers feel. They are not afraid because they believe air travel to be unsafe; they are afraid because they have surrendered control, and if something goes wrong all they can do is sit there clutching airsick bags or the in-flight magazine. To surrender control runs counter to the survival directive. Conversely, while a thinking, informed person may understand intellectually that travel by car is much more dangerous than flying, he or she is still apt to feel much more comfortable behind the wheel, because she/he has control . . . or at least an illusion of it.

18    This hidden hostility and anxiety toward the airline pilots of their lives may be one explanation why, like the Disney pictures which are released during

# An Album of Advertisements:
## Images of Culture

The advertisements that appear in this album reflect various ideas in the popular culture—what we value and what we desire. Advertising clearly is a powerful force in molding popular culture and taste. Consider what the advertisements in this album say about popular culture and how they embody forms of argument and persuasion that promote a product, person, or idea.

**Advocacy Advertising:** The AIDS awareness campaign of ALDO and YouthAIDS

### CONSIDERING THE ADVERTISEMENT

1. What is the effect of using a celebrity—Christina Aguilera—as an advocate in this advertisement? How does the designer present her within the frame of the ad?
2. Search in magazines or online for three other ads that use celebrities to promote a product or idea. Write an essay explaining why these ads are effective. If possible, download or scan these images into your essay.

I am your Christmas wish, the realization of your Christmas desire. I am the voice of Slezak, the soul of Sylva, the dramatic art of Sarah Bernhardt—I am the laugh of Lauder, the coon shouts of Stella Mayhew—I am Sousa and his entire band, Herbert and his orchestra—I am the

# EDISON PHONOGRAPH

I hold, on a little sapphire button, scarcely bigger than the point of a pin, the ability to produce exactly the kind of music you and each member of your family like best. No one in your family is too young, none will *ever* be too old to enjoy my presence. I am supreme as an entertainer—the greatest *kind* of Christmas gift—a gift for *all* the family.

And I am the greatest Christmas gift *of its kind*. For I have four great advantages: Exactly the right volume of sound for your home; the sapphire reproducing point that never wears out—no needles to be changed after each record; Amberol (four-and-one-half minute) Records rendering every composition *completely*, without cutting or hurrying; and home recording. This is a great feature: Talk to me, sing to me! I answer you back in your own words, in your own voice. I, the Edison Phonograph, am you *yourself*.

Go to an Edison dealer and hear and see me—be sure to have me in your home on Christmas Day.

There is an Edison Phonograph at a price to suit everybody's means, from $15.00 to $200.00; sold at the same prices everywhere in the United States. Edison Standard Records, 35c; Edison Amberol Records (play twice as long), 50c; Edison Grand Opera Records, 75c to $2.00.

Thomas A. Edison
INCORPORATED
11 Lakeside Ave., Orange, N.J.

**Classic Advertisement:** Edison Phonograph—a 1910 magazine advertisement for a phonograph, a device used to record and replay sound

**Contemporary Advertisement:** Apple iPod—advertisement
for a portable media player

## CONSIDERING THE ADVERTISEMENTS

1. Describe the images in each advertisement: How are they similar? How are they different? Who is the audience for each ad? What techniques are used to appeal to the audience? What cultural assumptions and ideals does each advertisement build on?
2. Using these classic and contemporary ads as a reference point, write an essay arguing for or against the proposition that the methods and goals of advertising have not changed or improved over time, even though the culture may have changed.

**International Advertising:** Budweiser in China

**CONSIDERING THE ADVERTISEMENT**

1. Explain the way in which this photograph captures the power of advertising to promote an American product overseas. What details hold your attention? Why is the poster advertising Budweiser so large?
2. In an essay, argue for or against the idea that advertising American products like Budweiser, Coke, or McDonald's overseas is a form of "cultural imperialism" that harms the societies of other countries.

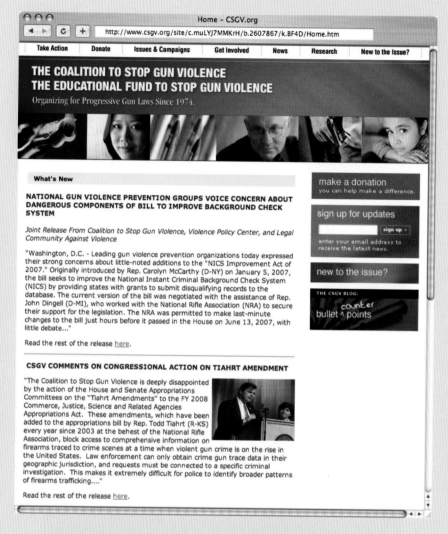

**Political Advertising:** The Coalition to Stop Gun Violence

## CONSIDERING THE ADVERTISEMENT

1. Explain the various details and visual elements that create the "message" in this screenshot taken from a Web site advocating progressive gun laws.
2. Search online for other Web sites that promote changes in local or national laws—for instance, banning same-sex marriage, supporting stem-cell research, or promoting "intelligent design" in school textbooks. In an essay, analyze the argumentative techniques underlying the verbal and nonverbal elements in the text you have selected. Attach or integrate the image into your essay.

**Mobile Outdoor Advertising:** NotinLA.com

## CONSIDERING THE ADVERTISEMENT

1. What seems to be the purpose behind this mobile ad? What evidence can you cite to support your response? Why would it be helpful to go to the Web site to decipher the ad's message?
2. In an argumentative essay, explain why you think this NotinLA.com ad is or is not successful.

*Thirty-five years ago,*
*Dave Thomas® opened the front door*
*and welcomed you inside.*

**Spokesperson Advertising:** Wendy's ad featuring its founder

## CONSIDERING THE ADVERTISEMENT

1. This advertisement features Dave Thomas, the deceased founder of Wendy's. How does the ad exploit the argumentative technique of *pathos* (appeal to emotion) and *ethos* (appeal to values and character)?
2. Write an essay in which you argue from one side or the other about the impact of fast-food advertising on American culture. In other words, do you think that the ads promoting the fast-food industry do more good or harm? Use the Wendy's ad and any others you locate to support your claim.

**Anti-Advertising:** God billboard.

## CONSIDERING THE ADVERTISEMENT

1. What is your response to this billboard ad? Are you surprised, shocked, or amused, and why? Who might have paid for the billboard ad? What is the ad's purpose? Why might some viewers find the ad controversial? Why might the ad be considered a humorous form of anti-advertising?
2. Write an essay in which you contend that various expressions of faith should or should not be used in advertising, or that God should or should not be used to promote a product, person, or idea.

school vacations in perpetuity, the old fairy tales also seem to go on forever. A parent who would raise his or her hands in horror at the thought of taking his/ her child to see *Dracula* or *The Changeling* (with its pervasive imagery of the drowning child) would be unlikely to object to the baby sitter reading "Hansel and Gretel" to the child before bedtime. But consider: the tale of Hansel and Gretel begins with deliberate abandonment (oh yes, the stepmother master-minds that one, but she is the symbolic mother all the same, and the father is a spaghetti-brained nurd who goes along with everything she suggests even though he knows it's wrong—thus we can see her as amoral, him as actively evil in the Biblical and Miltonian sense), it progresses to kidnapping (the witch in the candy house), enslavement, illegal detention, and finally justifiable homi-cide and cremation. Most mothers and fathers would never take their children to see *Survive,* that quickie Mexican exploitation flick about the rugby players who survived the aftermath of a plane crash in the Andes by eating their dead teammates, but these same parents find little to object to in "Hansel and Gretel," where the witch is fattening the children up so she can eat them. We give this stuff to the kids almost instinctively, understanding on a deeper level, perhaps, that such fairy stories are the perfect points of crystallization for those fears and hostilities.

Even anxiety-ridden air travelers have their own fairy tales—all those *Air-* 19 *port* movies, which, like "Hansel and Gretel" and all those Disney cartoons, show every sign of going on forever . . . but which should only be viewed on Thanksgivings, since all of them feature a large cast of turkeys.

My gut reaction to *Creature from the Black Lagoon* on that long-ago night was 20 a kind of terrible, waking swoon. The nightmare was happening right in front of me; every hideous possibility that human flesh is heir to was being played out on that drive-in screen.

Approximately twenty-two years later, I had a chance to see *Creature from* 21 *the Black Lagoon* again—not on TV, with any kind of dramatic build and mood broken up by adverts for used cars, K-Tel disco anthologies, and Underalls pantyhose, thank God, but intact, uncut . . . and even in 3-D. Guys like me who wear glasses have a hell of a time with 3-D, you know; ask anyone who wears specs how they like those nifty little cardboard glasses they give you when you walk in the door. If 3-D ever comes back in a big way, I'm going to take myself down to the local Pearle Vision Center and invest seventy bucks in a special pair of prescription lenses: one red, one blue. Annoying glasses aside, I should add that I took my son Joe with me—he was then five, about the age I had been myself, that night at the drive-in (and imagine my surprise—my *rueful* surprise—to discover that the movie which had so terrified me on that long-ago night had been rated G by the MPAA . . . just like the Disney pictures).

As a result, I had a chance to experience that weird doubling back in time 22 that I believe most parents only experience at the Disney films with their chil-dren, or when reading them the Pooh books or perhaps taking them to the Shrine or the Barnum & Bailey circus. A popular record is apt to create a par-ticular "set" in a listener's mind, precisely because of its brief life of six weeks to three months, and "golden oldies" continue to be played because they are the emotional equivalent of freeze-dried coffee. When the Beach Boys come on the radio singing "Help Me, Rhonda," there is always that wonderful second or two when I can re-experience the wonderful, guilty joy of copping my first feel (and if you do the mental subtraction from my present age of thirty-three, you'll see that I was a little backward in that respect). Movies and books do the same thing, although I would argue that the mental set, its depth and texture, tends to be a little richer, a little more complex, when re-experiencing films and a lot more complex when dealing with books.

23      With Joe that day I experienced *Creature from the Black Lagoon* from the other end of the telescope, but this particular theory of set identification still applied; in fact, it prevailed. Time and age and experience have all left their marks on me, just as they have on you; time is not a river, as Einstein theorized—it's a big . . . buffalo herd that runs us down and eventually mashes us into the ground, dead and bleeding, with a hearing-aid plugged into one ear and a colostomy bag instead of a .44 clapped on one leg. Twenty-two years later I knew that the Creature was really good old Ricou Browning, the famed underwater stunt-man, in a molded latex suit, and the suspension of disbelief, that mental clean-and-jerk, had become a lot harder to accomplish. But I did it, which may mean nothing, or which may mean (I hope!) that the buffalo haven't got me yet. But when that weight of disbelief was finally up there, the old feelings came flooding in, as they flooded in some five years ago when I took Joe and my daughter Naomi to their first movie, a reissue of *Snow White and the Seven Dwarfs*. There is a scene in that film where, after Snow White has taken a bite from the poisoned apple, the dwarfs take her into the forest, weeping copiously. Half the audience of little kids was also in tears; the lower lips of the other half were trembling. The set identification in that case was strong enough so that I was also surprised into tears. I hated myself for being so blatantly manipulated, but manipulated I was, and there I sat, blubbering into my beard over a bunch of cartoon characters. But it wasn't Disney that manipulated me; I did it myself. It was the kid inside who wept, surprised out of dormancy and into schmaltzy tears . . . but at least awake for awhile.

24      During the final two reels of *Creature from the Black Lagoon*, the weight of disbelief is nicely balanced somewhere above my head, and once again director Jack Arnold places the symbols in front of me and produces the old equation of the fairy tales, each symbol as big and as easy to handle as a child's alphabet block. Watching, the child awakes again and knows that this is what dying is like. Dying is when the Creature from the Black Lagoon dams up the exit. Dying is when the monster gets you.

25      In the end, of course, the hero and heroine, very much alive, not only survive but triumph—as Hansel and Gretel do. As the drive-in floodlights over the screen came on and the projector flashed its GOOD NIGHT, DRIVE SAFELY slide on that big white space (along with the virtuous suggestion that you ATTEND THE CHURCH OF YOUR CHOICE), there was a brief feeling of relief, almost of resurrection. But the feeling that stuck longest was the swooning sensation that good

old Richard Carlson and Julia Adams were surely going down for the third time, and the image that remains forever after is of the creature slowly and patiently walling its victims into the Black Lagoon; even now I can see it peering over that growing wall of mud and sticks.

Its eyes. Its ancient eyes.                                                              26

## COMPREHENSION

1. Why does King claim that it is harder for an author to successfully bring a horror tale to life than a standard "realistic" one? What special skills does the horror writer need?
2. Why are children the "perfect audience for horror" (paragraph 9)? What exists in the structure of most horror films that make them suitable for children?
3. King titles his essay "My Creature from the Black Lagoon" rather than using the original title *The Creature from the Black Lagoon*. Why?
4. Why does King think it is ironic that many Disney movies are G-rated while "horror" movies often contain warnings about content for children?
5. In paragraph 23, King remarks that he is pleased that he is still able to get a thrill from watching a horror movie even though he is an adult and understands the artifice behind the monster. Why does he feel this is a positive response? Why does he believe it would be beneficial for most adults to react this way?

## RHETORIC

1. In paragraph 9, King attempts to reproduce the sense of what it is like to think like a child. How does he achieve this effect? What is his purpose?
2. How does King structure paragraph 18 to compare and contrast horror movies with "fairy tales"? What is his rhetorical intent?
3. What vocabulary choices does King use in his introduction to set up his conversational style of writing? What relationship does King intend to create between the writer and reader by employing this type of discourse?
4. In paragraphs 4 and 5, King recounts a childhood anecdote. What is the purpose of describing the outing to the drive-in theater with his mother's boyfriend, Milt? How does King structure these two paragraphs so that they culminate rhetorically in a device similar to that employed in horror movies?
5. Although much of King's writing is informal, he does use references to popular culture, literature, and science in his writing. What is the significance and meaning of the following terms and phrases: *batrachian* (paragraph 3), *suspension of disbelief* (paragraph 8), *Döppler effects* (paragraph 11), *twi-night double-header* (paragraph 11), *possibility that human flesh is heir to* (paragraph 20), and *golden oldies* (paragraph 22)?

6. The conclusion is only five words: two sentence fragments. Why did King choose to end his essay this way?

7. King uses irony in his essay for comic effect; for example, in paragraph 25, what is the irony in the "sign-off" at the drive-in movie theater that reads: ATTEND THE CHURCH OF YOUR CHOICE?

## WRITING

1. Think of the first horror movie you recall vividly from your childhood. Write an expository essay about how the film scared you. Include both the dramatic elements on the screen and your own state of mind while you watched.

2. Select a horror or science fiction book you've read that has been adapted for the screen. Compare and contrast the effects of each version. Which was more captivating? More engaging? More horrifying? More believable? Explain your view.

3. Compare and contrast the benefits or drawbacks, or both, of an adult reading a story to a child versus taking a child to the movies.

4. **Writing an Argument:** In an essay, argue for or against the proposition that horror movies are scarier when viewed at the movie theater than on home video.

www.mhhe.com/ **mhreader** | For more information on Stephen King, go to: **More Resources > Ch. 9 Media & Pop Culture**

# Red, White, and Beer

## Dave Barry

*Dave Barry (b. 1947) was born in Armonk, New York. He graduated from Haverford College in 1969 and was a reporter and editor at the* Daily Local News *from 1971 to 1975 and subsequently a columnist for* The Miami Herald. *Besides writing his columns, Barry has written numerous books, all with his unique, amusing point of view. His books include* Stay Fit and Healthy Until You're Dead *(1985),* Dave Barry's Greatest Hits *(1988),* Dave Barry Turns 40 *(1990),* Dave Barry's Only Travel Guide You'll Ever Need *(1991), and* Boogers Are My Beat *(2002). Barry won the 1988 Pulitzer Prize for commentary. In the following piece, he comments on the relation between television commercials and patriotism.*

Lately I've been feeling very patriotic, especially during commercials. Like, 1
when I see those strongly pro-American Chrysler commercials, the ones where
the winner of the Bruce Springsteen Sound-Alike Contest sings about how The
Pride Is Back, the ones where Lee Iacocca himself comes striding out and practically challenges the president of Toyota to a knife fight, I get this warm, proud
feeling inside, the same kind of feeling I get whenever we hold routine naval
maneuvers off the coast of Libya.

But if you want to talk about *real* patriotism, of course, you have to talk 2
about beer commercials. I would have to say that Miller is the most patriotic
brand of beer. I grant you it tastes like rat saliva, but we are not talking about
taste here. What we are talking about, according to the commercials, is that
Miller is by God an *American* beer, "born and brewed in the U.S.A.," and the
men who drink it are American men, the kind of men who aren't afraid to per-
spire freely and shake a man's hand. That's mainly what happens in Miller
commercials: Burly American men go around, drenched in perspiration, shaking each other's hands in a violent and patriotic fashion.

You never find out exactly why these men spend so much time shaking 3
hands. Maybe shaking hands is just their simple straightforward burly masculine American patriotic way of saying to each other: "Floyd, I am truly sorry I
drank all that Miller beer last night and went to the bathroom in your glove
compartment." Another possible explanation is that, since there are never any
women in the part of America where beer commercials are made, the burly
men have become lonesome and desperate for any form of physical contact. I
have noticed that sometimes, in addition to shaking hands, they hug each other.
Maybe very late at night, after the David Letterman show, there are Miller commercials in which the burly men engage in slow dancing. I don't know.

I do know that in one beer commercial, I think this is for Miller—although it 4
could be for Budweiser, which is also a very patriotic beer—the burly men build
a house. You see them all getting together and pushing up a brand-new wall. Me,
I worry some about a house built by men drinking beer. In my experience, you
run into trouble when you ask a group of beer-drinking men to perform any task
more complex than remembering not to light the filter ends of cigarettes.

For example, in my younger days, whenever anybody in my circle of 5
friends wanted to move, he'd get the rest of us to help, and, as an inducement,
he'd buy a couple of cases of beer. This almost always produced unfortunate
results, such as the time we were trying to move Dick "The Wretch" Curry
from a horrible fourth-floor walk-up apartment in Manhattan's Lower East Side
to another horrible fourth-floor walk-up apartment in Manhattan's Lower East
Side, and we hit upon the labor-saving concept of, instead of carrying The
Wretch's possessions manually down the stairs, simply dropping them out the
window, down onto the street, where The Wretch was racing around, gathering
up the broken pieces of his life and shrieking at us to stop helping him move,
his emotions reaching a fever pitch when his bed, which had been swinging
wildly from a rope, entered the apartment two floors below his through what
had until seconds earlier been a window.

6    This is the kind of thinking you get, with beer. So I figure what happens, in the beer commercial where the burly men are building the house, is they push the wall up so it's vertical, and then, after the camera stops filming them, they just keep pushing, and the wall crashes down on the other side, possibly onto somebody's pickup truck. And then they all shake hands.

7    But other than that, I'm in favor of the upsurge in retail patriotism, which is lucky for me because the airwaves are saturated with pro-American commercials. Especially popular are commercials in which the newly restored Statue of Liberty—and by the way, I say Lee Iacocca should get some kind of medal for that, or at least be elected president—appears to be endorsing various products, as if she were Mary Lou Retton or somebody. I saw one commercial strongly suggesting that the Statue of Liberty uses Sure brand underarm deodorant.

8    I have yet to see a patriotic laxative commercial, but I imagine it's only a matter of time. They'll show some actors dressed up as hard-working country folk, maybe at a church picnic, smiling at each other and eating pieces of pie. At least one of them will be a black person. The Statue of Liberty will appear in the background. Then you'll hear a country-style singer singing:

Folks 'round here they love this land;
They stand by their beliefs;
An' when they git themselves stopped up;
They want some quick relief.

9    Well, what do you think? Pretty good commercial concept, huh?

10    Nah, you're right. They'd never try to pull something like that. They'd put the statue in the *foreground*.

## COMPREHENSION

1. What does Barry mean by "retail patriotism" (paragraph 7)? How does the essay's title illustrate this concept?
2. According to Barry, what makes beer commercials, especially those for Miller, patriotic?
3. In Barry's opinion, what do sexism, patriotism, and beer have in common?

## RHETORIC

1. Barry doesn't explicitly state his thesis anywhere in the essay. In your own words, what is his implied thesis? Use evidence from the essay to support your view.
2. Barry uses irony and humor very effectively in this piece. Cite some examples of his humor, and analyze how he achieves the desired effect.

3. The writer uses specific brand names in his essay. How does this device help strengthen his argument? Would eliminating them make the essay less persuasive? Why or why not?
4. Barry seems to digress from his point in paragraphs 4–6. Why does he do this? How does this digression serve the purpose of the piece?
5. Does the anecdote Barry uses in paragraph 5 ring true? Why or why not? What purpose does it serve in the essay? Does its plausibility affect the strength of Barry's argument?
6. How does paragraph 10 function as a conclusion? Is it in keeping with the essay's tone and style? Is it an effective device? Justify your response.

## WRITING

1. Barry's essay examines how television sells patriotism. Write an essay analyzing how television sells other abstract ideas, such as success, love, freedom, or democracy. Pattern your essay after Barry's, using humor. Also, use specific television commercials you have seen as examples.
2. Write an essay titled "Patriotism," using both denotative and connotative definitions of the word.
3. **Writing an Argument:** In an essay, argue for or against the claim that television advertising has had a harmful impact on American and global consumers.

| www.mhhe.com/ **mhreader** | For more information on Dave Barry, go to: **More Resources > Ch. 9 Media & Pop Culture** |

# Wonder Woman

## Gloria Steinem

*Gloria Steinem (b. 1934) was born and raised in Toledo, Ohio; she attended Smith College, receiving a BA in government in 1956. A noted feminist and political activist, Steinem in 1968 helped to found* New York *magazine; in 1971 she cofounded* Ms. *magazine and served as its editor. Whether campaigning for Robert Kennedy, defending raising money for the United Farm Workers, or championing women's reproductive rights, Steinem has been on the cutting edge of American politics and social activism for almost four decades. Her books include* The Thousand Indias *(1957),* Outrageous Acts and Everyday Rebellions *(1983),* Marilyn: Norma Jean *(1986),*

*Revolution from Within (1992), and Moving beyond Words (1994). In the follow-*
*ing essay, Steinem explains why the comic book heroine Wonder Woman (who was on*
*the first cover of Ms.) was such a formative influence during her childhood.*

1   Wonder Woman is the only female super-hero to be published continuously
since comic books began—indeed, she is one of the few to have existed at all or
to be anything other than part of a male super-hero group—but this may strike
many readers as a difference without much distinction. After all, haven't comic
books always been a little disreputable? Something that would never have been
assigned in school? The answer to those questions is yes, which is exactly why
they are important. Comic books have power—including over the child who
still lives within each of us—because they are *not* part of the "serious" grown-
up world.

2       I remember hundreds of nights reading comic books under the covers with
a flashlight; dozens of car trips while my parents told me I was ruining my eyes
and perhaps my mind ("brain-deadeners" was what my mother called them);
and countless hours spent hiding in a tree or some other inaccessible spot where
I could pore over their pages in sweet freedom. Because my family's traveling
meant I didn't go to school regularly until I was about twelve, comic books
joined cereal boxes and ketchup labels as the primers that taught me how to
read. They were even cheap enough to be the first things I bought on my own—
a customer who couldn't see over the countertop but whose dignity was greatly
enhanced by making a choice, counting out carefully hoarded coins, and completing a grown-up exchange.

3   I've always wondered if this seemingly innate drive toward independence in
children isn't more than just "a movement toward mastery," as psychologists
say. After all, each of us is the result of millennia of environment and heredity,
a unique combination that could never happen before—or again. Like a seed
that contains a plant, a child is already a unique person; an ancient spirit born
into a body too small to express itself, or even cope with the world. I remember
feeling the greatest love for my parents whenever they allowed me to express
my own will, whether that meant wearing an inappropriate hat for days on
end, or eating dessert before I had finished dinner.

4       Perhaps it's our memories of past competence and dreams for the future
that create the need for super-heroes in the first place. Leaping skyscrapers in a
single bound, seeing through walls, and forcing people to tell the truth by en-
circling them in a magic lasso—all would be satisfying fantasies at any age, but
they may be psychological necessities when we have trouble tying our shoes,
escaping a worldview composed mainly of belts and knees, and getting grown-
ups to *pay attention.*

5       The problem is that the super-heroes who perform magical feats—indeed,
even mortal heroes who are merely competent—are almost always men. A
female child is left to believe that, even when her body is as big as her spirit, she
will still be helping with minor tasks, appreciating the accomplishments of

others, and waiting to be rescued. Of course, pleasure is to be found in all these experiences of helping, appreciating, and being rescued; pleasure that should be open to boys, too. Even in comic books, heroes sometimes work in groups or are called upon to protect their own kind, not just helpless females. But the truth is that a male super-hero is more likely to be vulnerable, if only to create suspense, than a female character is to be powerful or independent. For little girls, the only alternative is suppressing a crucial part of ourselves by transplanting our consciousness into a male character—which usually means a white one, thus penalizing girls of color doubly, and boys of color, too. Otherwise, choices remain limited: in the case of girls, to an "ideal" life of sitting around like a Technicolor clotheshorse, getting into jams with villains, and saying things like, "Oh, Superman! I'll always be grateful to you"; in the case of boys of color, to identifying with villains who may be the only ethnic characters with any power; and in the case of girls of color, to making an impossible choice between parts of their identity. It hardly seems worth learning to tie our shoes.

I'm happy to say that I was rescued from this dependent fate at the age of seven or so; rescued (Great Hera!) by a woman. Not only did she have the wisdom of Athena and Aphrodite's power to inspire love, she was also faster than Mercury and stronger than Hercules. In her all-woman home on Paradise Island, a refuge of ancient Amazon culture protected from nosy travelers by magnetic thought-fields that created an area known to the world as the Bermuda Triangle, she had come to her many and amazing powers naturally. Together with her Amazon sisters, she had been trained in them from infancy and perfected them in Greek-style contests of dexterity, strength, and speed. The lesson was that each of us might have unknown powers within us, if we only believed and practiced them. (To me, it always seemed boring that Superman had bullet-proof skin, X-ray vision, and the ability to fly. Where was the contest?) Though definitely white, as were all her Amazon sisters, she was tall and strong, with dark hair and eyes—a relief from the weak, bosomy, blonde heroines of the 1940s.

Of course, this Amazon did need a few fantastic gadgets to help her once she entered a modern world governed by Ares, God of War, not Aphrodite, Goddess of Love: a magic golden lasso that compelled all within its coils to obey her command, silver bracelets that repelled bullets, and an invisible plane that carried her through time as well as space. But she still had to learn how to throw the lasso with accuracy, be agile enough to deflect bullets from her silver-encased wrists, and navigate an invisible plane.

Charles Moulton, whose name appeared on each episode as Wonder Woman's writer and creator, had seen straight into my heart and understood the fears of violence and humiliation hidden there. No longer did I have to pretend to like the "POW!" and "SPLAT!" of boys' comic books, from Captain Marvel to the Green Hornet. No longer did I have nightmares after looking at ghoulish images of torture and murder, bloody scenes made all the more realistic by steel-booted Nazis and fang-toothed Japanese who were caricatures of World War II enemies then marching in every newsreel. (Eventually, the sadism of boys' comic books was so extreme that it inspired Congressional hearings, and publishers were asked to limit the number of severed heads and dripping entrails—a reminder that television wasn't the first popular medium selling sadism to boys.) Best of all, I could stop pretending to enjoy the ridicule, bossing-around, and constant endangering of female characters. In these Amazon adventures, only the villains bought the idea that "masculine" meant aggression and "feminine" meant submission. Only the occasional female accomplice said things like "Girls want superior men to boss them around," and even they were usually converted to the joys of self-respect by the story's end.

9     This was an Amazon super-hero who never killed her enemies. Instead, she converted them to a belief in equality and peace, to self-reliance, and respect for the rights of others. If villains destroyed themselves, it was through their own actions or some unbloody accident. Otherwise, they might be conquered by force, but it was a force tempered by love and justice.

10    In short, she was wise, beautiful, brave, and explicitly out to change "a world torn by the hatreds and wars of men."

11    She was Wonder Woman.

12    Only much later, when I was in my thirties and modern feminism had begun to explain the political roots of women's status—instead of accepting some "natural" inferiority decreed by biology, God, or Freud—did I realize how hard Charles Moulton had tried to get an egalitarian worldview into comic book form. From Wonder Woman's birth myth as Princess Diana of Paradise Island, "that enlightened land," to her adventures in America disguised as Diana Prince, a be-spectacled army nurse and intelligence officer (a clear steal from Superman's Clark Kent), this female super-hero was devoted to democracy, peace, justice, and "liberty and freedom for all womankind."

13    One typical story centers on Prudence, a young pioneer in the days of the American Frontier, where Wonder Woman has been transported by the invisible plane that doubles as a time machine. After being rescued from a Perils of Pauline life, Prudence finally realizes her own worth, and also the worth of all women. "From now on," she says proudly to Wonder Woman, "I'll rely on myself, not on a man." Another story ends with Wonder Woman explaining her own long-running romance with Captain Steve Trevor, the American pilot whose crash-landing on Paradise Island was Aphrodite's signal that the strongest and wisest of all the Amazons must answer the call of a war-torn world. As Wonder Woman says of this colleague whom she so often rescues: "I can never love a dominant man."

14    The most consistent villain is Ares, God of War, a kind of metavillain who considers women "the natural spoils of war" and insists they stay home as the slaves of men. Otherwise, he fears women will spread their antiwar sentiments, create democracy in the world, and leave him dishonored and unemployed. That's why he keeps trying to trick Queen Hippolyte, Princess Diana's mother, into giving up her powers as Queen of the Amazons, thus allowing him to conquer Paradise Island and destroy the last refuge of ancient feminism. It is in memory of a past time when the Amazons did give in

to the soldiers of Ares, and were enslaved by them, that Aphrodite requires each Amazon to wear a pair of cufflike bracelets. If captured and bound by them (as Wonder Woman sometimes is in particularly harrowing episodes), an Amazon loses all her power. Wearing them is a reminder of the fragility of female freedom.

In America, however, villains are marked not only by their violence, but by their prejudice and lust for money. Thomas Tighe, woman-hating industrialist, is typical. After being rescued by Wonder Woman from accidental imprisonment in his own bank vault, he refuses to give her the promised reward of a million dollars. Though the money is needed to support Holliday College, the home of the band of college girls who aid Wonder Woman, Tighe insists that its students must first complete impossible tests of strength and daring. Only after Wonder Woman's powers allow them to meet every challenge does Tighe finally admit: "You win, Wonder Woman! . . . I am no longer a woman hater." She replies: "Then you're the real winner, Mr. Tighe! Because when one ceases to hate, he becomes stronger!"

Other villains are not so easily converted. Chief among them is Dr. Psycho, perhaps a parody of Sigmund Freud. An "evil genius" who "abhors women," the mad doctor's intentions are summed up in this scene-setting preface to an episode called "Battle for Womanhood": "With weird cunning and dark, forbidden knowledge of the occult, Dr. Psycho prepares to change the independent status of modern American women back to the days of the sultans and slave markets, clanking chains and abject captivity. But sly and subtle Psycho reckons without Wonder Woman!"

When I looked into the origins of my proto-feminist super-hero, I discovered that her pseudonymous creator had been a very non-Freudian psychologist named William Moulton Marston. Also a lawyer, businessman, prison reformer, and inventor of the lie-detector test (no doubt the inspiration for Wonder Woman's magic lasso), he had invented Wonder Woman as a heroine for little girls, and also as a conscious alternative to the violence of comic books for boys. In fact, Wonder Woman did attract some boys as readers, but the integrated world of comic book trading revealed her true status: at least three Wonder Woman comic books were necessary to trade for one of Superman. Among the many male super-heroes, only Superman and Batman were to be as long-lived as Wonder Woman, yet she was still a second-class citizen.

Of course, it's also true that Marston's message wasn't as feminist as it might have been. Instead of portraying the goal of full humanity for women and men, which is what feminism has in mind, he often got stuck in the subject/object, winner/loser paradigm of "masculine" versus "feminine," and came up with female superiority instead. As he wrote: "Women represent love; men represent force. Man's use of force without love brings evil and unhappiness. Wonder Woman proves that women are superior to men because they have love in addition to force." No wonder I was inspired but confused by the isolationism of Paradise Island: Did women have to live separately in order to be happy and courageous? No wonder even boys who could accept equality might have felt less than good about themselves in some of these stories: Were there *any* men who could escape the cultural instruction to be violent?

19      Wonder Woman herself sometimes got trapped in this either/or choice. As she muses to herself: "Some girls love to have a man stronger than they are to make them do things. Do I like it? I don't know, it's sort of thrilling. But isn't it more fun to make a man obey?" Even female villains weren't capable of being evil on their own. Instead, they were hyperfeminine followers of men's commands. Consider Priscilla Rich, the upper-class antagonist who metamorphoses into the Cheetah, a dangerous she-animal. "Women have been submissive to men," wrote Marston, "and taken men's psychology [force without love] as their own."

20      In those wartime years, stories could verge on a jingoistic, even racist patriotism. Wonder Woman sometimes forgot her initial shock at America's unjust patriarchal system and confined herself to defeating a sinister foreign threat by proving that women could be just as loyal and brave as men in service of their country. Her costume was a version of the Stars and Stripes. Some of her adversaries were suspiciously short, ugly, fat, or ethnic as a symbol of "unAmerican" status. In spite of her preaching against violence and for democracy, the good guys were often in uniform, and no country but the United States was seen as a bastion of freedom.

21      But Marston didn't succumb to stereotypes as often as most comic book writers of the 1940s. Though Prudence, his frontier heroine, is threatened by monosyllabic Indians, Prudence's father turns out to be the true villain, who has been cheating the Indians. And the irrepressible Etta Candy, one of Wonder Woman's band of college girls, is surely one of the few fat-girl heroines in comics.

22      There are other unusual rewards. Queen Hippolyte, for instance, is a rare example of a mother who is good, powerful, and a mentor to her daughter. She founds nations, fights to protect Paradise Island, and is a source of strength to Wonder Woman as she battles the forces of evil and inequality. Mother and daughter stay in touch through a sort of telepathic TV set, and the result is a team of equals who are separated only by experience. In the flashback episode in which Queen Hippolyte succumbs to Hercules, she is even seen as a sexual being. How many girl children grew to adulthood with no such example of a strong, sensual mother—except for these slender stories? How many mothers preferred sons, or believed the patriarchal myth that competition is "natural" between mothers and daughters, or tamed their daughters instead of encouraging their wildness and strength? We are just beginning to realize the sense of anger and loss in girls whose mothers had no power to protect them, or forced them to conform out of fear for their safety, or left them to identify only with their fathers if they had any ambition at all.

23      Finally, there is Wonder Woman's ability to unleash the power of selfrespect within the women around her; to help them work together and support each other. This may not seem revolutionary to male readers accustomed to stories that depict men working together, but for females who are usually seen as competing for the favors of men—especially little girls who may just be getting to the age when girlfriends betray each other for the approval of boys—this

discovery of sisterhood can be exhilarating indeed. Women get a rare message of independence, of depending on themselves, not even on Wonder Woman. "You saved yourselves," as she says in one of her inevitable morals at story's end. "I only showed you that you could."

Whatever the shortcomings of William Marston, his virtues became clear after 24 his death in 1947. Looking back at the post-Marston stories I had missed the first time around—for at twelve or thirteen, I thought I had outgrown Wonder Woman and had abandoned her—I could see how little her later writers understood her spirit. She became sexier-looking and more submissive, violent episodes increased, more of her adversaries were female, and Wonder Woman herself required more help from men in order to triumph. Like so many of her real-life sisters in the postwar era of conservatism and "togetherness" of the 1950s, she had fallen on very hard times.

By the 1960s, Wonder Woman had given up her magic lasso, her bullet- 25 deflecting bracelets, her invisible plane, and all her Amazonian powers. Though she still had adventures and even practiced karate, any attractive man could disarm her. She had become a kind of female James Bond, though much more boring because she was denied his sexual freedom. She was Diana Prince, a mortal who walked about in boutique, car-hop clothes and took the advice of a male mastermind named "I Ching."

It was in this sad state that I first rediscovered my Amazon super-hero in 26 1972. *Ms.* magazine had just begun, and we were looking for a cover story for its first regular issue to appear in July. Since Joanne Edgar and other of its founding editors had also been rescued by Wonder Woman in their childhoods, we decided to rescue Wonder Woman in return. Though it wasn't easy to persuade her publishers to let us put her original image on the cover of a new and unknown feminist magazine, or to reprint her 1940s Golden Age episodes inside, we finally succeeded. Wonder Woman appeared on newsstands again in all her original glory, striding through city streets like a colossus, stopping planes and bombs with one hand and rescuing buildings with the other.

Clearly, there were many nostalgic grown-ups and heroine-starved readers of 27 all ages. The consensus of response seemed to be that if we had all read more about Wonder Woman and less about Dick and Jane, we might have been a lot better off. As for her publishers, they, too, were impressed. Under the direction of Dorothy Woolfolk, the first woman editor of Wonder Woman in all her long history, she was returned to her original Amazon status—golden lasso, bracelets, and all.

One day some months after her rebirth, I got a phone call from one of Won- 28 der Woman's tougher male writers. "Okay," he said, "she's got all her Amazon powers back. She talks to the Amazons on Paradise Island. She even has a Black Amazon sister named Nubia. Now will you leave me alone?"

I said we would.                                                                    29

In the 1970s, Wonder Woman became the star of a television series. As played 30 by Lynda Carter, she was a little blue of eye and large of breast, but she still retained her Amazon powers, her ability to convert instead of kill, and her appeal for many young female viewers. There were some who refused to leave their TV sets on Wonder Woman night. A few young boys even began to dress up as Wonder Woman on Halloween—a true revolution.

31      In the 1980s, Wonder Woman's story line was revamped by DC Comics, which reinvented its male super-heroes Superman and Batman at about the same time. Steve Trevor became a veteran of Vietnam; he remained a friend, but was romantically involved with Etta Candy. Wonder Woman acquired a Katharine Hepburn–Spencer Tracy relationship with a street-smart Boston detective named Ed Indelicato, whose tough-guy attitude played off Wonder Woman's idealism. She also gained a friend and surrogate mother in Julia Kapatelis, a leading archaeologist and professor of Greek culture at Harvard University who can understand the ancient Greek that is Wonder Woman's native tongue, and be a model of a smart, caring, single mother for girl readers. Julia's teenage daughter, Vanessa, is the age of many readers and goes through all of their uncertainties, trials, and tribulations, but has the joy of having a powerful older sister in Wonder Woman. There is even Myndi Mayer, a slick Hollywood public relations agent who turns Wonder Woman into America's hero, and is also in constant danger of betraying Diana's idealistic spirit. In other words, there are many of the currents of society today, from single mothers to the worries of teenage daughters and a commercial culture, instead of the simpler plots of America's dangers in World War II.

32      You will see whether Wonder Woman carries her true Amazon spirit into the present. If not, let her publishers know. She belongs to you.

33  Since Wonder Woman's beginnings more than a half century ago, however, a strange thing has happened: the Amazon myth has been rethought as archaeological relics have come to light. Though Amazons had been considered figments of the imagination, perhaps the mythological evidence of man's fear of woman, there is a tentative but growing body of evidence to support the theory that some Amazon-like societies did exist. In Europe, graves once thought to contain male skeletons—because they were buried with weapons or were killed by battle wounds—have turned out to hold skeletons of females after all. In the jungles of Brazil, scientists have found caves of what appears to have been an all-female society. The caves are strikingly devoid of the usual phallic design and theme; they feature, instead, the triangular female symbol, and the only cave that does bear male designs is believed to have been the copulatorium, where Amazons mated with males from surrounding tribes, kept only the female children, and returned male infants to the tribe. Such archaeological finds have turned up not only along the Amazon River in Brazil, but at the foot of the Atlas Mountains in northwestern Africa, and on the European and Asiatic sides of the Black Sea.

34      There is still far more controversy than agreement, but a shared supposition of these myths is this: imposing patriarchy on the gynocracy of pre-history took many centuries and great cruelty. Rather than give up freedom and worship only male gods, some bands of women resisted. They formed all-woman cultures that survived by capturing men from local tribes, mating with them, and raising

their girl children to have great skills of body and mind. These bands became warriors and healers who were sometimes employed for their skills by patriarchal cultures around them. As a backlash culture, they were doomed, but they may also have lasted for centuries.

Perhaps that's the appeal of Wonder Woman, Paradise Island, and this comic 35 book message. It's not only a child's need for a lost independence, but an adult's need for a lost balance between women and men, between humans and nature. As the new Wonder Woman says to Vanessa, "Remember your *power*, little sister."

However simplified, that is Wonder Woman's message: Remember Our Power. 36

## COMPREHENSION

1. According to Steinem, why are children drawn to comic books and superheroes?
2. Why did Wonder Woman appeal especially to Steinem? What distinctions does she draw between the way boys and girls view action heroes?
3. The writer traces the development of Wonder Woman from her inception during the 1940s to the 1980s. How did Wonder Woman change over the years? How did she remain true to her creator's (William Marston) conception of her? What does Steinem think about these changes?

## RHETORIC

1. What is this essay's persuasive thesis?
2. At whom is this essay aimed—lovers of comic books, or women, or a general audience? On what do you base your conclusion?
3. In part, this is a personal essay. How does Steinem create her persona or self-image? Does the personal element enhance or detract from the analysis? Explain your response.
4. Sort out the complex cause-and-effect relationships in this essay. How does the comparative method reinforce the writer's analysis?
5. What types of evidence does the writer provide? Is it sufficient to convince readers? Where, if anywhere, would more detail be helpful?
6. Steinem divides the essay into five sections. What is her purpose? How successful is she in maintaining the essay's unity by employing this method?
7. What paragraphs form the writer's conclusion? How do they recapitulate and add to the substance of the overall essay?

## WRITING

1. Write a personal essay about your favorite action hero or heroine—drawn from the comics, television cartoons, or computer games. Explain why this figure appeals to you and what it reveals about the broader culture.

2. Compare and contrast the ways in which females and males approach action heroes. Refer to specific icons like the one in the *Terminator* film series or Buffy the Vampire Slayer on television to support your assessment.

3. **Writing an Argument:** Think about the numerous action or super-heroes that young children and adolescents encounter today in various media forms. Write an essay in which you contend that exposure to such superheroes either does or does not encourage violent behavior in young people.

| www.mhhe.com/ **mhreader** | For more information on Gloria Steinem, go to: **More Resources > Ch. 9 Media & Pop Culture** |

# Supersaturation, or, The Media Torrent and Disposable Feeling

## Todd Gitlin

*Todd Gitlin (b. 1943) was born and grew up in New York City. He received a PhD in sociology from the University of California at Berkeley and was president of Students for a Democratic Society (SDS) in the 1960s. Gitlin is professor of culture, journalism, and sociology at New York University and has held the chair in American civilization at the Ecole des Hautes Etudes en Sciences Sociales in Paris. Gitlin also lectures at home and abroad on contemporary culture and history. He is the North American editor of the Web site openDemocracy.net. Among his notable books are* Inside Prime Time *(1983),* The Twilight of Common Dreams: Why America Is Wracked by Culture Wars *(1995), and* Media Unlimited: How the Torrent of Images and Sounds Overwhelms Our Lives *(2001). In the selection from* Media Unlimited *that follows, Gitlin offers an overview of the ways in which the media influence our contemporary lives.*

1 On my bedroom wall hangs a print of Vermeer's *The Concert*, painted around 1660. A young woman is playing a spinet. A second woman, probably her maid, holds a letter. A cavalier stands between them, his back to us. A landscape is painted on the raised lid of the spinet, and on the wall hang two paintings, a landscape and *The Procuress*, a work by Baburen, another Dutch artist, depicting a man and two women in a brothel. As in many seventeenth-century Dutch paintings, the domestic space is decorated by paintings. In wealthy Holland, many homes, and not only bourgeois ones, featured such renderings of the outer world. These pictures were pleasing, but more: they were proofs of taste and prosperity, amusements and news at once.

Vermeer froze instants, but instants that spoke of the relative constancy of ₂ the world in which his subjects lived. If he had painted the same room in the same house an hour, a day, or a month later, the letter in the maid's hand would have been different, and the woman might have been playing a different selection, but the paintings on the far wall would likely have been the same. There might have been other paintings, etchings, and prints elsewhere in the house, but they would not have changed much from month to month, year to year.

In what was then the richest country in the world, "everyone strives to em- ₃ bellish his house with precious pieces, especially the room toward the street," as one English visitor to Amsterdam wrote in 1640, noting that he had observed paintings in bakeries, butcher's shops, and the workshops of blacksmiths and cobblers.[1] Of course, the number of paintings, etchings, and prints in homes varied considerably. One tailor owned five paintings, for example, while at the high end, a 1665 inventory of a lavish patrician's house in Amsterdam held two maps and thirteen paintings in one grand room, twelve paintings in his widow's bedroom, and seven in the maid's room. Still, compared with today's domestic imagery, the grandest Dutch inventories of that prosperous era were tiny.[2] Even in the better-off households depicted by Vermeer, the visual field inhabited by his figures was relatively scanty and fixed.[3]

Today, Vermeer's equivalent, if he were painting domestic scenes, or shoot- ₄ ing a spread for *Vanity Fair,* or directing commercials or movies, would also display his figures against a background of images; and if his work appeared on-screen, there is a good chance that he would mix in a soundtrack as well. Most of the images would be portraits of individuals who have never walked in the door—not in the flesh—and yet are recognized and welcomed, though not like actual persons. They would rapidly segue into others—either because they had been edited into a video montage, or because they appear on pages meant to be leafed through. Today's Vermeer would discover that the private space of the home offers up vastly more impressions of the larger world than was possible in 1660. In seventeenth-century Delft, painters did not knock on the door day and night offering fresh images for sale. Today, though living space has been set apart from working space, as would have been the case only for the wealthier burghers of Vermeer's time, the outside world has entered the home with a vengeance—in the profusion of media.

The flow of images and sounds through the households of the rich world, ₅ and the richer parts of the poor world, seems unremarkable today. Only a

[1]Peter Mundy, quoted by Geert Mak, *Amsterdam,* trans. Philipp Blom (Cambridge, Mass. Harvard University Press, 2000), p. 109.
[2]Simon Schama, *The Embarrassment of Riches: An Interpretation of Dutch Culture in the Golden Age* (New York: Knopf, 1987), pp. 313–19. Schama notes that research in the relevant archives is "still in its early days" (p. 315).
[3]Many bourgeois Dutch houses also featured a camera lucida, a mounted magnifying lens trained on objects in the vicinity. Because the lens was movable, motion could be simulated—distant objects being brought nearer and sent farther away. But because the apparatus was mounted in a fixed location, the range of objects in motion was limited to those actually visible from the window. (Svetlana Alpers, personal communication, October 8, 1999.)

visitor from an earlier century or an impoverished country could be startled by the fact that life is now played out against a shimmering multitude of images and sounds, emanating from television, videotapes, videodiscs, video games, VCRs, computer screens, digital displays of all sorts, always in flux, chosen partly at will, partly by whim, supplemented by words, numbers, symbols, phrases, fragments, all passing through screens that in a single minute can display more pictures than a prosperous seventeenth-century Dutch household contained over several lifetimes, portraying in one day more individuals than the Dutch burgher would have beheld in the course of years, and in one week more bits of what we have come to call "information" than all the books in all the households in Vermeer's Delft. And this is not yet to speak of our sonic surroundings: the music, voices, and sound effects from radios, CD players, and turntables. Nor is it to speak of newspapers, magazines, newsletters, and books. Most of the faces we shall ever behold, we shall behold in the form of images.

6          Because they arrive with sound, at home, in the car, the elevator, or the waiting room, today's images are capable of attracting our attention during much of the day. We may ignore most of them most of the time, take issue with them or shrug them off (or think we are shrugging them off), but we must do the work of dispelling them—and even then, we know we can usher them into our presence whenever we like. Iconic plenitude is the contemporary condition, and it is taken for granted. To grow up in this culture is to grow into an expectation that images and sounds will be there for us on command, and that the stories they compose will be succeeded by still other stories, all bidding for our attention, all striving to make sense, all, in some sense, *ours*. Raymond Williams, the first analyst to pay attention to the fact that television is not just pictures but flow, and not just flow but drama upon drama, pointed out more than a quarter century ago, long before hundred-channel cable TV and VCRs, that

> we have never as a society acted so much or watched so many others acting. . . .
> [W]hat is really new . . . is that drama . . . is built into the rhythms of everyday
> life. In earlier periods drama was important at a festival, in a season, or as a con-
> scious journey to a theater; from honouring Dionysus or Christ to taking in a
> show. What we have now is drama as habitual experience: more in a week, in
> many cases, than most human beings would previously have seen in a lifetime.[4]

7          Around the time Vermeer painted *The Concert*, Blaise Pascal, who worried about the seductive power of distraction among the French royalty, wrote that "near the persons of kings there never fail to be a great number of people who see to it that amusement follows business, and who watch all the time of their leisure to supply them with delights and games, so that there is no blank in it."[5] In this one respect, today almost everyone—even the poor—in the rich

---

[4]"Drama in a Dramatised Society," in Alan O'Connor, ed., *Raymond Williams on Television* (Toronto: Between the Lines, 1989 [1974]), pp. 3–5. *Flow* comes up in Williams's *Television: Technology and Cultural Form* (New York: Schocken, 1975), pp. 86 ff.

[5]*Pensées*, trans. W. F. Trotter (www.eserver.org/philosophy/pascal-pensees.txt), sec. 2, par. 142.

countries resembles a king, attended by the courtiers of the media offering a divine right of choice.

## Measures of Magnitude

Statistics begin—but barely—to convey the sheer magnitude of this in-touchness, access, exposure, plenitude, glut, however we want to think of it.

In 1999, a television set was on in the average American household more than seven hours a day, a figure that has remained fairly steady since 1983. According to the measurements of the A. C. Nielsen Company, the standard used by advertisers and the television business itself, the average individual watched television about four hours a day, not counting the time when the set was on but the individual in question was not watching. When Americans were asked to keep diaries of how they spend their time, the time spent actually watching dropped to a still striking three hours a day—probably an undercount. In 1995, of those who watched, the percentage who watched "whatever's on," as opposed to any specific program, was 43 percent, up from 29 percent in 1979.[6] Though cross-national comparisons are elusive because of differences in measurement systems, the numbers in other industrialized nations seem to be comparable—France, for example, averaging three and a half hours per person.[7] One survey of forty-three nations showed the United States ranking third in viewing hours, after Japan and Mexico. None of this counts time spent discussing programs, reading about their stars, or thinking about either.[8]

Overall, wrote one major researcher in 1990, "watching TV is the dominant leisure activity of Americans, consuming 40 percent of the average person's free time as a primary activity [when people give television their undivided attention]. Television takes up more than half of our free time if you count . . . watching TV while doing something else like eating or reading . . . [or] when you have the set on but you aren't paying attention to it."[9] Sex, race, income, age, and marital status make surprisingly little difference in time spent.[10] Neither, at this writing, has the Internet diminished total media use, even if you don't count the Web as part of the media. While Internet users do watch 28 percent less television, they spend more time than nonusers playing video games and listening to the radio and recorded music—obviously a younger crowd. Long-term users (four or more years) say they go on-line for more than two hours a

[6]Robert D. Putnam, *Bowling Alone: The Collapse and Revival of American Community* (New York: Simon and Schuster, 2000), p. 222, citing John P. Robinson and Geoffrey Godbey, *Time for Life: The Surprising Ways Americans Use Their Time,* 2nd ed. (University Park: Pennsylvania State University Press, 1999), pp. 136–53, 340–41, 222.
[7]This April 2001 figure for individuals fifteen and older comes from Mediamat (Mediametrie www.mediametria.fr/television/mediamat_mensuel/2001/avril.html).
[8]Putnam, *Bowling Alone,* p. 480, citing Eurodata TV (*One Television Year in the World: Audience Report,* April 1999).
[9]John P. Robinson, "I Love My TV," *American Demographics,* September 1990, p. 24.
[10]Robert Kubey and Mihaly Csikszentmihalyi, *Television and the Quality of Life: How Viewing Shapes Everyday Experience* (Hillsdale, N.J.: Lawrence Erlbaum Associates, 1990), pp. 71–73.

day, and boys and girls alike spend the bulk of their Internet time entertaining themselves with games, hobbies, and the like.[11] In other words, the Internet redistributes the flow of unlimited media but does not dry it up. When one considers the overlapping and additional hours of exposure to radio, magazines, newspapers, compact discs, movies (available via a range of technologies as well as in theaters), and comic books, as well as the accompanying articles, books, and chats about what's on or was on or is coming up via all these means, it is clear that the media flow into the home—not to mention outside—has swelled into a torrent of immense force and constancy, an accompaniment *to* life that has become a central experience *of* life.

11      The place of media in the lives of children is worth special attention—not simply because children are uniquely impressionable but because their experience shapes everyone's future; if we today take a media-soaked environment for granted, surely one reason is that we grew up in it and can no longer see how remarkable it is. Here are some findings from a national survey of media conditions among American children aged two through eighteen. The average American child lives in a household with 2.9 televisions, 1.8 VCRs, 3.1 radios, 2.6 tape players, 2.1 CD players, 1.4 video game players, and 1 computer. Ninety-nine percent of these children live in homes with one or more TVs, 97 percent with a VCR, 97 percent with a radio, 94 percent with a tape player, 90 percent with a CD player, 70 percent with a video game player, 69 percent with a computer. Eighty-eight percent live in homes with two or more TVs, 60 percent in homes with three or more. Of the 99 percent with a TV, 74 percent have cable or satellite service.[12] And so on, and on, and on.

12      The uniformity of this picture is no less astounding. A great deal about the lives of children depends on their race, sex, and social class, but access to major media does not. For TV, VCR, and radio ownership, rates do not vary significantly among white, black, and Hispanic children, or between girls and boys. For television and radio, rates do not vary significantly according to the income of the community.[13]

13      How accessible, then, is the media cavalcade at home? Of children eight to eighteen, 65 percent have a TV in their bedrooms, 86 percent a radio, 81 percent a tape player, 75 percent a CD player. Boys and girls are not significantly different in possessing this bounty, though the relative usages do vary by medium. Researchers also asked children whether the television was "on in their homes

[11]UCLA Center for Communication Policy, *The UCLA Internet Report: Surveying the Digital Future,* November 2000, pp. 10, 17, 18, 14 (www.ccp.ucla.edu).

[12]Donald F. Roberts, *Kids and Media @ the New Millennium* (Menlo Park, Calif.: Henry J. Kaiser Family Foundation, 1999), p. 9, table 1. There were 3,155 children in the sample, including oversamples of black and Hispanic children, to ensure that results in these minority populations would also be statistically significant. As best as a reader can discern, this was a reliable study, with a margin of error of no more than plus-or-minus five percentage points. Since the results for younger children, ages two to seven, come from parents' reports, they may well be conservative, since parents may be uninformed of the extent of their children's viewing or may be underplaying it in order not to feel ashamed before interviewers.

[13]Ibid, p. 11, tables 3-A, 3-B, 3-C.

even if no one is watching 'most of the time,' 'some of the time,' 'a little of the time,' or 'never.'" Homes in which television is on "most of the time" are termed *constant television households*. By this measure, 42 percent of all American households with children are constant television households. Blacks are more likely than whites or Hispanics to experience TV in their lives: 56 percent of black children live in constant television households (and 69 percent have a TV in their bedrooms, compared to 48 percent of whites). The lower the family education and the median income of the community, the greater the chance that a household is a constant television household.[14]

As for time, the average child spent six hours and thirty-two minutes per day exposed to media of all kinds, of which the time spent reading books and magazines—not counting schoolwork—averaged about forty-five minutes. For ages two to seven, the average for total media was four hours and seventeen minutes; for ages eight to thirteen, eight hours and eight minutes, falling to seven hours and thirty-five minutes for ages fourteen to eighteen.[15] Here, race and social class do count. Black children are most exposed, followed by Hispanics, then whites. At all age levels, the amount of exposure to all media varies inversely with class, from six hours and fifty-nine minutes a day for children in households where the median income for the zip code is under $25,000 to six hours and two minutes for children whose zip code median income is over $40,000. The discrepancy for TV exposure is especially pronounced, ranging from three hours and six minutes a day for children whose zip code incomes are under $25,000 to two hours and twenty-nine minutes for children whose zip code incomes are over $40,000.[16] Still, these differences are not vast. Given everything that divides the rich from the poor, the professional from the working class—differences in physical and mental health, infant mortality, longevity, safety, vulnerability to crime, prospects for stable employment, and so on—the class differences in media access and use are surprisingly slender. So are the differences between American and western European children, the latter averaging

[14]Ibid., pp. 13–15, tables 4, 5-A, 5-B, 6. In general, fewer western European or Israeli children than Americans have TVs in their bedrooms, but 70 percent in Great Britain do. Next highest in Europe is 64 percent in Denmark. The lows are 31 percent in Holland and 24 percent in Switzerland. Leen d'Haenens, "Old and New Media: Access and Ownership in the Home," in Sonia Livingstone and Moira Bovill, eds., *Children and Their Changing Media Environment: A European Comparative Study* (London: Lawrence Erlbaum Associates, 2001), p. 57.

[15]Roberts, *Kids and Media*, pp. 21–23, tables 8-C, 8-D.

[16]The same point applies to differences in media use throughout the prosperous world. As the economist Adair Turner writes: "European Internet penetration lags the US by 18 to 24 months. When cars or television sets were first introduced, the lag was more like 15 years. . . . The shortness of the lag also suggests that social concern about a 'digital divide,' whether within or between nations, is largely misplaced. . . . Time lags between different income groups in the penetration of personal computers, Internet connections or mobile phones are much shorter, once again because all these products are cheap. . . . At the global level the same scepticism about a digital divide should prevail. Africa may lag 15 years or so behind US levels of PC and Internet penetration, but it lags more like a century behind in basic literacy and health care." Adair Turner, "Not the e-conomy," *Prospect* (London), April 2001 (www.prospect-magazine.co.uk/highlights/essay_turner_april01).

six hours a day total, though in Europe only two and a quarter of those hours are spent with TV.[17]

15       All such statistics are crude, of course. Most of them register the time that people *say* they spend. They are—thankfully—not checked by total surveillance. Moreover, the meaning of *exposure* is hard to assess, since the concept encompasses rapt attention, vague awareness, oblivious coexistence, and all possible shadings in between. As the images glide by and the voices come and go, how can we assess what goes on in people's heads? Still, the figures do convey some sense of the media saturation with which we live—and so far we have counted only what can be counted at home. These numbers don't take into account the billboards, the TVs at bars and on planes, the Muzak in restaurants and shops, the magazines in the doctor's waiting room, the digital displays at the gas pump and over the urinal, the ads, insignias, and logos whizzing by on the sides of buses and taxis, climbing the walls of buildings, making announcements from caps, bags, T-shirts, and sneakers. To vary our experience, we can pay to watch stories about individuals unfold across larger-than-life-size movie screens, or visit theme parks and troop from image to image, display to display. Whenever we like, on foot or in vehicles, we can convert ourselves into movable nodes of communication, thanks to car radios, tape, CD, and game players, cell phones, beepers, Walkmen, and the latest in "personal communication systems"—and even if we ourselves refrain, we find ourselves drawn willy-nilly into the soundscape that others broadcast around us.

16       Crucially, who we are is how we live our time—or *spend* it, to use the term that registers its intrinsic scarcity. What we believe, or say we believe, is less important. We vote for a way of life with our time. And increasingly, when we are not at work or asleep, we are in the media torrent. (Sometimes at work, we are also there, listening to the radio or checking out sports scores, pin-ups, or headlines on the Internet.) Steadily more inhabitants of the wealthy part of the world have the means, incentives, and opportunities to seek private electronic companionship. The more money we have to spend, the more personal space each household member gets. With personal space comes solitude, but this solitude is instantly crowded with images and soundtracks. To a degree that was unthinkable in the seventeenth century, life experience has become an experience in the presence of media.

[17]Johannes W. J. Beentjes et al, "Children's Use of Different Media: For How Long and Why?" in Livingstone and Bovill, eds., *Children and Their Changing Media Environment*, p. 96.

## COMPREHENSION

1. What does Gitlin's title mean? How are the concepts of "supersaturation" and "disposable feeling" reflected in the essay?
2. Summarize Gitlin's treatment of Vermeer. Who was Vermeer? How, according to the writer, would Vermeer art be produced today?

3. List some of the facts and statistics that the writer presents to support his idea that we are caught in a "media torrent."

## RHETORIC

1. What is Gitlin's argument? Where does he state his claim most clearly? What appeals to logic, ethics, and emotion does he make? Does he rely on his own opinions? Justify your answer.
2. How does the writer maintain unity between the two parts of this essay? Why, for example, does he open his essay with the story of Vermeer? How does Vermeer serve as a unifying element? What other unifying motifs can you find?
3. What varieties of evidence does the writer provide to bolster his argument? Does he rely on anecdotal or actual evidence? How do you know?
4. The writer employs a range of rhetorical strategies in this essay. Point to places where he uses description, comparison and contrast, classification, definition, and causal analysis.
5. Is the author's style personal, informal, or formal? How does this style explain Gitlin's relationship to his audience and the expectations he holds of his readers?
6. What strategy does the writer use in his conclusion? Is this strategy effective? Why or why not?
7. What do Gitlin's footnotes add to the essay? Why are they important?

## WRITING

1. Write an essay in which you explain how one medium—television or the Internet, for example—has affected or changed your life. Make sure that you provide adequate detail or evidence.
2. Write a comparative essay in which you analyze the similarities and differences between an "old" and a "new" component of the media—actual books and recordings of books, or telephones and cell phones, for example.
3. **Writing an Argument:** Write an essay in which you either agree or disagree with Gitlin's claim that increasingly "we are in a media torrent." Use appeals to logic, ethics, and emotion to advance your claim. Make certain that you have adequate evidence to support your major and minor propositions.

www.mhhe.com/
**mhreader**

For more information on Todd Gitlin, go to:
**More Resources > Ch. 9 Media & Pop Culture**

# Escape from Wonderland: Disney and the Female Imagination

### Deborah Ross

*Deborah Ross is professor of English at Hawai'i Pacific University, where she teaches writing, literature, and humanities. She specializes in popular culture, especially from the perspective of gender. In the following research paper, published in a 2004 issue of* Marvels & Tales: Journal of Fairy-Tale Studies, *Ross analyzes a series of Disney films, all based on children's books and fairy tales; she evaluates the Disney ideology as it affects the imaginative and actual lives of girls.*

1   In 1989, Disney's little mermaid first asked the musical question, "When's it my turn?" She asked it again in 1996, when her movie was re-released in theaters, and she continues to ask it, frequently, in many of our living rooms. Never has a protagonist had so many turns to demand a turn: yet, seemingly, she remains unsatisfied. If even the heroine in a Disney "girls' movie" does not enjoy being a girl, how must the girls watching her feel about it?

2   Behind this gender question lurks a larger political one. If Ariel's feminist rhetoric is undercut by more conservative elements in her movie, so is the environmentalism of *The Lion King*, the multiculturalism of *Pocahontas*, the valuing of difference in *The Hunchback of Notre Dame*—in short, all the quasi-liberal sentiments that focus groups have no doubt caused to grace the surface of the last decade's Disney features. Ideology in Disney is a much vexed question, and I will not attempt here to untangle a knot which began forming for critics when Walt first denied having any politics back in the thirties, and which has only grown in mass and complexity since his death, as his corporation's management style has evolved to cope with a burgeoning staff of artists and technicians, changing public tastes, and changing perceptions of those tastes.

3   One generalization I do suggest, however, is that Disney the man and the corporation are known for a belief in control. The top-down management style Disney epitomizes—Auschwitz (Giroux 55), or Mouschwitz (Lewis 88), is a frequent analogy—thrives on homogeneity and rigid adherence to rules. These are features often decried in Disney production and product, both by critics of capitalism, such as Benjamin and Adorno,[1] and by far less radical proponents of individualism and open debate, from early Disney biographer Richard Schickel to educator Henry Giroux. Yet imagination, the company's major commodity,

---

[1] Miriam Hansen discusses Benjamin's and Adorno's objections to Disney in some detail. Jack Zipes's critique of Disney also occurs within a larger argument about the "freezing" of fairy tales into myths to perpetuate bourgeois, patriarchal values (see his Introduction and Chapter 3).

does not easily lend itself to a program of control. To encourage imagination in artists, and arouse it in viewers, is to invite unique self-expression rather than homogeneity, and spontaneity rather than predictability. Link imagination to the animated cartoon, an art form with roots in dada, surrealism, and radical politics, and matters could well get out of hand.[2]

I believe that this conflict between control and imaginative freedom is vis- 4 ible in the animated features that have come out of the Disney studios, from *Snow White and the Seven Dwarfs* to *Lilo and Stitch*. Of course, ambiguity is rarely viewed now as either a moral or an aesthetic flaw, and the presence of elements that contradict each other may well be preferable to consistent, monologic disapproval of imagination. Neither, however, do conflict and contradiction in themselves necessarily create a space for viewers to question values and exercise judgment. Much depends on how the elements relate to each other, or how an audience is likely to relate them. An audience even partially looking for guides to behavior along with entertainment will have to resolve apparent ambiguities into one suggested course of action. Giroux's attack on Disney rests on the contention that for children, these movies, however apparently bland, do have a didactic effect (18). For them, ambiguity at its best ultimately resolves into a connected but complex world view that embraces difference and spontaneity; at its worst, it can produce confusion and anxiety.

I wish to explore the overall impressions these films may give children 5 about the value of their own imaginations, and thus about their own value as unique individuals able to envision, and eventually to enact, change. In particular, to get back to Ariel, I am concerned about what girls may learn about this potentially explosive aspect of their characters that could so easily burst the bounds of traditional femininity. To help answer this question, I have chosen to examine the way various elements of image, story, and dialogue interact to influence the valuation of imagination in three of Disney's girls' movies: *Alice in Wonderland* (1951), *The Little Mermaid* (1989), and *Beauty and the Beast* (1991, re-released 2001).

I have chosen these three because, although one might be called "prefemi- 6 nist" and the other two "post-," all specifically concern young women who fantasize about a life more vivid and exciting than their reality. I will suggest that some of these films' discomfort with female imagination has roots far back in didactic narrative for girls by looking at Charlotte Lennox's 1759 novel, *The Female Quixote,* which concerns the fortunes of a young woman who might be considered the great-grandmother, or prototype, of the Disney heroine. Then, comparing the three Disney movies with their written fairy-tale sources, I will show how much more confusing a many-tongued message can become when it is told in pictures as well as words.

---

[2]Janet Wasko notes that Disney deliberately avoided the more "anarchistic and inventive" styles of animation employed at other studios (115). My own belief, on which my approach to Disney is based, is that where there is animation, anarchy can never be wholly suppressed. For discussion of the roots of animation in surrealism and dada, see Inez Hedges.

7    Girls have been learning from stories where to draw the line between fantasy and reality probably since the first story was told, but one sees this didactic purpose especially clearly beginning in the seventeenth century, when romances and literary fairy tales were first written specifically for, about, and even by women. Samuel Johnson was greatly concerned about the effects of fiction on "the young, the ignorant, and the idle," and Paul Hunter has shown that there was indeed a class of new readers early in the eighteenth century who were socially displaced and looking to novels for moral and social guidance as well as entertainment (Hunter 271–72). From that time till the present, conservative authors have used romances and novels to teach girls that their dreams are dangerous and of little relevance to their daily lives. Progressive or feminist authors, on the other hand, have encouraged young women readers' belief in fantasy to help them visualize what they want, perhaps as a first step toward going after it. For example, it can be argued (as I have done elsewhere) that European women's experience with romantic fiction gradually gained them the right, first, to refuse to cooperate in arranged marriages, and eventually, to choose husbands for themselves.[3]

8    Charlotte Lennox's *The Female Quixote* illustrates both these conservative and progressive plot patterns, for it both draws upon and criticizes earlier romances, which themselves often both celebrated and punished female imagination and expressiveness.[4] Therefore, like Disney's movies today, which also use material from the romance and fairy-tale tradition, Lennox's novel can be more muddling than enlightening to young people seeking instruction on the conduct of real life. As the title suggests, the premise is that a young girl is at least as likely to have her head turned by reading romances as Cervantes's knight-errant had been over a century before. Appropriately, the romances devoured by this quixote, Arabella, are the largely female-centered French romances of d'Urfé and Scudéry, which focus more on love than on questing, and in which males are present mainly either to carry off or rescue heroines. A reader who takes too literally stories in which women wield such power, albeit of a limited kind, will not adjust well to woman's lot: being ignored, submitting always to others' convenience, like Jane Austen in her letters, perpetually waiting to be "fetched" by a male relative (Austen 9–10). Thus Arabella's reading sets her up to make many ridiculous mistakes, and ultimately to be humbled, or humiliated, when she learns her own real unimportance.

9    The novel shows its author's ambivalence about Arabella's fantasy in several ways. Overtly, she presents it as an adolescent error the heroine must grow out of in order to find happiness. Yet her very frank satire of the world to which Arabella's cure forces her to conform leaves readers wondering, along with the heroine, whether the world of romance might not be preferable. Romances also receive

---

[3]I develop this argument in *The Excellence of Falsehood*. Marina Warner (169, 277–78) and Jack Zipes (21–23, 28) discuss the seventeenth-century *précieuses'* preoccupation with the issue of forced marriage.

[4]Warner discusses ambivalence about the old woman or "Mother Goose" figure who narrates fairy tales throughout the first half of *From the Beast to the Blonde,* and more specifically the power of the female voice in her discussion of "The Little Mermaid" (394).

implicit support from the central "real" narrative's resemblance to romance: beautiful heroine, beloved by the perfect man, whom after trials and separations she marries, presumably to live happily ever after. If the novel presents a romantic story under the guise of realism, then perhaps Arabella is not so quixotic after all.

*The Female Quixote* thus presents contradictory impressions about the worthiness of the heroine's desires, the degree to which those desires are ultimately fulfilled or frustrated, and the amount of satisfaction with the outcome the tone directs the reader to feel. Critics of our own time naturally enjoy this ambivalence (the novel has had a comeback of sorts in the last decades and is available in paperback), which particularly lends itself to feminist approaches of the *Madwoman in the Attic*, conformist text–radical subtext variety. Yet the fact that this novel might well make a madwoman out of any young female reader looking for a framework for understanding life should also be part of our critical awareness. Critics may find it a useful model for highlighting similar constellations of ideological paradox in other stories about women's imagination, stories which also leave their audiences struggling to integrate contradictory messages.  10

Disney's female quixotes are at least as sorely beset by ambiguity as Arabella. The heroines' fantasies reveal desires for many things, including novelty, excitement, power, sex, and knowledge. Some of these desires are ridiculed, others respected; some are fulfilled, others surrendered. And the paradoxes in the plots are further complicated by words and images that seem at times to be telling stories of their own.  11

The presence of conservative elements in Disney's *Alice in Wonderland* is not surprising, considering that it was released in 1951, when "Hollywood's dark prince" was still very much alive, fighting unions, castigating the League of Women Voters, and exerting strong control over the studio's output.[5] One would perhaps not expect, though, to find an American movie of the mid-twentieth century so much more stereotypically Victorian than its nineteenth-century British source.  12

Of course, Lewis Carroll's *Alice's Adventures in Wonderland* and *Through the Looking Glass* are not typical of Victorian children's literature. In particular, most girls' stories of this era promoted humility, devotion, punctuality, and tidiness, implying that adventure (as a countess once told Lennox's Arabella) is something a nice girl would be wise to avoid (Lennox 365). The Alice stories, on the other hand, present adventure as positive: whether wondrous or frightening, it leads the heroine in the direction of personal growth and control over her surroundings. Alice learns how to manage her size, how to talk back to a queen, and, finally, how to wear the crown of adulthood. Carroll celebrates childhood as a brief, fleeting time in which even girls may follow talking rabbits before being overtaken by the "dull reality" (115) of womanhood.  13

[5]I refer here to the title of Marc Eliot's Disney biography. Holly Allen and Michael Denning discuss politics at the Disney studio during the 1940s. For a full discussion of Disney's rather complex politics, see Steven Watts.

14     The Disney movie begins with the same positive message about girls' fantasies. In her opening conversation, Disney's Alice, like Carroll's, expresses the usual quixotic desires: to escape boredom (with lessons), to satisfy curiosity (about the white rabbit), and above all, to exert power. Things would be different "in my world," she notes, though her sister ridicules her ambition. Books, for one thing, would all have pictures—a remark given to Alice by Carroll in a way that almost invites someone to make an Alice movie. The first few minutes of the movie do seem to deliver what Alice wants by introducing such pictorial wonders as singing flowers and surrealistic insects.

15     Soon, however, the plot darkens, signaled by small but significant cuts and alterations in the original dialogue. Speaking with the Cheshire Cat, who tells her everyone in the neighborhood is mad, Alice speaks Carroll's line, "But I don't want to go among mad people" (63). The cat responds that everyone in Wonderland is mad, but he does not go on to say that Alice too is mad, so that already Disney's Alice is presented as out of her element, the lone sane and rational creature among lunatics.

16     After the mad tea party, in a section of plot invented for the movie, Disney's Alice has had enough craziness and wants to go home. Overjoyed to find what looks like a path—symbolic of her now acknowledged need for order and direction—she is reduced to helpless tears when it is erased by a fanciful broom creature. She then passively sits down to wait to be rescued, all the while lecturing herself about the importance of reason and patience, and berating herself for the curiosity that once again has led her into trouble. The movie takes a line from early in the story, "She generally gave herself very good advice (though she very seldom followed it)" (23), puts it in the first person, and makes it the center of a self-lacerating musical lament in which Alice abandons for good her fantasy of excitement and power to dwindle into a tiny, forlorn figure in the center of a large, dark frame. In the end of the movie, the defiance and assertiveness of the line, "You're only a pack of cards," are lost, as she utters it while fleeing for her life from the menacing gang of wonders she has created. She is saved, not by facing them down with dawning maturity and confidence, like the "real" Alice, but by waking up.[6]

17     British reviewers at the time of the movie's release, when the militantly innocuous Enid Blyton held sway over English children's imaginations, objected to Disney's "anarchic" alteration of what they saw as a serene and placid children's tale (Allan 137). But Carroll's story is in fact far more tolerant of anarchy, in the sense of irrationality, than the Disney version. The images used to tell the story further support this rationalist message. Despite Disney artist Claude Coats's comment that the staff had "let [them]selves go with some wild designs" (Allan 138), the visuals in fact are rather staid and restrained, mainly literal, representational renderings of the story done in the highly finished, realistic style for which the studio was famous. The fall down the rabbit hole, for

[6]Donald Britton comments that in the Disney cartoon universe, "children don't become adults; rather, adults kill children" (120).

example, which marks Alice's entry into the dream state, might have lent itself to surrealistic treatment like that of *Dumbo's* "Pink Elephants on Parade" sequence, but instead it is simply a serial listing in images of the objects Carroll mentions that Alice sees on her way down.

Surrealism does appear, briefly, in the visual puns formed by the caterpil- 18 lar's smoke (as he asks "why [k]not"), and in the wild proliferation of crockery at the tea party, the cups and saucers truly "animated" and seeming to breed like, well, rabbits. Yet the story-line ensures that just as this style reaches its climax, Alice is reaching the limits of her fear of imagination. What might have been delightful Daliesque creatures—telephone-ducks, drum-frogs—function rather to frighten the heroine at a point in the plot when she has rejected all this "nonsense" and is anxious to get home to write a book about it.[7] Writing a story, she has decided, is much safer than living one.

Thus all elements combine to entrap the unwary viewer: to entice her to 19 fantasize—even to pay money for the privilege—and then to make her feel, like Alice, guilty and ashamed.

Contrasting Alice's defeated whining with Ariel's anthem of independence in 20 *The Little Mermaid*, one is apt to feel girls have come a long way. Here, as Laura Sells and Marina Warner observe, the tale on which the movie is based is ostensibly more conservative than Disney's retelling (Sells 176, 177, 181; Warner 397, 403).[8] Hans Christian Andersen's story is a tragic celebration of feminine self-sacrifice. His mermaid fantasizes about becoming human partly because, like Alice, she is curious about a world she has only glimpsed (here, from below rather than from above). But that world interests her mainly because in it dwells a man who resembles a handsome statue she already adores. Her love is partly sexual, of course, since she needs to be human from the waist down to win the hero. But her ultimate desire is spiritual, for only by marrying a human can a mermaid, who normally lives three hundred years and then turns into sea foam, gain a soul and eternal life.

In pursuit of this desire Andersen's mermaid is willing to spend all she has: 21 her voice, her health, and eventually her life. She buys her new legs, from which blood oozes with every agonizing step, by letting the sea witch cut out her tongue. The permanent loss of her voice means playing dumb in more ways than one, as she can only listen demurely as the prince lectures her about her own world, the sea (166).[9] Failing to bring the prince to a proposal, she could save her own life by killing him, but she chooses instead to die. Her many acts of self-torture earn her a slight reprieve as she is turned into a spirit of the air, instead of sea-foam, and given a chance to gain a soul by performing more self-less deeds. Andersen gives her this reward, not for having a dream, but for

[7]Dali had been at the studio in 1946, and Robin Allan believes his influence was still apparent in *Alice* (137).
[8]See also Wasko 134.
[9]See Warner's discussion on the significance of this silence, and of the blood which in Andersen's tale connects pain with the dawning of female sexuality (387–408).

desiring martyrdom. No real authorial punishment is needed for a female quixote so intent on punishing herself.

22        Naturally in the Disney version the mutilation and blood would have to go.
But much more would have to be altered to make this tragic story look and sound
so convincingly like a triumph of adolescent self-will and entitlement, as befit the
close of the "me decade." (Warner comments on how often, while she can speak,
Ariel utters the verb "want" [403].) For example, instead of making the mermaid
love the human world because she loves a human, the movie has Ariel love a human mainly because she is already curious enough about his world to have collected a cave full of human souvenirs (in Andersen's story this collection belongs
to a mermaid sister). Like Alice before her initiation, Ariel imagines this other
world as in a sense more her own than her actual world. She believes it to be a
utopia of free movement: she dreams of legs first for "jumping" and "dancing"
and "strolling," and only secondarily for marrying.

23        There is nothing masochistic about this mermaid's fantasy; nor is she willing to sacrifice herself to fulfill it, though she is willing to gamble. Her voice, for
example, is not permanently lost but poured into a shell, ready to be returned
to her if she succeeds, and she has every intention of succeeding. Eighties heroine that she is, she means to have it all: voice, soul, legs, and husband.

24        For the most part, the movie seems to present this female quixote's fantasy
positively and reward her with her desire, as the older generation, in the person
of her father, learns to abandon prejudice and let teenagers live their own lives.
But there are undercurrents here, so to speak, that work against the theme of
imaginative freedom. The odd thing about Ariel's quixotism—what makes the
audience recognize it *as* quixotism—is that the exotic world of her fantasy is, to
us, boring and commonplace. Even a two-year-old viewer knows, as the heroine does not, that forks are not used to comb hair, and that human fathers do
indeed "reprimand their daughters," just like old King Triton. Thus we laugh at
Ariel's naïve reveries, as Andersen's listeners must have laughed at his mermaid's amazed reaction to birds (150). In the end, it seems ludicrous that Ariel
should put so much rebellious energy into becoming the girl next door.

25        The visual style of the movie makes Andersen's painful story seem oddly
encouraging by comparison. Andersen shifts points of view back and forth between the mermaids, who see our world as exotic, and his own audience, who
glamorize the unknown world below. He provides lavish descriptions of the
shore as well as the sea in order to reawaken his listeners' sense of wonder at
their own city lights, sunsets, forests, and hills (151–52). An outsider's desire to
live here thus becomes quite understandable. The movie contains no such balance, for beauty and splendor are mainly found "Under the Sea," the title of the
dizzying production number in which Sebastian the crab tries to convince Ariel
that there's no place like home. Here creatures and objects are surrealistically
combined and transformed into an underwater orchestra. Here in abundance
are the magical bubbles that have signaled fun with physics in Disney movies
from *Snow White* to *Dumbo* to *Cinderella* The world of humans, in contrast,
though picturesque, is static and finite. When Ariel takes a bath at Eric's palace,

while mundane, gossiping laundresses wash her clothes, one is forced to notice that bubbles here just don't *do* anything. Similarly, Grimsby's pipe, which Ariel mistakes for a musical instrument, produces more soot than smoke—nothing approaching the punning puffs from the caterpillar's hookah in *Alice,* or even the smoky ink that billows about in the sea witch's cave. Clearly, Sebastian is right: it is "better down where it's wetter."

The images the movie uses to tell the story thus give its trendy feminism a 26 reverse spin. Whatever Ariel might *say,* or sing, what we see her *do* is flee a world of infinite possibility to settle in the land of the banal. Her fantasy is a sort of anti-fantasy. Yes, she gets her legs, she makes her stand, she marches—but only down the aisle, to marry some guy named Eric.

Many fairy tales, and many more movies, end with a wedding, and for this reason 27 they often draw censure from critics, such as Janet Wasko (116) and Elizabeth Bell (114, 155), who would like to see our daughters presented with other options. Without question there ought to be more than one girls' story out there, relentlessly repeated with minor variations. I would also argue, however, that just as in life there are marriages and marriages, so in fiction living happily ever after is not always a euphemism for dying. When the marriage seems to grant the heroine true personal fulfillment and possibilities for further growth, the ending may actually seem like the beginning of a new life. Such is the case with *Beauty and the Beast,* a tale endowed by ancient archetypes with a feminine power that resists the attempts of individual authors, such as Madame Leprince de Beaumont in 1757, to tie its heroine down to mediocrity. With *The Little Mermaid* behind us, we might expect Disney's version to dole out a similarly dull and didactic message, clothed in mock-progressive nineties clichés of gender equality. But in Disney's *Beauty and the Beast,* thanks in part to the screenplay by Linda Woolverton (the first woman writer of a Disney animated feature), imagination flows freely in the words and the images, allowing the tale to work its magic.[10]

One problem with the plot that ends in marriage, of course, is its reduction 28 of the heroine to an object of desire, and therefore a heroine actually named Beauty would not, on the face of it, seem like a good role model. In this tale, however, with its roots penetrating beyond the Cupid and Psyche tale from Apuleius's *The Golden Ass* to very old stories about beast bridegrooms (Warner 275; Zipes 24–25), the heroine is more subject than object because her quest for a desirable mate drives the plot. (Apuleius intensifies the female point of view by having the tale narrated by an old woman [Warner 275].) Of course, the whole question of the story's sexual politics hinges on whether the heroine's desire can be consciously controlled, by herself or by others; whether, as is often said in Christian wedding ceremonies, love is an act of will rather than a feeling; whether, therefore, she can make herself love the one she "ought." Conservative versions of *Beauty and the Beast* do tend to assume such schooling of the will is possible, as Jack Zipes emphasizes (29–40). Nevertheless, an important feature

[10]See Bell 114; Murphy 133–34; Warner 313.

even in such versions is that the beast, though he may be dutifully or even cheerfully endured, cannot become a handsome prince until the heroine actively wants him, truly chooses him for reasons of her own. The young female audience is thus reassured that sex in conjunction with love is pleasant rather than frightening (Bettelheim 306; Warner 312–13); in other words, the beast of one's choice is not a beast at all.

29      At about the same time Charlotte Lennox was composing *The Female Quixote,* Madame Leprince de Beaumont, with similar concerns about young women's imaginations, was dressing this ancient tale in anti-romance, turning to her own purpose a Scudérian vocabulary of love that, to her readers, would be all too familiar. Beauty feels "esteem" for the Beast because of his "great service" to her, and eventually she comes to feel "tenderness" for him as she wants to care for him and ease his distress (Beaumont 37). Out of this tenderness comes a desire to marry him—including, one supposes, some sexual feeling. The romance code word for active sexual desire—"inclination"—never appears.[11] By telling her young readers that esteem and tenderness are the best basis for marriage, Beaumont warns them not to wait for the handsome, witty lover of their fantasies; in the closing words of the rewarding fairy: "You have preferred virtue before either wit or beauty, and you deserve to find one in whom all these are united" (47). In this way, the author joins the tradition of conservative writers who urge girls to face reality and, to the very limited extent they will be permitted to choose, to choose wisely.[12] Still, while schooling the reader in what she ought to desire, Beaumont cannot avoid conveying the importance of the heroine's will, for until Beauty desires the Beast, a beast he will remain.

30      The Disney movie reaches past Beaumont to draw upon older strains of the story. For example, here, as in some older versions, including that of Beaumont's immediate predecessor, Madame de Villeneuve (Warner 290–91), it is the Beast rather than Beauty who is supposed to learn self-control. The heroine is therefore permitted—even encouraged—to fantasize to her heart's content. Where Beaumont only noted that Beauty liked to read, Disney enlarges on Belle's taste in books, which turns out to be just like Arabella's: fairy tales and romances about swordfights, magic, a prince in disguise, and above all, a "she" at the center of the action. Nor is she content just to read about "adventure in the great wide somewhere." Given the chance to tour the Beast's library—ordinarily for Belle the greatest of temptations—she chooses instead to explore the forbidden west wing of his castle, as if somehow aware that she will find there the escape from "provincial life" she has been longing and singing for. For all her quixotism, however, Belle, unlike Arabella, is seen as "rather odd" only by her neighbors, not by her audience.

31      Certainly, as several commentators observe, the movie has its share of politically correct modern touches to underscore the heroine's self-determination (Warner 316–17; Zipes 46). Interestingly, however, each apparent innovation in

[11]See the Map of Tender in Scudéry's *Clelia* (1:42).
[12]See Warner 292–94.

fact draws on the French romance tradition that Belle and Arabella revere. Most notably, the movie makes contemporary-sounding statements about gender stereotypes by introducing a new character as foil to the Beast, the hypermasculine Gaston, who boasts in a Sigmund Romberg-ish aria, "I'm especially good at expectorating," "I use antlers in all of my decorating," and "every last inch of me's covered with hair." He is the real beast, of course, an animal who sneers at the Beast for being so openly in touch with his feminine side, "the Male Chauvinist Pig [. . .] that would turn the women of any primetime talkshow audience into beasts themselves" (Jeffords 170). But Gaston is not really new. He dates back, beyond the Cocteau movie often cited as his source, to the French romance villain who loves the heroine selfishly, determined to possess her by force: by winning her in a duel, carrying her off, or scheming to get her parents to give her to him. Gaston arranges to have Belle's eccentric father locked in a madhouse unless she agrees to marry him. Then he nearly kills the Beast under the illusion that the winner gets Belle as prize. The Beast, in contrast, is the romance hero who fights the villain to win the heroine's freedom, not her hand, which he will accept only as her gift. In fact, he would rather die than oppress her. By choosing the Beast over Gaston, Belle helps this ancient story confirm the value of a woman's equal right to a will of her own.

Gaston also helps this movie make another observation mistakenly thought 32 of as modern: that men and women aren't nearly as different as some men would like them to be. This idea is found in women's romantic writing from the seventeenth century on,[13] and it reverberates in Belle's opening song as she wishes for someone who understands her and shares her interests. Naturally she chooses to marry the gentleman who gives her the key to his extensive library, not the "positively primeval" clod who throws her book in the mud with a warning about what happens to society when women are taught to read. And in the end, when the spell is broken and the Beast resumes his original shape, he markedly resembles Belle, unruly bangs and all. By marrying a man who can help her get what she wants, and who wants the same things, symbolically she is marrying an aspect of herself.[14]

The Beast's oddly familiar new face is not the only image in the movie that 33 makes one feel the heroine's fantasy is a worthy one. Much creativity was lavished on the look of the castle that provides the atmosphere of old romance. Although for most of the movie it resembles a Gothic ruin, and Belle comes here at first as a prisoner, it is really a house of magic in which every object is alive, or "animated"—most famously the dinnerware that dances and sings "Be Our Guest." And the enchantment does not quite end with the breaking of the spell, but is rather replaced with a different kind of magic as the castle comes into its original baroque splendor with a seeming infinity of detail, something

[13]See for example the pastoral lyrics of Aphra Behn.
[14]See Clarissa Pinkola Estes for an interpretation of the Beast as an aspect of the heroine's own personality (272–73). Warner also discusses how the beast in modern versions of the tale, including Disney's, functions to help the heroine get in touch with her own inner beast, or sexuality (307–13).

new around every corner, and always a new corner, for the eye to explore. As Belle waltzes with her Prince around that gorgeous marble hall, the title tune welling up around them, one may see as well as feel that she's getting not just a husband, but more books than she can read in a lifetime, and a home as big and beautiful as her imagination.

34   Neither age, divorce, nor parenthood has yet made me cynical enough to see the ending of this movie without a sob of satisfaction. But then Disney did begin training me to react in just that way from a very early age (the first movie I ever saw, at the age of five, was *Sleeping Beauty*). Critics have been warning the public for decades about the Disney program to bring about the complete "invasion and control of children's imaginations" (Schickel 18), as well as the silencing of fairy tales' originally female voice (Warner 416–17); no doubt I am a cipher in the company's success. How much more complete the Disney conquest will become for our children and grandchildren, with the constant replay made possible by video and DVD, is definitely cause for concern.

35      The market forces that drive Disney today are dangerous, to be sure, as is the ideology of the market-place the movies promote, as Giroux and others warn. Fortunately, however, because the overriding goal is self-promotion—because Disney will absorb and use whatever works, or whatever sells the product—the movies lack the philosophical consistency of propaganda.[15] Thus films like *Beauty and the Beast,* which pays more than lip-service to the liberating potential of fantasy, can sometimes appear.

36      Nevertheless, the fact that many Disney movies implant seeds of guilt and fear to spring up along with children's developing imaginations is a serious problem. The mixed messages noticeable in *Alice* are present in earlier movies such as *Dumbo* and "The Sorcerer's Apprentice" in *Fantasia.* They continue in more recent examples such as *Hercules* and *The Hunchback of Notre Dame,* in which only evil and terrifying characters wield the transformative power that is, in essence, the animator's art; thus these movies almost identify themselves as products of black magic.[16] Some recent films seem almost to reject the notion of animation altogether, striking the eye most forcibly with stills such as the battlefield in *Mulan,* or the cathedral of Notre Dame—breathtaking, to be sure, but unlike the Beast's castle, completely static. Clearly the reluctance to embrace imagination with both arms is still present among the many and shifting ideas that make up the Disney ethos.

37      The inconsistencies found in these movies do not lighten either the parent's burden of guiding the young in their adventures with the media, or the critic's task of understanding the various manifestations of culture. On the contrary,

---

[15]Giroux notes inconsistent values among elements in the films (5, 91). Wasko emphasizes consistent elements that make "classic Disney" a recognizable "brand" (3, 152), but does not explore tensions among the elements she lists as consistent, such as "work ethic" vs. "escape fantasy" (114).
[16]A notable exception is *The Emperor's New Groove,* in which magic transformative potions intended as evil by the villain turn positive and bring about both the narrative and visual climax of the movie.

they oblige us to do more than count the number of profane words or violent acts or exposed body parts; and also to do more than catalogue plots, count the numbers of males and females, and quantify relative levels of aggression. Instead, we must watch carefully the interplay of elements within the films and notice how many stories are going on at one time. Watching the faces of our children as they watch, we will often find that imagination, in these movies, is like Alice's garden—just beyond a little locked door, the key to which is tantalizingly, frustratingly out of reach.

## WORKS CITED

*Alice in Wonderland.* Dir. Clyde Geronimi, Hamilton Luske, and Wilfred Jackson. Walt Disney Company, 1951.

Allan, Robin. "Alice in Disneyland." *Sight and Sound* 54 (Spring 1985): 136–38.

Allen, Holly, and Michael Denning. "The Cartoonists' Front." *South Atlantic Quarterly* 92.1 (1993): 89–117.

Andersen, Hans Christian. "The Little Mermaid." *Hans Christian Andersen: His Classic Fairy Tales.* Trans. Erik Haugaard. Garden City, NY: Doubleday, 1978. 149–70.

Apuleius. *Transformations of Lucius Otherwise Known as the Golden Ass.* Trans. Robert Graves. New York: Noonday, 1998.

Austen, Jane. *Selected Letters.* Oxford: Oxford UP, 1985.

Beaumont, Madame Leprince de. *Beauty and the Beast.* Trans. P. H. Muir. New York: Knopf, 1968.

*Beauty and the Beast.* Dir. Gary Trousdale and Kirk Wise. Walt Disney Company, 1991.

Behn, Aphra. *The Works of Aphra Behn: Poetry.* Ed. Janet Todd. Columbus: Ohio UP, 1992.

Bell, Elizabeth. "Somatexts at the Disney Shop." Bell, Haas, and Sells 107–24.

Bell, Elizabeth, Lynda Haas, and Laura Sells, eds. *From Mouse to Mermaid: The Politics of Film, Gender, and Culture.* Bloomington: Indiana UP, 1995.

Bettelheim, Bruno. *The Uses of Enchantment.* New York: Vintage, 1977.

Britton, Donald. "The Dark Side of Disneyland." *Mythomania: Fantasies, Fables, and Sheer Lies in Contemporary American Popular Art,* By Bernard Welt. Los Angeles: Art Issues, 1996. 113–26.

Carroll, Lewis. *Alice's Adventures in Wonderland and Through the Looking-Glass.* New York: New American Library, 1960.

*Cinderella.* Dir. Hamilton Luske and Wilfred Jackson. Walt Disney Company, 1950.

*Dumbo.* Dir. Ben Sharpsteen. Walt Disney Company, 1941.

Eliot, Marc. *Walt Disney: Hollywood's Dark Prince.* New York: Birch Lane, 1993.

*The Emperor's New Groove.* Dir. Mark Dindal. Walt Disney Company, 2000.

Estes, Clarissa Pinkola. *Women Who Run with the Wolves.* New York: Ballantine, 1992.

*Fantasia*. Dir. Ford Beebe and Bill Roberts. Walt Disney Company, 1942.

Gilbert, Sandra, and Susan Gubar. *The Madwoman in the Attic*. New Haven: Yale UP, 1979.

Giroux, Henry. *The Mouse That Roared: Disney and the End of Innocence*. Lanham, MD: Rowman, 1999.

Hansen, Miriam. "Of Mice and Ducks: Benjamin and Adorno on Disney." *South Atlantic Quarterly* 92.1 (1993): 27–61.

Hedges, Inez. *Languages of Revolt: Dada and Surrealist Literature and Film*. Durham: Duke UP, 1983.

*Hercules*. Dir. Ron Clements and John Musker. Walt Disney Company, 1997.

*The Hunchback of Notre Dame*. Dir. Gary Trousdale and Kirk Wise. Walt Disney Company, 1996.

Hunter. J. Paul. "'The Young, the Ignorant, and the Idle': Some Notes on Readers and the Beginnings of the English Novel." *Anticipations of the Enlightenment in England, France, and Germany*. Ed. Alan Charles Kors and Paul J. Korshin. Philadelphia: U of Pennsylvania P, 1987. 259–82.

Jeffords, Susan. "The Curse of Masculinity." Bell, Haas, and Sells 161–72.

Johnson, Samuel. *The Rambler*. Ed. W. J. Bate and Albrecht B. Strauss. New Haven: Yale UP, 1969.

Lennox, Charlotte. *The Female Quixote, 1759*. Boston: Pandora, 1986.

Lewis, Jon. "Disney after Disney." *Disney Discourse: Producing the Magic Kingdom*. Ed. Eric Smoodin. New York: Routledge, 1994.

*Lilo and Stitch*. Dir. Dean DeBlois and Chris Sanders (III). Walt Disney Company, 2002.

*The Lion King*. Dir. Rob Minkoff and Roger Allers. Walt Disney Company, 1994.

*The Little Mermaid*. Dir. John Musker and Ron Clements. Walt Disney Company, 1989.

*Mulan*. Dir. Tony Bancroft and Barry Cook. Walt Disney Company, 1998.

Murphy, Patrick D. "'The Whole Wide World Was Scrubbed Clean': The Androcentric Animation of Denatured Disney." Bell, Haas, and Sells 125–36.

*Pocahontas*. Dir. Mike Gabriel and Eric Goldberg. Walt Disney Company, 1995.

Ross, Deborah. *The Excellence of Falsehood*. Lexington: UP of Kentucky, 1991.

Schickel, Richard. *The Disney Version*. New York: Simon, 1968.

Scudéry, Madeleine de. *Clelia*. Trans. John Davies. London: Herringman, 1678.

Sells, Laura. "'Where Do the Mermaids Stand?' Voice and Body in *The Little Mermaid*." Bell, Haas, and Sells 175–92.

*The Sleeping Beauty*. Dir. Clyde Geronimi. Walt Disney Company, 1959.

*Snow White and the Seven Dwarfs*. Dir. David Hand. Walt Disney Company, 1938.

Warner, Marina. *From the Beast to the Blonde: On Fairy Tales and Their Tellers*. New York: Noonday, 1994.

Wasko, Janet. *Understanding Disney*. Cambridge, UK: Polity, 2001.

Watts, Steven. "Walt Disney: Art and Politics in the American Century." *Journal of American History* 82.1 (June 1995): 84–110.

Zipes, Jack. *Fairy Tale as Myth/Myth as Fairy Tale*. Lexington: UP of Kentucky, 1994.

# COMPREHENSION

1. How does Ross define the ideology inherent in Disney's films for girls?
2. Summarize the content of the three films that Ross discusses. What similarities and differences does Ross see among them?
3. According to the writer, what is a "female Quixote"? Where does she treat this concept directly and indirectly?

# RHETORIC

1. This essay appeared in a specialized scholarly journal. What "scholarly" elements appear in the paper? How does Ross adjust her style to this specialized audience? What strategies does she use to make the essay accessible to a wider audience?
2. Where does Ross state her claim most clearly? Analyze the varieties of evidence that she uses to support her claim and the minor propositions.
3. How does the writer organize her essay? What are the main divisions, and how do they cohere?
4. Why does Ross cite other scholars and writers? How does this strategy affect the power of her argument?
5. Ross elaborates a definition of the Disney "program" or ideology. What rhetorical strategies does she use to create this extended definition?
6. How effective do you find the concluding paragraph? Justify your response.

# WRITING

1. Select one Disney movie and write an analysis of its "program"—its ethical message or ideology.
2. In an expository essay, explain why children's stories or fairy tales have such a hold on young people's imaginations.
3. **Writing an Argument:** Write a persuasive essay on the benefits of children's literature and film—even the films that Walt Disney produced. Present at least three extended examples to support your claim.

www.mhhe.com/
**mhreader**

For more information on Deborah Ross, go to:
**More Resources > Ch. 9 Media & Pop Culture**

# Synthesis: Connections for Critical Thinking

1. Examine the role of the media in society and the responsibilities or duties to humanity of individuals associated with the media. Use at least three essays from this chapter to illustrate or support your thesis.

2. Define *popular culture,* using the essays of Barry, Gates, Ross, and Steinem as reference points, along with any additional essays that you consider relevant.

3. Compare and contrast Dove's views on television with those of Ross on film.

4. Use the essays of Warshow, Willis, Ross, and Gitlin to explore the connections of media representations to American cultural experience. What strategies do these writers use? Are their goals similar?

5. Use the essays of Gates and Barry to explore the importance of both the causes and effects of the media promoting particular lifestyles to the public.

6. Gates refers to the African American "style" of communicating through music, and Barry presents beer commercials as communicating the traditional "patriotic symbols" of America. Do these authors have similar or differing points of view regarding the issues they address? Refer specifically to selections in each essay to support your view.

7. After reading the essays of Warshow, Willis, Gates, and King, research the issue of the difference between popular entertainment and art. On the basis of your research, discuss whether there are legitimate criteria that distinguish the two forms. Apply these criteria to gangster films, rap music, and horror films.

8. Select several images of real "gangsters" from magazines, or print out images of true gangsters from the Internet. Compare and contrast them with advertisements depicting gangsters from contemporary crime movies such as *Pulp Fiction.* What are the similarities and differences in the subjects' dress, demeanor, facial expression, and so on? What can you conclude from your comparisons?

9. **Network:** Search the Internet using the keywords *television* and *teenagers.* Select three or four sites, and write an expository paper describing the various ways the authors interpret any of the major themes.

chapter *10*

# Literature and the Arts

*Why Do They Matter?*

Imagine a world without fiction, poetry, or drama, without music, art, or other fine arts. We are so accustomed to taking the arts in their totality for granted that it is hard for us to conceive of contemporary culture without them. Our fondness for stories or paintings or any other creative form might help us understand our culture or might even move us to action. Yet the value of various artistic forms doesn't derive exclusively from their ability to tell us something about life. The arts can also take us into an imaginative realm offering perhaps more intense experiences than anything we encounter in the "real" world.

Think of literature and the arts as an exercise in imaginative freedom. You are free to select the books you read, the music that appeals to you, the exhibitions and concerts you attend, and the entertainment software with which you interact. Some of your decisions might be serious and consequential to your education. Other decisions, perhaps to watch a few soap operas on a rainy afternoon or to buy the latest potboiler, are less important. The way you view the arts—whether as a temporary escape from conventional reality or as a way to learn something about the temper of civilization—is entirely a matter of taste. Regardless of your purpose or intent, you approach literature and the arts initially for the sheer exhilaration and pleasure they provide. Art, as Plato observed, is a dream for awakened minds.

The arts awaken you to the power and intensity of the creative spirit. At the same time, you make judgments and evaluations of the nature of your creative encounter. When you assert that you like this painting or dislike that poem, you are assessing the work and the value of the artistic experience. Clearly, you develop taste and become more equipped to discern the more subtle elements of art the more you are exposed to it. Perhaps you prefer to keep your experience of literature and the other arts a pleasurable pastime or an escape from reality. Or you may wish to participate in them as a creative writer, musician, painter, or photographer. Ultimately, you may come to view literature and the arts as a transformational experience, a voyage of discovery in which you encounter diverse peoples and cultures, learn to see the world in creative terms, and begin to perceive your own creative potential in a new light.

## Previewing the Chapter

As you read the essays in this chapter and respond to them in discussion and writing, consider the following questions:

- According to the author, what is the value of the art or literary form under discussion?
- What function does literature or art serve?
- Is the writer's perspective subjective or objective, and why?
- How does the author define his or her subject—whether it is poetry, fiction, art, or photography?
- Is the writer's experience of literature or art similar to or different from your own?
- In what ways do gender and race influence the writer's perspective on the subject?
- What is the main idea that the author wants to present about literature or the arts? Do you agree or disagree with this key concept?
- What have you learned about the importance of literature and the arts from reading these essays?

# Classic and Contemporary Images

## HOW DO WE EVALUATE A WORK OF ART?

*Using a Critical Perspective*   Although "greatness" in art and literature might be in the mind of the beholder, it could be argued that you need certain standards of excellence or judgment to determine the quality of any work. The artist's or writer's control of the medium, the projection of a unique vision, the evidence of a superlative style—all enter into the evaluation process. As you consider the following sculptures by Auguste Rodin and Jeff Koons, try to evaluate their relative worth. Which work reflects greater artistic control? What makes the sculpture appealing, and why? Which work strikes you as "new" or original, or modern? Explain your response and criteria for evaluation.

Auguste Rodin (1840–1917), a French sculptor famous for his bronze and marble figures, is thought by some critics to be one of the greatest portraitists in the history of sculpture. Yet he was also criticized in his time for the excessive realism and sensuousness of his figures. *Walking Man* hints at some of the objections contemporary critics lodged against Rodin's work.

Jeff Koons (b. 1955) is an American artist who, like Rodin, has had his admirers and detractors. Koons studied at the Art Institute of Chicago and elsewhere before becoming a commodities trader in New York City, which helped fund the materials for his art. *Rabbit* reflects Koons's fondness for popular culture and the way in which he takes consumer goods and repositions them as art objects.

# Classic and Contemporary Essays
## How Do We Know It's Good?

E. M. Forster and Francine Prose, one English and the other American, represent two generations and two different literary and cultural styles. Forster, educated at Kings College, Cambridge, was associated with the famous Bloomsbury Group of writers, artists, and bohemians. Prose, removed by geography and time from her predecessor, came to maturity in New York City and Cambridge, Massachusetts. Yet Forster and Prose share a hearty skepticism about the intellectual and artistic universe they inhabit. Each employs an ironic/satiric style—a common voice—to describe their respective artistic realms. Forster is more self-referential, adopting a self-effacing persona to confess his inability to look at pictures. Prose, although she also is an actor in her essay, is more other-directed, willing to attack "ignorance and vulgarity" whenever she sees it. Forster roots his observations in classical art: Michelangelo, Velasquez, van Gogh. In contrast, Prose focuses her eye on Hitler and a certain "First Lady," wondering about both their taste and their commitment to free artistic inquiry. However, both writers have the same purpose in mind—an objective shared by all the writers in this chapter: They want to establish what criteria we can use to determine if any work of art is good or bad, why literature and the arts matter, and what the arts tell us about ourselves, our culture, and our world.

# Not Looking at Pictures

### E. M. Forster

*E(dward) M(organ) Forster (1879–1970), English essayist, novelist, biographer, and
literary critic, wrote several notable works of fiction dealing with the constrictive effects
of social and national conventions on human relationships. These novels include* A
Room with a View *(1908),* Howard's End *(1910), and* A Passage to India *(1924).
In addition, his lectures on fiction, collected as* Aspects of the Novel *(1927), remain
graceful elucidations of the genre. In "Not Looking at Pictures," an essay taken from*
Two Cheers for Democracy *(1939), Forster offers a whimsical account of difficulties
when trying to evaluate art.*

Pictures are not easy to look at. They generate private fantasies, they furnish   1
material for jokes, they recall scraps of historical knowledge, they show landscapes where one would like to wander and human beings whom one would
like to resemble or adore, but looking at them is another matter, yet they must
have been painted to be looked at. They were intended to appeal to the eye, but
almost as if it were gazing at the sun itself the eye often reacts by closing as
soon as it catches sight of them. The mind takes charge instead and goes off on
some alien vision. The mind has such a congenial time that it forgets what set it
going. Van Gogh and Corot and Michelangelo are three different painters, but
if the mind is undisciplined and uncontrolled by the eye, they may all three induce the same mood; we may take just the same course through dreamland or
funland from them, each time, and never experience anything new.

I am bad at looking at pictures myself, and the late Roger Fry enjoyed going   2
to a gallery with me now and then, for this very reason. He found it an amusing
change to be with someone who scarcely ever saw what the painter had painted.
"Tell me, why do you like this, why do you prefer it to that?" he would ask, and
listen agape for the ridiculous answer. One day we looked at a fifteenth-century
Italian predella, where a St. George was engaged in spearing a dragon of the
plesiosaurus type. I laughed. "Now, *what* is there funny in this?" pounced Fry.
I readily explained. The fun was to be found in the expression upon the dragon's face. The spear had gone through its hooped-up neck once, and now startled it by arriving at a second thickness. "Oh dear, here it comes again, I hoped
that was all" it was thinking. Fry laughed too, but not at the misfortunes of the
dragon. He was amazed that anyone could go so completely off the lines. There
was no harm in it—but really, really! He was even more amazed when our en-
thusiasms coincided: "I fancy we are talking about different things," he would
say, and we always were; I liked the mountain-back because it reminded me of
a peacock, he because it had some structural significance, though not as much
as the sack of potatoes in the foreground.

3      Long years of wandering down miles of galleries have convinced me that there must be something rare in those colored slabs called "pictures," something which I am incapable of detecting for myself, though glimpses of it are to be had through the eyes of others. How much am I missing? And what? And are other modern sightseers in the same fix? Ours is an aural rather than a visual age, we do not get so lost in the concert hall, we seem able to hear music for ourselves, and to hear it as music, but in galleries so many of us go off at once into a laugh or a sigh or an amorous day-dream. In vain does the picture recall us. "What have your obsessions got to do with me?" it complains. "I am neither a theatre of varieties nor a spring-mattress, but paint. Look at my paint." Back we go—the picture kindly standing still meanwhile, and being to that extent more obliging than music—and resume the looking-business. But something is sure to intervene—a tress of hair, the half-open door of a summer-house, a Crivelli dessert, a Bosch fish-and-fiend salad—and to draw us away.

4      One of the things that helps us keep looking is composition. For many years now I have associated composition with a diagonal line, and when I find such a line I imagine I have gutted the picture's secret. Giorgione's Castelfranco Madonna has such a line in the lance of the warrior-saint, and Titian's Entombment at Venice has a very good one indeed. Five figures contribute to make up the diagonal; beginning high on the left with the statue of Moses, it passes through the heads of the Magdalene, Mary, and the dead Christ, and plunges through the body of Joseph of Arimathea into the ground. Making a right angle to it, flits the winged Genius of Burial. And to the right, apart from it, and perpendicular, balancing the Moses, towers the statue of Faith. Titian's Entombment is one of my easiest pictures. I look at photographs of it intelligently, and encourage the diagonal and the pathos to reinforce one another. I see, with more than usual vividness, the grim alcove at the back and the sinister tusked pedestals upon which the two statues stand. Stone shuts in flesh; the whole picture is a tomb. I hear sounds of lamentation, though not to the extent of shattering the general scheme; that is held together by the emphatic diagonal, which no emotion breaks. Titian was a very old man when he achieved this masterpiece; that too I realize, but not immoderately. Composition here really has been a help, and it is a composition which no one can miss: the diagonal slopes as obviously as the band on a threshing-machine, and vibrates with power.

5      Unfortunately, having no natural esthetic aptitude, I look for diagonals everywhere, and if I cannot find one thing the composition must be at fault. It is a word which I have learnt—a solitary word in a foreign language. For instance, I was completely baffled by Velasquez's Las Meninas. Wherever was the diagonal? Then the friend I was with—Charles Mauron, the friend who, after Roger Fry, has helped me with pictures most—set to work on my behalf, and cautiously underlined the themes. There is a wave. There is a half-wave. The wave starts up on the left, with the head of the painter, and curves down and up through the heads of the three girls. The half-wave starts with the head of Isabel de Velasco, and sinks out of the canvas through the dwarfs. Responding to these great curves, or inverting them, are smaller ones on the women's dresses or elsewhere. All

these waves are not merely pattern; they are doing other work too—e.g., helping to bring out the effect of depth in the room, and the effect of air. Important too is the pushing forward of objects in the extreme left and right foregrounds, the easel of the painter in the one case, the paws of a placid dog in the other. From these, the composition curves back to the central figure, the lovely child-princess. I put it more crudely than did Charles Mauron, nor do I suppose that his account would have been Velasquez's, or that Velasquez would have given any account at all. But it is an example of the way in which pictures should be tackled for the benefit of us outsiders: coolly and patiently, as if they were designs, so that we are helped at last to the appreciation of something non-mathematical. Here again, as in the case of the Entombment, the composition and the action reinforced one another. I viewed with increasing joy that adorable party, which had been surprised not only by myself but by the King and Queen of Spain. There they were in the looking-glass! Las Meninas has a snapshot quality. The party might have been taken by Philip IV, if Philip IV had had a Kodak. It is all so casual—and yet it is all so elaborate and sophisticated, and I suppose those curves and the rest of it help to bring this out, and to evoke a vanished civilization.

Besides composition there is color. I look for that, too, but with even less 6 success. Color is visible when thrown in my face—like the two cherries in the great grey Michael Sweertz group in the National Gallery. But as a rule it is only material for dream.

On the whole, I am improving, and after all these years, I am learning to get 7 myself out of the way a little, and to be more receptive, and my appreciation of pictures does increase. If I can make any progress at all, the average outsider should do better still. A combination of courage and modesty is what he wants. It is so unenterprising to annihilate everything that's made to a green thought, even when the thought is an exquisite one. Not looking at art leads to one goal only. Looking at it leads to so many.

## COMPREHENSION

1. Why does the author declare, "Pictures are not easy to look at" (paragraph 1)? Why is Forster himself "bad at looking at pictures" (paragraph 2)?
2. What does the author seem to like about art? Why does he persist in viewing artworks, despite his difficulties?
3. What does Forster say about "composition" and "color"?

## RHETORIC

1. What is Forster's purpose in writing this essay? What response does he expect of his audience? How do you know?
2. Identify these allusions in the essay: van Gogh, Corot, Michelangelo (paragraph 1); Roger Fry (paragraph 2); Crivelli, Bosch (paragraph 3); Giorgione, Titian (paragraph 4); and Velasquez (paragraph 5). What do these allusions tell us about the degree of Forster's expertise?

3. Analyze the material presented in the introduction and the strategies employed.
4. How does Forster employ illustration to help structure each paragraph in this essay?
5. Explain the author's use of comparison and contrast in this essay.
6. What elements contribute to the gently humorous tone of this essay?

### WRITING

1. Forster mentions "composition" and "color" as two aspects of art appreciation. Elaborate on these qualities and others in an essay explaining how you evaluate pictures.
2. Analyze a particular work of art based on a museum trip or an illustration.
3. **Writing an Argument:** Forster declares, "Ours is an aural rather than a visual age" (paragraph 3). Do you agree or disagree with his assertion, and why?

| www.mhhe.com/ mhreader | For more information on E. M. Forster, go to: **More Resources > Ch. 10 Literature & Arts** |

# The Universal in the Particular

### Francine Prose

*Francine Prose (b. 1947) was born in Brooklyn. She received degrees from Radcliffe College (BA 1968) and Harvard University (MA, 1969), and today is a widely published writer of fiction and nonfiction for children and adults. Prose has also taught writing at Harvard, the University of Arizona, Warren Wilson College, Johns Hopkins University, and elsewhere. Her fiction includes* Household Saints *(1981) and* Blue Angel *(2000), which was a National Book Award finalist. Her most recent nonfiction work is* Reading like a Writer *(2006). Prose's fiction for children typically reformulates Jewish tales and folklore, as in* Dybbuk: A Story Made in Heaven *(1996). In this essay, published in the* Virginia Quarterly Review *in 2004, Prose targets the aesthetic tastes of Hitler and a certain "First Lady" while asserting the primacy of artists and writers as defenders of free inquiry.*

1  Let me begin with two stories about the bad behavior of two world leaders—or, a world leader and the wife of another world leader—in art museums.

The first concerns Hitler's visit to Berlin's National Gallery in the 1920s. ₂
Enraged to discover that Germany did not possess any work by Michelangelo,
his favorite artist, Hitler was mildly consoled to find a painting by Caravaggio—
Michelangelo Merisi da Caravaggio—whom Hitler thought was the same person as Michelangelo Buonarroti. Next, he became enchanted by Correggio's
erotic depiction of Leda and the Swan, though when his guide discovered him,
transfixed before the painting, Hitler insisted he was only admiring the subtle
play of light and shadow. Finally, and most revealingly, he sought out
Rembrandt's *Man in a Golden Helmet,* an image which, Hitler claimed, proved
that Rembrandt was a true Aryan and that, despite the many works he'd done
in the Jewish Quarter, he had had no real interest in the Jews, after all.

The second, more recent story concerns the visit of the wife of an American ₃
president to a new museum of modern art in a great European city. The museum director was assigned to show the First Lady around. The director shep-
herded the First Lady through the museum for forty minutes, during which the
president's wife said nothing. Finally, she stopped in front of a great work of
modern art and said, "How much does that cost?" The director replied that it
was not for sale, that she did not know, that selling art was not her business.
Another forty minutes went by; again the First Lady said nothing. Finally, the
director showed her one of the museum's finest works, her own favorite piece,
a work of great passion, originality, and intensity. The First Lady was silent for
a moment. Then she said, "How much would I have to pay for that?"

On the surface, both stories are about ignorance and vulgarity, and about ₄
the fact that political power is rarely conducive to art appreciation. But they are
not the same story, and what makes them interesting and useful to us is not
their similarities so much as their differences, which I'll return to in a moment.

As a child, before I'd learned to distinguish between high and low art, between ₅
great and popular literature, one of my favorite novels was Ray Bradbury's
*Fahrenheit 451.* Its subject is book burning—451 degrees Fahrenheit is the temperature at which books catch fire—but I knew that the novel was science fiction. And when I heard about the burning of books by the Nazis, and about the
ruthless, systematic suppression of freedom of speech in other countries, all
that too seemed to me to be, in a way, science fiction. That is, it might as well
have been happening on another planet. I believed that nothing like that could
happen on our planet, because we had those beautiful documents, the Constitution of the United States and the Bill of Rights, to protect our basic freedoms
of speech and expression.

America is a young country, and so it has taken us longer to learn the pain- ₆
ful adult lessons that older countries learned decades and even centuries ago.
Now at last we are old enough to discover what it is like to have an administration with little interest in safeguarding the Constitution and the Bill of Rights,
in protecting our freedoms of speech and expression. In fact, it is against their
economic and political interests to do so. The word *patriotism* is increasingly
being used as a bludgeon with which to attack critics of the shameful war in
Iraq, as a gag to silence dissenters accused of being unpatriotic. There is no

need, as it turns out, to censor the press—throwing journalists into jail is an ugly and potentially unpopular business—since the corporations who own our newspapers and television stations are the same as those that finance our administration, and the news anchorman about to attend a dinner party with our secretary of defense is unlikely to ask him embarrassing questions.

7      Meanwhile, laws have been passed designed to have what we call a "chilling effect" on our determination to exert our constitutionally guaranteed freedoms. For example, the USA PATRIOT Act contains provisions requiring librarians and booksellers to respond to FBI requests for information about what ordinary American citizens are reading.

8      It's become increasingly clear to many American writers and indeed to many American people that something has to be done to resist and counteract this. But the question is, as always, what to do, and how to do it.

9      Last fall, I attended a reading by the great Israeli poet Aharon Shabtai. He is a controversial figure, often accused, in his own country, of being pro-Palestinian, when in fact he is simply pro-human. I admire his work, his courage, his willingness to face the criticism and contempt of his countrymen to stand up for what he believes is right, and what, indeed, is right. There was only one thing he said during his reading that troubled me. He said that his generation had grown up steeped in French philosophy, first Sartre, then Derrida, grown up believing in fine distinctions. But the need to make such distinctions had become paralyzing, incapacitating. The only distinction that mattered now, he said, was the one between good and evil.

10     I suppose I know what he meant, but still it made me uneasy, and, in fact, I disagree. So let's return, for a moment, to those stories about Hitler and the First Lady in the art museums. As I said earlier, it seems to me that the most significant things about these stories are not the similarities but the differences, because these differences, if we look closely, are keys—cautionary, analytical, predictive clues—to the culture, the methods, and the deepest beliefs of two very different regimes. Hitler's response to art was entirely about nationalism, repression, and anti-Semitism. Whereas the First Lady's reflected the heartfelt conviction that the world is a store in which everything—art, culture, passion, human life, if necessary—can be bought and sold and converted into profit.

11     As writers, we are inclined by sensibility to look beneath the surface, to analyze and make distinctions. And even as we insist on preserving our liberties, wherever they are threatened, we need to be conscious of, and hold on to, the freedom to make crucial distinctions, to see clearly, to think intelligently and logically, to avoid the siren songs of prejudice, ideology, nationalism, and sectarianism, of simplistic and reductive rhetoric and propaganda, regardless of their source. As writers, as citizens of the world, we need to remember—as Samuel Beckett said, echoing Chekhov, a century before—"in the particular is contained the universal." This seems especially important as political extremists encourage us to think about one another not as human beings but in categories that grow, daily, at once broader and more narrow, coarser, more ignorant, heartless, and brutal. As writers, trained to observe, we

need to stay exquisitely attuned to the chasm between our own observations of reality and the lies we are being told. And as lovers and producers of literature, we cannot forget what literature continues to teach us: that each of us is a unique entity with something—that mystery called human nature—in common that should be, for us, a bottomless well of empathy and compassion.

## COMPREHENSION

1. According to Prose, what are the similarities and differences in the two stories that she relates? Are the similarities or the differences more important to her, and why?
2. Prose speaks of her own education in art and literature as a child. What did she learn from this exposure?
3. What does the writer say about the connection between art and "preserving our liberties" (paragraph 11)?

## RHETORIC

1. What is your interpretation of Prose's title? How might it suggest a thesis or claim that she intends to make?
2. Why does Prose craft a very brief introductory paragraph? Do you find it effective or suggestive? Why or why not?
3. Why do you think Prose begins the body of her essay with the extended example of Hitler in the Berlin National Gallery? Why is she somewhat opaque in treating the First Lady in paragraph 3, not naming her?
4. After developing her comparative framework in paragraphs 2–5, the writer seemingly moves away from her subjects. How do you explain this shift in strategy?
5. Prose alludes to numerous artists, writers, and works. How do these examples serve to substantiate her claim?
6. What, ultimately, is the argument that Prose wants to advance in this essay? Where does the claim appear most clearly? What overall strategy of argumentation has she used?

## WRITING

1. Write an essay in which you reflect on the role(s) that artists should play in society and culture.
2. Identify a writer, artist, or media personality who has demonstrated a commitment to social and political change. If necessary, conduct online or library research on this figure, and then write an essay demonstrating how he or she contributes to the preservation of our liberties.
3. **Writing an Argument:** Write an essay agreeing or disagreeing with Prose's position that the duty of writers and artists is "to avoid the siren songs of prejudice, ideology, nationalism, and sectarianism . . . "

## Synthesis: Classic and Contemporary Questions for Comparison

1. Both Forster and Prose take art as their subject, but they seem to have different agendas or purposes. Summarize and critique these differences.
2. According to both writers, why is art important? How does each writer support this proposition?
3. Compare the style of each essay. Which writer's style seems more accessible to you, and why?
4. Imagine what Prose might say about Forster's "long years of wandering down miles of galleries." How do you think she would respond to the earlier writer's attempts to appreciate art?

# Hearing Voices

### Linda Hogan

*Linda Hogan (b. 1947) is a Chickasaw poet, novelist, short-story writer, and essayist. She was born in Denver, Colorado, and earned her MA at the University of Colorado. She has been a professor of American and American Indian studies at the University of Minnesota and the University of Colorado. She is one of three Indian writers who were commissioned to co-author a book celebrating the grand opening of the Smithsonian National Museum of the American Indian in 2004. Among her many books are the novel* Mean Spirit *(1990), which was a finalist for the Pulitzer Prize, and the poetry collection* The Book of Medicines *(1993), a finalist for the National Book Critics Circle Award. A versatile writer, she has also published* The Woman Who Watches over the World: A Native Memoir *(2000) and* The Mysterious Journey of the Gray Whale *(2000). In the essay that follows, Hogan offers reflections on the complex interactions of tribal stories, poetry, landscape, and the human condition.*

1 When Barbara McClintock was awarded a Nobel Prize for her work on gene transposition in corn plants, the most striking thing about her was that she made her discoveries by listening to what the corn spoke to her, by respecting the life of the corn and "letting it come."

McClintock says she learned "the stories" of the plants. She "heard" them. ₂ She watched the daily green journeys of growth from earth toward sky and sun. She knew her plants in the way a healer or mystic would have known them, from the inside, the inner voices of corn and woman speaking to one another.

As an Indian woman, I come from a long history of people who have lis- ₃ tened to the language of this continent, people who have known that corn grows with the songs and prayers of the people, that it has a story to tell, that the world is alive. Both in oral traditions and in mythology—the true language of inner life—account after account tells of the stones giving guidance, the trees singing, the corn telling of inner earth, the dragonfly offering up a tongue. This is true in the European traditions as well: Psyche received direction from the reeds and the ants, Orpheus knew the languages of earth, animals, and birds.

This intuitive and common language is what I seek for my writing, work in ₄ touch with the mystery and force of life, work that speaks a few of the many voices around us, and it is important to me that McClintock listened to the voices of corn. It is important to the continuance of life that she told the truth of her method and that it reminded us all of where our strength, our knowing, and our sustenance come from.

It is also poetry, this science, and I note how often scientific theories lead to ₅ the world of poetry and vision, theories telling us how atoms that were stars have been transformed into our living, breathing bodies. And in these theories, or maybe they should be called stories, we begin to understand how we are each many people, including the stars we once were, and how we are in essence the earth and the universe, how what we do travels clear around the earth and returns. In a single moment of our living, there is our ancestral and personal history, our future, even our deaths planted in us and already growing toward their fulfillment. The corn plants are there, and like all the rest we are forever merging our borders with theirs in the world collective.

Our very lives might depend on this listening. In the Chernobyl nuclear ac- ₆ cident, the wind told the story that was being suppressed by the people. It gave away the truth. It carried the story of danger to other countries. It was a poet, a prophet, a scientist.

Sometimes, like the wind, poetry has its own laws speaking for the life of ₇ the planet. It is a language that wants to bring back together what the other words have torn apart. It is the language of life speaking through us about the sacredness of life.

This life speaking life is what I find so compelling about the work of poets ₈ such as Ernesto Cardenal, who is also a priest and was the Nicaraguan Minister of Culture. He writes: "The armadilloes are very happy with this government. . . . Not only humans desired liberation/the whole ecology wanted it." Cardenal has also written "The Parrots," a poem about caged birds who were being sent to the United States as pets for the wealthy, how the cages were opened, the parrots allowed back into the mountains and jungles, freed like the people, "and sent back to the land we were pulled from."

9    How we have been pulled from the land! And how poetry has worked hard to set us free, uncage us, keep us from split tongues that mimic the voices of our captors. It returns us to our land. Poetry is a string of words that parades without a permit. It is a lockbox of words to put an ear to as we try to crack the safe of language, listening for the right combination, the treasure inside. It is life resonating. It is sometimes called Prayer, Soothsaying, Complaint, Invocation, Proclamation, Testimony, Witness. Writing is and does all these things. And like that parade, it is illegitimately insistent on going its own way, on being part of the miracle of life, telling the story about what happened when we were cosmic dust, what it means to be stars listening to our human atoms.

10   But don't misunderstand me. I am not just a dreamer. I am also the practical type. A friend's father, watching the United States stage another revolution in another Third World country, said, "Why doesn't the government just feed people and then let the political chips fall where they may?" He was right. It was easy, obvious, even financially more reasonable to do that, to let democracy be chosen because it feeds hunger. I want my writing to be that simple, that clear and direct. Likewise, I feel it is not enough for me just to write, but I need to live it, to be informed by it. I have found over the years that my work has more courage than I do. It has more wisdom. It teaches me, leads me places I never knew I was heading. And it is about a new way of living, of being in the world.

11   I was on a panel recently where the question was raised whether we thought literature could save lives. The audience, book people, smiled expectantly with the thought. I wanted to say, Yes, it saves lives. But I couldn't speak those words. It saves spirits maybe, hearts. It changes minds, but for me writing is an incredible privilege. When I sit down at the desk, there are other women who are hungry, homeless. I don't want to forget that, that the world of matter is still there to be reckoned with. This writing is a form of freedom most other people do not have. So, when I write, I feel a responsibility, a commitment to other humans and to the animal and plant communities as well.

12   Still, writing has changed me. And there is the powerful need we all have to tell a story, each of us with a piece of the whole pattern to complete. As Alice Walker says, We are all telling part of the same story, and as Sharon Olds has said, Every writer is a cell on the body politic of America.

13   Another Nobel Prize laureate is Betty William, a Northern Ireland cowinner of the 1977 Peace Prize. I heard her speak about how, after witnessing the death of children, she stepped outside in the middle of the night and began knocking on doors and yelling, behaviors that would have earned her a diagnosis of hysteria in our own medical circles. She knocked on doors that might have opened with weapons pointing in her face, and she cried out, "What kind of people have we become that we would allow children to be killed on our streets?" Within four hours the city was awake, and there were sixteen thousand names on petitions for peace. Now, that woman's work is a lesson to those of us who deal with language, and to those of us who are dealt into silence. She used language to begin the process of peace. This is the living, breathing power

of the word. It is poetry. So are the names of those who signed the petitions. Maybe it is this kind of language that saves lives.

Writing begins for me with survival, with life and with freeing life, saving 14 life, speaking life. It is work that speaks what can't be easily said. It originates from a compelling desire to live and be alive. For me, it is sometimes the need to speak for other forms of life, to take the side of human life, even our some-times frivolous living, and our grief-filled living, our joyous living, our violent living, busy living, our peaceful living. It is about possibility. It is based in the world of matter. I am interested in how something small turns into an image that is large and strong with resonance, where the ordinary becomes beautiful. I believe the divine, the magic, is here in the weeds at our feet, unacknowl-edged. What a world this is. Where else could water rise up to the sky, turn into snow crystals, magnificently brought together, fall from the sky all around us, pile up billions deep, and catch the small sparks of sunlight as they return again to water?

These acts of magic happen all the time; in Chaco Canyon, my sister has 15 seen a kiva, a ceremonial room in the earth, that is in the center of the canyon. This place has been uninhabited for what seems like forever. It has been with-out water. In fact, there are theories that the ancient people disappeared when they journeyed after water. In the center of it a corn plant was growing. It was all alone and it had been there since the ancient ones, the old ones who came before us all, those people who wove dog hair into belts, who witnessed the painting of flute players on the seeping canyon walls, who knew the stories of corn. And there was one corn plant growing out of the holy place. It planted itself yearly. With no water, no person to care for it, no overturning of the soil, this corn plant rises up to tell its story, and that's what this poetry is.

## COMPREHENSION

1. Why does Hogan specifically identify herself as an "Indian woman" (para-graph 3)? How does this identity influence her perception of the place of poetry in the life of a community or nation?
2. Where does the writer refer to "voices"? What types of voices does she hear, and why are they important?
3. What is the writer's definition of poetry? Why does she call poetry "life resonating" (paragraph 9)?

## RHETORIC

1. What is the significance of the title? How does the title resonate throughout the essay?
2. What persona does the writer create for herself in this essay? What is her purpose in presenting herself in the way she does? What tone does she adopt?

3. As we might expect of a poet, Hogan employs highly figurative language in this essay. Locate examples of allusion, imagery, symbolism, and metaphor, and explain their meaning.
4. Where does the writer use illustration to help explain both the writing and the nature of poetry? What do these concrete examples add to her extended definition of poetry?
5. How might this essay be considered an argument? What is Hogan's claim? Where does she appeal to ethics and emotion? Why does she refer to writers such as Ernesto Cardenal and Alice Walker to support her claim? Why does she refer to the Chernobyl nuclear accident (paragraph 6) and the United States staging revolutions in Third World nations (paragraph 10)?
6. How does the concluding paragraph serve as a coda for the essay?

## WRITING

1. Write your own definition of poetry, basing it on your personal experience, ethnic or racial background, and understanding of the world today.
2. Conduct additional research on Hogan's poetry. Select one or two of her poems, and write an analysis of them.
3. **Writing an Argument:** Argue for or against the proposition, advanced by Hogan, that poetry—or, more generally, literature—has the power to change minds and even save lives. Provide evidence to support your claim.

 www.mhhe.com/ **mhreader**        For more information on Linda Hogan, go to: **More Resources > Ch. 10 Literature & Arts**

# Orwell and Me

## Margaret Atwood

*Margaret Atwood (b. 1939) is arguably Canada's most famous contemporary writer—a poet, novelist, short-story writer, and essayist who explores the role of personal consciousness in a troubled world. Atwood received degrees from the University of Toronto (BA, 1961) and Radcliffe College (AM, 1962). Her second collection of poetry,* The Circle Game *(1966), brought her critical recognition. Atwood is even better known as a novelist; her fiction includes* Surfacing *(1973),* Life Before Man *(1979),* The Handmaid's Tale *(1985),* Cat's Eye *(1988),* The Blind Assassin *(2000), and*

The Tent *(2006). In the following selection, published in the Manchester* Guardian *in 2003, Atwood explains the relevance of one English writer for the post-9/11 world.*

I grew up with George Orwell. I was born in 1939, and *Animal Farm* was pub- 1
lished in 1945. Thus, I was able to read it at the age of nine. It was lying around
the house, and I mistook it for a book about talking animals, sort of like *Wind in
the Willows.* I knew nothing about the kind of politics in the book—the child's
version of politics then, just after the war, consisted of the simple notion that
Hitler was bad but dead. So I gobbled up the adventures of Napoleon and
Snowball, the smart, greedy, upwardly mobile pigs, and Squealer the spin-
doctor, and Boxer the noble but thick-witted horse, and the easily led, slogan-
chanting sheep, without making any connection with historical events.

To say that I was horrified by this book is an understatement. The fate of the 2
farm animals was so grim, the pigs so mean and mendacious and treacherous,
the sheep so stupid. Children have a keen sense of injustice, and this was the
thing that upset me the most: the pigs were so unjust. I cried my eyes out when
Boxer the horse had an accident and was carted off to be made into dog food,
instead of being given the quiet corner of the pasture he'd been promised.

The whole experience was deeply disturbing to me, but I am forever grate- 3
ful to Orwell for alerting me early to the danger flags I've tried to watch out for
since. In the world of *Animal Farm,* most speechifying and public palaver is
bullshit and instigated lying, and though many characters are good-hearted
and mean well, they can be frightened into closing their eyes to what's really
going on. The pigs browbeat the others with ideology, then twist that ideology
to suit their own purposes: their language games were evident to me even at
that age. As Orwell taught, it isn't the labels—Christianity, Socialism, Islam,
Democracy, Two Legs Bad, Four Legs Good, the works—that are definitive, but
the acts done in their name.

I could see, too, how easily those who have toppled an oppressive power 4
take on its trappings and habits. Jean-Jacques Rousseau was right to warn us that
democracy is the hardest form of government to maintain; Orwell knew that to
the marrow of his bones, because he had seen it in action. How quickly the precept "All Animals Are Equal" is changed into "All Animals Are Equal, but Some
Are More Equal Than Others." What oily concern the pigs show for the welfare
of the other animals, a concern that disguises their contempt for those they are
manipulating. With what alacrity do they put on the once-despised uniforms of
the tyrannous humans they have overthrown, and learn to use their whips.
How self-righteously they justify their actions, helped by the verbal web-
spinning of Squealer, their nimble-tongued press agent, until all power is in
their trotters, pretence is no longer necessary, and they rule by naked force. A
revolution often means only that: a revolving, a turn of the wheel of fortune, by
which those who were at the bottom mount to the top, and assume the choice
positions, crushing the former power-holders beneath them. We should beware
of all those who plaster the landscape with large portraits of themselves, like
the evil pig, Napoleon.

5    *Animal Farm* is one of the most spectacular Emperor-Has-No-Clothes books
of the 20th century, and it got George Orwell into trouble. People who run
counter to the current popular wisdom, who point out the uncomfortably obvious, are likely to be strenuously baa-ed at by herds of angry sheep. I didn't
have all that figured out at the age of nine, of course—not in any conscious
way. But we learn the patterns of stories before we learn their meanings, and
*Animal Farm* has a very clear pattern.

6    Then along came *Nineteen Eighty-Four,* which was published in 1949. Thus,
I read it in paperback a couple of years later, when I was in high school. Then I
read it again, and again: it was right up there among my favourite books, along
with *Wuthering Heights.* At the same time, I absorbed its two companions,
Arthur Koestler's *Darkness at Noon* and Aldous Huxley's *Brave New World.* I was
keen on all three of them, but I understood *Darkness at Noon* to be a tragedy about
events that had already happened, and *Brave New World* to be a satirical comedy,
with events that were unlikely to unfold in exactly that way. (Orgy-Porgy, indeed.) *Nineteen Eighty-Four* struck me as more realistic, probably because
Winston Smith was more like me—a skinny person who got tired a lot and was
subjected to physical education under chilly conditions (this was a feature of
my school)—and who was silently at odds with the ideas and the manner of life
proposed for him. (This may be one of the reasons *Nineteen Eighty-Four* is best
read when you are an adolescent: most adolescents feel like that.) I sympathi-
sed particularly with Winston's desire to write his forbidden thoughts down in
a deliciously tempting, secret blank book: I had not yet started to write, but I
could see the attractions of it. I could also see the dangers, because it's this
scribbling of his—along with illicit sex, another item with considerable allure
for a teenager of the 50s—that gets Winston into such a mess.

7    *Animal Farm* charts the progress of an idealistic movement of liberation towards a totalitarian dictatorship headed by a despotic tyrant; *Nineteen Eighty-
Four* describes what it's like to live entirely within such a system. Its hero,
Winston, has only fragmentary memories of what life was like before the present dreadful regime set in: he's an orphan, a child of the collectivity. His father
died in the war that has ushered in the repression, and his mother has disappeared, leaving him with only the reproachful glance she gave him as he betrayed her over a chocolate bar—a small betrayal that acts both as the key to
Winston's character and as a precursor to the many other betrayals in the book.

8    The government of Airstrip One, Winston's "country," is brutal. The constant surveillance, the impossibility of speaking frankly to anyone, the looming,
ominous figure of Big Brother, the regime's need for enemies and wars—
fictitious though both may be—which are used to terrify the people and unite
them in hatred, the mind-numbing slogans, the distortions of language, the destruction of what has really happened by stuffing any record of it down the
Memory Hole—these made a deep impression on me. Let me re-state that: they
frightened the stuffing out of me. Orwell was writing a satire about Stalin's
Soviet Union, a place about which I knew very little at the age of 14, but he did
it so well that I could imagine such things happening anywhere.

There is no love interest in *Animal Farm* but there is in *Nineteen Eighty-Four*.  9
Winston finds a soulmate in Julia; outwardly a devoted Party fanatic, secretly a
girl who enjoys sex and makeup and other spots of decadence. But the two lovers are discovered, and Winston is tortured for thought-crime—inner disloyalty
to the regime. He feels that if he can only remain faithful in his heart to Julia, his
soul will be saved—a romantic concept, though one we are likely to endorse.
But like all absolutist governments and religions, the Party demands that every
personal loyalty be sacrificed to it, and replaced with an absolute loyalty to Big
Brother. Confronted with his worst fear in the dreaded Room 101, where a
nasty device involving a cage-full of starving rats can be fitted to the eyes,
Winston breaks: "Don't do it to me," he pleads, "do it to Julia." (This sentence
has become shorthand in our household for the avoidance of onerous duties.
Poor Julia—how hard we would make her life if she actually existed. She'd
have to be on a lot of panel discussions, for instance.)

After his betrayal of Julia, Winston becomes a handful of malleable goo. He  10
truly believes that two and two make five, and that he loves Big Brother. Our
last glimpse of him is sitting drink-sodden at an outdoor cafe, knowing he's a
dead man walking and having learned that Julia has betrayed him, too, while
he listens to a popular refrain: "Under the spreading chestnut tree/I sold you
and you sold me . . ."

Orwell has been accused of bitterness and pessimism—of leaving us with a  11
vision of the future in which the individual has no chance, and where the brutal, totalitarian boot of the all-controlling Party will grind into the human face,
forever. But this view of Orwell is contradicted by the last chapter in the book,
an essay on Newspeak—the doublethink language concocted by the regime. By
expurgating all words that might be troublesome—"bad" is no longer permitted, but becomes "double-plus-ungood"—and by making other words mean
the opposite of what they used to mean—the place where people get tortured is
the Ministry of Love, the building where the past is destroyed is the Ministry of
Information—the rulers of Airstrip One wish to make it literally impossible for
people to think straight. However, the essay on Newspeak is written in standard English, in the third person, and in the past tense, which can only mean
that the regime has fallen, and that language and individuality have survived.
For whoever has written the essay on Newspeak, the world of *Nineteen Eighty-
Four* is over. Thus, it's my view that Orwell had much more faith in the resilience of the human spirit than he's usually been given credit for.

Orwell became a direct model for me much later in my life—in the real  12
1984, the year in which I began writing a somewhat different dystopia, *The
Handmaid's Tale*. By that time I was 44, and I had learned enough about real
despotisms—through the reading of history, travel, and my membership of
Amnesty International—so that I didn't need to rely on Orwell alone.

The majority of dystopias—Orwell's included—have been written by  13
men, and the point of view has been male. When women have appeared in
them, they have been either sexless automatons or rebels who have defied
the sex rules of the regime. They have acted as the temptresses of the male

protagonists, however welcome this temptation may be to the men them-selves. Thus Julia; thus the cami-knicker-wearing, orgy-porgy seducer of the Savage in *Brave New World*; thus the subversive femme fatale of Yevgeny Zamyatin's 1924 seminal classic, *We*. I wanted to try a dystopia from the fe-male point of view—the world according to Julia, as it were. However, this does not make *The Handmaid's Tale* a "feminist dystopia," except insofar as giving a woman a voice and an inner life will always be considered "femi-nist" by those who think women ought not to have these things.

14    The 20th century could be seen as a race between two versions of man-made hell—the jackbooted state totalitarianism of Orwell's *Nineteen Eight-Four* and the hedonistic ersatz paradise of *Brave New World*, where absolutely every-thing is a consumer good and human beings are engineered to be happy. With the fall of the Berlin Wall in 1989, it seemed for a time that *Brave New World* had won—from henceforth, state control would be minimal, and all we would have to do was go shopping and smile a lot, and wallow in pleasures, popping a pill or two when depression set in.

15    But with 9/11, all that changed. Now it appears we face the prospect of two contradictory dystopias at once—open markets, closed minds—because state surveillance is back again with a vengeance. The torturer's dreaded Room 101 has been with us for millennia. The dungeons of Rome, the Inquisition, the Star Chamber, the Bastille, the proceedings of General Pinochet and of the junta in Argentina—all have depended on secrecy and on the abuse of power. Lots of countries have had their versions of it—their ways of silencing troublesome dissent. Democracies have traditionally defined themselves by, among other things, openness and the rule of law. But now it seems that we in the west are tacitly legitimising the methods of the darker human past, upgraded techno-logically and sanctified to our own uses, of course. For the sake of freedom, freedom must be renounced. To move us towards the improved world—the utopia we're promised—dystopia must first hold sway.

16    It's a concept worthy of doublethink. It's also, in its ordering of events, strangely Marxist. First the dictatorship of the proletariat, in which lots of heads must roll; then the pie-in-the-sky classless society, which oddly enough never materialises. Instead, we just get pigs with whips.

17    I often ask myself: what would George Orwell have to say about it?

18    Quite a lot.

## COMPREHENSION

1.  This article is an edited extract of a talk that Atwood gave on BBC Radio. Why do you think her talk would be of interest to a radio audience?
2.  Summarize what you learn from Atwood's essay about George Orwell and his novels *Animal Farm* and *Nineteen Eighty-Four*.
3.  What does Atwood learn from Orwell? What does she think all of us should learn from him today in our "post-9/11 world"?

## RHETORIC

1. Why does Atwood begin on a personal note: "I grew up with George Or-well"? What do we learn about her as a person? How does this personal element influence the tone and development of the essay?
2. What is Atwood's main claim? What premises or warrants does she estab-lish, and how sound is the logic? Justify your response.
3. Atwood seems to speak from a position of authority. How does she estab-lish this sense of authority in the essay?
4. Why does Atwood summarize Orwell's two novels at considerable length? How does she use comparison and contrast to frame her discussion of the novels?
5. What causes and effects does Atwood analyze in this essay? What is her purpose here?
6. How does Atwood conclude her discussion of Orwell? How successful do you find the ending, and why?

## WRITING

1. Read *Animal Farm* or view the film version. Then write your own analysis of Orwell's work.
2. In a comparative essay, relate Atwood's article to Orwell's "Politics and the English Language" (see pages 92–102).
3. **Writing an Argument:** Atwood raises the question of whether writers and artists should warn us about dangers confronting society. Write a persua-sive essay in which you take a clear stand on this issue. Provide examples drawn from literature, art, and the media.

 www.mhhe.com/ **mhreader**   | For more information on Margaret Atwood, go to: **More Resources > Ch. 10 Literature & Arts**

# Regarding the Torture of Others

## Susan Sontag

*Susan Sontag (1933-2004), one of the most influential critics of her generation, was born in New York City and grew up in Tucson, Arizona, and Los Angeles. After gradu-ating from high school at the age of 15, she started studies at the University of California at Berkeley; subsequently, she received degrees from the University of Chicago and Harvard University. As an art critic as well as a political and cultural commentator, Sontag brought intellectual rigor to her subjects. The main body of her work in prose consists of two collections of essays,* Against Interpretation *(1966) and* Where the Stress Falls *(2001), as well as* Trip to Hanoi *(1968),* Illness as Metaphor *(1978), and* AIDS and Its Metaphors *(1988). In addition, Sontag wrote fiction, including* Volcano Lover *(1992) and* In America: A Novel *(2001), and several films and plays. In this essay, published in* The New York Times Magazine *in 2004, Sontag offers a meditation on the photographs of torture taken by American troops at Abu Ghraib prison in Baghdad.*

# I.

1  For a long time—at least six decades—photographs have laid down the tracks of how important conflicts are judged and remembered. The Western memory museum is now mostly a visual one. Photographs have an insuperable power to determine what we recall of events, and it now seems probable that the defining association of people everywhere with the war that the United States launched pre-emptively in Iraq last year will be photographs of the torture of Iraqi prisoners by Americans in the most infamous of Saddam Hussein's prisons, Abu Ghraib.

2      The Bush administration and its defenders have chiefly sought to limit a public-relations disaster—the dissemination of the photographs—rather than deal with the complex crimes of leadership and of policy revealed by the pictures. There was, first of all, the displacement of the reality onto the photographs themselves. The administration's initial response was to say that the president was shocked and disgusted by the photographs—as if the fault or horror lay in the images, not in what they depict. There was also the avoidance of the word "torture." The prisoners had possibly been the objects of "abuse," eventually of "humiliation"—that was the most to be admitted. "My impression is that what has been charged thus far is abuse, which I believe technically

An Iraqi detainee at Abu Ghraib: The horror of what is shown in the photographs cannot be separated from the horror that the photographs were taken.

is different from torture," Secretary of Defense Donald Rumsfeld said at a press conference. "And therefore I'm not going to address the 'torture' word."

Words alter, words add, words subtract. It was the strenuous avoidance of the ₃ word "genocide" while some 800,000 Tutsis in Rwanda were being slaughtered, over a few weeks' time, by their Hutu neighbors 10 years ago that indicated the American government had no intention of doing anything. To refuse to call what took place in Abu Ghraib—and what has taken place elsewhere in Iraq and in Afghanistan and at Guantánamo Bay—by its true name, torture, is as outrageous as the refusal to call the Rwandan genocide a genocide. Here is one of the definitions of torture contained in a convention to which the United States is a signatory: *"any act by which severe pain or suffering, whether physical or mental, is intentionally inflicted on a person for such purposes as obtaining from him or a third person information or a confession."* (The definition comes from the 1984 Convention Against Torture and Other Cruel, Inhuman or Degrading Treatment or Punishment. Similar definitions have existed for some time in customary law and in treaties, starting with Article 3—common to the four Geneva conventions of 1949—and many recent human rights conventions.) The 1984 convention declares, *"No exceptional circumstances whatsoever, whether a state of war or a threat of war, internal political instability or any other public emergency may be invoked as a justification of torture."* And all covenants on torture specify that it includes treatment intended to humiliate the victim, like leaving prisoners naked in cells and corridors.

Whatever actions this administration undertakes to limit the damage of the ₄ widening revelations of the torture of prisoners in Abu Ghraib and elsewhere— trials, courts-martial, dishonorable discharges, resignation of senior military figures and responsible administration officials and substantial compensation to the victims—it is probable that the "torture" word will continue to be banned. To acknowledge that Americans torture their prisoners would contradict everything this administration has invited the public to believe about the virtue of American intentions and America's right, flowing from that virtue, to undertake unilateral action on the world stage.

Even when the president was finally compelled, as the damage to America's ₅ reputation everywhere in the world widened and deepened, to use the "sorry" word, the focus of regret still seemed the damage to America's claim to moral superiority. Yes, President Bush said in Washington on May 6, standing alongside King Abdullah II of Jordan, he was "sorry for the humiliation suffered by the Iraqi prisoners and the humiliation suffered by their families." But, he went on, he was "equally sorry that people seeing these pictures didn't understand the true nature and heart of America."

To have the American effort in Iraq summed up by these images must seem, ₆ to those who saw some justification in a war that did overthrow one of the monster tyrants of modern times, "unfair." A war, an occupation, is inevitably a huge tapestry of actions. What makes some actions representative and others not? The issue is not whether the torture was done by individuals (i.e., "not by everybody")—but whether it was systematic. Authorized. Condoned. All acts are done by individuals. The issue is not whether a majority or a minority of Americans performs such acts but whether the nature of the policies prosecuted by this administration and the hierarchies deployed to carry them out makes such acts likely.

## II.

7 Considered in this light, the photographs are us. That is, they are representative of the fundamental corruptions of any foreign occupation together with the Bush adminstration's distinctive policies. The Belgians in the Congo, the French in Algeria, practiced torture and sexual humiliation on despised recalcitrant natives. Add to this generic corruption the mystifying, near-total unpreparedness of the American rulers of Iraq to deal with the complex realities of the country after its "liberation." And add to that the overarching, distinctive doctrines of the Bush administration, namely that the United States has embarked on an endless war and that those detained in this war are, if the president so decides, "unlawful combatants"—a policy enunciated by Donald Rumsfeld for Taliban and Qaeda prisoners as early as January 2002—and thus, as Rumsfeld said, "technically" they "do not have any rights under the Geneva Convention," and you have a perfect recipe for the cruelties and crimes committed against the thousands incarcerated without charges or access to lawyers in American-run prisons that have been set up since the attacks of Sept. 11, 2001.

8 So, then, is the real issue not the photographs themselves but what the photographs reveal to have happened to "suspects" in American custody? No: the horror of what is shown in the photographs cannot be separated from the horror that the photographs were taken—with the perpetrators posing, gloating, over their helpless captives. German soldiers in the Second World War took photographs of the atrocities they were committing in Poland and Russia, but snapshots in which the executioners placed themselves among their victims are exceedingly rare, as may be seen in a book just published, "Photographing the Holocaust," by Janina Struk. If there is something comparable to what these pictures show it would be some of the photographs of black victims of lynching taken between the 1880's and 1930's, which show Americans grinning beneath the naked mutilated body of a black man or woman hanging behind them from a tree. The lynching photographs were souvenirs of a collective action whose participants felt perfectly justified in what they had done. So are the pictures from Abu Ghraib.

9 The lynching pictures were in the nature of photographs as trophies—taken by a photographer in order to be collected, stored in albums, displayed. The pictures taken by American soldiers in Abu Ghraib, however, reflect a shift in the use made of pictures—less objects to be saved than messages to be disseminated, circulated. A digital camera is a common possession among soldiers. Where once photographing war was the province of photojournalists, now the soldiers themselves are all photographers—recording their war, their fun, their observations of what they find picturesque, their atrocities—and swapping images among themselves and e-mailing them around the globe.

What formerly was segregated as pornography, as the exercise of extreme sadomasochistic longings, is being normalized, by some, as high-spirited play or venting.

There is more and more recording of what people do, by themselves. At  10 least or especially in America, Andy Warhol's ideal of filming real events in real time—life isn't edited, why should its record be edited?—has become a norm for countless Webcasts, in which people record their day, each in his or her own reality show. Here I am—waking and yawning and stretching, brushing my teeth, making breakfast, getting the kids off to school. People record all aspects of their lives, store them in computer files and send the files around. Family life goes with the recording of family life—even when, or especially when, the family is in the throes of crisis and disgrace. Surely the dedicated, incessant home-videoing of one another, in conversation and monologue, over many years was the most astonishing material in "Capturing the Friedmans," the recent documentary by Andrew Jarecki about a Long Island family embroiled in pedophilia charges.

An erotic life is, for more and more people, that whither can be captured in  11 digital photographs and on video. And perhaps the torture is more attractive, as something to record, when it has a sexual component. It is surely revealing, as more Abu Ghraib photographs enter public view, that torture photographs are interleaved with pornographic images of American soldiers having sex with one another. In fact, most of the torture photographs have a sexual theme, as in those showing the coercing of prisoners to perform, or simulate, sexual acts among themselves. One exception, already canonical, is the photograph of the man made to stand on a box, hooded and sprouting wires, reportedly told he would be electrocuted if he fell off. Yet pictures of prisoners bound in painful positions, or made to stand with outstretched arms, are infrequent. That they count as torture cannot be doubted. You have only to look at the terror on the victim's face, although such "stress" fell within the Pentagon's limits of the acceptable. But most of the pictures seem part of a larger confluence of torture

Most of the pictures, like this one of soldiers who used their guard dogs to torture and humiliate prisoners, seem to depict part of a larger continence of torture and pornography.

and pornography: a young woman leading a naked man around on a leash is classic dominatrix imagery. And you wonder how much of the sexual tortures inflicted on the inmates of Abu Ghraib was inspired by the vast repertory of pornographic imagery available on the Internet—and which ordinary people, by sending out Webcasts of themselves, try to emulate.

## III.

12   To live is to be photographed, to have a record of one's life, and therefore to go on with one's life oblivious, or claiming to be oblivious, to the camera's nonstop attentions. But to live is also to pose. To act is to share in the community of actions recorded as images. The expression of satisfaction at the acts of torture being inflicted on helpless, trussed, naked victims is only part of the story. There is the deep satisfaction of being photographed, to which one is now more inclined to respond not with a stiff, direct gaze (as in former times) but with glee. The events are in part designed to be photographed. The grin is a grin for the camera. There would be something missing if, after stacking the naked men, you couldn't take a picture of them.

13       Looking at these photographs, you ask yourself, How can someone grin at the sufferings and humiliation of another human being? Set guard dogs at the genitals and legs of cowering naked prisoners? Force shackled, hooded prisoners to masturbate or simulate oral sex with one another? And you feel naïve for asking, since the answer is, self-evidently, People do these things to other people. Rape and pain inflicted on the genitals are among the most common forms of torture. Not just in Nazi concentration camps and in Abu Ghraib when it was run by Saddam Hussein. Americans, too, have done and do them when they are told, or made to feel, that those over whom they have

absolute power deserve to be humiliated, tormented. They do them when they are led to believe that the people they are torturing belong to an inferior race or religion. For the meaning of these pictures is not just that these acts were performed, but that their perpetrators apparently had no sense that there was anything wrong in what the pictures show.

Even more appalling, since the pictures were meant to be circulated and 14 seen by many people: it was all fun. And this idea of fun is, alas, more and more—contrary to what President Bush is telling the world—part of "the true nature and heart of America." It is hard to measure the increasing acceptance of brutality in American life, but its evidence is everywhere, starting with the video games of killing that are a principal entertainment of boys—can the video game "Interrogating the Terrorists" really be far behind?—and on to the violence that has become endemic in the group rites of youth on an exuberant kick. Violent crime is down, yet the easy delight taken in violence seems to have grown. From the harsh torments inflicted on incoming students in many American suburban high schools—depicted in Richard Linklater's 1993 film, "Dazed and Confused"—to the hazing rituals of physical brutality and sexual humiliation in college fraternities and on sports teams, America has become a country in which the fantasies and the practice of violence are seen as good entertainment, fun.

What formerly was segregated as pornography, as the exercise of extreme 15 sadomasochistic longings—as in Pier Paolo Pasolini's last, near-unwatchable film, "Salò" (1975), depicting orgies of torture in the Fascist redoubt in northern Italy at the end of the Mussolini era—is now being normalized, by some, as high-spirited play or venting. To "stack naked men" is like a college fraternity prank, said a caller to Rush Limbaugh and the many millions of Americans who listen to his radio show. Had the caller, one wonders, seen the photographs? No matter. The observation—or is it the fantasy?—was on the mark. What may still be capable of shocking some Americans was Limbaugh's response: "Exactly!" he exclaimed. "Exactly my point. This is no different than what happens at the Skull and Bones initiation, and we're going to ruin people's lives over it, and we're going to hamper our military effort, and then we are going to really hammer them because they had a good time." "They" are the American soldiers, the torturers. And Limbaugh went on: "You know, these people are being fired at every day. I'm talking about people having a good time, these people. You ever heard of emotional release?"

Shock and awe were what our military promised the Iraqis. And shock and 16 the awful are what these photographs announce to the world that the Americans have delivered: a pattern of criminal behavior in open contempt of international humanitarian conventions. Soldiers now pose, thumbs up, before the atrocities they commit, and send off the pictures to their buddies. Secrets of private life that, formerly, you would have given nearly anything to conceal, you now clamor to be invited on a television show to reveal. What is illustrated by these photographs is as much the culture of shamelessness as the reigning admiration for unapologetic brutality.

## IV.

17  The notion that apologies or professions of "disgust" by the president and the secretary of defense are a sufficient response is an insult to one's historical and moral sense. The torture of prisoners is not an aberration. It is a direct consequence of the with-us-or-against-us doctrines of world struggle with which the Bush administration has sought to change, change radically, the international stance of the United States and to recast many domestic institutions and prerogatives. The Bush administration has committed the country to a pseudoreligious doctrine of war, endless war—for "the war on terror" is nothing less than that. Endless war is taken to justify endless incarcerations. Those held in the extralegal American penal empire are "detainees"; "prisoners," a newly obsolete word, might suggest that they have the rights accorded by international law and the laws of all civilized countries. This endless "global war on terrorism"—into which both the quite justified invasion of Afghanistan and the unwinnable folly in Iraq have been folded by Pentagon decree—inevitably leads to the demonizing and dehumanizing of anyone declared by the Bush administration to be a possible terrorist: a definition that is not up for debate and is, in fact, usually made in secret.

18  The charges against most of the people detained in the prisons in Iraq and Afghanistan being nonexistent—the Red Cross reports that 70 to 90 percent of those being held seem to have committed no crime other than simply being in the wrong place at the wrong time, caught up in some sweep of "suspects"—the principal justification for holding them is "interrogation." Interrogation about what? About anything. Whatever the detainee might know. If interrogation is the point of detaining prisoners indefinitely, then physical coercion, humiliation and torture become inevitable.

19  Remember: we are not talking about that rarest of cases, the "ticking time bomb" situation, which is sometimes used as a limiting case that justifies torture of prisoners who have knowledge of an imminent attack. This is general or nonspecific information-gathering, authorized by American military and civilian administrators to learn more of a shadowy empire of evildoers about whom Americans know virtually nothing, in countries about which they are singularly ignorant: in principle, any information at all might be useful. An interrogation that produced no information (whatever information might consist of) would count as a failure. All the more justification for preparing prisoners to talk. Softening them up, stressing them out—these are the euphemisms for the bestial practices in American prisons where suspected terrorists are being held. Unfortunately, as Staff Sgt. Ivan (Chip) Frederick noted in his diary, a prisoner can get too stressed out and die. The picture of a man in a body bag with ice on his chest may well be of the man Frederick was describing.

20  The pictures will not go away. That is the nature of the digital world in which we live. Indeed, it seems they were necessary to get our leaders to acknowledge that they had a problem on their hands. After all, the conclusions of reports compiled by the International Committee of the Red Cross, and other

reports by journalists and protests by humanitarian organizations about the atrocious punishments inflicted on "detainees" and "suspected terrorists" in prisons run by the American military, first in Afghanistan and later in Iraq, have been circulating for more than a year. It seems doubtful that such reports were read by President Bush or Vice President Dick Cheney or Condoleezza Rice or Rumsfeld. Apparently it took the photographs to get their attention, when it became clear they could not be suppressed; it was the photographs that made all this "real" to Bush and his associates. Up to then, there had been only words, which are easier to cover up in our age of infinite digital self-reproduction and self-dissemination, and so much easier to forget.

So now the pictures will continue to "assault" us—as many Americans are   21
bound to feel. Will people get used to them? Some Americans are already say-ing they have seen enough. Not, however, the rest of the world. Endless war: endless stream of photographs. Will editors now debate whether showing more of them, or showing them uncropped (which, with some of the best-known im-ages, like that of a hooded man on a box, gives a different and in some instances more appalling view), would be in "bad taste" or too implicitly political? By "political," read: critical of the Bush administration's imperial project. For there can be no doubt that the photographs damage, as Rumsfeld testified, "the repu-tation of the honorable men and women of the armed forces who are coura-geously and responsibly and professionally defending our freedom across the globe." This damage—to our reputation, our image, our success as the lone superpower—is what the Bush administration principally deplores. How the protection of "our freedom"—the freedom of 5 percent of humanity—came to require having American soldiers "across the globe" is hardly debated by our elected officials.

Already the backlash has begun. Americans are being warned against in-   22
dulging in an orgy of self-condemnation. The continuing publication of the pic-tures is being taken by many Americans as suggesting that we do not have the right to defend ourselves: after all, they (the terrorists) started it. They—Osama bin Laden? Saddam Hussein? what's the difference?—attacked us first. Senator James Inhofe of Oklahoma, a Republican member of the Senate Armed Services Committee, before which Secretary Rumsfeld testified, avowed that he was sure he was not the only member of the committee "more outraged by the out-rage" over the photographs than by what the photographs show. "These pris-oners," Senator Inhofe explained, "you know they're not there for traffic violations. If they're in Cellblock 1-A or 1-B, these prisoners, they're murderers, they're terrorists, they're insurgents. Many of them probably have American blood on their hands, and here we're so concerned about the treatment of those individuals." It's the fault of "the media" which are provoking, and will con-tinue to provoke, further violence against Americans around the world. More Americans will die. Because of these photos.

There is an answer to this charge, of course. Americans are dying not   23
because of the photographs but because of what the photographs reveal to be happening, happening with the complicity of a chain of command—so

In this photograph,
Specialist Charles Graner,
who identified men in
another of the Abu Ghraib
photos, poses over
handcuffed detainees
lying on the floor.

Maj. Gen. Antonio Taguba implied, and Pfc. Lynndie England said, and (among others) Senator Lindsey Graham of South Carolina, a Republican, suggested, after he saw the Pentagon's full range of images on May 12. "Some of it has an elaborate nature to it that makes me very suspicious of whether or not others were directing or encouraging." Senator Graham said. Senator Bill Nelson, a Florida Democrat, said that viewing an uncropped version of one photo showing a stack of naked men in a hallway—a version that revealed how many other soldiers were at the scene, some not even paying attention—contradicted the Pentagon's assertion that only rogue soldiers were involved. "Somewhere along the line," Senator Nelson said of the torturers, "they were either told or winked at." An attorney for Specialist Charles Graner Jr., who is in the picture, has had his client identify the men in the uncropped version; according to *The Wall Street Journal*, Graner said that four of the men were military intelligence and one a civilian contractor working with military intelligence.

## V.

24  But the distinction between photograph and reality—as between spin and policy—can easily evaporate. And that is what the administration wishes to happen. "There are a lot more photographs and videos that exist," Rumsfeld acknowledged in his testimony. "If these are released to the public, obviously, it's going to make matters worse." Worse for the administration and its programs, presumably, not for those who are the actual—and potential?—victims of torture.

25      The media may self-censor but, as Rumsfeld acknowledged, it's hard to censor soldiers overseas, who don't write letters home, as in the old days, that can be opened by military censors who ink out unacceptable lines. Today's soldiers instead function like tourists, as Rumsfeld put it, "running around with digital cameras and taking these unbelievable photographs and then passing

them off, against the law, to the media, to our surprise." The administration's effort to withhold pictures is proceeding along several fronts. Currently, the argument is taking a legalistic turn: now the photographs are classified as evidence in future criminal cases, whose outcome may be prejudiced if they are made public. The Republican chairman of the Senate Armed Services Committee, John Warner of Virginia, after the May 12 slide show of image after image of sexual humiliation and violence against Iraqi prisoners, said he felt "very strongly" that the newer photos "should not be made public. I feel that it could possibly endanger the men and women of the armed forces as they are serving and at great risk."

But the real push to limit the accessibility of the photographs will come 26 from the continuing effort to protect the administration and cover up our misrule in Iraq—to identify "outrage" over the photographs with a campaign to undermine American military might and the purposes it currently serves. Just as it was regarded by many as an implicit criticism of the war to show on television photographs of American soldiers who have been killed in the course of the invasion and occupation of Iraq, it will increasingly be thought unpatriotic to disseminate the new photographs and further tarnish the image of America.

After all, we're at war. Endless war. And war is hell, more so than any of 27 the people who got us into this rotten war seem to have expected. In our digital hall of mirrors, the pictures aren't going to go away. Yes, it seems that one picture is worth a thousand words. And even if our leaders choose not to look at them, there will be thousands more snapshots and videos. Unstoppable.

## COMPREHENSION

1. Summarize Sontag's harsh condemnation of the Bush administration's prosecution of the Iraq war.
2. Sontag writes that the photographs coming out of Abu Ghraib "are us" (paragraph 7). What does she mean? Would you agree or disagree with the implications of her statement? Why?
3. Explain what Sontag finds to be uniquely powerful about photography as an art form.

## RHETORIC

1. Sontag structures her essay around the dual subjects of photography and the American involvement in Iraq. Explain what her purpose is and how she links these two subjects.
2. What is Sontag's claim and in what place(s) does she state it? Where does she make logical, ethical, and emotional appeals? Are you persuaded by her argument? Why or why not?
3. Sontag includes six illustrations in the essay similar to the far we have included here. What is her objective? Does she mention additional photographs? How do the photographs enhance the message?

4. Sontag divides her essay into five numbered sections. How does each section serve to advance her argument?
5. How does Sontag's use of connotation and definition—of *torture, enemy combatants, the erotic life,* and so forth—serve her purpose?
6. What conclusions does Sontag draw "regarding the torture of others"?

## WRITING

1. Write your own extended definition of torture, linking it to a specific situation like Abu Ghraib. Add clip art to support your definition.
2. Sontag alludes to the popular radio commentator Rush Limbaugh. Find out more about this personality, and in an expository essay explain why Limbaugh would disagree with Sontag's argument.
3. **Writing an Argument:** Conduct your own research on the Abu Ghraib incident, and then stake out an argumentative position on it. Develop logical, ethical, and emotional appeals to support your position. Provide clip art to augment your claim.

 www.mhhe.com/
**mhreader**    For more information on Susan Sontag, go to:
**More Resources > Ch. 10 Literature & Arts**

# Imprisoning Time in a Rectangle

## Lance Morrow

*Lance Morrow (b. 1939), an American journalist and nonfiction writer, was born in Philadelphia. After getting his undergraduate degree from Harvard University in 1963, he worked as a reporter for the* Washington Star *before joining the staff of* Time *magazine in 1965, where he currently is senior writer and essayist. His books include* The Chief: A Memoir of Fathers and Sons *(1984),* America: A Rediscovery *(1987),* Fishing the Tiber *(1988), and* Safari: Experiencing the World *(1992). After surviving a heart attack at the age of 53, he recorded his experience in* Heart: A Memoir *(1995). In the following essay, first printed in a special issue of* Time *(Fall 1989), Morrow offers insights into the art of photography and the importance of photojournalism.*

1  Balzac had a "vague dread" of being photographed. Like some primitive peoples, he thought the camera steals something of the soul—that, as he told a friend, "every body in its natural state is made up of a series of ghostly images

superimposed in layers to infinity, wrapped in infinitesimal films." Each time a photograph was made, he believed, another thin layer of the subject's being would be stripped off to become not life as before but a membrane of memory in a sort of translucent antiworld.

If that is what photography is up to, then the onion of the world is being peeled away, layer by layer—lenses like black holes gobbling up life's emanations. Mere images proliferate, while history pares down to a phosphorescence of itself. 2

The idea catches something of the superstition (sometimes justified, if you think about it) and the spooky metaphysics that go ghosting around photography. Taking pictures is a transaction that snatches instants away from time and imprisons them in rectangles. These rectangles become a collective public memory and an image-world that is located usually on the verge of tears, often on the edge of a moral mess. 3

It is possible to be entranced by photography and at the same time disquieted by its powerful capacity to bypass thought. Photography, as the critic Susan Sontag has pointed out, is an elegiac, nostalgic phenomenon. No one photographs the future. The instants that the photographer freezes are ever the past, ever receding. They have about them the brilliance or instancy of their moment but also the cello sound of loss that life makes when going irrecoverably away and lodging at last in the dreamworks. 4

The pictures made by photojournalists have the legitimacy of being news, fresh information. They slice along the hard edge of the present. Photojournalism is not self-conscious, since it first enters the room (the brain) as a battle report from the far-flung Now. It is only later that the artifacts of photojournalism sink into the textures of the civilization and tincture its memory: Jack Ruby shooting Lee Harvey Oswald, an image so raw and shocking, subsides at last into the ecology of memory where we also find thousands of other oddments from the time—John John saluting at the funeral, Jack and Jackie on Cape Cod, who knows?—bright shards that stimulate old feelings (ghost pangs, ghost tendernesses, wistfulness) but not thought really. The shocks turn into dreams. The memory of such pictures, flipped through like a disordered Rolodex, makes at last a cultural tapestry, an inventory of the kind that brothers and sisters and distant cousins may rummage through at family reunions, except that the greatest photojournalism has given certain memories the emotional prestige of icons. 5

If journalism—the kind done with words—is the first draft of history, what is photojournalism? Is it the first impression of history, the first graphic flash? Yes, but it is also (and this is the disturbing thing) history's lasting visual impression. The service that the pictures perform is splendid, and so powerful as to seem preternatural. But sometimes the power they possess is more than they deserve. 6

Call up Eddie Adams' 1968 photo of General Nguyen Ngoc Loan, the police chief of Saigon, firing his snub-nosed revolver into the temple of a Viet Cong officer. Bright sunlight, Saigon: the scrawny police chief's arm, 7 outstretched, goes by extension through the trigger finger into the V.C.'s brain. That photograph, and another in 1972 showing a naked young Vietnamese girl running in arms-outstretched terror up a road away from American napalm, outmanned the force of three U.S. Presidents and the most powerful Army in the world. The photographs were considered, quite ridiculously, to be a portrait of America's moral disgrace. Freudians spend years trying to call up the primal image-memories, turned to trauma, that distort a neurotic patient's psyche. Photographs sometimes have a way of installing the image and legitimizing the trauma: the very vividness of the image, the greatness of the photograph as journalism or even as art, forestalls examination.

8      Adams has always felt uncomfortable about his picture of Loan executing the Viet Cong officer. What the picture does not show is that a few moments earlier the Viet Cong had slaughtered the family of Loan's best friend in a house just up the road. All this occurred during the Tet offensive, a state of general mayhem all over South Viet Nam. The Communists in similar circumstances would not have had qualms about summary execution.

9      But Loan shot the man; Adams took the picture. The image went firing around the world and lodged in the conscience. Photography is the very dream of the Heisenberg uncertainty principle, which holds that the act of observing a physical event inevitably changes it. War is merciless, bloody, and by definition it occurs outside the orbit of due process. Loan's Viet Cong did not have a trial. He did have a photographer. The photographer's picture took on a life of its own and changed history.

10     All great photographs have lives of their own, but they can be as false as dreams. Somehow the mind knows that and sorts out the matter, and permits itself to enjoy the pictures without getting sunk in the really mysterious business that they involve.

11     Still, a puritan conscience recoils a little from the sheer power of photographs. They have lingering about them the ghost of the golden calf—the bright object too much admired, without God's abstract difficulties. Great photographs bring the mind alive. Photographs are magic things that traffic in mystery. They float on the surface, and they have a strange life in the depths of the mind. They bear watching.

## COMPREHENSION

1. What does Morrow mean by "the superstition . . . and the spooky metaphysics that go ghosting around photography" (paragraph 3)?
2. According to the author, how does photography deal with time? What is the relationship of photojournalism to truth?
3. Much of the essay deals with a famous photograph by Eddie Adams. (See page 153 for a reproduction of this photo.) Summarize the writer's analysis of this photograph.

## RHETORIC

1. Morrow's introductory paragraph contains an allusion to the French novelist and short-story writer Honoré de Balzac (1799–1850). What is his purpose? How does this opening paragraph set the stage for the body of the essay?
2. What claim does Morrow make about the impact of photography and history? What evidence does he provide to support this claim?
3. Identify the many instances of figurative language—images, metaphors, and symbols—employed by the writer. What is he attempting to achieve with this highly figurative style? How effective is this language in advancing his key propositions?
4. How does the writer apply a comparative method to advance his argument?
5. At what point does Morrow begin his conclusion? How does the conclusion reflect earlier motifs and ideas? Is the ending effective? Why or why not?

## WRITING

1. Select a famous photograph, and write an essay explaining how it captures a moment in time and history.
2. Compare and contrast photography with pictorial art. Analyze examples of paintings and photographs; integrate these images into your essay.
3. **Writing an Argument:** Argue for or against the well-known adage "The camera doesn't lie." Refer to Morrow's commentary to support your position on this proposition.

www.mhhe.com/
**mhreader**

For more information on Lance Morrow, go to:
**More Resources > Ch. 10 Literature & Arts**

# Saving the Life That Is Your Own: The Importance of Models in the Artist's Life

### Alice Walker

*Alice Walker (b. 1941) was born in Eatonton, Georgia, and now lives in San Francisco and Mendocino County, California. She attended Spelman College and graduated from*

*Sarah Lawrence College. A celebrated and prolific novelist, short-story writer, poet, and essayist, she has also been active in the civil rights movement. Walker often draws on both her own personal experience and historical records to reflect on the African American experience. Her books include* The Color Purple *(1976), which won the American Book Award and the Pulitzer Prize;* You Can't Keep a Good Woman Down *(1981);* Living in the World: Selected Essays, 1973–1987 *(1987);* The Temple of My Familiar *(1989);* By the Light of My Father's Smile *(1999); and* The Way Forward Is with a Broken Heart *(2001). The following essay, from* In Search of Our Mother's Gardens *(1983), offers a highly personalized and perceptive analysis of the importance of influence on both art and life.*

1   There is a letter Vincent van Gogh wrote to Emile Bernard that is very meaning-ful to me. A year before he wrote the letter, van Gogh had had a fight with his domineering friend Gauguin, left his company, and cut off, in desperation and anguish, his own ear. The letter was written in Saint-Remy, in the South of France, from a mental institution to which van Gogh had voluntarily commit-ted himself.

2       I imagine van Gogh sitting at a rough desk too small for him, looking out at the lovely Southern light, and occasionally glancing critically next to him at his own paintings of the landscape he loved so much. The date of the letter is December 1889. Van Gogh wrote:

> However hateful painting may be, and however cumbersome in the times we are living in, if anyone who has chosen this handicraft pursues it zealously, he is a man of duty, sound and faithful.
>
> Society makes our existence wretchedly difficult at times, hence our impo-tence and the imperfection of our work.
>
> . . . I myself am suffering under an absolute lack of models.
>
> But on the other hand, there are beautiful spots here. I have just done five size 30 canvasses, olive trees. And the reason I am staying on here is that my health is improving a great deal.
>
> What I am doing is hard, dry, but that is because I am trying to gather new strength by doing some rough work, and I'm afraid abstractions would make me soft.

3       Six months later, van Gogh—whose health was "improving a great deal"—committed suicide. He had sold one painting during his lifetime. Three times was his work noticed in the press. But these are just details.

4       The real Vincent van Gogh is the man who has "just done five size 30 can-vasses, olive trees." To me, in context, one of the most moving and revealing descriptions of how a real artist thinks. And the knowledge that when he spoke of "suffering under an absolute lack of models" he spoke of that lack in terms of both the intensity of his commitment and the quality and singularity of his work, which was frequently ridiculed in his day.

5       The absence of models, in literature as in life, to say nothing of painting, is an occupational hazard for the artist, simply because models in art, in behavior, in growth of spirit and intellects—even if rejected—enrich and enlarge one's

view of existence. Deadlier still, to the artist who lacks models, is the curse of ridicule, the bringing to bear on an artist's best work, especially his or her most original, most strikingly deviant, only a fund of ignorance and the presumption that, as an artist's critic, one's judgment is free of the restrictions imposed by prejudice, and is well informed, indeed, about all the art in the world that really matters.

What is always needed in the appreciation of art, or life, is the larger per- 6 spective. Connections made, or at least attempted, where none existed before, the straining to encompass in one's glance at the varied world the common thread, the unifying theme through immense diversity, a fearlessness of growth, of search, of looking, that enlarges the private and the public world. And yet, in our particular society, it is the narrowed and narrowing view of life that often wins.

Recently, I read at a college and was asked by one of the audience what I 7 considered the major difference between the literature written by black and by white Americans. I had not spent a lot of time considering this question, since it is not the difference between them that interests me, but, rather, the way black writers and white writers seem to me to be writing one immense story—the same story, for the most part—with different parts of this immense story coming from a multitude of different perspectives. Until this is generally recognized, literature will always be broken into bits, black and white, and there will always be questions, wanting neat answers, such as this.

Still, I answered that I thought, for the most part, white American writers 8 tended to end their books and their characters' lives as if there were no better existence for which to struggle. The gloom of defeat is thick.

By comparison, black writers seem always involved in a moral and/or 9 physical struggle, the result of which is expected to be some kind of larger freedom. Perhaps this is because our literary tradition is based on the slave narratives, where escape for the body and freedom for the soul went together, or perhaps this is because black people have never felt themselves guilty of global, cosmic sins.

This comparison does not hold up in every case, of course, and perhaps 10 does not really hold up at all. I am not a gatherer of statistics, only a curious reader, and this has been my impression from reading many books by black and white writers.

There are, however, two books by American women that illustrate what I 11 am talking about: *The Awakening,* by Kate Chopin, and *Their Eyes Were Watching God,* by Zora Neale Hurston.

The plight of Mme Pontellier is quite similar to that of Janie Crawford. Each 12 woman is married to a dull, society-conscious husband and living in a dull, propriety-conscious community. Each woman desires a life of her own and a man who loves her and makes her feel alive. Each woman finds such a man.

Mme Pontellier, overcome by the strictures of society and the existence of 13 her children (along with the cowardice of her lover), kills herself rather than defy the one and abandon the other. Janie Crawford, on the other hand, refuses to allow society to dictate behavior to her, enjoys the love of a much younger, freedom-loving man, and lives to tell others of her experience.

14     When I mentioned these two books to my audience, I was not surprised to learn that only one person, a young black poet in the first row, had ever heard of *Their Eyes Were Watching God* (*The Awakening* they had fortunately read in their "Women in Literature" class), primarily because it was written by a black woman, whose experience—in love and life—was apparently assumed to be unimportant to the students (and the teachers) of a predominantly white school.

15     Certainly, as a student, I was not directed toward this book, which would have urged me more toward freedom and experience than toward comfort and security, but was directed instead toward a plethora of books by mainly white male writers who thought most women worthless if they didn't enjoy bullfighting or hadn't volunteered for the trenches in World War I.

16     Loving both these books, knowing each to be indispensable to my own growth, my own life, I choose the model, the example, of Janie Crawford. And yet this book, as necessary to me and to other women as air and water, is again out of print. But I have distilled as much as I could of its wisdom in this poem about its heroine, Janie Crawford:

> I love the way Janie Crawford
> left her husbands
> the one who wanted to change her
> into a mule
> and the other who tried to interest her
> in being a queen.
> A woman, unless she submits,
> is neither a mule
> nor a queen
> though like a mule she may suffer
> and like a queen pace the floor.

17     It has been said that someone asked Toni Morrison why she writes the kind of books she writes, and that she replied: Because they are the kind of books I want to read.

18     This remains my favorite reply to that kind of question. As if anyone reading the magnificent, mysterious *Sula* or the grim, poetic *The Bluest Eye* would require more of a reason for their existence than for the brooding, haunting *Wuthering Heights,* for example, or the melancholy, triumphant *Jane Eyre.* (I am not speaking here of the most famous short line of that book, "Reader, I married him," as the triumph, but, rather, of the triumph of Jane Eyre's control over her own sense of morality and her own stout will, which are but reflections of her creator's, Charlotte Brontë, who no doubt wished to write the sort of books *she* wished to read.)

19     Flannery O'Connor has written that more and more the serious novelist will write, not what other people want, and certainly not what other people

expect, but whatever interests her or him. And that the direction taken, therefore, will be away from sociology, away from the "writing of explanation," of statistics, and further into mystery, into poetry, and into prophecy. I believe this is true, *fortunately true;* especially for "Third World Writers"; Morrison, Marquez, Ahmadi, Camara Laye make good examples. And not only do I believe it is true for serious writers in general, but I believe, as firmly as did O'Connor, that this is our only hope—in a culture so in love with flash, with trendiness, with superficiality, as ours—of acquiring a sense of essence, of timelessness, and of vision. Therefore, to write the books one wants to read is both to point in the direction of vision and, at the same time, to follow it.

When Toni Morrison said she writes the kind of books she wants to read, [20] she was acknowledging the fact that in a society in which "accepted literature" is so often sexist and racist and otherwise irrelevant or offensive to so many lives, she must do the work of two. She must be her own model as well as the artist attending, creating, learning from, realizing the model, which is to say, herself.

(It should be remembered that, as a black person, one cannot completely [21] identify with a Jane Eyre, or with her creator, no matter how much one admires them. And certainly, if one allows history to impinge on one's reading pleasure, one must cringe at the thought of how Heathcliff, in the New World far from Wuthering Heights, amassed his Cathy-dazzling fortune.) I have often been asked why, in my own life and work, I have felt such a desperate need to know and assimilate the experiences of earlier black women writers, most of them unheard of by you and by me, until quite recently; why I felt a need to study them and to teach them.

I don't recall the exact moment I set out to explore the works of black [22] women, mainly those in the past, and certainly, in the beginning, I had no desire to teach them. Teaching being for me, at that time, less rewarding than stargazing on a frigid night. My discovery of them—most of them out of print, abandoned, discredited, maligned, nearly lost—came about, as many things of value do, almost by accident. As it turned out—and this should not have surprised me—I found I was in need of something that only one of them could provide.

Mindful that throughout my four years at a prestigious black and then a [23] prestigious white college I had heard not one word about early black women writers, one of my first tasks was simply to determine whether they had existed. After this, I could breathe easier, with more assurance about the profession I myself had chosen.

But the incident that started my search began several years ago: I sat [24] down at my desk one day, in a room of my own, with key and lock, and began preparations for a story about voodoo, a subject that had always fascinated me. Many of the elements of this story I had gathered from a story my mother several times told me. She had gone, during the Depression, into town to apply for some government surplus food at the local commissary, and had been turned down, in a particularly humiliating way, by the white woman in charge.

25   My mother always told this story with a most curious expression on her face. She automatically raised her head higher than ever—it was always high— and there was a look of righteousness, a kind of holy *heat* coming from her eyes. She said she had lived to see this same white woman grow old and senile and so badly crippled she had to get about on *two* sticks.

26   To her, this was clearly the working of God, who, as in the old spiritual, ". . . may not come when you want him, but he's right on time!" To me, hearing the story for about the fiftieth time, something else was discernible: the possibilities of the story, for fiction.

27   What, I asked myself, would have happened if, after the crippled old lady died, it was discovered that someone, my mother perhaps (who would have been mortified at the thought, Christian that she is), had voodooed her?

28   Then, my thoughts sweeping me away into the world of hexes and conjurings of centuries past, I wondered how a larger story could be created out of my mother's story; one that would be true to the magnitude of her humiliation and grief, and to the white woman's lack of sensitivity and compassion.

29   My third quandary was: How could I find out all I needed to know in order to write a story that used *authentic* black witchcraft?

30   Which brings me back, almost, to the day I became really interested in black women writers. I say "almost" because one other thing, from my childhood, made the choice of black magic a logical and irresistible one for my story. Aside from my mother's several stories about root doctors she had heard of or known, there was the story I had often heard about my "crazy" Walker aunt.

31   Many years ago, when my aunt was a meek and obedient girl growing up in a strict, conventionally religious house in the rural South, she had suddenly thrown off her meekness and had run away from home, escorted by a rogue of a man permanently attached elsewhere.

32   When she was returned home by her father, she was declared quite mad. In the backwoods South at the turn of the century, "madness" of this sort was cured not by psychiatry but by powders and by spells. (One can see Scott Joplin's *Treemonisha* to understand the role voodoo played among black people of that period.) My aunt's madness was treated by the community conjurer, who promised, and delivered, the desired results. His treatment was a bag of white powder, bought for fifty cents, and sprinkled on the ground around her house, with some of it sewed, I believe, into the bodice of her nightgown.

33   So when I sat down to write my story about voodoo, my crazy Walker aunt was definitely on my mind.

34   But she had experienced her temporary craziness so long ago that her story had all the excitement of a might-have-been. I needed, instead of family memories, some hard facts about the *craft* of voodoo, as practiced by Southern

blacks in the nineteenth century. (It never once, fortunately, occurred to me that voodoo was not worthy of the interest I had in it, or was too ridiculous to study seriously.)

I began reading all I could find on the subject of "The Negro and His Folk- 35 ways and Superstitions." There were Botkin and Puckett and others, all white, most racist. How was I to believe anything they wrote, since at least one of them, Puckett, was capable of wondering, in his book, if "The Negro" had a large enough brain?

Well, I thought, where are the *black* collectors of folklore? Where is the *black* 36 anthropologist? Where is the *black* person who took the time to travel the back roads of the South and collect the information I need: how to cure heat trouble, treat dropsy, hex somebody to death, lock bowels, cause joints to swell, eyes to fall out, and so on. Where was this black person?

And that is when I first saw, in a *footnote* to the white voices of authority, 37 the name Zora Neale Hurston.

Folklorist, novelist, anthropologist, serious student of voodoo, also all- 38 around black woman, with guts enough to take a slide rule and measure random black heads in Harlem; not to prove their inferiority, but to prove that whatever their size, shape, or present condition of servitude, those heads contained all the intelligence anyone could use to get through this world.

Zora Hurston, who went to Barnard to learn how to study what she really 39 wanted to learn: the ways of her own people, and what ancient rituals, customs, and beliefs had made them unique.

Zora, of the sandy-colored hair and the daredevil eyes, a girl who escaped 40 poverty and parental neglect by hard work and a sharp eye for the main chance.

Zora, who left the South only to return to look at it again. Who went to root 41 doctors from Florida to Louisiana and said, "Here I am. I want to learn your trade."

Zora, who had collected all the black folklore I could ever use.                         42
*That Zora.*                                                                             43

And having found *that Zora* (like a golden key to a storehouse of varied 44 treasure), I was hooked.

What I had discovered, of course, was a model. A model, who, as it hap- 45 pened, provided more than voodoo for my story, more than one of the greatest novels America had produced—though, being America, it did not realize this. She had provided, as if she knew someday I would come along wandering in the wilderness, a nearly complete record of her life. And though her life sprouted an occasional wart, I am eternally grateful for that life, warts and all.

It is not irrelevant, nor is it bragging (except perhaps to gloat a little on the 46 happy relatedness of Zora, my mother and me), to mention here that the story I wrote, called "The Revenge of Hannah Kemhuff," based on my mother's experiences during the Depression, and on Zora Hurston's folklore collection of the

1920s, and on my own response to both out of a contemporary existence, was immediately published and was later selected, by a reputable collector of short stories, as one of the *Best Short Stories of 1974.*

47    I mention it because this story might never have been written, because the very bases of its structure, authentic black folklore, viewed from a black perspective, might have been lost.

48    Had it been lost, my mother's story would have had no historical underpinning, none I could trust, anyway. I would not have written the story, which I enjoyed writing as much as I've enjoyed writing anything in my life, had I not known that Zora had already done a thorough job of preparing the ground over which I was then moving.

49    In that story I gathered up the historical and psychological threads of the life my ancestors lived, and in the writing of it I felt joy and strength and my own continuity. I had that wonderful feeling writers get sometimes, not very often, of being *with* a great many people, ancient spirits, all very happy to see me consulting and acknowledging them, and eager to let me know, through the joy of their presence, that, indeed, I am not alone.

50    To take Toni Morrison's statement further, if that is possible, in my own work I write not only what I want to read—understanding fully and indelibly that if I don't do it no one else is so vitally interested, or capable of doing it to my satisfaction—I write all the things *I should have been able to read.* Consulting, as belatedly discovered models, those writers—most of whom, not surprisingly, are women—who understood that their experience as ordinary human beings was also valuable, and in danger of being misrepresented, distorted, or lost:

> Zora Hurston—novelist, essayist, anthropologist, autobiographer;
>
> Jean Toomer—novelist, poet, philosopher, visionary, a man who cared what women felt;
>
> Colette—whose crinkly hair enhances her French, part-black face; novelist, playwright, dancer, essayist, newspaperwoman, lover of women, men, small dogs; fortunate not to have been born in America;
>
> Anaïs Nin—recorder of everything, no matter how minute;
>
> Tillie Olson—a writer of such generosity and honesty, she literally saves lives;
>
> Virginia Woolf—who has saved so many of us.

51    It is, in the end, the saving of lives that we writers are about. Whether we are "minority" writers or "majority." It is simply in our power to do this.

52    We do it because we care. We care that Vincent van Gogh mutilated his ear. We care that behind a pile of manure in the yard he destroyed his life. We care that Scott Joplin's music *lives!* We care because we know this: *the life we save is our own.*

## COMPREHENSION

1. Explain the significance of Walker's title. How does it serve her purpose and guide readers to her thesis? What is her thesis?
2. According to the author, what is the importance of models in art? What is the relationship of models to life? List the models in Walker's life. Which of them stand out?
3. Paraphrase Walker's remarks on the relationship between black American and white American writing.

## RHETORIC

1. Walker uses many allusions in this essay. Identify as many as you can. What is the allusion in the title? Comment on the general effectiveness of her allusions.
2. Is the author's style and choice of diction suitable to her subject matter and to her audience? Why or why not?
3. Why does the author personalize her treatment of the topic? What does she gain? Is there anything lost?
4. Walker employs several unique structuring devices in this essay. Cite at least three, and analyze their utility.
5. Explain Walker's use of examples to reinforce her generalizations and to organize the essay.
6. Which paragraphs constitute Walker's conclusion? What is their effect?

## WRITING

1. Write an essay expanding the meaning of Walker's remark "What is always needed in the appreciation of art, or life, is the larger perspective" (paragraph 6).
2. If you were planning on a career as a writer, artist, actor, or musician, who would your models be, and why?
3. **Writing an Argument:** Argue for or against Walker's proposition that the absence of models in art and life is an "occupational hazard" (paragraph 5).

www.mhhe.com/
**mhreader**

For more information on Alice Walker, go to:
**More Resources > Ch. 10 Literature & Arts**

# The Beatles

## Ned Rorem

*Ned Rorem (b. 1923), an acclaimed composer and writer, was born in Richmond, Indiana. He studied at several conservatories before graduating from Juilliard School of Music in New York City with BA (1946) and MA (1948) degrees. Rorem also studied privately with the famous composers Aaron Copland and Virgil Thomson. During a long, distinguished career, Rorem has composed three symphonies, six operas, numerous concertos and chamber pieces, and more than 500 songs. His music has received many awards, including the Pulitzer Prize for* Air Music for Orchestra *(1976) and the Gold Medal from the American Academy of Arts and Letters. Rorem is the author of 17 books, among them five diaries, starting with* The Paris Diary *(1966). He has also written* Music from Inside Out *(1967) and* Other Entertainment *(1996). Rorem's knowledge of and fondness for music in all its forms—from classical to pop—is revealed in the following essay, written when the Beatles were at the height of their popularity in 1968.*

1   I never go to classical concerts any more, and I don't know anyone who does. It's hard still to care whether some virtuoso tonight will perform the *Moonlight Sonata* a bit better or a bit worse than another virtuoso performed it last night.

2       I do often attend what used to be called avant-garde recitals, though seldom with delight, and inevitably I look around and wonder: What am I doing here? What am I learning? Where are the poets and painters and even composers who used to flock to these things? Well, perhaps what I'm doing here is a duty, keeping an ear on my profession so as to justify the joys of resentment, to steal an idea or two, or just to show charity toward some friend on the program. But I learn less and less. Meanwhile the absent artists are home playing records; they are *reacting* again, finally, to something they no longer find at concerts.

3       Reacting to what? To the Beatles, of course—the Beatles, whose arrival has proved one of the most healthy events in music since 1950. They and their offshoots represent—as any nonspecialized intellectual will tell you—the finest communicable music of our time.

4       This music was already sprouting a decade ago through such innocent male sex symbols as Presley in America and Johnny Halliday in France, both of whom were then caricatured by the English in a movie called *Expresso Bongo*, a precursor of *Privilege*, about a none-too-bright rock singer. These young soloists (still functioning and making lots of money) were the parents of more sophisticated, more *committed*, soloists like Dylan and Donovan, who in turn spawned a horde of masculine offspring including twins (Simon and Garfunkel, the most cultured), quintuplets (Country Joe & The Fish, the most exotic), sextuplets

(The Association, the most nostalgic), even septuplets (Mothers of Invention, the most madly satirical). With much less frequency were born female descendants such as Janis Ian or Bobbie Gentry (each of whom has produced one, and only one, good song—and who may be forgotten or immortal by the time this is read) and the trio of Supremes. Unlike their "grandparents," all of these groups, plus some twenty other fairly good ones, write most of their own material, thus combining the traditions of 12th-century troubadours, 16th-century madrigalists, and 18th-century musical artisans who were always composer-performers— in short, combining all sung expression (except opera) as it was before the twentieth century.

Why are the Beatles superior? It is easy to say that most of their competition  5 (like most everything everywhere) is junk; more important, their betterness is consistent: each of the songs from their last three albums is memorable. The best of these memorable tunes—and the best is a large percentage ("Here, There and Everywhere," "Good Day Sunshine," "Michelle," "Norwegian Wood" are already classics)—compare with those by composers from great eras of song: Monteverdi, Schumann, Poulenc.

Good melody—even perfect melody—can be both defined and taught, as  6 indeed can the other three "dimensions" of music: rhythm, harmony, counterpoint (although rhythm is the only one that can exist alone). Melody may be described thus: a series of notes of varying pitch and length, which evolve into a recognizable musical shape. In the case of a melody (*tune* means the same thing) which is set to words, the musical line will flow in curves relating to the verse that propels it inevitably toward a "high" point, usually called climax, and thence to the moment of culmination. The *inevitable* element is what makes the melody good—or perfect. But perfection can be sterile, as witness the thousands of 32-bar models turned out yesterday in Tin Pan Alley, or today by, say, Jefferson Airplane. Can we really recall such tunes when divorced from their words?

Superior melody results from the same recipe, with the difference that cer-  7 tain of the ingredients are blessed with the Distortion of Genius. The Beatles' words often go against the music (the crushing poetry that opens "A Day in the Life" intoned to the blandest of tunes), even as Martha Graham's music often contradicts her dance (she gyrates hysterically to utter silence, or stands motionless while all hell breaks loose in the pit). Because the Beatles pervert with naturalness they usually build solid structures, whereas their rivals pervert with affectation, aping the gargoyles but not the cathedral.

The unexpected in itself, of course, is no virtue, though all great works seem  8 to contain it. For instance, to cite as examples only the above four songs: "Here, There, and Everywhere" would seem at mid-hearing to be no more than a charming college show ballad, but once concluded it has grown immediately memorable. Why? Because of the minute harmonic shift on the words "wave of her hand," as surprising, yet as satisfyingly *right* as that in a Monteverdi madrigal like "A un giro sol." The notation of the hyper-exuberant rhythms in "Good Day Sunshine" was as aggravatingly elusive to me as some by Charles Ives, until I realized it was made by *triplets over the bar*; the "surprise" here was that the Beatles had made so simple a process *sound* so complex to a professional ear, and yet (by a third convolution) be instantly imitable by any amateur "with a beat." "Michelle" changes key on the very second measure (which is also the second word): in itself this is "allowed"—Poulenc often did it, and certainly he was the most derivative and correct composer who ever lived; the point is that he *chose* to do it on just the second measure, and that the choice worked. Genius doesn't lie in not being derivative, but in making right choices instead of wrong ones. As for "Norwegian Wood," again it is the arch of the tune—a movement growing increasingly disjunct, an inverted pyramid formed by a zigzag—which proves the song unique and memorable, rather than merely original.

9      Newness per se has never been the basis—or even especially an ingredient—of the Beatles' work. On the contrary, they have revitalized music's basics (harmony, counterpoint, rhythm, melody) by using them again in the simplest manner, a manner directed away from intellectualism and toward the heart. The Beatles' instrumentation may superficially sound far-out, but it apes the flashier element of electronic background no more advanced than the echo-chamber sound tracks of 1930s horror movies. Their "newest" thing is probably a kind of prosodic liberty; their rendition—their *realization*—often sounds contrary to the verses' predictable look on paper. Yet even at that, are they much different from our definitive songwriters of the past? From Purcell, say, or Debussy? It is not in their difference but in their betterness that their superiority lies.

10     But their betterness is not always apparent. Again, like Stravinsky, they are already classifiable with retrospective periods. Inasmuch as they try to surpass or even consciously to redefine themselves with each period, they fail, as they mostly have with their *Magical Mystery Tour*. This isn't surprising with persons so public and hence so vulnerable. But where, from this almost complacent "civilization," can they go from here?

11     Well, where does any artist go? Merely on. Still, it should now be clear that they are not the sum of their parts, but four distinct entities. Paul, I guess, is a genius with tunes; though what, finally, is genius without training? John, it seems, is no less clever than James Joyce; though where, ultimately, can that lead, when he is no *more* clever? George, they say, has brought East to West; but what, really, can that prove, when even Kipling realized it's not the twain of deeds but of concepts which never seem to meet? And Ringo, to at least one taste, is cute as a bug; though anyone, actually, can learn quick to play percussion, as our own George Plimpton now is demonstrating.

12     We've become so hung up on what they *mean*, we can no longer hear what they're performing. Nor was Beethoven ever so Freudianized.

13     Just as twenty years ago one found oneself reading more books about Kafka than reading Kafka himself, so today one gets embarrassed at being overheard in deep discussion of the Beatles. I love them. But I love them not as symbolic layers of "the scene" (or whatever it's called), and even less as caricatures of themselves (which, like Mae West, they're inclined to become). I love them as the hearty barbaric troubadours they essentially are. As such I hope they will continue to

develop, together or apart, for they represent the most invigorating music of an era so civilized that it risks extinction less from fallout than from boredom.

## COMPREHENSION

1. Why does Rorem, a classically trained musician, like the Beatles? Why, according to the writer, are they superior to other pop groups?
2. Explain what the author means by *harmony, counterpoint, rhythm,* and *melody* (paragraph 6). Which songs does he cite as examples of these elements?
3. Is this an essay exclusively about the Beatles? Why or why not?

## RHETORIC

1. Does "The Beatles" have an explicitly stated thesis or claim? Why or why not? Is Rorem's purpose to inform, persuade, or both? Justify your answer.
2. How much do you think Rorem expects readers to know about music composition, as well as both popular and classical music? How can you tell? In what ways does he establish himself as an authority on these matters? What is his tone?
3. Which paragraphs constitute the writer's introduction? What is the organizing principle in these paragraphs? How do subsequent paragraphs come back to ideas first expressed in the introduction?
4. Why does Rorem divide the essay into two sections? What is the relationship between these sections?
5. How does the writer develop an extended definition of what constitutes good or memorable music? What rhetorical strategies does he employ?
6. Evaluate the writer's conclusion. Why does he refer to Kafka and Mae West in an essay ostensibly about music?

## WRITING

1. Select a musician or musical group. Explain what you like about the music and, if you can, what compositional elements the music reveals. Refer to other musicians to establish a comparative framework.
2. What types of music do you like? Write a classification essay answering this question.
3. **Writing an Argument:** Does Rorem convince you that the Beatles composed some of "the finest communicable music of our time" (paragraph 3)? Write an argumentative essay in which you either support or reject his claim.

www.mhhe.com/ **mhreader** | For more information on Ned Rorem, go to:
**More Resources > Ch. 10 Literature & Arts**

# Synthesis: Connections for Critical Thinking

1. Write an essay comparing and contrasting literature and any other art form. What merits does each form have? Are there any limitations in either form? Which do you find more satisfying? Which form is more accessible? Use at least three essays in this chapter to illustrate or support your thesis.
2. Write an essay exploring the importance of role models in art and literature. Refer to the essays by Walker, Rorem, and Morrow to address the issue.
3. Develop an extended definition of photography, using the essays by Sontag and Morrow to help refine your ideas.
4. Forster, Atwood, Rorem, Morrow, and other writers in this chapter provide extended examples of art and artists. How do they develop these illustrations? What strategies do they use? Are their goals similar or not? Explain your response.
5. Use the essays by Forster, Prose, and Rorem to explore the question of excellence in the arts. Answer this question: How do you know the work of art is good?
6. Examine the role of the artist in society and the artist's purpose in or duty to society. How would the writers in this chapter address this issue?
7. **Network:** Working as a group, discuss the two works by Orwell that appear in Atwood's essay. Go online to find out more about Orwell, and report your findings in group discussion.
8. **Network:** After visiting several Web sites, write an essay in which you explain the importance of photography and photojournalism. Connect your findings to the ideas presented by Morrow and Sontag in their essays.

chapter *11*

# Philosophy, Ethics, and Religion

*What Do We Believe?*

You do not have to be an academician in an ivory tower to think about religion and the destiny of humankind or about questions of right and wrong. All of us possess beliefs about human nature and conduct, about "rival conceptions of God" (to use C. S. Lewis's phrase), about standards of behavior and moral duty. In fact, as Robert Coles argues in an essay appearing in this chapter, even children make ethical choices every day and are attuned to the "moral currents and issues in the large society."

Most of us have a system of ethical and religious beliefs, a philosophy of sorts, although it may not be a fully logical and systematic philosophy, and we may not be conscious that it determines what we do in everyday life. This system of beliefs and values is transmitted to us by family members, friends, educators, religious figures, and representatives of social groups. Such a philosophical system is not unyielding or unchanging, because our typical conflicts and dilemmas often force us to test our ethical assumptions and our values. For example, you may believe in nonviolence, but what would you do if someone threatened physical harm to you or a loved one? Or you may oppose the death penalty but encounter an essay that causes you to reassess your position. Our beliefs about nonviolence, capital punishment, abortion, cheating, equality, and so on are often paradoxical and place us in a universe of ethical dilemmas.

Your ability to resolve such dilemmas and make complex ethical decisions depends on your storehouse of knowledge and experience and on how well formulated your philosophy or system of beliefs is. When you know what is truly important in your life, you can make choices and decisions carefully and responsibly. Growing up in a world with competing views on morality often makes these choices that much harder, for constellations of cultures, beliefs, and influences contribute to our own personal development. As Plato observes in his classic "The Allegory of the Cave," the idea of what is truly good and correct never appears without wisdom and effort.

In this context, religion is also intrinsically connected to our sense of morality and ethics. Our personal code of ethics often has a religious grounding. Our religion often determines the way in which we apply our ethics—for instance, it may determine our attitudes toward contraception, equality of the races or the sexes, and evolution. In all instances, competing religious and secular values may force us to make hard decisions about our positions on significant cultural issues.

In one essay in the first chapter, Virginia Woolf contemplates a seemingly insignificant creature—a moth—that tells her (and us) a great deal about life and death. All authors in this chapter seek the essence of the values and ideas that we develop during our brief time on this planet and that lend meaning and vitality to our lives.

## Previewing the Chapter

As you read the essays in this chapter and respond to them in discussion and writing, consider the following questions:

- On what ethical or religious problem or conflict does the author focus?
- Is the author's view of life optimistic or pessimistic? Why?
- Do you agree or disagree with the philosophical or religious perspective that the author adopts?
- Is there a clear solution to the issue the author investigates?
- Does the author present rational arguments or engage in emotional appeals and weak reasoning?
- Does the author approach ethical, theological, and philosophical issues in an objective or in a subjective way?
- How significant is the ethical or philosophical subject addressed by the author?
- What social, political, or racial issues are raised by the author?
- Are there religious dimensions to the essay? If so, how does religion reinforce the author's philosophical inquiry?
- How do these essays encourage you to examine your own attitudes and values? In reading them, what do you discover about your own system of beliefs and the beliefs of society at large?

## Classic and Contemporary Images

DO WE BELIEVE IN GOOD AND EVIL?

*Using a Critical Perspective*  Comment on the composition of each of these works of art. How does each artist present the supernatural beings depicted? What do you notice about the organization of the images? From what angle does the artist approach the depiction? What do the artists have in common? Is the overall impression or effect of each illustration the same or different? Explain.

Angels, supernatural beings who serve as messengers from God, are found in the literature and imagery of Judaism, Christianity, and Islam from ancient times to the present, as in the Islamic painting from India shown here.

In more recent times, the sculptor Jacob Epstein (1880–1959) created a bronze
statue of St. Michael for Coventry Cathedral in England. The ancient
cathedral at Coventry was destroyed by German bombs in 1940.
During the 1950s, a new cathedral was built near the ruins of the old one.
With his spear in hand and his wings outstretched, St. Michael
stands in triumph over the prone, chained figure of the devil.

## Classic and Contemporary Essays
### *Is Superstition a Form of Belief?*

Although most contemporary individuals who consider themselves "educated" deny any strong influence of superstition in their lives, both Margaret Mead and Letty Cottin Pogrebin suggest in their respective essays that neither contemporary ideas, with their reliance on science, nor higher education, with its focus on rational thinking, insulate us from at least a small amount of superstition into our lives. Mead discounts the notion that superstition is relegated to "primitive" societies or to the uneducated who have not been enlightened by a firm grounding in empiricism. The famed anthropologist suggests that we need superstition to provide coherence to our lives when other forms of belief and thought are not competent to satisfy us. In fact, in facing the unknown, we may turn to superstition as a welcome friend. How many of your fellow schoolmates, for example, will cross their fingers before an exam or keep a good-luck charm attached to their computer? Simply put, very few of us are so secure that we can rely on our own inner fortitude to ward off occasional fears or feelings of helplessness. Superstition, therefore, provides a framework to maintain a private sanctuary against the unknown. Pogrebin admits to being a "very rational person" who also "happen[s] to be superstitious." Although the particular rituals that inform her superstition were learned from her mother, who used them as a means of "imposing order," the function of superstition in her own life, Pogrebin claims, is to maintain coherence with the past: to feel the connection between herself and her mother. In other words, like Mead, Pogrebin contends that superstition helps us maintain a sense of security in an environment where we do not have complete control. By keeping the same rituals as her mother, Pogrebin senses her mother's protection. Does this mean that humans are flawed, weak creatures? If we consider the vicissitudes and uncertainties of modern life, perhaps the tendency of humans to have a bit of superstition in their worldview is a sign of intelligence.

# New Superstitions for Old

## Margaret Mead

*Margaret Mead (1901–1979), famed American anthropologist, was curator of ethnology at the American Museum of Natural History and a professor at Columbia University. Her field expeditions to Samoa, New Guinea, and Bali in the 1920s and 1930s produced several major studies, notably* Coming of Age in Samoa *(1928),* Growing Up in New Guinea *(1930), and* Sex and Temperament in Three Primitive Societies *(1935). In this essay, first published in* A Way of Seeing *(1970), Mead discusses the role that superstition plays in our daily life.*

Once in a while there is a day when everything seems to run smoothly and  1
even the riskiest venture comes out exactly right. You exclaim, "This is my lucky day!" Then as an afterthought you say, "Knock on wood!" Of course, you do not really believe that knocking on wood will ward off danger. Still, boasting about your own good luck gives you a slightly uneasy feeling—and you carry out the little protective ritual. If someone challenged you at that moment, you would probably say, "Oh, that's nothing. Just an old superstition."

But when you come to think about it, what is superstition?  2

In the contemporary world most people treat old folk beliefs as superstitions—  3
the belief, for instance, that there are lucky and unlucky days or numbers, that future events can be read from omens, that there are protective charms or that what happens can be influenced by casting spells. We have excluded magic from our current world view, for we know that natural events have natural causes.

In a religious context, where truths cannot be demonstrated, we accept  4
them as a matter of faith. Superstitions, however, belong to the category of beliefs, practices and ways of thinking that have been discarded because they are inconsistent with scientific knowledge. It is easy to say that other people are superstitious because they believe what we regard to be untrue. "Superstition" used in that sense is a derogatory term for the beliefs of other people that we do not share. But there is more to it than that. For superstitions lead a kind of half life in a twilight world where, sometimes, we partly suspend our disbelief and act as if magic worked.

Actually, almost every day, even in the most sophisticated home, some-  5
thing is likely to happen that evokes the memory of some old folk belief. The salt spills. A knife falls to the floor. Your nose tickles. Then perhaps, with a slightly embarrassed smile, the person who spilled the salt tosses a pinch over his left shoulder. Or someone recites the old rhyme, "Knife falls, gentleman calls." Or as you rub your nose you think, That means a letter. I wonder who's

writing? No one takes these small responses very seriously or gives them more than a passing thought. Sometimes people will preface one of these ritual acts— walking around instead of under a ladder or hastily closing an umbrella that has been opened inside a house—with such remarks as "I remember my great-aunt used to . . . " or "Germans used to say you ought not . . . " And then, having placed the belief at some distance away in time or space, they carry out the ritual.

6    Everyone also remembers a few of the observances of childhood—wishing on the first star; looking at the new moon over the right shoulder; avoiding the cracks in the sidewalk on the way to school while chanting, "Step on a crack, break your mother's back"; wishing on white horses, on loads of hay, on covered bridges, on red cars; saying quickly, "Bread-and-butter" when a post or a tree separated you from the friend you were walking with. The adult may not actually recite the formula "Star light, star bright . . . " and may not quite turn to look at the new moon, but his mood is tempered by a little of the old thrill that came when the observance was still freighted with magic.

7    Superstition can also be used with another meaning. When I discuss the religious beliefs of other peoples, especially primitive peoples, I am often asked, "Do they really have a religion, or is it all just superstition?" The point of contrast here is not between a scientific and a magical view of the world but between the clear, theologically defensible religious beliefs of members of civilized societies and what we regard as the false and childish views of the heathen who "bow down to wood and stone." Within the civilized religions, however, where membership includes believers who are educated and urbane and others who are ignorant and simple, one always finds traditions and practices that the more sophisticated will dismiss offhand as "just superstition" but that guide the steps of those who live by older ways. Mostly these are very ancient beliefs, some handed on from one religion to another and carried from country to country around the world.

8    Very commonly, people associate superstition with the past, with very old ways of thinking that have been supplanted by modern knowledge. But new superstitions are continually coming into being and flourishing in our society. Listening to mothers in the park in the 1930s, one heard them say, "Now, don't you run out into the sun, or Polio will get you." In the 1940s elderly people explained to one another in tones of resignation, "It was the Virus that got him down." And every year the cosmetics industry offers us new magic—cures for baldness, lotions that will give every woman radiant skin, hair coloring that will restore to the middle-aged the charm and romance of youth—results that are promised if we will just follow the simple directions. Families and individuals also have their cherished, private superstitions. You must leave by the back door when you are going on a journey, or you must wear a green dress when you are taking an examination. It is a kind of joke, of course, but it makes you feel safe.

9    These old half-beliefs and new half-beliefs reflect the keenness of our wish to have something come true or to prevent something bad from happening. We

do not always recognize new superstitions for what they are, and we still follow the old ones because someone's faith long ago matches our contemporary hopes and fears. In the past people "knew" that a black cat crossing one's path was a bad omen, and they turned back home. Today we are fearful of taking a journey and would give anything to turn back—and then we notice a black cat running across the road in front of us.

Child psychologists recognize the value of the toy a child holds in his hand 10 at bedtime. It is different from his thumb, with which he can close himself in from the rest of the world, and it is different from the real world to which he is learning to relate himself. Psychologists call these toys—these furry animals and old, cozy baby blankets—"transitional objects"; that is, objects that help the child move back and forth between the exactions of everyday life and the world of wish and dream.

Superstitions have some of the qualities of these transitional objects. They 11 help people pass between the areas of life where what happens has to be accepted without proof and the areas where sequences of events are explicable in terms of cause and effect, based on knowledge. Bacteria and viruses that cause sickness have been identified; the cause of symptoms can be diagnosed and a rational course of treatment prescribed. Magical charms no longer are needed to treat the sick; modern medicine has brought the whole sequence of events into the secular world. But people often act as if this change had not taken place. Laymen still treat germs as if they were invisible, malign spirits, and physicians sometimes prescribe antibiotics as if they were magic substances.

Over time, more and more of life has become subject to the controls of 12 knowledge. However, this is never a one-way process. Scientific investigation is continually increasing our knowledge. But if we are to make good use of this knowledge, we must not only rid our minds of old, superseded beliefs and fragments of magical practice, but also recognize new superstitions for what they are. Both are generated by our wishes, our fears and our feeling of helplessness in difficult situations.

Civilized peoples are not alone in having grasped the idea of superstitions— 13 beliefs and practices that are superseded but that still may evoke the different worlds in which we live—the sacred, the secular and the scientific. They allow us to keep a private world also, where, smiling a little, we can banish danger with a gesture and summon luck with a rhyme, make the sun shine in spite of storm clouds, force the stranger to do our bidding, keep an enemy at bay and straighten the paths of those we love.

## COMPREHENSION

1. Explain in your own words the religious context for this essay.
2. What point is Mead making about superstition in modern life? Where does she state her main idea?
3. Where does Mead define *superstition?* How does it differ from folk beliefs?

## RHETORIC

1. Explain what Mead means by "transitional objects" (paragraph 10). Why does she mention them?
2. Discuss the author's use of the pronouns *we* and *us* in the conclusion. Why does she state the conclusion in personal terms?
3. How does Mead use definition to differentiate *superstition* from *faith*? Explain the logic behind her distinction.
4. How does Mead use classification to describe the "worlds in which we live" (paragraph 13)? What are these worlds? What examples does she give of superstition in each of these worlds?
5. Look at paragraph 10. What is the purpose of this example? How does it figure in the context of Mead's essay?
6. Discuss the term *theologically defensible* as used in paragraph 7. Does Mead support this concept by example or evidence?

## WRITING

1. Write an essay about beliefs you once held that you have since abandoned. Why did you abandon them? What was the practical result?
2. Select a saying or phrase based in superstition or folk belief that you or a friend are fond of. Analyze its appeal.
3. **Writing an Argument:** This article was published in 1966. Have we made any progress toward banishing superstition since then? Will we ever live in a culture free of superstition? Do we want to? Answer these questions in an argumentative essay.

 www.mhhe.com/ **mhreader** | For more information on Margaret Mead, go to: **More Resources > Ch. 11 Ethics & Religion**

# Superstitious Minds

### LETTY COTTIN POGREBIN

*Letty Cottin Pogrebin (b. 1939) is deeply committed to women's issues, family politics, and the nonsexist rearing and education of children. A native of New York, she graduated from Brandeis University and from 1971 to 1987 was the editor of* Ms. *magazine, for which she remains a contributing editor. She has also contributed to such publications as* The New York Times *and* The Nation *and has written a number of books, including* Among Friends *(1986),* Debra Golda and Me: Being Female and Jewish in America *(1991), and* Getting Over Getting Older *(1996). Pogrebin lectures frequently and is a founder of the Women's Political Caucus as well as president of the Authors' Guild. In the following essay, she reminisces about her fearful, superstitious mother, whom she understands much better since becoming a mother herself.*

I am a very rational person. I tend to trust reason more than feeling. But I also   1
happen to be superstitious—in my fashion. Black cats and rabbits' feet hold no power for me. My superstitions are my mother's superstitions, the amulets and incantations she learned from her mother and taught me.

I don't mean to suggest that I grew up in an occult atmosphere. On the con-   2
trary, my mother desperately wanted me to rise above her immigrant ways and become an educated American. She tried to hide her superstitions, but I came to know them all: Slap a girl's cheeks when she first gets her period. Never take a picture of a pregnant woman. Knock wood when speaking about your good fortune. Eat the ends of bread if you want to have a boy. Don't leave a bride alone on her wedding day.

When I was growing up, my mother often would tiptoe in after I seemed to   3
be asleep and kiss my forehead three times, making odd noises that sounded like a cross between sucking and spitting. One night I opened my eyes and demanded an explanation. Embarrassed, she told me she was excising the "Evil Eye"—in case I had attracted its attention that day by being especially wonderful. She believed her kisses could suck out any envy or ill will that those less fortunate may have directed at her child.

By the time I was in my teens, I was almost on speaking terms with the Evil   4
Eye, a jealous spirit that kept track of those who had "too much" happiness and zapped them with sickness and misery to even the score. To guard against his mischief, my mother practiced rituals of interference, evasion, deference, and above all, avoidance of situations where the Evil Eye might feel at home.

This is why I wasn't allowed to attend funerals. This is also why my mother   5
hated to mend my clothes while I was wearing them. The only garment one should properly get sewn *into* is a shroud. To ensure that the Evil Eye did not confuse my pinafore with a burial outfit, my mother insisted that I chew a thread while she sewed, thus proving myself very much alive. Outwitting the Evil Eye also accounted for her closing the window shades above my bed whenever there was a full moon. The moon should only shine on cemeteries, you see; the living need protection from the spirits.

Because we were dealing with a deadly force, I also wasn't supposed to say   6
any words associated with mortality. This was hard for a 12-year-old who punctuated every anecdote with the verb "to die," as in "You'll die when you hear this!" or "If I don't get home by ten, I'm dead." I managed to avoid using such expressions in the presence of my mother until the day my parents brought home a painting I hated and we were arguing about whether it should be displayed on our walls. Unthinking, I pressed my point with a melodramatic

idiom: "That picture will hang over my dead body!" Without a word, my mother grabbed a knife and slashed the canvas to shreds.

7      I understand all this now. My mother emigrated in 1907 from a small Hungarian village. The oldest of seven children, she had to go out to work before she finished the eighth grade. Experience taught her that life was unpredictable and often incomprehensible. Just as an athlete keeps wearing the same T-shirt in every game to prolong a winning streak, my mother's superstitions gave her a means of imposing order on a chaotic system. Her desire to control the fates sprung from the same helplessness that makes the San Francisco 49ers' defensive more superstitious than its offensive team. Psychologists speculate this is because the defense has less control; they don't have the ball.

8      Women like my mother never had the ball. She died when I was 15, leaving me with deep regrets for what she might have been—and a growing understanding of who she was. *Superstitious* is one of the things she was. I wish I had a million sharp recollections of her, but when you don't expect someone to die, you don't store up enough memories. Ironically, her mystical practices are among the clearest impressions she left behind. In honor of this matrilineal heritage—and to symbolize my mother's effort to control her life as I in my way try to find order in mine—knock on wood and I do not let the moon shine on those I love. My children laugh at me, but they understand that these tiny rituals have helped keep my mother alive in my mind.

9      A year ago, I awoke in the night and realized that my son's window blinds had been removed for repair. Smiling at my own compulsion, I got a bed sheet to tack up against the moonlight and I opened his bedroom door. What I saw brought tears to my eyes. There, hopelessly askew, was a blanket my son, then 18, had taped to his window like a curtain.

10     My mother never lived to know David, but he knew she would not want the moon to shine upon him as he slept.

## COMPREHENSION

1. What is the function of superstition in the writer's life? What purpose did it serve in her mother's life?
2. What was Pogrebin's reaction to her mother's behavior while she was growing up? How does the adult feel?
3. How does the writer use superstitions now as an adult? Has she passed on these beliefs to her children? Explain.

## RHETORIC

1. Examine Pogrebin's first sentence. How does it prepare the reader for the content of the essay? How does its simplicity add to its force?
2. How do the accumulated examples in paragraph 2 illustrate the point of the paragraph?

3.  What is the writer's tone? Justify your answer.
4.  What is the point of paragraph 7? How does the comparison work to support Pogrebin's point?
5.  What is the purpose of the essay? Where does it become apparent? How do the other paragraphs reinforce it?
6.  Comment on the author's final sentence. What effect does it have on the reader? How does it help to hold the essay together?

## WRITING

1.  Children are often annoyed with or embarrassed by their parents' behavior or beliefs. Write an essay describing something your parents repeatedly said or did that caused you discomfort or confusion. Include how you now feel about their actions and any insight you may have since gained into their motives or feelings.
2.  Write an essay about superstition. Consider the meaning of the word. What connection, if any, does it have with religion? How do superstitions affect the people who believe in them? Why do they believe? What is the role of superstition in your family? Provide examples of superstitions.
3.  Write an essay in which you consider how your parents raised you—the values, opinions, and beliefs they instilled in you. Would you want to pass these on to your children? Why or why not?
4.  **Writing an Argument:** Argue for or against the proposition that children need superstition—Santa Claus, the Tooth Fairy, and so forth—in their lives.

www.mhhe.com/
**mhreader**

For more information on Letty Cottin Pogrebin, go to:
**More Resources > Ch. 11 Ethics & Religion**

## Synthesis: Classic and Contemporary Questions for Comparison

1.  Mead presents her argument regarding the benefits of superstition through an anthropological analysis of the subject, whereas Pogrebin employs a more personal approach, focusing on the role of superstition in her own life. What are the merits of each approach? Do the two essays together contribute to a greater understanding of the nature of superstition than either one alone?
2.  Both Mead and Pogrebin discuss the value of superstition in childhood. Why is childhood in particular a time in life when superstition can prove valuable? What is Mead's answer to this issue? How does it differ from Pogrebin's?

3. The tone of Mead's essay is objective, scientific, and critical. In addition, she never refers to personal experience, and we can assume she is writing from the perspective of someone who needs to maintain her professional status. Why would these factors influence her decision to contour her style so that she seems an observer of superstition rather than someone with superstitious leanings? On the other hand, why would Pogrebin choose to "personalize" her essay by referring to personal experience? Are these choices matters of style, audience, purpose, or a combination of these?

4. Mead seems more concerned with explicating her subject matter in academic terms. Note how she articulates the meaning of *folk beliefs, religion,* and *transitional objects.* How would you characterize the differences between an academically oriented argument such as Mead's and one intended for a more general audience such as Pogrebin's?

# I Listen to My Parents and I Wonder What They Believe

## Robert Coles

*Robert Coles (b. 1929), author and psychologist, won the Pulitzer Prize in general nonfiction for volumes 1 and 2 of* Children of Crisis, *in which he examines with compassion and intelligence the effects of the controversy over integration on children in the South. Walker Percy praised Coles because he "spends his time listening to people and trying to understand them." In its final form,* Children of Crisis *has five volumes, and Coles has widened its focus to include the children of the wealthy and the poor, the exploited and the exploiters. In collaboration with Jane Coles, he completed* Women in Crisis II *(1980). He has also written* The Secular Mind *(1999) and* Lives of Moral Leadership *(2000). Below, Coles demonstrates his capacity to listen to and to understand children.*

1  Not so long ago children were looked upon in a sentimental fashion as "angels," or as "innocents." Today, thanks to Freud and his followers, boys and girls are understood to have complicated inner lives; to feel love, hate, envy and rivalry in various and subtle mixtures; to be eager participants in the sexual and emotional politics of the home, neighborhood and school. Yet some of us parents still cling to the notion of childhood innocence in another way. We do not see that our children also make ethical decisions every day in their own lives, or realize how attuned they may be to moral currents and issues in the larger society.

2      In Appalachia I heard a girl of eight whose father owns coal fields (and gas stations, a department store and much timberland) wonder about "life" one

day: "I'll be walking to the school bus, and I'll ask myself why there's some who are poor and their daddies can't find a job, and there's some who are lucky like me. Last month there was an explosion in a mine my daddy owns, and everyone became upset. Two miners got killed. My daddy said it was their own fault, because they'll be working and they get careless. When my mother asked if there was anything wrong with the safety down in the mine, he told her no and she shouldn't ask questions like that. Then the Government people came and they said it was the owner's fault—Daddy's. But he has a lawyer and the lawyer is fighting the Government and the union. In school, kids ask me what I think, and I sure do feel sorry for the two miners and so does my mother—I know that. She told me it's just not a fair world and you have to remember that. Of course, there's no one who can be sure there won't be trouble; like my daddy says, the rain falls on the just and the unjust. My brother is only six and he asked Daddy awhile back who are the 'just' and the 'unjust,' and Daddy said there are people who work hard and they live good lives, and there are lazy people and they're always trying to sponge off others. But I guess you have to feel sorry for anyone who has a lot of trouble, because it's poured-down, heavy rain."

Listening, one begins to realize that an elementary-school child is no 3 stranger to moral reflection—and to ethical conflict. This girl was torn between her loyalty to her particular background, its values and assumptions, and to a larger affiliation—her membership in the nation, the world. As a human being whose parents were kind and decent to her, she was inclined to be thoughtful and sensitive with respect to others, no matter what their work or position in society. But her father was among other things a mineowner, and she had already learned to shape her concerns to suit that fact of life. The result: a moral oscillation of sorts, first toward nameless others all over the world and then toward her own family. As the girl put it later, when she was a year older: "You should try to have 'good thoughts' about everyone, the minister says, and our teacher says that too. But you should honor your father and mother most of all; that's why you should find out what they think and then sort of copy them. But sometimes you're not sure if you're on the right track."

*Sort of copy them.* There could be worse descriptions of how children acquire 4 moral values. In fact, the girl understood how girls and boys all over the world "sort of" develop attitudes of what is right and wrong, ideas of who the just and the unjust are. And they also struggle hard and long, and not always with success, to find out where the "right track" starts and ends. Children need encouragement or assistance as they wage that struggle.

In home after home that I have visited, and in many classrooms, I have met 5 children who not only are growing emotionally and intellectually but also are trying to make sense of the world morally. That is to say, they are asking themselves and others about issues of fair play, justice, liberty, equality. Those last words are abstractions, of course—the stuff of college term papers. And there are, one has to repeat, those in psychology and psychiatry who would deny elementary-school children access to that "higher level" of moral reflection. But any parent who has listened closely to his or her child knows that girls and boys are capable of wondering about matters of morality, and knows too that often it is their grown-up protectors (parents, relatives, teachers, neighbors) who are made uncomfortable by the so-called "innocent" nature of the questions children may ask or the statements they may make. Often enough the issue is not the moral capacity of children but the default of us parents who fail to respond to inquiries put to us by our daughters and sons—and fail to set moral standards for both ourselves and our children.

6    Do's and don't's are, of course, pressed upon many of our girls and boys. But a moral education is something more than a series of rules handed down, and in our time one cannot assume that every parent feels able—sure enough of her own or his own actual beliefs and values—to make even an initial explanatory and disciplinary effect toward a moral education. Furthermore, for many of us parents these days it is a child's emotional life that preoccupies us.

7    In 1963, when I was studying school desegregation in the South, I had extended conversations with Black and white elementary-school children caught up in a dramatic moment of historical change. For longer than I care to remember, I concentrated on possible psychiatric troubles, on how a given child was managing under circumstances of extreme stress, on how I could be of help—with "support," with reassurance, with a helpful psychological observation or interpretation. In many instances I was off the mark. These children weren't "patients"; they weren't even complaining. They were worried, all right, and often enough they had things to say that were substantive—that had to do not so much with troubled emotions as with questions of right and wrong in the real-life dramas taking place in their worlds.

8    Here is a nine-year-old white boy, the son of ardent segregationists, telling me about his sense of what desegregation meant to Louisiana in the 1960s: "They told us it wouldn't happen—never. My daddy said none of us white people would go into schools with the colored. But then it did happen, and when I went to school the first day I didn't know what would go on. Would the school stay open or would it close up? We didn't know what to do; the teacher kept telling us that we should be good and obey the law, but my daddy said the law was wrong. Then my mother said she wanted me in school even if there were some colored kids there. She said if we all stayed home she'd be a 'nervous wreck.' So I went.

9    "After a while I saw that the colored weren't so bad. I saw that there are different kinds of colored people, just like with us whites. There was one of the colored who was nice, a boy who smiled, and he played real good. There was another one, a boy, who wouldn't talk with anyone. I don't know if it's right that we all be in the same school. Maybe it isn't right. My sister is starting school next year, and she says she doesn't care if there's 'mixing of the races.' She says they told her in Sunday school that everyone is a child of God, and then a kid asked if that goes for the colored too and the teacher said yes, she thought so. My daddy said that it's true, God made everyone—but that doesn't mean we all have to be living together under the same roof in the home or the school. But my mother said we'll never know what God wants of us but we have to try to read His mind,

and that's why we pray. So when I say my prayers I ask God to tell me what's the right thing to do. In school I try to say hello to the colored, because they're kids, and you can't be mean or you'll be 'doing wrong,' like my grandmother says."

Children aren't usually long-winded in the moral discussions they have  10
with one another or with adults, and in quoting this boy I have pulled together comments he made to me in the course of several days. But everything he said was of interest to me. I was interested in the boy's changing racial attitudes. It was clear he was trying to find a coherent, sensible moral position too. It was also borne in on me that if one spends days, weeks in a given home, it is hard to escape a particular moral climate just as significant as the psychological one.

In many homes parents establish moral assumptions, mandates, priorities.  11
They teach children what to believe in, what not to believe in. They teach children what is permissible or not permissible—and why. They may summon up the Bible, the flag, history, novels, aphorisms, philosophical or political sayings, personal memories—all in an effort to teach children how to behave, what and whom to respect and for which reasons. Or they may neglect to do so, and in so doing teach their children *that*—a moral abdication, of sorts—and in this way fail their children. Children need and long for words of moral advice, instruction, warning, as much as they need words of affirmation or criticism from their parents about other matters. They must learn how to dress and what to wear, how to eat and what to eat; and they must also learn how to behave under X or Y or Z conditions, and why.

All the time, in 20 years of working with poor children and rich children,  12
Black children and white children, children from rural areas and urban areas and in every region of this county, I have heard questions—thoroughly intelligent and discerning questions—about social and historical matters, about personal behavior, and so on. But most striking is the fact that almost all those questions, in one way or another, are moral in nature: Why did the Pilgrims leave England? Why didn't they just stay and agree to do what the king wanted them to do? . . . Should you try to share all you've got or should you save a lot for yourself? . . . What do you do when you see others fighting—do you try to break up the fight, do you stand by and watch or do you leave as fast as you can? . . . Is it right that some people haven't got enough to eat? . . . I see other kids cheating and I wish I could copy the answers too; but I won't cheat, though sometimes I feel I'd like to and I get all mixed up. I go home and talk with my parents, and I ask them what should you do if you see kids cheating—pay no attention, or report the kids or do the same thing they are doing?

Those are examples of children's concerns—and surely millions of Ameri-  13
can parents have heard versions of them. Have the various "experts" on childhood stressed strongly enough the importance of such questions—and the importance of the hunger we all have, no matter what our age or background, to examine what we believe in, are willing to stand up for, and what we are determined to ask, likewise, of our children?

Children not only need our understanding of their complicated emotional  14
lives; they also need a constant regard for the moral issues that come their way

as soon as they are old enough to play with others and take part in the politics of
the nursery, the back yard and the schoolroom. They need to be told what they
must do and what they must not do. They need control over themselves and a
sense of what others are entitled to from them—cooperation, thoughtfulness, an
attentive ear and eye. They need discipline not only to tame their excesses of
emotion but discipline also connected to stated and clarified moral values. They
need, in other words, something to believe in that is larger than their own appetites and urges and, yes, bigger than their "psychological drives." They need
a larger view of the world, a moral context, as it were—a faith that addresses itself to the meaning of this life we all live and, soon enough, let go of.

15      Yes, it is time for us parents to begin to look more closely at what ideas our
children have about the world; and it would be well to do so before they become teenagers and young adults and begin to remind us, as often happens, of
how little attention we did pay to their moral development. Perhaps a nine-
year-old girl from a well-off suburban home in Texas put it better than anyone
else I've met:

> I listen to my parents, and I wonder what they believe in more than anything
> else. I asked my mom and my daddy once: What's the thing that means most to
> you? They said they didn't know but I shouldn't worry my head too hard with
> questions like that. So I asked my best friend, and she said she wonders if
> there's a God and how do you know Him and what does He want you to do—
> I mean, when you're in school or out playing with your friends. They talk about
> God in church, but is it only in church that He's there and keeping an eye on
> you? I saw a kid steal in a store, and I know her father has a lot of money—
> because I hear my daddy talk. But stealing's wrong. My mother said she's a
> "sick girl," but it's still wrong what she did. Don't you think?

16      There was more—much more—in the course of the months I came to
know that child and her parents and their neighbors. But those observations
and questions—a "mere child's"—reminded me unforgettably of the aching
hunger for firm ethical principles that so many of us feel. Ought we not begin
thinking about this need? Ought we not all be asking ourselves more intently
what standards we live by—and how we can satisfy our children's hunger for
moral values?

## COMPREHENSION

1. How does Coles's title capture the substance of his essay? What is his
   thesis?
2. According to Coles, why do parents have difficulty explaining ethics to
   their children? On what aspects of their children's development do they
   tend to concentrate? Why?
3. There is an implied contrast between mothers' and fathers' attitudes toward morality in Coles's essay. Explain this contrast, and cite examples for
   your explanation.

## RHETORIC

1. What point of view does Coles use here? How does that viewpoint affect the tone of the essay?
2. Compare Coles's sentence structure with the sentence structure of the children he quotes. How do they differ?
3. Does this essay present an inductive or a deductive argument? Give evidence for your answer.
4. How does paragraph 13 differ from paragraphs 3, 10, and 16? How do all four paragraphs contribute to the development of the essay?
5. Explain the line of reasoning in the first paragraph. Why does Coles allude to Freud? How is that allusion related to the final sentence of the paragraph?
6. What paragraphs constitute the conclusion of the essay? Why? How do they summarize Coles's argument?

## WRITING

1. Write an essay describing conflict between your parents' ethical views and your own.
2. Gather evidence, from conversations with friends and relatives, about an ethical issue such as poverty, world starvation, abortion, or capital punishment. Incorporate their opinions in your essay through direct and indirect quotation.
3. **Writing an Argument:** Coles asserts the need for clear ethical values. How have your parents provided such values? What kind of values will you give your children? Answer these questions in a brief argumentative essay.

www.mhhe.com/
**mhreader**

For more information on Robert Coles, go to:
**More Resources > Ch. 11 Ethics & Religion**

# Salvation

## Langston Hughes

*James Langston Hughes (1902–1967), poet, playwright, fiction writer, biographer, and essayist, was for more than 50 years one of the most productive and significant American authors. In* The Weary Blues *(1926),* Simple Speaks His Mind *(1950),* The Ways of White Folks *(1940),* Selected Poems *(1959), and dozens of other books, he strove, in his own words, "to explain the Negro condition in America." This essay, from his 1940 autobiography* The Big Sea, *reflects the sharp, humorous, often bitter- sweet insights contained in Hughes's examination of human behavior.*

1    I was saved from sin when I was going on thirteen. But not really saved. It hap- pened like this. There was a big revival at my Auntie Reed's church. Every night for weeks there had been much preaching, singing, praying, and shout- ing, and some very hardened sinners had been brought to Christ, and the mem- bership of the church had grown by leaps and bounds. Then just before the revival ended, they held a special meeting for children, "to bring the young lambs to the fold." My aunt spoke of it for days ahead. That night I was es- corted to the front row and placed on the mourners' bench with all the other young sinners, who had not yet been brought to Jesus.

2    My aunt told me that when you were saved you saw a light, and something happened to you inside! And Jesus came into your life! And God was with you from then on! She said you could see and hear and feel Jesus in your soul. I be- lieved her. I had heard a great many old people say the same thing and it seemed to me they ought to know. So I sat there calmly in the hot, crowded church, waiting for Jesus to come to me.

3    The preacher preached a wonderful rhythmical sermon, all moans and shouts and lonely cries and dire pictures of hell, and then he sang a song about the ninety and nine safe in the fold, but one little lamb was left out in the cold. Then he said: "Won't you come? Won't you come to Jesus? Young lambs, won't you come?" And he held out his arms to all us young sinners there on the mourners' bench. And the little girls cried. And some of them jumped up and went to Jesus right away. But most of us just sat there.

4    A great many old people came and knelt around us and prayed, old women with jet-black faces and braided hair, old men with work-gnarled hands. And the church sang a song about the lower lights are burning, some poor sinners to be saved. And the whole building rocked with prayer and song.

5    Still I kept waiting to *see* Jesus.

6    Finally all the young people had gone to the altar and were saved, but one boy and me. He was a rounder's son named Westley. Westley and I were sur- rounded by sisters and deacons praying. It was very hot in the church, and get- ting late now. Finally Westley said to me in a whisper: "God damn! I'm tired o' sitting here. Let's get up and be saved." So he got up and was saved.

7    Then I was left all alone on the mourners' bench. My aunt came and knelt at my knees and cried, while prayers and song swirled all around me in the little church. The whole congregation prayed for me alone, in a mighty wail of moans and voices. And I kept waiting serenely for Jesus, waiting, waiting—but he didn't come. I wanted to see him, but nothing happened to me. Nothing! I wanted something to happen to me, but nothing happened.

8    I heard the songs and the minister saying: "Why don't you come? My dear child, why don't you come to Jesus? Jesus is waiting for you. He wants you. Why don't you come? Sister Reed, what is this child's name?"

"Langston," my aunt sobbed.                                                           9

"Langston, why don't you come? Why don't you come and be saved? Oh,   10
Lamb of God! Why don't you come?"

Now it was really getting late. I began to be ashamed of myself, holding   11
everything up so long. I began to wonder what God thought about Westley,
who certainly hadn't seen Jesus either, but who was now sitting proudly on the
platform, swinging his knickerbockered legs and grinning down at me, surrounded by deacons and old women on their knees praying. God had not struck
Westley dead for taking his name in vain or for lying in the temple. So I decided
that maybe to save further trouble, I'd better lie, too, and say that Jesus had
come, and get up and be saved.

So I got up.                                                                         12

Suddenly the whole room broke into a sea of shouting, as they saw me rise.   13
Waves of rejoicing swept the place. Women leaped in the air. My aunt threw her
arms around me. The minister took me by the hand and led me to the platform.

When things quieted down, in a hushed silence, punctuated by a few   14
ecstatic "Amens," all the new young lambs were blessed in the name of God.
Then joyous singing filled the room.

That night, for the last time in my life but one—for I was a big boy twelve   15
years old—I cried. I cried, in bed alone, and couldn't stop. I buried my head under
the quilts, but my aunt heard me. She woke up and told my uncle I was crying
because the Holy Ghost had come into my life, and because I had seen Jesus. But I
was really crying because I couldn't bear to tell her that I had lied, that I had deceived everybody in the church, that I hadn't seen Jesus, and that now I didn't
believe there was a Jesus any more, since he didn't come to help me.

## COMPREHENSION

1. What does the title tell you about the subject of this essay? How would you
   state, in your own words, the thesis that emerges from the title and the essay?
2. How does Hughes recount the revival meeting he attended? What is the
   dominant impression?
3. Explain Hughes's shifting attitude toward salvation in this essay. Why is he
   disappointed in the religious answers provided by his church? What does
   he say about salvation in the last paragraph?

## RHETORIC

1. Key words and phrases in this essay relate to the religious experience. Locate
   five of these words and expressions, and explain their connotations.
2. Identify the level of language in the essay. How does Hughes employ
   language effectively?
3. Where is the thesis statement in the essay? Consider the following: the use
   of dialogue, the use of phrases familiar to you (idioms), and the sentence
   structure. Cite examples of these elements.

4. How much time elapses, and why is this important to the effect? How does the author achieve narrative coherence?

5. Locate details and examples in the essay that are especially vivid and interesting. Compare your list with what others have listed. What are the similarities? The differences?

6. What is the tone of the essay? What is the relationship between tone and point of view?

### WRITING

1. Describe a time in your life when you suppressed your feelings about religion because you thought friends or adults would misunderstand.

2. Write a narrative account of the most intense religious experience in your life.

3. **Writing an Argument:** In an argumentative essay, explain why you think or do not think that politicians today often profess their religious beliefs simply to satisfy voters and not because of firmly held religious sentiments.

 www.mhhe.com/ **mhreader** | For more information on Langston Hughes, go to: **More Resources > Ch. 11 Ethics & Religion**

# What's God Got to Do with It?

## Karen Armstrong

*Karen Armstrong (b. 1945), who was educated in an English convent and subsequently earned a doctorate from St. Anne's College, Oxford, is a renowned historian, public lecturer, and radio and television broadcaster. A former nun, Armstrong is the author of more than a dozen books on religion, among them* The Gospel according to Woman *(1987),* A History of God *(1993), and* Muhammad: A Prophet for Our Time *(2006). She also has written two autobiographies tracing her own spiritual journey:* Through the Narrow Gate *(1981) and* Beginning the World *(1983). Much of Armstrong's work, as the next essay indicates, explores the world's religions from ethical and cross-cultural perspectives.*

1   The activity that we call religion is complex. Religious and non-religious people alike often share the same misperceptions. Today in the West, it is often assumed that religion is all about the supernatural and that it is

inseparable from belief in an external, personalised deity. Critics claim that religion encourages escapist fantasies that cannot be verified. The explosion of terrorism (which is often given a religious justification) has convinced many people that religion is incurably violent. I have lost count of the number of times a taxi driver has informed me that religion has been the cause of all the wars in history.

Yet we find something very different when we look back to the period that the German philosopher Karl Jaspers called the "Axial Age" (c. 900 to 200 BCE) because it proved to be pivotal to the spiritual development of humanity. In this era, in four distinct regions of the world, the traditions that have continued to nourish humanity either came into being or put down roots. Hinduism, Buddhism and Jainism emerged in India; Confucianism and Taoism in China; monotheism was born in Israel; and philosophical rationalism developed in Greece. It was a period of astonishing creativity; we have never really succeeded in going beyond the insights of such sages as the Buddha, the mystics of the Upanishads, Confucius, Lao-tzu, and the great Hebrew prophets. Rabbinic Judaism, Christianity and Islam, for example, can be seen as a later flowering of the religion that had developed in Israel during the Axial Age.

Despite interesting and revealing differences in emphasis, these traditions all reached remarkably similar solutions. They can, perhaps, tell us something important about the structure of our humanity. The God of Israel was an important symbol of transcendence, but in the other Axial faiths the gods were not very important. Confucius discouraged speculation about spirits and the afterlife: how could you talk about other-worldly phenomena, when there was so much that you did not understand about earthly matters?

During the Indian Axial Age, the ancient Vedic deities retreated from the religious imagination. They were seen as unsatisfactory expressions of the sacred, and were either demoted to human status or seen as aspects of the psyche. Many of the Axial sages were reaching beyond the gods to a more impersonal transcendence—to Brahman, Nirvana or the Tao—that was also inseparable from humanity. Yogins and Taoists did not believe that their ecstatic trances represented an encounter with the supernatural, but regarded them as entirely natural to humanity. Later, the more sophisticated theologians in all three of the monotheistic religions would make similar claims about the experience of the reality that they called God.

None of these sages was interested in dogma or metaphysics. A person's theological opinions were a matter of total indifference to a teacher like the Buddha. He insisted that nobody should ever take any religious teaching, from however august a source, on faith or at second hand. One of the Buddha's disciples pestered him continuously about metaphysics: was there a God? Who created the world? He was so preoccupied with these matters that he neglected his yoga and ethical practice. The Buddha told him that he was like a man who had been shot with a poisoned arrow but refused to have any medical treatment until he discovered the name of his assailant and what village he came from: he would die before he got this perfectly useless information.

6      The Taoists were also wary of dogmatic conformity; they believed that the kind of certainty that many seek in religion was unrealistic and a sign of immaturity. Eventually, the Chinese preferred to synthesise the schools which had developed during their Axial Age, because no single tradition could have the monopoly of truth. In all four regions, when a sage started to insist upon strict orthodoxy, this was usually a sign that the Axial Age was drawing to a close.

7      The prophets of Israel were more like political commentators than theologians; they found the divine in analysis of current events rather than metaphysics. Jesus, as far as we know, spent no time discussing the trinity or original sin, which would later become so important to Christians; and the Koran dismisses theological dogmatism as *zannah*, self-indulgent guesswork that makes people stupidly quarrelsome and sectarian.

8      Religion was not about believing credal propositions, but about behaving in a way that changed you at a profound level. Human beings have always sought what the Greeks called *ekstasis*, a "stepping out" of the mundane, in moments when we feel deeply touched within and lifted momentarily beyond ourselves. The Axial sages all believed that if we stepped outside of our egotism and greed, we would transcend ourselves and achieve an enhanced humanity. Yoga, for instance, one of the great spiritual technologies of the Axial Age, was a formidable assault on the ego, designed to take the "I" out of the practitioner's thinking.

9   But the safest way to achieve this *ekstasis* was by the practice of compassion. Compassion—the ability to feel with another—was not simply the litmus test of any true religiosity, but the chief way of encountering the ineffable reality of Nirvana, Brahman, God and Tao. For the Buddha, compassion brought about *ceto-vimutti*, the "release of the mind" that was a synonym for the supreme enlightenment of Nirvana, a sacred realm of peace in the core of one's being.

10     All the Axial religions, in different ways, regarded what has been called the Golden Rule as the essence of religion: "Do not do to others what you would not like them to do to you." Confucius was the first to formulate this maxim. It was, he said, the thread that pulled all his teachings together and should be practised all day and every day. Five hundred years later, Rabbi Hillel was asked to sum up the whole of Jewish teaching while he stood on one leg. He replied: "That which is hateful to you, do not do to your neighbour. That is the Torah. The rest is commentary. Go and study it."

11     The Chinese sage Mo-tzu (c. 480–390) insisted that we had to have *jian ai*, "concern for everybody." The priestly authors of Leviticus urged the Israelites to love and honour the stranger; the Buddha taught layfolk and monks alike a method of meditation called "the Immeasurables," in which they systematically extended benevolent thoughts to the four corners of the world. Jesus told his disciples to love their enemies. This impartial sympathy would break down the barricades of egotism, because it was offered with little hope of any return.

12     If a ruler practised *jian ai*, Mo-tzu taught, war would be impossible. The Axial religions all developed in regions that were convulsed by violence on an

unprecedented scale. Iron weaponry meant that warfare had become more deadly; states had become more coercive; in the market place, merchants preyed on each other aggressively. In every case, throughout the Axial Age, the catalyst for religious change was always a disciplined revulsion towards this violence.

In the 9th century, the ritualists of India systematically extracted all the vio- 13 lence from the sacrificial ritual, and in seeking the cause of aggression in the psyche, discovered the inner self. Renouncers, Buddhists and Jains all insisted that *ahimsa*, "harmlessness," was an indispensable prerequisite to enlightenment. In the Tao Te Ching, Lao-tzu pointed out that violence could only elicit more violence. The sage-ruler must always seek to bring a military campaign to a speedy end: "Bring it to a conclusion, but do not intimidate." Some of the gospels present Jesus as a man of *ahimsa* who taught his followers to turn the other cheek.

Socrates, one of the greatest figures of the Axial Age, also condemned 14 retaliation as evil. In general, however, the Greeks did not eschew violence. Ultimately, they did not have a religious Axial Age. Their great transformation was philosophical, scientific and mathematical, and pagan religion continued to flourish in Greece until it was forcibly replaced by Christianity in the 5th century CE.

Compassion is an unpopular virtue. All too often, religious people have 15 preferred to be right rather than compassionate. They have shielded themselves from the demands of empathy by making secondary and peripheral goals— such as theological correctness or sexual orthodoxy—central to their faith. As the Chinese sages pointed out, vehement professions of belief were essentially egotistic, a pompous trumpeting of self, and, therefore, they impeded enlightenment. Denominational chauvinism, like nationalism, should also be seen as a form of collective egotism or, in monotheistic terms, idolatry.

Nevertheless, in our torn, conflicted world, we need to revive the Axial 16 ethos. This does not require orthodox belief and need not involve the supernatural. In the Axial Age, individualism was beginning to supersede the older tribal or communal expressions of identity. The sages were trying to moderate the clash of competing egos and they were all concerned about the plight of society. We are still rampant, chronic individualists, but our technology has created a global village, which is interconnected electronically, militarily, politically and economically. If we want to survive, it makes practical sense to cultivate *jian ai*. We need to apply the Golden Rule politically, and learn that other nations, however remote from our own, are as important as ours.

## COMPREHENSION

1. How does Armstrong answer the question posed by her title?
2. Identify the main religions mentioned by Armstrong. How are they alike and unlike? What idea or principle serves to unify them?
3. Armstrong writes of the Axial Age. Describe this period as she presents it. Why, according to Armstrong, is it important?

## RHETORIC

1. What is Armstrong's claim? What is her persuasive purpose, and what techniques of argumentation does she employ to convince the reader? How convinced are you?
2. How do the first two paragraphs serve as an introduction to the essay?
3. Explain the writer's use of definition, classification and division, and comparison and contrast to organize her essay.
4. Does this essay reflect inductive or deductive reasoning? Justify your answer.
5. Why does the writer divide the essay into two sections? What relationships do you detect between the parts? What transitions does she use?
6. Armstrong's conclusion suggests a certain causality linking periods of history. How persuasive do you find her presentation of these historic interconnections, and how effective do you find the conclusion?

## WRITING

1. Select a religion other than your own that Armstrong discusses, and write an explanatory essay in which you suggest ways in which this system of belief is relevant to some of today's most pressing global problems.
2. Conduct research on the Axial Age, and write an extended definition of this period.
3. **Writing an Argument:** Answer the question posed by Armstrong in her title, relying on logical and ethical appeals.

www.mhhe.com/
**mhreader**

For more information on Karen Armstrong, go to:
**More Resources > Ch. 11 Ethics & Religion**

# The Divine Revolution

## Václav Havel

*Václav Havel (b. 1936) was born into a well-to-do family in Prague. Because of his "bourgeois" background, he was denied entrance to a university and instead studied at a technical college. In the 1960s, Havel became interested in the theater. He subsequently enrolled in the Academy of Dramatic Arts and graduated in 1967. During the 1970s and 1980s, Havel was repeatedly arrested for his dissident activities. In November 1989, he formed a political opposition group, the Civic Forum, and, with the fall of communism, was elected by popular vote as the president of the Czech and Slovak Federal Republic. He resigned in 1992 but was elected president of the New Czech Republic in 1993. Among his plays are* The Beggar's Opera *(1976),* Largo Desolato *(1985), and* Temptation *(1986). He has also published numerous essays; a collection of letters to his wife while he was in prison,* Letters to Olga *(1988); and a collection of thoughts on life, literature, and politics titled* Disturbing the Peace *(1990). He has won numerous international prizes for his writing and humanitarian efforts. In the following essay, he disputes the importance of the "God of Technology" as an answer to our current problems, and instead calls for a new spiritual vision for the future.*

Humankind today is well aware of the spectrum of threats looming over its head. 1
We know that the number of people living on our planet is growing at a soaring rate and that within a relatively short time we can expect it to total in the tens of billions. We know that the already-deep abyss separating the planet's poor and rich could deepen further, and more and more dangerously, because of this rapid population growth. We also know that we've been destroying the environment on which our existence depends and that we are headed for disaster by producing weapons of mass destruction and allowing them to proliferate.

And yet, even though we are aware of these dangers, *we do almost nothing to* 2
*avert them.* It's fascinating to me how preoccupied people are today with catastrophic prognoses, how books containing evidence of impending crises become bestsellers, but how very little account we take of these threats in our everyday activities. Doesn't every schoolchild know that the resources of this planet are limited and that if they are expended faster than they are recovered, we are doomed? And still we continue in our wasteful ways and don't even seem perturbed. Quite the contrary: *Rising production is considered to be the main sign of national success,* not only in poor states where such a position could be justified, but also in wealthy ones, which are cutting the branch on which they sit with their ideology of indefinitely prolonged and senseless growth.

The most important thing we can do today is to study the reasons why hu- 3
mankind does little to address these threats and why it allows itself to be carried onward by some kind of perpetual motion, unaffected by self-awareness or a sense of future options. It would be unfair to ignore the existence of numerous projects for averting these dangers, or to deny that a lot already has been done. However, all attempts of this kind have one thing in common: *They do not touch the seed from which the threats I'm speaking of sprout,* but merely try to diminish their impact. (A typical example is the list of legal acts, ordinances, and international treaties stipulating how much toxic matter this or that plant may discharge into the environment.) I'm not criticizing these safeguards; I'm only saying that they are technical tricks that have no real effect on the substance of the matter.

What, then, is the substance of the matter? What could change the direction 4
of today's civilization?

It is my deep conviction that the only option is a change in the sphere of the 5
spirit, in the sphere of human conscience. It's not enough to invent new machines, new regulations, new institutions. We must develop a new understanding of the

true purpose of our existence on this earth. Only by making such a fundamental shift will we be able to create new models of behavior and a new set of values for the planet. In short, it appears to me that it would be better to start from the head rather than the tail.

6      Whenever I've gotten involved in a major global problem—the logging of rainforests, ethnic or religious intolerance, the brutal destruction of indigenous cultures—I've always discovered somewhere in the long chain of events that gave rise to it a basic lack of responsibility for the planet.

7      There are countless types of responsibility—more or less pressing, depending on who's involved. We feel responsible for our personal welfare, our families, our companies, our communities, our nations. And somewhere in the background there is, in every one of us, a small feeling of responsibility for the planet and its future. It seems to me that this last and deepest responsibility has become a very low priority—dangerously low, considering that the world today is more interlinked than ever before and that we are, for all intents and purposes, living one global destiny.

8      At the same time, our world is dominated by several great religious systems, whose differences seem to be coming to the fore with increasing sharpness and setting the stage for innumerable political and armed conflicts. In my opinion, this fact—which is attracting, understandably, a great deal of media attention—partly conceals a more important fact: that the civilization within which this religious tension is taking place is, in essence, a deeply atheistic one. Indeed, it is the first atheistic civilization in the history of humankind.

9      Perhaps the real issue is a crisis of respect for the moral order extended to us from above, or simply a crisis of respect for any kind of authority higher than our own earthly being, with its material and thoroughly ephemeral interests. Perhaps our lack of responsibility for the planet is only the logical consequence of the modern conception of the universe as a complex of phenomena controlled by certain scientifically identifiable laws, formulated for God-knows-what purpose. This is a conception that does not inquire into the meaning of existence and renounces any kind of metaphysics, including its own metaphysical roots.

10     In the process, we've lost our certainty that the universe, nature, existence, and our own lives are works of creation that have a definite meaning and purpose. This loss is accompanied by loss of the feeling that whatever we do must be seen in the light of a higher order of which we are part and whose authority we must respect.

11     In recent years the great religions have been playing an increasingly important role in global politics. Since the fall of communism, the world has become multipolar instead of bipolar, and many countries outside the hitherto dominant Euro-American cultural sphere have grown in self-confidence and influence. But the more closely tied we are by the bonds of a single global civilization, the more the various religious groups emphasize all the ways in which they differ from each other. This is an epoch of accentuated spiritual, religious, and cultural "otherness."

How can we restore in the human mind a shared attitude to what is above 12 if people everywhere feel the need to stress their otherness? Is there any sense in trying to turn the human mind to the heavens when such a turn would only aggravate the conflict among our various deities?

I'm not, of course, an expert on religion, but it seems to me that the major 13 faiths have much more in common than they are willing to admit. They share a basic point of departure—that this world and our existence are not freaks of chance but rather part of a mysterious, yet integral, act whose sources, direction, and purpose are difficult for us to perceive in their entirety. And they share a large complex of moral imperatives that this mysterious act implies. In my view, whatever differences these religions might have are not as important as these fundamental similarities.

Perhaps the way out of our current bleak situation could be found by 14 searching for what unites the various religions—a purposeful search for common principles. Then we could cultivate human coexistence while, at the same time, cultivating the planet on which we live, suffusing it with the spirit of this religious and ethical common ground—what I would call the common spiritual and moral minimum.

Could this be a way to stop the blind perpetual motion dragging us toward 15 hell? Can the persuasive words of the wise be enough to achieve what must be done? Or will it take an unprecedented disaster to provoke this kind of existential revolution—a universal recovery of the human spirit and renewed responsibility for the world?

## COMPREHENSION

1. What is the thesis of the essay?
2. What does Havel mean by the "divine revolution"? How does it differ from what we usually have in mind when we think of a revolution?
3. According to Havel, what is the major shortcoming of humankind today?

## RHETORIC

1. Havel's first paragraph contains the phrase "we know" three times. What function does the use of this repetition serve in introducing his subject?
2. Paragraph 4 is composed of two short questions. How does Havel employ these questions to make the paragraph a major transitional point in his essay? What argument grows from these questions?
3. Study paragraph 8. Where is the topic sentence located? How does Havel develop the ideas in this paragraph so that its placement is so effective?
4. Paragraph 12 is similar in form and rhetorical purpose to paragraph 4. It too is composed of two questions. How does paragraph 12 create another transition in logical development in the essay, and how do paragraphs 4 and 12 help create an overall rhetorical structure for the essay?

5. Havel makes liberal use of the words *could* and *perhaps* as he makes suggestions regarding how to improve the current state of civilization. How do these words affect the tone of his argument? What do they imply about his voice?

6. Havel refers to the contemporary world as being "senseless" (paragraph 2), "atheistic" (paragraph 8), "bleak" (paragraph 14), and "blind" (paragraph 15). Are these prognoses fact or opinion? Explain your view.

7. Havel concludes his essay with three questions. How do they reinforce the tone of the essay?

## WRITING

1. Write an expository essay exploring how the media exploit our spiritual crisis by obsessing over issues such as political scandals, marginal social behavior (as depicted on such shows as *The Jerry Springer Show*), and celebrity tragedies.

2. Write a 300-word summary of Havel's essay.

3. **Writing an Argument:** Argue for or against the view that Havel is much too pessimistic about the world today given the rise in awareness of and assistance toward homelessness, foster care, adoption, and other social and cultural issues.

www.mhhe.com/ **mhreader**

For more information on Václav Havel, go to:
**More Resources > Ch. 11 Ethics & Religion**

# The Allegory of the Cave

## Plato

*Plato (427–347 BCE), pupil and friend of Socrates, was one of the greatest philosophers of the ancient world. Plato's surviving works are all dialogues and epistles, many of the dialogues purporting to be conversations of Socrates and his disciples. Two key aspects of his philosophy are the dialectical method—represented by the questioning and probing of the particular event to reveal the general truth—and the existence of Forms. Plato's best-known works include the* Phaedo, Symposium, Phaedrus, *and* Timaeus. *The following selection, from the* Republic, *is an early description of the nature of Forms.*

And now, I said, let me show in a figure how far our nature is enlightened or  1
unenlightened: Behold! human beings living in an underground den, which
has a mouth open towards the light and reaching all along the den; here they
have been from their childhood, and have their legs and necks chained so
that they cannot move, and can only see before them, being prevented by the
chains from turning round their heads. Above and behind them a fire is blazing at a distance, and between the fire and the prisoners there is a raised
way; and you will see, if you look, a low wall built along the way, like the
screen which marionette players have in front of them, over which they show
the puppets.

I see.
                                                                                                2

And do you see, I said, men passing along the wall carrying all sorts of ves-  3
sels, and statues and figures of animals made of wood and stone and various
materials, which appear over the wall? Some of them are talking, others silent.

You have shown me a strange image, and they are strange prisoners.          4

Like ourselves, I replied; and they see only their own shadows, or the shad-  5
ows of one another, which the fire throws on the opposite wall of the cave?

True, he said; how could they see anything but the shadows if they were  6
never allowed to move their heads?

And of the objects which are being carried in like manner they would only  7
see the shadows?

Yes, he said.
                                                                                                8

And if they were able to converse with one another, would they not sup-  9
pose that they were naming what was actually before them?

Very true.
                                                                                                10

And suppose further that the prison had an echo which came from the  11
other side, would they not be sure to fancy when one of the passersby spoke
that the voice which they heard came from the passing shadow?

No question, he replied.
                                                                                                12

To them, I said, the truth would be literally nothing but the shadows of the  13
images.

That is certain.
                                                                                                14

And now look again, and see what will naturally follow if the prisoners are  15
released and disabused of their error. At first, when any of them is liberated
and compelled suddenly to stand up and turn his neck round and walk and
look towards the light, he will suffer sharp pains; the glare will distress him
and he will be unable to see the realities of which in his former state he had
seen the shadows; and then conceive some one saying to him, that what he saw
before was an illusion, but that now, when he is approaching nearer to being
and his eye is turned towards more real existence, he has a clearer vision—what
will be his reply? And you may further imagine that his instructor is pointing to
the objects as they pass and requiring him to name them—will he not be perplexed? Will he not fancy that the shadows which he formerly saw are truer
than the objects which are now shown to him?

Far truer.
                                                                                                16

17    And if he is compelled to look straight at the light, will he not have a pain in his eyes which will make him turn away to take refuge in the objects of vision which he can see, and which he will conceive to be in reality clearer than the things which are now being shown to him?

18    True, he said.

19    And suppose once more, that he is reluctantly dragged up a steep and rugged ascent, and held fast until he is forced into the presence of the sun himself, is he not likely to be pained and irritated? When he approaches the light his eyes will be dazzled and he will not be able to see anything at all of what are now called realities.

20    Not all in a moment, he said.

21    He will require to grow accustomed to the sight of the upper world. And first he will see the shadows best, next the reflections of men and other objects in the water, and then the objects themselves; then he will gaze upon the light of the moon and the stars and the spangled heaven; and he will see the sky and the stars by night better than the sun or the light of the sun by day?

22    Certainly.

23    Last of all he will be able to see the sun, and not mere reflections of him in the water, but he will see him in his own proper place, and not in another; and he will contemplate him as he is.

24    Certainly.

25    He will then proceed to argue that this is he who gives the season and the years, and is the guardian of all that is in the visible world, and in a certain way the cause of all things which he and his fellows have been accustomed to behold?

26    Clearly, he said, he would first see the sun and then reason about him.

27    And when he remembered his old habitation, and the wisdom of the den and his fellow-prisoners, do you not suppose that he would felicitate himself on the change, and pity them?

28    Certainly, he would.

29    And if they were in the habit of conferring honors among themselves on those who were quickest to observe the passing shadows and to remark which of them went before, and which followed after, and which were together; and who were therefore best able to draw conclusions as to the future, do you think that he would care for such honors and glories, or envy the possessors of them? Would he not say with Homer, Better to be the poor servant of a poor master, and to endure anything, rather than think as they do and live after their manner?

30    Yes, he said, I think that he would rather suffer anything than entertain these false notions and live in this miserable manner.

31    Imagine once more, I said, such an one coming suddenly out of the sun to be replaced in his old situation; would he not be certain to have his eyes full of darkness?

32    To be sure, he said.

33    And if there were a contest, and he had to compete in measuring the shadows with the prisoners who had never moved out of the den, while his sight

was still weak, and before his eyes had become steady (and the time which would be needed to acquire this new habit of sight might be very considerable) would he not be ridiculous? Men would say of him that up he went and down he came without his eyes; and that it was better not even to think of ascending; and if any one tried to loose another and lead him up to the light, let them only catch the offender, and they would put him to death.

No question, he said.                                                                                      34

This entire allegory, I said, you may now append, dear Glaucon, to the pre-   35
vious argument; the prison-house is the world of sight, the light of fire is the sun, and you will not misapprehend me if you interpret the journey upwards to be the ascent of the soul into the intellectual world according to my poor belief, which, at your desire, I have expressed—whether rightly or wrongly God knows. But, whether true or false, my opinion is that in the world of knowledge the idea of good appears last of all, and is seen only with an effort; and, when seen, is also inferred to be the universal author of all things beautiful and right, parent of light and of the lord of light in this visible world, and the immediate source of reason and truth in the intellectual; and that this is the power upon which he who would act rationally either in public or private life must have his eye fixed.

I agree, he said, as far as I am able to understand you.                                    36

Moreover, I said, you must not wonder that those who attain to this beauti-   37
ful vision are unwilling to descend to human affairs; for their souls are ever hastening into the upper world where they desire to dwell; which desire of theirs is very natural, if our allegory may be trusted.

Yes, very natural.                                                                                        38

And is there anything surprising in one who passes from divine contem-   39
plations to the evil state of man, misbehaving himself in a ridiculous manner; if, while his eyes are blinking and before he has become accustomed to the sur-rounding darkness, he is compelled to fight in courts of law, or in other places, about the images or the shadows of images of justice, and is endeavoring to meet the conceptions of those who have never yet seen absolute justice?

Anything but surprising, he replied.                                                          40

Any one who has common sense will remember that the bewilderments of   41
the eyes are of two kinds, and arise from two causes, either from coming out of the light or from going into the light, which is true of the mind's eye, quite as much as of the bodily eye; and he who remembers this when he sees any one whose vision is perplexed and weak, will not be too ready to laugh; he will first ask whether that soul of man has come out of the brighter light, and is unable to see because unaccustomed to the dark, or having turned from darkness to the day is dazzled by excess of light. And he will count the one happy in his condi-tion and state of being, and he will pity the other; or, if he have a mind to laugh at the soul which comes from below into the light, there will be more reason in this than in the laugh which greets him who returns from above out of the light into the den.

That, he said, is a very just distinction.                                                       42

# COMPREHENSION

1. What does Plato hope to convey to readers of his allegory?
2. According to Plato, do human beings typically perceive reality? To what does he compare the world?
3. According to Plato, what often happens to people who develop a true idea of reality? How well do they compete with others? Who is usually considered superior? Why?

# RHETORIC

1. Is the conversation portrayed here realistic? How effective is this conversational style at conveying information?
2. How do you interpret such details of this allegory as the chains, the cave, and the fire? What connotations do such symbols have?
3. How does Plato use conversation to develop his argument? What is Glaucon's role in the conversation?
4. Note examples of transition words that mark contrasts between the real and the shadow world. How does Plato use contrast to develop his idea of the true real world?
5. Plato uses syllogistic reasoning to derive human behavior from his allegory. Trace his line of reasoning, noting transitional devices and the development of ideas in paragraphs 5–14. Find and describe a similar line of reasoning.
6. In what paragraph does Plato explain his allegory? Why do you think he locates his explanation where he does?

# WRITING

1. Are Plato's ideas still influencing contemporary society? How do his ideas affect our evaluation of materialism, sensuality, sex, and love?
2. Write an allegory based on a sport, business, or space flight to explain how we act in the world.
3. **Writing an Argument:** In an extended essay, try to convince your audience that *The Matrix* films are based on Plato's essay.

| www.mhhe.com/ **mhreader** | For more information on Plato, go to: **More Resources > Ch. 11 Ethics & Religion** |

# Not about Islam?

## Salman Rushdie

*Salman Rushdie (b. 1947), a well-known novelist, essayist, and critic, was born in Bombay, India, into a middle-class Muslim family that relocated to Pakistan following the bloody Partition. He attended public school in Pakistan and England and graduated from Kings College at Cambridge University. Rushdie first received critical acclaim for* Midnight's Children *(1981) and* Shame *(1983). With the publication of his controversial novel* Satanic Verses *(1989) and the subsequent* fatwa, *or religious edict, issued by Ayatollah Khomeini ordering his death for blasphemy against Islam and his depiction of Muhammad, Rushdie went into hiding for several years. In 1998, the Islamic Republic of Iran announced that it would not carry out Rushdie's death sentence, but the* fatwa *remains in force. Rushdie's more recent work includes* Imaginary Homelands: Essays and Criticism *(1991),* The Moor's Last Sigh *(1995), and* Fury *(2001). In the selection that follows, published in* The New York Times *in 2001, shortly after the 9/11 attacks, Rushdie confronts the issue of Islamic terrorism.*

"This isn't about Islam." The world's leaders have been repeating this mantra   1
for weeks, partly in the virtuous hope of deterring reprisal attacks on innocent Muslims living in the West, partly because if the United States is to maintain its coalition against terror it can't afford to allege that Islam and terrorism are in any way related.

The trouble with this necessary disclaimer is that it isn't true. If this isn't   2
about Islam, why the worldwide Muslim demonstrations in support of Osama bin Laden and Al-Qaida? Why did those ten thousand men armed with swords and axes mass on the Pakistan-Afghanistan frontier, answering some mullah's call to jihad? Why are the war's first British casualties three Muslim men who died fighting on the Taliban side?

Why the routine anti-Semitism of the much-repeated Islamic slander that "the   3
Jews" arranged the hits on the World Trade Center and Pentagon, with the oddly self-deprecating explanation offered by the Taliban leadership among others; that Muslims could not have the technological know-how or organizational sophistication to pull off such a feat? Why does Imran Khan, the Pakistani ex–sports star turned politician, demand to be shown the evidence of Al-Qaida's guilt while apparently turning a deaf ear to the self-incriminating statements of Al-Qaida's own spokesmen (there will be a rain of aircraft from the skies, Muslims in the West are warned not to live or work in tall buildings, et cetera)? Why all the talk about U.S. military infidels desecrating the sacred soil of Saudi Arabia, if some sort of definition of what is sacred is not at the heart of the present discontents?

4      Let's start calling a spade a spade. Of course this is "about Islam." The
question is, what exactly does that mean? After all, most religious belief isn't
very theological. Most Muslims are not profound Quranic analysts. For a vast
number of "believing"Muslim men, "Islam" stands, in a jumbled, half-examined
way, not only for the fear of God—the fear more than the love, one suspects—
but also for a cluster of customs, opinions, and prejudices that include their
dietary practices; the sequestration or near-sequestration of "their" women;
the sermons delivered by their mullah of choice; a loathing of modern society
in general, riddled as it is with music, godlessness, and sex; and a more particularized loathing (and fear) of the prospect that their own immediate surroundings could be taken over—"Westoxicated"—by the liberal Western-style
way of life.

5      Highly motivated organizations of Muslim men (oh, for the voices of
Muslim women to be heard) have been engaged, over the last thirty years or so,
on growing radical political movements out of this mulch of "belief." These
Islamists—we must get used to this word, "Islamists," meaning those who are
engaged upon such political projects, and learn to distinguish it from the more
general and politically neutral "Muslim"—include the Muslim Brotherhood in
Egypt, the blood-soaked combatants of the FIS and GIA in Algeria, the Shia
revolutionaries of Iran, and the Taliban. Poverty is their great helper, and the
fruit of their efforts is paranoia. This paranoid Islam, which blames outsiders,
"infidels," for all the ills of Muslim societies, and whose proposed remedy is
the closing of those societies to the rival project of modernity, is presently the
fastest-growing version of Islam in the world.

6      This is not really to go along with Samuel Huntington's thesis about the
"clash of civilizations," for the simple reason that the Islamists' project is turned
not only against the West and "the Jews" but also against their fellow Islamists.
Whatever the public rhetoric, there's little love lost between the Taliban and
Iranian regimes. Dissensions between Muslim nations run at least as deep as, if
not deeper than, those nations' resentment of the West. Nevertheless, it would
be absurd to deny that this self-exculpatory, paranoiac Islam is an ideology
with widespread appeal.

7      Twenty years ago, when I was writing a novel about power struggles in a
fictionalized Pakistan, it was already de rigueur in the Muslim world to blame
all its troubles on the West and, in particular, the United States. Then as now,
some of these criticisms were well-founded; no room here to rehearse the geopolitics of the Cold War, and America's frequently damaging foreign policy
"tilts," to use the Kissinger term, toward (or away from) this or that temporarily useful (or disapproved-of) nation-state, or America's role in the installation
and deposition of sundry unsavory leaders and regimes. But I wanted then to
ask a question which is no less important now: suppose we say that the ills of
our societies are not primarily America's fault—that we are to blame for our
own failings? How would we understand them then? Might we not, by accepting our own responsibility for our problems, begin to learn to solve them for
ourselves?

It is interesting that many Muslims, as well as secularist analysts with roots 8 in the Muslim world, are beginning to ask such questions now. In recent weeks Muslim voices have everywhere been raised against the obscurantist "hijack" of their religion. Yesterday's hotheads (among them Yusuf Islam, a.k.a. Cat Stevens) are improbably repackaging themselves as today's pussycats. An Iraqi writer quotes an earlier Iraqi satirist: "The disease that is in us, is from us." A British Muslim writes that "Islam has become its own enemy." A Lebanese writer friend, returning from Beirut, tells me that, in the aftermath of September 11, public criticism of Islamism has become much more outspoken. Many commentators have spoken of the need for a Reformation in the Muslim world. I'm reminded of the way non-communist socialists used to distance themselves from the tyrannous "actually existing" socialism of the Soviets; nevertheless, the first stirrings of this counterproject are of great significance. If Islam is to be reconciled with modernity, these voices must be encouraged until they swell into a roar.

Many of them speak of another Islam, their personal, private faith, and the 9 restoration of religion to the sphere of the personal, its de-politicization, is the nettle that all Muslim societies must grasp in order to become modern. The only aspect of modernity in which the terrorists are interested is technology, which they see as a weapon that can be turned against its makers. If terrorism is to be defeated, the world of Islam must take on board the secularist-humanist principles on which the modern is based, and without which their countries' freedom will remain a distant dream.

## COMPREHENSION

1. What is Rushdie's response to statements that 9/11 was not "about Islam"?
2. What distinction does Rushdie draw between "Muslims" and "Islamists"? What, according to the writer, is the proper role of religion in the contemporary world?
3. Explain Rushdie's solution to some of the problems confronting Islamic nations today.

## RHETORIC

1. How would you describe Rushdie's tone? Identify words, phrases, and sentences that capture his attitude toward his subject. How does the fact that he writes in the immediate aftermath of the events of September 11, 2001, affect the tone? How do his personal difficulties bear on his approach to the subject?
2. What is the key claim that the writer makes in this essay? Is it stated or implied?
3. Where does Rushdie engage in rebuttal of his opponents' points? Does he refute these points clearly and adequately? Why or why not?

4. What reasons and evidence does the writer offer to support his contention that if Muslim nations accepted responsibility for their internal conditions rather than blaming the West, they could solve their own problems?
5. Where does the writer apply the comparative method to advance his argument?
6. How does Rushdie support his premise that Islamic societies want to become modernized and can do so if their religion returns to "the sphere of the personal" (paragraph 9)?

## WRITING

1. Write a personal essay in which you explain what you think the proper role of religion should be in the post–September 11 world.
2. Write a comparative essay in which you distinguish between "Islam" and "Islamists." Conduct research if necessary.
3. **Writing an Argument:** Take issue with Rushdie's claim that September 11, 2001, is "about Islam." Rebut his reasons, offering ideas and support for your alternative explanation.

www.mhhe.com/
**mhreader**

For more information on Salman Rushdie, go to:
**More Resources > Ch. 11 Ethics & Religion**

# The Rival Conceptions of God

## C. S. Lewis

*C(live) S(taples) Lewis (1898–1963) was born in Belfast, Ireland, but spent the most important years of his life as a lecturer in English at Oxford. His first book,* Dymer, *was published in 1926, but it was not until the publication of* The Pilgrim's Regress *in 1933 that he addressed the central work of his life: a passionate defense of the Christian faith. Lewis's immense output embraces science fiction, fantasy, children's books, theology, and literary criticism. Among his best-known works are* The Screwtape Letters *(1942),* The Lion, the Witch, and the Wardrobe *(1950), and* The Chronicles of Narnia *(1950–1956). In this essay, Lewis describes the reasoning that led to his conversion.*

1  I have been asked to tell you what Christians believe, and I am going to begin by telling you one thing that Christians do not need to believe. If you are a Christian you do not have to believe that all the other religions are simply

wrong all through. If you are an atheist you do have to believe that the main point in all the religions of the whole world is simply one huge mistake. If you are a Christian, you are free to think that all these religions, even the queerest ones, contain at least some hint of the truth. When I was an atheist I had to try to persuade myself that most of the human race have always been wrong about the question that mattered to them most; when I became a Christian I was able to take a more liberal view. But, of course, being a Christian does mean thinking that where Christianity differs from other religions, Christianity is right and they are wrong. As in arithmetic—there is only one right answer to a sum, and all other answers are wrong: but some of the wrong answers are much nearer being right than others.

The first big division of humanity is into the majority, who believe in some  2 kind of God or gods, and the minority who do not. On this point, Christianity lines up with the majority—lines up with ancient Greeks and Romans, modern savages, Stoics, Platonists, Hindus, Mohammedans, etc., against the modern Western European materialist.

Now I go on to the next big division. People who all believe in God can be  3 divided according to the sort of God they believe in. There are two very different ideas on this subject. One of them is the idea that He is beyond good and evil. We humans call one thing good and another thing bad. But according to some people that is merely our human point of view. These people would say that the wiser you become the less you would want to call anything good or bad, and the more clearly you would see that everything is good in one way and bad in another, and that nothing could have been different. Consequently, these people think that long before you got anywhere near the divine point of view the distinction would have disappeared altogether. We call a cancer bad, they would say, because it kills a man; but you might just as well call a successful surgeon bad because he kills a cancer. It all depends on the point of view. The other and opposite idea is that God is quite definitely "good" or "righteous," a God who takes sides, who loves love and hates hatred, who wants us to behave in one way and not in another. The first of these views—the one that thinks God beyond good and evil—is called Pantheism. It was held by the great Prussian philosopher Hegel and, as far as I can understand them, by the Hindus. The other view is held by Jews, Mohammedans and Christians.

And with this big difference between Pantheism and the Christian idea of  4 God, there usually goes another. Pantheists usually believe that God, so to speak, animates the universe as you animate your body: that the universe almost *is* God, so that if it did not exist He would not exist either, and anything you find in the universe is a part of God. The Christian idea is quite different. They think God invented and made the universe—like a man making a picture or composing a tune. A painter is not a picture, and he does not die if his picture is destroyed. You may say, "He's put a lot of himself into it," but you only mean that all its beauty and interest has come out of his head. His skill is not in the picture in the same way that it is in his head, or even in his hands. I expect you see how this difference between Pantheists and Christians hangs together with the other one. If you do not take the distinction between good and bad very seriously, then it is easy to say that anything you find in this world is a part of God. But, of course, if you think some things really bad, and God really good, then you cannot talk like that. You must believe that God is separate from the world and that some of the things we see in it are contrary to His will. Confronted with a cancer or a slum the Pantheist can say, "If you could only see it from the divine point of view, you would realize that this also is God." The Christian replies, "Don't talk damned nonsense."[1] For Christianity is a fighting religion. It thinks God made the world—that space and time, heat and cold, and all the colors and tastes, and all the animals and vegetables, are things that God "made up out of His head" as a man makes up a story. But it also thinks that a great many things have gone wrong with the world that God made and that God insists, and insists very loudly, on our putting them right again.

5       And, of course, that raises a very big question. If a good God made the world why has it gone wrong? And for many years I simply refused to listen to the Christian answers to this question, because I kept on feeling "whatever you say, and however clever your arguments are, isn't it much simpler and easier to say that the world was not made by any intelligent power? Aren't all your arguments simply a complicated attempt to avoid the obvious?" But then that threw me back into another difficulty.

6       My argument against God was that the universe seemed so cruel and unjust. But how had I got this idea of *just* and *unjust*? A man does not call a line crooked unless he has some idea of a straight line. What was I comparing this universe with when I called it unjust? If the whole show was bad and senseless from A to Z, so to speak, why did I, who was supposed to be part of the show, find myself in such violent reaction against it? A man feels wet when he falls into water, because man is not a water animal: a fish would not feel wet. Of course I could have given up my idea of justice by saying it was nothing but a private idea of my own. But if I did that, then my argument against God collapsed too—for the argument depended on saying that the world was really unjust, not simply that it did not happen to please my private fancies. Thus in the very act of trying to prove that God did not exist—in other words, that the whole of reality was senseless—I found I was forced to assume that one part of reality—namely my idea of justice—was full of sense. Consequently atheism turns out to be too simple. If the whole universe has no meaning, we should never have found out that it has no meaning: just as, if there were no light in the universe and therefore no creature with eyes, we should never know it was dark. *Dark* would be without meaning.

---

[1]One listener complained of the word *damned* as frivolous swearing. But I mean exactly what I say—nonsense that is *damned* is under God's curse, and will (apart from God's grace) lead those who believe it to eternal death.

## COMPREHENSION

1. Who is Lewis's audience? What is his purpose? How do you know?
2. Lewis divides humanity into a number of distinct categories. Name them, and discuss his purpose in establishing these categories.
3. What is Lewis's purpose in likening Christianity to arithmetic? In what sense is this apt? Where does he use a similar image?

## RHETORIC

1. Look up the following words from paragraph 2 in a dictionary or an encyclopedia: *Stoics, Platonists, Hindus,* and *Mohammedans.* What are the major tenets of their beliefs?
2. Explain Lewis's use of the word *damned* (paragraph 4). What is specific about his use of this word? Is it appropriate?
3. How does Lewis develop his argument? What line of reasoning does he follow? What transition markers does he use?
4. How does Lewis use definition to structure certain parts of his argument?
5. In which paragraph is Lewis making what he considers the one irrefutable argument in favor of the existence of God? Is this paragraph coherently reasoned in terms of the whole essay? Explain.
6. Why is Lewis's idea of justice critical to the evaluation of his thought? Is his use of the word *justice* idiosyncratic or objective? How does accepting his definition make an important difference in how a reader would respond to this piece?

## WRITING

1. The Western tradition is based, in large part, on the belief that Christianity is right and other religions are wrong. Is this belief as strong today as it was in the past? Does it still cohere as an argument?
2. Write an essay describing your religious beliefs and how they originated.
3. **Writing an Argument:** Argue for or against atheism.

For more information on C. S. Lewis, go to:

**More Resources > Ch. 11 Ethics & Religion**

# The Culture of Disbelief

### Stephen L. Carter

*Stephen L. Carter (b. 1954) received a BA from Stanford University in 1976 and graduated from Yale University Law School in 1979. He served as a law clerk for the U.S. Supreme Court and as a lawyer in private practice before becoming a professor of law at Yale University Law School in 1982. An African American who is opposed to affirmative action, he has become a controversial figure among proponents of the policy. His first book,* Reflections of an Affirmative Action Baby *(1991), outlines his views on the subject and draws on personal experience to show that, even though he was a beneficiary of affirmative action, such preference ultimately makes successful African Americans seem to have received preferential treatment. His second book,* The Culture of Disbelief: How American Law and Politics Trivialize Religious Devotion *(1993), addresses the ways he believes the law has recently operated against the spirit of American values in its effort to ban religion from political discourse and expression. The following essay succinctly sums up this argument.*

1   Contemporary American politics faces few greater dilemmas than deciding how to deal with the resurgence of religious belief. On the one hand, American ideology cherishes religion, as it does all matters of private conscience, which is why we justly celebrate a strong tradition against state interference with private religious choice. At the same time, many political leaders, commentators, scholars, and voters are coming to view any religious element in public moral discourse as a tool of the radical right for reshaping American society. But the effort to banish religion for politics' sake has led us astray: In our sensible zeal to keep religion from dominating our politics, we have created a political and legal culture that presses the religiously faithful to be other than themselves, to act publicly, and sometimes privately as well, as though their faith does not matter to them.

2   Recently, a national magazine devoted its cover story to an investigation of prayer: how many people pray, how often, why, how, and for what. A few weeks later came the inevitable letter from a disgruntled reader, wanting to know why so much space had been dedicated to such nonsense.[1]

3   Statistically, the letter writer was in the minority: by the magazine's figures, better than nine out of ten Americans believe in God and some four out of five

---

[1]"Taking to God," *Newsweek*, Jan. 6, 1992, p. 38; Letter to the Editor, *Newsweek*, Jan. 20, 1992, p. 10. The letter called the article a "theocratic text masquerading as a news article."

pray regularly.[2] Politically and culturally, however, the writer was in the American mainstream, for those who do pray regularly—indeed, those who believe in God—are encouraged to keep it a secret, and often a shameful one at that. Aside from the ritual appeals to God that are expected of our politicians, for Americans to take their religions seriously, to treat them as ordained rather than chosen, is to risk assignment to the lunatic fringe.

Yet religion matters to people, and matters a lot. Surveys indicate that Americans are far more likely to believe in God and to attend worship services regularly than any other people in the Western world. True, nobody prays on prime-time television unless religion is a part of the plot, but strong majorities of citizens tell pollsters that their religious beliefs are of great importance to them in their daily lives. Even though some popular histories wrongly assert the contrary, the best evidence is that this deep religiosity has always been a facet of the American character and that it has grown consistently through the nation's history.[3] And today, to the frustration of many opinion leaders in both the legal and political cultures, religion, as a moral force and perhaps a political one too, is surging. Unfortunately, in our public life, we prefer to pretend that it is not.

Consider the following events:

- When Hillary Rodham Clinton was seen wearing a cross around her neck at some of the public events surrounding her husband's inauguration as President of the United States, many observers were aghast, and one television commentator asked whether it was appropriate for the First Lady to display so openly a religious symbol. But if the First Lady can't do it, then certainly the President can't do it, which would bar from ever holding the office an Orthodox Jew under a religious compulsion to wear a yarmulke.
- Back in the mid-1980s, the magazine *Sojourners*—published by politically liberal Christian evangelicals—found itself in the unaccustomed position of defending the conservative evangelist Pat Robertson against secular liberals who, a writer in the magazine sighed, "see[m] to consider Robertson a dangerous neanderthal because he happens to believe that God can heal diseases."[4] The point is that the editors of *Sojourners,* who are no great admirers of Robertson, also believe that God can heal diseases. So do tens of millions of Americans. But they are not supposed to say so.

---

[2]"Talking to God," p. 39. The most recent Gallup data indicate that 96 percent of Americans say they believe in God, including 82 percent who describe themselves as Christians (56 percent Protestant, 25 percent Roman Catholic) and 2 percent who describe themselves as Jewish. (No other faith accounted for as much as 1 percent.) See Ari L. Goldman, "Religion Notes," *New York Times,* Feb. 27, 1993, p. 9.
[3]See, for example, Jon Butler, *Awash in a Sea of Faith* (Cambridge: Harvard University Press, 1990).
[4]Collum, "The Kingdom and the Power," *Sojourners,* Nov. 1986, p. 4. Some 82 percent of Americans believe that God performs miracles today. George Gallup, Jr., and Jim Castelli, *The People's Religion: American Faith in the '90s* (New York: Macmillan, 1989), p. 58.

- In the early 1980s, the state of New York adopted legislation that, in effect, requires an Orthodox Jewish husband seeking a divorce to give his wife a *get*—a religious divorce—without which she cannot remarry under Jewish law. Civil libertarians attacked the statute as unconstitutional. Said one critic, the "barriers to remarriage erected by religious law . . . only exist in the minds of those who believe in the religion."[5] If the barriers are religious, it seems, then they are not real barriers, they are "only" in the woman's mind—perhaps even a figment of the imagination.
- When the Supreme Court of the United States, ostensibly the final refuge of religious freedom, struck down a Connecticut statute requiring employers to make efforts to allow their employees to observe the sabbath, one Justice observed that the sabbath should not be singled out because all employees would like to have "the right to select the day of the week in which to refrain from labor."[6] Sounds good, except that, as one scholar has noted, "It would come as some surprise to a devout Jew to find that he has 'selected the day of the week in which to refrain from labor,' since the Jewish people have been under the impression for some 3,000 years that this choice was made by God."[7] If the sabbath is just another day off, then religious choice is essentially arbitrary and unimportant; so if one sabbath day is inconvenient, the religiously devout employee can just choose another.
- When President Ronald Reagan told religious broadcasters in 1983 that all laws passed since biblical times "have not improved on the Ten Commandments one bit," which might once have been considered a pardonable piece of rhetorical license, he was excoriated by political pundits, including one who charged angrily that Reagan was giving "short shrift to the secular laws and institutions that a president is charged with protecting."[8] And as for the millions of Americans who consider the Ten Commandments the fundaments on which they build their lives, well, they are no doubt subversive of these same institutions.

6      These examples share a common rhetoric that refuses to accept the notion that rational, public-spirited people can take religion seriously. It might be argued that such cases as these involve threats to the separation of church and state, the durable and vital doctrine that shields our public institutions from religious domination and our religious institutions from government domination. I am a great supporter of the separation of church and state . . . but that is not what these examples are about.

---

[5]Madeline Kochen, "Constitutional Implications of New York's 'Get' Statute," *New York Law Journal*, Oct. 27, 1983, p. 32.
[6]*Estate of Thornton v. Caldor, Inc.*, 472 U.S. 703, 711 (1985) (Justice Sandra Day O'Connor, concurring).
[7]Michael W. McConnell, "Religious Freedom at a Crossroads," *University of Chicago Law Review* 59 (1992):115.
[8]Robert G. Kaiser, "Hypocrisy: This Puffed-Up Piety Is Perfectly Preposterous," *Washington Post*, March 18, 1984, p. C1.

What matters about these examples is the *language* chosen to make the 7 points. In each example, as in many more that I shall discuss, one sees a trend in our political and legal cultures toward treating religious beliefs as arbitrary and unimportant, a trend supported by a rhetoric that implies that there is something wrong with religious devotion. More and more, our culture seems to take the position that believing deeply in the tenets of one's faith represents a kind of mystical irrationality, something that thoughtful, public-spirited American citizens would do better to avoid. If you must worship your God, the lesson runs, at least have the courtesy to disbelieve in the power of prayer; if you must observe your sabbath, have the good sense to understand that it is just like any other day off from work.

The rhetoric matters. A few years ago, my wife and I were startled by a 8 teaser for a story on a network news program, which asked what was meant to be a provocative question: "When is a church more than just a place of worship?" For those to whom worship is significant, the subtle arrangement of words is arresting: *more than* suggests that what follows ("just a place of worship") is somewhere well down the scale of interesting or useful human activities, and certainly that whatever the story is about is *more than* worship; and *just*—suggests that what follows ("place of worship") is rather small potatoes.

A friend tells the story of how he showed his résumé to an executive search 9 consultant—in the jargon, a corporate headhunter—who told him crisply that if he was serious about moving ahead in the business world, he should remove from the résumé any mention of his involvement with a social welfare organization that was connected with a church, but not one of the genteel mainstream denominations. Otherwise, she explained, a potential employer might think him a religious fanatic.

How did we reach this disturbing pass, when our culture teaches that reli- 10 gion is not to be taken seriously, even by those who profess to believe in it? Some observers suggest that the key moment was the Enlightenment, when the Western tradition sought to sever the link between religion and authority. One of the playwright Tom Stoppard's characters observes that there came "a calendar date—*a moment*—when the onus of proof passed from the atheist to the believer, when, quite suddenly, the noes had it."[9] To which the philosopher Jeffrey Stout appends the following comment: "If so, it was not a matter of majority rule."[10] Maybe not—but a strong undercurrent of contemporary American politics holds that religion must be kept in its proper place and, still more, in proper perspective. There are, we are taught by our opinion leaders, religious matters and important matters, and disaster arises when we confuse the two. Rationality, it seems, consists in getting one's priorities straight. (Ignore your religious law and marry at leisure.) Small wonder, then, that we have recently been treated to a book, coauthored by two therapists, one of them an ordained

---

[9]Tom Stoppard, *Jumpers*, quoted in Jeffrey Stout, *The Flight from Authority: Religion, Morality and the Quest for Autonomy* (South Bend, Ind.: University of Notre Dame Press, 1981), p. 150.
[10]Ibid

minister, arguing that those who would put aside, say, the needs of their families in order to serve their religions are suffering from a malady the authors called "toxic faith"—for no normal person, evidently, would sacrifice the things that most of us hold dear just because of a belief that God so intended it.[11] (One wonders how the authors would have judged the toxicity of the faith of Jesus, Moses, or Mohammed.)

11      We are trying, here in America, to strike an awkward but necessary balance, one that seems more and more difficult with each passing year. On the one hand, a magnificent respect for freedom of conscience, including the freedom of religious belief, runs deep in our political ideology. On the other hand, our understandable fear of religious domination of politics presses us, in our public personas, to be wary of those who take their religion too seriously. This public balance reflects our private selves. We are one of the most religious nations on earth, in the sense that we have a deeply religious citizenry; but we are also perhaps the most zealous in guarding our public institutions against explicit religious influences. One result is that we often ask our citizens to split their public and private selves, telling them in effect that it is fine to be religious in private, but there is something askew when those private beliefs become the basis for public action.

12      We teach college freshmen that the Protestant Reformation began the process of freeing the church from the state, thus creating the possibility of a powerful independent moral force in society. As defenders of the separation of church and state have argued for centuries, autonomous religions play a vital role as free critics of the institutions of secular society. But our public culture more and more prefers religion as something without political significance, less an independent moral force than a quietly irrelevant moralizer, never heard, rarely seen. "[T]he public sphere," writes the theologian Martin Marty, "does not welcome explicit Reformed witness—or any other particularized Christian witness."[12] Or, for that matter, any religious witness at all.

13      Religions that most need protection seem to receive it least. Contemporary America is not likely to enact legislation aimed at curbing the mainstream Protestant, Roman Catholic, or Jewish faiths. But Native Americans, having once been hounded from their lands, are now hounded from their religions, with the complicity of a Supreme Court untroubled when sacred lands are taken for road building or when Native Americans under a bona fide religious compulsion to use *peyote* in their rituals are punished under state antidrug regulations.[13] (Imagine the brouhaha if New York City were to try to take St. Patrick's Cathedral by eminent domain to build a new convention center, or if Kansas, a dry state, were to outlaw the religious use of wine.) And airports, backed by the Supreme Court, are happy to restrict solicitation by devotees of

[11]Stephen Arterburn and Jack Felton, *Toxic Faith: Understanding and Overcoming Religious Addiction* (Nashville, Tenn.: Oliver-Nelson Books, 1991).
[12]Martin E. Marty, "Reformed America and America Reformed," *Reformed Journal* (March 1989): 8, 10.
[13]*Employment Division, Department of Human Resources v. Smith*, 494 U.S. 872 (1990).

Krishna Consciousness, which travelers, including this one, find irritating.[14] (Picture the response should the airports try to regulate the wearing of crucifixes or yarmulkes on similar grounds of irritation.)

The problem goes well beyond our society's treatment of those who simply  14 want freedom to worship in ways that most Americans find troubling. An analogous difficulty is posed by those whose religious convictions move them to action in the public arena. Too often, our rhetoric treats the religious impulse to public action as presumptively wicked—indeed, as necessarily oppressive. But this is historically bizarre. Every time people whose vision of God's will moves them to oppose abortion rights are excoriated for purportedly trying to impose their religious views on others, equal calumny is implicitly heaped upon the mass protest wing of the civil rights movement, which was openly and unashamedly religious in its appeals as it worked to impose its moral vision on, for example, those who would rather segregate their restaurants.

One result of this rhetoric is that we often end up fighting the wrong battles.  15 Consider what must in our present day serve as the ultimate example of religion in the service of politics: the 1989 death sentence pronounced by the late Ayatollah Ruhollah Khomeini upon the writer Salman Rushdie for his authorship of *The Satanic Verses,* which was said to blaspheme against Islam. The death sentence is both terrifying and outrageous, and the Ayatollah deserved all the fury lavished upon him for imposing it. Unfortunately, for some critics the facts that the Ayatollah was a religious leader and that the "crime" was a religious one lends the sentence a particular monstrousness; evidently they are under the impression that writers who are murdered for their ideas are choosy about the motivations of their murderers, and that those whose writings led to their executions under, say, Stalin, thanked their lucky stars at the last instant of their lives that Communism was at least godless.

To do battle against the death sentence for Salman Rushdie—to battle  16 against the Ayatollah—one should properly fight against official censorship and intimidation, not against religion. We err when we presume that religious motives are likely to be illiberal, and we compound the error when we insist that the devout should keep their religious ideas—whether good or bad—to themselves. We do no credit to the ideal of religious freedom when we talk as though religious belief is something of which public-spirited adults should be ashamed.

The First Amendment to the Constitution, often cited as the place where  17 this difficulty is resolved, merely restates it. The First Amendment guarantees the "free exercise" of religion but also prohibits its "establishment" by the government. There may have been times in our history when we as a nation have tilted too far in one direction, allowing too much religious sway over politics. But in late-twentieth-century America, despite some loud fears about the influence of the weak and divided Christian right, we are upsetting the balance afresh by tilting too far in the other direction—and the courts are assisting in

---

[14]*International Society for Krishna Consciousness v. Lee,* 112 S. Ct. 2701 (1992)

the effort. For example, when a group of Native Americans objected to the Forest Service's plans to allow logging and road building in a national forest area traditionally used by the tribes for sacred rituals, the Supreme Court offered the back of its hand. True, said the Justices, the logging "could have devastating effects on traditional Indian religious practices." But that was just too bad: "government simply could not operate if it were required to satisfy every citizen's religious needs and desires."[15]

18      A good point: but what, exactly, are the protesting Indians left to do? Presumably, now that their government has decided to destroy the land they use for their sacred rituals, they are free to choose new rituals. Evidently, a small matter like the potential destruction of a religion is no reason to halt a logging project. Moreover, had the government decided instead to prohibit logging in order to preserve the threatened rituals, it is entirely possible that the decision would be challenged as a forbidden entanglement of church and state. Far better for everyone, it seems, for the Native Americans to simply allow their rituals to go quietly into oblivion. Otherwise, they run the risk that somebody will think they actually take their rituals seriously.

## The Price of Faith

19  When citizens do act in their public selves as though their faith matters, they risk not only ridicule, but actual punishment. In Colorado, a public school teacher was ordered by his superiors, on pain of disciplinary action, to remove his personal Bible from his desk where students might see it. He was forbidden to read it silently when his students were involved in other activities. He was also told to take away books on Christianity he had added to the classroom library, although books on Native American religious traditions, as well as on the occult, were allowed to remain. A federal appeals court upheld the instruction, explaining that the teacher could not be allowed to create a religious atmosphere in the classroom, which, it seems, might happen if the students knew he was a Christian.[16] One wonders what the school, and the courts, might do if, as many Christians do, the teacher came to school on Ash Wednesday with ashes in the shape of a cross imposed on his forehead—would he be required to wash them off? He just might. Early in 1993, a judge required a prosecutor arguing a case on Ash Wednesday to clean the ashes from his forehead, lest the jury be influenced by its knowledge of the prosecutor's religiosity.

20      Or suppose a Jewish teacher were to wear a yarmulke in the classroom. If the school district tried to stop him, it would apparently be acting within its authority. In 1986, after a Jewish Air Force officer was disciplined for wearing a yarmulke while on duty, in violation of a military rule against wearing headgear indoors, the Supreme Court shrugged: "The desirability of dress regulations in the military is decided by the appropriate military officials," the justices

[15]*Lyng v. Northwest Indian Cemetery Protective Association*, 485 U.S. 439 (1988).
[16]*Roberts v. Madigan*, 921 F. 2d 1047 (10th Cir. 1990).

explained, "and they are under no constitutional mandate to abandon their considered professional judgment."[17] The Congress quickly enacted legislation permitting the wearing of religious apparel while in uniform as long as "the wearing of the item would [not] interfere with the performance of the member's military duties," and—interesting caveat—as long as the item is "neat and conservative."[18] Those whose faiths require them to wear dreadlocks and turbans, one supposes, need not apply to serve their country, unless they are prepared to change religions.

Consider the matter of religious holidays. One Connecticut town recently   21 warned Jewish students in its public schools that they would be charged with *six* absences if they missed two days instead of the officially allocated one for Yom Kippur, the holiest observance in the Jewish calendar. And Alan Dershowitz of Harvard Law School, in his controversial book *Chutzpah*, castigates Harry Edwards, a Berkeley sociologist, for scheduling an examination on Yom Kippur, when most Jewish students would be absent. According to Dershowitz's account, Edwards answered criticism by saying: "That's how I'm going to operate. If the students don't like it, they can drop the class." For Dershowitz, this was evidence that "Jewish students [are] second-class citizens in Professor Edwards's classes."[19] Edwards has heatedly denied Dershowitz's description of events, but even if it is accurate, it is possible that Dershowitz has identified the right crime and the wrong villain. The attitude that Dershowitz describes, if it exists, might reflect less a personal prejudice against Jewish students than the society's broader prejudice against religious devotion, a prejudice that masquerades as "neutrality." If Edwards really dared his students to choose between their religion and their grade, and if that meant that he was treating them as second-class citizens, he was still doing no more than the courts have allowed all levels of government to do to one religious group after another—Jews, Christians, Muslims, Sikhs, it matters not at all. The consistent message of modern American society is that whenever the demands of one's religion conflict with what one has to do to get ahead, one is expected to ignore the religious demands and act . . . well . . . *rationally.*

Consider Jehovah's Witnesses, who believe that a blood transfusion from one   22 human being to another violates the biblical prohibition on ingesting blood. To accept the transfusion, many Witnesses believe, is to lose, perhaps forever, the possibility of salvation. As the Witnesses understand God's law, moreover, the issue is not whether the blood transfusion is given against the recipient's will, but whether the recipient is, at the time of the transfusion, actively protesting. This is the reason that Jehovah's Witnesses sometimes try to impede the physical access of medical personnel to an unconscious Witness: lack of consciousness is no defense. This is also the reason that Witnesses try to make the decisions on behalf of their children: a child cannot be trusted to protest adequately.

---

[17]*Goldman v Weinberger*, 475 U.S. 503 (1986).
[18]45 U.S.C. 774, as amended by Pub. L. No. 100-80, Dec. 4, 1987.
[19]Alan M. Dershowitz, *Chutzpah* (Boston: Little, Brown, 1991), pp. 329–30.

23    The machinery of law has not been particularly impressed with these arguments. There are many cases in which the courts have allowed or ordered transfusions to save the lives of unconscious Witnesses, even though the patient might have indicated a desire while conscious not to be transfused.[20] The machinery of modern medicine has not been impressed, either, except with the possibility that the Witnesses have gone off the deep end; at least one hospital's protocol apparently requires doctors to refer protesting Witnesses to psychiatrists.[21] Although the formal text of this requirement states as the reason the need to be sure that the Witness knows what he or she is doing, the subtext is a suspicion that the patient was not acting rationally in rejecting medical advice for religious reasons. After all, there is no protocol for packing *consenting* patients off to see the psychiatrist. But then, patients who consent to blood transfusions are presumably acting rationally. Perhaps, with a bit of gentle persuasion, the dissenting Witness can be made to act rationally too—even if it means giving up an important tenet of the religion.

24    And therein lies the trouble. In contemporary American culture, the religions are more and more treated as just passing beliefs—almost as fads, older, stuffier, less liberal versions of so-called New Age—rather than as the fundaments upon which the devout build their lives. (The noes have it!) And if religions *are* fundamental, well, too bad—at least if they're the *wrong* fundaments—if they're inconvenient, give them up! If you can't remarry because you have the wrong religious belief, well, hey, believe something else! If you can't take your exam because of a Holy Day, get a new Holy Day! If the government decides to destroy your sacred lands, just make some other lands sacred! If you must go to work on your sabbath, it's no big deal! It's just a day off! Pick a different one! If you can't have a blood transfusion because you think God forbids it, no problem! Get a new God! And through all of this trivializing rhetoric runs the subtle but unmistakable message: pray if you like, worship if you must, but whatever you do, do not on any account take your religion seriously.

[20]In every decided case that I have discovered involving efforts by Jehovah's Witness parents to prevent their children from receiving blood transfusions, the court has allowed the transfusion to proceed in the face of parental objection. I say more about transfusions of children of Witnesses, and about the rights of parents over their children's religious lives, in chapter 11 [of my book].
[21]See Ruth Macklin, "The Inner Workings of an Ethics Committee: Latest Battle over Jehovah's Witnesses," *Hastings Center Report* 18 (February/March 1988): 15.

## COMPREHENSION

1. Where does Carter articulate the thesis of his essay?
2. The author cites the First Amendment as being a significant historical reference in raising the debate regarding the relationship between government and religion in the United States. What is the First Amendment to the Constitution? What does it mean that the Constitution was amended?
3. In your own words, what is the meaning of the essay's title?

## RHETORIC

1. How does the opening line of the essay draw the reader into the concerns of the author?
2. What is the rhetorical function of the bulleted examples Carter uses in paragraph 5?
3. In paragraphs 8 and 9, the author introduces a personal tone to his essay. Does this add to or diminish his argument?
4. In paragraph 7, Carter places the word *language* in italics; while in other places, he refers to the use of rhetoric as a way of demeaning the religious impulse. For example, in paragraph 14, he states, "Too often, our rhetoric treats the religious impulse to public action as presumptively wicked." Why does Carter focus so much on the use of language as a tool in the attack on religion?
5. The author uses mainly anecdotal evidence to support his views, yet most social sciences claim that anecdotes are a poor form of evidence because they refer only to individual cases, and not to general trends. To what degree does Carter's strategy in using anecdotes strengthen or weaken his argument?
6. Carter devotes one section of his essay to "The Price of Faith." Why has he emphasized this religious issue by placing it in a separate category?
7. How does Carter use irony in his final paragraph? Why is this an effective way of both summing up his main points and drawing attention to them?

## WRITING

1. In a research paper, compare and contrast court rulings regarding perceived governmental infringements on Christian rights of worship versus Native American rights of worship.
2. Assume the role of CEO of a corporation. Write a policy statement in which you provide guidelines for acceptable and unacceptable displays of religious behavior and symbols.
3. **Writing an Argument:** Argue for or against the view that the strength of religious toleration among the American people renders any specific legislation regarding religion merely an academic exercise, with no true social effect.

www.mhhe.com/
**mhreader**

For more information on Stephen L. Carter, go to:
**More Resources > Ch. 11 Ethics & Religion**

# Synthesis: Connections for Critical Thinking

1. How do writers like Plato and Havel use figurative language to make philosophical points? Use specific examples from these authors' works to formulate your answer.

2. Explore the connection between Plato, the philosopher, and Coles, the psychiatrist. How do their essays complement each other? How does Coles's attitude toward existence reflect Plato's philosophy of the cave?

3. What distinguishes a "true" religious belief from a superstition? What are their various functions? Is one more valid than the other? Explain your answer with reference to Mead, Pogrebin, Hughes, and Armstrong.

4. Coles argues that the moral education of children is essential to a well-functioning society. What function does superstition serve in the lives of children that a pure moral education may fail to provide?

5. Based on your reading of Lewis, explain whether you think he would agree or disagree with Rushdie's observations about Islam.

6. What is the difference between philosophy and religion? Is it merely a matter of belief? Address this question in an essay, using support from writers in this chapter.

7. Write an essay titled "The Purpose of Life." Using examples and evidence from their works, choose three writers in this chapter to develop this theme.

8. **Network:** Join two religious newsgroups. Spend two weeks monitoring their messages. Compare and contrast their concerns, questions, perspectives, and beliefs.

9. **Network:** Working with classmates, create your own interactive blog or Web site displaying an excerpt from Rushdie's essay. Ask for personal responses from all its visitors, and report your findings.

10. **Network:** Visit a Web site with summaries of judicial rulings by the Supreme Court. Using the keyword *religion,* study three case histories and the Court's ruling on each.

11. **Network:** Research online the role of cults in American society, particularly among young people. Focus on finding specific superstitions they have that can inflict self-harm or harm on others. Using the essays by Mead and Pogrebin as sources, explore the differences between "good" and "bad" superstitions.

chapter *12*

# Health and Medicine

*What Are the Challenges?*

Today, medicine and the health sciences are recasting our lives and the world we know. From stem-cell research, to the abortion debate, to the AIDS epidemic, we are dealing with enormous medical challenges and controversies. At the same time, commonplace conditions ranging from starvation to the common cold continue to defy solutions. There are surely medical breakthroughs—new drugs, therapies, technologies, and delivery systems—that offer some cause for optimism. However, we must acknowledge the ongoing reality of illness, both physical and psychological, and the serious imbalance in individuals' access to health care.

It could be argued that medical science presents an unequal playing field to Americans and people worldwide, for health care clearly is a privilege rather than a right. For millions of people in the United States and billions around the world, health care is rudimentary or nonexistent. College students, of course, are among the privileged. They typically enjoy health insurance, access to campus clinics or affiliated hospitals, counseling and psychiatric intervention, and an entire network of other health care support systems. Health care at an American college or university is a model that we would wish for any culture, society, or nation.

Medicine and health care are also subjects for civic discourse, cultural argument, and political debate. Disputes over medicine—abortion, cloning, drug addiction, and more—are also part of everyday life. The subject was an integral part of the most recent U.S. presidential election and assuredly will resurface in future election cycles. And, of course, the media (as we discussed in an earlier chapter) exploit our fascination with health and medicine. Television shows feature extreme surgical makeovers and contests among oversized people competing to lose the most weight. Magazines and television promote potentially dangerous body images. On the Internet, people suffering from anorexia and other dietary disorders can find solace and support.

The writers in this chapter contend with some of the most pressing issues confronting medical science today. Some of the writers are physicians. Some authors personalize their subject; others offer objective analysis or compelling arguments. All raise moral and ethical issues as they deal with ways in which medicine is shaping our personalities and our lives.

## Previewing the Chapter

As you read the essays in this chapter and respond to them in discussion and writing, consider the following questions:

- What is the writer's subject? What perspective on medicine or health does she or he take?
- What is the writer's purpose: to explain, narrate, argue, or persuade?
- Do you find the writer's tone to be subjective or objective? Does the author have a personal motive in addressing the topic in the way he or she does?
- What moral, ethical, or religious issues does the writer raise in connection with medicine or health science?
- What logical, emotional, and ethical appeals does the author make to his or her audience?
- Which level of specialized knowledge—history, science, medicine, or some other area—does the author bring to bear on the subject? What level of authority does she or he bring to the topic?
- What cultural, economic, or political problems does the author connect to the medical topic under consideration?
- Do you agree or disagree with the author's thesis or claim, and why?
- Which essays appear similar in subject, thesis, or perspective?
- Which essays did you find most compelling or convincing, and why?
- Which ones changed your opinion or altered your thinking on the subject?

# Classic and Contemporary Images
## WHAT DOES MEDICAL RESEARCH TELL US?

*Using a Critical Perspective*   The medical universe has changed radically since 1632, when Rembrandt painted *The Anatomy Lesson of Professor Nicolaes Tulp*. Flash forward to 2004 and move from Holland to New York City, where photographer Gary Bramnick captured the release of conjoined twins after successful surgery. As you consider these visual texts, answer these questions: What is the main purpose of the artist or the photographer? What elements in each image contribute to the overall effect? How is the human subject portrayed, and which scene evokes the strongest emotional reaction? How does the much earlier scene relate to the contemporary one?

Rembrandt van Rijn (1606–1669) was the most gifted painter, draftsman, and etcher of Holland's Golden Age. *The Anatomy Lesson* (1632) is a group portrait of the Amsterdam surgeon's guild, whose members, led by Dr. Nicolaes Tulp, were unsurpassed in the surgical techniques of the period.

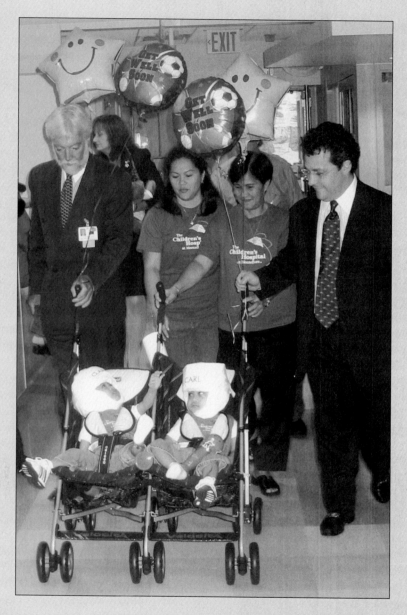

Clarence and Carl Aguirre, formerly conjoined twins who were separated by surgery, are followed by their mother Arlene Aguirre, center left, and grandmother Evelyn, center right, as they leave Children's Hospital at Montefiore in New York, flanked by the doctors who performed the surgery, Dr. James T. Goodrich, left, and Dr. David A. Staffenberg. Nurses loaded the boys into separate ambulances, which took off with a police escort for Blythedale Children's Hospital in Valhalla, where they and their mother have lived between operations at Montefiore.

# Classic and Contemporary Essays
## CAN WE AVOID EPIDEMICS?

We would like to think that the 21st century will avoid a plague like the one that swept through Asia and Europe during the 14th century. Yet the AIDS epidemic proves to be intractable and growing in sub-Saharan Africa, Asia, Russia, and the Indian subcontinent, while outbreaks of new potential epidemics like Ebola and SARS pose serious challenges for medical researchers and dangers for humankind. Plagues seem to be as old and persistent as civilization itself. Looking back to the 14th century, the noted historian Barbara Tuchman tells the story of the Black Death—the bubonic plague—that devastated Europe, resulting in the extinction of perhaps one-third of the population. With a historian's eye for narrative and detail, she describes the symptoms associated with plague, the process by which it spread inexorably from one nation to the next, and the religious, political, and cultural impact of the disease on the continent. Unlike Tuchman, the physician and writer Ronald J. Glasser deals with the present and with the possibility that we are facing new plague years. Like Tuchman, he traces the origins of "the emerging plagues" and their consequences for peoples around the world. But he also provides a pointed argument about the failure of the American health care system, as well as politicians, to recognize and deal rationally with diseases of potentially epidemic proportions. As you read these two essays, one looking backward in history and the other forward in time, consider the rhetorical strategies that Tuchman and Glasser employ to render their vision of the plague years in vivid and compelling ways.

# "This Is the End of the World": The Black Death

### Barbara Tuchman

*Barbara Tuchman (1912–1989) was born in New York City and graduated from Rad-cliffe College. A self-taught historian, she worked as a writer for* The Nation *magazine and during World War II served as an editor at the U.S. Office of War Information. Her book* The Guns of August *(1960), a narrative history of the outbreak of World War I, won the Pulitzer Prize. She won it again for her book* Stilwell and the American Experience in China: 1911–45 *(1971). Her other books included such best-sellers as* A Distant Mirror: The Calamitous 14th Century *(1978) and* The First Salute *(1989). In her later years, she was a lecturer at Harvard University and at the U.S. Naval War College. In this selection, excerpted from* A Distant Mirror, *Tuchman explains in her vivid narrative style the effects of the bubonic plague on Western Europe.*

In October 1347, two months after the fall of Calais, Genoese trading ships   1 put into the harbor of Messina in Sicily with dead and dying men at the oars. The ships had come from the Black Sea port of Caffa (now Feodosiya) in the Crimea, where the Genoese maintained a trading post. The diseased sailors showed strange black swellings about the size of an egg or an apple in the armpits and groin. The swellings oozed blood and pus and were followed by spreading boils and black blotches on the skin from internal bleeding. The sick suffered severe pain and died quickly within five days of the first symptoms. As the disease spread, other symptoms of continuous fever and spitting of blood appeared instead of the swellings or buboes. These victims coughed and sweated heavily and died even more quickly, within three days or less, sometimes in 24 hours. In both types everything that issued from the body—breath, sweat, blood from the buboes and lungs, bloody urine, and blood-blackened excrement—smelled foul. Depression and despair accompanied the physical symptoms, and before the end "death is seen seated on the face."

The disease was bubonic plague, present in two forms: one that infected the   2 bloodstream, causing the buboes and internal bleeding, and was spread by contact; and a second, more virulent pneumonic type that infected the lungs and was spread by respiratory infection. The presence of both at once caused the high mortality and speed of contagion. So lethal was the disease that cases were known of persons going to bed well and dying before they woke, of doctors catching the illness at a bedside and dying before the patient. So rapidly did it spread from one to another that to a French physician, Simon de Covino, it seemed as if one sick person "could infect the whole world." The malignity of the pestilence appeared more terrible because its victims knew no prevention and no remedy.

3     The physical suffering of the disease and its aspect of evil mystery were expressed in a strange Welsh lament which saw "death coming into our midst like black smoke, a plague which cuts off the young, a rootless phantom which has no mercy for fair countenance. Woe is me of the shilling in the armpit! It is seething, terrible . . . a head that gives pain and causes a loud cry . . . a painful angry knob . . . Great is its seething like a burning cinder . . . a grievous thing of ashy color." Its eruption is ugly like the "seeds of black peas, broken fragments of brittle sea-coal . . . the early ornaments of black death, cinders of the peelings of the cockle weed, a mixed multitude, a black plague like halfpence, like berries. . . ."

4     Rumors of a terrible plague supposedly arising in China and spreading through Tartary (Central Asia) to India and Persia, Mesopotamia, Syria, Egypt, and all of Asia Minor had reached Europe in 1346. They told of a death toll so devastating that all of India was said to be depopulated, whole territories covered by dead bodies, other areas with no one left alive. As added up by Pope Clement VI at Avignon, the total of reported dead reached 23,840,000. In the absence of a concept of contagion, no serious alarm was felt in Europe until the trading ships brought their black burden of pestilence into Messina while other infected ships from the Levant carried it to Genoa and Venice.

5     By January 1348 it penetrated France via Marseille, and North Africa via Tunis. Shipborne along coasts and navigable rivers, it spread westward from Marseille through the ports of Languedoc to Spain and northward up the Rhône to Avignon, where it arrived in March. It reached Narbonne, Montpellier, Carcassonne, and Toulouse between February and May, and at the same time in Italy spread to Rome and Florence and their hinterlands. Between June and August it reached Bordeaux, Lyon, and Paris, spread to Burgundy and Normandy, and crossed the Channel from Normandy into southern England. From Italy during the same summer it crossed the Alps into Switzerland and reached eastward to Hungary.

6     In a given area the plague accomplished its kill within four to six months and then faded, except in the larger cities, where, rooting into the close-quartered population, it abated during the winter, only to reappear in spring and rage for another six months.

7     In 1349 it resumed in Paris, spread to Picardy, Flanders, and the Low Countries, and from England to Scotland and Ireland as well as to Norway, where a ghost ship with a cargo of wool and a dead crew drifted offshore until it ran aground near Bergen. From there the plague passed into Sweden, Denmark, Prussia, Iceland, and as far as Greenland. Leaving a strange pocket of immunity in Bohemia, and Russia unattacked until 1351, it had passed from most of Europe by mid-1350. Although the mortality rate was erratic, ranging from one fifth in some places to nine tenths or almost total elimination in others, the overall estimate of modern demographers has settled—for the area extending from India to Iceland—around the same figure expressed in Froissart's casual words: "a third of the world died." His estimate, the common one at the time, was not

Burial of the plague victims. From Annales de Gilles de Muisit.

an inspired guess but a borrowing of St. John's figure for mortality from plague in Revelation, the favorite guide to human affairs of the Middle Ages.

A third of Europe would have meant about 20 million deaths. No one knows in truth how many died. Contemporary reports were an awed impression, not an accurate count. In crowded Avignon, it was said, 400 died daily; 7,000 houses emptied by death were shut up; a single graveyard received 11,000 corpses in six weeks; half the city's inhabitants reportedly died, including 9 cardinals or one third of the total, and 70 lesser prelates. Watching the endlessly passing death carts, chroniclers let normal exaggeration take wings and put the Avignon death toll at 62,000 and even at 120,000, although the city's total population was probably less than 50,000.

When graveyards filled up, bodies at Avignon were thrown into the Rhône until mass burial pits were dug for dumping the corpses. In London in such pits corpses piled up in layers until they overflowed. Everywhere reports speak of the sick dying too fast for the living to bury. Corpses were dragged out of homes and left in front of doorways. Morning light revealed new piles of bodies. In Florence the dead were gathered up by the Compagnia della Misericordia— founded in 1244 to care for the sick—whose members wore red robes and hoods masking the face except for the eyes. When their efforts failed, the dead lay putrid in the streets for days at a time. When no coffins were to be had, the bodies were laid on boards, two or three at once, to be carried to graveyards or common pits. Families dumped their own relatives into the pits, or buried them so hastily and thinly "that dogs dragged them forth and devoured their bodies."

Amid accumulating death and fear of contagion, people died without last rites and were buried without prayers, a prospect that terrified the last hours of the stricken. A bishop in England gave permission to laymen to make confession to each other as was done by the Apostles, "or if no man is present then even to a woman," and if no priest could be found to administer extreme unction, "then faith must suffice." Clement VI found it necessary to grant remissions of sin to all who died of the plague because so many were unattended by priests. "And no bells tolled," wrote a chronicler of Siena, "and nobody wept no matter what his loss because almost everyone expected death. . . . And people said and believed, 'This is the end of the world.'"

11     In Paris, where the plague lasted through 1349, the reported death rate was 800 a day, in Pisa 500, in Vienna 500 to 600. The total dead in Paris numbered 50,000 or half the population. Florence, weakened by the famine of 1347, lost three to four fifths of its citizens, Venice two thirds, Hamburg and Bremen, though smaller in size, about the same proportion. Cities, as centers of transportation, were more likely to be affected than villages, although once a village was infected, its death rate was equally high. At Givry, a prosperous village in Burgundy of 1,200 to 1,500 people, the parish register records 615 deaths in the space of fourteen weeks, compared to an average of thirty deaths a year in the previous decade. In three villages of Cambridgeshire, manorial records show a death rate of 47 percent, 57 percent, and in one case 70 percent. When the last survivors, too few to carry on, moved away, a deserted village sank back into the wilderness and disappeared from the map altogether, leaving only a grass-covered ghostly outline to show where mortals once had lived.

12     In enclosed places such as monasteries and prisons, the infection of one person usually meant that of all, as happened in the Franciscan convents of Carcassonne and Marseille, where every inmate without exception died. Of the 140 Dominicans at Montpellier only seven survived. Petrarch's brother Gherardo, member of a Carthusian monastery, buried the prior and 34 fellow monks one by one, sometimes three a day, until he was left alone with his dog and fled to look for a place that would take him in. Watching every comrade die, men in such places could not but wonder whether the strange peril that filled the air had not been sent to exterminate the human race. In Kilkenny, Ireland, Brother John Clyn of the Friars Minor, another monk left alone among dead men, kept a record of what had happened lest "things which should be remembered perish with time and vanish from the memory of those who come after us." Sensing "the whole world, as it were, placed within the grasp of the Evil One," and waiting for death to visit him too, he wrote, "I leave parchment to continue this work, if perchance any man survive and any of the race of Adam escape this pestilence and carry on the work which I have begun." Brother John, as noted by another hand, died of the pestilence, but he foiled oblivion.

13     The largest cities of Europe, with populations of about 100,000, were Paris and Florence, Venice and Genoa. At the next level, more than 50,000 were Ghent and Bruges in Flanders, Milan, Bologna, Rome, Naples, and Palermo, and Cologne. London hovered below 50,000, the only city in England except York with more than 10,000. At the level of 20,000 to 50,000 were Bordeaux, Toulouse, Montpellier, Marseille, and Lyon in France, Barcelona, Seville, and Toledo in

Spain, Siena, Pisa, and other secondary cities in Italy, and the Hanseatic trading cities of the Empire. The plague raged through them all, killing anywhere from one third to two thirds of their inhabitants. Italy, with a total population of 10 to 11 million, probably suffered the heaviest toll. Following the Florentine bankruptcies, the crop failures and workers' riots of 1346–47, the revolt of Cola di Rienzi that plunged Rome into anarchy, the plague came as the peak of successive calamities. As if the world were indeed in the grasp of the Evil One, its first appearance on the European mainland in January 1348 coincided with a fearsome earthquake that carved a path of wreckage from Naples up to Venice. Houses collapsed, church towers toppled, villages were crushed, and the destruction reached as far as Germany and Greece. Emotional response, dulled by horrors, underwent a kind of atrophy epitomized by the chronicler who wrote, "And in these days was burying without sorrowe and wedding without friendschippe."

In Siena, where more than half the inhabitants died of the plague, work  14 was abandoned on the great cathedral, planned to be the largest in the world, and never resumed, owing to loss of workers and master masons and "the melancholy and grief" of the survivors. The cathedral's truncated transept still stands in permanent witness to the sweep of death's scythe. Angolo di Tura, a chronicler of Siena, recorded the fear of contagion that froze every other instinct. "Father abandoned child, wife husband, one brother another," he wrote, "for this plague seemed to strike through the breath and sight. And so they died. And no one could be found to bury the dead for money or friendship. . . . And I, Angolo di Tura, called the Fat, buried my five children with my own hands, and so did many others likewise."

There were many to echo his account of inhumanity and few to balance it,  15 for the plague was not the kind of calamity that inspired mutual help. Its loathsomeness and deadliness did not herd people together in mutual distress, but only prompted their desire to escape each other. "Magistrates and notaries refused to come and make the wills of the dying," reported a Franciscan friar of Piazza in Sicily; what was worse, "even the priests did not come to hear their confessions." A clerk of the Archbishop of Canterbury reported the same of English priests who "turned away from the care of their benefices from fear of death." Cases of parents deserting children and children their parents were reported across Europe from Scotland to Russia. The calamity chilled the hearts of men, wrote Boccaccio in his famous account of the plague in Florence that serves as introduction to the *Decameron*. "One man shunned another . . . kinsfolk held aloof, brother was forsaken by brother, oftentimes husband by wife; nay, what is more, and scarcely to be believed, fathers and mothers were found to abandon their own children to their fate, untended, unvisited as if they had been strangers." Exaggeration and literary pessimism were common in the 14th century, but the Pope's physician, Guy de Chauliac, was a sober, careful observer who reported the same phenomenon: "A father did not visit his son, nor the son his father. Charity was dead."

Yet not entirely. In Paris, according to the chronicler Jean de Venette, the  16 nuns of the Hôtel Dieu or municipal hospital, "having no fear of death, tended the sick with all sweetness and humility." New nuns repeatedly took the places of those who died, until the majority "many times renewed by death now rest in peace with Christ as we may piously believe."

17     When the plague entered northern France in July 1348, it settled first in Normandy and, checked by winter, gave Picardy a deceptive interim until the next summer. Either in mourning or warning, black flags were flown from church towers of the worst-stricken villages of Normandy. "And in that time," wrote a monk of the abbey of Fourcarment, "the mortality was so great among the people of Normandy that those of Picardy mocked them." The same unneighborly reaction was reported of the Scots, separated by a winter's immunity from the English. Delighted to hear of the disease that was scourging the "southrons," they gathered forces for an invasion, "laughing at their enemies." Before they could move, the savage mortality fell upon them too, scattering some in death and the rest in panic to spread the infection as they fled.

18     In Picardy in the summer of 1349 the pestilence penetrated the castle of Coucy to kill Enguerrand's mother, Catherine, and her new husband. Whether her nine-year-old son escaped by chance or was perhaps living elsewhere with one of his guardians is unrecorded. In nearby Amiens, tannery workers, responding quickly to losses in the labor force, combined to bargain for higher wages. In another place villagers were seen dancing to drums and trumpets, and on being asked the reason, answered that, seeing their neighbors die day by day while their village remained immune, they believed they could keep the plague from entering "by the jollity that is in us. That is why we dance." Further north in Tournai on the border of Flanders, Gilles li Muisis, Abbot of St. Martin's, kept one of the epidemic's most vivid accounts. The passing bells rang all day and all night, he recorded, because sextons were anxious to obtain their fees while they could. Filled with the sound of mourning, the city became oppressed by fear, so that the authorities forbade the tolling of bells and the wearing of black and restricted funeral services to two mourners. The silencing of funeral bells and of criers' announcements of deaths was ordained by most cities. Siena imposed a fine on the wearing of mourning clothes by all except widows.

19     Flight was the chief recourse of those who could afford it or arrange it. The rich fled to their country places like Boccaccio's young patricians of Florence, who settled in a pastoral palace "removed on every side from the roads" with "wells of cool water and vaults of rare wines." The urban poor died in their burrows, "and only the stench of their bodies informed neighbors of their death." That the poor were more heavily afflicted than the rich was clearly remarked at the time, in the north as in the south. A Scottish chronicler, John of Fordun, stated flatly that the pest "attacked especially the meaner sort and common people—seldom the magnates." Simon de Covino of Montpellier made the same observation. He ascribed it to the misery and want and hard lives that made the poor more susceptible, which was half the truth. Close contact and lack of sanitation was the unrecognized other half. It was noticed too that the young died in greater proportion than the old. Simon de Covino compared the disappearance of youth to the withering of flowers in the fields.

In the countryside peasants dropped dead on the roads, in the fields, in their houses. Survivors in growing helplessness fell into apathy, leaving ripe wheat uncut and livestock untended. Oxen and asses, sheep and goats, pigs and chickens ran wild and they too, according to local reports, succumbed to the pest. English sheep, bearers of the precious wool, died throughout the country. The chronicler Henry Knighton, canon of Leicester Abbey, reported 5,000 dead in one field alone, "their bodies so corrupted by the plague that neither beast nor bird would touch them," and spreading an appalling stench. In the Austrian Alps wolves came down to prey upon sheep and then, "as if alarmed by some invisible warning, turned and fled back into the wilderness." In remote Dalmatia bolder wolves descended upon a plague-stricken city and attacked human survivors. For want of herdsmen, cattle strayed from place to place and died in hedgerows and ditches. Dogs and cats fell like the rest.

The dearth of labor held a fearful prospect because the 14th century lived close to the annual harvest both for food and for next year's seed. "So few servants and laborers were left," wrote Knighton, "that no one knew where to turn for help." The sense of a vanishing future created a kind of dementia of despair. A Bavarian chronicler of Neuberg on the Danube recorded that "Men and women . . . wandered around as if mad" and let their cattle stray "because no one had any inclination to concern themselves about the future." Fields went uncultivated, spring seed unsown. Second growth with nature's awful energy crept back over cleared land, dikes crumbled, salt water reinvaded and soured the lowlands. With so few hands remaining to restore the work of centuries, people felt, in Walsingham's words, that "the world could never again regain its former prosperity."

Though the death rate was higher among the anonymous poor, the known and the great died too. King Alfonso XI of Castile was the only reigning monarch killed by the pest, but his neighbor King Pedro of Aragon lost his wife, Queen Leonora, his daughter Marie, and a niece in the space of six months. John Cantacuzene, Emperor of Byzantium, lost his son. In France the lame Queen Jeanne and her daughter-in-law Bonne de Luxemburg, wife of the Dauphin, both died in 1349 in the same phase that took the life of Enguerrand's mother. Jeanne, Queen of Navarre, daughter of Louis X, was another victim. Edward III's second daughter, Joanna, who was on her way to marry Pedro, the heir of Castile, died in Bordeaux. Women appear to have been more vulnerable than men, perhaps because, being more housebound, they were more exposed to fleas. Boccaccio's mistress Fiammetta, illegitimate daughter of the King of Naples, died, as did Laura, the beloved—whether real or fictional—of Petrarch. Reaching out to us in the future, Petrarch cried, "Oh happy posterity who will not experience such abysmal woe and will look upon our testimony as a fable."

In Florence Giovanni Villani, the great historian of his time, died at 68 in the midst of an unfinished sentence: " . . . *e dure questo pistolenza fino a* . . . (in the midst of this pestilence there came to an end . . .)." Siena's master painters, the brothers

20

21

22

23

Ambrogio and Pietro Lorenzetti, whose names never appear after 1348, presumably perished in the plague, as did Andrea Pisano, architect and sculptor of Florence. William of Ockham and the English mystic Richard Rolle of Hampole both disappear from mention after 1349. Francisco Datini, merchant of Prato, lost both his parents and two siblings. Curious sweeps of mortality afflicted certain bodies of merchants in London. All eight wardens of the Company of Cutters, all six wardens of the Hatters, and four wardens of the Goldsmiths died before July 1350. Sir John Pulteney, master draper and four times Mayor of London, was a victim, likewise Sir John Montgomery, Governor of Calais.

24      Among the clergy and doctors the mortality was naturally high because of the nature of their professions. Out of 24 physicians in Venice, 20 were said to have lost their lives in the plague, although according to another account, some were believed to have fled or to have shut themselves up in their houses. At Montpellier, site of the leading medieval medical school, the physician Simon de Covino reported that, despite the great number of doctors, "hardly one of them escaped." In Avignon, Guy de Chauliac confessed that he performed his medical visits only because he dared not stay away for fear of infamy, but "I was in continual fear." He claimed to have contracted the disease but to have cured himself by his own treatment; if so, he was one of the few who recovered.

25      Clerical mortality varied with rank. Although the one-third toll of cardinals reflects the same proportion as the whole, this was probably due to their concentration in Avignon. In England, in strange and almost sinister procession, the Archbishop of Canterbury, John Stratford, died in August 1348, his appointed successor died in May 1349, and the next appointee three months later, all three within a year. Despite such weird vagaries, prelates in general managed to sustain a higher survival rate than the lesser clergy. Among bishops the deaths have been estimated at about one in twenty. The loss of priests, even if many avoided their fearful duty of attending the dying, was about the same as among the population as a whole.

26      Government officials, whose loss contributed to the general chaos, found, on the whole, no special shelter. In Siena four of the nine members of the governing oligarchy died, in France one third of the royal notaries, in Bristol 15 out of the 52 members of the Town Council or almost one third. Tax-collecting obviously suffered, with the result that Philip VI was unable to collect more than a fraction of the subsidy granted him by the Estates in the winter of 1347–48.

27      Lawlessness and debauchery accompanied the plague as they had during the great plague of Athens of 430 B.C., when according to Thucydides, men grew bold in the indulgence of pleasure: "For seeing how the rich died in a moment and those who had nothing immediately inherited their property, they reflected that life and riches were alike transitory and they resolved to enjoy themselves while they could." Human behavior is timeless. When St. John had his vision of plague in Revelation, he knew from some experience or race memory that those who survived "repented not of the work of their hands . . . . Neither repented they of their murders, nor of their sorceries, nor of their fornication, nor of their thefts."

## COMPREHENSION

1. The title of this essay suggests a religious theme. Why did intellectuals and religious leaders associate the bubonic plague with biblical prophecy?
2. Does this essay have a thesis, or does it merely record in detail a period in European history? If it does have a thesis, is it implied or expressed directly? Explain your answer.
3. Does Tuchman suggest that Europe was "fated" to endure the tragic consequences of the plague owing to a higher power, or does she attribute the disaster to a confluence of history and chance? Explain your answer.

## RHETORIC

1. Tuchman begins her essay by describing in detail the physical symptoms of the plague. What strategy lies behind this rhetorical decision?
2. Tuchman has a reputation as a historian whose goal was to bring "history to life." What methods does she use to realize this goal? Is she successful? Why or why not? What does the illustration on page 735 contribute?
3. Contemporary authors and filmmakers often select morbid themes for their sensational value or for financial gain, or both. For example, there is a plethora of "true-crime" stories, "re-creations" of natural disasters, and profiles of aberrant and murderous personalities such as Jeffrey Dahmer, Ted Bundy, and the "Hillside Strangler." Is this Tuchman's purpose? Explain why or why not.
4. Note the particular parts of speech Tuchman uses to begin paragraphs 5–7, 9, 11, 12, 14, 16–18, 20, 22, and 23. All begin with either conjunctions or prepositions. How do these grammatical devices help maintain the flow of Tuchman's narrative?
5. Tuchman makes references to a vast number of historical figures and specific locations in 14th-century Europe. What is her assumption about the educational level of her intended audience? About the specialization of her readership? Is it necessary to know something about the people and places she cites to appreciate the essay? Or is Tuchman writing a book of general interest, with the implicit supposition that different readers will extract their own level of appreciation from her narrative? Explain.
6. Tuchman uses direct quotations from the observers and chroniclers of the times. Examine the use of such sources in paragraphs 10, 13, 15–20, and 23, among others. How does Tuchman weave their observations into her own narrative so that the essay maintains unity and coherence? How does her use of these citations affect the strength of her writing?

## WRITING

1. Write a 300-word summary of Tuchman's essay.

2. For a research project, study Tuchman's philosophy regarding how history should be reported. Apply your research to her treatment of the Black Death.
3. **Writing an Argument:** Argue for or against the proposition that an epidemic as severe as the one that Tuchman describes could not possibly occur in the 21st century.

www.mhhe.com/
**mhreader**

For more information on Barbara Tuchman, go to:
**More Resources > Ch. 12 Health & Medicine**

# We Are Not Immune

## Ronald J. Glasser

*Ronald J. Glasser (b. 1940) is a Minneapolis specialist in pediatric nephrology and rheumatology. Additionally, he is a nonfiction writer and a novelist. His books in-clude* 365 Days *(1971), a collection of sketches about wounded and dying American soldiers fighting in the Vietnam War, and* Ward 402 *(1973), the story of a young girl dying of cancer. His nonfiction books include a study of cancer,* The Greatest Battle *(1976), and* The Light in the Skull: An Odyssey of Medical Discovery *(1997). In the following essay, which appeared in* Harper's Magazine *in 2004, Glasser dis-cusses current epidemics and the collapse of public health.*

1   Death is inevitable, but not disease. The difference may be as simple as washing our hands or keeping the wastes of industrialized farming out of the water sup-ply, but it is often much more complicated. Bacteria and viruses are no mean adversaries, nor are they easily defeated. If we fail to be watchful or to protect those most at risk, a public-health catastrophe is inevitable, and yet somewhere within the span of the last thirty years the idea of the common good has disap-peared from our national consciousness, giving way to the misconception that we no longer need concern ourselves with the welfare of our fellow citizens. It is a dangerous conceit, and it leads us toward a future infected with unprece-dented and unnecessary disease.

2       We have grown not so much complacent as narcotized, lulled into a sense of security by the almost daily pronouncements from corporate medicine and the pharmaceutical industry of ever better drugs and more "breakthrough" treat-ments. The spectacular progress of twentieth-century medicine, most recently the sequencing of the human genome, sponsors the widespread fancy that disease might someday be conquered, that genetic manipulation or nanotechnology

or some other science-fiction marvel might bring with it a cure for death. Long forgotten are the days when the loss of a child to diphtheria or whooping cough or yellow fever was a commonplace event, the days before widespread vaccination and government safety and health regulations; we no longer remember life before publicly funded sewage-treatment plants and the passage of the clean-air and -water acts. Public health is often invisible and unremarked when it works well; when it fails, our neighbors sicken and die.

A public-health system is only as strong as its weakest link; an epidemic  3 enforces, in the most rigorous fashion, the American credo that all men are created equal. If we allow one segment of our society to suffer and perish from preventable disease, little stands in the way of collective doom. Yet today, 44 million people in the United States are without health insurance; those who can afford to pay for it generally receive inferior treatment, despite the fact that Americans spend $1.4 trillion annually for their health care. Public-health departments across the country have never recovered from decades of cutbacks, despite injections of funding in response to specific emergencies such as AIDS or the threat of bioterrorism. Purchases of newer and more reliable diagnostic-testing equipment have been deferred; technical staff and other employees needed to support epidemiologic and testing programs have been downsized; vital on-site bacteriological and viral laboratories have been closed and the testing outsourced to the lowest bidder or simply abandoned.[1] State and local early-childhood services, prenatal care, immunization campaigns for the poor, alcohol-abuse and smoking-awareness campaigns, monitoring programs for lead and arsenic levels, as well as HIV/AIDS treatment programs, have been curtailed as health departments shift around available monies and reassign what few permanent staff members they have left in an attempt to keep the most critical programs in operation. Prevention becomes secondary to simply keeping people alive. Nor must we concern ourselves simply with the state of American public health; as distances collapse and human populations grow ever more mobile, so also new and deadly diseases (among them Ebola and the Marburg virus) find their way across deserts and oceans. AIDS took decades to escape its origins in central Africa; we should not expect the next simian retrovirus to take so long. SARS made its way from Asia to Toronto in a matter of weeks.

Medical historians describe the last few decades as the age of "the emerg-  4 ing plagues." Overpopulation, poverty, ecological devastation and global climate change, chemical pollution and industrial agriculture—all of these factors conspire to create the conditions for unprecedented death by infectious disease. Between 1977 and 1994, twenty-nine previously unknown human pathogens emerged, and it is estimated, moreover, that we have identified only 1 percent of the bacteria and 4 percent of the viruses on the planet. Tuberculosis, a disease that should have disappeared decades ago, has reemerged as an epidemic,

---

[1]More than 3,000 hospital beds and 35 hospitals have been eliminated in Minnesota over the last twenty years; the state has 16,511 licensed beds, of which only about 7,000 are staffed, and most of these are occupied every day. Nationally, between 1980 and 2000, 1,000 hospitals shut their doors.

and drug-resistant strains continue to spread throughout our cities. In 1995, 1.7 million American patients contracted hospital-spread infections; 88,000 of these patients died; 70 percent of the infections were drug-resistant.[2] Each year an estimated 76 million Americans fall ill to food-borne illnesses resulting in approximately 325,000 hospitalizations and 5,000 deaths. Influenza infects 10 to 20 percent of the U.S. population every year and kills 36,000; a virulent avian flu could kill millions. Such numbers, a mere sampling of those available, paint a grim portrait, and the view does not improve if we narrow the perspective.

5  During a two-week period in 1993 one of Milwaukee's two water-treatment plants malfunctioned. This waterworks supplied treated drinking water directly from Lake Michigan to at least half the population of Milwaukee and nine of its suburbs. The investigation that eventually followed revealed unprecedented increases in the density levels of the supposedly treated water during that two-week period. The gauges designed for continuous measurement of water purity had clearly not been functioning properly for periods as long as eight to twelve hours at a time. The precise reason for the failure remains obscure, but what is clear is that no alarms went off, no backup systems were brought online, and no one noticed the increases in turbidity that led to the largest waterborne epidemic ever to occur in the United States.

6      Within days of the plant's malfunction and continuing for an additional month, more than 403,000 people in the Milwaukee area developed fever, vomiting, and diarrhea. One hundred people died. The cause of the illness was *Cryptosporidium*, a single-celled microorganism that survives in bodies of standing water and has been known as a cause of diarrhea, abdominal cramping, nausea, vomiting, and fever since the 1970s. There is no medical treatment for the infection, and in otherwise healthy individuals the disease is usually self-limiting, though in a minority of cases the disease can lead to weeks of disability. In patients on immunosuppressive medications, those undergoing chemotherapy, or those with AIDS, the infection can be ruthless, unrelenting, and fatal.

7      The seriousness of *Cryptosporidium* in an immune-suppressed patient became clear at the beginning of the AIDS epidemic when physicians first found this strange and unexpected parasite in the blood and bone marrows of infected patients. Knowing that the organism was basically a disease of herd animals, the doctors contacted the preeminent expert on *Cryptosporidium* in the department of agriculture at the University of Iowa. When the professor was asked how infected sheep were treated, he hesitated. "There is no treatment," he answered. "We shoot them."

8      There are well over 1,400 documented microorganisms that can infect humans, of which fully one half first caused disease in animals. *Cryptosporidium*

[2]The failure of antibiotics to control common infections such as staph and strep is one of the most chilling of recent developments, one hastened by the reckless overprescription of physicians and by massive application of antibiotics to livestock that would otherwise perish in the lethal miasma created by industrial agriculture.

made the transfer to humans through the contamination of surface waters by runoff from farmlands and drainage ditches. Unfortunately, the cysts that spread the infection are highly resistant to chlorine and even remain viable in the laboratory after exposures to full-strength household bleaches. You can't kill the *Cryptosporidium* cysts, and while alive they remain astonishingly infectious. Disease has been known to occur through ingestion of as few as thirty cysts, and experimental data have shown that even a single cyst can pass on the disease to uninfected sheep as well as to humans. The only means of prevention for a contaminated water supply are filters of less than one micron placed within water-purification systems that physically remove the millions of heavy, dense cysts before they reach the household taps of public water supplies.

The failure of the main safety and backup gauges in Milwaukee was clearly  9 a disaster, but the most unnerving aspect of the Wisconsin epidemic was not the astronomical numbers of affected people or even the deaths; it was the fact that, in the midst of the worsening epidemic, it was not the federal government or any state or local health department or surveillance program or emergency-room database or managed-healthcare reporting system that alerted the public that an epidemic was in progress. It was a pharmacist, who happened to notice unusual sales of over-the-counter diarrhea medication. The local media reported the outbreak days before the health department took action, almost a week after the alarm was first raised.

The outbreak of *Cryptosporidium* in Milwaukee was more than the simple  10 malfunction of a few gauges in a midsized American city; to those concerned about the nation's ability to treat its people and control disease, it was a clear sign that our infectious-disease and medical surveillance and prevention programs were no longer working. Although the Milwaukee disaster was unusual for its size, waterborne outbreaks of disease are not uncommon. The Centers for Disease Control maintain a database on the subject, but the statistics are not very reliable because they depend on the voluntary reporting of state and local health officials. Some states choose not to make these reports; some states do not even have active disease-surveillance systems. But local failures can often have far broader consequences, as we learned from the 1999 outbreak of the West Nile virus in New York City. Mosquito surveillance and control was a local budget casualty that led to a national epidemic, and by last year West Nile had appeared in every state but Washington, Oregon, Alaska, and Hawaii; 14,163 people are known to have been infected and 564 have died. The discovery in 2002 that the virus was transmitted via organ transplantation, and possibly by blood transfusion, has led to fears that the national blood supply could be contaminated. Testing for West Nile raises the cost of blood by $4 to $7 a unit. And even as the virus spreads across the continent, federal funding is being cut; in 2004 the Mosquito Abatement for Safety and Health Act received zero funding, and none has been requested for 2005.

The United States has no single agency responsible for public health and  11 thus no coherent policy. As Laurie Garrett suggests in her monumental study, *Betrayal of Trust: The Collapse of Global Public Health*, it is no exaggeration to say that we simply lack a public-health system per se; what we do have is best described as "a hodgepodge of programs, bureaucracies, and failings."

12    The great public-health victories of the nineteenth and early twentieth centuries over yellow fever, cholera, encephalitis, smallpox, puerperal fever, and a host of other infectious diseases were largely the result of preventive measures enacted by visionary public officials: improved sanitation and nutrition (safe water and food, decent housing, paved streets, sewers), vigorous powers of quarantine to prevent contagion, mosquito control and the installation of window glass, and the creation of vaccination programs. Few advances were as important as the realization that merely washing one's hands could prevent the spread of disease. Life expectancy in the eighteenth century for an average male was about thirty years; by the early 1970s, it was seventy-five years. And as Garrett points out, most of that progress occurred prior to the invention of antibiotics, and "less than 4 percent of the total improvement in life expectancy since the 1700s can be credited to twentieth century advances in medical care." Ironically, the medical revolutions of the twentieth century have contributed to our overconfident and complacent neglect of the public-health infrastructure. We spend vast sums to lengthen the lives of terminally ill patients by a few days and refuse to make modest investments that would prevent millions of needless illnesses and deaths.

13    The peculiar dynamics of American politics, with its periodic spasms of irrational antigovernment hysteria, have ensured that few effective public-health policies fail to attract powerful political enemies, enemies that more often than not have succeeded in weakening the agencies charged by Congress with the responsibility for the health and well-being of the American people. Not even the CDC is immune from the virus of partisan politics; despite an overwhelming medical consensus, the agency has refused to take a position on the use of condoms to prevent AIDS and has curtailed the printing or distribution of any data on the control or treatment of sexually transmitted diseases that might offend the most conservative Christians. In response to political pressure from the NRA and threats from Congress to withhold funding, the CDC has also discontinued its definitive research documenting the public-health costs of handguns.

14    The Food and Drug Administration presents the same self-defeating pattern of regulatory behavior. In May of this year, the agency refused to approve a morning-after contraceptive pill for over-the-counter use, even after its own expert advisory panel recommended it. Far worse is the degree to which the FDA panders to its industrial constituency. Drugs receive approval without adequate testing; the agency dithers when patients begin to die; eventually it turns out that adverse findings were ignored or suppressed. Often more concerned for the well-being of the pharmaceutical industry than for the health of American citizens, the FDA challenges states that seek to purchase cheaper Canadian drugs for their citizens and ignores the ongoing concentration of drug and vaccine production into the hands of fewer and larger companies, which has led to greater consumer costs and vaccine shortages. The agency has

shown no inclination to pressure manufacturers into adopting new technologies that would allow the timely and safe development of new vaccines in response to emerging diseases. Not too long ago the FDA supported the pharmaceutical industry's wish to give antidepressant drugs to children despite the agency's own finding that such drugs might cause them to commit suicide.

Faced with alarming outbreaks of food-borne illness, the Department of 15 Agriculture has refused to enforce the use of any of the more definitive and reliable, though admittedly more costly, bacterial tests of meat and meat products to replace the pathetically ineffective "poke and sniff" test used in all government-monitored and -approved slaughterhouses and meat-processing plants. *E. coli,* salmonella, listeria, shigella, have all caused outbreaks of disease. What is astonishing is not that a million pounds of hamburger can be contaminated from one infected cow but that the federal government demands only "voluntary" recalls. Confronted with proof that mad cow disease has infected the American food supply, the agency has prohibited the routine testing of American cattle for the disease, using the newly available tests only in obviously diseased animals and then allowing the animals to be slaughtered and put into the food supply before the results of those tests are available. The USDA has dismissed the recommendations of some of the nation's most prominent professors of agriculture and veterinary medicine to institute a more rigorous and scientific method of testing for this disease, usually citing as an excuse the meat industry's concern that any testing will add an additional three to five cents a pound to consumer prices. The USDA is not so much a regulatory agency as it is an arm of the meat-industry lobby.

Americans, we know, pay too much for their health care, and compared with 16 other countries we receive a very poor return on our investment. The reasons are many, but they are not hard to understand: in essence, we have tended historically to view health care as a commodity like any other. But health is not a product; it is a public good. The evidence is clear that even when viewed through the reductive lens of purely economic self-interest, market-based, entrepreneurial medicine is a failure. Healing people after they fall ill is vastly more expensive than preventing the illness in the first place: every dollar spent preventing diphtheria, for instance, saves $27; every dollar spent on measles, mumps, and rubella saves $23. Yet policymakers have consistently preferred the most expensive and least efficient models of health care, proving once again that the apostles of privatization are motivated not by hard-nosed economics but by an incoherent ideology that is little more than a brittle mask concealing the most irrational species of self-interest.

For the last quarter century, especially after the election of Ronald Reagan 17 and his declaration that government itself is the problem that afflicts us, the public-health infrastructure of this country has been eviscerated. Between 1981 and 1993, public-health expenditures declined by 25 percent as a proportion of overall health spending; in 1992, less than 1 percent of all American health-care spending was devoted to public health. That trend has continued, even after the anthrax attacks of 2001, when politicians suddenly realized how vulnerable the nation was to biological attack.

18    Since then, it is true, the federal government has appropriated about $2 billion for bioterrorism response, an undertaking that if it were actually carried out would necessarily involve improving the public-health infrastructure. In theory, the bioterrorism money is channeled through the CDC, which distributes it to the states, which in turn disperse money to local health departments. Superficially, the gains are impressive: the CDC's budget for "public health preparedness and response for bioterrorism" increased from $49.9 million in 2001 to $918 million in 2002 and $870 million in 2003. Yet strangely enough, state and local public-health budgets have continued to decline. Public-health laboratories in California could lose 20 percent of their funding this year; the Alabama Department of Public Health expects to fire 250 people and to close regional labs and cut back on its flu-vaccination programs. State funding for AIDS prevention in Massachusetts has been cut by 40 percent over the last two years. Larimer County, Colorado, where last summer 500 people contracted the West Nile virus, received $100,000 in federal funds but lost $700,000 in state money. Overall, thirty-two states cut their public-health budgets between fiscal years 2002 and 2003. Michigan cut its spending by 24 percent, Massachusetts by 23 percent, and Montana, which received more federal bioterror money per capita than New York, cut its public-health budget by 19 percent. Many states, facing huge budget deficits, apparently took the federal money and simply cut their own appropriations. This should come as no surprise: in 2003 the states collectively faced a $66 billion shortfall, and in 2004 state deficits are estimated to be $78 billion. Federal investment will do no good if state politicians, struggling to cope with the economic effects of other federal policies, use those funds to reduce their own deficits.

19    The Trust for America's Health (TFAH), a nonprofit group that monitors public-health policy, in December released a comprehensive study of what the state health departments have accomplished with their "increased" funding. TFAH found that only twenty-four states had spent at least 90 percent of their 2002 bioterror funds, and only seventeen states had passed at least 50 percent of the money along to local health departments. Much of the money is mired in bureaucracy. A February GAO report revealed that the states were not much better prepared for bioterrorism (and by extension, a natural epidemic) than they were in 2001.

20    Of course, state health departments can hardly be blamed for their inability to correct a quarter century of neglect with what amounts to a mere $2,000 for every staffed hospital bed in America. Bioterrorism funds are being used simply to keep the lights on, and no one who has carefully observed the Bush Administration would expect it to follow through with its promises to rebuild the public-health system. In fact, the President's 2005 budget proposal calls for a $105 million decrease in state and local bioterrorism funding. The new budget also cuts $1.1 billion from the "Function 550" account, which finances disease-prevention programs and other public-health initiatives, and the federal Public Health Improvements Programs were cut by 64 percent.

Secretary of Health and Human Services Tommy Thompson has claimed   21
that preparing for bioterrorism will enable the government to respond to influenza and other infectious diseases; in fact, the reverse is true. Bioterrorism is a
remote threat and a massive attack is very unlikely, but it captures the imagination of weak-minded politicians and a populace raised on movies starring Bruce
Willis. The truly imminent biological threat, which all public-health experts
agree will inevitably strike, is an influenza pandemic. The 1918 pandemic killed
550,000 Americans and 30 million worldwide. A virulent flu would thus be
much worse than a bioterrorism attack, and it would strike every part of the
country more or less simultaneously. These facts are well known and understood, yet TFAH found that only thirteen states have a plan or at least a draft of
a plan to confront an influenza pandemic. Amazingly, the CDC itself has yet to
release a federal plan for such a pandemic; nor does the CDC require states to
report flu cases or even flu deaths.

Every year influenza epidemics emerge from areas such as the Guangdong region   22
of China, where large populations of farmers, pigs, and poultry share their
species' various strains of the influenza virus. When multiple strains of the virus
infect the same host, they begin to share genes, creating new mutations; when a
new strain emerges for which humans have no immunity, a pandemic can occur.

In response to a 1997 avian influenza outbreak that began to infect humans   23
but stopped short, for some reason, of becoming an epidemic, the World Health
Organization significantly expanded its flu-prevention activities and set up its
Global Agenda for Influenza Surveillance and Control, a program whose four
main objectives are to monitor the spread of influenza in animals and humans,
to identify each year's newest infective strain, to accelerate global pandemic
awareness, and to increase usage and speed development of an effective vaccine. Each year the WHO surveillance program puts its infectious-disease teams
along with its worldwide network of more than one hundred laboratories on
alert, hoping to detect outbreaks before they spread around the globe. Such
generalized surveillance is difficult and expensive, but the danger of emerging
infections and the continuing influenza threat have left the world health community with little choice.

In February 2003 the WHO issued a report about a group of patients with   24
severe influenza in Hong Kong. The index case was a physician from Guangdong province in China. A global alert was soon issued concerning similar illnesses in Singapore and Hanoi. The WHO sent Dr. Carlo Urbani, an Italian
infectious-disease specialist, to Hanoi to investigate. Urbani swiftly determined
that the disease was something unusual and that it was highly contagious and
virulent. Unlike influenza, which always begins with a runny nose, waves of
generalized aches and pains, and weakness, followed by days of fever and an
increasing cough before the onset of pneumonia, this disease progressed almost
immediately to severe pneumonia, respiratory collapse, and, for many, death.
We now know that these alerts were describing the SARS outbreak, which
nearly became a global pandemic. Working closely with the Vietnamese

authorities, Urbani and other specialists from the WHO, the CDC, and Doctors Without Borders were able to contain the disease in Hanoi, though tragically Urbani himself contracted SARS and died in a makeshift isolation ward in Bangkok. It was not long before the disease spread to Toronto. By late March, 6,800 people there had already been quarantined, with another 5,200 health-care staff working "in quarantine" at facilities that public-health officials had quickly set aside for treating suspected SARS cases. In the United States public-health officials were simply holding their breath and hoping for the best. Not only have cutbacks stripped rural areas of their hospitals and clinics but even the major cities now lack the number of acute-care and infectious-disease beds—not to mention the nursing staff, technicians, and isolation units—to deal with a bad year of influenza much less a full-fledged disease with what appeared to be the staggering demands of SARS.

25      What happened next was unprecedented: researchers quickly determined that the disease was caused by a new type of virus and very rapidly isolated the cause as a previously unknown coronavirus that had apparently jumped from an animal species to humans. It was not lost on the world's infectious-disease experts that what had taken physicians and scientists almost four years in the case of AIDS was accomplished for SARS in less than four months. It is no exaggeration to say that the billions of dollars so reluctantly pushed into viral research as a result of the efforts of AIDS activists in the 1980s and 1990s enabled the WHO to quickly find the cause of another viral plague. And it was the ability to share accurate information in real time via email and the Internet that allowed the WHO to hold the disease in check.

26      In the midst of all the tracking of potential contacts, the increased hospitalizations, the thousands of people in quarantine, the disease simply vanished at virtually the same time all over the world. Coronaviruses thrive in cold weather, and, like influenza, they spread during the winter months, which accounts for the yearly outbreaks of colds and upper-respiratory infections. The realization that SARS is a cold-weather virus is troubling, because it means that there has been no real victory, only a reprieve. It has to be assumed that SARS is still out there waiting for another winter.

27      The lesson of the SARS outbreak was that preparation, surveillance, and decisive action from public officials can prevent epidemics. The WHO response was exemplary—training, staffing, equipment, and funding were all in place, ready for an emergency—but we still lack a truly global early-warning system. In the United States we continue to be without an effective national warning system. As *Lancet* editor Richard Horten writes in *Health Wars*, his scathing critique of contemporary medicine, "No single agency—CDC, WHO, the military, or a nongovernmental organization (such as Médecins Sans Frontières)—currently has the resources, staff, or equipment to act as a rapid-response strike force during a civilian health emergency." If SARS had come to the United States, there is little hope that it could have been contained.

28      Today, we are no better prepared for a SARS epidemic than we were last year. "Homeland security," curiously interpreted to exclude the most plausible and

deadly threats facing our population, has remained the priority. The massive smallpox immunization program in 2002 was little more than a distraction and waste of precious funds. Meanwhile, we are afflicted with a government that has waged war all across the world to avenge the deaths of 3,000 terror victims, far fewer than die of influenza in a mild year; a government that insists on spending $50 billion to build a missile-defense system that does not work, a military-industrial make-work project designed to meet a threat that does not exist. The war in Iraq consumes almost $4 billion a month, twice the amount we have largely squandered on bioterrorism since 2001. We have grown so foolish and so incompetent that perhaps we do not deserve to survive. Perhaps it is simply time to die.

## COMPREHENSION

1. What does Glasser mean when he writes, "We have grown not so much complacent as narcotized" about medicine and illness (paragraph 2)? What examples does he give to support this assertion?
2. According to the author, what are some of the main examples of the age of the "emerging plagues" (paragraph 4)?
3. Explain Glasser's opinion of the state of American health care. How is health care policy affected by politics? What does the author conclude?

## RHETORIC

1. What is Glasser's claim? Where does it appear most clearly? How does the tone of the essay reinforce the claim?
2. The writer divides his essay into five sections. What is the topic of each section? How does each section relate to the unit that follows? How does Glasser maintain coherence?
3. What appeals to authority does the author make? How does he establish his own credibility?
4. What are the different types of evidence that the writer offers in this essay? What are the premises behind the evidence? How convincing is this evidence? Explain your answer.
5. What patterns of cause and effect does Glasser analyze? What is his purpose in using causal analysis?
6. Examine the first and last paragraphs. What similarities do you detect in content and tone? How do these beginning and ending paragraphs serve to frame the entire essay?

## WRITING

1. Write a personal essay in which you describe an instance when you did not receive proper or adequate health care.

2. Research one disease that Glasser mentions—for example influenza, AIDS, or SARS—and write an essay defining and describing the illness and its epidemic nature either in the United States or worldwide.

3. **Writing an Argument:** Write a response to the author, either agreeing with his views or refuting them. Be certain to deal with his concluding remark, "Perhaps it is simply time to die."

www.mhhe.com/
**mhreader**

For more information on Ronald J. Glasser, go to:
**More Resources > Ch. 12 Health & Medicine**

### Synthesis: Classic and Contemporary Questions for Comparison

1. Discuss Tuchman's and Glasser's essays in terms of style, method, and tone. What level of language do they employ? What forms of authority do they bring to bear on their subject? What rhetorical strategies do they use? How does the fact that one writer is a historian and the other a doctor affect their approach to the subject? Does one argue and the other explain, or do they both make similar assertions?

2. Compare Tuchman's view of the bubonic plague of the 14th century with Glasser's presentation of the new plague years.

3. In groups of three or four, conduct research on epidemics throughout history not mentioned by either Tuchman or Glasser. How do these epidemics serve to reinforce the assertions that the two writers make?

# I Worked Hard for That Furrowed Brow

### Ellen Goodman

*Ellen Goodman (b. 1941) is an award-winning journalist and associate editor of* The Boston Globe. *She was born in Newton, Massachusetts, and educated at Radcliffe College. She began working for* The Globe *in 1967 and started writing a weekly column in 1971, which today is syndicated in more than 400 newspapers across the United States. Starting with* Close to Home *(1979), Goodman has published five collections of her columns, dealing with a broad range of topics, including the status of women, health and reproductive issues, politics, and the family. In 1980 her columns*

*were awarded the Pulitzer Prize for Distinguished Commentary. Here, in a column
that appeared in 2002, she dissents from the current obsession with Botox and other
forms of cosmetic surgery.*

Just because the FDA has approved of Botox doesn't mean that I have to. In 1
fact, since 835,000 people have already had their foreheads injected with the
paralyzing fluid that keeps them from being able to frown, I figure that
somebody has to frown for them.

When I first read about Botox as a cosmetic, I thought there was something 2
vaguely charming about the idea. After all, the microbe created by the U.S. Army
to inflict botulism poisoning on our enemies was now being used for domestic
and aesthetic purposes. Talk about beating your swords into tweezers.

But even before the FDA gave the green light, we heard that Botox gather- 3
ings of women had become the Tupperware parties of the 21st century. Only
what's being preserved are the women, not the leftovers.

This is not, I promise you, a screed about the political incorrectness of plas- 4
tic surgery or vanity. Nor is it about how beauty is only skin deep.

Over the years, my attitudes—like my jaw line—have softened toward 5
women who choose to change their faces rather than live with them. I know
there's a line between those who "need" to be "fixed" and those who don't,
between those who need surgery—think burn victim—and those who need
therapy—think Michael Jackson. But I'm less inclined to draw it for anyone
else.

When 47-year-old Greta Van Susteren became the poster anchor for plastic 6
surgery, I thought the criticism was way over the top. As she said, "Having
plastic surgery isn't shoplifting." If it were, nearly every female-and-fifty face
on TV would be behind bars. After all, most of us choose, um, some self-
improvement. Where is the unacceptable point on the aesthetic slope between
braces and face lifts? Aging gracefully does not mean that you have to age
grayly. So, you tell me the cut-off between hair color and collagen.

Nevertheless. 7

As a woman of a certain age—the age targeted by the hefty $53 million ad 8
campaign being launched by Allergan, the maker of Botox—every time someone I know, or watch, has some "work" done, I have a vague feeling of being
deserted. It's as if they'd left a threatened neighborhood, the endangered, natural species free range, and sided with the image-makers.

Remember back when Gloria Steinem turned 40? (If you do, it's probably 9
too late for Botox, anyway.) She said: "This is what 40 looks like." At that time
it was a statement that said proudly: We are not your grandmother's 40-year-
old.

Of course, 40 never did necessarily look like Gloria. But what happens 10
when 50 is supposed to look like 40? Does that mean the whole standard of aging has changed? Do we think 60 should look like 50? Does, say, a 70-year-old
Barbara Walters actually change the future for older women on TV? Or is an
older woman only accepted if she doesn't look her age?

11     Chemical peels. Endoscopic lifts. Microfat injections. Eyelid lifts. Face lifts. Botox marketed to women the way Viagra is to men (never mind). How long is it before looking "your age" is regarded as a slatternly failure of effort? How long before any woman who doesn't try one of the above is dismissed as someone who is "letting herself go"?

12     I have always loved the expression, "letting yourself go." Where do you go, when you let yourself? To the recycle bin or to freedom? On Oscar night, in a sea of nipped and tucked, siliconed and surgeried women, the only seamed faces over 50 belonged to the likes of Judi Dench, Maggie Smith, and Helen Mirren. They are all character actors. Is that where they let themselves go? Into character?

13     In the past few years, I have found myself looking at older women as harbingers of the future. I'm looking for energy and confidence, and yes, attractiveness. Who do I want to be when I grow up? I am sure there are young women searching for the same clues. But there's no way to find them on the Botox party masks. This is the real symbolism of Botox. It eliminates lines temporarily by paralyzing muscles. It offers an actual trade-off. You trade the ability, literally, to express your emotions—furrow that brow, crinkle that eye—for a flawless appearance. In the search for approval from others, you hide what you are feeling. Especially anger.

14     This seems to my cranky eye and creased eyebrow to be exactly the opposite of my goal to become an outspoken, maybe even outrageous, laugh-out-loud, nothing-left-to-lose old lady. Spare me the Botox. I plan to remain the kind of character actor who wears her emotions, not on her sleeve or on her surgeon's bill, but on her face.

## COMPREHENSION

1. What does Goodman think about Botox? What other forms of cosmetic surgery does she mention? What is her attitude toward them?
2. Why does the author mention Michael Jackson? Who are Greta Van Susteren and Gloria Steinem (see page 593), and how do they differ in their approach to beauty?
3. What, finally, is the author's attitude toward aging?

## RHETORIC

1. A newspaper column places strict stylistic and formal demands on a writer. What journalistic elements do you find in this essay? What elements of style stand out?
2. Explain the tone of this essay. Where is Goodman serious? Where does she employ irony and satire? What is the overall effect?
3. What is the main idea of this essay? Which sentence serves as the thesis statement?

4. Analyze the essay as an argument and an attempt to persuade. What is the author's warrant, claim, and support? Does she engage in refutation? Why or why not?
5. What is the purpose and effect of the many questions that the author poses in this essay?
6. Where does Goodman use metaphors and other types of figurative language? What ideas do they convey?
7. How effective is the conclusion? Why?

## WRITING

1. Have you had cosmetic surgery, or do you know someone who has? Write an essay telling about the procedure and the result.
2. Write an essay that compares and contrasts the ways that men and women view cosmetic surgery.
3. **Writing an Argument:** Compose an answer to Goodman in which you offer a humorous defense of cosmetic surgery.

---

 **www.mhhe.com/ mhreader**   For more information on Ellen Goodman,, go to: **More Resources > Ch. 12 Health & Medicine**

---

# Between a Woman and Her Doctor

## Martha Mendoza

*Martha Mendoza (b. 1969) was born and raised in Los Angeles and attended college at the University of California at Santa Cruz (BA, 1988). Based in San Jose, Mendoza is a national investigative reporter for the Associated Press. Her work has appeared in the* Los Angeles Times, Houston Chronicle, Newsday, *and elsewhere. Mendoza is also the co-author of* The Bridge at No Gun Ri: A Hidden Nightmare from the Korean War *(2001). In 2000, she won a Pulitzer Prize for investigative reporting. In this essay, which appeared in* Ms. *magazine in 2004, Mendoza tells of her abortion while at the same time exploring broader medical, social, and legal issues.*

I could see my baby's amazing and perfect spine, a precise, pebbled curl of 1 vertebrae. His little round skull. The curve of his nose. I could even see his small leg floating slowly through my uterus.

2    My doctor came in a moment later, slid the ultrasound sensor around my growing, round belly and put her hand on my shoulder. "It's not alive," she said.

3    She turned her back to me and started taking notes. I looked at the wall, breathing deeply, trying not to cry.

4    I can make it through this, I thought. I can handle this.

5    I didn't know I was about to become a pariah.

6    I was 19 weeks pregnant, strong, fit and happy, imagining our fourth child, the newest member of our family. He would have dark hair and bright eyes. He'd be intelligent and strong—really strong, judging by his early kicks.

7    And now this. Not alive?

8    I didn't realize that pressures well beyond my uterus, beyond the too-bright, too-loud, too-small ultrasound room, extending all the way to board-rooms of hospitals, administrative sessions at medical schools and committee hearings in Congress, were going to deepen and expand my sorrow and pain.

9    On November 6, 2003, President Bush signed what he called a "partial birth abortion ban," prohibiting doctors from committing an "overt act" designed to kill a partially delivered fetus. The law, which faces vigorous challenges, is the most significant change to the nation's abortion laws since the U.S. Supreme Court ruled abortion legal in *Roe v. Wade* in 1973. One of the unintended consequences of this new law is that it put people in my position, with a fetus that is already dead, in a technical limbo.

10    Legally, a doctor can still surgically take a dead body out of a pregnant woman. But in reality, the years of angry debate that led to the law's passage, restrictive state laws and the violence targeting physicians have reduced the number of hospitals and doctors willing to do dilations and evacuations (D&Es) and dilations and extractions (intact D&Es), which involve removing a larger fetus, sometimes in pieces, from the womb.

11    At the same time, fewer medical schools are training doctors to do these procedures. After all, why spend time training for a surgery that's likely to be made illegal?

12    At this point, 74 percent of obstetrics and gynecology residency programs do *not* train all residents in abortion procedures, according to reproductive health researchers at the National Abortion Federation. Those that do usually teach only the first trimester abortion procedures such as dilation and curettage—D&C, the 15-minute uterine scraping. Fewer than 7 percent of obstetricians are trained to do D&Es, the procedure used on fetuses from about 13 to 19 weeks. Almost all the doctors doing them are over 50 years old.

13    "Finding a doctor who will do a D&E is getting very tough," says Ron Fitzsimmons, executive director of the National Coalition of Abortion Providers.

14    My doctor turned around and faced me. She told me that because dilation and evacuation is rarely offered in my community, I could opt instead to chemically induce labor over several days and then deliver the little body at my local maternity ward.

"It's up to you," she said.                                                                    15

I'd been through labor and delivery three times before, with great joy as    16
well as pain, and the notion of going through that profound experience only to
deliver a dead fetus (whose skin was already starting to slough off, whose skull
might be collapsing) was horrifying.

I also did some research, spoke with friends who were obstetricians and    17
gynecologists, and quickly learned this: Study after study shows D&Es are *safer*
than labor and delivery. Women who had D&Es were far less likely to have
bleeding requiring transfusion, infection requiring intravenous antibiotics,
organ injuries requiring additional surgery or cervical laceration requiring
repair and hospital readmission. A review of 300 second-trimester abortions
published in 2002 in the *American Journal of Obstetrics & Gynecology* found that
29 percent of women who went through labor and delivery had complications,
compared with just 4 percent of those who had D&Es.

The American Medical Association said D&Es, compared to labor and    18
delivery, "may minimize trauma to the woman's uterus, cervix and other vital
organs."

There was this fact, too: The intact D&E surgery makes less use of "grasping    19
instruments," which could damage the body of the fetus. If the body were intact,
doctors might be able to more easily figure out why my baby died in the womb.

I'm a healthy person. I run, swim and bike. I'm 37 years old and optimistic.    20
Good things happen to me. I didn't want to rule out having more kids, but I did
want to know what went wrong before I tried again.

We told our doctor we had chosen a dilation and evacuation.                     21

"I can't do these myself," said my doctor. "I trained at a Catholic hospital."    22

My doctor recommended a specialist in a neighboring county, but when I    23
called for an appointment, they said they couldn't see me for almost a week.

I could feel my baby's dead body inside of mine. This baby had thrilled me    24
with kicks and flutters, those first soft tickles of life bringing a smile to my face and
my hand to my rounding belly. Now this baby floated, limp and heavy, from one
side to the other, as I rolled in my bed. And within a day, I started to bleed. My
body, with or without a doctor's help, was starting to expel the fetus. Technically,
I was threatening a spontaneous abortion, the least safe of the available options.

I did what any pregnant patient would do. I called my doctor. And she    25
advised me to wait.

I lay in my bed, not sleeping day or night, trying not to lose this little baby's    26
body that my own womb was working to expel. Wait, I told myself. Just hold
on. Let a doctor take this out. I was scared. Was it going to fall out of my body
when I rose, in the middle of the night, to check on my toddler? Would it come
apart on its own and double me over, knock me to the floor, as I stood at the
stove scrambling eggs for my boys?

On my fourth morning, with the bleeding and cramping increasing,    27
I couldn't wait any more. I called my doctor and was told that since I wasn't
hemorrhaging, I should not come in. Her partner, on call, pedantically explained
that women can safely lose a lot of blood, even during a routine period.

28   I began calling labor and delivery units at the top five medical centers in my area. I told them I had been 19 weeks along. The baby is dead. I'm bleeding, I said. I'm scheduled for a D&E in a few days. If I come in right now, what could you do for me, I asked.

29   Don't come in, they told me again and again. "Go to your emergency room if you are hemorrhaging to avoid bleeding to death. No one here can do a D&E today, and unless you're really in active labor you're safer to wait."

30   More than 66,000 women each year in the U.S. undergo an abortion at some point between 13 and 20 weeks, according to the Centers for Disease Control and Prevention. The CDC doesn't specify the physical circumstances of the women or their fetuses. Other CDC data shows that 4,000 women miscarry in their second trimester. Again, the data doesn't clarify whether those 4,000 women have to go through surgery.

31   Here's what is clear: Most of those women face increasingly limited access to care. One survey showed that half of the women who got abortions after 15 weeks of gestation said they were delayed because of problems in affording, finding or getting to abortion services. No surprise there; abortion is not readily available in 86 percent of the counties in the U.S.

32   Although there are some new, early diagnostic tests available, the most common prenatal screening for neural tube defects or Down syndrome is done around the 16th week of pregnancy. When problems are found—some times life-threatening problems—pregnant women face the same limited options that I did.

33   At last I found one university teaching hospital that, at least over the telephone, was willing to take me.

34   "We do have one doctor who can do a D&E," they said. "Come in to our emergency room if you want."

35   But when I arrived at the university's emergency room, the source of the tension was clear. After examining me and confirming I was bleeding but not hemorrhaging, the attending obstetrician, obviously pregnant herself, defensively explained that only one of their dozens of obstetricians and gynecologists still does D&Es, and he was simply not available. Not today. Not tomorrow. Not the next day. No, I couldn't have his name. She walked away from me and called my doctor.

36   "You can't just dump these patients on us," she shouted into the phone, her high-pitched voice floating through the heavy curtains surrounding my bed. "You should be dealing with this yourself."

37   Shivering on the narrow, white exam table, I wondered what I had done wrong. Then I pulled back on my loose maternity pants and stumbled into the sunny parking lot, blinking back tears in the dazzling spring day, trying to understand the directions they sent me out with: Find a hotel within a few blocks from a hospital. Rest, monitor the bleeding. Don't go home—the 45-minute drive might be too far.

The next few days were a blur of lumpy motel beds, telephone calls to doc- 38 tors, cramps. The pre-examination for my D&E finally arrived. First, the hospital required me to sign a legal form consenting to terminate the pregnancy. Then they explained I could, at no cost, have the remains incinerated by the hospital pathology department as medical waste, or for a fee have them taken to a funeral home for burial or cremation.

They inserted sticks of seaweed into my cervix and told me to go home for 39 the night. A few hours later—when the contractions were regular, strong and frequent—I knew we needed to get to the hospital.

"The patient appeared to be in active labor," say my charts, "and I explained 40 this to the patient and offered her pain medication for vaginal delivery."

According to the charts, I was "adamant" in demanding a D&E. I remem- 41 ber that I definitely wanted the surgical procedure that was the safest option. One hour later, just as an anesthesiologist was slipping me into unconsciousness, I had the D&E and a little body, my little boy, slipped out. Around his neck, three times and very tight, was the umbilical cord, source of his life, cause of his death.

This past spring, as the wild flowers started blooming around the simple 42 cross we built for this baby, the Justice Department began trying to enforce the Bush administration's ban and federal courts in three different cities heard arguments regarding the new law. Doctors explained that D&Es are the safest procedure in many cases, and that the law is particularly cruel to mothers like me whose babies were already dead. In hopes of bolstering their case, prosecutors sent federal subpoenas to various medical centers, asking for records of D&Es. There's an attorney somewhere, someday, who may poke through the files of my loss.

I didn't watch the trial because I had another appointment to keep–another 43 ultrasound. Lying on the crisp white paper, watching the monitor, I saw new life, the incredible spine, tiny fingers waving slowly across my uterus, a perfect thigh. Best of all, there it was, a strong, four-chamber heart, beating steady and solid. A soft quiver, baby rolling, rippled across my belly.

"Everything looks wonderful," said my doctor. "This baby is doing great." 44

## COMPREHENSION

1. Explain the nature and extent of Mendoza's "sorrow and pain" (paragraph 8).
2. What is "D&E"? What is Mendoza's understanding of the procedure, and how does she react to it?
3. What elements of government policy does Mendoza discuss, and why?

## RHETORIC

1. Mendoza's title might contain more than one level of meaning. Would you agree or disagree? Explain.

2. Why does Mendoza begin with personal narrative and then switch to exposition? How does she sustain this back-and-forth movement between narration and exposition?
3. Do you think that Mendoza develops an argument in this essay or attempts
   to persuade readers to adopt a certain position regarding abortion? Or is
   she merely investigating, as a journalist, a procedure that she and many
   other women experience? Elaborate on your response.
4. Mendoza's essay appeared in a feminist magazine. Why would the article
   and the position that Mendoza stakes out appeal to *Ms.* readers?
5. What elements of investigative reporting do you find in this essay?
6. What is your response to the conclusion? What is Mendoza's purpose in
   using an emotional appeal at this end point in the essay?

## WRITING

1. Investigate "partial birth abortion," and write an essay analyzing the process.
2. Write a personal essay recounting an illness or painful medical procedure
   that you or someone close to you experienced.
3. **Writing an Argument:** Argue for or against the proposition that abortion
   should be strictly a matter "between a woman and her doctor."

| www.mhhe.com/ **mhreader** | For more information on Martha Mendoza, go to: **More Resources > Ch. 12 Health & Medicine** |

# The Terrifying Normalcy of AIDS

### Stephen Jay Gould

*Stephen Jay Gould (1941–2002), an acclaimed contemporary science writer, taught bi-*
*ology, geology, and the history of science at Harvard University, where he was Alexander*
*Agassiz Professor of Zoology. Born in New York City, he was educated at Antioch College*
*(BA, 1963) and Columbia University (PhD, 1967). He wrote a monthly column, "This*
*View of Life," for* Natural History *magazine and was the author of* Ever Since Darwin
*(1977),* Ontogeny and Phylogeny *(1977),* The Panda's Thumb *(1980),* Wonderful
Life *(1989),* Bully for Brontosaurus *(1991),* The Structure of Evolutionary Theory
*(2002), and other books. In this 1987 essay, Gould explains in clear, precise language why*
*AIDS is a "natural phenomenon" and warns against viewing it in moral terms.*

Disney's Epcot Center in Orlando, Fla., is a technological tour de force and a  1
conceptual desert. In this permanent World's Fair, American industrial giants
have built their versions of an unblemished future. These masterful entertain-
ments convey but one message, brilliantly packaged and relentlessly expressed:
progress through technology is the solution to all human problems. G.E.
proclaims from Horizons: "If we can dream it, we can do it." A.T.&T. speaks
from on high within its giant golf ball: We are now "unbounded by space and
time." United Technologies bubbles from the depths of Living Seas: "With the
help of modern technology, we feel there's really no limit to what can be
accomplished."

Yet several of these exhibits at the Experimental Prototype Community of  2
Tomorrow, all predating last year's space disaster, belie their stated message
from within by using the launch of the shuttle as a visual metaphor for technological triumph. The *Challenger* disaster may represent a general malaise, but it
remains an incident. The AIDS pandemic, an issue that may rank with nuclear
weaponry as the greatest danger of our era, provides a more striking proof that
mind and technology are not omnipotent and that we have not canceled our
bond to nature.

In 1984, John Platt, a biophysicist who taught at the University of Chicago  3
for many years, wrote a short paper for private circulation. At a time when
most of us were either ignoring AIDS, or viewing it as a contained and peculiar
affliction of homosexual men, Platt recognized that the limited data on the origin of AIDS and its spread in America suggested a more frightening prospect:
we are all susceptible to AIDS, and the disease has been spreading in a simple
exponential manner.

Exponential growth is a geometric increase. Remember the old kiddy prob-  4
lem: if you place a penny on square one of a checkerboard and double the number of coins on each subsequent square—2, 4, 8, 16, 32 ...—how big is the stack
by the sixty-fourth square? The answer: about as high as the universe is wide.
Nothing in the external environment inhibits this increase, thus giving to exponential processes their relentless character. In the real, noninfinite world, of
course, some limit will eventually arise, and the process slows down, reaches a
steady state, or destroys the entire system: the stack of pennies falls over, the
bacterial cells exhaust their supply of nutrients.

Platt noticed that data for the initial spread of AIDS fell right on an expo-  5
nential curve. He then followed the simplest possible procedure of extrapolat-
ing the curve unabated into the 1990's. Most of us were incredulous, accusing
Platt of the mathematical gamesmanship that scientists call "curve fitting." After all, aren't exponential models unrealistic? Surely we are not all susceptible
to AIDS. Is it not spread only by odd practices to odd people? Will it not, therefore, quickly run its short course within a confined group?

Well, hello 1987—worldwide data still match Platt's extrapolated curve. This  6
will not, of course, go on forever. AIDS has probably already saturated the
African areas where it probably originated, and where the sex ratio of afflicted

people is 1-to-1, male-female. But AIDS still has far to spread, and may be moving exponentially, through the rest of the world. We have learned enough about the cause of AIDS to slow its spread, if we can make rapid and fundamental changes in our handling of that most powerful part of human biology—our own sexuality. But medicine, as yet, has nothing to offer as a cure and precious little even for palliation.

7     This exponential spread of AIDS not only illuminates its, and our, biology, but also underscores the tragedy of our moralistic misperception. Exponential processes have a definite time and place of origin, an initial point of "inoculation"—in this case, Africa. We didn't notice the spread at first. In a population of billions, we pay little attention when one increases to two, or eight to sixteen, but when one million becomes two million, we panic, even though the *rate* of doubling has not increased.

8     The infection has to start somewhere, and its initial locus may be little more than an accident of circumstance. For a while, it remains confined to those in close contact with the primary source, but only by accident of proximity, not by intrinsic susceptibility. Eventually, given the power and lability of human sexuality, it spreads outside the initial group and into the general population. And now AIDS has begun its march through our own heterosexual community.

9     What a tragedy that our moral stupidity caused us to lose precious time, the greatest enemy in fighting an exponential spread, by down-playing the danger because we thought that AIDS was a disease of three irregular groups of minorities: minorities of life style (needle users), of sexual preference (homosexuals) and of color (Haitians). If AIDS had first been imported from Africa into a Park Avenue apartment, we would not have dithered as the exponential march began.

10    The message of Orlando—the inevitability of technological solutions—is wrong, and we need to understand why.

11    Our species has not won its independence from nature, and we cannot do all that we can dream. Or at least we cannot do it at the rate required to avoid tragedy, for we are not unbounded from time. Viral diseases are preventable in principle, and I suspect that an AIDS vaccine will one day be produced. But how will this discovery avail us if it takes until the millennium, and by then AIDS has fully run its exponential course and saturated our population, killing a substantial percentage of the human race? A fight against an exponential enemy is primarily a race against time.

12    We must also grasp the perspective of ecology and evolutionary biology and recognize, once we reinsert ourselves properly into nature, that AIDS represents the ordinary workings of biology, not an irrational or diabolical plague with a moral meaning. Disease, including epidemic spread, is a natural phenomenon, part of human history from the beginning. An entire subdiscipline of my profession, paleopathology, studies the evidence of ancient diseases preserved in the fossil remains of organisms. Human history has been marked by episodic plagues. More native peoples died of imported disease than ever fell before the gun during the era of colonial expansion. Our memories are short, and we have had a respite,

really, only since the influenza pandemic at the end of World War I, but AIDS must be viewed as a virulent expression of an ordinary natural phenomenon.

I do not say this to foster either comfort or complacency. The evolutionary 13 perspective is correct, but utterly inappropriate for our human scale. Yes, AIDS is a natural phenomenon, one of a recurring class of pandemic diseases. Yes, AIDS may run through the entire population, and may carry off a quarter or more of us. Yes, it may make no *biological* difference to Homo sapiens in the long run: there will still be plenty of us left and we can start again. Evolution cares as little for its agents—organisms struggling for reproductive success—as physics cares for individual atoms of hydrogen in the sun. But we care. These atoms are our neighbors, our lovers, our children and ourselves. AIDS is both a natural phenomenon and, potentially, the greatest natural tragedy in human history.

The cardboard message of Epcot fosters the wrong attitudes: we must both rein- 14 sert ourselves into nature and view AIDS as a natural phenomenon in order to fight properly. If we stand above nature and if technology is all-powerful, then AIDS is a horrifying anomaly that must be trying to tell us something. If so, we can adopt one of two attitudes, each potentially fatal. We can either become compla- cent, because we believe the message of Epcot and assume that medicine will soon generate a cure, or we can panic in confusion and seek a scapegoat for something so irregular that it must have been visited upon us to teach us a moral lesson.

But AIDS is not irregular. It is part of nature. So are we. This should 15 galvanize us and give us hope, not prompt the worst of all responses: a kind of "new-age" negativism that equates natural with what we must accept and cannot, or even should not, change. When we view AIDS as natural, and when we recognize both the exponential property of its spread and the accidental character of its point of entry into America, we can break through our destruc- tive tendencies to blame others and to free ourselves of concern.

If AIDS is natural, then there is no message in its spread. But by all that 16 science has learned and all that rationality proclaims, AIDS works by a *mechanism*—and we can discover it. Victory is not ordained by any principle of progress, or any slogan of technology, so we shall have to fight like hell, and be watchful. There is no message, but there is a mechanism.

## COMPREHENSION

1. What does Gould mean when he defines AIDS as a "natural phenomenon" (paragraph 12)? How does the title support this definition?
2. What does Gould mean by "our moral stupidity" in paragraph 9?
3. What connection does Gould make between our reaction to the AIDS crisis and our alienation from nature?

## RHETORIC

1. What is Gould's main idea? Where in the essay is it stated?

2. What is the purpose of paragraphs 1 and 2? How do they contribute to Gould's argument? How do they help establish the tone of the essay? What is the tone? What is the importance of Epcot Center to Gould's thesis?

3. Gould uses scientific terminology in his essay. Define the words *exponential* (paragraph 3) and *pandemic* and *phenomenon* (paragraph 13). Is this essay intended for a specialized audience? Justify your response.

4. Trace the progression of ideas in paragraphs 2–5. What transitions does Gould employ?

5. Does Gould use rhetorical strategies besides argument in his essay? Cite evidence of this varied rhetorical approach.

6. Explain the final sentence in Gould's conclusion. What is its relation to the paragraph as a whole?

## WRITING

1. Gould states that we must "reinsert ourselves into nature" (paragraph 14). What does he mean by this? How would this affect the way in which we deal with disease and death in our society? Explore this issue in a brief essay.

2. Write an extended definition of HIV/AIDS, attempting to avoid moralizing about the subject. Conduct research if necessary.

3. **Writing an Argument:** Write an essay in which you expand on Gould's belief that our moral stupidity has not only hindered society's recognition of the AIDS threat but continues to impede AIDS research and treatment.

 **www.mhhe.com/ mhreader**  For more information on Stephen Jay Gould, go to: **More Resources > Ch. 12 Health & Medicine**

# The Man Who Couldn't Stop Eating

### Atul Gawande

*Atul Gawande (b. 1965) was born in Brooklyn, the son of two physicians. After taking dual degrees at Stanford University (BA, BS, 1987), Gawande attended Balliol College, Oxford (MA, 1989) before enrolling in Harvard Medical School. He uses his experiences as a medical resident in his critically acclaimed collection of essays on medical science in* America, Complications: A Surgeon's Notes on an Imperfect Science *(2002). Gawande also is active in the public arena, serving first as an advisor to President Bill Clinton and then, beginning in 1993, as a senior advisor for the U.S. Department of*

*Health and Human Services. Gawande is a staff writer for* The New Yorker, *where this essay on obesity and obesity surgery first appeared, in the July 9, 2001 issue.*

At 7:30 A.M. on September 13, 1999, an anesthesiologist and two orderlies rolled    1
our patient, whom I will call Vincent Caselli, into the operating room, where his attending surgeon and I awaited him. Caselli was a short man of middle age—five feet seven, fifty-four years old. The son of Italian immigrants, he had worked as a heavy-machine operator and road-construction contractor. (He and his men had paved a rotary in my own neighborhood.) He had been married for thirty-five years; he and his wife had three girls, all grown now. And he weighed four hundred and twenty-eight pounds. Housebound, his health failing, he no longer had anything resembling a normal life. And so, although he was afraid of surgery, he had come for a Roux-en-Y gastric-bypass operation. It is the most drastic treatment we have for obesity. It is also among the strangest operations surgeons perform. It removes no disease, repairs no defect or injury. It is an operation that is intended to control a person's will—to manipulate his innards so that he does not overeat—and it is soaring in popularity. Some forty-five thousand patients underwent obesity surgery in 1999, and the number is expected to double by 2003.

For the very obese, general anesthesia alone is a dangerous undertaking;    2
major abdominal surgery can easily become a disaster. Obesity substantially increases the risk of respiratory failure, heart attacks, wound infections, hernias—almost every complication possible, including death. Nevertheless, Dr. Sheldon Randall, the attending surgeon, was relaxed, having done more than a thousand of these operations. I, the assisting resident, remained anxious. Watching Caselli struggle to shift himself from the stretcher onto the operating table and then stop halfway to catch his breath, I was afraid that he would fall in between. Once he was on the table, his haunches rolled off the sides, and I double-checked the padding that protected him from the table's sharp edges. He was naked except for his "universal"-size johnny, which covered him like a napkin, and a nurse put a blanket over his lower body for the sake of modesty. When we tried to lay him down, he lost his breath and started to turn blue, and the anesthesiologist had to put him to sleep sitting up. Only with the breathing tube and a mechanical ventilator in place were we able to lay him flat.

He was a mountain on the table. I am six feet two, but even with the table    3
as low as it goes I had to stand on a step stool; Dr. Randall stood on two stools stacked together. He nodded to me, and I cut down the middle of our patient's belly, through skin and then dense inches of glistening yellow fat, and we opened the abdomen. Inside, his liver was streaked with fat, too, and his bowel was covered by a thick apron of it, but his stomach looked ordinary—a smooth, grayish-pink bag the size of two fists. We put metal retractors in place to hold the wound open and keep the liver and the slithering loops of bowel out of the way. Working elbow deep, we stapled his stomach down to the size of an ounce. Before the operation, it could accommodate a quart of

food and drink; now it would hold no more than a shot glass. We then sewed the opening of this little pouch to a portion of bowel two feet past his duodenum—past the initial portion of the small bowel, where bile and pancreatic juices break food down. This was the bypass part of the operation, and it meant that what food the stomach could accommodate would be less readily absorbed.

4      The operation took us a little over two hours. Caselli was stable throughout, but his recovery was difficult. Patients are usually ready to go home three days after surgery; it was two days before Caselli even knew where he was. His kidneys failed for twenty-four hours, and fluid built up in his lungs. He became delirious, seeing things on the walls, pulling off his oxygen mask, his chest leads for the monitors, even yanking out the I.V. We were worried, and his wife and daughters were terrified, but gradually he pulled through.

5      By the third day after surgery, he was well enough to take sips of clear liquids (water, apple juice, ginger ale), up to one ounce every four hours. On my afternoon rounds, I asked him how he'd done. "O.K.," he said. We began giving him four-ounce servings of Carnation Instant Breakfast for protein and modest calories. He could finish only half, and that took him an hour. It filled him up and, when it did, he felt a sharp, unpleasant pain. This was to be expected, Dr. Randall told him. It would be a few days before he was ready for solid food. But he was doing well. He no longer needed I.V. fluids. And, after he'd had a short stay in a rehabilitation facility, we sent him home.

6      A couple of weeks later, I asked Dr. Randall how Caselli was getting on. "Just fine," the surgeon said. Although I had done a few of these cases with him, I had not seen how the patients progressed afterward. Would he really lose all that weight? I asked. And how much could he eat? Randall suggested that I see Caselli for myself. So one day that October, I gave him a call, and he invited me to stop by.

7      Vincent Caselli and his wife live in an unassuming saltbox house not far outside Boston. To get there, I took Route 1, past four Dunkin' Donuts, four pizzerias, three steak houses, two McDonald's, two Ground Rounds, a Taco Bell, a Friendly's, and an International House of Pancakes. (A familiar roadside vista, but that day it seemed a sad tour of our self-destructiveness.) I rang the doorbell, and a long minute passed. I heard a slow footfall coming toward the door, and Caselli, visibly winded, opened it. But he smiled broadly when he saw me and gave my hand a warm squeeze. He led me—his hand on table, wall, doorjamb for support—to a seat at a breakfast table in his flowered-wallpaper kitchen.

8      I asked him how things were going. "Real good," he said. He had no more pain from the operation, the incision had healed, and, though it had been only three weeks, he'd already lost forty pounds. But, at three hundred and ninety, and still stretching his size-64 slacks and size-XXXXXXL T-shirts (the largest he could find at the local big-and-tall store), he did not yet feel different. Sitting, he had to keep his legs apart to let his abdomen sag between them, and the weight of his body on the wooden chair forced him to shift every minute or two because

his buttocks would fall asleep. Sweat rimmed the folds of his forehead and made his thin salt-and-pepper hair stick to his pate. His brown eyes were rheumy, above dark bags. He breathed with a disconcerting wheeze.

We talked about his arrival home from the hospital. The first solid food he had tried was a spoonful of scrambled eggs. Just that much, he said, made him so full it hurt, "like something was ripping," and he threw it up. He was afraid that nothing solid would ever go down. But he gradually found that he could tolerate small amounts of soft foods—mashed potatoes, macaroni, even chicken if it was finely chopped and moist. Breads and dry meats, he found, got "stuck," and he'd have to put a finger down his throat and make himself vomit.

Caselli's battle with obesity, he explained, began in his late twenties. "I always had some weight on me," he said—he was two hundred pounds at nineteen, when he married Teresa (as I'll call her), and a decade later he reached three hundred. He would diet and lose seventy-five pounds, then put a hundred back on. By 1985, he weighed four hundred pounds. On one diet, he got down to a hundred and ninety, but he gained it all back. "I must have gained and lost a thousand pounds," he told me. He developed high blood pressure, high cholesterol, and diabetes. His knees and his back ached all the time, and he had limited mobility. He used to get season tickets to Boston Bruins games, and go out regularly to the track at Seekonk every summer to see the auto racing. Years ago, he drove in races himself. Now he could barely walk to his pickup truck. He hadn't been on an airplane since 1983, and it had been two years since he had been to the second floor of his own house, because he couldn't negotiate the stairs. "Teresa bought a computer a year ago for her office upstairs, and I've never seen it," he told me. He had to move out of their bedroom, upstairs, to a small room off the kitchen. Unable to lie down, he had slept in a recliner ever since. Even so, he could doze only in snatches, because of sleep apnea, which is a common syndrome among the obese and is thought to be related to excessive fat in the tongue and in the soft tissues of the upper airway. Every thirty minutes, his breathing would stop, and he'd wake up asphyxiating. He was perpetually exhausted.

There were other troubles, too, the kind that few people speak about. Good hygiene, he said, was nearly impossible. He could no longer stand up to urinate, and after moving his bowels he often had to shower in order to get clean. Skin folds would become chafed and red, and sometimes develop boils and infections. And, he reported, "Sex life is nonexistent. I have real hopes for it." For him, though, the worst part was his diminishing ability to earn a livelihood.

Vincent Caselli's father had come to Boston from Italy in 1914 to work in construction, and he soon established his own firm. In 1979, Vincent went into business for himself. He was skilled at operating heavy equipment—his specialty was running a Gradall, a thirty-ton, three-hundred-thousand-dollar hydraulic excavator—and he employed a team of men year-round to build roads and sidewalks. Eventually, he owned his own Gradall, a ten-wheel Mack dump truck, a backhoe, and a fleet of pickup trucks. But in the past three years he had become too big to operate the Gradall or keep up with the daily maintenance of the equipment. He had to run the business from his house, and pay others to do the heavy work; he enlisted a nephew to help manage the men and the contracts. Expenses rose, and since he could no longer go around to city halls himself, he found contracts harder to get. If Teresa hadn't had a job—she is the business manager for an assisted-living facility in Boston—they would have gone bankrupt.

13      Teresa, a freckled redhead, had been pushing him for a long time to diet and exercise. He, too, wanted desperately to lose weight, but the task of controlling himself, day to day, meal to meal, seemed beyond him. "I'm a man of habits," he told me. "I'm very prone to habits." And eating, he said, was his worst habit. But, then, eating is everyone's habit. What was different about his habit? I asked. Well, the portions he took were too big, and he could never leave a crumb on his plate. If there was pasta left in the pot, he'd eat that, too. But why, I wanted to know. Was it that he just loved food? He pondered this question for a moment. It wasn't love, he decided. "Eating felt good instantaneously," he said, "but it only felt good instantaneously." Was it excessive hunger that drove him? "I was never hungry," he said.

14      As far as I could tell, Caselli ate for the same reasons that everyone eats: because food tasted good, because it was seven o'clock and time for dinner, because a nice meal had been set out on the table. And he stopped eating for the same reason everyone stops: because he was full and eating was no longer pleasurable. The main difference seemed to be that it took an unusual quantity of food to make him full. (He could eat a large pizza as if it were a canape.) To lose weight, he faced the same difficult task that every dieter faces—to stop eating before he felt full, while the food still tasted good, and to exercise. These were things that he could do for a little while, and, with some reminding and coaching, for perhaps a bit longer, but they were not, he had found, things that he could do for long. "I am not strong," he said.

15      In the spring of 1999, Caselli developed serious infections in both legs: as his weight increased, and varicosities appeared, the skin thinned and broke down, producing open, purulent ulcers. Despite fevers and searing pain, it was only after persistent coaxing from his wife that he finally agreed to see his doctor. The doctor diagnosed a serious case of cellulitis, and he spent a week in the hospital receiving intravenous antibiotics.

16      At the hospital, he was given an ultrasound scan to check whether blood clots had formed in the deep veins of his legs. A radiologist came to give him the results. Caselli recounted the conversation to me. "He says, 'You don't have blood clots, and I'm really surprised. A guy like you, in the situation you're in, the odds are you're gonna have blood clots. That tells me you're a pretty healthy guy'"—but only, he went on, if Caselli did something about his weight. A little later, the infectious-disease specialist came by to inspect his wounds. "I'm going to tell you something," Caselli recalls the man saying. "I've been reading your whole file—where you were, what you were, how you were. You take that weight off—and I'm not telling you this to bust your ass—you take that weight off and you're a very healthy guy. Your heart is good. Your lungs are good. You're strong."

"I took that seriously," Caselli said. "You know, there are two different doc-  17
tors telling me this. They don't know me other than what they're reading from
their records. They had no reason to tell me this. But they knew the weight was
a problem. And if I could get it down somewhere near reality. . . ."

When he got home, he remained sick in bed for another two weeks.  18
Meanwhile, his business collapsed. Contracts stopped coming in entirely, and
he knew that when his men finished the existing jobs he would have to let them
go. Months before, his internist had suggested that he consider surgery and he
had dismissed the notion. But he didn't now. He went to see Dr. Randall, who
spoke with him frankly about the risks involved. There was a one-in-two-
hundred chance of death and a one-in-ten chance of a significant complication,
such as bleeding, infection, gastric ulceration, blood clots, or leakage into the
abdomen. The doctor also told him that it would change how he ate forever.
Unable to work, humiliated, ill, and in pain, Vincent Caselli decided that
surgery was his only hope.

It is hard to contemplate the human appetite without wondering if we have  19
any say over our lives at all. We believe in will—in the notion that we have a
choice over such simple matters as whether to sit still or stand up, to talk or not
talk, to have a slice of pie or not. Yet very few people, whether heavy or slim,
can voluntarily reduce their weight for long. The history of weight-loss treatment is one of nearly unremitting failure. Whatever the regimen—liquid diets,
high-protein diets, or grapefruit diets, the Zone, Atkins, or Dean Ornish diet—
people lose weight quite readily, but they do not keep it off. A 1993 National
Institutes of Health expert panel reviewed decades of diet studies and found
that between ninety and ninety-five per cent of people regained one-third to
two-thirds of any weight lost within a year—and all of it within five years.
Doctors have wired patients' jaws closed, inflated plastic balloons inside their
stomachs, performed massive excisions of body fat, prescribed amphetamines
and large amounts of thyroid hormone, even performed neurosurgery to destroy the hunger centers in the brain's hypothalamus—and still people do not
keep the weight off. Jaw wiring, for example, can produce substantial weight
loss, and patients who ask for the procedure are highly motivated; yet some still
take in enough liquid calories through their closed jaws to gain weight, and the
others regain it once the wires are removed. We are a species that has evolved to
survive starvation, not to resist abundance.

Children are the surprising exception to this history of failure. Nobody  20
would argue that children have more self-control than adults; yet in four ran-
domized studies of obese children between the ages of six and twelve, those
who received simple behavioral teaching (weekly lessons for eight to twelve
weeks, followed by monthly meetings for up to a year) ended up markedly less
overweight ten years later than those who didn't; thirty percent were no longer
obese. Apparently, children's appetites are malleable. Those of adults are not.

There are at least two ways that humans can eat more than they ought to at  21
a sitting. One is by eating slowly but steadily for far too long. This is what people
with Prader-Willi syndrome do. Afflicted with a rare inherited dysfunction of

the hypothalamus, they are incapable of experiencing satiety. And though they eat only half as quickly as most people, they do not stop. Unless their access to food is strictly controlled (some will eat garbage or pet food if they find nothing else), they become mortally obese.

22      The more common pattern, however, relies on rapid intake. Human beings are subject to what scientists call a "fat paradox." When food enters your stomach and duodenum (the upper portion of the small intestine), it triggers stretch receptors, protein receptors, and fat receptors that signal the hypothalamus to induce satiety. Nothing stimulates the reaction more quickly than fat. Even a small amount, once it reaches the duodenum, will cause a person to stop eating. Still we eat too much fat. How can this be? It turns out that foods can trigger receptors in the mouth which get the hypothalamus to accelerate our intake—and, again, the most potent stimulant is fat. A little bit on the tongue, and the receptors push us to eat fast, before the gut signals shut us down. The tastier the food, the faster we eat—a phenomenon called "the appetizer effect." (This is accomplished, in case you were wondering, not by chewing faster but by chewing less. French researchers have discovered that, in order to eat more and eat it faster, people shorten their "chewing time"—they take fewer "chews per standard food unit" before swallowing. In other words, we gulp.)

23      Apparently, how heavy one becomes is determined, in part, by how the hypothalamus and the brain stem adjudicate the conflicting signals from the mouth and the gut. Some people feel full quite early in a meal; others, like Vincent Caselli, experience the appetizer effect for much longer. In the past several years, much has been discovered about the mechanisms of this control. We now know, for instance, that hormones, like leptin and neuropeptide Y, rise and fall with fat levels and adjust the appetite accordingly. But our knowledge of these mechanisms is still crude at best.

24      Consider a 1998 report concerning two men, "BR" and "RH," who suffered from profound amnesia. Like the protagonist in the movie "Memento," they could carry on a coherent conversation with you, but, once they had been distracted, they recalled nothing from as recently as a minute before, not even that they were talking to you. (BR had had a bout of viral encephalitis; RH had had a severe seizure disorder for twenty years.) Paul Rozin, a professor of psychology at the University of Pennsylvania, thought of using them in an experiment that would explore the relationship between memory and eating. On three consecutive days, he and his team brought each subject his typical lunch (BR got meat loaf, barley soup, tomatoes, potatoes, beans, bread, butter, peaches, and tea; RH got veal parmigiana with pasta, string beans, juice, and apple crumb cake). Each day, BR ate all his lunch, and RH could not quite finish. Their plates were then taken away. Ten to thirty minutes later, the researchers would reappear with the same meal. "Here's lunch," they would announce. The men ate just as much as before. Another ten to thirty minutes later, the researchers again appeared with the same meal. "Here's lunch," they would say, and again the men would eat. On a couple of occasions, the researchers even offered RH a

fourth lunch. Only then did he decline, saying that his "stomach was a little tight." Stomach stretch receptors weren't completely ineffectual. Yet, in the absence of a memory of having eaten, social context alone—someone walking in with lunch—was enough to re-create appetite.

You can imagine forces in the brain vying to make you feel hungry or full. 25 You have mouth receptors, smell receptors, visions of tiramisu pushing one way and gut receptors another. You have leptins and neuropeptides saying you have either too much fat stored or too little. And you have your own social and personal sense of whether eating more is a good idea. If one mechanism is thrown out of whack, there's trouble.

Given the complexity of appetite and our imperfect understanding of it, we 26 shouldn't be surprised that appetite-altering drugs have had only meagre success in making people eat less. (The drug combination of fenfluramine and phentermine, or "fen-phen," had the most success, but it was linked to heart-valve abnormalities and was withdrawn from the market.) University researchers and pharmaceutical companies are searching intensively for a drug that will effectively treat serious obesity. So far, no such drug exists. Nonetheless, one treatment has been found to be effective, and, oddly enough, it turns out to be an operation.

At my hospital, there is a recovery-room nurse who is forty-eight years old 27 and just over five feet tall, with boyish sandy hair and an almost athletic physique. Over coffee one day at the hospital cafe, not long after my visit with Vincent Caselli, she revealed that she once weighed more than two hundred and fifty pounds. Carla (as I'll call her) explained that she had had gastric-bypass surgery some fifteen years ago.

She had been obese since she was five years old. She started going on diets 28 and taking diet pills—laxatives, diuretics, amphetamines—in junior high school. "It was never a problem losing weight," she said. "It was a problem keeping it off." She remembers how upset she was when, on a trip with friends to Disneyland, she found that she couldn't fit through the entrance turnstile. At the age of thirty-three, she reached two hundred and sixty-five pounds. One day, accompanying her partner, a physician, to a New Orleans medical convention, she found that she was too short of breath to walk down Bourbon Street. For the first time, she said, "I became fearful for my life—not just the quality of it but the longevity of it."

This was 1985. Doctors were experimenting with radical obesity surgery, 29 but there was dwindling enthusiasm for it. Two operations had held considerable promise. One, known as jejuno-ileal bypass—in which nearly all the small intestine was bypassed, so that only a minimum amount of food could be absorbed—was killing people. The other, stomach stapling, was proving not to be very effective over time; people tended to adapt to the tiny stomach, eating densely caloric foods more and more frequently.

Working in the hospital, however, Carla heard encouraging reports about 30 the gastric-bypass operation—stomach stapling plus a rerouting of the intestine so that food bypassed only the duodenum. She knew that the data about its success was still sketchy, that other operations had failed, but in May of 1986, after a year of thinking about it, she had the surgery.

31     "For the first time in my life, I experienced fullness," she told me. Six months after the operation, she was down to a hundred and eighty-five pounds. Six months after that, she weighed a hundred and thirty pounds. She lost so much weight that she had to have surgery to remove the aprons of skin that hung from her belly and thighs down to her knees. She was unrecognizable to anyone who had known her before, and even to herself. "I went to bars to see if I could get picked up—and I did," she said. "I always said no," she quickly added, laughing. "But I did it anyway."

32     The changes weren't just physical, though. She said she felt a profound and unfamiliar sense of will power. She no longer had to eat anything: "Whenever I eat, somewhere in the course of that time I end up asking myself, 'Is this good for you? Are you going to put on weight if you eat too much of this?' And I can just stop." She knew, intellectually, that the surgery was why she no longer ate as much as she used to. Yet she felt as if she were choosing not to do it.

33     Studies report this to be a typical experience of a successful gastric-bypass patient. "I do get hungry, but I tend to think about it more," another woman who had had the operation told me, and she described an internal dialogue very much like Carla's: "I ask myself, 'Do I really need this?' I watch myself." For many, this feeling of control extends beyond eating. They become more confident, even assertive—sometimes to the point of conflict. Divorce rates, for example, have been found to increase significantly after the surgery. Indeed, a few months after her operation, Carla and her partner broke up.

34     Carla's dramatic weight loss has proved to be no aberration. Published case series now show that most patients undergoing gastric bypass lose at least two-thirds of their excess weight (generally more than a hundred pounds) within a year. They keep it off, too: ten-year follow-up studies find an average regain of only ten to twenty pounds. And the health benefits are striking: patients are less likely to have heart failure, asthma, or arthritis; eighty per cent of those with diabetes are completely cured of it.

35     I stopped in to see Vincent Caselli one morning in January of 2000, about four months after his operation. He didn't quite spring to the door, but he wasn't winded this time. The bags under his eyes had shrunk. His face was more defined. Although his midriff was vast, it seemed smaller, less of a sack.

36     He told me that he weighed three hundred and forty-eight pounds—still far too much for a man who was only five feet seven inches tall, but ninety pounds less than he weighed on the operating table. And it had already made a difference in his life. Back in October, he told me, he missed his youngest daughter's wedding because he couldn't manage the walking required to get to the church. But by December he had lost enough weight to resume going to his East Dedham garage every morning. "Yesterday, I unloaded three tires off the truck," he said. "For me to do that three months ago? There's no way." He had climbed the stairs of his house for the first time since 1997. "One day around Christmastime, I say to myself, 'Let me try this. I gotta try this.' I went very

slow, one foot at a time." The second floor was nearly unrecognizable to him. The bathroom had been renovated since he last saw it, and Teresa had, naturally, taken over the bedroom, including the closets. He would move back up eventually, he said, though it might be a while. He still had to sleep sitting up in a recliner, but he was sleeping in four-hour stretches now—"Thank God," he said. His diabetes was gone. And although he was still unable to stand up longer than twenty minutes, his leg ulcers were gone, too. He lifted his pants legs to show me. I noticed that he was wearing regular Red Wing work boots—in the past, he had to cut slits along the sides of his shoes in order to fit into them.

"I've got to lose at least another hundred pounds," he said. He wanted to   37 be able to work, pick up his grandchildren, buy clothes off the rack at Filenes, go places without having to ask himself, "Are there stairs? Will I fit in the seats? Will I run out of breath?" He was still eating like a bird. The previous day, he'd had nothing all morning, a morsel of chicken with some cooked carrots and a small roast potato for lunch, and for dinner one fried shrimp, one teriyaki chicken strip, and two forkfuls of chicken-and-vegetable lo mein from a Chinese restaurant. He was starting up the business again, and, he told me, he'd gone out for a business lunch one day recently. It was at a new restaurant in Hyde Park—"beautiful"—and he couldn't help ordering a giant burger and a plate of fries. Just two bites into the burger, though, he had to stop. "One of the fellas says to me, 'Is that all you're going to eat?' And I say, 'I can't eat any more.' 'Really?' I say, 'Yeah, I can't eat any more. That's the truth.'"

I noticed, however, that the way he spoke about eating was not the way   38 Carla had spoken. He did not speak of stopping because he wanted to. He spoke of stopping because he had to. You want to eat more, he explained, but "you start to get that feeling in your insides that one more bite is going to push you over the top." Still, he often took that bite. Overcome by waves of nausea, pain, and bloating—the so-called dumping syndrome—he'd have to vomit. If there were a way to eat more, he would. This scared him, he admitted. "It's not right," he said.

Three months later, in April, Caselli invited me and my son to stop by his   39 garage in East Dedham. My son was four years old and, as Vince remembered my once saying, fascinated with all things mechanical. The garage was huge, cavernous, with a two-story roll-up door and metal walls painted yellow. There, in the shadows, was Vince's beloved Gradall, a handsome tank of a machine, as wide as a county road, painted yield-sign yellow, with shiny black tires that came up to my chest and his company name emblazoned in curlicue script along its flanks. On the chassis, six feet off the ground, was a glass-enclosed control cab and a thirty-foot telescoping boom, mounted on a three-hundred-and-sixty-degree swivel. Vince and a friend of his, a fellow heavy-equipment contractor I'll call Danny, were sitting on metal folding chairs in a sliver of sunlight, puffing fat Honduran cigars, silently enjoying the day. They both rose to greet us. Vince introduced me as "one of the doctors who did my stomach operation."

I let my son go off to explore the equipment and asked Vince how his busi-   40 ness was going. Not well, he said. Except for a few jobs in late winter plowing snow for the city in his pickup truck, he had brought in no income since the previous August. He'd had to sell two of his three pickup trucks, his Mack dump truck, and most of the small equipment for road building. Danny came to his defense. "Well, he's been out of action," he said. "And you see we're just coming into the summer season. It's a seasonal business." But we all knew that wasn't the issue.

41      Vince told me that he weighed about three hundred and twenty pounds. This was about thirty pounds less than when I had last seen him, and he was proud of that. "He don't eat," Danny said. "He eats half of what I eat." But Vince was still unable to climb up into the Gradall and operate it. And he was beginning to wonder whether that would ever change. The rate of weight loss was slowing down, and he noticed that he was able to eat more. Before, he could eat only a couple of bites of a burger, but now he could sometimes eat half of one. And he still found himself eating more than he could handle. "Last week, Danny and this other fellow, we had to do some business," he said. "We had Chinese food. Lots of days, I don't eat the right stuff—I try to do what I can do, but I ate a little bit too much. I had to bring Danny back to Boston College, and before I left the parking lot there I just couldn't take it anymore. I had to vomit.

42      "I'm finding that I'm getting back into that pattern where I've always got to eat," he went on. His gut still stopped him, but he was worried. What if one day it didn't? He had heard about people whose staples gave way, returning their stomach to its original size, or who managed to put the weight back on in some other way.

43      I tried to reassure him. I told him what I knew Dr. Randall had already told him during a recent appointment: that a small increase in the capacity of his stomach pouch was to be expected, and that what he was experiencing seemed normal. But could something worse happen? I didn't want to say.

44      Among the gastric-bypass patients I had talked with was a man whose story remains a warning and a mystery to me. He was forty-two years old, married, and had two daughters, both of whom were single mothers with babies and still lived at home, and he had been the senior computer-systems manager for a large local company. At the age of thirty-eight, he had had to retire and go on disability because his weight—which had been above three hundred pounds since high school—had increased to more than four hundred and fifty pounds and was causing unmanageable back pain. He was soon confined to his home. He could not walk half a block. He could stand for only brief periods. He went out, on average, once a week, usually for medical appointments. In December, 1998, he had a gastric bypass. By June of the following year, he had lost a hundred pounds.

45      Then, as he put it, "I started eating again." Pizzas. Boxes of sugar cookies. Packages of doughnuts. He found it hard to say how, exactly. His stomach was still tiny and admitted only a small amount of food at a time, and he experienced the severe nausea and pain that gastric-bypass patients get whenever they eat sweet or rich things. Yet his drive was stronger than ever. "I'd eat right

through pain—even to the point of throwing up," he told me." If I threw up, it was just room for more. I would eat straight through the day." He did not pass a waking hour without eating something. "I'd just shut the bedroom door. The kids would be screaming. The babes would be crying. My wife would be at work. And I would be eating." His weight returned to four hundred and fifty pounds, and then more. The surgery had failed. And his life had been shrunk to the needs of pure appetite.

He is among the five to twenty per cent of patients—the published reports 46 conflict on the exact number—who regain weight despite gastric-bypass surgery. (When we spoke, he had recently submitted to another, more radical gastric bypass, in the desperate hope that something would work.) In these failures, one begins to grasp the power that one is up against. An operation that makes overeating both extremely difficult and extremely unpleasant—which, for more than eighty per cent of patients, is finally sufficient to cause appetite to surrender and be transformed—can sometimes be defeated after all. Studies have yet to uncover a single consistent risk factor for this outcome. It could, apparently, happen to anyone.

It was a long time before I saw Vince Caselli again. Earlier this year, I called 47 him to ask about getting together, and he suggested that we go out to see a Boston Bruins game. A few days later, he picked me up at the hospital in his rumbling Dodge Ram. For the first time, he looked almost small in the outsized truck. He was down to about two hundred and fifty pounds. "I'm still no Gregory Peck," he said, but he was now one of the crowd—chubby, in an ordinary way. The rolls beneath his chin were gone. His face had a shape. His middle no longer rested between his legs. And, almost a year and a half after the surgery, he was still losing weight. At the FleetCenter, where the Bruins play, he walked up the escalator without getting winded. Our tickets were taken at the gate— the Bruins were playing the Pittsburgh Penguins—and we walked through the turnstiles. Suddenly, he stopped and said, "Look at that. I went right through, no problem. I never would have made it through there before." It was the first time he'd gone to an event like this in years.

We took our seats about two dozen rows up from the ice, and he laughed a 48 little about how easily he fit. The seats were as tight as coach class, but he was quite comfortable. (I, with my long legs, was the one who had trouble finding room.) Vince was right at home here. He had been a hockey fan his whole life, and could supply me with all the details: the Penguins' goalie Garth Snow was a local boy from Wrentham and a friend of one of Vince's cousins; Joe Thornton and Jason Allison were the Bruins' best forwards, but neither could hold a candle to the Penguins' Mario Lemieux. There were nearly twenty thousand people at the game, but within ten minutes Vince had found a friend from his barbershop sitting just a few rows away.

The Bruins won, and we left cheered and buzzing. Afterward, we went out 49 to dinner at a grill near the hospital. Vince told me that his business was finally up and running. He could operate the Gradall without difficulty, and he'd had full-time Gradall work for the past three months. He was even thinking of buying a new model. At home, he had moved back upstairs. He and Teresa had taken a vacation in the Adirondacks; they were going out evenings, and visiting their grandchildren.

50      I asked him what had changed since I saw him the previous spring. He could not say precisely, but he gave me an example. "I used to love Italian cookies, and I still do," he said. A year ago, he would have eaten to the point of nausea. "But now they're, I don't know, they're too sweet. I eat one now, and after one or two bites I just don't want it." It was the same with pasta, which had always been a problem for him. "Now I can have a bite and I'm satisfied."

51      Partly, it appeared that his taste in food had changed. He pointed to the nachos and buffalo wings and hamburgers on the menu, and said that, to his surprise, he no longer felt like eating any of them. "It seems like I lean toward protein and vegetables nowadays," he said, and he ordered a chicken Caesar salad. But he also no longer felt the need to stuff himself. "I used to be real reluctant to push food away," he told me. "Now it's just—it's different." But when did this happen? And how? He shook his head. "I wish I could pinpoint it for you," he said. He paused to consider. "As a human, you adjust to conditions. You don't think you are. But you are."

52      These days, it isn't the failure of obesity surgery that is prompting concerns but its success. Physicians have gone from scorning it to encouraging, sometimes imploring, their most severely overweight patients to undergo a gastric-bypass operation. That's not a small group. More than five million adult Americans meet the strict definition of morbid obesity. (Their "body mass index"—that is, their weight in kilograms divided by the square of their height in metres—is forty or more, which for an average man is roughly a hundred pounds or more overweight.) Ten million more weigh just under the mark but may nevertheless have obesity-related health problems that are serious enough to warrant the surgery. There are ten times as many candidates for obesity surgery right now as there are for heart-bypass surgery in a year. So many patients are seeking the procedure that established surgeons cannot keep up. The American Society of Bariatric Surgery has only five hundred members nationwide who perform gastric-bypass operations, and their waiting lists are typically months long. Hence the too familiar troubles associated with new and lucrative surgical techniques (the fee can be as much as twenty thousand dollars): newcomers are stampeding to the field, including many who have proper training but have not yet mastered the procedure, and others who have no training at all. Complicating matters further, individual surgeons are promoting a slew of variations on the standard operation which haven't been fully researched—the "duodenal switch," the "long limb" bypass, the laparoscopic bypass. And a few surgeons are pursuing new populations, such as adolescents and people who are only moderately obese.

53      Perhaps what's most unsettling about the soaring popularity of gastric-bypass surgery, however, is simply the world that surrounds it. Ours is a culture in which fatness is seen as tantamount to failure, and get-thin-quick

promises—whatever the risks—can have an irresistible allure. Doctors may recommend the operation out of concern for their patients' health, but the stigma of obesity is clearly what drives many patients to the operating room. "How can you let yourself look like that?" is society's sneering, unspoken question, and often its spoken one as well. Women suffer even more than men from the social sanction, and it's no accident that seven times as many women as men have had the operation. (Women are only an eighth more likely to be obese.)

Indeed, deciding not to undergo the surgery, if you qualify, is at risk of 54 being considered the unreasonable thing to do. A three-hundred-and-fifty-pound woman who did not want the operation told me of doctors browbeating her for her choice. And I have learned of at least one patient with heart disease being refused treatment by a doctor unless she had a gastric bypass. If you don't have the surgery, you will die, some doctors tell their patients. But we actually do not know this. Despite the striking improvements in weight and health, studies have not yet proved a corresponding reduction in mortality.

There are legitimate grounds for being wary of the procedure. As Paul Ern- 55 sberger, an obesity researcher at Case Western Reserve University, pointed out to me, many patients undergoing gastric bypass are in their twenties and thirties. "But is this really going to be effective and worthwhile over a forty-year span?" he asked. "No one can say." He was concerned about the possible long-term effects of nutritional deficiencies (for which patients are instructed to take a daily multivitamin). And he was concerned about evidence from rats that raises the possibility of an increased risk of bowel cancer.

We want progress in medicine to be clear and unequivocal, but of course it 56 rarely is. Every new treatment has gaping unknowns—for both patients and society—and it can be hard to decide what to do about them. Perhaps a simpler, less radical operation will prove effective for obesity. Perhaps the long-sought satiety pill will be found. Nevertheless, the gastric bypass is the one thing we have now that works. Not all the questions have been answered, but there are more than a decade of studies behind it. And so we forge ahead. Hospitals everywhere are constructing obesity-surgery centers, ordering reinforced operating tables, training surgeons and staff. At the same time, everyone expects that, one day, something new and better will be discovered that will make what we're now doing obsolete.

Across from me, in our booth at the grill, Vince Caselli pushed his chicken 57 Caesar salad aside only half eaten. "No taste for it," he said, and he told me he was grateful for that. The operation, he said, had given him his life back. But, after one more round of drinks, it was clear that he still felt uneasy.

"I had a serious problem and I had to take serious measures," he said. "I think 58 I had the best technology that is available at this point. But I do get concerned: Is this going to last my whole life? Someday, am I going to be right back to square one—or worse?" He fell silent for a moment, gazing into his glass. "Well, that's the cards that God gave me. I can't worry about stuff I can't control."

The most drastic treatment for morbid obesity may be the only one that 59 works.

## COMPREHENSION

1. How does Gawande account for the "soaring popularity of gastric-bypass surgery" (paragraph 53)? What are the ethical implications of this procedure for surgeons?
2. Gawande describes the patient he calls Vincent Caselli "a mountain on the table" (paragraph 3). Why is he a perfect candidate for gastric-bypass surgery? According to Gawande, what are the predictable outcomes, both positive and negative, of such surgery?
3. Summarize Gawande's analysis of Americans' eating habits, preoccupation with weight and weight loss, and obsession with medical procedures that will improve their body image.

## RHETORIC

1. What is Gawande's thesis, and how does he adjust the tone of this essay—his attitude toward the subject of gastric-bypass surgery—to complement the thesis?
2. Where does the writer indicate that he is a medical authority on the subject under discussion? How might this authoritative persona affect a reader's response?
3. Explain Gawande's use of process analysis in this article.
4. What types of evidence does Gawande provide to support his main points?
5. How does the story that Gawande tells about Vincent Caselli serve as a framework for the essay? If there were no narrative involving Caselli, would the essay be better or worse, in your opinion?
6. Trace the chain of causality that Gawande explores in this essay—a chain linking American culture, people's eating habits, and the medical profession.

## WRITING

1. Write an essay of causal analysis in which you explain why so many people in the United States overeat—and endure the consequences.
2. Physicians constantly confront ethical issues in their treatment of patients. Write an essay classifying three or more of these medical dilemmas, and suggest how you think doctors should respond to them.
3. **Writing an Argument:** Argue for or against the proposition that obesity should not be cured by surgical procedures but rather by self-control.

www.mhhe.com/
**mhreader**

For more information on Atul Gawande, go to:
**More Resources > Ch. 12 Health & Medicine**

# Sarcophagus

### Richard Selzer

*Richard Selzer (b. 1928) is a professional surgeon who started writing for several hours each night after he had already established a successful medical career. He was born in Troy, New York, and received degrees from Union College (BS, 1948) and Albany Medical College (MD, 1953). His first book of essays,* Mortal Essays: Notes on the Art of Surgery *(1974), established him as a prominent essayist specializing in the world of medicine and surgery. Selzer employs his elegant prose style in describing the often tragic, unpleasant, and painful world of medical patients. He is a contributor to popular magazines, and his essays have been collected in several books, among them* Confessions of a Knife *(1979),* Letters to a Young Doctor *(1982),* Taking the World in for Repairs *(1997), and* The Exact Location of the Soul *(2001). He has also contributed to a number of anthologies and written a book of stories,* Imagine a Woman *(1997). The following essay demonstrates Selzer's experience and expertise as a surgeon as well as his unique ability to describe the world of medicine in poetic and graceful terms.*

We are six who labor here in the night. No . . . seven! For the man horizontal   1
upon the table strives as well. But we do not acknowledge his struggle. It is our
own that preoccupies us.

I am the surgeon.                                                                 2

David is the anesthesiologist. You will see how kind, how soft he is. Each   3
patient is, for him, a preparation respectfully controlled. Blood pressure, pulse,
heartbeat, flow of urine, loss of blood, temperature, whatever is measurable,
David measures. And he is a titrator, adding a little gas, drug, oxygen, fluid,
blood in order to maintain the dynamic equilibrium that is the only state
compatible with life. He is in the very center of the battle, yet he is one step
removed; he has not known the patient before this time, nor will he deal with
the next of kin. But for him, the occasion is no less momentous.

Heriberto Paz is an assistant resident in surgery. He is deft, tiny, mercurial.   4
I have known him for three years. One day he will be the best surgeon in
Mexico.

Evelyn, the scrub nurse, is a young Irish woman. For seven years we have   5
worked together. Shortly after her immigration, she led her young husband
into my office to show me a lump on his neck. One year ago he died of Hodgkin's disease. For the last two years of his life, he was paralyzed from the waist
down. Evelyn has one child, a boy named Liam.

Brenda is a black woman of forty-five. She is the circulating nurse, who will   6
conduct the affairs of this room, serving our table, adjusting the lights, counting
the sponges, ministering to us from the unsterile world.

7   Roy is a medical student who is beginning his surgical clerkship. He has been assigned to me for the next six weeks. This is his first day, his first operation.

8   David is inducing anesthesia. In cases where the stomach is not empty through fasting, the tube is passed into the windpipe while the patient is awake. Such an "awake" intubation is called crashing. It is done to avoid vomiting and the aspiration of stomach contents into the lungs while the muscles that control coughing are paralyzed.

9   We stand around the table. To receive a tube in the windpipe while fully awake is a terrifying thing.

10   "Open your mouth wide," David says to the man. The man's mouth opens slowly to its fullest, as though to shriek. But instead, he yawns. We smile down at him behind our masks.

11   "OK. Open again. Real wide."

12   David sprays the throat of the man with a local anesthetic. He does this three times. Then, into the man's mouth. David inserts a metal tongue depressor which bears a light at the tip. It is called a laryngoscope. It is to light up the throat, reveal the glottic chink through which the tube must be shoved. All this while, the man holds his mouth agape, submitting to the hard pressure of the laryngoscope. But suddenly, he cannot submit. The man on the table gags, struggles to free himself, to spit out the instrument. In his frenzy his lip is pinched by the metal blade.

13   There is little blood.

14   "Suction," says David.

15   Secretions at the back of the throat obscure the view. David suctions them away with a plastic catheter.

16   "Open," commands David. More gagging. Another pass with the scope. Another thrust with the tube. Violent coughing informs us that the tube is in the right place. It has entered the windpipe. Quickly the balloon is inflated to snug it against the wall of the trachea. A bolus of Pentothal is injected into a vein in the man's arm. It takes fifteen seconds for the drug to travel from his arm to his heart, then on to his brain. I count them. In fifteen seconds, the coughing stops, the man's body relaxes. He is asleep.

17   "All set?" I ask David.

18   "Go ahead," he nods.

19   A long incision. You do not know how much room you will need. This part of the operation is swift, tidy. Fat . . . muscle . . . fascia . . . the peritoneum is snapped open and a giant shining eggplant presents itself. It is the stomach, black from the blood it contains and that threatens to burst it. We must open that stomach, evacuate its contents, explore.

20   Silk sutures are placed in the wall of the stomach as guidelines between which the incision will be made. They are like the pitons of a mountaineer. I cut again. No sooner is the cavity of the stomach achieved, than a columnar geyser of blood stands from the small opening I have made. Quickly, I slice open the whole front of the stomach. We scoop out handfuls of clot, great black gelatinous

masses that shimmy from the drapes to rest against our own bellies as though, having been evicted from one body, they must find another in which to dwell. Now and then we step back to let them slither to the floor. They are under our feet. We slip in them. "Jesus," I say. "He is bleeding all over North America." Now my hand is inside the stomach, feeling, pressing. There! A tumor spreads across the back wall of this stomach. A great hard crateous plain, the dreaded linitis plastica (leather bottle) that is not content with seizing one area, but infiltrates between the layers until the entire organ is stiff with cancer. It is that, of course, which is bleeding. I stuff wads of gauze against the tumor. I press my fist against the mass of cloth. The blood slows. I press harder. The bleeding stops.

A quick glance at Roy. His gown and gloves, even his mask, are sprinkled 21 with blood. Now is he dipped; and I, his baptist.

David has opened a second line into the man's veins. He is pumping blood 22 into both tubings.

"Where do we stand?" I ask him.                                                                                23

"Still behind. Three units." He checks the blood pressure.                                      24

"Low, but coming up," he says.                                                                            25

"Shall I wait 'til you catch up?"                                                                            26

"No. Go ahead. I'll keep pumping."                                                                       27

I try to remove my fist from the stomach, but as soon as I do, there is a fresh 28 river of blood.

"More light," I say. "I need more light."                                                                29

Brenda stands on a platform behind me. She adjusts the lamps.                            30

"More light," I say, like a man going blind.                                                           31

"That's it," she says. "There is no more light."                                                      32

"We'll go around from the outside," I say. Heriberto nods agreement. "Free 33 up the greater curvature first, then the lesser, lift the stomach up and get some control from behind."

I must work with one hand. The other continues as the compressor. It is the 34 tiredest hand of my life. One hand, then, inside the stomach, while the other creeps behind. Between them … a ridge of tumor. The left hand fumbles, gropes toward its mate. They swim together. I lift the stomach forward to find that *nothing* separates my hands from each other. The wall of the stomach has been eaten through by the tumor. One finger enters a large tubular structure. It is the aorta. The incision in the stomach has released the tamponade of blood and brought us to this rocky place.

"Curved aortic clamp."                                                                                          35

A blind grab with the clamp, high up at the diaphragm. The bleeding slack- 36 ens, dwindles. I release the pressure warily. A moment later there is a great bang of blood. The clamp has bitten through the cancerous aorta.

"Zero silk on a big Mayo needle."                                                                        37

I throw the heavy sutures, one after the other, into the pool of blood, hoping to 38 snag with my needle some bit of tissue to close over the rent in the aorta, to hold back the blood. There is no tissue. Each time, the needle pulls through the crumble of tumor. I stop. I repack the stomach. Now there is a buttress of packing both outside and inside the stomach. The bleeding is controlled. We wait. Slowly, something is gathering here, organizing. What had been vague and shapeless before is now declaring itself. All at once, I know what it is. There is nothing to do.

39    For what tool shall I ask? With what device fight off this bleeding? A knife? There is nothing here to cut. Clamps? Where place the jaws of a hemostat? A scissors? Forceps? Nothing. The instrument does not exist that knows such deep red jugglery. Not all my clever picks, my rasp . . . A miner's lamp, I think, to cast a brave glow.

40  David has been pumping blood steadily.

41    "He is stable at the moment," he says. "'Where do we go from here?'"

42    "No place. He's going to die. The minute I take away my pressure, he'll bleed to death."

43    I try to think of possibilities, alternatives. I cannot; there are none. Minutes pass. We listen to the cardiac monitor, the gassy piston of the anesthesia machine.

44    "More light!" I say. "Fix the light."

45    The light seems dim, aquarial, a dilute beam slanting through a green sea. At such a fathom the fingers are clumsy. There is pressure. It is cold.

46    "Dave," I say, "stop the transfusion." I hear my voice coming as from a great distance. "Stop it," I say again.

47    David and I look at each other, standing among the drenched rags, the smeared equipment.

48    "I can't," he says.

49    "Then I will," I say, and with my free hand I reach across the boundary that separates the sterile field from the outside world, and I close the clamp on the intravenous tubing. It is the act of an outlaw, someone who does not know right from wrong. But I know. I know that this is right to do.

50    "The oxygen." I say. "Turn it off."

51    "You want it turned off, you do it," he says.

52    "Hold this," I say to Heriberto, and I give over the packing to him. I step back from the table, and go to the gas tanks.

53    "This one?" I have to ask him.

54    "Yes," David nods.

55    I turn it off. We stand there, waiting, listening to the beeping of the electro-cardiograph. It remains even, regular, relentless. Minutes go by, and the sound continues. The man will not die. At last, the intervals on the screen grow longer, the shape of the curve changes, the rhythm grows wild, furious. The line droops, flattens. The man is dead.

56    It is silent in the room. Now we are no longer a team, each with his circumscribed duties to perform. It is Evelyn who speaks first.

57    "It is a blessing," she says. I think of her husband's endless dying.

58    "No," says Brenda. "Better for the family if they have a few days . . . to get used to the idea of it."

59    "But, look at all the pain he's been spared."

60    "Still, for the ones that are left, it's better to have a little time."

I listen to the two women murmuring, debating without rancor, speaking in  61
hushed tones of the newly dead as women have done for thousands of years.

"May I have the name of the operation?" It is Brenda, picking up her duties.  62
She is ready with pen and paper.

"Exploratory laparotomy. Attempt to suture malignant aorto-gastric  63
fistula."

"Is he pronounced?"                                                          64

"What time is it?"                                                           65

"Eleven-twenty."                                                             66

"Shall I put that down?"                                                     67

"Yes."                                                                       68

"Sew him up," I say to Heriberto. "I'll talk to the family."                69

To Roy I say, "You come with me."                                           70

Roy's face is speckled with blood. He seems to me a child with the measles.  71
What, in God's name, is he doing here?

From the doorway, I hear the voices of the others, resuming.                72

"Stitch," says Heriberto.                                                    73

Roy and I go to change our bloody scrub suits. We put on long white coats. In  74
the elevator, we do not speak. For the duration of the ride to the floor where the
family is waiting, I am reasonable. I understand that in its cellular wisdom, the
body of this man had sought out the murderous function of my scalpel, and
stretched itself upon the table to receive the final stabbing. For this little time, I
know that it is not a murder committed but a mercy bestowed. Tonight's knife
is no assassin, but the kind scythe of time.

We enter the solarium. The family rises in unison. There are so many! How  75
ruthless the eyes of the next of kin.

"I am terribly sorry . . . ," I begin. Their faces tighten, take guard. "There  76
was nothing we could do."

I tell them of the lesion, tell of how it began somewhere at the back of the  77
stomach; how, long ago, no one knows why, a cell lost the rhythm of the body,
fell out of step, sprang, furious, into rebellion. I tell of how the cell divided and
begat two of its kind, which begat four more and so on, until there was a whole
race of lunatic cells, which is called cancer.

I tell of how the cancer spread until it had replaced the whole back of the  78
stomach, invading, chewing until it had broken into the main artery of the body.
Then it was, I tell them, that the great artery poured its blood into the stomach.
I tell of how I could not stop the bleeding, how my clamps bit through the
crumbling tissue, how my stitches would not hold, how there was nothing to be
done. All of this I tell.

A woman speaks. She has not heard my words, only caught the tone of my  79
voice.

"Do you mean he is dead?"                                                    80

Should I say "passed away" instead of "died"? No. I cannot.                 81

"Yes," I tell her, "he is dead."                                            82

83      Her question and my answer unleash their anguish. Roy and I stand among the welter of bodies that tangle, grapple, rock, split apart to form new couplings. Their keening is exuberant, wild. It is more than I can stand. All at once, a young man slams his fist into the wall with great force.

84      "Son of a bitch!" he cries.

85      "Stop that!" I tell him sharply. Then, more softly, "Please try to control yourself."

86      The other men crowd about him, patting, puffing, grunting. They are all fat, with huge underslung bellies. Like their father's. A young woman in a nun's habit hugs each of the women in turn.

87      "Shit!" says one of the men.

88      The nun hears, turns away her face. Later, I see the man apologizing to her.

89      The women, too, are fat. One of them has a great pile of yellowish hair that has been sprayed and rendered motionless. All at once, she begins to whine. A single note, coming louder and louder. I ask a nurse to bring tranquilizer pills. She does, and I hand them out, one to each, as though they were the wafers of communion. They urge the pills upon each other.

90      "Go on, Theresa, take it. Make her take one."

91      Roy and I are busy with cups of water. Gradually it grows quiet. One of the men speaks.

92      "What's the next step?"

93      "Do you have an undertaker in mind?"

94      They look at each other, shrug. Someone mentions a name. The rest nod.

95      "Give the undertaker a call. Let him know. He'll take care of everything."

96      I turn to leave.

97      "Just a minute," one of the men calls. "Thanks, Doc. You did what you could."

98      "Yes," I say.

99  Once again in the operating room. Blood is everywhere. There is a wild smell, as though a fox had come and gone. The others, clotted about the table, work on. They are silent, ravaged.

100      "How did the family take it?"

101      "They were good, good."

102      Heriberto has finished reefing up the abdomen. The drapes are peeled back. The man on the table seems more than just dead. He seems to have gone beyond that, into a state where expression is possible—reproach and scorn. I study him. His baldness had advanced beyond the halfway mark. The remaining strands of hair had been gallantly dyed. They are, even now, neatly combed and crenellated. A stripe of black moustache rides his upper lip. Once, he had been spruce!

103      We all help lift the man from the table to the stretcher.

104      "On three," says David. "One . . . two . . . three."

105      And we heft him over, using the sheet as a sling. My hand brushes his shoulder. It is cool. I shudder as though he were infested with lice. He has become something that I do not want to touch.

More questions from the women. 106

"Is a priest coming?" 107

"Does the family want to view him?" 108

"Yes. No. Don't bother me with these things." 109

"Come on," I say to Roy. We go to the locker room and sit together on a 110
bench. We light cigarettes.

"Well?" I ask him. 111

"When you were scooping out the clots, I thought I was going to swoon." 112

I pause over the word. It is too quaint, too genteel for this time. I feel, at that 113
moment, a great affection for him.

"But you fought it." 114

"Yes. I forced it back down. But, almost . . . " 115

"Good," I say. Who knows what I mean by it? I want him to know that I 116
count it for something.

"And you?" he asks me. The students are not shy these days. 117

"It was terrible, his refusal to die." 118

I want him to say that it was right to call it quits, that I did the best I could. 119
But he says nothing. We take off our scrub suits and go to the shower. There are
two stalls opposite each other. They are curtained. But we do not draw the
curtains. We need to see each other's healthy bodies. I watch Roy turn his face
directly upward into the blinding fall of water. His mouth is open to receive it.
As though it were milk flowing from the breasts of God. For me, too, this water
is like a well in a wilderness.

In the locker room, we dress in silence. 120

"Well, goodnight." 121

Awkwardly our words come out in unison. 122

"In the morning . . . " 123

"Yes, yes, later." 124

"Goodnight." 125

I watch him leave through the elevator door. 126

For the third time I go to that operating room. The others have long since 127
finished and left. It is empty, dark. I turn on the great lamps above the table that
stands in the center of the room. The pediments of the table and the floor have
been scrubbed clean. There is no sign of the struggle. I close my eyes and see
again the great pale body of the man, like a white bullock, bled. The line of
stitches on his abdomen is a hieroglyph. Already, the events of this night are
hidden from me by these strange untranslatable markings.

## COMPREHENSION

1. What has the author implied by choosing his title for the essay? How is the
   title reinforced by the final paragraph?
2. Based upon Selzer's description of his work as a surgeon, to what other
   profession does he draw analogies? Explain.

3. Why do the other members of the operating team refuse to tamper with the medical apparatus, even after being ordered to do so by the surgeon?

## RHETORIC

1. What is the dramatic effect of telling the story in the present tense?
2. Selzer often eschews conventional sentence structure. For example in paragraph 16, he employs fragments: "Another pass with the scope. Another thrust with the tube." In paragraph 21, he uses odd syntax, "Now is he dipped; and I, his baptist." And some sentences are extremely short, such as paragraph 96: "I turn to leave." What is the cumulative effect of using such innovative sentence structure?
3. Why has the author divided his essay into six parts? What is the function of each part? How does he create drama via the juxtaposition of one section to the next?
4. Dialogue is used frequently in the essay. What is the function and effect of the dialogue?
5. Selzer's imagery is often vivid and original. How do the following excerpts contribute to the tone of the essay: "I understand that in its cellular wisdom, the body of this man had sought out the murderous function of my scalpel . . . . Tonight's knife is no assassin, but the kind scythe of time" (paragraph 74), and "There is a wild smell, as though a fox had come and gone" (paragraph 99).
6. There are several references to religion in the essay. Locate them, and explain what their cumulative effect is on the tone of the essay.
7. Mystery plays a significant part in the author's mood; for example, the final sentence reads, "Already, the events of this night are hidden from me by these strange untranslatable markings." What other passages reflect this mood of mystery in the essay? How does this mood affect the description of the essay's events, which are supposedly based on science?

## WRITING

1. We take for granted many things that are mysterious to us—for example, the acts of reading, writing, and breathing. Write a descriptive essay in which you reflect upon some basic activity that you have never analyzed before.
2. Write a critique of Selzer's essay, titling it "Religious Imagery in Selzer's 'Sarcophagus.'"
3. **Writing an Argument:** Explain why it is dangerous to treat physicians as supermen or superwomen, and why it is especially damaging to think that surgeons are gods or goddesses.

**www.mhhe.com/**
**mhreader**

For more information on Richard Selzer, go to:
**More Resources > Ch. 12 Health & Medicine**

# The Globalization of Eating Disorders

## Susan Bordo

**Susan Bordo** *(b. 1947) was born in Newark, New Jersey, and was educated at Carleton University (BA, 1972) and the State University of New York at Stony Brook (PhD, 1982). She is the Singletary Chair in the Humanities and a professor of English and women's studies at the University of Kentucky. A feminist philosopher and interdisciplinary scholar who focuses on Western culture's attitudes toward gender and the body, Bordo has written* The Flight to Objectivity: Essays on Cartesianism and Culture *(1987),* Unbearable Weight: Feminism, Western Culture, and the Body *(1993),* Twilight Zones: The Hidden Life of Cultural Images from Plato to O.J. *(1997), and* The Male Body: A New Look at Men in Public and in Private *(1999). In this selection, Bordo offers an overview of a new kind of epidemic, fueled by Western media images, that is affecting cultures around the world.*

The young girl stands in front of the mirror. Never fat to begin with, she's been on   1
a no-fat diet for a couple of weeks and has reached her goal weight: 115 lb., at
5'4—exactly what she should weigh, according to her doctor's chart. But in her
eyes she still looks dumpy. She can't shake her mind free of the "Lady Marmelade" video from Moulin Rouge. Christina Aguilera, Pink, L'il Kim, and Mya, each
one perfect in her own way: every curve smooth and sleek, lean-sexy, nothing to
spare. Self-hatred and shame start to burn in the girl, and envy tears at her stomach, enough to make her sick. She'll never look like them, no matter how much
weight she loses. Look at that stomach of hers, see how it sticks out? Those
thighs—they actually jiggle. Her butt is monstrous. She's fat, gross, a dough girl.

As you read the imaginary scenario above, whom did you picture standing in   2
front of the mirror? If your images of girls with eating and body image problems
have been shaped by *People* magazine and Lifetime movies, she's probably white,
North American, and economically secure. A child whose parents have never had
to worry about putting food on the family table. A girl with money to spare for
fashion magazines and trendy clothing, probably college-bound. If you're familiar
with the classic psychological literature on eating disorders, you may also have

read that she's an extreme "perfectionist" with a hyper-demanding mother, and that she suffers from "body-image distortion syndrome" and other severe perceptual and cognitive problems that "normal" girls don't share. You probably don't picture her as Black, Asian, or Latina.

3    Read the description again, but this time imagine twenty-something Tenisha Williamson standing in front of the mirror. Tenisha is black, suffers from anorexia, and feels like a traitor to her race. "From an African-American standpoint," she writes, "we as a people are encouraged to embrace our big, voluptuous bodies. This makes me feel terrible because I don't want a big, voluptuous body! I don't ever want to be fat—ever, and I don't ever want to gain weight. I would rather die from starvation than gain a single pound."[1] Tenisha is no longer an anomaly. Eating and body image problems are now not only crossing racial and class lines, but gender lines. They have also become a global phenomenon.

4    Fiji is a striking example. Because of their remote location, the Fiji islands did not have access to television until 1995, when a single station was introduced. It broadcasts programs from the United States, Great Britain, and Australia. Until that time, Fiji had no reported cases of eating disorders, and a study conducted by anthropologist Anne Becker showed that most Fijian girls and women, no matter how large, were comfortable with their bodies. In 1998, just three years after the station began broadcasting, 11 percent of girls reported vomiting to control weight, and 62 percent of the girls surveyed reported dieting during the previous months.[2]

5    Becker was surprised by the change; she had thought that Fijian cultural traditions, which celebrate eating and favor voluptuous bodies, would "withstand" the influence of media images. Becker hadn't yet understood that we live in an empire of images, and that there are no protective borders.

6    In Central Africa, for example, traditional cultures still celebrate voluptuous women. In some regions, brides are sent to fattening farms, to be plumped and massaged into shape for their wedding night. In a country plagued by AIDS, the skinny body has meant—as it used to among Italian Jewish, and Black Americans—poverty, sickness, death. "An African girl must have hips," says dress designer Frank Osodi, "We have hips. We have bums. We like flesh in Africa." For years, Nigeria sent its local version of beautiful to the Miss World Competition. The contestants did very poorly. Then a savvy entrepreneur went against local ideals and entered Agbani Darego, a light-skinned, hyper-skinny beauty. (He got his inspiration from M-Net, the South African network seen across Africa on satellite television, which broadcasts mostly American movies and television shows.) Agbani Darego won the Miss World Pageant, the first Black African to do so. Now, Nigerian teenagers fast and exercise, trying to become "lepa"—a popular slang phrase for the thin "it" girls that are all the rage. Said one: "People have realized that slim is beautiful."[3]

[1]From the Colours of Ana website (http://coloursofana.com//ss8.asp).
[2]Reported in Nancy Snyderman, *The Girl in the Mirror* (New York: Hyperion, 2002), p. 84.
[3]Norimistsu Onishi, "Globalization of Beauty Makes Slimness Trendy," *The New York Times*, Oct. 3, 2002.

How can mere images be so powerful? For one thing, they are never "just
pictures," as the fashion magazines continually maintain (disingenuously) in
their own defense. They speak to young people not just about how to be beautiful but also about how to become what the dominant culture admires, values,
rewards. They tell them how to be cool, "get it together," overcome their shame.
To girls who have been abused they may offer a fantasy of control and invul-
nerability, immunity from pain and hurt. For racial and ethnic groups whose
bodies have been deemed "foreign," earthy, and primitive, and considered
unattractive by Anglo-Saxon norms, they may cast the lure of being accepted as
"normal" by the dominant culture.

In today's world, it is through images—much more than parents, teachers,
or clergy—that we are taught how to be. And it is images, too, that teach us
how to see, that educate our vision in what's a defect and what is normal, that
give us the models against which our own bodies and the bodies of others are
measured. Perceptual pedagogy: "How To Interpret Your Body 101." It's
become a global requirement.

I was intrigued, for example, when my articles on eating disorders began to
be translated, over the past few years, into Japanese and Chinese. Among the
members of audiences at my talks, Asian women had been among the most insistent that eating and body image weren't problems for their people, and indeed, my initial research showed that eating disorders were virtually unknown
in Asia. But when, this year, a Korean translation of *Unbearable Weight* was published, I felt I needed to revisit the situation. I discovered multiple reports on
dramatic increases in eating disorders in China, South Korea, and Japan. "As
many Asian countries become Westernized and infused with the Western aesthetic of a tall, thin, lean body, a virtual tsunami of eating disorders has
swamped Asian countries," writes Eunice Park in *Asian Week* magazine. Older
people can still remember when it was very different. In China, for example,
where revolutionary ideals once condemned any focus on appearance and there
have been several disastrous famines, "little fatty" was a term of endearment
for children. Now, with fast food on every corner, childhood obesity is on the
rise, and the cultural meaning of fat and thin has changed. "When I was young,"
says Li Xiaojing, who manages a fitness center in Beijing, "people admired and
were even jealous of fat people since they thought they had a better life. . . . But
now, most of us see a fat person and think 'He looks awful.'"[4]

Clearly, body insecurity can be exported, imported, and marketed—just
like any other profitable commodity. In this respect, what's happened with
men and boys is illustrative. Ten years ago men tended, if anything, to see
themselves as better looking than they (perhaps) actually were. And then (as
I chronicle in detail in my book *The Male Body*) the menswear manufacturers,
the diet industries, and the plastic surgeons "discovered" the male body. And
now, young guys are looking in their mirrors, finding themselves soft and ill

---

[4]Reported in Elizabeth Rosenthal, "Beijing Journal: China's Chic Waistline: Convex to Concave,"
*The New York Times,* Dec. 9, 1999.

defined, no matter how muscular they are. Now they are developing the eating and body image disorders that we once thought only girls had. Now they are abusing steroids, measuring their own muscularity against the oiled and perfected images of professional athletes, body-builders, and *Men's Health* models. Now the industries in body-enhancement—cosmetic surgeons, manufacturers of anti-aging creams, spas and salons—are making huge bucks off men, too.

11      What is to be done? I have no easy answers. But I do know that we need to acknowledge, finally and decisively, that we are dealing here with a cultural problem. If eating disorders were biochemical, as some claim, how can we account for their gradual "spread" across race, gender, and nationality? And with mass media culture increasingly providing the dominant "public education" in our children's lives—and those of children around the globe—how can we blame families? Families matter, of course, and so do racial and ethnic traditions. But families exist in cultural time and space—and so do racial groups. In the empire of images, no one lives in a bubble of self-generated "dysfunction" or permanent immunity. The sooner we recognize that—and start paying attention to the culture around us and what it is teaching our children—the sooner we can begin developing some strategies for change.

## COMPREHENSION

1. How does Bordo define the "body-image distortion syndrome" (paragraph 2)?
2. Why have body image and weight problems become a global phenomenon? What is the main cause of this phenomenon?
3. How, according to the author, should we deal with the globalization of eating disorders?

## RHETORIC

1. How does the author establish herself as an authority on her subject? Do you think that she succeeds? Why or why not?
2. What is the writer's claim? Where does she place it, and why?
3. Bordo begins with an imaginary situation. Does this strategy enhance or detract from the validity of her argument? Justify your response.
4. The writer uses several rhetorical strategies to advance her argument. Identify places where she employs description, illustration, comparison and contrast, and causal analysis.
5. The writer has been praised for her readable or accessible style. Do you think that this essay is well written and thought provoking? Explain.
6. How does Bordo develop this selection as a problem-solution essay? Where does the solution appear, and how effective is its placement within the essay?

# WRITING

1. Write a causal essay analyzing young Americans' fascination with body image and the consequences of this preoccupation.
2. Why are women in the United States and around the world more susceptible to eating disorders than men? Answer this question in an analytical essay.
3. **Writing an Argument:** Write an essay titled "Body Images, Eating Disorders, and Cultural Imperialism." In this essay, argue for or against the proposition that American media are exporting potentially unhealthy images of the human body.

| | |
|---|---|
| www.mhhe.com/ **mhreader** | For more information on Susan Bordo, go to: **More Resources > Ch. 12 Health & Medicine** |

# Synthesis: Connections for Critical Thinking

1. Research the current status of public health in the United States and what is being done to prevent major outbreaks of disease. Refer to at least three essays in this chapter to support your findings and thesis.
2. Compare approaches to women's health issues as discussed by several writers in this chapter, notably Goodman, Mendoza, and Bordo.
3. Compare and contrast the strategies that Glasser, Goodman, and Bordo use to develop their arguments.
4. Referring to any three essays in this chapter, analyze some of the major moral, ethical, and religious issues raised by current medical research.
5. Compare and contrast the treatment of death in the essays by Tuchman, Glasser, and Selzer.
6. Compare and contrast the essays by Gawande and Bordo.
7. Research the subject of AIDS, and connect your findings to the essays by Tuchman, Glasser, and Gould.
8. Working with three other class members, develop a PowerPoint presentation informing your college about a health issue of campus concern.
9. **Network:** Compare and contrast two Web sites devoted to some aspect of medicine and health—for example, stem-cell research, abortion, funeral practices, cosmetic surgery, or dieting.
10. **Network:** Explore the World Health Organization Web site (www.who .int/en), and summarize what you find about global pandemics.

chapter *13*

# Nature and the Environment

*How Do We Relate to the Natural World?*

We are at a point in the history of civilization where consciousness of our fragile relationship with nature and the environment is high. Even as you spend an hour reading a few of the essays in this chapter, it is estimated that we are losing 3,000 acres of rain forest around the world and four species of plants or animals. From pollution, to the population explosion, to the depletion of the ozone layer, we seem to be confronted with ecological catastrophe. Nevertheless, as Rachel Carson reminds us, we have "an obligation to endure," to survive potential natural catastrophes by understanding and managing our relationship with the natural world.

Ecology, or the study of nature and the environment, as many of the essayists in this chapter attest, involves us in the conservation of the earth. It moves us to suppress our rapacious destruction of the planet. Clearly, the biological stability of the planet is increasingly precarious. More plants, insects, birds, and animals became extinct in the 20th century than in any era since the Cretaceous catastrophe more than 65 million years ago that led to the extinction of the dinosaurs. Within this ecological context, writers like Carson become our literary conscience, reminding us of how easily natural processes can break down unless we insist on a degree of ecological economy.

Of course, any modification of human behavior in an effort to conserve nature is a complex matter. To save the spotted owl in the Pacific Northwest, we must sacrifice the jobs of people in the timber industry. To reduce pollution, we must forsake gas and oil for alternate energy sources that are costly to develop. To reduce the waste stream, we must shift from a consumption to a conservation ethos. The ecological debate is complicated, but it is clear that the preservation of the myriad life cycles on earth is crucial, for we, too, could become an endangered species.

The language of nature is as enigmatic as the sounds of dolphins and whales communicating with their respective species. Writers like Barry Lopez and Rachel Carson and the vision expressed in the letter of Chief Seattle help us decipher the language of our environment. These writers encourage us to converse with nature, learn from it, and even revere it. All of us are guests on this planet; the natural world is our host. If we do not protect the earth, how can we guarantee the survival of civilization?

## Previewing the Chapter

As you read the essays in this chapter and respond to them in discussion and writing, consider the following questions:

- According to the author, what should our relationship to the natural world be?
- What claims or arguments does the author make about the importance of nature? Do you agree or disagree with these claims and arguments?
- What specific ecological problem does the author investigate?
- How does the author think that nature influences human behavior?
- What cultural factors are involved in our approach to the environment?
- Is the writer optimistic, pessimistic, or neutral in the assessment of our ability to conserve nature?
- Do you find that the author is too idealistic or sentimental in the depiction of nature? Why?
- Based on the author's essay, how does he or she qualify as a nature writer?
- How have you been challenged or changed by the essays in this chapter?

✺

# Classic and Contemporary Images:

## ARE WE DESTROYING OUR NATURAL WORLD?

*Using a Critical Perspective*   Imagine yourself to be part of each of the scenes depicted in these two illustrations. How do you feel, and why? Now examine the purpose of each image. What details do the artists emphasize to convey their feelings about our relationship to the natural world? What images does each artist create to capture your attention and direct your viewing and thinking toward a specific, dominant impression?

The painters of the Hudson River School such as John Frederick Kensett (1816–1872) celebrated American landscapes in their art, painting breathtaking scenes in meticulous detail. In *Along the Hudson* (1852), the beauty of the river is unspoiled.

Vehicles travel on the 405 Freeway where it intersects with the 10 West Freeway in Los Angeles. California could take the lead in the international effort to reduce global warming after the state's Air Resources Board gave approval to a package of regulations that would cut vehicle emissions by as much as 25 percent.

# Classic and Contemporary Essays
## DO WE OWN NATURE?

The simple yet passionate reflections of Chief Seattle regarding the destruction of a worldview are complemented by the more scholarly and learned meditations, nearly a century and a half later, of the esteemed naturalist and writer Barry Lopez. Chief Seattle mourns the death of a way of life, a way of thinking, and a way of being as he accepts that the cultural world of his people is doomed to disappear with the encroachment of "civilization." The white man exploits nature, uses nature, and perhaps most radically of all, perceives himself as apart from nature. This is in profound contrast to the ways of Chief Seattle's people, who saw themselves as in harmony with nature or, more specifically, as inseparable from it—as inseparable perhaps as from a part of their own bodies. Chief Seattle's address is simple. And so perhaps is his message, although one should not confuse simplicity with lack of profundity. Lopez, writing from the perspective of a 21st-century academic and naturalist, informs the reader of humans' ongoing "feud" with nature—not only by reflecting on his own experience and perceptions but by drawing on his "book" knowledge as well. He relates many relevant tales from other cultures and mythologies, and excavates the historical record when reflecting on the "stone horse" he finds hidden in the wilderness, a symbol of that union with nature that Chief Seattle wrote of so eloquently. Although they speak in very different levels of discourse and from different perspectives, their awe of nature has not been demolished despite many deliberate and random attempts to extinguish it.

# Letter to President Pierce, 1855

## Chief Seattle

*Chief Seattle (1786–1866) was the leader of the Dewamish and other Pacific Northwest tribes. The city of Seattle, Washington, bears his name. In 1854, Chief Seattle reluctantly agreed to sell tribal lands to the United States government and move to the government-established reservations. The authenticity of the following speech has been challenged by many scholars. However, most specialists agree that it contains the substance and perspective of Chief Seattle's attitude toward nature and the white race.*

We know that the white man does not understand our ways. One portion of the 1 land is the same to him as the next, for he is a stranger who comes in the night and takes from the land whatever he needs. The earth is not his brother, but his enemy, and when he has conquered it, he moves on. He leaves his fathers' graves, and his children's birthright is forgotten. The sight of your cities pains the eyes of the red man. But perhaps it is because the red man is a savage and does not understand.

There is no quiet place in the white man's cities. No place to hear the leaves 2 of spring or the rustle of insect's wings. But perhaps because I am a savage and do not understand, the clatter only seems to insult the ears. The Indian prefers the soft sound of the wind darting over the face of the pond, the smell of the wind itself cleansed by a mid-day rain, or scented with the piñon pine. The air is precious to the red man. For all things share the same breath—the beasts, the trees, the man. Like a man dying for many days, he is numb to the stench.

What is man without the beasts? If all the beasts were gone, men would die 3 from great loneliness of spirit, for whatever happens to the beasts also happens to man. All things are connected. Whatever befalls the earth befalls the sons of the earth.

It matters little where we pass the rest of our days; they are not many. A 4 few more hours, a few more winters, and none of the children of the great tribes that once lived on this earth, or that roamed in small bands in the woods, will be left to mourn the graves of a people once as powerful and hopeful as yours.

The whites, too, shall pass—perhaps sooner than other tribes. Continue to 5 contaminate your bed, and you will one night suffocate in your own waste. When the buffalo are all slaughtered, the wild horses all tamed, the secret corners of the forest heavy with the scent of many men, and the view of the ripe hills blotted by talking wires, where is the thicket? Gone. Where is the eagle? Gone. And what is it to say goodbye to the swift and the hunt, the end of living and the beginning of survival? We might understand if we knew what it was that the white man dreams, what he describes to his children on the long winter nights, what visions he burns into their minds, so they will wish for tomorrow. But we are savages. The white man's dreams are hidden from us.

## COMPREHENSION

1. What does Chief Seattle suggest is the major difference between the white man's relationship with nature and that of the red man?
2. Chief Seattle claims that perhaps the red man would understand the white man better if he understood better the "dreams" and "visions" of the white man. What does Chief Seattle suggest by these terms?
3. Chief Seattle refers to Native Americans as "savages." Why?

## RHETORIC

1. The author uses a number of sensory details in describing both nature and the white man's crimes against nature. How does the eliciting of sensations help determine the relationship between writer, text, and reader?
2. The letter is written simply, with simply constructed paragraphs and sentences. What does this style suggest about the writer's voice?
3. There is a noted absence of transitional expressions in the writing, that is, such linking words as *in addition, furthermore, nevertheless,* and *moreover.* How does this absence contribute to the directness of the writing?
4. The author uses the convention of the series, as in the following examples: "For all things share the same breath—the beasts, the trees, the man" (paragraph 2) and "When the buffalo are all slaughtered, the wild horses all tamed, the secret corners of the forest heavy with the scent of many men, and the view of the ripe hills blotted by talking wires" (paragraph 5). What is the rhetorical effect of this device?
5. Note the opening and closing sentences of the letter. How do they frame the letter? What do they suggest about one of its major themes?
6. Some scholars dispute the authenticity of the letter, attributing it to a white man who was attempting to articulate the essence of Chief Seattle's oratory in an effort to champion Native American causes. What elements of the letter resemble the rhetorical elements of a speech?

## WRITING

1. Write a 250-word summary in which you compare and contrast the major differences between the white man's and the red man's perception of and relationship to nature as conceived by Chief Seattle.
2. For a research project, trace the use of the word *savage* as it has been used to describe Native Americans.

3. **Writing an Argument:** Argue for or against the view that the charge by Chief Seattle that the white man is contemptuous of nature is still valid today. Use at least three points to support your thesis.

| www.mhhe.com/ **mhreader** | For more information on Chief Seattle, go to: **More Resources > Ch. 13 Nature & Environment** |

# The Stone Horse

## Barry Lopez

*Barry Lopez (b. 1945) was born in New York but spent much of his childhood in Southern California. He received a BA from the University of Notre Dame and an MAT from the University of Oregon in 1968. His early writings appeared in such magazines as* National Geographic, Antaeus, Wilderness, Science, *and* Harper's. *He has written both fiction and nonfiction including* Desert Notes: Reflections in the Eye of a Raven *(1976),* Of Wolves and Men *(1978),* Arctic Dreams: Imagination and Desire in a Northern Landscape *(1986),* Crossing Open Ground *(1988),* The Rediscovery of North America *(1991),* Crow & Weasel *(1999), and an autobiography,* About This Life *(1999). Lopez sees his role as a storyteller, someone who has the responsibility to create an atmosphere in which the wisdom of the work can reveal itself and "make the reader feel a part of something." In the following piece, from* Crossing Open Ground, *he focuses on an archaeological landmark to make a philosophical and moral inquiry into the way humans regard nature.*

### I

The deserts of southern California, the high, relatively cooler and wetter 1 Mojave and the hotter, dryer Sonoran to the south of it, carry the signatures of many cultures. Prehistoric rock drawings in the Mojave's Coso Range, probably the greatest concentration of petroglyphs in North America, are at least three thousand years old. Big-game-hunting cultures that flourished six or seven thousand years before that are known from broken spear tips, choppers, and burins left scattered along the shores of great Pleistocene lakes, long since evaporated. Weapons and tools discovered at China Lake may be thirty thousand years old; and worked stone from a quarry in the Calico Mountains is, some argue, evidence that human beings were here more than 200,000 years ago.

2      Because of the long-term stability of such arid environments, much of this prehistoric stone evidence still lies exposed on the ground, accessible to anyone who passes by—the studious, the acquisitive, the indifferent, the merely curious. Archaeologists do not agree on the sequence of cultural history beyond about twelve thousand years ago, but it is clear that these broken bits of chalcedony, chert, and obsidian, like the animal drawings and geometric designs etched on walls of basalt throughout the desert, anchor the earliest threads of human history, the first record of human endeavor here.

3      Western man did not enter the California desert until the end of the eighteenth century, 250 years after Coronado brought his soldiers into the Zuni pueblos in a bewildered search for the cities of Cibola. The earliest appraisals of the land were cursory, hurried. People traveled *through* it, en route to Santa Fe or the California coastal settlements. Only miners tarried. In 1823 what had been Spain's became Mexico's, and in 1848 what had been Mexico's became America's; but the bare, jagged mountains and dry lake beds, the vast and uniform plains of creosote bush and yucca plants, remained as obscure as the northern Sudan until the end of the nineteenth century.

4      Before 1940 the tangible evidence of twentieth-century man's passage here consisted of very little—the hard tracery of travel corridors; the widely scattered, relatively insignificant evidence of mining operations; and the fair expanse of irrigated fields at the desert's periphery. In the space of a hundred years or so the wagon roads were paved, railroads were laid down, and canals and high-tension lines were built to bring water and electricity across the desert to Los Angeles from the Colorado River. The dark mouths of gold, talc, and tin mines yawned from the bony flanks of desert ranges. Dust-encrusted chemical plants stood at work on the lonely edges of dry lake beds. And crops of grapes, lettuce, dates, alfalfa, and cotton covered the Coachella and Imperial valleys, north and south of the Salton Sea, and the Palo Verde Valley along the Colorado.

5      These developments proceeded with little or no awareness of earlier human occupations by cultures that preceded those of the historic Indians—the Mohave, the Chemehuevi, the Quechan. (Extensive irrigation began actually to change the climate of the Sonoran Desert, and human settlements, the railroads, and farming introduced many new, successful plants into the region.)

6      During World War II, the American military moved into the desert in great force, to train troops and to test equipment. They found the clear weather conducive to year-round flying, the dry air and isolation very attractive. After the war, a complex of training grounds, storage facilities, and gunnery and test ranges was permanently settled on more than three million acres of military reservations. Few perceived the extent or significance of the destruction of the aboriginal sites that took place during tank maneuvers and bombing runs or in the laying out of highways, railroads, mining districts, and irrigated fields. The few who intuited that something like an American Dordogne Valley lay exposed here were (only) amateur archaeologists; even they reasoned that the desert was too vast for any of this to matter.

After World War II, people began moving out of the crowded Los Angeles 7
basin into homes in Lucerne, Apple, and Antelope valleys in the western
Mojave. They emigrated as well to a stretch of resort land at the foot of the San
Jacinto Mountains that included Palm Springs, and farther out to old railroad
and military towns like Twenty-nine Palms and Barstow. People also began
exploring the desert, at first in military-surplus jeeps and then with a variety of
all-terrain and off-road vehicles that became available in the 1960s. By the mid-
1970s, the number of people using such vehicles for desert recreation had
increased exponentially. Most came and went in innocent curiosity; the few
who didn't wreaked a havoc all out of proportion to their numbers. The disturbance of previously isolated archaeological sites increased by an order of magnitude. Many sites were vandalized before archaeologists, themselves late to
the desert, had any firm grasp of the bounds of human history in the desert. It
was as though in the same moment an Aztec library had been discovered intact
various lacunae had begun to appear.

The vandalism was of three sorts: the general disturbance usually caused 8
by souvenir hunters and by the curious and the oblivious; the wholesale
stripping of a place by professional thieves for black-market sale and trade; and
outright destruction, in which vehicles were actually used to ram and trench an
area. By 1980, the Bureau of Land Management estimated that probably 35 percent of the archaeological sites in the desert had been vandalized. The destruction at some places by rifles and shotguns, or by power winches mounted on
vehicles, was, if one cared for history, demoralizing to behold.

In spite of public education, land closures, and stricter law enforcement in 9
recent years, the BLM estimates that, annually, about 1 percent of the archaeological record in the desert continues to be destroyed or stolen.


## II

A BLM archaeologist told me, with understandable reluctance, where to find the 10
intaglio. I spread my Automobile Club of Southern California map of Imperial
County out on his desk, and he traced the route with a pink felt-tip pen. The line
crossed Interstate 8 and then turned west along the Mexican border.

"You can't drive any farther than about here," he said, marking a small X. 11
"There's boulders in the wash. You walk up past them."

On a separate piece of paper he drew a route in a smaller scale that would 12
take me up the arroyo to a certain point where I was to cross back east, to another
arroyo. At its head, on higher ground just to the north, I would find the horse.

"It's tough to spot unless you know it's there. Once you pick it up . . ." He 13
shook his head slowly, in a gesture of wonder at its existence.

I waited until I held his eye. I assured him I would not tell anyone else how 14
to get there. He looked at me with stoical despair, like a man who had been
robbed twice, whose belief in human beings was offered without conviction.

I did not go until the following day because I wanted to see it at dawn. I ate 15
breakfast at four A.M. in El Centro and then drove south. The route was easy to

follow, though the last section of road proved difficult, broken and drifted over with sand in some spots. I came to the barricade of boulders and parked. It was light enough by then to find my way over the ground with little trouble. The contours of the landscape were stark, without any masking vegetation. I worried only about rattlesnakes.

16    I traversed the stone plain as directed, but, in spite of the frankness of the land, I came on the horse unawares. In the first moment of recognition I was without feeling. I recalled later being startled, and that I held my breath. It was laid out on the ground with its head to the east, three times life size. As I took in its outline I felt a growing concentration of all my senses, as though my attentiveness to the pale rose color of the morning sky and other peripheral images had now ceased to be important. I was aware that I was straining for sound in the windless air, and I felt the uneven pressure of the earth hard against my feet. The horse, outlined in a standing profile on the dark ground, was as vivid before me as a bed of tulips.

17    I've come upon animals suddenly before, and felt a similar tension, a precipitate heightening of the senses. And I have felt the inexplicable but sharply boosted intensity of a wild moment in the bush, where it is not until some minutes later that you discover the source of electricity—the warm remains of a grizzly bear kill, or the still moist tracks of a wolverine.

18    But this was slightly different. I felt I had stepped into an unoccupied corridor. I had no familiar sense of history, the temporal structure in which to think: This horse was made by Quechan people three hundred years ago. I felt instead a headlong rush of images: people hunting wild horses with spears on the Pleistocene veld of southern California; Cortés riding across the causeway into Montezuma's Tenochtitlán; a short-legged Comanche, astride his horse like some sort of ferret, slashing through cavalry lines of young men who rode like farmers; a hood exploding past my face one morning in a corral in Wyoming. These images had the weight and silence of stone.

19    When I released my breath, the images softened. My initial feeling, of facing a wild animal in a remote region, was replaced with a calm sense of antiquity. It was then that I became conscious, like an ordinary tourist, of what was before me, and thought: this horse was probably laid out by Quechan people. But when? I wondered. The first horses they saw, I knew, might have been those that came north from Mexico in 1692 with Father Eusebio Kino. But Cocopa people, I recalled, also came this far north on occasion, to fight with their neighbors, the Quechan. And *they* could have seen horses with Melchior Diaz, at the mouth of the Colorado River in the fall of 1540. So, it could be four hundred years old. (No one in fact knows.)

20    I still had not moved. I took my eyes off the horse for a moment to look south over the desert plain into Mexico, to look east past its head at the brightening sunrise, to situate myself. Then, finally, I brought my trailing foot slowly forward and stood erect. Sunlight was running like a thin sheet of water over the stony ground and it threw the horse into relief. It looked as though no hand had ever disturbed the stones that gave it its form.

The horse had been brought to life on ground called desert pavement, a  21
tight, flat matrix of small cobbles blasted smooth by sand-laden winds. The
uniform, monochromatic blackness of the stones, a patina of iron and magne-
sium oxides called desert varnish, is caused by long-term exposure to the sun.
To make this type of low-relief ground glyph, or intaglio, the artist either selectively turns individual stones over to their lighter side or removes areas of
stone to expose the lighter soil underneath, creating a negative image. This
horse, about eighteen feet from brow to rump and eight feet from withers to
hoof, had been made in the latter way, and its outline was bermed at certain
points with low ridges of stone a few inches high to enhance its three-dimensional qualities. (The left side of the horse was in full profile; each leg was
extended at 90 degrees to the body and fully visible, as though seen in three-
quarter profile.)

I was not eager to move. The moment I did I would be back in the flow of  22
time, the horse no longer quivering in the same way before me. I did not want
to feel again the sequence of quotidian events—to be drawn off into deliberation and analysis. A human being, a four-footed animal, the open land. That
was all that was present—and a "thoughtless" understanding of the very old
desires bearing on this particular animal: to hunt it, to render it, to fathom it, to
subjugate it, to honor it, to take it as a companion.

What finally made me move was the light. The sun now filled the shal-  23
low basin of the horse's body. The weighted line of the stone berm created
the illusion of a mane and the distinctive roundness of an equine belly. The
change in definition impelled me. I moved to the left, circling past its rump,
to see how the light might flesh the horse out from various points of view. I
circled it completely before squatting on my haunches. Ten or fifteen minutes later I chose another view. The third time I moved, to a point near the
rear hooves, I spotted a stone tool at my feet. I stared at it a long while, more
in awe than disbelief, before reaching out to pick it up. I turned it over in my
left palm and took it between my fingers to feel its cutting edge. It is always
difficult, especially with something so portable, to rechannel the desire to
steal.

I spent several hours with the horse. As I changed positions and as the an-  24
gle of the light continued to change I noticed a number of things. The angle at
which the pastern carried the hoof away from the ankle was perfect. Also,
stones had been placed within the image to suggest at precisely the right spot
the left shoulder above the foreleg. The line that joined thigh and hock was
similarly accurate. The muzzle alone seemed distorted—but perhaps these
stones had been moved by a later hand. It was an admirably accurate representation, but not what a breeder would call perfect conformation. There was the
suggestion of a bowed neck and an undershot jaw, and the tail, as full as a
winter coyote's, did not appear to be precisely to scale.

The more I thought about it, the more I felt I was looking at an individual  25
horse, a unique combination of generic and specific detail. It was easy to
imagine one of Kino's horses as a model, or a horse that ran off from one of

Coronado's columns. What kind of horses would these have been? I wondered. In the sixteenth century the most sought-after horses in Europe were Spanish, the offspring of Arabian stock and Barbary horses that the Moors brought to Iberia and bred to the older, eastern European strains brought in by the Romans. The model for this horse, I speculated, could easily have been a palomino, or a descendant of horses trained for lion hunting in North Africa.

26    A few generations ago, cowboys, cavalry quartermasters, and draymen would have taken this horse before me under consideration and not let up their scrutiny until they had its heritage fixed to their satisfaction. Today, the distinction between draft and harness horses is arcane knowledge, and no image may come to mind for a blue roan or a claybank horse. The loss of such refinement in everyday conversation leaves me unsettled. People praise the Eskimo's ability to distinguish among forty types of snow but forget the skill of others who routinely differentiate between overo and tobiano pintos. Such distinctions are made for the same reason. You have to do it to be able to talk clearly about the world.

27    For parts of two years I worked as a horse wrangler and packer in Wyoming. It is dim knowledge now; I would have to think to remember if a buckskin was a kind of dun horse. And I couldn't throw a double-diamond hitch over a set of panniers—the packer's basic tie-down—without guidance. As I squatted there in the desert, however, these more personal memories seemed tenuous in comparison with the sweep of this animal in human time. My memories had no depth. I thought of the Hittite cavalry riding against the Syrians 3,500 years ago. And the first of the Chinese emperors, Ch'in Shih Huang, buried in Shensi Province in 210 B.C. with thousands of life-size horses and soldiers, a terra-cotta guardian army. What could I know of what was in the mind of whoever made this horse? Was there some racial memory of it as an animal that had once fed the artist's ancestors and then disappeared from North America? And then returned in this strange alliance with another race of men?

28    Certainly, whoever it was, the artist had observed the animal very closely. Certainly the animal's speed had impressed him. Among the first things the Quechan would have learned from an encounter with Kino's horses was that their own long-distance runners—men who could run down mule deer—were no match for this animal.

29    From where I squatted I could look far out over the Mexican plain. Juan Bautista de Anza passed this way in 1774, extending El Camino Real into Alta California from Sinaloa. He was followed by others, all of them astride the magical horse; *gente de razón*, the people of reason, coming into the country of *los primitivos*. The horse, like the stone animals of Egypt, urged these memories upon me. And as I drew them up from some forgotten corner of my mind— huge horses carved in the white chalk downs of southern England by an Iron Age people; Spanish horses rearing and wheeling in fear before alligators in Florida—the images seemed tethered before me. With this sense of proportion,

a memory of my own—the morning I almost lost my face to a horse's hoof—now had somewhere to fit.

I rose up and began to walk slowly around the horse again. I had taken the ₃₀ first long measure of it and was now looking for a way to depart, a new angle of light, a fading of the image itself before the rising sun, that would break its hold on me. As I circled, feeling both heady and serene at the encounter, I realized again how strangely vivid it was. It had been created on a barren bajada between two arroyos, as nondescript a place as one could imagine. The only plant life here was a few wands of ocotillo cactus. The ground beneath my shoes was so hard it wouldn't take the print of a heavy animal even after a rain. The only sounds I heard here were the voices of quail.

The archaeologist had been correct. For all its forcefulness, the horse is ₃₁ inconspicuous. If you don't care to see it you can walk right past it. That pleases him, I think. Unmarked on the bleak shoulder of the plain, the site signals to no one; so he wants no protective fences here, no informative plaque, to act as beacons. He would rather take a chance that no motorcyclist, no aimless wanderer with a flair for violence and a depth of ignorance, will ever find his way here.

The archaeologist had given me something before I left his office that now ₃₂ seemed peculiar—an aerial photograph of the horse. It is widely believed that an aerial view of an intaglio provides a fair and accurate depiction. It does not. In the photograph the horse looks somewhat crudely constructed; from the ground it appears far more deftly rendered. The photograph is of a single moment, and in that split second the horse seems vaguely impotent. I watched light pool in the intaglio at dawn; I imagine you could watch it withdraw at dusk and sense the same animation I did. In those prolonged moments its shape and so, too, its general character change—noticeably The living quality of the image, its immediacy to the eye, was brought out by the light-in-time, not, at least here, in the camera's frozen instant.

Intaglios, I thought, were never meant to be seen by gods in the sky above. ₃₃ They were meant to be seen by people on the ground, over a long period of shifting light. This could even be true of the huge figures on the Plain of Nazca in Peru, where people could walk for the length of a day beside them. It is our own impatience that leads us to think otherwise.

This process of abstraction, almost unintentional, drew me gradually away ₃₄ from the horse. I came to a position of attention at the edge of the sphere of its influence. With a slight bow I paid my respects to the horse, its maker, and the history of us all, and departed.

## III

A short distance away I stopped the car in the middle of the road to make a ₃₅ few notes. I could not write down what I was thinking when I was with the horse. It would have seemed disrespectful, and it would have required another kind of attention. So now I patiently drained my memory of the details it had fastened itself upon. The road I'd stopped on was adjacent to the All American Canal, the major source of water for the Imperial and Coachella valleys. The water flowed west placidly. A disjointed flock of coots, small, dark birds with white bills, was paddling against the current, foraging in the rushes.

36    I was peripherally aware of the birds as I wrote, the only movement in the desert, and of a series of sounds from a village a half-mile away. The first sounds from this collection of ramshackle houses in a grove of cottonwoods were the distracted dawn voices of dogs. I heard them intermingled with the cries of a rooster. Later, the high-pitched voices of children calling out to each other came disembodied through the dry desert air. Now, a little after seven, I could hear someone practicing on the trumpet, the same rough phrases played over and over. I suddenly remembered how as children we had tried to get the rhythm of a galloping horse with hands against our thighs, or by fluttering our tongues against the roofs of our mouths.

37    After the trumpet, the impatient calls of adults summoning children. Sunday morning. Wood smoke hung like a lens in the trees. The first car starts—a cold eight-cylinder engine, of Chrysler extraction perhaps, goosed to life, then throttled back to murmur through dual mufflers, the obbligato music of a shade-tree mechanic. The rote bark of mongrel dogs at dawn, the jagged outcries of men and women, an engine coming to life. Like a thousand villages from West Virginia to Guadalajara.

38    I finished my notes—where was I going to find a description of the horses that came north with the conquistadors? Did their manes come forward prominently over the brow, like this one's, like the forelocks of Blackfeet and Assiniboin men in nineteenth-century paintings? I set the notes on the seat beside me.

39    The road followed the canal for a while and then arced north, toward Interstate 8. It was slow driving and I fell to thinking how the desert had changed since Anza had come through. New plants and animals—the MacDougall cottonwood, the English house sparrow, the chukar from India—have about them now the air of the native born. Of the native species, some—no one knows how many—are extinct. The populations of many others, especially the animals, have been sharply reduced. The idea of a desert impoverished by agricultural poisons and varmint hunters, by off-road vehicles and military operations, did not seem as disturbing to me, however, as this other horror, now that I had been those hours with the horse. The vandals, the few who crowbar rock art off the desert's walls, who dig up graves, who punish the ground that holds intaglios, are people who devour history. Their self-centered scorn, their disrespect for ideas and images beyond their ken, create the awful atmosphere of loose ends in which totalitarianism thrives, in which the past is merely curious or wrong.

40    I thought about the horse sitting out there on the unprotected plain. I enumerated its qualities in my mind until a sense of its vulnerability receded and it became an anchor for something else. I remembered that history, a history like this one, which ran deeper than Mexico, deeper than the Spanish, was a kind of

medicine. It permitted the great breadth of human expression to reverberate, and it did not urge you to locate its apotheosis in the present.

Each of us, individuals and civilizations, has been held upside down like 41 Achilles in the River Styx. The artist mixing his colors in the dim light of Altamira; an Egyptian ruler lying still now, wrapped in his byssus, stored against time in a pyramid; the faded Dorset culture of the Arctic; the Hmong and Samburu and Walbiri of historic time; the modern nations. This great, imperfect stretch of human expression is the clarification and encouragement, the urging and the reminder, we call history. And it is inscribed everywhere in the face of the land, from the mountain passes of the Himalayas to a nameless bajada in the California desert.

Small birds rose up in the road ahead, startled, and flew off. I prayed no 42 infidel would ever find that horse.

## COMPREHENSION

1. What is Lopez's primary purpose in this essay? How does its title relate to the purpose?
2. Does Lopez assume his audience has the same value position as he does? Does he assume it has a commensurate background in anthropology, history, and ecology? Explain your answer.
3. What provides Lopez with the most compelling evidence that humans have a history? Base your answer on his statement in paragraph 41: "This great, imperfect stretch of human expression is the clarification and encouragement, the origin and the reminder, we call history."

## RHETORIC

1. How would you characterize the tone of this essay? Does the tone remain constant or does it change? Can you connect the tone with Lopez's thesis?
2. Lopez has chosen to divide his essay into three sections. Why is that decision appropriate to his strategy? How does the structure relate to the overall development of his theme?
3. While Lopez inspects the "horse," he describes it in detail. Next, he experiences a change in emotion and thinking. How does his erudition concerning history and anthropology enrich his emotional response? Explain the rhetorical progression from description to response and reflection in paragraphs 19–28.
4. Define the following terms: *petroglyphs* (paragraph 1), *intaglio* (paragraph 10), *arroyo* (paragraph 12), *glyph* (paragraph 21), *pastern* (paragraph 24), *conquistadors* (paragraph 38), and *totalitarianism* (paragraph 39).
5. Why does Lopez end this substantial essay with such a brief conclusion? Why does he juxtapose the presence of "birds" and the fear of the "infidel" in his conclusion?

6. There is a marked change in atmosphere between sections II and III. What is this change? How does Lopez express it? What does it signify?
7. How does Lopez demonstrate a sense of authority over his subject matter? Does it stem naturally from the flow of his writing, or is it superimposed? Explain your response.

## WRITING

1. Write a descriptive/narrative essay about a personal experience in an environment that made you feel as though you were experiencing a place with implications greater than yourself—for example, a setting in nature, a church, sports arena or stadium during a game, or a concert.
2. Write an essay in which you argue for or against the public's right to gain access to archaeological sites for study.
3. **Writing an Argument:** Argue for or against the proposition that the American system of values encourages people to despoil, destroy, or neglect historical sites and structures.

www.mhhe.com/
**mhreader**

For more information on Barry Lopez, go to:
**More Resources > Ch. 13 Nature & Environment**

## Synthesis: Classic and Contemporary Questions for Comparison

1. Chief Seattle and Barry Lopez decry the destruction of nature as a physical and spiritual presence. In what ways are their stakes in this destruction the same? In what ways are they different? Does either writer have the power to effect a transformation in our attitude toward nature? Explain.
2. It has often been said that intellectual knowledge changes one's relationship with the world environment. In what ways has Lopez's "book learning" and erudition made him a different person from Chief Seattle? Base your response on the style and tone of each author.
3. Chief Seattle is literally the leader and spokesperson of a defeated nation. How does he preserve his dignity in the face of being conquered? How does he indicate to the white man that his "victory" is temporary? Lopez, on the other hand, is a successful member of his society: esteemed naturalist, award-winning writer, popular lecturer. What prevents him from reaping the benefits of his accomplishments? Explain by referring to the text.

# Why I Hunt

### Rick Bass

*Rick Bass (b. 1958) was born in Fort Worth, Texas, and grew up in the Texas hill country where his grandfather taught him how to hunt. His collection of essays,* The Deer Pasture *(1985), recounts his Texas years, the ethos of hunting, and the allure of the outdoors. Bass studied at Utah State University (BS, 1979) and worked as an oil and gas geologist in Mississippi for eight years. His time working in the oil fields of the deep South is documented in* Oil Notes *(1979). Bass has written more than a dozen works of nonfiction and fiction, many of them reflecting environmental issues and people's search for balance in the natural world. An environmental advocate and land conservationist, Bass lives in the remote Yaak Valley on the Montana-Canada border, a region depicted in books such as* Winter: Notes from Montana *(1991),* Brown Dog of the Yaak: Essays on Art and Activism *(1999), and* The Roadless Yaak: Reflections and Observations about One of Our Last Great Wild Places *(2002). Bass wrote this vivid and provocative essay on the allure of the hunt for* Sierra *magazine in 2001.*

I was a hunter before I came far up into northwest Montana, but not to the degree I am now. It astounds me sometimes to step back particularly at the end of autumn, the end of the hunting season, and take both mental and physical inventory of all that was hunted and all that was gathered from this life in the mountains. The woodshed groaning tight, full of firewood. The fruits and herbs and vegetables from the garden, canned or dried or frozen; the wild mushrooms, huckleberries, thimbleberries, and strawberries. And most precious of all, the flesh of the wild things that share with us these mountains and the plains to the east—the elk, the whitetail and mule deer; the ducks and geese, grouse and pheasant and Hungarian partridge and dove and chukar and wild turkey; the trout and whitefish. Each year the cumulative bounty seems unbelievable. What heaven is this into which we've fallen?

How my wife and I got to this valley—the Yaak—15 years ago is a mystery, a move that I've only recently come to accept as having been inevitable. We got in the truck one day feeling strangely restless in Mississippi, and we drove. What did I know? Only that I missed the West's terrain of space. Young and healthy, and not coincidentally new-in-love, we hit that huge and rugged landscape in full stride. We drove north until we ran out of country—until the road ended, and we reached Canada's thick blue woods—and then we turned west and traveled until we ran almost out of mountains: the backside of the Rockies, to the wet, west-slope rainforest.

We came over a little mountain pass—it was August and winter was already fast approaching—and looked down on the soft hills, the dense purples of the

spruce and fir forests, the ivory crests of the ice-capped peaks, and the slender ribbons of gray thread rising from the chimneys of the few cabins nudged close to the winding river below, and we fell in love with the Yaak Valley and the hard-logged Kootenai National Forest—the way people in movies fall with each other, star and starlet, as if a trap door has been pulled out from beneath them: tumbling through the air, arms windmilling furiously, and suddenly no other world but each other, no other world but this one and eyes for no one, or no place, else.

4      Right from the beginning, I could see that there was extraordinary bounty in this low-elevation forest, resting as it does in a magical seam between the Pacific Northwest and the northern Rockies. Some landscapes these days have been reduced to nothing but dandelions and fire ants, knapweed and thistle, where the only remaining wildlife are sparrows, squirrels, and starlings. In the blessed Yaak, however, not a single mammal has gone extinct since the end of the Ice Age. This forest sustains more types of hunters—carnivores—than any valley in North America. It is a predator's showcase, home not just to wolves and grizzlies, but wolverines, lynx, bobcat, marten, fisher, black bear, mountain lion, golden eagle, bald eagle, coyote, fox, weasel. In the Yaak, everything is in motion, either seeking its quarry, or seeking to avoid becoming quarry.

5      The people who have chosen to live in this remote valley—few phones, very little electricity, and long, dark winters—possess a hardness and a dreaminess both. They—we—can live a life of deprivation, and yet are willing to enter the comfort of daydreams and imagination. There is something mysterious happening here between the landscape and the people, a thing that stimulates our imagination, and causes many of us to set off deep into the woods in search of the unknown, and sustenance—not just metaphorical or spiritual sustenance, but the real thing.

6      Only about 5 percent of the nation and 15 to 20 percent of Montanans are hunters. But in this one valley, almost everyone is a hunter. It is not the peer pressure of the local culture that recruits us into hunting, nor even necessarily the economic boon of a few hundred pounds of meat in a cash-poor society. Rather, it is the terrain itself, and one's gradual integration into it, that summons the hunter. Nearly everyone who has lived here for any length of time

has ended up—sometimes almost against one's conscious wishes—becoming a hunter. This wild and powerful landscape sculpts us like clay. I don't find such sculpting an affront to the human spirit, but instead, wonderful testimony to our pliability, our ability to adapt to a place.

I myself love to hunt the deer, the elk, and the grouse—to follow them into ₇ the mouth of the forest, to disappear in their pursuit—to get lost following their snowy tracks up one mountain and down the next. One sets out after one's quarry with senses fully engaged, wildly alert: entranced, nearly hypnotized. The tiniest of factors can possess the largest significance—the crack of a twig, the shift of a breeze, a single stray hair caught on a piece of bark, a fresh-bent blade of grass.

Each year during such pursuits, I am struck more and more by the conceit ₈ that people in a hunter-gatherer culture might have richer imaginations than those who dwell more fully in an agricultural or even post-agricultural environment. What else is the hunt but a stirring of the imagination, with the quarry, or goal, or treasure lying just around the corner or over the next rise? A hunter's imagination has no choice but to become deeply engaged, for it is never the hunter who is in control, but always the hunted, in that the prey directs the predator's movements.

The hunted shapes the hunter; the pursuit and evasion of predator and ₉ prey are but shadows of the same desire. The thrush wants to remain a thrush. The goshawk wants to consume the thrush and in doing so, partly become the thrush—to take its flesh into its flesh. They weave through the tangled branches of the forest, zigging and zagging, the goshawk right on the thrush's tail, like a shadow. Or perhaps it is the thrush that is the shadow thrown by the light of the goshawk's fiery desire.

Either way, the escape maneuvers of the thrush help carve and shape and ₁₀ direct the muscles of the goshawk. Even when you are walking through the woods seeing nothing but trees, you can feel the unseen passage of pursuits that might have occurred earlier that morning, precisely where you are standing—

pursuits that will doubtless, after you are gone, sweep right back across that same spot again and again.

11      As does the goshawk, so too do human hunters imagine where their prey might be, or where it might go. They follow tracks hinting at not only distance and direction traveled, but also pace and gait and the general state of mind of the animal that is evading them. They plead to the mountain to deliver to them a deer, an elk. They imagine and hope that they are moving toward their goal of obtaining game.

12      When you plant a row of corn, there is not so much unknown. You can be fairly sure that, if the rains come, the corn is going to sprout. The corn is not seeking to elude you. But when you step into the woods, looking for a deer—well, there's nothing in your mind, or in your blood, or in the world, but imagination.

13      Most Americans neither hunt nor gather nor even grow their own food, nor make, with their own hands, any of their other necessities. In this post-agricultural society, too often we confuse anticipation with imagination. When we wander down the aisle of the supermarket searching for a chunk of frozen chicken, or cruise into Dillard's department store looking for a sweater, we can be fairly confident that grayish wad of chicken or that sweater is going to be there, thanks to the vigor and efficiency of a supply-and-demand marketplace. The imagination never quite hits second gear. Does the imagination atrophy, from such chronic inactivity? I suspect that it does.

14      All I know is that hunting—beyond being a thing I like to do—helps keep my imagination vital. I would hope never to be so blind as to offer it as prescription; I offer it only as testimony to my love of the landscape where I live—a place that is still, against all odds, its own place, quite unlike any other. I don't think I would be able to sustain myself as a dreamer in this strange landscape if I did not take off three months each year to wander the mountains in search of game; to hunt, stretching and exercising not just my imagination, but my spirit. And to wander the mountains, too, in all the other seasons. And to be nourished by the river of spirit that flows, shifting and winding, between me and the land.

# COMPREHENSION

1. Why did Bass and his wife fall in love with the Yaak Valley? What does this fondness for wild places tell us about his character and interests?
2. Explain the relationship between the people residing in the Yaak Valley and their fondness for hunting.
3. Does Bass apologize for his fondness for hunting? Explain your response.

# RHETORIC

1. Bass wrote this essay for the official magazine of the Sierra Club, of which he is an active member. Why would an organization whose goal is the preservation of wilderness and wildlife agree to publish an article advocating hunting? How does Bass anticipate objections to his argument?
2. What is Bass's claim and where does he state it? Does he rely on logical, ethical, or emotional appeal—or a combination—to advance his argument, and why?
3. What causal connection does Bass establish between landscape and human behavior? Where does he use comparison and contrast to distinguish this place and its people from other Americans?
4. Cite examples of Bass's descriptive skills. How does description enhance the appeal of the writer's argument?
5. What is the dominant impression that Bass creates of the Yaak Valley region?
6. Evaluate Bass's conclusion. How does it serve as a writer's justification for hunting?

# WRITING

1. Select a natural landscape that you know well and, including description as one rhetorical strategy, explain how this site affects the behavior of people and their ethical values.
2. Go online and locate the Web site for the Sierra Club. Summarize the organization's goals, and then evaluate whether Bass's essay conforms to these objectives.
3. **Writing an Argument:** What is the difference between killing the game that you consume and buying meat in a grocery store or supermarket? Is one act more ethical than the other? Compose an argumentative essay dealing with this issue.

www.mhhe.com/
**mhreader**

For more information on Rick Bass, go to:
**More Resources > Ch. 13 Nature & Environment**

# The Way to Rainy Mountain

## N. Scott Momaday

*N(avarre) Scott Momaday (b. 1934), Pulitzer Prize–winning poet, critic, and acade-
mician, was born in Lawton, Oklahoma, of Kiowa ancestry. He holds degrees from
the University of New Mexico and Stanford University and is a professor of English at
the University of Arizona. He is the author of* House Made of Dawn *(1968),* The
Way to Rainy Mountain *(1969),* The Names *(1976), and other works. "I am an
American Indian (Kiowa), and am vitally interested in American Indian art, history
and culture," Momaday has written. In this essay, he elevates personal experience and
landscape to the realm of poetry and tribal myth.*

1  A single knoll rises out of the plain in Oklahoma, north and west of the Wichita
Range. For my people, the Kiowas, it is an old landmark, and they gave it the
name Rainy Mountain. The hardest weather in the world is there. Winter brings
blizzards, hot tornadic winds arise in the spring, and in summer the prairie is
an anvil's edge. The grass turns brittle and brown, and it cracks beneath your
feet. There are green belts along the rivers and creeks, linear groves of hickory
and pecan, willow and witch hazel. At a distance in July or August the steam-
ing foliage seems almost to writhe in fire. Great green and yellow grasshoppers
are everywhere in the tall grass, popping up like corn to sting the flesh, and
tortoises crawl about on the red earth, going nowhere in the plenty of time.
Loneliness is an aspect of the land. All things in the plain are isolate; there is no
confusion of objects in the eye, but *one* hill or *one* tree or *one* man. To look upon
that landscape in the early morning, with the sun at your back, is to lose the
sense of proportion. Your imagination comes to life, and this, you think, is
where Creation was begun.

2      I returned to Rainy Mountain in July. My grandmother had died in the
spring, and I wanted to be at her grave. She had lived to be very old and at last
infirm. Her only living daughter was with her when she died, and I was told
that in death her face was that of a child.

3      I like to think of her as a child. When she was born, the Kiowas were living
the last great moment of their history. For more than a hundred years they had
controlled the open range from the Smoky Hill River to the Red, from the head-
waters of the Canadian to the fork of the Arkansas and Cimarron. In alliance
with the Comanches, they had ruled the whole of the southern Plains. War was
their sacred business, and they were among the finest horsemen the world has
ever known. But warfare for the Kiowas was preeminently a matter of disposition rather than of survival, and they never understood the grim, unrelenting
advance of the U.S. Cavalry. When at last, divided and ill-provisioned, they

were driven onto the Staked Plains in the cold rains of autumn, they fell into panic. In Palo Duro Canyon they abandoned their crucial stores to pillage and had nothing then but their lives. In order to save themselves, they surrendered to the soldiers at Fort Sill and were imprisoned in the old stone corral that now stands as a military museum. My grandmother was spared the humiliation of those high gray walls by eight or ten years, but she must have known from birth the affliction of defeat, the dark brooding of old warriors.

Her name was Aho, and she belonged to the last culture to evolve in North 4 America. Her forebears came down from the high country in western Montana nearly three centuries ago. They were a mountain people, a mysterious tribe of hunters whose language has never been positively classified in any major group. In the late seventeenth century they began a long migration to the south and east. It was a journey toward the dawn, and it led to a golden age. Along the way the Kiowas were befriended by the Crows, who gave them the culture and religion of the Plains. They acquired horses, and their ancient nomadic spirit was suddenly free of the ground. They acquired Tai-me, the sacred Sun Dance doll, from that moment the object and symbol of their worship, and so shared in the divinity of the sun. Not least, they acquired the sense of destiny, therefore courage and pride. When they entered upon the southern Plains they had been transformed. No longer were they slaves to the simple necessity of survival; they were a lordly and dangerous society of fighters and thieves, hunters and priests of the sun. According to their origin myth, they entered the world through a hollow log. From one point of view, their migration was the fruit of an old prophecy, for indeed they emerged from a sunless world.

Although my grandmother lived out her long life in the shadow of Rainy 5 Mountain, the immense landscape of the continental interior lay like memory in her blood. She could tell of the Crows, whom she had never seen, and of the Black Hills, where she had never been. I wanted to see in reality what she had seen more perfectly in the mind's eye, and traveled fifteen hundred miles to begin my pilgrimage.

Yellowstone, it seemed to me, was the top of the world, a region of deep 6 lakes and dark timber, canyons and waterfalls. But, beautiful as it is, one might have the sense of confinement there. The skyline in all directions is close at hand, the high wall of the woods and deep cleavages of shade. There is a perfect freedom in the mountains, but it belongs to the eagle and the elk, the badger and the bear. The Kiowas reckoned their stature by the distance they could see, and they were bent and blind in the wilderness.

Descending eastward, the highland meadows are a stairway to the plain. In 7 July the inland slope of the Rockies is luxuriant with flax and buckwheat, stone-crop and larkspur. The earth unfolds and the limit of the land recedes. Clusters of trees, and animals grazing far in the distance, cause the vision to reach away and wonder to build upon the mind. The sun follows a longer course in the day, and the sky is immense beyond all comparison. The great billowing clouds that sail upon it are shadows that move upon the grain like water, dividing light. Farther down, in the land of the Crows and Blackfeet, the plain is yellow. Sweet clover takes hold of the hills and bends upon itself to cover and seal the soil. There the Kiowas paused on their way; they had come to the place where they must change their lives. The sun is at home on the plains. Precisely there does it have the certain character of a god. When the Kiowas came to the land of the Crows, they could see the dark lees of the hills at dawn across the Bighorn River, the profusion of light on the grain shelves, the oldest deity ranging after the solstices. Not yet would they veer southward to the caldron of the land that lay below; they must wean their blood from the northern winter and hold the mountains a while longer in their view. They bore Tai-me in procession to the east.

8      A dark mist lay over the Black Hills, and the land was like iron. At the top of a ridge I caught sight of Devil's Tower upthrust against the gray sky as if in the birth of time the core of the earth had broken through its crust and the motion of the world was begun. There are things in nature that engender an awful quiet in the heart of man; Devil's Tower is one of them. Two centuries ago, because they could not do otherwise, the Kiowas made a legend at the base of the rock. My grandmother said:

> Eight children were there at play, seven sisters and their brother. Suddenly the boy was struck dumb; he trembled and began to run upon his hands and feet. His fingers became claws, and his body was covered with fur. Directly there was a bear where the boy had been. The sisters were terrified; they ran, and the bear after them. They came to the stump of a great tree, and the tree spoke to them. It bade them climb upon it, and as they did so it began to rise into the air. The bear came to kill them, but they were just beyond its reach. It reared against the tree and scored the bark all around with its claws. The seven sisters were borne into the sky, and they became the stars of the Big Dipper.

From that moment, and so long as the legend lives, the Kiowas have kinsmen in the night sky. Whatever they were in the mountains, they could be no more. However tenuous their well-being, however much they had suffered and would suffer again, they had found a way out of the wilderness.

9      My grandmother had a reverence for the sun, a holy regard that now is all but gone out of mankind. There was a wariness in her, and an ancient awe. She was a Christian in her later years, but she had come a long way about, and she never forgot her birthright. As a child she had been to the Sun Dances; she had taken part in those annual rites, and by them she had learned the restoration of her people in the presence of Tai-me. She was about seven when the last Kiowa Sun Dance was held in 1887 on the Washita River above Rainy Mountain Creek. The buffalo were gone. In order to consummate the ancient sacrifice—to impale the head of a buffalo bull upon the medicine tree—a delegation of old men journeyed into Texas, there to beg and barter for an animal from the Goodnight herd. She was ten when the Kiowas came together for the last time as a living Sun Dance culture. They could find no buffalo; they had to hang an old hide from the sacred tree. Before the dance could begin, a company of soldiers rode out from Fort Sill under orders to disperse the tribe. Forbidden without cause the essential act of their faith, having seen the wild herds slaughtered and left to rot upon

the ground, the Kiowas backed away forever from the medicine tree. That was
July 20, 1890, at the great bend of the Washita. My grandmother was there. Without bitterness, and for as long as she lived, she bore a vision of deicide.

Now that I can have her only in memory, I see my grandmother in the several   10
postures that were peculiar to her: standing at the wood stove on a winter morning and turning meat in a great iron skillet; sitting at the south window, bent
above her beadwork, and afterwards, when her vision failed, looking down for a
long time into the fold of her hands; going out upon a cane, very slowly as she
did when the weight of age came upon her; praying. I remember her most often
at prayer. She made long, rambling prayers out of suffering and hope, having
seen many things. I was never sure that I had the right to hear, so exclusive were
they of all mere custom and company. The last time I saw her she prayed standing by the side of her bed at night, naked to the waist, the light of a kerosene lamp
moving upon her dark skin. Her long, black hair, always drawn and braided in
the day, lay upon her shoulders and against her breasts like a shawl. I do not
speak Kiowa, and I never understood her prayers, but there was something inherently sad in the sound, some merest hesitation upon the syllables of sorrow.
She began in a high and descending pitch, exhausting her breath to silence;
then again and again—and always the same intensity of effort, of something
that is, and is not, like urgency in the human voice. Transported so in the dancing light among the shadows of her room, she seemed beyond the reach of time.
But that was illusion; I think I knew then that I should not see her again.

Houses are like sentinels in the plain, old keepers of the weather watch.   11
There, in a very little while, wood takes on the appearance of great age. All
colors wear soon away in the wind and rain, and then the wood is burned gray
and the grain appears and the nails turn red with rust. The windowpanes are
black and opaque; you imagine there is nothing within, and indeed there
are many ghosts, bones given up to the land. They stand here and there against
the sky, and you approach them for a longer time than you expect. They belong
in the distance; it is their domain.

Once there was a lot of sound in my grandmother's house, a lot of coming   12
and going, feasting and talk. The summers there were full of excitement and
reunion. The Kiowas are a summer people; they abide the cold and keep to
themselves, but when the season turns and the land becomes warm and vital
they cannot hold still; an old love of going returns upon them. The aged visitors
who came to my grandmother's house when I was a child were made of lean
and leather, and they bore themselves upright. They wore great black hats and
bright ample shirts that shook in the wind. They rubbed fat upon their hair and
wound their braids with strips of colored cloth. Some of them painted their
faces and carried the scars of old and cherished enmities. They were an old
council of warlords, come to remind and be reminded of who they were. Their
wives and daughters served them well. The women might indulge themselves;
gossip was at once the mark and compensation of their servitude. They made
loud and elaborate talk among themselves, full of jest and gesture, fright and
false alarm. They went abroad in fringed and flowered shawls, bright beadwork

and German silver. They were at home in the kitchen, and they prepared meals that were banquets.

13    There were frequent prayer meetings, and great nocturnal feasts. When I was a child I played with my cousins outside, where the lamplight fell upon the ground and the singing of the old people rose up around us and carried away into the darkness. There were a lot of good things to eat, a lot of laughter and surprise. And afterwards, when the quiet returned, I lay down with my grandmother and could hear the frogs away by the river and feel the motion of the air.

14    Now there is funeral silence in the rooms, the endless wake of some final word. The walls have closed in upon my grandmother's house. When I returned to it in mourning, I saw for the first time in my life how small it was. It was late at night, and there was a white moon, nearly full. I sat for a long time on the stone steps by the kitchen door. From there I could see out across the land; I could see the long row of trees by the creek, the low light upon the rolling plains, and the stars of the Big Dipper. Once I looked at the moon and caught sight of a strange thing. A cricket had perched upon the handrail, only a few inches away from me. My line of vision was such that the creature filled the moon like a fossil. It had gone there, I thought, to live and die, for there, of all places, was its small definition made whole and eternal. A warm wind rose up and purled like the longing within me.

15    The next morning I awoke at dawn and went out on the dirt road to Rainy Mountain. It was already hot, and the grasshoppers began to fill the air. Still, it was early in the morning, and the birds sang out of the shadows. The long yellow grass on the mountain shone in the bright light, and a scissortail hied above the land. There, where it ought to be, at the end of a long and legendary way, was my grandmother's grave. Here and there on the dark stones were ancestral names. Looking back once, I saw the mountain and came away.

## COMPREHENSION

1.  What is the significance of Momaday's title? How does the title help explain the author's purpose?
2.  Why does Momaday return to his grandmother's house and journey to her grave? In what ways was her life tied to the land?
3.  List the various myths and legends the author mentions in the essay. What subjects do they treat? How are these subjects interrelated?

## RHETORIC

1.  What is the method of development in the first paragraph? How does the introduction, with its focus on Rainy Mountain, serve as a vehicle for the central meanings in the essay?
2.  Locate and explain instances of sensory, metaphorical, and symbolic language in the essay. Why are these modes of language consistent with the subject and thesis elaborated by Momaday?

3. How does Momaday's use of abstract language affect the concrete vocabulary in the essay?
4. What forms of narrative and description serve to unify this selection? Are the narrative patterns strictly linear? Is the descriptive technique cinematic? Explain.
5. How do the land, the Kiowas, and Momaday's grandmother serve as reinforcing frames in the essay?
6. How does Momaday create mood in this essay? Explain specifically the mood at the conclusion.

## WRITING

1. Write about a person and place that, taken together, inspire a special reverence in you.
2. Momaday implies that myth—especially nature myths—is central to his life and the life of the Kiowas. What *is* myth? Do you think that myth is as prominent in general American culture as it is in Kiowa culture? In what ways does it operate? How can myth sustain the individual, community, and nation? Write an analytical essay on this subject.
3. **Writing An Argument:** Write an essay in which you discuss Momaday's implied assertion that white Americans destroyed a way of Kiowa life that was rooted in reverence for nature and landscape. Determine whether you support this view.

 www.mhhe.com/ **mhreader**  |  For more information on N. Scott Momaday, go to:
**More Resources > Ch. 13 Nature & Environment**

# The Environmental Issue from Hell

### Bill McKibben

*Bill McKibben (b. 1960) was born in Palo Alto, California. After receiving a BA from Harvard University (1982), McKibben became a staff writer for* The New Yorker *magazine. McKibben's chief concern is the impact of humans on the environment and the ways in which consumerism affects the global ecosystem. A prominent writer for the environmental movement, he has published several books, among them* The End of Nature *(1989),* The Age of Missing Information *(1992),* Long Distance: A Year of Living Strenuously *(2000), and* Enough: Staying Human in an Engineered Age

*(2003). In the essay that follows, which was published in* These Times *in 2001, McKibben argues for a new approach to global warming.*

1   When global warming first emerged as a potential crisis in the late 1980s, one academic analyst called it "the public policy problem from hell." The years since have only proven him more astute: Fifteen years into our understanding of climate change, we have yet to figure out how we're going to tackle it. And environmentalists are just as clueless as anyone else: Do we need to work on lifestyle or on lobbying, on photovoltaics or on politics? And is there a difference? How well we handle global warming will determine what kind of century we inhabit—and indeed what kind of planet we leave behind. The issue cuts close to home and also floats off easily into the abstract. So far it has been the ultimate "can't get there from here" problem, but the time has come to draw a road map—one that may help us deal with the handful of other issues on the list of real, world-shattering problems.

2   Typically, when you're mounting a campaign, you look for self-interest, you scare people by saying what will happen to us if we don't do something: All the birds will die, the canyon will disappear beneath a reservoir, we will choke to death on smog. But in the case of global warming, that doesn't exactly do the trick, at least in the time frame we're discussing. In temperate latitudes, climate change will creep up on us. Severe storms already have grown more frequent and more damaging. The progression of seasons is less steady. Some agriculture is less reliable. But face it: Our economy is so enormous that it takes those changes in stride. Economists who work on this stuff talk about how it will shave a percentage or two off the GNP over the next few decades. And most of us live lives so divorced from the natural world that we hardly notice the changes anyway. Hotter? Turn up the air-conditioning. Stormier? Well, an enormous percentage of Americans commute from remote-controlled garage to office parking garage—it may have been some time since they got good and wet in a rainstorm. By the time the magnitude of the change is truly in our faces, it will be too late to do much about it: There's such a lag time to increased levels of carbon dioxide in the atmosphere that we need to be making the switch to solar and wind and hydrogen power right now to prevent disaster decades away. Yesterday, in fact.

3   So maybe we should think of global warming in a different way—as the great moral crisis of our time, the equivalent of the civil rights movement of the 1960s.

4   Why a moral question? In the first place, no one's ever figured out a more effective way to screw the marginalized and poor of this planet than climate change. Having taken their dignity, their resources, and their freedom under a variety of other schemes, we now are taking the very physical stability on which their already difficult lives depend.

5   Our economy can absorb these changes for a while, but consider Bangladesh for a moment. In 1998 the sea level in the Bay of Bengal was higher than normal, just the sort of thing we can expect to become more frequent and severe.

The waters sweeping down the Ganges and the Brahmaputra rivers from the Himalayas could not drain easily into the ocean—they backed up across the country, forcing most of its inhabitants to spend three months in thigh-deep water. The fall rice crop didn't get planted. We've seen this same kind of disaster over the past few years in Mozambique and Honduras and Venezuela and other places.

And global warming is a moral crisis, too, if you place any value on the rest 6 of creation. Coral reef researchers indicate that these spectacularly intricate ecosystems are also spectacularly vulnerable. Rising water temperatures are likely to bleach them to extinction by mid-century. In the Arctic, polar bears are 20 percent scrawnier than they were a decade ago: As pack ice melts, so does the opportunity for hunting seals. All in all, the 21st century seems poised to see extinctions at a rate not observed since the last big asteroid slammed into the planet. But this time the asteroid is us.

It's a moral question, finally, if you think we owe any debt to the future. No 7 one ever has figured out a more thoroughgoing way to strip-mine the present and degrade what comes after—all the people who will ever be related to you. Ever. No generation yet to come will ever forget us—we are the ones present at the moment when the temperature starts to spike, and so far we have not reacted. If it had been done to us, we would loathe the generation that did it, precisely as we will one day be loathed.

But trying to launch a moral campaign is no easy task. In most moral crises, 8 there is a villain—some person or class or institution that must be overcome. Once the villain is identified, the battle can commence. But you can't really get angry at carbon dioxide, and the people responsible for its production are, well, us. So perhaps we need some symbols to get us started, some places to sharpen the debate and rally ourselves to action. There are plenty to choose from: our taste for ever bigger houses and the heating and cooling bills that come with them, our penchant for jumping on airplanes at the drop of a hat. But if you wanted one glaring example of our lack of balance, you could do worse than point the finger at sport utility vehicles.

SUVs are more than mere symbols. They are a major part of the prob- 9 lem—we emit so much more carbon dioxide now than we did a decade ago in part because our fleet of cars and trucks actually has gotten steadily less fuel efficient for the past 10 years. If you switched today from the average American car to a big SUV, and drove it for just one year, the difference in carbon dioxide that you produced would be the equivalent of opening your refrigerator door and then forgetting to close it for six years. SUVs essentially are machines for burning fossil fuel that just happen to also move you and your stuff around.

But what makes them such a perfect symbol is the brute fact that they are 10 simply unnecessary. Go to the parking lot of the nearest suburban supermarket and look around: The only conclusion you can draw is that to reach the grocery, people must drive through three or four raging rivers and up the side of a canyon. These are semi-military machines, armored trucks on a slight diet. While they do not keep their occupants appreciably safer, they do wreck whatever they plow into, making them the perfect metaphor for a heedless, supersized society.

11    That's why we need a much broader politics than the Washington lobbying that's occupied the big environmental groups for the past decade. We need to take all the brilliant and energetic strategies of local grassroots groups fighting dumps and cleaning up rivers and apply those tactics in the national and international arenas. That's why some pastors are starting to talk with their congregations about what cars to buy, and why some college seniors are passing around petitions pledging to stay away from the Ford Explorers and Excursions, and why some auto dealers have begun to notice informational picketers outside their showrooms on Saturday mornings urging customers to think about gas mileage when they look at cars.

12    The point is not that such actions by themselves—any individual actions—will make any real dent in the levels of carbon dioxide pouring into our atmosphere. Even if you got 10 percent of Americans really committed to changing their energy use, their solar homes wouldn't make much of a difference in our national totals. But 10 percent would be enough to change the politics around the issue, enough to pressure politicians to pass laws that would cause us all to shift our habits. And so we need to begin to take an issue that is now the province of technicians and turn it into a political issue, just as bus boycotts began to make public the issue of race, forcing the system to respond. That response is likely to be ugly—there are huge companies with a lot to lose, and many people so tied in to their current ways of life that advocating change smacks of subversion. But this has to become a political issue—and fast. The only way that may happen, short of a hideous drought or monster flood, is if it becomes a personal issue first.

## COMPREHENSION

1. According to McKibben, what are the causes of global warming?
2. What instances of ecological disaster does the writer say will occur if we do not change our habits?
3. Why is a new approach to the problem of global warming needed? What approach does McKibben suggest?

## RHETORIC

1. How does McKibben's title capture the tone of the essay? What is his purpose in writing the essay? Does he see his readers as hostile or sympathetic to his position? How do you know?
2. How does McKibben develop his introduction? Why does he pose questions? Where does he state his claim?
3. Does McKibben make his argument through appeals to reason, emotion, ethics—or a combination of these elements? Justify your response.

4. How does the writer contend with possible objections to his position on global warming?
5. Explain the pattern of cause and effect that McKibben uses to structure his essay.
6. What varieties of evidence does the writer present to support his claim? What extended illustration does he provide? How effective is it, and why?
7. In the concluding paragraph, McKibben issues a call to action. How does the body of the essay prepare the reader for this persuasive appeal?

## WRITING

1. Write an essay in which you explain your own sense of the causes and effects of global warming.
2. Research your state's policy toward global warming. Present your findings in a summary essay.
3. **Writing an Argument:** McKibben argues that SUVs are a primary cause of wastefulness and global warming and that both moral persuasion and political activism are required to change consumers' habits. Do you agree or disagree with his assertions? Write an argumentative essay responding to this issue.

www.mhhe.com/
**mhreader**
For more information on Bill McKibben, go to:
**More Resources > Ch. 13 Nature & Environment**

# The Obligation to Endure

## Rachel Carson

*Rachel Carson (1907–1964) was a seminal figure in the environmental movement. Born in Pennsylvania, she awakened public consciousness to environmental issues through her writing. Her style was both literary and scientific as she described nature's riches in such books as* The Sea around Us *(1951) and* The Edge of the Sea *(1954). Her last book,* Silent Spring *(1962), aroused controversy and concern with its indictment of insecticides. In the following excerpt from that important book, Carson provides compelling evidence of the damage caused by indiscriminate use of insecticides and the danger of disturbing the earth's delicate balance.*

1   The history of life on earth has been a history of interaction between living things and their surroundings. To a large extent, the physical form and the habits of the earth's vegetation and its animal life have been molded by the environment. Considering the whole span of earthly time, the opposite effect, in which life actually modifies its surroundings, has been relatively slight. Only within the moment of time represented by the present century has one species—man—acquired significant power to alter the nature of his world.

2   During the past quarter century this power has not only increased to one of disturbing magnitude but it has changed in character. The most alarming of all man's assaults upon the environment is the contamination of air, earth, rivers, and sea with dangerous and even lethal materials. This pollution is for the most part irrecoverable; the chain of evil it initiates not only in the world that must support life but in living tissues is for the most part irreversible. In this now universal contamination of the environment, chemicals are the sinister and little-recognized partners of radiation in changing the very nature of the world—the very nature of its life. Strontium 90, released through nuclear explosions into the air, comes to earth in rain or drifts down as fallout, lodges in soil, enters into the grass or corn or wheat grown there, and in time takes up its abode in the bones of a human being, there to remain until his death. Similarly, chemicals sprayed on croplands or forests or gardens lie long in soil, entering into living organisms, passing from one to another in a chain of poisoning and death. Or they pass mysteriously by underground streams until they emerge and, through the alchemy of air and sunlight, combine into new forms that kill vegetation, sicken cattle, and work unknown harm on those who drink from once pure wells. As Albert Schweitzer has said, "Man can hardly even recognize the devils of his own creation."

3   It took hundreds of millions of years to produce the life that now inhabits the earth—eons of time in which that developing and evolving and diversifying life reached a state of adjustment and balance with its surroundings. The environment, rigorously shaping and directing the life it supported, contained elements that were hostile as well as supporting. Certain rocks gave out dangerous radiation; even within the light of the sun, from which all life draws its energy, there were shortwave radiations with power to injure. Given time—time not in years but in millennia—life adjusts, and a balance has been reached. For time is the essential ingredient; but in the modern world there is no time.

4   The rapidity of change and the speed with which new situations are created follow the impetuous and heedless pace of man rather than the deliberate pace of nature. Radiation is no longer merely the background radiation of rocks, the bombardment of cosmic rays, the ultraviolet of the sun that have existed before there was any life on earth; radiation is now the unnatural creation of man's tampering with the atom. The chemicals to which life is asked to make its adjustment are no longer merely the calcium and silica and copper and all the rest of the minerals washed out of the rocks and carried in rivers to the sea; they

are the synthetic creations of man's inventive mind, brewed in his laboratories, and having no counterparts in nature.

To adjust to these chemicals would require time on the scale that is 5 nature's; it would require not merely the years of a man's life but the life of generations. And even this, were it by some miracle possible, would be futile, for the new chemicals come from our laboratories in an endless stream; almost five hundred annually find their way into actual use in the United States alone. The figure is staggering and its implications are not easily grasped— 500 new chemicals to which the bodies of men and animals are required somehow to adapt each year, chemicals totally outside the limits of biologic experience.

Among them are many that are used in man's war against nature. Since 6 the mid-1940s over 200 basic chemicals have been created for use in killing insects, weeds, rodents, and other organisms described in the modern vernacular as "pests"; and they are sold under several thousand different brand names.

These sprays, dusts, and aerosols are now applied almost universally to 7 farms, gardens, forests, and homes—nonselective chemicals that have the power to kill every insect, the "good" and the "bad," to still the song of birds and the leaping of fish in the streams, to coat the leaves with a deadly film, and to linger on in soil—all this though the intended target may be only a few weeds or insects. Can anyone believe it is possible to lay down such a barrage of poisons on the surface of the earth without making it unfit for all life? They should not be called "insecticides," but "biocides."

The whole process of spraying seems caught up in an endless spiral. Since 8 DDT was released for civilian use, a process of escalation has been going on in which ever more toxic materials must be found. This has happened because insects, in a triumphant vindication of Darwin's principle of the survival of the fittest, have evolved super races immune to the particular insecticide used, hence a deadlier one has always to be developed—and then a deadlier one than that. It has happened also because, for reasons to be described later, destructive insects often undergo a "flareback," or resurgence, after spraying in numbers greater than before. Thus the chemical war is never won, and all life is caught in its violent crossfire.

Along with the possibility of the extinction of mankind by nuclear war, the 9 central problem of our age has therefore become the contamination of man's total environment with such substances of incredible potential for harm— substances that accumulate in the tissues of plants and animals and even penetrate the germ cells to shatter or alter the very material of heredity upon which the shape of the future depends.

Some would-be architects of our future look toward a time when it will be 10 possible to alter the human germ plasm by design. But we may easily be doing so now by inadvertence, for many chemicals, like radiation, bring about gene mutations. It is ironic to think that man might determine his own future by something so seemingly trivial as the choice of an insect spray.

11      All this has been risked—for what? Future historians may well be amazed by our distorted sense of proportion. How could intelligent beings seek to control a few unwanted species by a method that contaminated the entire environment and brought the threat of disease and death even to their own kind? Yet this is precisely what we have done. We have done it, moreover, for reasons that collapse the moment we examine them. We are told that the enormous and expanding use of pesticides is necessary to maintain farm production. Yet is our real problem not one of *overproduction?* Our farms, despite measures to remove acreages from production and to pay farmers *not* to produce, have yielded such a staggering excess of crops that the American taxpayer in 1962 is paying out more than one billion dollars a year as the total carrying cost of the surplus-food storage program. And is the situation helped when one branch of the Agriculture Department tries to reduce production while another states, as it did in 1958, "It is believed generally that reduction of crop acreages under provisions of the Soil Bank will stimulate interest in use of chemicals to obtain maximum production on the land retained in crops."

12      All this is not to say there is no insect problem and no need of control. I am saying, rather, that control must be geared to realities, not to mythical situations, and that the methods employed must be such that they do not destroy us along with the insects.

13   The problem whose attempted solution has brought such a train of disaster in its wake is an accompaniment of our modern way of life. Long before the age of man, insects inhabited the earth—a group of extraordinarily varied and adaptable beings. Over the course of time since man's advent, a small percentage of the more than half a million species of insects have come into conflict with human welfare in two principal ways: as competitors for the food supply and as carriers of human disease.

14      Disease-carrying insects become important where human beings are crowded together, especially under conditions where sanitation is poor, as in times of natural disaster or war or in situations of extreme poverty and deprivation. Then control of some sort becomes necessary. It is a sobering fact, however, as we shall presently see, that the method of massive chemical control has had only limited success, and also threatens to worsen the very conditions it is intended to curb.

15      Under primitive agricultural conditions the farmer had few insect problems. These arose with the intensification of agriculture—the devotion of immense acreages to a single crop. Such a system set the stage for explosive increases in specific insect populations. Single-crop farming does not take advantage of the principles by which nature works; it is agriculture as an engineer might conceive it to be. Nature has introduced great variety into the landscape, but man has displayed a passion for simplifying it. Thus he undoes the built-in checks and balances by which nature holds the species within bounds. One important natural check is a limit on the amount of suitable habitat for

each species. Obviously then, an insect that lives on wheat can build up its population to much higher levels on a farm devoted to wheat than on one in which wheat is intermingled with other crops to which the insect is not adapted.

The same thing happens in other situations. A generation or more ago, 16 the towns of large areas of the United States lined their streets with the noble elm tree. Now the beauty they hopefully created is threatened with complete destruction as disease sweeps through the elms, carried by a beetle that would have only limited chance to build up large populations and to spread from tree to tree if the elms were only occasional trees in a richly diversified planting.

Another factor in the modern insect problem is one that must be viewed 17 against a background of geologic and human history: the spreading of thousands of different kinds of organisms from their native homes to invade new territories. This worldwide migration has been studied and graphically described by the British ecologist Charles Elton in his recent book *The Ecology of Invasions*. During the Cretaceous Period, some hundred million years ago, flooding seas cut many land bridges between continents and living things found themselves confined in what Elton calls "colossal separate nature reserves." There, isolated from others of their kind, they developed many new species. When some of the land masses were joined again, about 15 million years ago, these species began to move out into new territories—a movement that is not only still in progress but is now receiving considerable assistance from man.

The importation of plants is the primary agent in the modern spread of spe- 18 cies, for animals have almost invariably gone along with the plants, quarantine being a comparatively recent and not completely effective innovation. The United States Office of Plant Introduction alone has introduced almost 200,000 species and varieties of plants from all over the world. Nearly half of the 180 or so major insect enemies of plants in the United States are accidental imports from abroad, and most of them have come as hitchhikers on plants.

In new territory, out of reach of the restraining hand of the natural enemies 19 that kept down its numbers in its native land, an invading plant or animal is able to become enormously abundant. Thus it is no accident that our most troublesome insects are introduced species.

These invasions, both the naturally occurring and those dependent on hu- 20 man assistance, are likely to continue indefinitely. Quarantine and massive chemical campaigns are only extremely expensive ways of buying time. We are faced, according to Dr. Elton, "with a life-and-death need not just to find new technological means of suppressing this plant or that animal"; instead we need the basic knowledge of animal populations and their relations to their surroundings that will "promote an even balance and damp down the explosive power of outbreaks and new invasions."

Much of the necessary knowledge is now available but we do not use it. 21 We train ecologists in our universities and even employ them in our governmental agencies but we seldom take their advice. We allow the chemical death rain to fall as though there were no alternative, whereas in fact there are many, and our ingenuity could soon discover many more if given opportunity.

22      Have we fallen into a mesmerized state that makes us accept as inevitable that which is inferior or detrimental, as though having lost the will or the vision to demand that which is good? Such thinking, in the words of the ecologist Paul Shepard, "idealizes life with only its head out of water, inches above the limits of toleration of the corruption of its own environment. . . . Why should we tolerate a diet of weak poisons, a home in insipid surroundings, a circle of acquaintances who are not quite our enemies, the noise of motors with just enough relief to prevent insanity? Who would want to live in a world which is just not quite fatal?"

23      Yet such a world is pressed upon us. The crusade to create a chemically sterile, insect-free world seems to have engendered a fanatic zeal on the part of many specialists and most of the so-called control agencies. On every hand there is evidence that those engaged in spraying operations exercise a ruthless power. "The regulatory entomologists . . . function as prosecutor, judge and jury, tax assessor and collector and sheriff to enforce their own orders," said Connecticut entomologist Neely Turner. The most flagrant abuses go unchecked in both state and federal agencies.

24      It is not my contention that chemical insecticides must never be used. I do contend that we have put poisonous and biologically potent chemicals indiscriminately into the hands of persons largely or wholly ignorant of their potentials for harm. We have subjected enormous numbers of people to contact with these poisons, without their consent and often without their knowledge. If the Bill of Rights contains no guarantee that a citizen shall be secure against lethal poisons distributed either by private individuals or by public officials, it is surely only because our forefathers, despite their considerable wisdom and foresight, could conceive of no such problem.

25      I contend, furthermore, that we have allowed these chemicals to be used with little or no advance investigation of their effect on soil, water, wildlife, and man himself. Future generations are unlikely to condone our lack of prudent concern for the integrity of the natural world that supports all life.

26      There is still very limited awareness of the nature of the threat. This is an era of specialists, each of whom sees his own problem and is unaware of or intolerant of the larger frame into which it fits. It is also an era dominated by industry, in which the right to make a dollar at whatever cost is seldom challenged. When the public protests, confronted with some obvious evidence of damaging results of pesticide applications, it is fed little tranquilizing pills of half truth. We urgently need an end to these false assurances, to the sugar coating of unpalatable facts. It is the public that is being asked to assume the risks that the insect controllers calculate. The public must decide whether it wishes to continue on the present road, and it can do so only when in full

possession of the facts. In the words of Jean Rostand, "The obligation to endure gives us the right to know."

## COMPREHENSION

1. What does Carson mean by "the obligation to endure"?
2. What reasons does the author cite for the overpopulation of insects?
3. What remedies does Carson propose?

## RHETORIC

1. What tone does Carson use in her essay? Does she seem to be a subjective
   or an objective writer? Give specific support for your response.
2. How does the use of words such as *dangerous, evil, irrevocable,* and *sinister*
   help shape the reader's reaction to the piece? What emotional and ethical
   appeals do such words indicate?
3. Examine the ordering of ideas in paragraph 4, and consider how such an
   order serves to reinforce Carson's argument.
4. Paragraph 9 consists of only one (long) sentence. What is its function in the
   essay's scheme?
5. Examine Carson's use of expert testimony. How does it help strengthen her
   thesis?
6. How effectively does the essay's conclusion help tie up Carson's points?
   What is the writer's intent in this final paragraph? How does she accomplish this aim?

## WRITING

1. Write an essay in which you suggest solutions to the problems brought up
   in Carson's piece. You may want to suggest measures that the average citizen can take to eliminate the casual use of insecticides to control the insect
   population.
2. Write a biographical research paper on Carson that focuses on her involvement with nature and environmental issues.
3. **Writing an Argument:** Write an essay titled "Insects Are Not the Problem;
   Humanity Is." In this essay, argue that it is humanity's greed that has
   caused such an imbalance in nature as to threaten the planet's survival.

www.mhhe.com/
**mhreader**

For more information on Rachel Carson, go to:
**More Resources > Ch. 13 Nature &
Environment**

# Am I Blue?

## Alice Walker

*Alice Walker (b. 1944) was born in Eatonton, Georgia; attended Spelman College; and graduated from Sarah Lawrence College. Besides being a prolific novelist, short-story writer, poet, and essayist, she has also been active in the civil rights movement. She often draws on both her own history and historical records to reflect on the African American experience. Some of her well-known books are* The Color Purple *(1976),* You Can't Keep a Good Woman Down *(1981),* Living in the World: Selected Writings, 1973–1987 *(1987),* The Temple of My Familiar *(1989),* By the Light of My Father's Smile *(1999), and* The Way Forward Is with a Broken Heart *(2001). In the following essay from* Living in the World, *Walker questions the distinctions commonly made between human and animal.*

1   For about three years my companion and I rented a small house in the country that stood on the edge of a large meadow that appeared to run from the end of our deck straight into the mountains. The mountains, however, were quite far away, and between us and them there was, in fact, a town. It was one of the many pleasant aspects of the house that you never really were aware of this.

2   It was a house of many windows, low, wide, nearly floor to ceiling in the living room, which faced the meadow, and it was from one of these that I first saw our closest neighbor, a large white horse, cropping grass, flipping its mane, and ambling about— not over the entire meadow, which stretched well out of sight of the house, but over the five or so fenced-in acres that were next to the twenty-odd that we had rented. I soon learned that the horse, whose name was Blue, belonged to a man who lived in another town, but was boarded by our neighbors next door. Occasionally, one of the children, usually a stocky teenager, but sometimes a much younger girl or boy, could be seen riding Blue. They would appear in the meadow, climb up on his back, ride furiously for ten or fifteen minutes, then get off, slap Blue on the flanks, and not be seen again for a month or more.

3   There were many apple trees in our yard, and one by the fence that Blue could almost reach. We were soon in the habit of feeding him apples, which he relished, especially because by the middle of summer the meadow grasses—so green and succulent since January—had dried out from lack of rain, and Blue stumbled about munching the dried stalks half-heartedly. Sometimes he would stand very still just by the apple tree, and when one of us came out he would whinny, snort loudly, or stamp the ground. This meant, of course: I want an apple.

It was quite wonderful to pick a few apples, or collect those that had fallen to    4
the ground overnight, and patiently hold them, one by one, up to his large, toothy
mouth. I remained as thrilled as a child by his flexible dark lips, huge, cubelike
teeth that crunched the apples, core and all, with such finality, and his high, broad-
breasted *enormity;* beside which, I felt small indeed. When I was a child, I used to
ride horses, and was especially friendly with one named Nan until the day I was
riding and my brother deliberately spooked her and I was thrown, head first,
against the trunk of a tree. When I came to, I was in bed and my mother was bending worriedly over me; we silently agreed that perhaps horseback riding was not
the safest sport for me. Since then I have walked, and prefer walking to horseback
riding—but I had forgotten the depth of feeling one could see in horses' eyes.

I was therefore unprepared for the expression in Blue's. Blue was lonely.    5
Blue was horribly lonely and bored. I was not shocked that this should be the
case; five acres to tramp by yourself, endlessly, even in the most beautiful of
meadows—and his was—cannot provide many interesting events, and once the
rainy season turned to dry that was about it. No, I was shocked that I had forgotten that human animals and nonhuman animals can communicate quite
well; if we are brought up around animals as children we take this for granted.
By the time we are adults we no longer remember. However, the animals have
not changed. They are in fact *completed* creations (at least they seem to be, so
much more than we) who are not likely *to* change; it is their nature to express
themselves. What else are they going to express? And they do. And, generally
speaking, they are ignored.

After giving Blue the apples, I would wander back to the house, aware that    6
he was observing me. Were more apples not forthcoming then? Was that to be
his sole entertainment for the day? My partner's small son had decided he
wanted to learn how to piece a quilt; we worked in silence on our respective
squares as I thought . . .

Well, about slavery: about white children, who were raised by black people,    7
who knew their first all-accepting love from black women, and then, when they
were twelve or so, were told they must "forget" the deep levels of communication between themselves and "mammy" that they knew. Later they would be
able to relate quite calmly, "My old mammy was sold to another good family."
"My old mammy was _____." Fill in the blank. Many more years later a
white woman would say: "I can't understand these Negroes, these blacks. What
do they want? They're so different from us."

And about the Indians, considered to be "like animals" by the "settlers" (a    8
very benign euphemism for what they actually were), who did not understand
their description as a compliment.

And about the thousands of American men who marry Japanese, Korean,    9
Filipina, and other non-English-speaking women and of how happy they report
they are, *"blissfully,"* until their brides learn to speak English, at which point the
marriages tend to fall apart. What then did the men see, when they looked into
the eyes of the women they married, before they could speak English? Apparently only their own reflections.

10    I thought of society's impatience with the young. "Why are they playing the music so loud?" Perhaps the children have listened to much of the music of oppressed people their parents danced to before they were born, with its passionate but soft cries for acceptance and love, and they have wondered why their parents failed to hear.

11    I do not know how long Blue had inhabited his five beautiful, boring acres before we moved into our house; a year after we had arrived—and had also traveled to other valleys, other cities, other worlds—he was still there.

12    But then, in our second year at the house, something happened in Blue's life. One morning, looking out the window at the fog that lay like a ribbon over the meadow, I saw another horse, a brown one, at the other end of Blue's field. Blue appeared to be afraid of it, and for several days made no attempt to go near. We went away for a week. When we returned, Blue had decided to make friends and the two horses ambled or galloped along together, and Blue did not come nearly as often to the fence underneath the apple tree.

13    When he did, bringing his new friend with him, there was a different look in his eyes. A look of independence, of self-possession, of inalienable *horse*ness. His friend eventually became pregnant. For months and months there was, it seemed to me, a mutual feeling between me and the horses of justice, of peace. I fed apples to them both. The look in Blue's eyes was one of unabashed "this is *it*ness."

14    It did not, however, last forever. One day, after a visit to the city, I went out to give Blue some apples. He stood waiting, or so I thought, though not beneath the tree. When I shook the tree and jumped back from the shower of apples, he made no move. I carried some over to him. He managed to half-crunch one. The rest he let fall to the ground. I dreaded looking into his eyes—because I had of course noticed that Brown, his partner, had gone—but I did look. If I had been born into slavery, and my partner had been sold or killed, my eyes would have looked like that. The children next door explained that Blue's partner had been "put with him" (the same expression that old people used, I had noticed, when speaking of an ancestor during slavery who had been impregnated by her owner) so that they could mate and she conceive. Since that was accomplished, she had been taken back by her owner, who lived somewhere else.

15    Will she be back? I asked.

16    They didn't know.

17    Blue was like a crazed person. Blue *was*, to me, a crazed person. He galloped furiously, as if he were being ridden, around and around his five beautiful acres. He whinnied until he couldn't. He tore at the ground with his hooves. He butted himself against his single shade tree. He looked always and always toward the road down which his partner had gone. And then, occasionally, when he came up for apples, or I took apples to him, he looked at me. It was a look so piercing, so full of grief, a look so *human*, I almost laughed (I felt too sad to cry) to think there are people who do not know that animals suffer. People like me who have forgotten, and daily forget, all that animals try to tell us. "Everything you do to us will happen to you; we are your teachers, as you are ours. We are one lesson" is essentially it, I think. There are those who never once have even considered

animals' rights: those who have been taught that animals actually want to be used and abused by us, as small children "love" to be frightened, or women "love" to be mutilated and raped . . . . They are the great-grandchildren of those who honestly thought, because someone taught them this: "Woman can't think" and "niggers can't faint." But most disturbing of all, in Blue's large brown eyes was a new look, more painful than the look of despair: the look of disgust with human beings, with life; the look of hatred. And it was odd what the look of hatred did. It gave him, for the first time, the look of a beast. And what that meant was that he had put up a barrier within to protect himself from further violence; all the apples in the world wouldn't change that fact.

And so Blue remained, a beautiful part of our landscape, very peaceful to    18
look at from the window, white against the grass. Once a friend came to visit and said, looking out on the soothing view: "And it *would* have to be a *white* horse; the very image of freedom." And I thought, yes, the animals are forced to become for us merely "images" of what they once so beautifully expressed. And we are used to drinking milk from containers showing "contented" cows, whose real lives we want to hear nothing about, eating eggs and drumsticks from "happy" hens, and munching hamburgers advertised by bulls of integrity who seem to command their fate.

As we talked of freedom and justice one day for all, we sat down to steaks.    19
I am eating misery, I thought, as I took the first bite. And spit it out.

## COMPREHENSION

1. What is the major thesis of the essay? Is it stated explicitly in the text, or does one have to infer it? Explain.
2. In paragraph 5, Walker states that animals are "*completed* creations (at least they seem to be, so much more than we) who are not likely to change." What does she mean by making this distinction between animals and humans?
3. What is the significance of the title of the essay? Does it have more than one meaning? Explain your answer.

## RHETORIC

1. In paragraph 4, Walker creates a vivid description of Blue. How does she achieve this?
2. In paragraph 7, Walker makes a cognitive association between the relationship between humans and animals and the relationship between whites and blacks during slavery. Does this transition seem too abrupt, or is there a rhetorical reason for the immediate comparison? Explain.
3. Explore the other analogies Walker makes in paragraphs 7 and 8. Are they pertinent? What is the rhetorical effect of juxtaposing seemingly different realms to convey one central idea?

4. Walker often breaks the conventions of "college English." For example, paragraphs 8 and 9 both begin with the coordinating conjunction *and*. Paragraph 12 begins with the coordinating conjunction *but*. Paragraphs 15 and 16 are only one short sentence each. Explain the effect of each of these rhetorical devices. Find three other unusual rhetorical strategies—either on the paragraph or sentence level—and explain their effects.

5. In paragraphs 17 and 18, Walker speeds up the tempo of her writing by beginning many of the sentences with the conjunction *and*. What is the purpose and rhetorical effect of this strategy, and how does it mimic—in linguistic terms—Blue's altered emotional state?

6. Walker seems to have a profound empathy for animals, yet it is only at the end that she is repulsed by the thought of eating meat. What rhetorical strategy is she employing in the conclusion that helps bring closure to her meditation on Blue? Does it matter whether the culminating event actually occurred in her experience, or is it all right for an essayist to use poetic license for stylistic purposes?

## WRITING

1. Write a personal essay in which you describe your relationship with a favorite pet. Include your observations of, responses to, and attitude toward your pet. Compare and contrast this relationship to those you have with humans.

2. Some writers have argued that it matters little if certain "nonessential" endangered species become extinct if they interfere with "human progress." Argue for or against this proposition.

3. **Writing an Argument:** Argue for or against one of the following practices: **(a)** hunting for the sake of the hunt, **(b)** eating meat, or **(c)** keeping animals in zoos.

www.mhhe.com/
**mhreader**

For more information on Alice Walker, go to:
**More Resources > Ch. 13 Nature & Environment**

# The Greenest Campuses: An Idiosyncratic Guide

### Noel Perrin

*Noel Perrin (b. 1927) was born in New York City and worked as an editor before start-*
*ing a career as a college instructor at the University of North Carolina and then Dart-*
*mouth College, where he has taught since 1959. He has been awarded two Guggenheim*
*Fellowships, has been a contributor to numerous periodicals, and has authored more*
*than 10 books. His subject matter has ranged from the scholarly, such as* Dr. Bowdler's
Legacy *(1969) and* Giving Up the Gun: Japan's Reversion to the Sword, 1543–
1879 *(1979), to his experiences as a part-time farmer. Among the latter are* First Person
Plural *(1978),* Second Person Plural *(1980),* Third Person Plural *(1983), and* Last
Person Plural *(1991). His concerns about the environment have made him a popular*
*speaker on ecological issues. In the following essay, first published in* The Chronicle of
Higher Education *in April 2001, Perrin creates his own "best" college guide by*
*ranking institutions of higher learning according to their environmental awareness.*

About 1,100 American colleges and universities run at least a token environmental-   1
studies program, and many hundreds of those programs offer well-designed
and useful courses. But only a drastically smaller number practice even a portion of what they teach. The one exception is recycling. Nearly every institution
that has so much as one lonely environmental-studies course also does a little
halfhearted recycling. Paper and glass, usually.

There are some glorious exceptions to those rather churlish observations,   2
I'm glad to say. How many? Nobody knows. No one has yet done the necessary
research (though the National Wildlife Federation's Campus Ecology program
is planning a survey).

Certainly *U.S. News & World Report* hasn't. Look at the rankings in their   3
annual college issue. The magazine uses a complex formula something like this:
Institution's reputation, 25 percent; student-retention rate, 20 percent; faculty
resources, 20 percent; and so on, down to alumni giving, 5 percent. The lead
criterion may help explain why Harvard, Yale, and Princeton Universities so
frequently do a little dance at the top of the list.

But *U.S. News* has nothing at all to say about the degree to which a college   4
or university attempts to behave sustainably—that is, to manage its campus
and activities in ways that promote the long-term health of the planet. The
magazine is equally mum about which of the institutions it is ranking can serve
as models to society in a threatened world.

And, of course, the world is threatened. When the Royal Society in London   5
and the National Academy of Sciences in Washington issued their first-ever

joint statement, it ended like this: "The future of our planet is in the balance. Sustainable development can be achieved, but only if irreversible degradation of the environment can be halted in time. The next 30 years may be crucial." They said that in 1992. If all those top scientists are right, we have a little more than 20 years left in which to make major changes in how we live.

6    All this affects colleges. I have one environmentalist friend who loves to point out to the deans and trustees she meets that if we don't make such changes, and if the irreversible degradation of earth does occur, Harvard's huge endowment and Yale's lofty reputation will count for nothing.

7    But though *U.S. News* has nothing to say, fortunately there is a fairly good grapevine in the green world. I have spent considerable time in the past two years using it like an organic cell phone. By that means I have come up with a short, idiosyncratic list of green colleges, consisting of six that are a healthy green, two that are greener still, and three that I believe are the greenest in the United States.

8    Which approved surveying techniques have I used? None at all. Some of my evidence is anecdotal, and some of my conclusions are affected by my personal beliefs, such as that electric and hybrid cars are not just a good idea, but instruments of salvation.

9    Obviously I did not examine, even casually, all 1,100 institutions. I'm sure I have missed some outstanding performers. I hope I have missed a great many.

10    Now, here are the 11, starting with **Brown University.**

11    It is generally harder for a large urban university to move toward sustainable behavior than it is for a small-town college with maybe a thousand students. But it's not impossible. Both Brown, in the heart of Providence, R.I., and Yale University (by no means an environmental leader in other respects), in the heart of New Haven, Conn., have found a country way of dealing with food waste. Pigs. Both rely on pigs.

12    For the past 10 years, Brown has been shipping nearly all of its food waste to a Rhode Island piggery. Actually, not shipping it—just leaving it out at dawn each morning. The farmer comes to the campus and gets it. Not since Ralph Waldo Emerson took food scraps out to the family pig have these creatures enjoyed such a high intellectual connection.

13    But there is a big difference in scale. Where Emerson might have one pail of slops now and then, Brown generates 700 tons of edible garbage each year. Haulage fee: $0. Tipping fee: $0. (That's the cost of dumping the garbage into huge cookers, where it is heated for the pigs.) Annual savings to Brown: about $50,000. Addition to the American food supply: many tons of ham and bacon each year.

14    Of course, Brown does far more than feed a balanced diet to a lot of pigs. That's just the most exotic (for an urban institution) of its green actions. "Brown is Green" became the official motto of the university in August 1990. It was accurate then, and it remains accurate now.

Yale is the only other urban institution I'm aware of that supports a pig 15 population. Much of the credit goes to Cyril May, the university's environmental coordinator, just as much of the credit at Brown goes to its environmental coordinator, Kurt Teichert.

May has managed to locate two Connecticut piggeries. The one to which he 16 sends garbage presents problems. The farmer has demanded—and received—a collection fee. And he has developed an antagonistic relationship with some of Yale's food-service people. (There are a lot of them: The campus has 16 dining facilities.) May is working on an arrangement with the second piggery. But if it falls through, he says, "I may go back on semibended knee to the other."

Yale does not make the list as a green college, for reasons you will learn 17 later in this essay. But it might in a few more years

**Carleton College** is an interesting example of an institution turning green 18 almost overnight. No pig slops here; the dining halls are catered by Marriott. But change is coming fast.

In the summer of 1999, Carleton appointed its first-ever environmental 19 coordinator, a brand-new graduate named Rachel Smit. The one-year appointment was an experiment, with a cobbled-together salary and the humble title of "fifth-year intern." The experiment worked beyond anyone's expectation.

Smit began publishing an environmental newsletter called *The Green Bean* 20 and organized a small committee of undergraduates to explore the feasibility of composting the college's food waste, an effort that will soon begin. A surprised Marriott has already found itself serving organic dinners on Earth Day.

Better yet, the college set up an environmental-advisory committee of three 21 administrators, three faculty members, and three students to review all campus projects from a green perspective. Naturally, many of those projects will be buildings, and to evaluate them, Carleton is using the *Minnesota Sustainable Design Guide*, itself cowritten by Richard Strong, director of facilities.

The position of fifth-year intern is now a permanent one-year position, and 22 its salary is a regular part of the budget.

What's next? If Carleton gets a grant it has applied for, there will be a mas- 23 sive increase in environmental-studies courses and faculty seminars and, says the dean of budgets, "a whole range of green campus projects under the rubric of 'participatory learning.'"

And if Carleton doesn't get the grant? Same plans, slower pace. 24

Twenty years ago, **Dartmouth College** would have been a contender for 25 the title of greenest college in America, had such a title existed. It's still fairly green. It has a large and distinguished group of faculty members who teach environmental studies, good recycling, an organic farm that was used last summer in six courses, years of experience with solar panels, and a fair number of midlevel administrators (including three in the purchasing office) who are ardent believers in sustainability.

But the college has lost ground. Most troubling is its new $50-million 26 library, which has an actual anti-environmental twist: A portion of the roof requires steam from the power plant to melt snow off of it. The architect, Robert Venturi, may be famous, but he's no environmentalist.

27      Dartmouth is a striking example of what I shall modestly call Perrin's Law: No college or university can move far toward sustainability without the active support of at least two senior administrators. Dartmouth has no such committed senior administrators at all. It used to. James Hornig, a former dean of sciences, and Frank Smallwood, a former provost, were instrumental in creating the environmental-studies program, back in 1970. They are now emeriti. The current senior administrators are not in the least hostile to sustainability; they just give a very low priority to the college's practicing what it preaches.

28      **Emory University** is probably further into the use of nonpolluting and low-polluting motor vehicles than any other college in the country. According to Eric Gaither, senior associate vice president for business affairs, 60 percent of Emory's fleet is powered by alternative fuels. The facilities-management office has 40 electric carts, which maintenance workers use for getting around campus. The community-service office (security and parking) has its own electric carts and an electric patrol vehicle. There are five electric shuttle buses and 14 compressed–natural-gas buses on order, plus one natural-gas bus in service.

29      Bill Chace, Emory's president, has a battery-charging station for electric cars in his garage, and until recently an electric car to charge. Georgia Power, which lent the car, has recalled it, but Chace hopes to get it back. Meanwhile, he rides his bike to work most of the time.

30      How has Emory made such giant strides? "It's easy to do," says Gaither, "when your president wants you to."

31      If Carleton is a model of how a small college turns green, the **University of Michigan at Ann Arbor** is a model of how a big university does. Carleton is changing pretty much as an entity, while Michigan is more like the Electoral College—50 separate entities. The School of Natural Resources casts its 6 votes for sustainability, the English department casts its 12 for humanistic studies, the recycling coordinator casts her 1, the electric-vehicle program casts its 2, and so on. An institution of Michigan's size changes in bits and pieces.

32      Some of the bits show true leadership. For example, the university is within weeks of buying a modest amount of green power. It makes about half of its own electricity (at its heating plant) and buys the other half. Five percent of that other half soon will come from renewable sources: hydro (water power) and biomass (so-called fuel crops, which are grown specifically to be burned for power).

33      The supporters of sustainability at Michigan would like to see the university adopt a version of what is known as the Kyoto Protocol. The agreement, which the United States so far has refused to sign, requires that by 2012 each nation reduce its emission of greenhouse gases to 7 percent below its 1990 figure. Michigan's version of the protocol, at present a pipe dream, would require the university to do what the government won't—accept that reduction as a goal.

34      The immediate goal of "sustainabilists" at Ann Arbor is the creation of a universitywide environmental coordinator, who would work either in the president's or the provost's office.

Giants are slow, but they are also strong.                                    35

**Tulane University** has the usual programs, among green institutions, in     36
recycling, composting, and energy efficiency. But what sets it apart is the Tulane
Environmental Law Clinic, which is staffed by third-year law students. The director is a faculty member, and there are three law "fellows," all lawyers, who
work with the students. The clinic does legal work for environmental organizations across Louisiana and "most likely has had a greater environmental impact
than all our other efforts combined," says Elizabeth Davey, Tulane's first-ever
environmental coordinator.

At least two campuses of the **University of California** (Berkeley is not among   37
them) have taken a first and even a second step toward sustainable behavior.
First step: symbolic action, like installing a few solar panels, to produce clean
energy and to help educate students. With luck, one of those little solar arrays
might produce as much as a 20th of a percent of the electricity the university
uses. It's a start.

The two campuses are Davis and Santa Cruz, and I think Davis nudges         38
ahead of Santa Cruz. That is primarily because Davis the city and Davis the
university have done something almost miraculous. They have brought car culture at least partially under control, greatly reducing air pollution as a result.

The city has a population of about 58,000, which includes 24,000 students.   39
According to reliable estimates, there are something over 50,000 bikes in town
or on the campus, all but a few hundred owned by their riders. Most of the
bikes are used regularly on the city's 45 miles of bike paths (closed to cars) and
the 47 miles of bike lanes (cars permitted in the other lanes). The university
maintains an additional 14 miles of bike paths on its large campus

What happens on rainy days? "A surprising number continue to bike," says    40
David Takemoto-Weerts, coordinator of Davis's bicycle program.

If every American college in a suitable climate were to behave like Davis,   41
we could close a medium-sized oil refinery. Maybe we could even get rid of
one coal-fired power plant, and thus seriously improve air quality.

The **University of New Hampshire** is trying to jump straight from sym-     42
bolic gestures, like installing a handful of solar panels, to the hardest task of all
for an institution trying to become green—establishing a completely new mind-
set among students, administrators, and faculty and staff members. It may well
succeed.

Campuses that have managed to change attitudes are rare. Prescott Col-       43
lege, in Prescott, Ariz., and Sterling College, in Craftsbury Common, Vt., are
rumored to have done so, and there may be two or three others. They're not on
my list—because they're so small, because their students tend to be bright green
even before they arrive, and because I have limited space.

New Hampshire has several token green projects, including a tiny solar       44
array, able to produce one kilowatt at noon on a good day. And last April it inau-
gurated the Yellow Bike Cooperative. It is much smaller than anything that happens at Davis, where a bike rack might be a hundred yards long. But it's also

more original and more communitarian. Anyone in Durham—student, burger flipper, associate dean—can join the Yellow Bike program by paying a $5 fee.

45      What you get right away is a key that unlocks all 50 bikes owned by the cooperative. (They are repaired and painted by student volunteers.) Want to cross campus? Just go to the nearest bike rack, unlock a Yellow, and pedal off. The goal, says Julie Newman, of the Office of Sustainability Programs, is "to greatly decrease one-person car trips on campus."

46      But the main thrust at New Hampshire is consciousness-raising. When the subject of composting food waste came up, the university held a seminar for its food workers.

47      New Hampshire's striking vigor is partly the result of a special endow ment—about $12.8 million—exclusively for the sustainability office. Tom Kelly, the director, refuses to equate sustainability with greenness. Being green, in the sense of avoiding pollution and promoting reuse, is just one aspect of living sustainably, which involves "the balancing of economic viability with ecological health and human well-being," he says.

48      **Oberlin College** is an exception to Perrin's Law. The college has gotten deeply into environmental behavior without the active support of two or, indeed, any senior administrators. As at Dartmouth, the top people are not hostile; they just have other priorities.

49      Apparently, until this year, Oberlin's environmental-studies program was housed in a dreary cellar. Now it's in the $8.2-million Adam Joseph Lewis Environmental Studies Center, which is one of the most environmentally benign college buildings in the world. The money for it was raised as a result of a deal that the department chairman, David Orr, made with the administration: He could raise money for his own program, provided that he approached only people and foundations that had never shown the faintest interest in Oberlin.

50      It's too soon for a full report on the building. It is loaded with solar panels—690 of them, covering the roof (for a diagram of the building, see www.oberlin.edu/newserv/esc/escabout.html). In about a year, data will be available on how much energy the panels have saved and whether, as Orr hopes, the center will not only make all its own power, but even export some.

51      **Northland College,** in Wisconsin, also goes way beyond tokenism. Its McLean Environmental Living and Learning Center, a two-year-old residence hall for 114 students, is topped by a 120-foot wind tower that, with a good breeze coming off Lake Superior, can generate 20 kilowatts of electricity. The building also includes three arrays of solar panels. They are only token-size, generating a total of 3.2 kilowatts at most. But one array does heat most of the water for one wing of McLean, while the other three form a test project.

52      One test array is fixed in place—it can't be aimed. Another is like that sunflower in Blake's poem—it countest the steps of the sun. Put more prosaically, it tracks the sun across the sky each day. The third array does that and can also be tilted to get the best angle for each season of the year.

53      Inside the dorm is a pair of composting toilets—an experiment, to see if students will use them. Because no one is forced to try the new ones if they don't

want to—plenty of conventional toilets are close by—it means something when James Miller, vice president and dean of student development and enrollment, reports, "Students almost always choose the composting bathrooms."

From the start, the college's goal has been to have McLean operate so effi- 54 ciently that it consumes 40 percent less outside energy than would a conventional dormitory of the same dimensions. The building didn't reach that goal in its first year; energy use dropped only 34.2 percent. But anyone dealing with a new system knows to expect bugs at the beginning. There were some at Northland, including the wind generator's being down for three months. (As I write, it's turning busily.) Dean Miller is confident that the building will meet or exceed the college's energy-efficiency goal.

There is no room here to talk about the octagonal classroom structure made 55 of bales of straw, built largely by students. Or about the fact that Northland's grounds are pesticide- and herbicide-free.

If Oberlin is a flagrant exception to Perrin's Law, **Middlebury College** is a 56 strong confirmation. Middlebury is unique, as far as I know, in having not only senior administrators who strongly back environmentalism, but one senior administrator right inside the program. What Michigan wants, Middlebury has.

Nan Jenks-Jay, director of environmental affairs, reports directly to the pro- 57 vost. She is responsible for both the teaching side and the living-sustainably side of environmentalism. Under her are an environmental coordinator, Amy Self, and an academic-program coordinator, Janet Wiseman.

The program has powerful backers, including the president, John M. 58 McCardell Jr.; the provost and executive vice president, Ronald D. Liebowitz; and the executive vice president for facilities planning, David W. Ginevan. But everyone I talked with at Middlebury, except for the occasional student who didn't want to trouble his mind with things like returnable bottles—to say nothing of acid rain—seemed at least somewhat committed to sustainable living.

Middlebury has what I think is the oldest environmental-studies program 59 in the country; it began back in 1965. It has the best composting program I've ever seen. And, like Northland, it is pesticide- and herbicide-free.

Let me end as I began, with Harvard, Yale, and Princeton. And with *U.S. News*'s 60 consistently ranking them in the top five, accompanied from time to time by the California Institute of Technology, Stanford University, and the Massachusetts Institute of Technology.

What if *U.S. News* did a green ranking? What if it based the listings on one 61 of the few bits of hard data that can be widely compared: the percentage of waste that a college recycles?

Harvard would come out okay, though hardly at the top. The university 62 recycled 24 percent of its waste last year, thanks in considerable part to the presence of Rob Gogan, the waste manager. He hopes to achieve 28 percent this year. That's feeble compared with Brown's 35 percent, and downright puny against Middlebury's 64 percent.

63    But compared with Yale and Princeton, it's magnificent. Most of the information I could get from Princeton is sadly dated. It comes from the 1995 report of the Princeton Environmental Reform Committee, whose primary recommendation was that the university hire a full-time waste manager. The university has not yet done so. And if any administrators on the campus know the current recycling percentage, they're not telling.

64    And Yale—poor Yale! It does have a figure. Among the performances of the 20 or so other colleges and universities whose percentages I'm aware of, only Carnegie Mellon's is worse. Yale: 19 percent. Carnegie Mellon: 11 percent.

65    What should universities—and society—be shooting for? How can you ask? One-hundred-percent retrieval of everything retrievable, of course.

## COMPREHENSION

1. Why does Perrin call his essay an "idiosyncratic guide" when environmentalism has become a major issue in most municipalities, regions, and countries?
2. Is Perrin's purpose to inform, argue, or both? Does he have a clear-cut thesis, or does he leave it up to the reader to infer the thesis? Explain.
3. What information is Perrin's informal guide providing that is not offered in more conventional college rankings? Is he suggesting that parents and students consider "green rankings" in choosing which college to apply to? Explain.

## RHETORIC

1. What purpose might Perrin have for choosing to create a "green guide" for colleges when there are so many other institutions or items he could have selected for review, such as corporations, towns, cities, automobiles, and numerous household products? What makes colleges and universities a particularly apt target?
2. Usually, Ivy League colleges are at the top of college guide lists as most desirable. Where do they rank on Perrin's list? What ironic statement is Perrin making by providing their rankings on the "green scale"? What is he implying about American values, particularly as they pertain to education?
3. Colleges and universities often pride themselves on the renown of their faculties. Who are the people Perrin cites as models of academic worth? Why has he chosen them?
4. What is the ironic purpose behind the author mentioning "Perrin's Law" (paragraph 27)? Is it a true "law," like the law of gravity? What body of knowledge is the author satirizing by invoking such a law?
5. Perrin is not didactic, since he does not recommend that other colleges adopt the environmental measures his model colleges have chosen. Would

more direct advocacy on his part have strengthened his argument or weakened it, or not have had any effect? Explain.

6. In Perrin's conclusion, he changes his purpose from providing a purely informational assessment to offering a strong reprimand and recommendation. Why does he wait until the concluding paragraph to do so?

### WRITING

1. Describe an environmentally friendly practice conducted at your college or university. Is it truly helpful for the environment, or is it largely symbolic?
2. Compare and contrast the academically oriented courses and programs offered at your school with what your institution actually does in the way of helping the environment. Discuss which of the two priorities is more prominent, and why.
3. **Writing an Argument:** Argue for or against the proposition that a magazine such as *U.S. News & World Report* should include environmental awareness and practice in its formula for assessing the rankings of colleges.

|  www.mhhe.com/ **mhreader** | For more information on Noel Perrin, go to: **More Resources > Ch. 13 Nature & Environment** |

# The Last Americans: Environmental Collapse and the End of Civilization

## Jared Diamond

*Jared Diamond* (b. 1937), *who was born in Boston, is a physiologist, ecologist, and prolific writer who has published hundreds of popular and scientific articles. He has a BA from Harvard University (1958) and a PhD from Cambridge University (1961). Currently a professor of geography at UCLA and formerly professor of physiology at UCLA's School of Medicine, Diamond has conducted research in ecology and evolutionary biology in New Guinea and other southwest Pacific islands. As a field researcher and director of the World Wildlife Fund, Diamond helped to establish New Guinea's national park system. He received the Pulitzer Prize for* Guns, Germs, and Steel: The Fates of Human Societies *(1997). Another well-received book of Diamonds's is* Collapse: How Societies Choose to Fail or Succeed *(2004). In the following essay, which appeared in the June 2003 issue of* Harper's Magazine, *Diamond*

*examines the environmental crises and failures of previous societies and civilizations,
and how we might be able to learn lessons from these lost worlds.*

*I met a traveler from an antique land*
*Who said: Two vast and trunkless legs of stone*
*Stand in the desert . . . . Near them, on the sand,*
*Half sunk, a shattered visage lies, whose frown,*
*And wrinkled lip, and sneer of cold command,*
*Tell that its sculptor well those passions read*
*Which yet survive, stamped on these lifeless things,*
*The hand that mocked them, and the heart that fed:*
*And on the pedestal these words appear:*
*"My name is Ozymandias, king of kings:*
*Look on my works, ye Mighty, and despair!"*
*Nothing beside remains. Round the decay*
*Of that colossal wreck, boundless and bare*
*The lone and level sands stretch far away.*

*—"Ozymandias," Percy Bysshe Shelley*

1   One of the disturbing facts of history is that so many civilizations collapse. Few
people, however, least of all our politicians, realize that a primary cause of the
collapse of those societies has been the destruction of the environmental resources
on which they depended. Fewer still appreciate that many of those civilizations
share a sharp curve of decline. Indeed, a society's demise may begin only a
decade or two after it reaches its peak population, wealth, and power.

2   Recent archaeological discoveries have revealed similar courses of collapse
in such otherwise dissimilar ancient societies as the Maya in the Yucatán, the
Anasazi in the American Southwest, the Cahokia mound builders outside
St. Louis, the Greenland Norse, the statue builders of Easter Island, ancient
Mesopotamia in the Fertile Crescent, Great Zimbabwe in Africa, and Angkor
Wat in Cambodia. These civilizations, and many others, succumbed to various
combinations of environmental degradaton and climate change, aggression

from enemies taking advantage of their resulting weakness, and declining trade with neighbors who faced their own environmental problems. Because peak population, wealth, resource consumption, and waste production are accompanied by peak environmental impact—approaching the limit at which impact outstrips resources—we can now understand why declines of societies tend to follow swiftly on their peaks.

These combinations of undermining factors were compounded by cultural  3 attitudes preventing those in power from perceiving or resolving the crisis. That's a familiar problem today. Some of us are inclined to dismiss the importance of a healthy environment, or at least to suggest that it's just one of many problems facing us—an "issue." That dismissal is based on three dangerous misconceptions.

Foremost among these misconceptions is that we must balance the environ-  4 ment against human needs. That reasoning is exactly upside-down. Human needs and a healthy environment are not opposing claims that must be balanced; instead, they are inexorably linked by chains of cause and effect. We need a healthy environment because we need clean water, clean air, wood, and food from the ocean, plus soil and sunlight to grow crops. We need functioning natural ecosystems, with their native species of earthworms, bees, plants, and microbes, to generate and aerate our soils, pollinate our crops, decompose our wastes, and produce our oxygen. We need to prevent toxic substances from accumulating in our water and air and soil. We need to prevent weeds, germs, and other pest species from becoming established in places where they aren't native and where they cause economic damage. Our strongest arguments for a healthy environment are selfish: we want it for ourselves, not for threatened species like snail darters, spotted owls, and Furbish louseworts.

Another popular misconception is that we can trust in technology to solve  5 our problems. Whatever environmental problem you name, you can also name some hoped-for technological solution under discussion. Some of us have faith that we shall solve our dependence on fossil fuels by developing new technologies for hydrogen engines, wind energy, or solar energy. Some of us have faith that we shall solve our food problems with new or soon-to-be-developed genetically modified crops. Some of us have faith that new technologies will succeed in cleaning up the toxic materials in our air, water, soil, and foods without the horrendous cleanup expenses that we now incur.

Those with such faith assume that the new technologies will ultimately suc-  6 ceed, but in fact some of them may succeed and others may not. They assume that the new technologies will succeed quickly enough to make a big difference soon, but all of these major technological changes will actually take five to thirty years to develop and implement—if they catch on at all. Most of all, those with faith assume that new technology won't cause any new problems. In fact, technology merely constitutes increased power, which produces changes that can be either for the better or for the worse. All of our current environmental problems are unanticipated harmful consequences of our existing technology. There is no basis for believing that technology will miraculously stop causing new and unanticipated problems while it is solving the problems that it previously produced.

7     The final misconception holds that environmentalists are fear-mongering, overreacting extremists whose predictions of impending disaster have been proved wrong before and will be proved wrong again. Behold, say the optimists: water still flows from our faucets, the grass is still green, and the supermarkets are full of food. We are more prosperous than ever before, and that's the final proof that our system works.

8     Well, for a few billion of the world's people who are causing us increasing trouble, there isn't any clean water, there is less and less green grass, and there are no supermarkets full of food. To appreciate what the environmental problems of those billions of people mean for us Americans, compare the following two lists of countries. First ask some ivory-tower academic ecologist who knows a lot about the environment but never reads a newspaper and has no interest in politics to list the overseas countries facing some of the worst problems of environmental stress, overpopulation, or both. The ecologist would answer, "That's a nobrainer, it's obvious. Your list of environmentally stressed or overpopulated countries should surely include Afghanistan, Bangladesh, Burundi, Haiti, Indonesia, Iraq, Nepal, Pakistan, the Philippines, Rwanda, the Solomon Islands, and Somalia, plus others." Then ask a First World politician who knows nothing, and cares less, about the environment and population problems to list the world's worst trouble spots: countries where state government has already been overwhelmed and has collapsed, or is now at risk of collapsing, or has been wracked by recent civil wars; and countries that, as a result of their problems, are also creating problems for us rich First World countries, which may be deluged by illegal immigrants, or have to provide foreign aid to those countries, or may decide to provide them with military assistance to deal with rebellions and terrorists, or may even (God forbid) have to send in our own troops. The politician would answer, "That's a nobrainer, it's obvious. Your list of political trouble spots should surely include Afghanistan, Bangladesh, Burundi, Haiti, Indonesia, Iraq, Nepal, Pakistan, the Philippines, Rwanda, the Soloman Islands, and Somalia, plus others."

9     The connection between the two lists is transparent. Today, just as in the past, countries that are environmentally stressed, overpopulated or both are at risk of becoming politically stressed, and of seeing their governments collapse. When people are desperate and undernourished, they blame their government, which they see as responsible for failing to solve their problems. They try to emigrate at any cost. They start civil wars. They kill one another. They figure that they have nothing to lose, so they become terrorists, or they support or tolerate terrorism. The results are genocides such as the ones that already have exploded in Burundi, Indonesia, and Rwanda; civil wars, as in Afghanistan, Indonesia, Nepal, the Philippines, and the Solomon Islands; calls for the dispatch of First World troops, as to Afghanistan, Indonesia, Iraq, the Philippines, Rwanda, the Solomon Islands, and Somalia; the collapse of central government, as has already happened in Somalia; and overwhelming poverty, as in all of the countries on these lists.

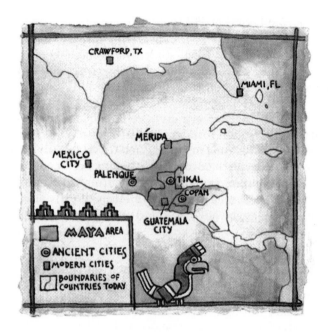

But what about the United States? Some might argue that the environ-   10
mental collapse of ancient societies is relevant to the modern decline of weak,
far-off, overpopulated Rwanda and environmentally devastated Somalia, but
isn't it ridiculous to suggest any possible relevance to the fate of our own
society? After all, we might reason, those ancients didn't enjoy the wonders
of modern environment-friendly technologies. Those ancients had the misfortune to suffer from the effects of climate change. They behaved stupidly
and ruined their own environment by doing obviously dumb things, like cutting down their forests, watching their topsoil erode, and building cities in
dry areas likely to run short of water. They had foolish leaders who didn't
have books and so couldn't learn from history, and who embroiled them in
destabilizing wars and didn't pay attention to problems at home. They were
overwhelmed by desperate immigrants, as one society after another collapsed, sending floods of economic refugees to tax the resources of the societies that weren't collapsing. In all those respects, we modern Americans are
fundamentally different from those primitive ancients, and there is nothing
that we could learn from them.

Or so the argument goes. It's an argument so ingrained both in our subcon-   11
scious and in public discourse that it has assumed the status of objective reality.
We think we are different. In fact, of course, all of those powerful societies of
the past thought that they too were unique, right up to the moment of their collapse. It's sobering to consider the swift decline of the ancient Maya, who 1,200
years ago were themselves the most advanced society in the Western Hemisphere,
and who, like us now, were then at the apex of their own power and numbers.

Two excellent recent books, David Webster's *The Fall of the Ancient Maya* and Richardson Gill's *The Great Maya Droughts,* help bring the trajectory of Maya civilization back to life for us. Their studies illustrate how even sophisticated societies like that of the Maya (and ours) can be undermined by details of rainfall, farming methods, and motives of leaders.

12  By now, millions of modern Americans have visited Maya ruins. To do so, one need only take a direct flight from the United States to the Yucatán capital of Mérida, jump into a rental car or minibus, and drive an hour on a paved highway. Most Maya ruins, with their great temples and monuments, lie surrounded by jungles (seasonal tropical forests), far from current human settlement. They are "pure" archaeological sites. That is, their locations became depopulated, so they were not covered up by later buildings as were so many other ancient cities, like the Aztec capital of Tenochtitlán—now buried under modern Mexico City—and Rome.

13      One of the reasons few people live there now is that the Maya homeland poses serious environmental challenges to would-be farmers. Although it has a somewhat unpredictable rainy season from May to October, it also has a dry season from January through April. Indeed, if one focuses on the dry months, one could describe the Yucatán as a "seasonal desert."

14      Complicating things, from a farmer's perspective, is that the part of the Yucatán with the most rain, the south, is also the part at the highest elevation above the water table. Most of the Yucatán consists of karst—a porous, sponge-like, limestone terrain—and so rain runs straight into the ground, leaving little or no surface water. The Maya in the lower-elevation regions of the north were able to reach the water table by way of deep sinkholes called cenotes, and the Maya in low coastal areas without sinkholes could reach it by digging wells up to 75 feet deep. Most Maya, however, lived in the south. How did they deal with their resulting water problem?

15      Technology provided an answer. The Maya plugged up leaks on karst promontories by plastering the bottoms of depressions to create reservoirs, which collected rain and stored it for use in the dry season. The reservoirs at the Maya city of Tikal, for example, held enough water to meet the needs of about 10,000 people for eighteen months. If a drought lasted longer than that, though, the inhabitants of Tikal were in deep trouble.

16      Maya farmers grew mostly corn, which constituted the astonishingly high proportion of about 70 percent of their diet, as deduced from isotope analyses of ancient Maya skeletons. They grew corn by means of a modified version of swidden slash-and-burn agriculture, in which forest is cleared, crops are grown in the resulting clearing for a few years until the soil is exhausted, and then the field is abandoned for fifteen to twenty years until regrowth of wild vegetation restores the soil's fertility. Because most of the land under a swidden agricultural system is fallow at any given time, it can support only modest population densities. Thus, it was a surprise for archaeologists to discover that ancient Maya population densities, judging from numbers of stone foundations of farmhouses,

were often far higher than what unmodified swidden agriculture could support: often 250 to 750 people per square mile. The Maya probably achieved those high populations by such means as shortening the fallow period and tilling the soil to restore soil fertility, or omitting the fallow period entirely and growing crops every year, or, in especially moist areas, growing two crops per year.

Socially stratified societies, ours included, consist of farmers who produce   17 food, plus nonfarmers such as bureaucrats and soldiers who do not produce food and are in effect parasites on farmers. The farmers must grow enough food to meet not only their own needs but also those of everybody else. The number of nonproducing consumers who can be supported depends on the society's agricultural productivity. In the United States today, with its highly efficient agriculture, farmers make up only 2 percent of our population, and each farmer can feed, on the average, 129 other people. Ancient Egyptian agriculture was efficient enough for an Egyptian peasant to produce five times the food required for himself and his family. But a Maya peasant could produce only twice the needs of himself and his family.

Fully 80 percent of May society consisted of peasants. Their inability to sup-   18 port many nonfarmers resulted from several limitations of their agriculture. It produced little protein, because corn has much lower protein content than wheat, and because the few edible domestic animals kept by the Maya (turkeys, ducks, and dogs) included no large animals like our cows and sheep. There was little use of terracing or irrigation to increase production. In the Maya area's humid climate, stored corn would rot or become infested after a year, so the Maya couldn't get through a longer drought by eating surplus corn accumulated in good years. And unlike Old World peoples with their horses, oxen, donkeys, and camels, the Maya had no animal-powered transport. Indeed, the Maya lacked not only pack animals and animal-drawn plows but also metal tools, wheels, and boats with sails. All of those great Maya temples were built by stone and wooden tools and human muscle power alone, and all overland transport went on the backs of human porters.

19    Those limitations on food supply and food transport may in part explain why Maya society remained politically organized in small kingdoms that were perpetually at war with one another and that never became unified into large empires like the Aztec empire of the Valley of Mexico (fed by highly productive agriculture) or the Inca empire of the Andes (fed by diverse crops carried on llamas). Maya armies were small and unable to mount lengthy campaigns over long distances. The typical Maya kingdom held a population of only up to 50,000 people, within a radius of two or three days' walk from the king's palace. From the top of the temple of some Maya kingdoms, one could see the tops of the temples of other kingdoms.

20    Presiding over the temple was the king himself, who functioned both as head priest and as political leader. It was his responsibility to pray to the gods, to perform astronomical and calendrical rituals, to ensure the timely arrival of the rains on which agriculture depended, and thereby to bring prosperity. The king claimed to have the supernatural power to deliver those good things because of his asserted family relationship to the gods. Of course, that exposed him to the risk that his subjects would become disillusioned if he couldn't fulfill his boast of being able to deliver rains and prosperity.

21    Those are the basic outlines of Classic Maya society, which for all its limitations lasted more than 500 years. Indeed, the Maya themselves believed that it had lasted for much longer. Their remarkable Long Count calendar had its starting date (analogous to January 1, A.D. 1 of our calendar) backdated into the remote preliterate past, at August 11, 3114 B.C. The first physical evidence of civilization within the Maya area, in the form of villagers and pottery, appeared around 1400 B.C., substantial buildings around 500 B.C., and writing around 400 B.C. The so-called Classic period of Maya history arose around A.D. 250, when evidence for the first kings and dynasties emerged. From then, the Maya population increased almost exponentially, to reach peak numbers in the eighth century A.D. The largest monuments were erected toward the end of that century. All the indicators of a complex society declined throughout the ninth century, until the last date on any monument was A.D. 909. This decline of Maya population and architecture constitutes what is known as the Classic Maya collapse.

22    What happened? Let's consider in more detail a city whose ruins now lie in western Honduras at the world-famous site of Copán. The most fertile ground in the Copán area consists of five pockets of flat land along a river valley with a total area of only one square mile; the largest of those five pockets, known as the Copán pocket, has an area of half a square mile. Much of the land around Copán consists of steep hills with poor soil. Today, corn yields from valley-bottom fields are two or three times those of fields on hill slopes, which suffer rapid erosion and lose most of their productivity within a decade of farming.

23    To judge by the number of house sites, population growth in the Copán valley rose steeply from the fifth century up to a peak estimated at around

27,000 people between A.D. 750 and 900. Construction of royal monuments glorifying kings became especially massive from A.D. 650 onward. After A.D. 700, nobles other than kings got into the act and began erecting their own palaces, increasing the burden that the king and his own court already imposed on the peasants. The last big buildings at Copán were put up around A.D. 800; the last date on an incomplete altar possibly bearing a king's name is A.D. 822.

Archaeological surveys of different types of habitats in the Copán valley 24 show that they were occupied in a regular sequence. The first area farmed was the large Copán pocket of bottomland, followed by occupation of the other four bottomland pockets. During that time the human population was growing, but the hills remained uninhabited. Hence that increased population must have been accommodated by intensifying production in the bottomland pockets: probably some combination of shorter fallow periods and double-cropping. By A.D. 500, people had started to settle the hill slopes, but those sites were occupied only briefly. The percentage of Copán's total population that was in the hills, rather than in the valleys, peaked in the year 575 and then declined, as the population again became concentrated in the pockets.

What caused that pullback of population from the hills? From excavation of 25 building foundations on the valley floor we know that they became covered with sediment during the eighth century, meaning that the hill slopes were becoming eroded and probably also leached of nutrients. The acidic hill soils being carried down into the valley would have reduced agricultural yields. The reason for that erosion of the hillsides is clear: the forests that formerly covered them and protected their soil were being cut down. Dated pollen samples show that the pine forests originally covering the hilltops were eventually all cleared, to be burned for fuel. Besides causing sediment accumulation in the valleys and depriving valley inhabitants of wood supplies, that deforestation may have begun to cause a "man-made drought" in the valley bottom, because forests play a major role in water cycling, such that massive deforestation tends to result in lowered rainfall.

Hundreds of skeletons recovered from Copán archaeological sites have 26 been studied for signs of disease and poor nutrition, such as porous bones and stress lines in the teeth. Those skeletal signs show that the health of Copán's inhabitants deteriorated from A.D. 650 to 850, among both the elite and commoners, though the health of commoners was worse.

Recall that Copán's population was growing rapidly while the hills were 27 being occupied. The subsequent abandonment of all of those hill fields meant that the burden of feeding the extra population formerly dependent on the hills now fell increasingly on the valley floor, and that more and more people were competing for the food grown on that one square mile of bottomland. That would have led to fighting among the farmers themselves for the best land, or for any land, just as in modern Rwanda. Because the king was failing to deliver on his promises of rain and prosperity, he would have been the scapegoat for this agricultural failure, which explains why the last that we hear of any king is A.D. 822, and why the royal palace was burned around A.D. 850.

28    Datable pieces of obsidian, the sharp rock from which the Maya made their stone tools, suggest that Copán's total population decreased more gradually than did its signs of kings and nobles. The estimated population in the year A.D. 950 was still around 15,000, or 55 percent of the peak population of 27,000. That population continued to dwindle, until there are few signs of anyone in the Copán valley after around A.D. 1235. The reappearance of pollen from forest trees thereafter provides independent evidence that the valley became virtually empty of people.

29    The Maya history that I have just related, and Copán's history in particular, illustrate why we talk about "the Maya collapse." But the story grows more complicated, for at least five reasons. There was not only that enormous Classic collapse but also at least two smaller pre-Classic collapses, around A.D. 150 and 600, as well as some post-Classic collapses. The Classic collapse was obviously not complete, because hundreds of thousands of Maya survived, in areas with stable water supplies, to meet and fight the Spaniards. The collapse of population (as gauged by numbers of house sites and of obsidian tools) was in some cases much slower than the decline in numbers of Long Count dates. Many apparent collapses of cities were nothing more than "power cycling"; i.e., particular cities becoming more powerful at the expense of neighboring cities, then declining or getting conquered by neighbors, without changes in the whole population. Finally, cities in different parts of the Maya area rose and fell on different trajectories.

30    Some archaeologists focus on these complications and don't want to recognize a Classic Maya collapse at all. But this overlooks the obvious fact that cries out for explanation: the disappearance of between 90 and 99 percent of the Maya population after A.D. 800, and of the institution of the kingship, Long Count calendars, and other complex political and cultural institutions. Before we can understand those disappearances, however, we need first to understand the roles of warfare and of drought.

31    Archaeologists for a long time believed the ancient Maya to be gentle and peaceful people. We now know that Maya warfare was intense, chronic, and unresolvable, because limitations of food supply and transportation made it impossible for any Maya principality to unite the whole region in an empire. The archaeological record shows that wars became more intense and frequent toward the time of the Classic collapse. That evidence comes from discoveries of several types since the Second World War: archaeological excavations of massive fortifications surrounding many Maya sites; vivid depictions of warfare and captives on stone monuments and on the famous painted murals discovered in 1946 at Bonampak; and the decipherment of Maya writing, much of which proved to consist of royal inscriptions boasting of conquests. Maya kings fought to capture and torture one another; an unfortunate loser was a Copán king with the to us unforgettable name of King 18 Rabbit.

32    Maya warfare involved well-documented types of violence: wars among separate kingdoms; attempts of cities within a kingdom to secede by revolting against the capital; and civil wars resulting from frequent violent attempts by

would be kings to usurp the throne. All of these events were described or depicted on monuments, because they involved kings and nobles. Not considered worthy of description, but probably even more frequent, were fights between commoners over land, as overpopulation became excessive and land became scarce.

The other phenomenon important to understanding all of these collapses is the repeated occurrence of droughts, as inferred by climatologists from evidence of lake evaporation preserved in lake sediments, and as summarized by Gill in *The Great Maya Droughts*. The rise of Maya civilization may have been facilitated by a rainy period beginning around 250 B.C., until a temporary drought after A.D. 125 was associated with a pre-Classic collapse at some sites. That collapse was followed by the resumption of rainy conditions and the buildup of Classic Maya cities, briefly interrupted by another drought around 600 corresponding to a decline at Tikal and some other sites. Finally, around A.D. 750 there began the worst drought in the past 7,000 years, peaking around the year A.D. 800, and suspiciously associated with the Classic collapse.

The area most affected by the Classic collapse was the southern highlands, probably for the two reasons already mentioned: it was the area with the densest population, and it also had the most severe water problems because it lay too high above the water table for cenotes or wells to provide water. The southern highlands lost more than 99 percent of its population in the course of the Classic collapse. When Cortés and his Spanish army marched in 1524 and 1525 through an area formerly inhabited by millions of Maya, he nearly starved because he encountered so few villagers from whom to acquire corn. The Spaniards passed within only a few miles of the abandoned ruins of the great Classic cities of Tikal and Palenque, but still they heard or saw nothing of them.

We can identify increasingly familiar strands in the Classic Maya collapse. One consisted of population growth outstripping available resources: the dilemma foreseen by Thomas Malthus in 1798. As Webster succinctly puts it in *The Fall of the Ancient Maya*, "Too many farmers grew too many crops on too much of the landscape." While population was increasing, the area of usable farmland paradoxically was decreasing from the effects of deforestation and hillside erosion.

The next strand consisted of increased fighting as more and more people fought over fewer resources. Maya warfare, already endemic, peaked just before the collapse. That is not surprising when one reflects that at least 5 million people, most of them farmers, were crammed into an area smaller than the state of Colorado. That's a high population by the standards of ancient farming societies, even if it wouldn't strike modern Manhattan-dwellers as crowded.

Bringing matters to a head was a drought that, although not the first one the Maya had been through, was the most severe. At the time of previous droughts, there were still uninhabited parts of the Maya landscape, and people in a drought area or dust bowl could save themselves by moving to another site. By the time of the Classic collapse, however, there was no useful unoccupied land in the vicinity on which to begin anew, and the whole population

could not be accommodated in the few areas that continued to have reliable water supplies.

38      The final strand is political. Why did the kings and nobles not recognize and solve these problems? A major reason was that their attention was evidently focused on the short-term concerns of enriching themselves, waging wars, erecting monuments, competing with one another, and extracting enough food from the peasants to support all those activities. Like most leaders throughout human history, the Maya kings and nobles did not have the leisure to focus on long-term problems, insofar as they perceived them.

39   What about those same strands today? The United States is also at the peak of its power, and it is also suffering from many environmental problems. Most of us have become aware of more crowding and stress. Most of us living in large American cities are encountering increased commuting delays, because the number of people and hence of cars is increasing faster than the number of free-way lanes. I know plenty of people who in the abstract doubt that the world has a population problem, but almost all of those same people complain to me about crowding, space issues, and traffic experienced in their personal lives.

40      Many parts of the United States face locally severe problems of water restriction (especially southern California, Arizona, the Everglades, and, in-creasingly, the Northeast); forest fires resulting from logging and forest-management practices throughout the intermontane West; and losses of farmlands to salinization, drought, and climate change in the northern Great Plains. Many of us frequently experience problems of air quality, and some of us also experience problems of water quality and taste. We are losing economi-cally valuable natural resources. We have already lost American chestnut trees, the Grand Banks cod fishery, and the Monterey sardine fishery; we are in the process of losing swordfish and tuna and Chesapeake Bay oysters and elm trees; and we are losing topsoil.

The list goes on: All of us are experiencing personal consequences of our ⁴¹
national dependence on imported energy, which affects us not only through
higher gas prices but also through the current contraction of the national economy, itself the partial result of political problems associated with our oil dependence. We are saddled with expensive toxic cleanups at many locations, most
notoriously near Montana mines, on the Hudson River, and in the Chesapeake
Bay. We also face expensive eradication problems resulting from hundreds of
introduced pest species—including zebra mussels, Mediterranean fruit flies,
Asian longhorn beetles, water hyacinth, and spotted knapweed—that now affect our agriculture, forests, waterways, and pastures.

These particular environmental problems, and many others, are enor- ⁴²
mously expensive in terms of resources lost, cleanup and restoration costs, and
the cost of finding substitutes for lost resources: a billion dollars here, 10 billion
there, in dozens and dozens of cases. Some of the problems, especially those of
air quality and toxic substances, also exact health costs that are large, whether
measured in dollars or in lost years or in quality of life. The cost of our home-
grown environmental problems adds up to a large fraction of our gross national
product, even without mentioning the costs that we incur from environmental
problems overseas, such as the military operations that they inspire. Even the
mildest of bad scenarios for our future include a gradual economic decline, as
happened to the Roman and British empires. Actually, in case you didn't notice
it, our economic decline is already well under way. Just check the numbers for
our national debt, yearly government budget deficit, unemployment statistics,
and the value of your investment and pension funds.

The environmental problems of the United States are still modest compared with ⁴³
those of the rest of the world. But the problems of environmentally devastated,
overpopulated, distant countries are now our problems as well. We are accustomed to thinking of globalization in terms of us rich, advanced First Worlders
sending our good things, such as the Internet and Coca-Cola, to those poor backward Third Worlders. Globalization, however, means nothing more than
improved worldwide communication and transportation, which can convey
many things in either direction; it is not restricted to good things carried only
from the First to the Third World. They in the Third World can now, intentionally
or unintentionally, send us their bad things: terrorists; diseases such as AIDS,
SARS, cholera, and West Nile fever, carried inadvertently by passengers on trans-
continental airplanes; unstoppable numbers of immigrants, both legal and illegal,
arriving by boat, truck, train, plane, and on foot; and other consequences of their
Third World problems. We in the United States are no longer the isolated Fortress America to which some of us aspired in the 1930s; instead, we are tightly
and irreversibly connected to overseas countries. The United States is the world's
leading importer, and it is also the world's leading exporter. Our own society
opted long ago to become interlocked with the rest of the world.

That's why political stability anywhere in the world now affects us, our ⁴⁴
trade routes, and our overseas markets and suppliers. We are so dependent on

the rest of the world that if a decade ago you had asked a politician to name the countries most geopolitically irrelevant to U.S. interests because of their being so remote, poor, and weak, the list would have begun with Afghanistan and Somalia, yet these countries were subsequently considered important enough to warrant our dispatching U.S. troops. The Maya were "globalized" only within the Yucatán: the southern Yucatán Maya affected the northern Yucatán Maya and may have had some effects on the Valley of Mexico, but they had no contact with Somalia. That's because Maya transportation was slow, short-distance, on foot or else in canoes, and had low cargo capacity. Our transport today is much more rapid and has much higher cargo capacity. The Maya lived in a globalized Yucatán; we live in a globalized world.

45  If all of this reasoning seems straightforward when expressed so bluntly, one has to wonder: Why don't those in power today get the message? Why didn't the leaders of the Maya, Anasazi, and those other societies also recognize and solve their problems? What were the Maya thinking while they watched loggers clearing the last pine forests on the hills above Copán? Here, the past really is a useful guide to the present. It turns out that there are at least a dozen reasons why past societies failed to *anticipate* some problems before they developed, or failed to *perceive* problems that had already developed, or failed even to try to solve problems that they did perceive. All of those dozen reasons still can be seen operating today. Let me mention just three of them.

46       First, it's difficult to recognize a slow trend in some quantity that fluctuates widely up and down anyway, such as seasonal temperature, annual rainfall, or

economic indicators. That's surely why the Maya didn't recognize the oncoming drought until it was too late, given that rainfall in the Yucatán varies several-fold from year to year. Natural fluctuations also explain why it's only within the last few years that all climatologists have become convinced of the reality of climate change, and why our president still isn't convinced but thinks that we need more research to test for it.

Second, when a problem *is* recognized, those in power may not attempt to  47
solve it because of a clash between their short-term interests and the interests of the rest of us. Pumping that oil, cutting down those trees, and catching those fish may benefit the elite by bringing them money or prestige and yet be bad for society as a whole (including the children of the elite) in the long run. Maya kings were consumed by immediate concerns for their prestige (requiring more and bigger temples) and their success in the next war (requiring more followers), rather than for the happiness of commoners or of the next generation. Those people with the greatest power to make decisions in our own society today regularly make money from activities that may be bad for society as a whole and for their own children; those decision-makers include Enron executives, many land developers, and advocates of tax cuts for the rich.

Finally, it's difficult for us to acknowledge the wisdom of policies that clash  48
with strongly held values. For example, a belief in individual freedom and a distrust of big government are deeply ingrained in Americans, and they make sense under some circumstances and up to a certain point. But they also make it hard for us to accept big government's legitimate role in ensuring that each individual's freedom to maximize the value of his or her land holdings doesn't decrease the value of the collective land of all Americans.

Not all societies make fatal mistakes. There are parts of the world where societ-  49
ies have unfolded for thousands of years without any collapse, such as Java, Tonga, and (until 1945) Japan. Today, Germany and Japan are successfully managing their forests, which are even expanding in area rather than shrinking. The Alaskan salmon fishery and the Australian lobster fishery are being managed sustainably. The Dominican Republic, hardly a rich country, nevertheless has set aside a comprehensive system of protected areas encompassing most of the country's natural habitats.

Is there any secret to explain why some societies acquire good environmen-  50
tal sense while others don't? Naturally, part of the answer depends on accidents of individual leaders' wisdom (or lack thereof). But part also depends upon whether a society is organized so as to minimize built-in clashes of interest between its decision-making elites and its masses. Given how our society is organized, the executives of Enron, Tyco, and Adelphi correctly calculated that their own interests would be best promoted by looting the company coffers, and that they would probably get away with most of their loot. A good example of a society that minimizes such clashes of interest is the Netherlands, whose citizens have perhaps the world's highest level of environmental awareness and of membership in environmental organizations. I never understood why,

until on a recent trip to the Netherlands I posed the question to three of my Dutch friends while driving through their countryside.

51        Just look around you, they said. All of this farmland that you see lies below sea level. One fifth of the total area of the Netherlands is below sea level, as much as 22 feet below, because it used to be shallow bays, and we reclaimed it from the sea by surrounding the bays with dikes and then gradually pumping out the water. We call these reclaimed lands "polders." We began draining our polders nearly a thousand years ago. Today, we still have to keep pumping out the water that gradually seeps in. That's what our windmills used to be for, to drive the pumps to pump out the polders. Now we use steam, diesel, and electric pumps instead. In each polder there are lines of them, starting with those farthest from the sea, pumping the water in sequence until the last pump finally deposits it into a river or the ocean. And all of us, rich or poor, live down in the polders. It's not the case that rich people live safely up on top of the dikes while poor people live in the polder bottoms below sea level. If the dikes and pumps fail, we'll all drown together.

52        Throughout human history, all peoples have been connected to some other peoples, living together in virtual polders. For the ancient Maya, their polder consisted of most of the Yucatán and neighboring areas. When the Classic Maya cities collapsed in the southern Yucatán, refugees may have reached the northern Yucatán, but probably not the Valley of Mexico, and certainly not Florida. Today, our whole world has become one polder, such that events in even Afghanistan and Somalia affect Americans. We do indeed differ from the Maya, but not in ways we might like: we have a much larger population, we have more potent destructive technology, and we face the risk of a worldwide rather than a local decline. Fortunately, we also differ from the Maya in that we know their fate, and they did not. Perhaps we can learn.

## COMPREHENSION

1. Explain the significance of Shelley's poem "Ozymandias" for Diamond's essay.
2. What are the three "dangerous misconceptions" (paragraph 3) about the environment that Diamond discusses?
3. List all the civilizations that Diamond mentions in this essay. Which civilization does he emphasize? According to Diamond, why did previous civilizations fail, and how do these collapses provide guides to the state of contemporary American civilization?

## RHETORIC

1. State Diamond's argument or major proposition. Where does his claim appear most clearly? What minor propositions does he develop? How does he deal with opposing viewpoints?

2. What types of evidence does the writer provide to support his claim?
3. Why does Diamond divide his essay into so many sections? What relationships do you detect between and among these sections?
4. Where does Diamond use comparison and contrast and causal analysis to organize parts of his essay?
5. How does classification operate as a rhetorical element in this article?
6. Assess the relative effectiveness of Diamond's conclusion. How does the ending serve as a coda for the entire essay?

## WRITING

1. Write an essay focusing on a local environmental problem. Analyze the ways in which this environmental problem affects the lives of nearby residents.
2. Select one civilization that Diamond mentions. Conduct research on this civilization, and then write a report on the environmental factors that led to the decline of that society.
3. **Writing an Argument:** Write a persuasive essay in which you warn readers about three environmental dangers confronting the United States today.

www.mhhe.com/
**mhreader**

For more information on Jared Diamond, go to:
**More Resources > Ch. 13 Nature & Environment**

## Synthesis: Connections for Critical Thinking

1. Using support from the works of Lopez, Carson, Chief Seattle, and others, write a causal-analysis essay tracing our relationship to the land. To what extent have history, greed, and fear helped shape our attitude? Can this attitude be changed? How?
2. Consider the empathy and sensitivity Walker has toward animals. How do her attitude and perceptions coincide with the view expressed by Bass and Chief Seattle concerning the natural world?
3. Write a letter to the op-ed page of a newspaper objecting to a governmental ruling harmful to the environment. State the nature of the policy, its possible dangers, and your reasons for opposing it. Use support from McKibben, Diamond, and any other writers in this chapter. Extra reading or research may be necessary.
4. Consider why we fear nature. Why do we consider it an enemy, an alien, something to be destroyed? How would Momaday, Walker, Lopez, and Chief Seattle respond to this question? Do you agree or disagree with them?

5. Both Lopez and Diamond use narration and description to explore our relationship to the land. How do they approach their subject in terms of language, attitude, and style?

6. Choose an author in this chapter whose essay, in your opinion, romanticizes nature. Compare his or her attitude with that of a writer with a more pragmatic approach to the subject. Compare the two views, and specify the elements in their writing that contribute to the overall strength of their arguments.

7. Perrin uses enumeration and illustration to structure his essay. What are some of the strengths and weaknesses of employing traditional and orderly means of presenting one's thoughts?

8. Write an essay titled "Nature's Revenge" in which you examine the consequences of environmental abuse. Consider the short- as well as the long-term effects on the quality of life. Use support from any three writers in this chapter to defend your opinion.

9. Write specifically about our relationship to other living creatures on our planet. Is it one of exploitation, cooperation, or tyranny? How does this relationship influence how we treat each other? Explore the answers to these questions in an essay. Use the works of Lopez, Walker, and Chief Seattle to support your thesis.

10. **Network:** Join a newsgroup on the Web devoted to addressing a specific environmental issue—for example, atomic waste, overdevelopment, or environmental regulations and deregulations. Follow the conversation of the newsgroup for one month. Write an essay describing what the chief concerns of the newsgroup members are, how they address issues regarding the environment, and what specific actions they recommend or take over the course of your membership.

11. **Network:** Visit the Web site of the Environmental Protection Agency. Write a report describing the agency's announcements, speeches, activities, and proposals.

12. **Network:** Create your own interactive Web site focusing on the environment. Present, in its headline, this request: "In a statement of 100 words, please explain whether we are doing enough to reverse the destruction to our environment." Check back in a month, and write a report summarizing the responses.

 chapter *14*

# Science and Technology
*What Can Science Teach Us?*

Contrary to popular assumptions, contemporary science and technology are not dry subjects but rather are bodies of specialized knowledge concerned with the great how and why questions of our time. In fact, we are currently in the midst of a whole series of scientific revolutions that will radically transform our lives in the 21st century. The essential problem for humankind is to make sense of all this revolutionary scientific and technological knowledge, invest it with value, use it ethically, and make it serve our cultural and global needs.

As you will see in the essays in this chapter, human beings are always the ultimate subject of scientific investigation. Science and mathematics attempt to understand the physical, biological, and chemical events that shape our lives. Whenever we switch on a light or turn on a computer, take an aspirin or start the car, we see that science and technology have intervened effectively in our lives. Often the specialized knowledge of science forces us to make painful decisions, and the misuse of science can have disastrous results. As Terry Tempest Williams demonstrates in her highly personal essay "The Clan of One-Breasted Women," science can have dire, unforeseen ethical implications.

The technology that arises from science affects everyday decisions as well as the larger culture. Nowhere is the impact of science more apparent than in the field of biotechnology. As Dinesh D'Souza observes in his essay on the biotech revolution, science is intended to serve us, to help us with our common dilemmas. At the same time, biotechnology reminds us that despite advances, we are still mortals confronting ethical dilemmas. Even as knowledge flows from research laboratories, these mortal paradoxes tend to perplex and goad us as we seek scientific solutions to the complex problems of our era.

Science and technology as specialized bodies of knowledge can send contradictory messages because science and technology are socially constructed and reflect the contours of culture. How we manage the revolution in science—how we harness nuclear power or battle the ravages of AIDS—will determine the health of civilization in our century.

## Previewing the Chapter

As you read the essays in this chapter and respond to them in discussion and writing, consider the following questions:

- Does the author take a personal or an objective approach to the subject? What is the effect?
- What area of scientific or technological inquiry does the writer focus on?
- What scientific conflicts arise in the course of the essay?
- Is the writer a specialist, a layperson, a journalist, or a commentator? How does the background of the writer affect the tone of the essay?
- What assumptions does the author make about his or her audience? How much specialized knowledge must you bring to the essay?
- How do social issues enter into the author's presentation?
- What gender issues are raised by the author?
- How have your perceptions of the author's topic been changed or enhanced? What new knowledge have you gained? Does the writer contradict any of your assumptions or beliefs?
- Is the writer optimistic or pessimistic about the state of technology or science? How do you know?

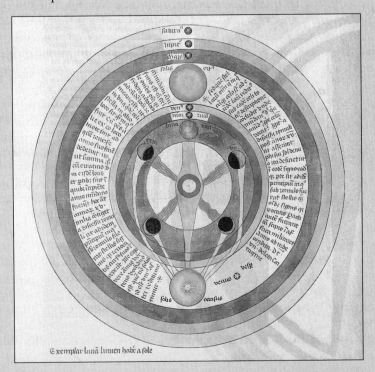

# Classic and Contemporary Images

## WHERE IS SCIENCE TAKING US?

*Using a Critical Perspective*  Make a series of observations about each of these images. Where does your eye rest in each one? How many objects and details do you see? What reasonable inferences can you draw about the relationship of the artist who created the 15th-century image to the culture and historical period? What purpose did the scientists who created and control the Hubble Space Telescope have? What purposes do the 15th-century artist and 20th-century scientist have in common? Argue for or against the proposition that art can actually capture the advances in science, technology, and humanity that we have experienced over time.

During the Renaissance in Europe, scientists such as Nicolaus Copernicus (1473–1543) and Galileo Galilei (1564–1642) revolutionized the way Europeans viewed the universe and their place in it by proving that the earth and the planets revolve around the sun, thus changing forever the worldview exemplified by the 15th-century Flemish depiction of the movements of the sun and moon shown here.

Galileo's primitive telescope was a distant forerunner of the powerful
Hubble Space Telescope, launched in 1990, which is able to take
photographs of extremely distant stars and other phenomenon,
such as the gaseous pillars shown here, as it orbits the earth.

# Classic and Contemporary Essays
## HOW HAS NATURE EVOLVED?

Evolution seems to be more highly and hotly debated each year, insinuating itself into educational, political, scientific, and religious debates. Unfortunately, extreme positions on evolution tend to obscure what is valuable about the concept. The idea or theory of evolution is rooted in scientific creativity and the scientific method. Scientists are observers and collectors of information, and they use facts to build an explanation of the natural world and our place in it. Darwin looked carefully at nature and the physical world, as the following selection on natural selection illustrates. In his autobiography, Darwin observed that he "collected facts on a wholesale scale" before arriving at his theory of natural selection, and this inductive approach, at the heart of *On the Origin of Species* (1859), typifies his method of inquiry. But does evolutionary theory explain all the facts—all of humankind's problems? Does evolution mark the progress of human civilization, or are dimensions needed to explain our relationship to the world and the world's events? Natalie Angier, one of the most lucid and persuasive contemporary science writers, tackles these questions and more in an essay prompted by the events of September 11, 2001. Basing her ideas on recent studies in evolutionary biology and other sciences, Angier presents Darwin in a new light, finding his theories generally sufficient to explain our responses to 9/11 but also suggesting that an added dimension to human behavior—beyond Darwin—is required to fully explain our struggle for existence and meaning in the modern world.

# Natural Selection

## Charles Darwin

*Charles Darwin (1809–1882) was born in England and studied medicine at Edinburgh. He also studied for the ministry at Cambridge but soon turned his interest to natural history. Through his friendship with a well-known botanist, he was given the opportunity to take a five-year cruise around the world (1831–1836) aboard the H.M.S.* Beagle, *serving as a naturalist. This started Darwin on a career of accumulating and assimilating data that resulted in the formulation of his concept of evolution. He spent the remainder of his life carefully and methodically working over the information from his copious notes. He first published his findings in 1858 and a year later published his influential* Origin of Species. *This seminal work was supplemented and elaborated on in many later books, including* The Descent of Man *(1871). The following selection demonstrates the methodical and meticulous method Darwin used in developing his concepts.*

In order to make it clear how, as I believe, natural selection acts, I must beg   1
permission to give one or two imaginary illustrations. Let us take the case of a wolf, which preys on various animals, securing some by craft, some by strength, and some by fleetness; and let us suppose that the fleetest prey, a deer for instance, had from any change in the country increased in numbers, or that other prey had decreased in numbers, during that season of the year when the wolf is hardest pressed for food. I can under such circumstances see no reason to doubt that the swiftest and slimmest wolves would have the best chance of surviving, and so be preserved or selected, provided always that they retained strength to master their prey at this or at some other period of the year, when they might be compelled to prey on other animals. I can see no more reason to doubt this, than that man can improve the fleetness of his greyhounds by careful and methodical selection, or by that unconscious selection which results from each man trying to keep the best dogs without any thought of modifying the breed.

Even without any change in the proportional numbers of the animals on   2
which our wolf preyed, a cub might be born with an innate tendency to pursue certain kinds of prey. Nor can this be thought very improbable; for we often observe great differences in the natural tendencies of our domestic animals; one cat, for instance, taking to catch rats, another mice; one cat, according to Mr. St. John, bringing home winged game, another hares or rabbits, and another hunting on marshy ground and almost nightly catching woodcocks or snipes. The tendency to catch rats rather than mice is known to be inherited. Now, if any slight innate change of habit or of structure benefited an individual wolf, it would have the best chance of surviving and of leaving offspring. Some of its

young would probably inherit the same habits or structure, and by the repetition of this process, a new variety might be formed which would either supplant or coexist with the parent-form of wolf. Or, again, the wolves inhabiting a mountainous district, and those frequenting the lowlands, would naturally be forced to hunt different prey; and from the continued preservation of the individuals best fitted for the two sites, two varieties might slowly be formed. These varieties would cross and blend where they met; but to this subject of intercrossing we shall soon have to return. I may add, that, according to Mr. Pierce, there are two varieties of the wolf inhabiting the Catskill Mountains in the United States, one with a light greyhound-like form, which pursues deer, and the other more bulky, with shorter legs, which more frequently attacks the shepherd's flocks.

3      Let us now take a more complex case. Certain plants excrete a sweet juice, apparently for the sake of eliminating something injurious from their sap; this is effected by glands at the base of the stipules in some Leguminosae, and at the back of the leaf of the common laurel. This juice, though small in quantity, is greedily sought by insects. Let us now suppose a little sweet juice or nectar to be excreted by the inner bases of the petals of a flower. In this case insects in seeking the nectar would get dusted with pollen, and would certainly often transport the pollen from one flower to the stigma of another flower. The flowers of two distinct individuals of the same species would thus get crossed; and the act of crossing, we have good reason to believe (as will hereafter be more fully alluded to), would produce very vigorous seedlings, which consequently would have the best chance of flourishing and surviving. Some of these seedlings would probably inherit the nectar-excreting power. Those individual flowers which had the largest glands or nectaries, and which excreted most nectar, would be oftenest visited by insects, and would be oftenest crossed; and so in the long-run would gain the upper hand. Those flowers, also, which had their stamens and pistils placed, in relation to the size and habits of the particular insects which visited them, so as to favor in any degree the transportal of their pollen from flower to flower, would likewise be favored or selected. We might have taken the case of insects visiting flowers for the sake of collecting pollen instead of nectar; and as pollen is formed for the sole object of fertilization, its destruction appears a simple loss to the plant; yet if a little pollen were carried, at first occasionally and then habitually, by the pollen-devouring insects from flower to flower, and a cross thus effected, although nine-tenths of the pollen were destroyed, it might still be a great gain to the plant; and those individuals which produced more and more pollen, and had larger and larger anthers, would be selected.

4      When our plant, by this process of the continued preservation or natural selection of more and more attractive flowers, had been rendered highly attractive to insects, they would, unintentionally on their part, regularly carry pollen from flower to flower; and that they can most effectually do this, I could easily show by many striking instances. I will give only one—not as a very striking case, but as likewise illustrating one step in the separation of the sexes of plants, presently to be alluded to. Some holly-trees bear only male flowers, which have

four stamens producing rather a small quantity of pollen, and a rudimentary pistil; other holly-trees bear only female flowers; these have a full-sized pistil, and four stamens with shriveled anthers, in which not a grain of pollen can be detected. Having found a female tree exactly sixty yards from a male tree, I put the stigmas of twenty flowers, taken from different branches, under the microscope, and on all, without exception, there were pollen-grains, and on some a profusion of pollen. As the wind had set for several days from the female to the male tree, the pollen could not thus have been carried. The weather had been cold and boisterous, and therefore not favorable to bees; nevertheless every female flower which I examined had been effectually fertilized by the bees, accidentally dusted with pollen, having flown from tree to tree in search of nectar. But to return to our imaginary case: as soon as the plant had been rendered so highly attractive to insects that pollen was regularly carried from flower to flower, another process might commence. No naturalist doubts the advantage of what has been called the "physiological division of labor"; hence we may believe that it would be advantageous to a plant to produce stamens alone in one flower or on one whole plant, and pistils alone in another flower or on another plant. In plants under culture and placed under new conditions of life, sometimes the male organs and sometimes the female organs become more or less impotent; now if we suppose this to occur in ever so slight a degree under nature, then as pollen is already carried regularly from flower to flower, and as a more complete separation of the sexes of our plant would be advantageous on the principle of the division of labor, individuals with this tendency more and more increased, would be continually favored or selected, until at last a complete separation of the sexes would be effected.

Let us now turn to the nectar-feeding insects in our imaginary case: we may 5 suppose the plant of which we have been slowly increasing the nectar by continued selection, to be a common plant; and that certain insects depended in main part on its nectar for food. I could give many facts, showing how anxious bees are to save time; for instance, their habit of cutting holes and sucking the nectar at the bases of certain flowers, which they can, with a very little more trouble, enter by the mouth. Bearing such facts in mind, I can see no reason to doubt that an accidental deviation in the size and form of the body, or in the curvature and length of the proboscis, etc., far too slight to be appreciated by us, might profit a bee or other insect, so that an individual so characterized would be able to obtain its food more quickly, and so have a better chance of living and leaving descendants. Its descendants would probably inherit a tendency to a similar slight deviation of structure. The tubes of the corollas of the common red and incarnate clovers (Trifolium pratense and incarnatum) do not on a hasty glance appear to differ in length; yet the hive-bee can easily suck the nectar out of the incarnate clover, but not out of the common red clover, which is visited by humble-bees alone; so that the whole fields of the red clover offer in vain an abundant supply of precious nectar to the hive-bee. Thus it might be a great advantage to the hive-bee to have a slightly longer or differently constructed proboscis. On the other hand, I have found by experiment that the fertility of clover greatly depends on bees visiting and moving parts of the corolla, so as to push the pollen on to the stigmatic surface. Hence, again, if humble-bees were to become rare in any country, it might be a great advantage to the red clover to have a shorter or more deeply divided tube to its corolla, so that the hive-bee could visit its flowers. Thus I can understand how a flower and a bee might slowly become, either simultaneously or one after the other, modified and adapted in the most perfect manner to each other, by the continued preservation of individuals presenting mutual and slightly favorable deviations of structure.

6      I am well aware that this doctrine of natural selection, exemplified in the above imaginary instances, is open to the same objections which were at first urged against Sir Charles Lyell's noble views on "the modern changes of the earth, as illustrative of geology"; but we now very seldom hear the action, for instance, of the coast-waves, called a trifling and insignificant cause, when applied to the excavation of gigantic valleys or to the formation of the longest lines of inland cliffs. Natural selection can act only by the preservation and accumulation of infinitesimally small inherited modifications, each profitable to the preserved being; and as modern geology has almost banished such views as the excavation of a great valley by a single diluvial wave, so will natural selection, if it be a true principle, banish the belief of the continued creation of new organic beings, or of any great and sudden modification in their structure.

## COMPREHENSION

1. What does Darwin mean by the term *natural selection?*
2. What is Darwin attempting to refute by his concept of natural selection? Where in the essay is this refutation articulated?
3. Explain what Darwin means by the "physiological division of labor" (paragraph 4).
4. Define the following terms: *innate* (paragraph 2), *stamens* and *pistils* (paragraph 3), *rudimentary* (paragraph 4), *incarnate* (paragraph 5), and *doctrine* (paragraph 6).

## RHETORIC

1. In the introduction, Darwin makes an analogy between the needs of humans and those of nature. What is this analogy, and why is it important in devising his argument?
2. What is the tone of the essay? Consider such phrases as "beg permission" (paragraph 1) and "Let us now" (paragraph 3).
3. Darwin uses two "imaginary illustrations" in an attempt to prove his point. What are they, and why are these hypothetical illustrations more effective than real-life ones for his purpose?
4. Darwin tends to use extremely long sentences when he wishes to illustrate a process. For example, the sentence in paragraph 3 that begins "We might

have taken" is 101 words long. Deconstruct this sentence by paying special attention to its punctuation, its logical succession of clauses, and its effect on the reader of describing so many processes within its boundaries. What is the relationship between its rhetorical style and purpose?

5. Who is the implied audience for the essay? Cite specific aspects of the rhetoric that led you to your conclusion.

6. What gives Darwin his authority? Specifically, how is his authority linked to the specialized vocabulary of the essay and to the way Darwin uses language to articulate natural processes?

7. Darwin uses the argumentative technique of disarming potential critics in the final paragraph. What is the rhetorical function of this device? Does it strengthen or weaken his argument? Explain your view.

## WRITING

1. Write a précis of the essay, focusing on the major points Darwin is trying to assert in his theory of natural selection.

2. **Writing an Argument:** In an essay, argue for or against the proposition that in order to agree with or refute Darwin's ideas of natural selection, one would have to have at least as much experience in observing nature as Darwin obviously had.

3. **Writing an Argument:** Argue for or against the view that Darwin's theory can have disastrous consequences for the human species if applied to politics, sociology, or economics.

| www.mhhe.com/ **mhreader** | For more information on Charles Darwin, go to: **More Resources > Ch. 14 Science & Technology** |

# Of Altruism, Heroism and Nature's Gifts in the Face of Terror

## Natalie Angier

*Natalie Angier (b. 1958) grew up in New York City and graduated from Barnard College in 1978. She started her career a founding staff member of* Discover *magazine, covering topics in biology. In 1990 she became a reporter for* The New York Times. *Her work as a* Times *science correspondent led to a Pulitzer Prize in 1991. She is also the recipient of the Lewis Thomas Award and was one of only seven journalists to receive four stars in the* Forbes Media Guide *that rated 500 reporters. Angier has also published in* The Atlantic, Parade, Washington Monthly, *and* Reader's Digest. *Her books include* The Beauty of the Beastly: New Views on the Nature of Life *(1995) and the national best-seller* Women: An Intimate Geography *(1999). In the following essay, which appeared in* The New York Times *one week after the terrorist attacks of September 11, 2001, Angier writes that evolution offers hopeful prospects for human nature.*

1  For the worldless, formless, expectant citizens of tomorrow, here are some post-cards of all that matters today:

2     Minutes after terrorists slam jet planes into the towers of the World Trade Center, streams of harrowed humanity crowd the emergency stairwells, heading in two directions. While terrified employees scramble down, toward exit doors and survival, hundreds of New York firefighters, each laden with 70 to 100 pounds of lifesaving gear, charge upward, never to be seen again.

3     As the last of four hijacked planes advances toward an unknown but surely populated destination, passengers huddle together and plot resistance against their captors, an act that may explain why the plane fails to reach its target, crashing instead into an empty field outside Pittsburgh.

4     Hearing of the tragedy whose dimensions cannot be charted or absorbed, tens of thousands of people across the nation storm their local hospitals and blood banks, begging for the chance to give blood, something of themselves to the hearts of the wounded—and the heart of us all—beating against the void.

5     Altruism and heroism. If not for these twin radiant badges of our humanity, there would be no us, and we know it. And so, when their vile opposite threatened to choke us into submission last Tuesday, we rallied them in quantities so great we surprised even ourselves.

6     Nothing and nobody can fully explain the source of the emotional genius that has been everywhere on display. Politicians have cast it as evidence of the indomitable spirit of a rock-solid America; pastors have given credit to a more celestial source. And while biologists in no way claim to have discovered the key to human nobility, they do have their own spin on the subject. The altruistic impulse, they say, is a nondenominational gift, the birthright and defining characteristic of the human species.

7     As they see it, the roots of altruistic behavior far predate *Homo sapiens*, and that is why it seems to flow forth so readily once tapped. Recent studies that model group dynamics suggest that a spirit of cooperation will arise in nature under a wide variety of circumstances.

8     "There's a general trend in evolutionary biology toward recognizing that very often the best way to compete is to cooperate," said Dr. Barbara Smuts, a professor of anthropology at the University of Michigan, who has published papers on the evolution of altruism. "And that, to me, is a source of some solace and comfort."

9     Moreover, most biologists concur that the human capacity for language and memory allows altruistic behavior—the desire to give, and to sacrifice for the sake of others—to flourish in measure far beyond the cooperative spirit seen in other species.

With language, they say, people can learn of individuals they have never   10
met and feel compassion for their suffering, and honor and even emulate their
heroic deeds. They can also warn one another of any selfish cheaters or malign
tricksters lurking in their midst.

"In a large crowd, we know who the good guys are, and we can talk about,   11
and ostracize, the bad ones," said Dr. Craig Packer, a professor of ecology and
evolution at the University of Minnesota. "People are very concerned about
their reputation, and that, too, can inspire us to be good."

Oh, better than good.   12

"There's a grandness in the human species that is so striking, and so pro-   13
foundly different from what we see in other animals," he added. "We are an
amalgamation of families working together. This is what civilization is derived
from."

At the same time, said biologists, the very conditions that encourage hero-   14
ics and selflessness can be the source of profound barbarism as well. "Moral
behavior is often a within-group phenomenon," said Dr. David Sloan Wilson, a
professor of biology at the State University of New York at Binghamton. "Altruism is practiced within your group, and often turned off toward members of
other groups."

The desire to understand the nature of altruism has occupied evolutionary   15
thinkers since Charles Darwin, who was fascinated by the apparent existence of
altruism among social insects. In ant and bee colonies, sterile female workers
labor ceaselessly for their queen, and will even die for her when the nest is
threatened. How could such seeming selflessness evolve, when it is exactly
those individuals that are behaving altruistically that fail to breed and thereby
pass their selfless genes along?

By a similar token, human soldiers who go to war often are at the beginning   16
of their reproductive potential, and many are killed before getting the chance to
have children. Why don't the stay-at-homes simply outbreed the do-gooders
and thus bury the altruistic impulse along with the casualties of combat?

The question of altruism was at least partly solved when the British evolu-   17
tionary theorist William Hamilton formulated the idea of inclusive fitness: the
notion that individuals can enhance their reproductive success not merely by
having young of their own, but by caring for their genetic relatives as well.
Among social bees and ants, it turns out, the sister workers are more closely
related to one another than parents normally are to their offspring; thus it be-
hooves the workers to care more about current and potential sisters than to fret
over their sterile selves.

The concept of inclusive fitness explains many brave acts observed in na-   18
ture. Dr. Richard Wrangham, a primatologist at Harvard, cites the example of
the red colobus monkey. When they are being hunted by chimpanzees, the male
monkeys are "amazingly brave," Dr. Wrangham said. "As the biggest and
strongest members of their group, they undoubtedly could escape quicker than
the others." Instead, the males jump to the front, confronting the chimpanzee
hunters while the mothers and offspring jump to safety. Often, the much bigger

chimpanzees pull the colobus soldiers off by their tails and slam them to their deaths.

19      Their courageousness can be explained by the fact that colobus monkeys live in multimale, multifemale groups in which the males are almost always related. So in protecting the young monkeys, the adult males are defending their kin.

20      Yet, as biologists are learning, there is more to cooperation and generosity than an investment in one's nepotistic patch of DNA. Lately, they have accrued evidence that something like group selection encourages the evolution of traits beneficial to a group, even when members of the group are not related.

21      In computer simulation studies, Dr. Smuts and her colleagues modeled two types of group-living agents that would behave like herbivores: one that would selfishly consume all the food in a given patch before moving on, and another that would consume resources modestly rather than greedily, thus allowing local plant food to regenerate.

22      Researchers had assumed that cooperators could collaborate with genetically unrelated cooperators only if they had the cognitive capacity to know goodness when they saw it.

23      But the data suggested otherwise. "These models showed that under a wide range of simulated environmental conditions you could get selection for prudent, cooperative behavior," Dr. Smuts said, even in the absence of cognition or kinship. "If you happened by chance to get good guys together, they remained together because they created a mutually beneficial environment."

24      This sort of win-win principle, she said, could explain all sorts of symbiotic arrangements, even among different species—like the tendency of baboons and impalas to associate together because they use each other's warning calls.

25      Add to this basic mechanistic selection for cooperation the human capacity to recognize and reward behaviors that strengthen the group—the tribe, the state, the church, the platoon—and selflessness thrives and multiplies. So, too, does the need for group identity. Classic so-called minimal group experiments have shown that when people are gathered together and assigned membership in arbitrary groups, called, say, the Greens and the Reds, before long the members begin expressing amity for their fellow Greens or Reds and animosity toward those of the wrong "color."

26      "Ancestral life frequently consisted of intergroup conflict," Dr. Wilson of SUNY said. "It's part of our mental heritage."

27      Yet he does not see conflict as inevitable. "It's been shown pretty well that where people place the boundary between us and them is extremely flexible and strategic," he said. "It's possible to widen the moral circle, and I'm optimistic enough to believe it can be done on a worldwide scale."

28      Ultimately, though, scientists acknowledge that the evolutionary framework for self-sacrificing acts is overlaid by individual choice. And it is there, when individual firefighters or office workers or airplane passengers choose the altruistic path, that science gives way to wonder.

29      Dr. James J. Moore, a professor of anthropology at the University of California at San Diego, said he had studied many species, including many different primates.

"We're the nicest species I know," he said. "To see those guys risking their lives, climbing over rubble on the chance of finding one person alive, well, you wouldn't find baboons doing that." The horrors of last week notwithstanding, he said, "the overall picture to come out about human nature is wonderful."

"For every 50 people making bomb threats now to mosques," he said, "there are 500,000 people around the world behaving just the way we hoped they would, with empathy and expressions of grief. We are amazingly civilized." 30

True, death-defying acts of heroism may be the province of the few. For the rest of us, simple humanity will do. 31

## COMPREHENSION

1. According to Angier, how should we view the events of September 11, 2001, from the perspective of evolutionary science? What else can we learn about human nature that cannot be explained by evolutionary biology? What does she say about Darwin?
2. Explain the relationship, as the writer presents it, between altruism and heroism. What does she mean by the "win-win principle" (paragraph 24)?
3. What experiments does the author cite to support her main ideas?

## RHETORIC

1. Which paragraphs constitute the author's introduction? What strategy does she employ to start her essay? Why is this introduction especially compelling?
2. What is Angier's claim? What types of evidence does she offer to support her argument? Where does she appeal to reason, ethics, and emotion? Does she engage in refutation? Why or why not?
3. How does the author use comparison and contrast to organize this selection? How does definition serve to advance the essay and the argument?
4. Explain the writer's tone. Is she objective or subjective? Is she optimistic or pessimistic? What other attitudes toward her subject can you detect? Justify your response.
5. Where does the writer use figurative language? What is the effect?
6. Angier's concluding paragraph is brief. Do you find it effective? Why or why not?

## WRITING

1. Using the data provided by Angier in her essay, and any additional research you may want to conduct, write an essay on the events of 9/11 from the perspective of evolutionary biology.

2.  Write a comparison/contrast essay on altruism and heroism, explaining why they are unique to the human species. Be certain to provide sufficient examples to support your thesis.

3.  **Writing an Argument:** In an essay, argue for or against the idea that the way we respond to crises confirms that we have evolved as a species. Provide evidence. Incorporate appeals to reason, ethics, and emotion. Refute those who might oppose your main and minor propositions.

www.mhhe.com/
**mhreader**

For more information on Natalie Angier, go to:
**More Resources > Ch. 14 Science & Technology**

## Synthesis: Classic and Contemporary Questions for Comparison

1.  How do Darwin and Angier approach the subject of evolution? Do they have the same or different priorities, and why? Are they writing for the same audience? Use examples from both selections to support your response.

2.  Analyze the language used in the two essays. What is similar or different about the style and diction of the two pieces? How does each use details? Is one essay more accessible to the modern reader? Why or why not?

3.  How do both essays reflect the scientific method? Is one selection more "scientific" in its approach than the other? Explain your response.

# Nutcracker.com

### David Sedaris

*David Sedaris (b. 1957), who was born in Johnson City, New York, and grew up in Raleigh, North Carolina, is a well-known humorist, essayist, diarist, short-story writer, and radio commentator. After graduating from the Art Institute of Chicago in 1987, Sedaris held several temporary jobs, ranging from a cleaner of apartments to an elf in SantaLand at Macy's. His stint on National Public Radio's* Morning Edition *established Sedaris as a popular if quirky humorist and led to his first collection of essays,* Barrel Fever (2000). *Termed by* Entertainment Weekly *"a crackpot in the best sense of the word," Sedaris has also written* Naked (1997), Me Talk Pretty One Day (2000), Dress Your Family in Corduroy and Denim (2004), *and other works. In this essay, Sedaris humorously explains why he is a technophobe.*

It was my father's dream that one day the people of the world would be con-  1
nected to one another through a network of blocky, refrigerator-size computers,
much like those he was helping develop at IBM. He envisioned families of the
future gathered around their mammoth terminals, ordering groceries and paying their taxes from the comfort of their own homes. A person could compose
music, design a doghouse, and . . . something more, something even better. "A
person could . . . he could . . ."

When predicting this utopia, he would eventually reach a point where  2
words failed him. His eyes would widen and sparkle at the thought of this inde-
scribable something more. "I mean, my God," he'd say, "just think about it."

My sisters and I preferred not to. I didn't know about them, but I was hop-  3
ing the people of the world might be united by something more interesting, like
drugs or an armed struggle against the undead. Unfortunately, my father's
team won, so computers it is. My only regret is that this had to happen during
my lifetime.

Somewhere in the back of my mind is a dim memory of standing in some  4
line holding a perforated card. I remember the cheap, slightly clinical feeling it
gave me, and recall thinking that the computer would never advance much
further than this. Call me naive, but I seem to have underestimated the universal desire to sit in a hard plastic chair and stare at a screen until your eyes cross.
My father saw it coming, but this was a future that took me completely by surprise. There were no computers in my high school, and the first two times I attempted college, people were still counting on their fingers and removing their
shoes when the numbers got above ten. I wasn't really aware of computers until the mid-1980s. For some reason, I seemed to know quite a few graphic designers whose homes and offices pleasantly stank of Spray Mount. Their floors
were always collaged with stray bits of paper, and trapped flies waved for help
from the gummy killing fields of their tabletops. I had always counted on these
friends to loan me the adhesive of my choice, but then, seemingly overnight,
their Scotch tape and rubber cement were gone, replaced with odorless computers and spongy mouse pads. They had nothing left that I wanted to borrow,
and so I dropped them and fell in with a group of typesetters who ultimately
betrayed me as well.

Thanks to my complete lack of office skills, I found it fairly easy to avoid  5
direct contact with the new technology. The indirect contact was disturbing
enough. I was still living in Chicago when I began to receive creepy Christmas
newsletters designed to look like tabloids and annual reports. Word processors
made writing fun. They did not, however, make reading fun, a point made
painfully evident by such publications as *The Herald Family Tribune* and *Wassup
with the Wexlers!*

Friends who had previously expressed no interest in torture began send-  6
ing letters composed to resemble Chinese take-out menus and the Dead Sea
Scrolls. Everybody had a font, and I was told that I should get one, too. The
authors of these letters shared an enthusiasm with the sort of people who now
arrived at dinner parties hoisting expensive new video cameras and suggesting

that, after dessert, we all sit down and replay the evening on TV. We, the regular people of the world, now had access to the means of production, but still I failed to see what all the fuss was about. A dopey letter is still a dopey letter, no matter how you dress it up; and there's a reason regular people don't appear on TV: we're boring.

7      By the early 1990s I was living in New York and working for a house-cleaning company. My job taught me that regardless of their purported virtues, computers are a pain in the ass to keep clean. The pebbled surface is a magnet for grease and dirt, and you can pretty much forget about reaming out the gaps in the keyboard. More than once I accidentally pushed a button and recoiled in terror as the blank screen came to life with exotic tropical fish or swarms of flying toasters. Equally distressing was the way people used the slanted roofs of their terminals to display framed photographs and great populations of plush and plastic creatures, which would fall behind the desk the moment I began cleaning the screen. There was never any place to plug in the vacuum, as every outlet was occupied by some member of the computer family. Cords ran wild, and everyone seemed to own one of those ominous foot-long power strips with the blinking red light that sends the message YOU MUST LEAVE US ALONE. I was more than happy to comply, and the complaints came rolling in.

8      Due to my general aversion to machines and a few pronounced episodes of screaming, I was labeled a technophobe, a term that ranks fairly low on my scale of fightin' words. The word *phobic* has its place when properly used, but lately it's been declawed by the pompous insistence that most animosity is based upon fear rather than loathing. No credit is given for distinguishing between these two very different emotions. I fear snakes. I hate computers. My hatred is entrenched, and I nourish it daily. I'm comfortable with it, and no community outreach program will change my mind.

9      I hate computers for getting their own section in the *New York Times* and for lengthening commercials with the mention of a Web site address. Who really wants to find out more about Procter & Gamble? Just buy the toothpaste or laundry detergent, and get on with it. I hate them for creating the word *org* and I hate them for e-mail, which isn't real mail but a variation of the pointless notes people used to pass in class. I hate computers for replacing the card catalog in the New York Public Library and I hate the way they've invaded the movies. I'm not talking about their contribution to the world of special effects. I have nothing against a well-defined mutant or full-scale alien invasion—that's *good* technology. I'm talking about their actual presence *in* any given movie. They've become like horses in a western—they may not be the main focus, but everybody seems to have one. Each tiresome new thriller includes a scene in which the hero, trapped by some version of the enemy, runs for his desk in a desperate race against time. Music swells and droplets of sweat rain down onto the keyboard as he sits at his laptop, frantically pawing for answers. It might be different if he were flagging down a passing car or trying to phone for help, but typing, in and of itself, is not an inherently dramatic activity.

I hate computers for any number of reasons, but I despise them most for 10 what they've done to my friend the typewriter. In a democratic country you'd think there would be room for both of them, but computers won't rest until I'm making my ribbons from torn shirts and brewing Wite-Out in my bathtub. Their goal is to place the IBM Selectric II beside the feather quill and chisel in the museum of antiquated writing implements. They're power hungry, and someone needs to stop them.

When told I'm like the guy still pining for his eight-track tapes, I say, "You 11 have eight-tracks? Where?" In reality I know nothing about them, yet I feel it's important to express some solidarity with others who have had the rug pulled out from beneath them. I don't care if it can count words or rearrange paragraphs at the push of a button, I don't want a computer. Unlike the faint scurry raised by fingers against a plastic computer keyboard, the smack and clatter of a typewriter suggests that you're actually building something. At the end of a miserable day, instead of grieving my virtual nothing, I can always look at my loaded wastepaper basket and tell myself that if I failed, at least I took a few trees down with me.

When forced to leave my house for an extended period of time, I take my 12 typewriter with me, and together we endure the wretchedness of passing through the X-ray scanner. The laptops roll merrily down the belt, while I'm instructed to stand aside and open my bag. To me it seems like a normal enough thing to be carrying, but the typewriter's declining popularity arouses suspicion and I wind up eliciting the sort of reaction one might expect when traveling with a cannon.

"It's a typewriter," I say. "You use it to write angry letters to airport au- 13 thorities."

The keys are then slapped and pounded, and I'm forced to explain that if you 14 want the words to appear, you first have to plug it in and insert a sheet of paper.

The goons shake their heads and tell me I really should be using a com- 15 puter. That's their job, to stand around in an ill-fitting uniform and tell you how you should lead your life. I'm told the exact same thing later in the evening when the bellhop knocks on my hotel door. The people whose televisions I can hear have complained about my typing, and he has come to make me stop. To hear him talk, you'd think I'd been playing the kettledrum. In the great scheme of things, the typewriter is not nearly as loud as he makes it out to be, but there's no use arguing with him. "You know," he says, "you really should be using a computer."

You have to wonder where you've gone wrong when twice a day you're 16 offered writing advice from men in funny hats. The harder I'm pressured to use a computer, the harder I resist. One by one, all of my friends have deserted me and fled to the dark side. "How can I write you if you don't have an e-mail ad-dress?" they ask. They talk of their B-trees and Disk Doctors and then have the nerve to complain when I discuss bowel obstructions at the dinner table.

*Who needs them?* I think. I figured I'd always have my family and was dev- 17 astated when my sister Amy brought home a candy-colored laptop. "I only use it for e-mail," she said. Coming from her, these words made me physically ill.

"It's fun," she said. "People send you things. Look at this." She pushed a button, and there, on the screen, was a naked man lying facedown on a carpet. His hair was graying and his hands were cuffed behind his doughy back. A woman entered the room. You couldn't see her face, just her legs and feet, which were big and mean-looking, forced into sharp-toed shoes with high, pencil-thin heels. The man on the carpet shifted position, and when his testicles came into view, the woman reacted as if she had seen an old balding mouse, one that she had been trying to kill for a long time. She stomped on the man's testicles with the toes of her shoes and then she turned around and stomped on them with the heels. She kicked them mercilessly and, just when I thought she'd finished, she got her second wind and started all over again.

18      I'd never realized that a computer could act so much like a TV set. No one had ever told me that the picture could be so clear, that the cries of pain could be heard so distinctly. This, I thought, was what my father had been envisioning all those years ago when words had failed him, not necessarily this scene, but something equally capable of provoking such wonder.

19      "Again?" Amy pushed a button and, our faces bathed in the glow of the screen, we watched the future a second time.

## COMPREHENSION

1. What distinguishes the author from his father and his sister Amy?
2. Why does Sedaris hate computers? Does he actually enjoy being a "technophobe"? How do you know?
3. What sort of writer is Sedaris? Why doesn't he want to use computers to help him in the writing process?

## RHETORIC

1. How do you interpret the title? How does the title prepare us for the tone of this selection?
2. Sedaris employs a personal voice in this essay. What does the "I" point of view contribute to the selection?
3. What comic strategies does the author develop? What details stand out? Does comedy serve to support or undercut his claim?
4. How does Sedaris argue his case? Does he actually have a case, or a cause, or is his purpose simply to amuse the reader? How do you know?
5. What principle of classification appears in the essay, and how does this rhetorical strategy serve the author's purpose?
6. How does the writer use comparison and contrast, narration, and description to develop the essay?
7. Explain the impact and significance of the concluding scene. How does the tone alter here? What is the final effect? What is the writer's parting message to his readers?

### WRITING

1. In a personal essay employing narration and description as well as analysis, describe the impact of computers on your family life. Use a comic approach to the subject.
2. Write an analysis of the elements of humor that appear in Sedaris's essay. Why is comedy an appropriate strategy for dealing with the subject of computer technology?
3. **Writing an Argument:** Write an essay about why you love or hate computers. Use ironic humor to undercut your argument—to convince readers that your opinions are actually the opposite of what you proclaim.

**www.mhhe.com/
mhreader**   For more information on David Sedaris, go to:
**More Resources > Ch. 14 Science and Technology**

# How Computers Change
# the Way We Think

### Sherry Turkle

*Sherry Turkle (b. 1948), born and raised in New York City, attended Harvard University where she received her BA (1970), MA (1973), and PhD (1976). A professor in the Program in Science, Technology, and Society at the Massachusetts Institute of Technology, Turkle observes: "I study the sociology of sciences of mind, a study of the interactions among technical, literary, and popular discourses about the self as they develop in specific social contexts." The results of Turkle's research appear in* Psychoanalytic Politics: Freud's French Revolution *(1992),* The Second Self: Computers and the Human Spirit *(1984), and* Life on the Screen: Identity in the Age of the Internet *(1995). "My work on computation," Turkle states, "begins with the premise that we live in a nascent computer culture that will exert an analogous influence on the way we think"—an idea she explores in the following essay, which appeared in a 2004 issue of* The Chronicle of Higher Education.

The tools we use to think change the ways in which we think. The invention of   1
written language brought about a radical shift in how we process, organize, store, and transmit representations of the world. Although writing remains our primary information technology, today when we think about the impact of technology on our habits of mind, we think primarily of the computer.

2      My first encounters with how computers change the way we think came soon after I joined the faculty at the Massachusetts Institute of Technology in the late 1970s, at the end of the era of the slide rule and the beginning of the era of the personal computer. At a lunch for new faculty members, several senior professors in engineering complained that the transition from slide rules to calculators had affected their students' ability to deal with issues of scale. When students used slide rules, they had to insert decimal points themselves. The professors insisted that that required students to maintain a mental sense of scale, whereas those who relied on calculators made frequent errors in orders of magnitude. Additionally, the students with calculators had lost their ability to do "back of the envelope" calculations, and with that, an intuitive feel for the material.

3      That same semester, taught a course in the history of psychology. There, I experienced the impact of computational objects on students' ideas about their emotional lives. My class had read Freud's essay on slips of the tongue, with its famous first example: The chairman of a parliamentary session opens a meeting by declaring it closed. The students discussed how Freud interpreted such errors as revealing a person's mixed emotions. A computer-science major disagreed with Freud's approach. The mind, she argued, is a computer. And in a computational dictionary—like we have in the human mind—"closed" and "open" are designated by the same symbol, separated by a sign for opposition. "Closed" equals "minus open." To substitute "closed" for "open" does not require the notion of ambivalence or conflict.

4      "When the chairman made that substitution," she declared, "a bit was dropped; a minus sign was lost. There was a power surge. No problem."

5      The young woman turned a Freudian slip into an information-processing error. An explanation in terms of meaning had become an explanation in terms of mechanism.

6      Such encounters turned me to the study of both the instrumental and the subjective sides of the nascent computer culture. As an ethnographer and psychologist, I began to study not only what the computer was doing for us, but what it was doing to us, including how it was changing the way we see ourselves, our sense of human identity.

7      In the 1980s, I surveyed the psychological effects of computational object in everyday life—largely the unintended side effects of people's tendency to project thoughts and feelings onto their machines. In the 20 years since, computational objects have become more explicitly designed to have emotional and cognitive effects. And those "effects by design" will become even stronger in the decade to come. Machines are being designed to serve explicitly as companions, pets, and tutors. And they are introduced in school settings for the youngest children.

8      Today, starting in elementary school, students use e-mail, word processing, computer simulations, virtual communities, and PowerPoint software. In the process, they are absorbing more than the content of what appears on their screens. They are learning new ways to think about what it means to know and understand.

What follows is a short and certainly not comprehensive list of areas where 9
I see information technology encouraging changes in thinking. There can be no
simple way of cataloging whether any particular change is good or bad. That is
contested terrain. At every step we have to ask, as educators and citizens,
whether current technology is leading us in directions that serve our human
purposes. Such questions are not technical; they are social, moral, and political.
For me, addressing that subjective side of computation is one of the more significant challenges for the next decade of information technology in higher education. Technology does not determine change, but it encourages us to take
certain directions. If we make those directions clear, we can more easily exert
human choice.

**Thinking about privacy.** Today's college students are habituated to a 10
world of online blogging, instant messaging, and Web browsing that leaves
electronic traces. Yet they have had little experience with the right to privacy.
Unlike past generations of Americans, who grew up with the notion that the
privacy of their mail was sacrosanct, our children are accustomed to electronic
surveillance as part of their daily lives.

I have colleagues who feel that the increased incursions on privacy have 11
put the topic more in the news, and that this is a positive change. But middle-
school and high-school students tend to be willing to provide personal information online with no safeguards, and college students seem uninterested in
violations of privacy and in increased governmental and commercial surveillance. Professors find that students do not understand that in a democracy, privacy is a right, not merely a privilege. In 10 years, ideas about the relationship
of privacy and government will require even more active pedagogy. (One might
also hope that increased education about the kinds of silent surveillance that
technology makes possible may inspire more active political engagement with
the issue.)

**Avatars or a self?** Chat rooms, role-playing games, and other technological 12
venues offer us many different contexts for presenting ourselves online. Those
possibilities are particularly important for adolescents because they offer what
Erik Erikson described as a moratorium, a time out or safe space for the personal experimentation that is so crucial for adolescent development. Our dangerous world—with crime, terrorism, drugs, and AIDS—offers little in the way
of safe spaces. Online worlds can provide valuable spaces for identity play.

But some people who gain fluency in expressing multiple aspects of self 13
may find it harder to develop authentic selves. Some children who write narratives for their screen avatars may grow up with too little experience of how to
share their real feelings with other people. For those who are lonely yet afraid
of intimacy, information technology has made it possible to have the illusion of
companionship without the demands of friendship.

**From powerful ideas to PowerPoint.** In the 1970s and early 1980s, some 14
educators wanted to make programming part of the regular curriculum for K–12
education. They argued that because information technology carries ideas, it
might as well carry the most powerful ideas that computer science has to offer.

It is ironic that in most elementary schools today, the ideas being carried by information technology are not ideas from computer science like procedural thinking, but more likely to be those embedded in productivity tools like PowerPoint presentation software.

15    PowerPoint does more than provide a way of transmitting content. It carries its own way of thinking, its own aesthetic—which not surprisingly shows up in the aesthetic of college freshmen. In that aesthetic, presentation becomes its own powerful idea.

16    To be sure, the software cannot be blamed for lower intellectual standards. Misuse of the former is as much a symptom as a cause of the latter. Indeed, the culture in which our children are raised is increasingly a culture of presentation, a corporate culture in which appearance is often more important than reality. In contemporary political discourse, the bar has also been lowered. Use of rhetorical devices at the expense of cogent argument regularly goes without notice. But it is precisely because standards of intellectual rigor outside the educational sphere have fallen that educators must attend to how we use, and when we introduce, software that has been designed to simplify the organization and processing of information.

17    In *The Cognitive Style of PowerPoint* (Graphics Press, 2003), Edward R. Tufts suggests that PowerPoint equates bulleting with clear thinking. It does not teach students to begin a discussion or construct a narrative. It encourages presentation, not conversation. Of course, in the hands of a master teacher, a PowerPoint presentation with few words and powerful images can serve as the jumping-off point for a brilliant lecture. But in the hands of elementary-school students, often introduced to PowerPoint in the third grade, and often infatuated with its swooshing sounds, animated icons, and flashing text, a slide show is more likely to close down debate than open it up.

18    Developed to serve the needs of the corporate boardroom, the software is designed to convey absolute authority. Teachers used to tell students that clear exposition depended on clear outlining, but presentation software has fetishized the outline at the expense of the content.

19    Narrative, the exposition of content, takes time. PowerPoint, like so much in the computer culture, speeds up the pace.

20    **Word processing vs. thinking.** The catalog for the Vermont Country Store advertises a manual typewriter, which the advertising copy says "moves at a pace that allows time to compose your thoughts." As many of us know, it is possible to manipulate text on a computer screen and see how it looks faster than we can think about what the words mean.

21    Word processing has its own complex psychology. From a pedagogical point of view, it can make dedicated students into better writers because it allows them to revise text, rearrange paragraphs, and experiment with the tone and shape of an essay. Few professional writers would part with their computers; some claim that they simply cannot think without their hands on the keyboard. Yet the ability to quickly fill the page, to see it before you can think it, can make bad writers even worse.

A seventh grader once told me that the typewriter she found in her mother's 22 attic is "cool because you have to type each letter by itself. You have to know what you are doing in advance or it comes out a mess." The idea of thinking ahead has become exotic.

**Taking things at interface value.** We expect software to be easy to use, and 23 we assume that we don't have to know how a computer works. In the early 1980s, most computer users who spoke of transparency meant that, as with any other machine, you could "open the hood" and poke around. But only a few years later, Macintosh users began to use the term when they talked about seeing their documents and programs represented by attractive and easy-to-interpret icons. They were referring to an ability to make things work without needing to go below the screen surface. Paradoxically, it was the screen's opacity that permitted that kind of transparency. Today, when people say that something is transparent, they mean that they can see how to make it work, not that they know how it works. In other words, transparency means epistemic opacity.

The people who built or bought the first generation of personal computers 24 understood them down to the bits and bytes. The next generation of operating systems were more complex, but they still invited that old-time reductive understanding. Contemporary information technology encourages different habits of mind. Today's college students are already used to taking things at (inter) face value; their successors in 2014 will be even less accustomed to probing below the surface.

**Simulation and its discontents.** Some thinkers argue that the new opacity 25 is empowering, enabling anyone to use the most sophisticated technological tools and to experiment with simulation in complex and creative ways. But it is also true that our tools carry the message that they are beyond our understanding. It is possible that in daily life, epistemic opacity can lead to passivity.

I first became aware of that possibility in the early 1990s, when the first genera- 26 tion of complex simulation games were introduced and immediately became popular for home as well as school use. SimLife teaches the principles of evolution by getting children involved in the development of complex ecosystems; in that sense it is an extraordinary learning tool. During one session in which I played SimLife with Tim, a 13-year-old, the screen before us flashed a message: "Your orgot is being eaten up." "What's an orgot?" I asked. Tim didn't know. "I just ignore that," he said confidently. "You don't need to know that kind of stuff to play."

For me, that story serves as a cautionary tale. Computer simulations enable 27 their users to think about complex phenomena as dynamic, evolving systems. But they also accustom us to manipulating systems whose core assumptions we may not understand and that may not be true.

We live in a culture of simulation. Our games, our economic and political sys- 28 tems, and the ways architects design buildings, chemists envisage molecules, and surgeons perform operations all use simulation technology. In 10 years the degree to which simulations are embedded in every area of life will have increased exponentially. We need to develop a new form of media literacy: readership for the culture of simulation.

29    We come to written text with habits of readership based on centuries of civilization. At the very least, we have learned to begin with the journalist's traditional questions: who, what, when, where, why, and how. Who wrote these words, what is their message, why were they written, and how are they situated in time and place, politically and socially? A central project for higher education during the next 10 years should be creating programs in information-technology literacy, with the goal of teaching students to interrogate simulations in much the same spirit, challenging their built-in assumptions.

30    Despite the ever-increasing complexity of software, most computer environments put users in worlds based on constrained choices. In other words, immersion in programmed worlds puts us in reassuring environments where the rules are clear. For example, when you play a video game, you often go through a series of frightening situations that you escape by mastering the rules—you experience life as a reassuring dichotomy of scary and safe. Children grow up in a culture of video games, action films, fantasy epics, and computer programs that all rely on that familiar scenario of almost losing but then regaining total mastery: There is danger. It is mastered. A still-more-powerful monster appears. It is subdued. Scary. Safe.

31    Yet in the real world, we have never had a greater need to work our way out of binary assumptions. In the decade ahead, we need to rebuild the culture around information technology. In that new sociotechnical culture, assumptions about the nature of mastery would be less absolute. The new culture would make it easier, not more difficult, to consider life in shades of gray, to see moral dilemmas in terms other than a battle between Good and Evil. For never has our world been more complex, hybridized, and global. Never have we so needed to have many contradictory thoughts and feelings at the same time. Our tools must help us accomplish that, not fight against us.

32    Information technology is identity technology. Embedding it in a culture that supports democracy, freedom of expression, tolerance, diversity, and complexity of opinion is one of the next decade's greatest challenges. We cannot afford to fail.

33    When I first began studying the computer culture, a small breed of highly trained technologists thought of themselves as "computer people." That is no longer the case. If we take the computer as a carrier of a way of knowing, a way of seeing the world and our place in it, we are all computer people now.

## COMPREHENSION

1. According to Turkle, in what ways do computers change the ways we think?
2. What does Turkle mean by "the instrumental and subjective sides of nascent computer culture" (paragraph 6)? What examples of these two sides does she offer?
3. What are some of the challenges facing the "sociotechnical culture" Turkle says we are entering?

## RHETORIC

1. Turkle published this essay in a weekly newspaper designed for people in higher education. What stylistic elements suggest that she gears her writing to this specialized audience? How does she make the article accessible to a broader, secondary audience?
2. What is Turkle's thesis, and where does she state it?
3. How does Turkle use classification to advance her thesis and organize the essay? Where does she employ process and causal analysis?
4. What comparative points does the writer draw between actual and virtual reality?
5. Turkle's paragraphs are relatively brief, some no more than two or three sentences. Why does she employ this method? Does this strategy ruin the coherence of the essay or weaken the emphasis on certain ideas? Why or why not?
6. In the final analysis, does Turkle prove the point made in the final paragraph, that "we are all computer people now"?

## WRITING

1. Using Turkle's essay as a model, write a classification essay on the ways that computers are changing the way we think.
2. Select one area where information technology is changing our processes and habits of thought, and write an essay explaining this phenomenon.
3. **Writing an Argument:** Do you agree or disagree with Turkle's assertion that information technology can foster democracy? Write a persuasive essay that articulates your position on the issue.

www.mhhe.com/ **mhreader**

For more information on Sherry Turkle, go to: **More Resources > Ch. 14 Science & Technology**

# Can We Know the Universe? Reflections on a Grain of Salt

### Carl Sagan

*Carl Edward Sagan (1931–1996) received BA, BS, MA, and PhD degrees from the University of Chicago. Probably the most popular scientist in America in the 1970s and 1980s, he was the host of several television series on science and wrote a number of best-selling books on science, including* The Dragons of Eden *(1977) and* Broca's Brain *(1979). The former earned him a Pulitzer Prize for general nonfiction in 1978. He also contributed hundreds of papers to scientific journals. Besides writing, Sagan served as a full-time professor at Cornell University and a visiting professor at dozens of other institutions of higher learning in the United States and abroad. He was also an activist for many philanthropic causes and served as an advisor to groups such as the Council for a Livable World Education Fund, the Children's Health Fund, and the American Committee on U.S.–Soviet Relations. Despite controversies surrounding the speculative nature of his work, Carl Sagan was one of modern science's most popular spokespersons. Sagan's philosophy may be summed up in a statement he made in a* Time *magazine interview. "We make our world significant by the courage of our questions and by the depth of our answers."*

*Nothing is rich but the inexhaustible wealth of nature. She shows us only surfaces, but she is a million fathoms deep.*

—*Ralph Waldo Emerson*

1   Science is a way of thinking much more than it is a body of knowledge. Its goal is to find out how the world works, to seek what regularities there may be, to penetrate to the connections of things—from subnuclear particles, which may be the constituents of all matter, to living organisms, the human social community, and thence to the cosmos as a whole. Our intuition is by no means an infallible guide. Our perceptions may be distorted by training and prejudice or merely because of the limitations of our sense organs, which, of course, perceive directly but a small fraction of the phenomena of the world. Even so straightforward a question as whether in the absence of friction a pound of lead falls faster than a gram of fluff was answered incorrectly by Aristotle and almost everyone else before the time of Galileo. Science is based on experiment, on a willingness to challenge old dogma, on an openness to see the universe as it really is. Accordingly, science sometimes requires courage—at the very least the courage to question the conventional wisdom.

2   Beyond this the main trick of science is to *really* think of something: the shape of clouds and their occasional sharp bottom edges at the same altitude everywhere in the sky; the formation of a dewdrop on a leaf; the origin of a name or a word—Shakespeare, say, or "philanthropic"; the reason for human social customs—the incest taboo, for example; how it is that a lens in sunlight can make paper burn; how a "walking stick" got to look so much like a twig; why the Moon seems to follow us as we walk; what prevents us from digging a hole down to the center of the Earth; what the definition is of "down" on a spherical Earth; how it is possible for the body to convert yesterday's lunch into today's muscle and sinew; or how far is up—does the universe go on forever, or if it does not, is there any meaning to the question of what lies on the other side? Some of these questions are pretty easy. Others, especially the last, are mysteries to which no one even today knows the answer. They are natural

questions to ask. Every culture has posed such questions in one way or another. Almost always the proposed answers are in the nature of "Just So Stories," attempted explanations divorced from experiment, or even from careful comparative observations.

But the scientific cast of mind examines the world critically as if many 3 alternative worlds might exist, as if other things might be here which are not. Then we are forced to ask why what we see is present and not something else. Why are the Sun and the Moon and the planets spheres? Why not pyramids, or cubes, or dodecahedra? Why not irregular, jumbly shapes? Why so symmetrical, worlds? If you spend any time spinning hypotheses, checking to see whether they make sense, whether they conform to what else we know, thinking of tests you can pose to substantiate or deflate your hypotheses, you will find yourself doing science. And as you come to practice this habit of thought more and more you will get better and better at it. To penetrate into the heart of the thing—even a little thing, a blade of grass, as Walt Whitman said—is to experience a kind of exhilaration that, it may be, only human beings of all the beings on this planet can feel. We are an intelligent species and the use of our intelligence quite properly gives us pleasure. In this respect the brain is like a muscle. When we think well, we feel good. Understanding is a kind of ecstasy.

But to what extent can we *really* know the universe around us? Sometimes 4 this question is posed by people who hope the answer will be in the negative, who are fearful of a universe in which everything might one day be known. And sometimes we hear pronouncements from scientists who confidently state that everything worth knowing will soon be known—or even is already known—and who paint pictures of a Dionysian or Polynesian age in which the zest for intellectual discovery has withered, to be replaced by a kind of subdued languor, the lotus eaters drinking fermented coconut milk or some other mild hallucinogen. In addition to maligning both the Polynesians, who were intrepid explorers (and whose brief respite in paradise is now sadly ending), as well as the inducements to intellectual discovery provided by some hallucinogens, this contention turns out to be trivially mistaken.

Let us approach a much more modest question: not whether we can know 5 the universe or the Milky Way Galaxy or a star or a world. Can we know, ultimately and in detail, a grain of salt? Consider one microgram of table salt, a speck just barely large enough for someone with keen eyesight to make out without a microscope. In that grain of salt there are about $10^{16}$ sodium and chlorine atoms. This is a 1 followed by 16 zeros, 10 million billion atoms. If we wish to know a grain of salt, we must know at least the three-dimensional positions of each of these atoms. (In fact, there is much more to be known—for example, the nature of the forces between the atoms—but we are making only a modest calculation.) Now, is this number more or less than the number of things which the brain can know?

How much *can* the brain know? There are perhaps $10^{11}$ neurons in the brain, 6 the circuit elements and switches that are responsible in their electrical and chemical activity for the functioning of our minds. A typical brain neuron has perhaps a thousand little wires, called dendrites, which connect it with its fellows. If, as seems likely, every bit of information in the brain corresponds to one of these connections, the total number of things knowable by the brain is no more than $10^{14}$, one hundred trillion. But this number is only one percent of the number of atoms in our speck of salt.

7      So in this sense the universe is intractable, astonishingly immune to any human attempt at full knowledge. We cannot on this level understand a grain of salt, much less the universe.

8      But let us look a little more deeply at our microgram of salt. Salt happens to be a crystal in which, except for defects in the structure of the crystal lattice, the position of every sodium and chlorine atom is predetermined. If we could shrink ourselves into this crystalline world, we would see rank upon rank of atoms in an ordered array, a regularly alternating structure—sodium, chlorine, sodium, chlorine, specifying the sheet of atoms we are standing on and all the sheets above us and below us. An absolutely pure crystal of salt could have the position of every atom specified by something like 10 bits of information.[1] This would not strain the information-carrying capacity of the brain.

9      If the universe had natural laws that governed its behavior to the same degree of regularity that determines a crystal of salt, then, of course, the universe would be knowable. Even if there were many such laws, each of considerable complexity, human beings might have the capability to understand them all. Even if such knowledge exceeded the information-carrying capacity of the brain, we might store the additional information outside our bodies—in books, for example, or in computer memories—and still, in some sense, know the universe.

10     Human beings are, understandably, highly motivated to find regularities, natural laws. The search for rules, the only possible way to understand such a vast and complex universe, is called science. The universe forces those who live in it to understand it. Those creatures who find everyday experience a muddled jumble of events with no predictability, no regularity, are in grave peril. The universe belongs to those who, at least to some degree, have figured it out.

11     It is an astonishing fact that there *are* laws of nature, rules that summarize conveniently—not just qualitatively but quantitatively—how the world works. We might imagine a universe in which there are no such laws, in which the $10^{80}$ elementary particles that make up a universe like our own behave with utter and uncompromising abandon. To understand such a universe we would need a brain at least as massive as the universe. It seems unlikely that such a universe could have life and intelligence, because beings and brains require some

---

[1]Chlorine is a deadly poison gas employed on European battlefields in World War I. Sodium is a corrosive metal which burns upon contact with water. Together they make a placid and unpoisonous material, table salt. Why each of these substances has the properties it does is a subject called chemistry, which requires more than 10 bits of information to understand.

degree of internal stability and order. But even if in a much more random universe there were such beings with an intelligence much greater than our own, there could not be much knowledge, passion or joy.

Fortunately for us, we live in a universe that has at least important parts that are knowable. Our common-sense experience and our evolutionary history have prepared us to understand something of the workaday world. When we go into other realms, however, common sense and ordinary intuition turn out to be highly unreliable guides. It is stunning that as we go close to the speed of light our mass increases indefinitely, we shrink toward zero thickness in the direction of motion, and time for us comes as near to stopping as we would like. Many people think that this is silly, and every week or two I get a letter from someone who complains to me about it. But it is a virtually certain consequence not just of experiment but also of Albert Einstein's brilliant analysis of space and time called the Special Theory of Relativity. It does not matter that these effects seem unreasonable to us. We are not in the habit of traveling close to the speed of light. The testimony of our common sense is suspect at high velocities.

Or consider an isolated molecule composed of two atoms shaped something like a dumbbell—a molecule of salt, it might be. Such a molecule rotates about an axis through the line connecting the two atoms. But in the world of quantum mechanics, the realm of the very small, not all orientations of our dumbbell molecule are possible. It might be that the molecule could be oriented in a horizontal position, say, or in a vertical position, but not at many angles in between. Some rotational positions are forbidden. Forbidden by what? By the laws of nature. The universe is built in such a way as to limit, or quantize, rotation. We do not experience this directly in everyday life; we would find it startling as well as awkward in sitting-up exercises, to find arms outstretched from the sides or pointed up to the skies permitted but many intermediate positions forbidden. We do not live in the world of the small, on the scale of $10^{-13}$ centimeters, in the realm where there are twelve zeros between the decimal place and the one. Our common-sense intuitions do not count. What does count is experiment—in this case observations from the far infrared spectra of molecules. They show molecular rotation to be quantized.

The idea that the world places restrictions on what humans might do is frustrating. Why *shouldn't* we be able to have intermediate rotational positions? Why *can't* we travel faster than the speed of light? But so far as we can tell, this is the way the universe is constructed. Such prohibitions not only press us toward a little humility; they also make the world more knowable. Every restriction corresponds to a law of nature, a regularization of the universe. The more restrictions there are on what matter and energy can do, the more knowledge human beings can attain. Whether in some sense the universe is ultimately knowable depends not only on how many natural laws there are that encompass widely divergent phenomena, but also on whether we have the openness and the intellectual capacity to understand such laws.

Our formulations of the regularities of nature are surely dependent on how the brain is built, but also, and to a significant degree, on how the universe is built.

15    For myself, I like a universe that includes much that is unknown and, at the same time, much that is knowable. A universe in which everything is known would be static and dull, as boring as the heaven of some weak-minded theologians. A universe that is unknowable is no fit place for a thinking being. The ideal universe for us is one very much like the universe we inhabit. And I would guess that this is not really much of a coincidence.

## COMPREHENSION

1.  What is the thesis of the essay? In what paragraph is this thesis most clearly expressed?
2.  Why does Sagan say, in paragraph 12, that in many circumstances, "common sense and ordinary intuition turn out to be highly unreliable guides"?
3.  Why does Sagan say, in his conclusion, that "the ideal universe for us is one very much like the universe we inhabit"?

## RHETORIC

1.  What is the function of the epigram by Emerson? How does it relate to the essay proper?
2.  Many of the paragraphs in the essay begin with coordinating conjunctions (a structure frowned on by many high school English teachers). What is Sagan's rhetorical purpose in using them as connecting devices?
3.  What specific clues are there in the essay that Sagan's tone is one of excitement and celebration regarding science?
4.  Sagan refers often to what he calls "a law of nature." Where and how in the essay does he explain, describe, or define this term?
5.  The essay begins abruptly with an explanation of the concept of science. What purpose is served by diving into the subject so dramatically?
6.  What is the intended effect of combining the terms *universe* and *grain of salt* in the title and subtitle? How does the author exploit this juxtaposition in his essay?
7.  Examine the italicized words in the essay. Why has Sagan chosen to italicize these words? Explain.

## WRITING

1.  Write a personal essay in which you describe how you felt when you suddenly understood a particular topic in school that had previously eluded you.

2. For a research paper, select one of the items Sagan enumerates in paragraph 2, such as "the formation of a dewdrop on a leaf," the origin of the name *Shakespeare* or the word *philanthropic*, "the incest taboo," or "how a 'walking stick' got to look so much like a twig." Write an expository essay on your topic.
3. **Writing an Argument:** Argue for or against the proposition that scientific knowledge takes the mystery out of life.

| www.mhhe.com/ **mhreader** | For more information on Carl Sagan, go to: **More Resources > Ch. 14 Science & Technology** |

# Staying Human

### Dinesh D'Souza

*Dinesh D'Souza, a leading conservative thinker, was born in Bombay, India, and came to the United States for his high school education. He graduated from Dartmouth College (BA, 1983) and subsequently wrote for several magazines, notably the* National Review, *before becoming a policy analyst for the Reagan administration. His books include* Illiberal Education: The Politics of Race and Sex on Campus *(1991),* The End of Racism: Principles for a Multicultural Society *(1995),* The Virtue of Prosperity: Finding Values in an Age of Techno-Affluence *(2001), and* What's So Great about America *(2002). D'Souza has been a visiting scholar at the Hoover Institution and a research scholar at the American Enterprise Institute. In the following essay, written for the* National Review *in 2001, D'Souza offers a wide-ranging assessment of our emerging "techno-utopia."*

*We are as gods, and we might as well get good at it.*
                                                    —*Kevin Kelly, author and techno-utopian*

The most important technological advance of recent times is not the Internet, 1 but rather the biotech revolution—which promises to give us unprecedented power to transform human nature. How should we use that power? A group of cutting-edge scientists, entrepreneurs, and intellectuals has a bold answer. This group—I call them the techno-utopians—argues that science will soon give us the means to straighten the crooked timber of humanity, and even to remake our species into something "post-human."

One of the leading techno-utopians is Lee Silver, who teaches molecular biol- 2 ogy at Princeton University. Silver reports that biotechnology is moving beyond cloning to offer us a momentous possibility: designer children. He envisions that, in the not too distant future, couples who want to have a child will review a long list of traits on a computer screen, put together combinations of "virtual children," decide on the one they want, click on the appropriate selection, and thus—in effect—design their own offspring. "Parents are going to be able to give their children . . . genes that increase athletic ability, genes that increase musical talents . . . and ultimately genes that affect cognitive abilities."

3　　But even this, the techno-utopians say, is a relatively small step: People living today can determine the genetic destiny of all future generations. Some writers, including physicist Stephen Hawking, have suggested that genetic engineering could be used to reduce human aggression, thus solving the crime problem and making war less likely. James Watson, co-discoverer of the structure of DNA, argues that if biological interventions could be used to "cure what I feel is a very serious disease—that is, stupidity—it would be a great thing for people." Silver himself forecasts a general elevation of intellectual, athletic, temperamental, and artistic abilities so that we can over time create "a special group of mental beings" who will "trace their ancestry back to Homo sapiens," but who will be "as different from humans as humans are from the primitive worms with tiny brains that first crawled along the earth's surface."

4　　These ideas might seem implausible, but they are taken very seriously by some of the best minds in the scientific community. The confidence of the techno-utopians is based on stunning advances that have made cloning and genetic engineering feasible. In theoretical terms, biotechnology crossed a major threshold with James Watson and Francis Crick's 1953 discovery of the structure of DNA, but practical applications were slow in coming. In 1997, an obscure animal-husbandry laboratory in Scotland cloned a sheep named Dolly; today, the knowledge and the means of cloning human beings already exist, and the only question is whether we are going to do it. And why stop there? As the scientific journal *Nature* editorialized shortly after the emergence of Dolly, "The growing power of molecular genetics confronts us with future prospects of being able to change the nature of our species."

5　　In 1999, neurobiologist Joe Tsien boosted the intelligence of mice by inserting extra copies of a gene that enhances memory and learning; these mouse genes are virtually identical to those found in human beings. Gene therapy has already been successfully carried out in people, and now that the Human Genome Project has made possible a comprehensive understanding of the human genetic code, scientists will possess a new kind of power: the power to design our children, and even to redesign humanity itself.

## The Hitler Scenario

6　The fact that these things are possible does not, of course, mean that they should be done. As one might expect, cloning and genetic engineering are attracting criticism. The techno-utopians have not yet made their products and services available to consumers; but one can reasonably expect that a society that is anxious about eating genetically modified tomatoes is going to be vastly more anxious about a scheme to engineer our offspring and our species.

A recent book communicating that sense of outrage is Jeremy Rifkin's *The* 7 *Biotech Century*. Rifkin alleges that we are heading for a nightmarish future "where babies are genetically designed and customized in the womb, and where people are identified, stereotyped and discriminated against on the basis of their genotype." How can living beings be considered sacred, Rifkin asks, if they are treated as nothing more than "bundles of genetic information"? Biotechnology, he charges, is launching us into a new age of eugenics. In Rifkin's view, the Nazi idea of the superman is very much alive, but now in a different form: the illusion of the "perfect child."

Although Rifkin has a propensity for inflammatory rhetoric, he is raising 8 some important concerns: The new technology is unprecedented, so we should be very cautious in developing it. It poses grave risks to human health. Cloning and genetic engineering are unnatural; human beings have no right to do this to nature and to ourselves.

These criticisms meet with derision on the part of the techno-utopians. 9 Every time a major new technology is developed, they say, there are people who forecast the apocalypse. The techno-utopians point out that the new technology will deliver amazing medical benefits, including cures for genetic diseases. How can it be ethical, they ask, to withhold these technologies from people who need and want them?

Lee Silver, the biologist, is annoyed at critics such as Rifkin who keep rais- 10 ing the specter of Hitler and eugenics. "It is individuals and couples, not governments, who will seize control of these new technologies," Silver writes. The premise of the techno-utopians is that if the market produces a result, it is good. In this view, what is wrong with the old eugenics is not that it sought to eliminate defective types and produce a superior kind of being, but that it sought to do so in a coercive and collectivist way. The new advocates of biotechnology speak approvingly of what they term "free-market eugenics."

The champions of biotechnology concede that cloning and genetic engi- 11 neering should not be permitted in human beings until they are safe. But "safe," they say, does not mean "error-free"; it means safe compared with existing forms of reproduction. And they are confident that the new forms of reproduction will soon be as safe as giving birth the natural way.

The techno-utopians are also not very concerned that the availability of 12 enhancement technologies will create two classes in society, the genetically advantaged and the genetically disadvantaged. They correctly point to the fact that two such classes exist now, even in the absence of new therapies. Physicist Freeman Dyson says that genetic enhancement might be costly at first, but won't remain permanently expensive: "Most of our socially important technologies, such as telephones, automobiles, television, and computers, began as expensive toys for the rich and afterwards became cheap enough for ordinary people."

Dyson is right that time will make genetic enhancements more widely avail- 13 able, just as cars and TV sets are now. But the poor family still drives a second-hand Plymouth while the rich family can afford a new Porsche. This may not be highly significant when it comes to cars, because both groups can still get around fairly well. What about when it comes to genetic advantages conferred at birth? Democratic societies can live with inequalities conferred by the lottery of nature, but can they countenance the deliberate introduction of biological alterations that give some citizens a better chance to succeed than others?

14      The techno-utopians have not, to my knowledge, addressed this concern. They emphasize instead that it is well established in law, and widely recognized in society, that parents have a right to determine what is best for their children. "There are already plenty of ways in which we design our children," remarks biologist Gregory Stock. "One of them is called piano lessons. Another is called private school." Stock's point is that engineering their children's genes is simply one more way in which parents can make their children better people.

15      Some people might find it weird and unnatural to fix their child in the same way they fix their car—but, say the techno-utopians, this is purely a function of habit. We're not used to genetic engineering, so it seems "unnatural" to us. But think about how unnatural driving a car seemed for people who previously got around on horses and in carriages. "The smallpox virus was part of the natural order," Silver wryly observes, "until it was forced into extinction by human intervention." Diseases and death are natural; life-saving surgery is unnatural.

## Not Sacred after All?

16  Nor are the techno-utopians worried about diminishing the sanctity of human life because, they say, it isn't intrinsically sacred. "This is not an ethical argument but a religious one," says Silver. "There is no logic to it." Biologist David Baltimore, a Nobel laureate, argues that "statements about morally and ethically unacceptable practices" have no place in the biotechnology debate "because those are subjective grounds and therefore provide no basis for discussion." Silver and Baltimore's shared assumption is that the moralists are talking about values while they, the hard scientists, are dealing in facts.

17      In this view, the subjective preferences of those who seek to mystify human life do not square with the truths about human biology taught by science. The cells of human beings, Silver points out, are not different in their chemical makeup from the cells of horses and bacteria. If there is such a thing as human dignity, Silver argues, it derives exclusively from consciousness, from our ability to perceive and apprehend our environment. "The human mind," Silver writes, "is much more than the genes that brought it into existence." Somehow the electrochemical reactions in our brain produce consciousness, and it is this consciousness, Silver contends, that is the source of man's autonomy and power. While genes fully control the activity of all life forms, Silver writes that in human beings "master and slave have switched positions." Consciousness enables man to complete his dominance over nature by prevailing over his human nature. Silver concludes that, in a bold assertion of will, we can defeat the program of our genes, we can take over the reins of evolution, we can choose the

genetic code we want for our children, and we can collectively determine the future of our species.

This triumphant note is echoed by many techno-utopians. Biotech, writes 18 journalist Ronald Bailey, "will liberate future generations from today's limitations and offer them a much wider scope of freedom." Physicist Gregory Benford is even more enthusiastic: "It is as though prodigious, bountiful Nature for billions of years has tossed off variations on its themes like a careless, prolific Picasso. Now Nature finds that one of its casual creations has come back with a piercing, searching vision, and its own pictures to paint."

These are ringing statements. But do they make sense? Clearly there are 19 many problems with Silver's definition of human dignity as based in consciousness. Animals are conscious; do they deserve the same dignity as human beings? Moreover, are human beings entitled to dignity only when they are conscious? Do we lose our right to be respected, and become legitimate subjects for discarding medical experiments, when we fall asleep, or into a coma? Surely Silver would disavow these conclusions. They do, however, flow directly from his definition, which is, in fact, just as heavily freighted with values as are the statements of his opponents.

There is, behind the proclamations of scientific neutrality, an ideology that 20 needs to be spelled out, a techno-Nietzschean doctrine that proclaims: We are molecules, but molecules that know how to rebel. Our values do not derive from nature or nature's God; rather, they arise from the arbitrary force of our wills. And now our wills can make the most momentous choice ever exercised on behalf of our species: the choice to reject our human nature. Why should we remain subject to the constraints of our mortality and destiny? Wealth and technology have given us the keys to unlimited, indeed godlike, power: the dawn of the post-human era.

What is one to make of all this? In many respects, we should celebrate the 21 advent of technologies that enable us to alleviate suffering and extend life. I have no problem with genetic therapy to cure disease; I am even willing to endorse therapy that not only cures illness in patients but also prevents it from being transmitted to the next generation. Under certain circumstances, I can see the benefits of cloning. The cloning of animals can provide organs for transplant as well as animals with medicinal properties ("drugstores on the hoof"). Even human cloning seems defensible when it offers the prospect of a biological child to married couples who might not otherwise be able to have one.

## Creating the Perfect Child

But there is a seduction contained in these exercises in humanitarianism: They 22 urge us to keep going, to take the next step. And when we take that step, when we start designing our children, when we start remaking human beings, I think we will have crossed a perilous frontier. Even cloning does not cross this frontier, because it merely replicates an existing genetic palate. It is unconvincing to argue, as some techno-utopians do, that giving a child a heightened genetic capacity for music or athletics or intelligence is no different from giving a child piano, swimming, or math lessons. In fact, there is a big difference. It is one thing to take a person's given nature and given capacity, and seek to develop it, and quite another to shape that person's nature in accordance with one's will.

23   There is no reason to object to people's attempting brain implants and somatic gene enhancements on themselves. Perhaps, in some cases, these will do some good; others may end up doing injury. But at least these people have, through their free choices, done it to themselves. The problem arises when people seek to use enhancement technologies to shape the destiny of others, and especially their children.

24   But, argues Lee Silver, we have the right to terminate pregnancy and control our children's lives in every other way; why shouldn't parents be permitted to alter their child's genetic constitution? In the single instance of gene therapy to cure disease, I'd agree—because, in this one limited case, we can trust the parents to make a decision that there is every rational reason to believe their offspring would decide in the identical manner, were they in a position to make the choice. No child would say, "I can't believe my parents did that to me. I would have chosen to have Parkinson's disease."

25   But I would contend that in no other case do people have the right to bend the genetic constitution of their children—or anyone else—to their will. But they might, in good conscience, be tempted to do so; and this temptation must be resisted. Indeed, it must be outlawed—because what the techno-utopians want does, in fact, represent a fundamental attack on the value of human life, and the core principle of America.

## Rescuing Humanity and the American Idea

26   The scientific-capitalist project at the heart of the American experiment was an attempted "conquest of nature." Never did the early philosophers of science, like Francis Bacon, or the American Founders conceive that this enterprise would eventually seek to conquer human nature. Their goal was to take human nature as a given, as something less elevated than the angels, and thus requiring a government characterized by separation of offices, checks and balances, limited power. At the same time, the Founders saw human nature as more elevated than that of other animals. They held that human beings have claims to dignity and rights that do not extend to animals: Human beings cannot be killed for sport or rightfully governed without their consent.

27   The principles of the Founders were extremely far-reaching. They called into question the legitimacy of every existing government, because at the time of the American founding, no government in the world was entirely based on the consent of the governed. The ideals of the Founders even called into question their own practices, such as slavery. It took the genius of Abraham Lincoln, and the tragedy of the Civil War, to compel the enforcement of the central principle of the Declaration of Independence: that we each have an inalienable right to life, liberty, and the pursuit of happiness, and that these rights shall not be abridged without our consent.

The attempt to enhance and redesign other human beings represents a fla- 28 grant denial of this principle that is the basis of our dignity and rights. Indeed, it is a restoration of the principle underlying slavery, and the argument between the defenders and critics of genetic enhancement is identical in principle, and very nearly in form, to the argument between Stephen Douglas and Abraham Lincoln on the issue of human enslavement.

In that tempestuous exchange, which laid the groundwork for the Civil 29 War, Douglas argued for the pro-choice position. He wanted to let each new territory decide for itself whether it wanted slavery. He wanted the American people to agree to disagree on the issue. He advocated for each community a very high value: the right to self-determination.

Lincoln challenged him on the grounds that choice cannot be exercised 30 without reference to the content of the choice. How can it make sense to permit people to choose to enslave another human being? How can self-determination be invoked to deny others the same? A free people can disagree on many things, but it cannot disagree on the distinction between freedom and despotism. Lincoln summarized Douglas's argument as follows: "If any one man choose to enslave another, no third man shall be allowed to object."

Lincoln's argument was based on a simple premise: "As I would not be a 31 slave, so I would not be a master." Lincoln rejects in principle the subordination implied in the master-slave relationship. Those who want freedom for themselves, he insists, must also show themselves willing to extend it to others. At its deepest level, Lincoln's argument is that the legitimacy of popular consent is itself dependent on a doctrine of natural rights that arises out of a specific understanding of human nature and human dignity. "Slavery," he said, "is founded in the selfishness of man's nature-opposition to it, in his love of justice. These principles are in eternal antagonism; and when brought into collision so fiercely . . . convulsions must ceaselessly follow." What Lincoln is saying is that self-interest by itself is too base a foundation for the new experiment called America. Selfishness is part of our nature, but it is not the best part of our nature. It should be subordinated to a nobler ideal. Lincoln seeks to dedicate America to a higher proposition: the proposition that all men are created equal. It is the denial of this truth, Lincoln warns, that will bring on the cataclysm.

Let me restate Lincoln's position for our current context. We speak of 32 "our children," but they are not really ours; we do not own them. At most, we own ourselves. It is true that *Roe v. Wade* gives us the right to kill our unborn in the womb. The right to abortion has been defended, both by its advocates and by the Supreme Court, as the right of a woman to control her own body. This is not the same as saying the woman has ownership of the fetus, that the fetus is the woman's property. The Supreme Court has said that as long as the fetus is occupying her womb, she can treat it as an unwelcome intruder, and get rid of it. (Even here, technology is changing the shape of the debate by moving up the period when the fetus can survive outside the womb.) But once a woman decides to carry the pregnancy to term, she has already exercised her choice. She has chosen to give birth to the child, which is in the process of becoming an independent human being with its own dignity and rights.

## No Place for Parental Tyranny

33　As parents, we have been entrusted with our children, and it is our privilege and responsibility to raise them as best we can. Undoubtedly we will infuse them with our values and expectations, but even so, the good parent will respect the child's right to follow his own path. There is something perversely restrictive about parents who apply relentless pressure on their children to conform to their will—to follow the same professional paths that they did, or to become the "first doctor in the family." These efforts, however well intentioned, are a betrayal of the true meaning of parenthood. Indeed, American culture encourages a certain measure of adolescent rebellion against parental expectations, precisely so that young people making the transition to independence can "find themselves" and discover their own identity.

34　Consequently, parents have no right to treat their children as chattels; but this is precisely the enterprise that is being championed by the techno-utopians. Some of these people profess to be libertarians, but they are in fact totalitarians. They speak about freedom and choice, although what they advocate is despotism and human bondage. The power they seek to exercise is not over "nature" but over other human beings.

35　Parents who try to design their children are in some ways more tyrannical than slaveowners, who merely sought to steal the labor of their slaves. Undoubtedly some will protest that they only wish the best for their children, that they are only doing this for their own good. But the slaveowners made similar arguments, saying that they ruled the Negroes in the Negroes' own interest. The argument was as self-serving then as it is now. What makes us think that in designing our children it will be their objective good—rather than our desires and preferences—that will predominate?

36　The argument against slavery is that you may not tyrannize over the life and freedom of another person for any reason whatsoever. Even that individual's consent cannot overturn "inalienable" rights: One does not have the right to sell oneself into slavery. This is the clear meaning of the American proposition. The object of the American Revolution that is now spreading throughout the world has always been the affirmation, not the repudiation, of human nature. The Founders envisioned technology and capitalism as providing the framework and the tools for human beings to live richer, fuller lives. They would have scorned, as we should, the preposterous view that we are the servants of our technology. They would have strenuously opposed, as we should, the effort on the part of the techno-utopians to design their offspring; to alter, improve, and perfect human nature; or to relinquish our humanity in pursuit of some post-human ideal.

37　Mary Shelley's 1818 novel *Frankenstein* describes a monster that is the laboratory creation of a doctor who refuses to accept the natural limits of humanity. He wants to appropriate to himself the traditional prerogatives of the deity, such as control over human mortality. He even talks about making "a new species" with "me as its creator and source." In his rhetoric, Frankenstein sounds very much like today's techno-utopians. And, contrary to what most people think, the real monster in the novel isn't the lumbering, tragic creature; it is the doctor who creates him. This is the prophetic message of Shelley's work: In seeking to become gods, we are going to make monsters of ourselves.

## COMPREHENSION

1. What is the meaning of D'Souza's title? According to the writer, what are the dangers we face in our effort to "stay human"? What must we do to retain our essential humanity?
2. What aspects of the biotech revolution does the author treat? What is his opinion of each?
3. What does the writer mean by the "Hitler Scenario" and the "American Idea"?

## RHETORIC

1. What is D'Souza's purpose? What is his tone? Does he seem reasonable or unnecessarily argumentative? Objective or biased? How do you know? For what type of audience does he seem to be writing?
2. D'Souza begins his essay by introducing the ideas of such "leading techno-utopians" as Lee Silver, Stephen Hawking, James Watson and Francis Crick, and Joe Tsien. It this an effective opening strategy? Why or why not?
3. Explain the author's claim. What minor propositions does he provide? Where does he advance logical, ethical, and emotional appeals? Cite instances in which he employs refutation to advance his argument. What faults does he find with the techno-utopians?
4. Consider the essay's section headings. How do they serve to focus the content of each section? What characterizes the progression of ideas from section to section? How does the author's decision to divide the essay into sections help him to construct his argument?
5. Does D'Souza reveal any of his own biases in this essay? Explain.
6. In the concluding paragraph, D'Souza alludes to Mary Shelley's novel *Frankenstein*. Does this allusion flow naturally from the introduction and body? Why or why not?

## WRITING

1. Write a 300-word summary of this essay, transcribing all of the main aspects of D'Souza's argument.

2. Write your own survey of the biotech revolution. Refer to some of the topics and ideas mentioned by D'Souza in his essay.
3. **Writing an Argument:** Select one aspect of the biotech revolution—for instance, cloning or stem-cell research—and write an argumentative essay supporting or opposing developments in the field.

www.mhhe.com/ **mhreader**     For more information on Dinesh D'Souza, go to: **More Resources > Ch. 14 Science & Technology**

# Anybody Out There?

## Oliver Sacks

*Oliver Sacks (b. 1933), a well-known neurologist, was born in London and immigrated to the United States in 1960. He was educated at Queens College, Oxford, where he received a BA (1954) and subsequent degrees in chemistry and medicine. Sacks has practiced and taught medicine, surgery, and neurology at several institutions, including Albert Einstein College of Medicine, Bronx Psychiatric Hospital, and New York University Medical Center. An award-winning physician and science writer, Sacks has written numerous books, including* Awakenings *(1973), which was made into a film starring Robin Williams and Robert De Niro;* The Man Who Mistook His Wife for a Hat, and Other Clinical Tales *(1985);* An Anthropologist on Mars *(1995);* Uncle Tungsten: Memories of a Chemical Boyhood *(2001); and* Vintage Sacks *(2004). In this essay, published in* Natural History *in 2002, Sacks speculates about the existence of life forms in the universe.*

1   One of the first books I read as a boy was H. G. Wells's 1901 fable, *The First Men in the Moon.* The two men, Cavor and Bedford, land in a crater, apparently barren and lifeless, just before the lunar dawn; then, as the sun rises, they realize there is an atmosphere. They spot small pools and eddies of water, and then little round objects scattered on the ground. One of them, as it is warmed by the sun, bursts open and reveals a sliver of green. ("'A seed,' said Cavor . . . And then . . . very softly, 'Life!'") They light a piece of paper and throw it onto the surface of the Moon. It glows and sends up a thread of smoke, indicating that the atmosphere, though thin, is rich in oxygen and will support life as they know it.

2      Here, then, was how Wells conceived the prerequisites of life: water, sunlight (a source of energy), and oxygen. "A Lunar Morning," the eighth chapter in his book, was my first introduction to astrobiology.

It was apparent, even in Wells's day, that most of the planets in our solar ₃
system were not possible homes for life. The only reasonable surrogate for the
Earth was Mars, which was known to be a solid planet of reasonable size, in
stable orbit, not too distant from the sun, and so, it was thought, having a range
of surface temperatures compatible with the presence of liquid water.

But free oxygen gas—how could that occur in a planet's atmosphere? What ₄
would keep it from being mopped up by ferrous iron and other oxygen-hungry
chemicals on the surface unless, somehow, it was continuously pumped out in
huge quantities, enough to oxidize all the surface minerals and keep the atmosphere charged as well?

It was the blue-green algae, or cyanobacteria, that infused the Earth's atmo- ₅
sphere with oxygen, a process that took between a billion and two billion years.
The fossil record shows that cyanobacteria go back three and a half billion
years. Yet, amazingly, some of them still thrive today in odd corners of the
world, forming strange, cushion-shaped colonies called stromatolites. It is an
extraordinary experience to go to Shark Bay in western Australia, where stromatolites flourish in the hypersaline waters, to watch them slowly bubbling
oxygen, and to reflect that, three billion years ago, this was how the Earth was
transformed. The cyanobacteria invented photosynthesis: by capturing the energy of the sun, they were able to combine carbon dioxide (massively present in
the Earth's early atmosphere) with water to create complex molecules—sugars,
carbohydrates—which the bacteria could then store and tap for energy as
needed. This process generated free oxygen as a byproduct—a waste product
that was to determine the future course of evolution.

Although free oxygen in a planet's atmosphere would be an infallible ₆
marker of life, and one that, if present, should be readily detected in the spectra
of extrasolar planets, it is not a prerequisite for life. Planets, after all, get started
without free oxygen, and may remain without it all their lives. Anaerobic organisms swarmed before oxygen was available, perfectly at home in the atmosphere of the early Earth, converting nitrogen to ammonia, sulfur to hydrogen
sulfide, carbon dioxide to formaldehyde, and so forth. (From formaldehyde
and ammonia the bacteria could make every organic compound they needed.)

There may be planets in our solar system and elsewhere that lack an atmo- ₇
sphere of oxygen but are nonetheless teeming with anaerobes. And such anaerobes
need not live on the surface of the planet; they could occur well below the surface,
in boiling vents and sulfurous hot pots, as they do on Earth today, to say nothing
of subterranean oceans and lakes. (There is thought to be such a subsurface ocean
on Jupiter's moon Europa, locked beneath a shell of ice several miles thick, and its
exploration is one of the astrobiological priorities of this century. Curiously, Wells,
in *The First Men in the Moon,* imagines life originating in a central sea in the middle
of the Moon and then spreading outward to its inhospitable periphery.)

It is not clear whether life has to "advance"—whether evolution must take ₈
place—if there is a satisfactory status quo. Brachiopods—lampshells—for

instance, have remained virtually unchanged since they first appeared in the Cambrian Period, more than 500 million years ago. But there does seem to be a drive for organisms to become more highly organized and more efficient in retaining energy, at least when environmental conditions are changing rapidly, as they were before the Cambrian. The evidence indicates that the first primitive anaerobes on Earth were prokaryotes: small, simple cells—just cytoplasm, usually bounded by a cell wall, but with little if any internal structure.

9      By degrees, however—and the process took place with glacial slowness—prokaryotes became more complex, acquiring internal structure, nuclei, mitochondria, and so on. The microbiologist Lynn Margulis of the University of Massachusetts, Amherst, has convincingly suggested that these complex so-called eukaryotes arose when prokaryotes began incorporating other prokaryotes within their own cells. The incorporated organisms at first became symbiotic and later came to function as essential organelles of their hosts, enabling the resultant organisms to use what was originally a noxious poison: oxygen.

10     Primitive as they are, prokaryotes are still highly sophisticated organisms with formidable genetic and metabolic machinery. Even the simplest ones manufacture more than five hundred proteins, and their DNA includes at least half a million base pairs. Hence it is certain that still more primitive life forms must have preceded the prokaryotes.

11     Perhaps, as the physicist Freeman Dyson of the Institute for Advanced Study in Princeton has suggested, there were "pro-genotes" capable of metabolizing, growing, and dividing but lacking any genetic mechanism for precise replication. And before them there must have been millions of years of purely chemical, prebiotic evolution—the synthesis, over eons, of formaldehyde and cyanide, of amino acids and peptides, of proteins and self-replicating molecules. Perhaps that chemistry took place in the minute vesicles, or globules, that develop when fluids at very different temperatures meet, as may well have happened around the boiling midocean vents of the Archaean sea.

12  Life as we know it is not imaginable without proteins, and proteins are built from peptides, and ultimately from amino acids. It is easy to imagine that amino acids were abundant in the early Earth, either formed as a result of lightning discharges or brought to the planet by comets and meteors.

13     The real problem is to get from amino acids and other simple compounds to peptides, nucleotides, proteins, and so on. It is unlikely that such delicate chemical syntheses would occur in "some warm little pond," as Darwin imagined, or on the surface of a primordial sea. Instead, they would probably require unusual conditions of heat and concentration, as well as the presence of special catalysts and energy-rich compounds to make them proceed. The biochemist Christian de Duve of Rockefeller University suggests that complex organic sulfur compounds played a crucial role in providing chemical energy, and that these compounds may have formed spontaneously early in Earth's history, perhaps in the hot, acidic, sulfurous depths of the seafloor vents (where, it is increasingly believed, life probably originated). De Duve imagines this purely

chemical world as the precursor of an "RNA world," believed by many to represent the first form of self-replicating life. He thinks that the movement from one to the other was both inevitable and fast.

The two preeminent evolutionary changes in the early history of life on Earth—  14
from prokaryote to eukaryote, from anaerobe to aerobe—took the better part of two billion years. And there then had to pass another 1,200 or 1,300 million years before life rose above the microscopic forms, and the first "higher," multicellular organisms appeared. So if the Earth's history is anything to go by, we should not expect to find any higher life on a planet that is still young. Even if extraterrestrial life has appeared, and all goes well, should take billions of years for evolutionary processes to move it along to the multicellular stage.

Moreover, all those "stages" of evolution—including the evolution of intel-  15
ligent, conscious beings from the first multicellular forms—may have happened against daunting odds. Stephen Jay Gould spoke of life as "a glorious accident"; Richard Dawkins of Oxford University likens evolution to "climbing Mount Improbable." And life, once started, is subject to vicissitudes of all kinds: from meteors and volcanic eruptions to global overheating and cooling; from dead ends in evolution to mysterious mass extinctions; and finally (if things get that far) the fateful proclivities of a species like ourselves.

We know there are microfossils in some of the Earth's most ancient rocks,  16
rocks more than three and a half billion years old. So life must have appeared within 100 or 200 million years after the Earth had cooled off sufficiently for water to become liquid. That astonishingly rapid transformation makes one think that life may develop readily, perhaps inevitably, as soon as the right physical and chemical conditions appear.

But can one argue from a single example? Can one speak confidently of  17
"earthlike" planets, or is the Earth physically, chemically, and geologically unique? And even if there are other "habitable" planets, what are the chances that life, with its thousands of physical and chemical coincidences and contingencies, will emerge? Life may be a one-off event.

Opinion here varies as widely as it can. The French biochemist Jacques Monod  18
regarded life as a fantastically improbable accident, unlikely to have arisen anywhere else in the universe. In his book *Chance and Necessity*, he writes, "The universe was not pregnant with life." De Duve takes issue with this, and sees the origin of life as determined by a large number of steps, most of which must have had a "high likelihood of taking place under the prevailing conditions." Indeed, de Duve believes that there is not merely unicellular life throughout the universe but complex, intelligent life, too, on trillions of planets. How are we to align ourselves between these utterly opposite but theoretically defensible positions?

What we need, what we must have, is hard evidence of life on another planet  19
or heavenly body. Mars is the obvious candidate: it was wet and warm there once, with lakes and hydrothermal vents and perhaps deposits of clay and iron ore. It is especially in such places that we should look, suggests Malcolm Walter, an expert on fossil bacteria that date from the Earth's earliest epochs. If the

evidence shows that life once existed on Mars, we will then need to know, crucially, whether it originated there or was transported (as would have been readily possible) from the young, teeming, volcanic Earth. If we can determine that life originated independently on Mars (if Mars, for instance, once harbored DNA nucleotides different from our own), we will have made an incredible discovery—one that will alter our view of the universe and enable us to perceive it, in the words of the physicist Paul Davies, as a "biofriendly" one. It would help us to gauge the probability of finding life elsewhere instead of bombinating in a vacuum of data, caught between the poles of inevitability and uniqueness.

20     In just the past twenty years life has been discovered in previously unexpected places on our own planet, such as the life-rich black smokers of the ocean depths, where organisms thrive in conditions biologists would once have dismissed as utterly deadly. Life is much tougher, much more resilient, than we once thought. It now seems to me quite possible that microorganisms or their remains will be found on Mars and perhaps on some of the satellites of Jupiter and Saturn.

21  It seems far less likely, many orders of magnitude less likely, that we will find any evidence of higher-order, intelligent life forms, at least in our own solar system. But who knows? Given the vastness and age of the universe at large, the innumerable stars and planets it must contain, and our radical uncertainties about life's origin and evolution, the possibility cannot be ruled out. And though the rate of evolutionary and geochemical processes is incredibly slow, that of technological progress is incredibly fast. Who is to say (if humanity survives) what we may not be capable of, or discover, in the next thousand years?

22     For myself, since I cannot wait, I turn to science fiction on occasion—and, not least, back to my favorite Wells. Although it was written a hundred years ago, "A Lunar Morning" has the freshness of a new dawn, and it remains for me, as when I first read it, the most poetic evocation of how it may be when, finally, we encounter alien life.

## COMPREHENSION

1. What is Sacks's answer to the question he poses in the title?
2. Explain the connection between the writer's boyhood reading and his interest in life elsewhere in the universe.
3. List and define some of the scientific evidence and scientific principles Sacks mentions in his essay.

## RHETORIC

1. Why does Sacks begin with an anecdote about his boyhood? How might this strategy appeal to readers of *Natural History*, where the essay first appeared?
2. In what ways does Sacks demonstrate his expertise and authority as a scientist in this essay? What tone does he take in presenting this information?

3. What is Sacks's thesis? What types of evidence does he offer to support his main idea?
4. Identify the main sections in this essay and the transitions Sacks uses to link them.
5. Where does Sacks use definition, comparison and contrast, process analysis, and causal analysis? Does he mix patterns successfully? Why or why not?
6. Examine the conclusion. Why does Sacks ask questions, and why does he end on a provisional note?

### WRITING

1. In an expository essay, examine the popularity of science fiction in literature and/or film. How does science fiction present the notion of life in the universe? Be certain to develop examples to support your thesis.
2. Conduct research on H. G. Wells, and then write an evaluative paper in which you highlight the ways in which he predicted the future.
3. **Writing an Argument:** Do you think that extraterrestrial life exists? Answer this question in an argumentative essay.

www.mhhe.com/
**mhreader**

For more information on Oliver Sacks, go to:
**More Resources > Ch. 14 Science & Technology**

# The Clan of One-Breasted Women

## Terry Tempest Williams

*Terry Tempest Williams (b. 1955) is the author of many books of nonfiction, including* A Journey to Navajoland *(1984),* Coyote's Canyon *(1989),* Refuge: An Unnatural History of Family and Place *(1991),* An Unspoken Hunger *(1994), and* Desert Quartet *(1995). Williams was identified by* Newsweek *magazine as someone who will have "a considerable impact on the political, economic and environmental issues facing the western states in this decade." She is the recipient of a Lannan Fellowship in creative nonfiction and was chosen by the periodical* UTNE Reader *as a "visionary," one of the UTNE 100 "who could change your life." She is Naturalist-in-Residence at the Utah Museum of Natural History in Salt Lake City. The following essay—published in 1989 in* Witness—*describes the pernicious intergenerational effects of nuclear testing.*

1　I belong to a Clan of One-Breasted Women. My mother, my grandmothers, and six aunts have all had mastectomies. Seven are dead. The two who survive have just completed rounds of chemotherapy and radiation.

2　I've had my own problems: two biopsies for breast cancer and a small tumor between my ribs diagnosed as "a border-line malignancy."

3　This is my family history.

4　Most statistics tell us breast cancer is genetic, hereditary, with rising percentages attached to fatty diets, childlessness, or becoming pregnant after thirty. What they don't say is living in Utah may be the greatest hazard of all.

5　We are a Mormon family with roots in Utah since 1847. The word-of-wisdom, a religious doctrine of health, kept the women in my family aligned with good foods: no coffee, no tea, tobacco, or alcohol. For the most part, these women were finished having their babies by the time they were thirty. And only one faced breast cancer prior to 1960. Traditionally, as a group of people, Mormons have a low rate of cancer.

6　Is our family a cultural anomaly? The truth is we didn't think about it. Those who did, usually the men, simply said, "bad genes." The women's attitude was stoic. Cancer was part of life. On February 16, 1971, the eve before my mother's surgery, I accidentally picked up the telephone and overheard her ask my grandmother what she could expect.

7　"Diane, it is one of the most spiritual experiences you will ever encounter."

8　I quietly put down the receiver.

9　Two days later, my father took my three brothers and me to the hospital to visit her. She met us in the lobby in a wheelchair. No bandages were visible. I'll never forget her radiance, the way she held herself in a purple velour robe and how she gathered us around her.

10　"Children, I am fine. I want you to know I felt the arms of God around me."

11　We believed her. My father cried. Our mother, his wife, was thirty-eight years old.

12　Two years ago, after my mother's death from cancer, my father and I were having dinner together. He had just returned from St. George where his construction company was putting in natural gas lines for towns in southern Utah. He spoke of his love for the country: the sandstoned landscape, bare-boned and beautiful. He had just finished hiking the Kolob trail in Zion National Park. We got caught up in reminiscing, recalling with fondness our walk up Angel's Landing on his fiftieth birthday and the years our family had vacationed there. This was a remembered landscape where we had been raised.

13　Over dessert, I shared a recurring dream of mine. I told my father that for years, as long as I could remember, I saw this flash of light in the night in the desert. That this image had so permeated my being, I could not venture south without seeing it again, on the horizon, illuminating buttes and mesas.

14　"You did see it," he said.

15　"Saw what?" I asked, a bit tentative.

16　"The bomb. The cloud. We were driving home from Riverside, California. You were sitting on your mother's lap. She was pregnant. In fact, I remember the date,

September 7, 1957. We had just gotten out of the Service. We were driving north, past Las Vegas. It was an hour or so before dawn, when this explosion went off. We not only heard it, but felt it. I thought the oil tanker in front of us had blown up. We pulled over and suddenly, rising from the desert floor, we saw it, clearly, this golden-stemmed cloud, the mushroom. The sky seemed to vibrate with an eerie pink glow. Within a few minutes, a light ash was raining on the car."

I stared at my father. This was new information to me. [17]

"I thought you knew that," my father said. "It was a common occurrence in [18] the fifties."

It was at this moment I realized the deceit I had been living under. Children [19] growing up in the American Southwest, drinking contaminated milk from contaminated cows, even from the contaminated breasts of their mother, my mother—members, years later, of the Clan of One-Breasted Women.

It is a well-known story in the Desert West, "The Day We Bombed Utah," or [20] perhaps, "The Years We Bombed Utah."[1] Above ground atomic testing in Nevada took place from January 27, 1951, through July 11, 1962. Not only were the winds blowing north, covering "low use segments of the population" with fallout and leaving sheep dead in their tracks, but the climate was right.[2] The United States of the 1950s was red, white, and blue. The Korean War was raging. McCarthyism was rampant. Ike was in and the Cold War was hot. If you were against nuclear testing, you were for a Communist regime.

Much has been written about this "American nuclear tragedy." Public [21] health was secondary to national security. The Atomic Energy Commissioner, Thomas Murray said, "Gentlemen, we must not let anything interfere with this series of tests, nothing."[3]

Again and again, the American public was told by its government, in spite of [22] burns, blisters, and nausea, "It has been found that the tests may be conducted with adequate assurance of safety under conditions prevailing at the bombing reservations."[4] Assuaging public fears was simply a matter of public relations. "Your best action," an Atomic Energy Commission booklet read, "is not to be worried about fallout." A news release typical of the times stated, "We find no basis for concluding that harm to any individual has resulted from radioactive fallout."[5]

On August 30, 1979, during Jimmy Carter's presidency, a suit was filed [23] entitled "Irene Allen vs. the United States of America." Mrs. Allen was the first to be alphabetically listed with twenty-four test cases, representative of nearly 1200 plaintiffs seeking compensation from the United States government for cancers caused from nuclear testing in Nevada.

[1]Fuller, John G., *The Day We Bombed Utah* (New York: New American Library, 1984). [This and subsequent notes in the selection are the author's.]
[2]Discussion on March 14, 1988, with Carole Gallagher, photographer and author, *Nuclear Towns: The Secret War in the American Southwest*, published by Doubleday, Spring, 1990.
[3]Szasz, Ferenc M., "Downwind from the Bomb," *Nevada Historical Society Quarterly*, Fall 1987, Vol. XXX, No. 3, p. 185.
[4]Fradkin, Philip L., *Fallout* (Tucson: University of Arizona Press, 1989), 98.
[5]Ibid., 109.

24      Irene Allen lived in Hurricane, Utah. She was the mother of five children and had been widowed twice. Her first husband with their two oldest boys had watched the tests from the roof of the local high school. He died of leukemia in 1956. Her second husband died of pancreatic cancer in 1978.

25      In a town meeting conducted by Utah Senator Orrin Hatch, shortly before the suit was filed, Mrs. Allen said, "I am not blaming the government, I want you to know that, Senator Hatch. But I thought if my testimony could help in any way so this wouldn't happen again to any of the generations coming up after us . . . I am really happy to be here this day to bear testimony of this."[6]

26      God-fearing people. This is just one story in an anthology of thousands.

27      On May 10, 1984, Judge Bruce S. Jenkins handed down his opinion. Ten of the plaintiffs were awarded damages. It was the first time a federal court had determined that nuclear tests had been the cause of cancers. For the remaining fourteen test cases, the proof of causation was not sufficient. In spite of the split decision, it was considered a landmark ruling.[7] It was not to remain so for long.

28      In April 1987, the 10th Circuit Court of Appeals overturned Judge Jenkins' ruling on the basis that the United States was protected from suit by the legal doctrine of sovereign immunity, the centuries-old idea from England in the days of absolute monarchs.[8]

29      In January 1988, the Supreme Court refused to review the Appeals Court decision. To our court system, it does not matter whether the United States Government was irresponsible, whether it lied to its citizens or even that citizens died from the fallout of nuclear testing. What matters is that our government is immune. "The King can do no wrong."

30  In Mormon culture, authority is respected, obedience is revered, and independent thinking is not. I was taught as a young girl not to "make waves" or "rock the boat."

31      "Just let it go—" my mother would say. "You know how you feel, that's what counts."

32      For many years, I did just that—listened, observed, and quietly formed my own opinions within a culture that rarely asked questions because they had all the answers. But one by one, I watched the women in my family die common, heroic deaths. We sat in waiting rooms hoping for good news, always receiving the bad. I cared for them, bathed their scarred bodies and kept their secrets. I watched beautiful women become bald as cytoxan, cisplatin and adriamycin were injected into their veins. I held their foreheads as they vomited green-black bile and I shot them with morphine when the pain

---

[6]Town meeting held by Senator Orrin Hatch in St. George, Utah, April 17, 1979, transcript, 26–28.
[7]Fradkin, Op. cit., 228.
[8]U.S. vs. Allen, 816 Federal Reporter, 2d/1417 (10th Circuit Court 1987), cert. denied, 108 S. CT. 694 (1988).

became inhuman. In the end, I witnessed their last peaceful breaths, becoming a midwife to the rebirth of their souls. But the price of obedience became too high.

The fear and inability to question authority that ultimately killed rural com-   33 munities in Utah during atmospheric testing of atomic weapons was the same fear I saw being held in my mother's body. Sheep. Dead sheep. The evidence is buried.

I cannot prove that my mother, Diane Dixon Tempest, or my grandmoth-   34 ers, Lettie Romney Dixon and Kathryn Blackett Tempest, along with my aunts contracted cancer from nuclear fallout in Utah. But I can't prove they didn't.

My father's memory was correct, the September blast we drove through   35 in 1957 was part of Operation Plumbbob, one of the most intensive series of bomb tests to be initiated. The flash of light in the night in the desert I had always thought was a dream developed into a family nightmare. It took fourteen years, from 1957 to 1971, for cancer to show up in my mother—the same time, Howard L. Andrews, an authority on radioactive fallout at the National Institutes of Health, says radiation cancer requires to become evident.[9] The more I learn about what it means to be a "downwinder," the more questions I drown in.

What I do know, however, is that as a Mormon woman of the fifth genera-   36 tion of Latter-day Saints. I must question everything, even if it means losing my faith, even if it means becoming a member of a border tribe among my own people. Tolerating blind obedience in the name of patriotism or religion ultimately takes our lives.

When the Atomic Energy Commission described the country north of the   37 Nevada Test Site as "virtually uninhabited desert terrain," my family members were some of the "virtual uninhabitants."

One night, I dreamed women from all over the world circling a blazing fire in   38 the desert. They spoke of change, of how they hold the moon in their bellies and wax and wane with its phases. They mocked at the presumption of even-tempered beings and made promises that they would never fear the witch inside themselves. The women danced wildly as sparks broke away from the flames and entered the night sky as stars.

And they sang a song given to them by Shoshoni grandmothers:   39

Ah ne nah, nah
nin nah nah—
Ah ne nah, nah
nin nah nah—
Nyaga mutzi
oh ne nay—

[9]Fradkin, Op. cit. 116.

Nyaga mutzi
oh ne nay—[10]

40    The women danced and drummed and sang for weeks, preparing themselves for what was to come. They would reclaim the desert for the sake of their
children, for the sake of the land.

41    A few miles downwind from the fire circle, bombs were being tested. Rabbits felt the tremors. Their soft leather pads on paws and feet recognized the
shaking sands while the roots of mesquite and sage were smoldering. Rocks
were hot from the inside out and dust devils hummed unnaturally. And each
time there was another nuclear test, ravens watched the desert heave. Stretch
marks appeared. The land was losing its muscle.

42    The women couldn't bear it any longer. They were mothers. They had suffered labor pains but always under the promise of birth. The red hot pains
beneath the desert promised death only as each bomb became a stillborn. A
contract had been broken between human beings and the land. A new contract was being drawn by the women who understood the fate of the earth as
their own.

43    Under the cover of darkness, ten women slipped under the barbed wire
fence and entered the contaminated country. They were trespassing. They
walked toward the town of Mercury in moonlight, taking their cues from coyote, kit fox, antelope squirrel, and quail. They moved quietly and deliberately
through the maze of Joshua trees. When a hint of daylight appeared they rested,
drinking tea and sharing their rations of food. The women closed their eyes.
The time had come to protest with the heart, that to deny one's genealogy with
the earth was to commit treason against one's soul.

44    At dawn, the women draped themselves in mylar, wrapping long stream-
ers of silver plastic around their arms to blow in the breeze. They wore clear
masks that became the faces of humanity. And when they arrived on the edge
of Mercury, they carried all the butterflies of a summer day in their wombs.
They paused to allow their courage to settle.

45    The town which forbids pregnant women and children to enter because of
radiation risks to their health was asleep. The women moved through the streets
as winged messengers, twirling around each other in slow motion, peeking inside homes and watching the easy sleep of men and women. They were
astonished by such stillness and periodically would utter a shrill note or low cry
just to verify life.

46    The residents finally awoke to what appeared as strange apparitions. Some
simply stared. Others called authorities, and in time, the women were appre-
hended by wary soldiers dressed in desert fatigues. They were taken to a white,

[10]This song was sung by the Western Shoshone women as they crossed the line at the Nevada
Test Site on March 18, 1988, as part of their "Reclaim the Land" action. The translation they gave
was: "Consider the rabbits how gently they walk on the earth. Consider the rabbits how gently
they walk on the earth. We remember them. We can walk gently also. We remember them. We
can walk gently also."

square building on the other edge of Mercury. When asked who they were and why they were there, the women replied, "We are mothers and we have come to reclaim the desert for our children."

The soldiers arrested them. As the ten women were blindfolded and hand- 47 cuffed, they began singing:

> You can't forbid us everything
> You can't forbid us to think—
> You can't forbid our tears to flow
> And you can't stop the songs that we sing.

The women continued to sing louder and louder, until they heard the voices 48 of their sisters moving across the mesa.

> Ah ne nah, nah
> nin nah nah—
> Ah ne nah, nah
> nin nah nah—
> Nyaga mutzi
> oh ne nay—
> Nyaga mutzi
> oh ne nay—

"Call for re-enforcement," one soldier said.                                            49

"We have," interrupted one woman. "We have—and you have no idea of 50 our numbers."

On March 18, 1988, I crossed the line at the Nevada Test Site and was arrested 51 with nine other Utahns for trespassing on military lands. They are still conducting nuclear tests in the desert. Ours was an act of civil disobedience. But as I walked toward the town of Mercury, it was more than a gesture of peace. It was a gesture on behalf of the Clan of One-Breasted Women.

As one officer cinched the handcuffs around my wrists, another frisked my 52 body. She found a pen and a pad of paper tucked inside my left boot.

"And these?" she asked sternly.                                                         53

"Weapons," I replied.                                                                   54

Our eyes met. I smiled. She pulled the leg of my trousers back over my boot. 55

"Step forward, please," she said as she took my arm.                                    56

We were booked under an afternoon sun and bussed to Tonapah, Nevada. It 57 was a two-hour ride. This was familiar country to me. The Joshua trees standing their ground had been named by my ancestors who believed they looked like prophets pointing west to the promised land. These were the same trees that bloomed each spring, flowers appearing like white flames in the Mojave. And I recalled a full moon in May when my mother and I had walked among them, flushing out mourning doves and owls.

The bus stopped short of town. We were released. The officials thought it 58 was a cruel joke to leave us stranded in the desert with no way to get home.

What they didn't realize is that we were home, soul-centered and strong, women who recognized the sweet smell of sage as fuel for our spirits.

## COMPREHENSION

1. What is the subject of the essay? How did you arrive at your answer?
2. The credo of the United States promotes "life, liberty, and the pursuit of happiness." In her essay, what does Williams imply is the major antagonist to this philosophy?
3. Define the following words and terms: *doctrine* (paragraph 5), *anomaly* (paragraph 6), *buttes* and *mesas* (paragraph 13), *plaintiffs* (paragraph 23), and *sovereign* (paragraph 28).

## RHETORIC

1. Williams often uses quotation marks to signal irony in her writing. What is the perverse irony in the following expressions: "low use segments of the population (paragraph 20)," "downwinder" (paragraph 35), and "virtually uninhabited desert terrain" (paragraph 37)?
2. Although this is a highly personal essay and reveals a profound and emotional personal experience, Williams also relies on evidence from secondary source material to support her thesis. What is the effect of using such sources in terms of the author's authority and believability?
3. The essay is divided into four segments. What is the main subject of each one?
4. Williams uses extended metaphor, personification, and comparison and contrast in paragraphs 41 and 42. Explain how she incorporates these three rhetorical devices and what their relevance is to the overarching theme of the essay.
5. Williams provides a revelation to the reader in paragraph 16 that determines to a large degree the focus of her essay. What was the rhetorical purpose in waiting so long to reveal it?
6. Literary critics often state that one of the essential elements of powerful drama is some profound change that the main protagonist undergoes. What change in perspective did Williams undergo, and what was its implication for her attitudes and actions toward society?
7. Despite profound tragedy and continuous frustration in her life, Williams ends her essay on a positive note. Where is this change in tone most evident? What images reflect her ultimate triumph?

## WRITING

1. In an expository essay, analyze the dangers that nuclear proliferation poses for humanity?
2. For a research project, study public policy in the 1950s and 1960s regarding aboveground nuclear testing, and report on whether the American govern-

ment foresaw that some individuals likely would suffer dire physical infirmities as a result of such procedures.

3. **Writing an Argument:** Argue for or against the proposition that technology is never value-free.

| | |
|---|---|
| www.mhhe.com/ **mhreader** | For more information on Terry Tempest Williams, go to: **More Resources > Ch. 14 Science & Technology** |

## Synthesis: Connections for Critical Thinking

1. Using the essays of D'Souza and Williams, discuss the need for strict ethics among scientists in regards to their concern over the well-being of the general populace.
2. Imagine a conversation between Sedaris and Turkle. What would they say to each other?
3. Compare the process of natural selection as advanced by Darwin with the concept of evolution as defined by Sacks.
4. Rent the videotape or DVD version of the television series *Cosmos*, which was based on a novel by Carl Sagan. Compare the ideas set forth in the film with those in Sagan's essay "Can We Know the Universe? Reflections on a Grain of Salt."
5. Compare and contrast the expository methods Darwin uses to explain the process of natural selection and the narrative technique Sedaris uses to describe his technophobia.
6. Using Williams's essay on the pernicious effects of technology and Angier's views on how we are "selected" to survive tragedies like 9/11 as prompts for meditation and thought on the subject, explore how technology can be either a friend or a foe of humankind.
7. **Network:** Search the Web for two sites: one promoting the idea of evolution, the other promoting the idea of creationism. Compare and contrast the approach of each site as well as responses by the visitors to each site.
8. **Network:** Have your class create a private chat room with screen names that do not divulge the gender of the participants. Discuss the pros and cons of computers as described by Sedaris. Have a host tally the nature of the responses, reveal the gender of the students who participated, and discuss any differences between the responses of the male and female students.
9. **Network:** Do a search of the Web using the keywords *cloning* and *children*. Analyze three hits to demonstrate the ethical and religious controversies raised by the subject.

# Glossary of Terms

**Abstract/concrete**  patterns of language reflect an author's word choice. Abstract words (for example, *wisdom, power,* and *beauty*) refer to general ideas, qualities, or conditions. Concrete words name material objects and items associated with the five senses—words like *rock, pizza,* and *basketball.* Both abstract and concrete language are useful in communicating ideas. Generally, you should not be too abstract in writing. It is best to employ concrete words, naming things that can be seen, touched, smelled, heard, or tasted in order to support generalizations, topic sentences, or more abstract ideas.

**Acronym**  is a word formed from the first or first few letters of several words, as in OPEC (Organization of Petroleum Exporting Countries).

**Action**  in narrative writing is the sequence of happenings or events. This movement of events may occupy just a few minutes or extend over a period of years or centuries.

**Alliteration**  is the repetition of initial consonant sounds in words placed closely next to each other, as in "what a *t*ale of *t*error now their *t*urbulency *t*ells." Prose that is highly rhythmical or "poetic" often makes use of this method.

**Allusion**  is a literary, biographical, or historical reference, whether real or imaginary. It is a "figure of speech" (a fresh, useful comparison) employed to illuminate an idea. A writer's prose style can be made richer through this economical method of evoking an idea or emotion, as in E. M. Forster's biblical allusion in this sentence: "Property produces men of weight, and it was a man of weight who failed to get into the Kingdom of Heaven."

**Analogy**  is a form of comparison that uses a clear illustration to explain a difficult idea or function. It is unlike a formal comparison in that its subjects of comparison are from different categories or areas. For example, an analogy likening "division of labor" to the activity of bees in a hive makes the first concept more concrete by showing it to the reader through the figurative comparison with the bees. Analogy in exposition can involve a few sentences, a paragraph or set of paragraphs, or an entire essay. Analogies can also be used in argumentation to heighten an appeal to emotion, but they cannot actually *prove* anything.

**Analysis** is a method of exposition in which a subject is broken up into its parts to explain their nature, function, proportion, or relationship. Analysis thus explores connections and processes within the context of a given subject. (See *causal analysis* and *process analysis*.)

**Anecdote** is a brief, engaging account of some happening, often historical, biographical, or personal. As a technique in writing, anecdote is especially effective in creating interesting essay introductions and also in illuminating abstract concepts in the body of the essay.

**Antecedent** in grammar refers to the word, phrase, or clause to which a pronoun refers. In writing, antecedent also refers to any happening or thing that is prior to another, or to anything that logically precedes a subject.

**Antithesis** is the balancing of one idea or term against another for emphasis.

**Antonym** is a word whose meaning is opposite to that of another word.

**Aphorism** is a short, pointed statement expressing a general truism or an idea in an original or imaginative way. Marshall McLuhan's statement that "the medium is the message" is a well-known contemporary aphorism.

**Archaic** language is vocabulary or usage that belongs to an earlier period and is old-fashioned today. The word *thee* for *you* is an archaism still in use in certain situations.

**Archetypes** are special images or symbols that, according to Carl Jung, appeal to the total racial or cultural understanding of a people. Such images or symbols as the mother archetype, the cowboy in American film, a sacred mountain, or spring as a time of renewal tend to trigger the "collective unconscious" of the human race.

**Argumentation** is a formal variety of writing that offers reasons for or against something. Its goal is to persuade or convince the reader through logical reasoning and carefully controlled emotional appeal. Argumentation as a formal mode of writing contains many properties that distinguish it from exposition. (See *assumption, deduction, evidence, induction, logic, persuasion, proposition,* and *refutation.*)

**Assonance** is defined generally as likeness or rough similarity of sound. Its specific definition is a partial rhyme in which the stressed vowel sounds are alike but the consonant sounds are unlike, as in *late* and *make*. Although more common to poetry, assonance can also be detected in highly rhythmic prose.

**Assumption** in argumentation is anything taken for granted or presumed to be accepted by the audience and therefore unstated. Assumptions in argumentative writing can be dangerous because the audience might not always accept the idea implicit in them. (See *begging the question*.)

**Audience** is that readership toward which an author directs his or her essay. In composing essays, writers must acknowledge the nature of their expected readers—whether specialized or general, minimally educated or highly educated, sympathetic or unsympathetic toward the writer's opinions, and so forth. Failure to focus on the writer's true audience can lead to confusion in language and usage, presentation of inappropriate content, and failure to appeal to the expected reader.

**Balance** in sentence structure refers to the assignment of equal treatment in the arrangement of coordinate ideas. It is often used to heighten a contrast of ideas.

**Begging the question** is an error or a fallacy in reasoning and argumentation in which the writer assumes as a truth something for which evidence or proof is actually needed.

**Causal analysis** is a form of writing that examines causes and effects of events or conditions as they relate to a specific subject. Writers can investigate the causes of a particular effect or the effects of a particular cause or combine both methods. Basically, however, causal analysis looks for connections between things and reasons behind them.

**Characterization** is the creation of people involved in the action. It is used especially in narrative or descriptive writing. Authors use techniques of dialogue, description, reportage, and observation in attempting to present vivid and distinctive characters.

**Chronology or chronological order** is the arrangement of events in the order in which they happened. Chronological order can be used in such diverse narrative situations as history, biography, scientific process, and personal account. Essays that are ordered by chronology move from one step or point to the next in time.

**Cinematic technique** in narration, description, and occasionally exposition is the conscious application of film art to the development of the contemporary essay. Modern writers often are aware of such film techniques as montage (the process of cutting and arranging film so that short scenes are presented in rapid succession), zoom (intense enlargement of subject), and various forms of juxtaposition, and use these methods to enhance the quality of their essays.

**Classification** is a form of exposition in which the writer divides a subject into categories and then groups elements in each of those categories according to their relationships with one another. Thus a writer using classification takes a topic, divides it into several major groups, and then often subdivides those groups, moving always from larger categories to smaller ones.

**Cliché** is an expression that once was fresh and original but that has lost much of its vitality through overuse. Because expressions like "as quick as a wink" and "blew her stack" are trite or common today, they should be avoided in writing.

**Climactic ordering** is the arrangement of a paragraph or essay so that the most important items are saved for last. The effect is to build slowly through a sequence of events or ideas to the most critical part of the composition.

**Coherence** is a quality in effective writing that results from the careful ordering of each sentence in a paragraph and each paragraph in the essay. If an essay is coherent, each part will grow naturally and logically from those parts that come before it. Following careful chronological, logical, spatial, or sequential order is the most natural way to achieve coherence in writing. The main devices used in achieving coherence are transitions, which help connect one thought with another.

**Colloquial language** is conversational language used in certain types of informal and narrative writing but rarely in essays, business writing, or research writing. Expressions like "cool," "pal," or "I can dig it" often have a place in conversational settings. However, they should be used sparingly in essay writing for special effects.

**Comparison/contrast** as an essay pattern treats similarities and differences between two subjects. Any useful comparison involves two items from the same class. Moreover, there must be a clear reason for the comparison or contrast. Finally, there must be a balanced treatment of the various comparative or contrasting points between the two subjects.

**Conclusions** are the endings of essays. Without a conclusion, an essay would be incomplete, leaving the reader with the feeling that something important has been left out. There are numerous strategies for conclusions available to writers: summarizing main points in the essay, restating the main idea, using an effective quotation, offering the reader the climax to a series of events, returning to the beginning and echoing it, offering a solution to a problem, emphasizing the topic's significance, or setting a new frame of reference by generalizing from the main thesis. A conclusion should end the essay in a clear, convincing, emphatic way.

**Concrete**  (see *abstract/concrete.*)

**Conflict**  in narrative writing is the clash or opposition of events, characters, or ideas that makes the resolution of action necessary.

**Connotation/denotation**  are terms specifying the way a word has meaning. Connotation refers to the "shades of meaning" that a word might have because of various emotional associations it calls up for writers and readers alike. Words like *patriotism, pig,* and *rose* have strong connotative overtones to them. Denotation refers to the "dictionary" definition of a word—its exact meaning. Good writers understand the connotative and denotative value of words and control the shades of meaning that many words possess.

**Context**  is the situation surrounding a word, group of words, or sentence. Often the elements coming before or after a certain confusing or difficult construction will provide insight into the meaning or importance of that item.

**Coordination**  in sentence structure refers to the grammatical arrangement of parts of the same order or equality in rank.

**Declarative sentences**  make a statement or assertion.

**Deduction**  is a form of logic that begins with a generally stated truth or principle and then offers details, examples, and reasoning to support the generalization. In other words, deduction is based on reasoning from a known principle to an unknown principle, from the general to the specific, or from a premise to a logical conclusion. (See *syllogism.*)

**Definition**  in exposition is the extension of a word's meaning through a paragraph or an entire essay. As an extended method of explaining a word, this type of definition relies on other rhetorical methods, including detail, illustration, comparison and contrast, and anecdote.

**Denotation**  (see *connotation/denotation.*)

**Description**  in the prose essay is a variety of writing that uses details of sight, sound, color, smell, taste, and touch to create a word picture and to explain or illustrate an idea.

**Development**  refers to the way a paragraph or an essay elaborates or builds upon a topic or theme. Typical development proceeds either from general illustrations to specific ones or from one generalization to another. (See *horizontal/vertical.*)

**Dialogue**  is the reproduction of speech or conversation between two or more persons in writing. Dialogue can add concreteness and vividness to an essay and can also help reveal character. A writer who reproduces dialogue in an essay must use it for a purpose and not simply as a decorative device.

**Diction**  is the manner of expression in words, choice of words, or wording. Writers must choose vocabulary carefully and precisely to communicate a message and also to address an intended audience effectively; this is good diction.

**Digression** is a temporary departure from the main subject in writing. Any digression in the essay must serve a purpose or be intended for a specific effect.

**Discourse (forms of)** relates conventionally to the main categories of writing—narration, description, exposition and argumentation. In practice, these forms of discourse often blend or overlap. Essayists seek the ideal fusion of forms of discourse in the treatment of their subject.

**Division** is that aspect of classification in which the writer divides some large subject into categories. Division helps writers split large and potentially complicated subjects into parts for orderly presentation and discussion.

**Dominant impression** in description is the main impression or effect that writers attempt to create for their subject. It arises from an author's focus on a single subject and from the feelings the writer brings to that subject.

**Editorializing** is to express personal opinions about the subject of the essay. An editorial tone can have a useful effect in writing, but at other times an author might want to reduce editorializing in favor of a better balanced or more objective tone.

**Effect** is a term used in causal analysis to describe the outcome or expected result of a chain of happenings.

**Emphasis** indicates the placement of the most important ideas in key positions in the essay. As a major principle, emphasis relates to phrases, sentences, and paragraphs—the construction of the entire essay. Emphasis can be achieved by repetition, subordination, careful positioning of thesis and topic sentences, climactic ordering, comparison and contrast, and a variety of other methods.

**Episodic** relates to that variety of narrative writing that develops through a series of incidents or events.

**Essay** is the name given to a short prose work on a limited topic. Essays take many forms, ranging from personal narratives to critical or argumentative treatments of a subject. Normally, an essay will convey the writer's personal ideas about the subject.

**Etymology** is the origin and development of a word—tracing a word back as far as possible.

**Evidence** is material offered to support an argument or a proposition. Typical forms of evidence are facts, details, and expert testimony.

**Example** is a method of exposition in which the writer offers illustrations in order to explain a generalization or a whole thesis. (See *illustration*.)

**Exclamatory sentences** in writing express surprise or strong emotion.

**Expert testimony** as employed in argumentative essays and in expository essays is the use of statements by authorities to support a writer's position or idea. This method often requires careful quotation and acknowledgment of sources.

**Exposition** is a major form of discourse that informs or explains. Exposition is the form of expression required in much college writing, for it provides facts and information, clarifies ideas, and establishes meaning. The primary methods of exposition are *illustration, comparison and contrast, analogy, definition, classification, causal analysis,* and *process analysis* (see entries).

**Extended metaphor** is a figurative comparison that is used to structure a significant part of the composition or the whole essay. (See *figurative language* and *metaphor*.)

**Fable**  is a form of narrative containing a moral that normally appears clearly at the end.

**Fallacy**  in argumentation is an error in logic or in the reasoning process. Fallacies occur because of vague development of ideas, lack of awareness on the part of writers of the requirements of logical reasoning, or faulty assumptions about the proposition.

**Figurative language**  as opposed to literal language is a special approach to writing that departs from what is typically a concrete, straightforward style. It is the use of vivid, imaginative statements to illuminate or illustrate an idea. Figurative language adds freshness, meaning, and originality to a writer's style. Major figures of speech include *allusion, hyperbole, metaphor, personification,* and *simile* (see entries).

**Flashback**  is a narrative technique in which the writer begins at some point in the action and then moves into the past in order to provide crucial information about characters and events.

**Foreshadow**  is a technique that indicates beforehand what is to occur at a later point in the essay.

**Frame**  in narration and description is the use of a key object or pattern—typically at the start and end of the essay—that serves as a border or structure for the substance of the composition.

**General/specific words**  are the basis of writing, although it is wise in college composition to keep vocabulary as specific as possible. General words refer to broad categories and groups, whereas specific words capture with force and clarity the nature of the term. General words refer to large classes, concepts, groups, and emotions; specific words are more particular in providing meanings. The distinction between general and specific language is always a matter of degree.

**Generalization**  is a broad idea or statement. All generalizations require particulars and illustrations to support them.

**Genre**  is a type or form of literature—for example, short fiction, novel, poetry, or drama.

**Grammatical structure**  is a systematic description of language as it relates to the grammatical nature of a sentence.

**Horizontal/vertical**  paragraph and essay development refers to the basic way a writer moves either from one generalization to another in a carefully related series of generalizations (horizontal) or from a generalization to a series of specific supporting examples (vertical).

**Hortatory style**  is a variety of writing designed to encourage, give advice, or urge to good deeds.

**Hyperbole**  is a form of figurative language that uses exaggeration to overstate a position.

**Hypothesis**  is an unproven theory or proposition that is tentatively accepted to explain certain facts. A working hypothesis provides the basis for further investigation or argumentation.

**Hypothetical examples**  are illustrations in the form of assumptions that are based on the hypothesis. As such, they are conditional rather than absolute or certain facts.

**Identification**  as a method of exposition refers to focusing on the main subject of the essay. It involves the clear location of the subject within the context or situation of the composition.

**Idiomatic language** is the language or dialect of a people, region, or class—the individual nature of a language.

**Ignoring the question** in argumentation is a fallacy that involves the avoidance of the main issue by developing an entirely different one.

**Illustration** is the use of one or more examples to support an idea. Illustration permits the writer to support a generalization through particulars or specifics.

**Imagery** is clear, vivid description that appeals to the sense of sight, smell, touch, sound, or taste. Much imagery exists for its own sake, adding descriptive flavor to an essay. However, imagery (especially when it involves a larger pattern) can also add meaning to an essay.

**Induction** is a method of logic consisting of the presentation of a series of facts, pieces of information, or instances in order to formulate or build a likely generalization. The key is to provide prior examples before reaching a logical conclusion. Consequently, as a pattern of organization in essay writing, the inductive method requires the careful presentation of relevant data and information before the conclusion is reached at the end of the paper.

**Inference** involves arriving at a decision or opinion by reasoning from known facts or evidence.

**Interrogative sentences** are sentences that ask or pose a question.

**Introduction** is the beginning or opening of an essay. The introduction should alert the reader to the subject by identifying it, set the limits of the essay, and indicate what the thesis (or main idea) will be. Moreover, it should arouse the reader's interest in the subject. Among the devices available in the creation of good introductions are making a simple statement of thesis; giving a clear, vivid description of an important setting; posing a question or series of questions; referring to a relevant historical event; telling an anecdote; using comparison and contrast to frame the subject; using several examples to reinforce the statement of the subject; and presenting a personal attitude about a controversial issue.

**Irony** is the use of language to suggest the opposite of what is stated. Writers use irony to reveal unpleasant or troublesome realities that exist in life or to poke fun at human weaknesses and foolish attitudes. In an essay there may be verbal irony, in which the result of a sequence of ideas or events is the opposite of what normally would be expected. A key to the identification of irony in an essay is our ability to detect where the author is stating the opposite of what he or she actually believes.

**Issue** is the main question upon which an entire argument rests. It is the idea that the writer attempts to prove.

**Jargon** is special words associated with a specific area of knowledge or a particular profession. Writers who employ jargon either assume that readers know specialized terms or take care to define terms for the benefit of the audience.

**Juxtaposition** as a technique in writing or essay organization is the placing of elements—either similar or contrasting—close together, positioning them side by side in order to illuminate the subject.

**Levels of language** refer to the kinds of language used in speaking and writing. Basically, there are three main levels of language—formal, informal, and colloquial. Formal English, used in writing or speech, is the type of English employed to address special groups and professional people. Informal English is the sort of writing found in newspapers, magazines, books, and essays. It is popular English for an educated audience but still more formal than colloquial (conversational) English. Finally, colloquial English is spoken (and occasionally written) English used in conversations with friends, employees, and peer group members; it is characterized by the use of slang, idioms, ordinary language, and loose sentence structure.

**Linear order**   in paragraph development means the clear line of movement from one point to another.

**Listing**   is a simple technique of illustration in which facts or examples are used to support a topic or generalization.

**Logic**   as applied to essay writing is correct reasoning based on induction or deduction. The logical basis of an essay must offer reasonable criteria or principles of thought, present these principles in an orderly manner, avoid faults in reasoning, and result in a complete and satisfactory outcome in the reasoning process.

**Metaphor**   is a type of figurative language in which an item from one category is compared briefly and imaginatively with an item from another area. Writers use such implied comparisons to assign meaning in a fresh, vivid, and concrete way.

**Metonymy**   is a figure of language in which a thing is not designated by its own name but by another associated with or suggested by it, as in "The Supreme Court has decided" (meaning the judges of the Supreme Court have decided).

**Mood**   is the creation of atmosphere in descriptive writing.

**Motif**   in an essay is any series of components that can be detected as a pattern. For example, a particular detail, idea, or image can be elaborated upon or designed to form a pattern or motif in the essay.

**Myth**   in literature is a traditional story or series of events explaining some basic phenomenon of nature; the origin of humanity; or the customs, institutions, and religious rites of a people. Myth often relates to the exploits of gods, goddesses, and heroes.

**Narration**   as a form of essay writing is the presentation of a story in order to illustrate an idea.

**Non sequitur**   in argumentation is a conclusion or inference that does not follow from the premises or evidence on which it is based. The non sequitur thus is a type of logical fallacy.

**Objective/subjective**   writing refers to the attitude that writers take toward their subject. When writers are objective, they try not to report their personal feelings about the subject; they attempt to be detached, impersonal, and unbiased. Conversely, subjective writing reveals an author's personal attitudes and emotions. For many varieties of college writing, such as business or laboratory reports, term papers, and literary analyses, it is best to be as objective as possible. But for many personal essays in composition courses, the subjective touch is fine. In the hands of skilled writers, the objective and subjective tones often blend.

**Onomatopoeia**   is the formation of a word by imitating the natural sound associated with the object or action, as in *buzz* or *click*.

**Order**   is the arrangement of information or materials in an essay. The most common ordering techniques are *chronological order* (time in sequence), *spatial order* (the arrangement of descriptive details), *process order* (a step-by-step approach to an activity), *deductive order* (a thesis followed by information to support it), and *inductive order* (evidence and examples first, followed by the thesis in the form of a conclusion). Some rhetorical patterns, such as comparison and contrast, classification, and argumentation, require other ordering methods. Writers should select those ordering principles that permit them to present materials clearly.

**Overstatement** is an extravagant or exaggerated claim or statement.

**Paradox** is a statement that seems to be contradictory but actually contains an element of truth.

**Paragraph** is a unit in an essay that serves to present and examine one aspect of a topic. Composed normally of a group of sentences (one-sentence paragraphs can be used for emphasis or special effect), the paragraph elaborates an idea within the larger framework of the essay and the thesis unifying it.

**Parallelism** is a variety of sentence structure in which there is balance or coordination in the presentation of elements. "I came, I saw, I conquered" is a standard example of parallelism, presenting both pronouns and verbs in a coordinated manner. Parallelism can appear in a sentence, a group of sentences, or an entire paragraph.

**Paraphrase** as a literary method is the process of rewording the thought or meaning expressed in something that has been said or written before.

**Parenthetical** refers to giving qualifying information or explanation. This information normally is marked off or placed within parentheses.

**Parody** is ridiculing the language or style of another writer or composer. In parody, a serious subject tends to be treated in a nonsensical manner.

**Periphrasis** is the use of many words where one or a few would do; it is a roundabout way of speaking or writing.

**Persona** is the role or characterization that writers occasionally create for themselves in a personal narrative.

**Personification** is giving an object, a thing, or an idea lifelike or human characteristics, as in the common reference to a car as "she." Like all forms of figurative language, personification adds freshness to description and makes ideas vivid by setting up striking comparisons.

**Persuasion** is the form of discourse, related to argumentation, that attempts to move a person to action or to influence an audience toward a particular belief.

**Point of view** is the angle from which a writer tells a story. Many personal and informal essays take the *first-person* (or "I") point of view, which is natural and fitting for essays in which the author wants to speak in a familiar way to the reader. On the other hand, the *third-person* point of view ("he," "she," "it," "they") distances the reader somewhat from the writer. The third-person point of view is useful in essays in which the writers are not talking exclusively about themselves, but about other people, ideas, and events.

**Post hoc, ergo propter hoc** in logic is the fallacy of thinking that a happening that follows another must be its result. It arises from a confusion about the logical causal relationship.

**Process analysis** is a pattern of writing that explains in a step-by-step way how something is done, how it is put together, how it works, or how it occurs. The subject can be a mechanical device, a product, an idea, a natural phenomenon, or a historical sequence. However, in all varieties of process analysis, the writer traces all important steps, from beginning to end.

**Progression**   is the forward movement or succession of acts, events, or ideas presented in an essay.

**Proportion**   refers to the relative emphasis and length given to an event, an idea, a time, or a topic within the whole essay. Basically, in terms of proportion, the writer gives more emphasis to a major element than to a minor one.

**Proposition**   is the main point of an argumentative essay—the statement to be defended, proved, or upheld. It is like a *thesis* (see entry) except that it presents an idea that is debatable or can be disputed. The *major proposition* is the main argumentative point; *minor propositions* are the reasons given to support or prove the issue.

**Purpose**   is what the writer wants to accomplish in an essay. Writers having a clear purpose will know the proper style, language, tone, and materials to utilize in designing an effective essay.

**Refutation**   in argumentation is a method by which writers recognize and deal effectively with the arguments of their opponents. Their own argument will be stronger if they refute—prove false or wrong—all opposing arguments.

**Repetition**   is a simple method of achieving emphasis by repeating a word, a phrase, or an idea.

**Rhetoric**   is the art of using words effectively in speaking or writing. It is also the art of literary composition, particularly in prose, including both figures of speech and such strategies as *comparison and contrast, definition,* and *analysis.*

**Rhetorical question**   is a question asked only to emphasize a point, introduce a topic, or provoke thought, but not to elicit an answer.

**Rhythm**   in prose writing is a regular recurrence of elements or features in sentences, creating a patterned emphasis, balance, or contrast.

**Sarcasm**   is a sneering or taunting attitude in writing, designed to hurt by evaluating or criticizing. Basically, sarcasm is a heavy-handed form of *irony* (see entry). Writers should try to avoid sarcastic writing and to use more acceptable varieties of irony and satire to criticize their subject.

**Satire**   is the humorous or critical treatment of a subject in order to expose the subject's vices, follies, stupidities, and so forth. The intention of such satire is to reform by exposing the subject to comedy or ridicule.

**Sensory language**   is language that appeals to any of the five senses—sight, sound, touch, taste, or smell.

**Sentimentality**   in prose writing is the excessive display of emotion, whether intended or unintended. Because sentimentality can distort the true nature of a situation or an idea, writers should use it cautiously, or not at all.

**Series**   as a technique in prose is the presentation of several items, often concrete details or similar parts of grammar such as verbs or adjectives, in rapid sequence.

**Setting**   in narrative and descriptive writing is the time, place, environment, background, or surroundings established by an author.

**Simile** is a figurative comparison using *like* or *as*.

**Slang** is a kind of language that uses racy or colorful expressions associated more often with speech than with writing. It is colloquial English and should be used in essay writing only to reproduce dialogue or to create a special effect.

**Spatial order** in descriptive writing is the careful arrangement of details or materials in space—for example, from left to right, top to bottom, or near to far.

**Specific words** (see *general/specific words.*)

**Statistics** are facts or data of a numerical kind, assembled and tabulated to present significant information about a given subject. As a technique of illustration, statistics can be useful in analysis and argumentation.

**Style** is the specific or characteristic manner of expression, execution, construction, or design of an author. As a manner or mode of expression in language, it is the unique way each writer handles ideas. There are numerous stylistic categories—such as literary, formal, argumentative, and satiric—but ultimately, no two writers have the same style.

**Subjective** (see *objective/subjective.*)

**Subordination** in sentence structure is the placing of a relatively less important idea in an inferior grammatical position to the main idea. It is the designation of a minor clause that is dependent upon a major clause.

**Syllogism** is an argument or form of reasoning in which two statements or premises are made and a logical conclusion is drawn from them. As such, it is a form of deductive logic—reasoning from the general to the particular. The *major premise* presents a quality of class ("All writers are mortal"). The *minor premise* states that a particular subject is a member of that class ("Ernest Hemingway was a writer"). The conclusion states that the qualities of the class and the member of the class are the same. ("Hemingway was mortal").

**Symbol** is something—normally a concrete image—that exists in itself but also stands for something else or has greater meaning. As a variety of figurative language, the symbol can be a strong feature in an essay, operating to add depth of meaning and even to unify the composition.

**Synonym** is a word that means roughly the same as another word. In practice, few words are exactly alike in meaning. Careful writers use synonyms to vary word choice without ever moving too far from the shade of meaning intended.

**Theme** is the central idea in an essay; it is also termed the *thesis*. Everything in an essay should support the theme in one way or another.

**Thesis** is the main idea in an essay. The *thesis sentence,* appearing only in the essay (normally somewhere in the first paragraph) serves to convey the main idea to the reader in a clear and emphatic manner.

**Tone** is the writer's attitude toward his or her subject or material. An essay writer's tone may be objective, subjective, comic, ironic, nostalgic, critical, or a reflection of numerous other attitudes. Tone is the voice that writers give to an essay.

**Topic sentence** is the main idea that a paragraph develops. Not all paragraphs contain topic sentences; often the topic is implied.

**Transition** is the linking of ideas in sentences, paragraphs, and larger segments of an essay in order to achieve *coherence* (see entry). Among the most common techniques to achieve smooth transitions are (1) repeating a key word or phrase, (2) using a pronoun to refer to a key word or phrase, (3) relying on traditional connectives such as *thus, however, moreover, for example, therefore, finally,* or *in conclusion,* (4) using parallel structure (see *parallelism*), and (5) creating a sentence or paragraph that serves as a bridge from one part of an essay to another. Transition is best achieved when a writer presents ideas and details carefully and in logical order.

**Understatement**   is a method of making a weaker statement than is warranted by truth, accuracy, or importance.

**Unity**   is a feature in an essay whereby all material relates to a central concept and contributes to the meaning of the whole. To achieve a unified effect in an essay, the writer must design an effective introduction and conclusion, maintain consistent tone or point of view, develop middle paragraphs in a coherent manner, and above all stick to the subject, never permitting unimportant or irrelevant elements to enter.

**Usage**   is the way in which a word, phrase, or sentence is used to express a particular idea; it is the customary manner of using a given language in speaking or writing.

**Vertical**   (see *horizontal/vertical.*)

**Voice**   is the way you express your ideas to the reader, the tone you take in addressing your audience. Voice reflects your attitude toward both your subject and your readers. (See *tone.*)

# *Credits*

Orwell, George. "Politics and the English Language" reprinted from *Shooting and Elephant and Other Essays* by George Orwell. Copyright © 1946 by Sonia Brownell Orwell and renewed 1974 by Sonia Orwell. Reprinted by permission of Harcourt, Inc. and Bill Hamilton as Literary Executor of the Estate of the late Sonia Brownell Orwell and Secker and Warburg, Ltd.

Oyama, Richard. "You Spoke Japanese" copyright © 1989 by Richard Oyama. Reprinted by permission of the author. Richard Oyama teaches at the California College of Arts and Crafts.

Perrin, Noel. "The Greenest Campuses: An Idiosyncratic Guide" by Noel Perrin. Copyright © 2001 by Noel Perrin. Originally appeared in *Chronicle of Higher Education*. Reprinted by permission of the author.

Pivarnik, Greg. "MySpace Is Not Responsible for Your Kids" by Greg Pivarnik. Copyright © 2007 by *The Daily Campus*. Reprinted by permission of *The Daily Campus*.

Pogrebin, Letty Cottin. "Superstitious Minds" copyright © 1988 by Letty Cottin Pogrebin. Reprinted by permission of Ms. Magazine.

Posner, Richard. "Security Versus Civil Liberties" by Richard A. Posner. First published in *The Atlantic Monthly*, December 2001. Reprinted by permission of the author.

Prose, Francine. "The Universal in the Particular" by Francine Prose. Copyright © 2004 by Francine Prose. First appeared in *Virginia Quarterly Review*. Reprinted with permission of the Denise Shannon Literary Agency, Inc. All rights reserved.

Quindlen, Anna. "Sex Ed" from *Living Out Loud* by Anna Quindlen. Copyright © 1987 by Anna Quindlen. Used by permission of Random House, Inc.

Reed, Ishmael. "The Patriot Act of the 18th Century" by Ishmael Reed from *Time Magazine*, July 5, 2004. Copyright © 2004 *Time*, Inc. Reprinted by permission.

Reed, Ishmael. "America: The Multinational Society" from *Writin' Is Fightin': Forty-Three Years of Boxing on Paper* by Ishmael Reed. Copyright © Ishmael Reed. Reprinted by permission of Lowenstein Associates.

Reich, Richard. "Why the Rich Are Getting Richer, and the Poor, Poorer" from *The Work of Nations* by Robert B. Reich, copyright © 1991 by Robert B. Reich. Used by permission of Alfred A. Knopf, a division of Random House, Inc.

Rodriguez, Richard. "Family Values" by Richard Rodriguez. Copyright © 1992 by Richard Rodriguez. Originally appeared in *The Los Angeles Times*. Reprinted by permission of Georges Borchardt, Inc. on behalf of the author.

Rodriguez, Richard. "The Lonely, Good Company of Books" by Richard Rodriguez. Copyright © 1981 by Richard Rodriguez. Reprinted by permission of Georges Borchardt, Inc. on behalf of the author.

Rorem, Ned. "The Beatles" from *A Ned Rorem Reader* by Ned Rorem. Copyright © 2001 by Ned Rorem. Reprinted by permission of Yale University Press.

Rosenzweig, Paul. "Face Facts: Patriot Act Aids Security, Not Abuse" by Paul Rosenzweig from *Christian Science Monitor*, July 29, 2004. Copyright © 2004 by Christian Science Publishing Society. Reproduced with permission of Christian Science Publishing Society via Copyright Clearance Center.

Ross, Deborah. "Escape from Wonderland: Disney and the Female Imagination" by Deborah Ross, *Marvels and Tales: Journal of Fairy-Tale Studies*, Vol. 18, No. 1 (2004), pp. 53–66. Reprinted by permission of Wayne State University.

Roush, Wade. "Fakesters" by Wade Roush. *Technology Review*, November 1, 2006. Reprinted by permission of MIT *Technology Review* via Copyright Clearance Center.

Rushdie, Salman. "Not about Islam?" from *Step Across This Line* by Salman Rushdie, copyright © 2002 by Salman Rushdie. Used by permission of Random House, Inc.

Sabin, Heloisa. "Animal Research Saves Lives" by Heloisa Sabin. Originally appeared in *The Wall Street Journal*, October 18, 1995. Reprinted by permission of Americans for Medical Research on behalf of the author.

Sacks, Oliver. "Anybody Out There?" by Oliver Sacks. First published in *Natural History*, November, 2002. Copyright © 2002 by Oliver Sacks. Reprinted by permission of The Wylie Agency.

Sagan, Carl. "Can We Know the Universe? Reflections on a Grain of Salt" from *Broca's Brain* by Carl Sagan, copyright © 1979 by Carl Sagan. Reprinted with permission from Democritus Properties, LLC.

# Index

**I-1**